Contents

II	**Travel information**
II	Driving abroad – a cautionary tale
IV	Driving regulations
VII	Ski resorts

1	**Route planning maps**
1	Key map · Distance table

17	**Road maps**
17	Key map

121	**City plans and urban area maps**
121	Legends to city plans and urban area maps

Alicante C	121	Madrid U	135
Amsterdam CU	122	Madrid C	136
Antwerpen Antwerp C	121	Málaga C	136
Athina Athens U	122	Marseille Marseilles C	136
Athina Athens C	123	Milano Milan CU	137
Barcelona CU	123	Moskva Moscow CU	138
Basel C	123	München Munich CU	138
Beograd Belgrade C	125	Nápoli Naples CU	139
Berlin CU	124	Oslo U	139
Bordeaux CU	125	Oslo C	140
Bruxelles Brussels U	125	Paris C	140
Bruxelles Brussels C	126	Paris U	141
Budapest CU	126	Praha Prague CU	142
Dublin CU	127	Roma Rome CU	143
Düsseldorf C	127	Rotterdam C	142
Düsseldorf (Ruhrgebiet) U	128	Sankt Peterburg	
Edinburgh C	127	St Petersburg U	142
Firenze Florence C	129	Sevilla Seville C	144
Frankfurt C	129	Stockholm CU	145
Genève Geneva C	129	Strasbourg CU	144
Génova Genoa C	129	Stuttgart C	144
Göteborg Gothenburg C	130	Torino Turin U	146
Granada C	130	Torino Turin C	147
Hamburg CU	130	Venézia Venice C	146
Helsinki CU	131	Warszawa Warsaw CU	147
İstanbul U	131	Wien Vienna U	147
København Copenhagen CU	132	Wien Vienna C	148
Köln Cologne C	132	Zagreb C	148
Lisboa Lisbon CU	133	Zürich C	148
London C	133		
London U	134	C City street plan	
Luxembourg C	135	U Urban area map	
Lyon CU	135		

149	**Index to road maps**

.philips-maps.co.uk

published in 1998 as Philip's Multiscale Europe by
...'s, a division of Octopus Publishing Group Ltd
...octopusbooks.co.uk
...lite House,
...ctoria Embankment
...on EC4Y 0DZ
...hachette UK Company
...hachette.co.uk

...teenth edition 2017
...mpression 2017

This product includes mapping data licensed from
Ordnance Survey®, with the permission of the
Controller of Her Majesty's Stationery Office
© Crown copyright 2017. All rights reserved.
Licence number 100011710

... is a registered Trade Mark of the Northern Ireland
Department of Finance and Personnel. This product
includes mapping data licensed from Ordnance Survey of
Northern Ireland®, reproduced with the permission of Land
...roperty Services under delegated authority from the Controller of
Majesty's Stationery Office, © Crown Copyright 2017.

...ghts reserved. Apart from any fair dealing for the purpose of private
...research, criticism or review, as permitted under the Copyright
...gns and Patents Act, 1988, no part of this publication may be
...duced, stored in a retrieval system, or transmitted in any form
...any means, electronic, electrical, mechanical, optical,
...ocopying, recording, or otherwise, without prior written permission.

...quiries should be addressed to the Publisher.

Cartography by Philip's
Copyright © Philip's 2017

Printed in China

*Nielsen BookScan Travel Publishing Year Book 2015 data

**Independent research survey, from research carried out by Outlook
Research Limited, 2005/06.

Photographic acknowledgements:
Pages II and III: all photographs by Stephen Mesquita

Legend to route planning

	Motorway with selected jun...
	tunnel, under construction
	Toll motorway
	Pre-pay motorway
	Main through route
	Other major road
	Other road
25	European road number
56	Motorway number
55	National road number
56	Distances – in kilometres
	International boundary
	National boundary
LE HAVRE	Car ferry and destination
1089	Mountain pass, international airport, height in metres

	Town – population		Town – with Low Emission Zone
MOSKVA ▣	5 million +	■	5 million +
BERLIN ◫	2–5 million	■	2–5 million
MINSK ◱	1–2 million	■	1–2 million
Oslo ◉	500000–1million	●	500000–1million
Århus ◉	200000–500000	●	200000–500000
Turku ◉	100000–200000	●	100000–200000
Gävle ◉	50000–100000	●	50000–100000
Nybro ○	20000–50000	●	20000–50000
Ikast ○	10000–20000	●	10000–20000
Skjern ○	5000–10000	●	5000–10000
Lillesand ○	0–5000	●	0–5000

Scale

0   20   40   60   80 miles

1: 3 200 000
1cm = 32km   1 in = 50.51 miles

0   20   40   60   80   100   120   140 km

Legend to road maps pages 18–120

7 8	Motorway with junctions – full, restricted access
◇ ◇	services, rest or parking area
	tunnel
	under construction
I	Toll Motorway – with toll barrier
A CH CZ H SK	Pre-pay motorway
	'Vignette' must be purchased before travel
	Principal trunk highway – single / dual carriageway
	tunnel
	under construction
	Other main highway – single / dual carriageway
	Other important road
	Other road
E25	European road number
A49	Motorway number
135	National road number
Col Bayard 1248	Mountain pass
	Scenic route, gradient – arrow points uphill
143	Distances – in kilometres
	major
28	minor
	Principal railway
	tunnel
	Ferry route
	Short ferry route
	International boundary
	National boundary

In France, some national routes
have become departmental roads
and have been assigned new road
numbers. This means that road
signs are subject to change.
The new road numbers are
shown in this atlas

HEATHROW ✈	Airport	SANTA CRUZ ✚	Religious building
KNOSSOS ⌂	Ancient monument		Ski resort
	Beach	DISNEYLAND PARIS	Theme park
SCHLOSS LAHNECK ⌂	Castle or house	POMPEI	World Heritage site
GROTTE DE HAN-SUR-LESSE ⌂	Cave	PARQUE JURASSICO ✦	Other place of interest
GIVERNY ✿	Park or garden	1754▲	Spot height
	National park	**Sevilla**	World Heritage town
	Natural park	**Verona**	Town of tourist interest
		■ ●	Town with Low Emission Zone

Scales

1: 753 800 · Pages 18–110 and 120
1cm = 7.5km   1 inch = 12 miles

0   5   10   15   20 miles
0   5   10   15   20   25   30   35 km

1: 1 507 600 · Pages 111–119
1cm = 15km, 1 inch = 24 miles

0   10   20   30   40 miles
0   10   20   30   40   50   60   70 km

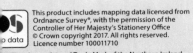
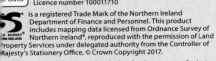

Driving abroad –
a cautionary tale

by Stephen Mesquita,
Philip's On the Road Correspondent

15/06/2016 07:10:39 LS300W *******

At last, you're on holiday. You can relax, leave your troubles behind you and soak in the sun, the food and the way of life. That's all true, of course – if you don't have to drive.

When you're driving in a strange country, relaxing is the last thing you should be doing. In fact, when you're driving on roads you don't know – and on the 'wrong' side of the road – you need to pay attention at all times and be ultra defensive.

Take one of my favourite places to visit – the very end of the heel of Italy. If you're only used to the UK's roads, driving there is a whole different kettle of fish. Or *'un altro paio di maniche'* (another pair of sleeves), as it should be.

These are the idyllic images you might have :

- Empty roads with great views.
- Timeless pastoral scenes.
- Village locals wandering down the middle of the street.
- Driving down to empty beaches for a swim before breakfast (only if you're really keen).

But the reality's a lot different. It's not that the Southern Italians are any better or worse drivers than we are. But there are different laws, different conventions, different road conditions and different driving styles.

5/06/2016 07:05:10 LS300W ******* Timeless pastoral scenes

2016 08:54:36 LS300W **Wandering down middle of street

15/06/2016 07:01:38 LS300W ******* Empty beaches

So here is my survival guide. Of course, this is only one small region of Europe. But I'm sure that wherever you're driving, some of this may ring bells – and perhaps even be useful.

Here are my Top 10 Tips from last year's holiday, illustrated with real-time dashcam video...

1 Being overtaken

Overtaking is more of a national sport on the continent than it is in the UK. What's disconcerting is the way that the overtaking car pulls in so sharply after overtaking. It takes a bit of getting used to but it's generally not (quite) as dangerous as it looks.

13/06/2016 08:43:35 LS300W *******

2 Tailgating

It's probably no worse than in the UK; but tailgating can still be intimidating and distracting. If you feel threatened, try to pull off the road if it's safe to do it. Or try my favourite ploy – go round a roundabout twice to escape your tailgater.

3 Motorway Slip Roads

Beware short slip roads on to motorways. They give merging motorists little chance to join the traffic at anything other than a snail's pace, leading them into narrow lanes of fast traffic. Not for the faint-hearted. Check your mirror as often as you can.

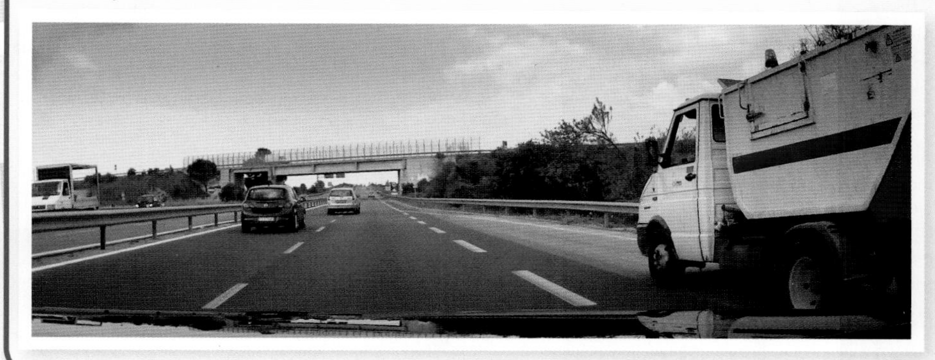

4 Oncoming traffic driving on your side of the road

On narrow country roads, this is a hazard everywhere. It's probably worse in the UK than it is in Southern Italy. But, as the picture shows, it can produce some heart-stopping moments.

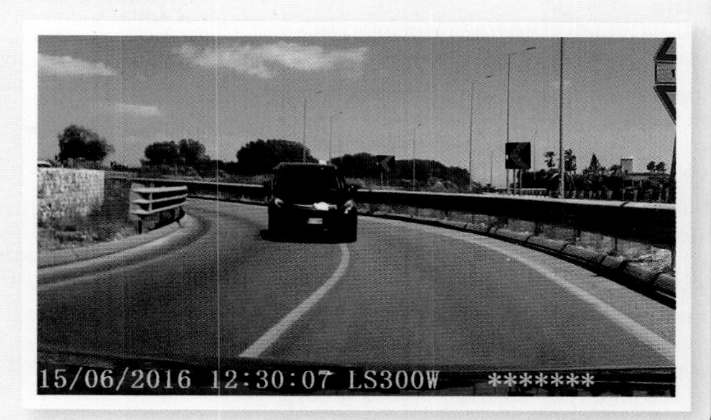

5 Pulling out of side roads and hoping

Pulling out of side roads and hoping. A lot of this goes on at crossroads in small towns and villages. Given the configuration of the roads, there's not much you can do about it – except be very cautious, even when it's your right of way or, as here, the traffic lights only work at certain times of day

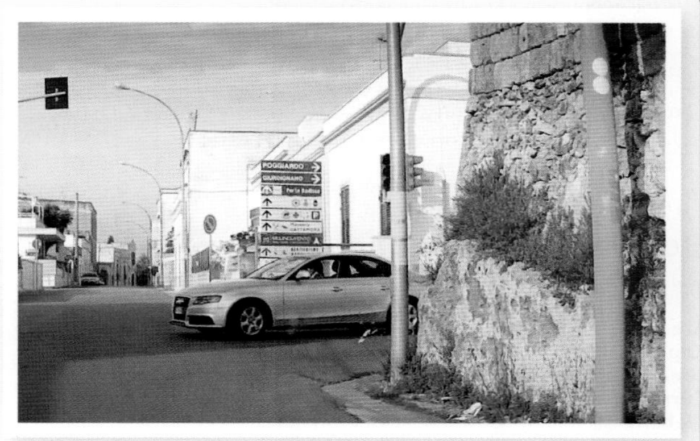

6 Petrol stations

Many country petrol stations are unmanned. Those that are manned sometimes charge you more for the privilege of having someone serve you. It may be worth it: the unmanned ones are not easy to operate. In a richly comic episode, I had to seek assistance to discover that I had paid for €40 of petrol at a pump some distance from the one at which my car was parked.

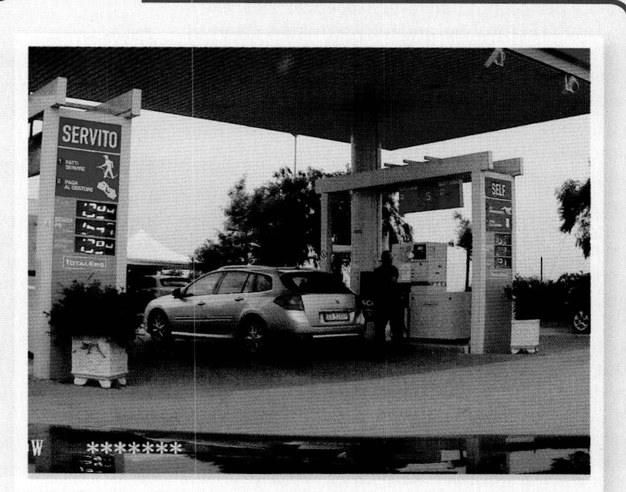

7 Parking Meters

In this region, almost every town has the blue road markings which indicate that, if you want to park here, you'll need to buy a ticket. You'll need coins – many don't accept notes or credit cards. No change is given. If you're lucky, as you put the coins in, the expiry time is shown. If you're unlucky, this panel will be dirty or scratched so that you can't read it. The times you need to pay for vary from town to town, depending on the time of year (always in the tourist season) and the time of day (siesta time is sometimes not charged). A crash course in the language is recommended. In 11 days, I spent over €65 on meters.

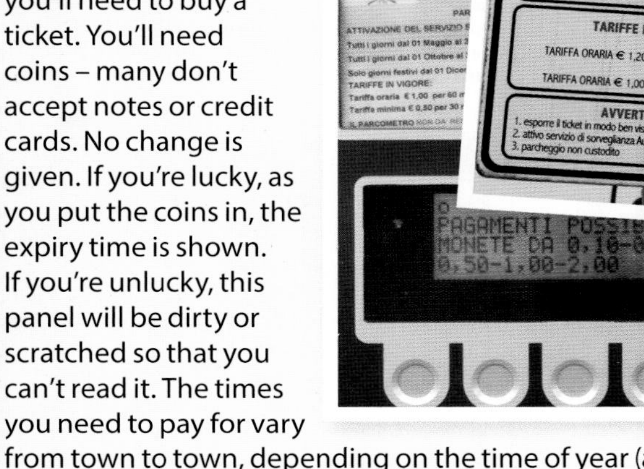

8 Sat Nav – beware of speed limits

Even though I'm an atlas publisher, I would strongly recommend you take a sat nav – as well as this atlas, of course. It really reduces the stress of navigating on unfamiliar roads (it's not so good for route planning). But beware if your sat nav tells you the speed limit – those on the screen seem to bear little resemblance to the signs at the side of the road.

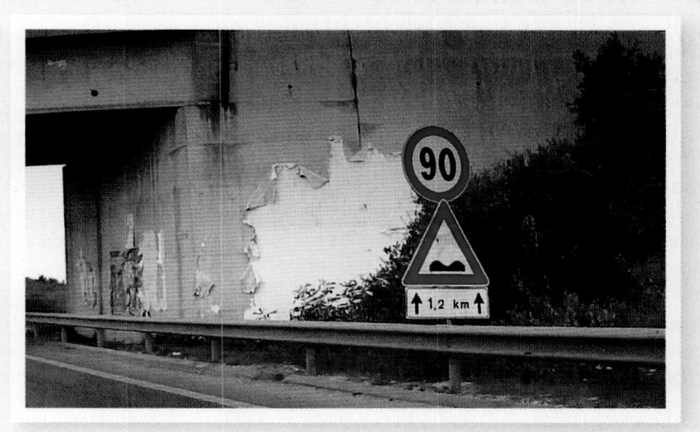

9 Speed limits Part 2

Even relying on the roadside signs, it can be hard to work out the speed limits. Can you work out what's happening here (answer at the foot of the page)?

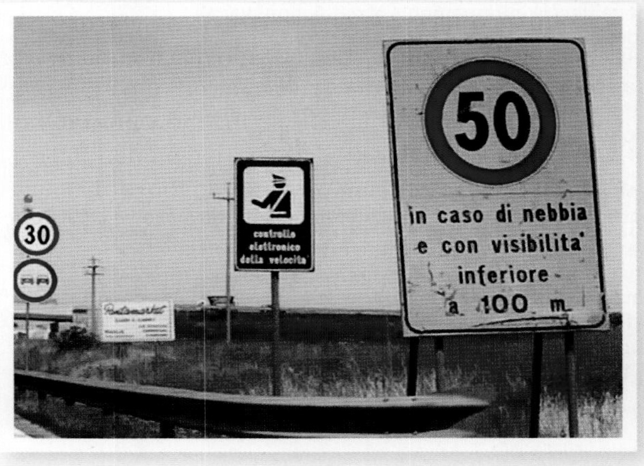

10 Cameras

These pictures cost me €200. They show me at the wheel of my stylish Fiat 500 (that's what the website said anyway) being distracted by two cyclists as they went through a red light. The red light is hidden in the hedge. This deserted spot in the middle of the countryside boasts the only traffic camera ever seen in the region. I stupidly had my eye on the cyclists, not the light. First I received a bill from Hertz for €47.90 – which I innocently thought was for the 'offence'. But no, it was for supplying my name and address (with almost every word misspelt) to the local authority. A year later, a bill arrived from said local authority, for €145 if paid within 5 days (or €220 if not).

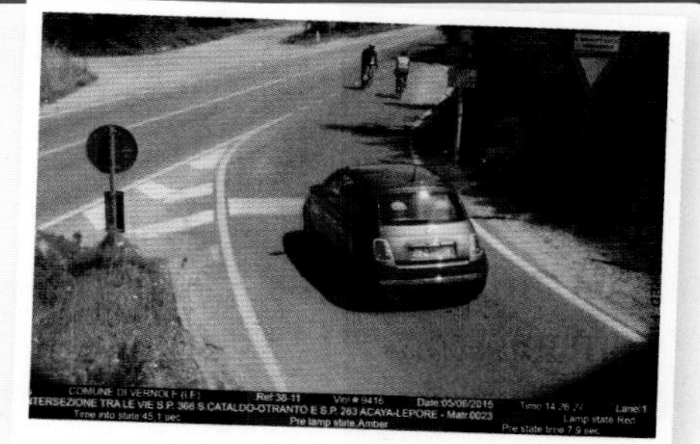

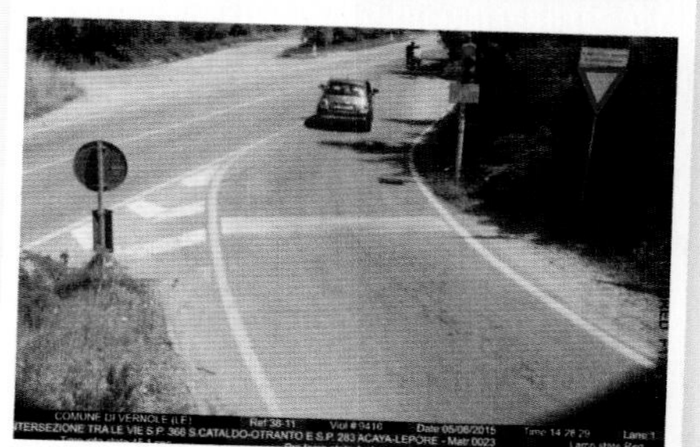

And I haven't even got to that most thrilling part of your holiday 'At the Car Hire Desk' (damage waiver rip-off's, not getting the car you ordered, should you photograph the car, and is it worth having another driver), documentation (the code you have to get now from the DVLA if you're hiring a car) and taking a spare pair of glasses. And do watch how much you drink. See the next section for all the rules and regulations for each country, including the alcohol limits. If in doubt, don't drink and drive. Now turn over and read the driving laws of the country you're going to. Buon Viaggio.

Answer to point 9: the speed limit is normally 90kph but it's 50kph when it's foggy or visibility is less than 100m.

Driving regulations

Vehicle
A national vehicle identification plate is always required when taking a vehicle abroad.

Fitting headlamp converters or beam deflectors when taking a right-hand drive car to a country where driving is on the right (every country in Europe except the UK and Ireland) is compulsory.

Within the EU, if not driving a locally hired car, it is compulsory to have either Europlates or a country of origin (eg GB) sticker. Outside the EU (and in Andorra) a sticker is compulsory, even with Europlates.

Documentation
All countries require that you carry a valid passport, vehicle registration document, hire certificate or letter of authority for the use of someone else's vehicle, full driving licence/International Driving Permit and insurance documentation (and/or green card outside the EU). Some non-EU countries also require a visa. Minimum driving ages are often higher for people holding foreign licences. New exit checks at the Eurotunnel and ferry terminals mean that drivers taking their vehicles from the UK should allow extra time. Drivers of vehicles over three years old should ensure that the MOT is up to date.

EHIC cards are free and give you entitlement to healthcare in other EU countries and Switzerland. *www.gov/european-health-insurance-card.*

Licence
A photo licence is preferred; with an old-style paper licence, an International Driving Permit (IDP) should also be carried. In some countries an IDP is compulsory, whatever form of licence is held. Non-EU drivers should always have both a licence and IDP. UK (except NI) drivers should check in advance whether a hire company will wish to check for endorsements and vehicle categories. If so, visit *https://www.gov.uk/view-driving-licence* to create a digital code (valid for 72 hours) that allows their details to be shared. For more information, contact the DVLA (0300 790 6802, *www.dft.gov.uk/dvla*).

Insurance
Third-party cover is compulsory across Europe. Most insurance policies give only basic cover when driving abroad, so you should check that your policy provides at least third-party cover for the countries in which you will be driving and upgrade it to the level that you require. You may be forced to take out extra cover at the frontier if you cannot produce acceptable proof that you have adequate insurance. Even in countries in which a green card is not required, carrying one is recommended for extra proof of insurance.

Motorcycles
It is compulsory for all motorcyclists and passengers to wear crash helmets. In France it may become compulsory for all motorcyclists and passengers to wear a minimum amount of reflective gear.

Other
In countries in which visibility vests are compulsory one for each person should be carried in the passenger compartment, or panniers on a motorbike, where they can be reached easily.

Warning triangles should also be carried in the passenger compartment.

The penalties for infringements of regulations vary considerably from one country to another. In many countries the police have the right to impose on-the-spot fines (ask for a receipt). Penalties can be severe for serious infringements, particularly for exceeding the blood-alcohol limit; in some countries this can result in immediate imprisonment.

In some countries, vignettes for toll roads are being replaced by electronic tags. See country details.

Please note that driving regulations often change, and that it has not been possible to cover all the information for every type of vehicle. The figures given for capitals' populations are for the whole metropolitan area.

The symbols used are:
- 🏛 Motorway
- ⚠ Dual carriageway
- ⚠ Single carriageway
- 🚗 Surfaced road
- 🚗 Unsurfaced or gravel road
- 🏭 Urban area
- ⊙ Speed limit in kilometres per hour (kph). These are the maximum speeds for the types of roads listed. In some places and under certain conditions they may be considerably lower. Always obey local signs.

🔗 Seat belts	Additional documents required
🧍 Children	Mobile phones
🍷 Blood alcohol level	LEZ Low Emission Zone
△ Warning triangle	Q▪ Dipped headlights
▪▪ First aid kit	❄ Winter driving
🔦 Spare bulb kit	★ Other information
▮ Fire extinguisher	
⊖ Minimum driving age	

The publishers have made every effort to ensure that the information given here was correct at the time of going to press. No responsibility can be accepted for any errors or their consequences.

Andorra Principat d'Andorra (AND)
Area 468 sq km (181 sq miles)
Population 85,500
Capital Andorra la Vella (44,000)
Languages Catalan (official), French, Castilian, Portuguese
Currency Euro = 100 cents
Website http://visitandorra.com

⊙ 🏛	⚠	⚠	🏭
n/a	90	60/90	50

- 🔗 Compulsory
- 🧍 Under 10 and below 150 cm must travel in an EU-approved restraint system adapted to their size in the rear. Airbag must be deactivated if a child is in the front passenger seat.
- 🍷 0.05%
- △ Compulsory
- ▪▪ Recommended
- 🔦 Compulsory
- ▮ Recommended
- ⊖ 18
- ▯ Not permitted whilst driving
- Q▪ Compulsory for motorcycles during day and for other vehicles during poor daytime visibility.
- ❄ Winter tyres or snow chains compulsory in poor conditions or when indicated by signs
- ★ Visibility vests compulsory

Austria Österreich (A)
Area 83,859 sq km (32,377 sq miles)
Population 8,663,000
Capital Vienna / Wien (2,600,000)
Languages German (official)
Currency Euro = 100 cents
Website www.austria.gv.at

⊙ 🏛	⚠	⚠	🏭
130	100	100	50
If towing trailer under 750kg / over 750 kg			
100	100	100/80	50

- 🔗 Compulsory
- 🧍 Under 14 and under 150cm cannot travel as a front or rear passenger unless they use a suitable child restraint; under 14 over 150cm must wear adult seat belt
- 🍷 0.049% • 0.01% if licence held less than 2 years
- △ Compulsory
- ▪▪ Compulsory
- 🔦 Recommended
- ▮ Recommended
- ⊖ 18 (16 for motorbikes under 50 cc, 20 for over 50 cc)
- ▯ Only allowed with hands-free kit
- LEZ LEZ On A12 motorway non-compliant vehicles banned and certain substances banned, night-time speed restrictions; Steiermark province has LEZs affecting lorries
- Q▪ Must be used during the day by all road users. Headlamp converters compulsory
- ❄ Winter tyres compulsory 1 Nov–15 Apr
- ★ On-the-spot fines imposed
- ★ Radar detectors and dashboard cameras prohibited
- ★ To drive on motorways or expressways, a motorway sticker must be purchased at the border or main petrol station. These are available for 10 days, 2 months or 1 year. Vehicles 3.5 tonnes or over must display an electronic tag.
- ★ Visibility vests compulsory

Belarus (BY)
Area 207,600 sq km (80,154 sq miles)
Population 9,499,000
Capital Minsk (2,101,000)
Languages Belarusian, Russian (both official)
Currency Belarusian ruble = 100 kopek
Website www.belarus.by/en/government

⊙ 🏛	⚠	⚠	🏭
110	90	90	60*
If towing trailer under 750kg			
90	70	70	

*In residential areas limit is 20 km/h • Vehicle towing another vehicle 50 kph limit • If full driving licence held for less than two years, must not exceed 70 kph

- 🔗 Compulsory in front seats, and rear seats if fitted
- 🧍 Under 12 not allowed in front seat and must use appropriate child restraint
- 🍷 0.00%
- △ Compulsory
- ▪▪ Compulsory
- 🔦 Recommended
- ▮ Compulsory
- ⊖ 18
- ▯ Visa, vehicle technical check stamp, international driving permit, green card, health insurance. Even with a green card, local third-party insurance may be imposed at the border
- ▯ Use prohibited
- Q▪ Compulsory during the day Nov–Mar and at all other times in conditions of poor visibility or when towing or being towed
- ❄ Winter tyres compulsory; snow chains recommended
- ★ A temporary vehicle import certificate must be purchased on entry and driver must be registered
- ★ Fees payable for driving on highways
- ★ It is illegal for vehicles to be dirty
- ★ On-the-spot fines imposed
- ★ Radar-detectors prohibited
- ★ Vehicles registered outside Eurasion Economic Union or over 3.5 tons are required to use BelToll device for automatic payment of motorway tolls. See **www.beltoll.by/index.php/en**

Belgium Belgique (B)
Area 30,528 sq km (11,786 sq miles)
Population 11,260,000
Capital Brussels/Bruxelles (1,166,000)
Languages Dutch, French, German (all official)
Currency Euro = 100 cents
Website www.belgium.be/en

⊙ 🏛	⚠	⚠	🏭
120*	120*	90	50**
If towing trailer			
90	90	60	50
Over 3.5 tonnes			
90	90	60	50

*Minimum speed of 70kph may be applied in certain conditions on motorways and some dual carriageways
**Near schools, hospitals and churches the limit may be 30kph

- 🔗 Compulsory
- 🧍 All under 19s under 135cm must wear an appropriate child restraint. Airbags must be deactivated if a rear-facing child seat is used in the front
- 🍷 0.049% △ Compulsory ▪▪ Recommended
- 🔦 Recommended ▮ Compulsory ⊖ 18
- ▯ Only allowed with a hands-free kit
- Q▪ Mandatory at all times for motorcycles and advised during the day in poor conditions for other vehicles
- ★ Cruise control must be deactivated on motorways where indicated
- ★ On-the-spot fines imposed
- ★ Radar detectors prohibited
- ★ Sticker indicating maximum recommended speed for winter tyres must be displayed on dashboard if using them
- ★ Visibility vest compulsory

Bosnia & Herzegovina
Bosna i Hercegovina (BIH)
Area 51,197 km² (19,767 mi²) **Population** 3,872,000
Capital Sarajevo (688,000)
Languages Bosnian/Croatian/Serbian
Currency Convertible Marka = 100 convertible pfenniga
Website www.fbihvlada.gov.ba/english/index.php

⊙ 🏛	⚠	⚠	🏭
130	100	80	50

- 🔗 Compulsory if fitted
- 🧍 Under 12s must sit in rear using an appropriate child restraint. Under-2s may travel in a rear-facing child seat in the front only if the airbags have been deactivated.
- 🍷 0.03% △ Compulsory
- ▪▪ Compulsory
- 🔦 Compulsory
- ▮ Compulsory for LPG vehicles
- ⊖ 18
- ▯ Visa, International Driving Permit, green card
- ▯ Prohibited
- Q▪ Compulsory for all vehicles at all times
- ❄ Winter tyres compulsory 15 Nov–15 Apr; snow chains recommended
- ★ GPS must have fixed speed camera function deactivated; radar detectors prohibited.
- ★ On-the-spot fines imposed
- ★ Visibility vest, tow rope or tow bar compulsory
- ★ Spare wheel compulsory, except for two-wheeled vehicles

Bulgaria Bulgariya (BG)
Area 110,912 sq km (42,822 sq miles)
Population 7,202,000 **Capital** Sofia (1,543,000)
Languages Bulgarian (official), Turkish
Currency Lev = 100 stotinki
Website www.government.bg

⊙ 🏛	⚠	⚠	🏭
130	90	90	50
If towing trailer			
100	70	70	50

- 🔗 Compulsory in front and rear seats
- 🧍 Under 3s not permitted in vehicles with no child restraints; 3–10 year olds must sit in rear
- 🍷 0.05% △ Compulsory ▪▪ Compulsory
- 🔦 Recommended ▮ Compulsory ⊖ 18
- ▯ Photo driving licence preferred; a paper licence must be accompanied by an International Driving Permit. Green card or insurance specific to Bulgaria.
- ▯ Only allowed with a hands-free kit
- Q▪ Compulsory
- ❄ Snow chains should be carried from 1 Nov–1 Mar.
- ★ Fee at border
- ★ GPS must have fixed speed camera function deactivated; radar detectors prohibited
- ★ On-the-spot fines imposed
- ★ Road tax stickers (annual, monthly or weekly) must be purchased at the border and displayed prominently with the vehicle registration number written on them.
- ★ Visibility vest compulsory

Croatia Hrvatska (HR)
Area 56,538 km² (21,829 mi²)
Population 4,285,000 **Capital** Zagreb (1,113,000)
Languages Croatian **Currency** Kuna = 100 lipa
Website https://vlada.gov.hr/

⊙ 🏛	⚠	⚠	🏭
130	110	90	50
Under 24			
⊙ 120	100	90	50
If towing			
⊙ 110	80	80	50

- 🔗 Compulsory if fitted
- 🧍 Children under 12 not permitted in front seat and must use appropriate child seat or restraint in rear.
- 🍷 0.05%, 0.00 % for drivers under 24
- △ Compulsory ▪▪ Compulsory
- 🔦 Compulsory ▮ Recommended ⊖ 18
- ▯ Green card recommended
- ▯ Only allowed with hands-free kit
- Q▪ Compulsory
- ❄ Winter tyres, snow chains and shovel compulsory in winter
- ★ On-the-spot fines imposed
- ★ Radar detectors prohibited
- ★ Tow bar and rope compulsory
- ★ Visibility vest compulsory

Czechia Česko (CZ)
Area 78,864 sq km (30,449 sq miles)
Population 10,553,000 **Capital** Prague/Praha (2,156,000)
Languages Czech (official), Moravian
Currency Czech Koruna = 100 haler
Website www.vlada.cz/en/

⊙ 🏛	⚠	⚠	🏭
130	90	90	50
If towing			
80	80	80	50

- 🔗 Compulsory in front seats and, if fitted, in rear
- 🧍 Children under 36 kg and 150 cm must use appropriate child restraint. Only front-facing child retraints are permitted in the front in vehicles with airbags fitted. Airbags must be deactivated if a rear-facing child seat is used in the front.
- 🍷 0.00% △ Compulsory ▪▪ Compulsory
- 🔦 Compulsory ▮ Compulsory
- ⊖ 18 (17 for motorcycles under 125 cc)
- ▯ Only allowed with a hands-free kit
- LEZ Two-stage LEZ in Prague for vehicles over 3.5 and 6 tonnes. Permit system.
- Q▪ Compulsory at all times
- ❄ Winter tyres compulsory November-March, roads are icy/snow-covered or snow is expected
- ★ GPS must have fixed speed camera function deactivated; radar detectors prohibited
- ★ On-the-spot fines imposed
- ★ Replacement fuses must be carried
- ★ Spectacles or contact lens wearers must carry a spare pair in their vehicle at all times
- ★ Vignette needed for motorway driving, available for 1 year, 60 days, 15 days. Toll specific to lorries introduced 2006, those over 12 tonnes must buy an electronic tag
- ★ Visibility vest compulsory

Denmark Danmark (DK)
Area 43,094 sq km (16,638 sq miles)
Population 5,707,000 **Languages** Danish (official)
Capital Copenhagen / København (2,016,000)
Currency Krone = 100 øre **Website** www.denmark.dk/en

⊙ 🏛	⚠	⚠	🏭
110-130	80-90	80	50*
If towing			
80	70	70	50*

*Central Copenhagen 40 kph

- 🔗 Compulsory front and rear
- 🧍 Under 135cm must use appropriate child restraint; in front permitted only in an appropriate rear-facing seat with any airbags disabled.
- 🍷 0.05% △ Compulsory ▪▪ Recommended
- 🔦 Recommended ▮ Recommended ⊖ 18
- ▯ Only allowed with a hands-free kit
- LEZ Aalborg, Arhus, Copenhagen, Frederiksberg and Odense. Proofs of emissions compliance or compliant filter needed to obtain sticker. Non-compliant vehicles banned.
- Q▪ Must be used at all times
- ★ On-the-spot fines imposed
- ★ Radar detectors prohibited
- ★ Tolls apply on the Storebaeltsbroen and Oresundsbron bridges.
- ★ Visibility vest recommended

Estonia Eesti (EST)
Area 45,100 sq km (17,413 sq miles)
Population 1,316,000 **Capital** Tallinn (543,000)
Languages Estonian (official), Russian
Currency Euro = 100 cents
Website valitsus.ee/en

⊙ 🏛	⚠	⚠	🏭
n/a	90*	90	50
If full driving licence held for less than two years			
90	90	90	50

*In summer, the speed limit on some dual carriageways may be raised to 100/110 kph

- 🔗 Compulsory if fitted
- 🧍 Children too small for adult seatbelts must wear a seat restraint appropriate to their size. Rear-facing safety seats must not be used in the front if an air bag is fitted unless this has been deactivated.
- 🍷 0.00% △ 2 compulsory ▪▪ Compulsory
- 🔦 Recommended ▮ Compulsory ⊖ 18
- ▯ Only allowed with a hands-free kit
- Q▪ Compulsory at all times
- ❄ Winter tyres are compulsory from Dec–Mar. Studded winter tyres are allowed from 15 Oct–31 Mar, but this can be extended to start 1 October and/or end 30 Apr
- ★ A toll system is in operation in Tallinn
- ★ On-the-spot fines imposed

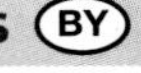

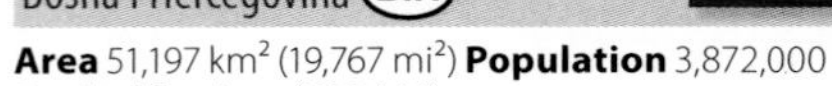

Finland Suomi (FIN)

rea 338,145 sq km (130,557 sq miles)
opulation 5,489,000 **Capital** Helsinki (1,442,000)
anguages Finnish, Swedish (both official)
urrency Euro = 100 cents
Vebsite http://valtioneuvosto.fi/en/frontpage

	120	100	80-100	20/50
Vans, lorries and if towing				
	80	80	60	20/50

100 in summer • If towing a vehicle by rope, cable or rod, nax speed limit 60 kph • Maximum of 80 kph for vans and orries • Speed limits are often lowered in winter

- Compulsory in front and rear
- Below 135 cm must use a child restraint or seat
- 0.05% Compulsory Recommended
- Recommended Recommended
- 18 (motorbikes below 125cc 16)
- Only allowed with hands-free kit
- Must be used at all times
- Winter tyres compulsory Dec–Feb
- ★ On-the-spot fines imposed ★ Radar-detectors prohibited ★ Visibility vest compulsory

France (F)

rea 551,500 sq km (212,934 sq miles)
opulation 64,570,000 **Capital** Paris (12,405,000)
anguages French (official), Breton, Occitan
urrency Euro = 100 cents
Vebsite www.diplomatie.gouv.fr/en/

	130	110	90	50
On wet roads or if full driving licence held for less than 2 years				
	110	100	80	50
f towing below / above 3.5 tonnes gross				
	110/90	100/90	90/80	50

0kph on all roads if fog reduces visibility to less than 50m
Licence will be lost and driver fined for exceeding speed mit by over 50kph

- Compulsory in front seats and, if fitted, in rear
- In rear, 4 or under must have a child safety seat (rear facing if up to 9 months); if 5–10 must use an appropriate restraint system. Under 10 permitted in the front only if rear seats are fully occupied by other under 10s or there are no rear safety belts. In front, if child is in rear-facing child seat, any airbag must be deactivated.
- 0.05%. If towing or with less than 2 years with full driving licence, 0.00% • All drivers/motorcyclists must carry an unused breathalyser to French certification standards, showing an NF number.
- Compulsory Recommended
- Recommended 18
- Use not permitted whilst driving
- LEZ An LEZ operates in the Mont Blanc tunnel. Cars and vans registered before 1997 and motorcycles before 1999 are banned from anywhere inside the Paris Boulevard Périphérique between 8 am and 8 pm on weekdays. Classic cars over 30 years old are exempt.
- Compulsory in poor daytime visibility and at all times for motorcycles
- Winter tyres recommended. Carrying snow chains recommended in winter, to be fitted if driving on snow-covered roads, in accordance with signage.
- ★ GPS must have fixed speed camera function deactivated; radar-detection equipment is prohibited
- ★ On-the-spot fines imposed
- ★ Tolls on motorways. Electronic tag needed if using automatic tolls.
- ★ Visibility vests, to be worn at the roadside in case of emergency or breakdown, must be carried for all vehicle occupants. ★ Motorcyclists and passengers must have four reflective stickers on their helmets (front, back and both sides) and carry visibility vests to be worn at the roadside in case of emergency or breakdown.

Germany Deutschland (D)

rea 357,022 sq km (137,846 sq miles)
opulation 81,459,000 **Capital** Berlin (5,871,000)
anguages German (official) **Currency** Euro = 100 cents
Vebsite www.bundesregierung.de

	*	*	100	50
f towing				
	80	80	80	50

no limit, 130 kph recommended

- Compulsory
- Change children item: Aged 3–12 and under 150cm must use an appropriate child seat or restraint and sit in the rear. In the front, if child under 3 is in a rear-facing seat, airbags must be deactivated.
- 0.05%, 0.0% for drivers 21 or under or with less than two years full licence
- Compulsory Compulsory Recommended
- Recommended 18 (motorbikes: 16 if under 50cc)
- Use permitted only with hands-free kit – also applies to drivers of motorbikes and bicycles
- LEZ More than 60 cities have or are planning LEZs. Proof of compliance needed to acquire sticker. Non-compliant vehicles banned.
- Compulsory during poor daytime visibility and tunnels; recommended at other times. Compulsory at all times for motorcyclists.
- Winter tyres compulsory in all winter weather conditions; snow chains recommended
- ★ GPS must have fixed speed camera function deactivated; radar detectors prohibited ★ On-the-spot fines imposed ★ Tolls on autobahns for lorries ★ Visibility vest compulsory

Greece Ellas (GR)

Area 131,957 sq km (50,948 sq miles)
Population 10,955,000
Capital Athens / Athina (3,754,000)
Languages Greek (official)
Currency Euro = 100 cents
Website www.primeminister.gr/english

	130	110	90	50
Motorbikes, and if towing				
	90	70	70	40

- Compulsory in front seats and, if fitted, in rear
- Under 12 or below 135cm must use appropriate child restraint. In front if child is in rear-facing child seat, any airbags must be deactivated.
- 0.05%, 0.00% for drivers with less than 2 years' full licence and motorcyclists
- Compulsory Compulsory
- Recommended Compulsory 18
- Not permitted.
- Compulsory during poor daytime visibility and at all times for motorcycles
- Snow chains permitted on ice- or snow-covered roads
- ★ Radar-detection equipment is prohibited
- ★ Tolls on several newer motorways.

Hungary Magyarország (H)

Area 93,032 sq km (35,919 sq miles)
Population 9,856,000
Capital Budapest (3,304,000)
Languages Hungarian (official)
Currency Forint = 100 filler
Website www.kormany.hu/en

	130	110	90	50
If towing				
	80	70	70	50

- Compulsory
- Under 135cm and over 3 must be seated in rear and use appropriate child restraint. Under 3 allowed in front only in rear-facing child seat with any airbags deactivated.
- 0.00% Compulsory Compulsory
- Compulsory Recommended 17
- Only allowed with a hands-free kit
- LEZ Budapest has vehicle restrictions on days with heavy dust and is planning an LEZ.
- Compulsory during the day outside built-up areas; compulsory at all times for motorcycles
- Snow chains compulsory where conditions dictate
- ★ Electronic vignette system in use for tolls on several motorways
- ★ Many motorways are toll and operate electronic vignette system with automatic number plate recognition, tickets are available for 4 days, 7 days, 1 month, 1 year
- ★ On-the-spot fines issued
- ★ Radar detectors prohibited
- ★ Tow rope recommended
- ★ Visibility vest compulsory

Iceland Ísland (IS)

Area 103,000 sq km (39,768 sq miles)
Population 333,000
Capital Reykjavík (210,000)
Languages Icelandic
Currency Krona = 100 aurar
Website www.government.is/

	n/a	90	80	50

- Compulsory in front and rear seats
- Under 12 or below 150cm not allowed in front seat and must use appropriate child restraint.
- 0.05% Compulsory Compulsory
- Compulsory Compulsory
- 18; 21 to drive a hire car; 25 to hire a jeep
- Only allowed with a hands-free kit
- Compulsory at all times
- Winter tyres compulsory c.1 Nov–14 Apr (variable)
- ★ Driving off marked roads is forbidden
- ★ Highland roads are not suitable for ordinary cars
- ★ On-the-spot fines imposed

Ireland Eire (IRL)

Area 70,273 sq km (27,132 sq miles)
Population 4,635,000
Capital Dublin (1,801,000)
Languages Irish, English (both official)
Currency Euro = 100 cents
Website www.gov.ie/en/

	120	100	80	50
If towing				
	80	80	80	50

- Compulsory where fitted. Driver responsible for ensuring passengers under 17 comply
- Children 3 and under must be in a suitable child restraint system. Airbags must be deactivated if a rear-facing child seat is used in the front. Those under 150 cm and 36 kg must use appropriate child restraint.
- 0.05% • 0.02% for novice and professional drivers
- Compulsory Recommended
- Recommended Recommended
- 17 (16 for motorbikes up to 125cc; 18 for over 125cc; 18 for lorries; 21 bus/minibus)
- Only allowed with a hands-free kit
- Compulsory for motorbikes at all times and in poor visibility for other vehicles
- ★ Driving is on the left
- ★ GPS must have fixed speed camera function deactivated; radar detectors prohibited
- ★ On-the-spot fines imposed
- ★ Tolls are being introduced on some motorways; the M50 Dublin has barrier-free tolling with number-plate recognition.

Italy Italia (I)

Area 301,318 sq km (116,338 sq miles)
Population 60,671,000
Capital Rome / Roma (4,321,000)
Languages Italian (official)
Currency Euro = 100 cents
Website www.italia.it

	130	110	90	50
If towing				
	80	70	70	50
Less than three years with full licence				
	100	90	90	50
When wet				
	100	90	80	50

Some motorways with emergency lanes have speed limit of 150 kph

- Compulsory in front seats and, if fitted, in rear
- Under 12 not allowed in front seats except in child safety seat; children under 3 must have special seat in the back. For foreign-registered cars, the country of origin's legislation applies.
- 0.05%, but 0.00% for professional drivers or with less than 3 years full licence
- Compulsory Recommended
- Compulsory Recommended
- 18 (14 for mopeds, 16 up to 125cc, 20 up to 350cc)
- Only allowed with hands-free kit
- LEZ Most northern and several southern regions operate seasonal LEZs and many towns and cities have various schemes that restrict access. There is an LEZ in the Mont Blanc tunnel
- Compulsory outside built-up areas, in tunnels, on motorways and dual carriageways and in poor visibility; compulsory at all times for motorcycles
- Snow chains compulsory where signs indicate 15 Oct–15 Apr
- ★ On-the-spot fines imposed
- ★ Radar-detection equipment is prohibited
- ★ Tolls on motorways. Blue lanes accept credit cards; yellow lanes restricted to holders of Telepass pay-toll device.
- ★ Visibility vest compulsory

Kosovo Republika e Kosoves / Republika Kosovo (RKS)

Area 10,887 sq km (4203 sq miles)
Population 1,859,000
Capital Pristina (504,000)
Languages Albanian, Serbian (both official), Bosnian, Turkish, Roma
Currency Euro (Serbian dinar in Serb enclaves)
Website www.kryeministri-ks.net/?page=2,1

	130	80	80	50

- Compulsory
- Under 12 must sit in rear seats
- 0.03%, 0.00% for professional, business and commercial drivers
- Compulsory Compulsory
- Compulsory Compulsory
- 18 (16 for motorbikes less than 125 cc, 14 for mopeds)
- International driving permit, locally purchased third-party insurance (green card is not recognised), documents with proof of ability to cover costs and valid reason for visiting. Visitors from many non-EU countries require a visa.
- Only allowed with a hands-free kit
- Compulsory at all times
- Winter tyres or snow chains compulsory in poor winter weather conditions

Latvia Latvija (LV)

Area 64,589 sq km (24,942 sq miles)
Population 1,974,000
Capital Riga (1,018,000)
Languages Latvian (official), Russian
Currency Euro = 100 cents
Website www.mk.gov.lv/en

	n/a	100	90	50
If towing				
	n/a	80	80	50

In residential areas limit is 20kph • If full driving licence held for less than two years, must not exceed 80 kph

- Compulsory in front seats and if fitted in rear
- If under 12 years and 150cm must use child restraint in front and rear seats
- 0.05%, 0.02% with less than 2 years experience
- Compulsory Compulsory
- Recommended Compulsory
- 18
- Only allowed with hands-free kit
- Must be used at all times all year round
- Winter tyres compulsory for vehicles up to 3.5 tonnes Dec–Feb, but illegal May–Sept
- ★ On-the-spot fines imposed
- ★ Pedestrians have priority
- ★ Radar-detection equipment prohibited
- ★ Visibility vests compulsory

Lithuania Lietuva (LT)

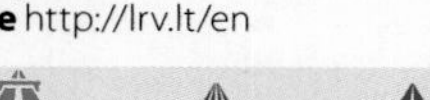

Area 65,200 sq km (25,173 sq miles)
Population 2,876,000
Capital Vilnius (543,000)
Languages Lithuanian (official), Russian, Polish
Currency Euro = 100 cents
Website http://lrv.lt/en

	130	110	90	50
If towing				
	n/a	70	70	50
If licence held for less than two years				
	130	90	70	50

In winter speed limits are reduced by 10–20 km/h

- Compulsory
- Under 12 or below 135 cm not allowed in front seats unless in a child safety seat; under 3 must use appropriate child seat and sit in rear
- 0.04% • 0.02% if full licence held less than 2 years
- Compulsory
- Compulsory
- Recommended
- Compulsory
- 18
- Licences without a photograph must be accompanied by photographic proof of identity, e.g. a passport
- Only allowed with a hands-free kit
- Must be used at all times
- Winter tyres compulsory 10 Nov–1 Apr
- ★ On-the-spot fines imposed
- ★ Visibility vest compulsory

Luxembourg (L)

Area 2,586 sq km (998 sq miles)
Population 563,000
Capital Luxembourg (107,000)
Languages Luxembourgian / Letzeburgish (official), French, German
Currency Euro = 100 cents
Website www.luxembourg.public.lu/en/

	130/110	90	90	50
If towing				
	90	75	75	50

If full driving licence held for less than two years, must not exceed 75 kph • In 20 km/h zones, pedestrians have right of way.

- Compulsory
- Children under 3 must use an appropriate restraint system. Airbags must be disabled if a rear-facing child seat is used in the front. Children 3–18 and/or under 150cm must use a restraint system appropriate to their size. If over 36kg a seatbelt may be used in the back only
- 0.05%, 0.02 for young drivers, drivers with less than 2 years experience and drivers of taxis and commercial vehicles
- Compulsory
- Compulsory (buses)
- Compulsory
- Compulsory (buses, transport of dangerous goods)
- 18
- Use permitted only with hands-free kit
- Compulsory for motorcyclists and in poor visibility for other vehicles
- Winter tyres compulsory in winter weather
- ★ On-the-spot fines imposed
- ★ Visibility vest compulsory

Macedonia Makedonija (MK)

Area 25,713 sq km (9,927 sq miles)
Population 2,069,000
Capital Skopje (507,000)
Languages Macedonian (official), Albanian
Currency Denar = 100 deni
Website www.vlada.mk/?language=en-gb

	120	100	80	50
Newly qualified drivers or if towing				
	100	80	60	50

- Compulsory
- Under 12 not allowed in front seats
- 0.05% • 0.00% for business, commercial and professional drivers and with less than 2 years experience
- Compulsory
- Compulsory
- Compulsory
- Recommended; compulsory for LPG vehicles
- 18 (mopeds 16)
- International driving permit; visa
- Use not permitted whilst driving
- Compulsory at all times
- Winter tyres or snow chains compulsory 15 Nov–15 Mar
- ★ GPS must have fixed speed camera function deactivated; radar detectors prohibited
- ★ Novice drivers may only drive between 11pm and 5am if there is someone over 25 with a valid licence in the vehicle.
- ★ On-the-spot fines imposed
- ★ Tolls apply on many roads
- ★ Tow rope compulsory
- ★ Visibility vest must be kept in the passenger compartment and worn to leave the vehicle in the dark outside built-up areas

Moldova (MD)

Area 33,851 sq km (13,069 sq miles)
Population 3,418,000 **Capital** Chisinau (736,000)
Languages Moldovan / Romanian (official)
Currency Leu = 100 bani **Website** www.moldova.md

	90	90	90	60
If towing or if licence held under 1 year				
	70	70	70	60

- Compulsory in front seats and, if fitted, in rear seats
- Under 12 not allowed in front seats
- 0.00% · Compulsory · Compulsory
- Recommended · Compulsory
- 18 (mopeds and motorbikes, 16; vehicles with more than eight passenger places, taxis or towing heavy vehicles, 21)
- International Driving Permit (preferred), visa
- Only allowed with hands-free kit
- Must use dipped headlights at all times
- Winter tyres recommended Nov–Feb

Montenegro Crna Gora (MNE)

Area 14,026 sq km, (5,415 sq miles)
Population 677,000
Capital Podgorica (187,000)
Languages Serbian (of the Ijekavian dialect)
Currency Euro = 100 cents
Website www.gov.me/en/homepage

	n/a	100	80	50

80kph speed limit if towing a caravan

- Compulsory in front and rear seats
- Under 12 not allowed in front seats. Under-5s must use an appropriate child seat.
- 0.03 % · Compulsory · Compulsory
- Compulsory · Compulsory
- 18 (16 for motorbikes less than 125cc; 14 for mopeds)
- Prohibited
- Must be used at all times
- From mid-Nov to March, driving wheels must be fitted with winter tyres
- ★ An 'eco' tax vignette must be obtained when crossing the border and displayed in the upper right-hand corner of the windscreen
- ★ On-the-spot fines imposed
- ★ Tolls on some primary roads and in the Sozina tunnel between Lake Skadar and the sea
- ★ Visibility vest compulsory

Netherlands Nederland (NL)

Area 41,526 sq km (16,033 sq miles)
Population 17,000,000
Capital Amsterdam 2,431,000 • administrative capital 's-Gravenhage (The Hague) 1,051,000
Languages Dutch (official), Frisian
Currency Euro = 100 cents **Website** www.government.nl

	130	80/100	80/100	50

- Compulsory
- Under 3 must travel in the back, using an appropriate child restraint; 3–18 and under 135cm must use an appropriate child restraint. A rear-facing child seat may be used in front only if airbags are deactivated.
- 0.05%, 0.02% with less than 5 years experience or moped riders under 24
- Compulsory · Recommended
- Recommended · Recommended · 18
- Only allowed with a hands-free kit
- LEZ About 20 cities operate or are planning LEZs. A national scheme is planned.
- Recommended in poor visibility and on open roads. Compulsory for motorcycles.
- ★ On-the-spot fines imposed
- ★ Radar-detection equipment is prohibited

Norway Norge (N)

Area 323,877 sq km (125,049 sq miles)
Population 5,215,000 **Capital** Oslo (1,718,000)
Languages Norwegian (official), Lappish, Finnish
Currency Krone = 100 øre **Website** www.norway.org.uk

	90/100	80	80	30/50
If towing trailer with brakes				
	80	80	80	50
If towing trailer without brakes				
	60	60	60	50

- Compulsory in front seats and, if fitted, in rear
- Children less than 150cm tall must use appropriate child restraint. Children under 4 must use child safety seat or safety restraint (cot). A rear-facing child seat may be used in front only if airbags are deactivated.
- 0.01% · Compulsory · Recommended
- Recommended · Recommended
- 18 (heavy vehicles 18/21)
- Only allowed with a hands-free kit
- LEZ Oslo (administered through national road-toll scheme), with plans for other cities
- Must be used at all times
- Winter tyres or summer tyres with snow chains compulsory for snow- or ice-covered roads
- ★ On-the-spot fines imposed
- ★ Radar-detectors are prohibited
- ★ Tolls apply on some bridges, tunnels and access roads into Bergen, Oslo, Trondheim and Stavangar. Several use electronic fee collection only.
- ★ Visibility vest compulsory

Poland Polska (PL)

Area 323,250 sq km (124,807 sq miles)
Population 38,484,000
Capital Warsaw / Warszawa (3,106,000)
Languages Polish (official) **Currency** Zloty = 100 groszy
Website www.premier.gov.pl/en.html

Motor-vehicle only roads[1], under/over 3.5 tonnes				
	130[2]/80[2]	110/80	100/80	n/a
Motor-vehicle only roads[1] if towing				
	n/a	80	80	n/a
Other roads, under 3.5 tonnes				
	n/a	100	90	50/60[3]
Other roads, 3.5 tonnes or over				
	n/a	80	70	50/60[3]
Other roads, if towing				
	n/a	60	60	30

[1]Indicated by signs with white car on blue background. [2]Minimum speed 40 kph. [3]50 kph 05.00–23.00; 60 kph 23.00–05.00; 20 kph in marked residential areas

- Compulsory in front seats and, if fitted, in rear
- Under 12 and below 150 cm must use an appropriate child restraint. Rear-facing child seats not permitted in vehicles with airbags.
- 0.02% · Compulsory · Recommended
- Recommended · Compulsory
- 18 (mopeds and motorbikes under 125cc – 16)
- Only allowed with a hands-free kit
- Compulsory for all vehicles
- Snow chains permitted only on roads completely covered in snow
- ★ On-the-spot fines imposed
- ★ Radar-detection equipment is prohibited
- ★ Vehicles over 3.5 tonnes (including cars towing caravans) must have a VIAbox for the electronic toll system
- ★ Visibility vests compulsory for drivers of Polish-registered vehicles

Portugal 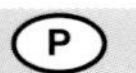(P)

Area 88,797 sq km (34,284 sq miles)
Population 10,427,000
Capital Lisbon / Lisboa (2,822,000)
Languages Portuguese (official)
Currency Euro = 100 cents
Website www.portugal.gov.pt/en.aspx

	120*	90/100	90	50/20
If towing				
	100*	90	80	50

*50kph minimum; 90kph maximum if licence held under 1 year

- Compulsory in front seats and, if fitted, in rear
- Under 12 and below 135cm must travel in the rear in an appropriate child restraint; rear-facing child seats permitted in front only if airbags deactivated
- 0.05%, 0.02% for drivers with less than 3 years with a full licence
- Compulsory · Recommended
- Recommended · Recommended
- 18 (motorcycles under 50cc 17)
- MOT certificate for vehicles over 3 years old, photographic proof of identity (e.g. driving licence or passport) must be carried at all times.
- Only allowed with hands-free kit
- LEZ An LEZ prohibits vehicles without catalytic converters from certain parts of Lisbon. There are plans to extend the scheme city-wide
- Compulsory for motorcycles, compulsory for other vehicles in poor visibility and tunnels
- Visibility vest compulsory
- ★ On-the-spot fines imposed
- ★ Radar-detectors prohibited
- ★ Tolls on motorways; do not use green lanes, these are reserved for auto-payment users. Some motorways require an automatic toll device.
- ★ Wearers of spectacles or contact lenses should carry a spare pair

Romania (RO)

Area 238,391 sq km (92,042 sq miles)
Population 19,511,000 **Capital** Bucharest / Bucuresti (2,272,000) **Languages** Romanian (official), Hungarian
Currency Romanian leu = 100 bani
Website www.gov.ro

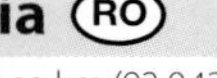

Cars and motorcycles				
	120/130	100	90	50
Vans				
	110	90	80	40
Motorcycles				
	100	80	80	50

For motor vehicles with trailers or if full driving licence has been held for less than one year, speed limits are 20kph lower than those listed above • Jeep-like vehicles: 70kph outside built-up areas but 60kph in all areas if diesel. For mopeds, the speed limit is 45 kph.

- Compulsory
- Under 12s not allowed in front and must use an appropriate restraint in the rear
- 0.00% · Compulsory · Compulsory
- Compulsory · Compulsory · 18
- Only allowed with hands-free kit
- Compulsory outside built-up areas, compulsory everywhere for motorcycles
- Winter tyres compulsory Nov–Mar if roads are snow- or ice-covered, especially in mountainous areas
- ★ Electronic road tax system; price depends on emissions category and length of stay
- ★ Compulsory road tax can be paid for at the border, post offices and some petrol stations
- ★ It is illegal for vehicles to be dirty
- ★ On-the-spot fines imposed
- ★ Tolls on motorways
- ★ Visibility vest compulsory

Russia Rossiya (RUS)

Area 17,075,000 sq km (6,592,800 sq miles)
Population 144,192,000
Capital Moscow / Moskva (11,504,000)
Languages Russian (official), and many others
Currency Russian ruble = 100 kopeks
Website government.ru/en/

	110	90	90	60/20
If licence held for under 2 years				
	70	70	70	60/20

- Compulsory if fitted
- Under 12s permitted only in an appropriate child restraint
- 0.03 % · Compulsory · Compulsory
- Compulsory · Compulsory · 18
- International Driving Permit with Russian translation, visa, green card endorsed for Russia, International Certificate for Motor Vehicles
- Only allowed with a hands-free kit
- Compulsory during the day
- Winter tyres compulsory December-February
- ★ On-the-spot fines imposed
- ★ Picking up hitchhikers is prohibited
- ★ Radar detectors/blockers prohibited
- ★ Road tax payable at the border

Serbia Srbija (SRB)

Area 77,474 sq km, 29,913 sq miles
Population 7,042,000
Capital Belgrade / Beograd (1,167,000)
Languages Serbian **Currency** Dinar = 100 paras
Website www.srbija.gov.rs

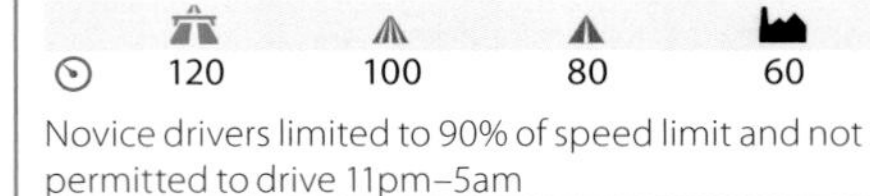

	120	100	80	60

Novice drivers limited to 90% of speed limit and not permitted to drive 11pm–5am

- Compulsory in front and rear seats
- Age 3–12 must be in rear seats and wear seat belt or appropriate child restraint; under 3 in rear-facing child seat permitted in front only if airbag deactivated
- 0.03%, but 0.0% for commercial drivers, motorcyclists, or if full licence held less than 1 year
- Compulsory · Compulsory
- Compulsory · Compulsory
- 18 (16 for motorbikes less than 125cc; 14 for mopeds)
- International Driving Permit, green card or locally bought third-party insurance
- Compulsory
- Winter tyres compulsory Nov–Apr for vehicles up to 3.5 tonnes. Carrying snow chains recommended in winter as these may have to be fitted if driving on snow-covered roads, in accordance with signage.
- ★ 3-metre tow bar or rope
- ★ 80km/h speed limit if towing a caravan
- ★ Spare wheel compulsory
- ★ On-the-spot fines imposed
- ★ Radar detectors prohibited
- ★ Tolls on motorways and some primary roads
- ★ Visibility vest compulsory

Slovakia Slovenska Republika (SK)

Area 49,012 sq km (18,923 sq miles)
Population 5,416,000 **Capital** Bratislava (660,000)
Languages Slovak (official), Hungarian
Currency Euro = 100 cents
Website www.government.gov.sk

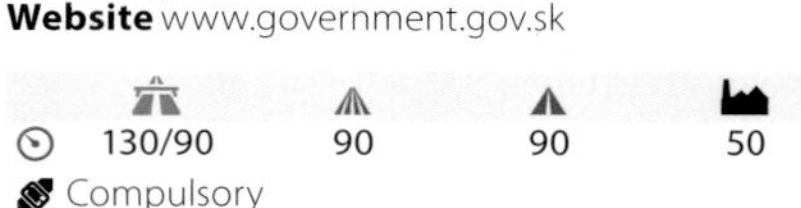

	130/90	90	90	50

- Compulsory
- Under 12 or below 150cm must be in rear in appropriate child restraint
- 0.0% · Compulsory · Compulsory
- Compulsory · Recommended
- 18 (15 for mopeds)
- International driving permit, proof of health insurance
- Only allowed with a hands-free kit
- Compulsory at all times
- Winter tyres compulsory
- ★ On-the-spot fines imposed
- ★ Radar-detection equipment is prohibited
- ★ Tow rope recommended
- ★ Vignette required for motorways, car valid for 1 year, 30 days, 7 days; lorry vignettes carry a higher charge.
- ★ Visibility vests compulsory

Slovenia Slovenija (SLO)

Area 20,256 sq km (7,820 sq miles)
Population 2,063,000 **Capital** Ljubljana (279,000)
Languages Slovene **Currency** Euro = 100 cents
Website www.gov.si

	130	90*	90*	50
If towing				
	80	80*	80*	50

*70kph in urban areas

- Compulsory
- Below 150cm must use appropriate child restraint. A rear-facing baby seat may be used in front only if airbags are deactivated.
- 0.05%, but 0.0% for commercial drivers, under 21s or with less than one year with a full licence
- Compulsory · Compulsory
- Compulsory · Recommended
- 18 (motorbikes up to 125cc – 16, up to 350cc – 18)
- Licences without photographs must be accompanied by an International Driving Permit
- Only allowed with hands-free kit
- Must be used at all times
- Snow chains or winter tyres compulsory mid-Nov to mid-March, and in wintery conditions at other times
- ★ On-the-spot fines imposed
- ★ Vignettes valid for variety of periods compulsory for vehicles below 3.5 tonnes for toll roads. Write your vehicle registration number on the vignette before displaying it. For heavier vehicles electronic tolling system applies; several routes are cargo-traffic free during high tourist season.
- ★ Visibility vest compulsory

Spain España (E)

Area 497,548 sq km (192,103 sq miles)
Population 46,423,000
Capital Madrid (6,489,000)
Languages Castilian Spanish (official), Catalan, Galician, Basque **Currency** Euro = 100 cents
Website www.lamoncloa.gob.es/lang/en

	120*	100*	90	50
If towing				
	80	80	70	50

*Urban motorways and dual carriageways 80 kph

- Compulsory
- Under 135cm and below 12 must use appropriate child restraint
- 0.05%, 0.03% if less than 2 years full licence or if vehicle is over 3.5 tonnes or carries more than 9 passengers
- Two compulsory (one for in front, one for behind)
- Recommended
- Compulsory · Recommended
- 18 (21 for heavy vehicles; 16 for motorbikes up to 125cc
- Compulsory for motorcycles and in poor daytime visibility for other vehicles.
- Snow chains recommended for mountainous areas in winter
- ★ Drivers who wear spectacles or contact lenses must carry a spare pair
- ★ Radar-detection equipment is prohibited
- ★ Spare wheel compulsory
- ★ Tolls on motorways
- ★ Visibility vest compulsory

Sweden Sverige (S)

Area 449,964 sq km (173,731 sq miles)
Population 9,875,000
Capital Stockholm (2,192,000)
Languages Swedish (official), Finnish
Currency Swedish krona = 100 ore
Website www.sweden.gov.se

	90–120	80	70–100	30–60
If towing trailer with brakes				
	80	80	70	50

- Compulsory in front and rear seats
- Under 15 or below 135cm must use an appropriate child restraint and may sit in the front only if airbag is deactivated; rear-facing baby seat permitted in front only if airbag deactivated.
- 0.02% · Compulsory · Recommended
- Recommended · Recommended · 18
- Licences without a photograph must be accompanie by photographic proof of identity, e.g. a passport
- LEZ Gothenberg, Helsingborg, Lund, Malmo, Mölndal and Stockholm have LEZs, progressively prohibiting vehicles 6 or more years old.
- Must be used at all times
- 1 Dec–31 Mar winter tyres, anti-freeze and shovel compulsory
- ★ On-the-spot fines imposed
- ★ Radar-detection equipment is prohibited

Switzerland Schweiz (CH)

Area 41,284 sq km (15,939 sq miles)
Population 8,212,000
Capital Bern (407,000)
Languages French, German, Italian, Romansch (all officia
Currency Swiss Franc = 100 centimes / rappen
Website www.admin.ch

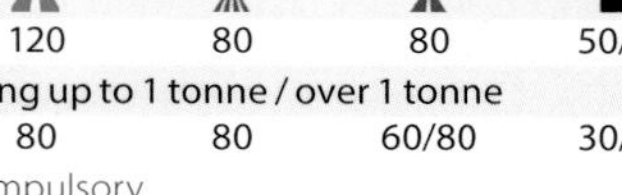

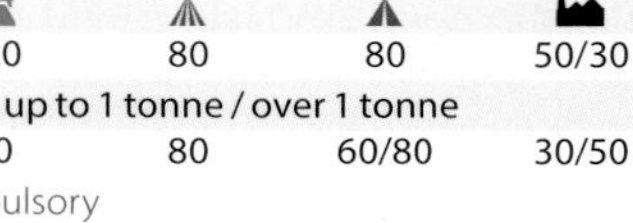

	120	80	80	50/30
If towing up to 1 tonne / over 1 tonne				
	80	80	60/80	30/50

- Compulsory
- Up to 12 years or below 150 cm must use an appropriate child restraint. Children 6 and under must sit in the rear.
- 0.05%, but 0.0% for commercial drivers or with less tha three years with a full licence
- Compulsory · Recommended
- Recommended · Recommended
- 18 (mopeds up to 50cc – 16)
- Only allowed with a hands-free kit
- Compulsory
- Winter tyres recommended Nov–Mar; snow chains compulsory in designated areas in poor winter weath

- ★ GPS must have fixed speed camera function deactivated; radar detectors prohibited
- ★ Motorways are all toll and for vehicles below 3.5 tonnes a vignette must be purchased at the border. The vignette is valid for one calendar year. Vehicles over 3.5 tonnes must have an electronic tag for travel on any road.
- ★ On-the-spot fines imposed
- ★ Pedestrians have right of way
- ★ Picking up hitchhikers is prohibited on motorways and main roads
- ★ Spectacles or contact lens wearers must carry a spare pair in their vehicle at all times

Turkey Türkiye (TR)

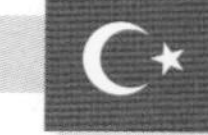

Area 774,815 sq km (299,156 sq miles)
Population 79,464,000
Capital Ankara (5,150,000)
Languages Turkish (official), Kurdish
Currency New Turkish lira = 100 kurus
Website www.mfa.gov.tr/default.en.mfa

⊙	120	90	90	50
If towing				
⊙	80	80	80	40

- Compulsory if fitted
- Under 150 cm and below 36kg must use suitable child restraint. If above 136 cm may sit in the back without child restraint. Under 3s can only travel in the front in a rear facing seat if the airbag is deactivated. Children 3–12 may not travel in the front seat.
- 0.00%
- Two compulsory (one in front, one behind)
- Compulsory   Compulsory
- Compulsory   18
- International driving permit advised, and required for use with licences without photographs; note that Turkey is in both Europe and Asia, green card/UK insurance that covers whole of Turkey or locally bought insurance, e-visa obtained in advance.
- Prohibited
- Compulsory in daylight hours
- ★ Spare wheel compulsory
- ★ On-the-spot fines imposed
- ★ Several motorways, and the Bosphorus bridges are toll roads
- ★ Tow rope and tool kit must be carried

Ukraine Ukraina (UA)

Area 603,700 sq km (233,088 sq miles)
Population 44,429,000
Capital Kiev / Kyviv (3,375,000)
Languages Ukrainian (official), Russian
Currency Hryvnia = 100 kopiykas
Website www.kmu.gov.ua/control/en

⊙	130	110	90	60
If towing				
⊙	80	80	80	60

Speed limit in pedestrian zone 20 kph

- Compulsory in front and rear seats
- Under 12 and below 145cm must use an appropriate child restraint and sit in rear
- 0.02% – if use of medication can be proved. Otherwise 0.00%
- Compulsory   Compulsory
- Optional   Compulsory   18
- International Driving Permit, visa, International Certificate for Motor Vehicles, green card
- No legislation
- Compulsory in poor daytime and from Oct–Apr
- Winter tyres compulsory Nov–Apr in snowy conditions
- ★ A road tax is payable on entry to the country.
- ★ On-the-spot fines imposed
- ★ Tow rope and tool kit recommended

United Kingdom (GB)

Area 241,857 sq km (93,381 sq miles)
Population 65,716,000 **Capital** London (13,880,000)
Languages English (official), Welsh (also official in Wales), Gaelic
Currency Sterling (pound) = 100 pence
Website www.direct.gov.uk

⊙	112	112	96	48
If towing				
⊙	96	96	80	48

- Compulsory in front seats and if fitted in rear seats
- Under 3 not allowed in front seats except with appropriate restraint, and in rear must use child restraint if available; in front 3–12 or under 135cm must use appropriate child restraint, in rear must use appropriate child restraint (or seat belt if no child restraint is available, e.g. because two occupied restraints prevent fitting of a third).
- 0.08% (England, Northern Ireland, Wales), 0.05% (Scotland)
- Recommended   Recommended
- Recommended   Recommended
- 17 (16 for mopeds)
- Only allowed with hands-free kit
- LEZ London's LEZ operates by number-plate recognition; non-compliant vehicles face hefty daily charges. Foreign-registered vehicles must register.
- ★ Driving is on the left
- ★ On-the-spot fines imposed
- ★ Smoking is banned in all commercial vehicles
- ★ Some toll motorways and bridges

Ski resorts

The resorts listed are popular ski centres, therefore road access to most is normally good and supported by road clearing during snow falls. However, mountain driving is never predictable and drivers should make sure they take suitable snow chains as well as emergency provisions and clothing. Listed for each resort are: the atlas page and grid square; the resort/minimum piste altitude (where only one figure is shown, they are at the same height) and maximum altitude of its own lifts; the number of lifts and gondolas (the total for lift-linked resorts); the season start and end dates (snow cover allowing); whether snow is augmented by cannon; the nearest town (with its distance in km) and, where available, the website and/or telephone number of the local tourist information centre or ski centre ('00' prefix required for calls from the UK).

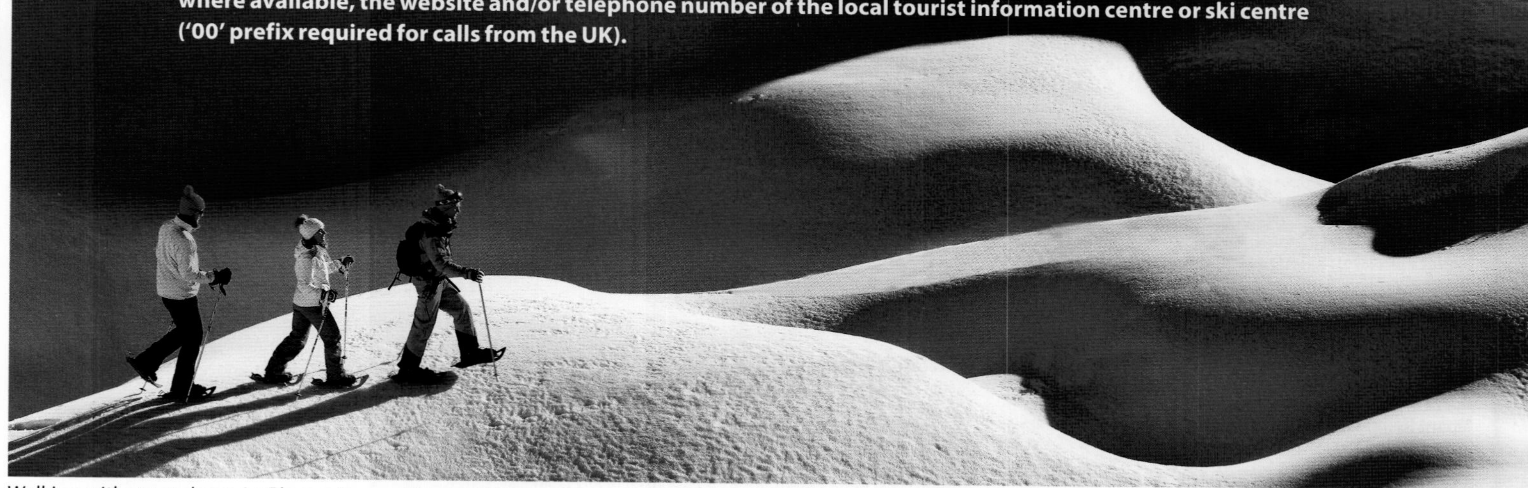

Walking with snow shoes, La Plagne, France blickwinkel / Alamy

The ❄ symbol indicates resorts with snow cannon

Andorra

Pyrenees

Pas de la Casa / Grau Roig 91 A4 ❄ 2050–2640m • 31 lifts • Dec–Apr • Andorra La Vella (30km) 💻www.pasdelacasa.com • *Access via Envalira Pass (2407m), highest in Pyrenees, snow chains essential.*

Austria

Alps

Bad Gastein 72 A3 ❄ 1050/1100–2700m • 50 lifts • Dec–Mar • St Johann im Pongau (45km) ℹ+43 6432 3393 0 💻www.gastein.com

Bad Hofgastein 72 A3 ❄ 860–2295m • 50 lifts • Dec–Mar • St Johann im Pongau (40km) ℹ+43 6432 3393 0 💻www.gastein.com/en/region-villages/bad-hofgastein

Bad Kleinkirchheim 72 B3 ❄ 1070–2310m • 27 lifts • Dec–Mar • Villach (35km) ℹ+43 4240 8212 💻www.badkleinkirchheim.at

Ehrwald 71 A5 ❄ 1000–2965m • 24 lifts • Dec–Apr • Imst (30km) ℹ+43 5673 2395 💻www.wetterstein-bahnen.at/en

Innsbruck 71 A6 ❄ 574/850–3200m • 59 lifts • Dec–Apr • Innsbruck ℹ+ 43 512 56 2000 💻www.innsbruck.info/en/ • *Motorway normally clear. The motorway through to Italy and through the Arlberg Tunnel are both toll roads.*

Ischgl 71 A5 ❄ 1340/1380–2900m • 101 lifts • Dec–May • Landeck (25km) ℹ+43 50990 100 💻www.ischgl.com • *Car entry to resort prohibited between 2200hrs and 0600hrs.*

Kaprun 72 A2 ❄ 885/770–3030m, • 25 lifts • Nov–Apr • Zell am See (10km) ℹ+43 6542 770 💻www.zellamsee-kaprun.com

Kirchberg in Tirol 72 A2 ❄ 860–2000m • 197 lifts • Nov–Apr • Kitzbühel (6km) ℹ+43 57507 2100 💻www.kitzbueheler-alpen.com/en • *Easily reached from Munich International Airport (120 km)*

Kitzbühel (Brixen im Thale) 72 A2 ❄ 800/1210–2000m • 197 lifts • Dec–Apr • Wörgl (40km) ℹ+43 57057 2200 💻www.kitzbueheler-alpen.com/en

Lech/Oberlech 71 A5 ❄ 1450–2810m • 66 lifts • Dec–Apr • Bludenz (50km) ℹ+43 5583 2161 0 💻www.lechzuers.com • *Roads normally cleared but keep chains accessible because of altitude.*

Mayrhofen 72 A1 ❄ 630–2500m • 57 lifts • Dec–Apr • Jenbach (35km) ℹ+43 5285 6760 💻www.mayrhofen.at • *Chains rarely required.*

Obertauern 72 A3 ❄ 1740/1640–2350m • 26 lifts • Dec–Apr • Radstadt (20km) ℹ+43 6456 7252 💻www.obertauern.com • *Roads normally cleared but chain accessibility recommended. Camper vans and caravans not allowed; park these in Radstadt*

Saalbach Hinterglemm 72 A2 ❄ 1030/1100–2100m • 70 lifts • Nov–Apr • Zell am See (19km) ℹ+43 6541 6800-68 💻www.saalbach.com • *Both village centres are pedestrianised and there is a good ski bus service during the daytime*

St Anton am Arlberg 71 A5 ❄ 1300–2810m • 41 lifts • Dec–Apr • Innsbruck (104km) ℹ+43 5446 22690 💻www.stantonamarlberg.com

Schladming 72 A3 ❄ 745–1900m • 85 lifts • Dec–Mar • Schladming ℹ+ 43 36 87 233 10 💻www.schladming-dachstein.at

Serfaus 71 A5 ❄ 1427/1200–2820m • 67 lifts • Dec–Apr • Landeck (30km) ℹ+43 5476 6239 💻www.serfaus-fiss-ladis.at • *Private vehicles banned from village. Use Dorfbahn Serfaus, an underground funicular which runs on an air cushion.*

Sölden 71 B6 ❄ 1380–3250m, • 33 lifts • Sep-Apr (glacier); Nov-Apr (main area) • Imst (50km) ℹ+43 57200 200 💻www.soelden.com • *Roads normally cleared but snow chains recommended because of altitude. The route from Italy and the south over the Timmelsjoch via Obergurgl is closed Oct–May and anyone arriving from the south should use the Brenner Pass motorway.*

Zell am See 72 A2 ❄ 750–1950m • 53 lifts • Dec–Mar • Zell am See ℹ+43 6542 770 💻www.zellamsee-kaprun.com • *Low altitude, so good access and no mountain passes to cross.*

Zell im Zillertal (Zell am Ziller) 72 A1 ❄ 580/930–2410m • 22 lifts • Dec–Apr • Jenbach (25km) ℹ+43 5282 7165–226 💻www.zillertalarena.com

Zürs 71 A5 ❄ 1720/1700–2450m • 97 lifts • Dec–Apr • Bludenz (30km) ℹ+43 5583 2245 💻www.lech-zuers.at • *Roads normally cleared but keep chains accessible because of altitude. Village has garage with 24-hour self-service gas/petrol, breakdown service and wheel chains supply.*

France

Alps

Alpe d'Huez 79 A5 ❄ 1860–3330m • 85 lifts • Dec–Apr • Grenoble (63km) 💻www.alpedhuez.com • *Snow chains may be required on access road to resort.*

Avoriaz 70 B1 ❄ 1800/1100–2280m • 35 lifts • Dec–May • Morzine (14km) ℹ+33 4 50 74 72 72 💻www.morzine-avoriaz.com • *Chains may be required for access road from Morzine. Car-free resort, park on edge of village. Horse-drawn sleigh service available.*

Chamonix-Mont-Blanc 70 C1 ❄ 1035–3840m • 49 lifts • Dec–Apr • Martigny (38km) ℹ+33 4 50 53 99 98 • 💻www.chamonix.com

Chamrousse 79 A4 ❄ 1700–2250m • 26 lifts • Dec–Apr • Grenoble (30km) 💻www.chamrousse.com • *Roads normally cleared, keep chains accessible because of altitude.*

Châtel 70 B1 ❄ 1200/1110–2200m • 41 lifts • Dec–Apr • Thonon-Les-Bains (35km) ℹ+33 4 50 73 22 44 💻http://info.chatel.com/english-version.html

Courchevel 70 C1 ❄ 1750/1300–2470m • 67 lifts • Dec–Apr • Moûtiers (23km) 💻www.courchevel.com • *Roads normally cleared but keep chains accessible. Traffic 'discouraged' within the four resort bases.*

Flaine 70 B1 ❄ 1600–2500m • 26 lifts • Dec–Apr • Cluses (25km) ℹ+33 4 50 90 80 01 💻www.flaine.com • *Keep chains accessible for D6 from Cluses to Flaine. Car access for depositing luggage and passengers only. 1500-space car park outside resort. Near Sixt-Fer-á-Cheval.*

La Clusaz 69 C6 ❄ 1100–2600m • 55 lifts • Dec–Apr • Annecy (32km) 💻www.laclusaz.com • *Roads normally clear but keep chains accessible for final road from Annecy.*

La Plagne 70 C1 ❄ 2500/1250–3250m • 109 lifts • Dec–Apr Moûtiers (32km) 💻www.la-plagne.com • *Ten different centres up to 2100m altitude. Road access via Bozel, Landry or Aime normally cleared. Linked to Les Arcs by cablecar*

Les Arcs 70 C1 ❄ 1600/1200–3230m • 77 lifts • Dec–May • Bourg-St-Maurice (15km) ℹ+33 4 79 07 12 57 💻www.lesarcs.com • *Four base areas up to 2000 metres; keep chains accessible. Pay parking at edge of each base resort. Linked to La Plagne by cablecar*

Les Carroz d'Araches 70 B1 ❄ 1140–2500m • 80 lifts • Dec–Apr • Cluses (13km) 💻www.lescarroz.com

Les Deux-Alpes 79 B5 ❄ 1650/1300–3600m • 55 lifts • Dec–Apr • Grenoble (75km) ℹ+33 4 76 79 22 00 💻www.les2alpes.com/en • *Roads normally cleared, however snow chains recommended for D213 up from valley road (D1091).*

Les Gets 70 B1 ❄ 1170/1000–2000m • 52 lifts • Dec–Apr • Cluses (18km) ℹ+33 4 50 75 80 80 💻www.lesgets.com

Les Ménuires 69 C6 ❄ 1815/1850–3200m • 40 lifts • Dec–Apr • Moûtiers (27km) 💻www.lesmenuires.com • *Keep chains accessible for D117 from Moûtiers.*

Les Sept Laux Prapoutel 69 C6 ❄ 1350–2400m, • 24 lifts • Dec–Apr • Grenoble (38km) 💻www.les7laux.com (French only) • *Roads normally cleared, however keep chains accessible for mountain road up from the A41 motorway. Near St Sorlin d'Arves.*

Megève 69 C6 ❄ 1100/1050–2350m • 79 lifts • Dec–Apr • Sallanches (12km) 💻www.megeve.com • *Horse-drawn sleigh rides available.*

Méribel 69 C6 ❄ 1400/1100–2950m • 61 lifts • Dec–May • Moûtiers (18km) ℹ+33 4 79 08 60 01 💻www.meribel.net • *Keep chains accessible for 18km to resort on D90 from Moûtiers.*

Morzine 70 B1 ❄ 1000–2460m • 67 lifts, • Dec–Apr • Thonon-Les-Bains (30km) ℹ+33 4 50 74 72 72 💻www.morzine-avoriaz.com

Pra Loup 79 B5 ❄ 1600/1500–2500m • 53 lifts • Dec–Apr • Barcelonnette (10km) ℹ+33 4 92 84 10 04 💻www.praloup.com • *Roads normally cleared but chains accessibility recommended.*

Risoul 79 B5 ❄ 1850/1650–2750m • 59 lifts • Dec–Apr • Briançon (40km) ℹ+33 4 92 46 02 60 💻www.risoul.com • *Keep chains accessible. Near Guillestre. Linked with Vars Les Claux*

St-Gervais Mont-Blanc 70 C1 ❄ 850/1150–2350m • 27 lifts • Dec–Apr • Sallanches (10km) ℹ+33 4 50 47 76 08 💻www.saintgervais.com/en

Serre Chevalier 79 B5 ❄ 1350/1200–2800m • 77 lifts • Dec–Apr • Briançon (10km) ℹ+ 33 4 92 24 98 98 💻www.serre-chevalier.com • *Made up of 13 small villages along the valley road, which is normally cleared.*

Tignes 70 C1 ❄ 2100/1550–3450m • 87 lifts • Jan–Dec • Bourg St Maurice (26km) ℹ+33 4 79 40 04 40 💻www.tignes.net • *Keep chains accessible because of altitude.*

Val d'Isère 70 C1 ❄ 1850/1550–3450m • 87 lifts • Dec–Apr • Bourg-St-Maurice (30km) ℹ+33 4 79 06 06 60 💻www.valdisere.com • *Roads normally cleared but keep chains accessible.*

Val Thorens 69 C6 ❄ 2300/1850–3200m • 29 lifts • Dec–Apr • Moûtiers (37km) ℹ+33 4 79 00 08 08 💻www.valthorens.com • *Chains essential – highest ski resort in Europe. Obligatory paid parking on edge of resort.*

Valloire 69 C6 ❄ 1430–2600m • 34 lifts • Dec–Apr • Modane (20km) ℹ+33 4 79 59 03 96 💻www.valloire.net • *Road normally clear up to the Col du Galbier, to the south of the resort, which is closed from 1st November to 1st June. Linked to Valmeinier.*

Valmeinier 69 C6 ❄ 1500–2600m • 34 lifts • Dec–Apr • St Michel de Maurienne (47km) ℹ+33 4 79 59 53 69 💻www.valmeinier.com • *Access from north on D1006 / D902. Col du Galbier, to the south of the resort closed from 1st November to 1st June. Linked to Valloire.*

Valmorel 69 C6 ❄ 1400–2550m • 90 lifts • Dec–Apr • Moûtiers (15km) ℹ+33 4 79 09 85 55 💻www.valmorel.com • *Near St Jean-de-Belleville. Linked with ski areas of Doucy-Combelouvière and St François-Longchamp.*

Vars Les Claux 79 B5 ❄ 1850/1650–2750m • 59 lifts • Dec–Apr • Briançon (40km) ℹ+33 4 92 46 51 31 💻www.vars.com/en/winter • *Four base resorts up to 1850 metres. Keep chains accessible. Linked with Risoul.*

Villard de Lans 79 A4 ❄ 1050/1160–2170m • 28 lifts • Dec–Apr • Grenoble (32km) ℹ+33 4 76 95 10 38 💻www.villarddelans.com

Pyrenees

Font-Romeu 91 A5 ❄ 1800/1600–2200m • 25 lifts • Nov–Apr • Perpignan (87km) ℹ+33 4 68 30 68 30 💻www.font-romeu.fr • *Roads normally cleared but keep chains accessible.*

Saint-Lary Soulan 77 D3 ❄ 830/1650/1700–2515m • 31 lifts • Dec–Mar • Tarbes (75km) ℹ+33 5 62 39 50 81 💻www.saintlary.com • *Access roads constantly cleared of snow.*

Vosges

La Bresse-Hohneck 60 B2 ❄ 500/900–1350m • 33 lifts • Dec–Mar • Cornimont (6km) ℹ+33 3 29 25 41 29 💻www.labresse.net

Germany

Alps

Garmisch-Partenkirchen 71 A6 ❄ 700–2830m • 38 lifts • Dec–Apr • Munich (95km) ☎ +49 8821 180 700 • 🖥 www.gapa.de • *Roads usually clear, chains rarely needed.*

Oberaudorf 62 C3 ❄ 480–1850m • 30 lifts • Dec–Apr • Kufstein (15km) 🖥 www.oberaudorf.de • *Motorway normally kept clear. Near Bayrischzell.*

Oberstdorf 71 A5 815m • 26 lifts • Dec–Apr • Sonthofen (15km) ☎ +49 8322 7000 • 🖥 www.oberstdorf.de/en

Rothaargebirge

Winterberg 51 B4 ❄ 700/620–830m • 19 lifts • Dec–Mar • Brilon (30km) ☎ +49 2981 925 00 • 🖥 www.winterberg.de (German and Dutch only) • *Roads usually cleared, chains rarely required.*

Greece

Central Greece

Mount Parnassos: Kelaria-Fterolakka 116 D4 1640–2260m • 16 lifts • Dec–Apr • Amfiklia 🖥 +30 22340 22694-5 🖥 www.parnassos-ski.gr

Mount Parnassos: Gerondovrahos 116 D4 1800–1900m • 3 lifts • Dec–Apr • Amfiklia ☎ +30 29444 70371

Peloponnisos

Mount Helmos: Kalavrita Ski Centre 117 D4 1650–2100m • 7 lifts • Dec–Apr • Kalavrita ☎ +30 276920 24451-2 🖥 www.kalavrita-ski.gr

Mount Menalo: Ostrakina 117 E4 1500–1600m • 4 lifts • Dec–Mar • Tripoli ☎ +30 27960 22227

Macedonia

Mount Falakro: Agio Pnevma 116 A6 1720/1620–2230m • 9 lifts • Dec–Apr • Drama ☎ + 30 25210 23691

Mount Vasilitsa: Vasilitsa 116 B3 1750/1800–2113m • 8 lifts • Dec–Mar • Konitsa ☎ +30 24620 84850 🖥 www.vasilitsa.com (Greek only)

Mount Vermio: Seli 116 B4 1500–1900m • 11 lifts • Dec–Mar • Kozani ☎ +30 23310 26237 🖥 www.seli-ski.gr (in Greek)

Mount Vermio: Tria-Pente Pigadia 116 B3 1420–2005m • 7 lifts • Dec–Mar • Ptolemaida ☎ +30 23320 44464 🖥 www.3-5pigadia.gr (Greek only)

Mount Verno: Vigla 116 B3 1650–1900m • 5 lifts • Dec–Mar • Florina ☎ +30 23850 22354 🖥 www.vigla-ski.gr (in Greek)

Mount Vrondous: Lailias 116 A5 1600–1850m • 4 lifts • Dec–Mar • Serres ☎ +30 23210 53790

Thessalia

Mount Pilio: Agriolefkes 116 C5 1300–1500m • 4 lifts • Dec–Mar • Volos ☎ +30 24280 73719

Italy

Alps

Bardonecchia 79 A5 ❄ 1312–2750m • 21 lifts • Dec–Apr • Bardonecchia ☎ + 39 122 99032 🖥 www.bardonecchiaski.com • *Resort reached through the 11km Frejus tunnel from France, roads normally cleared.*

Bórmio 71 B5 ❄ 1200/1230–3020m • 24 lifts • Dec–Apr • Tirano (40km) 🖥 www.bormio.com • *Tolls payable in Ponte del Gallo Tunnel, open 0800hrs–2000hrs.*

Breuil-Cervinia 70 C2 ❄ 2050–3500m • 21 lifts • Jan–Dec • Aosta (54km) ☎ +39 166 944311 🖥 www.cervinia.it • *Snow chains strongly recommended. Bus from Milan airport.*

Courmayeur 70 C1 ❄ 1200–2760m • 21 lifts • Dec–Apr • Aosta (40km) ☎ +39 165 841612 🖥 www.courmayeurmontblanc.it • *Access through the Mont Blanc tunnel from France. Roads constantly cleared.*

Limone Piemonte 80 B1 ❄ 1000/1050–2050m • 29 lifts • Dec–Apr • Cuneo (27km) 🖥 www.limonepiemonte.it • *Roads normally cleared, chains rarely required.*

Livigno 71 B5 ❄ 1800–3000m • 31 lifts • Nov–May • Zernez (CH) (27km) ☎ +39 342 052200 🖥 www.livigno.com • *Keep chains accessible. The direction of traffic through Munt la Schera Tunnel to/from Zernez is regulated on Saturdays. Check in advance.*

Sestrière 79 B5 ❄ 2035/1840–2840m • 92 lifts • Dec–Apr • Oulx (22km) ☎ +39 122 755444 🖥 www.sestriere-online.com • *One of Europe's highest resorts; although roads are normally cleared keep chains accessible.*

Appennines

Roccaraso – Aremogna 103 B7 ❄ 1285/1240–2140m • 24 lifts • Dec–Apr • Castel di Sangro (7km) ☎ +39 864 62210 🖥 www.roccaraso.net (in Italian)

Dolomites

Andalo – Fai della Paganella 71 B5 ❄ 1042/1050/2125m • 19 lifts • Dec–Apr • Trento (40km) 🖥 www.visitdolomitipaganella.it ☎ +39 461 585836

Arabba 72 B1 ❄ 1600/1450–2950m • 29 lifts • Dec–Mar • Brunico (45km) ☎ +39 436 780019 🖥 www.arabba.it • *Roads normally cleared but keep chains accessible.*

Cortina d'Ampezzo 72 B2 ❄ 1224/1050–2930m • 37 lifts • Dec–Apr • Belluno (72km) 🖥 www.cortina.dolomiti.org • *Access from north on route 51 over the Cimabanche Pass may require chains.*

Corvara (Alta Badia) 72 B1 ❄ 1568–2500m • 56 lifts • Dec–Apr • Brunico (38km) 🖥 www.altabadia.it • *Roads normally clear but keep chains accessible.*

Madonna di Campiglio 71 B5 ❄ 1550/1500–2600m • 72 lifts • Dec–Apr • Trento (60km) ☎ +39 465 447501 🖥 www.campigliodolomiti.it/homepage • *Roads normally cleared but keep chains accessible. Linked to Folgarida and Marilleva.*

Moena di Fassa (Sorte/Ronchi) 72 B1 ❄ 1184/1450–2520m • 8 lifts • Dec–Apr • Bolzano (40km) ☎ +39 462 609770 🖥 www.fassa.com

Selva di Val Gardena/Wolkenstein Groden 72 B1 ❄ 1563/1570–2450m • 81 lifts • Dec–Apr • Bolzano (40km) ☎ +39 471 777777 🖥 www.valgardena.it • *Roads normally cleared but keep chains accessible.*

Norway

Hemsedal 32 B5 ❄ 700/640–1450m • 24 lifts • Nov–May • Honefoss (150km) ☎ +47 32 055030 🖥 www.hemsedal.com • *Be prepared for extreme weather conditions.*

Slovakia

Chopok (Jasna-Chopok) 65 B5 ❄ 900/950–1840m • 17 lifts • Dec–Apr • Jasna ☎ +421 907 886644 🖥 www.jasna.sk

Donovaly 65 B5 ❄ 913–1360m • 17 lifts • Nov–Apr • Ruzomberok ☎ +421 48 4199900 🖥 www.parksnow.sk/zima

Martinské Hole 65 A4 1250/1150–1456m • 8 lifts • Nov–May • Zilina ☎ +421 43 430 6000 🖥 www.martinky.com (in Slovak only)

Plejsy 65 B6 470–912m • 9 lifts • Dec–Mar • Krompachy ☎ +421 53 429 8015 🖥 www.plejsy.sk

Strbske Pleso 65 A6 1380–1825m • 7 lifts • Dec–Mar • Poprad ☎ +421 917 682 260 🖥 www.vt.sk

Slovenia

Julijske Alpe

Kanin (Bovec) 72 B3 460/1600–2389m • 5 lifts • Dec–Apr • Bovec ☎ +386 5 384 1919 🖥 www.boveckanin.si

Kranjska Gora 72 B3 ❄ 800–1210m • 19 lifts • Dec–Mar • Kranjska Gora ☎ +386 4 5809 440 🖥 www.kranjska-gora.si

Vogel 72 B3 570–1800m • 11 lifts • Dec–Apr • Bohinjska Bistrica ☎ +386 4 5729 712 🖥 www.vogel.si

Kawiniške Savinjske Alpe

Krvavec 73 B4 1450–1970m • 10 lifts • Dec–Apr • Kranj ☎ 386 4 25 25 911 🖥 www.rtc-krvavec.si

Pohorje

Rogla 73 B5 1517/1050–1500m • 13 lifts • Dec–Apr • Slovenska Bistrica ☎ +386 3 75 77 100 🖥 www.rogla.eu

Spain

Pyrenees

Baqueira-Beret/Bonaigua 90 A3 ❄ 1500–2500m • 33 lifts • Dec–Apr • Vielha (15km) ☎ +34 902 415 415 🖥 www.baqueira.es • *Roads normally clear but keep chains accessible. Near Salardú.*

Sistema Penibetico

Sierra Nevada 100 D3 ❄ 2100–3300m • 24 lifts • Dec–May • Granada (32km) ☎ +34 902 70 80 90 🖥 http://sierranevada.es • *Access road designed to be avalanche safe and is snow cleared.*

Sweden

Idre Fjäll 115 F9 590–890m • 33 lifts • Nov–Apr • Mora (140km) ☎ +46 253 41000 🖥 www.idrefjall.se • *Be prepared for extreme weather conditions.*

Sälen 34 A5 360m • 100 lifts • Nov–Apr • Malung (70km) ☎ +46 771 84 00 00 🖥 www.skistar.com/salen • *Be prepared for extreme weather conditions.*

Switzerland

Alps

Adelboden 70 B2 1353m • 94 lifts • Dec–Apr • Frutigen (15km) 🖥 www.adelboden.ch • *Linked with Lenk.*

Arosa 71 B4 1800m • 16 lifts • Dec–Apr • Chur (30km) ☎ +41 81 378 70 20 🖥 www.arosa.ch • *Roads cleared but keep chains accessible due to high altitude.*

Crans Montana 70 B2 ❄ 1500–3000m • 34 lifts • Dec–Apr, Jul–Oct • Sierre (15km) • *Roads normally cleared but keep chains accessible for ascent from Sierre.*

Davos 71 B4 ❄ 1560/1100–2840m • 55 lifts • Nov–Apr • Davos. ☎ +41 81 415 21 21 🖥 www.davos.ch • *Linked with Klosters*

Engelberg 70 B3 ❄ 1000/1050–3020m • 26 lifts • Nov–May • Luzern (39km) ☎ +41 41 639 77 77 🖥 www.engelberg.ch • *Straight access road normally cleared.*

Flums (Flumserberg) 71 A4 ❄ 1400/1000–2220m • 17 lifts • Dec–Apr • Buchs (25km) ☎ +41 81 720 18 18 🖥 www.flumserberg.ch • *Roads normally cleared, but 1000-metre vertical ascent; keep chains accessible.*

Grindelwald 70 B3 ❄ 1050–2950m • 20 lifts • Dec–Apr • Interlaken (20km) ☎ +41 33 854 12 12 🖥 www.jungfrauregion.ch

Gstaad – Saanenland 70 B2 ❄ 1050/950–3000m • 74 lifts • Dec–Apr • Gstaad ☎ +41 33 748 81 81 🖥 www.gstaad.ch • *Linked to Anzère.*

Klosters 71 B4 ❄ 1191/1110–2840m • 55 lifts • Dec–Apr • Davos (10km). ☎ +41 81 410 20 20 🖥 www.davos.ch/klosters • *Linked with Davos. Roads normally clear but keep chains accessible.*

Leysin 70 B2 ❄ 2263/1260–2330m • 16 lifts • Dec–Apr • Aigle (6km) ☎ +41 24 493 33 00 🖥 www.leysin.ch

Mürren 70 B2 ❄ 1650–2970m • 12 lifts • Dec–Apr • Interlaken (18km) ☎ +41 33 856 86 86 🖥 www.mymurren.ch • *No road access. Park in Strechelberg (1500 free places) and take the two-stage cable car.*

Nendaz 70 B2 ❄ 1365/1400–3300m • 20 lifts • Nov–Apr • Sion (16km) ☎ +41 27 289 55 89 🖥 www.nendaz.ch • *Roads normally cleared, however keep chains accessible for ascent from Sion. Near Vex.*

Saas-Fee 70 B2 ❄ 1800–3500m • 23 lifts • Jan–Dec • Brig (35km) ☎ +41 27 958 18 58 🖥 www.saas-fee.ch/en/ • *Roads normally cleared but keep chains accessible because of altitude.*

St Moritz 71 B4 ❄ 1856/1730–3300m • 24 lifts • Nov–May • Chur (89km) ☎ +41 81 837 33 33 🖥 www.stmoritz.ch • *Roads normally cleared but keep chains accessible.*

Samnaun 71 B5 ❄ 1846/1400–2900m • 40 lifts • Dec–May • Scuol (30km) ☎ +41 81 861 88 30 🖥 www.engadin.com • *Roads normally cleared but keep chains accessible.*

Verbier 70 B2 ❄ 1500–3330m • 17 lifts • Nov–Apr • Martigny (27km) ☎ +41 27 775 38 38 🖥 www.verbier.ch • *Roads normally cleared.*

Villars-Gryon 70 B2 ❄ 1253/1200–2100m • 16 lifts • Dec–Apr, Jun–Jul • Montreux (35km) ☎ +41 24 495 32 32 🖥 www.villars.ch • *Roads normally cleared but keep chains accessible for ascent from N9. Near Bex.*

Wengen 70 B2 ❄ 1270–2320m • 19 lifts • Dec–Apr • Interlaken (12km) ☎ +41 33 856 85 85 🖥 http://wengen.ch • *No road access. Park at Lauterbrunnen and take mountain railway.*

Zermatt 70 B2 ❄ 1620–3900m • 40 lifts, • all year • Brig (42km) ☎ +41 27 966 81 00 🖥 www.zermatt.ch • *Cars not permitted in resort, park in Täsch (3km) and take shuttle train.*

Turkey

North Anatolian Mountains

Uludag 118 B4 1770–2320m • 15 lifts • Dec–Mar • Bursa (36km) ☎ +90 224 285 21 11 🖥 http://skiingturkey.com/resorts/uludag.html

To the best of the Publisher's knowledge the information in this table was correct at the time of going to press. No responsibility can be accepted for any errors or their consequences.

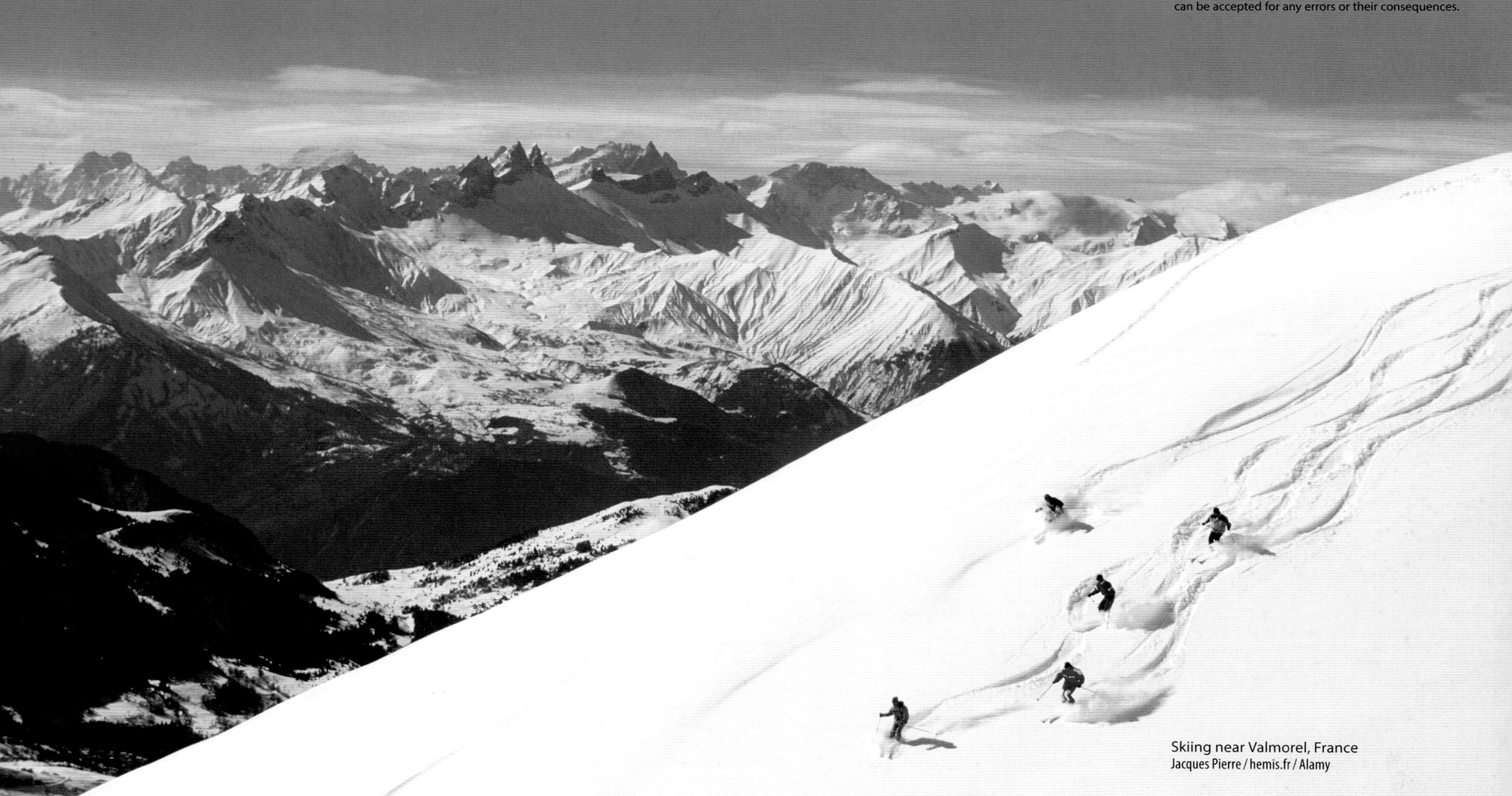

Skiing near Valmorel, France
Jacques Pierre / hemis.fr / Alamy

1 : 3 200 000 map pages

Map index showing regions of Europe numbered 1–16, with country and city labels including:

ICELAND (Reykjavik), NORWAY (Hammerfest, Narvik, Trondheim, Bergen, Stavanger), SWEDEN (Gothenburg, Stockholm), FINLAND (Helsinki), RUSSIA (Saint Petersburg, Moscow), ESTONIA (Tallinn), LATVIA (Riga), LITHUANIA (Kaliningrad, Minsk), BELARUS (Gdansk), POLAND (Berlin, Warsaw), UKRAINE (Kiev, Kraków), DENMARK (Copenhagen), UNITED KINGDOM (Edinburgh, London), IRELAND (Dublin), NETHERLANDS (Amsterdam, Rotterdam, Antwerp), BELGIUM (Brussels), GERMANY (Hamburg, Düsseldorf, Cologne, Frankfurt, Luxembourg, Stuttgart, Munich), CZECHIA (Prague), SLOVAKIA, AUSTRIA (Vienna), HUNGARY (Budapest), FRANCE (Paris, Strasbourg, Bordeaux, Lyon, Marseilles), SWITZ (Zürich, Basel, Geneva), ANDORRA, PORTUGAL (Lisbon), SPAIN (Madrid, Seville, Alicante, Málaga, Granada, Barcelona), GIBRALTAR, ITALY (Milan, Genoa, Turin, Venice, Florence, Rome, Naples), SLOVENIA, CROATIA (Zagreb), BOSNIA HERZEGOVINA (Sarajevo), SERBIA (Belgrade), MONTENEGRO, KOSOVO, MACEDONIA (Tirana), ALBANIA, ROMANIA (Bucharest), MOLDOVA, BULGARIA (Sofia), GREECE (Athens), TURKEY (Istanbul, Ankara), CYPRUS, MALTA, SAN MARINO, MONACO.

Distances

Calais

548	**Dublin**				
726	346	**Edinburgh**			
575	1123	1301	**Frankfurt**		
1342	477	176	1067	**Göteborg**	
1189	760	477	1486	485	582	**Hamburg**

> Dublin → Goteborg = 477 km
> Distances shown in blue involve at least one ferry journey

Amsterdam (km)

City	Amsterdam	Athina	Barcelona	Bergen	Berlin	Bruxelles	Bucuresti	Budapest	Calais	Dublin	Edinburgh	Frankfurt	Göteborg	Hamburg	Helsinki	Istanbul	København	Köln	Lisboa	London	Luxembourg	Madrid	Marseille	Milano	Moskva	München	Oslo	Paris	Praha	Roma	Sevilla	Sofiya	Stockholm	Warszawa	Wien	Zurich
Athina	2945																																			
Barcelona	1505	3192																																		
Bergen	1484	3742	2803																																	
Berlin	650	2412	1863	1309																																
Bruxelles	197	2895	1308	1586	764																															
Bucuresti	2245	1219	2644	3037	1707	2181																														
Budapest	1420	1530	1999	2212	882	1358	852																													
Calais	367	3100	1269	1783	956	215	2398	1573																												
Dublin	533	3630	1817	270	1504	763	3021	2196	548																											
Edinburgh	1093	3826	1995	176	1696	941	3124	2299	726	346																										
Frankfurt	441	2499	1313	1508	550	383	1804	979	575	1123	1301																									
Göteborg	1029	3080	2362	819	668	1145	1734	1550	1342	477	176	1067																								
Hamburg	447	2719	1780	1023	286	563	2014	1189	760	477	1486	485	582																							
Helsinki	1560	2539	2338	1063	475	1239	1834	1009	1431	1318	1236	1598	505	1113																						
Istanbul	2756	1145	2990	3653	2223	2706	690	1341	2911	3537	3657	2314	2891	2530	2350																					
København	965	2782	2090	1103	370	1081	2077	1252	1278	752	479	795	284	518	803	2593																				
Köln	256	2684	1376	1427	566	198	1983	1158	390	938	1116	180	986	404	1517	2499	714																			
Lisboa	2331	4460	1268	3723	2869	3141	3917	3222	2069	2617	2795	2400	3282	2700	3817	4342	3014	2339																		
London	480	3200	1387	458	1074	333	2591	1766	118	430	608	693	122	878	1991	3107	1188	508	2187																	
Luxembourg	406	2661	1190	1613	749	209	2052	1227	424	972	1150	240	1172	590	1703	2472	900	186	2160	542																
Madrid	1790	3809	617	3183	2364	1600	3262	2622	1528	1634	2254	1930	2742	2160	3276	3589	2473	1798	651	1646	1628															
Marseille	1210	2683	509	2435	1541	1030	2154	1505	1063	1588	1789	1023	1994	1412	2525	2479	1722	1006	1777	1182	822	1126														
Milano	1085	2182	1038	2141	1060	890	1668	992	1072	1620	1798	683	1700	1118	1535	1993	1428	868	2315	1190	679	1655	538													
Moskva	2457	2930	3655	2223	1821	2585	1761	2099	2800	3348	3526	2312	1665	2115	1160	2605	2325	2387	4875	2918	2852	4224	3270	3027												
München	839	2106	1340	1788	594	789	1497	672	994	1524	1720	398	1347	765	1069	1907	969	580	2545	1094	555	2010	1011	473	2305											
Oslo	1347	3372	2680	503	960	1463	2667	1842	1660	773	729	1385	316	900	697	3089	590	1304	3604	1778	1490	3063	2312	2018	1823	1559										
Paris	510	2917	988	1922	1051	320	2307	1482	281	829	1007	591	1481	899	2012	2727	1209	495	1821	399	351	1280	782	857	2903	810	1799									
Praha	950	2067	1750	1675	345	888	1362	537	1097	1635	1816	512	1013	652	770	1878	715	690	2870	1205	753	2329	1399	853	1853	388	1305	1061								
Roma	1691	1140	1385	2706	1502	1520	1904	1263	1678	2226	2404	1289	2265	1683	1977	2237	1993	1474	2653	1796	1285	2002	876	606	3362	918	2583	1389	1309							
Sevilla	2347	4223	1031	3736	2894	2150	3709	3010	2078	2626	2804	2344	3295	2713	3826	4034	3023	2318	401	2196	2178	550	1540	2078	4774	2371	3613	1830	2781	2446						
Sofiya	2206	828	2453	3103	1673	2156	391	790	2361	2891	3087	1764	2341	1980	1800	550	2043	1949	3706	2461	1922	3037	1929	1443	2252	1367	2632	2177	1328	1687	3484					
Stockholm	1393	3418	2726	1063	1006	1509	2713	1888	1673	2254	1069	1431	505	946	167	3185	590	1350	3650	1824	1536	3109	2358	2064	1228	1600	530	1845	1351	2629	3659	2679				
Warszawa	1256	2128	2366	1909	606	1350	1473	648	1542	2110	2268	1136	1274	886	361	1989	956	1152	3480	1680	1345	2960	2015	1469	1245	996	1506	1677	616	1853	3397	1439	1612			
Wien	1168	1772	1856	1970	640	1114	1067	242	1308	1954	2034	731	1308	947	1088	1583	1010	916	3100	1524	993	2473	1353	818	2137	430	1600	1240	295	1126	2876	1033	1646	727		
Zurich	816	2426	1030	1938	863	619	1810	985	804	1352	1530	464	1497	915	2164	2323	1433	589	2296	922	410	1647	699	292	2552	303	1815	592	691	898	2061	1173	1861	1307	743	

km

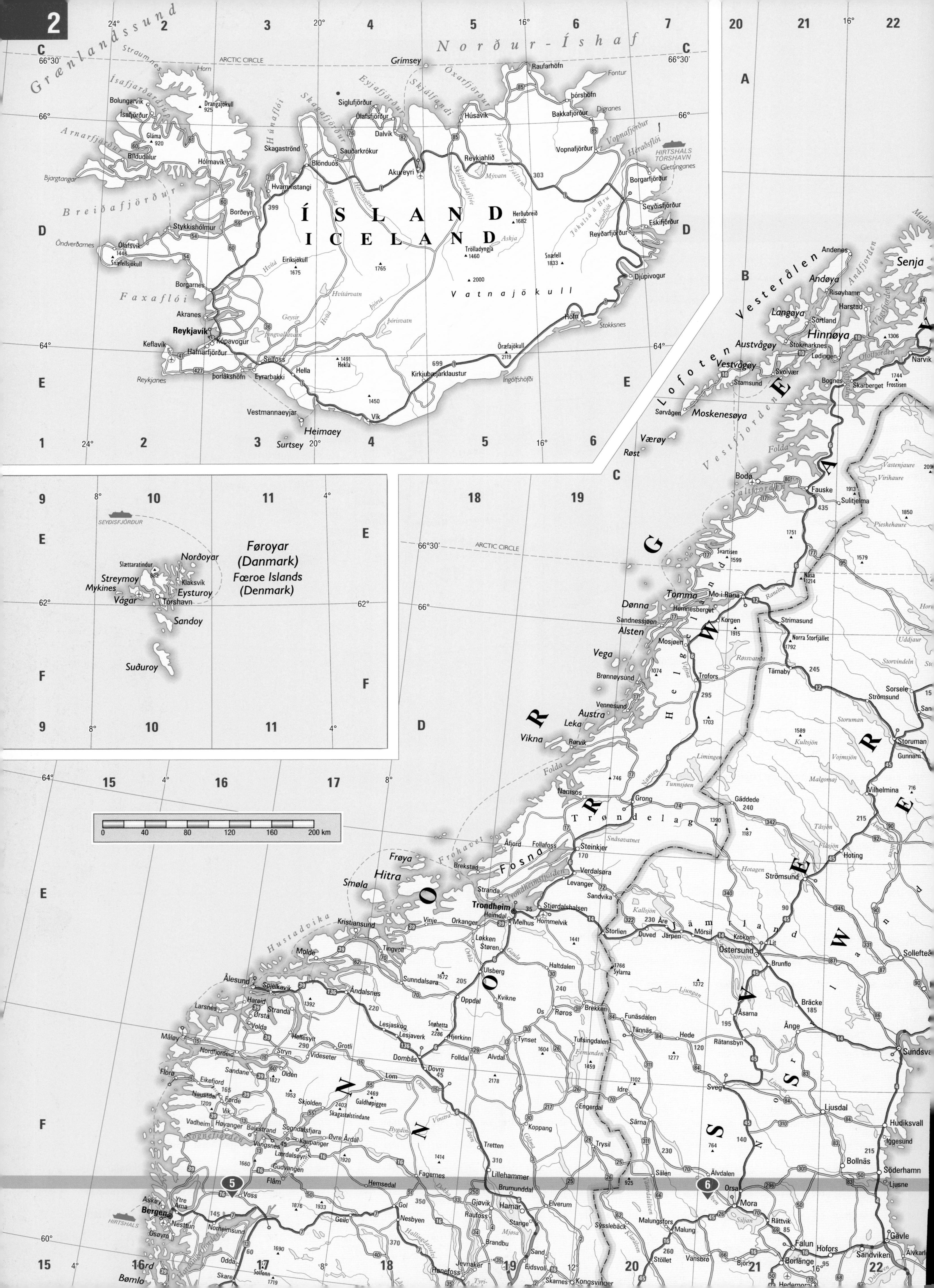

Grænlandssund
Norður-Íshaf
ARCTIC CIRCLE
Grímsey
Raufarhöfn
Fontur
Þórshöfn
Digranes
Bakkafjörður
Vopnafjörður
Héraðsflói
HIRTSHALS
TÓRSHAVN
Borgarfjörður
Seyðisfjörður
Eskifjörður
Reyðarfjörður
Djúpivogur
Höfn
Stokksnes
Öræfajökull
Ingólfshöfði
Kirkjubæjarklaustur
Vík
Heimaey
Surtsey
Vestmannaeyjar
Hella
Selfoss
Eyrarbakki
Þorlákshöfn
Reykjanes
Keflavík
Hafnarfjörður
Kópavogur
Reykjavík
Akranes
Borgarnes
Faxaflói
Snæfellsjökull
Ólafsvík
Öndverðarnes
Stykkishólmur
Breiðafjörður
Bjargtangar
Bíldudalur
Gláma
Arnarfjörður
Ísafjörður
Bolungarvík
Drangajökull
Horn
Straumnes
Ísafjarðardjúp
Hólmavík
Borðeyri
Hvammstangi
Húnaflói
Skagaströnd
Blönduós
Sauðárkrókur
Skagafjörður
Siglufjörður
Ólafsfjörður
Dalvík
Eyjafjörður
Akureyri
Skjálfandi
Öxarfjörður
Húsavík
Reykjahlíð
Mývatn
Herðubreið
Askja
Trölladyngja
Snæfell
Vatnajökull
Eiríksjökull
Hvítárvatn
Geysir
Þingvallavatn
Þórisvatn
Hekla
ÍSLAND
ICELAND
Føroyar (Danmark)
Færoe Islands (Denmark)
SEYÐISFJÖRÐUR
Norðoyar
Slættaratindur
Streymoy
Mykines
Vágar
Klaksvík
Eysturoy
Tórshavn
Sandoy
Suðuroy
NORGE
SVERIGE
Vesterålen
Lofoten
Andenes
Andøya
Senja
Risøyhamn
Harstad
Langøya
Sortland
Hinnøya
Austvågøy
Stokmarknes
Lødingen
Vestvågøy
Svolvær
Narvik
Bognes
Skarberget
Frostisen
Stamsund
Sørvågen
Moskenesøya
Værøy
Røst
Vestfjorden
Bodø
Fauske
Sulitjelma
Saltfjorden
Svartisen
Mo i Rana
Tomma
Dønna
Sandnessjøen
Hemnesberget
Korgen
Alsten
Mosjøen
Vega
Brønnøysund
Trofors
Helgeland
Vennesund
Austra
Leka
Vikna
Rørvik
Namsos
Grong
Gäddede
Trøndelag
Steinkjer
Follafoss
Åfjord
Frøya
Hitra
Smøla
Frohavet
Brekstad
Fosna
Verdalsøra
Levanger
Stranda
Trondheimsfjorden
Trondheim
Heimdal
Stjørdalshalsen
Hommelvik
Melhus
Kristiansund
Hustadvika
Orkanger
Løkken
Støren
Storlien
Duved
Järpen
Åre
Mörsil
Krokom
Östersund
Lit
Jämtland
Brunflo
Molde
Tingvoll
Ålesund
Spjelkavik
Åndalsnes
Sunndalsøra
Oppdal
Kvikne
Haltdalen
Sylarna
Røros
Os
Brekken
Funäsdalen
Tännäs
Hede
Rätansbyn
Larsnes
Hareid
Ørsta
Volda
Stranda
Hellesylt
Lesjaskog
Lesjaverk
Snøhetta
Hjerkinn
Tynset
Alvdal
Folldal
Dombås
Dovre
Måløy
Nordfjordeid
Stryn
Grotli
Videseter
Olden
Florø
Eikefjord
Naustdal
Førde
Lom
Galdhøpiggen
Skagastølstindane
Vik
Vadheim
Høyanger
Balestrand
Sogndalsfjøra
Kaupanger
Øvre Årdal
Sognefjorden
Vangsnes
Lærdalsøyri
Gudvangen
Flåm
Hemsedal
Fagernes
Tretten
Lillehammer
Brumunddal
Koppang
Engerdal
Trysil
Idre
Särna
Sälen
Älvdalen
Orsa
Mora
Askøy
Ytre Arna
Bergen
Nesttun
Voss
Gol
Geilo
Nesbyen
Gjøvik
Hamar
Raufoss
Stange
Elverum
Mjøsa
Norheimsund
Os
Odda
Bømlo
Skare
Sauda
Hønefoss
Jevnaker
Brandbu
Sand
Eidsvoll
Kongsvinger
Skarnes
Sysslebäck
Malungsfors
Malung
Stöllet
Vansbro
Rättvik
Siljan
Falun
Borlänge
Hofors
Sandviken
Gävle
Ljusne
Söderhamn
Bollnäs
Iggesund
Hudiksvall
Ljusdal
Sveg
Ånge
Bräcke
Sundsvall
Asarna
Sollefteå
Hoting
Strömsund
Vilhelmina
Storuman
Gunnarn
Sorsele
Strömsund
Tärnaby
Strimasund
Norra Storfjället
Røssvatnet
Limingen
Tunnsjøen
Kultsjön
Vojmsjön
Malgomaj
Kallsjön
Storsjön
Femunden
Hälsingland
Ljungan
Ljusnan
Indalsälven
Ångermanälven
Uddjaur
Storvindeln
Pieskehaure
Virihaure
Vastenjaure
Ranelva
0 40 80 120 160 200 km

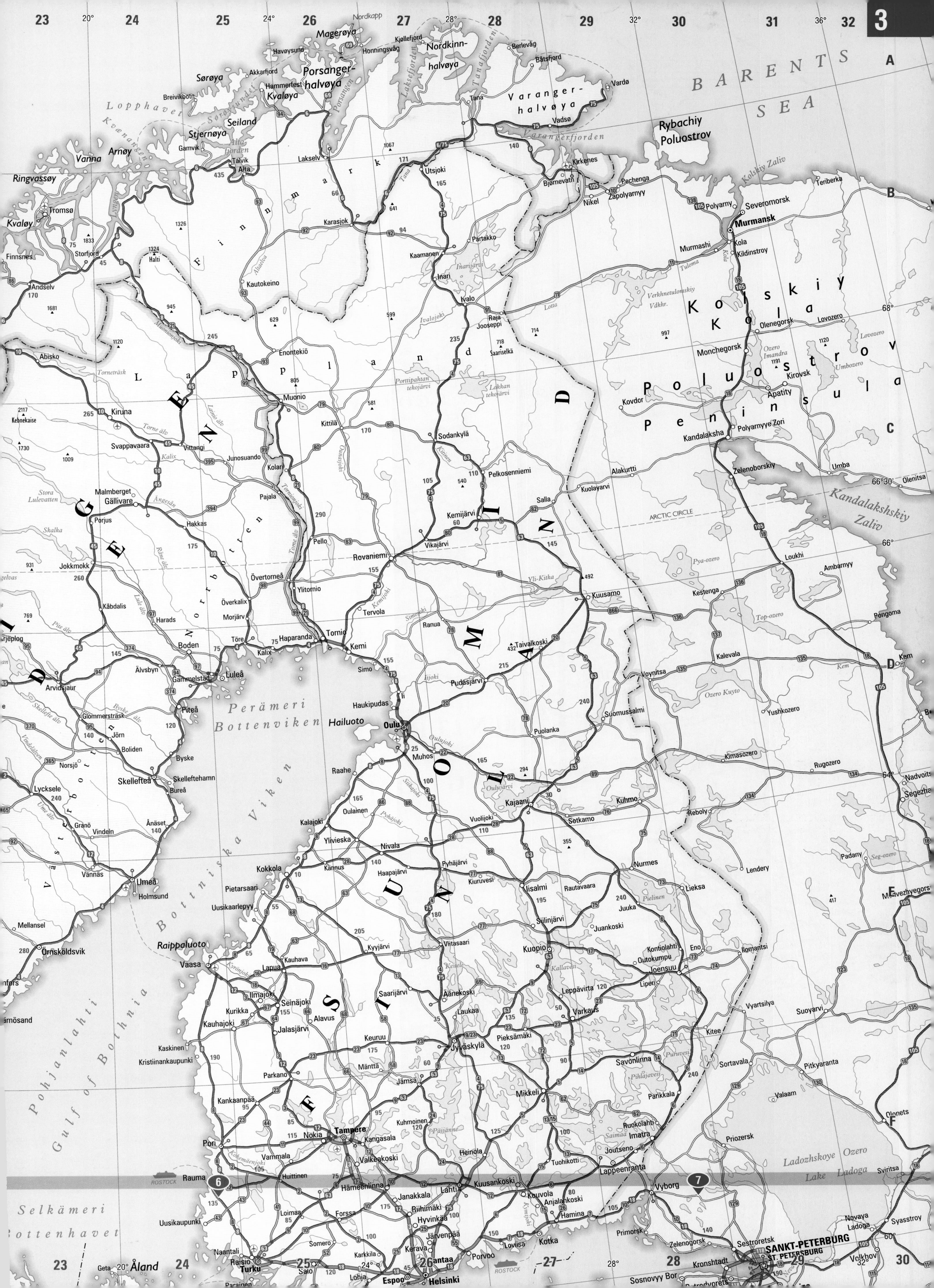

BARENTS SEA
Nordkapp
Magerøya
Havøysund
Honningsvåg
Kjøllefjord
Nordkinn-halvøya
Berlevåg
Båtsfjord
Vardø
Varanger-halvøya
Vadsø
Varangerfjorden
Tana
Porsanger-halvøya
Sørøya
Akkarfjord
Hammerfest
Kvaløya
Seiland
Stjernøya
Loppahavet
Breivikbotn
Gamvik
Talvik
Alta
Altafjorden
Arnøy
Vanna
Ringvassøy
Tromsø
Kvaløy
Storfjord
Finnsnes
Andselv
Lakselv
Karasjok
Kautokeino
Halti
Finnmark
Utsjoki
Kaamanen
Partakko
Inari
Inarijärvi
Ivalo
Raja Jooseppi
Saariselkä
Kirkenes
Bjørnevatn
Nikel
Zapolyarnyy
Pechenga
Rybachiy Poluostrov
Kolskiy Zaliv
Teriberka
Polyarnyy
Severomorsk
Murmansk
Murmashi
Kola
Kildinstroy
Tuloma
Verkhnetulomskiy Vdkhr.
Kolskiy Poluostrov
Kola Peninsula
Olenegorsk
Lovozero
Monchegorsk
Ozero Imandra
Kirovsk
Apatity
Kovdor
Polyarnyye Zori
Kandalaksha
Umba
Olenitsa
Zelenoborskiy
Kandalakshskiy Zaliv
Alakurtti
Kuolayarvi
ARCTIC CIRCLE
Loukhi
Ambarnyy
Kestenga
Pongoma
Top-ozero
Pya-ozero
Kalevala
Kem
Voynitsa
Ozero Kuyto
Yushkozero
Kimasozero
Rugozero
Nadvoitsy
Segezha
Reboly
Padany
Lendery
Medvezhyegorsk
Vyartsilya
Suoyarvi
Sortavala
Pitkyaranta
Valaam
Olonets
Ladozhskoye Ozero
Lake Ladoga
Sviritsa
Priozersk
Vyborg
Zelenogorsk
Sestroretsk
Kronshtadt
SANKT-PETERBURG
ST. PETERSBURG
Novaya Ladoga
Syasstroy
Volkhov
Sosnovyy Bor
Abisko
Torneträsk
Kiruna
Kebnekaise
Svappavaara
Vittangi
Junosuando
Malmberget
Gällivare
Porjus
Stora Lulevatten
Jokkmokk
Hakkas
Pajala
Norrbotten
Kåbdalis
Harads
Överkalix
Morjärv
Boden
Älvsbyn
Gammelstad
Luleå
Arvidsjaur
Arjeplog
Glommersträsk
Jörn
Boliden
Piteå
Byske
Norsjö
Skellefteå
Skelleftehamn
Bureå
Lycksele
Granö
Vindeln
Ånäset
Vännäs
Umeå
Holmsund
Västerbotten
Mellansel
Örnsköldsvik
Härnösand
Övertorneå
Ylitornio
Haparanda
Töre
Kalix
Tornio
Kemi
Simo
Enontekiö
Muonio
Kittilä
Kolari
Pello
Sodankylä
Pelkosenniemi
Kemijärvi
Vikajärvi
Salla
Rovaniemi
Tervola
Ranua
Kuusamo
Taivalkoski
Pudasjärvi
Ii
Haukipudas
Hailuoto
Oulu
Muhos
Suomussalmi
Puolanka
Raahe
Oulujärvi
Kajaani
Sotkamo
Kuhmo
Vuolijoki
Oulainen
Kalajoki
Ylivieska
Nivala
Haapajärvi
Pyhäjärvi
Kiuruvesi
Iisalmi
Rautavaara
Nurmes
Lieksa
Kokkola
Kannus
Pietarsaari
Uusikaarlepyy
Juuka
Pielinen
Siilinjärvi
Juankoski
Kuopio
Kontiolahti
Outokumpu
Eno
Ilomantsi
Joensuu
Liperi
Leppävirta
Varkaus
Kitee
Savonlinna
Parikkala
Pihlajavesi
Puruvesi
Viitasaari
Kyyjärvi
Kauhava
Lapua
Vaasa
Raippaluoto
Ilmajoki
Seinäjoki
Kurikka
Kauhajoki
Alavus
Saarijärvi
Äänekoski
Laukaa
Jalasjärvi
Keuruu
Jyväskylä
Pieksämäki
Mikkeli
Kaskinen
Kristiinankaupunki
Parkano
Mänttä
Jämsä
Kankaanpää
Kuhmoinen
Päijänne
Tampere
Nokia
Kangasala
Valkeakoski
Pori
Vammala
Huittinen
Heinola
Ruokolahti
Imatra
Joutseno
Tuohikotti
Lappeenranta
Rauma
Hämeenlinna
Janakkala
Lahti
Kuusankoski
Kouvola
Anjalankoski
Hamina
Riihimäki
Hyvinkää
Loimaa
Forssa
Uusikaupunki
Järvenpää
Kerava
Porvoo
Loviisa
Kotka
Somero
Karkkila
Naantali
Raisio
Turku
Salo
Lohja
Espoo
Vantaa
Helsinki
Parainen
Åland
Geta
ROSTOCK
SUOMI FINLAND
SVERIGE
Perämeri
Bottenviken
Bottniska Viken
Pohjanlahti
Gulf of Bothnia
Selkämeri
Bottenhavet

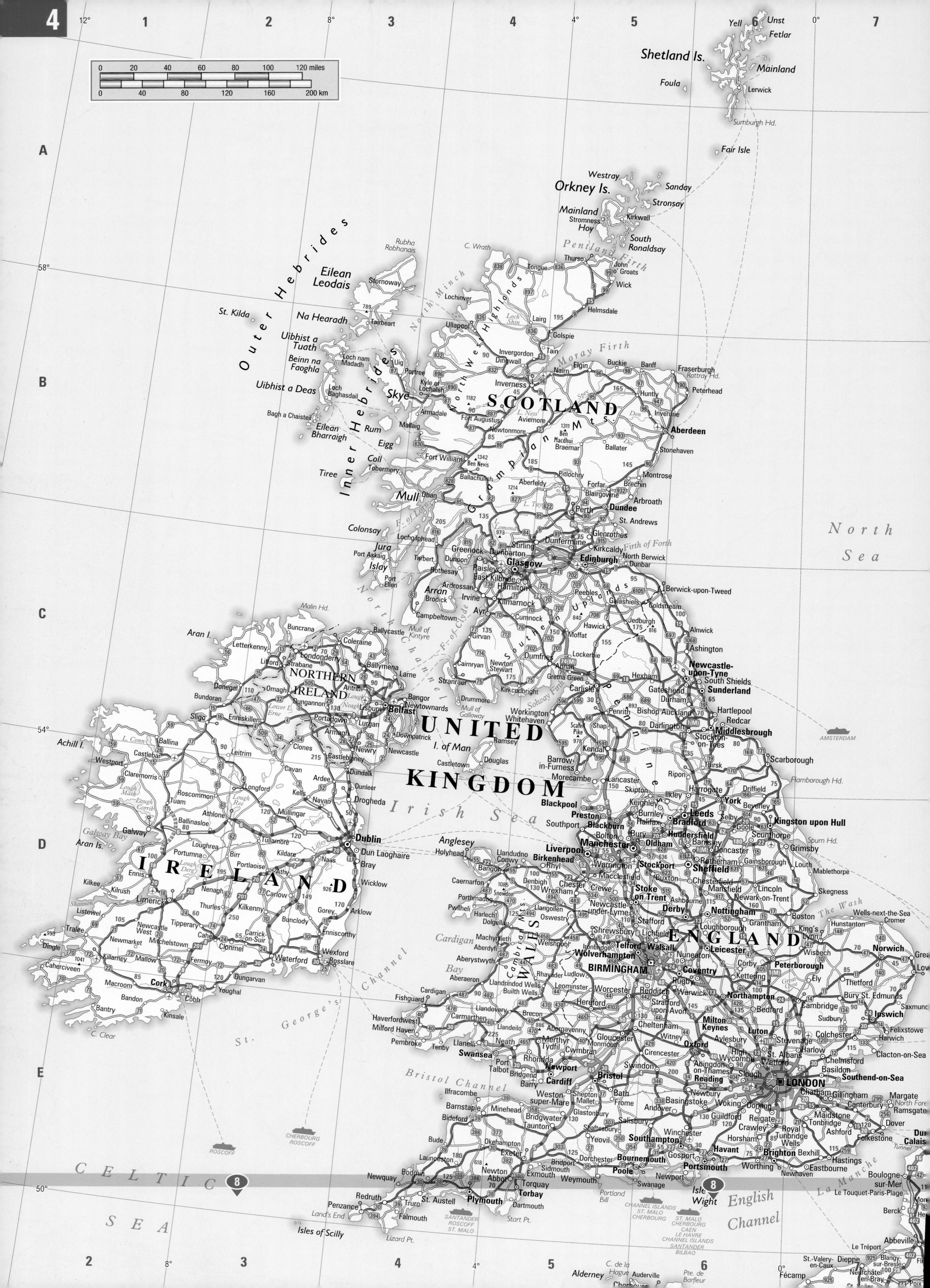

4
0 20 40 60 80 100 120 miles
0 40 80 120 160 200 km
Shetland Is.
Unst
Yell
Fetlar
Mainland
Foula
Lerwick
Sumburgh Hd.
Fair Isle
Orkney Is.
Westray
Sanday
Stronsay
Mainland
Stromness
Hoy
Kirkwall
South Ronaldsay
Pentland Firth
Outer Hebrides
Eilean Leodais
St. Kilda
Na Hearadh
Uibhist a Tuath
Beinn na Faoghla
Uibhist a Deas
Eilean Bharraigh
Inner Hebrides
Skye
Rum
Eigg
Coll
Tiree
Mull
Colonsay
Jura
Islay
Arran
SCOTLAND
Grampian Mts.
North West Highlands
Southern Uplands
Moray Firth
Firth of Forth
North Minch
Inverness
Aberdeen
Dundee
Perth
Stirling
Glasgow
Edinburgh
Fort William
Ben Nevis
North Sea
NORTHERN IRELAND
Belfast
Londonderry
IRELAND
Dublin
Cork
Limerick
Galway
Waterford
Wexford
Irish Sea
North Channel
St. George's Channel
Celtic Sea
UNITED KINGDOM
I. of Man
Douglas
Anglesey
WALES
Cambrian Mts.
Cardigan Bay
Bristol Channel
Cardiff
Swansea
ENGLAND
Pennines
Newcastle-upon-Tyne
Sunderland
Middlesbrough
Leeds
Bradford
York
Kingston upon Hull
Liverpool
Manchester
Sheffield
Nottingham
Leicester
BIRMINGHAM
Coventry
Bristol
Southampton
Portsmouth
Brighton
Plymouth
LONDON
The Wash
English Channel
La Manche
Isle of Wight
Isles of Scilly
AMSTERDAM
ROSCOFF
CHERBOURG ROSCOFF
SANTANDER ROSCOFF ST. MALO
CHANNEL ISLANDS ST. MALO CHERBOURG
Alderney
Calais
Boulogne-sur-Mer
Abbeville
8

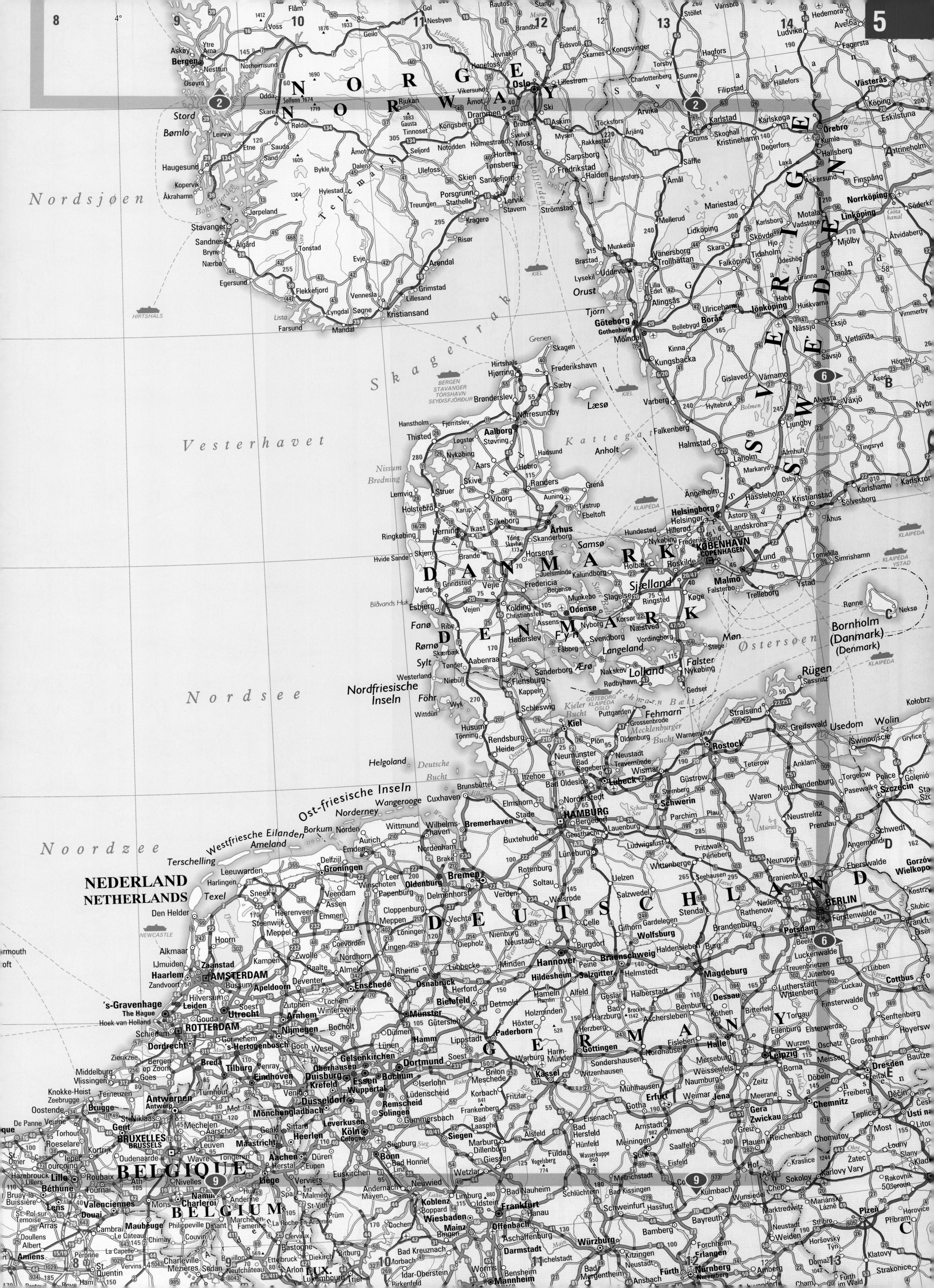
NORGE
NORWAY
SVERIGE
SWEDEN
DANMARK
DENMARK
DEUTSCHLAND
GERMANY
NEDERLAND
NETHERLANDS
BELGIQUE
BELGIUM
LUX.
Nordsjøen
Vesterhavet
Nordsee
Noordzee
Skagerrak
Kattegat
Østersøen
Deutsche Bucht
Mecklenburger Bucht
Fehmarn Bælt
Kieler Bucht
Nordfriesische Inseln
Ost-friesische Inseln
Westfriesche Eilanden
Bornholm (Danmark) (Denmark)
Oslo
Bergen
Stavanger
Kristiansand
Göteborg
Gothenburg
København
Copenhagen
Malmö
Helsingborg
Aalborg
Århus
Odense
Hamburg
Bremen
Hannover
Berlin
Kiel
Lübeck
Rostock
Schwerin
Magdeburg
Leipzig
Dresden
Kassel
Dortmund
Düsseldorf
Köln
Frankfurt
Amsterdam
Rotterdam
's-Gravenhage
The Hague
Utrecht
Bruxelles
Brussels
Antwerpen
Lille
Liège
Szczecin
Plzeň
Rügen
Fehmarn
Helgoland
Sjælland
Fyn
Lolland
Falster
Møn
Læsø
Anholt
Samsø
Langeland
Ærø
Fanø
Rømø
Sylt
Föhr
Texel
Terschelling
Ameland
Borkum
Norderney
Wangerooge
Usedom
Wolin
8
9
10
11
12
13
14

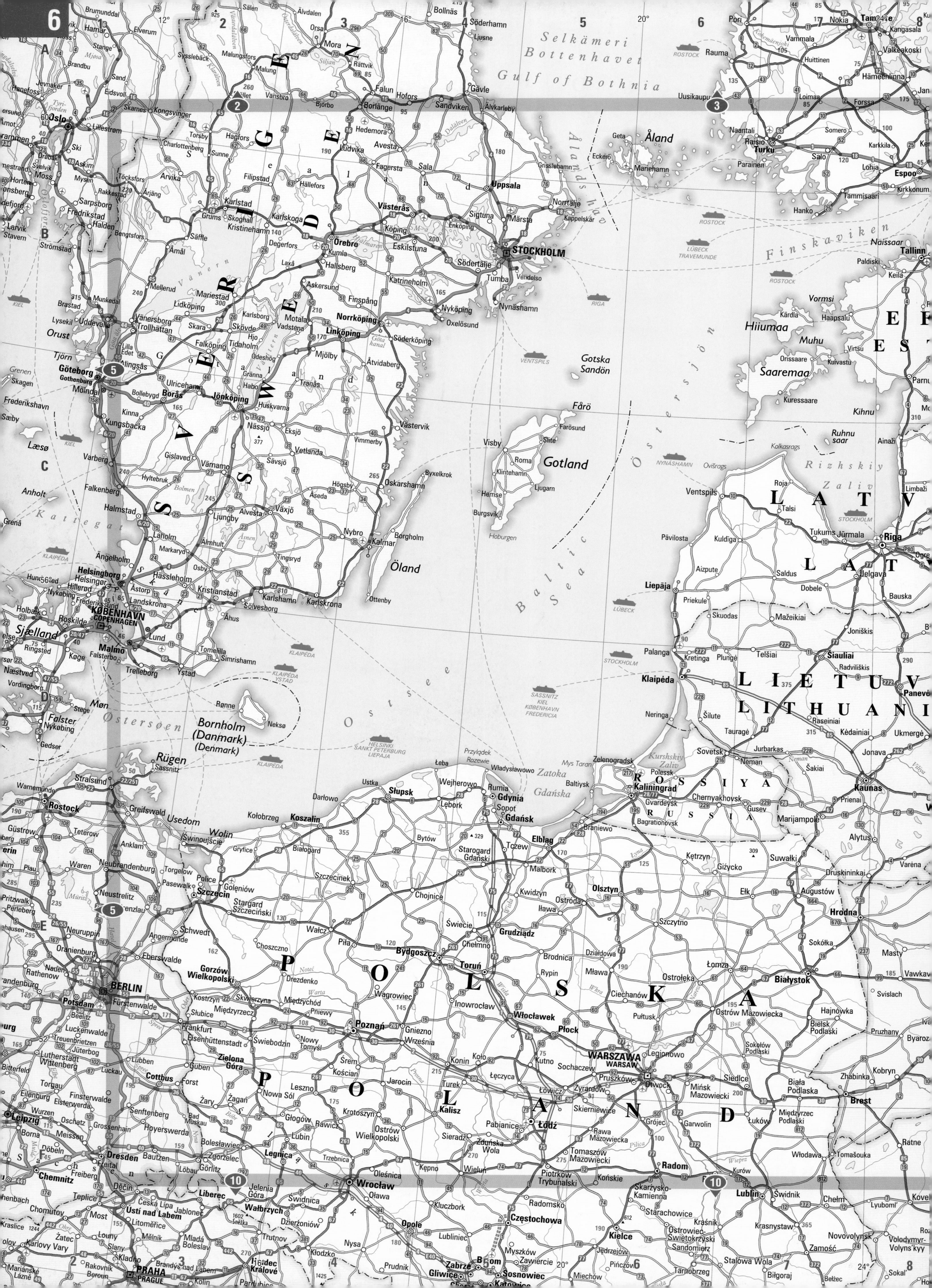
Selkämeri
Bottenhavet
Gulf of Bothnia
Finskaviken
Östersjön
Baltic Sea
Ostsee
Østersøen
Kattegat
Zatoka Gdańska
Kurshskiy Zaliv
Rizhskiy Zaliv
SVERIGE
SWEDEN
POLSKA
POLAND
LATVIA
LIETUVA
LITHUANIA
ROSSIYA
RUSSIA
ESTONIA
Åland
Mariehamn
Gotland
Visby
Fårö
Gotska Sandön
Öland
Bornholm (Danmark) (Denmark)
Rønne
Nexø
Hiiumaa
Saaremaa
Muhu
Vormsi
Kihnu
Ruhnu saar
Sjælland
Læsø
Anholt
Rügen
Usedom
Wolin
Orust
Tjörn
STOCKHOLM
Uppsala
Västerås
Örebro
Norrköping
Linköping
Jönköping
Göteborg
Gothenburg
Borås
Halmstad
Helsingborg
Malmö
Lund
Kristianstad
Karlskrona
Kalmar
Växjö
Karlstad
Gävle
Falun
Borlänge
Mora
Söderhamn
Bollnäs
Sundsvall
Södertälje
Nyköping
Nynäshamn
Norrtälje
Oslo
Hamar
Moss
Fredrikstad
Sarpsborg
Halden
KØBENHAVN
COPENHAGEN
Helsingør
Roskilde
Køge
Næstved
Trelleborg
Ystad
Turku
Espoo
Tampere
Pori
Rauma
Hanko
Hämeenlinna
Tallinn
Haapsalu
Pärnu
Kuressaare
Riga
Jūrmala
Ventspils
Liepāja
Jelgava
Klaipėda
Palanga
Šiauliai
Panevėžys
Kaunas
Marijampolė
Alytus
Kaliningrad
Sovetsk
Gusev
Chernyakhovsk
Hrodna
Brest
Gdańsk
Gdynia
Sopot
Słupsk
Koszalin
Kołobrzeg
Szczecin
Świnoujście
Elbląg
Olsztyn
Bydgoszcz
Toruń
Grudziądz
Poznań
Gniezno
Włocławek
Płock
WARSZAWA
WARSAW
Łódź
Kalisz
Białystok
Łomża
Siedlce
Lublin
Radom
Kielce
Częstochowa
Wrocław
Opole
Legnica
Zielona Góra
Gorzów Wielkopolski
Piła
Suwałki
Ełk
Rostock
Stralsund
Greifswald
Neubrandenburg
BERLIN
Potsdam
Frankfurt
Cottbus
Dresden
Leipzig
Chemnitz
PRAHA
PRAGUE
Liberec
Ústí nad Labem
Hradec Králové
Katowice
Gliwice
Zabrze
Sosnowiec
ROSTOCK
TRAVEMUNDE
LÜBECK
KIEL
RIGA
VENTSPILS
NYNÄSHAMN
STOCKHOLM
KLAIPĖDA
SASSNITZ
HELSINKI
SANKT PETERBURG
LIEPAJA
12°
16°
20°
24°

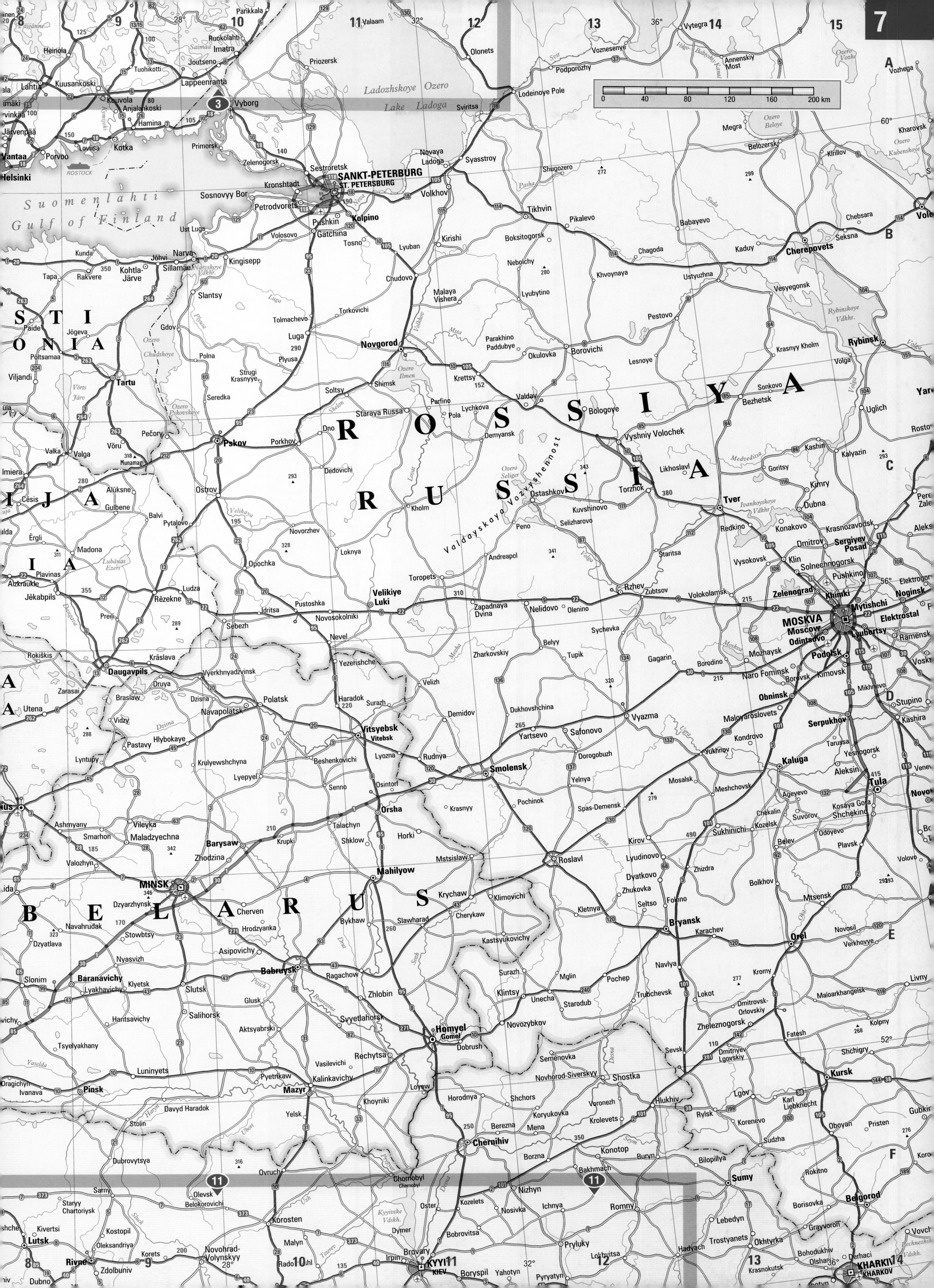
ROSSIYA
RUSSIA
BELARUS
SANKT-PETERBURG
ST. PETERSBURG
MOSKVA
Moscow
MINSK
KYYIV
KIEV
KHARKIV
KHARKOV
Helsinki
Vantaa
Porvoo
Kotka
Hamina
Kouvola
Lahti
Heinola
Kuusankoski
Lappeenranta
Imatra
Vyborg
Primorsk
Zelenogorsk
Sestroretsk
Kronshtadt
Sosnovyy Bor
Petrodvorets
Pushkin
Kolpino
Gatchina
Tosno
Ust Luga
Kingisepp
Narva
Sillamäe
Jõhvi
Kohtla-Järve
Rakvere
Tapa
Kunda
Paide
Jõgeva
Põltsamaa
Viljandi
Tartu
Võru
Valga
Valka
Cēsis
Gulbene
Alūksne
Balvi
Madona
Ērgli
Pļaviņas
Aizkraukle
Jēkabpils
Rēzekne
Ludza
Preiļi
Daugavpils
Krāslava
Rokiškis
Zarasai
Utena
Suomenlahti
Gulf of Finland
Ladozhskoye Ozero
Lake Ladoga
Ozero Chudskoye
Ozero Pskovskoye
Ozero Ilmen
Ozero Seliger
Rybinskoye Vdkhr.
Ivankovskoye Vdkhr.
Valdayskaya Vozvyshennost
Priozersk
Olonets
Lodeinoye Pole
Podporozhy
Vytegra
Voznesenye
Annenskiy Most
Vozhega
Kharovsk
Megra
Belozersk
Kirillov
Cherepovets
Chebsara
Seksna
Kaduy
Babayevo
Chagoda
Pikalevo
Tikhvin
Boksitogorsk
Volkhov
Novaya Ladoga
Syasstroy
Svirtsa
Shugozero
Kirishi
Lyuban
Chudovo
Malaya Vishera
Nebolchy
Lyubytino
Khvoynaya
Ustyuzhna
Vesyegonsk
Pestovo
Krasnyy Kholm
Rybinsk
Volga
Uglich
Kashin
Kalyazin
Bezhetsk
Sonkovo
Lesnoye
Borovichi
Okulovka
Parakhino Paddubye
Novgorod
Luga
Tolmachevo
Torkovichi
Slantsy
Gdov
Plyusa
Strugi Krasnyye
Polna
Seredka
Pskov
Porkhov
Dno
Soltsy
Shimsk
Staraya Russa
Parfino
Pola
Lychkova
Demyansk
Valday
Bologoye
Krettsy
Vyshniy Volochek
Likhoslavl
Torzhok
Ostashkov
Kuvshinovo
Selizharovo
Peno
Andreapol
Toropets
Tver
Redkino
Konakovo
Dubna
Kimry
Goritsy
Dmitrov
Sergiyev Posad
Krasnozavodsk
Klin
Solnechnogorsk
Pushkino
Zelenograd
Khimki
Mytishchi
Noginsk
Elektrostal
Lyubertsy
Odintsovo
Podolsk
Volokolamsk
Zubtsov
Rzhev
Staritsa
Vysokovsk
Olenino
Nelidovo
Zapadnaya Dvina
Velikiye Luki
Novosokolniki
Pustoshka
Idritsa
Sebezh
Nevel
Opochka
Novorzhev
Loknya
Kholm
Dedovichi
Ostrov
Pytalovo
Pečory
Sychevka
Belyy
Tupik
Zharkovskiy
Gagarin
Borodino
Mozhaysk
Naro Fominsk
Borovsk
Klimovsk
Obninsk
Maloyaroslavets
Serpukhov
Stupino
Kashira
Mikhnevo
Kaluga
Tarussa
Yasnogorsk
Aleksin
Tula
Kosaya Gora
Shchekino
Kondrovo
Yukhnov
Mosalsk
Meshchovsk
Sukhinichi
Kozelsk
Chekalin
Suvorov
Agevevo
Odoyevo
Belev
Plavsk
Volovo
Mtsensk
Orel
Novosil
Verkhovye
Livny
Maloarkhangelsk
Kolpny
Shchigry
Kursk
Fatesh
Zheleznogorsk
Dmitrovsk-Orlovskiy
Kromy
Lokot
Trubchevsk
Navlya
Bryansk
Karachev
Bolkhov
Zhizdra
Lyudinovo
Kirov
Dyatkovo
Zhukovka
Seltso
Fokino
Kletnya
Roslavl
Spas-Demensk
Yelnya
Dorogobuzh
Safonovo
Yartsevo
Vyazma
Dukhovshchina
Demidov
Velizh
Smolensk
Rudnya
Pochinok
Krasnyy
Pochep
Mglin
Unecha
Starodub
Surazh
Klintsy
Novozybkov
Kastsyukovichy
Klimovichi
Cherykaw
Krychaw
Mstsislaw
Slawharad
Bykhaw
Mahilyow
Horki
Shklow
Orsha
Talachyn
Krupki
Barysaw
Zhodzina
Smarhon
Maladzyechna
Vileyka
Ashmyany
Valozhyn
Dzyarzhynsk
Cherven
Hrodzyanka
Asipovichy
Babruysk
Ragachow
Zhlobin
Svyetlahorsk
Rechytsa
Homyel
Gomel
Dobrush
Kalinkavichy
Mazyr
Yelsk
Khoyniki
Loyew
Vasilevichi
Aktsyabrski
Hlusk
Salihorsk
Slutsk
Klyetsk
Lyakhavichy
Baranavichy
Nyasvizh
Stowbtsy
Navahrudak
Dzyatlava
Slonim
Hantsavichy
Tsyelyakhany
Luninyets
Pinsk
Ivanava
Davyd Haradok
Stolin
Dubrovytsya
Sarny
Olevsk
Belokorovichi
Korosten
Ovruch
Chornobyl
Chernobyl
Novohrad-Volynskyy
Korets
Rivne
Zdolbuniv
Kostopil
Lutsk
Kivertsi
Dubno
Malyn
Dymer
Brovary
Irpin
Boryspil
Yahotyn
Pyryatyn
Bobrovitsa
Kozelets
Oster
Nosivka
Nizhyn
Ichnya
Pryluky
Lokhvitsa
Romny
Chernihiv
Horodnya
Shchors
Mena
Berezna
Borzna
Koryukovka
Semenovka
Novhorod-Siverskyy
Shostka
Voronezh
Krolevets
Konotop
Bakhmach
Buryn
Hlukhiv
Bilopillya
Sumy
Lebedyn
Trostyanets
Okhtyrka
Hadyach
Krasnokutsk
Bohodukhiv
Olshany
Derhaci
Vovchansk
Sudzha
Korenevo
Rylsk
Lgov
Karl Liebknecht
Sevsk
Dmitriyev Lgovskiy
Oboyan
Pristen
Gubkin
Belgorod
Borisovka
Grayvoron
Rokitno
Polatsk
Navapolatsk
Vitsyebsk
Vitebsk
Haradok
Surazh
Yezerishche
Lyozna
Beshenkovichi
Senno
Lyepyel
Krulyewshchyna
Hlybokaye
Pastavy
Braslaw
Druya
Dzisna
Vyerkhnyadzvinsk
Lyntupy
Vidzy
0 40 80 120 160 200 km

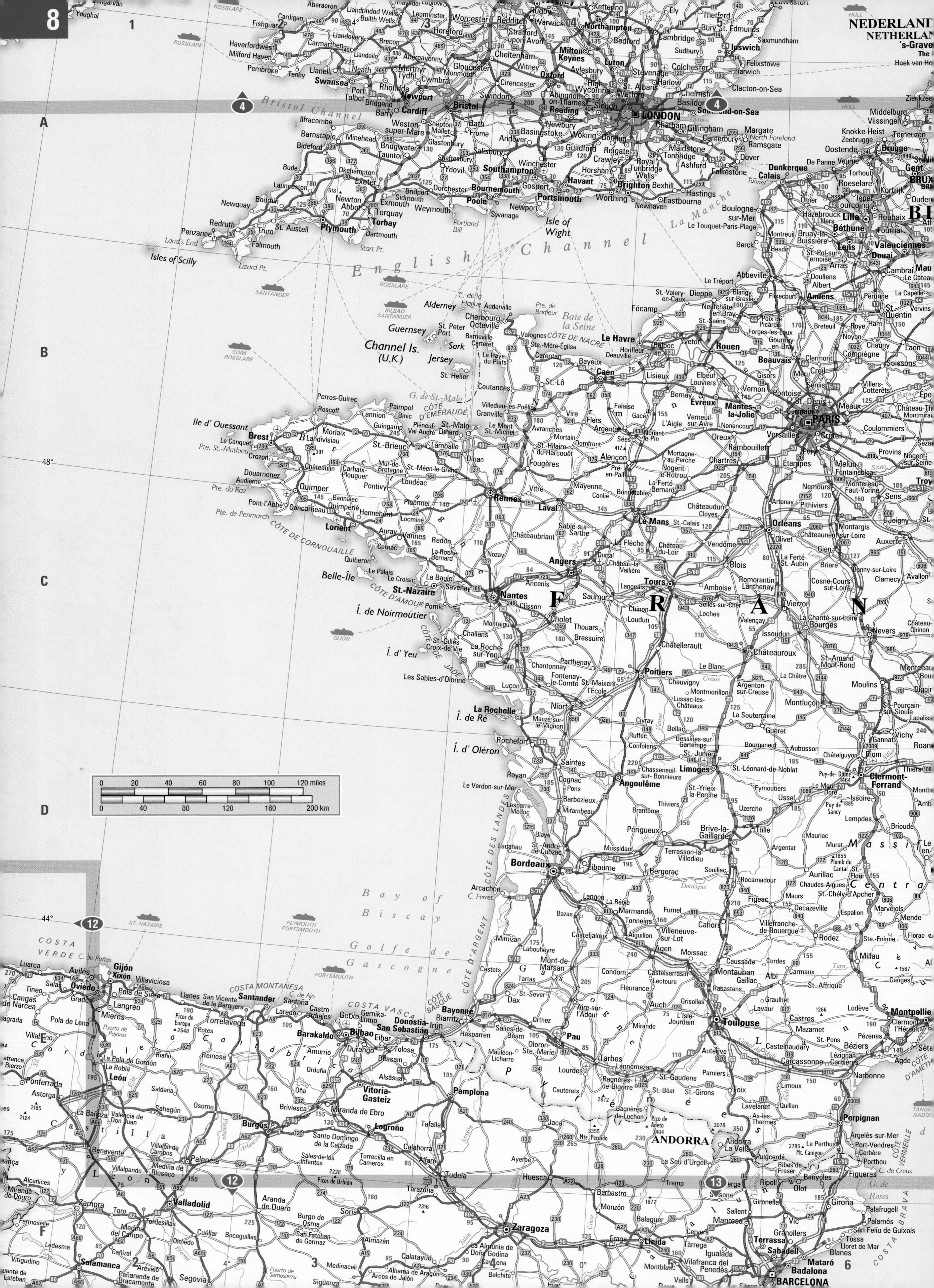
NEDERLAND
NETHERLANDS
Bristol Channel
English Channel
La Manche
Isles of Scilly
Land's End
Lizard Pt.
Start Pt.
Isle of Wight
Channel Is. (U.K.)
Alderney
Guernsey
Jersey
Sark
St. Peter Port
St. Helier
Baie de la Seine
CÔTE DE NACRE
G. de St.-Malo
CÔTE D'EMERAUDE
CÔTE DE CORNOUAILLE
CÔTE D'AMOUR
CÔTE DE JADE
CÔTE DES LANDES
CÔTE D'ARGENT
CÔTE BASQUE
Ile d' Ouessant
Belle-Île
Î. de Noirmoutier
Î. d' Yeu
Î. de Ré
Î. d' Oléron
Bay of Biscay
Golfe de Gascogne
COSTA VERDE
COSTA MONTAÑESA
COSTA VASCA
COSTA BRAVA
CÔTE VERMEILLE
FRANCE
ANDORRA
Massif Central
Pyrénées
LONDON
PARIS
BARCELONA
Swansea
Cardiff
Newport
Bristol
Bath
Swindon
Oxford
Reading
Southampton
Bournemouth
Poole
Portsmouth
Brighton
Plymouth
Torbay
Exeter
Dover
Folkestone
Canterbury
Margate
Southend-on-Sea
Cambridge
Ipswich
Northampton
Milton Keynes
Luton
Gloucester
Cheltenham
Worcester
Hereford
Calais
Dunkerque
Lille
Amiens
Rouen
Le Havre
Caen
Cherbourg-Octeville
Brest
Quimper
Lorient
St.-Brieuc
St.-Malo
Rennes
Laval
Le Mans
Angers
Nantes
St.-Nazaire
Tours
Orléans
Chartres
Poitiers
La Rochelle
Niort
Angoulême
Limoges
Bordeaux
Arcachon
Clermont-Ferrand
Montpellier
Toulouse
Pau
Bayonne
Biarritz
Perpignan
Narbonne
Carcassonne
Béziers
Bilbao
San Sebastián
Donostia-Irún
Santander
Oviedo
Gijón
León
Burgos
Vitoria-Gasteiz
Pamplona
Logroño
Zaragoza
Lleida
Girona
Valladolid
Salamanca
Segovia
Tarragona
ROSSLARE
SANTANDER
BILBAO SANTANDER
CORK ROSSLARE
GIJÓN
ST. NAZAIRE
PLYMOUTH PORTSMOUTH
PORTSMOUTH
HULL
Tunnel
A
B
C
D
E
F
1
2
3
4
5
6
4
12
13
48°
44°
0 20 40 60 80 100 120 miles
0 40 80 120 160 200 km

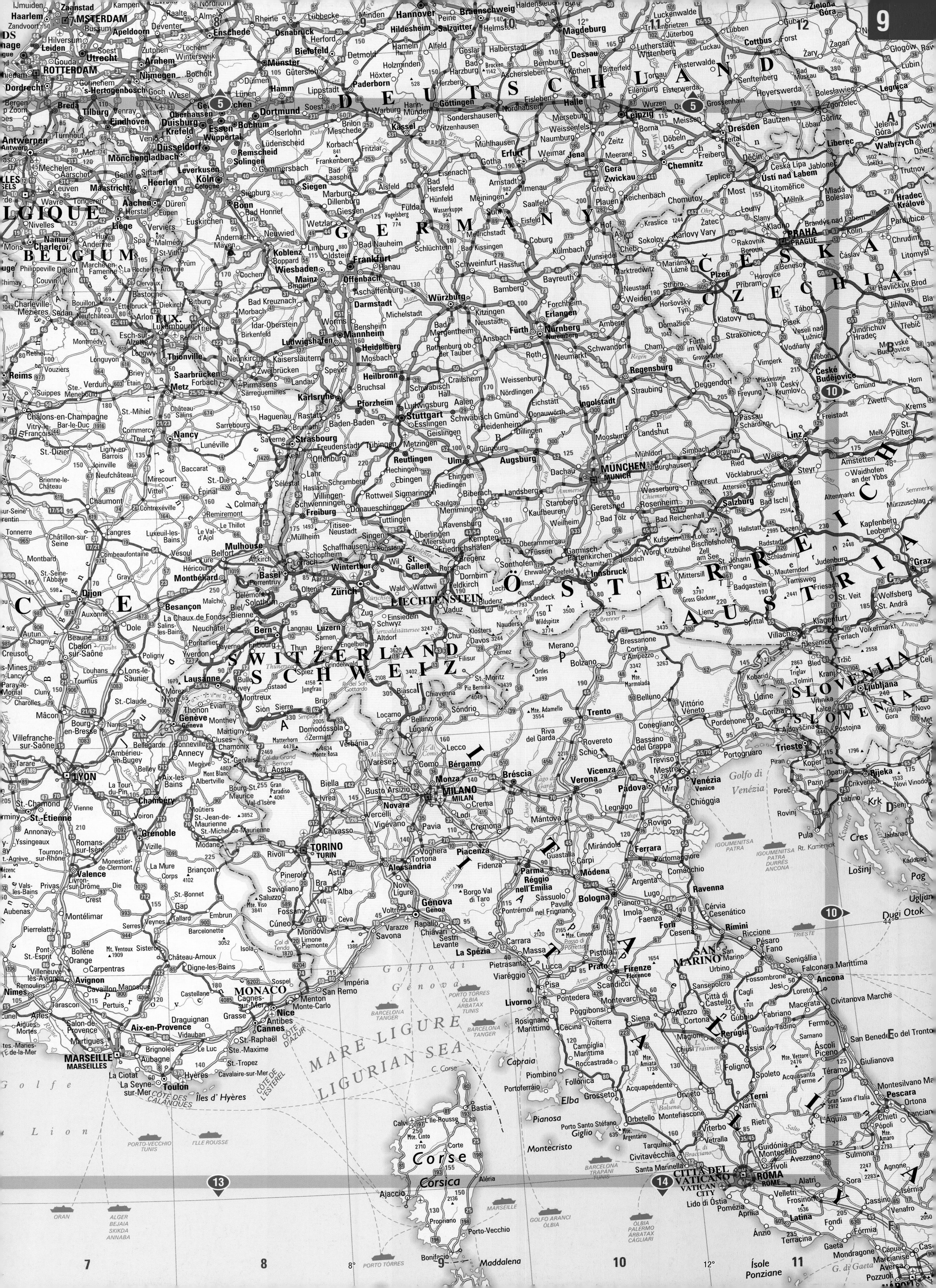
DEUTSCHLAND
GERMANY
BELGIQUE
BELGIUM
LUX.
ČESKÁ
CZECHIA
ÖSTERREICH
AUSTRIA
SWITZERLAND
SCHWEIZ
LIECHTENSTEIN
SLOVENIJA
SLOVENIA
ITALIA
ITALY
SAN MARINO
MONACO
CITTÀ DEL VATICANO
VATICAN CITY
MARE LIGURE
LIGURIAN SEA
Golfo di Génova
Golfo di Venézia
Golfe du Lion
Corse
Corsica
AMSTERDAM
ROTTERDAM
Antwerpen
Düsseldorf
Köln
Frankfurt
Hannover
Braunschweig
Magdeburg
Leipzig
Dresden
Stuttgart
München
Nürnberg
Praha
Linz
Salzburg
Innsbruck
Zürich
Bern
Basel
Genève
Lausanne
Lyon
Dijon
Strasbourg
Metz
Nancy
Marseille
Nice
Torino
Milano
Génova
Venézia
Trieste
Ljubljana
Bologna
Firenze
Roma
Pisa
Livorno
Ancona
Verona
Pádova
Bréscia
Bérgamo
Toulon
Grenoble
Avignon
Rijeka
Graz
7
8
9
10
11
12
5
10
13
14

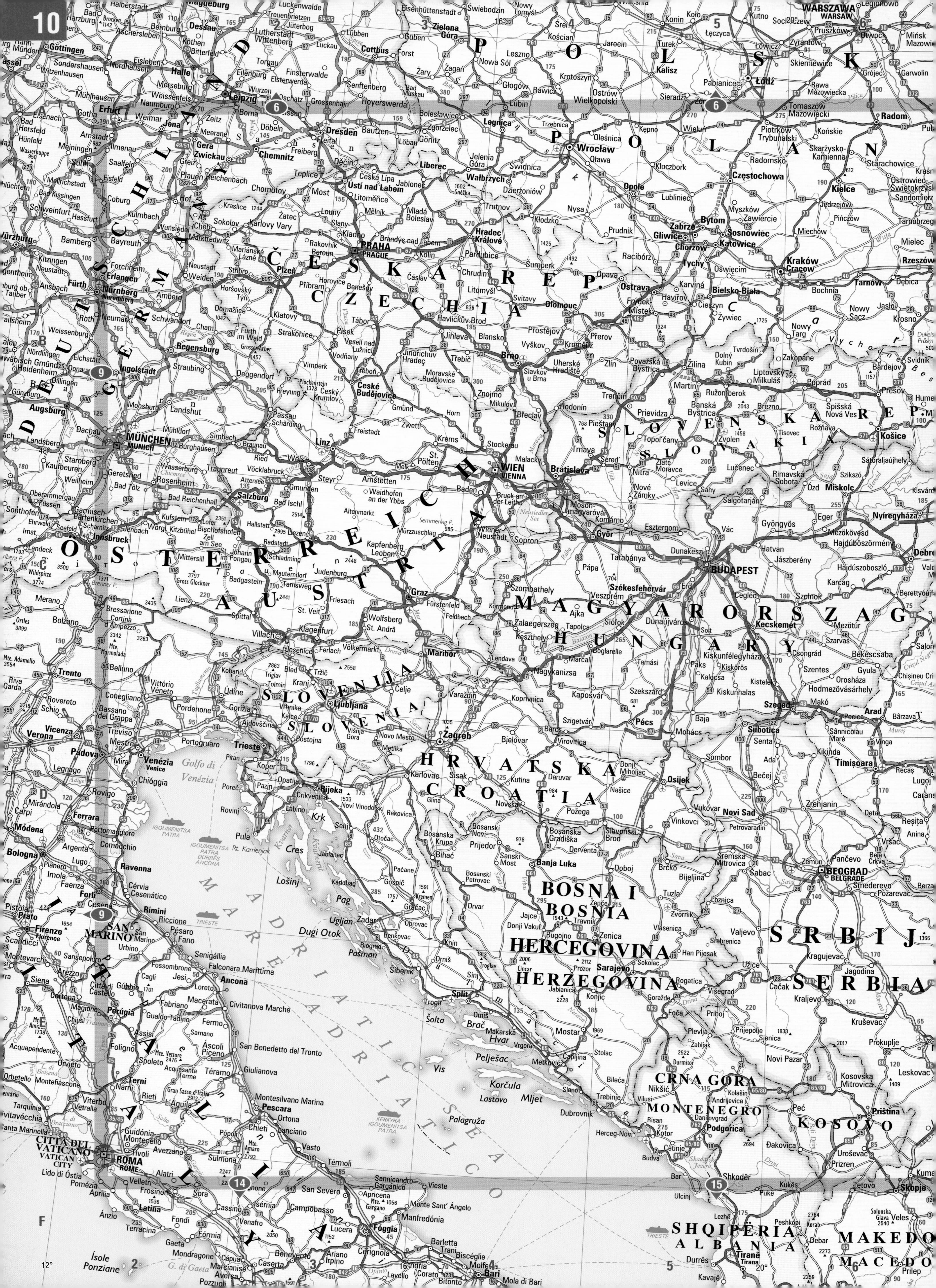
POLSKA
POLAND
DEUTSCHLAND
GERMANY
ČESKÁ REP.
CZECHIA
SLOVENSKÁ REP.
SLOVAKIA
ÖSTERREICH
AUSTRIA
MAGYARORSZÁG
HUNGARY
SLOVENIJA
SLOVENIA
HRVATSKA
CROATIA
BOSNA I HERCEGOVINA
BOSNIA HERZEGOVINA
SRBIJA
SERBIA
CRNA GORA
MONTENEGRO
KOSOVO
SHQIPËRIA
ALBANIA
MAKEDO
MACEDO
ITALIA
ITALY
MARE ADRIATICO
ADRIATIC SEA
Golfo di Venézia
WARSZAWA
WARSAW
Łódź
Wrocław
Kraków
Cracow
Katowice
Częstochowa
Poznań
Leipzig
Dresden
Chemnitz
Erfurt
Halle
Nürnberg
Nuremberg
München
Munich
Augsburg
Regensburg
Ingolstadt
PRAHA
PRAGUE
Brno
Ostrava
Olomouc
Plzeň
České Budějovice
Hradec Králové
Liberec
WIEN
VIENNA
Linz
Salzburg
Innsbruck
Graz
Klagenfurt
Bratislava
Košice
Žilina
BUDAPEST
Győr
Debrecen
Miskolc
Szeged
Pécs
Székesfehérvár
Kecskemét
Ljubljana
Maribor
Zagreb
Rijeka
Split
Osijek
Novi Sad
BEOGRAD
BELGRADE
Subotica
Timişoara
Arad
Banja Luka
Sarajevo
Mostar
Dubrovnik
Podgorica
Priština
Skopje
Tiranë
Trieste
Venézia
Venice
Verona
Pádova
Bologna
Firenze
Ancona
Perúgia
Pescara
ROMA
ROME
CITTÀ DEL VATICANO
VATICAN CITY
SAN MARINO
Fóggia
Bari
6
9
14
15
1
2
3
4
5
6
A
B
C
D
E
F
12°
20°

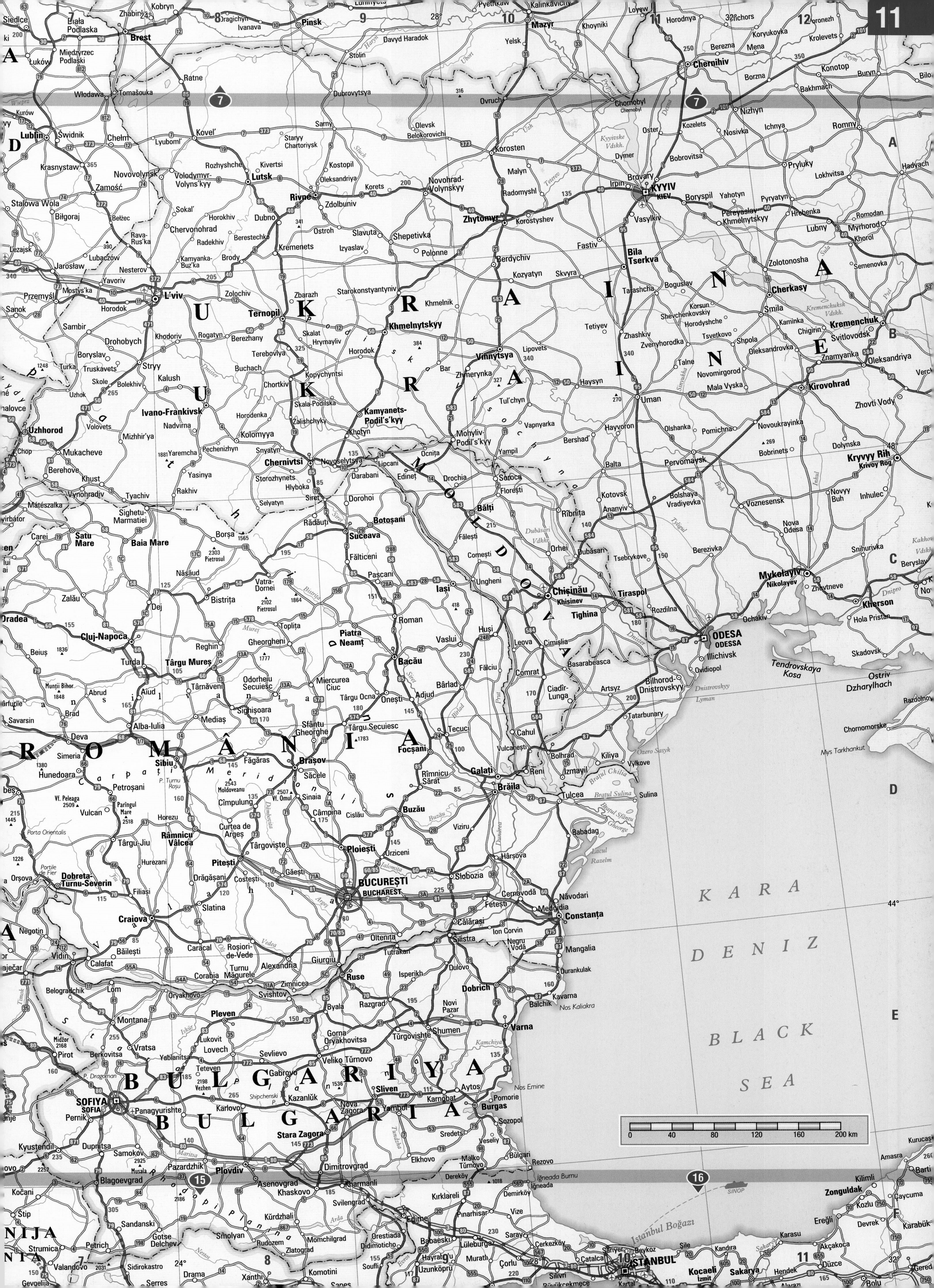
Brest
Pinsk
Mazyr
Chernihiv
Lublin
Kovel'
Lutsk
Rivne
Korosten
KYYIV
KIEV
Zhytomyr
L'viv
Ternopil
Khmelnytskyy
Vinnytsya
Bila Tserkva
Cherkasy
Kremenchuk
Kirovohrad
Uman
Ivano-Frankivsk
Uzhhorod
Chernivtsi
Kamyanets-Podil's'kyy
Kryvyy Rih
Mykolayiv
Kherson
ODESA
ODESSA
Chişinău
Khisinev
Tiraspol
Tighina
Bălţi
Iaşi
Suceava
Botoşani
Bacău
Cluj-Napoca
Târgu Mureş
Braşov
Sibiu
Galaţi
Brăila
Buzău
Ploieşti
BUCUREŞTI
BUCHAREST
Constanţa
Craiova
Piteşti
Ruse
Varna
Pleven
SOFIYA
SOFIA
Plovdiv
Burgas
Stara Zagora
Dobrich
Shumen
ISTANBUL
U K R A I N A
M O L D O V A
R O M Â N I A
B U L G A R I Y A
B U L G A R I A
KARA DENIZ
BLACK SEA
0 40 80 120 160 200 km

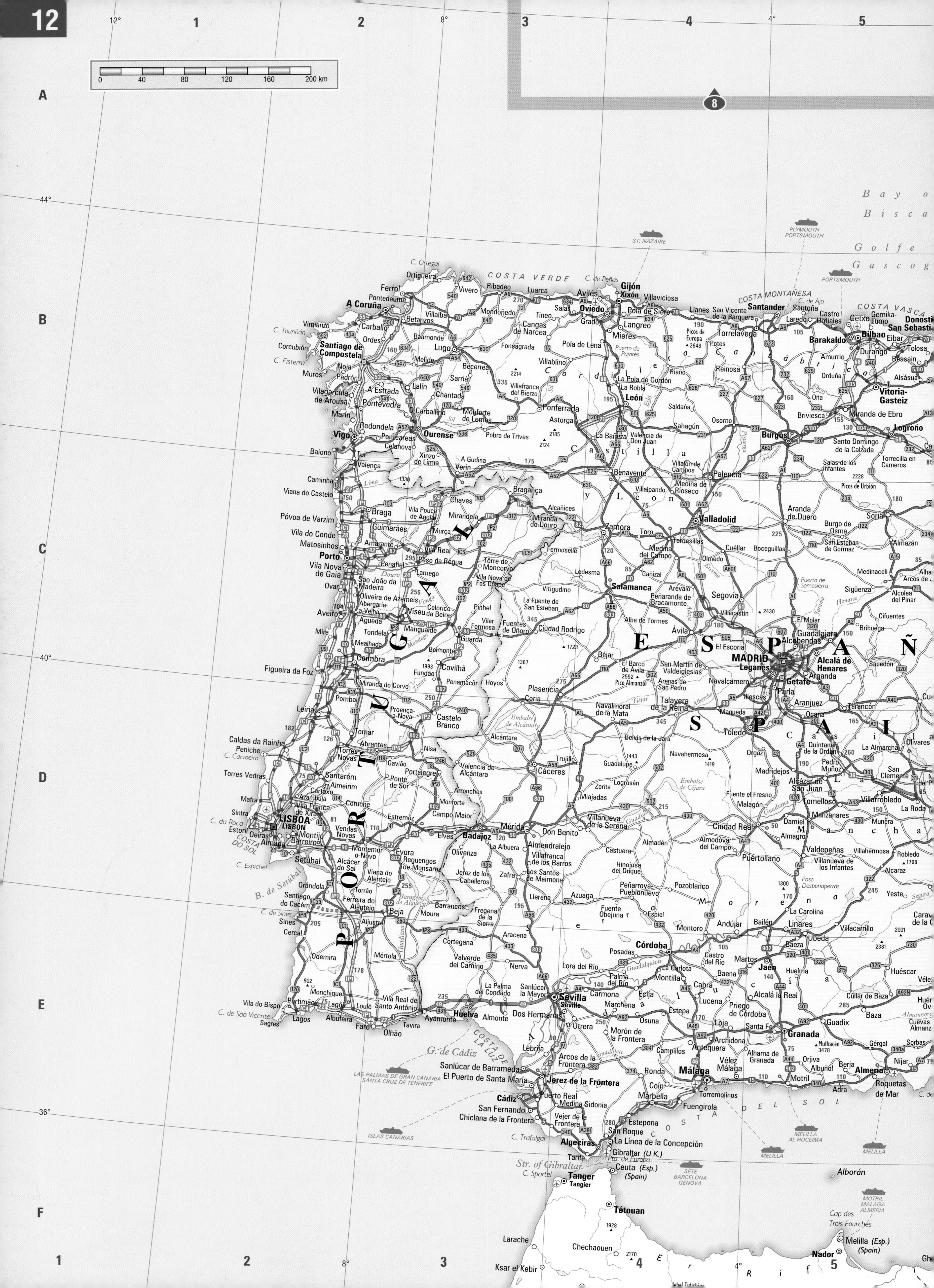

0 40 80 120 160 200 km
12° 8° 4°
44° 40° 36°
1 2 3 4 5
A B C D E F
8
Bay of Biscay
Golfe de Gascogne
PLYMOUTH PORTSMOUTH
ST. NAZAIRE
PORTSMOUTH
C. Ortegal
Ortigueira
COSTA VERDE
C. de Peñas
Ferrol
Pontedeume
A Coruña
Vivero
Ribadeo
Luarca
Avilés
Gijón Xixón
Villaviciosa
COSTA MONTAÑESA
C. de Ajo
COSTA VASCA
Oviedo
Salas
Tineo
Cangas de Narcea
Mondoñedo
Villalba
Betanzos
Carballo
Vimianzo
C. Touriñán
Corcubión
Santiago de Compostela
C. Fisterra
Muros
Noia
Padrón
Vilagarcía de Arousa
A Estrada
Pontevedra
Marín
Redondela
Vigo
Baiona
Ponteareas
Celanova
Tui
Valença
Lalín
Chantada
O Carballiño
Ourense
Xinzo de Limia
Verín
A Gudiña
Lugo
Baamonde
Melide
Becerreá
Sarria
Monforte de Lemos
Pobra de Trives
Fonsagrada
Villablino
Villafranca del Bierzo
Ponferrada
Astorga
Pola de Lena
Grado
Langreo
Mieres
Pola de Siero
Puerto de Pajares
La Pola de Gordón
La Robla
León
Riaño
Llanes
San Vicente de la Barquera
Picos de Europa
Potes
Torrelavega
Santander
Santoña
Laredo
Castro Urdiales
Getxo
Gernika-Lumo
Bilbao
Barakaldo
Eibar
Donostia San Sebastián
Tolosa
Durango
Beasain
Amurrio
Orduña
Alsasua
Vitoria-Gasteiz
Reinosa
Aguilar de Campoo
Oña
Briviesca
Miranda de Ebro
Logroño
Saldaña
Sahagún
Osorno
Burgos
Santo Domingo de la Calzada
La Bañeza
Valencia de Don Juan
Cordillera Cantábrica
Castilla y León
Villalón de Campos
Medina de Rioseco
Palencia
Benavente
Villalpando
Salas de los Infantes
Torrecilla en Cameros
Picos de Urbión
Aranda de Duero
Soria
Burgo de Osma
San Esteban de Gormaz
Valladolid
Zamora
Toro
Tordesillas
Medina del Campo
Cuéllar
Boceguillas
Olmedo
Alcañices
Miranda do Douro
Bragança
Chaves
Mirandela
Vila Pouca de Aguiar
Murça
Vila Real
Peso da Régua
Lamego
Torre de Moncorvo
Vila Nova de Fos Côa
Fermoselle
Ledesma
Salamanca
Vitigudino
Cañizal
Arévalo
Peñaranda de Bracamonte
Segovia
Villacastín
Puerto de Somosierra
Medinaceli
Sigüenza
Alcolea del Pinar
Almazán
Caminha
Viana do Castelo
Póvoa de Varzim
Braga
Guimarães
Vila do Conde
Matosinhos
Porto
Amarante
Penafiel
Vila Nova de Gaia
Espinho
Ovar
São João da Madeira
Oliveira de Azeméis
Albergaria-a-Velha
Aveiro
Viseu
Celorico da Beira
Águeda
Tondela
Mangualde
Mira
Mealhada
Guarda
Pinhel
Vilar Formoso
Fuentes de Oñoro
Ciudad Rodrigo
La Fuente de San Esteban
Alba de Tormes
Ávila
El Escorial
Guadalajara
Alcobendas
MADRID
Leganés
Getafe
Alcalá de Henares
Arganda
Parla
Aranjuez
Illescas
Sacedón
Cifuentes
Brihuega
El Molar
Belmonte
Coimbra
Figueira da Foz
Covilhã
Fundão
Penamacor
Hoyos
Béjar
El Barco de Ávila
Pico Almanzor
San Martín de Valdeiglesias
Arenas de San Pedro
Navalcarnero
Plasencia
Coria
Miranda do Corvo
Pombal
Leiria
Proença-a-Nova
Castelo Branco
Navalmoral de la Mata
Talavera de la Reina
Maqueda
Toledo
Ocaña
Tarancón
Quintanar de la Orden
Pedro Muñoz
Embalse de Alcántara
Alcántara
Belvís de la Jara
Caldas da Rainha
Peniche
C. Carvoeiro
Tomar
Abrantes
Torres Novas
Gavião
Nisa
Torres Vedras
Santarém
Almeirim
Ponte de Sor
Portalegre
Valencia de Alcántara
Cáceres
Trujillo
Guadalupe
Navahermosa
Orgaz
Madridejos
Alcázar de San Juan
Tomelloso
Villarrobledo
La Roda
San Clemente
La Almarcha
Olivares
Mafra
Cartaxo
Azambuja
Coruche
Arronches
Monforte
Sintra
C. da Roca
Estoril
Oeiras
LISBOA LISBON
Vila Franca de Xira
Almada
Barreiro
Montijo
COSTA DO SOL
Setúbal
C. Espichel
B. de Setúbal
Vendas Novas
Montemor-o-Novo
Estremoz
Campo Maior
Elvas
Badajoz
Mérida
Don Benito
Villanueva de la Serena
Miajadas
Zorita
Logrosán
Embalse de Cíjara
Ciudad Real
Almagro
Daniel
Manzanares
Munera
Fuente el Fresno
Malagón
Almodóvar del Campo
Puertollano
Almadén
Castuera
Valdepeñas
Villahermosa
Robledo
Villanueva de los Infantes
Alcaraz
Évora
Reguengos de Monsaraz
Alcácer do Sal
Viana do Alentejo
Olivenza
La Albuera
Almendralejo
Villafranca de los Barros
Los Santos de Maimona
Zafra
Jerez de los Caballeros
Hinojosa del Duque
Peñarroya-Pueblonuevo
Pozoblanco
Paso Despeñaperros
Grândola
Santiago do Cacém
C. de Sines
Sines
Torrão
Ferreira do Alentejo
Barragem de Alqueva
Beja
Moura
Barrancos
Fregenal de la Sierra
Llerena
Azuaga
Fuente Obejuna
Espiel
Montoro
Andújar
Bailén
Linares
La Carolina
Úbeda
Villacarrillo
Yeste
Cercal
Aljustrel
Mértola
Odemira
Aracena
Cortegana
Valverde del Camino
Nerva
Córdoba
Posadas
Castro del Río
Martos
Jaén
Baeza
Huelma
Lora del Río
Palma del Río
La Carlota
Montilla
Baena
Cabra
Lucena
Priego de Córdoba
Alcalá la Real
Huéscar
Monchique
Vila do Bispo
C. de São Vicente
Sagres
Portimão
Lagoa
Lagos
Albufeira
Loulé
Faro
Olhão
Tavira
Vila Real de Santo António
Ayamonte
Huelva
Almonte
La Palma del Condado
Sanlúcar la Mayor
Sevilla
Dos Hermanas
Carmona
Écija
Marchena
Estepa
Utrera
Osuna
Morón de la Frontera
Loja
Santa Fe
Granada
Guadix
Baza
Cúllar de Baza
COSTA DE LA LUZ
G. de Cádiz
Lebrija
Sanlúcar de Barrameda
El Puerto de Santa María
Arcos de la Frontera
Jerez de la Frontera
Cádiz
Puerto Real
San Fernando
Chiclana de la Frontera
Medina Sidonia
Vejer de la Frontera
Campillos
Antequera
Archidona
Alhama de Granada
Vélez Málaga
Málaga
Torremolinos
Fuengirola
Marbella
Ronda
Coín
Estepona
Orjiva
Albuñol
Motril
Adra
Berja
Almería
Níjar
Roquetas de Mar
Gérgal
Sorbas
Mulhacén
COSTA DEL SOL
LAS PALMAS DE GRAN CANARIA SANTA CRUZ DE TENERIFE
ISLAS CANARIAS
C. Trafalgar
San Roque
Algeciras
La Línea de la Concepción
Gibraltar (U.K.)
Pta. de Europa
Tarifa
Str. of Gibraltar
C. Spartel
Tanger Tangier
Ceuta (Esp.) (Spain)
SETE BARCELONA GENOVA
MELILLA AL HOCEIMA
MELILLA
Alborán
MOTRIL MALAGA ALMERIA
Cap des Trois Fourches
Melilla (Esp.) (Spain)
Nador
Tétouan
Larache
Chechaouen
Ksar el Kebir
Er Rif
PORTUGAL
ESPAÑA
SPAIN
Castilla-La Mancha
Sierra Morena
Andalucía

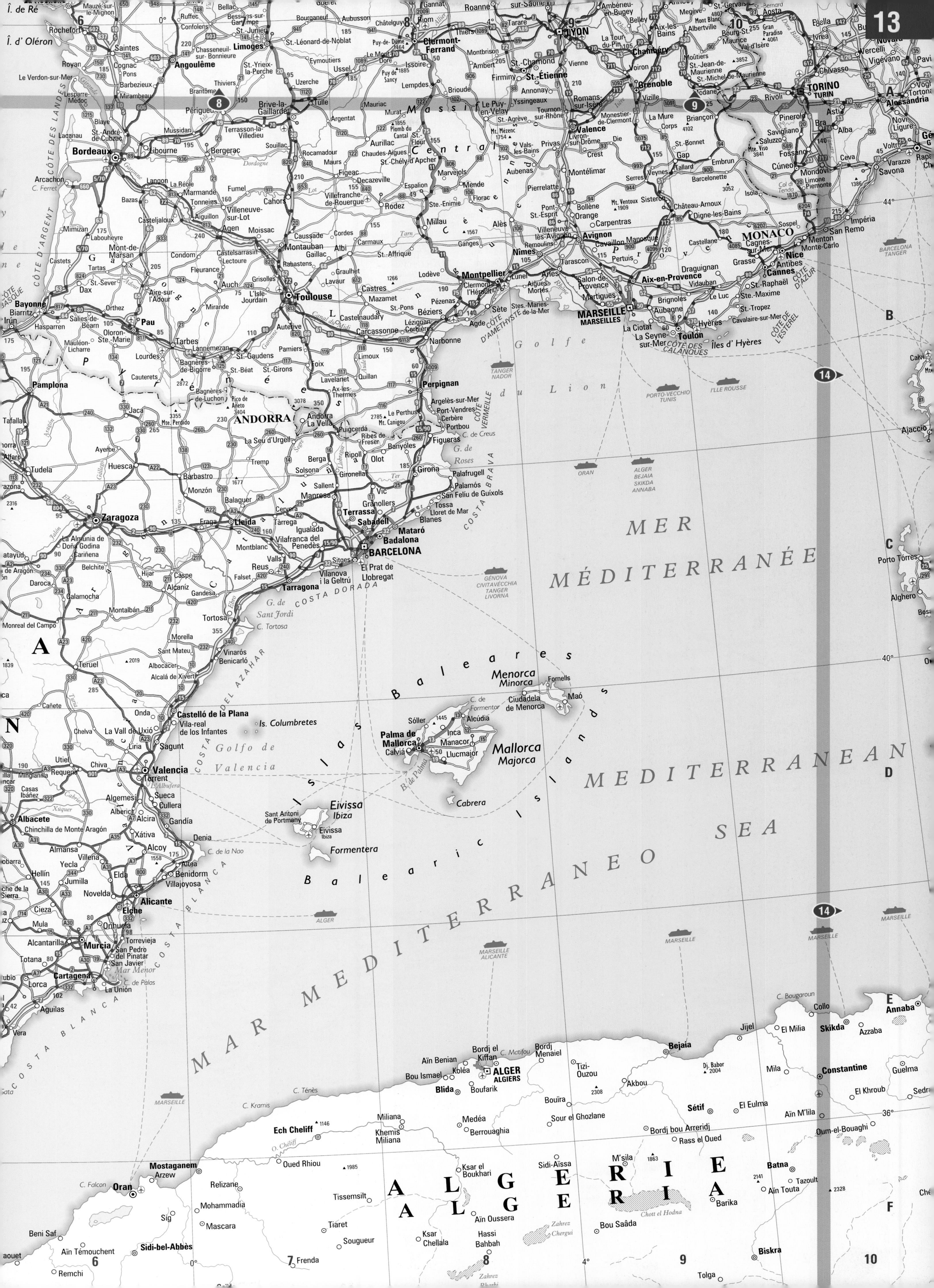
MER
MÉDITERRANÉE
MEDITERRANEAN
SEA
MAR MEDITERRANEO
MAR MEDITERRANEO
Golfe du Lion
Islas Baleares
Balearic Islands
Menorca
Minorca
Mallorca
Majorca
Eivissa
Ibiza
Formentera
Cabrera
Is. Columbretes
Golfo de Valencia
G. de Sant Jordi
G. de Roses
COSTA BRAVA
COSTA DORADA
COSTA DEL AZAHAR
COSTA BLANCA
CÔTE VERMEILLE
CÔTE D'AMÉTHYSTE
CÔTE DES CALANQUES
CÔTE D'AZUR
CÔTE DE L'ESTÉREL
CÔTE DES LANDES
CÔTE D'ARGENT
Massif Central
Pyrénées
Cévennes
Provence
Catalunya
Aragón
ANDORRA
MONACO
ALGERIE
ALGERIA
BARCELONA
MARSEILLE
MARSEILLES
ALGER
ALGIERS
LYON
TORINO
TURIN
Bordeaux
Toulouse
Montpellier
Perpignan
Nice
Cannes
Toulon
Aix-en-Provence
Avignon
Nîmes
Valence
Grenoble
Clermont-Ferrand
Limoges
Angoulême
Pau
Bayonne
Pamplona
Zaragoza
Lleida
Tarragona
Girona
Valencia
Castelló de la Plana
Alicante
Murcia
Cartagena
Albacete
Palma de Mallorca
Oran
Mostaganem
Bejaia
Skikda
Annaba
Constantine
Sétif
Biskra
Batna
Ech Cheliff
Blida
Sidi-bel-Abbès
6
7
8
9
10
A
B
C
D
E
F

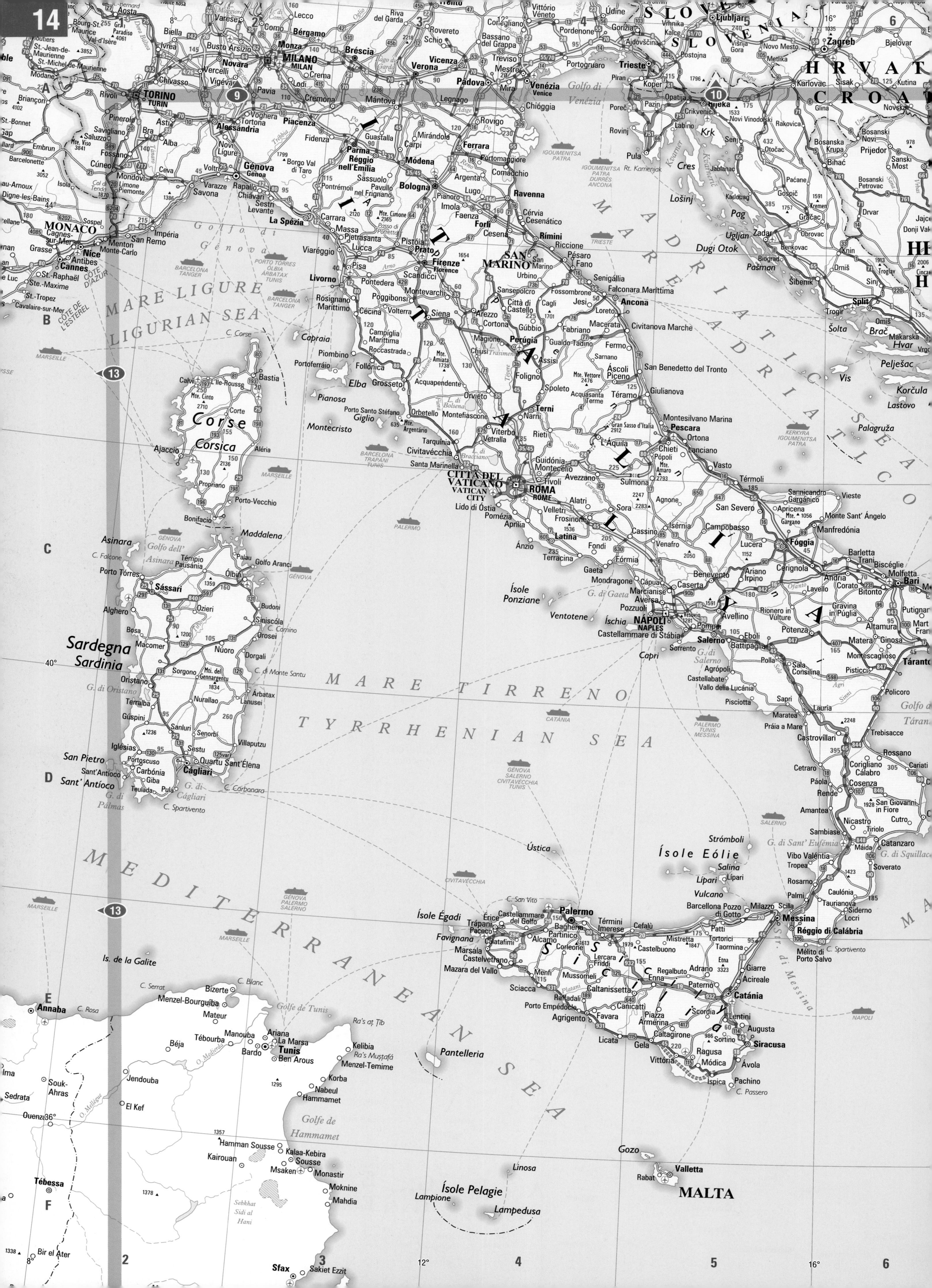

Aosta
Lecco
Bérgamo
Bréscia
Verona
Vicenza
Pádova
Venézia
Venice
Treviso
Trieste
Údine
Ljubljana
Zagreb
SLOVENIA
HRVATSKA
CROATIA
Novara
MILANO
MILAN
Vercelli
Biella
Ivrea
Pavia
Cremona
Mántova
TORINO
TURIN
Asti
Alessandria
Piacenza
Parma
Réggio nell'Emília
Módena
Bologna
Ferrara
Rovigo
Chióggia
Golfo di Venézia
Génova
Genoa
Savona
Rapallo
La Spézia
Carrara
Massa
Lucca
Pisa
Livorno
Firenze
Florence
Prato
Pistóia
Siena
Arezzo
Ravenna
Forlì
Cesena
Rímini
SAN MARINO
Pésaro
Urbino
Ancona
Perúgia
Assisi
Foligno
Spoleto
Terni
Viterbo
Grosseto
Civitavécchia
CITTÀ DEL VATICANO
VATICAN CITY
ROMA
ROME
Lido di Óstia
Latina
Frosinone
L'Áquila
Téramo
Pescara
Chieti
Campobasso
Fóggia
Bari
Barletta
Bénevento
Caserta
NÁPOLI
NAPLES
Salerno
Potenza
Matera
Táranto
Cosenza
Catanzaro
Réggio di Calábria
Messina
Palermo
Trápani
Marsala
Agrigento
Caltanissetta
Catánia
Siracusa
Ragusa
Enna
MONACO
Monte-Carlo
Nice
Cannes
San Remo
Impéria
Corse
Corsica
Ajaccio
Bastia
Bonifacio
Porto-Vecchio
Sardegna
Sardinia
Sássari
Ólbia
Alghero
Núoro
Oristano
Cágliari
Iglésias
Carbónia
Elba
Capraia
Montecristo
Giglio
Ísole Ponziane
Ventotene
Íschia
Capri
Ústica
Ísole Eólie
Strómboli
Lípari
Salina
Vulcano
Ísole Égadi
Favignana
Pantelleria
Linosa
Lampedusa
Lampione
Ísole Pelagie
Gozo
Valletta
Rabat
MALTA
ITALIA
ITALY
SICILIA
MARE LIGURE
LIGURIAN SEA
MARE TIRRENO
TYRRHENIAN SEA
MEDITERRANEAN SEA
MARE ADRIATICO
ADRIATIC SEA
Golfo di Génova
Golfo di Táranto
G. di Squillace
G. di Sant' Eufémia
G. di Salerno
G. di Gaeta
Golfe de Tunis
Golfe de Hammamet
Bizerte
Tunis
Ben Arous
La Marsa
Ariana
Béja
Jendouba
El Kef
Kelibia
Nabeul
Hammamet
Sousse
Monastir
Mahdia
Kairouan
Sfax
Annaba
Souk-Ahras
Tébessa
Is. de la Galite
Split
Zadar
Rijeka
Pula
Šibenik
Brač
Hvar
Korčula
Vis
Lastovo
Palagruža
Krk
Cres
Lošinj
Dugi Otok

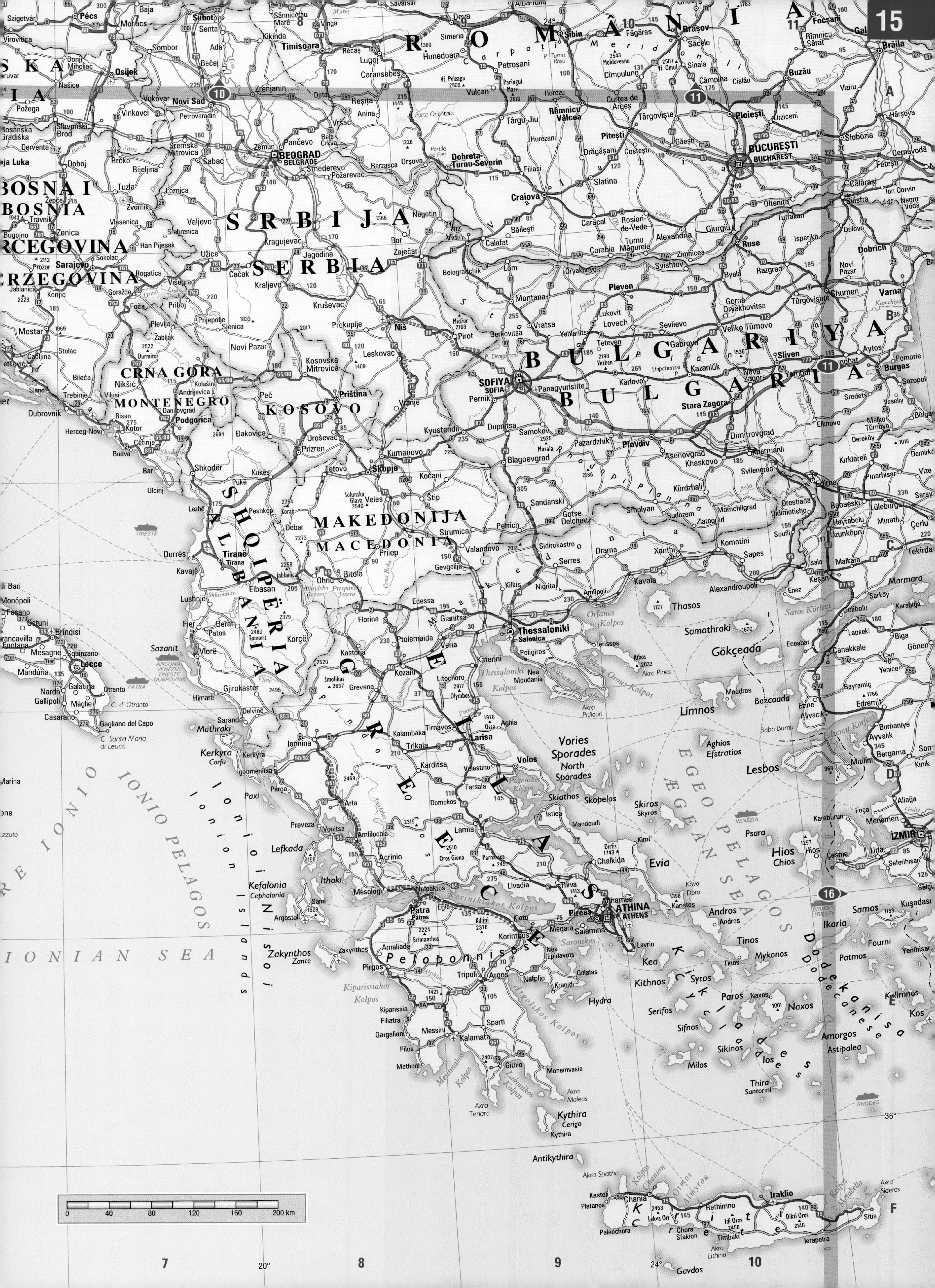

ROMÂNIA
SRBIJA
SERBIA
BOSNA I HERCEGOVINA
BOSNIA HERZEGOVINA
CRNA GORA
MONTENEGRO
KOSOVO
SHQIPËRIA
ALBANIA
MAKEDONIJA
MACEDONIA
BULGARIYA
BULGARIA
ELLAS
GREECE
Pécs
Szigetvár
Baja
Subotica
Senta
Sombor
Osijek
Novi Sad
Vukovar
Vinkovci
Zrenjanin
Kikinda
Timişoara
Lugoj
Caransebeş
Reşiţa
Hunedoara
Deva
Sibiu
Făgăraş
Braşov
Săcele
Sinaia
Câmpina
Buzău
Focşani
Râmnicu Sărat
Brăila
Ploieşti
Urziceni
Târgovişte
Piteşti
Râmnicu Vâlcea
Târgu-Jiu
Drobeta-Turnu-Severin
Craiova
Slatina
Caracal
Roşiori-de-Vede
Alexandria
Giurgiu
BUCUREŞTI
BUCHAREST
Slobozia
Călăraşi
Cernavodă
Feteşti
Silistra
Oltenita
Turnu Măgurele
Calafat
Vidin
Lom
Montana
Vratsa
Pleven
Lovech
Ruse
Razgrad
Shumen
Varna
Dobrich
Veliko Tŭrnovo
Tŭrgovishte
Gabrovo
Kazanlŭk
Sliven
Yambol
Burgas
Aytos
Pomorie
Sozopol
Stara Zagora
Nova Zagora
Haskovo
Dimitrovgrad
Kŭrdzhali
Plovdiv
Pazardzhik
Smolyan
SOFIYA
SOFIA
Pernik
Dupnitsa
Kyustendil
Blagoevgrad
Sandanski
Petrich
Karlovo
Berkovitsa
BEOGRAD
BELGRADE
Pančevo
Smederevo
Požarevac
Šabac
Valjevo
Užice
Čačak
Kragujevac
Kraljevo
Kruševac
Niš
Prokuplje
Leskovac
Vranje
Pirot
Zaječar
Negotin
Bor
Jagodina
Novi Pazar
Kosovska Mitrovica
Priština
Peć
Prizren
Uroševac
Đakovica
Podgorica
Nikšić
Kotor
Budva
Bar
Ulcinj
Herceg-Novi
Dubrovnik
Trebinje
Mostar
Sarajevo
Zenica
Tuzla
Zvornik
Doboj
Banja Luka
Bijeljina
Foča
Skopje
Tetovo
Kumanovo
Veles
Štip
Kočani
Strumica
Prilep
Bitola
Ohrid
Gevgelija
Valandovo
Shkodër
Lezhë
Durrës
Tiranë
Tirana
Kavajë
Elbasan
Lushnjë
Fier
Berat
Vlorë
Korçë
Gjirokastër
Sarandë
Himarë
Ionnina
Igoumenitsa
Kerkyra
Corfu
Paxi
Preveza
Lefkada
Kefalonia
Ithaki
Zakynthos
Zante
Patra
Patras
Pirgos
Tripoli
Argos
Kalamata
Sparti
Korinthos
Peloponnisos
Kythira
Antikythira
Kozani
Kastoria
Florina
Edessa
Veria
Katerini
Thessaloniki
Salonica
Serres
Drama
Kavala
Xanthi
Komotini
Alexandroupoli
Larisa
Trikala
Karditsa
Kalambaka
Volos
Lamia
Agrinio
Mesolongi
Nafpaktos
Thiva
Chalkida
ATHINA
ATHENS
Pireas
Thasos
Samothraki
Gökçeada
Limnos
Lesbos
Mitilini
Aghios Efstratios
Vories Sporades
North Sporades
Skiathos
Skopelos
Skiros
Evia
Andros
Tinos
Mykonos
Syros
Kea
Kithnos
Serifos
Sifnos
Paros
Naxos
Milos
Ios
Thira
Santorini
Amorgos
Astipalea
Ikaria
Samos
Fourni
Patmos
Kalimnos
Kos
Hios
Chios
Psara
Hydra
Kiklades
Cyclades
Dodekanisa
Dodecanese
Iraklio
Chania
Rethimno
Sitia
Ierapetra
Gavdos
Edirne
Kırklareli
Lüleburgaz
Tekirdağ
Keşan
Uzunköprü
Çanakkale
Biga
Edremit
Ayvalık
Bergama
Aliağa
Menemen
İZMIR
Çeşme
Kuşadası
Lecce
Brindisi
Otranto
Gallipoli
IONIAN SEA
IONIO PELAGOS
Ionioi Nisoi
Ionian Islands
EGEO PELAGOS
AEGEAN SEA
0
40
80
120
160
200 km
7
8
9
10
11
20°
24°
36°
A
B
C
D
E
F

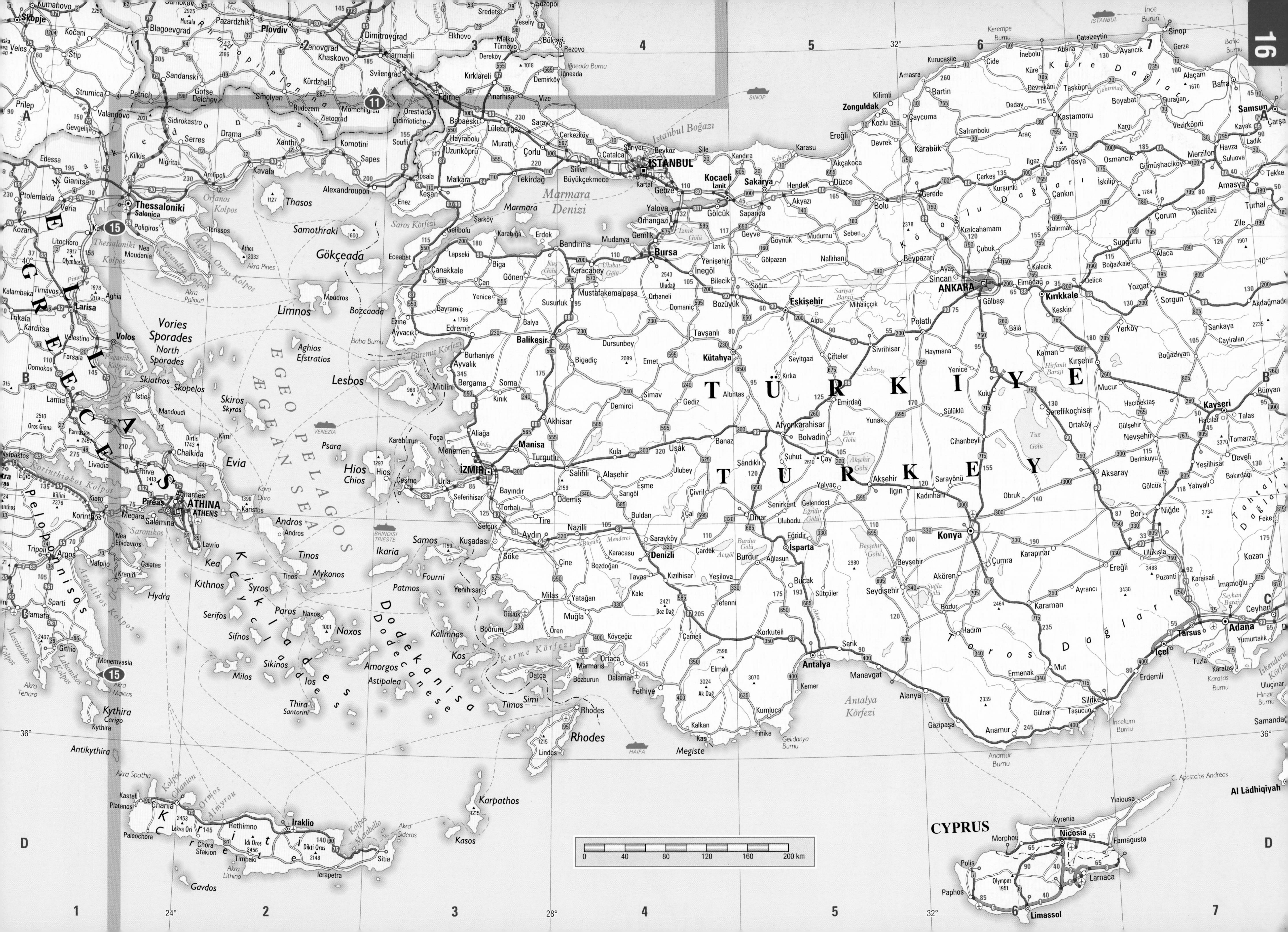
TÜRKIYE
TURKEY
GREECE
ELLAS
CYPRUS
EGEO PELAGOS
ÆGEAN SEA
Marmara Denizi
Küre Dağları
Köroğlu Dağları
Toros Dağları
Rhodopi Planina
Makedonia
Kikladhes
Cyclades
Dodekanisa
Dodecanese
Peloponnisos
Kriti
Crete
İSTANBUL
ANKARA
İZMIR
ATHINA
ATHENS
Thessaloniki
Salonica
Bursa
Eskişehir
Konya
Antalya
Adana
Kayseri
Samsun
Sinop
Zonguldak
Kastamonu
Çorum
Amasya
Kırıkkale
Yozgat
Aksaray
Niğde
Nevşehir
Kırşehir
Afyonkarahisar
Kütahya
Uşak
Manisa
Balıkesir
Denizli
Isparta
Burdur
Muğla
Aydın
Bilecik
Sakarya
Kocaeli
İzmit
Tekirdağ
Edirne
Kırklareli
Çanakkale
Karaman
Tarsus
İçel
Plovdiv
Skopje
Larisa
Volos
Iraklio
Chania
Rethimno
Nicosia
Limassol
Larnaca
Famagusta
Kyrenia
Paphos
Lesbos
Limnos
Hios
Chios
Samos
Ikaria
Rhodes
Karpathos
Kasos
Naxos
Paros
Mykonos
Tinos
Andros
Evia
Thasos
Samothraki
Gökçeada
Bozcaada
Skiros
Skyros
Vories Sporades
North Sporades
Kythira
Gavdos
Antalya Körfezi
Saros Körfezi
Edremit Körfezi
Kerme Körfezi
İstanbul Boğazı
Tuz Gölü
Al Lādhiqīyah
0 40 80 120 160 200 km

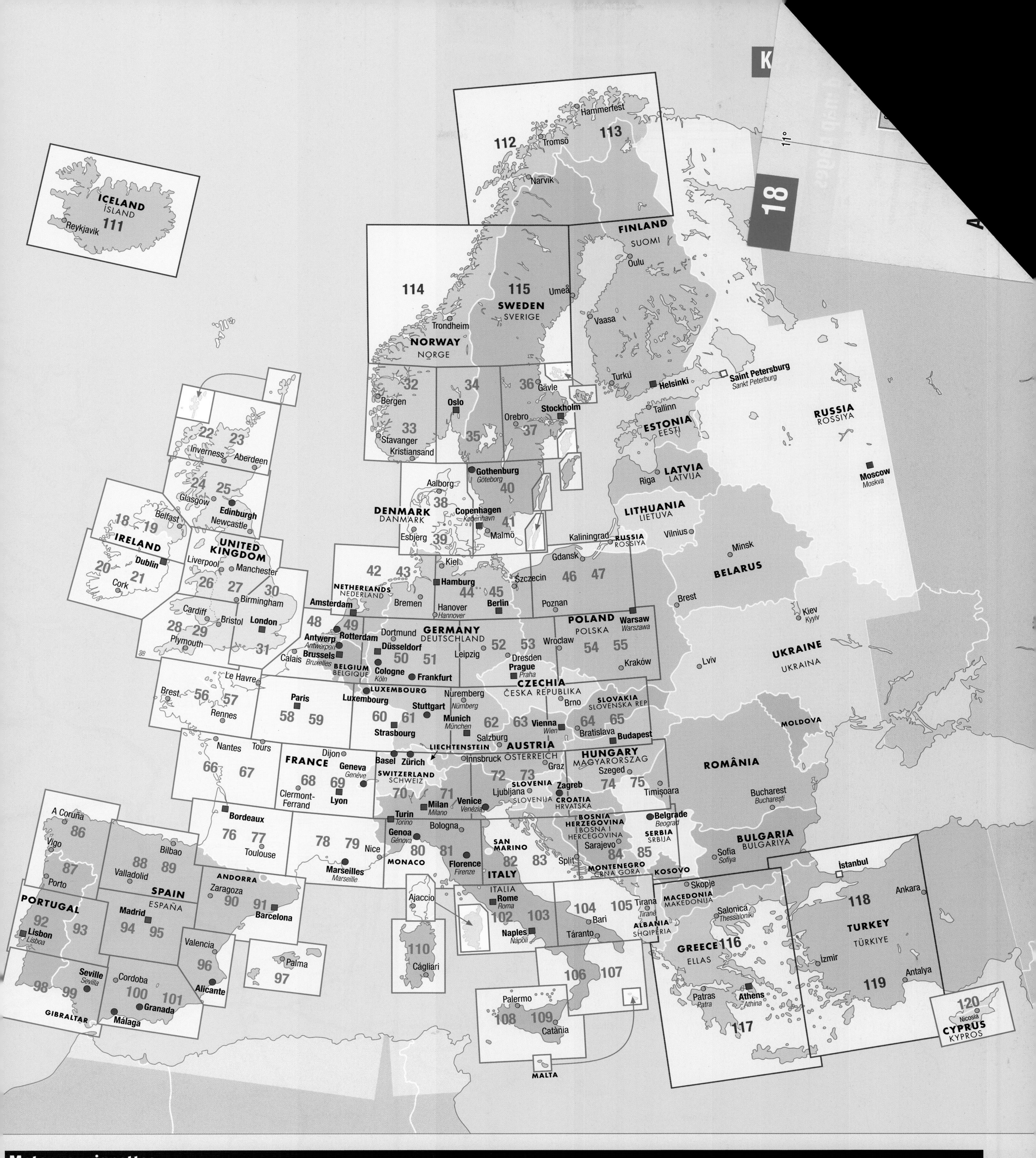

Motorway vignettes

Some countries require you to purchase (and in some cases display) a vignette before using motorways.

In Austria you will need to purchase and display a vignette on the inside of your windscreen. Vignettes are available for purchase at border crossings and petrol stations. More details from www.asfinag.at/toll/toll-sticker

In Belarus all vehicles over 3.5 tonnes and cars and vans under 3.5 tonnes registered outside the Eurasion Economic Union are required to have a BelToll unit installed. This device exchanges data with roadside gantries, enabling motorway tolls to be automatically deducted from the driver's account. http://www.beltoll.by/index.php/en/beltoll-system/five-steps#

In Czechia, you can buy a vignette at the border and also at petrol stations. Make sure you write your vehicle registration number on the vignette before displaying it. The roads without toll are indicated by a traffic sign saying "Bez poplatku". More details from www.motorway.cz

In Hungary a new e-vignette system was introduced in 2008. It is therefore no longer necessary to display the vignette, though you should make doubly sure the information you give on your vehicle is accurate. Vignettes are sold at petrol stations throughout the country. Buy online at http://toll-charge.hu/

In Slovakia, an electronic vignette must purchased before using the motorways. Vignettes may be purchased online, via a mobile app or at Slovak border crossings and petrol stations displaying the 'eznamka' logo. More details from https://eznamka.sk/selfcare/home/

In Switzerland, you will need to purchase and display a vignette before you drive on the motorway. Bear in mind you will need a separate vignette if you are towing a caravan. www.ezv.admin.ch/zollinfo_privat/04338/04340/04916/index.html?lang=en

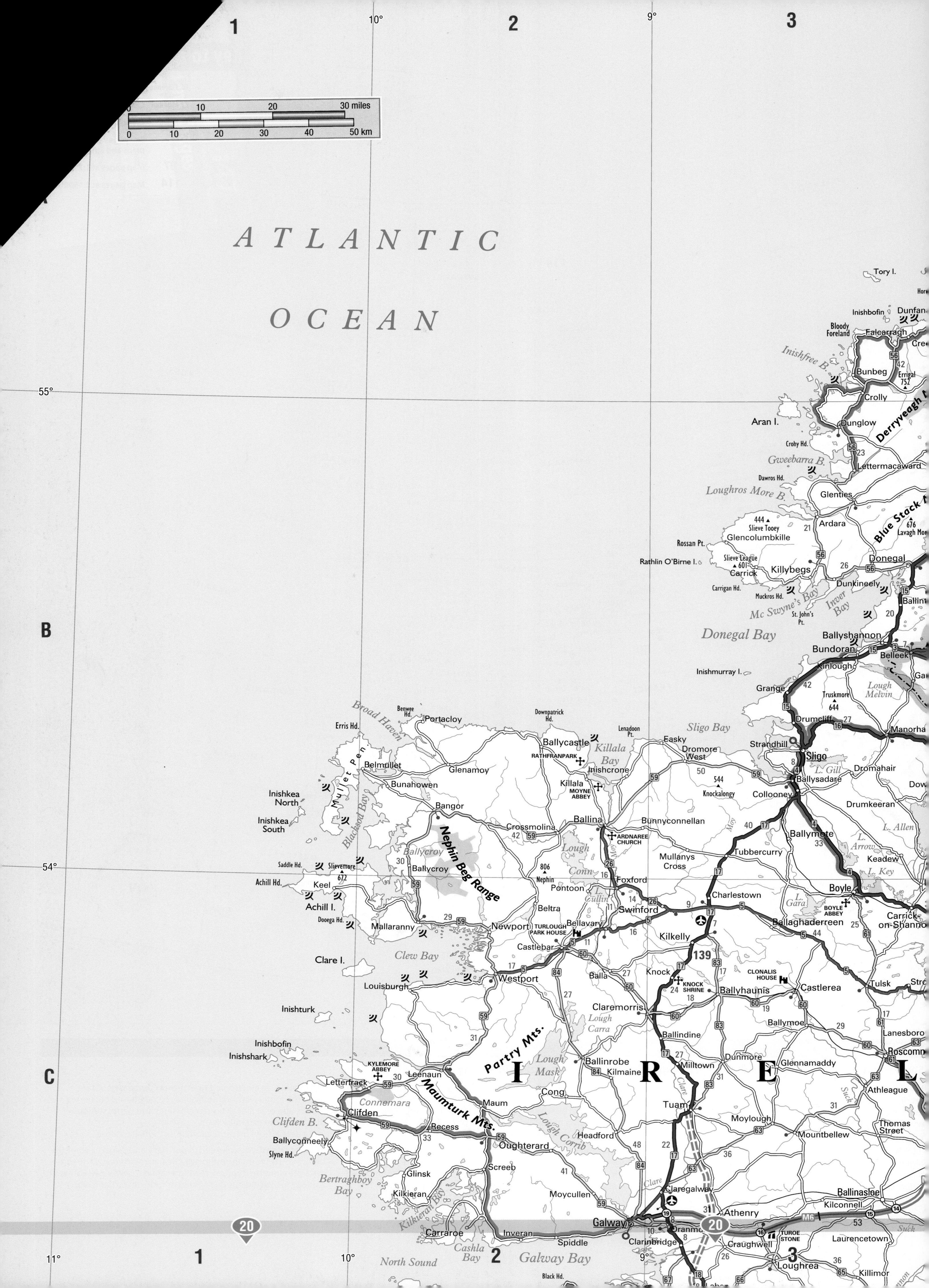

1
2
3
10°
9°
0
10
20
30 miles
0
10
20
30
40
50 km
ATLANTIC
OCEAN
55°
54°
B
C
11°
10°
20
Tory I.
Inishbofin
Dunfanaghy
Bloody Foreland
Falcarragh
Inishfree B.
Bunbeg
Errigal 752
Crolly
Aran I.
Dunglow
Derryveagh Mts.
Crohy Hd.
Gweebarra B.
Lettermacaward
Dawros Hd.
Loughros More B.
Glenties
444 Slieve Tooey
Glencolumbkille
Ardara
Blue Stack Mts.
676 Lavagh More
Rossan Pt.
Slieve League 601
Carrick
Killybegs
Donegal
Rathlin O'Birne I.
Carrigan Hd.
Muckros Hd.
Dunkineely
Mc Swyne's Bay
St. John's Pt.
Inver Bay
Donegal Bay
Ballyshannon
Bundoran
Belleek
Kinlough
Lough Melvin
Inishmurray I.
Grange
Truskmore 644
Drumcliff
Manorhamilton
Sligo Bay
Strandhill
Sligo
L. Gill
Dromahair
Ballysadare
Collooney
Drumkeeran
L. Allen
Ballymote
L. Arrow
Keadew
L. Key
Boyle
BOYLE ABBEY
Carrick-on-Shannon
Broad Haven
Benwee Hd.
Portacloy
Erris Hd.
Downpatrick Hd.
Lenadoon Pt.
Ballycastle
RATHFRANPARK
Killala Bay
Easky
Dromore West
Mullet Pen.
Belmullet
Glenamoy
Inishcrone
Killala
MOYNE ABBEY
544 Knockalongy
Bunahowen
Inishkea North
Inishkea South
Blacksod Bay
Bangor
Nephin Beg Range
Crossmolina
Ballina
ARDNAREE CHURCH
Bunnyconnellan
Moy
Tubbercurry
Lough Conn
Mullanys Cross
Ballycroy
Saddle Hd.
Slievemore 672
Achill Hd.
Keel
Achill I.
806 Nephin
Pontoon
L. Cullin
Foxford
Swinford
Charlestown
Gara
Dooega Hd.
Mallaranny
Newport
Beltra
TURLOUGH PARK HOUSE
Bellavary
Kilkelly
Ballaghaderreen
Clew Bay
Castlebar
Clare I.
Westport
Balla
Knock
KNOCK SHRINE
CLONALIS HOUSE
Castlerea
Tulsk
Louisburgh
Ballyhaunis
Claremorris
Lough Carra
Inishturk
Ballymoe
Lanesborough
Ballindine
Inishbofin
Inishshark
Partry Mts.
Lough Mask
Ballinrobe
Kilmaine
Milltown
Dunmore
Glennamaddy
Roscommon
KYLEMORE ABBEY
Leenaun
Letterfrack
Maumturk Mts.
I R E L
Cong
Athleague
Connemara
Maum
Tuam
Clare
Suck
Clifden
Clifden B.
Recess
Lough Corrib
Headford
Moylough
Thomas Street
Mountbellew
Ballyconneely
Slyne Hd.
Oughterard
Glinsk
Screeb
Bertraghboy Bay
Kilkieran
Kilkieran Bay
Moycullen
Claregalway
Ballinasloe
Kilconnell
Athenry
Galway
M6
Carraroe
Inveran
Spiddle
Clarinbridge
Oranmore
TUROE STONE
Craughwell
Laurencetown
Cashla Bay
Galway Bay
North Sound
Loughrea
Killimor
Black Hd.

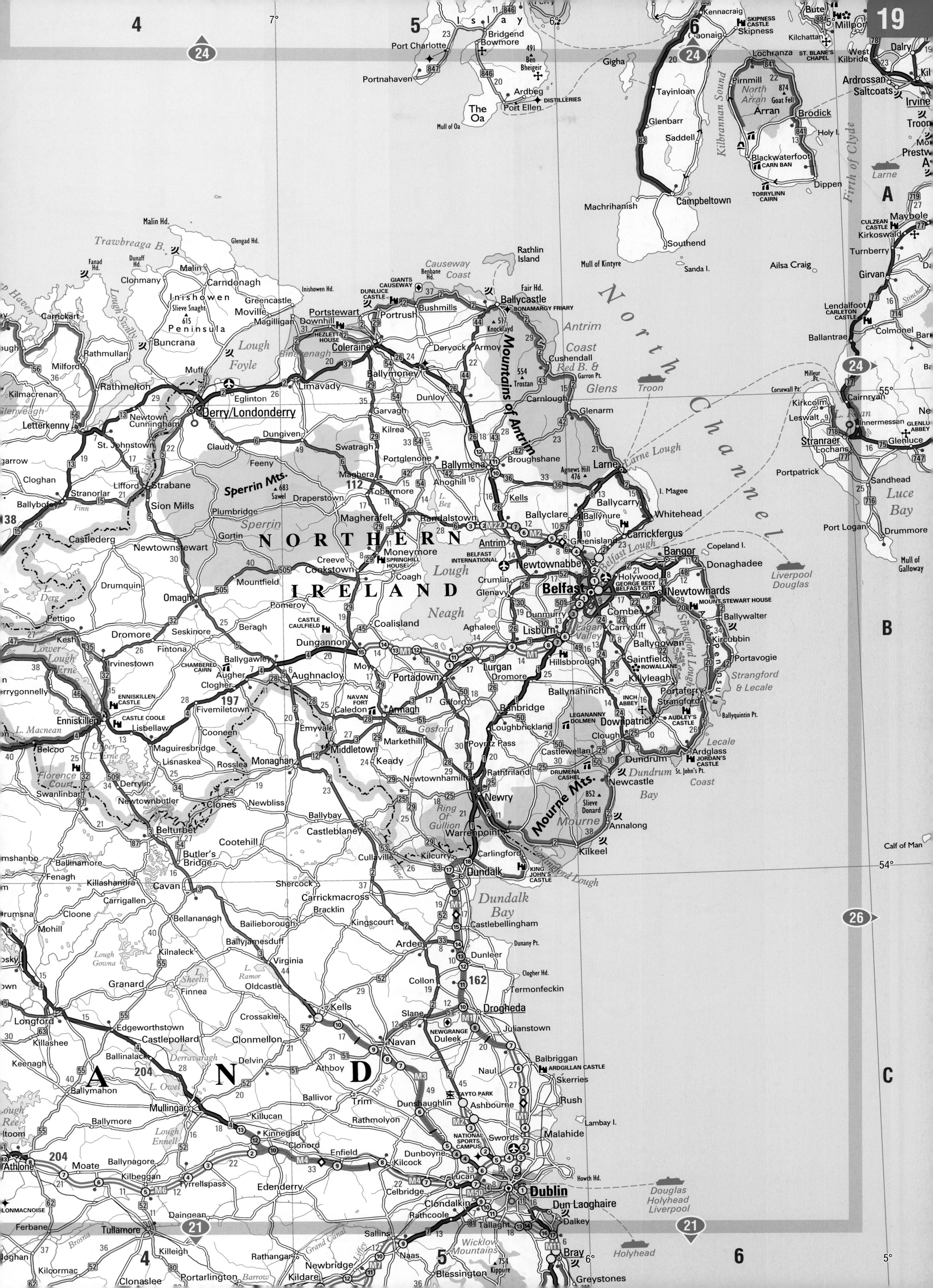
Islay
Port Charlotte
Bridgend
Bowmore
Portnahaven
Ben Bheigeir
Ardbeg
Port Ellen
DISTILLERIES
The Oa
Mull of Oa
Kennacraig
SKIPNESS CASTLE
Skipness
Claonaig
Gigha
Tayinloan
Glenbarr
Saddell
Kilbrannan Sound
Lochranza
Pirnmill
North Arran
Goat Fell
Arran
Brodick
Holy I.
Blackwaterfoot
CARN BAN
TORRYLINN CAIRN
Dippen
Campbeltown
Machrihanish
Southend
Mull of Kintyre
Sanda I.
Bute
Millport
Kilchattan
ST. BLANE'S CHAPEL
West Kilbride
Dalry
Ardrossan
Saltcoats
Irvine
Troon
Prestwick
Firth of Clyde
Larne
Maybole
CULZEAN CASTLE
Kirkoswald
Turnberry
Girvan
Ailsa Craig
Lendalfoot
CARLETON CASTLE
Colmonell
Ballantrae
Milleur Pt.
Corsewall Pt.
Kirkcolm
Leswalt
Cairnryan
L. Ryan
Innermessan
GLENLUCE ABBEY
Glenluce
Stranraer
Lochans
Portpatrick
Sandhead
Luce Bay
Port Logan
Drummore
Mull of Galloway
Rathlin Island
Causeway Coast
Benbane Hd.
GIANTS CAUSEWAY
DUNLUCE CASTLE
Bushmills
Ballycastle
BONAMARGY FRIARY
Fair Hd.
Knocklayd
Portstewart
Portrush
Downhill
HEZLETT HOUSE
Coleraine
Dervock
Armoy
Mountains of Antrim
Antrim Coast
Cushendall
Red B. & Garron Pt.
Glens
Trostan
Troon
Ballymoney
Dunloy
Carnlough
Glenarm
North Channel
Malin Hd.
Trawbreaga B.
Glengad Hd.
Fanad Hd.
Dunaff Hd.
Malin
Clonmany
Carndonagh
Inishowen Peninsula
Slieve Snaght
Inishowen Hd.
Greencastle
Moville
Magilligan
Lough Swilly
Buncrana
Lough Foyle
Binevenagh
Rathmullan
Milford
Muff
Eglinton
Limavady
Rathmelton
Kilmacrenan
Glenveagh
Letterkenny
Newtown Cunningham
Derry/Londonderry
Dungiven
Garvagh
Kilrea
Claudy
St. Johnstown
Swatragh
Portglenone
Ballymena
Broughshane
Larne Lough
Agnews Hill
Feeny
Sperrin Mts.
Sawel
Maghera
Tobermore
Ahoghill
Kells
I. Magee
Whitehead
Lifford
Strabane
Stranorlar
Ballybofey
Finn
Clogher
Sion Mills
Plumbridge
Draperstown
Magherafelt
Randalstown
L. Beg
Ballyclare
Ballycarry
Ballynure
Carrickfergus
Sperrin
Gortin
NORTHERN IRELAND
Castlederg
Newtownstewart
Antrim
BELFAST INTERNATIONAL
Greenisland
Belfast Lough
Bangor
Copeland I.
Donaghadee
Moneymore
SPRINGHILL HOUSE
Creeve
Cookstown
Coagh
Lough Neagh
Newtownabbey
Holywood
GEORGE BEST BELFAST CITY
Belfast
Liverpool Douglas
Drumquin
L. Derg
Mountfield
Omagh
Crumlin
Glenavy
Newtownards
MOUNT STEWART HOUSE
Pettigo
Pomeroy
Dunmurry
Comber
Ballywalter
Dromore
Seskinore
Beragh
CASTLE CAULFIELD
Coalisland
Aghalee
Lisburn
Lagan Valley
Carryduff
Strangford Lough
Ards Peninsula
Kircubbin
Kesh
Lower Lough Erne
Irvinestown
Fintona
Dungannon
Ballygowan
Portavogie
Ballygawley
CHAMBERED CAIRN
Augher
Aughnacloy
Moy
Lurgan
Hillsborough
Saintfield
ROWALLANE
Killyleagh
Strangford & Lecale
Clogher
Portadown
Dromore
ENNISKILLEN CASTLE
NAVAN FORT
Gilford
Ballynahinch
INCH ABBEY
Portaferry
Strangford
Enniskillen
Fivemiletown
Caledon
Armagh
Banbridge
LEGANANNY DOLMEN
Downpatrick
AUDLEY'S CASTLE
Ballyquintin Pt.
CASTLE COOLE
Lisbellaw
Emyvale
Gosford
Loughbrickland
L. Macnean
Cooneen
Markethill
Poyntz Pass
Clough
Lecale
Belcoo
Upper L. Erne
Maguiresbridge
Lisnaskea
Rosslea
Monaghan
Middletown
Keady
Castlewellan
Dundrum
Ardglass
JORDAN'S CASTLE
Florence Court
Derrylin
Newtownhamilton
Rathfriland
DRUMENA CASHEL
St. John's Pt.
Dundrum Bay
Coast
Swanlinbar
Newtownbutler
Clones
Newbliss
Newry
Mourne Mts.
Slieve Donard
Newcastle
Ring of Gullion
Mourne
Ballybay
Castleblaney
Warrenpoint
Annalong
Belturbet
Cootehill
Kilcurry
Carlingford
Kilkeel
Calf of Man
Ballinamore
Butler's Bridge
Cullaville
Fane
Dundalk
KING JOHN'S CASTLE
Carlingford Lough
Fenagh
Killashandra
Cavan
Shercock
Carrickmacross
Dundalk Bay
Carrigallen
Bracklin
Cloone
Bellananagh
Bailieborough
Kingscourt
Castlebellingham
Mohill
Ballyjamesduff
Ardee
Dunany Pt.
Kilnaleck
Dunleer
Lough Gowna
Virginia
L. Ramor
Oldcastle
L. Sheelin
Granard
Finnea
Collon
Clogher Hd.
Termonfeckin
Kells
Slane
Drogheda
Crossakiel
Longford
Edgeworthstown
NEWGRANGE
Duleek
Julianstown
Killashee
Castlepollard
Clonmellon
Navan
L. Derravaragh
Keenagh
Ballinalack
Delvin
Athboy
Balbriggan
ARDGILLAN CASTLE
Naul
Skerries
IRELAND
Ballymahon
L. Owel
Boyne
TAYTO PARK
Ballivor
Trim
Dunshaughlin
Ashbourne
Rush
Mullingar
Killucan
Ballymore
Rathmolyon
Lambay I.
Lough Ennell
Kinnegad
NATIONAL SPORTS CAMPUS
Swords
Malahide
Clonard
Enfield
Dunboyne
Athlone
Moate
Ballynagore
Kilbeggan
Kilcock
Tyrrellspass
Howth Hd.
Edenderry
Lucan
Celbridge
Dublin
Douglas Holyhead Liverpool
CLONMACNOISE
Daingean
Clondalkin
Dun Laoghaire
Rathcoole
Dalkey
Ferbane
Tullamore
Tallaght
Brosna
Killeigh
Sallins
Grand Canal
Liffey
Wicklow Mountains
Kippure
Bray
Holyhead
Rathangan
Naas
Kilcormac
Newbridge
Portarlington
Barrow
Clonaslee
Kildare
Blessington
Greystones

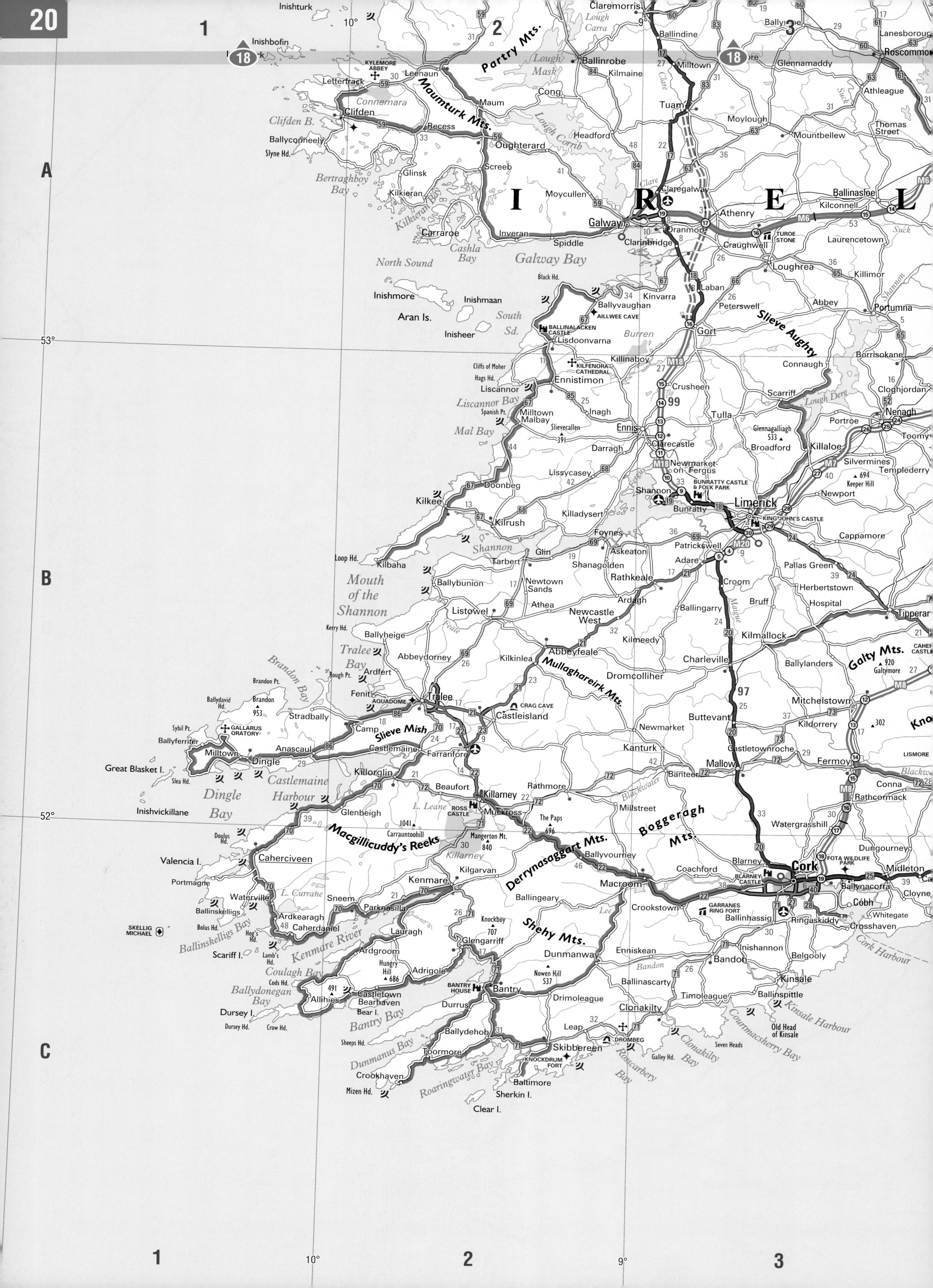

I R E L
Inishturk
Inishbofin
Claremorris
Lough Carra
Ballindine
Ballinrobe
Lough Mask
Partry Mts.
Kilmaine
Milltown
Glennamaddy
Roscommon
Lanesborough
Athleague
Kylemore Abbey
Leenaun
Letterfrack
Maumturk Mts.
Connemara
Clifden
Clifden B.
Maum
Cong
Tuam
Moylough
Mountbellew
Thomas Street
Recess
Ballyconneely
Slyne Hd.
Oughterard
Lough Corrib
Headford
Screeb
Glinsk
Bertraghboy Bay
Kilkieran
Kilkieran Bay
Moycullen
Claregalway
Athenry
Ballinasloe
Kilconnell
Galway
Oranmore
Clarinbridge
Turoe Stone
Laurencetown
Carraroe
Inveran
Spiddle
Cashla Bay
North Sound
Galway Bay
Craughwell
Loughrea
Killimor
Black Hd.
Kinvarra
Laban
Inishmore
Inishmaan
Aran Is.
Inisheer
South Sd.
Ballyvaughan
Aillwee Cave
Peterswell
Abbey
Portumna
Ballinalacken Castle
Lisdoonvarna
Burren
Gort
Slieve Aughty
Cliffs of Moher
Hags Hd.
Kilfenora Cathedral
Killinaboy
Connaugh
Borrisokane
Ennistimon
Liscannor
Liscannor Bay
Crusheen
Scarriff
Lough Derg
Cloghjordan
Spanish Pt.
Milltown Malbay
Inagh
Nenagh
Slievecallen 391
Ennis
Tulla
Glennagalliagh 533
Portroe
Mal Bay
Clarecastle
Broadford
Killaloe
Toomyvara
Darragh
Newmarket-on-Fergus
Silvermines
Templederry
Lissycasey
Keeper Hill 694
Bunratty Castle & Folk Park
Doonbeg
Shannon
Newport
Limerick
Kilkee
Bunratty
King John's Castle
Kilrush
Killadysert
Foynes
Cappamore
Shannon
Askeaton
Patrickswell
Glin
Loop Hd.
Kilbaha
Tarbert
Shanagolden
Adare
Pallas Green
Croom
Herbertstown
Rathkeale
Mouth of the Shannon
Ballybunion
Newtown Sands
Ardagh
Bruff
Hospital
Athea
Ballingarry
Listowel
Newcastle West
Tipperary
Kerry Hd.
Ballyheige
Kilmallock
Kilmeedy
Tralee Bay
Abbeyfeale
Galty Mts.
Galtymore 920
Abbeydorney
Kilkinlea
Mullaghareirk Mts.
Charleville
Ballylanders
Brandon Bay
Rough Pt.
Ardfert
Dromcolliher
Brandon Pt.
Ballydavid Hd.
Brandon 953
Fenit
Aquadome
Tralee
Mitchelstown
Crag Cave
Castleisland
Buttevant
Stradbally
Camp
Slieve Mish
Sybil Pt.
Gallarus Oratory
Kildorrery
Newmarket
Ballyferriter
Castlemaine
Castletownroche
Anascaul
Farranfore
Kanturk
Milltown
Dingle
Great Blasket I.
Slea Hd.
Castlemaine Harbour
Killorglin
Banteer
Mallow
Fermoy
Lismore
Dingle Bay
Beaufort
Rathmore
Conna
Killarney
Rathcormack
Inishvickillane
Glenbeigh
L. Leane
Ross Castle
Muckross
Millstreet
Blackwater
Boggeragh Mts.
The Paps 696
Watergrasshill
Carrauntoohill 1041
Macgillicuddy's Reeks
Mangerton Mt. 840
Derrynasaggart Mts.
Doulus Hd.
Valencia I.
Caherciveen
Killarney
Ballyvourney
Dungourney
Kilgarvan
Blarney
Fota Wildlife Park
Cork
Midleton
Portmagne
Kenmare
Coachford
Macroom
Blarney Castle
Ballynacorra
Cloyne
Waterville
L. Currane
Sneem
Ballingeary
Cobh
Ballinskelligs
Parknasilla
Crookstown
Garranes Ring Fort
Ballinhassig
Ringaskiddy
Whitegate
Skellig Michael
Ardkearagh
Caherdaniel
Knockboy 707
Shehy Mts.
Crosshaven
Bolus Hd.
Hog's Hd.
Ballinskelligs Bay
Lauragh
Glengarriff
Kenmare River
Dunmanway
Enniskean
Inishannon
Cork Harbour
Scariff I.
Lamb's Hd.
Ardgroom
Bandon
Bandon
Belgooly
Coulagh Bay
Hungry Hill 686
Adrigole
Nowen Hill 537
Cods Hd.
Kinsale
Ballinascarty
Ballydonegan Bay
Allihies
Castletown Bearhaven
Bantry House
Bantry
Drimoleague
Timoleague
Ballinspittle
Bear I.
Durrus
Clonakilty
Kinsale Harbour
Dursey I.
Bantry Bay
Dursey Hd.
Crow Hd.
Old Head of Kinsale
Courtmacsherry Bay
Leap
Ballydehob
Drombeg
Clonakilty Bay
Sheeps Hd.
Dunmanus Bay
Toormore
Skibbereen
Seven Heads
Galley Hd.
Knockdrum Fort
Rosscarbery Bay
Crookhaven
Roaringwater Bay
Baltimore
Mizen Hd.
Sherkin I.
Clear I.
A
B
C
1
2
3
10°
9°
53°
52°

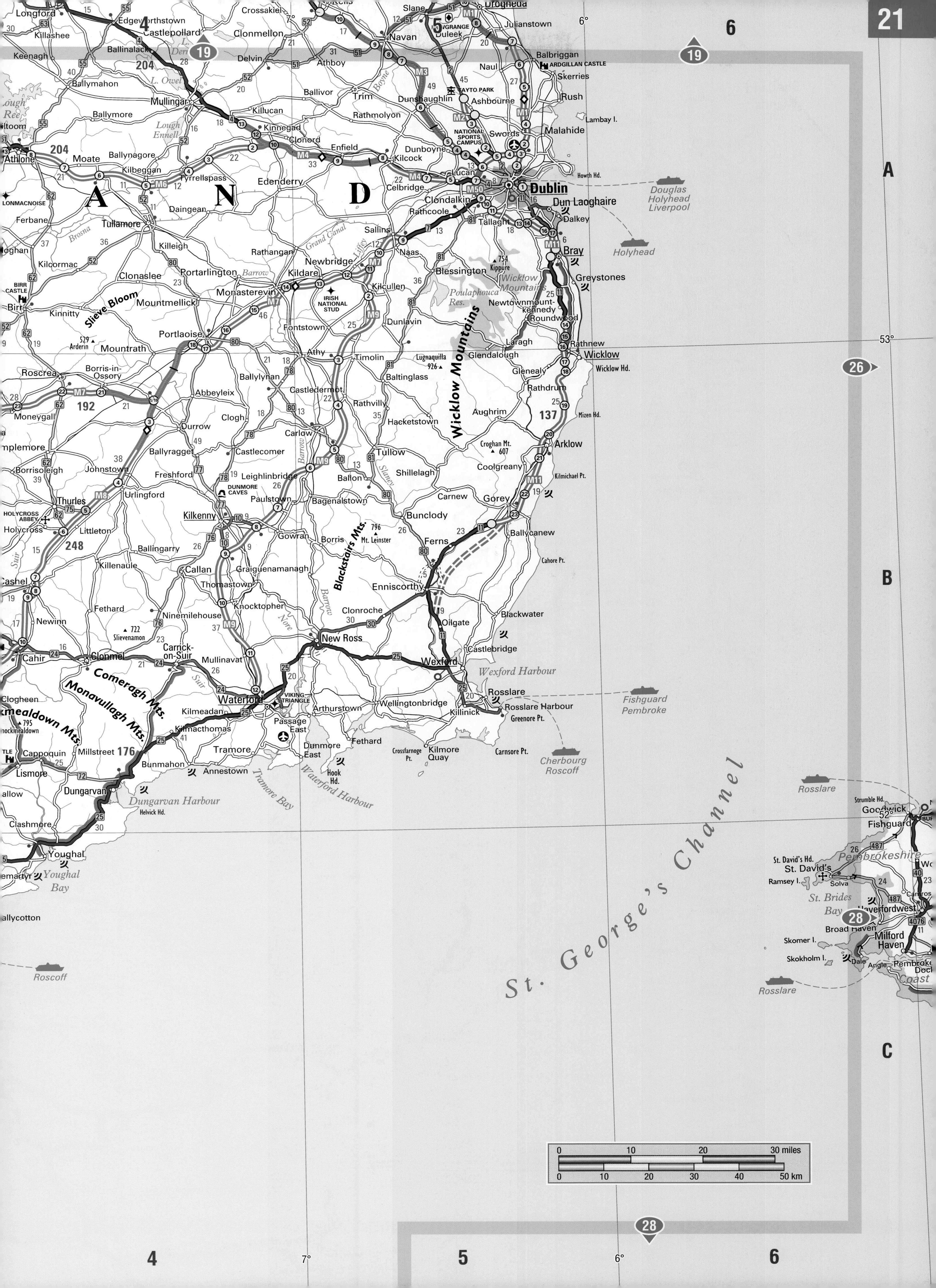

Longford
Edgeworthstown
Castlepollard
Crossakiel
Clonmellon
Slane
Drogheda
Julianstown
Navan
Duleek
Killashee
Keenagh
Ballinalack
Delvin
Athboy
Balbriggan
ARDGILLAN CASTLE
Skerries
Naul
Ballymahon
L. Owel
Ballivor
Trim
Dunshaughlin
TAYTO PARK
Ashbourne
Rush
Mullingar
Killucan
Rathmolyon
Lambay I.
Ballymore
Lough Ennell
Kinnegad
Clonard
Enfield
NATIONAL SPORTS CAMPUS
Swords
Malahide
Athlone
Moate
Ballynagore
Dunboyne
Kilcock
Kilbeggan
Tyrrellspass
Edenderry
Celbridge
Lucan
Howth Hd.
Dublin
Douglas
Holyhead
Liverpool
Dun Laoghaire
Dalkey
A
N
D
Clondalkin
Rathcoole
Tallaght
CLONMACNOISE
Ferbane
Daingean
Tullamore
Brosna
Grand Canal
Sallins
Killeigh
Rathangan
Naas
Bray
Holyhead
Kilcormac
Newbridge
Liffey
Blessington
Kippure
Greystones
Clonaslee
Portarlington
Barrow
Kildare
Kilcullen
Wicklow Mountains
BIRR CASTLE
Birr
Monasterevin
IRISH NATIONAL STUD
Poulaphouca Res.
Newtownmount-kennedy
Roundwood
Slieve Bloom
Mountmellick
Kinnitty
Dunlavin
Fontstown
Wicklow Mountains
Portlaoise
Arderin
Mountrath
Athy
Laragh
Timolin
Lugnaquilla
Glendalough
Rathnew
Wicklow
Wicklow Hd.
53°
Roscrea
Borris-in-Ossory
Ballylynan
Baltinglass
Glenealy
Castledermot
Rathdrum
Abbeyleix
Rathvilly
Aughrim
Mizen Hd.
Moneygall
Clogh
Hacketstown
Durrow
Carlow
Arklow
Templemore
Croghan Mt.
Ballyragget
Castlecomer
Tullow
Coolgreany
Borrisoleigh
Johnstown
Freshford
Leighlinbridge
Shillelagh
Kilmichael Pt.
Ballon
DUNMORE CAVES
Urlingford
Paulstown
Carnew
Gorey
Thurles
Bagenalstown
Bunclody
HOLYCROSS ABBEY
Kilkenny
Holycross
Littleton
Gowran
Borris
Blackstairs Mts.
Mt. Leinster
Ferns
Ballycanew
Ballingarry
Killenaule
Callan
Graiguenamanagh
Cahore Pt.
Cashel
Thomastown
Enniscorthy
Fethard
Ninemilehouse
Knocktopher
Clonroche
Blackwater
Newinn
Oilgate
Slievenamon
Carrick-on-Suir
New Ross
Castlebridge
Cahir
Clonmel
Mullinavat
Wexford
Comeragh Mts.
Wexford Harbour
Monavullagh Mts.
Waterford
VIKING TRIANGLE
Rosslare
Fishguard
Pembroke
Clogheen
Knockmealdown Mts.
Kilmeadan
Arthurstown
Wellingtonbridge
Rosslare Harbour
Killinick
Greenore Pt.
Kilmacthomas
Passage East
Fethard
Dunmore East
Crossfarnoge Pt.
Kilmore Quay
Carnsore Pt.
Cappoquin
Millstreet
Tramore
Cherbourg
Roscoff
Lismore
Bunmahon
Annestown
Hook Hd.
Tramore Bay
Waterford Harbour
Dungarvan
Dungarvan Harbour
Helvick Hd.
Rosslare
Strumble Hd.
Goodwick
Fishguard
Clashmore
Youghal
Youghal Bay
Pembrokeshire
St. David's Hd.
St. David's
Ramsey I.
Solva
St. Brides Bay
Haverfordwest
Ballycotton
Broad Haven
Milford Haven
Skomer I.
Skokholm I.
Dale
Angle
Pembroke Dock
Coast
St. George's Channel
Roscoff
Rosslare
0 10 20 30 miles
0 10 20 30 40 50 km
4
5
6
7°
6°
A
B
C
19
26
28

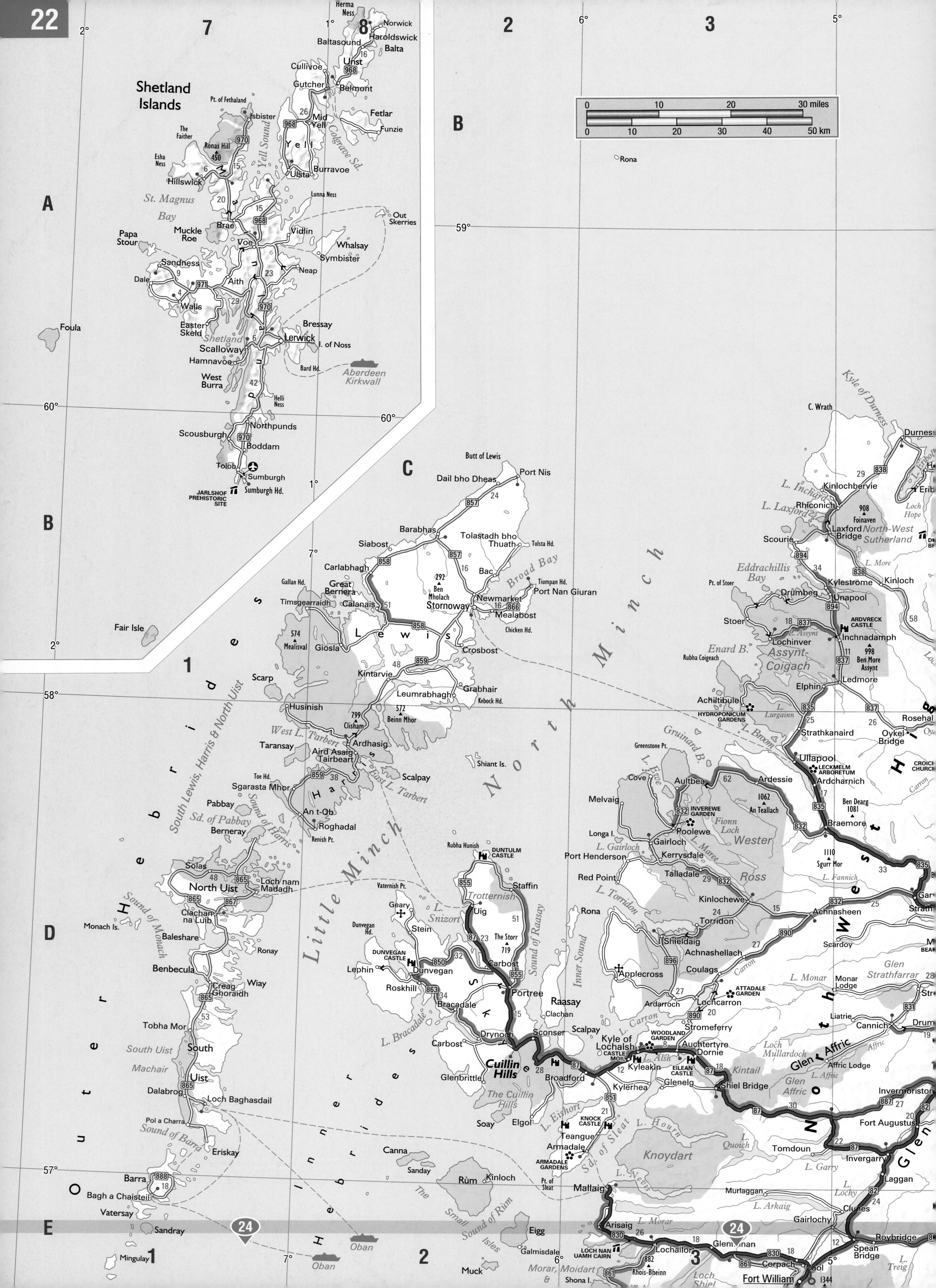
Shetland Islands
Herma Ness
Norwick
Haroldswick
Baltasound
Balta
Unst
Cullivoe
Gutcher
Belmont
Fetlar
Funzie
Mid Yell
Yell
Colgrave Sd.
Yell Sound
Burravoe
Ulsta
Pt. of Fethaland
Isbister
The Faither
Ronas Hill 450
Esha Ness
Hillswick
St. Magnus Bay
Lunna Ness
Out Skerries
Brae
Muckle Roe
Papa Stour
Vidlin
Voe
Whalsay
Symbister
Sandness
Neap
Dale
Aith
Walls
Foula
Easter Skeld
Bressay
Lerwick
I. of Noss
Scalloway
Hamnavoe
West Burra
Bard Hd.
Aberdeen Kirkwall
Helli Ness
Northpunds
Scousburgh
Boddam
Tolob
Sumburgh
Sumburgh Hd.
JARLSHOF PREHISTORIC SITE
Fair Isle
Rona
0 10 20 30 miles
0 10 20 30 40 50 km
C. Wrath
Kyle of Durness
Durness
Butt of Lewis
Port Nis
Dail bho Dheas
Kinlochbervie
L. Inchard
Rhiconich
L. Laxford
Foinaven
Laxford Bridge
North-West Sutherland
Loch Hope
Scourie
Barabhas
Tolastadh bho Thuath
Tolsta Hd.
Siabost
Carlabhagh
Broad Bay
Eddrachillis Bay
L. More
Kylestrome
Kinloch
Gallan Hd.
Great Bernera
Ben Mholach
Tiumpan Hd.
Port Nan Giuran
Pt. of Stoer
Drumbeg
Unapool
Timsgearraidh
Calanais
Stornoway
Newmarket
Mealabost
Stoer
ARDVRECK CASTLE
Inchnadamph
L. Assynt
Lochinver
Mealisval
Lewis
Chicken Hd.
Giosla
Crosbost
Enard B.
Rubha Coigeach
Assynt-Coigach
Ben More Assynt
Kintarvie
Grabhair
Elphin
Ledmore
Scarp
Leumrabhagh
Kebock Hd.
Achiltibuie
HYDROPONICUM GARDENS
L. Lurgainn
Rosehal
Husinish
Clisham
Beinn Mhor
Strathkanaird
Oykel Bridge
West L. Tarbert
Ardhasig
Taransay
Aird Asaig
Tairbeart
Gruinard B.
L. Broom
Greenstone Pt.
Ullapool
LECKMELM ARBORETUM
CROICK CHURCH
Shiant Is.
Harris
East L. Tarbert
Scalpay
Toe Hd.
Sgarasta Mhor
Cove
L. Ewe
Aultbea
Ardessie
Ardcharnich
Pabbay
Sd. of Pabbay
Sound of Harris
An t-Ob
Roghadal
Renish Pt.
Melvaig
INVEREWE GARDEN
An Teallach
Ben Dearg
Braemore
South Lewis, Harris & North Uist
Berneray
Fionn Loch
Poolewe
Wester Ross
Longa I.
Gairloch
L. Gairloch
L. Maree
Kerrysdale
Rubha Hunish
DUNTULM CASTLE
Port Henderson
Sgurr Mor
L. Fannich
Solas
North Uist
Loch nam Madadh
Red Point
Talladale
Staffin
Vaternish Pt.
Kinlochewe
Trotternish
Geary
L. Snizort
Uig
L. Torridon
Achnasheen
Sound of Monach
Clachan na Luib
Monach Is.
Baleshare
Dunvegan Hd.
Stein
The Storr
Sound of Raasay
Rona
Torridon
Shieldaig
Achnashellach
Scardoy
DUNVEGAN CASTLE
Dunvegan
Lephin
Carbost
Inner Sound
Applecross
Coulags
Glen Strathfarrar
L. Monar
Monar Lodge
Ronay
Benbecula
Wiay
Creag Ghoraidh
Roskhill
Bracadale
Portree
Raasay
Clachan
Ardarroch
L. Carron
ATTADALE GARDEN
Lochcarron
Liatrie
Cannich
Stromeferry
Tobha Mor
L. Bracadale
Carbost
Drynoch
Sconser
Scalpay
Kyle of Lochalsh
WOODLAND GARDEN
Auchtertyre
Dornie
Loch Mullardoch
Glen Affric
Affric Lodge
South Uist
Machair
Cuillin Hills
CASTLE MOIL
Kyleakin
L. Alsh
EILEAN CASTLE
Kintail
Uist
Glenbrittle
Broadford
Kylerhea
Glenelg
Shiel Bridge
Dalabrog
Loch Baghasdail
The Cuillin Hills
Invermoriston
Pol a Charra
Sound of Barra
L. Eishort
KNOCK CASTLE
L. Hourn
Fort Augustus
Soay
Elgol
Teangue
Eriskay
Armadale
ARMADALE GARDENS
Sd. of Sleat
Knoydart
L. Quoich
Tomdoun
Invergarry
Canna
Sanday
L. Garry
Laggan
Barra
Rùm
Kinloch
Pt. of Sleat
Mallaig
L. Nevis
L. Lochy
Bagh a Chaisteil
Murlaggan
L. Arkaig
Clunes
Vatersay
Sound of Rùm
The Small Isles
Arisaig
L. Morar
Gairlochy
Sandray
Eigg
Roybridge
Oban
Galmisdale
LOCH NAN UAMH CAIRN
Lochailort
Glenfinnan
Spean Bridge
Mingulay
Oban
Muck
Morar, Moidart &
Rhois-Bheinn
Corpach
Caol
Fort William
L. Treig
Shona I.
Loch Shiel
Outer Hebrides
Inner Hebrides
Little Minch
North Minch
North West Highlands
Glen
A
B
C
D
E
1
2
3
7
8
24

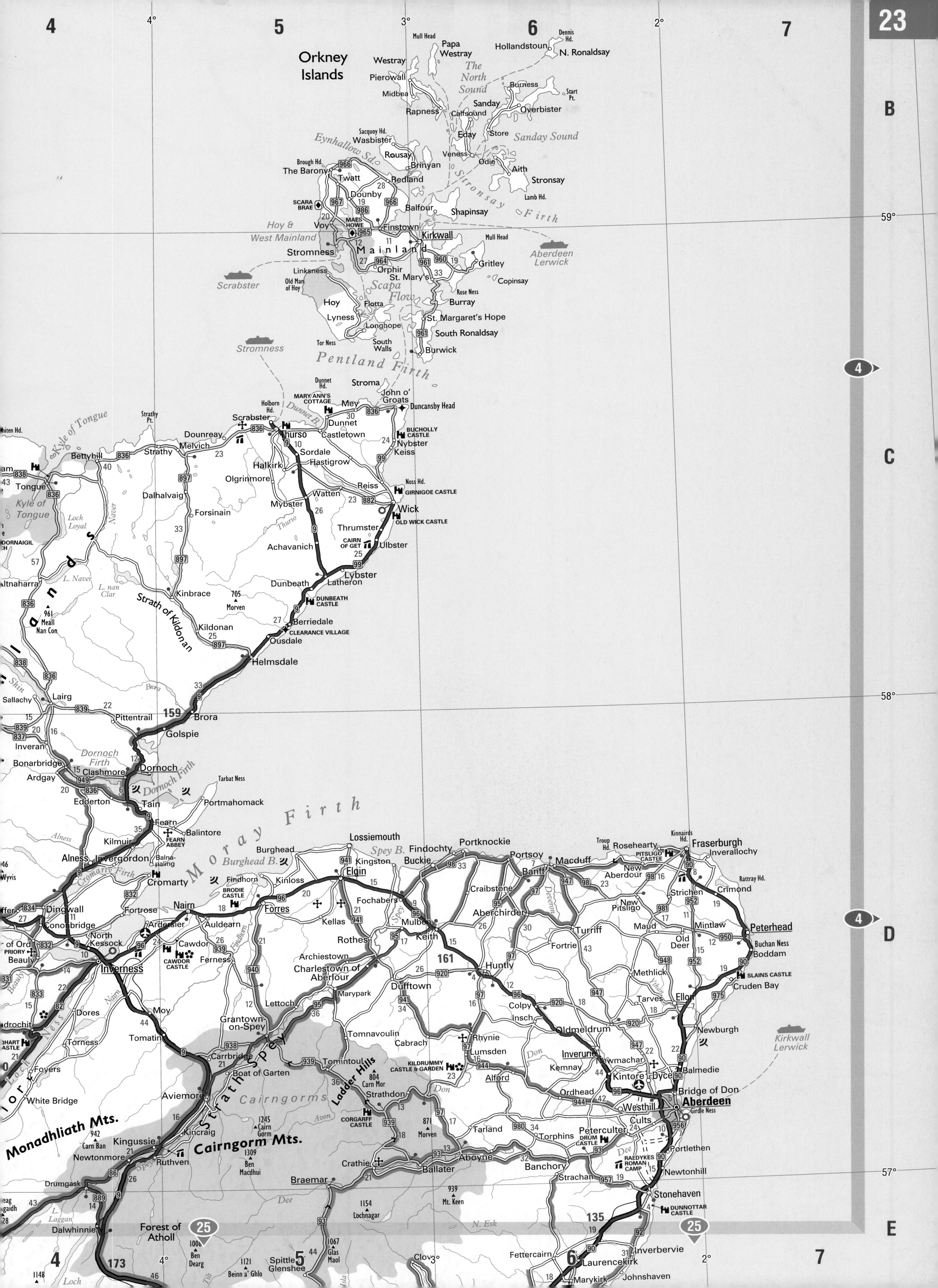

23
Orkney Islands
Mull Head
Papa Westray
Westray
Pierowall
Midbea
Rapness
Dennis Hd.
Hollandstoun
N. Ronaldsay
The North Sound
Burness
Start Pt.
Sanday
Calfsound
Overbister
Eday
Store
Sanday Sound
Sacquoy Hd.
Wasbister
Eynhallow Sd.
Rousay
Veness
Odie
Brough Hd.
The Barony
Brinyan
Aith
Twatt
Redland
Stronsay
Stronsay Firth
Dounby
SCARA BRAE
Balfour
Shapinsay
Lamb Hd.
MAES HOWE
Hoy & West Mainland
Voy
Finstown
Kirkwall
Mull Head
Stromness
Mainland
Aberdeen Lerwick
Gritley
Orphir
St. Mary's
Copinsay
Linksness
Old Man of Hoy
Scrabster
Scapa Flow
Rose Ness
Burray
Hoy
Flotta
Lyness
St. Margaret's Hope
Longhope
South Ronaldsay
South Walls
Tor Ness
Burwick
Stromness
Pentland Firth
Dunnet Hd.
Stroma
MARY ANN'S COTTAGE
Holborn Hd.
Dunnet B.
Mey
John o' Groats
Duncansby Head
Strathy Pt.
Kyle of Tongue
Scrabster
Thurso
Dunnet
Castletown
BUCHOLLY CASTLE
Nybster
Keiss
Dounreay
Melvich
Bettyhill
Strathy
Sordale
Hastigrow
Halkirk
Tongue
Olgrinmore
Reiss
Noss Hd.
GIRNIGOE CASTLE
Kyle of Tongue
Dalhalvaig
Watten
Mybster
Wick
OLD WICK CASTLE
Loch Loyal
Forsinain
Thurso
Thrumster
Naver
CAIRN OF GET
Ulbster
Achavanich
Lybster
Latheron
Dunbeath
Altnaharra
L. Naver
L. nan Clar
Kinbrace
Morven
DUNBEATH CASTLE
Strath of Kildonan
Berriedale
Meall Nan Con
Kildonan
CLEARANCE VILLAGE
Ousdale
Helmsdale
Brora
Shin
Lairg
Sallachy
Pittentrail
Brora
Golspie
Inveran
Dornoch Firth
Bonarbridge
Clashmore
Dornoch
Ardgay
Dornoch Firth
Tarbat Ness
Edderton
Tain
Portmahomack
Moray Firth
Fearn
Balintore
FEARN ABBEY
Alness
Kilmuir
Alness
Invergordon
Balnapaling
Cromarty Firth
Cromarty
Lossiemouth
Burghead
Burghead B.
Spey B.
Findochty
Portknockie
Kingston
Buckie
Portsoy
Macduff
Banff
Troup Hd.
Rosehearty
PITSLIGO CASTLE
Kinnairds Hd.
Fraserburgh
Inverallochy
Aberdour
New Aberdour
Elgin
Findhorn
Kinloss
BRODIE CASTLE
Craibstone
Strichen
Rattray Hd.
Crimond
Dingwall
Conon Bridge
Fortrose
Nairn
Forres
Fochabers
Spey
Aberchirder
Deveron
New Pitsligo
Mulben
Keith
Turriff
Maud
Mintlaw
Peterhead
North Kessock
Ardersier
Auldearn
Kellas
Rothes
Fortrie
Old Deer
Buchan Ness
Boddam
PRIORY
Beauly
Inverness
Cawdor
CAWDOR CASTLE
Ferness
Archiestown
Charlestown of Aberlour
Huntly
Methlick
SLAINS CASTLE
Cruden Bay
Dufftown
Tarves
Ellon
Findhorn
Marypark
Colpy
Lettoch
Moy
Dores
Grantown-on-Spey
Insch
Oldmeldrum
Newburgh
Tomnavoulin
Rhynie
Torness
Tomatin
Cabrach
Lumsden
Kirkwall Lerwick
Foyers
Carrbridge
Tomintoul
Inverurie
Newmachar
Balmedie
Boat of Garten
Ladder Hills
KILDRUMMY CASTLE & GARDEN
Kemnay
Carn Mor
Alford
Kintore
Dyce
White Bridge
Aviemore
Strath Spey
Cairngorms
Strathdon
Don
Ordhead
Bridge of Don
Aberdeen
Westhill
Girdle Ness
Monadhliath Mts.
Cairn Gorm
Avon
CORGARFF CASTLE
Morven
Tarland
Cults
Kincraig
Torphins
Peterculter
Carn Ban
Kingussie
Cairngorm Mts.
DRUM CASTLE
Portlethen
Newtonmore
Ben Macdhui
Ruthven
Crathie
Ballater
Aboyne
Banchory
Dee
RAEDYKES ROMAN CAMP
Newtonhill
Drumgask
Braemar
Strachan
Stonehaven
Mt. Keen
Dee
Lochnagar
DUNNOTTAR CASTLE
L. Laggan
N. Esk
Dalwhinnie
Forest of Atholl
Ben Dearg
Glas Maol
Beinn a' Ghlo
Spittle of Glenshee
Clova
Fettercairn
Inverbervie
Laurencekirk
Johnshaven
Marykirk
Loch
59°
58°
57°
4°
3°
2°
4
5
6
7
B
C
D
E

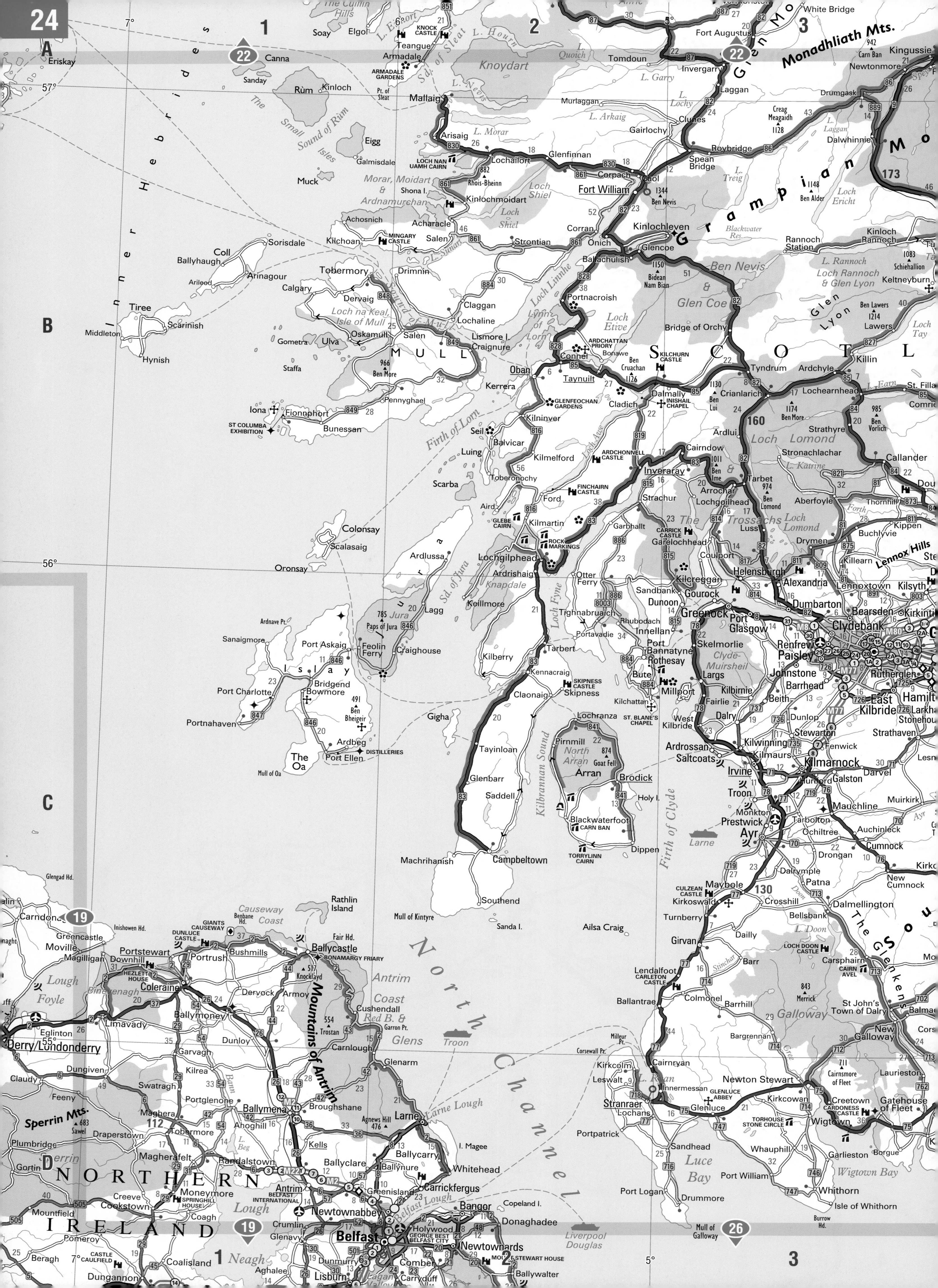

Inner Hebrides
Eriskay
Canna
Sanday
Rùm
Kinloch
The Small Isles
Sound of Rùm
Eigg
Muck
Galmisdale
Soay
Elgol
Teangue
Armadale
Armadale Gardens
Sd. of Sleat
Knock Castle
Knoydart
L. Hourn
L. Nevis
Mallaig
Arisaig
L. Morar
Loch nan Uamh Cairn
Lochailort
Glenfinnan
Morar, Moidart & Ardnamurchan
Shona I.
Kinlochmoidart
Loch Shiel
Achosnich
Acharacle
Kilchoan
Mingary Castle
Salen
Strontian
Coll
Sorisdale
Ballyhaugh
Arinagour
Arileod
Tiree
Scarinish
Middleton
Hynish
Tobermory
Drimnin
Calgary
Dervaig
Sound of Mull
Loch na Keal, Isle of Mull
Gometra
Ulva
Oskamull
Salen
Claggan
Lochaline
Lismore I.
Craignure
MULL
Staffa
Ben More
Iona
Fionnphort
Bunessan
St Columba Exhibition
Pennyghael
Oban
Kerrera
Firth of Lorn
Seil
Balvicar
Luing
Scarba
Kilninver
Kilmelford
Toberonochy
Ford
Aird
Kilmartin
Glebe Cairn
Rock Markings
Lochgilphead
Ardrishaig
Knapdale
Colonsay
Scalasaig
Oronsay
Jura
Ardlussa
Sd. of Jura
Lagg
Paps of Jura
Feolin Ferry
Craighouse
Ardnave Pt.
Sanaigmore
Port Askaig
Islay
Bridgend
Bowmore
Ben Bheigeir
Port Charlotte
Portnahaven
Ardbeg
Port Ellen
Distilleries
The Oa
Mull of Oa
Gigha
Keillmore
Kilberry
Tarbert
Kennacraig
Skipness Castle
Skipness
Claonaig
Tayinloan
Glenbarr
Saddell
Campbeltown
Machrihanish
Southend
Mull of Kintyre
Sanda I.
Kilbrannan Sound
Lochranza
Pirnmill
North Arran
Goat Fell
Arran
Brodick
Holy I.
Blackwaterfoot
Carn Ban
Torrylinn Cairn
Dippen
Firth of Clyde
Ailsa Craig
Fort Augustus
White Bridge
Tomdoun
L. Quoich
L. Garry
Invergarry
Glen Mor
Laggan
Monadhliath Mts.
Kingussie
Newtonmore
Carn Ban
Murlaggan
L. Arkaig
L. Lochy
Gairlochy
Clunes
Spean Bridge
Roybridge
Creag Meagaidh
Drumgask
L. Laggan
Dalwhinnie
Grampian Mountains
Corpach
Caol
Fort William
Ben Nevis
L. Treig
Ben Alder
Loch Ericht
Kinlochleven
Corran
Onich
Glencoe
Blackwater Res.
Rannoch Station
Kinloch Rannoch
L. Rannoch
Schiehallion
Keltneybur
Ballachulish
Bidean Nam Bian
Ben Nevis & Glen Coe
Portnacroish
Loch Linnhe
Loch Etive
Bridge of Orchy
Glen Lyon
Ben Lawers
Lawers
Loch Tay
Ardchattan Priory
Connel
Bonawe
Ben Cruachan
Kilchurn Castle
Taynuilt
SCOTLAND
Tyndrum
Ardchyle
Killin
Glenfeochan Gardens
Cladich
Dalmally
Inishail Chapel
Ben Lui
Crianlarich
Lochearnhead
L. Earn
St. Fillans
Comrie
Ben More
Ben Vorlich
Strathyre
Ardlui
Loch Lomond
Stronachlachar
L. Katrine
Callander
Loch Awe
Ardchonnell Castle
Cairndow
Inveraray
Ben Ime
Tarbet
Arrochar
Lochgoilhead
Aberfoyle
Thornhill
Doune
Finchairn Castle
Strachur
The Trossachs
Loch Lomond
Luss
Kippen
Buchlyvie
Garbhallt
Carrick Castle
Garelochhead
Drymen
Lennox Hills
Coulport
Helensburgh
Killearn
Alexandria
Otter Ferry
Sandbank
Kilcreggan
Gourock
Dunoon
Lennoxtown
Kilsyth
Dumbarton
Bearsden
Kirkintilloch
Clydebank
Loch Fyne
Tighnabruaich
Rhubodach
Greenock
Port Glasgow
Portavadie
Innellan
Port Bannatyne
Rothesay
Renfrew
Paisley
Skelmorlie
Clyde-Muirsheil
Largs
Johnstone
Barrhead
Rutherglen
Bute
Millport
Kilchattan
St. Blane's Chapel
Kilbirnie
Beith
East Kilbride
Hamilton
Larkhall
Stonehouse
Fairlie
West Kilbride
Dalry
Dunlop
Stewarton
Strathaven
Ardrossan
Saltcoats
Kilwinning
Kilmaurs
Fenwick
Kilmarnock
Irvine
Galston
Darvel
Troon
Hurlford
Mauchline
Muirkirk
Monkton
Prestwick
Tarbolton
Ayr
Ochiltree
Auchinleck
Larne
Drongan
Cumnock
Dalrymple
Culzean Castle
Maybole
Patna
Kirkoswald
Crosshill
New Cumnock
Dalmellington
Turnberry
Bellsbank
L. Doon
Girvan
Dailly
Loch Doon Castle
Barr
Carsphairn
The Glenkens
Lendalfoot
Carleton Castle
Cairn Avel
Merrick
Ballantrae
Colmonell
Barrhill
Galloway
St John's Town of Dalry
Bargrennan
New Galloway
Milleur Pt.
Corsewall Pt.
Kirkcolm
Cairnryan
Leswalt
L. Ryan
Innermessan
Newton Stewart
Cairnsmore of Fleet
Laurieston
Stranraer
Lochans
Glenluce Abbey
Glenluce
Kirkcowan
Creetown
Cardoness Castle
Gatehouse of Fleet
Torhouse Stone Circle
Wigtown
Portpatrick
Sandhead
Luce Bay
Whauphill
Garlieston
Wigtown Bay
Port William
Port Logan
Drummore
Whithorn
Isle of Whithorn
Mull of Galloway
Burrow Hd.
North Channel
Troon
Liverpool
Douglas
Glengad Hd.
Carndonagh
Greencastle
Moville
Inishowen Hd.
Magilligan
Lough Foyle
Eglinton
Derry/Londonderry
Limavady
Causeway Coast
Benbane Hd.
Giants Causeway
Dunluce Castle
Portstewart
Portrush
Bushmills
Downhill
Hezlett House
Coleraine
Rathlin Island
Fair Hd.
Ballycastle
Bonamargy Friary
Knocklayd
Dervock
Armoy
Ballymoney
Antrim Coast
Mountains of Antrim
Trostan
Cushendall
Red B. & Garron Pt.
Glens
Carnlough
Glenarm
Dunloy
Garvagh
Kilrea
Dungiven
Claudy
Feeny
Swatragh
Portglenone
Ballymena
Broughshane
Larne Lough
Agnews Hill
Larne
Sperrin Mts.
Sawel
Maghera
Ahoghill
Draperstown
Tobermore
Plumbridge
Magherafelt
Kells
Ballycarry
I. Magee
Randalstown
Ballyclare
Ballynure
Whitehead
Gortin
NORTHERN IRELAND
Moneymore
Springhill House
Antrim
Belfast International
Greenisland
Carrickfergus
Cookstown
Coagh
Lough Neagh
Newtownabbey
Belfast Lough
Bangor
Copeland I.
Mountfield
Crumlin
Holywood
Donaghadee
Pomeroy
Glenavy
Belfast
George Best Belfast City
Newtownards
Beragh
Castle Caulfield
Coalisland
Aghalee
Dunmurry
Mount Stewart House
Comber
Dungannon
Lisburn
Carryduff
Ballywalter

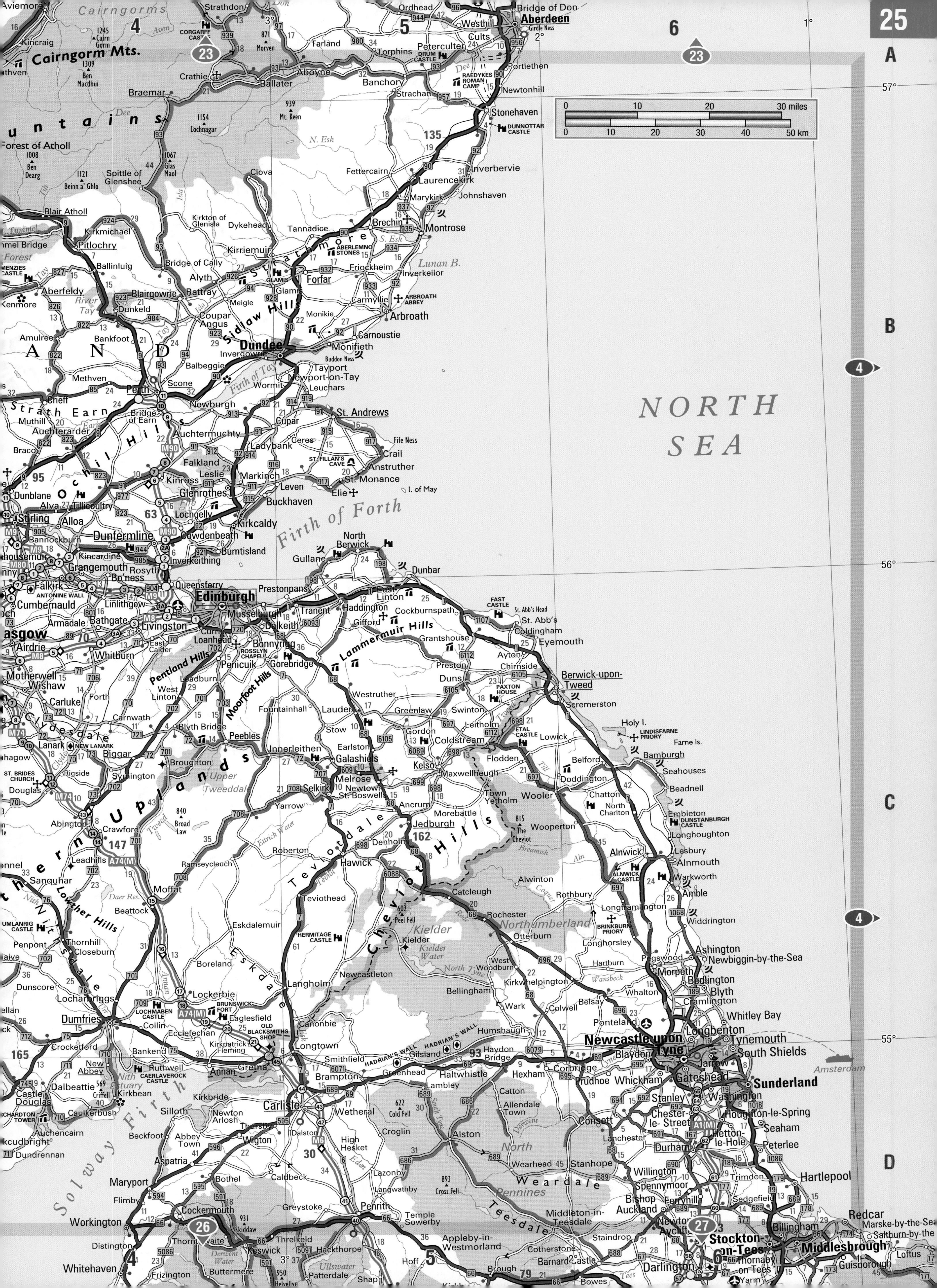

NORTH SEA
Aberdeen
Bridge of Don
Westhill
Cults
Peterculter
Portlethen
Newtonhill
Stonehaven
DUNNOTTAR CASTLE
Inverbervie
Laurencekirk
Johnshaven
Montrose
Brechin
Forfar
Arbroath
ARBROATH ABBEY
Carnoustie
Monifieth
Dundee
Tayport
Newport-on-Tay
Leuchars
St. Andrews
Fife Ness
Crail
Anstruther
St. Monance
Elie
I. of May
Firth of Forth
Kirkcaldy
Burntisland
Cowdenbeath
Dunfermline
Inverkeithing
Queensferry
Edinburgh
Musselburgh
Dalkeith
Prestonpans
Tranent
Haddington
North Berwick
Gullane
Dunbar
East Linton
Cockburnspath
St. Abb's Head
St. Abb's
Coldingham
Eyemouth
Berwick-upon-Tweed
Scremerston
Holy I.
LINDISFARNE PRIORY
Farne Is.
Bamburgh
Seahouses
Beadnell
Embleton
DUNSTANBURGH CASTLE
Longhoughton
Alnmouth
Alnwick
Warkworth
Amble
Widdrington
Ashington
Newbiggin-by-the-Sea
Morpeth
Bedlington
Blyth
Cramlington
Whitley Bay
Longbenton
Tynemouth
South Shields
Newcastle upon Tyne
Gateshead
Jarrow
Sunderland
Washington
Houghton-le-Spring
Seaham
Peterlee
Durham
Chester-le-Street
Hartlepool
Billingham
Stockton-on-Tees
Middlesbrough
Redcar
Marske-by-the-Sea
Saltburn-by-the-Sea
Guisborough
Loftus
Darlington
Newton Aycliffe
Bishop Auckland
Spennymoor
Amsterdam
Cairngorm Mts.
Braemar
Ballater
Aboyne
Banchory
Pitlochry
Blair Atholl
Aberfeldy
Blairgowrie
Dunkeld
Perth
Crieff
Auchterarder
Kinross
Glenrothes
Stirling
Alloa
Falkirk
Grangemouth
Cumbernauld
Livingston
Bathgate
Motherwell
Wishaw
Lanark
Peebles
Galashiels
Melrose
Kelso
Coldstream
Jedburgh
Hawick
Selkirk
Moffat
Lockerbie
Langholm
Dumfries
Annan
Gretna
Carlisle
Brampton
Haltwhistle
Hexham
Corbridge
Penrith
Keswick
Cockermouth
Workington
Maryport
Whitehaven
Wigton
Alston
Kielder
Otterburn
Rothbury
Wooler
The Cheviot
Cheviot Hills
Lammermuir Hills
Pentland Hills
Moorfoot Hills
Sidlaw Hills
Ochil Hills
Southern Uplands
Lowther Hills
Teviotdale
Eskdale
Nithsdale
Clydesdale
Weardale
Teesdale
North Pennines
Solway Firth
Northumberland
Strathmore
Strath Earn
Firth of Tay
HADRIAN'S WALL
Kielder Water
0 10 20 30 miles
0 10 20 30 40 50 km
57°
56°
55°
1°
2°
3°
A
B
C
D
4
5
6

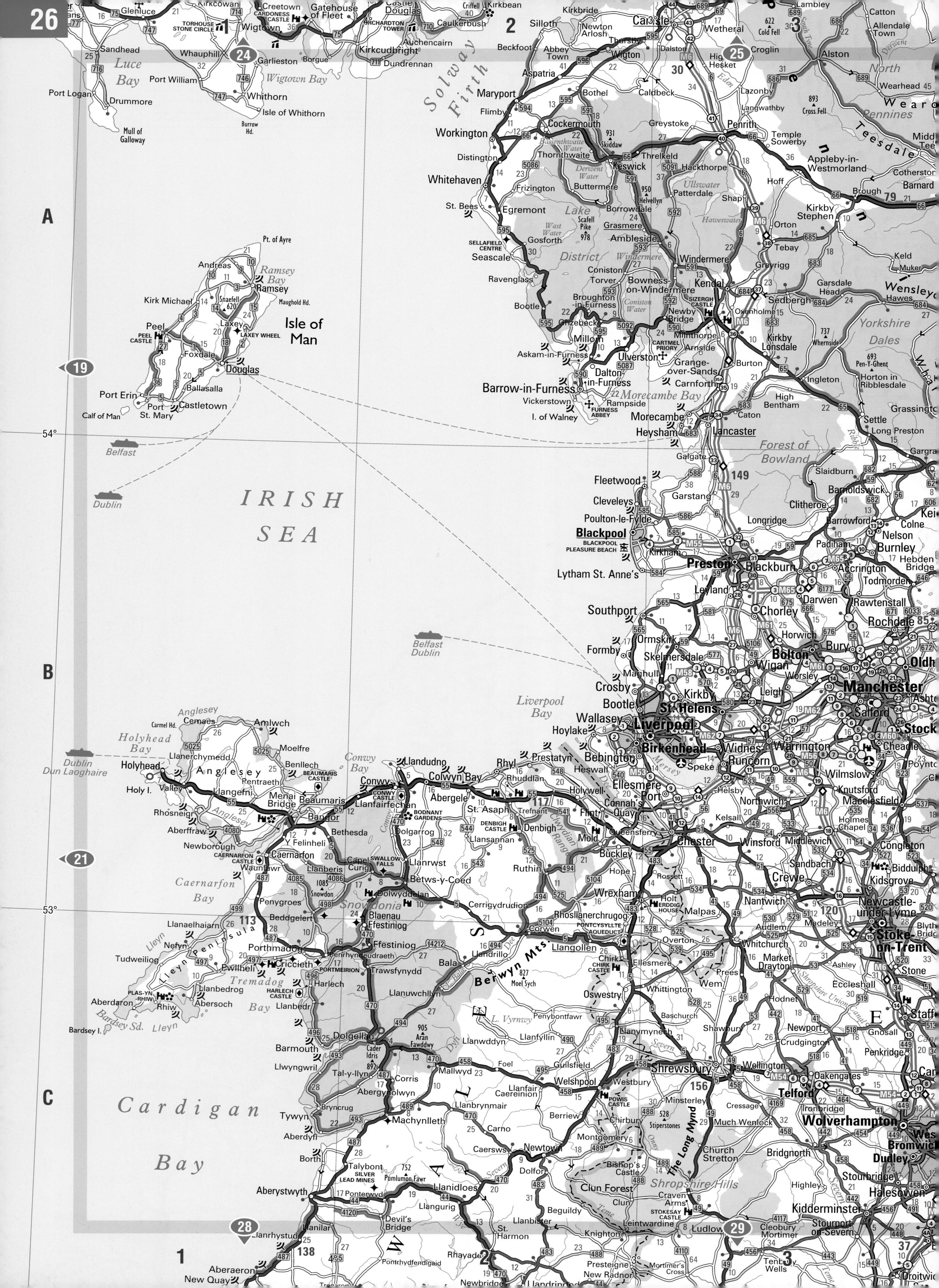

A
B
C
1
2
3
24
25
19
21
28
29
149
156
113
117
138
120
54°
53°
IRISH
SEA
Cardigan
Bay
Isle of
Man
Anglesey
Liverpool
Bay
Caernarfon
Bay
Tremadog
Bay
Luce
Bay
Wigtown Bay
Solway
Firth
Morecambe Bay
Ramsey
Bay
Holyhead
Bay
Conwy
Bay
Lake
District
North
Pennines
Yorkshire
Dales
Forest of
Bowland
Snowdonia
Berwyn Mts.
Shropshire Hills
Clun Forest
The Long Mynd
Lleyn Peninsula
WALES
Belfast
Dublin
Belfast
Dublin
Dublin
Dun Laoghaire
Glenluce
Sandhead
Port Logan
Drummore
Mull of
Galloway
Port William
Whithorn
Isle of Whithorn
Burrow
Hd.
Garlieston
Wigtown
Kirkcowan
Creetown
Gatehouse
of Fleet
Castle
Douglas
Kirkcudbright
Dundrennan
Auchencairn
Torhouse
Stone Circle
Cardoness
Castle
Orchardton
Tower
Caulkerbush
Criffell
Kirkbean
Silloth
Kirkbride
Newton
Arlosh
Carlisle
Wetheral
Lambley
Catton
Allendale
Town
Alston
Beckfoot
Abbey
Town
Wigton
Thursby
Dalston
High
Hesket
Croglin
Aspatria
Maryport
Bothel
Caldbeck
Lazonby
Wearhead
Flimby
Cockermouth
Greystoke
Langwathby
Cross Fell
Workington
Penrith
Temple
Sowerby
Teesdale
Distington
Skiddaw
Threlkeld
Thornthwaite
Keswick
Hackthorpe
Appleby-in-
Westmorland
Cotherstone
Whitehaven
Frizington
Buttermere
Ullswater
Patterdale
Shap
Hoff
Brough
Barnard
St. Bees
Egremont
Helvellyn
Borrowdale
Haweswater
Orton
Kirkby
Stephen
Sellafield
Centre
Seascale
Gosforth
Scafell
Pike
Grasmere
Ambleside
Tebay
Windermere
Keld
Muker
Ravenglass
Coniston
Torver
Bowness-
on-Windermere
Gayrigg
Kendal
Garsdale
Head
Sedbergh
Hawes
Wensley
Bootle
Broughton
-in-Furness
Newby
Bridge
Sizergh
Castle
Oxenholme
Grizebeck
Millom
Cartmel
Priory
Arnside
Milnthorpe
Kirkby
Lonsdale
Whernside
Askam-in-Furness
Ulverston
Grange-
over-Sands
Burton
Pen-Y-Ghent
Horton in
Ribblesdale
Ingleton
Dalton
-in-Furness
Barrow-in-Furness
Carnforth
High
Bentham
Vickerstown
Furness
Abbey
Rampside
I. of Walney
Grassington
Morecambe
Caton
Settle
Long Preston
Heysham
Lancaster
Galgate
Slaidburn
Fleetwood
Cleveleys
Garstang
Barnoldswick
Clitheroe
Poulton-le-Fylde
Longridge
Barrowford
Colne
Nelson
Blackpool
Blackpool
Pleasure Beach
Kirkham
Padiham
Burnley
Preston
Blackburn
Accrington
Hebden
Bridge
Lytham St. Anne's
Leyland
Todmorden
Darwen
Rawtenstall
Southport
Chorley
Rochdale
Horwich
Bury
Ormskirk
Bolton
Formby
Skelmersdale
Wigan
Worsley
Oldham
Maghull
Crosby
Kirkby
Leigh
Manchester
Bootle
St. Helens
Salford
Wallasey
Hoylake
Liverpool
Birkenhead
Stockport
Widnes
Warrington
Cheadle
Bebington
Speke
Runcorn
Wilmslow
Prestatyn
Heswall
Ellesmere
Port
Rhyl
Rhuddlan
Holywell
Llandudno
Colwyn Bay
Conwy
Conwy
Castle
Abergele
St. Asaph
Trefnant
Flint
Connah's
Quay
Helsby
Northwich
Knutsford
Macclesfield
Cemaes
Amlwch
Carmel Hd.
Moelfre
Llanerchymedd
Benllech
Beaumaris
Castle
Holyhead
Pentraeth
Holy I.
Valley
Llangefni
Menai
Bridge
Beaumaris
Llanfairfechan
Bodnant
Gardens
Denbigh
Castle
Denbigh
Llansannan
Mold
Queensferry
Chester
Kelsall
Winsford
Middlewich
Holmes
Chapel
Congleton
Rhosneigr
Bangor
Bethesda
Dolgarrog
Aberffraw
Y Felinheli
Llanrwst
Ruthin
Buckley
Hope
Sandbach
Biddulph
Kidsgrove
Newborough
Caernarfon
Castle
Caernarfon
Waunfawr
Llanberis
Capel
Curig
Swallow
Falls
Betws-y-Coed
Snowdon
Rossett
Crewe
Wrexham
Nantwich
Holt
Erddig
House
Malpas
Newcastle-
under-Lyme
Penygroes
Dolwyddelan
Cerrigydrudion
Beddgelert
Blaenau
Ffestiniog
Rhosllanerchrugog
Pontcysyllte
Aqueduct
Audlem
Madeley
Stoke-
on-Trent
Llanaelhaiarn
Corwen
Overton
Whitchurch
Nefyn
Porthmadog
Ffestiniog
Llangollen
Tudweiliog
Pwllheli
Criccieth
Penrhyndeudraeth
Portmeirion
Llandrillo
Chirk
Chirk
Castle
Ellesmere
Market
Drayton
Stone
Trawsfynydd
Bala
Moel Sych
Prees
Wem
Ashley
Harlech
Harlech
Castle
Llanbedr
Llanuwchllyn
Oswestry
Whittington
Eccleshall
Plas-yn-
Rhiw
Aberdaron
Llanbedrog
Abersoch
Rhiw
L. Vyrnwy
Penybontfawr
Hodnet
Baschurch
Stafford
Bardsey I.
Bardsey Sd.
Dolgellau
Aran
Fawddwy
Llanwddyn
Llanfyllin
Llanymynech
Shawbury
Newport
Gnosall
Barmouth
Cader
Idris
Crudgington
Penkridge
Llwyngwril
Tal-y-llyn
Corris
Mallwyd
Foel
Guilsfield
Shrewsbury
Wellington
Oakengates
Cannock
Welshpool
Westbury
Telford
Abergynolwyn
Llanfair
Caereinion
Powis
Castle
Minsterley
Cressage
Ironbridge
Tywyn
Bryncrug
Machynlleth
Llanbrynmair
Carno
Berriew
Chirbury
Stiperstones
Much Wenlock
Wolverhampton
West
Bromwich
Aberdyfi
Caersws
Montgomery
Church
Stretton
Bridgnorth
Dudley
Borth
Newtown
Talybont
Silver
Lead Mines
Plumlumon Fawr
Dolfor
Bishop's
Castle
Stourbridge
Aberystwyth
Ponterwyd
Llanidloes
Clun
Craven
Arms
Highley
Halesowen
Llangurig
Beguildy
Stokesay
Castle
Kidderminster
Devil's
Bridge
Llanbister
Leintwardine
Stourport-
on-Severn
Llanrhystud
Lanilar
St.
Harmon
Knighton
Ludlow
Cleobury
Mortimer
Pontrhydfendigaid
Rhayader
Presteigne
Mortimer's
Cross
Tenbury
Wells
Droitwich
Aberaeron
New Quay
New Radnor
Newbridge
Severn
Wye
Dee
Mersey
Eden
Teme
Dyfi
Vyrnwy
Onny
Ribble
Lune
Derwent Water
Bassenthwaite
Water
Wast
Water
Coniston
Water
Windermere
Shropshire Union Canal

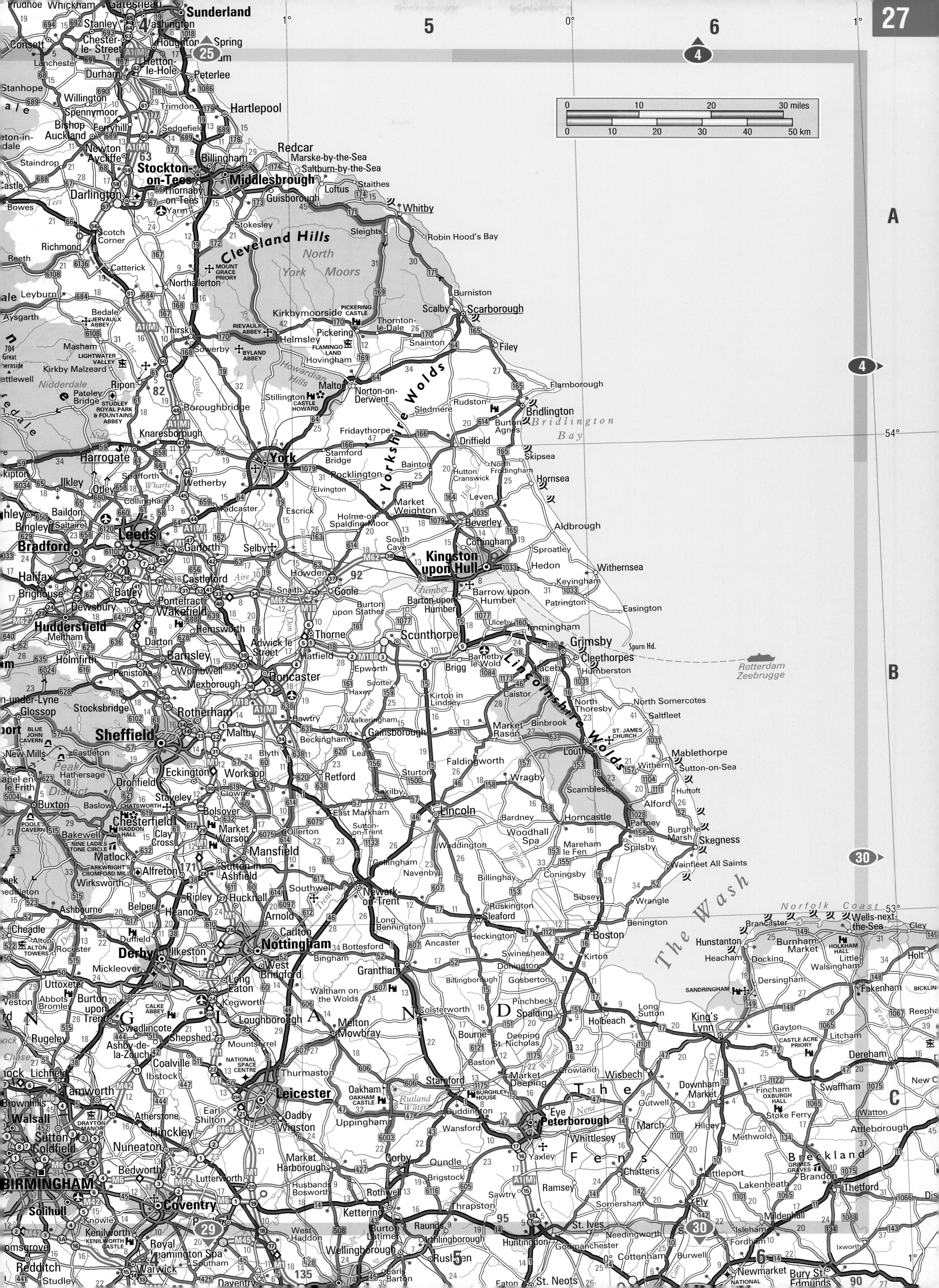

0 10 20 30 miles
0 10 20 30 40 50 km
A
B
C
5
6
Sunderland
Washington
Houghton
Spring
Chester-le-Street
Stanley
Consett
Lanchester
Durham
Hetton-le-Hole
Peterlee
Stanhope
Willington
Spennymoor
Trimdon
Hartlepool
Bishop Auckland
Ferryhill
Sedgefield
Newton Aycliffe
Billingham
Redcar
Marske-by-the-Sea
Saltburn-by-the-Sea
Staindrop
Stockton-on-Tees
Middlesbrough
Thornaby on-Tees
Darlington
Loftus
Staithes
Guisborough
Whitby
Yarm
Bowes
Scotch Corner
Stokesley
Sleights
Robin Hood's Bay
Richmond
Cleveland Hills
North York Moors
Reeth
Catterick
MOUNT GRACE PRIORY
Northallerton
Leyburn
Burniston
Bedale
JERVAULX ABBEY
Aysgarth
Kirkbymoorside
PICKERING CASTLE
Scalby
Scarborough
Thirsk
RIEVAULX ABBEY
Pickering
Thornton-le-Dale
Snainton
Helmsley
Filey
Masham
Sowerby
BYLAND ABBEY
FLAMINGO LAND
Hovingham
LIGHTWATER VALLEY
Kirkby Malzeard
Howardian Hills
Flamborough
Nidderdale
Ripon
Malton
Norton-on-Derwent
Pateley Bridge
Stillington
CASTLE HOWARD
Rudston
STUDLEY ROYAL PARK & FOUNTAINS ABBEY
Boroughbridge
Sledmere
Bridlington
Yorkshire Wolds
Burton Agnes
Bridlington Bay
54°
Knaresborough
Fridaythorpe
Driffield
Harrogate
York
Stamford Bridge
Skipsea
Spofforth
Bainton
North Frodingham
Ilkley
Otley
Wetherby
Pocklington
Hutton Cranswick
Hornsea
Elvington
Collingham
Leven
Market Weighton
Baildon
Tadcaster
Escrick
Aldbrough
Saltaire
Holme-on-Spalding-Moor
Beverley
Bingley
Leeds
Garforth
Selby
South Cave
Cottingham
Sproatley
Bradford
Kingston upon Hull
Hedon
Withernsea
Halifax
Castleford
Howden
Keyingham
Brighouse
Batley
Pontefract
Snaith
Goole
Humber
Barrow upon Humber
Dewsbury
Wakefield
Burton upon Stather
Barton-upon-Humber
Patrington
Easington
Huddersfield
Hemsworth
Ulceby
Immingham
Meltham
Darton
Thorne
Adwick le Street
Scunthorpe
Grimsby
Spurn Hd.
Holmfirth
Barnsley
Hatfield
Barnetby le Wold
Cleethorpes
Rotterdam Zeebrugge
Penistone
Wombwell
Epworth
Brigg
Humberston
Mexborough
Doncaster
Laceby
Haxey
Scotter
Kirton in Lindsey
Caistor
Stocksbridge
Rotherham
North Somercotes
Glossop
North Thoresby
Saltfleet
Bawtry
Walkeringham
Sheffield
Maltby
Gainsborough
Binbrook
Market Rasen
Lincolnshire Wolds
ST. JAMES CHURCH
BLUE JOHN CAVERN
Beckingham
New Mills
Castleton
Blyth
Louth
Mablethorpe
Peak District
Hathersage
Eckington
Worksop
Retford
Faldingworth
Withern
Sutton-on-Sea
Dronfield
Sturton
Wragby
Huttoft
Buxton
Baslow
CHATSWORTH
Staveley
Clowne
Saxilby
Scamblesby
Alford
Bolsover
East Markham
Lincoln
Bardney
Horncastle
Partney
POOLE'S CAVERN
Chesterfield
HADDON HALL
Market Warsop
Sutton-on-Trent
Burgh le Marsh
Bakewell
Clay Cross
Ollerton
Woodhall Spa
Skegness
NINE LADIES STONE CIRCLE
Waddington
Mareham le Fen
Spilsby
Matlock
Mansfield
ARKWRIGHT'S CROMFORD MILL
Alfreton
Sutton-in-Ashfield
Collingham
Wainfleet All Saints
Wirksworth
Navenby
Coningsby
Billinghay
Southwell
Newark-on-Trent
The Wash
Belper
Ripley
Hucknall
Sibsey
Wrangle
Ashbourne
Heanor
Ruskington
Norfolk Coast
Arnold
Sleaford
Long Bennington
53°
Benington
Brancaster
Wells-next-the-Sea
Cheadle
Carlton
Heckington
Boston
Duffield
Hunstanton
Burnham Market
Cley
ALTON TOWERS
Alton
Rocester
Derby
Ilkeston
Nottingham
Bottesford
Ancaster
Swineshead
Kirton
Heacham
Docking
HOLKHAM HALL
Little Walsingham
Holt
Mickleover
West Bridgford
Bingham
Grantham
Donington
Uttoxeter
Long Eaton
Billingborough
Gosberton
Dersingham
Fakenham
Abbots Bromley
Burton upon Trent
CALKE ABBEY
Kegworth
Waltham on the Wolds
SANDRINGHAM
Pinchbeck
Spalding
Long Sutton
King's Lynn
Reepham
Swadlincote
Loughborough
Colsterworth
Holbeach
Melton Mowbray
Bourne
Deeping St. Nicholas
Gayton
Rugeley
Shepshed
CASTLE ACRE PRIORY
Litcham
Ashby-de-la-Zouch
Mountsorrel
Baston
Dereham
Lichfield
Coalville
NATIONAL SPACE CENTRE
Thurmaston
Ibstock
Stamford
Market Deeping
Crowland
Wisbech
Downham Market
Swaffham
New Buckenham
Tamworth
Oakham
OAKHAM CASTLE
BURGHLEY HOUSE
Fincham
Rutland Water
Leicester
OXBURGH HALL
Brownhills
DRAYTON MANOR
Atherstone
Earl Shilton
Oadby
Duddington
Eye
Outwell
Stoke Ferry
Walsall
Uppingham
Wansford
Peterborough
March
Watton
Hinckley
Wigston
Hilgay
Attleborough
Sutton Coldfield
Whittlesey
Methwold
The Fens
Nuneaton
Market Harborough
Corby
Oundle
Yaxley
Breckland
Bedworth
Chatteris
GRIMES GRAVES
Brandon
Lutterworth
Husbands Bosworth
Brigstock
Littleport
Lakenheath
BIRMINGHAM
Ramsey
Thetford
Coventry
Rothwell
Sawtry
Solihull
Thrapston
Somersham
Ely
Mildenhall
Knowle
Kettering
Kenilworth
KENILWORTH CASTLE
West Haddon
Burton Latimer
Raunds
St. Ives
Needingworth
Isleham
Fordham
Bromsgrove
Royal Leamington Spa
Irthlingborough
Huntingdon
Godmanchester
Ixworth
Wellingborough
Rushden
Cottenham
Burwell
Redditch
Warwick
Southam
Earls Barton
Newmarket
Bury St. Edmunds
Studley
Daventry
St. Neots
NATIONAL

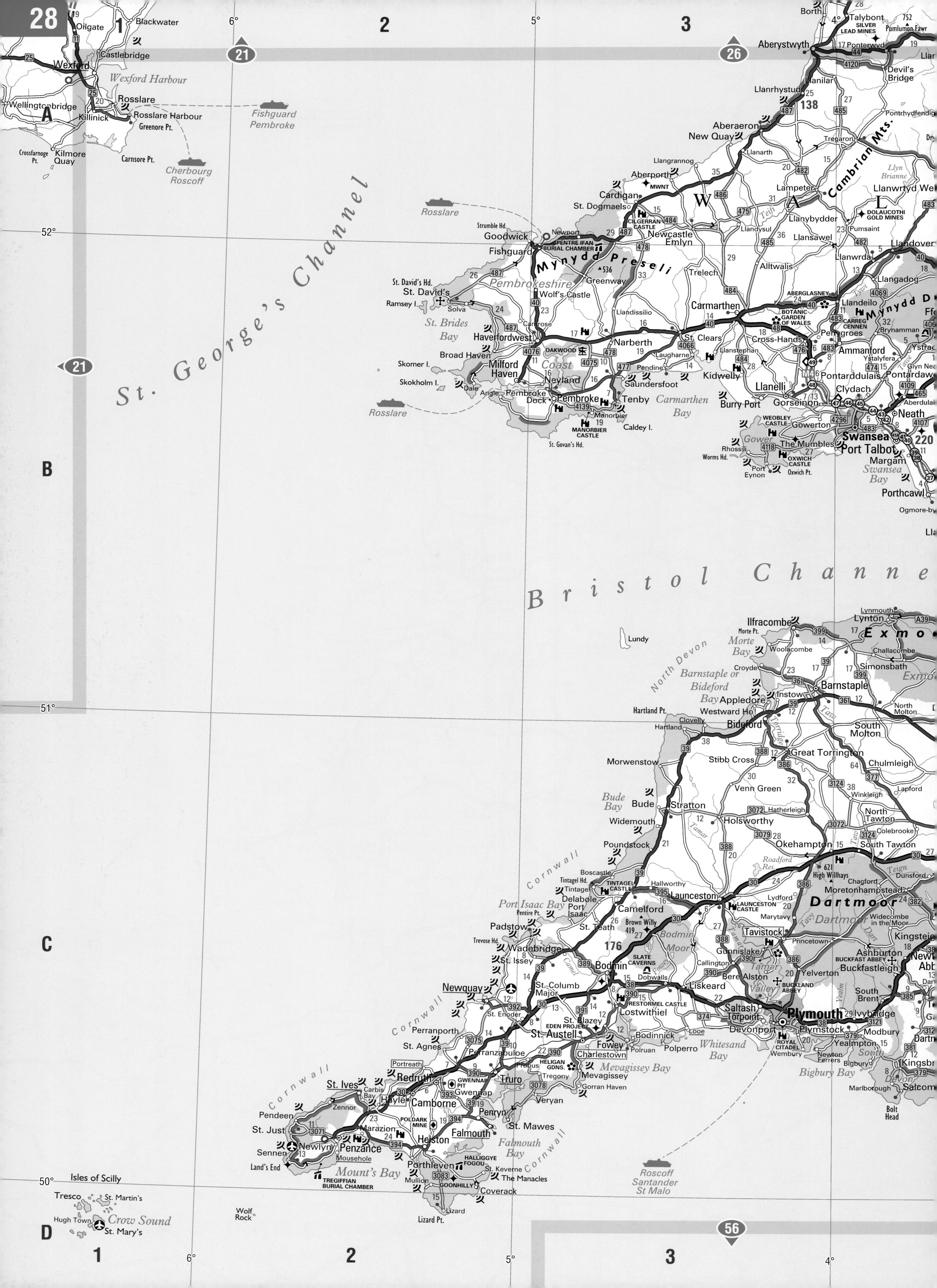
1
2
3
6°
5°
4°
A
B
C
D
21
26
56
52°
51°
50°
St. George's Channel
Bristol Channel
Oilgate
Blackwater
Castlebridge
Wexford
Wexford Harbour
Rosslare
Wellingtonbridge
Killinick
Rosslare Harbour
Greenore Pt.
Crossfarnoge Pt.
Kilmore Quay
Carnsore Pt.
Fishguard
Pembroke
Cherbourg
Roscoff
Rosslare
Borth
Talybont
SILVER LEAD MINES
752
Pumlumon Fawr
Aberystwyth
Ponterwyd
Devil's Bridge
Llanrhystud
Llanilar
138
Aberaeron
New Quay
Tregaron
Cambrian Mts.
Llanarth
Llangrannog
Aberporth
MWNT
Cardigan
Lampeter
Llyn Brianne
Llanwrtyd Wells
W
A
L
St. Dogmaels
CILGERRAN CASTLE
Llanybydder
DOLAUCOTHI GOLD MINES
Strumble Hd.
Goodwick
Newport
PENTRE IFAN BURIAL CHAMBER
Newcastle Emlyn
Llandysul
Llansawel
Pumsaint
Llandovery
Mynydd Preseli
536
Alltwalis
Llanwrda
Greenway
Trelech
Llangadog
St. David's Hd.
St. David's
Ramsey I.
Solva
Pembrokeshire
Wolf's Castle
Carmarthen
ABERGLASNEY
Llandeilo
BOTANIC GARDEN OF WALES
CARREG CENNEN
Mynydd D
St. Brides Bay
Camrose
Llandissilio
Brynamman
Haverfordwest
St. Clears
Pennygroes
OAKWOOD
Narberth
Cross-Hands
Ammanford
Broad Haven
Coast
Laugharne
Llanstephan
Pontarddulais
Pontardawe
Skomer I.
Milford Haven
Neyland
Pendine
Kidwelly
Skokholm I.
Dale
Angle
Pembroke Dock
Saundersfoot
Llanelli
Clydach
Pembroke
Tenby
Carmarthen Bay
Burry Port
Gorseinon
Neath
Manorbier
MANORBIER CASTLE
Caldey I.
WEOBLEY CASTLE
Gowerton
St. Govan's Hd.
Gower
The Mumbles
Swansea
220
Rhossili
Port Talbot
Worms Hd.
OXWICH CASTLE
Margam
Port Eynon
Oxwich Pt.
Swansea Bay
Porthcawl
Ogmore-by
Lynmouth
Lynton
Ilfracombe
Exmo
Morte Pt.
Lundy
Morte Bay
Woolacombe
Challacombe
North Devon
Croyde
Simonsbath
Barnstaple or Bideford Bay
Instow
Barnstaple
Appledore
Westward Ho!
North Molton
Hartland Pt.
Hartland
Clovelly
Bideford
South Molton
Morwenstow
Stibb Cross
Great Torrington
Chulmleigh
Venn Green
Bude Bay
Bude
Stratton
Hatherleigh
Winkleigh
Lapford
Widemouth
Holsworthy
North Tawton
Tamar
Colebrooke
Poundstock
Okehampton
South Tawton
Roadford Res.
Boscastle
Cornwall
621
High Willhays
Chagford
Dunsford
Tintagel Hd.
Tintagel
TINTAGEL CASTLE
Hallworthy
Moretonhampstead
Delabole
Launceston
Lydford
Dartmoor
Port Isaac Bay
Port Isaac
LAUNCESTON CASTLE
Pentire Pt.
Camelford
Marytavy
Widecombe in the Moor
Padstow
St. Teath
Brown Willy
419
Bodmin Moor
Tavistock
Kingsteig
Trevose Hd.
Wadebridge
176
Gunnislake
Princetown
Ashburton
St. Issey
SLATE CAVERNS
BUCKFAST ABBEY
Buckfastleigh
Bodmin
Callington
Dobwalls
Bere Alston
Yelverton
Newquay
St. Columb Major
Liskeard
BUCKLAND ABBEY
Tamar Valley
South Brent
St. Enoder
RESTORMEL CASTLE
Lostwithiel
Saltash
Torpoint
Plymouth
Ivybridge
Perranporth
St. Blazey
EDEN PROJECT
Devonport
Plymstock
Modbury
St. Agnes
St. Austell
Looe
Bodinnick
Fowey
Polruan
Polperro
Whitesand Bay
ROYAL CITADEL
Wembury
Yealmpton
Perranzabuloe
Charlestown
Newton Ferrers
Bigbury
Portreath
Probus
HELIGAN GDNS.
Mevagissey Bay
Mevagissey
Bigbury Bay
Redruth
GWENNAP PIT
Gwennap
Truro
Tregony
Kingsbr
St. Ives
Carbis Bay
Gorran Haven
Marlborough
Salcom
Hayle
Camborne
Veryan
Zennor
Pendeen
Penryn
POLDARK MINE
St. Mawes
Bolt Head
St. Just
Marazion
Newlyn
Penzance
Helston
Falmouth
Falmouth Bay
Sennen
Mousehole
HALLIGGYE FOGOU
Land's End
Mount's Bay
Porthleven
St. Keverne
TREGIFFIAN BURIAL CHAMBER
Mullion
GOONHILLY
The Manacles
Coverack
Roscoff
Santander
St Malo
Isles of Scilly
Tresco
St. Martin's
Hugh Town
Crow Sound
St. Mary's
Wolf Rock
Lizard
Lizard Pt.

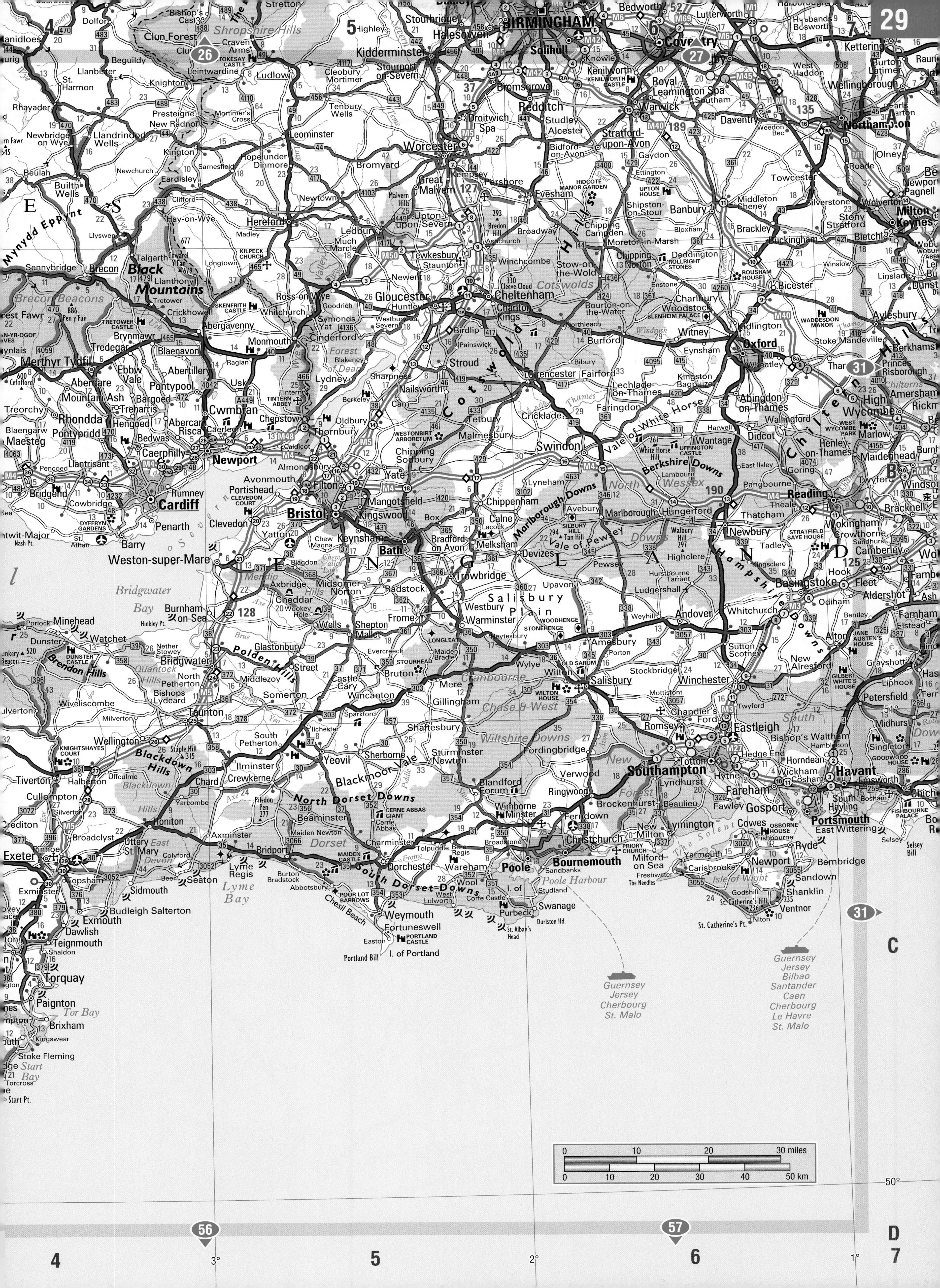
BIRMINGHAM
Coventry
Solihull
Kidderminster
Halesowen
Stourbridge
Bedworth
Lutterworth
Kettering
Bromsgrove
Redditch
Kenilworth
Royal Leamington Spa
Warwick
Daventry
Wellingborough
Northampton
Droitwich Spa
Worcester
Stratford-upon-Avon
Great Malvern
Pershore
Evesham
Hereford
Ledbury
Tewkesbury
Leominster
Ludlow
Bromyard
Shropshire Hills
Clun Forest
Knighton
Llandrindod Wells
Builth Wells
Hay-on-Wye
Brecon
Black Mountains
Brecon Beacons
Abergavenny
Monmouth
Ross-on-Wye
Gloucester
Cheltenham
Cotswolds
Stow-on-the-Wold
Chipping Norton
Banbury
Brackley
Buckingham
Milton Keynes
Bicester
Oxford
Witney
Aylesbury
Chiltern Hills
High Wycombe
Amersham
Marlow
Henley-on-Thames
Maidenhead
Reading
Windsor
Bracknell
Wokingham
Camberley
Basingstoke
Fleet
Aldershot
Farnham
Alton
Newbury
Hungerford
Berkshire Downs
Vale of White Horse
Abingdon-on-Thames
Didcot
Wantage
Wallingford
Swindon
Marlborough
Marlborough Downs
Vale of Pewsey
Devizes
Chippenham
Calne
Melksham
Trowbridge
Bradford on Avon
Bath
Bristol
Kingswood
Keynsham
Clevedon
Portishead
Weston-super-Mare
Newport
Cardiff
Cwmbran
Caerphilly
Pontypool
Merthyr Tydfil
Aberdare
Rhondda
Maesteg
Bridgend
Barry
Penarth
Chepstow
Stroud
Cirencester
Tetbury
Malmesbury
Mendip Hills
Cheddar
Wells
Shepton Mallet
Frome
Warminster
Salisbury Plain
Andover
Salisbury
Amesbury
Winchester
Hampshire Downs
Romsey
Eastleigh
Southampton
Fareham
Gosport
Portsmouth
Havant
Petersfield
Chichester
Isle of Wight
Newport
Cowes
Ryde
Sandown
Shanklin
Ventnor
Lymington
Christchurch
Bournemouth
Poole
Swanage
Wareham
Dorchester
Weymouth
Bridport
Lyme Regis
Lyme Bay
South Dorset Downs
North Dorset Downs
Blackmoor Vale
Yeovil
Sherborne
Shaftesbury
Cranbourne Chase & West Wiltshire Downs
Blandford Forum
Wimborne Minster
Ringwood
New Forest
Taunton
Bridgwater
Bridgwater Bay
Burnham-on-Sea
Glastonbury
Street
Polden Hills
Quantock Hills
Brendon Hills
Minehead
Watchet
Wellington
Blackdown Hills
Tiverton
Honiton
Chard
Crewkerne
Exeter
Exmouth
Sidmouth
Budleigh Salterton
Dawlish
Teignmouth
Torquay
Paignton
Tor Bay
Brixham
Start Bay
Guernsey
Jersey
Cherbourg
St. Malo
Bilbao
Santander
Caen
Le Havre
ENGLAND
0 10 20 30 miles
0 10 20 30 40 50 km
4
5
6
7
C
D

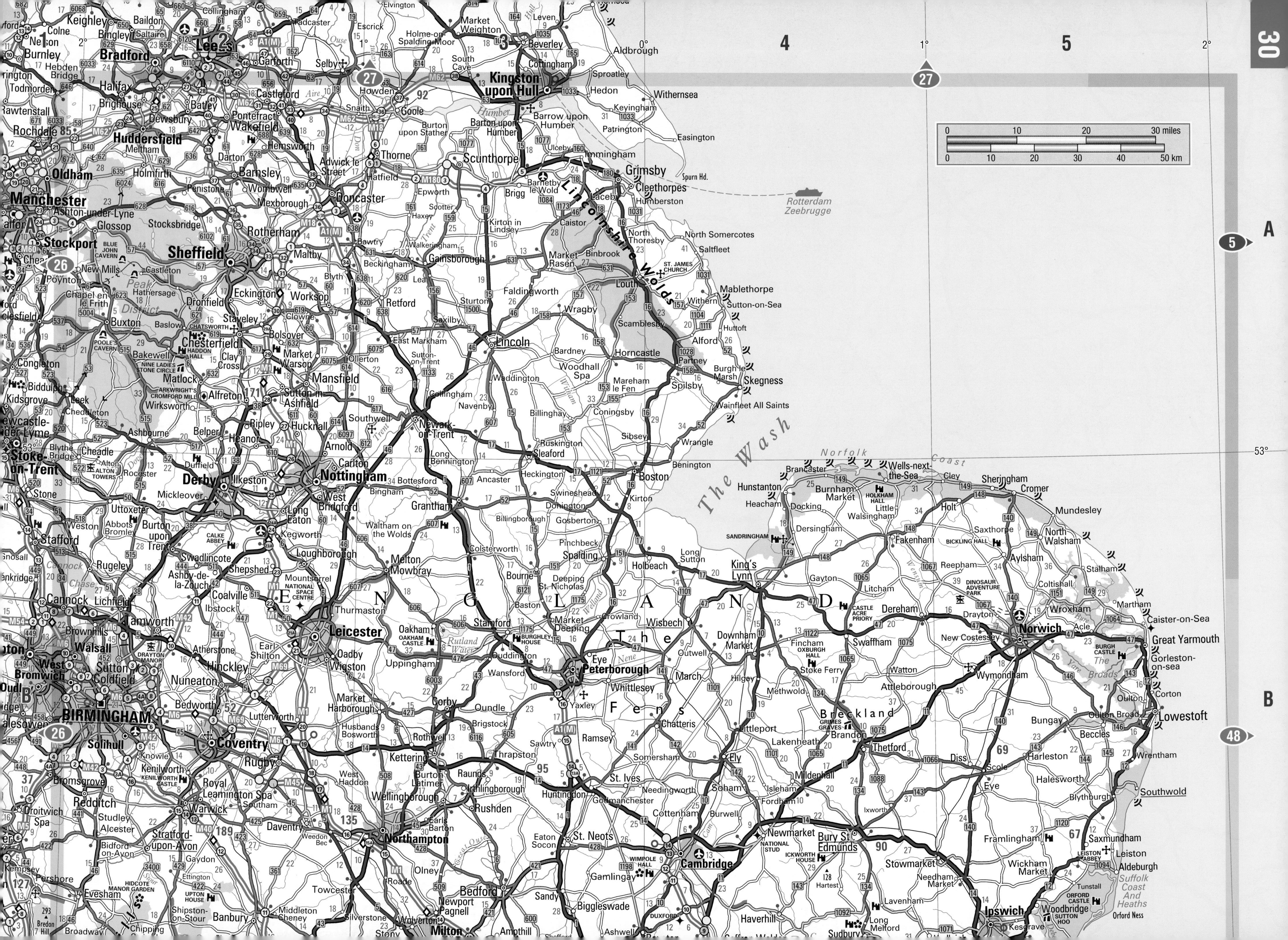

0 10 20 30 miles
0 10 20 30 40 50 km
4
5
A
B
5
48
27
26
0°
1°
2°
53°
Rotterdam
Zeebrugge
Spurn Hd.
The Wash
Norfolk Coast
Lincolnshire Wolds
ENGLAND
The Fens
Breckland
The Broads
Suffolk Coast And Heaths
Peak District
Cannock Chase
Leeds
Bradford
Halifax
Huddersfield
Wakefield
Castleford
Pontefract
Selby
Goole
Howden
Kingston upon Hull
Beverley
Cottingham
Hedon
Withernsea
Barton-upon-Humber
Scunthorpe
Grimsby
Cleethorpes
Immingham
Brigg
Caistor
Market Rasen
Louth
Mablethorpe
Sutton-on-Sea
Alford
Skegness
Wainfleet All Saints
Spilsby
Horncastle
Woodhall Spa
Coningsby
Boston
Sleaford
Lincoln
Gainsborough
Retford
Worksop
Doncaster
Thorne
Barnsley
Rotherham
Sheffield
Chesterfield
Mansfield
Newark-on-Trent
Grantham
Nottingham
Derby
Matlock
Bakewell
Buxton
Glossop
Manchester
Stockport
Oldham
Rochdale
Burnley
Keighley
Macclesfield
Congleton
Leek
Stoke-on-Trent
Stafford
Uttoxeter
Burton upon Trent
Ashby-de-la-Zouch
Loughborough
Melton Mowbray
Leicester
Oakham
Stamford
Spalding
Holbeach
Long Sutton
King's Lynn
Hunstanton
Wells-next-the-Sea
Sheringham
Cromer
Holt
Fakenham
Aylsham
North Walsham
Mundesley
Norwich
Great Yarmouth
Gorleston-on-sea
Lowestoft
Beccles
Bungay
Southwold
Halesworth
Saxmundham
Leiston
Aldeburgh
Orford Ness
Woodbridge
Ipswich
Stowmarket
Bury St Edmunds
Newmarket
Cambridge
Ely
Thetford
Diss
Wymondham
Dereham
Swaffham
Downham Market
Wisbech
March
Peterborough
Huntingdon
St. Neots
St. Ives
Bedford
Milton Keynes
Northampton
Kettering
Corby
Wellingborough
Rushden
Market Harborough
Rugby
Coventry
Nuneaton
Hinckley
Tamworth
Lichfield
Walsall
West Bromwich
Sutton Coldfield
Birmingham
Solihull
Redditch
Bromsgrove
Kenilworth
Warwick
Royal Leamington Spa
Stratford-upon-Avon
Evesham
Banbury
Daventry
Towcester
Biggleswade
Haverhill
Sudbury

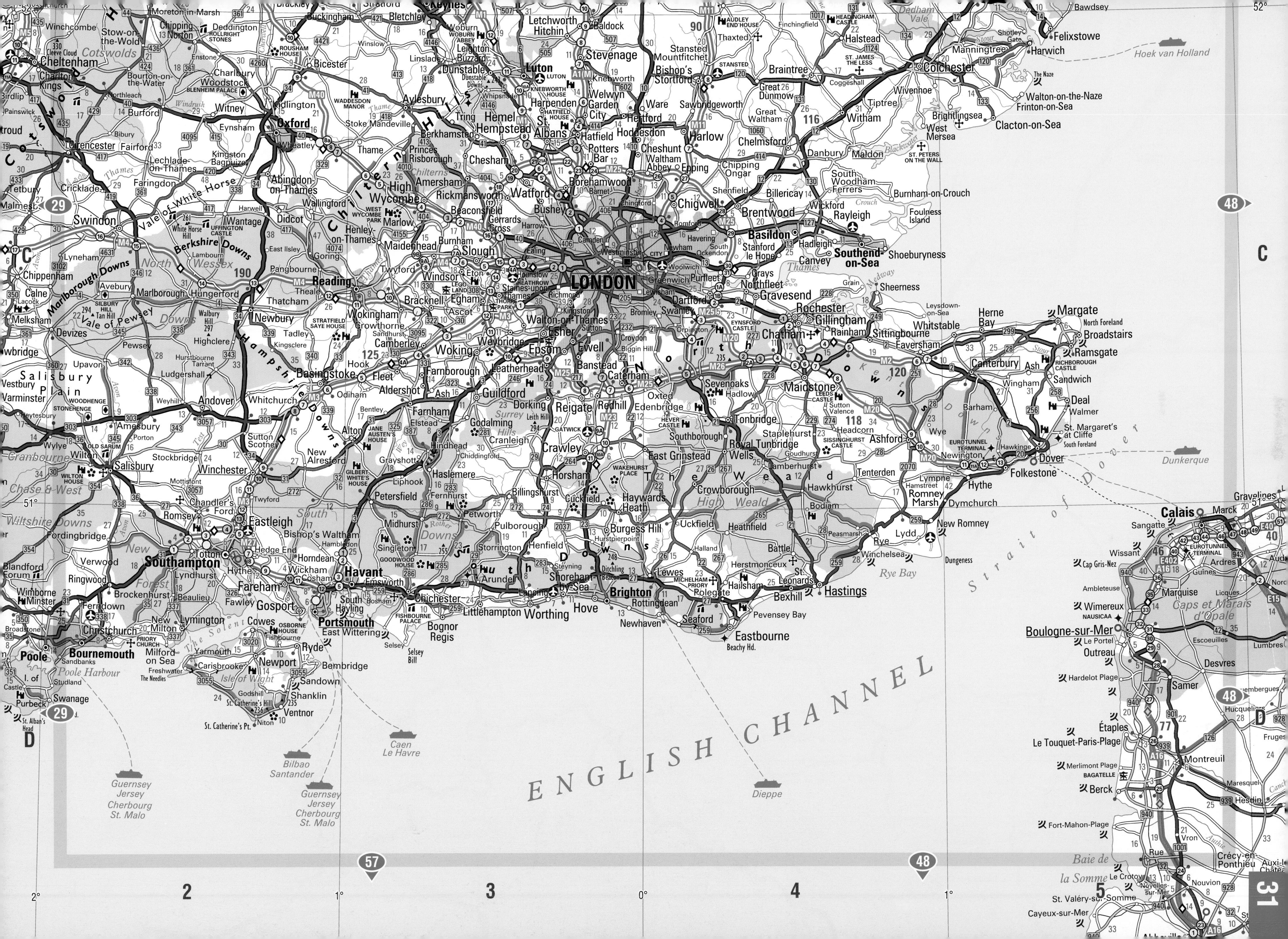
ENGLISH CHANNEL
Strait of Dover
LONDON
Oxford
Reading
Southampton
Portsmouth
Brighton
Hastings
Dover
Folkestone
Canterbury
Margate
Ramsgate
Broadstairs
Maidstone
Rochester
Gillingham
Chatham
Southend-on-Sea
Basildon
Chelmsford
Colchester
Harwich
Felixstowe
Clacton-on-Sea
Luton
Stevenage
Watford
Slough
Guildford
Crawley
Eastbourne
Worthing
Bournemouth
Poole
Salisbury
Winchester
Swindon
Cheltenham
Newbury
Basingstoke
Isle of Wight
Newport
Calais
Boulogne-sur-Mer
Dunkerque
Dieppe
Caen
Le Havre
Bilbao
Santander
Guernsey
Jersey
Cherbourg
St. Malo
Hoek van Holland
Le Touquet-Paris-Plage
Montreuil
Étaples
Berck
Baie de la Somme
Caps et Marais d'Opale
Chiltern Hills
North Downs
South Downs
The Weald
Vale of White Horse
Berkshire Downs
Marlborough Downs
Vale of Pewsey
Salisbury Plain
Hampshire Downs
Cotswolds
New Forest
The Solent
Poole Harbour
Rye Bay
29
48
57
2
3
4
5
C
D
52°
51°
2°
1°
0°

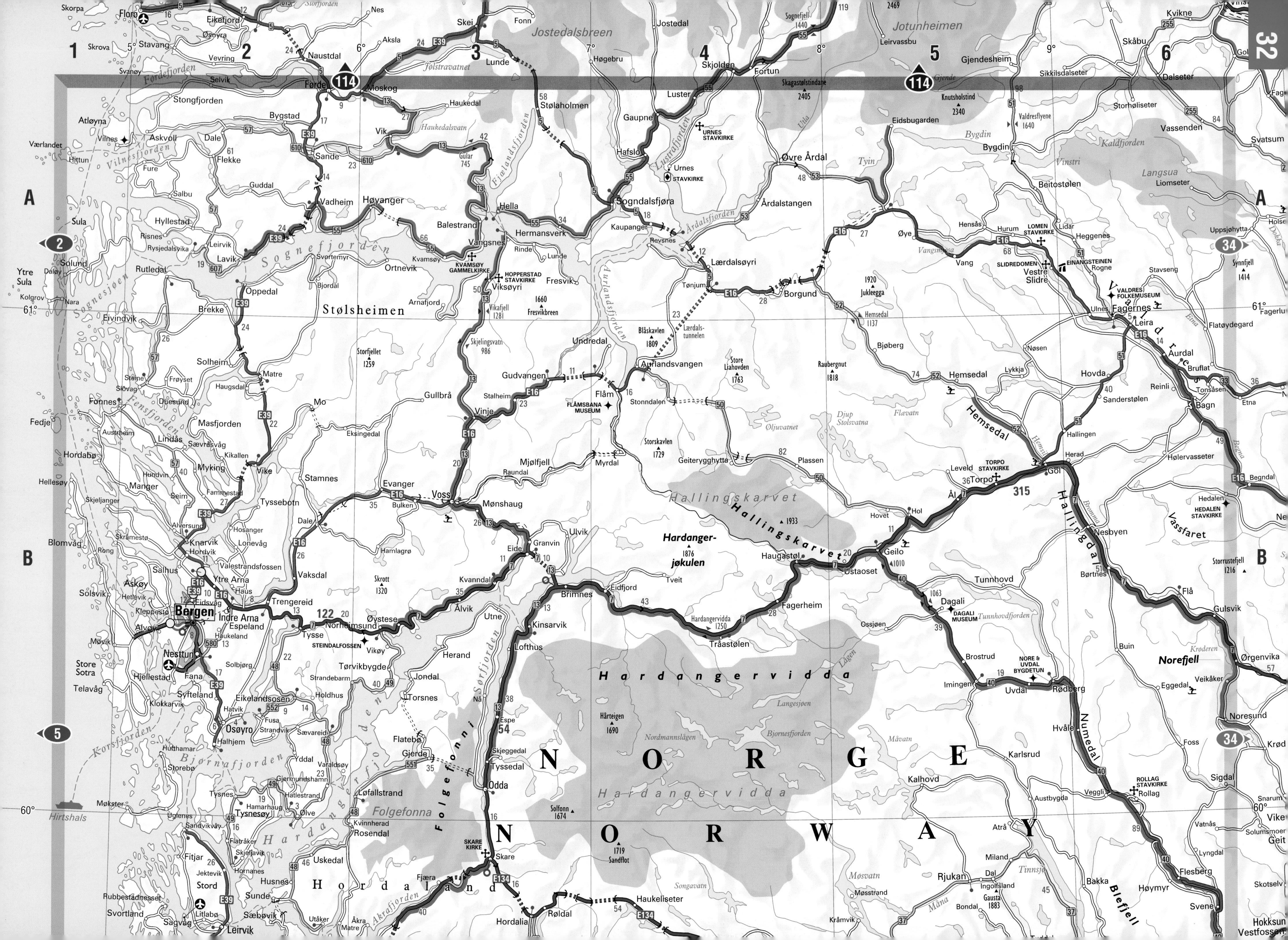
NORGE
NORWAY
Hardangervidda
Hallingskarvet
Hardangerjøkulen
Folgefonna
Folgefonni
Jostedalsbreen
Jotunheimen
Stølsheimen
Sognefjorden
Hardangerfjorden
Sørfjorden
Aurlandsfjorden
Bjørnafjorden
Fjærlandsfjorden
Lustrafjorden
Årdalsfjorden
Hallingdal
Numedal
Hemsedal
Valdres
Hordaland
Vassfaret
Norefjell
Blefjell
Bergen
Voss
Odda
Geilo
Gol
Fagernes
Flåm
FLÅMSBANA MUSEUM
Lærdalsøyri
Sogndalsfjøra
Førde
Høyanger
Vik
Vikøyri
HOPPERSTAD STAVKIRKE
KVAMSØY GAMMELKIRKE
URNES STAVKIRKE
TORPO STAVKIRKE
HEDALEN STAVKIRKE
ROLLAG STAVKIRKE
SKARE KIRKE
LOMEN STAVKIRKE
SLIDREDOMEN
EINANGSTEINEN
VALDRES FOLKEMUSEUM
DAGALI MUSEUM
NORE & UVDAL BYGDETUN
STEINDALFOSSEN
Gudvangen
Eidfjord
Ulvik
Kinsarvik
Lofthus
Norheimsund
Øystese
Osøyro
Stord
Leirvik
Rjukan
Uvdal
Rødberg
Nesbyen
Flå
Ål
Hol
Haugastøl
Myrdal
Aurlandsvangen
Årdalstangen
Øvre Årdal
Fortun
Skjolden
Luster
Gaupne
Hafslo
Kaupanger
Balestrand
Vangsnes
Hermansverk
Dale
Vaksdal
Stamnes
Mo
Evanger
Jondal
Rosendal
Sunde
Husnes
Røldal
Haukeliseter
Hordalia
Fjæra
Skare
Tyssedal
Utne
Granvin
Eide
Mønshaug
Vinje
Stalheim
Nesttun
Fana
Askøy
Knarvik
Lindås
Masfjorden
Manger
Fedje
Florø
Naustdal
Moskog
Skei
Lunde
Fonn
Stølaholmen
Sande
Vadheim
Lavik
Askvoll
Hyllestad
Sula
Solund
Ytre Sula
Bygdin
Beitostølen
Vang
Øye
Borgund
Torpo
Leveld
Vestre Slidre
Sikkilsdalseter
Gjendesheim
Eidsbugarden
Bagn
Aurdal
Leira
Gulsvik
Veggli
Ustaoset
Dagali
Imingen
Tunnhovd
Kalhovd
Atrå
Svene
Flesberg
Sigdal
Noresund
Hokksund
Vestfossen
Hirtshals
E16
E39
E134
114
34
2
5
A
B
1
2
3
4
5
6
60°
61°

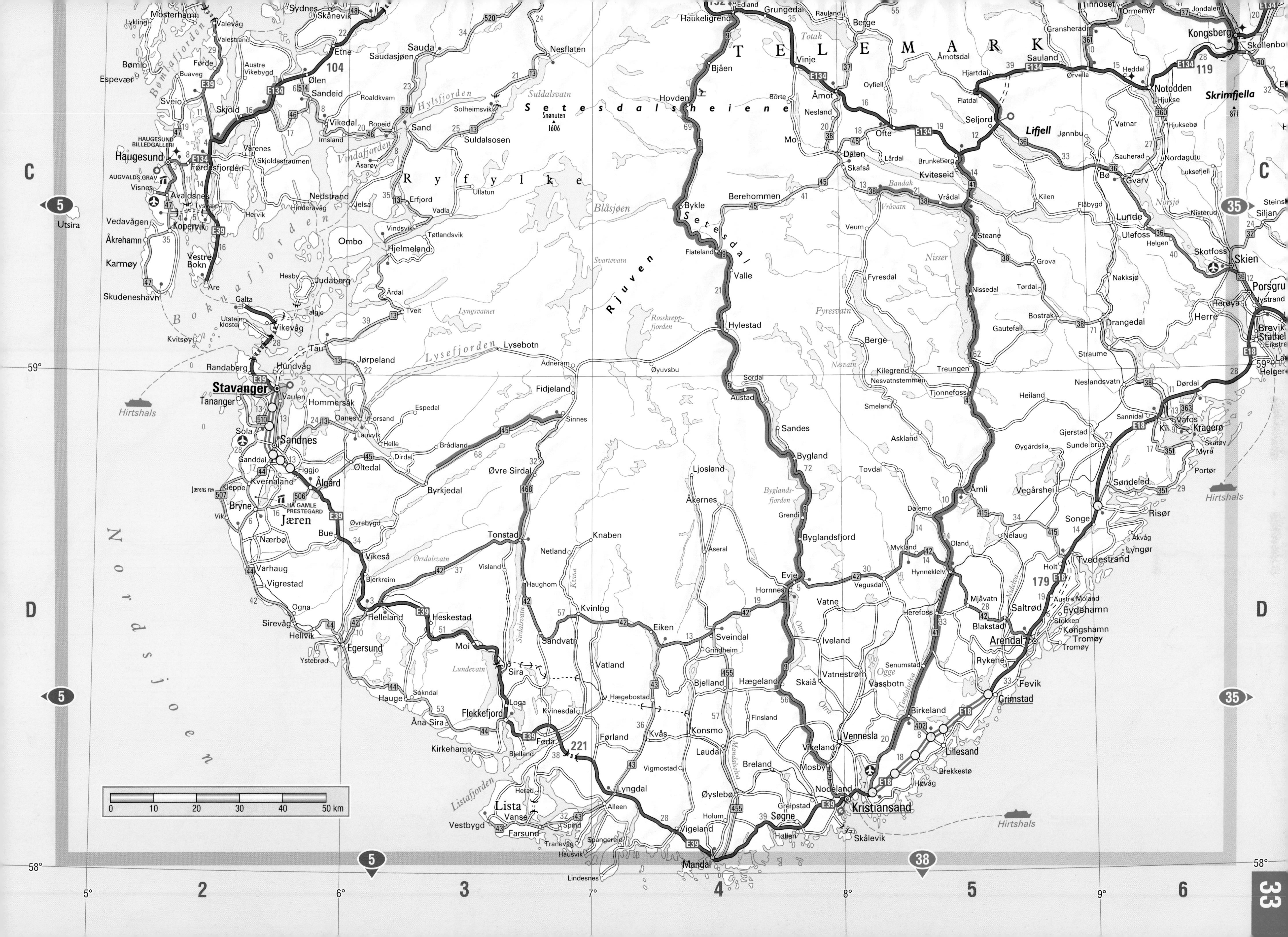

T E L E M A R K
R y f y l k e
S e t e s d a l s h e i e n e
Setesdal
Riuven
N o r d s j o e n
Stavanger
Kristiansand
Haugesund
Arendal
Grimstad
Mandal
Skien
Porsgrunn
Kongsberg
Notodden
Sandnes
Egersund
Flekkefjord
Lillesand
Tvedestrand
Kragerø
Risør
Farsund
Lista
Kopervik
Skudeneshavn
Karmøy
Sauda
Bygland
Valle
Bykle
Haukeligrend
Vinje
Seljord
Dalen
Åmli
Evje
Vennesla
Søgne
Øvre Sirdal
Jæren
Bryne
Lindesnes
Hirtshals
Skrimfjella
Lifjell
Totak
Nisser
Bandak
Suldalsvatn
Lysefjorden
Boknafjorden
Snønuten 1606
0 10 20 30 40 50 km
59°
58°

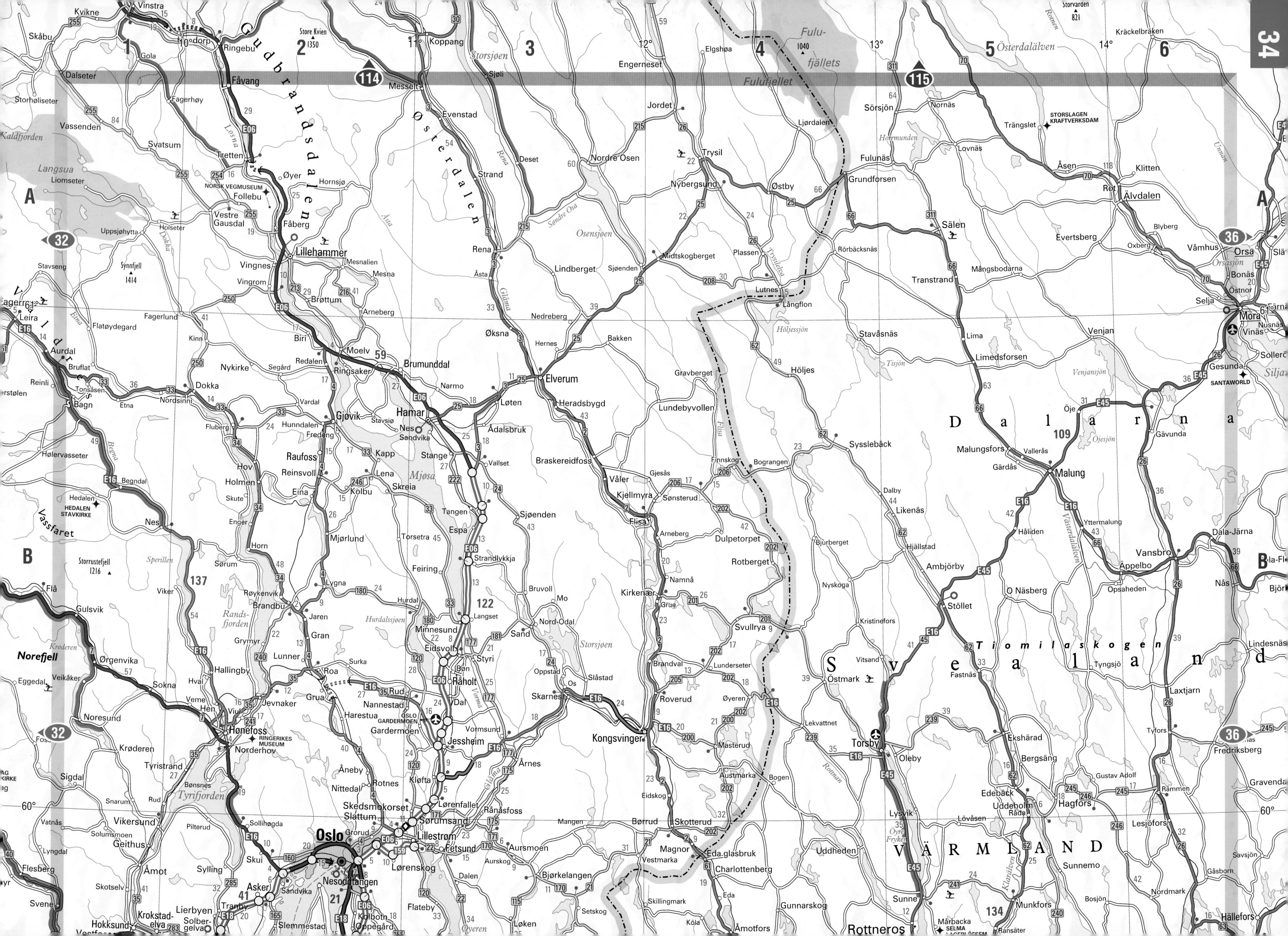
Gudbrandsdalen
Østerdalen
Dalarna
Svealand
Värmland
Tiomilaskogen
Fulufjället
Fulu-fjällets
Oslo
Lillehammer
Hamar
Gjøvik
Elverum
Kongsvinger
Hønefoss
Lillestrøm
Jessheim
Eidsvoll
Brumunddal
Rena
Trysil
Sälen
Malung
Mora
Orsa
Älvdalen
Vansbro
Torsby
Hagfors
Munkfors
Sunne
Rottneros
Mårbacka
Hällefors
Fredriksberg
Lesjöfors
Charlottenberg
Eda glasbruk
Magnor
Skotterud
Flisa
Kirkenær
Asker
Sandvika
Nesoddtangen
Drøbak
Krokstad-elva
Hokksund
Geithus
Åmot
Vikersund
Sokna
Noresund
Nesbyen
Fagernes
Bagn
Aurdal
Dokka
Raufoss
Kapp
Lena
Skreia
Moelv
Biri
Ringsaker
Stange
Løten
Mjøsa
Randsfjorden
Tyrifjorden
Storsjøen
Osensjøen
Femunden
Höljes
Stöllet
Ambjörby
Likenäs
Sysslebäck
Ekshärad
Uddeholm
Gardermoen
Norefjell
Vassfaret
Storsjøen
Österdalälven
Västerdalälven
Klarälven
Glåma
Siljan
HEDALEN STAVKIRKE
NORSK VEGMUSEUM
RINGERIKES MUSEUM
STORSLAGEN KRAFTVERKSDAM
SANTAWORLD
SELMA LAGERLÖFSEM
Store Kvien 1350
Synnfjell 1414
Storrustefjell 1216
60°
12°
13°
14°

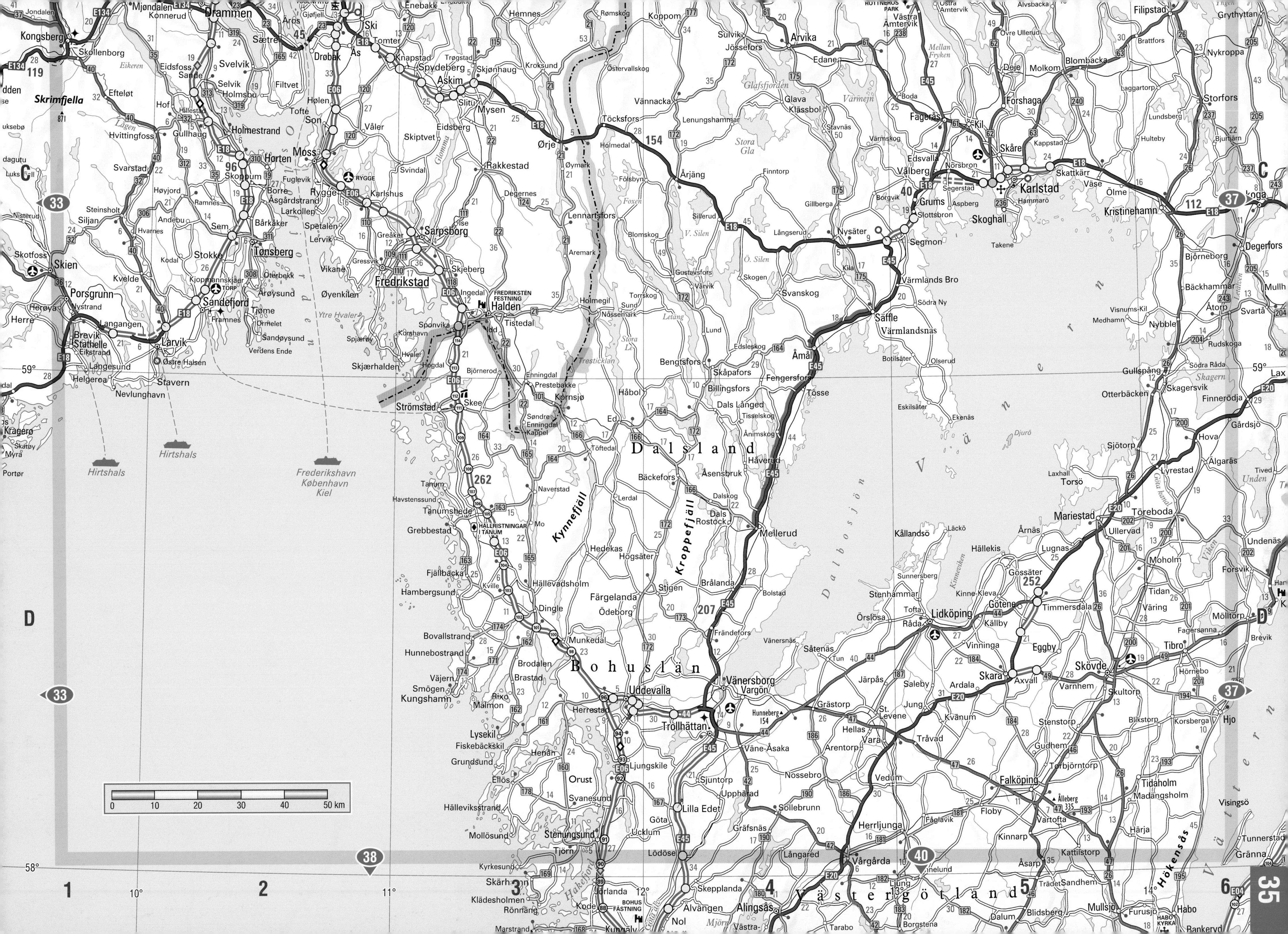
Vänern
Dalbosjön
Vättern
Dalsland
Bohuslän
Västergötland
Kroppefjäll
Kynnefjäll
Hökensås
Skrimfjella
Karlstad
Kristinehamn
Säffle
Åmål
Mellerud
Vänersborg
Trollhättan
Uddevalla
Lidköping
Skara
Skövde
Mariestad
Falköping
Alingsås
Arvika
Årjäng
Strömstad
Halden
Fredrikstad
Sarpsborg
Moss
Horten
Tønsberg
Sandefjord
Larvik
Porsgrunn
Skien
Drammen
Kongsberg
Frederikshavn
København
Kiel
Hirtshals
0
10
20
30
40
50 km

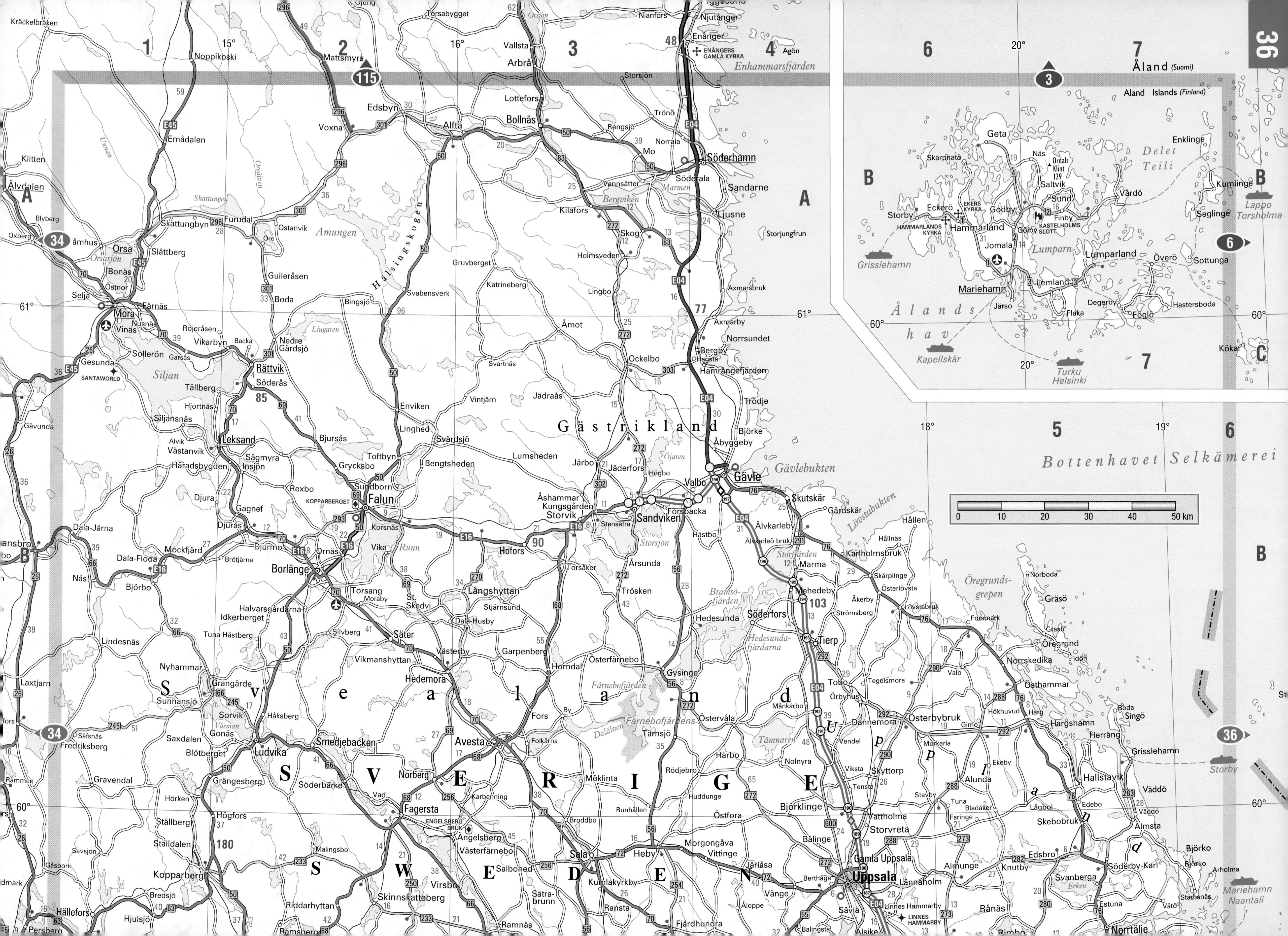
Åland (Suomi)
Aland Islands (Finland)
Bottenhavet Selkämerei
Gävlebukten
Lövstabukten
Öregrundsgrepen
Ålands hav
Enhammarsfjärden
0 10 20 30 40 50 km
Gästrikland
Uppland
Dalarna
SVERIGE
SVEDEN
SWEDEN
Söderhamn
Bollnäs
Alfta
Edsbyn
Arbrå
Vallsta
Lottefors
Ljusne
Sandarne
Skog
Kilafors
Mora
Orsa
Rättvik
Leksand
Falun
Borlänge
Gävle
Sandviken
Hofors
Avesta
Hedemora
Säter
Ludvika
Smedjebacken
Fagersta
Norberg
Sala
Heby
Uppsala
Gamla Uppsala
Tierp
Söderfors
Skutskär
Älvkarleby
Östhammar
Öregrund
Hallstavik
Norrtälje
Östervåla
Storvik
Kopparberg
Hällefors
Mariehamn
Jomala
Hammarland
Eckerö
Godby
Geta
Saltvik
Sund
Vårdö
Lumparland
Lemland
Föglö
Kökar
Sottunga
Kumlinge
Grisslehamn
Kapellskär
Turku Helsinki
Mariehamn Naantali
Lappo Torsholma
Siljan
Storsjön
Runn
Färnebofjärden
Dalälven
Hälsingskogen
E4
E16
E45
50
56
70
272
1
2
3
4
5
6
7
15°
16°
18°
19°
20°
60°
61°

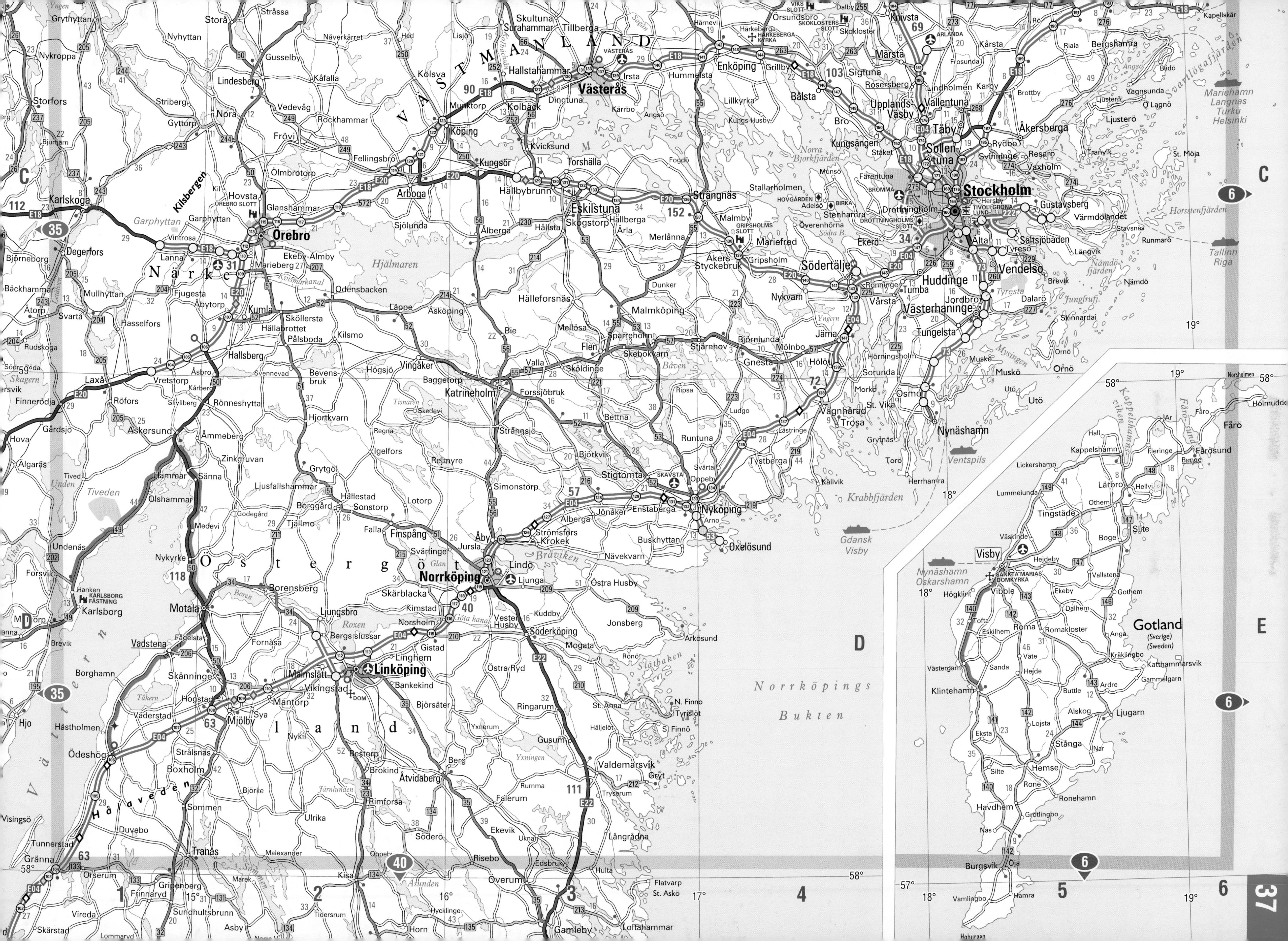
Stockholm
Västerås
Örebro
Eskilstuna
Södertälje
Nyköping
Norrköping
Linköping
Motala
Gotland
Visby
Nynäshamn
Hjälmaren
Norrköpings Bukten
Kilsbergen
Västmanland
Närke
Östergötland

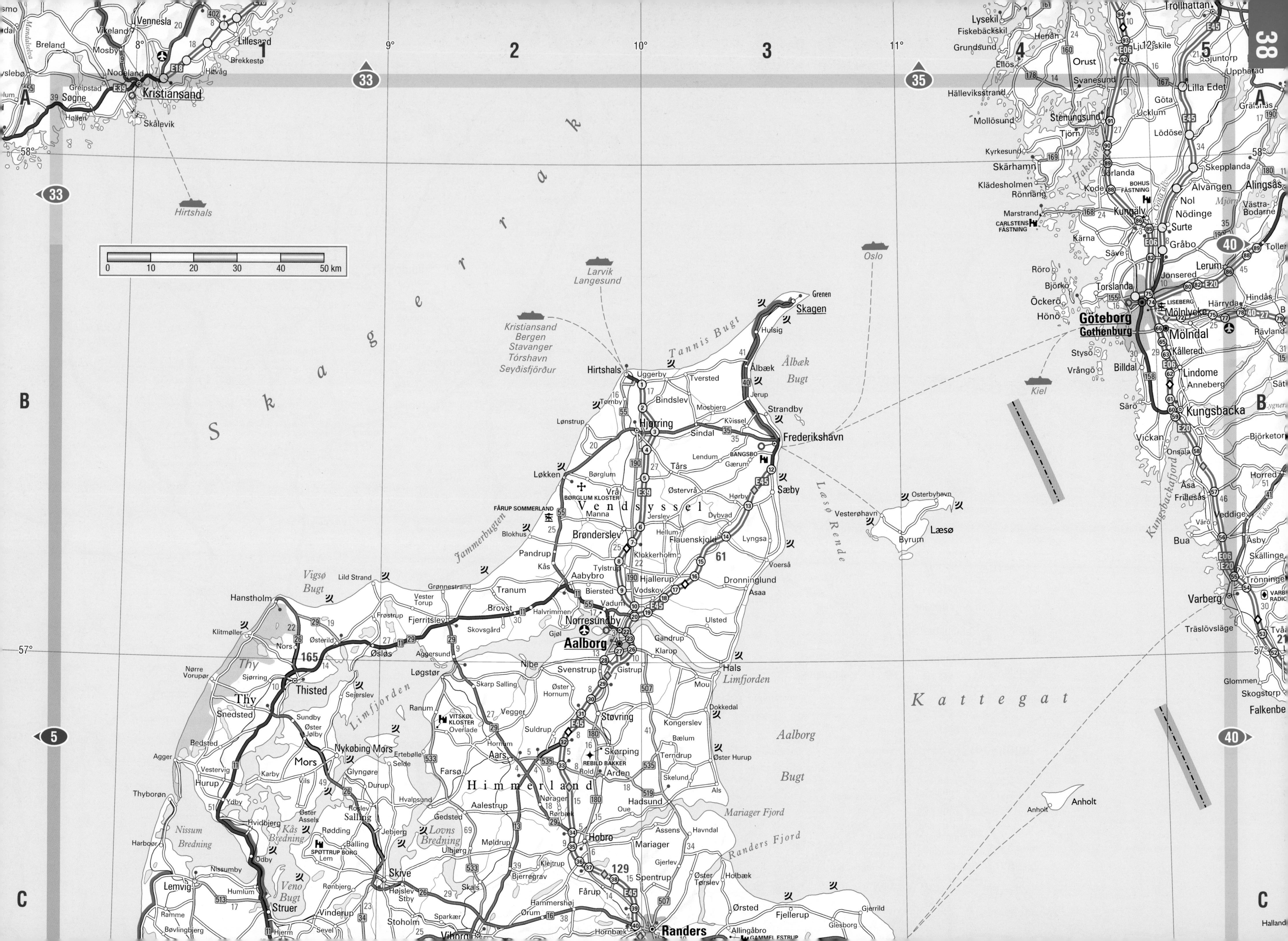
1
2
3
4
5
A
B
C
33
35
40
5
8°
9°
10°
11°
12°
58°
57°
0
10
20
30
40
50 km
Skagerrak
Kattegat
Kristiansand
Vennesla
Lillesand
Søgne
Hirtshals
Larvik
Langesund
Kristiansand
Bergen
Stavanger
Tórshavn
Seyðisfjörður
Oslo
Kiel
Tannis Bugt
Ålbæk Bugt
Læsø Rende
Læsø
Byrum
Vesterøhavn
Østerbyhavn
Grenen
Skagen
Hulsig
Ålbæk
Strandby
Frederikshavn
Sæby
Hjørring
Sindal
Tversted
Bindslev
Løkken
Brønderslev
Vendsyssel
Jammerbugten
Vigsø Bugt
Hanstholm
Thisted
Thy
Fjerritslev
Brovst
Aabybro
Nørresundby
Aalborg
Limfjorden
Dronninglund
Hals
Aalborg Bugt
Støvring
Skørping
Himmerland
Aars
Hobro
Hadsund
Mariager
Mariager Fjord
Randers Fjord
Randers
Skive
Viborg
Struer
Lemvig
Nykøbing Mors
Mors
Nissum Bredning
Anholt
Lysekil
Orust
Stenungsund
Kungälv
Göteborg
Gothenburg
Mölndal
Kungsbacka
Varberg
Trollhättan
Alingsås
Lilla Edet
Falkenbe
Halland

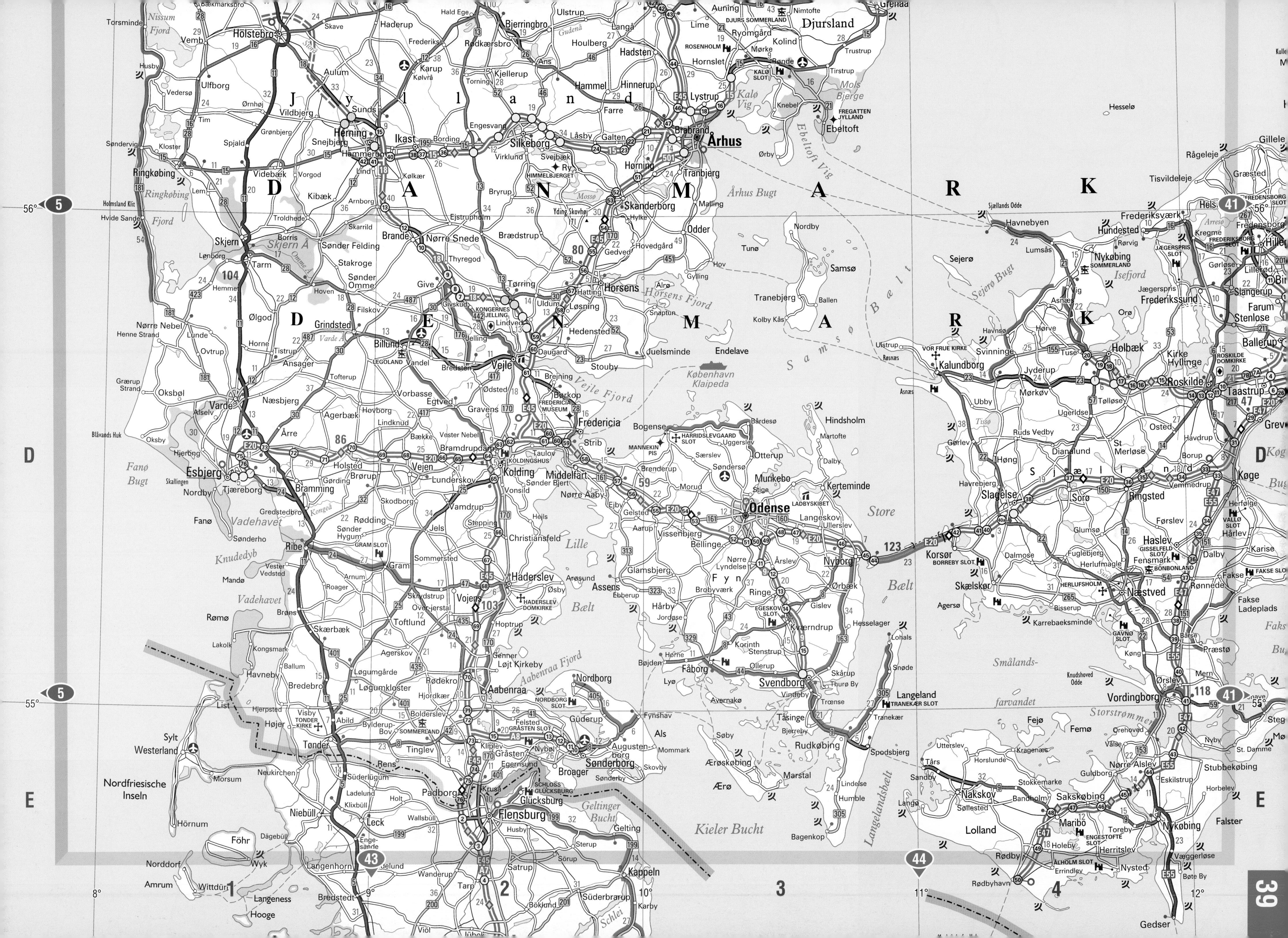
DANMARK
Jylland
Sjælland
Fyn
Djursland
Holstebro
Herning
Ikast
Silkeborg
Århus
Skanderborg
Horsens
Vejle
Fredericia
Kolding
Esbjerg
Ribe
Haderslev
Aabenraa
Sønderborg
Flensburg
Tønder
Odense
Svendborg
Nyborg
Middelfart
Faaborg
Slagelse
Korsør
Næstved
Kalundborg
Holbæk
Roskilde
Køge
Vordingborg
Nakskov
Lolland
Falster
Langeland
Ærø
Als
Samsø
Sylt
Föhr
Nordfriesische Inseln
Kieler Bucht
Lille Bælt
Store Bælt
Samsø Bælt
Smålands-farvandet
Vadehavet
Fanø
Rømø
Legoland
Billund
Skjern
Ringkøbing
Varde
Grindsted
Vejen
Nykøbing
Maribo
Sakskøbing
Ebeltoft
Grenaa

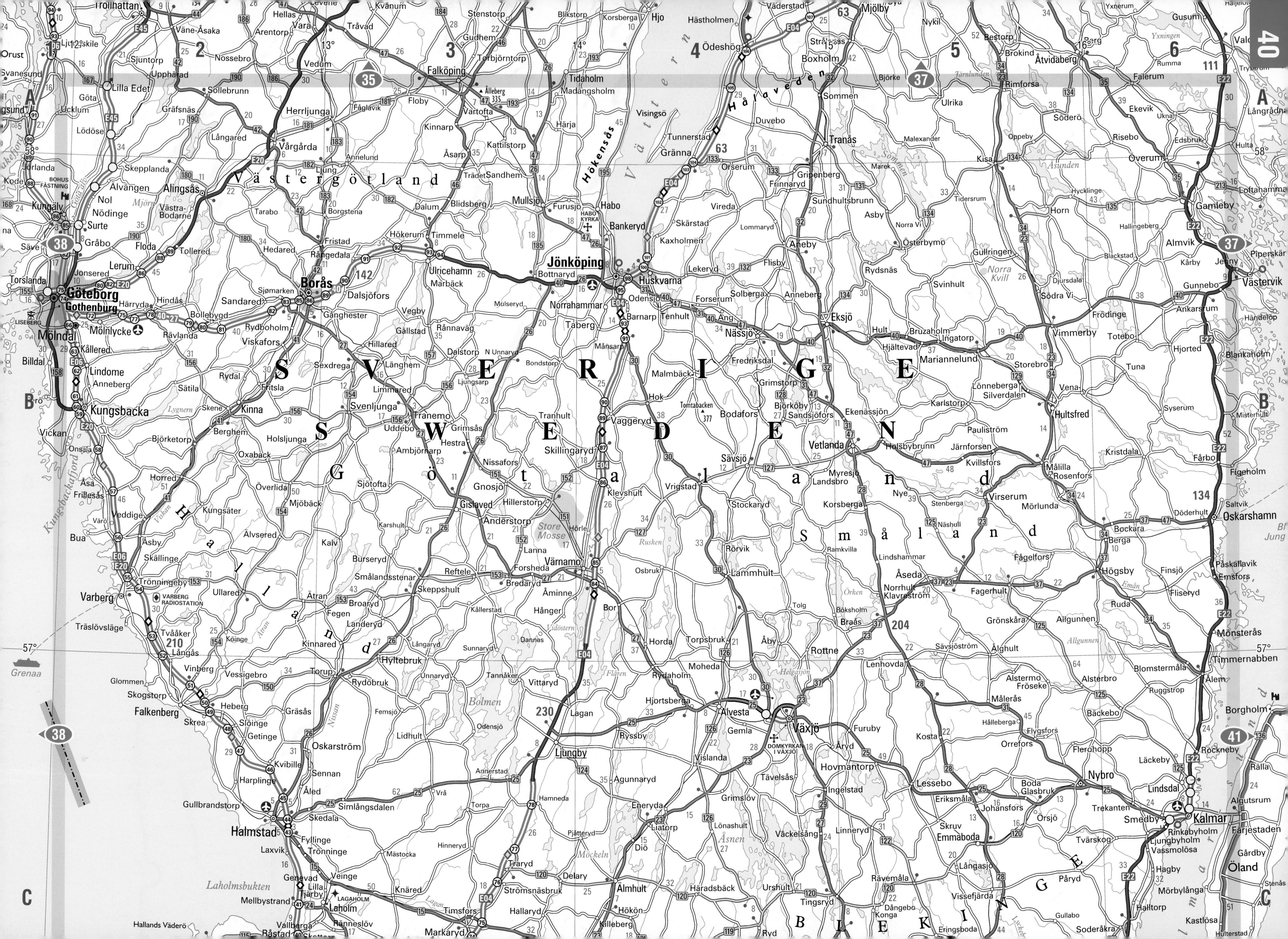
SVERIGE
SWEDEN
Västergötland
Småland
Halland
Blekinge
Vättern
Hökensås
Hålaveden
Göteborg
Gothenburg
Trollhättan
Mölndal
Kungälv
Kungsbacka
Alingsås
Borås
Ulricehamn
Falköping
Vårgårda
Herrljunga
Tidaholm
Jönköping
Huskvarna
Bankeryd
Habo
Mullsjö
Gränna
Tranås
Eksjö
Nässjö
Vetlanda
Sävsjö
Värnamo
Gislaved
Anderstorp
Gnosjö
Vaggeryd
Skillingaryd
Hultsfred
Vimmerby
Västervik
Oskarshamn
Mönsterås
Kalmar
Nybro
Emmaboda
Lessebo
Växjö
Alvesta
Ljungby
Älmhult
Markaryd
Halmstad
Falkenberg
Varberg
Laholm
Öland
Åtvidaberg
Mjölby
Ödeshög
Hjo
Kisa
Gamleby
Högsby
Åseda
Lenhovda
Tingsryd
Urshult
Laholmsbukten
Kungsbackafjord
Grenaa
Store Mosse
Bolmen
Åsnen
57°
58°
13°
14°
15°
16°
E20
E22
E45
E04
E06
35
37
38
41
63
111
134
142
204
210
230

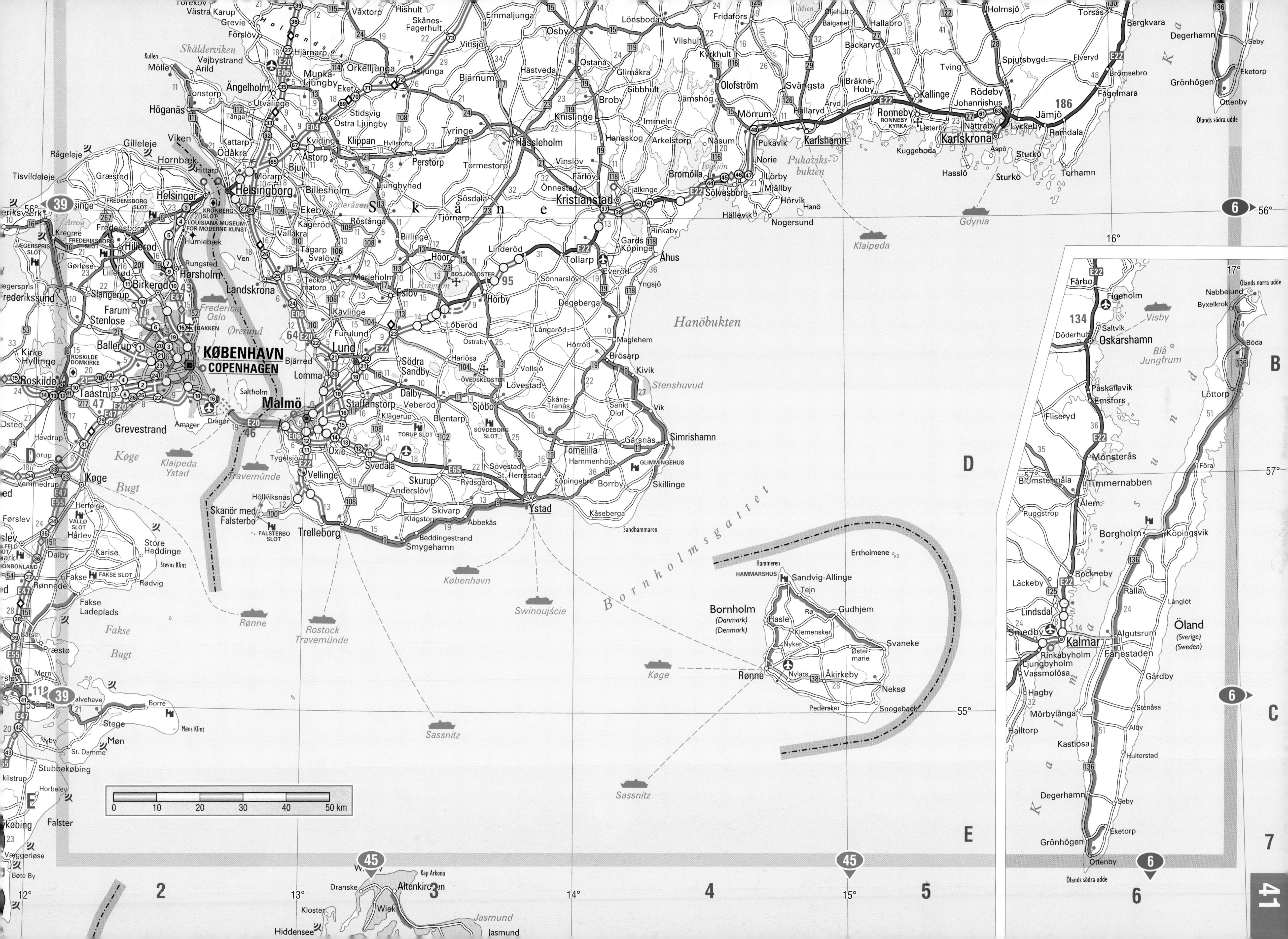

KØBENHAVN
COPENHAGEN
Malmö
Helsingborg
Helsingør
Lund
Landskrona
Trelleborg
Ystad
Simrishamn
Kristianstad
Åhus
Sölvesborg
Karlshamn
Ronneby
Karlskrona
Hässleholm
Höör
Hörby
Eslöv
Ängelholm
Höganäs
Klippan
Örkelljunga
Svedala
Skanör med Falsterbo
Hillerød
Roskilde
Køge
Øresund
Skåne
Hanöbukten
Bornholmsgattet
Bornholm
(Danmark)
(Denmark)
Rønne
Nexø
Gudhjem
Svaneke
Åkirkeby
Hasle
Sandvig-Allinge
Ertholmene
Öland
(Sverige)
(Sweden)
Kalmar
Borgholm
Färjestaden
Oskarshamn
Mönsterås
Grönhögen
Ölands södra udde
Ölands norra udde
Köpingsvik
Kalmarsund
Sassnitz
Swinoujście
Rostock
Travemünde
Klaipeda
Gdynia
Visby
København
Køge Bugt
Fakse Bugt
Møn
Stege
Falster
Kap Arkona
Altenkirchen
Dranske
Hiddensee
Jasmund
0
10
20
30
40
50 km

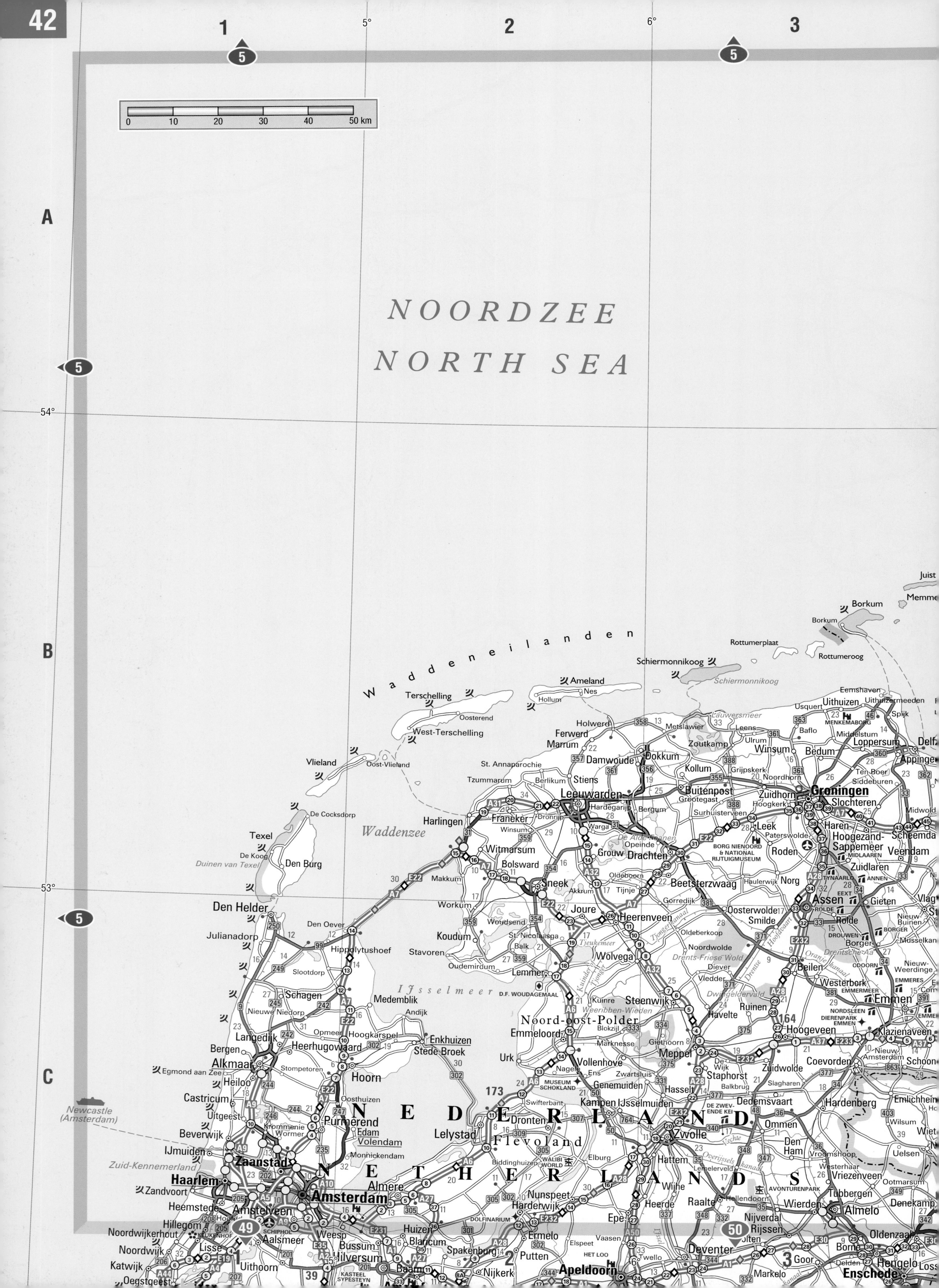

1
2
3
5°
6°
A
B
C
0
10
20
30
40
50 km
NOORDZEE
NORTH SEA
54°
53°
Waddeneilanden
Juist
Memmert
Borkum
Rottumerplaat
Rottumeroog
Schiermonnikoog
Ameland
Hollum
Nes
Terschelling
Oosterend
West-Terschelling
Vlieland
Oost-Vlieland
De Cocksdorp
Texel
De Koog
Den Burg
Duinen van Texel
Waddenzee
Harlingen
Den Helder
Julianadorp
Den Oever
Hippolytushoef
Slootdorp
Schagen
Medemblik
Andijk
Nieuwe Niedorp
Langedijk
Opmeer
Hoogkarspel
Enkhuizen
Stede Broek
Heerhugowaard
Bergen
Alkmaar
Stompetoren
Egmond aan Zee
Heiloo
Hoorn
Castricum
Uitgeest
Oosthuizen
Beverwijk
Krommenie
Wormer
Purmerend
Edam
Volendam
Monnickendam
IJmuiden
Zaanstad
Zuid-Kennemerland
Haarlem
Zandvoort
Heemstede
Amstelveen
Amsterdam
Almere
Hillegom
Noordwijkerhout
Noordwijk
Lisse
Aalsmeer
Katwijk
Oegstgeest
Uithoorn
Weesp
Bussum
Hilversum
Huizen
Blaricum
Baarn
Spakenburg
Nijkerk
Putten
Ermelo
Harderwijk
Nunspeet
Elspeet
Vaasen
Apeldoorn
Epe
Heerde
Wijhe
Raalte
Deventer
Rijssen
Nijverdal
Markelo
Goor
Borne
Hengelo
Enschede
Oldenzaal
Almelo
Wierden
Tubbergen
Denekamp
Ootmarsum
Vriezenveen
Uelsen
Den Ham
Vroomshoop
Ommen
Hardenberg
Dedemsvaart
Zwolle
Hattem
Kampen
IJsselmuiden
Genemuiden
Elburg
Biddinghuizen
Dronten
Lelystad
Flevoland
Swifterbant
Urk
Emmeloord
Noord-oost-Polder
Vollenhove
Blokzijl
Marknesse
Ens
Giethoorn
Steenwijk
Meppel
Hasselt
Staphorst
Zwartsluis
Havelte
Ruinen
Hoogeveen
Zuidwolde
Coevorden
Emmen
Klazienaveen
Schoonebeek
Westerbork
Beilen
Dwingeloo
Diever
Vledder
Wolvega
Heerenveen
Lemmer
Joure
Sneek
Bolsward
Workum
Koudum
Stavoren
Woudsend
Balk
Oudemirdum
Makkum
Witmarsum
Franeker
Leeuwarden
Harlingen
Dronrijp
Grouw
Drachten
Beetsterzwaag
Oosterwolde
Smilde
Assen
Rolde
Gieten
Borger
Norg
Roden
Zuidlaren
Veendam
Hoogezand-Sappemeer
Haren
Groningen
Slochteren
Appingedam
Delfzijl
Winsum
Bedum
Loppersum
Uithuizen
Uithuizermeeden
Eemshaven
Usquert
Baflo
Zoutkamp
Lauwersmeer
Kollum
Dokkum
Damwoude
Ferwerd
Holwerd
Marrum
Stiens
Buitenpost
Grootegast
Zuidhorn
Leek
Surhuisterveen
Tzummarum
St. Annaparochie
Berlikum
IJsselmeer
NEDERLAND
NETHERLANDS
Newcastle (Amsterdam)

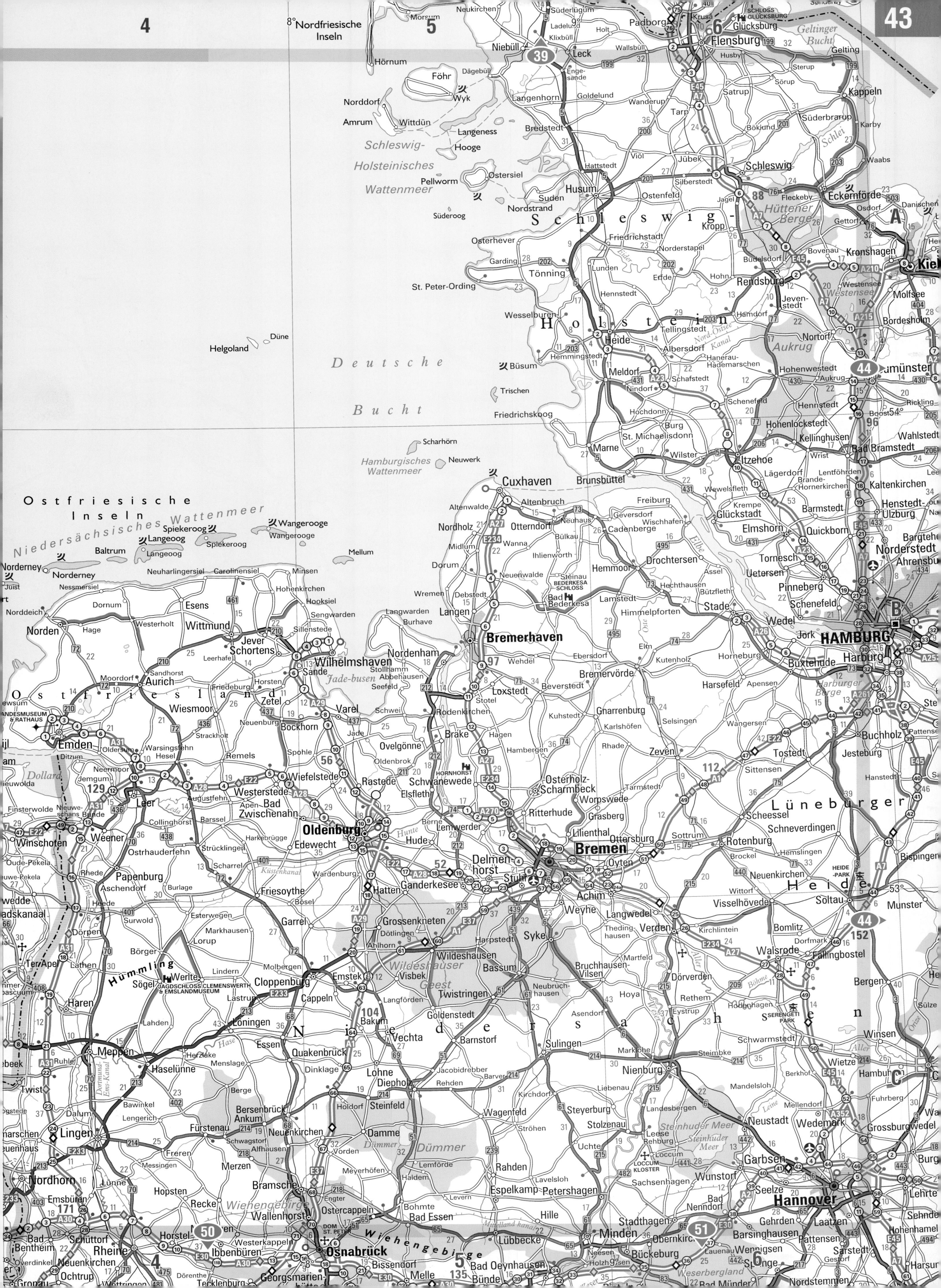
4
5
6
Nordfriesische Inseln
Föhr
Amrum
Schleswig-Holsteinisches Wattenmeer
Pellworm
Helgoland
Deutsche Bucht
Hamburgisches Wattenmeer
Ostfriesische Inseln
Niedersächsisches Wattenmeer
Wangerooge
Spiekeroog
Langeoog
Baltrum
Norderney
Schleswig-Holstein
Flensburg
Niebüll
Leck
Husum
Schleswig
Eckernförde
Kiel
Rendsburg
Heide
Büsum
Neumünster
Itzehoe
Cuxhaven
Brunsbüttel
Glückstadt
Elmshorn
Pinneberg
Norderstedt
HAMBURG
Stade
Buxtehude
Harburg
Bremerhaven
Nordenham
Wilhelmshaven
Jever
Wittmund
Esens
Norden
Aurich
Ostfriesland
Emden
Leer
Papenburg
Oldenburg
Delmenhorst
Bremen
Verden
Achim
Rotenburg
Zeven
Bremervörde
Buchholz
Lüneburger Heide
Soltau
Walsrode
Cloppenburg
Vechta
Diepholz
Meppen
Lingen
Nordhorn
Niedersachsen
Nienburg
Steinhuder Meer
Hannover
Garbsen
Minden
Osnabrück
Bad Oeynhausen
Rheine
Ibbenbüren
Dümmer
Wiehengebirge
Hümmling
Jade-busen
Dollard
50
51
39
44

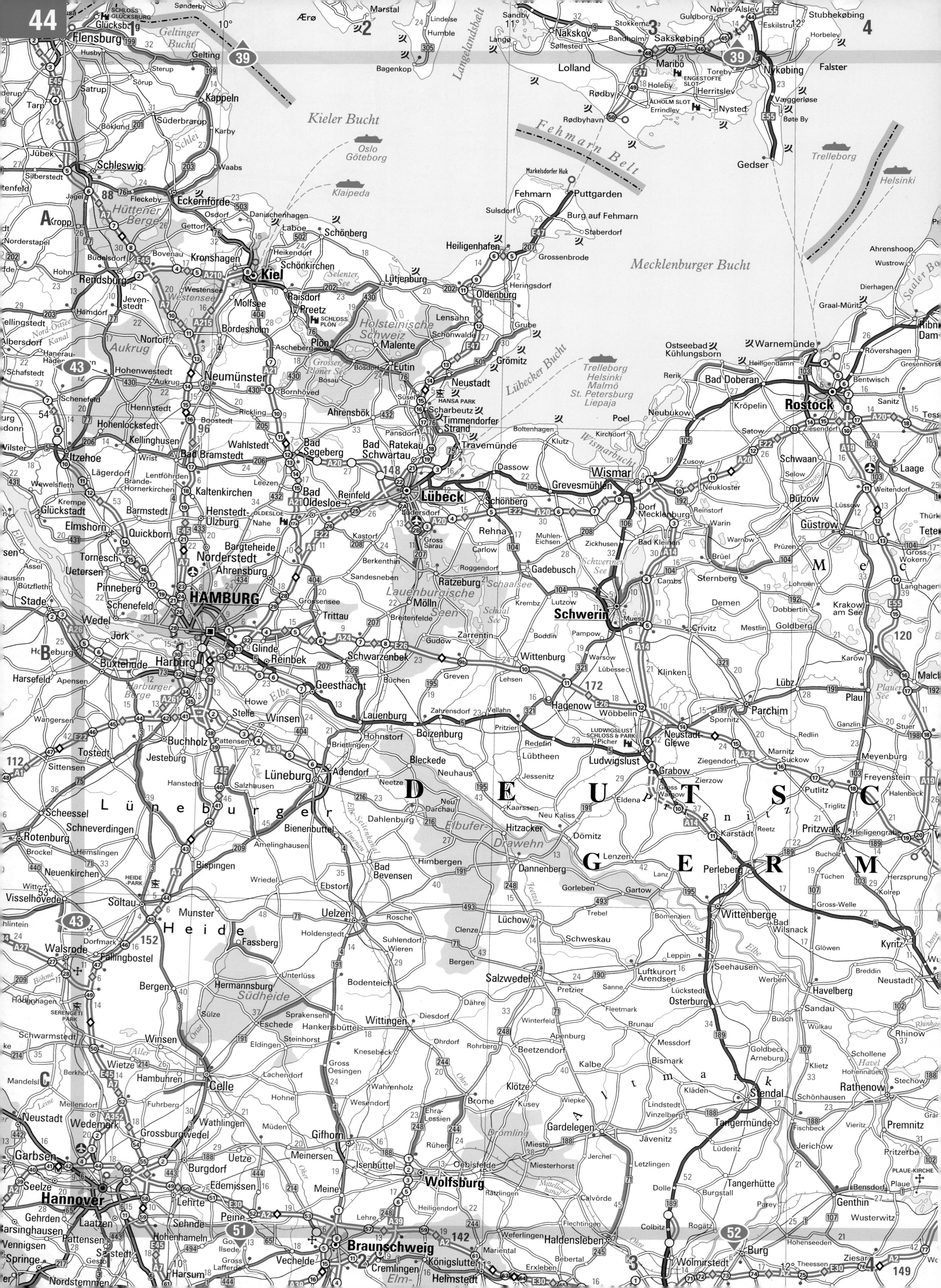
Flensburg
Glücksburg
Ærø
Marstal
Nakskov
Lolland
Maribo
Sakskøbing
Nykøbing
Falster
Rødby
Rødbyhavn
Nysted
Gedser
Kieler Bucht
Fehmarn Belt
Trelleborg
Helsinki
Oslo
Göteborg
Klaipeda
Kappeln
Schleswig
Eckernförde
Hüttener Berge
Kropp
Rendsburg
Kiel
Kronshagen
Laboe
Schönberg
Heiligenhafen
Fehmarn
Puttgarden
Burg auf Fehmarn
Mecklenburger Bucht
Lütjenburg
Oldenburg
Preetz
Plön
Holsteinische Schweiz
Malente
Eutin
Neumünster
Nortorf
Aukrug
Westensee
Bordesholm
Grömitz
Neustadt
Lübecker Bucht
Ostseebad Kühlungsborn
Warnemünde
Bad Doberan
Rostock
Graal-Müritz
Ahrenshoop
Itzehoe
Kellinghusen
Bad Bramstedt
Bad Segeberg
Bad Schwartau
Travemünde
Lübeck
Wismar
Schwaan
Laage
Güstrow
Bützow
Glückstadt
Elmshorn
Kaltenkirchen
Henstedt-Ulzburg
Quickborn
Norderstedt
Bargteheide
Ahrensburg
Bad Oldesloe
Reinfeld
Gadebusch
Grevesmühlen
Pinneberg
Uetersen
Wedel
Stade
HAMBURG
Ratzeburg
Mölln
Lauenburgische Seen
Schwerin
Sternberg
Crivitz
Goldberg
Harburg
Buxtehude
Reinbek
Geesthacht
Schwarzenbek
Zarrentin
Wittenburg
Hagenow
Parchim
Lübz
Plau
Buchholz
Winsen
Lauenburg
Boizenburg
Ludwigslust
Neustadt Glewe
Grabow
Lüneburg
Bleckede
Hitzacker
Dömitz
Perleberg
Pritzwalk
Meyenburg
Lüneburger Heide
D E U T S C H L A N D
Rotenburg
Soltau
Munster
Uelzen
Bad Bevensen
Dannenberg
Lüchow
Wittenberge
Kyritz
Walsrode
Bergen
Fassberg
Hermannsburg
Südheide
Salzwedel
Osterburg
Havelberg
Celle
Wittingen
Gifhorn
Wolfsburg
Klötze
Gardelegen
Stendal
Tangermünde
Rathenow
Altmark
Neustadt
Wedemark
Burgdorf
Lehrte
Peine
Hannover
Braunschweig
Helmstedt
Haldensleben
Wolmirstedt
Burg
Genthin
Premnitz

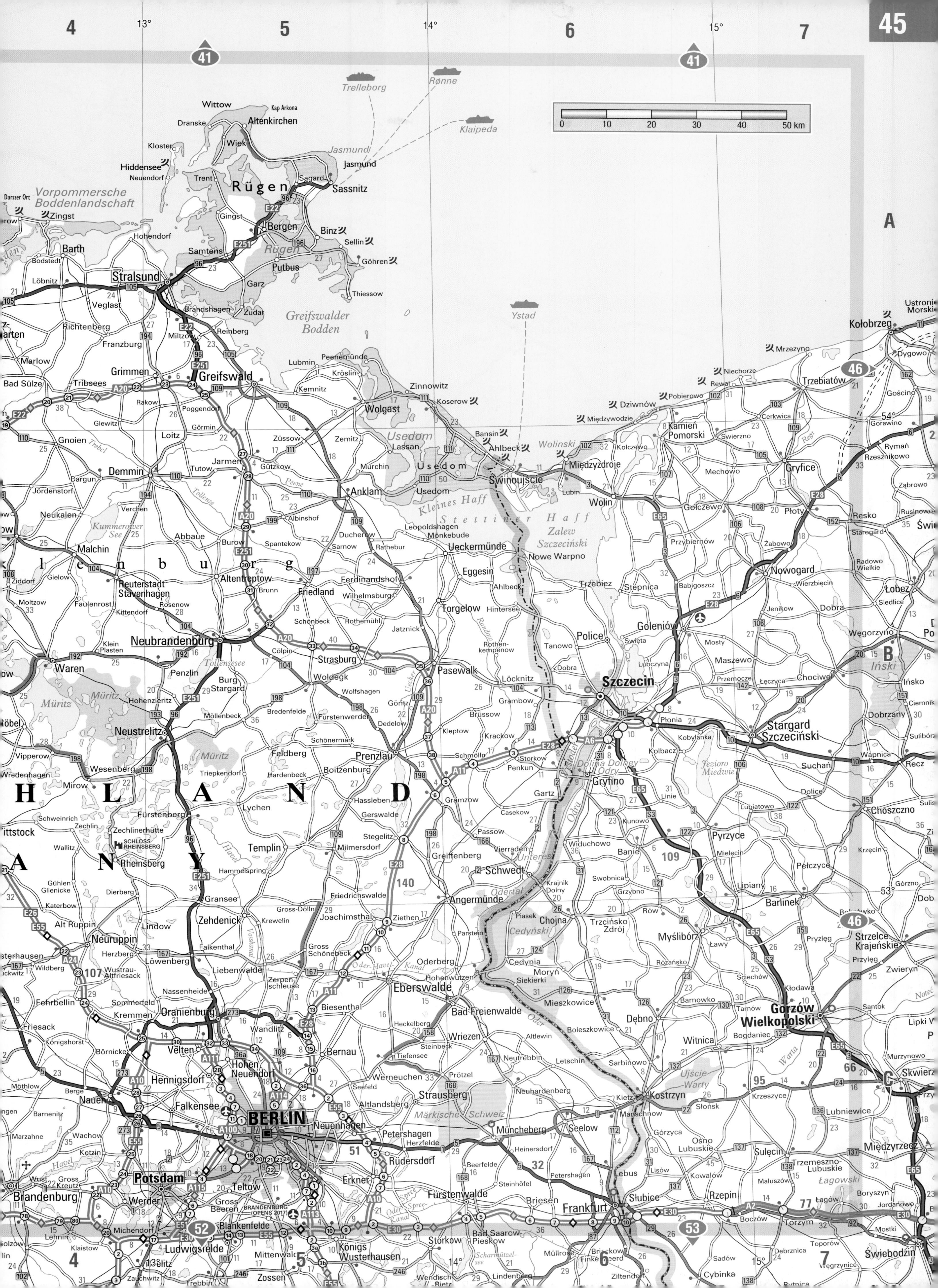
4
13°
5
14°
6
15°
7
41
Trelleborg
Rønne
Klaipeda
Ystad
0 10 20 30 40 50 km
Wittow
Kap Arkona
Dranske
Altenkirchen
Wiek
Kloster
Hiddensee
Neuendorf
Jasmund
Trent
Rügen
Sagard
Sassnitz
Darsser Ort
Vorpommersche Boddenlandschaft
Zingst
Gingst
Bergen
Binz
Sellin
Hohendorf
Barth
Samtens
Putbus
Göhren
Bodstedt
Stralsund
Garz
Thiessow
Löbnitz
Veglast
Brandshagen
Zudar
Greifswalder Bodden
Richtenberg
Reinberg
Franzburg
Miltzow
Marlow
Grimmen
Lubmin
Peenemünde
Kröslin
Greifswald
Bad Sülze
Tribsees
Kemnitz
Zinnowitz
Wolgast
Koserow
Rakow
Poggendorf
Glewitz
Görmin
Loitz
Gnoien
Züssow
Zemitz
Usedom
Lassan
Bansin
Ahlbeck
Jarmen
Gützkow
Murchin
Demmin
Dargun
Tutow
Świnoujście
Anklam
Jördenstorf
Kleines Haff
Stettiner Haff
Zalew Szczeciński
Verchen
Neukalen
Kummerower See
Albinshof
Leopoldshagen
Mönkebude
Abbaue
Ducherow
Spantekow
Burow
Sarnow
Rathebur
Ueckermünde
Nowe Warpno
Malchin
Eggesin
Ahlbeck
Ferdinandshof
Gielow
Ziddorf
Reuterstadt Stavenhagen
Altentreptow
Brunn
Friedland
Wilhelmsburg
Moltzow
Faulenrost
Rosenow
Kittendorf
Torgelow
Hintersee
Schönbeck
Rothemühl
Jatznick
Klein Plasten
Neubrandenburg
Cölpin
Strasburg
Rothenkempenow
Waren
Penzlin
Tollensesee
Burg Stargard
Woldegk
Pasewalk
Löcknitz
Müritz
Hohenzieritz
Wolfshagen
Bredenfelde
Göritz
Grambow
Möllenbeck
Fürstenwerder
Dedelow
Brüssow
Neustrelitz
Kleptow
Schönermark
Krackow
Vipperow
Feldberg
Prenzlau
Schmölln
Storkow
Penkun
Wredenhagen
Wesenberg
Triepkendorf
Hardenbeck
Boitzenburg
Mirow
Gramzow
Gartz
Lychen
Hassleben
Casekow
Schweinrich
Zechlin
Fürstenberg
Gerswalde
Zechlinerhütte
Schloss Rheinsberg
Stegelitz
Passow
Wallitz
Templin
Milmersdorf
Vierraden
Rheinsberg
Greiffenberg
Hammelspring
Schwedt
Gühlen Glienicke
Dierberg
Friedrichswalde
Angermünde
Gransee
Katerbow
Gross-Dölln
Joachimsthal
Ziethen
Alt Ruppin
Lindow
Zehdenick
Krewelin
Parstein
Neuruppin
Falkenthal
Herzberg
Gross Schönebeck
Wildberg
Wustrau-Altfriesack
Löwenberg
Oderberg
Liebenwalde
Zerpenschleuse
Eberswalde
Hohenwutzen
Fehrbellin
Sommerfeld
Nassenheide
Biesenthal
Kremmen
Oranienburg
Bad Freienwalde
Friesack
Wandlitz
Heckelberg
Königshorst
Wriezen
Altlewin
Börnicke
Velten
Bernau
Steinbeck
Hohen Neuendorf
Neutrebbin
Letschin
Hennigsdorf
Tiefensee
Möthlow
Werneuchen
Prötzel
Berge
Nauen
Seefeld
Neuhardenberg
Falkensee
Strausberg
Barnenitz
Altlandsberg
Kietz
Kostrzyn
BERLIN
Märkische Schweiz
Neuenhagen
Marzahne
Wachow
Petershagen
Herzfelde
Müncheberg
Seelow
Manschnow
Ketzin
Rüdersdorf
Heinersdorf
Potsdam
Erkner
Petershagen
Lebus
Gross Kreutz
Wust
Teltow
Beerfelde
Brandenburg
Werder
Fürstenwalde
Steinhöfel
Briesen
Frankfurt
Słubice
Gross Beeren
Blankenfelde
Lehnin
Michendorf
Bad Saarow Pieskow
Storkow
Ludwigsfelde
Mittenwalde
Königs Wusterhausen
Zossen
Müllrose
Klaistow
Beelitz
Zauchwitz
Trebbin
Kołobrzeg
Ustronie Morskie
Mrzeżyno
Dygowo
Niechorze
Rewal
Pobierowo
Trzebiatów
Gościno
Dziwnów
Międzywodzie
Cerkwica
Gorawino
Kamień Pomorski
Świerzno
Rymań
Rzesznikowo
Wolin
Kołczewo
Międzyzdroje
Mechowo
Gryfice
Lubin
Wolin
Golczewo
Płoty
Resko
Rusinowo
Przybiernów
Żabowo
Starogard
Radowo Wielkie
Trzebież
Stepnica
Babigoszcz
Nowogard
Wierzbięcin
Łobez
Siedlice
Jenikow
Dobra
Police
Goleniów
Tanowo
Święta
Mosty
Węgorzyno
Dobra
Maszewo
Lubczyna
Przemocze
Łęczyca
Chociwel
Ińsko
Szczecin
Dobrzany
Płonia
Stargard Szczeciński
Kobylanka
Kolbacz
Jezioro Miedwie
Suchań
Wapnica
Recz
Dolina Dolnej Odry
Gryfino
Linie
Dolice
Choszczno
Lubiatowo
Kunowo
Pyrzyce
Widuchowo
Banie
Mielęcin
Krzęcin
Pełczyce
Krajnik Dolny
Swobnica
Lipiany
Górzno
Barlinek
Piasek
Chojna
Trzcińsko Zdrój
Rów
Cedyński
Myślibórz
Ławy
Strzelce Krajeńskie
Przylęg
Cedynia
Moryń
Siekierki
Różańsko
Ściechów
Zwieryn
Mieszkowice
Barnówko
Kłodawa
Santok
Dębno
Tarnów
Gorzów Wielkopolski
Boleszkowice
Bogdaniec
Witnica
Sarbinowo
Ujście Warty
Skwierzyna
Krzeszyce
Słońsk
Lubniewice
Górzyca
Ośno Lubuskie
Sulęcin
Trzemeszno-Lubuskie
Międzyrzecz
Lisów
Kowalów
Maluszów
Łagowskie
Boryszyn
Rzepin
Jordanowo
Łagów
Boczów
Torzym
Mostki
Sadów
Debrznica
Toporów
Świebodzin
Cybinka
Ziltendorf
Brieskow-Finkenheerd
Lindenberg
A
B
C
46
52
53
D
N
Y

1 16° 2 17° 3

41 6

Scale: 0 10 20 30 40 50 km

A

Słowiński
Łeba J. Sarbsko
Czolpino Jezioro Łebsko Sasino
Rowy Smołdzino Wicko Cecenowo
Żelazno
Jarosławiec Duninowo J. Wicko Główczyce 49 213
Ustka Objazda Żelkowo Gorzyno
Postomino Lubuczewo Damnica Potęgowo E28 Lębork 107
ZAMEK W. SŁUPSKU Redzikowo Mianowice Pogorzelice
Darłowo Sycewice **Słupsk** Cewice Linia
MUZEUM DARŁOWO Stary Jarosław Dębnica Kaszubska Łupawa
Dąbki Łazy Sławno Kwakowo Sierakowice
Łaby 203 E28 Ostrowiec Korzybie Barcino Czarna-Dąbrówka Gowidlino
Mielno Jamno Sianów Lejkowo Dolina Unichowo Sulęczyno
Ustronie Morskie Sarbinowo Kępice Suchorze Kołczygłowy Stężyca
Kołobrzeg Koszalin Bonin Nacław Polanów 209 Borzytuchom Bytów
Dobrzyca ZAMEK W. KOSZALINIE Manowo Tuchomie Korne
Dygowo Biesiekierz Mostowo Dretyń Studzienice Lipusz
Trzebiatów Karlino Niedalino Rosnowo Piaszczyna Borzyszkowy Sominy
Gorawino Białogard Dargin Miastko Lipnica Dziemiany Wdzydze
Gryfice Świdwin Tychowo Drzewiany Upiłka Laska Brusy
Rabino Tychówka Bobolice Koczała Karsin
Resko Sława Połczyn-Zdrój Białowąs Grzmiąca Biały Bór Swornegacie
Nowogard Świdwin ZAMEK W. POŁCZYNIE Barwice Brzeze Konarzyny Charzykowy
Łobez Drawski Kluczewo Ostropole Szczecinek Rzeczenica Chojnice
Drawsko Pomorskie Złocieniec Czaplinek Silnowo Czarne Człuchów Tuchola
Węgorzyno ZAMEK W. ZŁOCIEŃCU Broczyno Borne Sulinowo Lotyń Barkowo Debrzno Zamarte
Iński Wierzchowo Okonek Cierznie Kamień Krajeński Gostycyn
Ińsko Nadarzyce Sypniewo Lędyczek Lipka Sępólno Krajeńskie
Stargard Szczeciński Sośnica Podgaje Jastrowie Złotów Więcbork Koronowo
Mirosławiec Zdbice Krajenka Sypniewo Sośno Makowarsko
Kalisz Pomorski Piecnik Szwecja Płytnica Mrocza
Recz Drawno Marcinkowice Kłębowiec Wałcz Krepsko Łobżenica
Choszczno Tuczno Gostomia Piła Wysoka Wyrzysk Nakło nad Notecią
Suliszewo Człopa Szydłowo Dobrzyca Grabówno Osiek nad Notecią Paterek **Bydgoszcz**
Pyrzyce Zieleniec Trzcianka Ujście Miasteczko Krajeńskie Białośliwie Sadki Białe Błota
Barlinek Osieczno Szczuczarz Stobno Szamocin Smogulec Szubin
Bierzwnik Siedlisko Chodzież Margonin Kcynia Łabiszyn
Strzelce Krajeńskie Dobiegniew Kuźnica Żelichowska Czarnków Sarbia Gołańcz Wapno Żnin
Przyłęg Krzyż Wielkopolski Huta Budzyń Damasławek Rogowo
Drezdenko Wieleń Lubasz Czeszewo Mieścisko Janowiec Wielkopolski Gąsawa
Gorzów Wielkopolski Zwierzyn Miały Ryczywół Wągrowiec Rogoźno
Santok Lipki Wielkie Chojno Połajewo Ludomy Skoki Kłecko
Skwierzyna Gościm Wronki Obrzycko Oborniki Gniezno
Międzychód Sieraków Wróblewo Ostroróg Szamotuły Murowana Goślina Pobiedziska
Przytoczna Gorzyń Sierakowski Nojewo Chludowo Kiszkowo
Lubniewice Kwilcz Pniewy Kaźmierz Rokietnica Owińska Słowo
Międzyrzecz Pszczew Lwówek Duszniki Tarnowo Podgórne Trzemeszno
Trzemeszno-Lubuskie Bolewice Lusówko **Poznań** Swarzędz Kostrzyn Nekla Czerniejewo
Łagów Nowy Tomyśl Buk Komorniki Luboń Środa Wielkopolski Września
Świebodzin Zbąszynek Zbąszyń Grodzisk Wielkopolski Mosina Kórnik Miłosław

B **C**

Puszcza Notecka Puszcza Pszczewski Łagowski

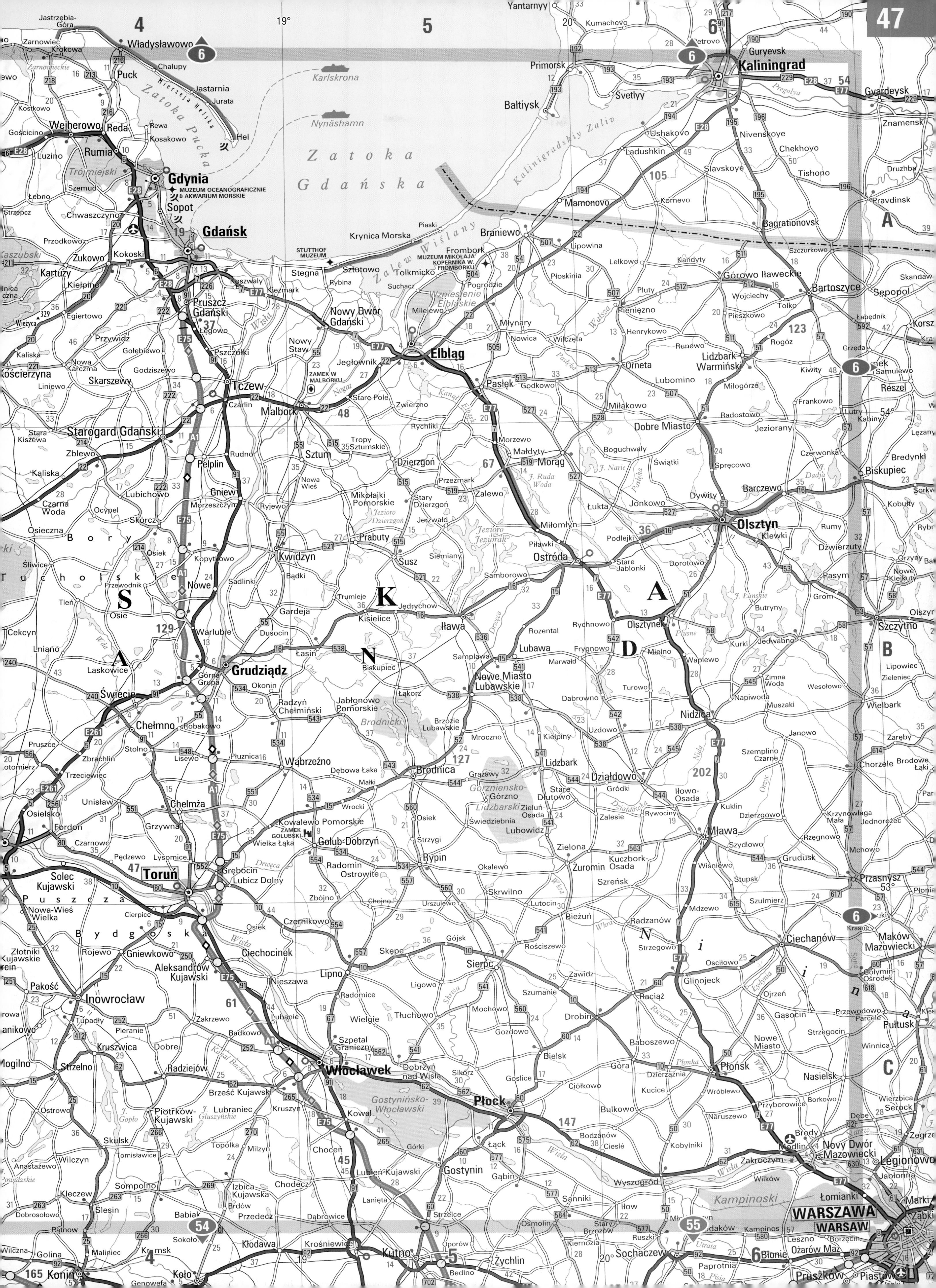
4
5
6
19°
20°
Zatoka Gdańska
Zatoka Pucka
Kaliningradskiy Zaliv
Zalew Wiślany
Mierzeja Helska
Karlskrona
Nynäshamn
Jastrzębia-Góra
Władysławowo
Żarnowiec
Krokowa
Puck
Chałupy
Jastarnia
Jurata
Hel
Wejherowo
Reda
Rewa
Kosakowo
Rumia
Luzino
Gdynia
MUZEUM OCEANOGRAFICZNE & AKWARIUM MORSKIE
Sopot
Gdańsk
Trójmiejski
Szemud
Łebno
Chwaszczyno
Przodkowo
Żukowo
Kokoski
Kartuzy
Kiełpino
Pruszcz Gdański
Koszwały
Kiezmark
Stegna
Sztutowo
STUTTHOF MUZEUM
Krynica Morska
Piaski
Tolkmicko
Frombork
MUZEUM MIKOŁAJA KOPERNIKA W FROMBORKU
Braniewo
Pogrodzie
Wzniesienie Elbląskie
Nowy Dwór Gdański
Nowy Staw
Elbląg
Jegłownik
ZAMEK W MALBORKU
Malbork
Stare Pole
Tczew
Czarlin
Pszczółki
Łęgowo
Przywidz
Gołębiewo
Godziszewo
Skarszewy
Nowa Karczma
Kościerzyna
Liniewo
Starogard Gdański
Stara Kiszewa
Zblewo
Kaliska
Pelplin
Rudno
Gniew
Morzeszczyn
Lubichowo
Czarna Woda
Ocypel
Skórcz
Osieczna
Bory Tucholskie
Osiek
Kopytkowo
Nowe
Przewodnik
Tleń
Osie
Warlubie
Cekcyn
Lniano
Laskowice
Grudziądz
Górna Grupa
Świecie
Chełmno
Robakowo
Stolno
Lisewo
Płużnica
Wąbrzeźno
Dębowa Łąka
Małki
Unisław
Chełmża
Grzywna
Fordon
Czarnowo
Pędzewo
Łysomice
Toruń
Solec Kujawski
Puszcza Bydgoska
Nowa Wieś Wielka
Cierpice
Złotniki Kujawskie
Rojewo
Gniewkowo
Aleksandrów Kujawski
Pakość
Inowrocław
Tupadły
Pieranie
Kruszwica
Dobre
Radziejów
Strzelno
Mogilno
Ostrowo
Piotrków Kujawski
Lubraniec
Brześć Kujawski
Skulsk
Wilczyn
Topólka
Tomisławice
Sompolno
Izbica Kujawska
Kleczew
Ślesin
Babiak
Brdów
Przedecz
Sokoło
Kłodawa
Krośniewice
Kutno
Żychlin
Bedlno
Konin
Koło
Golina
Maliniec
Genowefa
Kramsk
Pątnow
Sztum
Tropy Sztumskie
Dzierzgoń
Nowa Wieś
Mikołajki Pomorskie
Stary Dzierzgoń
Jezioro Dzierzgoń
Przezmark
Zalewo
Jerzwałd
Prabuty
Kwidzyn
Ryjewo
Susz
Siemiany
Sadlinki
Badki
Gardeja
Trumieje
Kisielice
Jędrychowo
Iława
Dusocin
Łasin
Biskupiec
Radzyń Chełmiński
Jabłonowo Pomorskie
Okonin
Łąkorz
Brodnicki
Brzozie Lubawskie
Kowalewo Pomorskie
ZAMEK GOLUBSKI
Golub-Dobrzyń
Wielka Łąka
Radomin
Ostrowite
Grębocin
Lubicz Dolny
Zbójno
Chojno
Czernikowo
Osiek
Ciechocinek
Nieszawa
Lipno
Skępe
Radomice
Wielgie
Tłuchowo
Szpetal Graniczny
Włocławek
Dobrzyń nad Wisłą
Kowal
Kruszyn
Gostynińsko-Włocławski
Choceń
Lubień Kujawski
Lanięta
Dąbrowice
Strzelce
Gostynin
Górki
Łąck
Gąbin
Płock
Brodnica
Grążawy
Górzno
Górznieńsko-Lidzbarski
Osiek
Strzygi
Rypin
Okalewo
Skrwilno
Urszulewo
Gójsk
Sierpc
Ligowo
Mochowo
Gozdowo
Bielsk
Goslice
Sikórz
Pasłęk
Godkowo
Młynary
Nowica
Wilczęta
Zwierzno
Rychliki
Morzewo
Małdyty
Morąg
J. Ruda Woda
Miłomłyn
Jezioro Jeziorak
Piławki
Ostróda
Samborowo
Stare Jabłonki
Rozental
Lubawa
Samplawa
Nowe Miasto Lubawskie
Marwałd
Frygnowo
Rychnowo
Olsztynek
Dąbrówno
Uzdowo
Kiełpiny
Mroczno
Lidzbark
Stare Dłutowo
Zieluń-Osada
Świedziebnia
Lubowidz
Działdowo
Gródki
Iłowo-Osada
Rywociny
Zalesie
Zielona
Żuromin
Kuczbork-Osada
Szreńsk
Lutocin
Bieżuń
Radzanów
Strzegowo
Rościszewo
Zawidz
Szumanie
Raciąż
Drobin
Baboszewo
Góra
Dzierzążnia
Ciółkowo
Kucice
Bulkowo
Cieślé
Bodzanów
Kobylniki
Wyszogród
Sanniki
Iłów
Osmolin
Stary Brzozów
Kiernozia
Sochaczew
Młodzieszyn
Ruszki
Paprotnia
Primorsk
Baltiysk
Svetlyy
Yantarnyy
Kumachevo
Petrovo
Kaliningrad
Guryevsk
Pregolya
Gvardeysk
Znamensk
Ushakovo
Ladushkin
Nivenskoye
Chekhovo
Tishono
Slavskoye
Mamonovo
Kornevo
Bagrationovsk
Pravdinsk
Druzhba
Lipowina
Lelkowo
Kandyty
Płoskinia
Pieniężno
Pluty
Górowo Iławeckie
Wojciechy
Pieszkowo
Bartoszyce
Sępopol
Skandawa
Łabędnik
Korsze
Tolko
Rogóż
Henrykowo
Orneta
Runowo
Lidzbark Warmiński
Lubomino
Kiwity
Samulewo
Reszel
Miłakowo
Dobre Miasto
Radostowo
Frankowo
Lutry
Kabiny
Jeziorany
Łężany
Boguchwały
Świątki
J. Narie
Sprecowo
Czerwonka
Bredynki
Biskupiec
Łukta
Jonkowo
Dywity
Barczewo
Kobułty
Olsztyn
Klewki
Rumy
Podlejki
Dorotowo
Dźwierzuty
Pasym
Nowe Kiejkuty
Grom
Butryny
Szczytno
Kurki
Jedwabno
J. Łańskie
Mielno
Waplewo
Turowo
Zimna Woda
Wesołowo
Napiwoda
Muszaki
Wielbark
Nidzica
Janowo
Zaręby
Szemplino Czarne
Chorzele
Brodowe Łąki
Kuklin
Dzierzgowo
Krzynowłoga Mała
Jednorożec
Mława
Rzęgnowo
Szydłowo
Grudusk
Mchowo
Wiśniewo
Stupsk
Przasnysz
Szulmierz
Mdzewo
Ciechanów
Krasne
Maków Mazowiecki
Ościsłowo
Glinojeck
Gołymin-Ośrodek
Ojrzeń
Gąsocin
Przewodowo-Parcele
Pułtusk
Strzegocin
Nowe Miasto
Winnica
Płońsk
Nasielsk
Wróblewo
Przyborowice
Borkowo
Serock
Naruszewo
Brody
Modlin
Nowy Dwór Mazowiecki
Legionowo
Zakroczym
Jabłonna
Łomianki
Wilków
Kampinoski
Kampinos
Leszno
Borzęcin
Ożarów Maz.
Błonie
Pruszków
Piastów
WARSZAWA
WARSAW
Marki
Ząbki
Gąbin
Skrwa
Wkra
Drwęca
Wisła
Nogat
Pasłęka
Łyna
Kanał Elbląski
Nida
Płonka
Orzyc
Narew
Kanał Bachorze
Utrata
Pisia
J. Gopło
J. Głuszyńskie
Wda
Osa
Żarnowieckie
Kaszubski
Wieżyca
Sarbinowo
Świerczewo
Przyborowo
Sokołowo
Pszczółki
Lubichowo
S
A
K
N
D
A
N
i
z
i
n
a
A
B
C
6
54
55
123
127
129
147
202
36
37
45
47
48
61
67
105

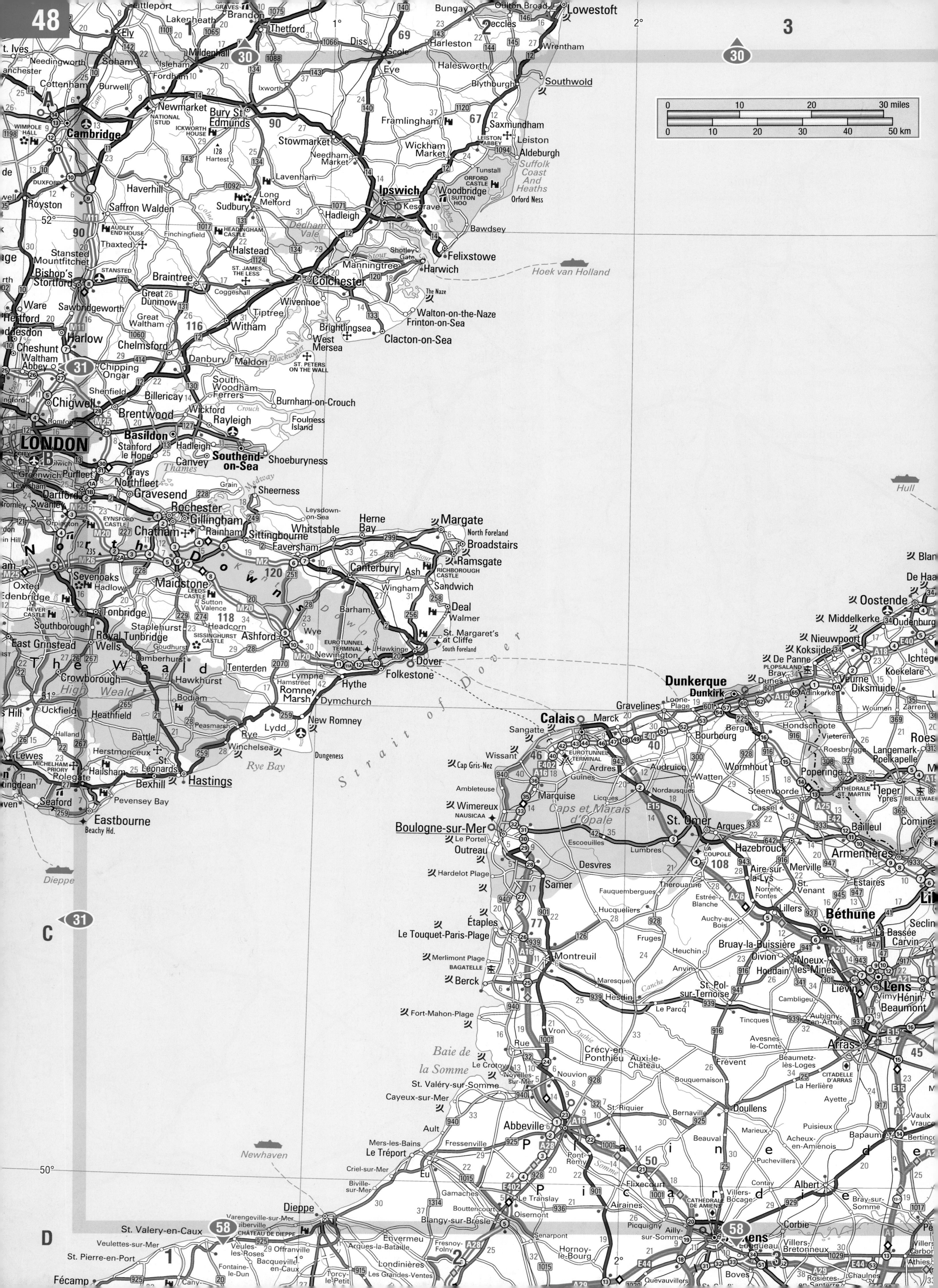
Littleport
Brandon
Lakenheath
Thetford
Bungay
Oulton Broad
Lowestoft
Ely
Diss
Harleston
Beccles
Wrentham
Mildenhall
Soham
Isleham
Fordham
Scole
Eye
Halesworth
Southwold
Blythburgh
St. Ives
Needingworth
Cottenham
Burwell
Ixworth
Newmarket
Bury St Edmunds
Framlingham
Saxmundham
Leiston
Aldeburgh
Cambridge
Stowmarket
Needham Market
Wickham Market
Tunstall
Suffolk Coast And Heaths
Orford Ness
Woodbridge
Haverhill
Lavenham
Ipswich
Kesgrave
Royston
Saffron Walden
Sudbury
Long Melford
Hadleigh
Dedham Vale
Bawdsey
Thaxted
Finchingfield
Halstead
Felixstowe
Shotley Gate
Harwich
Manningtree
Stansted Mountfitchet
Bishop's Stortford
Braintree
Coggeshall
Colchester
Hoek van Holland
The Naze
Ware
Sawbridgeworth
Great Dunmow
Wivenhoe
Tiptree
Walton-on-the-Naze
Frinton-on-Sea
Hertford
Witham
Brightlingsea
Clacton-on-Sea
Harlow
Chelmsford
West Mersea
Cheshunt
Waltham Abbey
Chipping Ongar
Danbury
Maldon
South Woodham Ferrers
Shenfield
Billericay
Burnham-on-Crouch
Chigwell
Brentwood
Wickford
Rayleigh
Foulness Island
LONDON
Basildon
Stanford le Hope
Hadleigh
Canvey
Southend-on-Sea
Shoeburyness
Greenwich
Purfleet
Grays
Thames
Northfleet
Gravesend
Sheerness
Dartford
Swanley
Rochester
Gillingham
Leysdown-on-Sea
Herne Bay
Margate
Chatham
Rainham
Sittingbourne
Whitstable
North Foreland
Broadstairs
Faversham
Ramsgate
North Downs
Canterbury
Sevenoaks
Maidstone
Ash
Sandwich
Wingham
Oxted
Edenbridge
Hadlow
Tonbridge
Barham
Deal
Walmer
Southborough
Royal Tunbridge Wells
Staplehurst
Headcorn
Ashford
Wye
St. Margaret's at Cliffe
South Foreland
East Grinstead
Newington
Hawkinge
Dover
The Weald
Tenterden
Folkestone
Crowborough
Hawkhurst
Lympne
Hythe
High Weald
Romney Marsh
Dymchurch
Bodiam
Uckfield
Heathfield
New Romney
Lydd
Battle
Rye
Winchelsea
Dungeness
Lewes
Herstmonceux
Hailsham
St. Leonards
Hastings
Rye Bay
Bexhill
Seaford
Pevensey Bay
Eastbourne
Beachy Hd.
Strait of Dover
Dieppe
Newhaven
Hull
Dunkerque
Dunkirk
Gravelines
Calais
Marck
Sangatte
Wissant
Cap Gris-Nez
Guînes
Ardres
Audruicq
Bourbourg
Bergues
Wormhout
Watten
Marquise
Ambleteuse
Wimereux
Caps et Marais d'Opale
Boulogne-sur-Mer
Le Portel
Outreau
St. Omer
Arques
Hardelot Plage
Desvres
Samer
Lumbres
Hazebrouck
Aire-sur-la-Lys
Thérouanne
Fauquembergues
Étaples
Le Touquet-Paris-Plage
Hucqueliers
Fruges
Montreuil
Merlimont Plage
Berck
Hesdin
Fort-Mahon-Plage
Vron
Baie de la Somme
Le Crotoy
Rue
Crécy-en-Ponthieu
Auxi-le-Château
St. Valéry-sur-Somme
Cayeux-sur-Mer
Nouvion
Abbeville
Ault
Mers-les-Bains
Le Tréport
Eu
Criel-sur-Mer
Dieppe
St. Valery-en-Caux
Veulettes-sur-Mer
St. Pierre-en-Port
Fécamp
Envermeu
Blangy-sur-Bresle
Oisemont
Airaines
Picquigny
Flixecourt
Doullens
Bernaville
Amiens
Albert
Corbie
Bapaume
Arras
Lens
Liévin
Béthune
Lillers
Bruay-la-Buissière
Houdain
St. Pol-sur-Ternoise
Frévent
Armentières
Bailleul
Poperinge
Ieper
Ypres
Steenvoorde
Cassel
Hondschoote
Veurne
Diksmuide
De Panne
Koksijde
Nieuwpoort
Middelkerke
Oostende
Oudenburg
Merville
St. Venant
Estaires
La Bassée
Carvin
Noeux-les-Mines
Divion
Aubigny-en-Artois
Avesnes-le-Comte
Beaumetz-lès-Loges
Pas-de-Calais
Picardie
Somme
Villers-Bocage
Villers-Bretonneux
Poix
Londinières
Arques-la-Bataille
Offranville
30 miles
50 km

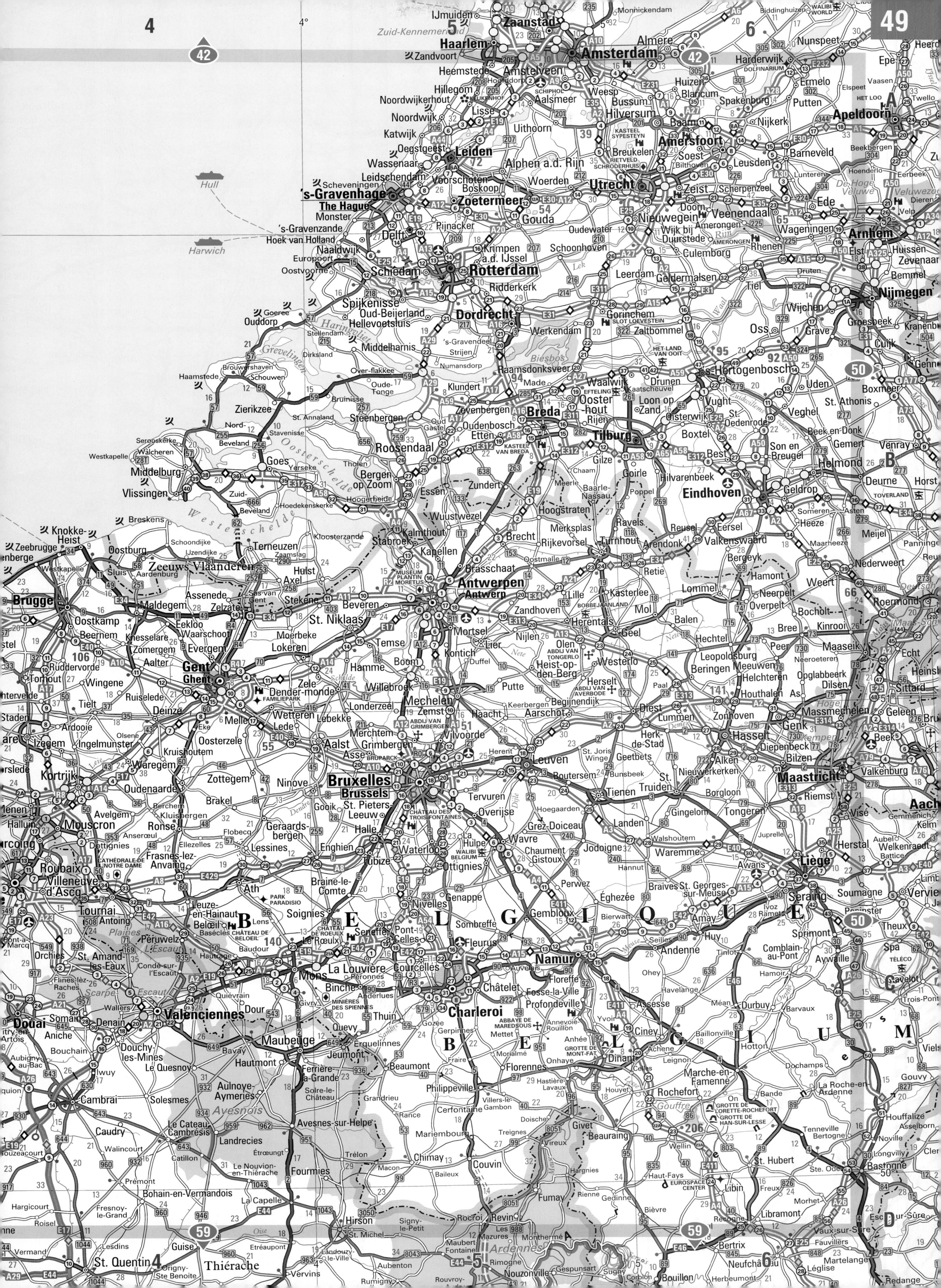
IJmuiden
Zaanstad
Monnickendam
Zuid-Kennemerland
Haarlem
Zandvoort
Amsterdam
Almere
Nunspeet
Harderwijk
Heemstede
Amstelveen
Hillegom
Weesp
Huizen
Blaricum
Ermelo
Noordwijkerhout
Aalsmeer
Bussum
Spakenburg
Putten
Noordwijk
Lisse
Hilversum
Baarn
Nijkerk
Apeldoorn
Katwijk
Uithoorn
Amersfoort
Oegstgeest
Leiden
Soest
Barneveld
Wassenaar
Alphen a.d. Rijn
Breukelen
Leusden
Leidschendam
Voorschoten
Woerden
Utrecht
Zeist
Scherpenzeel
Hull
's-Gravenhage
The Hague
Scheveningen
Zoetermeer
Gouda
Nieuwegein
Veenendaal
Ede
Monster
Delft
Pijnacker
Oudewater
Wijk bij Duurstede
Wageningen
Arnhem
's-Gravenzande
Hoek van Holland
Harwich
Naaldwijk
Krimpen a.d. IJssel
Schoonhoven
Culemborg
Rhenen
Huissen
Zevenaar
Europoort
Oostvoorne
Schiedam
Rotterdam
Leerdam
Geldermalsen
Tiel
Ridderkerk
Spijkenisse
Oud-Beijerland
Hellevoetsluis
Dordrecht
Gorinchem
Nijmegen
Wijchen
Goeree
Ouddorp
Haringvliet
Werkendam
Zaltbommel
Oss
Grave
Groesbeek
Middelharnis
Dirksland
Cuijk
Grevelingen
Strijen
Numansdorp
Biesbos
Brouwershaven
Schouwen
Over-flakkee
Raamsdonksveer
Waalwijk
Drunen
's-Hertogenbosch
Uden
Haamstede
Oude-Tonge
Made
Klundert
Efteling
Kaatsheuvel
Vught
Boxmeer
Zierikzee
Bruinisse
Zevenbergen
Breda
Oosterhout
Loon op Zand
St. Athonis
Veghel
Steenbergen
Oudenbosch
Etten
Tilburg
Oisterwijk
St. Oedenrode
Nord-Beveland
Stavenisse
Boxtel
Beek en Donk
Gemert
Venray
Walcheren
Oosterschelde
Roosendaal
Gilze
Best
Son en Breugel
Westkapelle
Middelburg
Goes
Yerseke
Tholen
Bergen op Zoom
Goirle
Hilvarenbeek
Helmond
Vlissingen
Zuid-Beveland
Essen
Zundert
Baarle-Nassau
Poppel
Eindhoven
Geldrop
Deurne
Hoedekenskerke
Hoogerheide
Hoogstraten
Westerschelde
Breskens
Knokke-Heist
Zeebrugge
Schoondijke
Kloosterzande
Wuustwezel
Ravels
Reusel
Eersel
Heeze
Meijel
Kalmthout
Merksplas
Turnhout
Arendonk
Valkenswaard
Oostburg
Terneuzen
Stabroek
Kapellen
Brecht
Rijkevorsel
Sluis
Zeeuws Vlaanderen
Aardenburg
Hulst
Axel
Brasschaat
Retie
Bergeyk
Hamont
Nederweert
Brugge
Maldegem
Assenede
Zelzate
Stekene
Beveren
Antwerpen
Antwerp
Lille
Kasterlee
Lommel
Neerpelt
Weert
Oostkamp
Eekloo
Waarschoot
St. Niklaas
Zandhoven
Herentals
Mol
Overpelt
Roermond
Beernem
Knesselare
Moerbeke
Mortsel
Nijlen
Balen
Bocholt
Zomergem
Evergem
Lokeren
Temse
Kontich
Lier
Olen
Geel
Hechtel
Bree
Kinrooi
Ruddervoorde
Aalter
Boom
Duffel
Westerlo
Leopoldsburg
Peer
Maaseik
Torhout
Wingene
Gent
Ghent
Hamme
Heist-op-den-Berg
Beringen
Opglabbeek
Dilsen
Tielt
Ruiselede
Dender-monde
Zele
Willebroek
Putte
Herselt
Houthalen
As
Sittard
Deinze
Wetteren
Lebbeke
Mechelen
Zemst
Haacht
Aarschot
Keerbergen
Begijnendijk
Diest
Zonhoven
Genk
Massmechelen
Geleen
Staden
Ardooie
Melle
Lede
Londerzeel
Lummen
Izegem
Ingelmunster
Oosterzele
Aalst
Merchtem
Grimbergen
Vilvoorde
Herk-de-Stad
Hasselt
Diepenbeek
Beek
Kruishoutem
Waregem
Asse
Leuven
Geetbets
Bilzen
Kortrijk
Zottegem
Ninove
Bruxelles
Brussels
Boutersem
Bunsbeek
Nieuwerkerken
Maastricht
Valkenburg
Oudenaarde
Tervuren
Tienen
St. Truiden
Borgloon
Riemst
Menen
Avelgem
Brakel
Gooik
St. Pieters Leeuw
Overijse
Hoegaarden
Gingelom
Tongeren
Aachen
Halluin
Mouscron
Ronse
Geraards-bergen
Halle
Grez-Doiceau
Landen
Visé
Kluisbergen
Ellezelles
Lessines
Enghien
Waterloo
La Hulpe
Wavre
Walshoutem
Herstal
Welkenraedt
Tourcoing
Frasnes-lez-Anvaing
Tubize
Chaumont Gistoux
Jodoigne
Waremme
Liège
Roubaix
Villeneuve-d'Ascq
Ath
Braine-le-Comte
Ottignies
Hannut
Awans
Perwez
Éghezée
Braives
St. Georges-sur-Meuse
Seraing
Soumagne
Verviers
Tournai
Antoing
Leuze-en-Hainaut
Soignies
Nivelles
Genappe
Amay
Péruwelz
Belœil
Sombreffe
Gembloux
Bierwart
Theux
Sprimont
Orchies
St. Amand-les-Eaux
Le Rœulx
Seneffe
Fleurus
Huy
Andenne
Comblain-au-Pont
Aywaille
Spa
Condé-sur-l'Escaut
Mons
La Louvière
Courcelles
Namur
Ohey
Hamoir
Flines-lez-Raches
Binche
Châtelet
Floreffe
Fosse-la-Ville
Profondeville
Assesse
Havelange
Durbuy
Trois-Ponts
Douai
Somain
Wallers
Valenciennes
Quiévrain
Dour
Thuin
Charleroi
Ciney
Barvaux
Aniche
Denain
Maubeuge
Gerpinnes
Mettet
Yvoir
Baillonville
Bouchain
Douchy-les-Mines
Bavay
Erquelinnes
Anhée
Dinant
Achêne
Hotton
Aubigny-au-Bac
Hautmont
Jeumont
Florennes
Onhaye
Leignon
Le Quesnoy
Beaumont
Marche-en-Famenne
Dochamps
Gouvy
Iwuy
Ferrière-la-Grande
Philippeville
Hastière-Lavaux
Houyet
La Roche-en-Ardenne
Cambrai
Solesmes
Aulnoye-Aymeries
Solre-le-Château
Grandrieu
Villers-le-Gambon
Rochefort
Cerfontaine
Doische
Houffalize
Caudry
Le Cateau-Cambrésis
Avesnes-sur-Helpe
Givet
Beauraing
Tenneville
Bertogne
Landrecies
Avesnois
Mariembourg
Treignes
Vireux
Wellin
Noville
Walincourt
Étroeungt
Chimay
Trélon
Catillon
Le Nouvion-en-Thiérache
Fourmies
Couvin
Hargnies
Haut-Fays
St. Hubert
Longville
Bastogne
Prémont
Bohain-en-Vermandois
Macon
Baileux
Fumay
Libin
Freux
La Capelle
Rienne
Gedinne
Morhet
Hargicourt
Fresnoy-le-Grand
Bièvre
Libramont
Roisel
Hirson
Signy-le-Petit
Rocroi
Revin
Recogne
Vaux-sur-Sûre
St. Michel
Les Mazures
Monthermé
Bertrix
Fauvillers
Vermand
Guise
Étréaupont
Maubert-Fontaine
Ardennes
Neufchâteau
Martelange
St. Quentin
Origny-Ste Benoite
Thiérache
Landouzy-la-Ville
Aubenton
Vervins
Rimogne
Nouzonville
Gespunsart
Sugny
Bouillon
Herbeumont
Léglise
Redange
Rumigny
Rouvroy
B E L G I Q U E
B E L G I U M

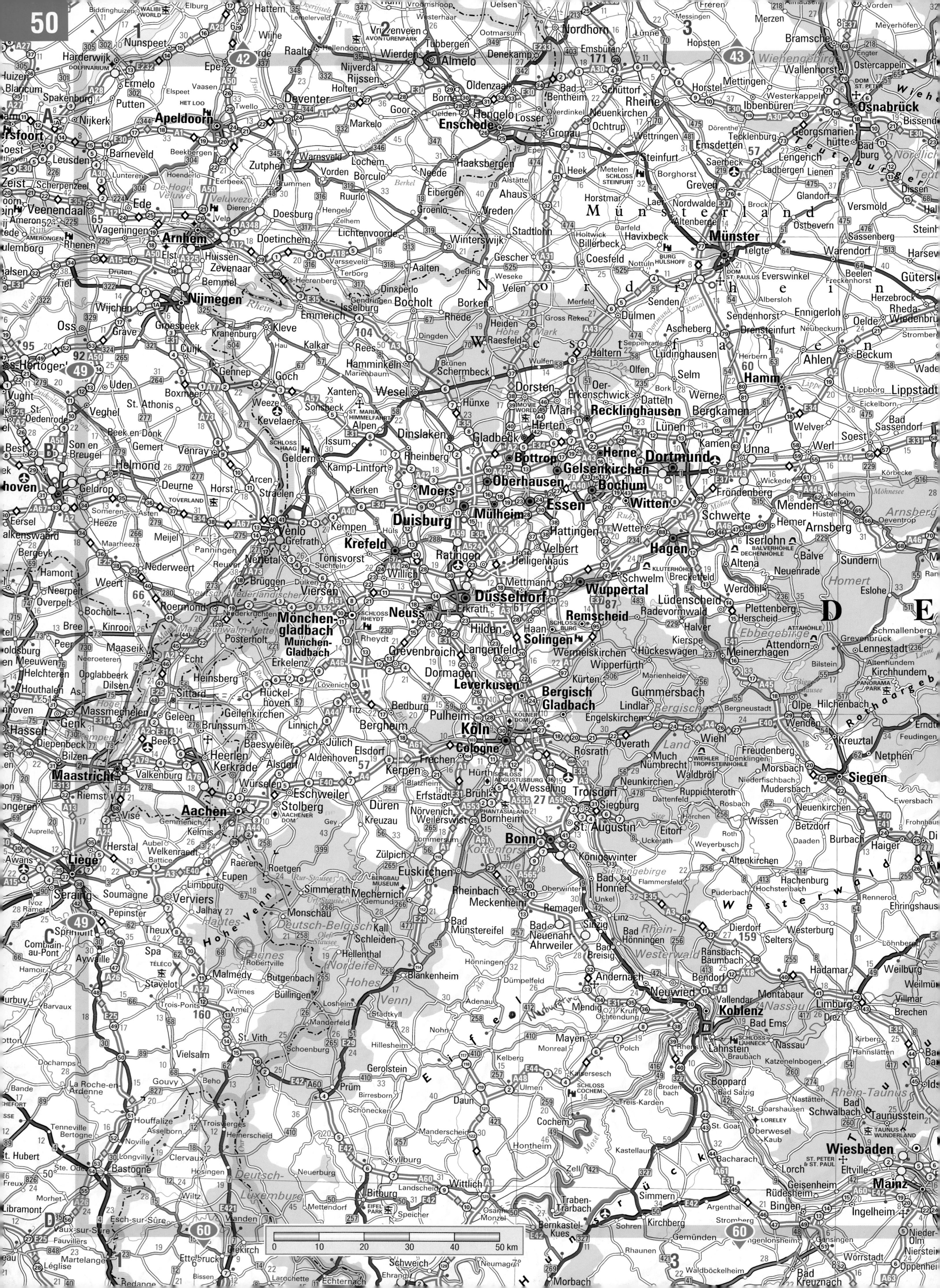

Apeldoorn
Deventer
Almelo
Nordhorn
Enschede
Hengelo
Osnabrück
Rheine
Münster
Münsterland
Arnhem
Nijmegen
Bocholt
Wesel
Dorsten
Recklinghausen
Hamm
Dortmund
Unna
Bottrop
Gelsenkirchen
Herne
Oberhausen
Bochum
Essen
Moers
Duisburg
Mülheim
Witten
Hagen
Krefeld
Venlo
Ratingen
Velbert
Iserlohn
Arnsberg
Düsseldorf
Wuppertal
Mönchengladbach
Neuss
Remscheid
Solingen
Lüdenscheid
Leverkusen
Bergisch Gladbach
Köln
Cologne
Gummersbach
Siegen
Maastricht
Aachen
Düren
Bonn
Liège
Eupen
Verviers
Euskirchen
Koblenz
Neuwied
Limburg
Wiesbaden
Mainz
Bingen
Bastogne
Wittlich
Bitburg
Cochem
D
E
Nordrhein-Westfalen
Eifel
Westerwald
Hunsrück
Sauerland
Rothaargebirge
Siebengebirge
Hohes Venn
Rhein-Taunus
0 10 20 30 40 50 km
42
43
49
60

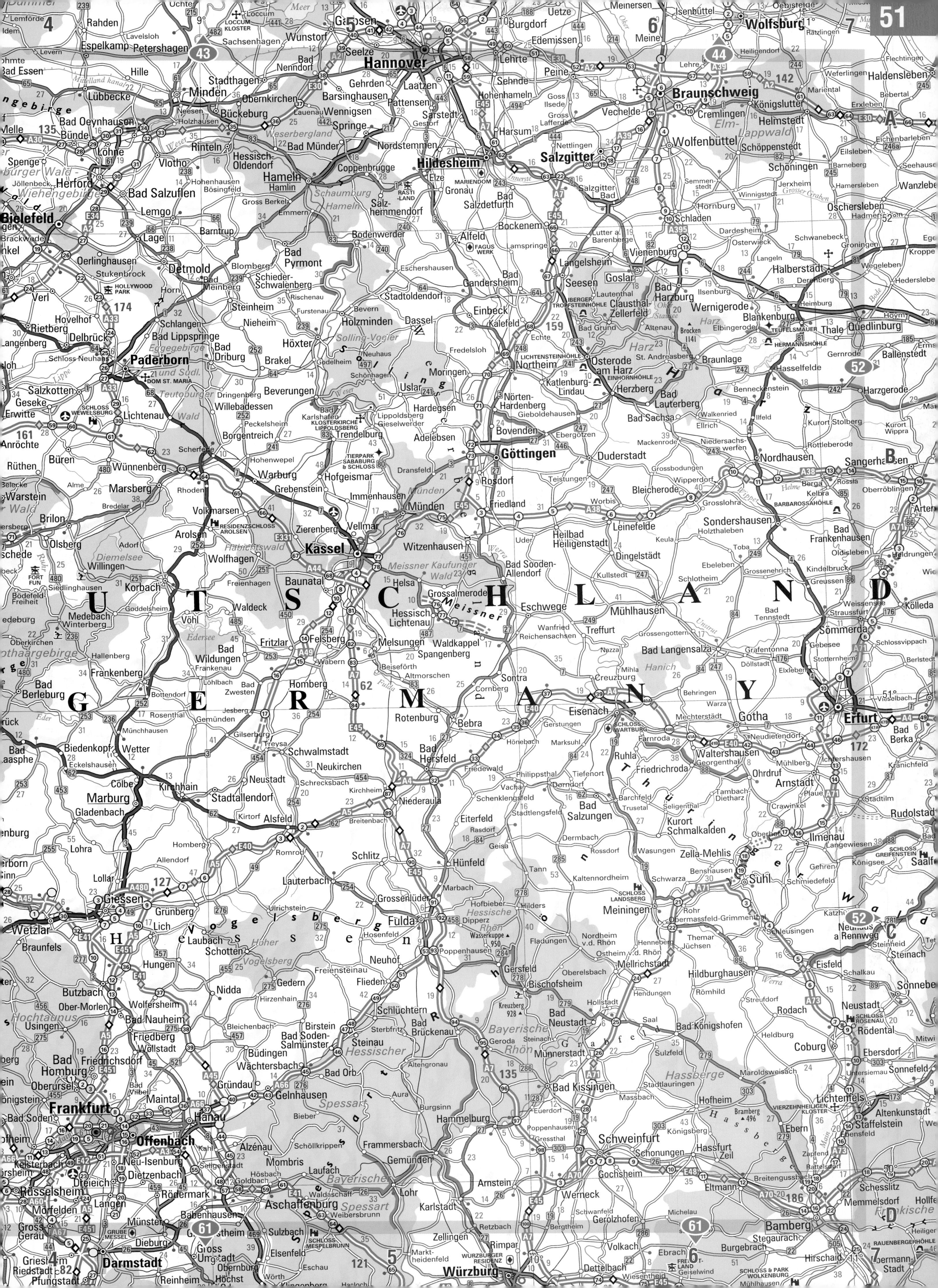
Hannover
Wolfsburg
Braunschweig
Salzgitter
Hildesheim
Wolfenbüttel
Helmstedt
Haldensleben
Minden
Bielefeld
Herford
Bad Salzuflen
Detmold
Paderborn
Hameln
Göttingen
Kassel
Marburg
Giessen
Fulda
Frankfurt
Offenbach
Darmstadt
Hanau
Aschaffenburg
Würzburg
Schweinfurt
Bamberg
Coburg
Erfurt
Eisenach
Gotha
Suhl
Meiningen
Nordhausen
Halberstadt
Quedlinburg
Wernigerode
Goslar
Osterode am Harz
Northeim
Einbeck
Holzminden
Höxter
Warburg
Mühlhausen
Eschwege
Bad Hersfeld
Alsfeld
Wetzlar
Bad Homburg
Rüsselsheim
Bad Kissingen
Lichtenfels
Sondershausen
Sangerhausen
Oschersleben
Peine
Celle
Uelzen
Meine
Burgdorf
Lehrte
Edemissen
Rinteln
Vlotho
Lemgo
Lippe
Harz
Rhön
Spessart
Vogelsberg
Thüringer Wald
Hessische Rhön
Bayerische Rhön
Hassberge
Solling
Meissner
Weserbergland
Teutoburger Wald
Eggegebirge
Diemelsee
Edersee
Hochtaunus
D E U T S C H L A N D
G E R M A N Y
4
5
6
7
A
B
C
D

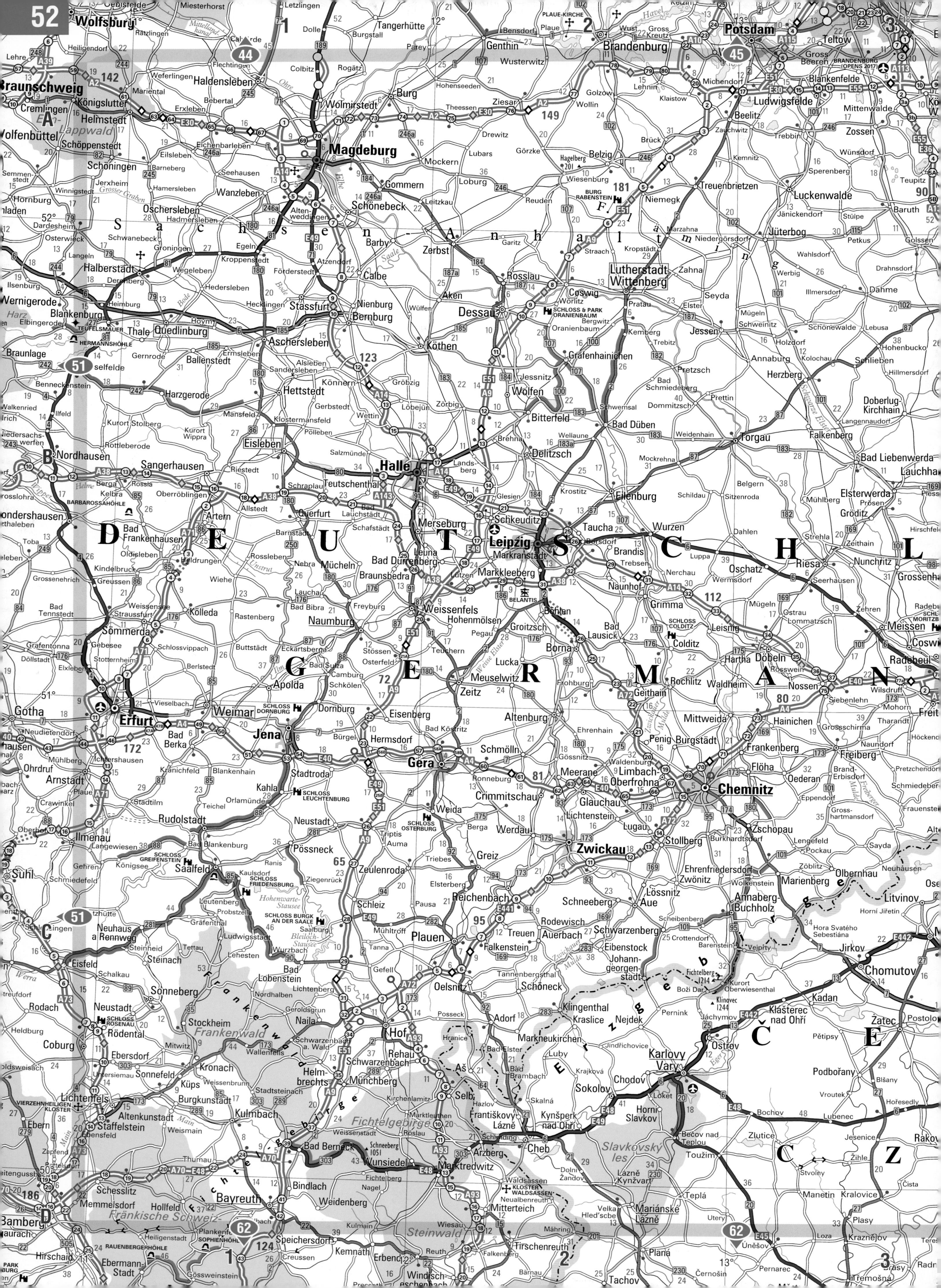

Wolfsburg
Braunschweig
Königslutter
Helmstedt
Wolfenbüttel
Schöppenstedt
Schöningen
Haldensleben
Magdeburg
Wolmirstedt
Burg
Genthin
Tangerhütte
Brandenburg
Potsdam
Teltow
Ludwigsfelde
Beelitz
Zossen
Belzig
Treuenbrietzen
Luckenwalde
Jüterbog
Lutherstadt Wittenberg
Zerbst
Gommern
Schönebeck
Oschersleben
Halberstadt
Wernigerode
Blankenburg
Thale
Quedlinburg
Aschersleben
Staßfurt
Bernburg
Köthen
Dessau
Roßlau
Coswig
Bitterfeld
Wolfen
Delitzsch
Halle
Eisleben
Hettstedt
Sangerhausen
Nordhausen
Sondershausen
Querfurt
Merseburg
Leipzig
Markranstädt
Schkeuditz
Taucha
Eilenburg
Wurzen
Torgau
Riesa
Oschatz
Grimma
Borna
Döbeln
Meissen
Naumburg
Weissenfels
Zeitz
Apolda
Weimar
Erfurt
Jena
Gera
Altenburg
Gotha
Arnstadt
Ilmenau
Rudolstadt
Saalfeld
Pössneck
Schleiz
Greiz
Plauen
Zwickau
Chemnitz
Hof
Kulmbach
Bayreuth
Marktredwitz
Cheb
Karlovy Vary
Sokolov
Chomutov
Coburg
Bamberg
Lichtenfels
Kronach
Sonneberg
Suhl
D E U T S C H L A N D
S a c h s e n - A n h a l t
F l ä m i n g
Frankenwald
Fichtelgebirge
Erzgebirge
Harz
Č E
C Z

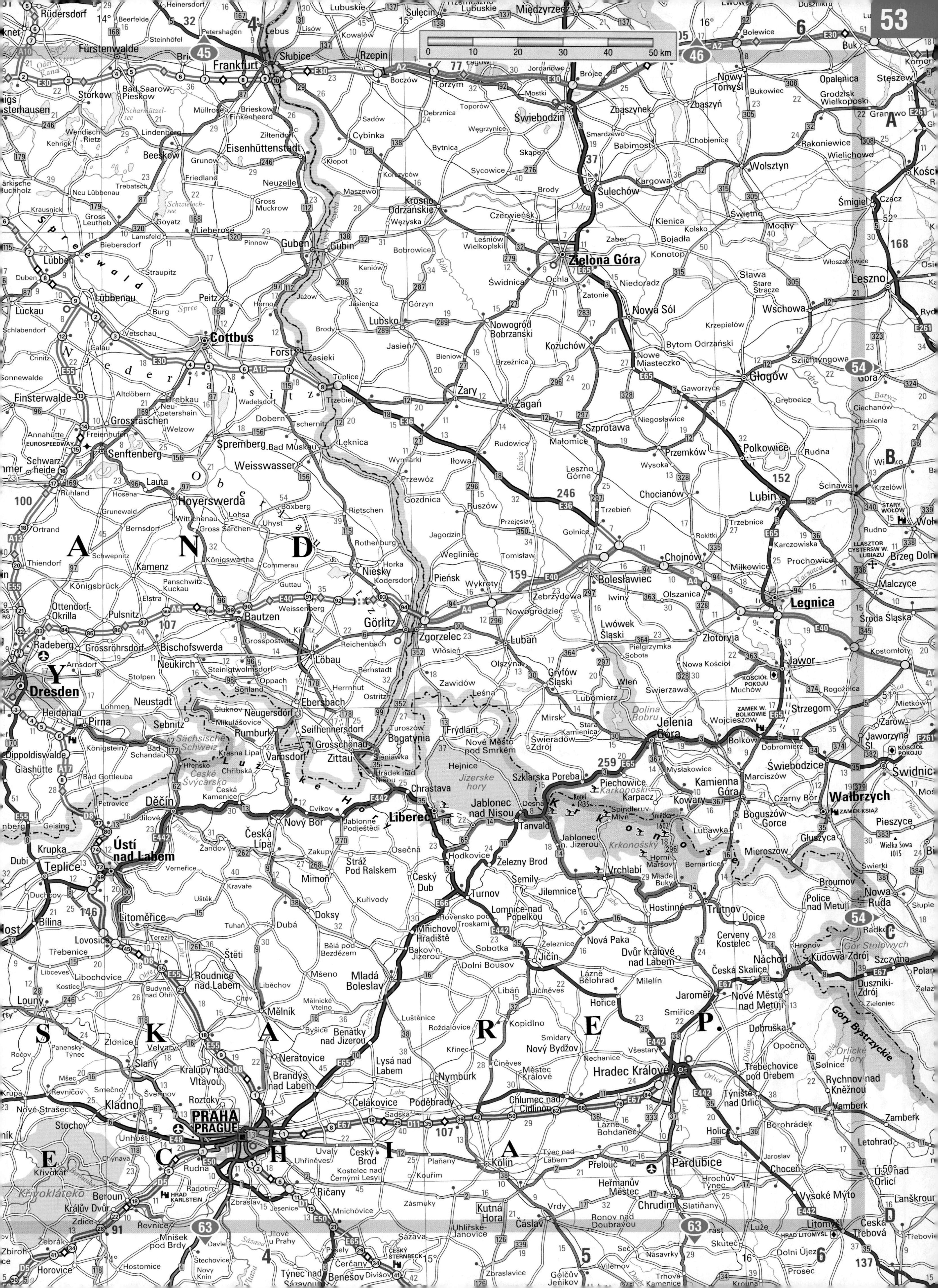
0 10 20 30 40 50 km
Rüdersdorf
Fürstenwalde
Frankfurt
Słubice
Lebus
Petershagen
Heinersdorf
Beerfelde
Steinhöfel
Storkow
Bad Saarow-Pieskow
Müllrose
Brieskow-Finkenheerd
Eisenhüttenstadt
Beeskow
Lindenberg
Grunow
Friedland
Neuzelle
Ziltendorf
Wendisch Rietz
Kehrigk
Neu Lübbenau
Krausnick
Gross Leutheb
Trebatsch
Goyatz
Lamsfeld
Lieberose
Biebersdorf
Gross Muckrow
Schwielochsee
Scharmützelsee
Pinnow
Guben
Gubin
Lübben
Duben
Lübbenau
Straupitz
Luckau
Peitz
Burg
Spree
Horno
Cottbus
Vetschau
Calau
Schlabendorf
Crinitz
Sonnewalde
Forst
Zasieki
Finsterwalde
Altdöbern
Drebkau
Neu-petershain
Welzow
Grossräschen
Annahütte
Freienhufen
EUROSPEEDWAY
Senftenberg
Schwarzheide
Ruhland
Lauta
Hosena
Hoyerswerda
Spremberg
Bad Muskau
Weisswasser
Tschernitz
Dobern
Wadelsdorf
Tuplice
Trzebiel
Łęknica
Spreewald
Niederlausitz
Oberlausitz
Grunewald
Wittichenau
Lohsa
Boxberg
Uhyst
Gross Särchen
Bernsdorf
Ortrand
Thiendorf
Schwepnitz
Kamenz
Königswartha
Commerau
Königsbrück
Panschwitz-Kuckau
Guttau
Elstra
Ottendorf-Okrilla
Pulsnitz
Bautzen
Weissenberg
Radeberg
Grossröhrsdorf
Bischofswerda
Arnsdorf
Neukirch
Stolpen
Dresden
Heidenau
Pirna
Lohmen
Neustadt
Sebnitz
Königstein
Bad Schandau
Dippoldiswalde
Glashütte
Bad Gottleuba
Sächsische Schweiz
Steinigtwolmsdorf
Sohland
Oppach
Löbau
Kittlitz
Grosspostwitz
Reichenbach
Bernstadt
Herrnhut
Ostritz
Ebersbach
Neugersdorf
Seifhennersdorf
Großschönau
Zittau
Rumburk
Šluknov
Mikulášovice
Krasná Lípa
Varnsdorf
Chřibská
Hřensko
České Švýcarsko
Česká Kamenice
Děčín
Petrovice
Geising
Jílové
Ústí nad Labem
Krupka
Teplice
Dubí
Duchcov
Bílina
Litoměřice
Lovosice
Třebenice
Terezín
Libceves
Libochovice
Kostice
Budyně nad Ohří
Roudnice nad Labem
Louny
Štětí
Mělník
Zlonice
Panenský Týnec
Slaný
Velvary
Kralupy nad Vltavou
Roztoky
Kladno
Nové Strašecí
Revničov
Smečno
Švermov
Stochov
Unhošť
Chýnava
Křivoklát
Křivoklátsko
Beroun
Králův Dvůr
Zdice
Žebrák
Zbiroh
Hořovice
Hostomice
Řevnice
Mníšek pod Brdy
Davle
Štěchovice
Nový Knín
Radotín
Zbraslav
Rudna
HRAD KARLŠTEJN
PRAHA PRAGUE
Jesenice
Jílové u Prahy
Týnec nad Sázavou
Benešov
Poříčí
Čerčany
Divišov
ČESKÝ ŠTERNBERK
Sázava
Mnichovice
Říčany
Uhříněves
Úvaly
Český Brod
Kostelec nad Černými Lesy
Kouřim
Zásmuky
Plaňany
Kolín
Kutná Hora
Čáslav
Uhlířské Janovice
Zbraslavice
Golčův Jeníkov
Vrdy
Ronov nad Doubravou
Vilémov
Seč
Nasavrky
Skuteč
Chrudim
Slatiňany
Heřmanův Městec
Přelouč
Týnec nad Labem
Pardubice
Hrochův Týnec
Holice
Chlumec nad Cidlinou
Lázně Bohdaneč
Poděbrady
Sadská
Čelákovice
Lysá nad Labem
Brandýs nad Labem
Neratovice
Nymburk
Městec Králové
Činěves
Křinec
Rožďalovice
Benátky nad Jizerou
Byšice
Mělnické Vtelno
Luštěnice
Mladá Boleslav
Bakov n. Jizerou
Mšeno
Bělá pod Bezdězem
Doksy
Dubá
Tuhaň
Kravaře
Úštěk
Liběchov
Citov
Česká Lípa
Žandov
Verneřice
Zákupy
Mimoň
Stráž pod Ralskem
Ralsko
Nový Bor
Cvikov
Jablonné v Podještědí
Osečná
Český Dub
Hodkovice
Liberec
Chrastava
Hrádek nad Nisou
Bogatynia
Turoszów
Sieniawka
Frýdlant
Nové Město pod Smrkem
Świeradów Zdrój
Hejnice
Jizerské hory
Jablonec nad Nisou
Tanvald
Desná
Szklarska Poręba
Piechowice
Karkonosze
Karpacz
Kowary
Špindlerův Mlýn
Sněžka
Kotel
Krkonošsky
Krkonoše
Horní Maršov
Mladé Buky
Jablonec n. Jizerou
Vrchlabí
Jilemnice
Semily
Železný Brod
Turnov
Lomnice nad Popelkou
Rovensko pod Troskami
Mnichovo Hradiště
Sobotka
Dolní Bousov
Jičín
Libáň
Jičíněves
Kopidlno
Železnice
Nová Paka
Lázně Bělohrad
Hořice
Miletín
Dvůr Králové nad Labem
Hostinné
Trutnov
Úpice
Bernartice
Lubawka
Mieroszów
Červený Kostelec
Náchod
Hronov
Česká Skalice
Jaroměř
Smiřice
Nové Město nad Metují
Dobruška
Opočno
Nový Bydžov
Smidary
Nechanice
Všestary
Hradec Králové
Třebechovice pod Orebem
Týniště nad Orlicí
Rychnov nad Kněžnou
Solnice
Orlické Hory
Vamberk
Borohrádek
Zamberk
Letohrad
Jaroslav
Choceň
Ústí nad Orlicí
Vysoké Mýto
Lanškroun
Litomyšl
HRAD LITOMYŠL
Česká Třebová
Luže
Dolní Újezd
Prosec
Třebovice
Polička
Police nad Metují
Broumov
Nowa Ruda
Radków
Kudowa-Zdrój
Szczytna
Duszniki-Zdrój
Zieleniec
Góry Stołowych
Góry Bystrzyckie
Słupiec
Świerki
Głuszyca
Wielka Sowa 1015
Pieszyce
ZAMEK KSIĄŻ
Wałbrzych
Boguszów-Gorce
Czarny Bór
Kamienna Góra
Marciszów
Świebodzice
Świdnica
Dobromierz
Bolków
Wojcieszów
ZAMEK W BOLKOWIE
Strzegom
Jelenia Góra
Mysłakowice
Stara Kamienica
Mirsk
Dolina Bobru
Gryfów Śląski
Lubomierz
Wleń
Świerzawa
Muchów
KOŚCIÓŁ POKOJU
Jawor
Nowa Kościoł
Pielgrzymka
Sobota
Złotoryja
Lwówek Śląski
Olszyna
Lubań
Leśna
Zawidów
Włosień
Zgorzelec
Görlitz
Niesky
Horka
Kodersdorf
Rothenburg
Rietschen
Pieńsk
Węgliniec
Jagodzin
Przejęsław
Tomisław
Wykroty
Nowogrodziec
Żebrzydowa
Bolesławiec
Iwiny
Olszanica
Chojnów
Golnice
Trzebień
Gozdnica
Przewóz
Ruszów
Wymiarki
Iłowa
Żary
Żagań
Szprotawa
Małomice
Niegosławice
Leszno Górne
Chocianów
Wysoka
Przemków
Rudowica
Kwisa
Tuplice
Brody
Lubsko
Jasień
Bieniów
Nowogród Bobrzański
Brzeźnica
Kożuchów
Nowe Miasteczko
Bytom Odrzański
Głogów
Gaworzyce
Polkowice
Lubin
Rudna
Ścinawa
Krzelów
STARY WOŁÓW
Wołów
Rokitki
Trzebnice
Karczowiska
Miłkowice
Prochowice
LLASZTOR CYSTERSW W. LUBIĄŻU
Brzeg Dolny
Malczyce
Legnica
Środa Śląska
Kostomłoty
Rogoźnica
Mietków
Żarów
Jaworzyna Śl.
Ciechanów
Chobienia
Grębocice
Szlichtyngowa
Wschowa
Krzepielów
Leszno
Sława
Stare Strącze
Włoszakowice
Konotop
Kolsko
Mochy
Bojadła
Nowa Sól
Niedoradz
Zatonie
Ochla
Zielona Góra
Świdnica
Górzyn
Jasienica
Jaźów
Kaniów
Bobrowice
Leśniów Wielkoplski
Czerwieńsk
Krosno Odrzańskie
Wężyska
Maszewo
Korczyców
Kłopot
Cybinka
Sadów
Debrznica
Bytnica
Toporów
Węgrzynice
Sycowice
Skąpe
Świebodzin
Smardzewo
Babimost
Sulechów
Brody
Odra
Klenica
Kargowa
Zbąszynek
Zbąszyń
Chobienice
Wolsztyn
Rakoniewice
Wielichowo
Grodzisk Wielkopolski
Granowo
Opalenica
Stęszew
Bukowiec
Nowy Tomyśl
Brójce
Jordanowo
Mostki
Torzym
Boczów
Rzepin
Kowalów
Lisów
Lubuskie
Sulęcin
Międzyrzecz
Bolewice
Buk
Komorniki
Kościan
Czacz
Śmigiel
Świętno
Bukowiec
Rydzyna
Osieczna
SAXONY
ANDY
BOHEMIA
SKA
REP.
CZECHIA

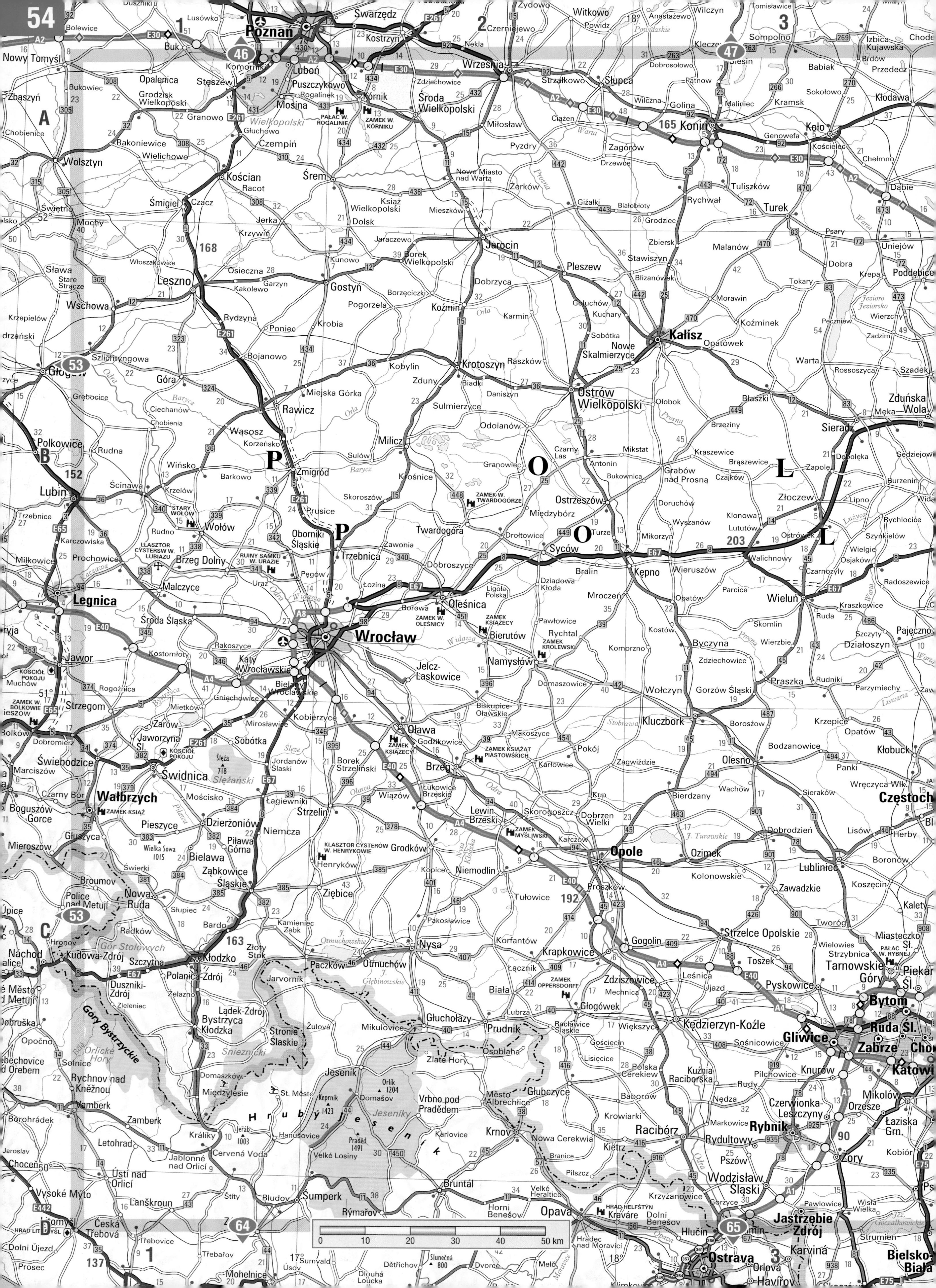
Poznań
Swarzędz
Kostrzyn
Września
Nowy Tomyśl
Buk
Opalenica
Stęszew
Luboń
Komorniki
Puszczykowo
Mosina
Kórnik
Środa Wielkopolski
Zbąszyń
Grodzisk Wielkopolski
Granowo
Wielkopolski
PAŁAC W. ROGALINIE
ZAMEK W. KÓRNIKU
Czempiń
Rakoniewice
Wielichowo
Wolsztyn
Kościan
Śrem
Nowe Miasto nad Wartą
Śmigiel
Książ Wielkopolski
Dolsk
Jarocin
Leszno
Gostyń
Borek Wielkopolski
Pleszew
Wschowa
Sława
Koźmin
Rydzyna
Krobia
Poniec
Kalisz
Nowe Skalmierzyce
Głogów
Szlichtyngowa
Bojanowo
Góra
Kobylin
Krotoszyn
Zduny
Ostrów Wielkopolski
Rawicz
Miejska Górka
Sulmierzyce
Odolanów
Polkowice
Wąsosz
Milicz
Rudna
Lubin
Żmigród
Ścinawa
Wołów
Trzebnica
Oborniki Śląskie
Prusice
Twardogóra
Syców
Ostrzeszów
Międzybórz
Kępno
Wieruszów
Brzeg Dolny
Legnica
Malczyce
Oleśnica
Wrocław
Środa Śląska
Bierutów
Namysłów
Jawor
Kąty Wrocławskie
Jelcz-Laskowice
Strzegom
Oława
Brzeg
Kluczbork
Byczyna
Wołczyn
Świebodzice
Świdnica
Sobótka
Ślęża
Wałbrzych
Dzierżoniów
Strzelin
Grodków
Niemodlin
Opole
Bielawa
Ząbkowice Śląskie
Ziębice
Nysa
Otmuchów
Paczków
Kłodzko
Nowa Ruda
Krapkowice
Gogolin
Strzelce Opolskie
Kędzierzyn-Koźle
Gliwice
Zabrze
Bytom
Ruda Śl.
Katowice
Rybnik
Racibórz
Wodzisław Śląski
Jastrzębie Zdrój
Żory
Ostrava
Opava
Krnov
Jeseník
Hrubý Jeseník
Bruntál
Šumperk
Głuchołazy
Prudnik
Głubczyce
Bystrzyca Kłodzka
Duszniki-Zdrój
Polanica-Zdrój
Kudowa-Zdrój
Náchod
Hronov
Góry Bystrzyckie
Konin
Koło
Słupca
Turek
Sieradz
Zduńska Wola
Wieluń
Złoczew
Kłobuck
Częstochowa
Olesno
Lubliniec
Praszka
Działoszyn
Pajęczno
Tarnowskie Góry
Pyskowice
P O L S K A
0 10 20 30 40 50 km

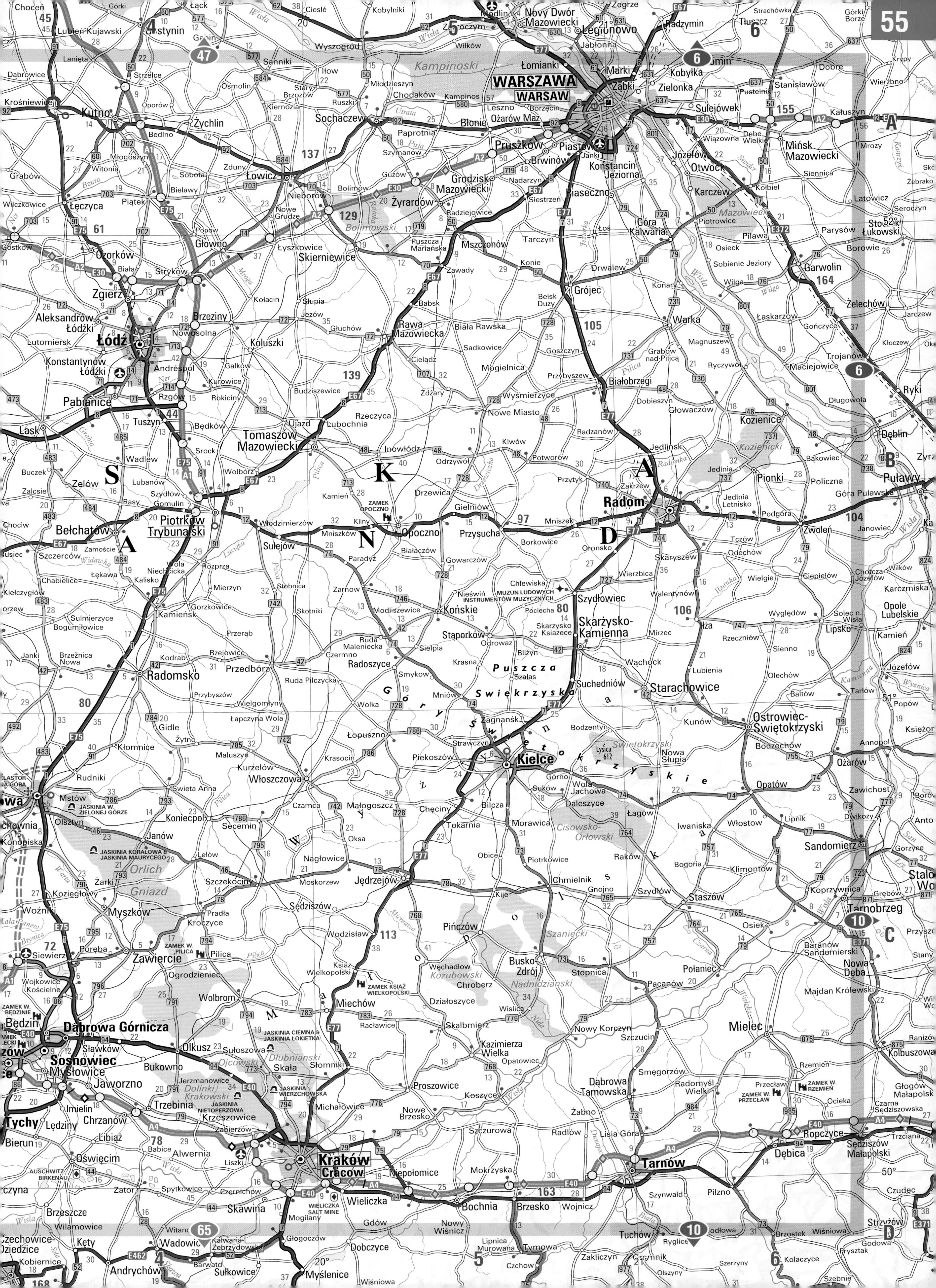

WARSZAWA
WARSAW
Kampinoski
Nowy Dwór Mazowiecki
Legionowo
Zegrze
Radzymin
Tłuszcz
Łomianki
Marki
Ząbki
Kobyłka
Zielonka
Sulejówek
Kałuszyn
Mińsk Mazowiecki
Józefów
Otwock
Karczew
Konstancin-Jeziorna
Piaseczno
Pruszków
Piastów
Brwinów
Błonie
Ożarów Maz.
Grodzisk Mazowiecki
Żyrardów
Sochaczew
Łowicz
Kutno
Żychlin
Gostynin
Lubień Kujawski
Łęczyca
Głowno
Ozorków
Zgierz
Stryków
Aleksandrów Łódzki
Łódź
Konstantynów Łódzki
Andrespol
Brzeziny
Koluszki
Pabianice
Rzgów
Tuszyn
Łask
Skierniewice
Rawa Mazowiecka
Mszczonów
Grójec
Góra Kalwaria
Garwolin
Żelechów
Warka
Białobrzegi
Kozienice
Dęblin
Ryki
Puławy
Tomaszów Mazowiecki
Piotrków Trybunalski
Bełchatów
Zelów
Wolbórz
Sulejów
Opoczno
Przysucha
Radom
Pionki
Zwoleń
Skaryszew
Szydłowiec
Końskie
Stąporków
Skarżysko-Kamienna
Iłża
Lipsko
Opole Lubelskie
Starachowice
Ostrowiec-Świętokrzyski
Suchedniów
Kielce
Puszcza Świętokrzyska
Góry Świętokrzyskie
Łysica 612
Nowa Słupia
Opatów
Sandomierz
Kamieńsk
Radomsko
Przedbórz
Włoszczowa
Jędrzejów
Chęciny
Daleszyce
Chmielnik
Staszów
Tarnobrzeg
Nowa Dęba
Mielec
Połaniec
Busko-Zdrój
Pińczów
Kazimierza Wielka
Miechów
Wolbrom
Zawiercie
Myszków
Koniecpol
Szczekociny
Mstów
Olsztyn
Będzin
Dąbrowa Górnicza
Sosnowiec
Mysłowice
Jaworzno
Olkusz
Trzebinia
Chrzanów
Tychy
Bieruń
Oświęcim
Kraków
Cracow
Wieliczka
Niepołomice
Bochnia
Brzesko
Tarnów
Dąbrowa Tarnowska
Dębica
Ropczyce
Sędziszów Małopolski
Skawina
Kalwaria Zebrzydowska
Wadowice
Andrychów
Kęty
Myślenice
Dobczyce
Czechowice-Dziedzice
Kolbuszowa
S K A N D A

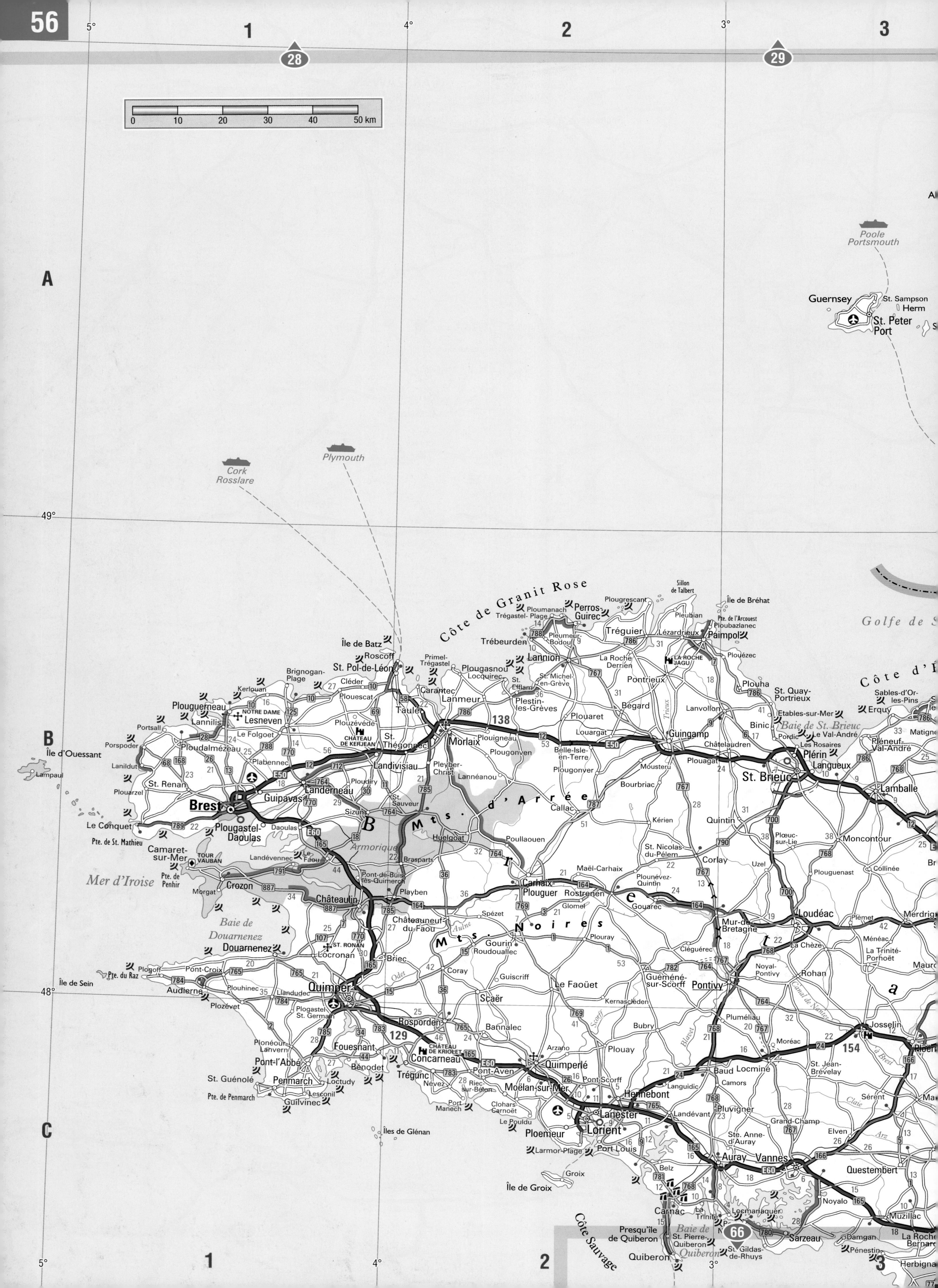

0 10 20 30 40 50 km

Poole
Portsmouth

Guernsey St. Sampson
Herm
St. Peter
Port

A

Plymouth

Cork
Rosslare

49°

Côte de Granit Rose
Sillon
de Talbert
Plougrescant
Île de Bréhat
Ploumanach Perros-
Trégastel- Plage Guirec
Pte. de l'Arcouest
Ploubazlanec
Golfe de S
Pleubian
Île de Batz 14
Roscoff Pleumeur-
Bodou Tréguier Lézardrieux Paimpol
Primel- 788 9 786 31   Plouézec
St. Pol-de-Léon Trégastel Trébeurden 786 La Roche
Brignogan- Cléder Plouasnou Lannion Derrien Plouha 786
Plage Locquirec St. 767 Plouaret Pontrieux St. Quay-
Plouguerneau Roscoff 27 Plouescat Carantec Efflam Bégard Lanvollon Portrieux
Kerlouan 16 10 Lanmeur 36 Plouaret 31 Sables-d'Or-
Plouvédé 58 Taulé 786 Plestin- Guingamp 41 les-Pins Erquy
Lannilis Le Folgoet 69 138 les-Grèves E50 Châtelaudren Binic Baie de St. Brieuc
NOTRE DAME 125 St. 12 Belle-Isle- Louargat 33 Matigne
Lesneven 788 14 Thégonnec Plouigneau 53 en-Terre Mousteru Plouaga Les Rosaires Pléneuf-
Portsall 24 CHÂTEAU Morlaix Plougonven Plérin Val-André
Ploudalmézeau DE KERJEAN 56 Plougonver Plouaget 24 Langueux 768
Lanildut Plabennec Landivisiau Pleyber- Lannéanou Bourbriac St. Brieuc Lamballe
Lampaul 168 785 Christ 21 767 28 31
Plouarzel 68 Plouédern 712 30 St. Callac Kérien Quintin 700
St. Renan 23 21 13 Ploudiry Sauveur 787 Ploeuc-
Brest Landerneau 11 d' A r r é e 51 St. Nicolas 790 sur-Lie Moncontour
Guipavas 764 29 Poullaouen du-Pélem 38 Collinée
Le Conquet 789 22 770 Sizun 764 32 764 Maël-Carhaix Corlay Uzel Plouguenast
Plougastel- Armorique B Huelgoat 21 Plounévez- 13 767 Ménéac
Daoulas Daoulas Brasparts 22 36 Carhaix- Quintin 24 Loudéac
Camaret- TOUR Landévennec Le Plouguer Rostrenen Gouarec 164 19 Plémet Merdrig
sur-Mer VAUBAN Faou 791 44 Pont-de-Buis Playben e Mur-de- 22 La Chèze
Pte. de lès-Quimerch 36 Spézet 769 Glomel Bretagne Ménéac
Penhir Mer d'Iroise Crozon 887 34 36 164 Noires Cléguérec 18 La Trinité-
Morgat Châteaulin 685 Châteauneuf- Gourin Plouray 782 Noyal- Porhoët
Baie de 887 du-Faou 27 Mts. Guéméné- 767 764 Pontivy Rohan Maur
Douarnenez 25 ST. RONAN Briec 42 Roudouallec sur-Scorff Pontivy a
Plogoff Douarnenez 107 Locronan 165 Coray Guiscriff Le Faouët 53 Pluméliau 32 Josselin
Pont-Croix 20 765 15 Scaër Bubry 768 20 767 Moréac 22 154
Pte. du Raz 784 Plouhinec Quimper 36 Kernascléden 769 22 24 Rohan
Audierne 35 Llandudec Rosporden 765 Bannalec Plouay 41 Locminé 166
Plozévet 784 Plogastel 129 824 Arzano Baud St. Jean- 16
St. Germain 46 Fouesnant 783 CHÂTEAU Quimperlé 768 Brévelay 17
Plonéour- 28 165 DE KRIOUET Pont-Aven 26 16 Pluvigner Camors Sérent
Lanvern 34 Bénodet Concarneau E60 Moëlan-sur-Mer Pont Scorff 24 Landévant 768 28 Claie
Pont-l'Abbé 27 Trégunc 783 Névez Hennebont Languidic Grand-Champ
St. Guénolé Loctudy Riec Clohars 765 11 Locminé 767
Penmarch Lesconil Carnoét Le Pouldu Pluvigner Elven 26
Pte. de Penmarch Guilvinec Port Lorient Ste. Anne- Vannes
Manech Ploemeur d'Auray Questembert
Îles de Glénan Larmor-Plage Lanester Auray 166 13
Port Louis 165 Noyalo 165
Groix Belz 781 768 14 Muzillac
Île de Groix Carnac Locmariaquer 780 Damgan La Roche
Presqu'île Trinité 66 Sarzeau Bernard
Côte de Quiberon Baie de Pénestin
Sauvage Quiberon St. Gildas- St. Pierre
Quiberon de-Rhuys

B

C

48°

5° 4° 3°
1 2 3

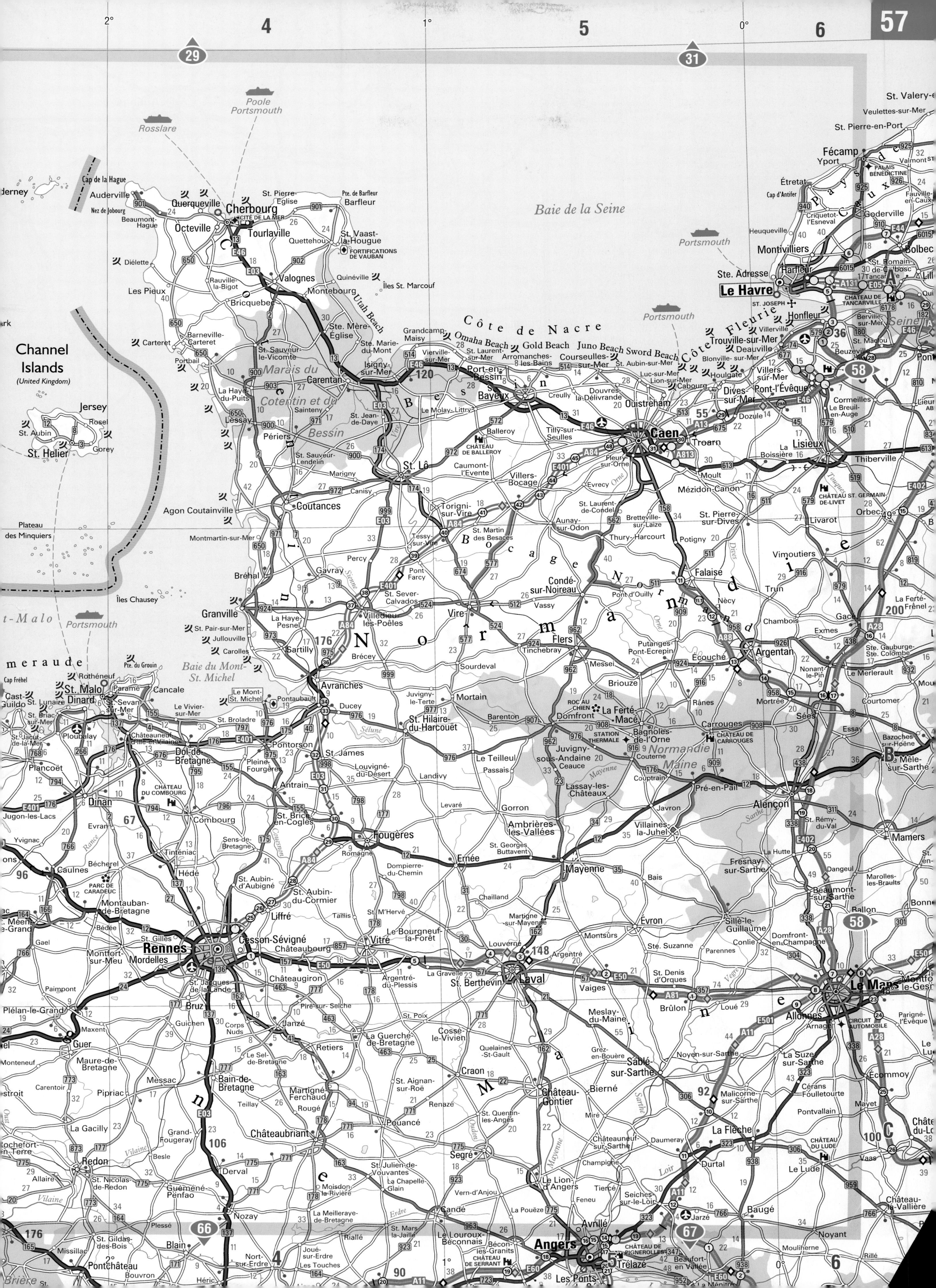
4
5
6
2°
1°
0°
29
31
58
66
67
Poole
Portsmouth
Rosslare
Channel Islands
(United Kingdom)
Jersey
St. Aubin
St. Helier
Rosel
Gorey
Plateau des Minquiers
Îles Chausey
Baie de la Seine
Côte de Nacre
Côte Fleurie
Pays de Caux
Omaha Beach
Gold Beach
Juno Beach
Sword Beach
Utah Beach
Cap de la Hague
Auderville
Nez de Jobourg
Beaumont-Hague
Querqueville
Cherbourg
Cité de la Mer
Octeville
Tourlaville
St. Pierre-Eglise
Pte. de Barfleur
Barfleur
Quettehou
St. Vaast-la-Hougue
Fortifications de Vauban
Diélette
Les Pieux
Rauville-la-Bigot
Valognes
Quinéville
Îles St. Marcouf
Montebourg
Bricquebec
Ste. Mère-Église
Ste. Marie-du-Mont
Carteret
Barneville-Carteret
St. Sauveur-le-Vicomte
Portbail
Marais du Cotentin et du Bessin
Carentan
Isigny-sur-Mer
Grandcamp-Maisy
Vierville-sur-Mer
St. Laurent-sur-Mer
Port-en-Bessin
Arromanches-les-Bains
Courseulles-sur-Mer
St. Aubin-sur-Mer
Luc-sur-Mer
Lion-sur-Mer
Bayeux
Creully
Douvres-la-Délivrande
Ouistreham
Cabourg
Houlgate
Dives-sur-Mer
La Haye-du-Puits
Lessay
Sainteny
St. Jean-de-Daye
Périers
Le Molay-Littry
Balleroy
Château de Balleroy
Tilly-sur-Seulles
Caen
Troarn
St. Sauveur-Lendelin
Marigny
St. Lô
Caumont-l'Evente
Villers-Bocage
Fleury-sur-Orne
Evrecy
Coutances
Canisy
Agon Coutainville
Torigni-sur-Vire
Aunay-sur-Odon
St. Laurent-de-Condel
Bretteville-sur-Laize
Thury-Harcourt
St. Martin des Besaces
Montmartin-sur-Mer
Tessy-sur-Vire
Percy
Gavray
Pont Farcy
Bréhal
Condé-sur-Noireau
Pont d'Ouilly
Falaise
Potigny
Granville
St. Pair-sur-Mer
Jullouville
Carolles
La Haye-Pesnel
St. Sever-Calvados
Villedieu-les-Poëles
Vire
Vassy
Flers
Tinchebray
Sartilly
Brécey
Avranches
Pte. du Grouin
Baie du Mont-St. Michel
Le Mont-St. Michel
Pontaubault
Sourdeval
Mortain
Juvigny-le-Tertre
St. Hilaire-du-Harcouët
Barenton
Ducey
Sélune
Messei
Briouze
Putanges-Pont-Ecrepin
Écouché
Argentan
Rânes
Roc au Chien
La Ferté-Macé
Domfront
Bagnoles-de-l'Orne
Station Thermale
Couterne
Carrouges
Château de Carrouges
Juvigny-sous-Andaine
Ceauce
Lassay-les-Châteaux
Passais
Le Teilleul
Normandie Maine
Couptrain
Pré-en-Pail
Alençon
Javron
Villaines-la-Juhel
Gorron
Ambrières-les-Vallées
St. Georges Buttavent
Ernée
Mayenne
Bais
Évron
Montsûrs
Martigné-sur-Mayenne
Chailland
Louverné
Laval
St. Berthevin
La Gravelle
Argentré
Vaiges
St. Denis d'Orques
Ste. Suzanne
Brûlon
Meslay-du-Maine
Loué
Le Mans
Allonnes
Arnage
Circuit Automobile
Cancale
Rothéneuf
St. Malo
Paramé
Dinard
St. Lunaire
St. Briac-sur-Mer
St. Jacut-de-la-Mer
Ploubalay
Cast-Guildo
St. Servan-sur-Mer
Le Vivier-sur-Mer
St. Broladre
Châteauneuf-d'Ille-et-Vilaine
Dol-de-Bretagne
Pontorson
Plancoët
Dinan
Jugon-les-Lacs
Pleine-Fougères
St. James
Louvigné-du-Désert
Landivy
Château du Combourg
Combourg
Antrain
St. Brice-en-Coglès
Fougères
Romagné
Tinténiac
Hédé
Bécherel
Caulnes
Parc de Caradeuc
Montauban-de-Bretagne
St. Aubin-d'Aubigné
St. Aubin-du-Cormier
Liffré
Dompierre-du-Chemin
Rennes
Cesson-Sévigné
Châteaubourg
Vitré
Le Bourgneuf-la-Forêt
St. Gilles
Mordelles
Montfort-sur-Meu
Bédée
Gael
Paimpont
Plélan-le-Grand
Maxent
Guer
Bruz
Guichen
St. Jacques-de-la-Lande
Châteaugiron
Argentré-du-Plessis
Janzé
Piré-sur-Seiche
Retiers
La Guerche-de-Bretagne
Cossé-le-Vivien
Craon
Quelaines-St-Gault
Château-Gontier
Bierné
Grez-en-Bouère
Sablé-sur-Sarthe
Maure-de-Bretagne
Bain-de-Bretagne
Messac
Pipriac
Carentoir
La Gacilly
Martigné-Ferchaud
Rougé
St. Aignan-sur-Roë
Renazé
Pouancé
Châteaubriant
St. Quentin-les-Anges
Segré
Redon
Grand-Fougeray
Derval
Guémené-Penfao
St. Nicolas-de-Redon
Allaire
St. Julien-de-Vouvantes
La Chapelle-Glain
Moisdon-la-Rivière
Vern-d'Anjou
Le Lion-d'Angers
Châteauneuf-sur-Sarthe
Champigné
Nozay
La Meilleraye-de-Bretagne
Candé
La Pouëze
Plessé
St. Gildas-des-Bois
Missillac
Pontchâteau
Blain
Nort-sur-Erdre
Joué-sur-Erdre
Les Touches
Riaillé
St. Mars-la-Jaille
Le Louroux-Béconnais
Bécon-les-Granits
Château de Serrant
Angers
Avrillé
Trélazé
Les Ponts
Château de Pignerolles
Beaufort-en-Vallée
Feneu
Tiercé
Seiches-sur-le-Loir
Durtal
La Flèche
Daumeray
Baugé
Jarzé
Noyant
Mouliherne
Le Lude
Château du Lude
Vaas
Château-la-Vallière
Pontvallain
Mayet
Écommoy
La Suze-sur-Sarthe
Cérans Foulletourte
Malicorne-sur-Sarthe
Noyen-sur-Sarthe
Parigné-l'Évêque
Sillé-le-Guillaume
Conlie
Domfront-en-Champagne
Parennes
Beaumont-sur-Sarthe
Fresnay-sur-Sarthe
Dangeul
Marolles-les-Braults
Ballon
St. Rémy-du-Val
Mamers
La Hutte
Bazoches-sur-Hoëne
Le Mêle-sur-Sarthe
Sées
Essay
Courtomer
Mortrée
Le Merlerault
Nonant-le-Pin
Chambois
Exmes
St. Gauburge-Ste. Colombe
Gacé
La Ferté-Frênel
Trun
Vimoutiers
Nècy
Livarot
St. Pierre-sur-Dives
Mézidon-Canon
Moult
Lisieux
La Boissière
Thiberville
Château St. Germain-de-Livet
Orbec
Dozulé
Le Breuil-en-Auge
Cormeilles
Pont-l'Évêque
Villers-sur-Mer
Blonville-sur-Mer
Deauville
Trouville-sur-Mer
Villerville
Honfleur
Beuzeville
Berville-sur-Mer
St. Maclou
Château de Tancarville
Le Havre
Ste. Adresse
St. Joseph
Harfleur
Montivilliers
St. Romain-de-Colbosc
Tancarville
Bolbec
Goderville
Heuqueville
Criquetot-l'Esneval
Cap d'Antifer
Étretat
Fécamp
Yport
Palais Bénédictine
Valmont
Fauville-en-Caux
St. Pierre-en-Port
Veulettes-sur-Mer
St. Valery-en-Caux
Bocage Normand
Normandie
Manche
Portsmouth
Émeraude

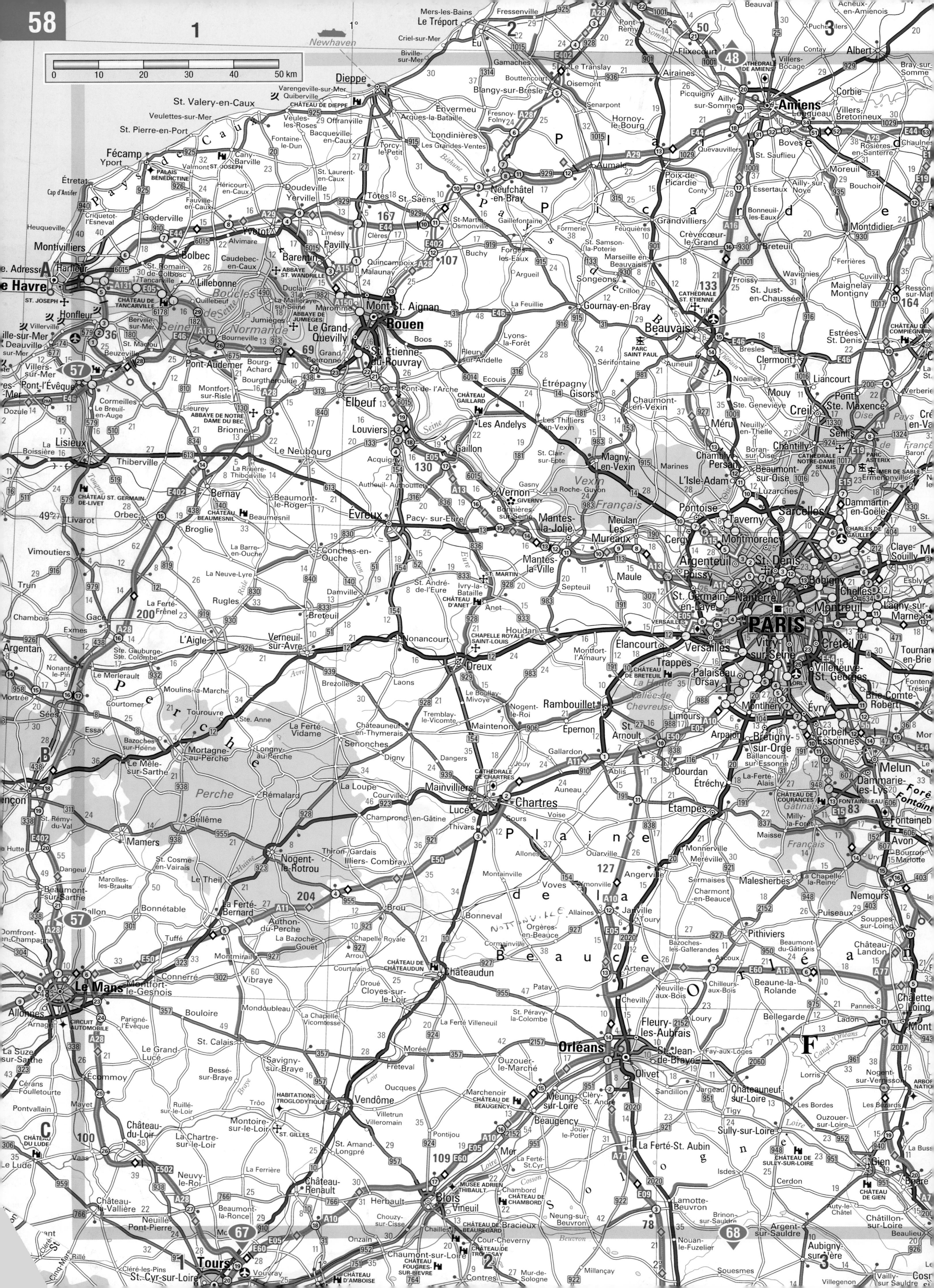
1
2
3
Newhaven
0 10 20 30 40 50 km
Mers-les-Bains
Le Tréport
Fressenville
Criel-sur-Mer
Eu
Biville-sur-Mer
Gamaches
Le Translay
Oisemont
Blangy-sur-Bresle
Bouttencourt
Dieppe
Varengeville-sur-Mer
Quiberville
CHÂTEAU DE DIEPPE
St. Valery-en-Caux
Veulettes-sur-Mer
St. Pierre-en-Port
Veules-les-Roses
Offranville
Arques-la-Bataille
Envermeu
Bacqueville-en-Caux
Londinières
Les Grandes-Ventes
Fontaine-le-Dun
Torcy-le-Petit
Fécamp
Yport
Cany-Barville
Valmont
ST. JOSEPH
PALAIS BÉNÉDICTINE
Étretat
Cap d'Antifer
Criquetot-l'Esneval
Héricourt-en-Caux
Fauville-en-Caux
Doudeville
Yerville
St. Laurent-en-Caux
Tôtes
St. Saëns
Neufchâtel-en-Bray
Gaillefontaine
Goderville
Yvetot
Alvimare
Heuqueville
Montivilliers
Bolbec
Caudebec-en-Caux
ABBAYE ST. WANDRILLE
Barentin
Pavilly
Limésy
Clères
Quincampoix
Malaunay
Buchy
Forges-les-Eaux
Argueil
Le Havre
Harfleur
St. Romain-de-Colbosc
Tancarville
CHÂTEAU DE TANCARVILLE
Lillebonne
Honfleur
Villerville
Trouville-sur-Mer
Deauville
Boucles de la Seine Normande
Jumièges
ABBAYE DE JUMIÈGES
Duclair
La Mailleraye-sur-Seine
Maromme
Mont-St. Aignan
Rouen
Le Grand-Quevilly
St. Étienne-du-Rouvray
Grand Couronne
Boos
Bourneville
Berville-sur-Mer
Beuzeville
St. Maclou
Pont-Audemer
Bourg-Achard
Bourgtheroulde
Villers-sur-Mer
Pont-l'Évêque
Dozulé
Cormeilles
Le Breuil-en-Auge
Montfort-sur-Risle
Lieurey
ABBAYE DE NOTRE DAME DU BEC
Brionne
Elbeuf
Pont-de-l'Arche
Louviers
CHÂTEAU GAILLARD
Les Andelys
Lisieux
Boissière
Thiberville
La Rivière-Thibouville
Le Neubourg
Acquigny
Gaillon
Bernay
Beaumont-le-Roger
CHÂTEAU ST. GERMAIN-DE-LIVET
Livarot
Orbec
CHÂTEAU BEAUMESNIL
Beaumesnil
Évreux
Pacy-sur-Eure
Vernon
Giverny
Bonnières-sur-Seine
Mantes-la-Jolie
Mantes-la-Ville
Vimoutiers
Broglie
Conches-en-Ouche
La Barre-en-Ouche
La Neuve-Lyre
Rugles
Damville
St. André-de-l'Eure
Ivry-la-Bataille
CHÂTEAU D'ANET
Anet
Breteuil
Trun
Chambois
Gacé
Exmes
La Ferté-Frênel
L'Aigle
Verneuil-sur-Avre
Nonancourt
Dreux
Houdan
CHAPELLE ROYALE SAINT-LOUIS
Argentan
Nonant-le-Pin
Ste. Gauburge-Ste. Colombe
Le Merlerault
Moulins-la-Marche
Mortrée
Sées
Courtomer
Tourouvre
Brezolles
Laons
Le Boullay-Mivoye
Tremblay-le-Vicomte
Nogent-le-Roi
Maintenon
Épernon
Rambouillet
Essay
Bazoches-sur-Hoëne
Mortagne-au-Perche
Le Mêle-sur-Sarthe
Ste. Anne
La Ferté-Vidame
Châteauneuf-en-Thymerais
Senonches
Longny-au-Perche
Digny
Dangers
Perche
Rémalard
La Loupe
Courville
Mainvilliers
Lucé
Chartres
CATHÉDRALE DE CHARTRES
Jouy
Gallardon
Auneau
Alençon
St. Rémy-du-Val
Bellême
Mamers
Champrond-en-Gâtine
Thivars
Sours
Voise
Thiron-Gardais
Illiers-Combray
Nogent-le-Rotrou
St. Cosme-en-Vairais
Dangeul
Marolles-les-Braults
Le Theil
Beaumont-sur-Sarthe
Bonnétable
La Ferté-Bernard
Authon-du-Perche
Brou
Bonneval
Montainville
Allonnes
Voves
Ymonville
Plaine de la Beauce
Allaines
Orgères-en-Beauce
Janville
Toury
Angerville
Ouarville
Domfront-en-Champagne
Tuffé
Chapelle Royale
La Bazoche-Gouet
Montmirail
Arrou
Cormainville
Courtalain
CHÂTEAU DE CHÂTEAUDUN
Châteaudun
Artenay
Le Mans
Montfort-le-Gesnois
Connerré
Vibraye
Droué
Cloyes-sur-le-Loir
Patay
Chevilly
Allonnes
Arnage
CIRCUIT AUTOMOBILE
Parigné-l'Évêque
Bouloire
Mondoubleau
La Chapelle-Vicomtesse
La Ferté Villeneuil
St. Péravy-la-Colombe
Fleury-les-Aubrais
La Suze-sur-Sarthe
Le Grand-Lucé
St. Calais
Bessé-sur-Braye
Savigny-sur-Braye
Morée
Fréteval
Ouzouer-le-Marché
Orléans
St. Jean-de-Braye
Olivet
Cérans-Foulletourte
Écommoy
Pontvallain
Mayet
Ruillé-sur-le-Loir
Trôo
HABITATIONS TROGLODYTIQUES
Vendôme
Oucques
Marchenoir
CHÂTEAU DE BEAUGENCY
Meung-sur-Loire
Cléry-St. André
Villetrun
Villeromain
Beaugency
Jouy-le-Potier
Château-du-Loir
Montoire-sur-le-Loir
La Chartre-sur-le-Loir
ST. GILLES
St. Amand-Longpré
Pontijou
Mer
La Ferté-St. Cyr
La Ferté-St. Aubin
Le Lude
Vaas
Neuvy-le-Roi
La Ferrière
Château-Renault
MUSÉE ADRIEN THIBAULT
Chambord
CHÂTEAU DE CHAMBORD
Blois
Vineuil
Herbault
Château-la-Vallière
Beaumont-la-Ronce
Neuillé-Pont-Pierre
Chouzy-sur-Cisse
Chailles
CHÂTEAU DE BEAUREGARD
CHÂTEAU DE Bracieux
Cour-Cheverny
Neung-sur-Beuvron
Lamotte-Beuvron
Nouan-le-Fuzelier
Rillé
Cléré-les-Pins
St.-Cyr-sur-Loire
Tours
Vouvray
Onzain
Chaumont-sur-Loire
CHÂTEAU FOUGÈRES-SUR-BIÈVRE
CHÂTEAU DE TROUSSAY
CHÂTEAU D'AMBOISE
Contres
Mur-de-Sologne
Millançay
Souesmes
Sologne
Pont-Remy
Flixecourt
Airaines
CATHÉDRALE DE AMIENS
Picquigny
Ailly-sur-Somme
Amiens
Longueau
Villers-Bretonneux
Corbie
Villers-Bocage
Contay
Albert
Beauval
Acheux-en-Amienois
Puchevillers
Bray-sur-Somme
Senarpont
Hornoy-le-Bourg
Quevauvillers
Boves
St. Saufflieu
Rosières-en-Santerre
Chaulnes
Aumale
Poix-de-Picardie
Conty
Essertaux
Ailly-sur-Noye
Moreuil
Bouchoir
Plateau de Picardie
Grandvilliers
Feuquières
Formerie
Bonneuil-les-Eaux
Montdidier
Crèvecœur-le-Grand
Breteuil
St. Samson-la-Poterie
Marseille en Beauvaisis
Songeons
Crillon
Froissy
St. Just-en-Chaussée
Wavignies
Ferrières
Maignelay Montigny
Cuvilly
Ressons-sur-Matz
CATHÉDRALE ST. ETIENNE
Beauvais
Tillé
Gournay-en-Bray
Pays de Bray
La Feuillie
Lyons-la-Forêt
Fleury-sur-Andelle
Ecouis
Sérifontaine
PARC SAINT PAUL
Auneuil
Bresles
Clermont
Estrées-St. Denis
CHÂTEAU DE COMPIÈGNE
Étrépagny
Gisors
Chaumont-en-Vexin
Noailles
Mouy
Liancourt
Pont-Ste. Maxence
Les Thilliers-en-Vexin
Méru
Ste. Geneviève
Creil
Senlis
CATHÉDRALE NOTRE-DAME SENLIS
PARC ASTERIX
MER DE SABLE
Ermenonville
Neuilly-en-Thelle
Chantilly
Boran-sur-Oise
Chambly
Persan
Beaumont-sur-Oise
Luzarches
Magny-en-Vexin
Vexin Français
Marines
L'Isle-Adam
Gasny
La Roche-Guyon
Meulan
Les Mureaux
Pontoise
Cergy
Taverny
Sarcelles
Montmorency
Dammartin-en-Goële
CHARLES DE GAULLE
Argenteuil
St. Denis
Poissy
Bobigny
Claye-Souilly
Chelles
Lagny-sur-Marne
St. Germain-en-Laye
Nanterre
PARIS
Montreuil
Versailles
VERSAILLES
Septeuil
Maule
Élancourt
Vitry-sur-Seine
Créteil
Montfort-l'Amaury
Trappes
Palaiseau
Orsay
ORLY
Villeneuve-St. Georges
CHÂTEAU DE BRETEUIL
La Haute Vallée de Chevreuse
Limours
Montlhéry
Évry
Brie-Comte-Robert
St. Arnoult
Arpajon
Brétigny-sur-Orge
Ballancourt-sur-Essonne
Corbeil-Essonnes
Melun
Dammarie-les-Lys
Dourdan
Ablis
Étréchy
La Ferté-Alais
CHÂTEAU DE COURANCES
Gâtinais
FONTAINEBLEAU
Milly-la-Forêt
Fontainebleau
Étampes
Maisse
Avon
Monnerville
Méréville
Malesherbes
La Chapelle-la-Reine
Nemours
Sermaises
Charmont-en-Beauce
Puiseaux
Souppes-sur-Loing
Pithiviers
Beaumont-du-Gâtinais
Château-Landon
Bazoches-les-Gallerandes
Ascoux
Neuville-aux-Bois
Chilleurs-aux-Bois
Beaune-la-Rolande
Forêt d'Orléans
Châlette-sur-Loing
Loury
Bellegarde
Ladon
Montargis
Fay-aux-Loges
Canal d'Orléans
Lorris
Nogent-sur-Vernisson
ARBORETUM
Jargeau
Châteauneuf-sur-Loire
Sandillon
Tigy
Les Bordes
Les Bézards
Ouzouer-sur-Loire
Sully-sur-Loire
CHÂTEAU DE SULLY-SUR-LOIRE
Isdes
Gien
CHÂTEAU DE GIEN
Briare
Cerdon
Autry-le-Châtel
Brinon-sur-Sauldre
Argent-sur-Sauldre
Châtillon-sur-Loire
Beaulieu
Aubigny-sur-Nère
Villegenon
Vailly-sur-Sauldre
Sologne
Orléanais
Plaine de la Beauce
Pays de Caux
Pays de Bray
Plateau de Picardie
Perche

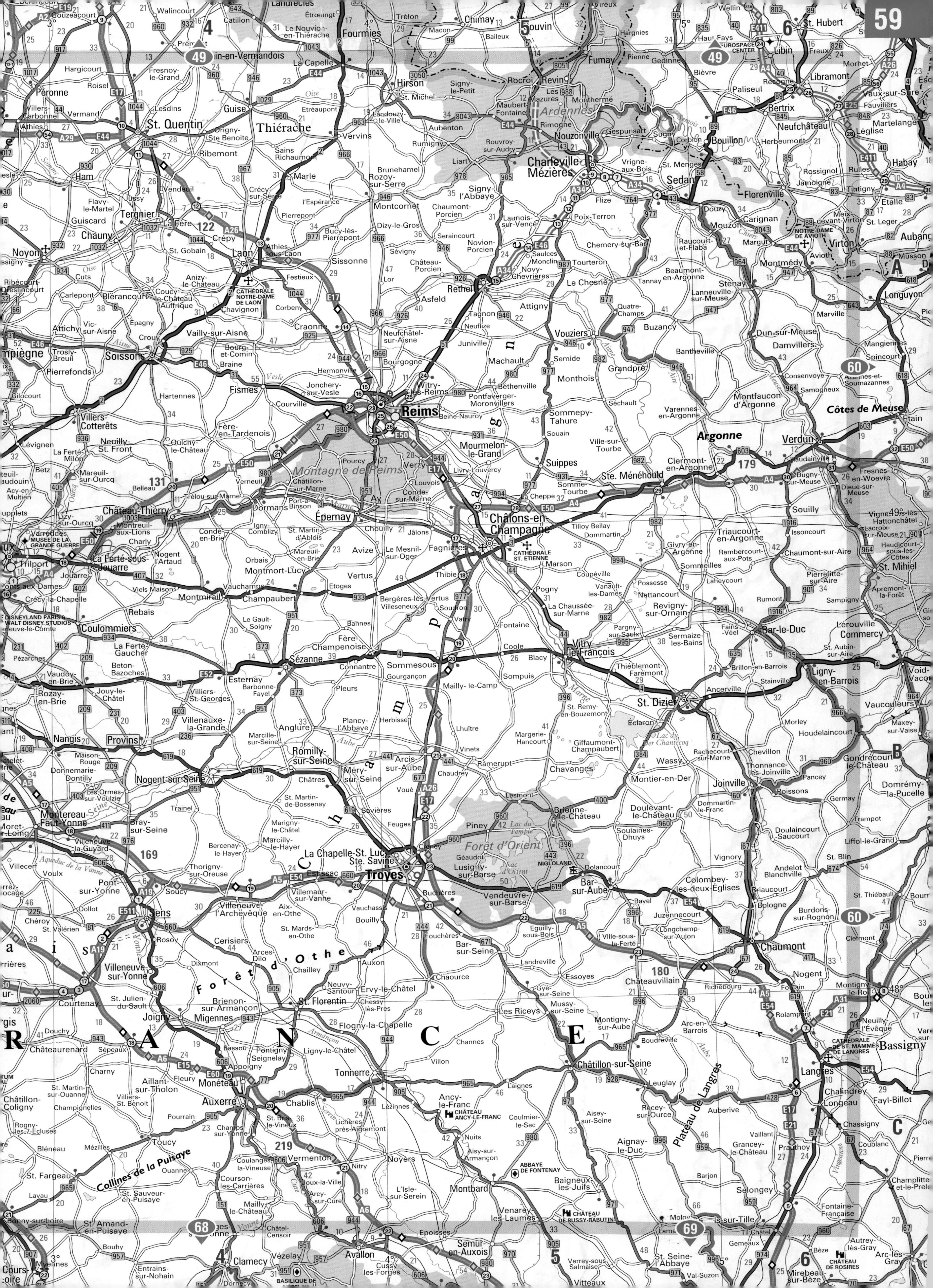

St. Quentin
Thiérache
Guise
Fourmies
Chimay
Hirson
Vervins
Rocroi
Revin
Fumay
Libin
St. Hubert
Libramont
Bertrix
Neufchâteau
Bouillon
Ardennes
Charleville-Mézières
Sedan
Florenville
Habay
Etalle
Virton
Aubange
Montmédy
Longuyon
Péronne
Ham
Tergnier
La Fère
Chauny
Noyon
Laon
Cathédrale Notre-Dame de Laon
Marle
Montcornet
Rethel
Vouziers
Stenay
Soissons
Compiègne
Reims
Fismes
Villers-Cotterêts
Montagne de Reims
Épernay
Châlons-en-Champagne
Cathédrale St. Etienne
Ste. Ménehould
Argonne
Verdun
Côtes de Meuse
St. Mihiel
Château-Thierry
Musée de la Grande Guerre
Disneyland Paris & Walt Disney Studios
La Ferté-sous-Jouarre
Meaux
Coulommiers
Montmirail
Sézanne
Vitry-le-François
Bar-le-Duc
Commercy
St. Dizier
Lac du Der Chantecoq
Provins
Nangis
Nogent-sur-Seine
Romilly-sur-Seine
Montereau-Fault-Yonne
Troyes
Forêt d'Orient
Lac du Temple
Nigloland
Bar-sur-Aube
Joinville
Chaumont
Langres
Cathédrale de St. Mammès de Langres
Bassigny
Plateau de Langres
Sens
Forêt d'Othe
Joigny
Auxerre
Chablis
Tonnerre
Châtillon-sur-Seine
Château Ancy-le-Franc
Abbaye de Fontenay
Montbard
Château de Bussy-Rabutin
Collines de la Puisaye
Avallon
Vézelay
Basilique de Vézelay
Clamecy
Semur-en-Auxois
Château de Rosières
Champagne
France

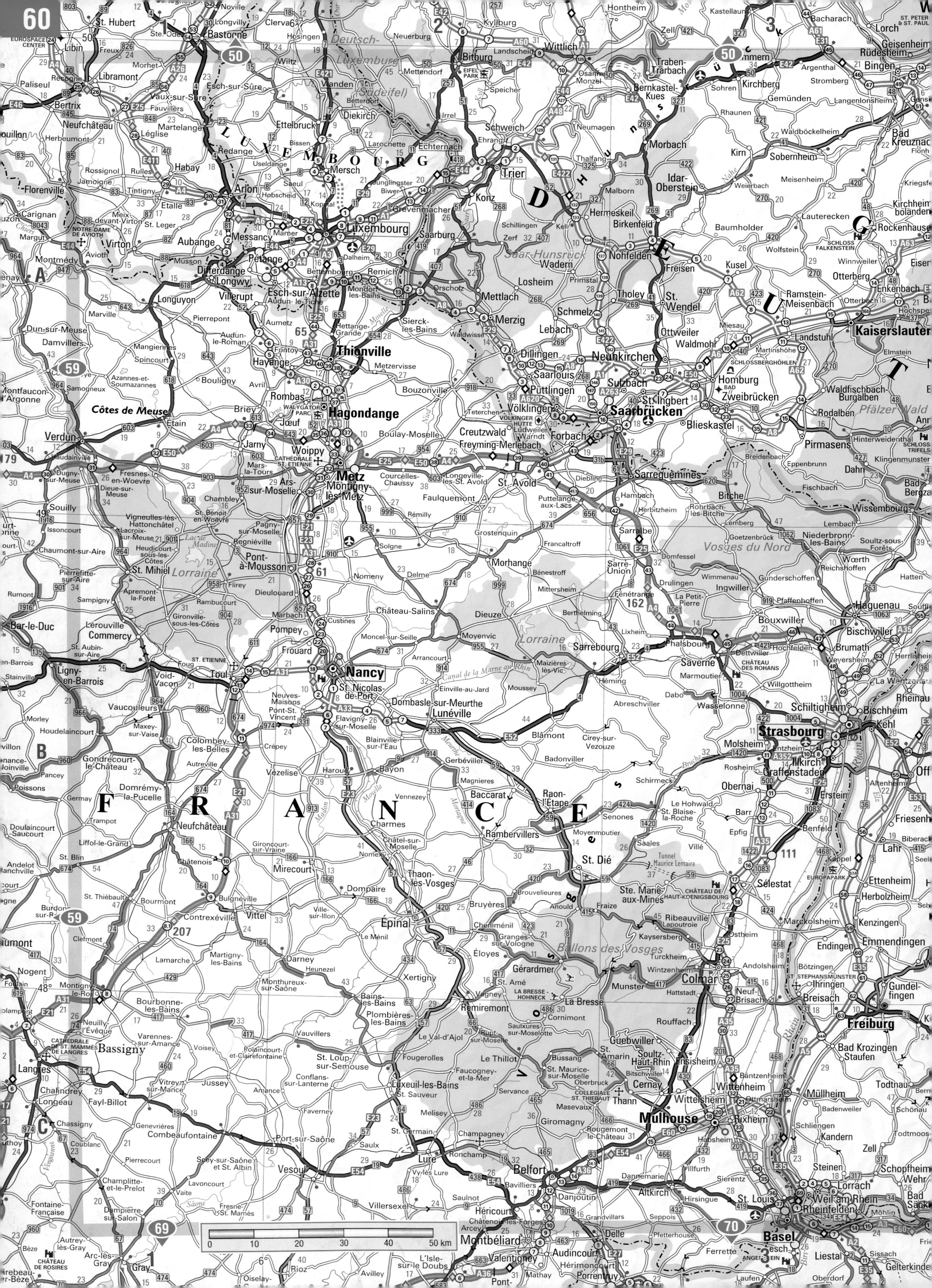

LUXEMBOURG
DEUTSCHLAND
FRANCE
VOSGES
HUNSRÜCK
Luxembourg
Trier
Saarbrücken
Kaiserslautern
Metz
Nancy
Thionville
Hagondange
Strasbourg
Mulhouse
Basel
Freiburg
Colmar
Épinal
Belfort
Montbéliard
Verdun
Arlon
Bastogne
Sarreguemines
Sarrebourg
Lunéville
Saverne
Haguenau
St. Dié
Vesoul
Langres
Neufchâteau
Bar-le-Duc
Toul
Pont-à-Mousson
Forbach
St. Avold
Homburg
Pirmasens
Zweibrücken
Neunkirchen
Bitburg
Wittlich
Idar-Oberstein
Bad Kreuznach
Bingen
Lorrach
Côtes de Meuse
Lorraine
Vosges du Nord
Pfälzer Wald
Ballons des Vosges
Saar-Hunsrück
Deutsch-Luxemburg (Südeifel)
Canal de la Marne au Rhin
0 10 20 30 40 50 km
50
59
61
65
69
70

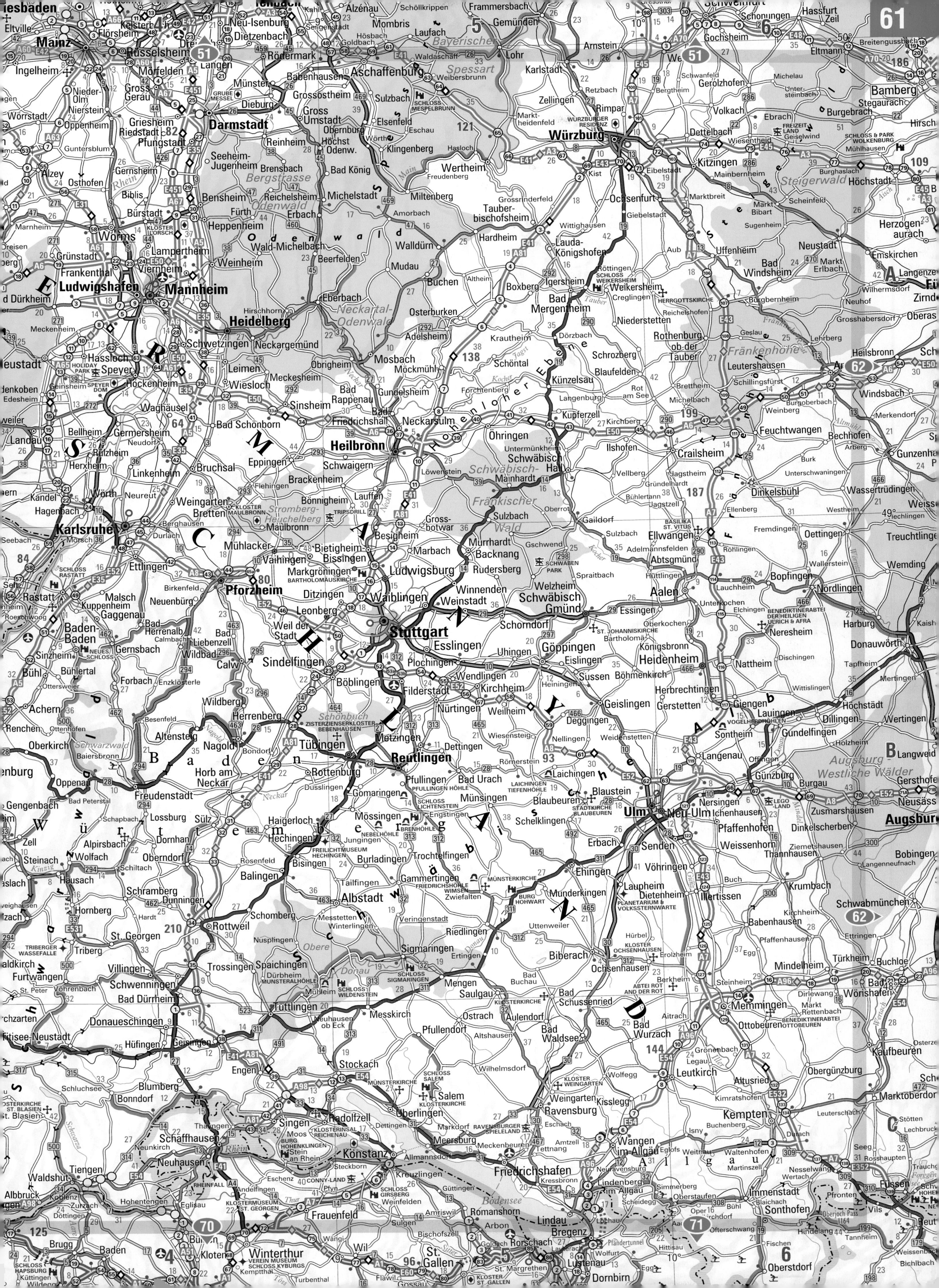
Wiesbaden
Mainz
Rüsselsheim
Darmstadt
Aschaffenburg
Würzburg
Schweinfurt
Bamberg
Kitzingen
Ochsenfurt
Wertheim
Tauberbischofsheim
Worms
Ludwigshafen
Mannheim
Heidelberg
Bad Mergentheim
Rothenburg ob der Tauber
Speyer
Heilbronn
Schwäbisch Hall
Crailsheim
Ansbach
Dinkelsbühl
Karlsruhe
Pforzheim
Ludwigsburg
Stuttgart
Esslingen
Göppingen
Schwäbisch Gmünd
Aalen
Nördlingen
Baden-Baden
Tübingen
Reutlingen
Heidenheim
Ulm
Neu-Ulm
Günzburg
Augsburg
Freudenstadt
Rottweil
Villingen
Schwenningen
Sigmaringen
Biberach
Memmingen
Kempten
Ravensburg
Friedrichshafen
Konstanz
Singen
Schaffhausen
Winterthur
St. Gallen
Bregenz
Lindau
Füssen
Oberstdorf
Spessart
Odenwald
Bergstrasse
Schwarzwald
Schwäbische Alb
Steigerwald
Frankenhöhe
Hohenloher Ebene
Allgäu
Bodensee
51
62
70
71
5
6
4
A
B
C

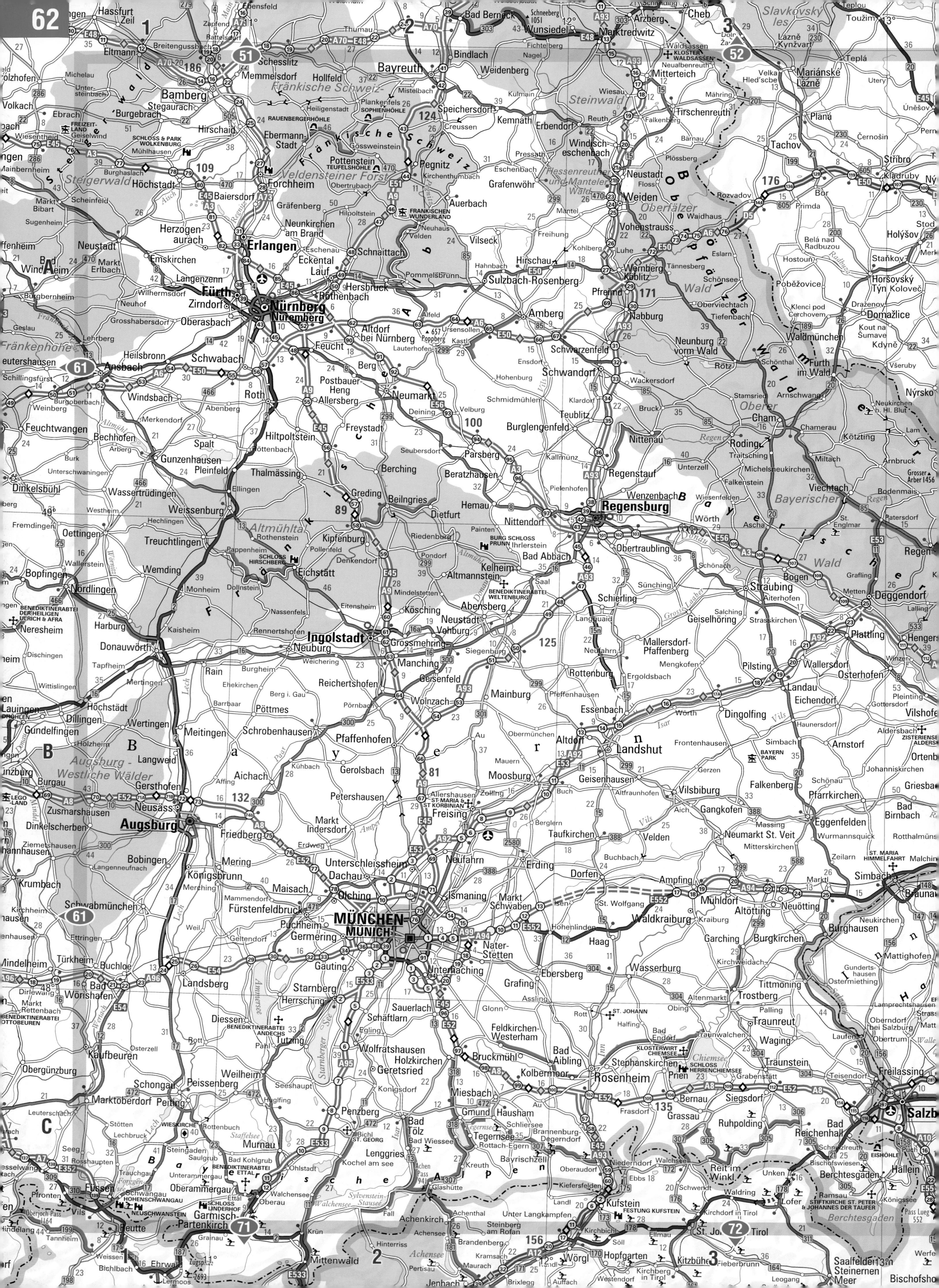
Hassfurt
Zeil
Eltmann
Bamberg
Schesslitz
Memmelsdorf
Hollfeld
Bayreuth
Bindlach
Weidenberg
Bad Berneck
Wunsiedel
Marktredwitz
Arzberg
Cheb
Slavkovský les
Lázně Kynžvart
Mariánské Lázně
Teplá
Toužim
Mitterteich
Waldsassen
Fränkische Schweiz
Steinwald
Tirschenreuth
Speichersdorf
Kemnath
Erbendorf
Windisch-eschenbach
Neustadt
Weiden
Oberpfälzer Wald
Tachov
Planá
Stříbro
Kladruby
Bor
Rozvadov
Primda
Vohenstrauss
Waidhaus
Holýšov
Staňkov
Horšovský Týn
Domažlice
Pobĕžovice
Pegnitz
Auerbach
Grafenwöhr
Vilseck
Hirschau
Sulzbach-Rosenberg
Amberg
Pottenstein
Gössweinstein
Ebermann-Stadt
Forchheim
Höchstadt
Steigerwald
Burgebrach
Ebrach
Schlüsselfeld
Erlangen
Herzogen-aurach
Neunkirchen am Brand
Eckental
Lauf
Hersbruck
Schnaittach
Fürth
Nürnberg
Nuremberg
Zirndorf
Oberasbach
Schwabach
Ansbach
Neustadt
Bad Windsheim
Heilsbronn
Windsbach
Roth
Altdorf bei Nürnberg
Feucht
Neumarkt
Postbauer-Heng
Allersberg
Freystadt
Hilpoltstein
Nabburg
Pfreimd
Schwarzenfeld
Schwandorf
Neunburg vorm Wald
Rötz
Waldmünchen
Furth im Wald
Cham
Roding
Nittenau
Teublitz
Burglengenfeld
Parsberg
Beratzhausen
Velburg
Regenstauf
Regensburg
Hemau
Nittendorf
Bad Abbach
Kelheim
Riedenburg
Dietfurt
Beilngries
Berching
Greding
Thalmässing
Spalt
Gunzenhausen
Pleinfeld
Weissenburg
Treuchtlingen
Eichstätt
Kipfenburg
Dinkelsbühl
Feuchtwangen
Wassertrüdingen
Oettingen
Nördlingen
Bopfingen
Wemding
Monheim
Harburg
Donauwörth
Neuburg
Ingolstadt
Grossmehring
Manching
Vohburg
Neustadt
Abensberg
Altmannstein
Schierling
Mallersdorf-Pfaffenberg
Geiselhöring
Straubing
Bogen
Deggendorf
Plattling
Viechtach
Bayerischer Wald
Wörth
Obertraubling
Rottenburg
Mainburg
Siegenburg
Geisenfeld
Wolnzach
Reichertshofen
Pfaffenhofen
Schrobenhausen
Pöttmes
Rain
Höchstädt
Dillingen
Lauingen
Gundelfingen
Wertingen
Meitingen
Augsburg - Westliche Wälder
Aichach
Gersthofen
Neusäss
Augsburg
Friedberg
Bobingen
Königsbrunn
Mering
Schwabmünchen
Krumbach
Türkheim
Buchloe
Landsberg
Bad Wörishofen
Mindelheim
Kaufbeuren
Marktoberdorf
Obergünzburg
Schongau
Peiting
Peissenberg
Weilheim
Murnau
Füssen
Oberammergau
Garmisch-Partenkirchen
Mittenwald
Landshut
Essenbach
Altdorf
Moosburg
Freising
Erding
Dorfen
Vilsbiburg
Dingolfing
Landau
Eggenfelden
Pfarrkirchen
Simbach
Braunau
Mühldorf
Altötting
Neuötting
Burghausen
Waldkraiburg
Haag
Wasserburg
Trostberg
Traunreut
Traunstein
Dachau
Olching
Fürstenfeldbruck
Germering
München
Munich
Gauting
Starnberg
Unterhaching
Ismaning
Unterschleissheim
Ebersberg
Grafing
Wolfratshausen
Holzkirchen
Bad Tölz
Penzberg
Miesbach
Tegernsee
Bad Aibling
Rosenheim
Kolbermoor
Prien
Chiemsee
Bernau
Siegsdorf
Ruhpolding
Bad Reichenhall
Freilassing
Salzburg
Berchtesgaden
Hallein
Kufstein
Wörgl
Kitzbühel
St. Johann
Tirol
Lofer
Reit im Winkl
Saalfelden
Achensee
Schwaz
Reutte
Ehrwald
Zugspitze
A

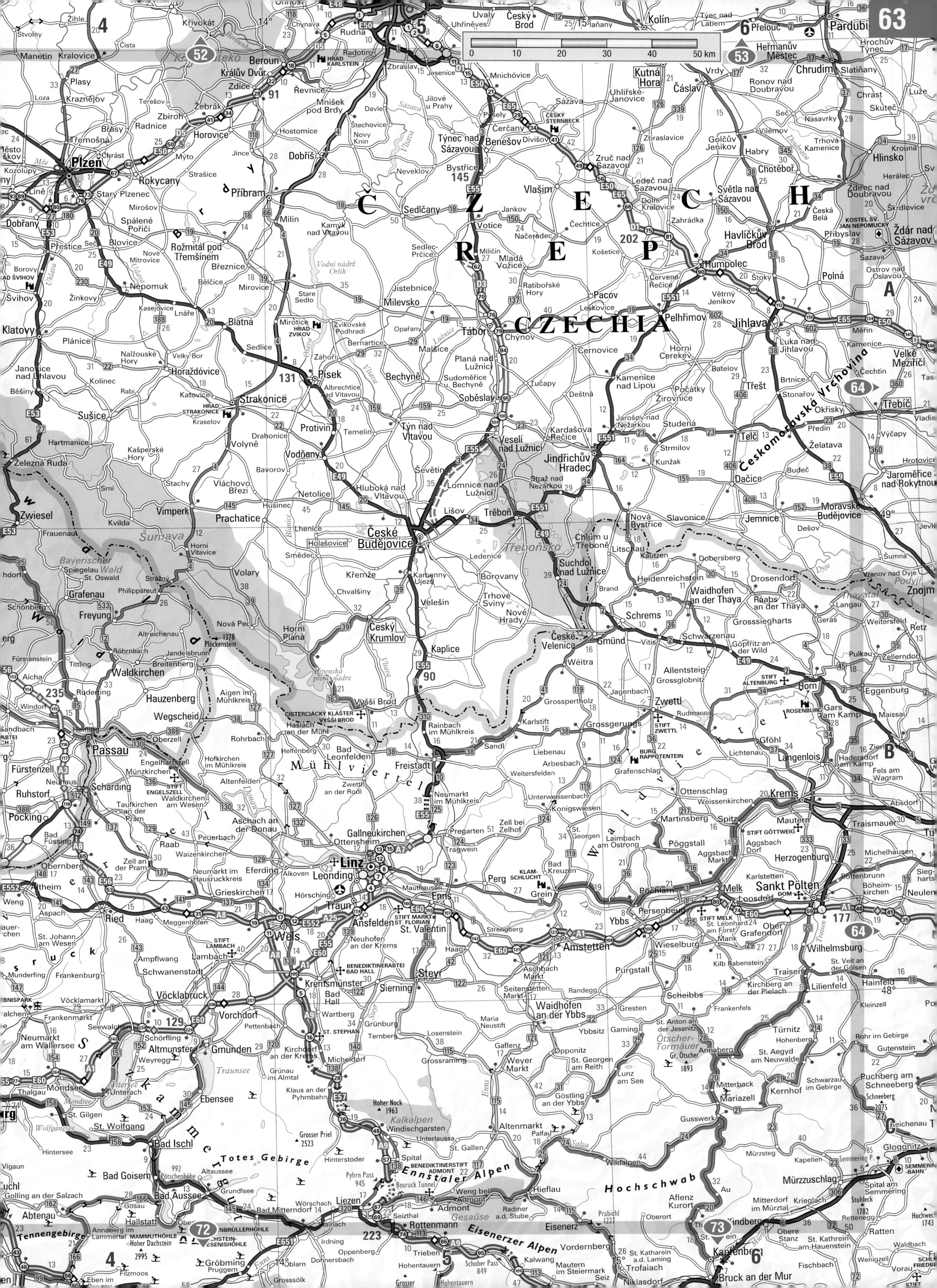
ČESKÁ REPUBLIKA
CZECHIA
Českomoravská Vrchovina
Brdy
Šumava
Bayerischer Wald
Třeboňsko
Mühlviertel
Waldviertel
Salzkammergut
Totes Gebirge
Ennstaler Alpen
Hochschwab
Eisenerzer Alpen
Kalkalpen
Tennengebirge
Plzeň
Beroun
Králův Dvůr
Zdice
Žebrák
Hořovice
Rokycany
Příbram
Dobříš
Rudná
Radotín
Zbraslav
Jesenice
Řevnice
Mníšek pod Brdy
Benešov
Týnec nad Sázavou
Kutná Hora
Kolín
Čáslav
Přelouč
Pardubice
Chrudim
Hlinsko
Havlíčkův Brod
Žďár nad Sázavou
Humpolec
Jihlava
Pelhřimov
Pacov
Vlašim
Votice
Sedlčany
Milevsko
Tábor
Chýnov
Písek
Strakonice
Blatná
Nepomuk
Horažďovice
Klatovy
Sušice
Vimperk
Prachatice
Volary
Vodňany
Protivín
Týn nad Vltavou
Hluboká nad Vltavou
České Budějovice
Soběslav
Veselí nad Lužnicí
Jindřichův Hradec
Třeboň
Lišov
Kaplice
Český Krumlov
Vyšší Brod
Horní Planá
Dačice
Telč
Třešť
Moravské Budějovice
Jaroměřice nad Rokytnou
Třebíč
Velké Meziříčí
Znojmo
Nová Bystřice
Slavonice
Jemnice
České Velenice
Gmünd
Waidhofen an der Thaya
Zwettl
Horn
Krems
Melk
Sankt Pölten
Linz
Leonding
Traun
Ansfelden
Enns
Steyr
Wels
Amstetten
Ybbs
Waidhofen an der Ybbs
Scheibbs
Lilienfeld
Mariazell
Mürzzuschlag
Kapfenberg
Bruck an der Mur
Leoben
Eisenerz
Liezen
Rottenmann
Bad Aussee
Bad Ischl
Bad Goisern
Hallstatt
Gmunden
Vöcklabruck
Mondsee
St. Wolfgang
St. Gilgen
Ried
Schärding
Passau
Freyung
Grafenau
Zwiesel
Waldkirchen
Hauzenberg
Wegscheid
Freistadt
Bad Leonfelden
Rohrbach
Aschach an der Donau
Eferding
Gallneukirchen
Perg
Grein
Kremsmünster
Windischgarsten
Spital
Admont
Sankt Valentin
Wilhelmsburg
Herzogenburg
Traismauer
Langenlois
Eggenburg
Retz
Zellerndorf
Raabs an der Thaya
Drosendorf
Schrems
Litschau
Allentsteig
Heidenreichstein
Ottenschlag
Pöggstall
Weitra
Karlstift
Sandl
Rainbach im Mühlkreis
Neumarkt im Mühlkreis
Pregarten
Hoher Nock 1963
Grosser Priel 2523
Hoher Dachstein 2995
Ötscher 1893
0 10 20 30 40 50 km
52
53
64
72
73
E50
E55
E49
E53
E551
E65
E59
E60
E552
E56
E57
D1
D3
D5
A1
A7
A8
A9
A25
S6
49°
48°
15°
14°
Totes Gebirge
Gesäuse
Semmering

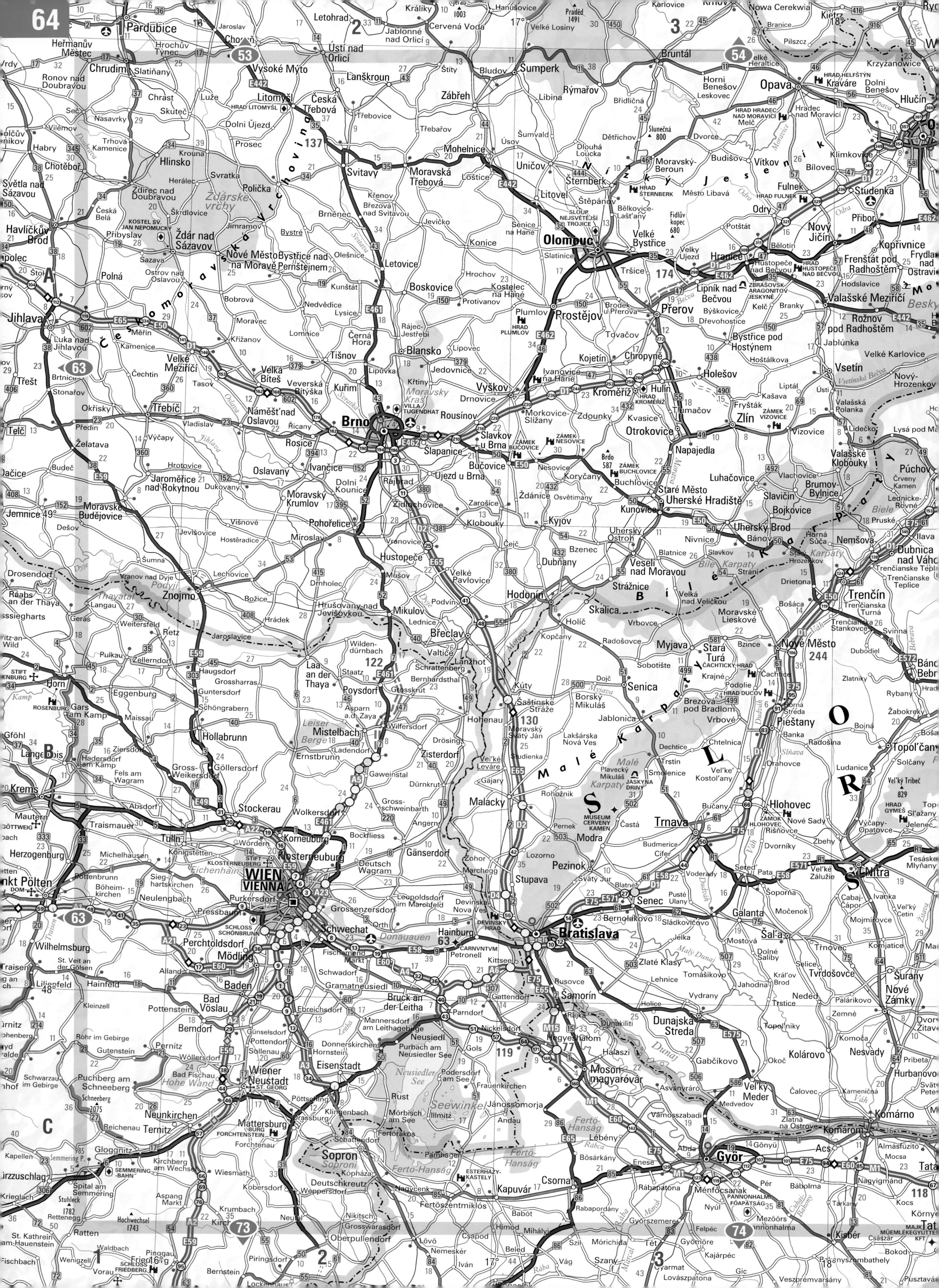
Pardubice
Hermanův Městec
Chrudim
Vysoké Mýto
Litomyšl
Česká Třebová
Ústí nad Orlicí
Letohrad
Králíky
Jablonné nad Orlicí
Červená Voda
Hanušovice
Praděd 1491
Velké Losiny
Karlovice
Nowa Cerekwia
Kietrz
Pilszcz
Krzyżanowice
Bruntál
Šumperk
Lanškroun
Štíty
Bludov
Zábřeh
Rýmařov
Horní Benešov
Opava
Kravåre
Dolní Benešov
Hlučín
Hradec nad Moravicí
Mohelnice
Svitavy
Moravská Třebová
Úsov
Uničov
Šternberk
Moravský Beroun
Bílovec
Fulnek
Studenka
Odry
Příbor
Nový Jičín
Kopřivnice
Frenštát pod Radhoštěm
Hlinsko
Polička
Žďárské vrchy
Žďár nad Sázavou
Nové Město na Moravě
Bystřice nad Pernštejnem
Letovice
Boskovice
Konice
Litovel
Olomouc
Hranice
Lipník nad Bečvou
Valašské Meziříčí
Rožnov pod Radhoštěm
Havlíčkův Brod
Chotěboř
Světla nad Sázavou
Polná
Jihlava
Třešť
Velké Meziříčí
Velká Bíteš
Tišnov
Blansko
Prostějov
Přerov
Kojetín
Chropyně
Holešov
Bystřice pod Hostýnem
Vsetín
Třebíč
Náměšť nad Oslavou
Brno
Vyškov
Kroměříž
Hulín
Zlín
Otrokovice
Telč
Slavkov u Brna
Bučovice
Rosice
Ivančice
Oslavany
Šlapanice
Napajedla
Luhačovice
Vizovice
Dačice
Jaroměřice nad Rokytnou
Moravský Krumlov
Židlochovice
Uherské Hradiště
Staré Město
Kunovice
Uherský Brod
Moravské Budějovice
Pohořelice
Hustopeče
Kyjov
Veselí nad Moravou
Dubňany
Hodonín
Strážnice
Bílé Karpaty
Znojmo
Mikulov
Břeclav
Valtice
Lednice
Skalica
Holíč
Myjava
Stará Turá
Senica
Nové Mesto
Trenčín
Piešťany
Hlohovec
Trnava
Malé Karpaty
Malacky
Modra
Pezinok
Senec
Bratislava
Nitra
Galanta
Šaľa
Dunajská Streda
Šamorín
Komárno
Nové Zámky
Kolárovo
Hollabrunn
Stockerau
Mistelbach
Poysdorf
Laa an der Thaya
Krems
Tulln
Korneuburg
Klosterneuburg
WIEN
VIENNA
Schwechat
Hainburg
Mödling
Baden
Bad Vöslau
Wiener Neustadt
Neunkirchen
Eisenstadt
Neusiedl
Neusiedler See
Bruck an der Leitha
Mattersburg
Sopron
Mosonmagyaróvár
Győr
Kapuvár
Csorna
Hegyeshalom
St. Pölten
Wilhelmsburg
Semmering
Gloggnitz
Mürzzuschlag
Kisbér
Pannonhalma
SLOVENSKO

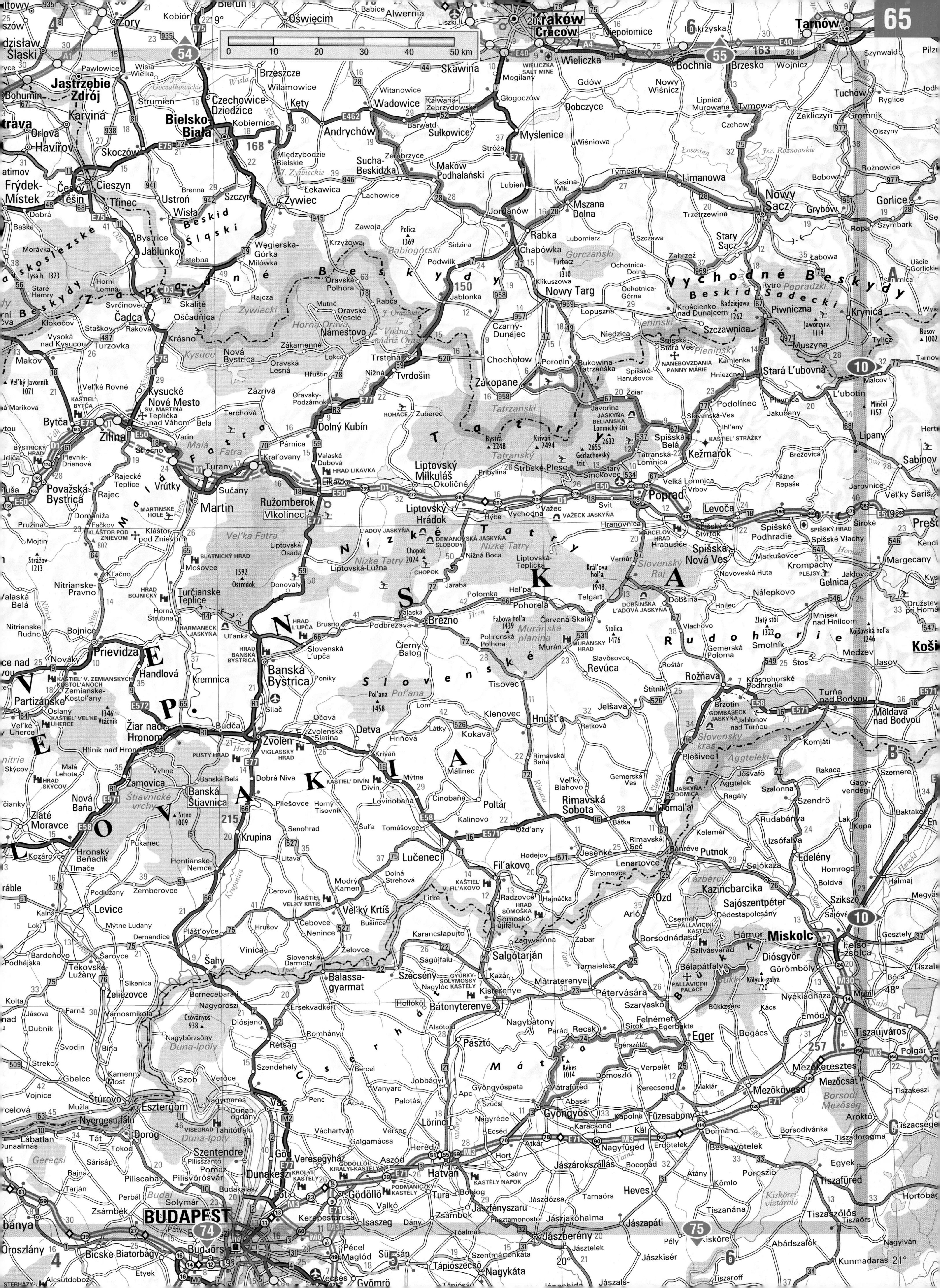
0 10 20 30 40 50 km
Kraków
Cracow
Oświęcim
Wieliczka
Bochnia
Tarnów
Brzesko
Żory
Jastrzębie Zdrój
Karviná
Havířov
Bielsko-Biała
Czechowice-Dziedzice
Wadowice
Andrychów
Myślenice
Skawina
Cieszyn
Český Těšín
Třinec
Frýdek-Místek
Żywiec
Sucha Beskidzka
Limanowa
Nowy Sącz
Gorlice
Grybów
Rabka
Nowy Targ
Zakopane
Krynica
Muszyna
Piwniczna
Szczawnica
Beskid Śląski
Vychodné Beskydy
Beskid Sądecki
Čadca
Námestovo
Tvrdošín
Trstená
Dolný Kubín
Žilina
Bytča
Kysucké Nové Mesto
Martin
Vrútky
Považská Bystrica
Ružomberok
Vlkolínec
Liptovský Mikuláš
Liptovský Hrádok
Poprad
Kežmarok
Levoča
Spišská Nová Ves
Stará L'ubovňa
Sabinov
Tatry
Nízke Tatry
Veľká Fatra
Malá Fatra
Slovenský Raj
Brezno
Banská Bystrica
Zvolen
Prievidza
Handlová
Kremnica
Žiar nad Hronom
Partizánske
Banská Štiavnica
Krupina
Detva
Lučenec
Rimavská Sobota
Revúca
Rožňava
Tornal'a
Fil'akovo
Veľký Krtíš
Levice
Šahy
Štúrovo
Esztergom
Vác
Salgótarján
Balassagyarmat
Ózd
Miskolc
Eger
Gyöngyös
Hatvan
Gödöllő
Mezőkövesd
Tiszaújváros
Jászberény
Heves
Tiszafüred
Füzesabony
BUDAPEST
Budaörs
Dunakeszi
Szentendre
Mátra
Cserhát
Bükk
Slovenské Rudohorie
SLOVENSKA

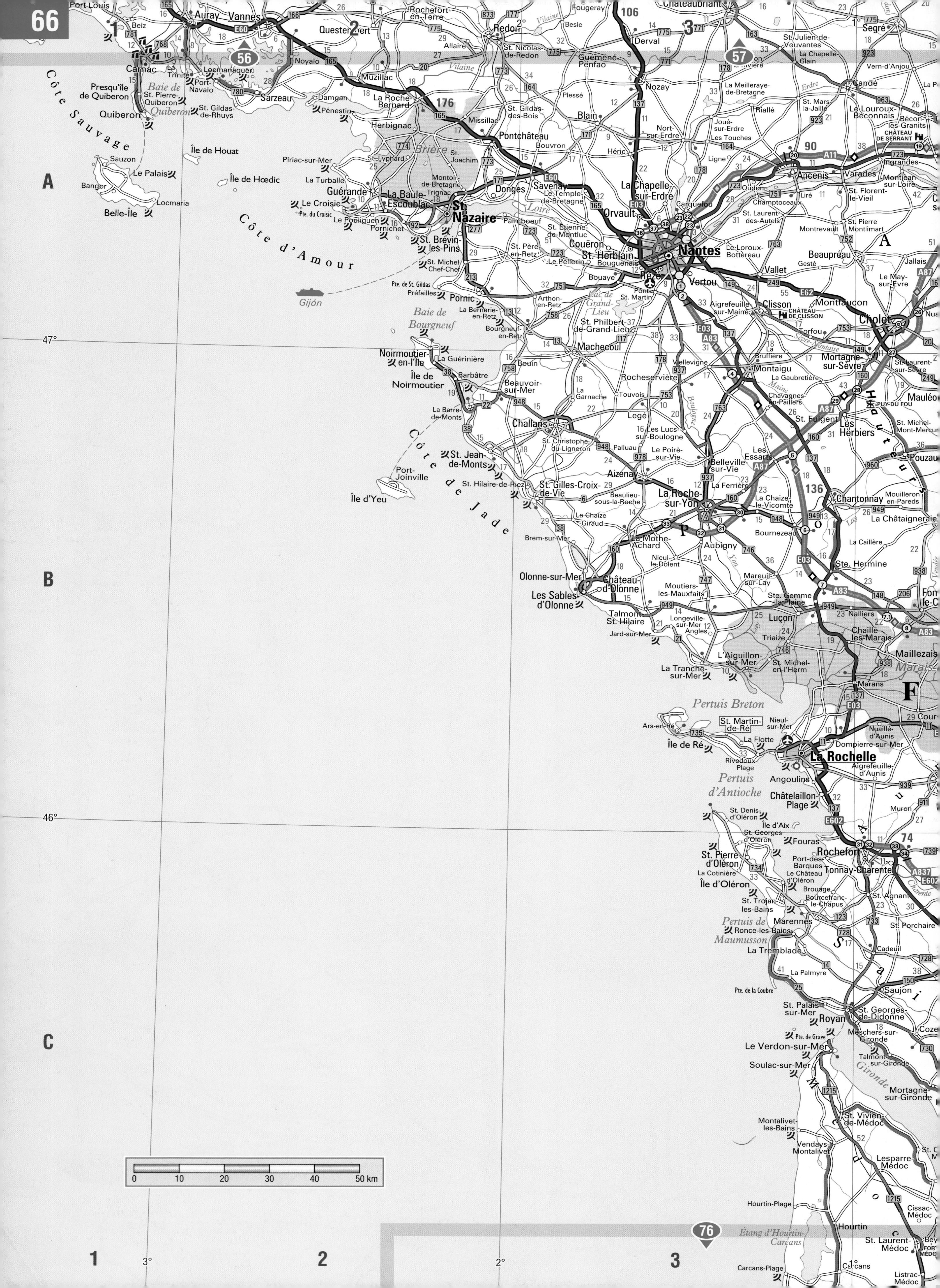
Port Louis
Auray
Vannes
Rochefort-en-Terre
Questembert
Redon
Fougeray
Châteaubriant
Segré
Belz
Carnac
La Trinité
Locmariaquer
Port-Navalo
Sarzeau
Noyalo
Muzillac
Allaire
St. Nicolas-de-Redon
Guémené-Penfao
Derval
Nozay
St. Julien-de-Vouvantes
La Chapelle-Glain
Vern-d'Anjou
Presqu'île de Quiberon
St. Pierre-Quiberon
Baie de Quiberon
St. Gildas-de-Rhuys
Quiberon
Damgan
Pénestin
La Roche-Bernard
Plessé
Blain
La Meilleraye-de-Bretagne
Candé
Côte Sauvage
Herbignac
Missillac
St. Gildas-des-Bois
Nort-sur-Erdre
Joué-sur-Erdre
Les Touches
Riaillé
St. Mars-la-Jaille
Le Louroux-Béconnais
Bécon-les-Granits
Château de Serrant
Île de Houat
Pontchâteau
Bouvron
Héric
Sauzon
Piriac-sur-Mer
St. Lyphard
Brière
St. Joachim
Ligné
Ancenis
Varades
Ingrandes
Le Palais
Île de Hœdic
La Turballe
Montoir-de-Bretagne
Donges
Savenay
La Chapelle-sur-Erdre
Oudon
St. Florent-le-Vieil
Montjean-sur-Loire
Bangor
Guérande
La Baule-Escoublac
Trignac
Le Temple-de-Bretagne
Carquefou
Champtoceaux
Liré
Locmaria
Le Croisic
Pte. du Croisic
St. Nazaire
Orvault
St. Laurent-des-Autels
Belle-Île
Le Pouliguen
Pornichet
Paimboeuf
St. Étienne-de-Montluc
Montrevault
St. Pierre-Montlimart
Côte d'Amour
St. Brévin-les-Pins
Couëron
St. Père-en-Retz
St. Herblain
Nantes
Le Loroux-Bottereau
Beaupréau
St. Michel-Chef-Chef
Le Pellerin
Bouguenais
Rezé
Vertou
Vallet
Gesté
Jallais
Le May-sur-Èvre
Pte. de St. Gildas
Préfailles
Pornic
Bouaye
Pont-St. Martin
Gijón
Arthon-en-Retz
Lac de Grand-Lieu
Aigrefeuille-sur-Maine
Clisson
Château de Clisson
Montfaucon
Cholet
Baie de Bourgneuf
La Bernerie-en-Retz
Bourgneuf-en-Retz
St. Philbert-de-Grand-Lieu
Torfou
Sèvre Nantaise
47°
Machecoul
Noirmoutier-en-l'Île
La Guérinière
Vieillevigne
Bruffière
Montaigu
Mortagne-sur-Sèvre
St. Laurent-sur-Sèvre
Île de Noirmoutier
Barbâtre
Bouin
Rocheservière
La Gaubretière
Beauvoir-sur-Mer
La Garnache
Touvois
Chavagnes-en-Paillers
Mauléon
Le Puy du Fou
La Barre-de-Monts
Legé
Les Herbiers
St. Fulgent
St. Michel-Mont-Mercure
Challans
Les Lucs-sur-Boulogne
St. Christophe-du-Ligneron
Palluau
Le Poiré-sur-Vie
Les Essarts
Pouzauges
Côte de Jade
St. Jean-de-Monts
Belleville-sur-Vie
Aizenay
La Ferrière
Port-Joinville
St. Hilaire-de-Riez
St. Gilles-Croix-de-Vie
Beaulieu-sous-la-Roche
La Roche-sur-Yon
La Chaize-le-Vicomte
Chantonnay
Mouilleron-en-Pareds
Île d'Yeu
La Chaize-Giraud
La Châtaigneraie
Brem-sur-Mer
La Mothe-Achard
Bournezeau
Aubigny
La Caillère
Nieul-le-Dolent
Mareuil-sur-Lay
Ste. Hermine
Olonne-sur-Mer
Château-d'Olonne
Les Sables-d'Olonne
Moutiers-les-Mauxfaits
Ste. Gemme-la-Plaine
Talmont-St. Hilaire
Longeville-sur-Mer
Angles
Luçon
Nalliers
Jard-sur-Mer
Triaize
Chaillé-les-Marais
Maillezais
L'Aiguillon-sur-Mer
St. Michel-en-l'Herm
La Tranche-sur-Mer
Marans
Pertuis Breton
Ars-en-Ré
St. Martin-de-Ré
Nieul-sur-Mer
Nuaillé-d'Aunis
Île de Ré
La Flotte
Dompierre-sur-Mer
Rivedoux-Plage
La Rochelle
Aigrefeuille-d'Aunis
Pertuis d'Antioche
Angoulins
Châtelaillon-Plage
Muron
46°
St. Denis-d'Oléron
Île d'Aix
St. Georges-d'Oléron
Fouras
St. Pierre-d'Oléron
Rochefort
Port-des-Barques
Tonnay-Charente
La Cotinière
Le Château d'Oléron
Île d'Oléron
Brouage
Bourcefranc-le-Chapus
St. Trojan-les-Bains
St. Agnant
Marennes
St. Porchaire
Pertuis de Maumusson
Ronce-les-Bains
La Tremblade
Cadeuil
La Palmyre
Pte. de la Coubre
Saujon
St. Palais-sur-Mer
Royan
St. Georges-de-Didonne
Meschers-sur-Gironde
Pte. de Grave
Le Verdon-sur-Mer
Talmont-sur-Gironde
Gironde
Soulac-sur-Mer
Mortagne-sur-Gironde
St. Vivien-de-Médoc
Montalivet-les-Bains
Vendays-Montalivet
Lesparre-Médoc
Médoc
Hourtin-Plage
Cissac-Médoc
Hourtin
Étang d'Hourtin-Carcans
St. Laurent-Médoc
Carcans-Plage
Carcans
Listrac-Médoc
Pays de la Loire
Poitou-Charentes
A
B
C
F
1
2
3
56
57
76
3°
2°
1°
0
10
20
30
40
50 km

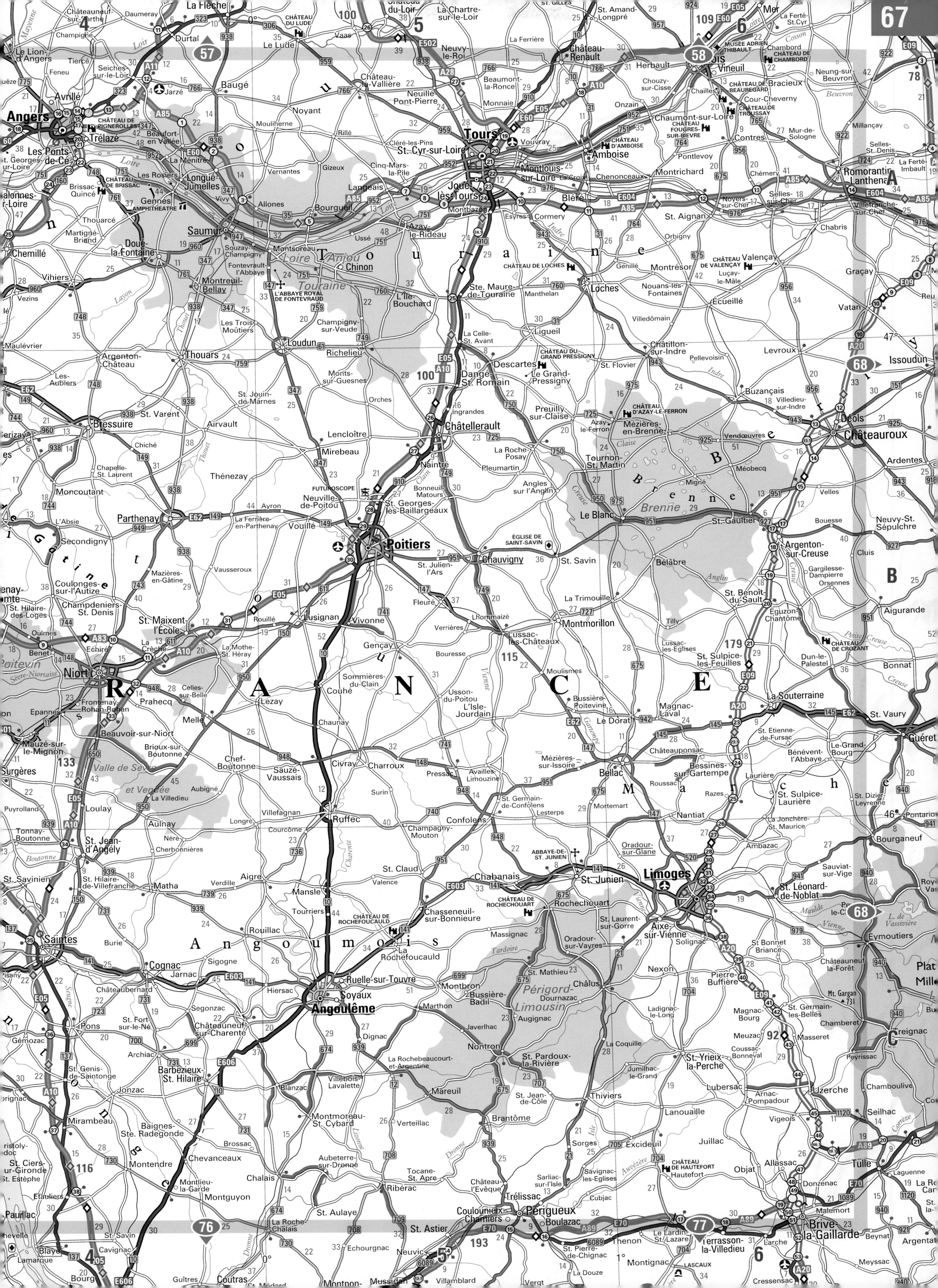
La Flèche
Châteauneuf-sur-Sarthe
Durtal
Le Lude
Château-du-Loir
La Chartre-sur-le-Loir
St. Amand-Longpré
Mer
Château-Renault
Blois
Angers
Trélazé
Les Ponts-de-Cé
Baugé
Beaufort-en-Vallée
Château-la-Vallière
Neuillé-Pont-Pierre
Tours
St. Cyr-sur-Loire
Vouvray
Amboise
Montlouis-sur-Loire
Joué-lès-Tours
Chenonceaux
Montrichard
Contres
Romorantin-Lanthenay
Selles-sur-Cher
St. Aignan
Valençay
Vatan
Issoudun
Saumur
Longué-Jumelles
Gennes
Doué-la-Fontaine
Montreuil-Bellay
Chinon
Azay-le-Rideau
Montbazon
Loches
Ste. Maure-de-Touraine
L'Île-Bouchard
Richelieu
Loudun
Thouars
Descartes
Le Grand-Pressigny
Châtellerault
Buzançais
Déols
Châteauroux
Bressuire
Parthenay
Mirebeau
Futuroscope
Neuville-de-Poitou
Poitiers
Chauvigny
Le Blanc
St. Gaultier
Argenton-sur-Creuse
Mézières-en-Brenne
Brenne
Montmorillon
Lussac-les-Châteaux
Lusignan
Vivonne
St. Maixent-l'École
Niort
Melle
Civray
Ruffec
Confolens
Bellac
Le Dorat
La Souterraine
Guéret
St. Jean-d'Angély
Cognac
Jarnac
Saintes
Angoulême
La Rochefoucauld
Rochechouart
St. Junien
Limoges
Aixe-sur-Vienne
St. Léonard-de-Noblat
Eymoutiers
Châlus
Nontron
Brantôme
St. Yrieix-la-Perche
Uzerche
Tulle
Brive-la-Gaillarde
Périgueux
Ribérac
Barbezieux-St. Hilaire
Jonzac
Pons
Blaye
Coutras
Terrasson-la-Villedieu
Touraine
Angoumois
Marche
Périgord-Limousin
FRANCE
57
58
68
76
77

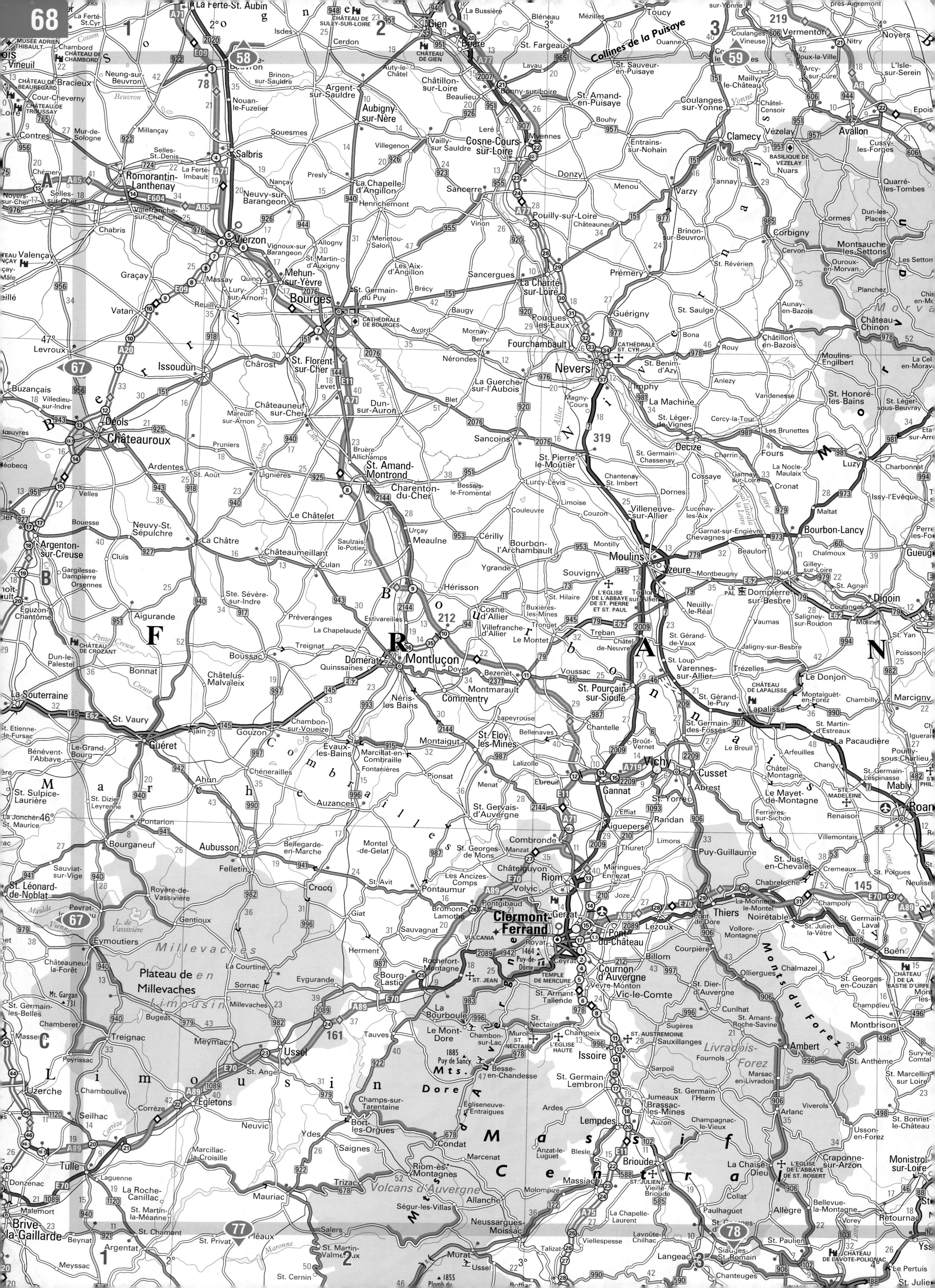
La Ferté-St. Aubin
La Ferté-St.Cyr
MUSÉE ADRIEN THIBAULT
Chambord
CHÂTEAU DE CHAMBORD
Vineuil
Neung-sur-Beuvron
Beuvron
CHÂTEAU DE BEAUREGARD
Bracieux
Cour-Cheverny
CHÂTEAU DE TROUSSAY
Mur-de-Sologne
Contres
Millançay
Nouan-le-Fuzelier
Selles-St.-Denis
Salbris
Romorantin-Lanthenay
La Ferté-Imbault
Chémery
Selles-sur-Cher
Noyers-sur-Cher
Villefranche-sur-Cher
Neuvy-sur-Barangeon
Nançay
Chabris
Vierzon
Valençay
Graçay
Vignoux-sur-Barangeon
Mehun-sur-Yèvre
Massay
Quincy
Lury-sur-Arnon
Reuilly
Vatan
Levroux
Issoudun
Chârost
Buzançais
Villedieu-sur-Indre
Déols
Châteauroux
Ardentes
Pruniers
Mareuil-sur-Arnon
Châteauneuf-sur-Cher
Velles
Bouesse
Neuvy-St. Sépulchre
Argenton-sur-Creuse
Gargilesse-Dampierre
Orsennes
Éguzon-Chantôme
Cluis
La Châtre
Ste. Sévère-sur-Indre
Aigurande
CHÂTEAU DE CROZANT
Dun-le-Palestel
Bonnat
Boussac
Châtelus-Malvaleix
La Souterraine
St. Vaury
Guéret
Ajain
Gouzon
St. Étienne-de-Fursac
Bénévent-l'Abbaye
Le-Grand-Bourg
St. Sulpice-Laurière
St. Dizier-Leyrenne
Ahun
Pontarion
Bourganeuf
Aubusson
Sauviat-sur-Vige
St. Léonard-de-Noblat
Royère-de-Vassivière
Peyrat-le-Château
Eymoutiers
Gentioux
Millevaches
Plateau de Millevaches
Limousin
Châteauneuf-la-Forêt
Mt. Gargan
St. Germain-les-Belles
Chamberet
Treignac
Bugeat
Meymac
Ussel
Uzerche
Chamboulive
Seilhac
Corrèze
Égletons
Neuvic
Tulle
Marcillac-la-Croisille
Laguenne
La Roche-Canillac
St. Martin-la-Méanne
Donzenac
Malemort
Brive-la-Gaillarde
Beynat
Argentat
St. Chamant
St. Privat
Pléaux
Meyssac
Gien
CHÂTEAU DE SULLY-SUR-LOIRE
CHÂTEAU DE GIEN
Briare
Isdes
Cerdon
Brinon-sur-Sauldre
Argent-sur-Sauldre
Aubigny-sur-Nère
Châtillon-sur-Loire
Beaulieu
Cosne-Cours-sur-Loire
Souesmes
Villegenon
Vailly-sur-Sauldre
Presly
La Chapelle-d'Angillon
Henrichemont
Sancerre
Allogny
Menetou-Salon
St. Martin-d'Auxigny
Les Aix-d'Angillon
St. Germain-du-Puy
Bourges
CATHÉDRALE DE BOURGES
Avord
Baugy
Brécy
Mornay-Berry
St. Florent-sur-Cher
Levet
Dun-sur-Auron
Nérondes
Lignières
St. Amand-Montrond
Charenton-du-Cher
Bruère-Allichamps
Le Châtelet
Châteaumeillant
Saulzais-le-Potier
Culan
Urçay
Meaulne
Préveranges
La Chapelaude
Treignat
Estivareilles
Domérat
Quinssaines
Montluçon
Néris-les-Bains
Chambon-sur-Voueize
Évaux-les-Bains
Marcillat-en-Combraille
Chénerailles
Auzances
Combrailles
Bellegarde-en-Marche
Felletin
Crocq
Montel-de-Gelat
St. Avit
Giat
La Courtine
Sornac
Millevaches
Eygurande
Bourg-Lastic
Herment
Sauvagnat
Tauves
La Bourboule
Le Mont-Dore
Puy de Sancy
Mts. Dore
Besse-en-Chandesse
Champs-sur-Tarentaine
Bort-les-Orgues
Ydes
Saignes
Condat
Riom-ès-Montagnes
Trizac
Mauriac
Volcans d'Auvergne
Ségur-les-Villas
Allanche
Salers
St. Martin-Valmeroux
Neussargues-Moissac
Murat
St. Cernin
Plomb du Cantal
Massif Central
Mts. d'Auvergne
Bléneau
St. Fargeau
Collines de la Puisaye
Toucy
St. Sauveur-en-Puisaye
St. Amand-en-Puisaye
Bonny-sur-Loire
Bouhy
Myennes
Entrains-sur-Nohain
Donzy
Menou
Pouilly-sur-Loire
Vinon
Châteauneuf
Varzy
Clamecy
Vézelay
BASILIQUE DE VÉZELAY
Coulanges-sur-Yonne
Mailly-le-Château
Vermenton
Avallon
Noyers
L'Isle-sur-Serein
Tannay
Brinon-sur-Beuvron
Corbigny
Lormes
Montsauche-les-Settons
Ouroux-en-Morvan
Prémery
La Charité-sur-Loire
Sancergues
Pougues-les-Eaux
Guérigny
St. Saulge
Fourchambault
Nevers
CATHÉDRALE ST. CYR
Imphy
La Machine
St. Benin-d'Azy
Châtillon-en-Bazois
Château-Chinon
Moulins-Engilbert
St. Honoré-les-Bains
Luzy
Decize
Cercy-la-Tour
La Guerche-sur-l'Aubois
Sancoins
St. Pierre-le-Moûtier
Magny-Cours
Lurcy-Lévis
Chantenay-St. Imbert
Dornes
Bourbon-l'Archambault
Cérilly
Ygrande
Hérisson
Souvigny
Moulins
Yzeure
Villeneuve-sur-Allier
Lucenay-lès-Aix
Chevagnes
Bourbon-Lancy
Dompierre-sur-Besbre
Digoin
LE PAL
Neuilly-le-Réal
Cosne-d'Allier
Villefranche-d'Allier
Le Montet
Buxières-les-Mines
Tronget
Montmarault
Commentry
Doyet
Bezenet
St. Pourçain-sur-Sioule
Varennes-sur-Allier
Lapalisse
CHÂTEAU DE LAPALISSE
Le Donjon
Jaligny-sur-Besbre
Montaiguët-en-Forez
Marcigny
Chantelle
St. Germain-des-Fossés
Montaigut
St. Éloy-les-Mines
Lapeyrouse
Pionsat
Menat
Ébreuil
Gannat
Vichy
Cusset
St. Yorre
Abrest
La Pacaudière
Le Mayet-de-Montagne
Châtel-Montagne
Roanne
Renaison
St. Gervais-d'Auvergne
Aigueperse
Randan
Combronde
Manzat
Châtelguyon
Riom
Volvic
Ennezat
Maringues
Thuret
Puy-Guillaume
St. Just-en-Chevalet
Pontaumur
Pontgibaud
Clermont-Ferrand
VULCANIA
Puy-de-Dôme
Royat
Gerzat
Lezoux
Thiers
Noirétable
Pont-du-Château
Billom
Cournon-d'Auvergne
Vic-le-Comte
Rochefort-Montagne
Olliergues
Monts du Forez
Boën
Montbrison
St. Nectaire
Champeix
Issoire
Sauxillanges
Ambert
Livradois-Forez
St. Germain-Lembron
Jumeaux
Brassac-les-Mines
Arlanc
Ardes
Lempdes
Brioude
Blesle
Massiac
La Chaise-Dieu
Craponne-sur-Arzon
Allègre
Paulhaguet
Langeac
Monistrol-sur-Loire
Retournac
Yssingeaux
CHÂTEAU DE LAVOÛTE-POLIGNAC
St. Paulien
Champdieu
Sury-le-Comtal
St. Bonnet-le-Château
Usson-en-Forez
St. Anthème
St. Germain-Laval
Chalmazel
Berry
Sologne
Brenne
Nivernais
Bourbonnais
Limousin
Creuse
Loire
Allier
Cher
Indre
Yonne
Vienne

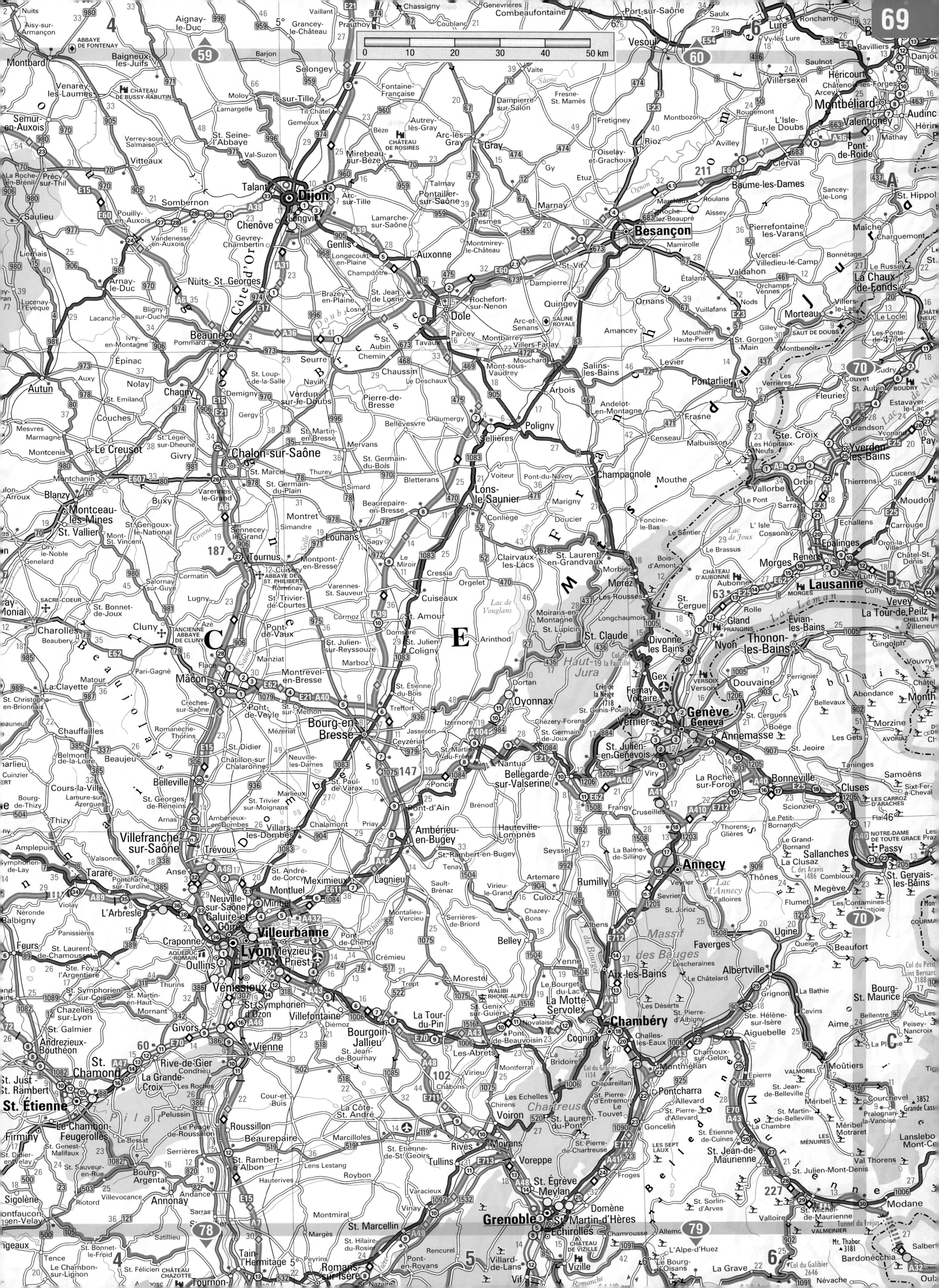
0 10 20 30 40 50 km
Dijon
Besançon
Lyon
Villeurbanne
Genève
Geneva
Lausanne
Grenoble
Chambéry
Annecy
St. Étienne
Mâcon
Chalon-sur-Saône
Bourg-en-Bresse
Lons-le-Saunier
Dole
Beaune
Montbard
Autun
Le Creusot
Montceau-les-Mines
Vesoul
Lure
Montbéliard
Héricourt
Pontarlier
La Chaux-de-Fonds
Le Locle
Yverdon-les-Bains
Vevey
Montreux
Thonon-les-Bains
Évian-les-Bains
Annemasse
Nyon
Oyonnax
Bellegarde-sur-Valserine
Aix-les-Bains
Albertville
Voiron
Vienne
Villefranche-sur-Saône
Tournus
Louhans
Poligny
Arbois
Champagnole
St. Claude
Gray
Auxonne
Nuits-St. Georges
Cluny
Charolles
Roanne
Tarare
Givors
Rive-de-Gier
Annonay
Romans-sur-Isère
Bourgoin-Jallieu
La Tour-du-Pin
Belley
Ambérieu-en-Bugey
Nantua
Gex
Divonne-les-Bains
Rumilly
Bonneville
Cluses
Sallanches
Ugine
Modane
Bardonècchia
Saulieu
Semur-en-Auxois
Baume-les-Dames
Ornans
Morteau
Valdahon
Salins-les-Bains
Morez
Les Rousses
Orbe
Vallorbe
Morges
Renens
Côte-d'Or
Bresse
Dombes
Beaujolais
Chablais
Jura
Haut-Jura
Massif des Bauges
Chartreuse
Maurienne
Belledonne
Pilat
Lac Léman
Lac d'Annecy
Lac du Bourget
Lac de Joux
Lac de Vouglans
Saône
Doubs
Rhône
Ain
Isère
59
60
70
78
79
4
5
6
A
B
C
E

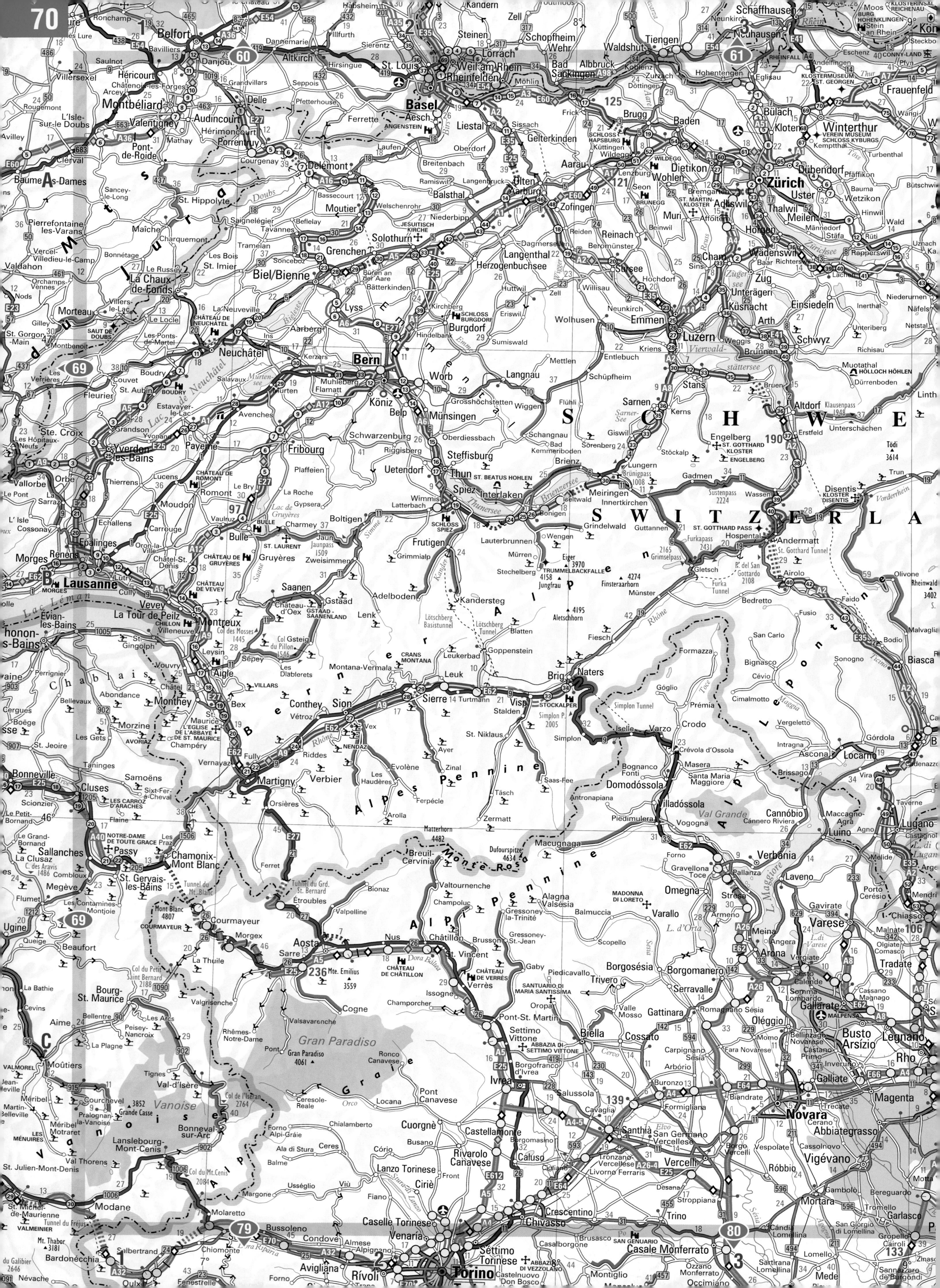

Belfort
Montbéliard
Valentigney
Audincourt
Porrentruy
Delle
Altkirch
Basel
St. Louis
Lörrach
Weil am Rhein
Rheinfelden
Liestal
Delémont
Moutier
Solothurn
Grenchen
Biel/Bienne
La Chaux-de-Fonds
Le Locle
Neuchâtel
Lac de Neuchâtel
Bern
Köniz
Belp
Münsingen
Thun
Spiez
Interlaken
Burgdorf
Langenthal
Herzogenbuchsee
Aarau
Olten
Aarburg
Zofingen
Brugg
Baden
Dietikon
Wohlen
Zürich
Winterthur
Bülach
Kloten
Dübendorf
Uster
Wetzikon
Thalwil
Meilen
Horgen
Wädenswil
Rapperswil
Zürichsee
Frauenfeld
Schaffhausen
Neuhausen
Waldshut
Tiengen
Bad Säckingen
Zug
Cham
Luzern
Vierwaldstättersee
Emmen
Sarnen
Stans
Schwyz
Brunnen
Altdorf
Einsiedeln
Andermatt
St. Gotthard Pass
St. Gotthard Tunnel
Airolo
Disentis
Fribourg
Payerne
Yverdon-les-Bains
Romont
Bulle
Gruyères
Lausanne
Renens
Morges
Vevey
Montreux
Lac Léman
Évian-les-Bains
Thonon-les-Bains
Aigle
Monthey
Martigny
Sion
Sierre
Leuk
Visp
Brig
Naters
Zermatt
Saas-Fee
Matterhorn 4482
Dufourspitze 4634
Monte Rosa
Jungfrau 4158
Eiger 3970
Finsteraarhorn 4274
Aletschhorn 4195
Grindelwald
Lauterbrunnen
Kandersteg
Adelboden
Gstaad
Saanen
Frutigen
Meiringen
Brienz
Brienzersee
Thunersee
Engelberg
Simplon
Simplon Tunnel
Domodóssola
Villadóssola
Verbania
Lago Maggiore
Locarno
Ascona
Bellinzona
Biasca
Lugano
Varese
Luino
Cannóbio
Stresa
Omegna
Arona
Gallarate
Busto Arsízio
Legnano
Rho
Magenta
Novara
Vigévano
Abbiategrasso
Mortara
Vercelli
Santhià
Biella
Ivrea
Aosta
Courmayeur
Mont Blanc 4807
Chamonix-Mont Blanc
Sallanches
Megève
Cluses
Bonneville
Ugine
Bourg-St. Maurice
Moûtiers
Val-d'Isère
Courchevel
Méribel
Val Thorens
Modane
Bardonécchia
Susa
Torino
Rívoli
Venaria
Chivasso
Casale Monferrato
Trino
Ciriè
Gran Paradiso 4061
Alpi Pennine
Alpes Pennine
Alpi Graie
Alpi Lepontine
Berner Alpen
Emmental
Jura
Vanoise
SCHWEIZ
SWITZERLAND
60
61
69
79
80

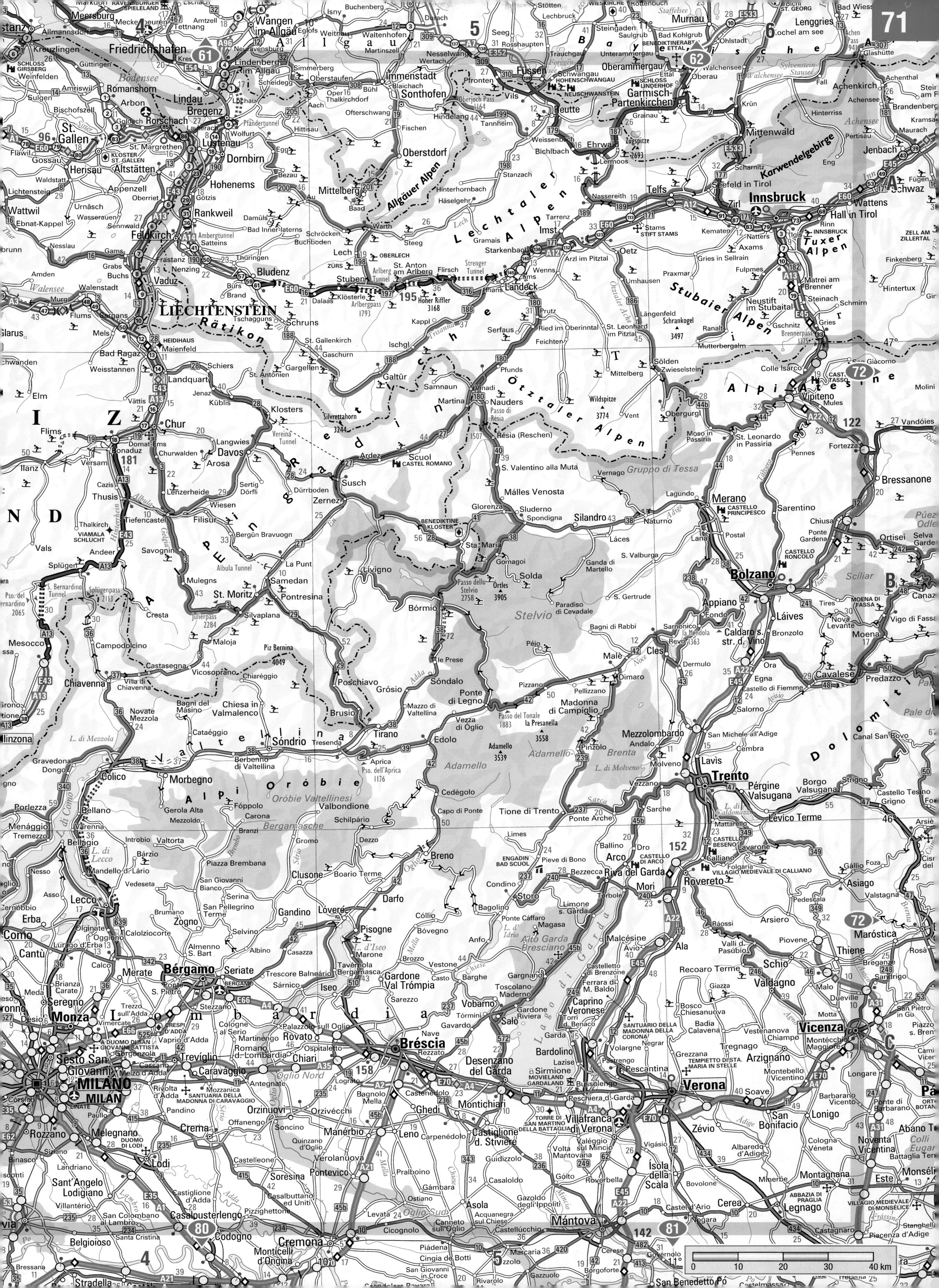
Meersburg
Friedrichshafen
Wangen im Allgäu
Allgäu
Bayerische
Murnau
Lenggries
Kreuzlingen
Bodensee
Lindau
Bregenz
Rorschach
Immenstadt
Sonthofen
Füssen
Oberammergau
Garmisch-Partenkirchen
Reutte
St. Gallen
Herisau
Dornbirn
Lustenau
Altstätten
Oberstdorf
Allgäuer Alpen
Mittenwald
Karwendelgebirge
Jenbach
Schwaz
Innsbruck
Hall in Tirol
Wattens
Telfs
Seefeld in Tirol
Zirl
Hohenems
Rankweil
Feldkirch
Lechtaler Alpen
Imst
Landeck
Bludenz
Vaduz
LIECHTENSTEIN
Rätikon
St. Anton am Arlberg
Lech
Stubaier Alpen
Tuxer Alpen
Ötztaler Alpen
Sölden
Schrankogel 3497
Wildspitze 3774
Bad Ragaz
Landquart
Klosters
Chur
Davos
Arosa
Thusis
Flims
Scuol
Zernez
Rätische Alpen
St. Moritz
Samedan
Pontresina
Piz Bernina 4049
Livigno
Bórmio
Ortles 3905
Stelvio
Merano
Bolzano
Bressanone
Vipiteno
Alpi Atesine
Silandro
Glorenza
Passo dello Stelvio 2758
Chiavenna
Poschiavo
Tirano
Sóndrio
Valtellina
Edolo
Adamello 3539
Ponte di Legno
Madonna di Campiglio
Cles
Malè
Cavalese
Ortisei
Dolomiti
Trento
Pérgine Valsugana
Levico Terme
Rovereto
Riva del Garda
Arco
Tione di Trento
Alpi Orobie
Colico
Morbegno
Lecco
Bellagio
L. di Como
Como
Cantù
Monza
Bérgamo
Lombardia
MILANO
MILAN
Sesto San Giovanni
Lodi
Crema
Melegnano
Treviglio
Chiari
Rovato
Iseo
L. d'Iseo
Lovere
Brescia
Salò
Desenzano del Garda
Lago di Garda
Malcésine
Bardolino
Verona
Villafranca di Verona
Peschiera d. Garda
Vicenza
Schio
Valdagno
Thiene
Asiago
Marostica
Legnago
Mántova
Cremona
Codogno
Casalpusterlengo
Ghedi
Montichiari
Orzinuovi
Soave
San Bonifacio
Isola della Scala
0 10 20 30 40 km

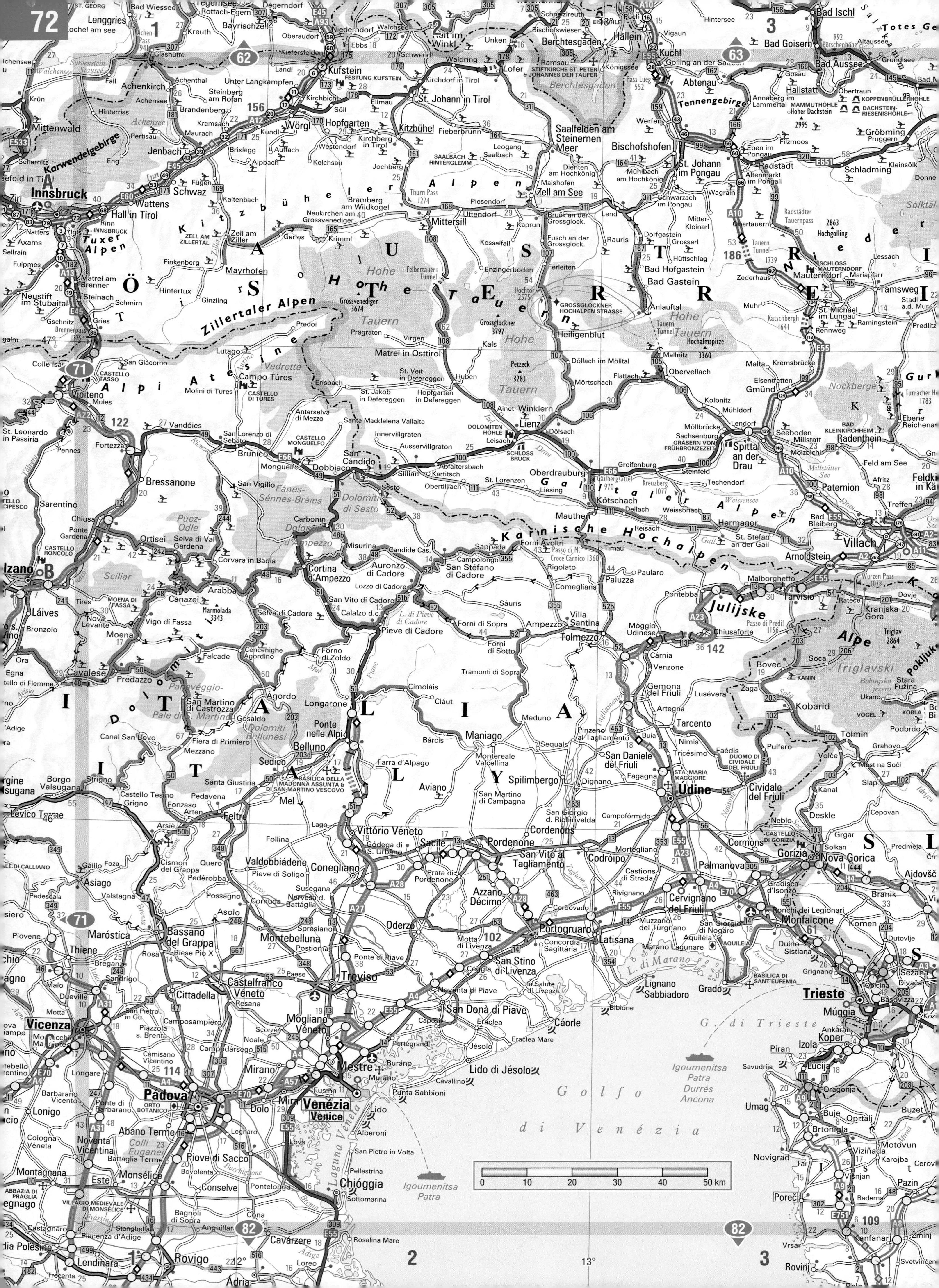

72
1
2
3
Innsbruck
Hall in Tirol
Schwaz
Jenbach
Wörgl
Kufstein
Kitzbühel
St. Johann in Tirol
Saalfelden am Steinernen Meer
Bischofshofen
Zell am See
Mittersill
Lienz
Spittal an der Drau
Villach
Bad Ischl
Bad Aussee
Hallein
Berchtesgaden
Radstadt
Schladming
Bad Gastein
Heiligenblut
Matrei in Osttirol
Kitzbüheler Alpen
Tuxer Alpen
Karwendelgebirge
Zillertaler Alpen
Hohe Tauern
Grossglockner 3797
Gailtaler Alpen
Karnische Hochalpen
ÖSTERREICH
Alpi Atesine
Vipiteno
Bressanone
Brunico
Bolzano
Cortina d'Ampezzo
Dolomiti
Belluno
Feltre
Pieve di Cadore
Tolmezzo
Údine
Cividale del Friuli
Gorizia
Nova Gorica
Monfalcone
Trieste
Koper
Pordenone
Conegliano
Vittório Véneto
Treviso
Castelfranco Véneto
Bassano del Grappa
Vicenza
Padova
Mestre
Venézia
Venice
Chióggia
Rovigo
Portogruaro
Latisana
Lignano Sabbiadoro
Grado
Lido di Jésolo
San Donà di Piave
Cáorle
Golfo di Venézia
G. di Trieste
Julijske Alpe
Triglavski
ITALIA
ITALY
Piran
Izola
Umag
Poreč
Rovinj
Igoumenitsa Patra Durrës Ancona
Igoumenitsa Patra
0 10 20 30 40 50 km
12°
13°

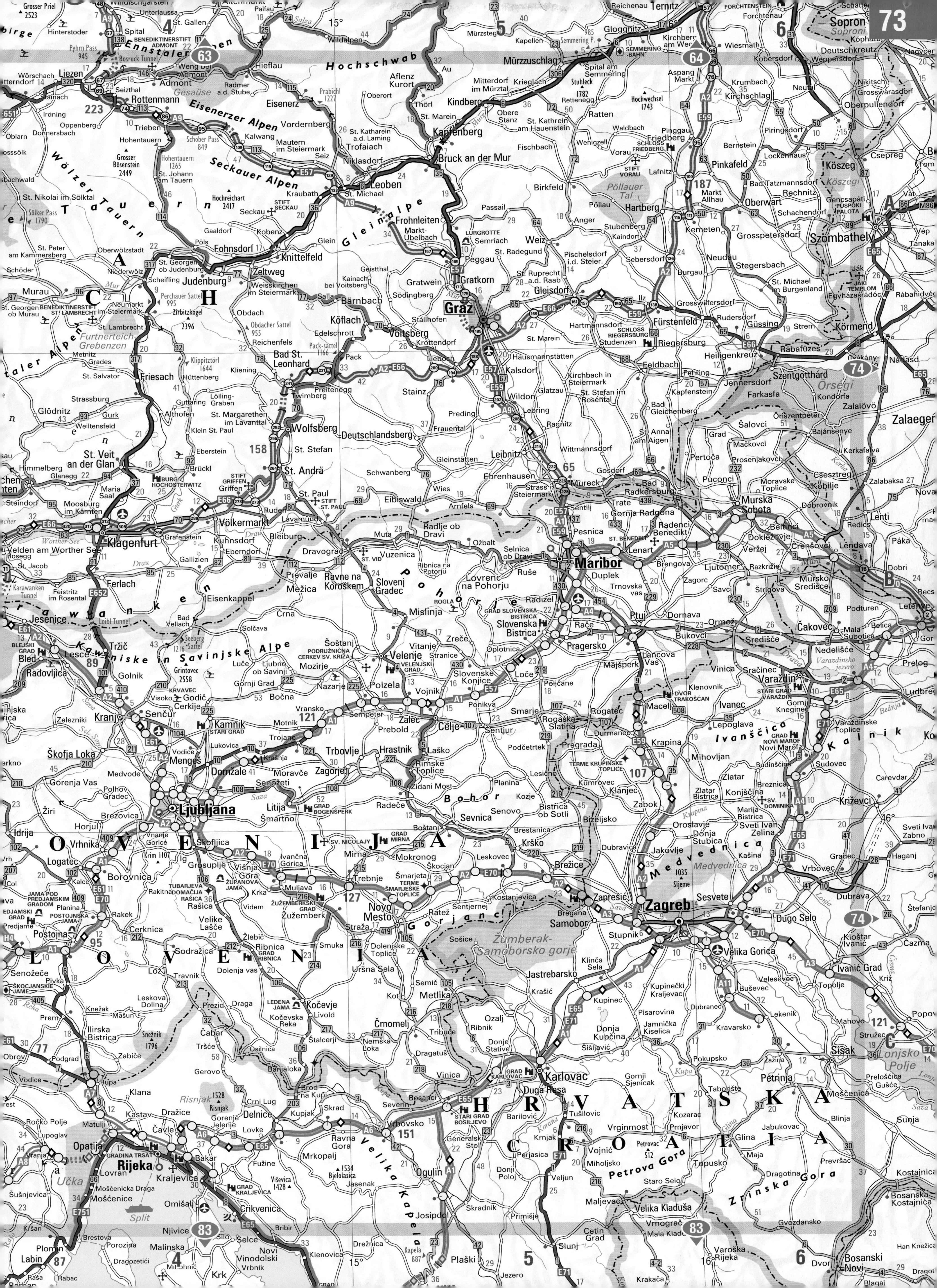
Grosser Priel
Hinterstoder
Spital
St. Gallen
Palfau
Wildalpen
Hochschwab
Mürzsteg
Gloggnitz
Ternitz
Reichenau
Sopron
Forchtenstein
Ennstaler Alpen
Liezen
Admont
Hieflau
Mürzzuschlag
Semmering
Wiesmath
Kirchberg am Wechsel
Rottenmann
Eisenerz
Eisenerzer Alpen
Kindberg
Kapfenberg
Bruck an der Mur
Trofaiach
Leoben
Seckauer Alpen
Friedberg
Pinkafeld
Köszeg
Oberwart
Hartberg
Szombathely
Wölzer Tauern
Gleinalpe
Frohnleiten
Weiz
Fohnsdorf
Knittelfeld
Judenburg
Zeltweg
Murau
Gratkorn
Gleisdorf
Ilz
Fürstenfeld
Graz
Köflach
Voitsberg
Körmend
Bad St. Leonhard
Friesach
Wolfsberg
Deutschlandsberg
Leibnitz
Szentgotthárd
Őrség
Zalaegerszeg
St. Veit an der Glan
St. Andrä
St. Paul
Völkermarkt
Klagenfurt
Villach
Mureck
Bad Radkersburg
Murska Sobota
Gornja Radgona
Lenti
Bleiburg
Dravograd
Ravne na Koroškem
Slovenj Gradec
Pohorje
Maribor
Ptuj
Ljutomer
Lendava
Ferlach
Karawanken
Eisenkappel
Jesenice
Bled
Tržič
Kamniško-Savinjske Alpe
Velenje
Slovenska Bistrica
Čakovec
Varaždin
Kranj
Kamnik
Celje
Krapina
Ivanščica
Kalnik
Škofja Loka
Domžale
Trbovlje
Zagorje
Ljubljana
Litija
Bohor
Sevnica
Krško
Križevci
SLOVENIJA
SLOVENIA
Vrhnika
Logatec
Grosuplje
Novo Mesto
Zaprešić
Medvednica
Zagreb
Sesvete
Dugo Selo
Postojna
Gorjanci
Žumberak-Samoborsko gorje
Samobor
Velika Gorica
Ivanić Grad
Kočevje
Metlika
Črnomelj
Jastrebarsko
Sisak
Karlovac
Opatija
Rijeka
Delnice
Vrbovsko
Ogulin
HRVATSKA
CROATIA
Petrinja
Velika Kapela
Petrova Gora
Zrinska Gora
Crikvenica
Velika Kladuša
Slunj
Krk
Labin
Bosanski Novi
Učka
Risnjak
Snežnik
Lonjsko Polje

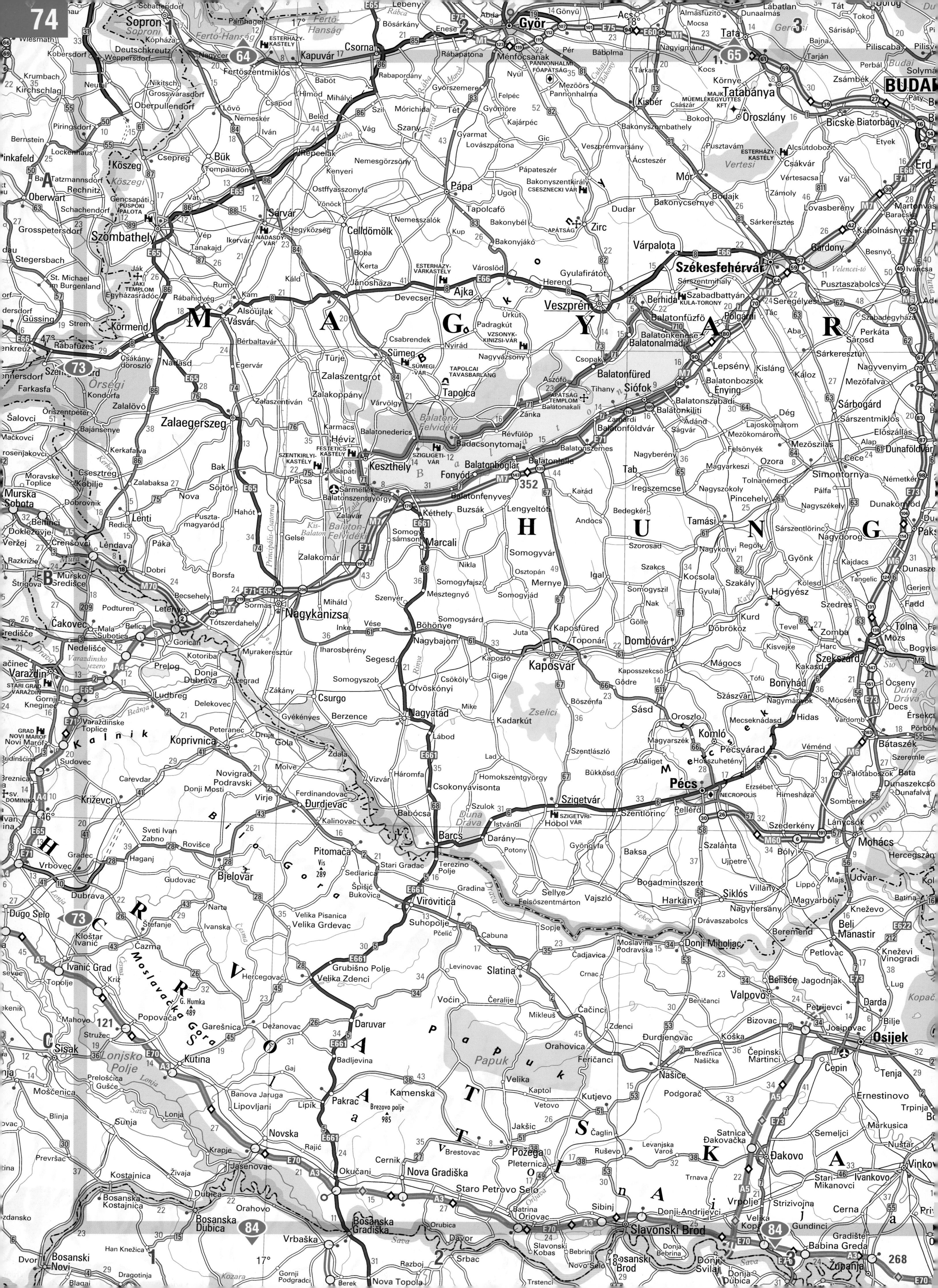

Sopron
Győr
Tata
Tatabánya
Csorna
Kapuvár
Mosonmagyaróvár
Fertő-Hanság
Nagycenk
Fertőszentmiklós
Ménfőcsanak
Pannonhalma
Kisbér
Oroszlány
Bicske
Biatorbágy
BUDAPEST
Kőszeg
Bük
Szombathely
Sárvár
Celldömölk
Pápa
Zirc
Mór
Várpalota
Székesfehérvár
Veszprém
Ajka
Herend
Jánosháza
Vasvár
Körmend
Oberwart
Güssing
Rábafüzes
Őrség
Zalaegerszeg
Sümeg
Tapolca
Keszthely
Hévíz
Balatonfüred
Siófok
Balatonalmádi
Balatonfűzfő
Berhida
Polgárdi
Tihany
Fonyód
Balatonboglár
Balatonlelle
Badacsonytomaj
Zalakaros
Marcali
Nagykanizsa
Letenye
Lenti
Lendava
Murska Sobota
Čakovec
Varaždin
Koprivnica
Križevci
Đurđevac
Bjelovar
Csurgó
Nagyatád
Barcs
Kaposvár
Dombóvár
Tamási
Enying
Simontornya
Sárbogárd
Dunaföldvár
Paks
Tolna
Szekszárd
Bonyhád
Komló
Pécs
Pécsvárad
Mohács
Szigetvár
Siklós
Harkány
Villány
Bóly
Bátaszék
Virovitica
Slatina
Daruvar
Pakrac
Lipik
Kutina
Sisak
Novska
Nova Gradiška
Okučani
Požega
Našice
Osijek
Valpovo
Belišće
Đakovo
Slavonski Brod
Bosanski Brod
Bosanska Gradiška
Bosanska Dubica
Bosanski Novi
Županja
Vinkovci
Beli Manastir
Donji Miholjac
Orahovica
Papuk
Bilo Gora
Moslavačka Gora
Kalnik
Mecsek
Zselic
Bakony
Vértes
Balaton
MAGYARORSZÁG
HUNGARY
HRVATSKA
SLAVONIJA
Dráva
Duna
Sava
Mura
Rába
Sió
64
65
73
84
268

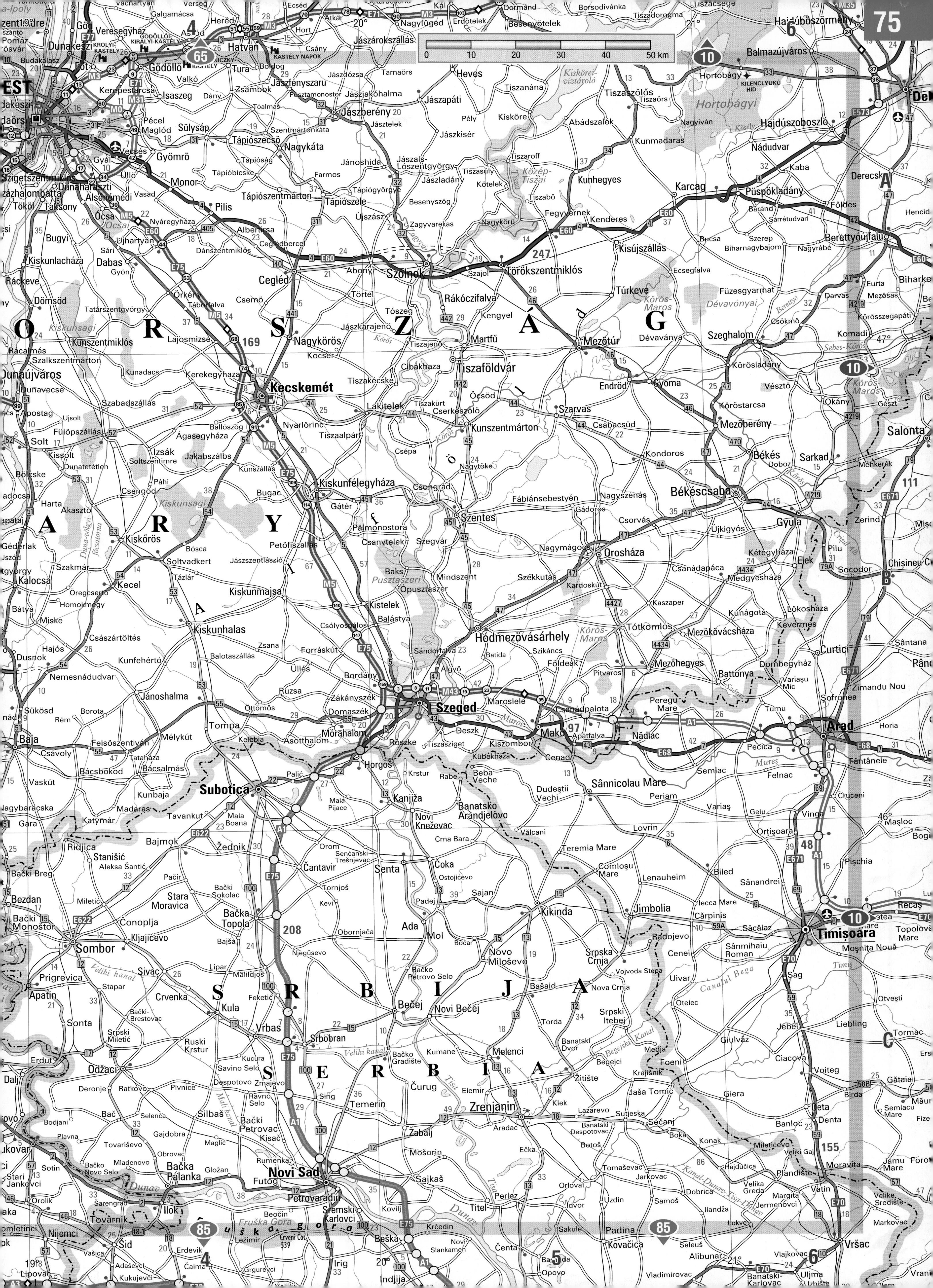
0 10 20 30 40 50 km
ORSZÁG
MAGYARORSZÁG
SRBIJA
SERBIA
Budapest
Gödöllő
Hatvan
Heves
Jászberény
Cegléd
Szolnok
Törökszentmiklós
Karcag
Püspökladány
Hajdúszoboszló
Berettyóújfalu
Kecskemét
Nagykőrös
Tiszaföldvár
Mezőtúr
Szarvas
Gyoma
Kunszentmárton
Kiskunfélegyháza
Csongrád
Szentes
Békés
Békéscsaba
Gyula
Orosháza
Hódmezővásárhely
Szeged
Makó
Kiskunhalas
Kiskőrös
Kalocsa
Baja
Dunaújváros
Salonta
Arad
Timișoara
Subotica
Sombor
Kikinda
Zrenjanin
Novi Sad
Senta
Bečej
Vršac
Kiskunsági
Hortobágyi
Dévaványai
Körös-Maros
Pusztaszeri
Duna
Tisza
Maros
Mureș
Dunav
Fruška Gora
Tisza-tó

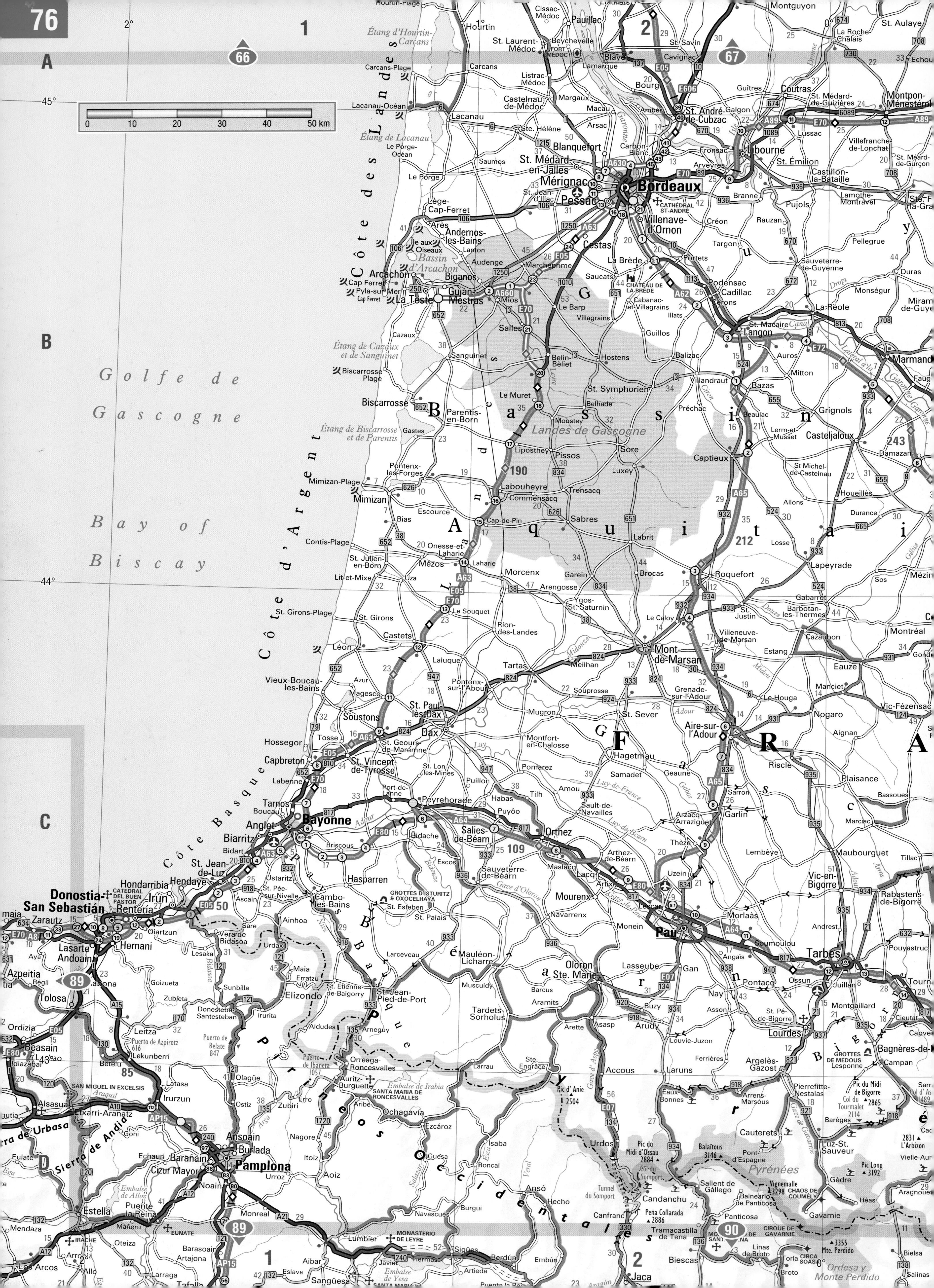

Golfe de Gascogne
Bay of Biscay
Côte des Landes
Côte d'Argent
Côte Basque
Landes
Bassin d'Arcachon
Landes de Gascogne
Aquitaine
Pays Basque
Béarn
Bigorre
Pirineos Occidentales
Pyrénées
Sierra de Urbasa
Sierra de Andia
FRANCE
Étang d'Hourtin-Carcans
Étang de Lacanau
Étang de Cazaux et de Sanguinet
Étang de Biscarrosse et de Parentis
Bordeaux
Mérignac
Pessac
St. Médard-en-Jalles
Blanquefort
Villenave-d'Ornon
Cestas
Libourne
St. Émilion
St. André-de-Cubzac
Pauillac
Blaye
Margaux
Arcachon
La Teste
Gujan-Mestras
Biganos
Andernos-les-Bains
Lège-Cap-Ferret
Lacanau
Lacanau-Océan
Hourtin
Carcans
Langon
Cadillac
Podensac
La Brède
La Réole
Marmande
Bazas
Casteljaloux
Biscarrosse
Parentis-en-Born
Mimizan
Mimizan-Plage
Labouheyre
Pissos
Sabres
Morcenx
Roquefort
Mont-de-Marsan
Tartas
Dax
St. Paul-lès-Dax
Soustons
Hossegor
Capbreton
St. Vincent-de-Tyrosse
Bayonne
Anglet
Biarritz
St. Jean-de-Luz
Hendaye
Hondarribia
Irun
Donostia-San Sebastián
Rentería
Hernani
Tolosa
Cambo-les-Bains
Hasparren
St. Jean-Pied-de-Port
Mauléon-Licharre
Sauveterre-de-Béarn
Salies-de-Béarn
Orthez
Peyrehorade
St. Sever
Hagetmau
Aire-sur-l'Adour
Nogaro
Eauze
Vic-Fézensac
Riscle
Plaisance
Maubourguet
Vic-en-Bigorre
Rabastens-de-Bigorre
Tarbes
Lourdes
Bagnères-de-Bigorre
Argelès-Gazost
Cauterets
Luz-St. Sauveur
Pau
Lescar
Morlaàs
Oloron-Ste. Marie
Navarrenx
Mourenx
Laruns
Arudy
Tardets-Sorholus
Canfranc
Candanchu
Jaca
Biescas
Pamplona
Burlada
Ansoain
Baranain
Noain
Cizur Mayor
Estella
Puente la Reina
Los Arcos
Lumbier
Sangüesa
Aoiz
Elizondo
Leitza
Beasain
Alsasua
Irurzun
Roncal
Ansó
Hecho
Tunnel du Somport
Pic du Midi d'Ossau 2884
Pic du Midi de Bigorre 2865
Col du Tourmalet 2114
Balaïtous 3146
Vignemale 3298
Mte. Perdido 3355
Pic d'Anie 2504
Cirque de Gavarnie
Gavarnie
Ordesa y Monte Perdido
0 10 20 30 40 50 km
45°
44°
43°
2°
A B C D
1 2
66 67 89 90

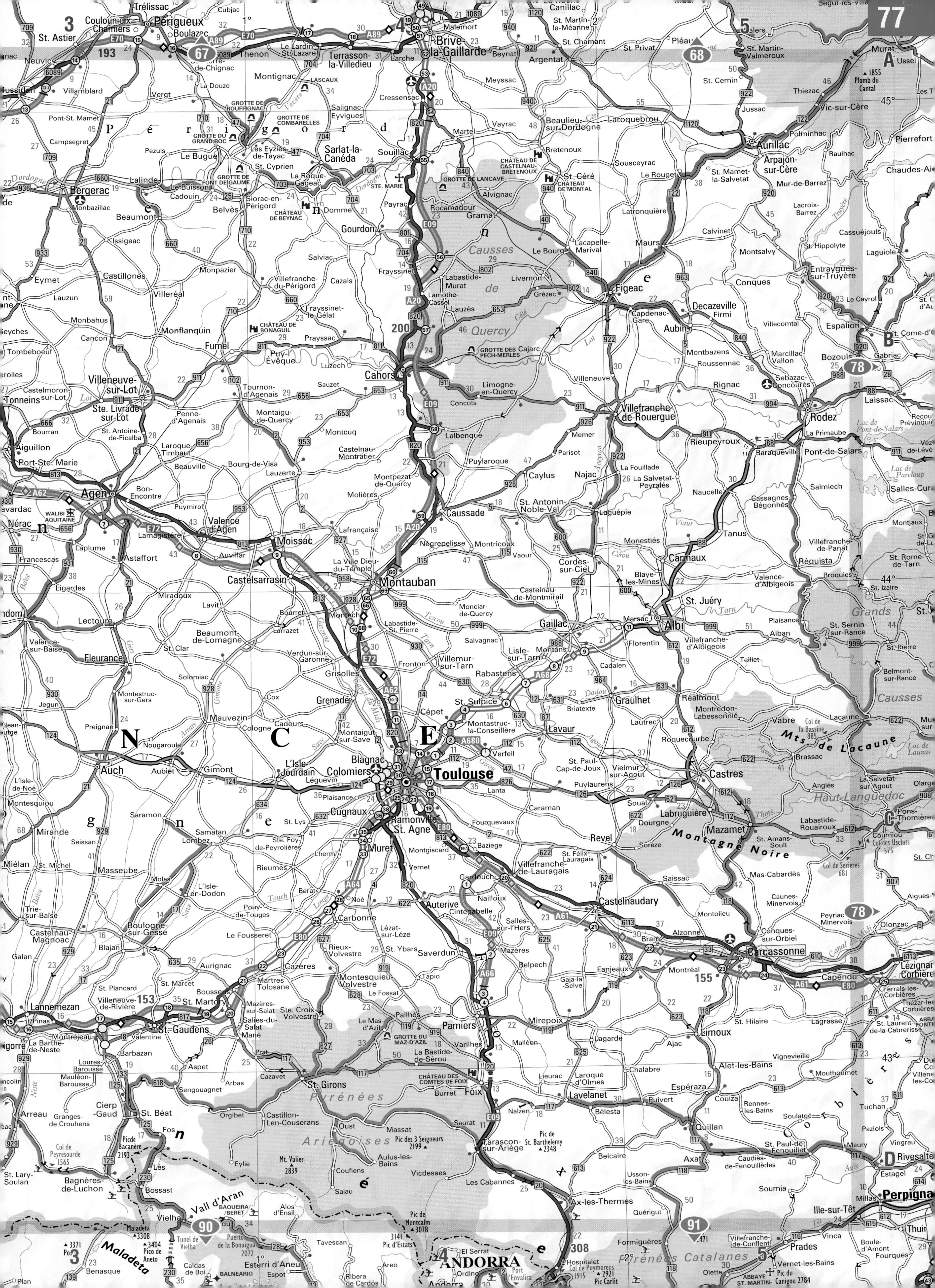
Trélissac
Coulounieix-Chamiers
Périgueux
Boulazac
St. Astier
Neuvic
Thenon
Terrasson-la-Villedieu
Le Lardin-St. Lazare
Brive-la-Gaillarde
Malemort
Larche
Beynat
Argentat
Canillac
St. Martin-la-Méanne
St. Chamant
St. Privat
Pléaux
Salers
St. Martin-Valmeroux
Murat
Ussel
Plomb du Cantal
Thiezac
Vic-sur-Cère
St. Cernin
Jussac
Aurillac
Arpajon-sur-Cère
Polminhac
Pierrefort
Raulhac
Chaudes-Aigues
St. Pierre-de-Chignac
Montignac
LASCAUX
La Douze
Vergt
Villamblard
Pont-St. Mamet
Campsegret
GROTTE DE ROUFFIGNAC
GROTTE DE COMBARELLES
GROTTE DU GRAND ROC
Les Eyzies-de-Tayac
St. Cyprien
Le Bugue
Pezuls
Sarlat-la-Canéda
Salignac-Eyvigues
Cressensac
Souillac
Martel
Vayrac
Meyssac
Beaulieu-sur-Dordogne
Laroquebrou
Bretenoux
CHÂTEAU DE CASTELNAU-BRETENOUX
St. Céré
CHÂTEAU DE MONTAL
Sousceyrac
Le Rouget
St. Mamet-la-Salvetat
Mur-de-Barrez
Lacroix-Barrez
Bergerac
Monbazillac
Lalinde
Le Buisson
Cadouin
GROTTE DE FONT DE GAUME
Siorac-en-Périgord
Belvès
CHÂTEAU DE BEYNAC
La Roque-Gageac
Domme
STE. MARIE
GROTTE DE LANCAVE
Rocamadour
Payrac
Alvignac
Gramat
Gourdon
Beaumont
Issigeac
Castillonès
Monpazier
Villeréal
Eymet
Lauzun
Salviac
Cazals
Villefranche-du-Périgord
Frayssinet
Labastide-Murat
Lamothe-Cassel
Lauzès
Causses
Quercy
Livernon
Grèzec
Le Bourg
Lacapelle-Marival
Latronquière
Maurs
Calvinet
Montsalvy
Cassuéjouls
Laguiole
St. Hippolyte
Entraygues-sur-Truyère
Figeac
Conques
Decazeville
Firmi
Capdenac-Gare
Aubin
Villecomtal
Espalion
Le Cayrol
St. Come-d'Olt
Monbahus
Seyches
Cancon
Tombeboeuf
Monflanquin
CHÂTEAU DE BONAGUIL
Fumel
Frayssinet-le-Gélat
Prayssac
Puy-l'Évêque
Luzech
GROTTE DES PECH-MERLES
Cajarc
Montbazens
Roussennac
Marcillac-Vallon
Bozouls
Gabriac
Villeneuve-sur-Lot
Castelmoron-sur-Lot
Tonneins
Ste. Livrade-sur-Lot
Tournon-d'Agenais
Sauzet
Cahors
Limogne-en-Quercy
Villeneuve
Rignac
Sebazac-Concourès
Laissac
Rodez
Concots
Villefranche-de-Rouergue
Penne-d'Agenais
Montaigu-de-Quercy
Montcuq
Castelnau-Montratier
Lalbenque
Memer
Rieupeyroux
La Primaube
Baraqueville
Pont-de-Salars
Aiguillon
St. Antoine-de-Ficalba
Bourran
Laroque-Timbaut
Port-Ste. Marie
Beauville
Bourg-de-Visa
Lauzerte
Montpezat-de-Quercy
Puylaroque
Parisot
Caylus
Najac
La Fouillade
La Salvetat-Peyralès
Naucelle
Salmiech
Salles-Curan
Agen
Bon-Encontre
Puymirol
Molières
Caussade
St. Antonin-Noble-Val
Laguépie
Cassagnes-Bégonhès
Nérac
WALIBI AQUITAINE
Valence-d'Agen
Lamagistère
Moissac
Lafrançaise
Negrepelisse
Montricoux
Vaour
Cordes-sur-Ciel
Monestiés
Carmaux
Tanus
Villefranche-de-Panat
Réquista
Montjaux
Laplume
Astaffort
Auvillar
Francescas
Castelsarrasin
La Ville Dieu-du-Temple
Montauban
Blaye-les-Mines
Valence-d'Albigeois
St. Rome-de-Tarn
Broquiès
Ligardes
Castelnau-de-Montmirail
St. Juéry
St. Izaire
Miradoux
Lavit
Montech
Monclar-de-Quercy
Marsac
Albi
Lectoure
Bourret
Larrazet
Labastide-St. Pierre
Gaillac
Plaisance
St. Sernin-sur-Rance
Grands
Alban
Beaumont-de-Lomagne
Valence-sur-Baïse
St. Clar
Salvagnac
Florentin
Villefranche-d'Albigeois
Fleurance
Verdun-sur-Garonne
Villemur-sur-Tarn
Lisle-sur-Tarn
Montans
Cadalen
Teillet
Belmont-sur-Rance
Solomiac
Grisolles
Fronton
Rabastens
Graulhet
Réalmont
Montredon-Labessonnié
Lacaune
Causses
Montestruc-sur-Gers
Cox
Grenade
Cépet
St. Sulpice
Briatexte
Jegun
Mauvezin
Cologne
Cadours
Montaigut-sur-Save
Montastruc-la-Conseillère
Lavaur
Lautrec
Roquecourbe
Vabre
Col de la Bassine
Mts. de Lacaune
Brassac
Lac de Lauzas
Preignan
Nougaroulet
Verfeil
St. Paul-Cap-de-Joux
Vielmur-sur-Agout
Castres
Auch
Aubiet
Gimont
L'Isle-Jourdain
Blagnac
Colomiers
Léguevin
Toulouse
Lanta
Puylaurens
La Salvetat-sur-Agout
Anglès
Haut-Languedoc
L'Isle-de-Noé
Montesquiou
Plaisance
Cugnaux
Caraman
Soual
Labruguière
Mazamet
Pons-Thomières
Saramon
Samatan
St. Lys
Ramonville-St. Agne
Fourquevaux
Revel
Dourgne
Sorèze
Montagne Noire
Labastide-Rouairoux
St. Amans-Soult
Courniou
Col des Usclats
Mirande
Seissan
Lombez
Ste. Foy-de-Peyrolières
Muret
Lherm
Montgiscard
Baziège
Villefranche-de-Lauragais
St. Félix-Lauragais
Miélan
St. Michel
Masseube
Rieumes
Vernet
Mas-Cabardès
Col de Serieres
Molas
L'Isle-en-Dodon
Bérat
Noé
Auterive
Gardouch
Nailloux
Cintegabelle
Castelnaudary
Saissac
Caunes-Minervois
Aigues-Vives
Trie-sur-Baïse
Pouy-de-Touges
Carbonne
Lézat-sur-Lèze
Salles-sur-l'Hers
Montolieu
Peyriac-Minervois
Olonzac
Boulogne-sur-Gesse
Castelnau-Magnoac
Le Fousseret
Rieux-Volvestre
St. Ybars
Saverdun
Mazères
Belpech
Bram
Alzonne
Conques-sur-Orbiel
Carcassonne
Lézignan-Corbières
Galan
Blajan
Aurignac
Cazères
Montesquieu-Volvestre
Tapio
Gaja-la-Selve
Fanjeaux
Montréal
Capendu
Ferrals-les-Corbières
Thézan-les-Corbières
St. Plancard
St. Marcet
Boussens
Martres-Tolosane
Le Fossat
Lagrasse
St. Laurent-de-la-Cabrerisse
Lannemezan
Villeneuve-de-Rivière
St. Martory
Mazères-sur-Salat
Salies-du-Salat
Mane
Ste. Croix-Volvestre
Pailhès
Le Mas-d'Azil
GROTTE DU MAZ-D'AZIL
Pamiers
Varilhes
Mirepoix
Limoux
St. Hilaire
Pinas
Montréjeau
St.-Gaudens
Valentine
La Barthe-de-Neste
Barbazan
Loures-Barousse
Mauléon-Barousse
Aspet
Arbas
Prat
Cazavet
St. Girons
La Bastide-de-Sérou
CHÂTEAU DES COMTES DE FOIX
Foix
Burret
Malléon
Lagarde
Lieurac
Laroque-d'Olmes
Lavelanet
Chalabre
Ajac
Alet-les-Bains
Vignevieille
Mouthoumet
Espéraza
Couiza
Rennes-les-Bains
Puivert
Bélesta
Arreau
Granges-de Crouhens
Cierp-Gaud
St. Béat
Sengouagnet
Orgibet
Castillon-Len-Couserans
Pyrénées
Ariégoises
Oust
Massat
Saurat
Nalzen
Pic de St. Barthelemy
Pic des 3 Seigneurs
Tarascon-sur-Ariège
Quillan
Soulatgé
Tuchan
Paziols
Col de Peyresourde
St. Lary-Soulan
Bagnères-de-Luchon
Picde Bacanère
Fos
Eylie
Mt. Valier
Couflens
Aulus-les-Bains
Vicdessos
Belcaire
Axat
Caudiès-de-Fenouillèdes
St. Paul-de-Fenouillet
Maury
Vingrau
Rivesaltes
Estagel
Bossast
Les
Les Cabannes
Usson-les-Bains
Sournia
Perpignan
Vall d'Aran
BAQUEIRA/BERET
Vielha
Tunel de Vielha
Alos d'Ensil
Pic de Montcalm
Ax-les-Thermes
Quérigut
Ille-sur-Têt
Millas
Thuir
Maladeta
Pico de Aneto
Puerto de la Bonaigua
Salau
Tavescan
Pic d'Estats
El Serrat
ANDORRA
Port d'Envalira
Formiguères
Pyrénées Catalanes
Villefranche-de-Conflent
Prades
Vinca
Boule-d'Amont
Fourques
Benasque
Caldas de Boi
BALNEARIO
Esterri d'Aneu
Espot
Areo
Ribera de Cardós
Ordino
Andorra
L'Hospitalet
Col de Puymorens
Pic Carlit
Olette
ABBAYE ST. MARTIN
Pic du Canigou
Vernet-les-Bains
Plan

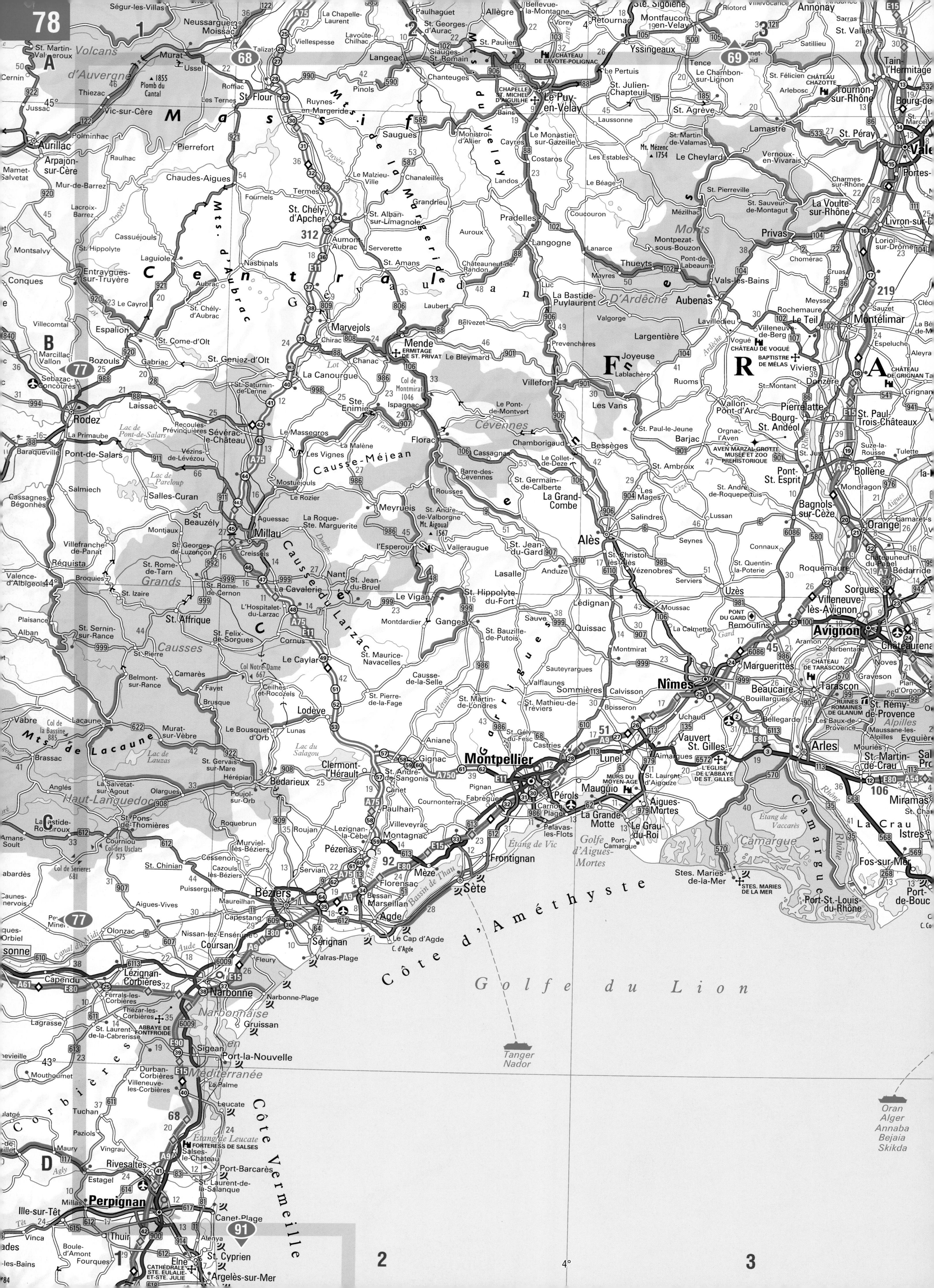

Massif Central
Mts du Velay
Mts de la Margeride
Mts. d'Aubrac
Monts d'Ardèche
Causse-Méjean
Causse du Larzac
Cévennes
Garrigues
Grands Causses
Mts de Lacaune
Haut-Languedoc
Corbières
Camargue
Volcans d'Auvergne
FRANCE
Côte d'Améthyste
Golfe du Lion
Côte Vermeille
Golfe d'Aigues-Mortes
Étang de Vaccarès
Étang de Leucate
Narbonnaise en Méditerranée
Alpilles
Tanger
Nador
Oran
Alger
Annaba
Bejaia
Skikda
Aurillac
Murat
St. Flour
Le Puy-en-Velay
Yssingeaux
Annonay
Tournon-sur-Rhône
Valence
Privas
Aubenas
Montélimar
Mende
Marvejols
St. Chély-d'Apcher
Langogne
Millau
Rodez
Espalion
Sévérac-le-Château
St. Affrique
Lodève
Florac
Le Vigan
Ganges
Alès
Uzès
Orange
Avignon
Nîmes
Arles
Tarascon
Beaucaire
Montpellier
Lunel
Aigues-Mortes
Sète
Agde
Pézenas
Béziers
Narbonne
Perpignan
Rivesaltes
Argelès-sur-Mer
St. Cyprien
Elne
Port-la-Nouvelle
Gruissan
Bédarieux
Clermont-l'Hérault
Bagnols-sur-Cèze
Pont-St. Esprit
Bollène
Carpentras
Istres
Fos-sur-Mer
Port-St.-Louis-du-Rhône
Stes. Maries-de-la-Mer
Miramas
St. Rémy-de-Provence
La Grande Motte
Le Grau-du-Roi
Frontignan
Mèze
Palavas-les-Flots
Villeneuve-lès-Avignon
Sorgues
Pont-St. Esprit
Les Vans
Largentière
Le Cheylard
Lamastre
La Voulte-sur-Rhône
Pierrelatte
Viviers
Le Teil
Mt. Aigoual 1567
Mt. Mézenc 1754
Plomb du Cantal 1855
Château de Vogüé
Château de Grignan
Château de Tarascon
Pont du Gard
Aven Marzal-Grotte Musée et Zoo Préhistorique
Forteresse de Salses
Abbaye de Fontfroide
Cathédrale Ste. Eulalie-et-Ste. Julie
L'Église de l'Abbaye de St. Gilles
Ruines romaines de Glanum
Murs du Moyen-Age
Ermitage de St. Privat
Chapelle St. Michel d'Aiguilhe
Château de Lavoûte-Polignac
A75
A9
A7
A54
A61
A750
E11
E15
E80
68
69
77
91
1
2
3
A
B
C
D
45°
44°
43°
4°

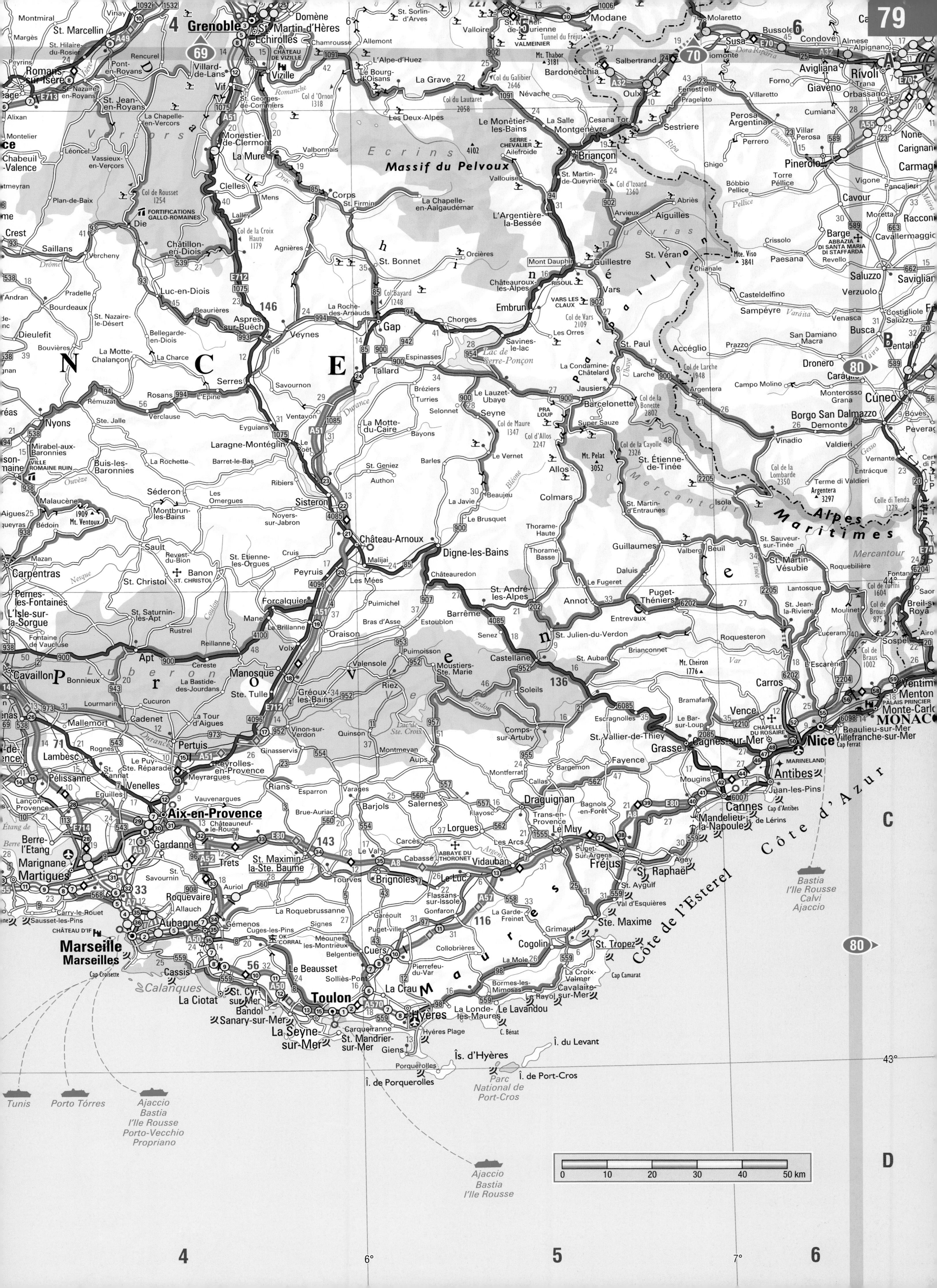

Grenoble
St. Martin-d'Hères
Échirolles
Domène
Vizille
Romans-sur-Isère
St. Marcellin
Vercors
Massif du Pelvoux
Ecrins
Briançon
Modane
Bardonècchia
Susa
Avigliana
Rívoli
Pinerolo
Saluzzo
Cuneo
Borgo San Dalmazzo
Dronero
Barcelonnette
Embrun
Gap
Guillestre
Queyras
Mt. Viso 3841
Lac de Serre-Ponçon
Die
Nyons
Sisteron
Château-Arnoux
Digne-les-Bains
Forcalquier
Manosque
Apt
Carpentras
Cavaillon
L'Isle-sur-la-Sorgue
Luberon
Mt. Ventoux 1909
Pertuis
Aix-en-Provence
Marseille
Marseilles
Aubagne
Cassis
La Ciotat
Bandol
Toulon
La Seyne-sur-Mer
Hyères
Îs. d'Hyères
Î. de Porquerolles
Î. de Port-Cros
Î. du Levant
Parc National de Port-Cros
Brignoles
Draguignan
Fréjus
St. Raphaël
Ste. Maxime
St. Tropez
Cannes
Antibes
Grasse
Cagnes-sur-Mer
Nice
Villefranche-sur-Mer
Beaulieu-sur-Mer
Menton
MONACO
Monte-Carlo
Alpes Maritimes
Mercantour
Côte d'Azur
Côte de l'Esterel
Castellane
Moustiers-Ste. Marie
Riez
Barrême
Colmars
Allos
Entrevaux
Puget-Théniers
Martigues
Marignane
Berre-l'Étang
Gardanne
Trets
St. Maximin-la-Ste. Baume
Vidauban
Le Muy
Lorgues
Salernes
Barjols
Cuers
Le Lavandou
Bormes-les-Mimosas
Cogolin
Grimaud
Calanques
Tunis
Porto Tórres
Ajaccio
Bastia
l'Ile Rousse
Porto-Vecchio
Propriano
Calvi
PROVENCE
0 10 20 30 40 50 km
4
5
6
6°
7°
43°
C
D
80

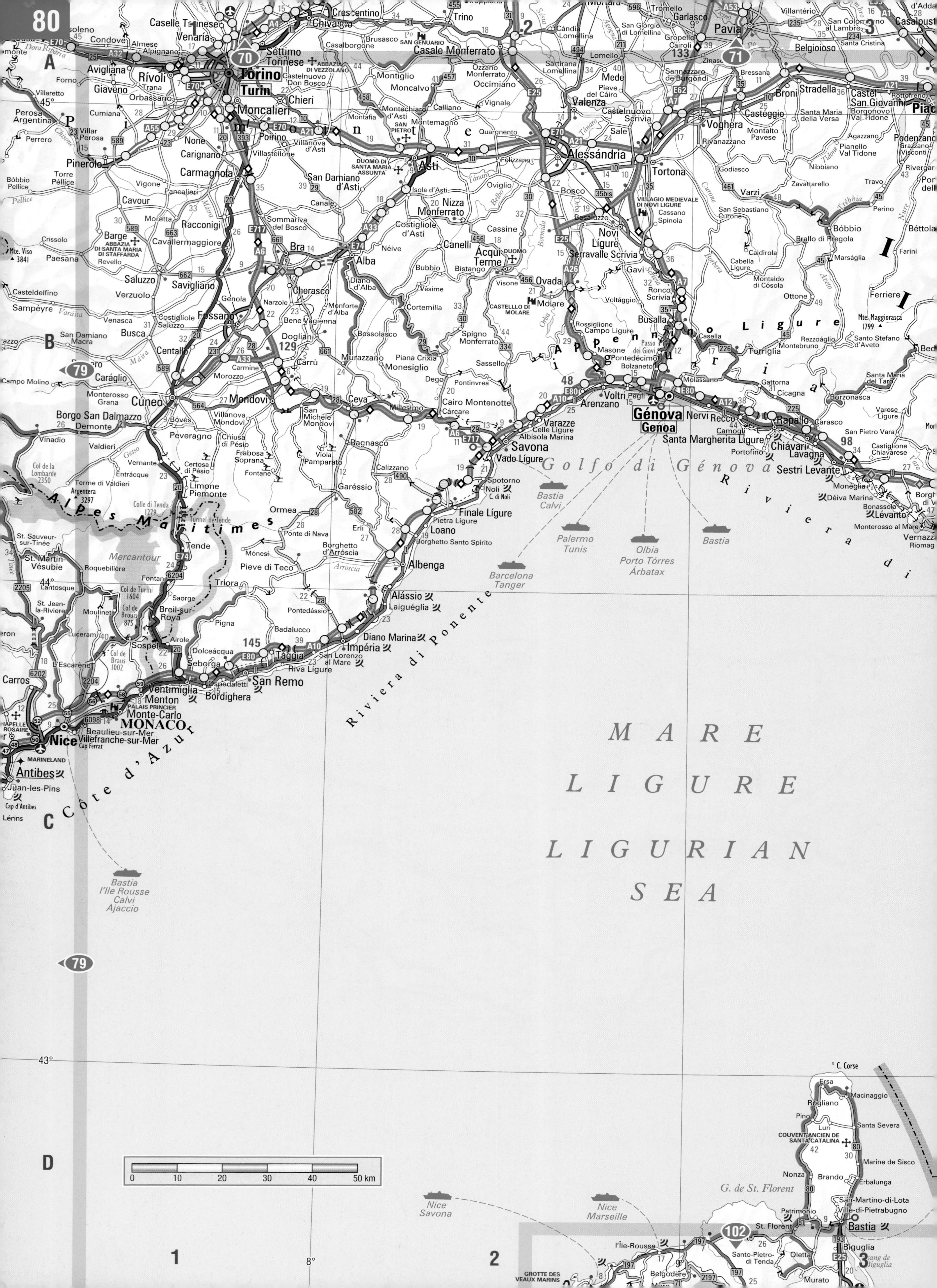
Torino
Turin
Moncalieri
Chieri
Rívoli
Pinerolo
Carmagnola
Asti
Alessándria
Tortona
Valenza
Casale Monferrato
Pavia
Voghera
Novi Lígure
Ovada
Acqui Terme
Alba
Bra
Cuneo
Mondovì
Saluzzo
Savigliano
Fossano
Ceva
Savona
Varazze
Génova
Genoa
Rapallo
Chiavari
Sestri Levante
Albenga
Alássio
Impéria
San Remo
Ventimiglia
Bordighera
Menton
Monte-Carlo
MONACO
Nice
Antibes
Golfo di Génova
Riviera di Ponente
Riviera di Levante
Côte d'Azur
Alpes Maritimes
Appennino Ligure
MARE LIGURE
LIGURIAN SEA
Bastia
Calvi
Palermo
Tunis
Olbia
Porto Tórres
Árbatax
Barcelona
Tanger
Bastia
l'Ile Rousse
Calvi
Ajaccio
Nice
Savona
Nice
Marseille
St. Florent
l'Île-Rousse
G. de St. Florent
C. Corse
0 10 20 30 40 50 km
A
B
C
D
1
2
3
79
70
71
102

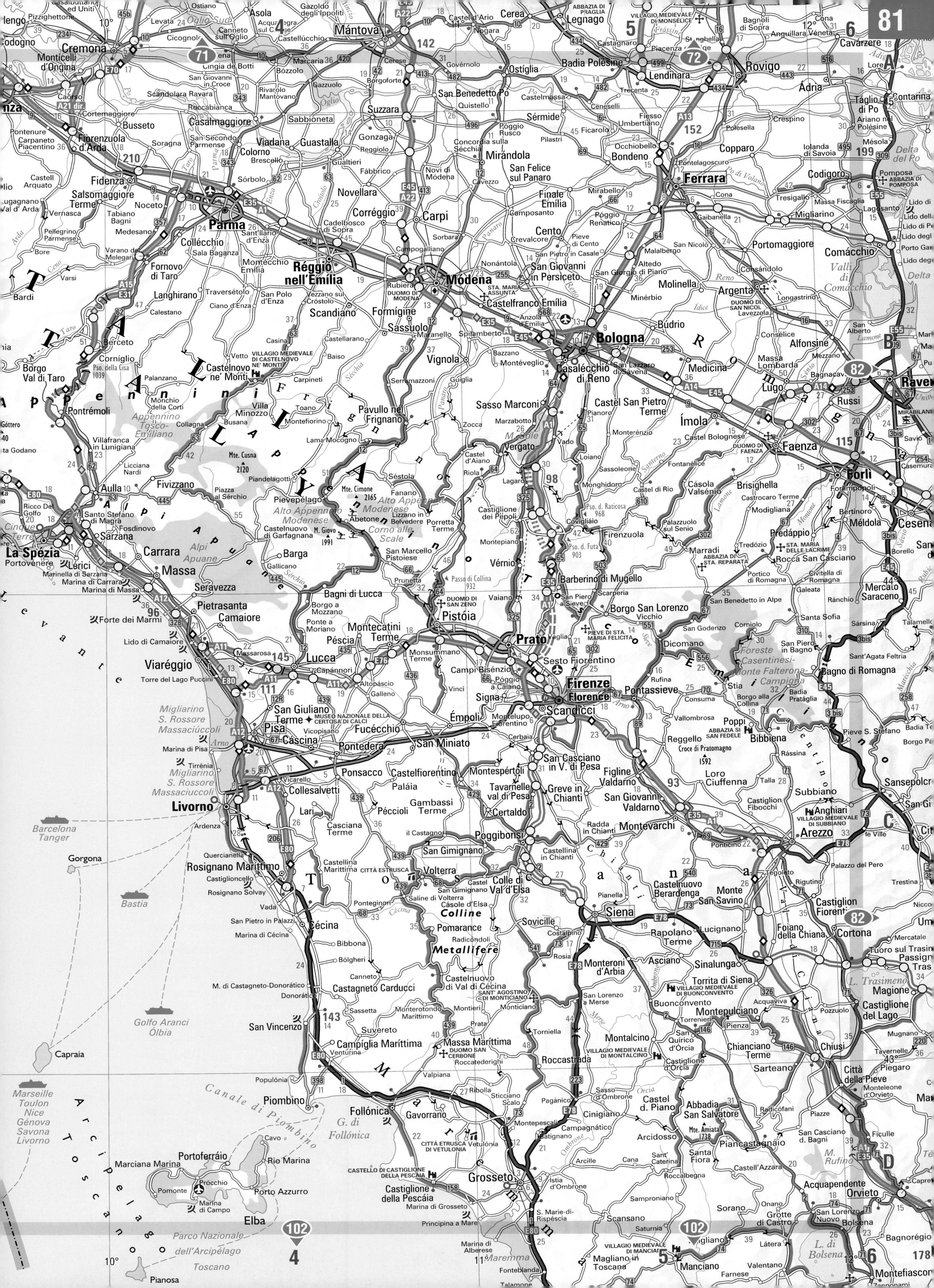

Cremona
Mántova
Legnago
Badia Polésine
Lendinara
Rovigo
Ádria
Cavárzere
Ostíglia
Suzzara
San Benedetto Po
Casalmaggiore
Sabbioneta
Busseto
Fiorenzuola d'Arda
Viadana
Guastalla
Gonzaga
Colorno
Mirándola
Concordia sulla Sécchia
San Felice sul Panaro
Bondeno
Copparo
Ferrara
Codigoro
Pompósa
Fidenza
Salsomaggiore Terme
Parma
Novellara
Corréggio
Carpi
Finale Emília
Cento
Comácchio
Portomaggiore
Réggio nell'Emília
Modena
San Giovanni in Persiceto
Molinella
Argenta
Castelfranco Emília
Scandiano
Formígine
Sassuolo
Vignola
Bologna
Budrio
Medicina
Lugo
Ravenna
Casalécchio di Reno
Castel San Pietro Terme
Ímola
Faenza
Forlì
Cesena
Berceto
Borgo Val di Taro
Pontrémoli
Castelnovo ne' Monti
Pavullo nel Frignano
Sasso Marconi
Vergato
Aulla
Fivizzano
Pievepélago
Abetone
Mte. Cimone 2165
Mte. Cusna 2120
Porretta Terme
Castiglione dei Pépoli
Firenzuola
Marradi
La Spézia
Carrara
Massa
Sarzana
Lérici
Portovénere
Castelnuovo di Garfagnana
Barga
Bagni di Lucca
Pietrasanta
Camaiore
Viaréggio
Lucca
Montecatini Terme
Péscia
Pistóia
Prato
Sesto Fiorentino
Firenze Florence
Scandicci
Pontassieve
Borgo San Lorenzo
Barberino di Mugello
Vicchio
Dicomano
Bibbiena
Poppi
Arezzo
Pisa
Cascina
Pontedera
Fucécchio
Émpoli
San Miniato
Livorno
Collesalvetti
Rosignano Maríttimo
Cécina
Volterra
San Gimignano
Poggibonsi
Colle di Val d'Elsa
Siena
Montevarchi
San Giovanni Valdarno
Figline Valdarno
Greve in Chianti
San Casciano in V. di Pesa
Castelnuovo Berardenga
Sinalunga
Montepulciano
Chianciano Terme
Chiusi
Cortona
Castiglion Fiorentino
Castiglione del Lago
L. Trasimeno
Montalcino
Buonconvento
Piombino
Follónica
Massa Maríttima
Campíglia Maríttima
San Vincenzo
Castagneto Carducci
Grosseto
Castiglione della Pescáia
Portoferráio
Elba
Marciana Marina
Porto Azzurro
Capraia
Gorgona
Pianosa
Orbetello
Orvieto
Bolsena
L. di Bolsena
Pitigliano
Manciano
Magliano in Toscana
Scansano
Roccastrada
Abbadia San Salvatore
Piancastagnáio
Castel d. Piano
Mar Ligure
Alpi Apuane
Appennino Tosco-Emiliano
Colline Metallifere
Arcipelago Toscano
Canale di Piombino
G. di Follónica
Golfo Aranci Ólbia
Bastia
Barcelona Tanger
Marseille Toulon Nice Génova Savona Livorno
Parco Nazionale dell'Arcipélago Toscano
Levante
Toscana
Emília-Romagna
Maremma
71
72
82
102
4
5
6
A
B
C
D
10°
11°
12°

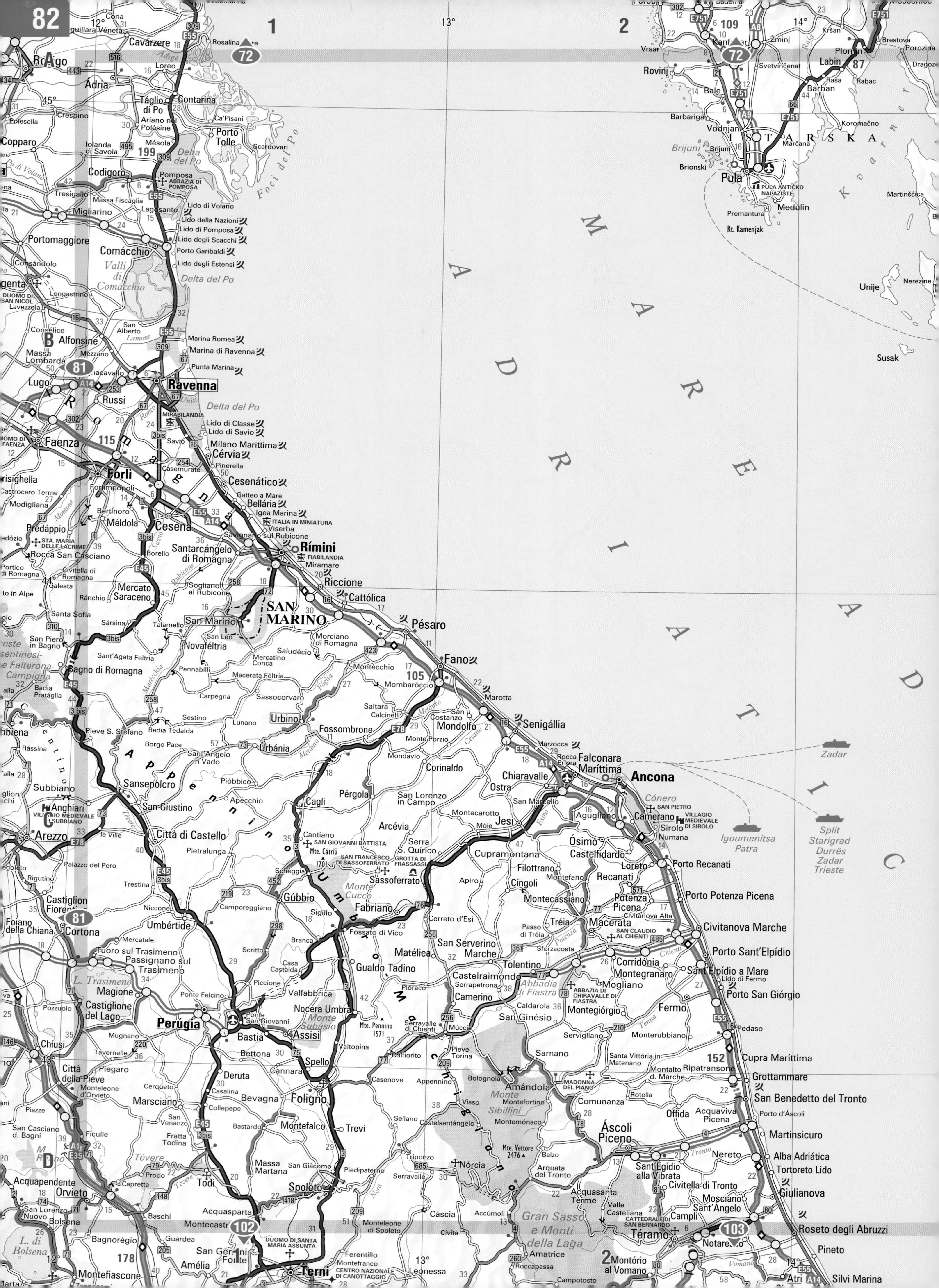
1
2
12°
13°
14°
A
B
C
D
72
81
102
103
M A R E
A D R I A T I C O
A D R I A T I C
I S T A R S K A
Kvarner
Cavàrzere
Loreo
Àdria
Contarina
Táglio di Po
Ariano nel Polésine
Porto Tolle
Scardovari
Ca'Pisani
Mésola
Delta del Po
Foci del Po
Copparo
Iolanda di Savoia
Codigoro
Pomposa
ABBAZIA DI POMPOSA
Tresigallo
Massa Fiscáglia
Migliarino
Lagosanto
Lido di Volano
Lido delle Nazioni
Lido di Pomposa
Lido degli Scacchi
Porto Garibaldi
Lido degli Estensi
Portomaggiore
Comácchio
Valli di Comácchio
Consándolo
Longastrino
DUOMO DI SAN NICOL
Lavezzola
Conselice
Alfonsine
San Alberto
Marina Romea
Marina di Ravenna
Punta Marina
Massa Lombarda
Mezzano
Lugo
Bagnacavallo
Ravenna
Russi
Faenza
MIRABILANDIA
Lido di Classe
Lido di Savio
Savio
Milano Marittima
Cérvia
Pinerella
Forlì
Forlimpopoli
Cesenático
Gatteo a Mare
Bellária
Igea Marina
ITALIA IN MINIATURA
Viserba
Brisighella
Castrocaro Terme
Modigliana
Bertinoro
Méldola
Cesena
Predáppio
STA. MARIA DELLE LACRIME
Rocca San Casciano
Civitella di Romagna
Galeata
Savignano sul Rubicone
Santarcángelo di Romagna
Borello
Rímini
FIABILANDIA
Miramare
Riccione
Cattólica
Mercato Saraceno
Ránchio
Sogliano al Rubicone
Santa Sofia
Sársina
Talamello
San Marino
SAN MARINO
San Leo
Novafeltria
Pésaro
Morciano di Romagna
Saludécio
Mercatino Conca
San Piero in Bagno
Sant'Agata Feltria
Bagno di Romagna
Badia Prataglia
Pennabilli
Macerata Féltria
Carpegna
Sassocorvaro
Montécchio
Mombaróccio
Fano
Marotta
Saltara
Calcinelli
Urbino
Fossombrone
Lunano
Sestino
Badia Tedalda
Pieve S. Stefano
Borgo Pace
Sant'Angelo in Vado
Urbánia
San Costanzo
Mondolfo
Senigállia
Monte Porzio
Mondavio
Corinaldo
Marzocca
Rocca Priora
Falconara Maríttima
Ancona
Chiaravalle
Ostra
Zadar
Cónero
SAN PIETRO
VILLAGIO MEDIEVALE DI SIROLO
Camerano
Sirolo
Numana
Igoumenitsa
Patra
Split
Starigrad
Durrës
Zadar
Trieste
Bibbiena
Rássina
Subbiano
Anghiari
Sansepolcro
San Giustino
Appennino Umbro-Marchigiano
Pióbbico
Apécchio
Cagli
Pérgola
San Lorenzo in Campo
Arcévia
Montecarotto
Móie
Jesi
San Marcello
Agugliano
Arezzo
Città di Castello
Pietralunga
Cantiano
SAN GIOVANNI BATTISTA
Mte. Cátria
SAN FRANCESCO DI SASSOFERRATO
GROTTA DI FRASSASSI
Sassoferrato
Serra S. Quírico
Cupramontana
Ósimo
Castelfidardo
Loreto
Porto Recanati
Palazzo del Pero
Rigutino
Castiglion Fiorentino
Trestina
Scheggia
Gúbbio
Monte Cucco
Apiro
Filottrano
Cíngoli
Montefano
Recanati
Montecassiano
Potenza Picena
Porto Potenza Picena
Foiano della Chiana
Cortona
Niccone
Umbértide
Camporeggiano
Sigillo
Fabriano
Cerreto d'Esi
Fossato di Vico
Passo di Tréia
Tréia
Macerata
Civitanova Alta
Civitanova Marche
SAN CLAUDIO AL CHIENTI
Mercatale
Tuoro sul Trasimeno
Passignano sul Trasimeno
Scritto
Branca
Matélica
San Severino Marche
Sforzacosta
Porto Sant'Elpídio
L. Trasimeno
Magione
Casa Castalda
Gualdo Tadino
Tolentino
Corridónia
Montegranaro
Sant'Elpídio a Mare
Lido di Fermo
Castiglione del Lago
Ponte Felcino
Piccione
Valfabbrica
Castelraimondo
Serrapetrona
Abbadia di Fiastra
ABBAZIA DI CHIARAVALLE DI FIASTRA
Mogliano
Porto San Giórgio
Perúgia
Ponte San Giovanni
Nocera Umbra
Monte Subásio
Pióraco
Camerino
Caldarola
San Ginésio
Montegiórgio
Fermo
Chiusi
Mugnano
Bastia
Assisi
Mte. Pennino
Serravalle di Chienti
Múccia
Servigliano
Monterubbiano
Pedaso
Tavernelle
Bettona
Spello
Valtopina
Colfiorito
Pieve Torina
Sarnano
Santa Vittória in Matenano
Montalto d. Marche
Ripatransone
Cupra Maríttima
Città della Pieve
Piegaro
Monteleone d'Orvieto
Deruta
Cannara
Casenove
Appennino
Bolognola
Amándola
MADONNA DEL PIANO
Grottammare
San Benedetto del Tronto
Porto d'Áscoli
Cerqueto
Marsciano
Casalina
Bevagna
Foligno
Visso
Monte Sibillini
Montefortino
Comunanza
Rotella
Offida
Acquaviva Picena
Piazze
San Venanzo
Collepepe
Montefalco
Trevi
Sellano
Castelsantángelo
Montemónaco
Áscoli Piceno
Martinsicuro
San Casciano d. Bagni
Fículle
Fratta Todina
Bastardo
Mte. Vettore
Alba Adriática
Tortoreto Lido
Monte Rufeno
Massa Martana
San Giácomo
Piediluco
Tripónzo
Nórcia
Balzo
Sant'Egídio alla Vibrata
Nereto
Acquapendente
Orvieto
Capretta
Prodo
Todi
Spoleto
Serravalle
Arquata del Tronto
Civitella di Tronto
Giulianova
San Lorenzo Nuovo
Bolsena
Acquasparta
Baschi
Montecastrilli
Cáscia
Accúmoli
Acquasanta Terme
Valle Castellana
Mosciano Sant'Angelo
Campli
L. di Bolsena
Bagnorégio
Guardea
DUOMO DI SANTA MARIA ASSUNTA
Monteleone di Spoleto
Cívita
Gran Sasso e Monti della Laga
CATTEDRALE DI SAN BERNARDO
Téramo
Notaresco
Roseto degli Abruzzi
Montefiascone
Amélia
San Gemini Fonte
Terni
Ferentillo
Montefranco
CENTRO NAZIONALE DI CANOTTAGGIO
Leonessa
Amatrice
Roccapassa
Campotosto
Montório al Vomano
Pineto
Atri
Silvi Marina
Rovinj
Vrsar
Kanfanar
Žminj
Svetvinčenat
Kršan
Plomin
Brestova
Porozina
Labin
Rabac
Rasa
Barban
Bale
Barbariga
Vodnjan
Koromačno
Brijuni
Brionski
Marčana
Pula
PULA ANTIČKO NALAZIŠTE
Medulin
Premantura
Rt. Kamenjak
Martinšćica
Unije
Nerezine
Susak
Rosolina Mare
Rovigo
Polesella
Crespino
45°

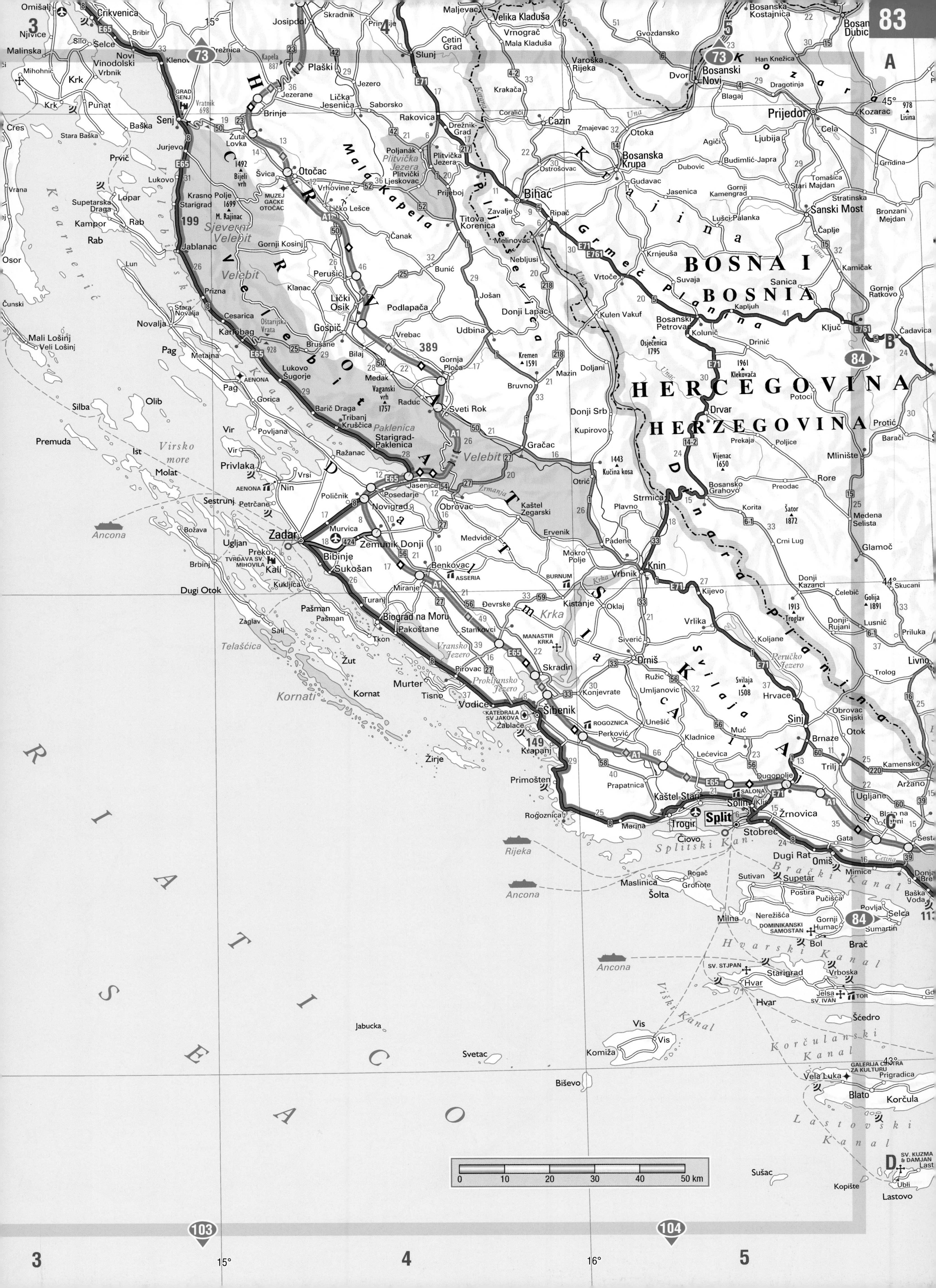

HRVATSKA
BOSNA I HERCEGOVINA
BOSNIA HERZEGOVINA
MARE ADRIATICO
Velebit
Sjeverni Velebit
Mala Kapela
Plješevica
Grmeč Planina
Krajina
Dinara planina
Svilaja
Kvarnerić
Virsko more
Splitski Kan.
Brački Kanal
Hvarski Kanal
Viški Kanal
Korčulanski Kanal
Lastovski Kanal
Kornati
Telašćica
Plitvička Jezera
Paklenica
Vransko Jezero
Prokljansko Jezero
Peručko Jezero
Krka
Zrmanja
Una
Unac
Sana
Cetina
Crikvenica
Omišalj
Njivice
Šilo
Šelce
Malinska
Novi Vinodolski
Bribir
Mihohnić
Krk
Vrbnik
Punat
Baška
Stara Baška
Cres
Senj
Jurjevo
Žuta Lovka
Brinje
Jezerane
Josipdol
Plaški
Skradnik
Slunj
Cetin Grad
Maljevac
Velika Kladuša
Vrnograč
Mala Kladuša
Gvozdansko
Bosanska Kostajnica
Bosanski Dubica
Varoška Rijeka
Dvor
Bosanski Novi
Han Knežica
Kozara
Dragotinja
Blagaj
Prijedor
Kozarac
Cela
Ljubija
Agići
Budimlić-Japra
Otoka
Zmajevac
Cazin
Coralići
Krakača
Rakovica
Drežnik-Grad
Poljanak
Plitvička Jezera
Plitvički Ljeskovac
Otočac
Švica
Vrhovine
Ličko Lešce
Lička Jesenica
Saborsko
Jezero
Lukovo
Prvič
Krasno Polje
Starigrad
Lopar
Rab
Supetarska Draga
Kampor
Vrana
Osor
Lun
Jablanac
Gornji Kosinj
Perušić
Klanac
Lički Osik
Gospić
Podlapača
Bunić
Udbina
Vrebac
Gornja Ploča
Medak
Bilaj
Brušane
Karlobag
Cesarica
Prizna
Stara Novalja
Novalja
Pag
Metajna
Mali Lošinj
Veli Lošinj
Čunski
Lukovo Šugorje
Barič Draga
Tribanj Kruščica
Starigrad-Paklenica
Sveti Rok
Raduč
Gračac
Titova Korenica
Prijeboj
Melinovac
Zavalje
Bihać
Ripač
Ostrošovac
Bosanska Krupa
Gudavac
Jasenica
Dubovic
Gornji Kamengrad
Stari Majdan
Tomašica
Stratinska
Sanski Most
Lušci Palanka
Bronzani Mejdan
Čaplje
Kamičak
Sanica
Gornje Ratkovo
Ključ
Čadavica
Krnjeuša
Suvaja
Vrtoče
Nebljusi
Donji Lapac
Kulen Vakuf
Bosanski Petrovac
Kolunić
Kapljuh
Drinić
Jošan
Mazin
Doljani
Bruvno
Donji Srb
Kupirovo
Drvar
Potoci
Prekaja
Poljice
Protić
Barači
Mliništė
Rore
Preodac
Bosansko Grahovo
Otrić
Strmica
Plavno
Korita
Medena Selista
Crni Lug
Glamoč
Padene
Knin
Vrbnik
Kistanje
Oklaj
Kijevo
Donji Kazanci
Čelebić
Skucani
Vrlika
Koljane
Donji Rujani
Lusnić
Priluka
Livno
Trolog
Siverić
Drniš
Ružić
Umljanović
Hrvace
Sinj
Obrovac Sinjski
Otok
Brnaze
Trilj
Kamensko
Aržano
Ugljane
Žrnovica
Dugopolje
Mokro Polje
Ervenik
Kaštel Žegarski
Obrovac
Medviđe
Benkovac
Jasenice
Posedarje
Novigrad
Poličnik
Nin
Vrsi
Ražanac
Povljana
Vir
Privlaka
Olib
Silba
Premuda
Ist
Molat
Sestrunj
Petrčane
Zadar
Božava
Ugljan
Preko
Kali
Brbinj
Dugi Otok
Kukljica
Bibinje
Sukošan
Murvica
Zemunik Donji
Miranje
Turanj
Pašman
Biograd na Moru
Pakoštane
Tkon
Zaglav
Sali
Žut
Kornat
Murter
Tisno
Pirovac
Stankovci
Đevrske
Skradin
Vodice
Šibenik
Zablaće
Krapanj
Konjevrate
Unešić
Perković
Kladnice
Lećevica
Muć
Primošten
Rogoznica
Prapatnica
Marina
Kaštel Stari
Trogir
Split
Solin
Klis
Stobreč
Čiovo
Dugi Rat
Omiš
Gata
Mimice
Žirje
Maslinica
Šolta
Rogač
Grohote
Sutivan
Supetar
Postira
Pučišća
Milna
Nerežišća
Gornji Humac
Bol
Brač
Sumartin
Selca
Povlja
Baška Voda
Starigrad
Vrboska
Hvar
Jelsa
Ščedro
Vis
Komiža
Biševo
Svetac
Jabucka
Vela Luka
Blato
Prigradica
Korčula
Sušac
Kopište
Ubli
Lastovo
Ancona
Rijeka
Krka
MANASTIR KRKA
KATEDRALA SV JAKOVA
ROGOZNICA
SALONA
ASSERIA
BURNUM
AENONA
TVRDAVA SV. MIHOVILA
MUZEJ GACKE OTOČAC
DOMINIKANSKI SAMOSTAN
SV. STJPAN
SV. IVAN
GALERIJA CENTRA ZA KULTURU
SV. KUZMA & DAMJAN
Bijeli vrh 1492
M. Rajinac 1699
Vaganski vrh 1757
Kremen 1591
Kučina kosa 1443
Osječenica 1795
Klekovača 1961
Vijenac 1650
Šator 1872
Troglav 1913
Golija 1891
Svilaja 1508
Vratnik 698
Oštarijska Vrata 928
Kapela 887
E65
E71
E761
A1
73
84
103
104
15°
16°
45°
44°
43°
A
B
C
D
3
4
5
0 10 20 30 40 50 km

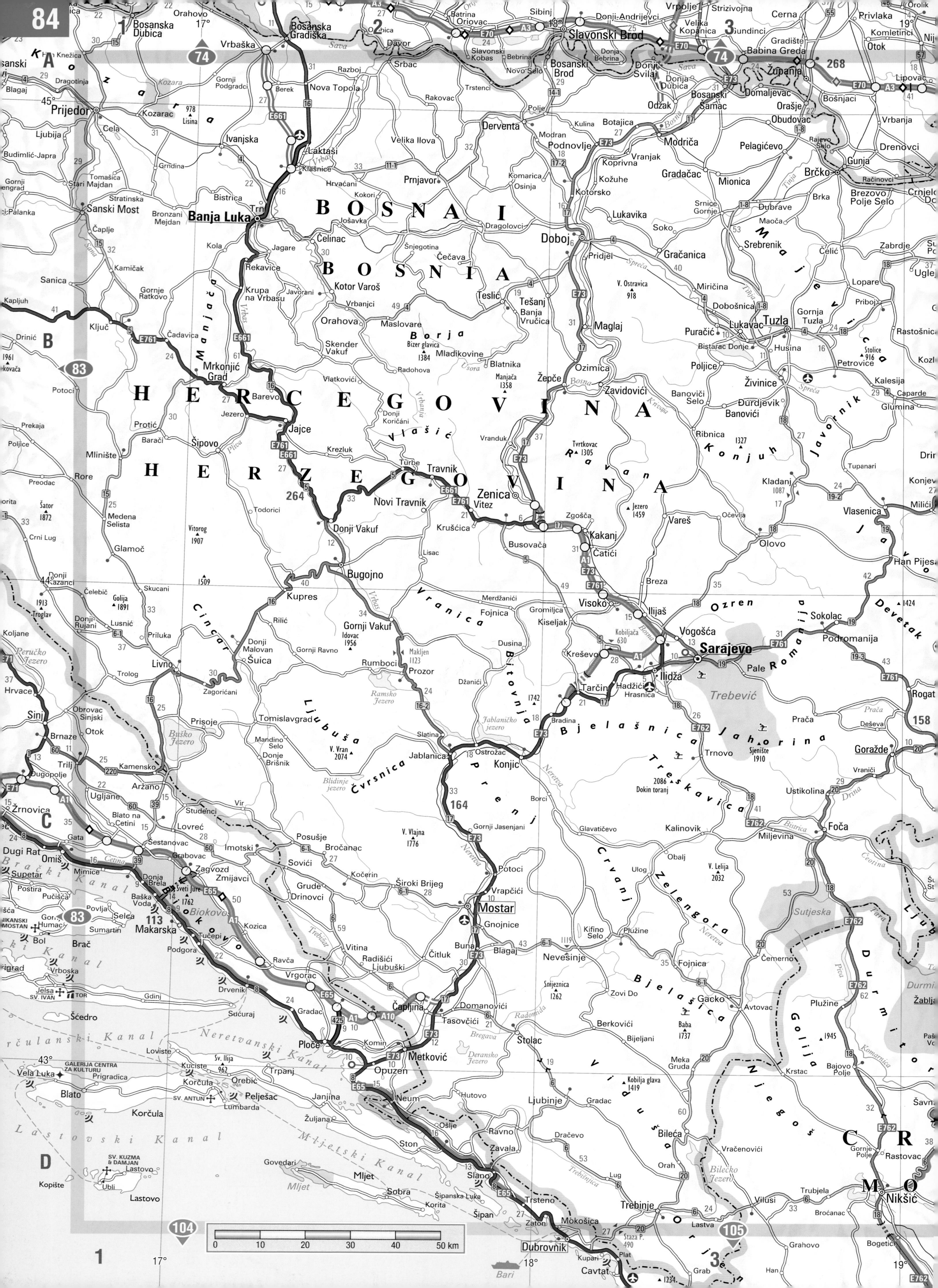

84
Bosanska Dubica
Orahovo
Bosanska Gradiška
Oriovac
Sibinj
Donji Andrijevci
Vrpolje
Strizivojna
Cerna
Privlaka
Slavonski Brod
Slavonski Kobas
Bosanski Brod
Davor
Srbac
Velika Kopanica
Gundinci
Gradište
Babina Greda
Županja
Otok
Komletinci
Lipovac
Vrbaška
Razboj
Nova Topola
Berek
Gornji Podgradci
Prijedor
Kozarac
Ljubija
Cela
Ivanjska
Laktaši
Klašnice
Rakovac
Trstenci
Derventa
Modran
Podnovlje
Kulina
Botajica
Odžak
Bosanski Šamac
Domaljevac
Orašje
Obudovac
Bošnjaci
Drenovci
Vrbanja
Gunja
Brčko
Modriča
Pelagićevo
Gradačac
Mionica
Vranjak
Koprivna
Kožuhe
Kotorsko
Velika Ilova
Prnjavor
Hrvaćani
Kokori
Komarica
Osinja
Sanski Most
Stratinska
Bistrica
Bronzani Mejdan
Banja Luka
Jošavka
Dragolovci
Doboj
Lukavika
Brezovo Polje Selo
Brka
Dubrave
Maoča
Srebrenik
Soko
Gračanica
BOSNA I
BOSNIA
Čelinac
Jagare
Kola
Šnjegotina
Čečava
Kamičak
Rekavice
Kotor Varoš
Krupa na Vrbasu
Javorani
Teslić
Tešanj
Banja Vručica
Pridjel
Miričina
Dobošnica
Lukavac
Tuzla
Gornja Tuzla
Puračić
Lopare
Priboj
Sanica
Gornje Ratkovo
Vrbanjci
Ključ
Čadavica
Orahova
Maslovare
Borja
Bizer glavica
Mladikovine
Skender Vakuf
Maglaj
Bistarac Donje
Husina
Poljice
Petrovice
Živinice
Kalesija
Mrkonjić Grad
Radohova
Blatnika
Ozimica
Žepče
Zavidovići
Banovići Selo
Đurđjevik
Banovići
Manjača
HERCEGOVINA
HERZEGOVINA
Barevo
Jezero
Jajce
Donji Korićani
Vlašić
Vlatkovići
Potoci
Protić
Barači
Šipovo
Mliništa
Krezluk
Turbe
Travnik
Vranduk
Tvrtkovac
Ravna
Ribnica
Konjuh
Javornik
Kladanj
Tupanari
Rore
Preodac
Novi Travnik
Zenica
Vitez
Kruščica
Busovača
Zgošća
Kakanj
Ćatići
Jezero
Vareš
Očevlja
Olovo
Vlasenica
Šator
Vitorog
Todorici
Donji Vakuf
Medena Selista
Crni Lug
Glamoč
Bugojno
Lisac
Breza
Han Pijesak
Donji Kazanci
Čelebić
Golija
Troglav
Skucani
Kupres
Vranica
Merdžanići
Fojnica
Gromiljca
Kiseljak
Visoko
Ilijaš
Ozren
Sokolac
Devetak
Donji Rujani
Lusnić
Priluka
Rilić
Gornji Vakuf
Idovac
Kobiljača
Vogošća
Podromanija
Koljane
Peručko Jezero
Cincar
Donji Malovan
Šuica
Gornji Ravno
Makljen
Rumboći
Dusina
Kreševo
Sarajevo
Ilidža
Pale
Romanija
Livno
Trolog
Prozor
Bitovnja
Hadžići
Hrasnica
Tarčin
Trebević
Rogatica
Hrvace
Sinj
Obrovac Sinjski
Zagorićani
Ramsko Jezero
Džanići
Otok
Prisoje
Tomislavgrad
Jablaničko jezero
Bradina
Bjelašnica
Jahorina
Prača
Deševa
Brnaze
Buško Jezero
Mandino Selo
Donje Brišnik
Ljubuša
V. Vran
Slatina
Jablanica
Ostrožac
Konjic
Trnovo
Treskavica
Sjenište
Goražde
Trilj
Kamensko
Čvrsnica
Prenj
Dokin toranj
Vraniči
Ustikolina
Dugopolje
Aržano
Ugljane
Blidinje jezero
Borci
Žrnovica
Blato na Cetini
Studenci
Vir
Lovreć
Gornji Jasenjani
Glavatičevo
Kalinovik
Miljevina
Foča
Gata
Sestanovac
Grabovac
Posušje
V. Vlajna
Dugi Rat
Omiš
Imotski
Bročanac
Obalj
Ulog
V. Lelija
Supetar
Mimice
Zagvozd
Zmijavci
Sovići
Kočerin
Potoci
Zelengora
Crvanj
Postira
Donja Brela
Sveti Jure
Grude
Drinovci
Široki Brijeg
Vrapčići
Sutjeska
Pučišća
Baška Voda
Mostar
Povlja
Selca
Makarska
Biokovo
Kozica
Gnojnice
Kifino Selo
Plužine
Humac
Sumartin
Tučepi
Podgora
Vitina
Radišići
Ljubuški
Čitluk
Buna
Blagaj
Nevesinje
Fojnica
Čemerno
Durmitor
Bol
Brač
Ravča
Vrgorac
Snježnica
Zovi Do
Bjelašica
Gacko
Žabljak
Vrboska
Jelsa
Drvenik
Čapljina
Domanovići
Avtovac
Pluzine
Gdinj
Sućuraj
Gradac
Tasovčići
Stolac
Berkovići
Bijeljani
Baba
Šćedro
Kanal
Neretvanski Kanal
Ploče
Komin
Metković
Deransko Jezero
Bregava
Golija
Loviste
Sv. Ilija
Opuzen
Meka Gruda
Krstac
Bajovo Polje
Vela Luka
Kuciste
Korčula
Orebić
Trpanj
Kobilja glava
Blato
Pelješac
Lumbarda
Janjina
Neum
Hutovo
Ljubinje
Gradac
Vidušа
Njegoš
Korčula
Žuljana
Ošlje
Ravno
Dračevo
Bileća
Lastovski Kanal
Mljetski Kanal
Ston
Zavala
Vračenovići
Gornje Polje
Rastovac
Govedari
Lastovo
Mljet
Slano
Orah
Bilećko Jezero
Lug
Kopište
Ubli
Lastovo
Sobra
Šipanska Luka
Korita
Šipan
Trsteno
Trebinje
Vilusi
Trubjela
Nikšić
Brocanac
Zaton
Mokošica
Lastva
Orjen
Dubrovnik
Kupari
Cavtat
Plat
Grab
Grahovo
Bogetići
Bari
Han
0 10 20 30 40 50 km

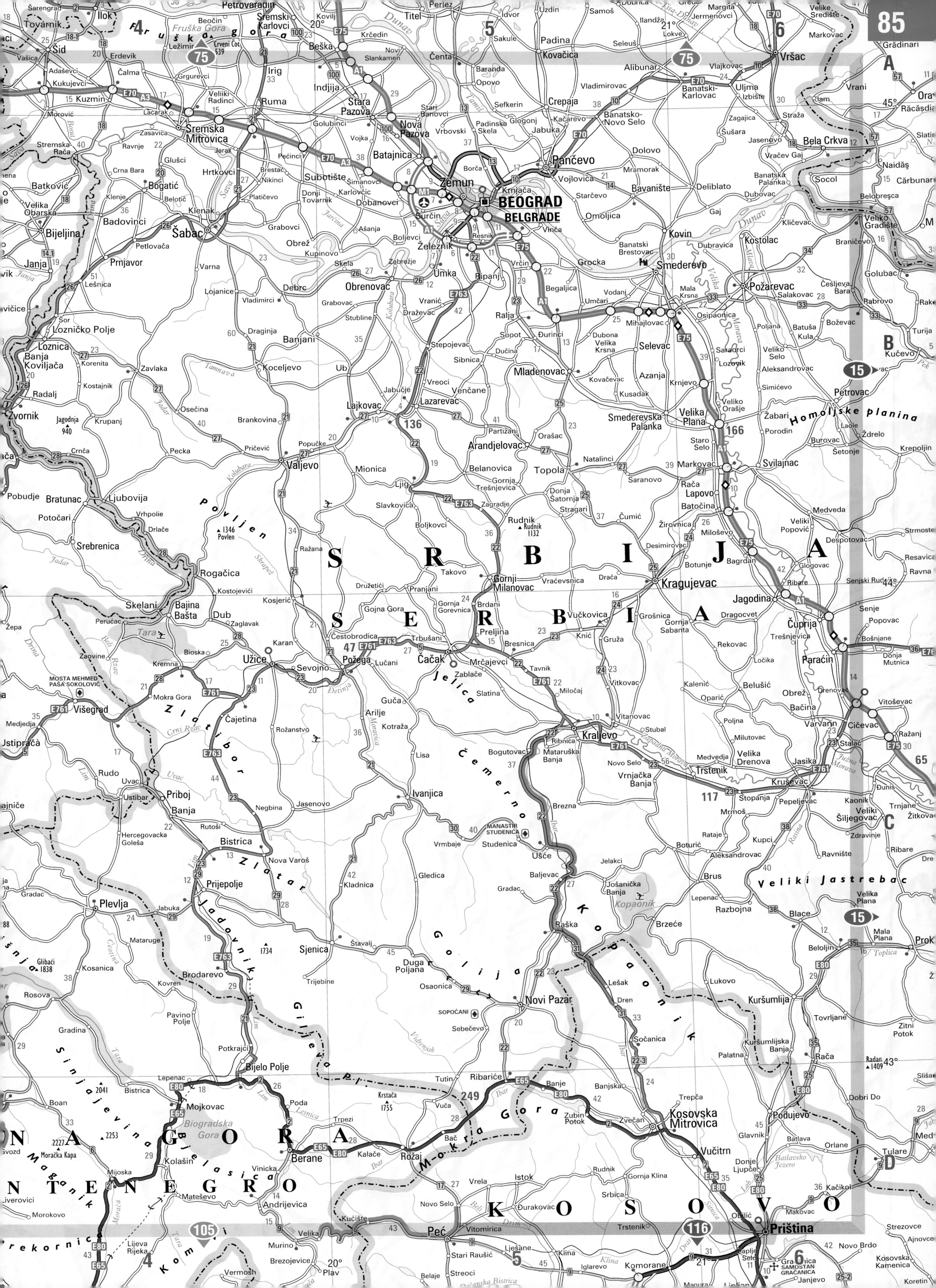
SRBIJA
SERBIA
CRNA GORA
MONTENEGRO
KOSOVO
BEOGRAD
BELGRADE
Zemun
Pančevo
Novi Sad
Petrovaradin
Sremski Karlovci
Fruška Gora
Šid
Sremska Mitrovica
Ruma
Inđija
Stara Pazova
Nova Pazova
Batajnica
Surčin
Obrenovac
Šabac
Bogatić
Bijeljina
Loznica
Banja Koviljača
Zvornik
Krupanj
Valjevo
Ljubovija
Bratunac
Srebrenica
Bajina Bašta
Užice
Požega
Čačak
Gornji Milanovac
Kragujevac
Kraljevo
Jagodina
Ćuprija
Paraćin
Kruševac
Trstenik
Vrnjačka Banja
Ivanjica
Arilje
Kosjerić
Zlatibor
Čajetina
Priboj
Prijepolje
Nova Varoš
Sjenica
Novi Pazar
Raška
Tutin
Kopaonik
Golija
Brus
Kuršumlija
Blace
Prokuplje
Podujevo
Priština
Kosovska Mitrovica
Vučitrn
Peć
Istok
Rožaje
Berane
Bijelo Polje
Mojkovac
Kolašin
Andrijevica
Plav
Pljevlja
Višegrad
Mokra Gora
Lazarevac
Ljig
Mionica
Arandjelovac
Topola
Mladenovac
Smederevo
Smederevska Palanka
Velika Plana
Požarevac
Kostolac
Vršac
Bela Crkva
Kovin
Svilajnac
Despotovac
Homoljske planina
Veliki Jastrebac
Sinjajevina
Bjelasica
Biogradska Gora
Mokra Gora
Čemerno
Jelica
Povljen
Tara
Drina
Dunav
Sava
Morava
Ibar
Lim
Kladovo
MANASTIR STUDENICA
SOPOĆANI
MOSTA MEHMED PAŠA SOKOLOVIĆ
SAMOSTAN GRAČANICA
A1
E70
E75
E763
E761
E65
E80
75
105
116
15
4
5
6
A
B
C
D

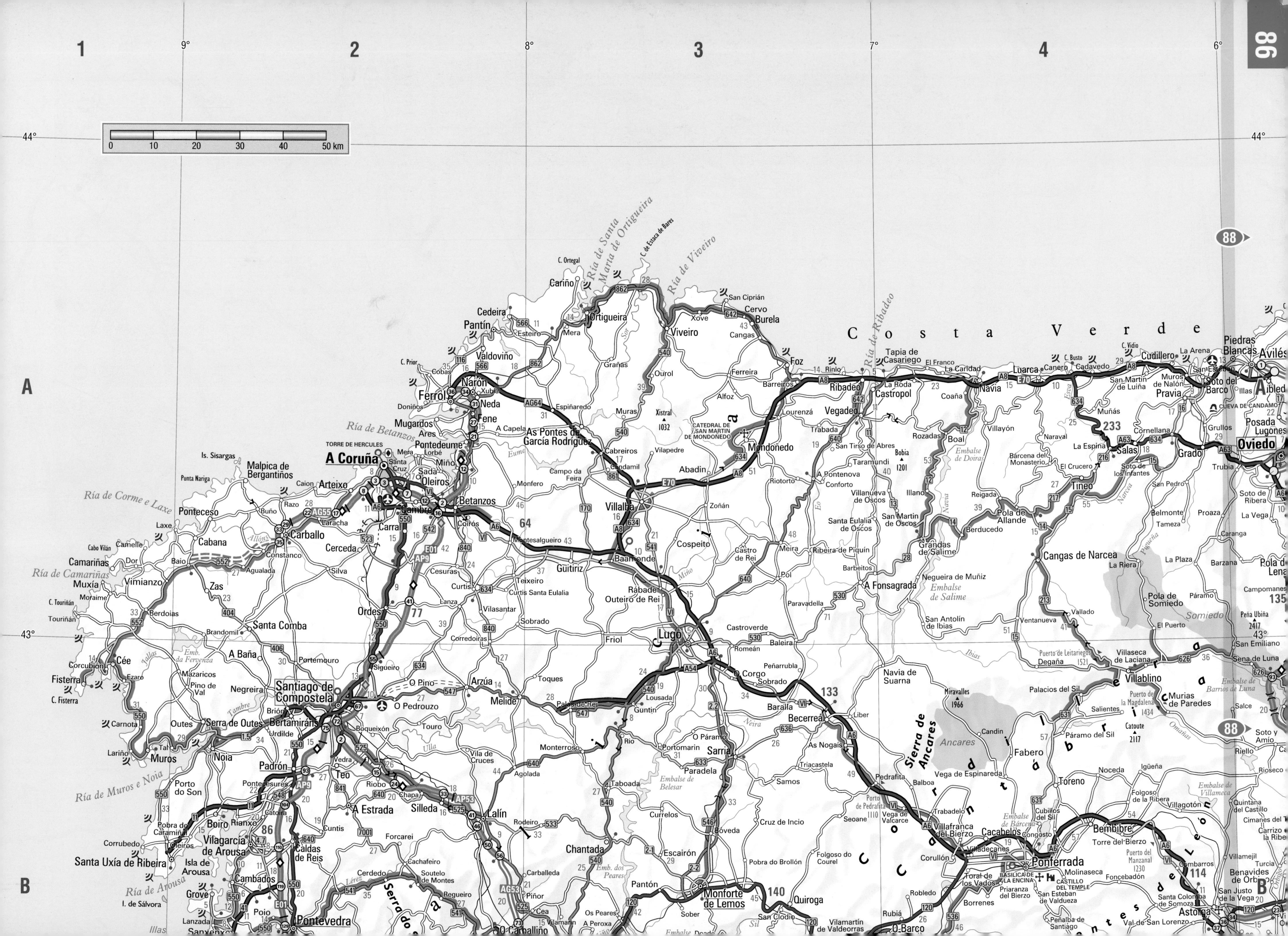
1
2
3
4
A
B
9°
8°
7°
6°
44°
43°
0
10
20
30
40
50 km
88
Costa Verde
Ría de Santa Marta de Ortigueira
Ría de Viveiro
Ría de Ribadeo
Ría de Betanzos
Ría de Corme e Laxe
Ría de Camariñas
Ría de Muros e Noia
Ría de Arousa
C. Ortegal
C. de Estaca de Bares
C. Prior
C. Fisterra
C. Touriñán
Cabo Vilán
Punta Nariga
Is. Sisargas
I. de Sálvora
C. Vidio
C. Busto
TORRE DE HERCULES
A Coruña
Ferrol
Narón
Neda
Fene
Mugardos
Ares
Pontedeume
Miño
Sada
Oleiros
Betanzos
Cambre
Carral
Arteixo
Laracha
Carballo
Malpica de Bergantiños
Ponteceso
Laxe
Cabana
Camariñas
Muxía
Vimianzo
Zas
Santa Comba
Fisterra
Corcubión
Cée
Carnota
Muros
Noia
Outes
Serra de Outes
Negreira
A Baña
Santiago de Compostela
Bertamiráns
Padrón
Teo
A Estrada
Silleda
Lalín
Melide
Arzúa
O Pedrouzo
Ordes
Cerceda
Curtis
Sobrado
Guitiriz
Villalba
Baamonde
Rábade
Outeiro de Rei
Lugo
Friol
Palas de Rei
Guntín
Portomarín
Sarria
Monforte de Lemos
Quiroga
Chantada
Taboada
Monterroso
Agolada
Boiro
Rianxo
Vilagarcía de Arousa
Caldas de Reis
Cambados
Grove
Isla de Arousa
Pontevedra
Santa Uxía de Ribeira
Porto do Son
Cedeira
Pantín
Valdoviño
Cariño
Ortigueira
As Pontes de García Rodríguez
Viveiro
Xove
Burela
Cervo
San Ciprián
Foz
Barreiros
Ribadeo
Mondoñedo
CATEDRAL DE SAN MARTIN DE MONDOÑEDO
Abadin
Xistral 1032
Vegadeo
Castropol
Tapia de Casariego
Navia
Luarca
Cudillero
Pravia
Soto del Barco
Piedras Blancas
Avilés
Oviedo
Grado
Salas
Tineo
Cangas de Narcea
Pola de Allande
Grandas de Salime
A Fonsagrada
Embalse de Salime
Pola de Somiedo
Villablino
Murias de Paredes
Sierra de Ancares
Becerreá
Baralla
Pedrafita
Villafranca del Bierzo
Cacabelos
Ponferrada
Bembibre
Toreno
Fabero
Astorga
O Barco
Borrenes
Miravalles 1966
Catoute 2117
Peña Ubiña 2417
CUEVA DE CANDAMO
CASTILLO DEL TEMPLE
BASILICA DE LA ENCINA
Cordillera Cantábrica
Montes de León
Serra do

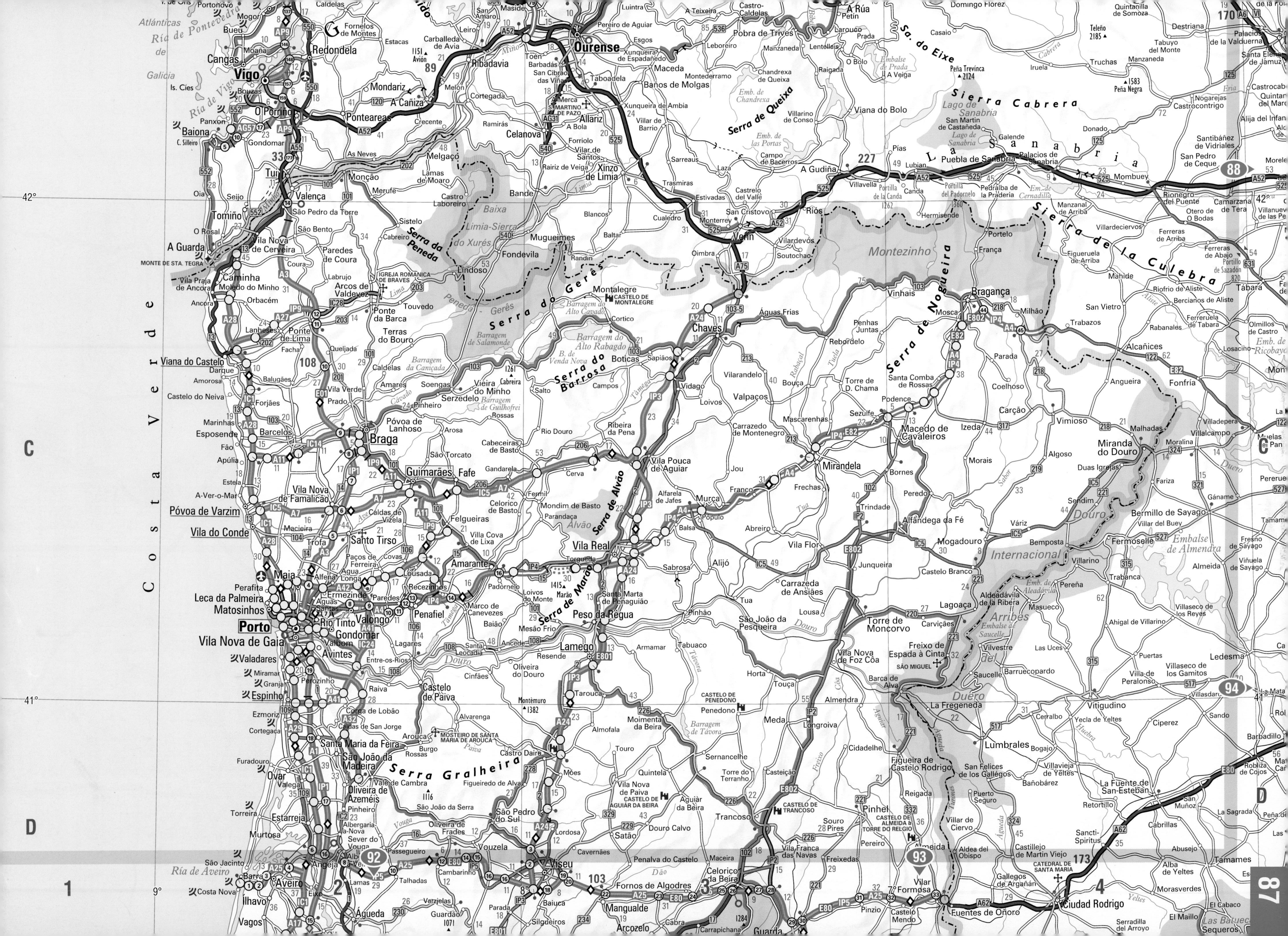
Porto
Vila Nova de Gaia
Matosinhos
Leca da Palmeira
Braga
Guimarães
Vila Real
Chaves
Bragança
Mirandela
Lamego
Viseu
Ourense
Vigo
Valença
Viana do Castelo
Póvoa de Varzim
Vila do Conde
Aveiro
Ciudad Rodrigo
Miranda do Douro
Macedo de Cavaleiros
Peso da Régua
Amarante
Penafiel
Espinho
Ovar
Águeda
Guarda
Trancoso
Mangualde
Celanova
Xinzo de Limia
Verín
A Gudiña
Puebla de Sanabria
Sierra de la Culebra
Serra de Nogueira
Serra do Gerês
Serra do Barroso
Serra de Alvão
Serra de Marão
Serra da Peneda
Serra Gralheira
Sierra Cabrera
Montezinho
Costa Verde
Douro
Arribes del Duero
Internacional
Baixa Limia-Serra do Xurés
Peneda - Gerês
Serra de Queixa
Sa. do Eixe
La Sanabria

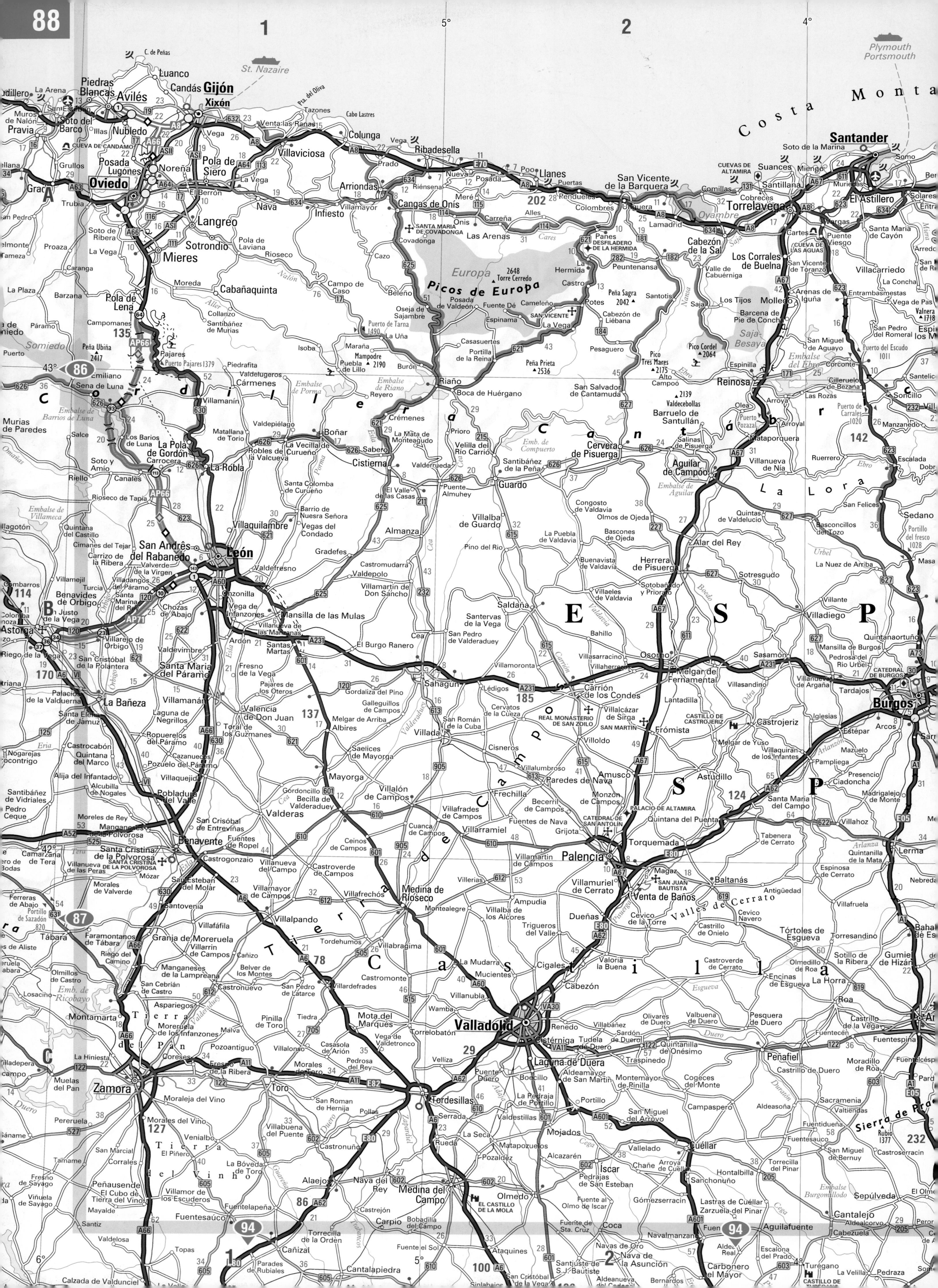
1
2
5°
4°
St. Nazaire
Plymouth
Portsmouth
Costa Monta
C. de Peñas
Luanco
Candás
Gijón
Xixón
Piedras Blancas
Avilés
La Arena
San Esteban
Muros de Nalón
Soto del Barco
Pravia
Nubledo
Illas
Venta las Ranas
Tazones
Cabo Lastres
Colunga
Vega
Villaviciosa
Ribadesella
Posada
Lugones
Noreña
Pola de Siero
La Vega
Oviedo
Grado
Trubia
Grullos
Arriondas
Nava
Infiesto
Villamayor
Cangas de Onís
Llanes
Posada
Nueva
Prado
Riensena
Meré
Poo
Puertas
Pendueles
Colombres
Unquera
San Vicente de la Barquera
Comillas
Santillana
Suances
Miengo
Santander
Soto de la Marina
Somo
Torrelavega
Cobreces
El Astillero
Oyambre
Lamadrid
Cuevas de Altamira
Langreo
Sotrondio
Mieres
Soto de Ribera
La Vega
Proaza
Pola de Laviana
Rioseco
Santa María de Covadonga
Covadonga
Las Arenas
Carreña
Alles
Onís
Cares
Panes
Desfiladero de la Hermida
Peuntenansa
Cabezón de la Sal
Puente Viesgo
Cartes
Vargas
Santa María de Cayón
Los Corrales de Buelna
Cueva de las Aguas
San Vicente de Toranzo
Villacarriedo
La Concha
Valle de Cabuérniga
Hermida
Castro
Europa
2648 Torre Cerredo
Picos de Europa
Posada de Valdeón
Fuente Dé
Cameleño
San Vicente
Potes
Espinama
La Vega
Peña Sagra 2042
Santotis
Cabezón de Liébana
Los Tijos
Molledo
Arenas de Iguña
Entrambasmestas
Vega de Pas
Valnera 1718
Barcena de Pie de Concha
Saja-Besaya
San Pedro del Romeral
San Miguel de Aguayo
Puerto del Escudo 1011
Pola de Lena
Cabañaquinta
Moreda
Collanzo
Santibáñez de Murias
Campo de Caso
Beleño
Oseja de Sajambre
Puerto de Tarna 1490
La Uña
Casasuertes
Portilla de la Reina
Pesaguero
Pico Tres Mares 2175
Pico Cordel 2064
Alto Campoo
Espinilla
Reinosa
Corconte
Embalse del Ebro
Cilleruelo de Bezana
Soncillo
La Plaza
Barzana
Campomanes
Somiedo
Peña Ubiña 2417
Puerto Pajares 1379
Pajares
Pedrafita
Valdelugueros
Cármenes
Isoba
Maraña
Mampodre 2190
Puebla de Lillo
Burón
Riaño
Boca de Huérgano
Peña Prieta 2536
San Salvador de Cantamuda
2139 Valdecebollas
Barruelo de Santullán
Puerto Pozazal
Olea
Arroyo
Las Rozas
Puerto de Carrales 1020
Manzanedo
Embalse de Riaño
Embalse de Porma
Reyero
Emiliano
Sena de Luna
Embalse de Barrios de Luna
Villamanín
Valdepiélago
Murias de Paredes
Los Barrios de Luna
La Pola de Gordón
Matallana de Torio
Boñar
La Vecilla de Curueño
Robles de la Valcueva
Sabero
Cistierna
Crémenes
La Mata de Monteagudo
Prioro
Velilla del Río Carrión
Emb. de Compuerto
Cervera de Pisuerga
Salinas de Pisuerga
Aguilar de Campóo
Mataporquera
Villanueva de Nía
Ruerrero
Escalada
Cordillera Cantábrica
Salce
Soto y Amío
Carrocera
La Robla
Santibáñez de la Peña
Valderrueda
Guardo
Puente Almuhey
Riello
Canales
Rioseco de Tapia
Santa Colomba de Curueño
El Valle de las Casas
Barrio de Nuestra Señora
Vegas del Condado
Villaquilambre
Almanza
Villalba de Guardo
Congosto de Valdavia
Olmos de Ojeda
La Lora
Quintas de Valdelucio
Basconcillos del Tozo
Sedano
Portillo del fresco 1028
San Felices
Embalse de Aguilar
Embalse de Villameca
Quintana del Castillo
Cimanes del Tejar
Carrizo de la Ribera
San Andrés del Rabanedo
León
Valverde de la Virgen
Gradefes
Pino del Río
La Puebla de Valdavia
Bascones de Ojeda
Alar del Rey
Herrera de Pisuerga
La Nuez de Arriba
Masa
Buenavista de Valdavia
Valdefresno
Castromudarra
Valdepolo
Villamartín de Don Sancho
Sotresgudo
Sotobañado y Priorato
Villaleles de Valdavia
Benavides de Órbigo
Villadangos del Páramo
Santa Marina del Rey
Hospital de Órbigo
San Justo de la Vega
Astorga
Turcia
Onzonilla
Vega de Infanzones
Chozas de Abajo
Mansilla de las Mulas
Villanueva de las Manzanas
Saldaña
Santervas de la Vega
Villadiego
Villante
Quintanaortuño
Villarejo de Órbigo
Valdevimbre
Ardón
Santas Martas
El Burgo Ranero
Cea
San Pedro de Valderaduey
Bahillo
Villasarracino
Villaherreros
Osorno
Melgar de Fernamental
Sasamón
Mansilla de Burgos
Pedrosa del Río Urbel
Catedral de Burgos
Tardajos
Burgos
Riego de la Vega
San Cristóbal de la Polantera
Santa María del Páramo
Fresno de la Vega
Pajares de los Oteros
Gordaliza del Pino
Villamoronta
Sahagún
Lédigos
Carrión de los Condes
Villasandino
Villanueva de Argaña
Villamañán
Palacios de la Valduerna
La Bañeza
Santa Elena de Jamuz
Laguna de Negrillos
Valencia de Don Juan
Galleguillos de Campos
Melgar de Arriba
Albires
Villada
San Román de la Cuba
Cervatos de la Cueza
Real Monasterio de San Zoilo
San Martín
Villalcázar de Sirga
Frómista
Castillo de Castrojeriz
Castrojeriz
Iglesias
Estépar
Arcos
Castrocabón
Quintana del Marco
Nogarejas
Pozuelo del Páramo
Roperuelos del Páramo
Cazanuecos
Toral de los Guzmanes
Saelices de Mayorga
Cisneros
Villoldo
Melgar de Yuso
Villaquirán de los Infantes
Pampliega
Mazuelo
Villaquejida
Alija del Infantado
Alcubilla de Nogales
Santibáñez de Vidriales
Pedro Ceque
Pobladura del Valle
Mayorga
Gordoncillo
Becilla de Valderaduey
Villalón de Campos
Villafrades de Campos
Frechilla
Villaumbrosso
Paredes de Nava
Amusco
Astudillo
Presencio
Ciadoncha
Madrigalejo del Monte
Monzón de Campos
Becerril de Campos
Palacio de Altamira
Santa María del Campo
Villahoz
Moreles de Rey
Manganeses de la Polvorosa
San Crisóbal de Entreviñas
Valderas
Cuanca de Campos
Fuentes de Nava
Catedral de San Antolín
Grijota
Quintana del Puente
Tabanera de Cerrato
Lerma
Camarzana de Tera
Benavente
Fuentes de Ropel
Santa Cristina de la Polvorosa
Ceinos de Campos
Villarramiel
Torquemada
Quintanilla de la Mata
Villanueva de las Peras
Mózar
Castrogonzalo
Villanueva del Campo
Castroverde de Campos
Villamartín de Campos
Palencia
Villerías
Magaz
San Juan Bautista
Baltanás
Antigüedad
Espinosa de Cerrato
Nebreda
Morales de Valverde
San Esteban del Molar
Santovenia
Villamayor de Campos
Villafrechós
Medina de Rioseco
Montealegre
Villalba de los Alcores
Ampudia
Villamuriel de Cerrato
Venta de Baños
Valles de Cerrato
Cevico de la Torre
Cevico Navero
Villafruela
Ferreras de Abajo
Portillo de Sazadón 820
Tábara
Faramontanos de Tábara
Villafáfila
Granja de Moreruela
Villarrín de Campos
Villalpando
Tordehumos
Villabrágima
Trigueros del Valle
Dueñas
Castillo de Onielo
Tórtoles de Esgueva
Torresandino
Riego del Camino
Manganeses de la Lampreana
Cañizo
Belver de los Montes
La Mudarra
Mucientes
Cigales
Valoria la Buena
Castroverde de Cerrato
Olmedillo de Roa
Sotillo de la Ribera
Gumiel de Hizán
Olmillos de Castro
Emb. de Ricobayo
San Cebrián de Castro
Castronuevo
San Pedro de Latarce
Castromonte
Villardefrades
Villanubla
Cabezón
Encinas de Esgueva
La Horra
Losacino
Montamarta
Tierra del Pan
Asprariegos
Moreruela de los Infanzones
Malva
Pinilla de Toro
Tiedra
Mota del Marqués
Wamba
Valladolid
Renedo
Olivares de Duero
Valbuena de Duero
Pesquera de Duero
Roa
Castrillo de la Vega
Villabáñez
Sardón de Duero
Fuentecén
La Hiniesta
Pozoantiguo
Villalonso
Casasola de Arión
Vega de Valdetronco
Torrelobatón
Cistérniga
Tudela de Duero
Quintanilla de Onésimo
Peñafiel
Fuentespina
Coreses
Fresno de la Ribera
Morales de Toro
Pedrosa del Rey
Velliza
Laguna de Duera
Traspinedo
Moradillo de Roa
Fuentelcésped
Muelas del Pan
Zamora
Toro
Puente Duero
Boecillo
Aldeamayor de San Martín
Montemayor de Pinilla
Cogeces del Monte
Castrillo de Duero
Moraleja del Vino
San Román de Hornija
Pollos
Tordesillas
La Pedraja de Portillo
Portillo
Campaspero
Aldeasoña
Sacramenia
Valtiendas
Perreruela
Morales del Vino
Villabuena del Puente
Serrada
Valdestillas
Mojados
San Miguel del Arroyo
Fuentidueña
Sierra de Pradales
Rubio 1377
Venialbo
Tierra del Vino
San Marcial
El Piñero
La Seca
Matapozuelos
Cuéllar
Fuentesauco
San Miguel de Bernuy
Castroserracín
Tamame
Corrales
Castronuño
Rueda
Pozaldez
Alcazarén
Valleado
Torrecilla del Pinar
La Bóveda de Toro
Iscar
Chañe
Arroyo de Cuéllar
Hontalbilla
Fresno de Sayago
Viñuela de Sayago
Peñausende
El Cubo de Tierra del Vino
Villamor de los Escuderos
Alaejos
Nava del Rey
Medina del Campo
Olmedo
Pedrajas de San Esteban
Sanchonuño
Embalse Burgomillodo
Sepúlveda
Mayalde
Fuentelapeña
Castrejón
El Castillo de la Mota
Fuente al Olmo de Iscar
Gómezserracín
Lastras de Cuéllar
Zarzuela del Pinar
Santiz
Fuentesaúco
Carpio
Bobadilla del Campo
Fuente de Sta. Cruz
Coca
Cantalejo
Aldealcorvo
Cabezuela
Valdelosa
Torrecilla de la Orden
Navalmanzano
Fuente el Sauz
Aguilafuente
Topas
Cañizal
Fuente el Sol
Ataquines
Navas de Oro
Nava de la Asunción
Aldea Real
Escalona del Prado
Turégano
Parades de Rubiales
Cantalapiedra
San Cristóbal de la Vega
Santiuste de S.J. Bautiste
Carbonero el Mayor
La Velilla
Pedraza
Castillo de Turégano
Calzada de Valdunciel
6°
5°
ESPAÑA
Campos
Tierra de Campos
Castilla
A
B
C
86
87
94

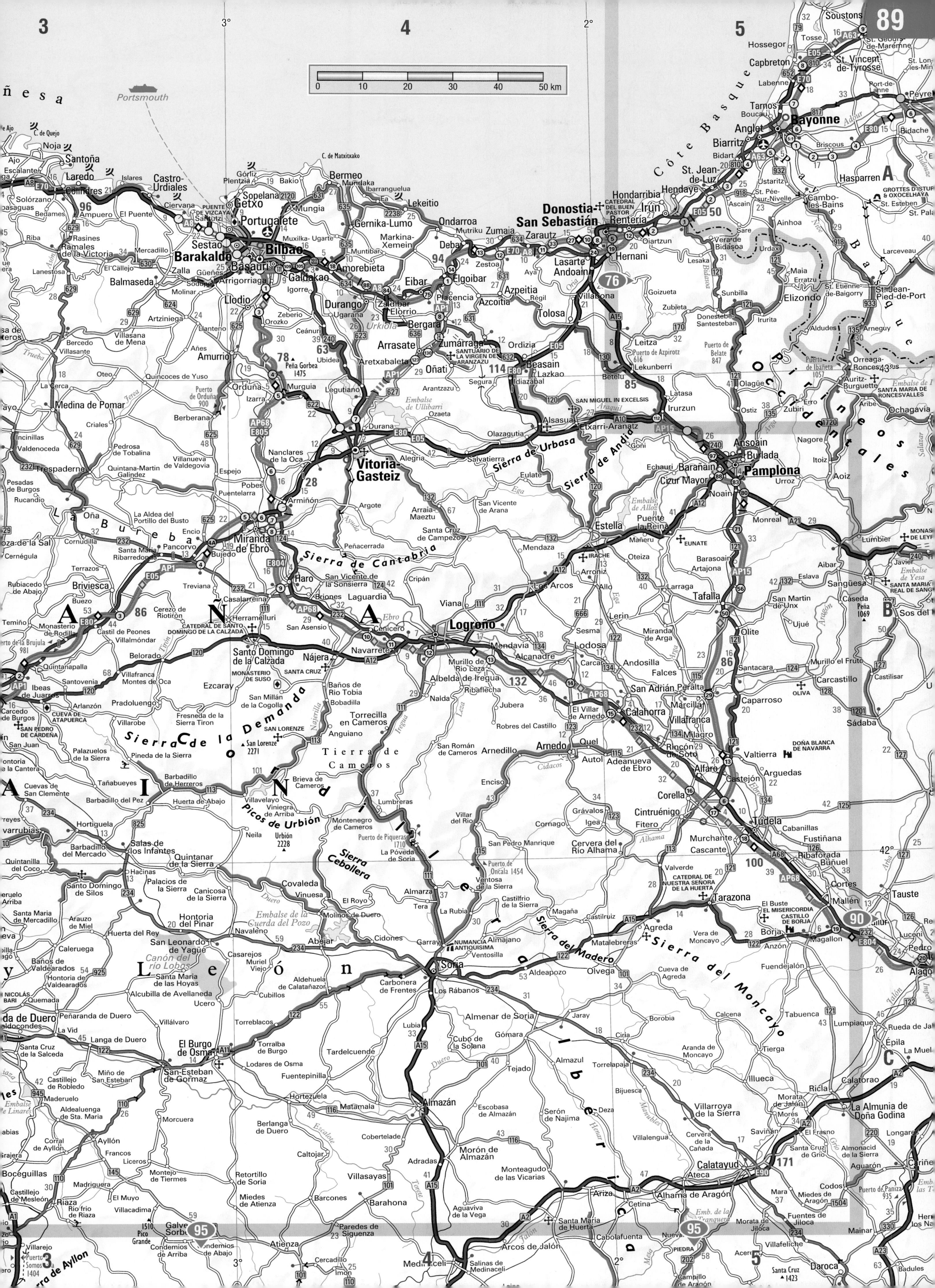
3
4
5
0 10 20 30 40 50 km
Portsmouth
Côte Basque
Pays Basque
Pirineos Occidentales
Sierra de Urbasa
Sierra de Andía
Sierra de Cantabria
Sierra de la Demanda
Sierra Cebollera
Picos de Urbión
Tierra de Cameros
Sierra del Madero
Sierra del Moncayo
Sistema Ibérico
Castilla y León
España
La Bureba
Bayonne
Anglet
Biarritz
St.-Jean-de-Luz
Hendaye
Irún
Hondarribia
Donostia-San Sebastián
Rentería
Hernani
Zarautz
Zumaia
Getaria
Ondarroa
Lekeitio
Bermeo
Mundaka
Gernika-Lumo
Getxo
Portugalete
Sestao
Barakaldo
Bilbao
Basauri
Galdakao
Amorebieta
Durango
Eibar
Elgoibar
Bergara
Arrasate
Oñati
Zumárraga
Azpeitia
Azcoitia
Tolosa
Beasain
Ordizia
Alsasua
Llodio
Amurrio
Orduña
Laredo
Castro-Urdiales
Santoña
Noja
Colindres
Ampuero
Balmaseda
Medina de Pomar
Trespaderne
Vitoria-Gasteiz
Miranda de Ebro
Briviesca
Haro
Laguardia
Logroño
Navarrete
Nájera
Santo Domingo de la Calzada
Ezcaray
Viana
Los Arcos
Estella
Puente la Reina
Pamplona
Burlada
Ansoain
Noain
Tafalla
Olite
Lodosa
Calahorra
Alfaro
Corella
Tudela
Cintruénigo
Cascante
Tarazona
Borja
Mallén
Agreda
Olvega
Soria
Almazán
El Burgo de Osma
San Esteban de Gormaz
Ayllón
Calatayud
Ateca
Épila
La Almunia de Doña Godina
Medinaceli
Arcos de Jalón
Sangüesa
Lumbier
Elizondo
Saint-Jean-Pied-de-Port
Cambo-les-Bains
Hasparren
Capbreton
Hossegor
Soustons
Arnedo
Arnedillo
Enciso
Ágreda
Ricla
Daroca
Ariza
Alhama de Aragón
Salas de los Infantes
Quintanar de la Sierra
Covaleda
Vinuesa
Molinos de Duero
Santo Domingo de Silos
Aranda de Moncayo
Illueca
Morata de Jalón
Tabuenca
Borobia
Gómara
Almenar de Soria
Berlanga de Duero
Langa de Duero
Castilla y León
Urbión 2228
San Lorenzo 2271
Peña Gorbea 1475
Puerto de Piqueras 1710
Puerto de Oncala 1454
Embalse de Ullíbarri
Embalse de la Cuerda del Pozo
Cañón del río Lobos
42°
3°
2°
A
B
C
95
90
76
85
100
171
86
28
63
78
94
114
132

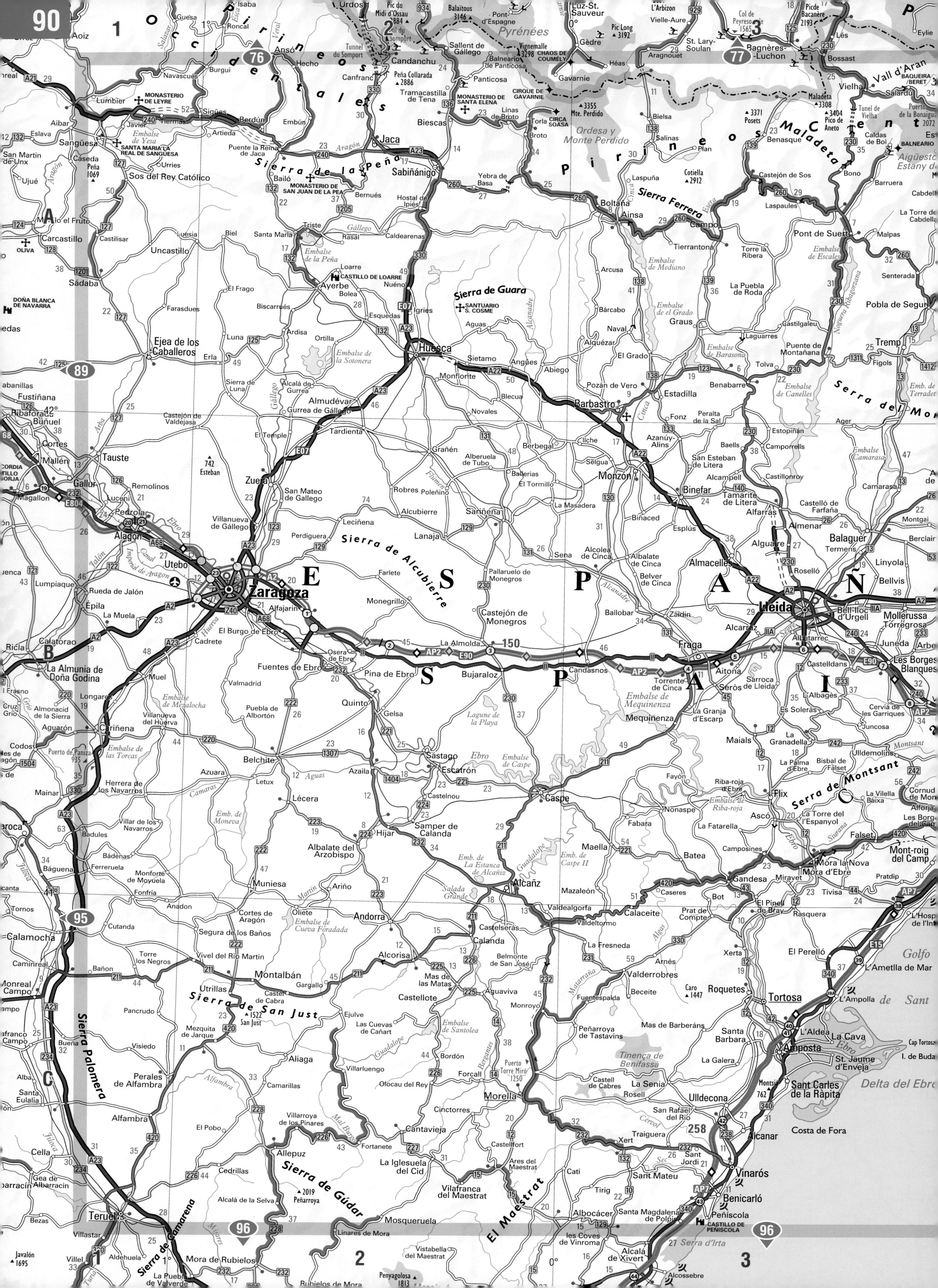
Pirineos Occidentales
Pirineos Centrales
Pyrénées
Aoiz
Roncal
Isaba
Ansó
Hecho
Navascués
Burgui
Lumbier
MONASTERIO DE LEYRE
Sigües
Berdún
Embún
Aibar
Javier
Tiermas
Sangüesa
Eslava
Embalse de Yesa
SANTA MARÍA LA REAL DE SANGÜESA
San Martín de Unx
Caseda
Peña 1069
Ujué
Urdos
Pic du Midi d'Ossau 2884
Col du Somport
Tunnel du Somport
Candanchu
Canfranc
Peña Collarada 2886
Tramacastilla de Tena
Balaïtous 3146
Pont-d'Espagne
Sallent de Gállego
Balneario de Panticosa
Panticosa
Vignemalle 3298
CHAOS DE COUMÉLY
Gavarnie
CIRQUE DE GAVARNIE
MONASTERIO DE SANTA ELENA
Biescas
Líneas de Broto
Torla
CIRCA SOASA
3355 Mte. Perdido
Ordesa y Monte Perdido
Broto
Luz-St. Sauveur
Gèdre
Héas
Pic Long 3192
L'Arbizon
Vielle-Aure
St. Lary-Soulan
Aragnouet
Col de Peyresourde 1565
Bagnères-de-Luchon
Picde Bacanère 2193
Bossost
Lès
Eylie
Vielha
Vall d'Aran
BAQUEIRA BERET
Salardú
Maladeta 3308
Túnel de Vielha
Puerto de la Bonaigua 2072
3404 Pico de Aneto
3371 Posets
Caldas de Boi
BALNEARIO
Aigüestortes Estany de
Bielsa
Salinas
Plan
Benasque
Maladeta
Jaca
Puente la Reina de Jaca
Artieda
Urriés
Sierra de la Peña
Sabiñánigo
Sos del Rey Católico
Bailó
MONASTERIO DE SAN JUAN DE LA PEÑA
Bernués
Hostal de Ipiés
Yebra de Basa
Laspuña
Cotiella 2912
Sierra Ferrera
Castejón de Sos
Bono
Barruera
Cabdella
Laspaules
Boltaña
Aínsa
Campo
Tierrantona
Pont de Suert
Malpas
La Torre de Cabdella
Torre la Ribera
Embalse de Escales
Senterada
Pobla de Segur
Mallo el Fruto
Carcastillo
OLIVA
Castilisar
Luesia
Biel
Santa María
Triste
Rasal
Gállego
Caldearenas
Embalse de la Peña
Loarre
CASTILLO DE LOARRE
Ayerbe
Bolea
Nueno
Uncastillo
Sádaba
DOÑA BLANCA DE NAVARRA
El Frago
Farasdués
Biscarrués
Esquedas
Igriés
Sierra de Guara
SANTUARIO S. COSME
Arcusa
Embalse de Mediano
La Puebla de Roda
Bárcabo
Embalse de el Grado
Graus
Naval
Alquézar
El Grado
Laguarres
Castilgaleu
Embalse de Barasona
Puente de Montañana
Tremp
Figols
Tolva
Ejea de los Caballeros
Luna
Ardisa
Ortilla
Embalse de la Sotonera
Huesca
Sietamo
Angües
Aguas
Monflorite
Abiego
Pozán de Vero
Estadilla
Benabarre
Embalse de Canelles
Serra del Montsec
Erla
Sierra de Luna
Alcalá de Gurrea
Almudévar
Gurrea de Gállego
Blecua
Barbastro
Fonz
Peralta de la Sal
Emb. de Terradets
Fustiñana
Ribaforada
Buñuel
Cortes
Mallén
Castejón de Valdejasa
El Temple
Tardienta
Novales
Ilche
Azanúy-Alins
Estopiñán
Ager
Berbegal
Baells
Camporrells
Embalse Camarasa
Tauste
742 Esteban
Zuera
Grañén
Alberuela de Tubo
Ballerias
El Tormillo
Selgua
Monzón
San Esteban de Litera
Alcampell
Castillonroy
Camarasa
Gallur
Remolinos
San Mateo de Gallego
Robres
Poleñino
Flumen
Tamarite de Litera
Binéfar
Alfarràs
Castelló de Farfaña
Montgai
Magallon
Luceni
Pedrola
Alcubierre
Sariñena
La Masadera
Binaced
Almenar
Alagón
Villanueva de Gállego
Leciñena
Lanaja
Esplús
Balaguer
Termens
Berclair
Perdiguera
Sierra de Alcubierre
Sena
Alcolea de Cinca
Albalate de Cinca
Alguaire
Roselló
Linyola
Bellvís
Utebo
Canal Imperial de Aragón
Lumpiaque
Rueda de Jalón
Épila
La Muela
Zaragoza
Alfajarín
Farlete
Monegrillo
Pallaruelo de Monegros
Belver de Cinca
Almacelles
Lleida
Bell-lloc d'Urgell
Mollerussa
Torregrosa
ESPAÑA
Castejón de Monegros
Ballobar
Zaidín
Alcarràs
Albatàrrec
Juneda
Arbeca
Les Borges Blanques
Ricla
Calatorao
La Almunia de Doña Godina
El Burgo de Ebro
Cadrete
Osera de Ebro
La Almolda
Fuentes de Ebro
Pina de Ebro
Bujaraloz
Candasnos
Fraga
Torrente de Cinca
Aitona
Sarroca de Lleida
Seròs
Castelldans
Muel
Valmadrid
Longares
Embalse de Mezalocha
Almonacid de la Sierra
Villanueva del Huerva
Quinto
Gelsa
Puebla de Albortón
Laguna de la Playa
Embalse de Mequinenza
Mequinenza
La Granja d'Escarp
L'Albagés
Es Soleràs
Cervià de les Garrigues
Juncosa
Aguarón
Cariñena
Embalse de las Torcas
Puerto de Paniza 935
Belchite
Sástago
Escatrón
Embalse de Caspe
Maials
La Granadella
Ulldemolins
Montsant
Herrera de los Navarros
Azuara
Letux
Azaila
Castelnou
Caspe
Fayón
Riba-roja d'Ebre
Embalse de Riba-roja
La Palma d'Ebre
Bisbal de Falset
Serra de Montsant
Flix
Mainar
Emb. de Moneva
Lécera
Samper de Calanda
Nonaspe
Fabara
Asco
La Torre de l'Espanyol
La Vilella Baixa
Cornudella de Montsant
Villar de los Navarros
Badules
Híjar
Albalate del Arzobispo
Maella
La Fatarella
Batea
Falset
Bádenas
Báguena
Ferreruela
Monforte de Moyuela
Muniesa
Emb. de La Estanca de Alcañiz
Emb. de Caspe II
Camposines
Mont-roig del Camp
Móra la Nova
Móra d'Ebre
Fonfría
Ariño
Alcañiz
Mazaleón
Gandesa
Miravet
Pratdip
Tornos
Anadón
Cortes de Aragón
Oliete
Embalse de Cueva Foradada
Salada Grande
Valdealgorfa
Caseres
Bot
El Pinell de Bray
Tivissa
Calamocha
Cutanda
Segura de los Baños
Andorra
Castelserás
Valdeltormo
Calaceite
Prat de Comte
Rasquera
L'Hospitalet de l'Infant
Torre los Negros
Vivel del Río Martín
Calanda
Belmonte de San José
La Fresneda
Xerta
El Perelló
Golfo de Sant Jordi
Caminreal
Baños
Montalbán
Alcorisa
Mas de las Matas
Arnes
L'Ametlla de Mar
Monreal del Campo
Utrillas
Castel de Cabra
Gargallo
Castellote
Aguaviva
Valderrobres
Caro 1447
Roquetes
Tortosa
L'Ampolla
Sierra de San Just
1522 San Just
Pancrudo
Ejulve
Embalse de Santolea
Monroyo
Fuentespalda
Beceite
Peñarroya de Tastavins
Mas de Barberáns
Santa Bárbara
Amposta
L'Aldea
La Cava
Cap Tortosa
I. de Buda
Mezquita de Jarque
Las Cuevas de Cañart
Guadalope
Bordón
Puerto Torre Miró 1250
Tinença de Benifassà
La Galera
St. Jaume d'Enveja
Delta del Ebro
Sierra Palomera
Visiedo
Aliaga
Villarluengo
Forcall
Castell de Cabres
La Sènia
Ulldecona
Sant Carles de la Ràpita
Montsià 762
Perales de Alfambra
Camarillas
Olocau del Rey
Morella
Rosell
Alba
Santa Eulalia
Alfambra
El Pobo
Villarroya de los Pinares
Cinctorres
Cantavieja
San Rafael del Río
Cérvol
Traiguera
Alcanar
Costa de Fora
Cella
Fortanete
Castellfort
Xert
Sant Jordi
Vinaròs
Gea de Albarracín
Allepuz
Cedrillas
Sierra de Gúdar
La Iglesuela del Cid
Ares del Maestrat
Catí
Sant Mateu
Tirig
Benicarló
Alcalá de la Selva
2019 Peñarroya
Vilafranca del Maestrat
El Maestrat
Albocàsser
Santa Magdalena de Polpís
Peñíscola
CASTILLO DE PEÑISCOLA
Teruel
Bezas
Mosqueruela
Villastar
Linares de Mora
Les Coves de Vinromà
Alcalà de Xivert
Serra d'Irta
Javalón 1695
Villel
Aldehuela
Sierra de Camarena
Mora de Rubielos
Vistabella del Maestrat
La Puebla de Valverde
Rubielos de Mora
Penyagolosa 1813
Alcossebre
42°
0°
1
2
3
A
B
C
76
77
89
95
96
258
150

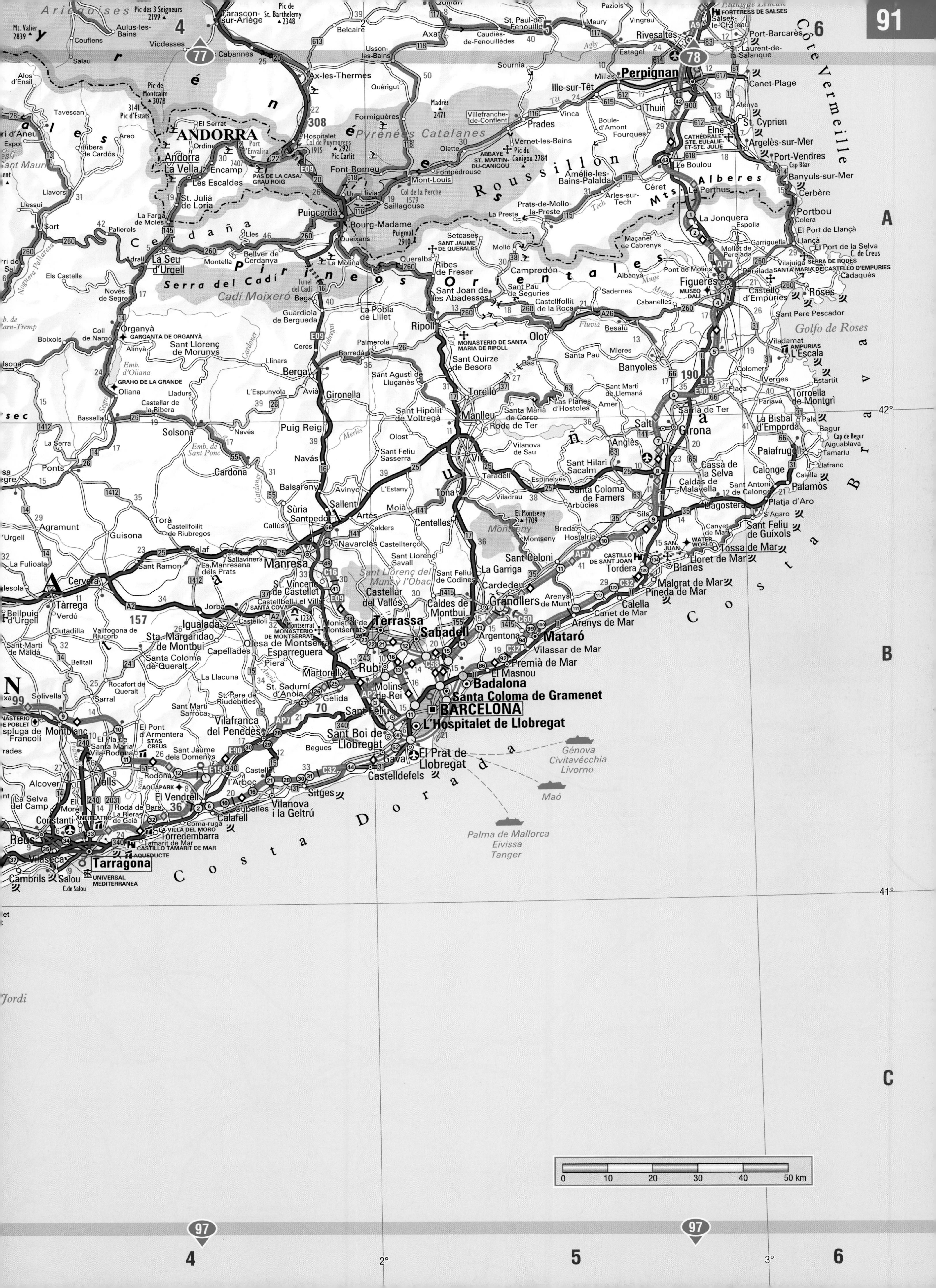

ANDORRA
Andorra la Vella
Encamp
Les Escaldes
St. Julià de Loria
El Serrat
Ordino
Port d'Envalira
Pas de la Casa/Grau Roig
Tarascon-sur-Ariège
Aulus-les-Bains
Vicdessos
Ax-les-Thermes
Quérigut
Formiguères
Font-Romeu
Mont-Louis
Puigcerdà
Bourg-Madame
Saillagouse
Llívia
L'Hospitalet
Col de Puymorens
Pic Carlit
Pyrénées Catalanes
Axat
Belcaire
Usson-les-Bains
St. Paul-de-Fenouillet
Caudiès-de-Fenouillèdes
Maury
Vingrau
Rivesaltes
Salses-le-Château
Forteresse de Salses
Port-Barcarès
St. Laurent-de-la-Salanque
Estagel
Millas
Sournia
Perpignan
Canet-Plage
Ille-sur-Têt
Thuir
Prades
Vinca
Villefranche-de-Conflent
Vernet-les-Bains
Olette
Abbaye St. Martin-du-Canigou
Pic du Canigou 2784
Fontpédrouse
Col de la Perche
Madrès 2471
Boule-d'Amont
Fourques
Elne
Cathédrale Ste. Eulalie-et-Ste. Julie
St. Cyprien
Argelès-sur-Mer
Port-Vendres
Cap Béar
Banyuls-sur-Mer
Cerbère
Portbou
Côte Vermeille
Le Boulou
Céret
Amélie-les-Bains-Palalda
Arles-sur-Tech
Prats-de-Mollo-la-Preste
La Preste
Roussillon
Mts. Albères
Le Perthus
La Jonquera
Colera
El Port de Llançà
Llançà
El Port de la Selva
C. de Creus
Serra de Rodes
Sant Maria de Castello d'Empuries
Cadaqués
Vilajuiga
Garriguella
Espolla
Maçanet de Cabrenys
Figueres
Museo Dalí
Castello d'Empúries
Roses
Sant Pere Pescador
Golfo de Roses
Viladamat
Ampurias
L'Escala
Estartit
Torroella de Montgrí
Verges
Colomers
Flaça
La Bisbal d'Empordà
Pals
Begur
Cap de Begur
Aiguablava
Tamariu
Llafranc
Palafrugell
Calella
Calonge
Palamós
Platja d'Aro
S'Agaro
Sant Feliu de Guíxols
Tossa de Mar
Lloret de Mar
Blanes
Malgrat de Mar
Pineda de Mar
Calella
Canet de Mar
Arenys de Mar
Arenys de Munt
Mataró
Vilassar de Mar
Premià de Mar
El Masnou
Badalona
Santa Coloma de Gramenet
BARCELONA
L'Hospitalet de Llobregat
El Prat de Llobregat
Gavà
Castelldefels
Sitges
Vilanova i la Geltrú
Cubelles
Calafell
El Vendrell
Coma-ruga
Torredembarra
Tamarit de Mar
Castillo Tamarit de Mar
Aqueducte
Tarragona
Salou
C. de Salou
Cambrils
Vilaseca
Reus
Constantí
Universal Mediterranea
Costa Dorada
Costa Brava
Gènova
Civitavècchia
Livorno
Maó
Palma de Mallorca
Eivissa
Tanger
Girona
Salt
Sarrià de Ter
Banyoles
Besalú
Olot
Castellfollit de la Roca
Sant Joan de les Abadesses
Ripoll
Monasterio de Santa Maria de Ripoll
Camprodon
Molló
Setcases
Sant Jaume de Queralbs
Queralbs
Ribes de Freser
Sant Pau de Seguries
Sant Quirze de Besora
Torelló
Manlleu
Vic
Tona
Taradell
Seva
Viladrau
Montseny
El Montseny 1709
Sant Celoni
Hostalric
Breda
Tordera
Castillo de Sant Joan
Santa Coloma de Farners
Arbúcies
Anglès
Cassà de la Selva
Llagostera
Caldas de Malavella
Sils
La Garriga
Cardedeu
Granollers
Argentona
Sant Feliu de Codines
Caldes de Montbui
Sabadell
Terrassa
Rubí
Molins de Rei
Sant Feliu
Sant Boi de Llobregat
Martorell
Esparreguera
Olesa de Montserrat
Monistrol de Montserrat
Monasterio de Montserrat
Castellbell i el Vilar
Sant Vicenç de Castellet
Castellar del Vallès
Sant Llorenç del Munt y l'Obac
Manresa
Navarcles
Sallent
Artés
Moià
Centelles
Súria
Callús
Sant Fruitós de Bages
Balsareny
Avinyó
L'Estany
Navás
Puig Reig
Gironella
Berga
Avià
Cercs
Guardiola de Berguedà
La Pobla de Lillet
Borredà
Sant Agustí de Lluçanès
Olost
Sant Feliu Sasserra
Sant Hipòlit de Voltregà
Roda de Ter
Santa Maria de Corco
Les Planes d'Hostoles
Amer
Sant Martí de Llemaná
Sant Hilari Sacalm
Vilanova de Sau
Espinelves
Solsona
Cardona
Navés
Emb. de Sant Ponç
Sant Llorenç de Morunys
Lladurs
Castellar de la Ribera
Bassella
Oliana
Graho de la Grande
Emb. d'Oliana
Organyà
Garganta de Organyà
Alinyà
Coll de Nargó
Boixols
La Seu d'Urgell
Adrall
Montella
Bellver de Cerdanya
La Molina
Serra del Cadí
Cadí Moixeró
Túnel del Cadí
Baga
Cerdaña
Lles
Pallerols
La Farga de Moles
Sort
Llavorsí
Tavescan
Alos d'Ensil
Pic de Montcalm 3078
Pic d'Estats 3141
Areo
Ribera de Cardós
Els Castells
Novés de Segre
Pirineos Orientales
Pyrénées
Ponts
Agramunt
Torà
Castellfollit de Riubregos
Guisona
Calaf
Sant Ramon
Cervera
Tàrrega
Verdú
Bellpuig d'Urgell
Ciutadilla
Vallfogona de Riucorb
Igualada
Jorba
La Manresana dels Prats
Sta. Margarida de Montbui
Santa Coloma de Queralt
Capellades
Piera
La Llacuna
Rocafort de Queralt
Sarral
Solivella
Montblanc
L'Espluga de Francolí
Valls
Alcover
La Selva del Camp
El Pla de Santa Maria
Vila-Rodona
Rodona
Roda de Barà
La Riera de Gaià
L'Arboç
Castellet
El Pont d'Armentera
Sant Jaume dels Domenys
Vilafranca del Penedès
Sant Martí Sarroca
Sant Pere de Riudebitlles
Sant Sadurní d'Anoia
Gelida
Begues
Aquapark
Costa Dorada
0 10 20 30 40 50 km

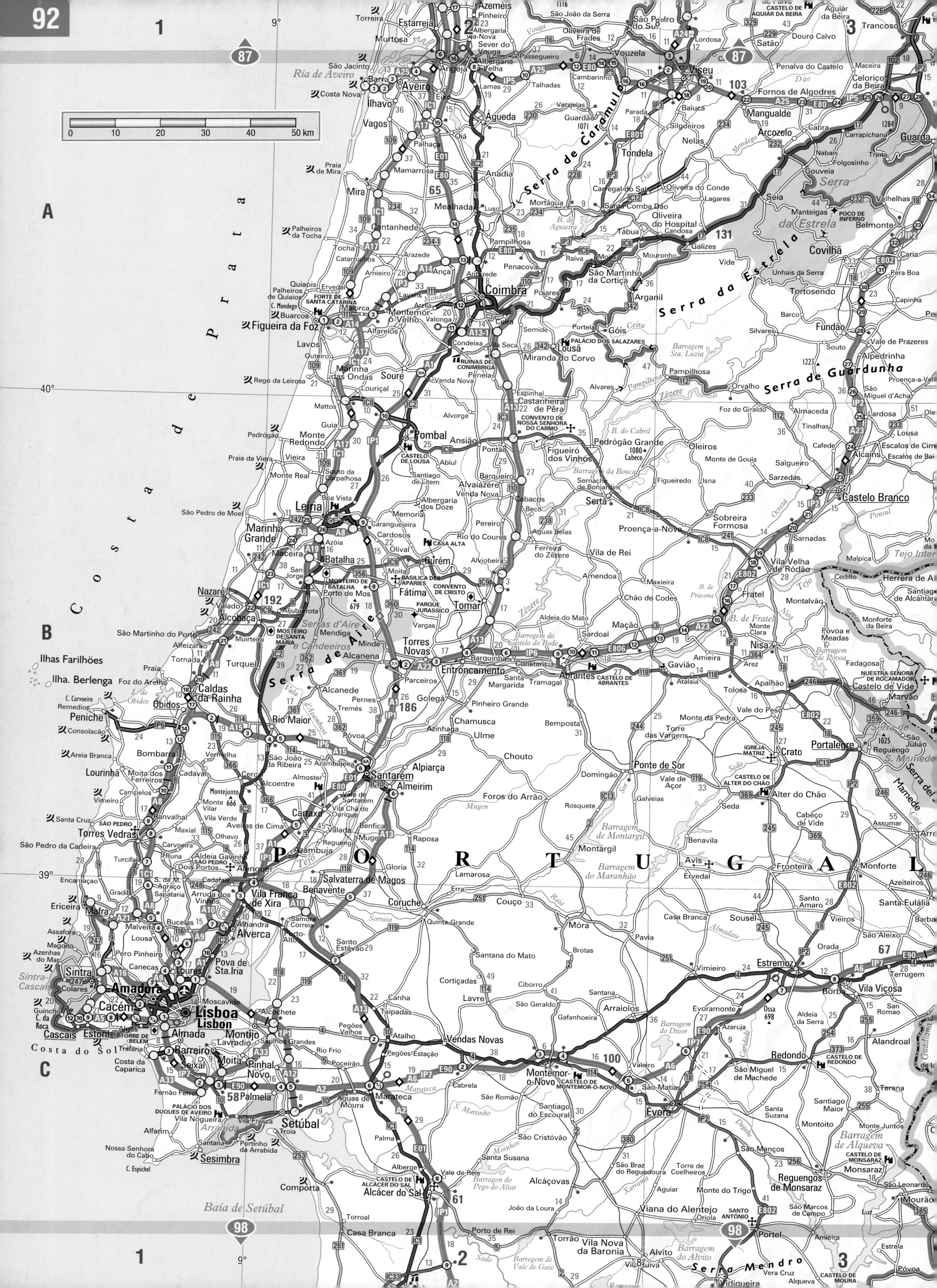
1
2
3
A
B
C
87
98
0 10 20 30 40 50 km
9°
40°
39°
Costa de Prata
P O R T U G A L
Ría de Aveiro
Costa do Sol
Baía de Setúbal
Serra de Caramulo
Serra da Estrela
Serra de Guardunha
Serra de Aire
Serras d'Aire e Candeeiros
Serra Mendro
Torreira
Estarreja
Murtosa
Azeméis
Oliveira de Frades
Vouzela
São Pedro do Sul
Viseu
Trancoso
Aguiar da Beira
Sátão
Penalva do Castelo
Celorico da Beira
Fornos de Algodres
Mangualde
Guarda
São Jacinto
Barra
Aveiro
Costa Nova
Ílhavo
Vagos
Águeda
Albergaria-a-Velha
Sever do Vouga
Angeja
Eixo
Talhadas
Guardão
Tondela
Nelas
Silgueiros
Arcozelo
Gouveia
Seia
Manteigas
Belmonte
Covilhã
Praia de Mira
Mira
Mamarrosa
Anadia
Mealhada
Mortágua
Santa Comba Dão
Carregal do Sal
Oliveira do Conde
Oliveira do Hospital
Lagares
Palheiros da Tocha
Cantanhede
Tocha
Pampilhosa
Penacova
Tábua
Galizes
Unhais da Serra
Tortosendo
Quiaios
Palheiros de Quiaios
C. Mondego
Buarcos
Figueira da Foz
FORTE DE SANTA CATARINA
Montemor-o-Velho
Coimbra
Condeixa
RUÍNAS DE CONIMBRIGA
Penela
Lousã
PALÁCIO DOS SALAZARES
Miranda do Corvo
Arganil
Góis
São Martinho da Cortiça
Fundão
Alpedrinha
Pampilhosa
Lavos
Rego da Leirosa
Marinha das Ondas
Soure
Louriçal
Pombal
CASTELO DE LOUSA
Ansião
Castanheira de Pêra
CONVENTO DE NOSSA SENHORA DO CARMO
Pedrógão Grande
Figueiró dos Vinhos
Oleiros
Castelo Branco
Alcains
Monte Redondo
Praia da Vieira
Monte Real
São Pedro de Moel
Marinha Grande
Leiria
Batalha
MOSTEIRO DE BATALHA
Porto de Mos
Fátima
BASÍLICA DES APARIES
Ourém
Tomar
CONVENTO DE CRISTO
PARQUE JURASSICO
Sertã
Proença-a-Nova
Vila de Rei
Vila Velha de Ródão
Nazaré
Alcobaça
MOSTEIRO DE SANTA MARIA
São Martinho do Porto
Torres Novas
Alcanena
Entroncamento
Abrantes
CASTELO DE ABRANTES
Mação
Nisa
Castelo de Vide
Marvão
Ilhas Farilhões
Ilha. Berlenga
Peniche
Óbidos
Caldas da Rainha
Rio Maior
Golegã
Chamusca
Ponte de Sor
Crato
Portalegre
Alter do Chão
CASTELO DE ALTER DO CHÃO
Lourinhã
Bombarral
Cadaval
Santarém
Almeirim
Alpiarça
Cartaxo
Torres Vedras
Azambuja
Alenquer
Salvaterra de Magos
Benavente
Coruche
Montargil
Avis
Fronteira
Monforte
Ericeira
Mafra
Vila Franca de Xira
Alverca
Sintra
Amadora
Cacém
Cascais
Estoril
Lisboa
Lisbon
TORRE DE BELÉM
Almada
Barreiro
Montijo
Seixal
Moita
Pinhal Novo
Palmela
Setúbal
Sesimbra
C. Espichel
Vendas Novas
Montemor-o-Novo
CASTELO DE MONTEMOR-O-NOVO
Arraiolos
Mora
Estremoz
Borba
Vila Viçosa
Redondo
CASTELO DE REDONDO
Évora
Reguengos de Monsaraz
Monsaraz
Alcácer do Sal
CASTELO DE ALCÁCER DO SAL
Alcáçovas
Viana do Alentejo
Portel
Vila Nova da Baronia
Alvito
Comporta
Torrão
CASTELO DE MOURA

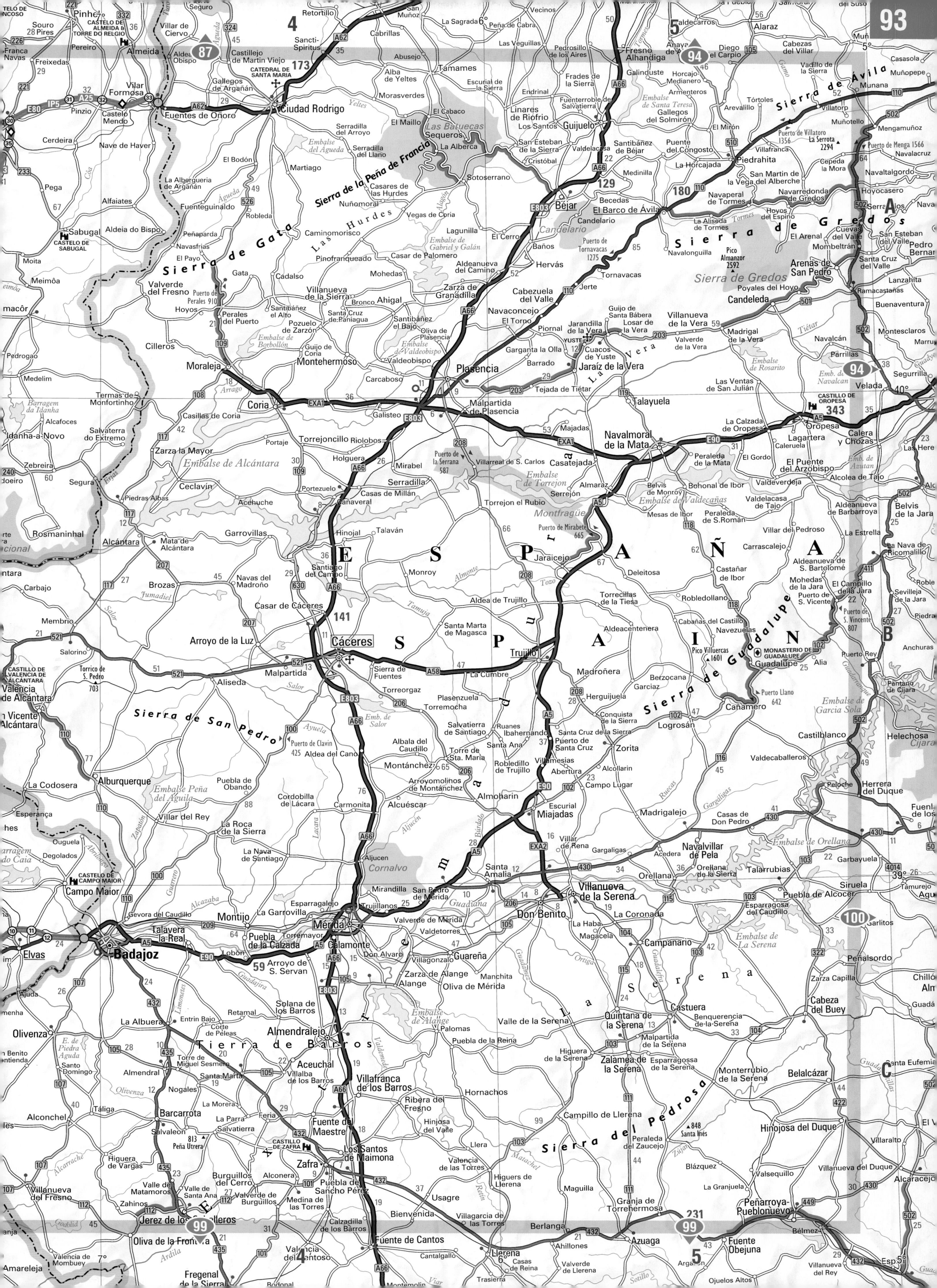

ESPAÑA
Sierra de la Peña de Francia
Sierra de Gata
Las Hurdes
Sierra de Ávila
Sierra de Gredos
La Vera
Sierra de Guadalupe
Sierra de San Pedro
Tierra de Barros
La Serena
Sierra del Pedrosa
Extremadura
Ciudad Rodrigo
Fuentes de Oñoro
Almeida
Vilar Formoso
Sabugal
Béjar
Guijuelo
Piedrahita
El Barco de Ávila
Arenas de San Pedro
Candeleda
Plasencia
Jaraíz de la Vera
Jarandilla de la Vera
Yuste
Navalmoral de la Mata
Oropesa
Calera y Chozas
Coria
Moraleja
Montehermoso
Cáceres
Trujillo
Guadalupe
Monasterio de Guadalupe
Miajadas
Mérida
Badajoz
Elvas
Campo Maior
Alburquerque
Valencia de Alcántara
Alcántara
Don Benito
Villanueva de la Serena
Almendralejo
Zafra
Castillo de Zafra
Jerez de los Caballeros
Olivenza
Fregenal de la Sierra
Llerena
Azuaga
Peñarroya-Pueblonuevo
Fuente Obejuna
Castuera
Zalamea de la Serena
Cabeza del Buey
Herrera del Duque
Logrosán
Montfragüe
Embalse de Alcántara
Embalse de Valdecañas
Embalse de Orellana
Embalse de La Serena
Embalse de Cijara
Cornalvo
Puerto de Tornavacas 1275
Pico Almanzor 2592
Pico Villuercas 1601
Puerto de Mirabete 665
Puerto de Perales 910
Castillo de Oropesa
Castelo de Sabugal
Catedral de Santa Maria
4
5
87
94
99
100

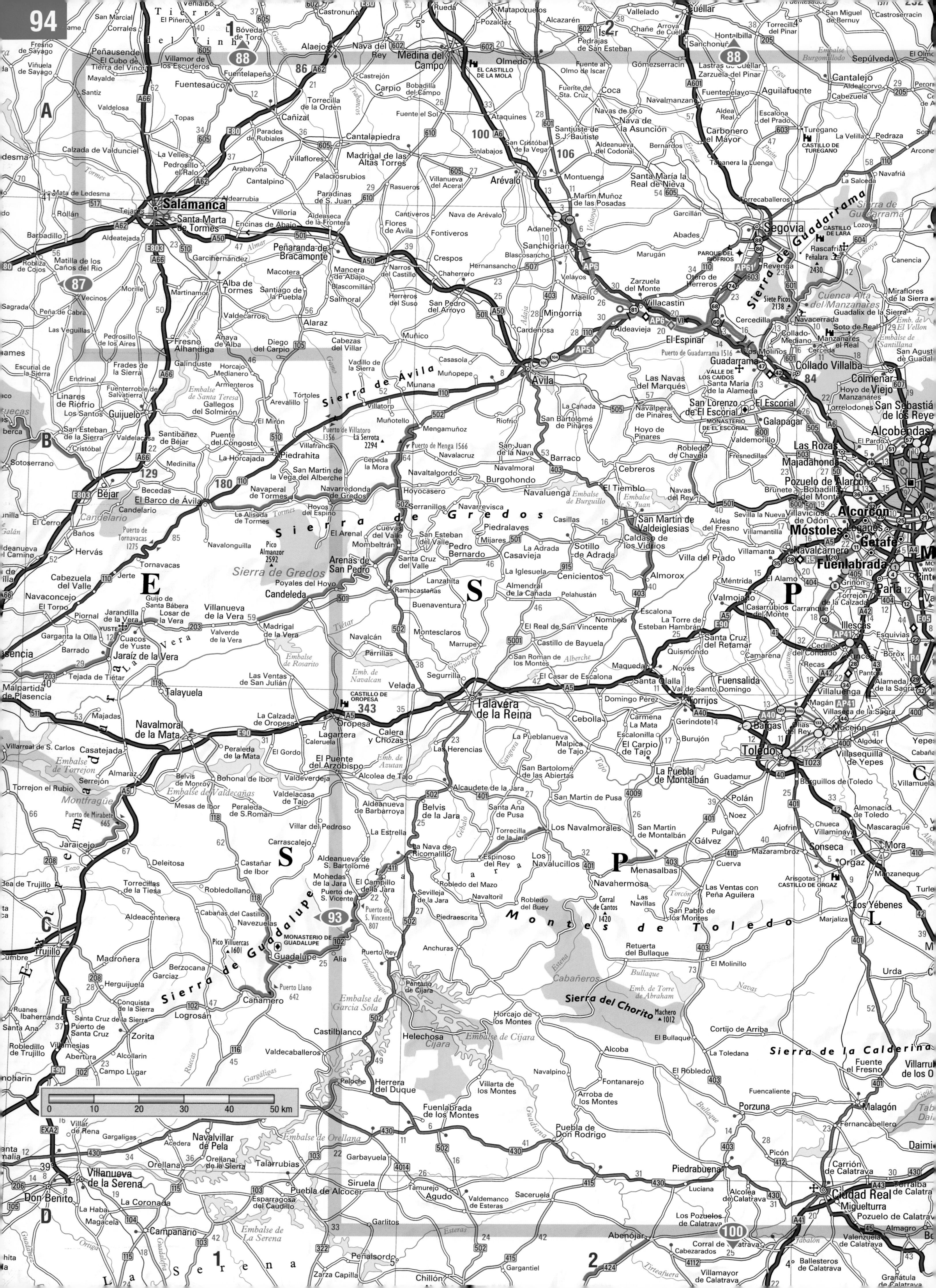

88
87
100
93
A
B
C
D
1
2
Salamanca
Santa Marta de Tormes
Medina del Campo
Segovia
Ávila
Talavera de la Reina
Toledo
Ciudad Real
Alcorcón
Móstoles
Getafe
Fuenlabrada
Alcobendas
Majadahonda
Las Rozas
Collado Villalba
Colmenar Viejo
Guadarrama
El Escorial
San Lorenzo de El Escorial
Galapagar
Navalcarnero
Illescas
Parla
Pinto
Leganés
Pozuelo de Alarcón
Boadilla del Monte
Villaviciosa de Odón
Arévalo
Peñaranda de Bracamonte
Alba de Tormes
Béjar
Piedrahita
El Barco de Ávila
Arenas de San Pedro
Candeleda
Jaraíz de la Vera
Navalmoral de la Mata
Oropesa
Trujillo
Guadalupe
Don Benito
Villanueva de la Serena
Campanario
Cuéllar
Coca
Olmedo
Cantalejo
Sepúlveda
Turégano
Villacastín
El Espinar
Las Navas del Marqués
Cebreros
El Tiemblo
San Martín de Valdeiglesias
Cadalso de los Vidrios
Almorox
Escalona
Maqueda
Torrijos
Bargas
Mocejón
Sonseca
Orgaz
Mora
Los Yébenes
Malagón
Porzuna
Piedrabuena
Miguelturra
Almagro
Fuente el Fresno
Urda
Consuegra
Menasalbas
Navahermosa
Los Navalmorales
La Puebla de Montalbán
Belvís de la Jara
Alcaudete de la Jara
Sevilleja de la Jara
Puerto de San Vicente
Herrera del Duque
Castilblanco
Fuenlabrada de los Montes
Puebla de Don Rodrigo
Siruela
Agudo
Talarrubias
Navalvillar de Pela
Orellana
Zorita
Logrosán
Cañamero
Madroñera
Deleitosa
Almaraz
Casatejada
Talayuela
Hervás
Baños
Guijuelo
Fuentesaúco
Cantalapiedra
Madrigal de las Altas Torres
Fontiveros
Sanchidrián
Mingorria
Santa María la Real de Nieva
Nava de la Asunción
Montuenga
Sierra de Guadarrama
Sierra de Ávila
Sierra de Gredos
Pico Almanzor 2592
Sierra de Guadalupe
Montes de Toledo
Sierra del Chorito
Sierra de la Calderina
Embalse de Cíjara
Embalse de García Sola
Embalse de Orellana
Embalse de La Serena
Embalse de Valdecañas
Embalse de Rosarito
Embalse de Burguillo
Embalse de Santa Teresa
Monfragüe
Cabañeros
La Jara
La Vera
La Serena
Extremadura
Tierra del Vino
E
S
P
L
MONASTERIO DE GUADALUPE
CASTILLO DE OROPESA
CASTILLO DE LA MOLA
CASTILLO DE TURÉGANO
CASTILLO DE LARA
CASTILLO DE ORGAZ
VALLE DE LOS CAÍDOS
MONASTERIO DE EL ESCORIAL
PARQUE DEL RIOFRÍO
Puerto de Guadarrama 1516
Puerto de Villatoro 1356
Puerto de Menga 1566
Puerto de Tornavacas 1275
Puerto de Mirabete 665
Puerto Llano 642
Pico Villuercas 1601
Peñalara 2430
Siete Picos 2138
La Serrota 2294
Corral de Cantos 1420
Machero 1012
0 10 20 30 40 50 km

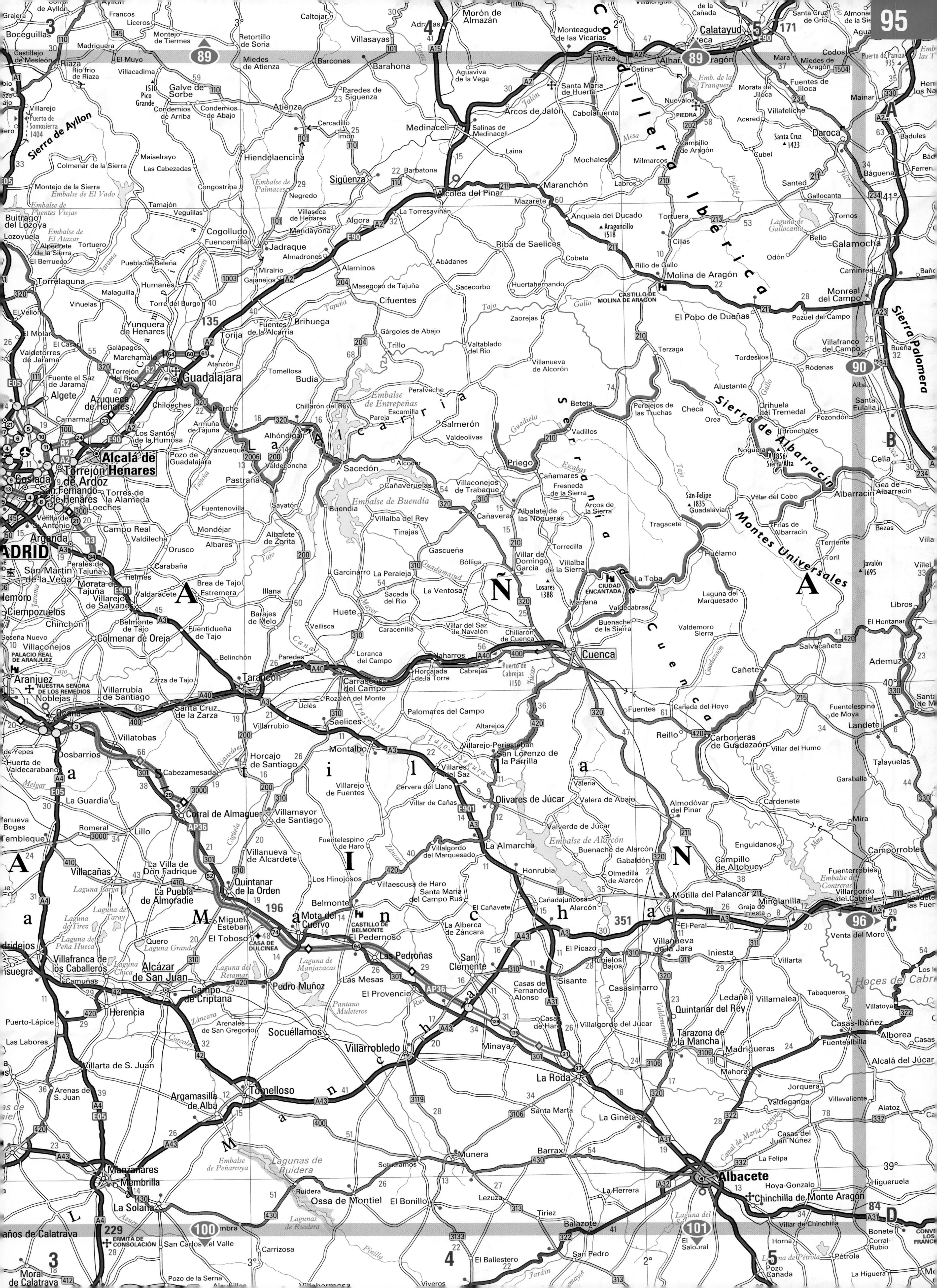

Boceguillas
Riaza
Sierra de Aylion
Atienza
Medinaceli
Calatayud
Ateca
Alhama de Aragón
Ariza
Monteagudo de las Vicarias
Morón de Almazán
Arcos de Jalón
Cordillera Ibérica
Daroca
Sigüenza
Alcolea del Pinar
Maranchón
Molina de Aragón
Castillo de Molina de Aragón
Calamocha
Monreal del Campo
Sierra Palomera
Jadraque
Cogolludo
Torrelaguna
Buitrago del Lozoya
Cifuentes
Brihuega
Guadalajara
Alcalá de Henares
Torrejón de Ardoz
Coslada
San Fernando de Henares
Arganda
Madrid
La Alcarria
Embalse de Entrepeñas
Sacedón
Embalse de Buendía
Priego
Beteta
Serranía de Cuenca
Sierra de Albarracín
Albarracín
Montes Universales
Ciudad Encantada
Cuenca
Huete
Pastrana
Tarancón
Aranjuez
Ocaña
Chinchón
Colmenar de Oreja
Villarejo de Salvanés
Cañete
Landete
Carboneras de Guadazaón
Motilla del Palancar
Minglanilla
Villagordo del Cabriel
Olivares de Júcar
Embalse de Alarcón
Alarcón
La Almarcha
Belmonte
Castillo de Belmonte
Mota del Cuervo
El Toboso
Quintanar de la Orden
Corral de Almaguer
Villacañas
Madridejos
Alcázar de San Juan
Campo de Criptana
Herencia
Pedro Muñoz
Las Pedroñas
San Clemente
Villarrobledo
Socuéllamos
Tomelloso
Argamasilla de Alba
Manzanares
Membrilla
La Solana
Lagunas de Ruidera
Ossa de Montiel
Munera
La Roda
Minaya
Quintanar del Rey
Tarazona de la Mancha
Madrigueras
Casas-Ibáñez
Albacete
Chinchilla de Monte Aragón
La Gineta
Barrax
Balazote
Alcalá del Júcar
Iniesta
Villanueva de la Jara
Sisante
Casasimarro
La Mancha
Castilla
Hoces del Cabriel
Ermita de Consolación
Moral de Calatrava
San Carlos del Valle
Valdepeñas
89
90
96
100
101

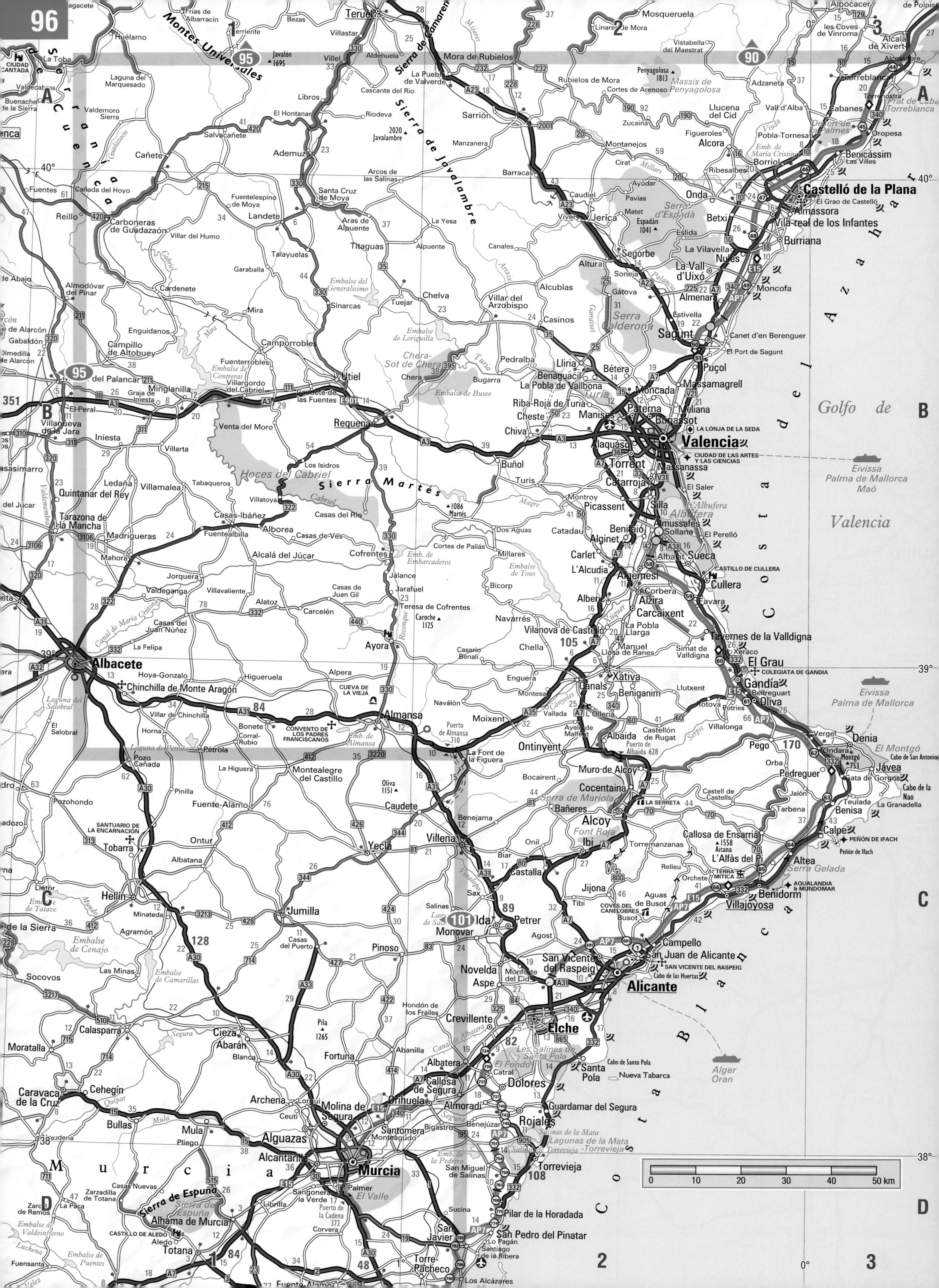
Teruel
Montes Universales
Serranía de Cuenca
Sierra de Camarena
Sierra de Javalambre
Mora de Rubielos
Rubielos de Mora
Mosqueruela
Linares de Mora
Vistabella del Maestrat
Penyagolosa 1813
Massís de Penyagolosa
Les Coves de Vinromà
Alcalà de Xivert
Alcossebre
Torreblanca
Prat de Cabanes Torreblanca
Cabanes
Oropesa
Benicàssim
Castelló de la Plana
El Grao de Castelló
Almassora
Vila-real de los Infantes
Burriana
Nules
Moncofa
La Vall d'Uixó
Almenara
Sagunt
Canet d'en Berenguer
El Port de Sagunt
Puçol
Massamagrell
Meliana
Valencia
La Lonja de la Seda
Ciudad de las Artes y las Ciencias
Golfo de Valencia
Eivissa Palma de Mallorca Maó
Costa del Azahar
Serra d'Espadà
Sierra Calderona
Onda
Betxí
Segorbe
Jerica
Altura
Lliria
Bétera
Moncada
Paterna
Burjassot
Manises
Torrent
Catarroja
Massanassa
El Saler
Silla
L'Albufera
Almussafes
Sollana
El Perelló
Sueca
Cullera
Castillo de Cullera
Alzira
Carcaixent
Algemesí
Tavernes de la Valldigna
Xàtiva
Gandía
Colegiata de Gandia
Oliva
Denia
El Montgó
Cabo de San Antonio
Jávea
Cabo de la Nao
Teulada
Benisa
Calpe
Peñón de Ifach
Altea
Serra Gelada
Benidorm
Villajoyosa
Aqualandia & Mundomar
Terra Mítica
L'Alfàs del Pi
Callosa de Ensarriá
Alcoy
Font Roja
Cocentaina
Muro de Alcoy
Serra de Mariola
Bañeres
Ibi
Castalla
Jijona
Ontinyent
Albaida
La Font de la Figuera
Almansa
Convento de los Padres Franciscanos
Cueva de la Vieja
Villena
Caudete
Yecla
Jumilla
Petrer
Elda
Monóvar
Novelda
Aspe
San Vicente del Raspeig
San Juan de Alicante
Campello
Alicante
Cabo de las Huertas
Elche
Crevillente
Santa Pola
Cabo de Santo Pola
Nueva Tabarca
Les Salines de Santa Pola
El Fondo
Alger Oran
Costa Blanca
Dolores
Guardamar del Segura
Rojales
Orihuela
Callosa de Segura
Almoradí
Torrevieja
Lagunas de la Mata Torrevieja
Pilar de la Horadada
San Pedro del Pinatar
San Javier
Torre-Pacheco
Los Alcázares
Murcia
Molina de Segura
Alcantarilla
Alguazas
Mula
Bullas
Cehegín
Caravaca de la Cruz
Calasparra
Moratalla
Cieza
Abarán
Sierra de Espuña
Alhama de Murcia
Castillo de Aledo
Totana
Hellín
Tobarra
Santuario de la Encarnación
Albacete
Chinchilla de Monte Aragón
La Roda
Madrigueras
Tarazona de la Mancha
Quintanar del Rey
Casas-Ibáñez
Alcalá del Júcar
Ayora
Cofrentes
Requena
Utiel
Chiva
Buñol
Cheste
Hoces del Cabriel
Sierra Martés
Venta del Moro
Minglanilla
Iniesta
Villanueva de la Jara
Cañete
Carboneras de Guadazaón
Landete
Ademuz
Chelva
Alcublas
Carlet
Alginet
L'Alcudia
Canals
Murcia
Costa Blanca
Costa del Azahar
0 10 20 30 40 50 km

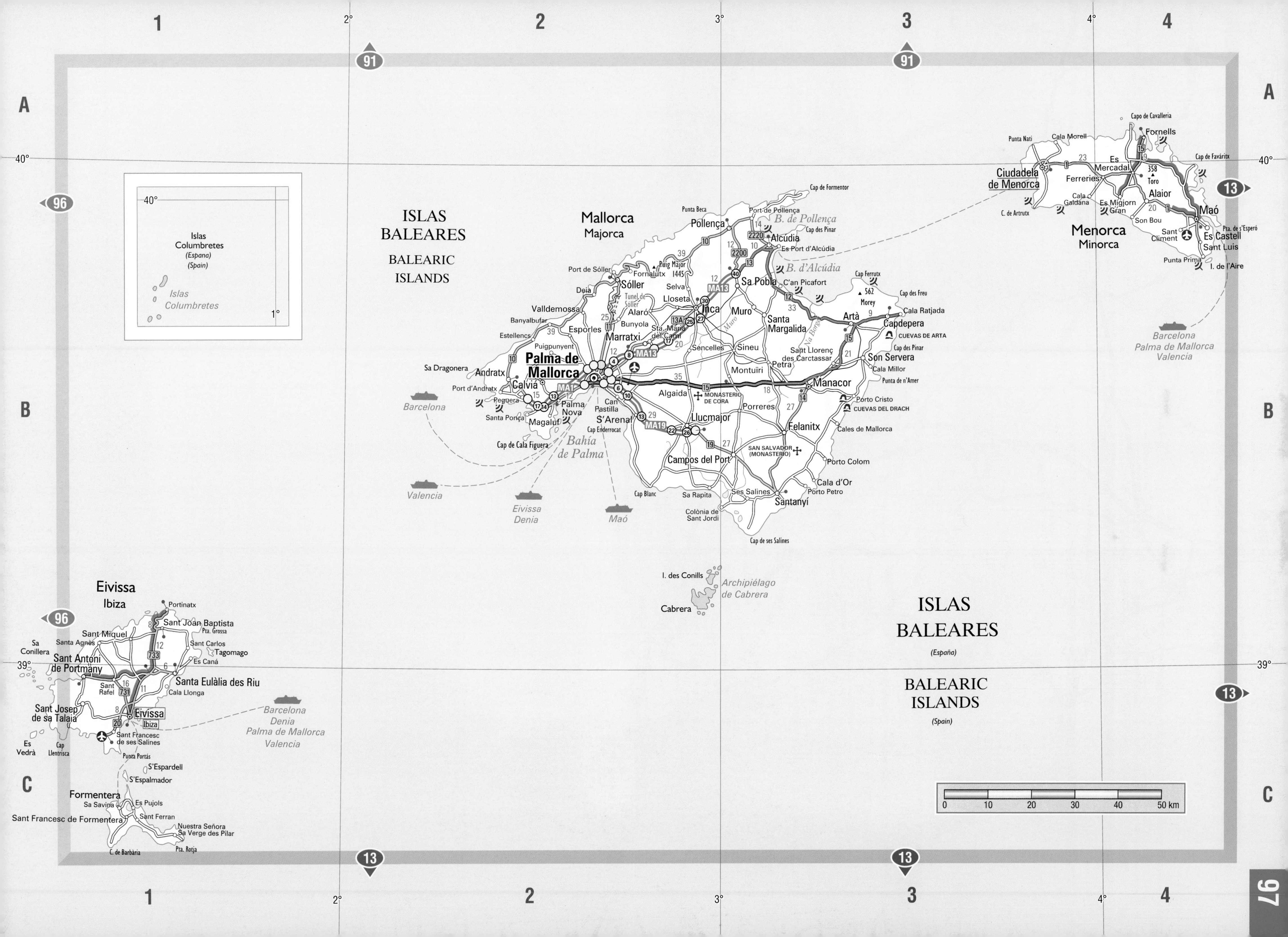

ISLAS BALEARES
BALEARIC ISLANDS
ISLAS BALEARES
(España)
BALEARIC ISLANDS
(Spain)
Islas Columbretes
(Espana)
(Spain)
Mallorca
Majorca
Menorca
Minorca
Eivissa
Ibiza
Formentera
Palma de Mallorca
Pollença
Port de Pollença
B. de Pollença
Alcúdia
Es Port d'Alcúdia
B. d'Alcúdia
Cap de Formentor
Cap des Pinar
Punta Beca
Port de Sóller
Sóller
Fornalutx
Puig Major
Deià
Valldemossa
Banyalbufar
Estellencs
Esporles
Puigpunyent
Sa Dragonera
Andratx
Port d'Andratx
Calvià
Peguera
Santa Ponça
Magaluf
Palma Nova
Cap de Cala Figuera
Bahía de Palma
Can Pastilla
S'Arenal
Cap Enderrocat
Marratxi
Bunyola
Alaró
Lloseta
Selva
Inca
Sa Pobla
C'an Picafort
Muro
Santa Margalida
Sineu
Sencelles
Sta. Maria del Camí
Algaida
Montuïri
Petra
Sant Llorenç des Carctassar
Artà
Capdepera
Cala Ratjada
Cap des Freu
Cap Ferrutx
Morey
CUEVAS DE ARTA
Son Servera
Cala Millor
Punta de n'Amer
Manacor
Porto Cristo
CUEVAS DEL DRACH
Cales de Mallorca
Porreres
Llucmajor
MONASTERIO DE CORA
Felanitx
SAN SALVADOR (MONASTERIO)
Porto Colom
Cala d'Or
Porto Petro
Santanyí
Ses Salines
Campos del Port
Sa Rapita
Colònia de Sant Jordi
Cap Blanc
Cap de ses Salines
I. des Conills
Cabrera
Archipiélago de Cabrera
Ciudadela de Menorca
Punta Nati
Cala Morell
Capo de Cavalleria
Fornells
Cap de Favàritx
Ferreries
Es Mercadal
Toro
Alaior
Es Migjorn Gran
Cala Galdana
C. de Artrutx
Son Bou
Maó
Es Castell
Sant Lluis
Sant Climent
Pta. de s'Esperó
Punta Prima
I. de l'Aire
Portinatx
Sant Joan Baptista
Pta. Grossa
Sant Miquel
Santa Agnès
Sant Carlos
Tagomago
Es Caná
Sa Conillera
Sant Antoni de Portmany
Sant Rafel
Santa Eulàlia des Riu
Cala Llonga
Sant Josep de sa Talaia
Eivissa
Ibiza
Sant Francesc de ses Salines
Es Vedrà
Cap Llentrisca
Punta Portás
S'Espardell
S'Espalmador
Sa Savina
Es Pujols
Sant Ferran
Sant Francesc de Formentera
Nuestra Señora Sa Verge des Pilar
Pta. Rotja
C. de Barbària
Barcelona
Valencia
Eivissa
Denia
Maó
Barcelona
Palma de Mallorca
Valencia
Barcelona
Denia
Palma de Mallorca
Valencia
0 10 20 30 40 50 km

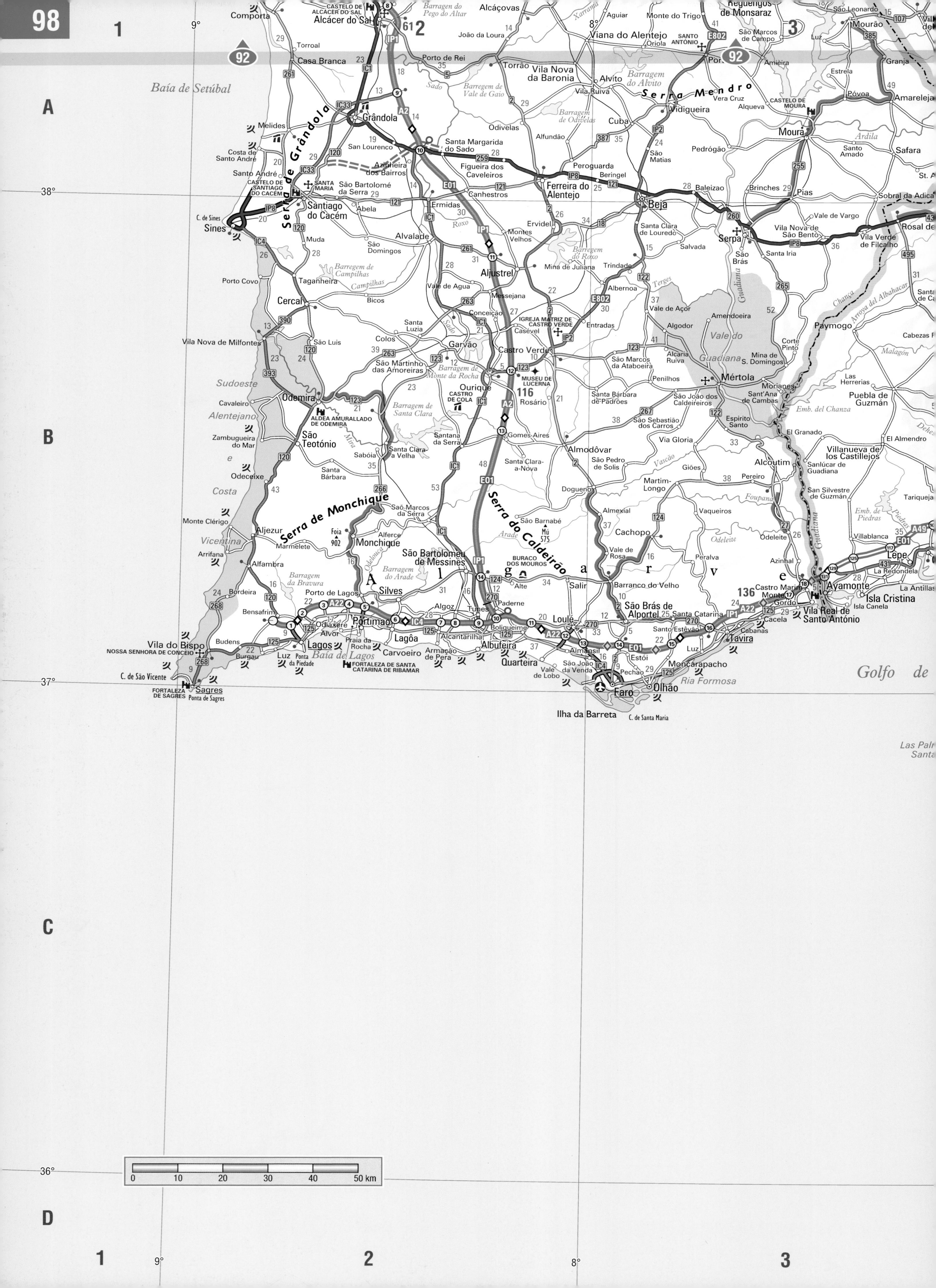
1
2
3
A
B
C
D
9°
8°
38°
37°
36°
92
Baía de Setúbal
Comporta
Alcácer do Sal
Alcáçovas
Aguiar
Monte do Trigo
Reguengos de Monsaraz
São Leonardo
Mourão
Torroal
João da Loura
Viana do Alentejo
Oriola
Santo António
São Marcos de Campo
Casa Branca
Porto de Rei
Torrão
Vila Nova da Baronia
Alvito
Barragem do Alvito
Amieira
Granja
Estrela
Barragem de Vale de Gaio
Vila Ruiva
Serra Mendro
Vidigueira
Vera Cruz
Alqueva
Castelo de Moura
Póvoa
Amareleja
Grândola
Odivelas
Barragem de Odivelas
Cuba
Moura
Melides
Serra de Grândola
Alfundão
Ardila
San Lourenço
Santa Margarida do Sado
São Matias
Pedrógão
Santo Amado
Safara
Costa de Santo André
Azinheira dos Barros
Figueira dos Caveleiros
Peroguarda
Beringel
Santo André
Castelo de Santiago do Cacém
Santa Maria
São Bartolomé da Serra
Ferreira do Alentejo
Canhestros
Baleizao
Brinches
Pias
Sobral da Adiça
Santiago do Cacém
Ermidas
Beja
C. de Sines
Sines
Abela
Roxo
Ervidel
Santa Clara de Louredo
Serpa
Vale de Vargo
Vila Nova de São Bento
Vila Verde de Filcalho
Rosal de
Muda
Alvalade
Montes Velhos
Salvada
São Brás
Santa Iria
São Domingos
Barragem do Roxo
Barregem de Campilhas
Aljustrel
Mina de Juliana
Trindade
Porto Covo
Taganheira
Campilhas
Vale de Agua
Albernoa
Terges
Guadiana
Chança
Arroyo del Albahacar
Bicos
Messejana
Cercal
Conceição
Igreja Matriz de Castro Verde
Entradas
Vale de Açor
Amendoeira
Santa Luzia
Casével
Algodor
Vale do Guadiana
Paymogo
Cabezas
Vila Nova de Milfontes
São Luis
Colos
Garvão
Castro Verde
Corte Pinto
Malagón
São Martinho das Amoreiras
São Marcos da Ataboeira
Alcaria Ruiva
Mina de S. Domingos
Barragem de Monte da Rocha
Ourique
Museu de Lucerna
Sudoeste
Penilhos
Mértola
Las Herrerias
Castro de Cola
Rosário
Santa Bárbara de Padrões
Morianes
Sant'Ana de Cambas
Puebla de Guzmán
Cavaleiro
Odemira
Aldea Amurallado de Odemira
Barragem de Santa Clara
São João dos Caldeireiros
Emb. del Chanza
Alentejano
Mira
São Sebastião dos Carros
Espirito Santo
Zambugueira do Mar
São Teotónio
Santana da Serra
Gomes Aires
Almodôvar
Via Gloria
El Granado
Villanueva de los Castillejos
El Almendro
Sabóia
Santa Clara-a-Velha
São Pedro de Solis
Vascão
Alcoutim
Sanlúcar de Guadiana
Odeceixe
Santa Bárbara
Santa Clara-a-Nova
Gilões
Pereiro
Martim-Longo
Costa
Dogueno
Foupana
San Silvestre de Guzmán
Tariqueja
Serra de Monchique
São Marcos da Serra
Serra do Caldeirão
Almexial
Vaqueiros
Emb. de Piedras
Monte Clérigo
Aljezur
Foia 902
Alferce
São Barnabé
Mú 575
Cachopo
Odeleite
Villablanca
Vicentina
Marmelete
Monchique
Arade
Vale de Rosa
Peralva
Lepe
Arrifana
São Bartolomeu de Messines
Buraco dos Mouros
Azinhal
La Redondela
Alfambra
Barragem da Bravura
Barragem do Arade
Algarve
Alte
Salir
Barranco do Velho
La Antilla
Bordeira
Porto de Lagos
Silves
Castro Marim
Monte Gordo
Ayamonte
Isla Cristina
Bensafrim
Odiáxere
Portimão
Algoz
Tunes
Paderne
Loulé
São Brás de Alportel
Santa Catarina
Cacela
Vila Real de Santo António
Isla Canela
Alvor
Lagoa
Alcantarilha
Boliqueime
Santo Estêvão
Cabanas
Vila do Bispo
Budens
Lagos
Praia da Rocha
Carvoeiro
Armação de Pera
Albufeira
Quarteira
Almansil
Estói
Tavira
Luz
Nossa Senhora de Conceição
Burgau
Ponta da Piedade
Baía de Lagos
Fortaleza de Santa Catarina de Ribamar
Vale de Lobo
São João da Venda
Pechão
Moncarapacho
Ria Formosa
Golfo de
C. de São Vicente
Fortaleza de Sagres
Sagres
Ponta de Sagres
Faro
Olhão
Ilha da Barreta
C. de Santa Maria
Las Palmas
0
10
20
30
40
50 km

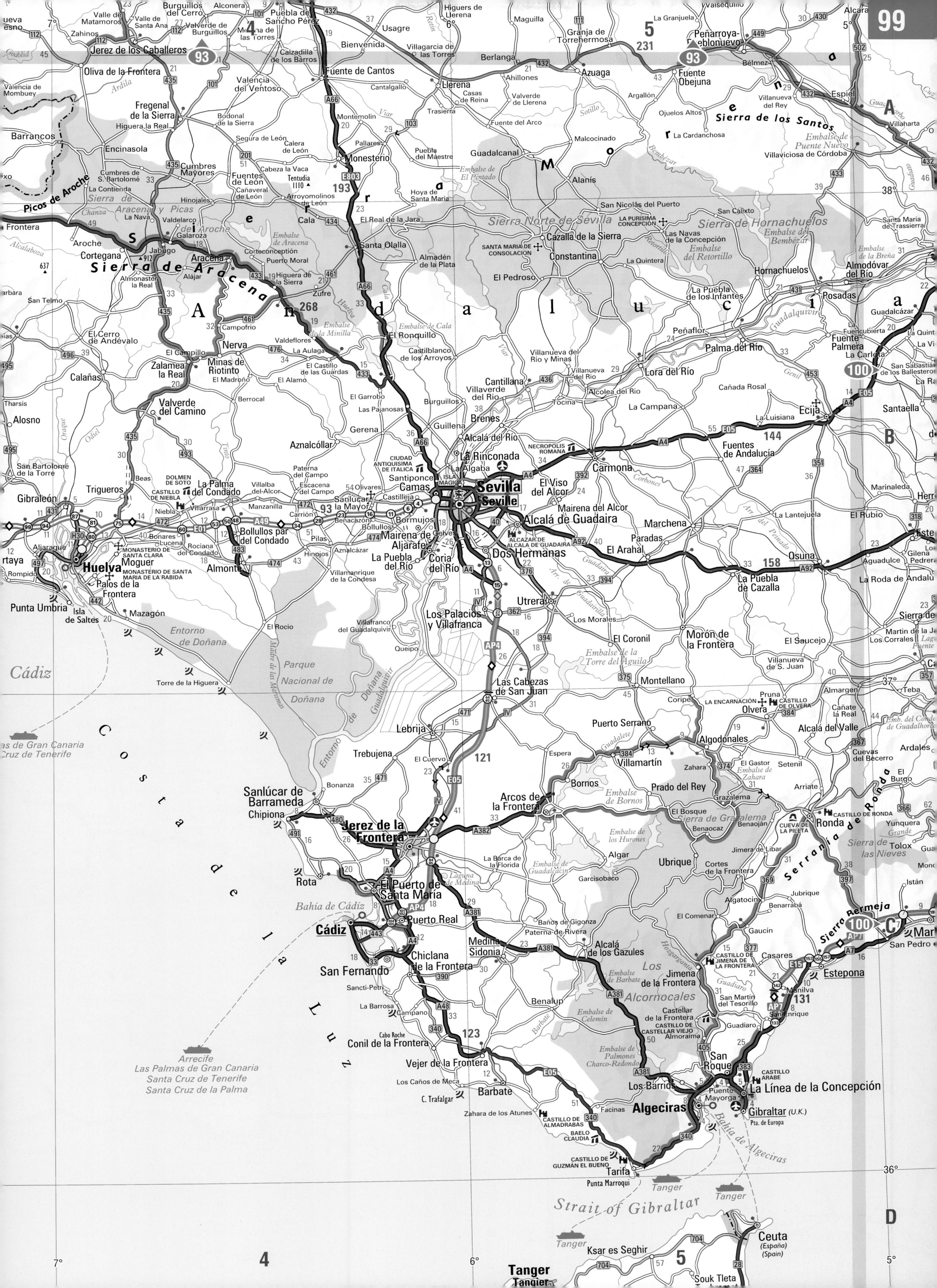

Jerez de los Caballeros
Oliva de la Frontera
Fregenal de la Sierra
Higuera la Real
Barrancos
Encinasola
Cumbres Mayores
Fuente de Cantos
Llerena
Monesterio
Usagre
Bienvenida
Berlanga
Azuaga
Fuente Obejuna
Peñarroya-Pueblonuevo
Bélmez
Espiel
Villaharta
Sierra de los Santos
Villaviciosa de Córdoba
Guadalcanal
Malcocinado
Alanís
Tentudía 1110
Picos de Aroche
Sierra de Aracena y Picos de Aroche
Sierra de Aracena
Aroche
Cortegana
Jabugo
Aracena
Alájar
Santa Olalla
Almadén de la Plata
El Real de la Jara
Cazalla de la Sierra
Constantina
Sierra Norte de Sevilla
Sierra de Hornachuelos
Las Navas de la Concepción
San Nicolás del Puerto
El Pedroso
Hornachuelos
Almodóvar del Río
Posadas
Guadalcázar
Fuente Palmera
La Carlota
Palma del Río
Peñaflor
Lora del Río
Andalucía
Sierra Morena
Nerva
Minas de Riotinto
Zalamea la Real
Calañas
Valverde del Camino
El Ronquillo
Castilblanco de los Arroyos
Cantillana
Villaverde del Río
Villanueva del Río y Minas
Alcolea del Río
Tocina
Burguillos
Brenes
Guillena
Gerena
Aznalcóllar
Alcalá del Río
La Rinconada
La Algaba
Santiponce
Camas
Sevilla
Seville
Carmona
El Viso del Alcor
Mairena del Alcor
Alcalá de Guadaira
Dos Hermanas
Coria del Río
La Puebla del Río
Mairena de Aljarafe
Bormujos
Sanlúcar la Mayor
Olivares
Pilas
Hinojos
Villamanrique de la Condesa
Bollullos par del Condado
La Palma del Condado
Niebla
Trigueros
Gibraleón
Huelva
Moguer
Palos de la Frontera
Punta Umbría
Isla de Saltes
Mazagón
Almonte
El Rocío
Écija
Fuentes de Andalucía
La Campana
Marchena
Paradas
El Arahal
Osuna
La Puebla de Cazalla
Utrera
Los Palacios y Villafranca
El Coronil
Morón de la Frontera
Montellano
El Saucejo
Las Cabezas de San Juan
Lebrija
Trebujena
Parque Nacional de Doñana
Entorno de Doñana
Cádiz
Costa de la Luz
Olvera
Puerto Serrano
Algodonales
Villamartín
Zahara
Setenil
Prado del Rey
Bornos
Arcos de la Frontera
Grazalema
Sierra de Grazalema
El Bosque
Ubrique
Ronda
Serranía de Ronda
Sierra de las Nieves
Sanlúcar de Barrameda
Chipiona
Jerez de la Frontera
Rota
El Puerto de Santa María
Bahía de Cádiz
Puerto Real
Cádiz
San Fernando
Chiclana de la Frontera
Medina Sidonia
Alcalá de los Gazules
Los Alcornocales
Jimena de la Frontera
Benalup
Conil de la Frontera
Vejer de la Frontera
Barbate
C. Trafalgar
Zahara de los Atunes
Tarifa
Punta Marroquí
Algeciras
Los Barrios
San Roque
La Línea de la Concepción
Gibraltar (U.K.)
Bahía de Algeciras
Estepona
Sierra Bermeja
Manilva
Strait of Gibraltar
Tanger
Tangier
Ksar es Seghir
Ceuta (España) (Spain)
Souk Tleta
Arrecife
Las Palmas de Gran Canaria
Santa Cruz de Tenerife
Santa Cruz de la Palma

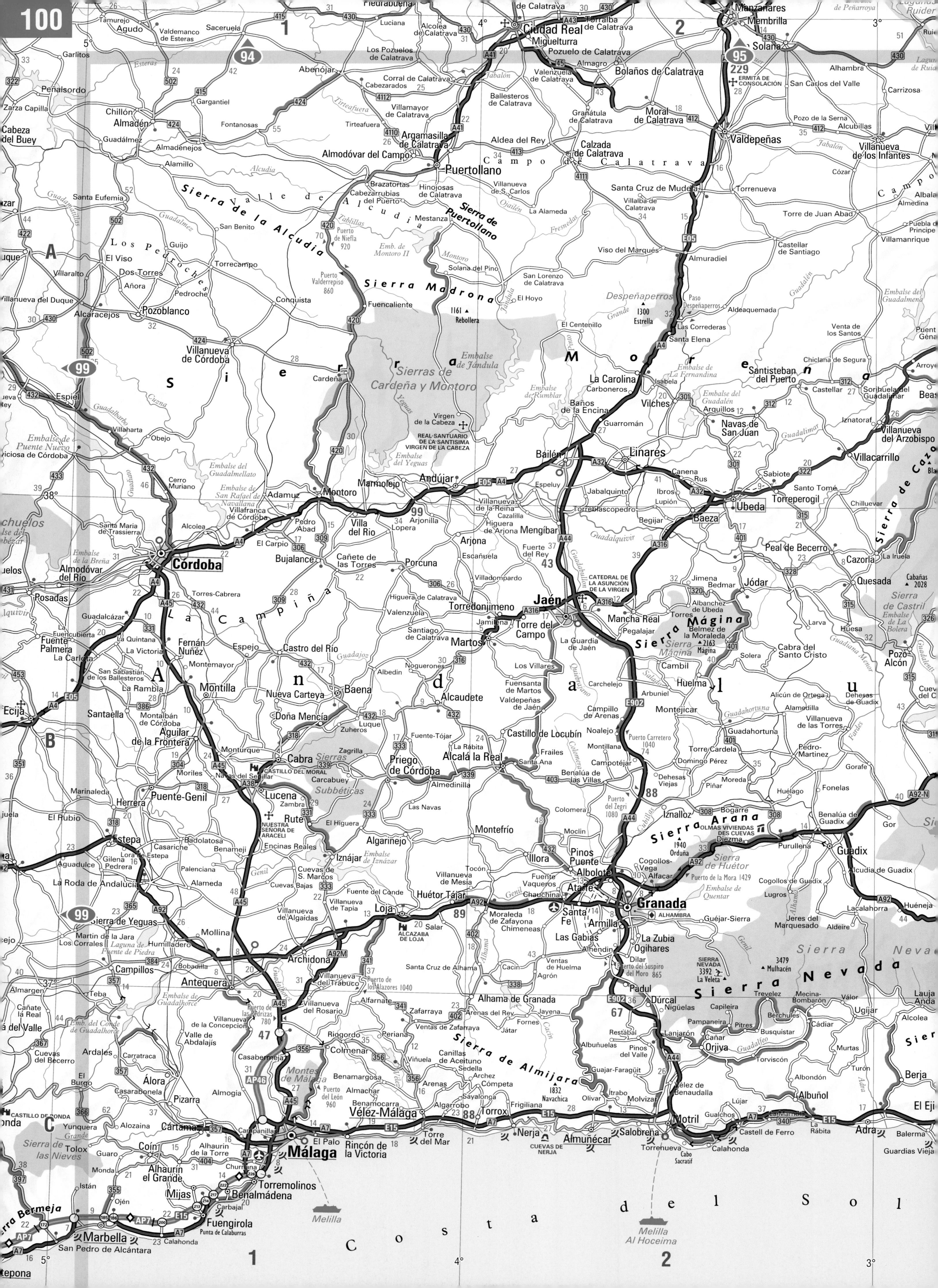
Ciudad Real
Miguelturra
Pozuelo de Calatrava
Torralba de Calatrava
Manzanares
Membrilla
Solana
Almagro
Bolaños de Calatrava
Valenzuela de Calatrava
Alhambra
Ermita de Consolación
San Carlos del Valle
Carrizosa
Tamurejo
Agudo
Valdemanco de Esteras
Saceruela
Luciana
Alcolea de Calatrava
Los Pozuelos de Calatrava
Garlitos
Peñalsordo
Abenójar
Corral de Calatrava
Cabezarados
Ballesteros de Calatrava
Gargantiel
Zarza Capilla
Chillón
Almadén
Fontanosas
Villamayor de Calatrava
Tirteafuera
Granátula de Calatrava
Moral de Calatrava
Pozo de la Serna
Alcubillas
Cabeza del Buey
Guadalmez
Almadenejos
Argamasilla de Calatrava
Aldea del Rey
Calzada de Calatrava
Valdepeñas
Villanueva de los Infantes
Almodóvar del Campo
Puertollano
Campo de Calatrava
Alamillo
Cózar
Santa Eufemia
Brazatortas
Cabezarrubias del Puerto
Hinojosas de Calatrava
Villanueva de S. Carlos
Santa Cruz de Mudela
Torrenueva
Almedina
Valle de Alcudia
Sierra de la Alcudia
Sierra de Puertollano
Mestanza
La Alameda
Villalba de Calatrava
Torre de Juan Abad
Puebla del Príncipe
San Benito
Puerto de Niefla 920
Emb. de Montoro II
Viso del Marqués
Castellar de Santiago
Villamanrique
Los Pedroches
Guijo
El Viso
Torrecampo
Dos Torres
Añora
Villaralto
Pedroche
Solana del Pino
San Lorenzo de Calatrava
Almuradiel
Villanueva del Duque
Conquista
Puerto Valderrepiso 860
Sierra Madrona
El Hoyo
Despeñaperros
Paso Despeñaperros
Aldeaquemada
Alcaracejos
Pozoblanco
Fuencaliente
1161 Rebollera
1300 Estrella
El Centenillo
Las Correderas
Santa Elena
Venta de los Santos
Villanueva de Córdoba
Sierra Morena
Sierras de Cardeña y Montoro
Embalse de Jándula
Chiclana de Segura
Santisteban del Puerto
Cardeña
La Carolina
Carboneros
Isabela
Embalse de La Fernandina
Castellar
Sorihuela del Guadalimar
Espiel
Embalse del Rumblar
Baños de la Encina
Vilches
Embalse del Guadalén
Arquillos
Navas de San Juan
Iznatoraf
Villanueva del Arzobispo
Villaharta
Obejo
Virgen de la Cabeza
Real Santuario de la Santísima Virgen de la Cabeza
Guarromán
Embalse de Puente Nuevo
Villaviciosa de Córdoba
Embalse del Yeguas
Bailén
Linares
Villacarrillo
Cerro Muriano
Embalse del Guadalmellato
Embalse de San Rafael de Navallana
Adamuz
Montoro
Marmolejo
Andújar
Espeluy
Canena
Rus
Sabiote
Santo Tomé
Jabalquinto
Ibros
Lupión
Úbeda
Torreperogil
Chilluevar
Villafranca de Córdoba
Villanueva de la Reina
Cazalilla
Torreblascopedro
Begíjar
Baeza
Sierra de Cazorla
Santa María de Trassierra
Alcolea
Pedro Abad
Villa del Río
Arjonilla
Lopera
Higuera de Arjona
Arjona
Mengíbar
El Carpio
Escañuela
Fuerte del Rey
Peal de Becerro
Cazorla
La Iruela
Embalse de la Breña
Córdoba
Almodóvar del Río
Bujalance
Cañete de las Torres
Porcuna
Villardompardo
Catedral de la Asunción de la Virgen
Jimena
Bedmar
Jódar
Quesada
Cabañas 2028
Posadas
Torres-Cabrera
Higuera de Calatrava
Torredonjimeno
Jaén
Albanchez de Úbeda
Sierra de Castril
Guadalcázar
La Campiña
Valenzuela
Jamilena
Torre del Campo
Mancha Real
Torres
Larva
Huesa
Embalse de La Bolera
Fuente Palmera
La Quintana
Fernán Núñez
Espejo
Castro del Río
Santiago de Calatrava
Martos
La Guardia de Jaén
Pegalajar
Sierra Mágina
Belmez de la Moraleda
2163 Mágina
Cabra del Santo Cristo
Pozo Alcón
La Victoria
La Carlota
Montemayor
Noguerones
Los Villares
Cambil
Solera
San Sebastián de los Ballesteros
La Rambla
Montilla
Nueva Carteya
Albedín
Baena
Alcaudete
Fuensanta de Martos
Valdepeñas de Jaén
Carchelejo
Huelma
Arbuniel
Montejícar
Alicún de Ortega
Dehesas de Guadix
Écija
Santaella
Montalbán de Córdoba
Doña Mencía
Zuheros
Luque
Campillo de Arenas
Noalejo
Alamedilla
Villanueva de las Torres
Guadahortuna
Aguilar de la Frontera
Monturque
Cabra
Zagrilla
Fuente-Tójar
Priego de Córdoba
La Rábita
Alcalá la Real
Castillo de Locubín
Frailes
Santa Ana
Montillana
Campotéjar
Puerto Carretero 1040
Torre Cardela
Domingo Pérez
Pedro-Martínez
Moriles
Navas del Selpillar
Castillo del Moral
Carcabuey
Subbéticas
Almedinilla
Benalúa de las Villas
Dehesas Viejas
Moreda
Piñar
Gorafe
Marinaleda
Puente-Genil
Herrera
Lucena
Zambra
Rute
Las Navas
Colomera
Puerto del Zegrí 1080
Iznalloz
Huélago
Fonelas
Benalúa de Guadix
Gor
El Rubio
Nuestra Señora de Araceli
El Higuera
Algarinejo
Montefrío
Moclín
Sierra Arana
Olmas viviendas des cuevas
Diezma
Bogarre
1940 Orduña
Estepa
Badolatosa
Casariche
Benamejí
Encinas Reales
Iznájar
Embalse de Iznájar
Illora
Pinos Puente
Albolote
Cogollos Vega
Alfacar
Sierra de Huétor
Puerto de la Mora 1429
Purullena
Guadix
Alcudia de Guadix
Aguadulce
Gilena
Pedrera
Lora de Estepa
Palenciana
Cuevas de S. Marcos
Cuevas Bajas
Tocón
Villanueva de Mesía
Fuente Vaquero
Atarfe
Embalse de Quéntar
Cogollos de Guadix
Lugros
La Roda de Andalucía
Alameda
Fuente del Conde
Huétor Tájar
Chauchina
Santa Fe
Granada
Alhambra
Güéjar-Sierra
Huéneja
Lacalahorra
Sierra de Yeguas
Villanueva de Tapia
Villanueva de Algaidas
Loja
Salar
Alcazaba de Loja
Moraleda de Zafayona
Chimeneas
Armilla
La Zubia
Ogíjares
Jeres del Marquesado
Aldeire
Martín de la Jara
Los Corrales
Humilladero
Laguna de Fuente de Piedra
Mollina
Archidona
Las Gabias
Alhendín
Sierra Nevada
Campillos
Bobadilla
Santa Cruz de Alhama
Cacín
Ventas de Huelma
Agrón
Dílar
Puerto del Suspiro del Moro 865
La Veleta 3392
3479 Mulhacén
Almargen
Teba
Antequera
Villanueva del Trabuco
Puerto de los Alazores 1040
Padul
Dúrcal
Nigüelas
Trevelez
Mecina-Bombarón
Válor
Lauja
Cañete la Real
Embalse de Guadalhorce
Villanueva del Rosario
Alfarnate
Alhama de Granada
Jayena
Capileira
Pampaneira
Pitres
Bérchules
Ugíjar
Alcolea
Almargen
Villanueva de la Concepción
Puerto de las Pedrizas 780
Zafarraya
Ventas de Zafarraya
Arenas del Rey
Fornes
Játar
Restábal
Lanjarón
Busquístar
Cádiar
Emb. del Conde de Guadalhorce
Valle de Abdalajís
Riogordo
Periana
Sierra de Almijara
Albuñuelas
Pinos del Valle
Cañar
Órgiva
Murtas
Cuevas del Becerro
Ardales
Carratraca
Colmenar
Viñuela
Canillas de Aceituno
Sedella
Guajar-Faragüit
Torviscón
Turón
El Burgo
Álora
Casabermeja
Montes de Málaga
Benamargosa
Arenas
Archez
Cómpeta
Vélez de Benaudalla
Albondón
Berja
Casarabonela
Almogía
Pizarra
Puerto del León 960
Almachar
Benamocarra
Sayalonga
1832 Navachica
Ítrabo
Molvízar
Albuñol
Castillo de Ronda
Ronda
Yunquera
Alozaina
Cártama
Vélez-Málaga
Algarrobo
Torrox
Frigiliana
Olivar
Lújar
Gualchos
La Mamola
El Ejido
Sierra de las Nieves
Tolox
Guaro
Coín
Alhaurín de la Torre
Churriana
El Palo
Málaga
Rincón de la Victoria
Torre del Mar
Nerja
Cuevas de Nerja
Almuñécar
Salobreña
Motril
Torrenueva
Cabo Sacratif
Calahonda
Castell de Ferro
La Rábita
Adra
Balerma
Guardias Viejas
Monda
Alhaurín el Grande
Torremolinos
Istán
Ojén
Mijas
Benalmádena
Carbajal
Fuengirola
Punta de Calaburras
Sierra Bermeja
Marbella
Calahonda
San Pedro de Alcántara
Estepona
Melilla
Melilla Al Hoceima
Costa del Sol
A
B
C
1
2
94
95
99
229
5°
4°
3°
38°
37°

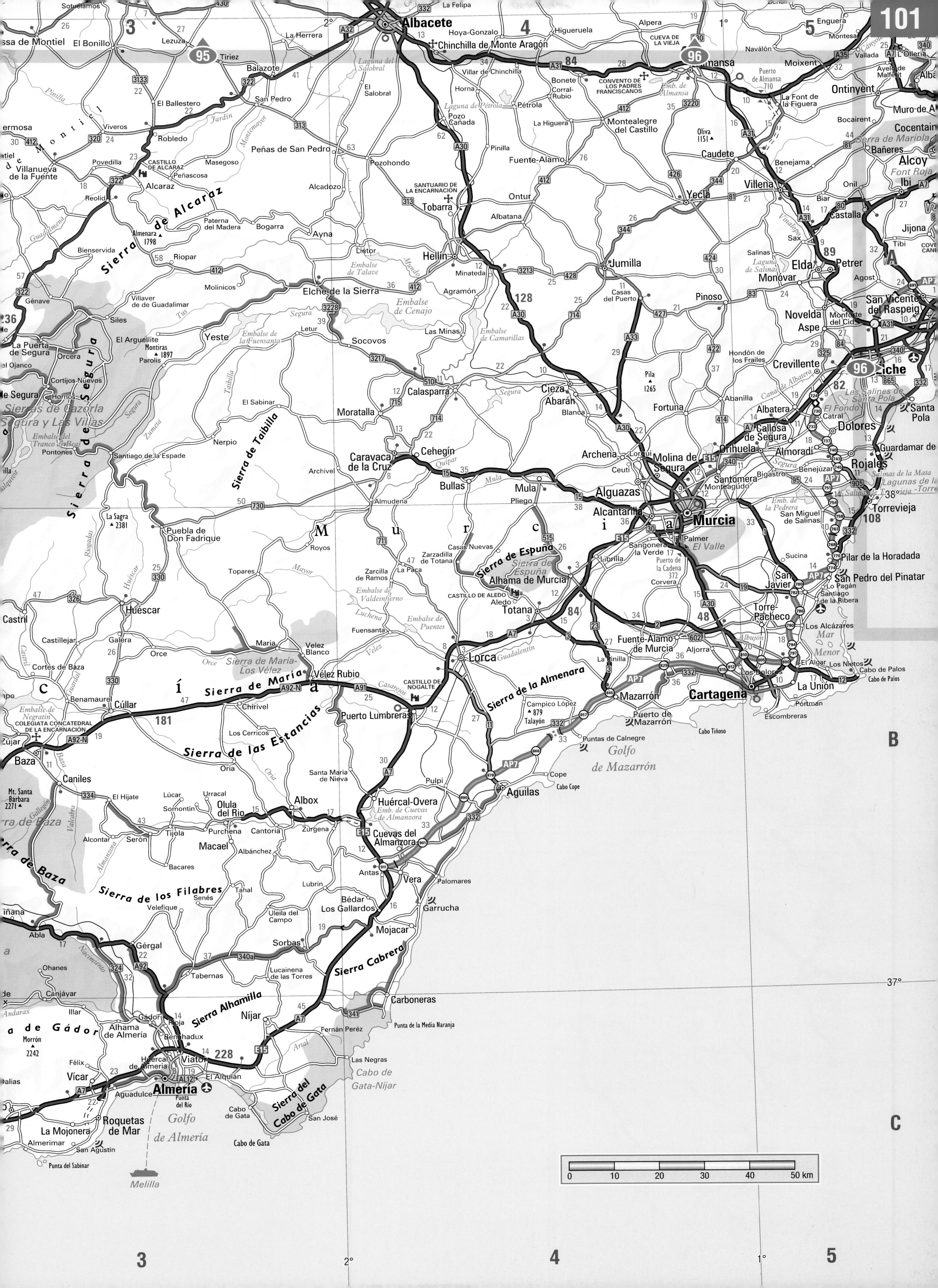
Albacete
Chinchilla de Monte Aragón
Hoya-Gonzalo
Higueruela
Alpera
Almansa
Enguera
Montesa
Vallada
L'Olleria
Navalón
Moixent
Ontinyent
Alcoy
Cocentaina
Muro de A.
Bocairent
Sierra de Mariola
Bañeres
Benejama
Villena
Caudete
Yecla
Biar
Castalla
Onil
Ibi
Jijona
Tibi
Sax
Elda
Petrer
Monóvar
Agost
Pinoso
Salinas
Novelda
Aspe
Monforte del Cid
San Vicente del Raspeig
Elche
Crevillente
Hondón de los Frailes
Albatera
Callosa de Segura
Dolores
Catral
Santa Pola
Rojales
Guardamar de
Almoradí
Benejúzar
Bigastro
Orihuela
Torrevieja
San Miguel de Salinas
Pilar de la Horadada
San Pedro del Pinatar
San Javier
Santiago de la Ribera
Los Alcázares
Mar Menor
Torre-Pacheco
Cartagena
La Unión
Cabo de Palos
Los Nietos
El Algar
Portman
Escombreras
Cabo Tiñoso
Mazarrón
Puerto de Mazarrón
Puntas de Calnegre
Golfo de Mazarrón
Aguilas
Cope
Cabo Cope
Pulpi
Puerto Lumbreras
Lorca
Totana
Alhama de Murcia
Sierra de Espuña
Sierra de la Almenara
Fuente-Álamo de Murcia
Murcia
Molina de Segura
Alguazas
Alcantarilla
Santomera
Monteagudo
Archena
Ceutí
Mula
Pliego
Bullas
Cehegín
Caravaca de la Cruz
Calasparra
Moratalla
Cieza
Abarán
Blanca
Fortuna
Abanilla
Jumilla
Hellín
Tobarra
Ontur
Albatana
Fuente-Álamo
Pétrola
Pozo Cañada
Montealegre del Castillo
La Higuera
Bonete
Corral-Rubio
Villar de Chinchilla
Horna
Pinilla
Pozohondo
Peñas de San Pedro
Alcadozo
Ayna
Liétor
Agramón
Minateda
Elche de la Sierra
Socovos
Letur
Yeste
Las Minas
Riopar
Molinicos
Alcaraz
Sierra de Alcaraz
Robledo
Viveros
Povedilla
Villanueva de la Fuente
El Bonillo
Lezuza
Tiriez
Balazote
San Pedro
El Ballestero
La Herrera
El Salobral
Masegoso
Peñascosa
Paterna del Madera
Bogarra
Bienservida
Villaverde de Guadalimar
Siles
La Puerta de Segura
Orcera
Génave
Sierra de Segura
Sierras de Cazorla Segura y Las Villas
Pontones
Santiago de la Espada
Nerpio
Sierra de Taibilla
El Sabinar
La Sagra 2381
Puebla de Don Fadrique
Huéscar
Castril
Castilléjar
Galera
Orce
María
Sierra de María-Los Vélez
Vélez Blanco
Vélez Rubio
Sierra de María
Cúllar
Benamaurel
Baza
Caniles
Chirivel
Sierra de las Estancias
Oria
Albox
Huércal-Overa
Olula del Río
Macael
Serón
Tíjola
Purchena
Cantoria
Zurgena
Cuevas del Almanzora
Antas
Vera
Garrucha
Palomares
Bédar
Los Gallardos
Mojacar
Sierra de los Filabres
Sorbas
Tabernas
Gérgal
Abla
Sierra Cabrera
Carboneras
Sierra Alhamilla
Níjar
Fernán Pérez
Las Negras
Cabo de Gata-Níjar
Sierra del Cabo de Gata
San José
Cabo de Gata
Almería
Golfo de Almería
Roquetas de Mar
Vícar
Aguadulce
La Mojonera
Almerimar
San Agustín
Punta del Sabinar
Melilla
Sierra de Gádor
Alhama de Almería
Benahadux
Huércal de Almería
Viator
El Alquián
Gádor
Rioja
Cartagena
Murcia
M u r c i a
A92-N
A92
A91
A7
AP7
A30
A31
A33
E15
0 10 20 30 40 50 km
3
4
5
B
C
1°
2°
37°

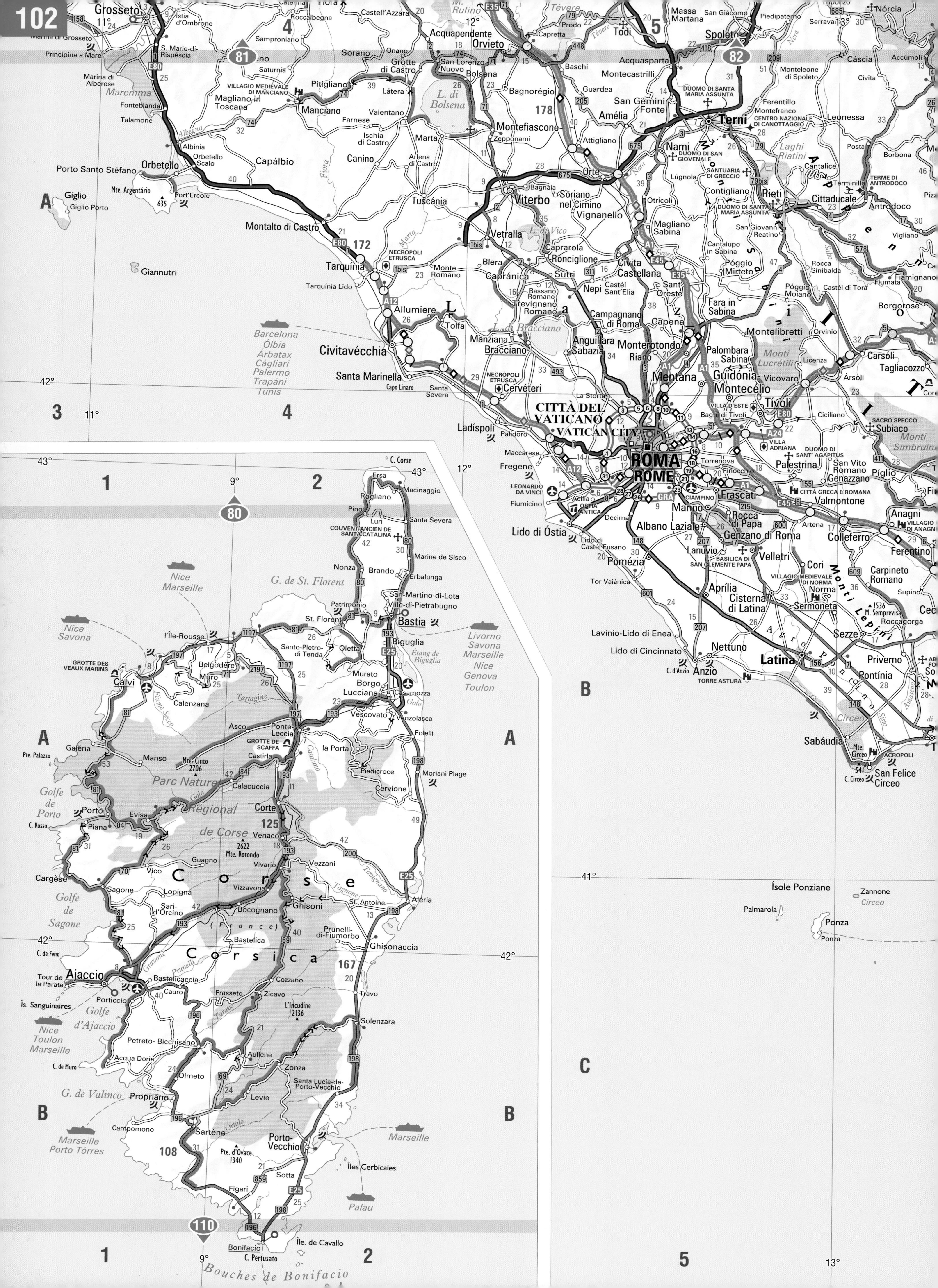

Grosseto
Ístia d'Ombrone
Marina di Grosseto
Principina a Mare
S. Marie-di-Rispéscia
81
Marina di Alberese
Maremma
Fonteblanda
Talamone
Magliano in Toscana
VILLAGGIO MEDIEVALE DI MANCIANO
Manciano
Saturnia
Roccalbegna
Semproniano
Sorano
Pitigliano
Látera
Grotte di Castro
Onano
Castell'Azzara
Acquapendente
Orvieto
San Lorenzo Nuovo
Bolsena
L. di Bolsena
Valentano
Farnese
Ischia di Castro
Canino
Marta
Ariena di Castro
Bagnorégio
Montefiascone
Zepponami
Albinia
Orbetello Scalo
Orbetello
Porto Santo Stéfano
Capálbio
Mte. Argentário
Port'Ercole
Gíglio
Giglio Porto
Giannutri
Montalto di Castro
Tuscánia
Tarquínia
Tarquínia Lido
172
NECROPOLI ETRUSCA
Monte Romano
Viterbo
Bagnaia
Vetralla
L. di Vico
Caprarola
Ronciglione
Soriano nel Cimino
Vignanello
Blera
Capránica
Sutri
Bassano Romano
Trevignano Romano
Nepi
Castel Sant'Elia
Civita Castellana
Allumiere
Tolfa
Civitavécchia
Barcelona
Ólbia
Árbatax
Cágliari
Palermo
Trápani
Tunis
Santa Marinella
Capo Linaro
Santa Severa
Manziana
Bracciano
L. di Bracciano
Anguillara Sabazia
Campagnano di Roma
NECROPOLI ETRUSCA
Cerveteri
Ladíspoli
Palidoro
Maccarese
Fregene
LEONARDO DA VINCI
Fiumicino
Acilia
OSTIA ANTICA
Lido di Óstia
Lido di Castel Fusano
Decima
CITTÀ DEL VATICANO
VATICAN CITY
ROMA
ROME
La Storta
CIAMPINO
Marino
Rocca di Papa
Albano Laziale
Genzano di Roma
Lanuvio
BASILICA DI SAN CLEMENTE PAPA
Velletri
Pomézia
Tor Vaiánica
Aprília
Cisterna di Latina
Lavinio-Lido di Enea
Lido di Cincinnato
Nettuno
Anzio
C. d'Anzio
TORRE ASTURA
Latina
Sabáudia
Mte. Circeo
ACROPOLI
San Felice Circeo
C. Circeo
Sermoneta
Sezze
Priverno
Pontínia
Monti Lepini
Agro Pontino
Cori
VILLAGGIO MEDIEVALE DI NORMA
Norma
Carpineto Romano
Supino
Roccagorga
M. Semprevisa
Colleferro
Artena
Valmontone
CITTÀ GRECA & ROMANA
Anagni
VILLAGGIO DI ANAGNI
Ferentino
Frascati
Palestrina
DUOMO DI SANT' AGAPITUS
San Vito Romano
Genazzano
Píglio
Tívoli
VILLA D'ESTE
Bagni di Tívoli
VILLA ADRIANA
Guidónia-Montecélio
Mentana
Monterotondo
Palombara Sabina
Monti Lucrétili
Licenza
Vicovaro
Riano
Capena
Fara in Sabina
Montelibretti
Orvinio
Sant'Oreste
Póggio Mirteto
Cantalupo in Sabina
Magliano Sabina
Otrícoli
Rieti
Cittaducale
Antrodoco
Terni
Narni
DUOMO DI SAN GIOVENALE
SANTUARIA DI GRECCIO
Contigliano
Lúgnola
Orte
Attigliano
Amélia
San Gémini Fonte
Guardea
Acquasparta
Montecastrilli
Todi
Baschi
Spoleto
82
Massa Martana
San Giácomo
Piediparterno
Serravalle
Nórcia
Cáscia
Monteleone di Spoleto
Leonessa
Posta
Borbona
Cantalice
TERME DI ANTRODOCO
Vigliano
Rocca Sinibalda
Póggio Moiano
Castel di Tora
Borgorose
Carsóli
Tagliacozzo
Ársoli
Subiaco
SACRO SPECCO
Monti Simbruini
Íole Ponziane
Zannone
Palmarola
Ponza
C. Corse
Ersa
Macinaggio
Rogliano
Pino
Luri
Santa Severa
COUVENT ANCIEN DE SANTA CATALINA
Marine de Sisco
Nonza
Brando
Erbalunga
G. de St. Florent
Nice
Marseille
Patrimonio
San-Martino-di-Lota
Ville-di-Pietrabugno
St. Florent
Bastia
Livorno
Savona
Marseille
Nice
Genova
Toulon
Nice
Savona
l'Île-Rousse
Santo-Pietro-di Tenda
Oletta
Biguglia
Étang de Biguglia
GROTTE DES VEAUX MARINS
Calvi
Belgodère
Muro
Calenzana
Tartagine
Murato
Borgo
Lucciana
Casamozza
Vescovato
Venzolasca
Folelli
Asco
Ponte-Leccia
GROTTE DE SCAFFA
Castirla
Galéria
Pte. Palazzo
Manso
Mte. Cinto
2706
la Porta
Piedicroce
Cervione
Moriani Plage
Parc Naturel Régional de Corse
Calacuccia
Golfe de Porto
Porto
C. Rosso
Piana
Evisa
Corte
Venaco
Mte. Rotondo
Vezzani
Guagno
Vico
Vivario
Cargèse
Sagone
Lopigna
Vizzavona
Golfe de Sagone
Sari-d'Orcino
Bocognano
Ghisoni
St. Antoine
Aléria
Prunelli-di-Fiumorbo
Ghisonaccia
Corse
(France)
Corsica
Bastelica
C. de Feno
Tour de la Parata
Ajaccio
Îs. Sanguinaires
Porticcio
Golfe d'Ajaccio
Bastelicaccia
Cauro
Cozzano
Frasseto
Zicavo
L'Incudine
2136
Travo
Solenzara
Nice
Toulon
Marseille
Petreto-Bicchisano
Acqua Doria
C. de Muro
Aullène
Olmeto
Zonza
Santa Lucia-de-Porto-Vecchio
G. de Valinco
Propriano
Levie
Campomoro
Sartène
Marseille
Porto Tòrres
Porto-Vecchio
Pte. d'Ovace
1340
Îles Cerbicales
Sotta
Figari
Palau
110
Bonifacio
C. Pertusato
Île. de Cavallo
Bouches de Bonifacio

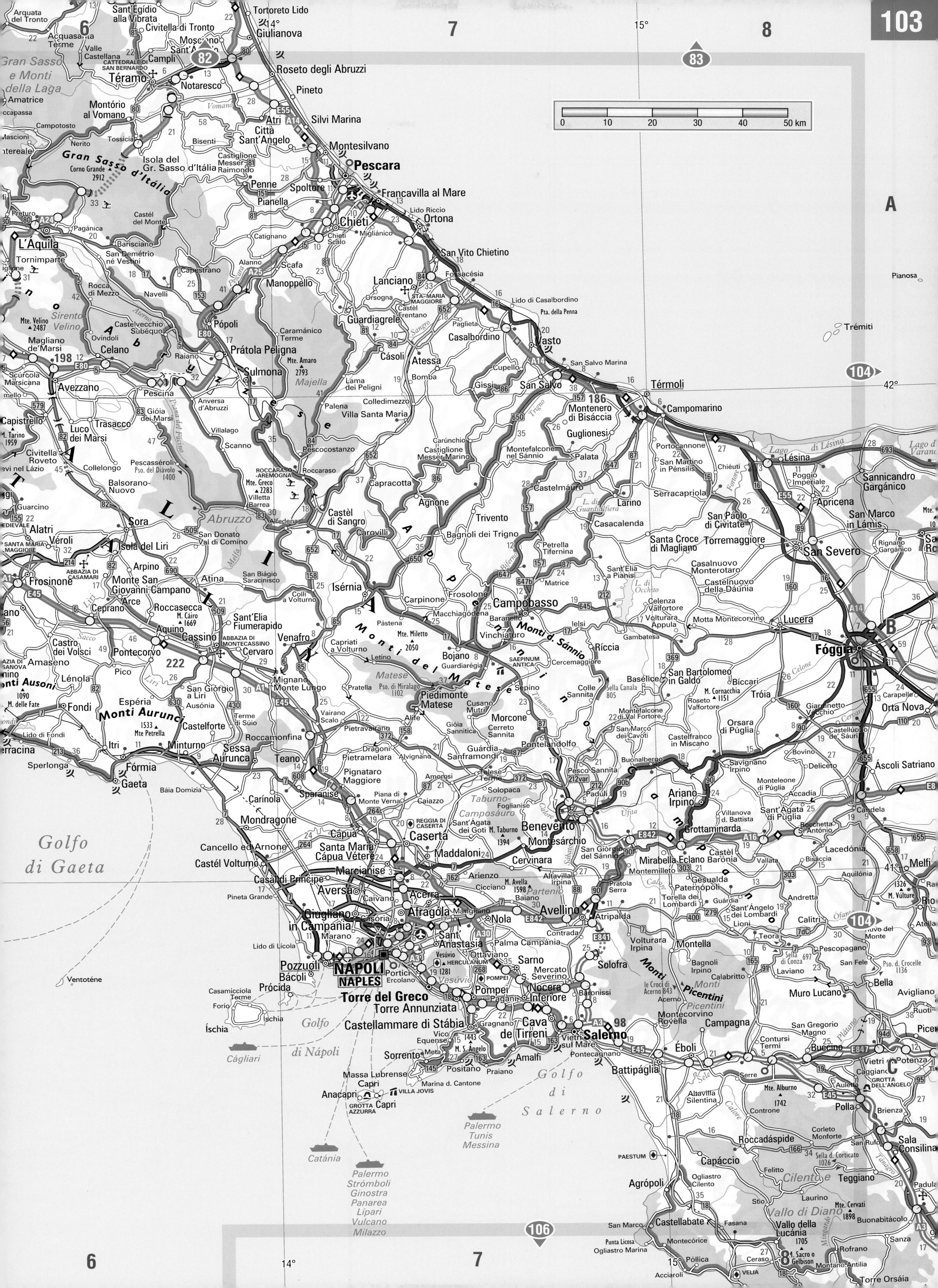
6
7
8
A
B
C
82
83
104
106
0 10 20 30 40 50 km
14°
15°
42°
Arquata del Tronto
Sant'Egidio alla Vibrata
Tortoreto Lido
Civitella di Tronto
Giulianova
Acquasanta Terme
Valle Castellana
Campli
Mosciano Sant'Angelo
Gran Sasso e Monti della Laga
Téramo
Roseto degli Abruzzi
Notaresco
Pineto
Amatrice
Montório al Vomano
Atri
Silvi Marina
Campotosto
Città Sant'Angelo
Montesilvano
Tossicia
Bisenti
Gran Sasso d'Itália
Isola del Gr. Sasso d'Itália
Castiglione Messer Raimondo
Pescara
Corno Grande 2912
Penne
Spoltore
Francavilla al Mare
Pianella
Lido Riccio
Ortona
Chieti
Castél del Monte
L'Aquila
Paganica
Catignano
Migliánico
San Vito Chietino
Tornimparte
Barisciano
San Demétrio né Vestini
Alanno
Scafa
Capestrano
Manoppello
Lanciano
Fossacésia
Rocca di Mezzo
Navelli
Orsogna
Lido di Casalbordino
Pta. della Penna
Sirento Velino
Mte. Velino 2487
Castelvecchio Subéquo
Caramánico Terme
Guardiagrele
Castel Frentano
Paglieta
Casalbordino
Magliano de'Marsi
Ovindoli
Celano
Pópoli
Prátola Peligna
Vasto
Cásoli
Atessa
San Salvo Marina
Tremiti
Pianosa
Mte. Amaro 2793
Sulmona
Majella
Bomba
Cupello
San Salvo
Términi
Tèrmoli
Scúrcola Marsicana
Avezzano
Pescina
Lama dei Peligni
Gissi
Montenero di Bisáccia
Campomarino
Anversa d'Abruzzi
Colledimezzo
Palena
Villa Santa Maria
Capistrello
Luco dei Marsi
Trasacco
Gióia dei Marsi
Villalago
Guglionesi
Civitella Roveto
Scanno
Carúnchio
Castiglione Messer Marino
Montefalcone nel Sánnio
Palata
Portocannone
San Martino in Pénsilis
Chiéuti
Lésina
Lago di Lésina
Poggio Imperiale
Sannicandro Gargánico
Pescocostanzo
Pescasséroli
Pso. del Diávolo 1400
Collelongo
Roccaraso
Capracotta
Castelmáuro
Serracapriola
Balsorano-Nuovo
Mte. Greco 2283
Villetta Barrea
Agnone
Larino
Apricena
San Marco in Lámis
Guarcino
Abruzzo
Alfedena
Castèl di Sangro
Trivento
Casacalenda
San Páolo di Civitate
Alatri
Sora
Véroli
San Donato Val di Comino
Carovilli
Bagnoli dei Trigno
Santa Croce di Magliano
Torremaggiore
San Severo
Rignano Gargánico
Isola del Liri
Petrella Tifernina
Abbazia di Casamari
Arpino
San Biágio Saracinisco
Sant'Elia a Pianisi
Casalnuovo Monterotaro
Frosinone
Monte San Giovanni Campano
Atina
Isérnia
Colli a Volturno
Matrice
Castelnuovo della Dáunia
Arce
Carpinone
Frosolone
Campobasso
Celenza Valfortore
Ceprano
Roccasecca
M. Cáiro 1669
Sant'Elia Fiumerapido
Macchiagodena
Baranello
Volturara Appula
Motta Montecorvino
Lucera
Aquino
Cassino
Abbazia di Montecassino
Pástena
Monti d. Sánnio
Vinchiaturo
Iélsi
Castro dei Volsci
Pontecorvo
Cervaro
Venafro
Mte. Miletto 2050
Gambatesa
Fóggia
Amaseno
Pico
Capriati a Volturno
Letino
Bojano
Guardiarégia
Ríccia
Cercemaggiore
Monti Ausoni
Lénola
San Giorgio a Liri
Mignano Monte Lungo
Matese
Monti del Matese
Pso. di Miralago 1102
Sepino
San Bartolomeo in Galdo
Baselice
Biccari
Espéria
Ausónia
Terme di Súio
Pratella
Piedimonte Matese
Colle Sannita
Sella Canala 805
M. Cornacchia 1151
Tróia
Fondi
Monti Aurunci
Castelforte
Vairano Scalo
Cusano Mutri
Morcone
Roseto Valfortore
Giardinetto Vecchio
Orta Nova
1533 Mte Petrella
Alife
Gióia Sannitica
Cerreto Sannita
Montefalcone di Val Fortore
San Marco dei Cavoti
Orsara di Púglia
Castelluccio de' Sáuri
Lido di Fondi
Itri
Minturno
Sessa Aurunca
Roccamonfina
Pietravairano
Guárdia Sanframondi
Pontelandolfo
Castelfranco in Miscano
Sperlonga
Fórmia
Gaeta
Teano
Dragoni
Pietramelara
Alvignano
Buonalbergo
Savignano Irpino
Bovino
Deliceto
Áscoli Satriano
Pignataro Maggiore
Amorosi
Telese Terme
Pesco Sannita
Ariano Irpino
Monteleone di Púglia
Báia Domizia
Sparanise
Piana di Monte Verna
Solopaca
Paduli
Accadia
Carínola
Caiazzo
Taburno-Camposauro
Foglianise
Villanova d. Battista
Sant'Ágata di Púglia
Candela
Mondragone
Reggia di Caserta
Sant'Ágata dei Goti
M. Taburno 1394
Benevento
Grottaminarda
Rocchetta Sant'Antonio
Golfo di Gaeta
Cápua
Caserta
Montesárchio
Santa Maria Cápua Vétere
Maddaloni
San Giorgio del Sánnio
Mirabella Eclano
Castèl Baronia
Vallata
Bisaccia
Lacedónia
Melfi
Cancello ed Arnone
Castél Volturno
Marcianise
Cervinara
Montemiletto
Aquilónia
Casal di Príncipe
Arienzo
Altavilla Irpina
Pratola Serra
Gesualda
Paternópoli
Pineta Grande
Aversa
Cicciano
M. Avella 1598
Baiano
Partenio
Torella dei Lombardi
Andretta
M. Vulture 1326
Caivano
Acerra
Guárdia dei Lombardi
Sant'Ángelo dei Lombardi
Giugliano in Campania
Afragola
Marigliano
Nola
Avellino
Atripalda
Calitri
Marano
Sant'Anastasia
Palma Campánia
Contrada
Lioni
Teora
Ruvo del Monte
Lido di Licola
Vesúvio 1281
Ottaviano
Volturara Irpina
Montella
Sella di Conza 697
Pescopagano
Pozzuoli
Herculanum
Sarno
Solofra
Monti Picentini
Bagnoli Irpino
Pso. d. Crocelle 1136
Ventoténe
Bácoli
Napoli
Naples
Portici
Ercolano
Pompei
Mercato S. Severino
Laviano
Pesce Fele
Bella
Prócida
Casamicciola Terme
Torre del Greco
Nocera Inferiore
Baronissi
Le Croci di Acerno 843
Calabritto
Muro Lucano
Avigliano
Forio
Ischia
Torre Annunziata
Pagani
Acerno
Montecorvino Rovella
Íschia
Golfo di Nápoli
Castellammare di Stábia
Gragnano
Cava de Tirreni
Salerno
Campagna
San Gregorio Magno
Vico Equense
M. S. Angelo 1443
Vietri sul Mare
Contursi Terme
Buccino
Vietri di Potenza
Cágliari
Sorrento
Meta
Positano
Amalfi
Pontecagnano
Éboli
Battipáglia
Serre
Caggiano
Massa Lubrense
Marina d. Cantone
Praiano
Golfo di Salerno
Mte. Alburno 1742
Auletta
Grotta dell'Angelo
Capri
Anacapri
Villa Jovis
Grotta Azzurra
Altavilla Silentina
Controne
Polla
Brienza
Palermo
Tunis
Messina
Corleto Monforte
Roccadáspide
San Rufo
Sala Consilina
Paestum
Capáccio
Sella d. Corticato 1026
Catánia
Felitto
Cilento e Vallo di Diano
Teggiano
Strómboli
Ginostra
Panarea
Lípari
Vulcano
Milazzo
Agrópoli
Ogliastro Cilento
Stio
Laurino
Mte. Cervati 1898
Buonabitácolo
Castellabate
San Marco
Fasana
Vallo della Lucánia
Padula
Punta Licosa
Ogliastro Marina
Montecórice
Mte. Sacro o Gelbison 1705
Rofrano
Sanza
Póllica
Ceraso
Velia
Acciaroli
Montano Antilia
Torre Orsáia
Monti del Sánnio
Appennino Sannita
Abruzzo
Lázio

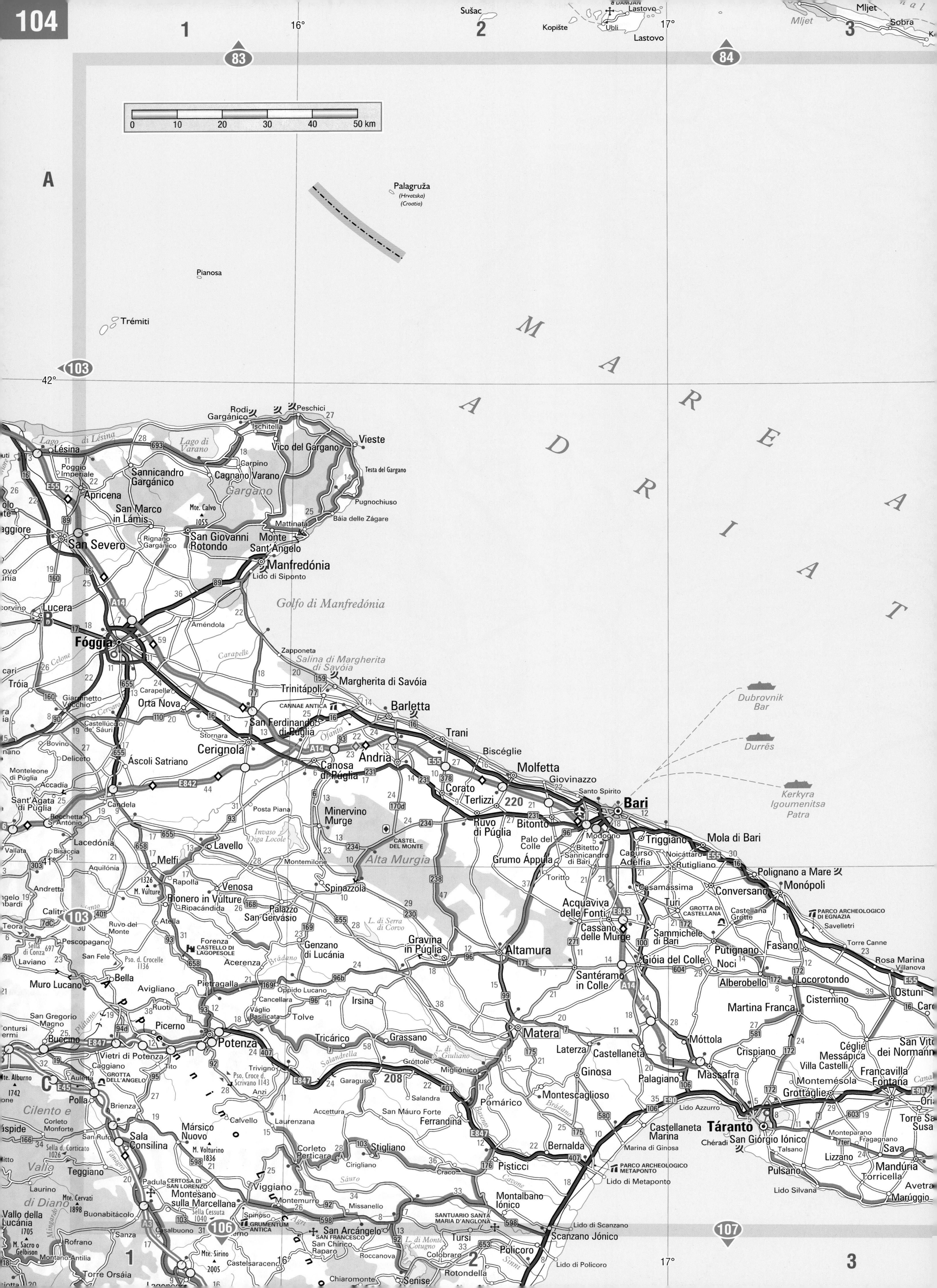
1
2
3
16°
17°
83
84
103
106
107
A
B
C
42°
0 10 20 30 40 50 km
Sušac
Lastovo
Kopište
Ubli
Mljet
Sobra
Palagruža
(Hrvatska)
(Croatia)
Pianosa
Trémiti
MARE ADRIATICO
MARE ADRIATICO
Rodi Gargánico
Peschici
Ischitella
Vieste
Lago di Lésina
Lésina
Lago di Varano
Vico del Gargano
Carpino
Poggio Imperiale
Sannicandro Gargánico
Cagnano Varano
Testa del Gargano
Gargano
Apricena
Pugnochiuso
San Marco in Lámis
Mte. Calvo 1055
Mattinata
Báia delle Zágare
San Severo
Rignano Gargánico
San Giovanni Rotondo
Monte Sant'Angelo
Manfredónia
Lido di Siponto
Golfo di Manfredónia
Lucera
Fóggia
Améndola
Zapponeta
Salina di Margherita di Savóia
Margherita di Savóia
Trinitápoli
Tróia
Giardinetto Vecchio
Carapelle
Orta Nova
Cannae Antica
Barletta
San Ferdinando di Púglia
Castellúccio de' Sauri
Stornara
Trani
Bovino
Cerignola
Canosa di Púglia
Ándria
Bisceglie
Deliceto
Áscoli Satriano
Molfetta
Giovinazzo
Santo Spirito
Bari
Monteleone di Púglia
Accadia
Corato
Terlizzi
Candela
Sant'Ágata di Púglia
Rocchetta S. António
Posta Piana
Minervino Murge
Ruvo di Púglia
Bitonto
Modugno
Triggiano
Mola di Bari
Lacedónia
Lavello
Invaso Diga Locone
Castel del Monte
Palo del Colle
Bitetto
Sannicandro di Bari
Capurso
Adelfia
Noicáttaro
Rutigliano
Polignano a Mare
Monópoli
Vallata
Bisaccia
Aquilónia
Melfi
Montemilone
Alta Murgia
Grumo Áppula
Toritto
Casamássima
Conversano
Rapolla
Venosa
Spinazzola
Turi
Grotta di Castellana
Castellana Grotte
Parco Archeologico di Egnazia
Savelletri
Andretta
Calitri
M. Vúlture
Rionero in Vúlture
Ripacándida
Palazzo San Gervásio
Acquaviva delle Fonti
Cassano delle Murge
Sammichele di Bari
Putignano
Fasano
Torre Canne
Rosa Marina
Villanova
L. di Serra di Corvo
Ruvo del Monte
Atella
Forenza
Castello di Lagopesole
Genzano di Lucánia
Gravina in Púglia
Altamura
Gióia del Colle
Noci
Alberobello
Locorotondo
Ostuni
Pescopagano
Laviano
San Fele
Pso. d. Crocelle 1136
Acerenza
Santéramo in Colle
Cisternino
Muro Lucano
Bella
Avigliano
Pietragalla
Oppido Lucano
Cancellara
Irsina
Martina Franca
San Gregorio Magno
Ruoti
Vaglio Basilicata
Tolve
Matera
Móttola
Crispiano
Céglie Messápica
San Vito dei Normanni
Buccino
Picerno
Potenza
Tricárico
Grassano
L. di S. Giuliano
Laterza
Castellaneta
Villa Castelli
Francavilla Fontana
Vietri di Potenza
Caggiano
Grotta dell'Angelo
Tito
Trivigno
Pso. Croce d. Scrivano 1143
Anzi
Grottole
Miglionico
Ginosa
Palagiano
Massafra
Monteméssola
Grottáglie
Mte. Alburno 1742
Auletta
Polla
Brienza
Garaguso
Salandra
Montescaglioso
Pomárico
Lido Azzurro
Cilento e
Corleto Monforte
Calvello
Laurenzana
Accettura
San Máuro Forte
Ferrandina
Táranto
San Giórgio Iónico
Castellaneta Marina
Chéradi
Monteparano
Fragagnano
Torre Santa Susanna
Sala Consilina
Sella d. Corticato 1026
Mársico Nuovo
M. Volturino 1836
Corleto Perticara
Stigliano
Bernalda
Marina di Ginosa
Talsano
Lizzano
Sava
Vallo
Teggiano
Cirigliano
Craco
Pisticci
Parco Archeologico Metaponto
Pulsano
Mandúria
Lido di Metaponto
Torricella
Laurino
di Diano
Mte. Cervati 1898
Padula
Certosa di San Lorenzo
Montesano sulla Marcellana
Viggiano
Montemurro
Missanello
Montalbano Iónico
Lido Silvana
Maruggio
Avetrana
Vallo della Lucánia
Buonabitácolo
Sella Cessuta 1040
Spinoso
Grumentum Antica
San Arcángelo
Santuario Santa Maria d'Anglona
Lido di Scanzano
Scanzano Jónico
M. Sacro o Gelbison
Sanza
Casalbuono
San Francesco
San Chírico Raparo
L. di Monte Cotugno
Tursi
Policoro
Rofrano
Montano Antilia
Mte. Sirino 2005
Castelsaraceno
Roccanova
Colobraro
Lido di Policoro
Torre Orsáia
Rotondella
Chiaromonte
Senise
Dubrovnik
Bar
Durrës
Kerkyra
Igoumenitsa
Patra
Appennino Lucano

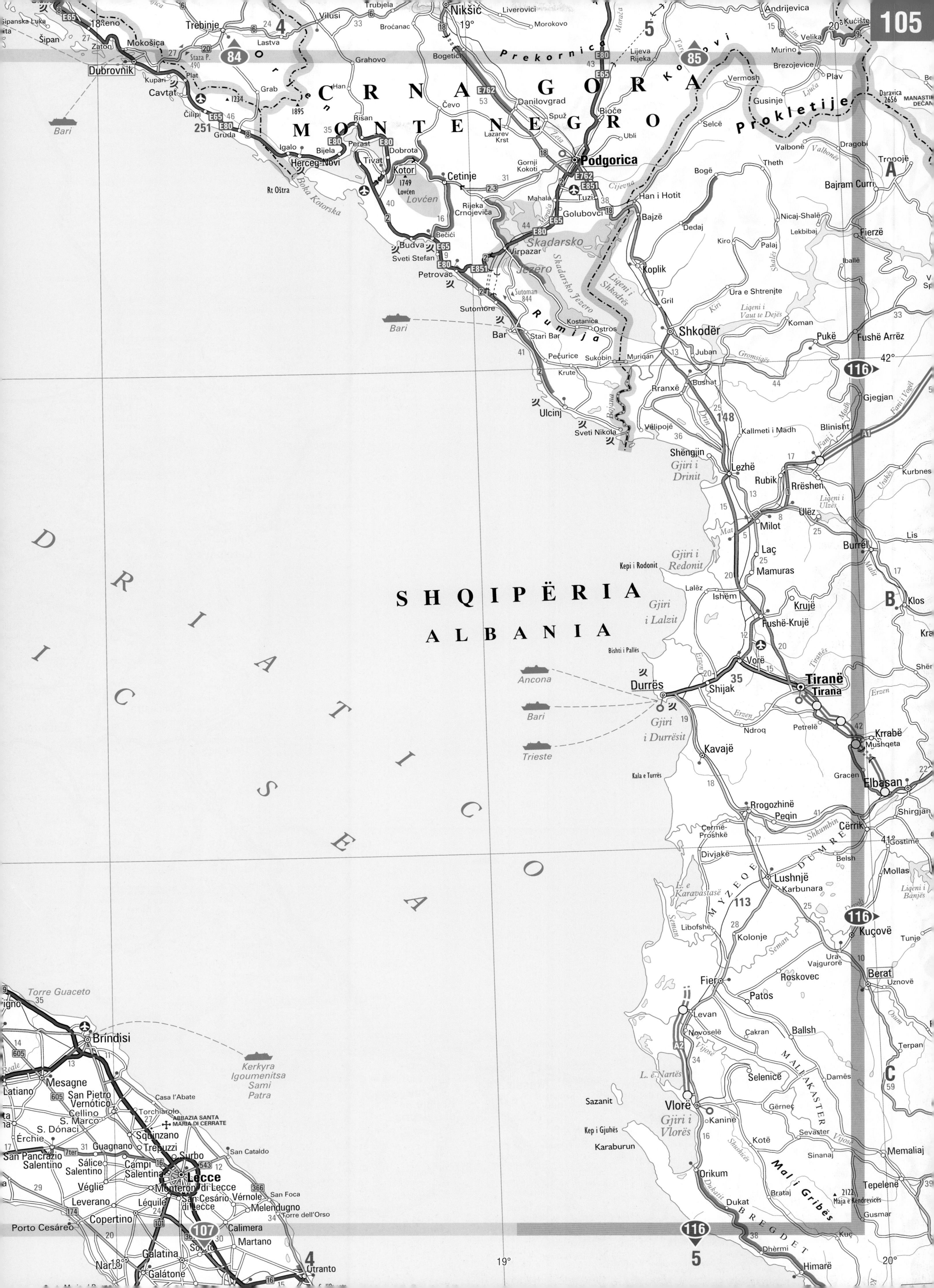
CRNA GORA
MONTENEGRO
SHQIPËRIA
ALBANIA
ADRIATICO
MARE
Dubrovnik
Cavtat
Trebinje
Mokošica
Šipan
Herceg-Novi
Igalo
Bijela
Risan
Perast
Tivat
Kotor
Dobrota
Lovćen
Cetinje
Budva
Sveti Stefan
Bečići
Petrovac
Sutomore
Bar
Stari Bar
Ulcinj
Sveti Nikola
Nikšić
Danilovgrad
Podgorica
Tuzi
Golubovci
Virpazar
Skadarsko Jezero
Rumija
Prekornica
Komovi
Prokletije
Andrijevica
Plav
Gusinje
Vermosh
Bajram Curri
Tropojë
Fierzë
Koplik
Shkodër
Bushat
Lezhë
Shëngjin
Gjiri i Drinit
Rubik
Rrëshen
Milot
Laç
Mamuras
Burrel
Gjiri i Rodonit
Kepi i Rodonit
Gjiri i Lalzit
Krujë
Fushë-Krujë
Vorë
Tiranë
Tirana
Durrës
Shijak
Gjiri i Durrësit
Kavajë
Krrabë
Mushqeta
Elbasan
Rrogozhinë
Peqin
Cërrik
Divjakë
Lushnjë
Myzeqe
Kuçovë
Berat
Fier
Patos
Roskovec
Levan
Ballsh
Mallakaster
Selenicë
Vlorë
Gjiri i Vlorës
Kaninë
Sazanit
Karaburun
Orikum
Mali i Gribës
Tepelenë
Memaliaj
Dukat
Bregdet
Dhërmi
Himarë
Ancona
Bari
Trieste
Kerkyra Igoumenitsa Sami Patra
Brindisi
Torre Guaceto
Mesagne
San Pietro Vernotico
Cellino S. Marco
Squinzano
Trepuzzi
Surbo
Lecce
Campi Salentina
Guagnano
San Pancrazio Salentino
Véglie
Leverano
Copertino
Monteroni di Lecce
San Cesário di Lecce
Vérnole
Melendugno
Calimera
Martano
Galatina
Soleto
Galatone
Nardò
Porto Cesáreo
Otranto
Torre dell'Orso
San Foca
San Cataldo
84
85
107
116
4
5
18°
19°
20°
41°
42°
A
B
C

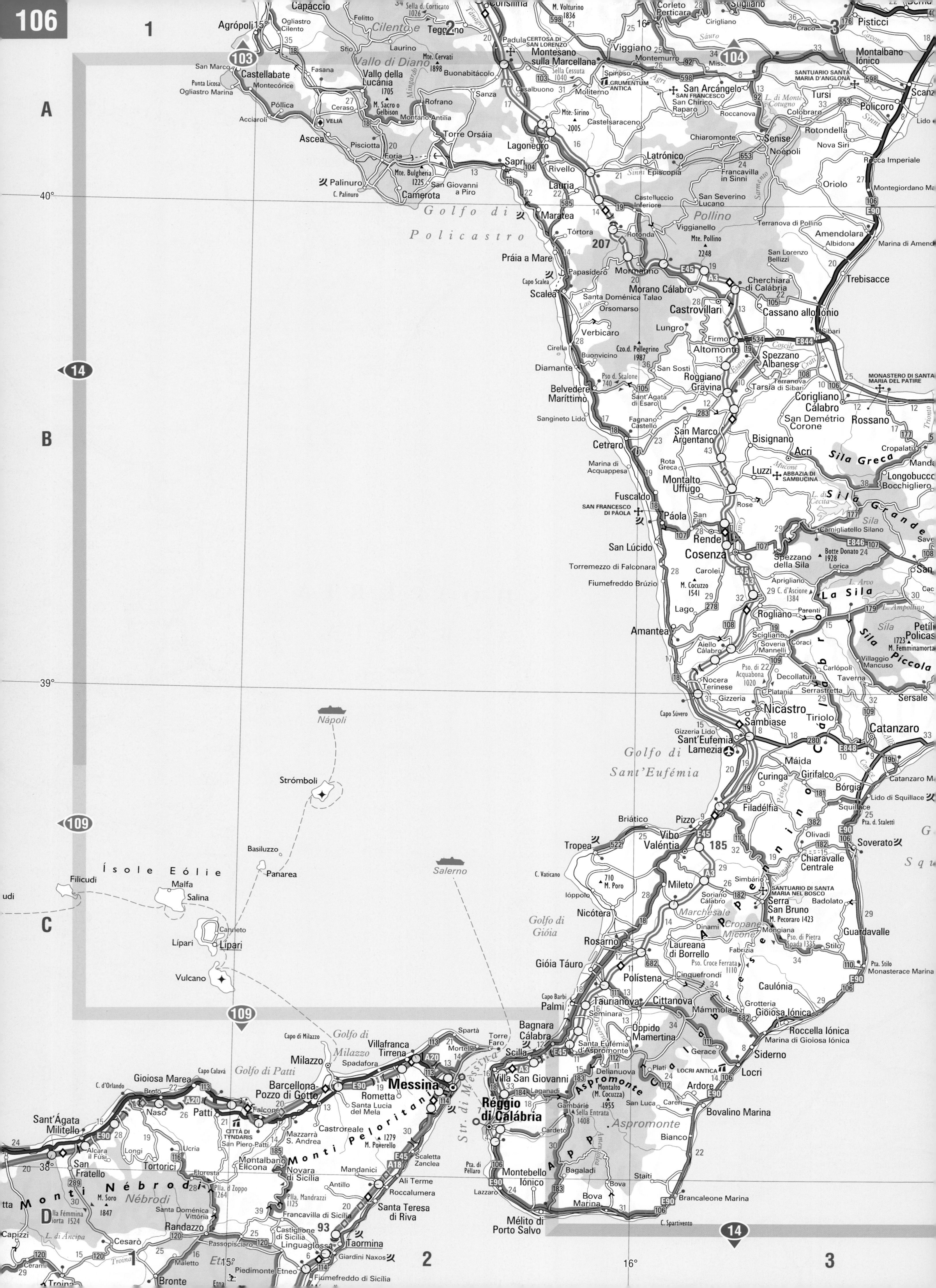
1
2
3
A
B
C
D
103
104
14
109
Capáccio
Agrópoli
Ogliastro Cilento
Felitto
Cilento e
Teggiano
Padula
Certosa di San Lorenzo
M. Volturino 1836
Corleto Perticara
Sugliano
Cirigliano
Pisticci
Craco
Montalbano Iónico
San Marco
Castellabate
Punta Licosa
Ogliastro Marina
Montecórice
Póllica
Acciaroli
Fasana
Vallo di Diano
Vallo della Lucánia
Mte. Cervati 1898
Buonabitácolo
Montesano sulla Marcellana
Viggiano
Montemurro
Spinoso
Grumentum antica
Moliterno
Sanza
Casalbuono
San Arcángelo
San Francesco
San Chirico Raparo
Roccanova
Santuario Santa Maria d'Anglona
Tursi
Policoro
Colobraro
M. Sacro o Gelbison 1705
Ceraso
Rofrano
Montano Antilia
Velia
Ascea
Torre Orsáia
Pisciotta
Foria
Mte. Bulgheria 1225
Palinuro
C. Palinuro
Camerota
San Giovanni a Piro
Sapri
Lagonegro
Mte. Sirino 2005
Castelsaraceno
Latrónico
Episcopia
Chiaromonte
Senise
Noépoli
Rotondella
Nova Siri
Rocca Imperiale
Francavilla in Sinni
Rivello
Lauria
Castelluccio Inferiore
San Severino Lucano
Oriolo
Montegiordano Marina
40°
Golfo di
Policastro
Maratea
Tórtora
Rotonda
Viggianello
Pollino
Mte. Pollino 2248
Terranova di Pollino
Amendolara
Albidona
Marina di Amendolara
207
Práia a Mare
Papasidero
Mormanno
San Lorenzo Bellizzi
Trebisacce
Capo Scalea
Scalea
Morano Cálabro
Cherchiara di Calábria
Santa Doménica Talao
Orsomarso
Castrovillari
Cassano allo Iónio
Verbicaro
Lungro
Sibari
Cirella
Cz.o d. Pellegrino 1987
Firmo
Altomonte
Spezzano Albanese
Diamante
Buonvicino
San Sosti
Roggiano Gravina
Terranova da Sibari
Tarsia
Monastero di Santa Maria del Patire
Pso d. Scalone 740
Belvedere Maríttimo
Sant'Ágata di Esaro
Corigliano Cálabro
San Demétrio Corone
Rossano
Sangineto Lido
Fagnano Castello
Cropalati
San Marco Argentano
Bisignano
Cetraro
Acri
Sila Greca
Marina di Acquappesa
Rota Greca
Luzzi
Abbazia di Sambucina
Longobucco
Bocchigliero
Montalto Uffugo
Fuscaldo
San Francesco di Páola
Páola
San Fili
Rose
Sila Grande
Camigliatello Silano
Rende
Cosenza
San Lúcido
Spezzano della Sila
Botte Donato 1928
Lorica
Torremezzo di Falconara
Carolei
Fiumefreddo Brúzio
M. Cocuzzo 1541
Aprigliano
C. d'Ascione 1384
La Sila
Lago
Rogliano
Parenti
Amantea
Sila
M. Femminamorta 1723
Scigliano
Soveria Mannelli
Cóvaci
Aiello Cálabro
Villaggio Mancuso
Sila Piccola
Carlópoli
Taverna
39°
Nocera Terinese
Pso. di Acquabona 1020
Decollatura
Serrastretta
Platania
Gizzeria
Sersale
Capo Súvero
Nicastro
Tiriolo
Sambiase
Catanzaro
Gizzeria Lido
Sant'Eufemia Lamezia
Golfo di
Sant'Eufémia
Máida
Curinga
Girifalco
Bórgia
Catanzaro Marina
Lido di Squillace
Squillace
Pta. d. Staletti
Filadélfia
Nápoli
Strómboli
Briático
Pizzo
Tropea
Vibo Valéntia
185
Olivadi
Soverato
Chiaravalle Centrale
Basiluzzo
Panarea
Salerno
Ísole Eólie
Filicudi
Malfa
Salina
C. Vaticano
M. Poro 710
Ióppolo
Mileto
Soriano Cálabro
Simbário
Santuario di Santo Maria nel Bosco
Serra San Bruno
Badolato
M. Pecoraro 1423
Nicótera
Golfo di Gióia
Canneto
Lípari
Marchesale
Dinami
Mongiana
Pso. di Pietra Spada 1335
Guardavalle
Stilo
Rosarno
Laureana di Borrello
Fabrizia
Gióia Táuro
Pso. Croce Ferrata 1110
Pta. Stilo
Monasterace Marina
Vulcano
Políстena
Cinquefrondi
Caulónia
Capo Barbi
Palmi
Taurianova
Cittanova
Seminara
Mámmola
Grotteria
Gioiosa Iónica
Oppido Mamertina
Bagnara Cálabra
Roccella Iónica
Marina di Gioiosa Iónica
Capo di Milazzo
Golfo di Milazzo
Villafranca Tirrena
Spartà
Torre Faro
Mortelle
Scilla
Santa Eufémia d'Aspromonte
Gerace
Siderno
Milazzo
Spadafora
Delianuova
Platì
Locri antica
Locri
Capo Calavà
Golfo di Patti
Gioiosa Marea
C. d'Orlando
Brolo
Barcellona-Pozzo di Gotto
Messina
Rometta
Villa San Giovanni
Aspromonte
Montalto (M. Cocuzza) 1955
Ardore
Naso
Patti
Falcone
Santa Lucia del Mela
Laganadi
Réggio di Calábria
Gambàrie
San Luca
Careri
Bovalino Marina
Sant'Ágata Militello
Città di Tyndaris
San Piero Patti
Castroreale
Mazzarrà S. Andrea
M. Poverello 1279
Str. di Messina
Sella Entrata 1408
Cardeto
Bianco
Alcara li Fusi
Longi
Ucria
Monti Peloritani
Scaletta Zanclea
San Fratello
Tortorici
Montalbano Elicona
Novara di Sicilia
Mandanici
Pta. di Péllaro
Montebello Iónico
Bagaladi
Staiti
Floresta
Pila. d'Zoppo 1264
Antillo
Roccalumera
Lazzaro
Bova
Monti Nébrodi
Nébrodi
M. Soro 1847
Santa Doménica Vittória
Plla. Mandrazzi 1125
Santa Teresa di Riva
Bova Marina
Brancaleone Marina
Serra della Fémmina Morta 1524
Randazzo
Francavilla di Sicilia
Mélito di Porto Salvo
C. Spartivento
Capizzi
L. di Áncipa
Cesarò
Castiglione di Sicilia
Linguaglossa
Taormina
Giardini Naxos
Passopisciaro
Maletto
Piedimonte Etneo
Fiumefreddo di Sicilia
Bronte
Troina
Etna
15°
16°
38°
Appennino Calabro
Aspromonte

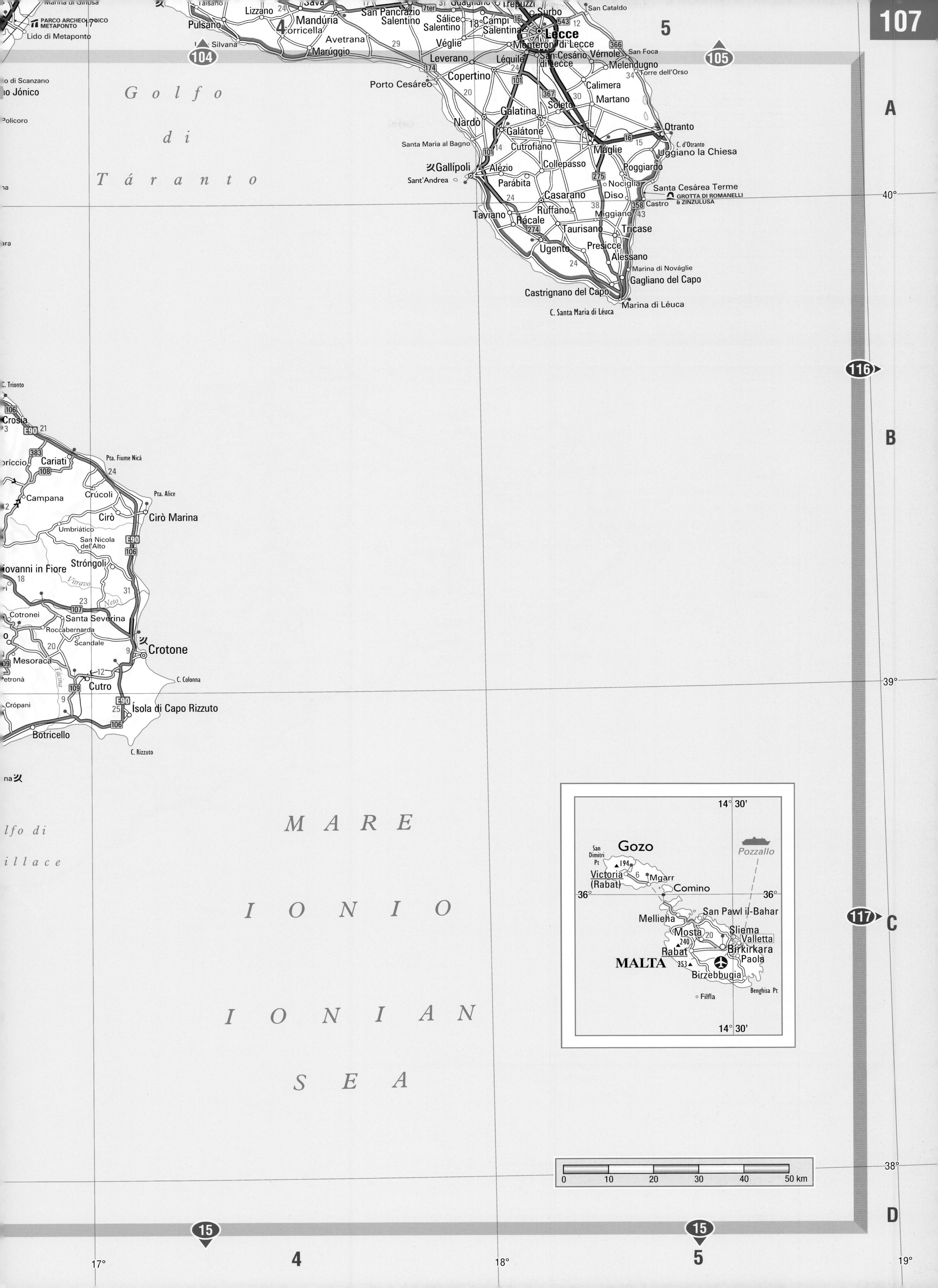

Marina di Ginosa
PARCO ARCHEOLOGICO METAPONTO 17
Lido di Metaponto
o di Scanzano
o Jónico
Policoro
a
104

Taisano
Lizzano 24
Sava
Pulsano
Manduria
Torricella
Avetrana
29
Marúggio
Leverano
174
Copertino
Porto Cesáreo
20
Nardó
Santa Maria al Bagno
Galatina
Galátone
Cutrofiano
101 14
Gallípoli
Sant'Andrea
Alézio
Parábita
24
Casarano
Ruffano
Taviano
Rácale
274
Ugento
24
Castrignano del Capo
C. Santa Maria di Léuca

San Pancrazio Salentino
Sálice Salentino
Véglie
Léquile
Soleto
San Cataldo

Campi Salentina
Monteroni di Lecce
San Cesário di Lecce
Calimera
Martano
Otranto
16 15
Máglie
Collepasso
Poggiardo
275
Nociglia
Diso
38 358 Castro
Miggiano 43
Taurisano
Presicce
Alessano
Marina di Nováglie
Gagliano del Capo
Marina di Léuca

Lecce 12
543
Squrbo
366
San Foca
Melendugno
34 Torre dell'Orso
C. d'Otranto
Uggiano la Chiesa
Santa Cesárea Terme
GROTTA DI ROMANELLI & ZINZULUSA

5

105

116

B

C. Trionto
106
Crosia
E90 21
oríccio
Cariati
383
108
Campana
Crúcoli
Cirò
Cirò Marina
Umbriático
San Nicola dell'Alto
Giovanni in Fiore
Stróngoli
E90 106
Cotronei
Santa Severina
Roccabernarda
Scandale
Mesoraca
Petrónà
Crópani
Botricello
C. Rizzuto

G o l f o
d i
T á r a n t o

Pta. Fiume Nicá
24
Pta. Alice
Vitravo
31
Neto
23
9
Crotone
12
C. Colonna
109
Cutro
E90
25
Ísola di Capo Rizzuto
106

lfo di
illace
na

39°

M A R E

I O N I O

I O N I A N

S E A

MALTA

Gozo
San Dimitri Pt
Victoria (Rabat)
▲194
6 Mgarr
Comino
Melieha
Mosta
240
Rabat
253
Birzebbugia
Filfla

14° 30'
Pozzallo
San Pawl il-Bahar
Sliema
20 Valletta
Birkirkara
Paola
Benghisa Pt

36°
14° 30'

117

C

40°

A

38°

D

0 10 20 30 40 50 km

15
17° 4 18° 15 5 19°

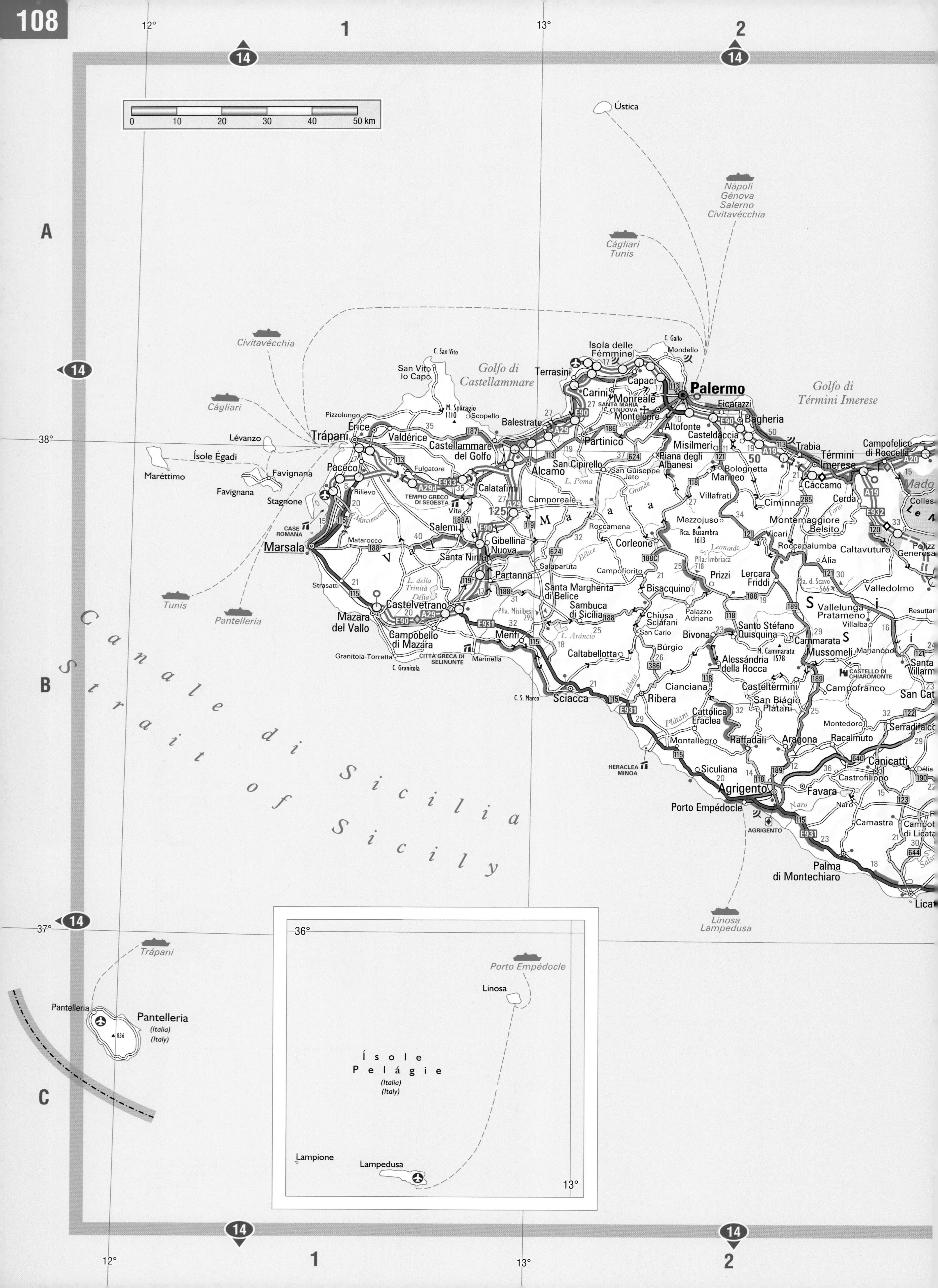

0 10 20 30 40 50 km
Ústica
Nápoli
Génova
Salerno
Civitavécchia
Cágliari
Tunis
Civitavécchia
Cágliari
Tunis
Pantelleria
Golfo di Castellammare
Golfo di Términi Imerese
Isola delle Fémmine
C. Gallo
Mondello
Terrasini
Palermo
Carini
Capaci
Monreale
Montelepre
Ficarazzi
Bagheria
Altofonte
Casteldáccia
Misilmeri
Trabia
Términi Imerese
Campofelice di Roccella
Cáccamo
Cerda
Partinico
Piana degli Albanesi
Marineo
Bolognetta
Villafrati
Ciminna
C. San Vito
San Vito lo Capo
M. Spáragio 1110
Scopello
Balestrate
Pizzolungo
Érice
Valdérice
Trápani
Lévanzo
Ísole Égadi
Maréttimo
Favignana
Favignana
Paceco
Castellammare del Golfo
Alcamo
San Cipirello
San Giuseppe Jato
L. Poma
Fulgatore
Rilievo
Stagnone
Calatafimi
TEMPIO GRECO DI SEGESTA
Vita
Camporeale
CASE ROMANA
Marsala
Matarocco
Salemi
Gibellina Nuova
Santa Ninfa
Roccamena
Corleone
Mezzojuso
Rca. Busambra 1613
Montemaggiore Belsito
Vicari
Roccapalumba
Caltavuturo
Ália
Valledolmo
Campofiorito
Salaparuta
Prizzi
Lercara Friddi
Strasatti
Partanna
L. della Trinità Délia
Santa Margherita di Belice
Bisacquino
Castelvetrano
Mazara del Vallo
Campobello di Mazara
Granitola-Torretta
C. Granitola
CITTÀ GRECA DI SELINUNTE
Marinella
Menfi
Plla. Misilbesi 295
Sambuca di Sicília
L. Aráncio
Chiusa Sclafani
San Carlo
Palazzo Adriano
Bivona
Santo Stéfano Quisquina
Búrgio
Caltabellotta
Alessándria della Rocca
M. Cammarata 1578
Cammarata
Vallelunga Pratameno
Villalba
Mussomeli
Marianópoli
CASTELLO DI CHIAROMONTE
Campofranco
Casteltérmini
San Biágio Plátani
Cianciana
Ribera
C. S. Marco
Sciacca
Cattólica Eraclea
Montallegro
Raffadali
Aragona
Montedoro
Racalmuto
Canicattì
Castrofilippo
HERACLEA MINOA
Siculiana
Agrigento
Favara
Naro
Porto Empédocle
AGRIGENTO
Camastra
Palma di Montechiaro
Linosa
Lampedusa
Val di Mazara
Sicilia
Canale di Sicilia
Strait of Sicily
Trápani
Pantelleria
Pantelleria (Italia) (Italy)
836
Porto Empédocle
Linosa
Ísole Pelágie (Italia) (Italy)
Lampione
Lampedusa
A
B
C
1
2
12°
13°
36°
37°
38°
14

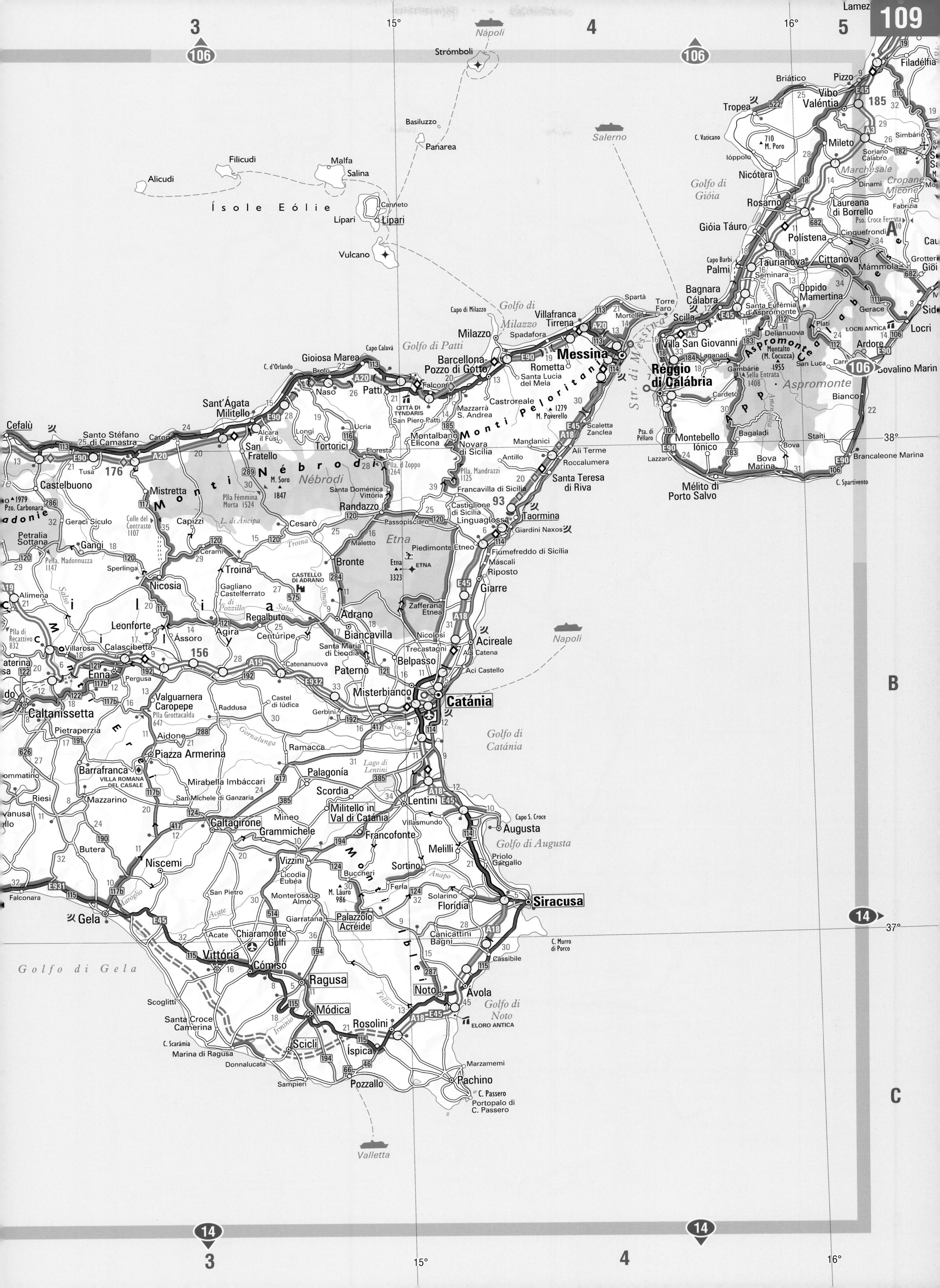

3
4
5
15°
16°
38°
37°
B
C
A
106
14
Nápoli
Strómboli
Basiluzzo
Panarea
Salerno
Filicudi
Alicudi
Malfa
Salina
Ísole Eólie
Canneto
Lípari
Vulcano
Lamez
Filadélfia
Pizzo
Briático
Vibo Valéntia
Tropea
C. Vaticano
M. Poro
Mileto
Soriano Cálabro
Simbário
Ióppolo
Nicótera
Golfo di Gióia
Rosarno
Laureana di Borrello
Fabrízia
Marchesale
Dinami
Gióia Táuro
Polístena
Cinquefrondi
Pso. Croce Ferrata
Capo Barbi
Palmi
Taurianova
Cittanova
Mámmola
Grotteria
Gióiosa
Seminara
Óppido Mamertina
Bagnara Cálabra
Sparta
Torre Faro
Scilla
Santa Eufémia d'Aspromonte
Delianuova
Gerace
Platì
Locri
LOCRI ANTICA
Ardore
Bovalino Marina
Villa San Giovanni
Laganadi
Montalto (M. Cocuzza)
Gambárie
Sella Entrata
San Luca
Aspromonte
Réggio di Calábria
Cardeto
Bianco
Pta. di Péllaro
Lazzaro
Montebello Iónico
Bagaladi
Bova
Staiti
Brancaleone Marina
Bova Marina
Mélito di Porto Salvo
C. Spartivento
Str. di Messina
Capo di Milazzo
Golfo di Milazzo
Villafranca Tirrena
Milazzo
Spadafora
Messina
Mortelle
Rometta
Santa Lucia del Mela
Monti Peloritani
Golfo di Patti
Capo Calavá
Gioiosa Marea
C. d'Orlando
Brolo
Naso
Patti
Falcone
Barcellona-Pozzo di Gotto
CITTÀ DI TYNDARIS
San Piero Patti
Castroreale
Mazzarrà S. Andrea
M. Poverello
Scaletta Zanclea
Sant'Ágata Militello
Alcara il Fusi
Longi
Ucria
Tortorici
Floresta
Montalbano Elicona
Novara di Sicilia
Mandanici
Alì Terme
Roccalumera
Antillo
Plla. Mandrazzi
Santa Teresa di Riva
Cefalù
Santo Stéfano di Camastra
Caronia
San Fratello
Monti Nébrodi
Nébrodi
Plla. d'Zoppo
M. Soro
Santa Doménica Vittória
Francavilla di Sicilia
Tusa
Castelbuono
Mistretta
Plla Fémmina Morta
Randazzo
Castiglione di Sicilia
Linguaglossa
Taormina
Giardini Naxos
Pzo. Carbonara
Madonie
Geraci Siculo
Colle del Contrasto
Capizzi
L. di Áncipa
Cesarò
Passopisciaro
Petralia Sottana
Gangi
Cerami
Troina
Maletto
Etna
Piedimonte Etneo
Fiumefreddo di Sicília
Máscali
Riposto
Pella. Madonnuzza
Sperlinga
Nicosia
Bronte
CASTELLO DI ADRANO
Giarre
Alimena
Gagliano Castelferrato
L. di Pozzillo
Salso
Simeto
Zafferana Etnea
Adrano
Regalbuto
Leonforte
Agira
Ássoro
Centúripe
Biancavilla
Nicolosi
Acireale
Pila di Recattivo
Villarosa
Calascibetta
Santa Maria di Licodia
Trecastagni
Aci Catena
Aci Castello
Enna
Pergusa
Catenanuova
Belpasso
Paternò
Misterbianco
Catánia
Caltanissetta
Valguarnera Caropepe
Plla Grottacalda
Raddusa
Castel di Iúdica
Gerbini
Golfo di Catánia
Pietraperzia
Aidone
Gornalunga
Ramacca
Piazza Armerina
Lago di Lentini
Barrafranca
VILLA ROMANA DEL CASALE
Mirabella Imbáccari
Palagonía
Scordia
Riesi
Mazzarino
San Michele di Ganzaria
Lentini
Capo S. Croce
Augusta
Caltagirone
Mineo
Militello in Val di Catánia
Villasmundo
Grammichele
Francofonte
Golfo di Augusta
Butera
Melilli
Priolo Gargallo
Niscemi
Vizzini
Licodia Eubea
Buccheri
Sortino
Monti Iblei
Anapo
M. Lauro
Ferla
San Pietro
Monterosso Almo
Solarino
Floridia
Siracusa
Falconara
Gela
Giarratana
Palazzolo Acréide
Acate
Chiaramonte Gulfi
Canicattini Bagni
C. Murro di Porco
Vittória
Cómiso
Cassibile
Golfo di Gela
Ragusa
Noto
Avola
Golfo di Noto
Scoglitti
Módica
Tellaro
ELORO ANTICA
Santa Croce Camerina
Irminio
Rosolini
C. Scarámia
Marina di Ragusa
Scicli
Íspica
Donnalucata
Marzamemi
Pachino
Sampieri
Pozzallo
C. Passero
Portopalo di C. Passero
Valletta
Napoli

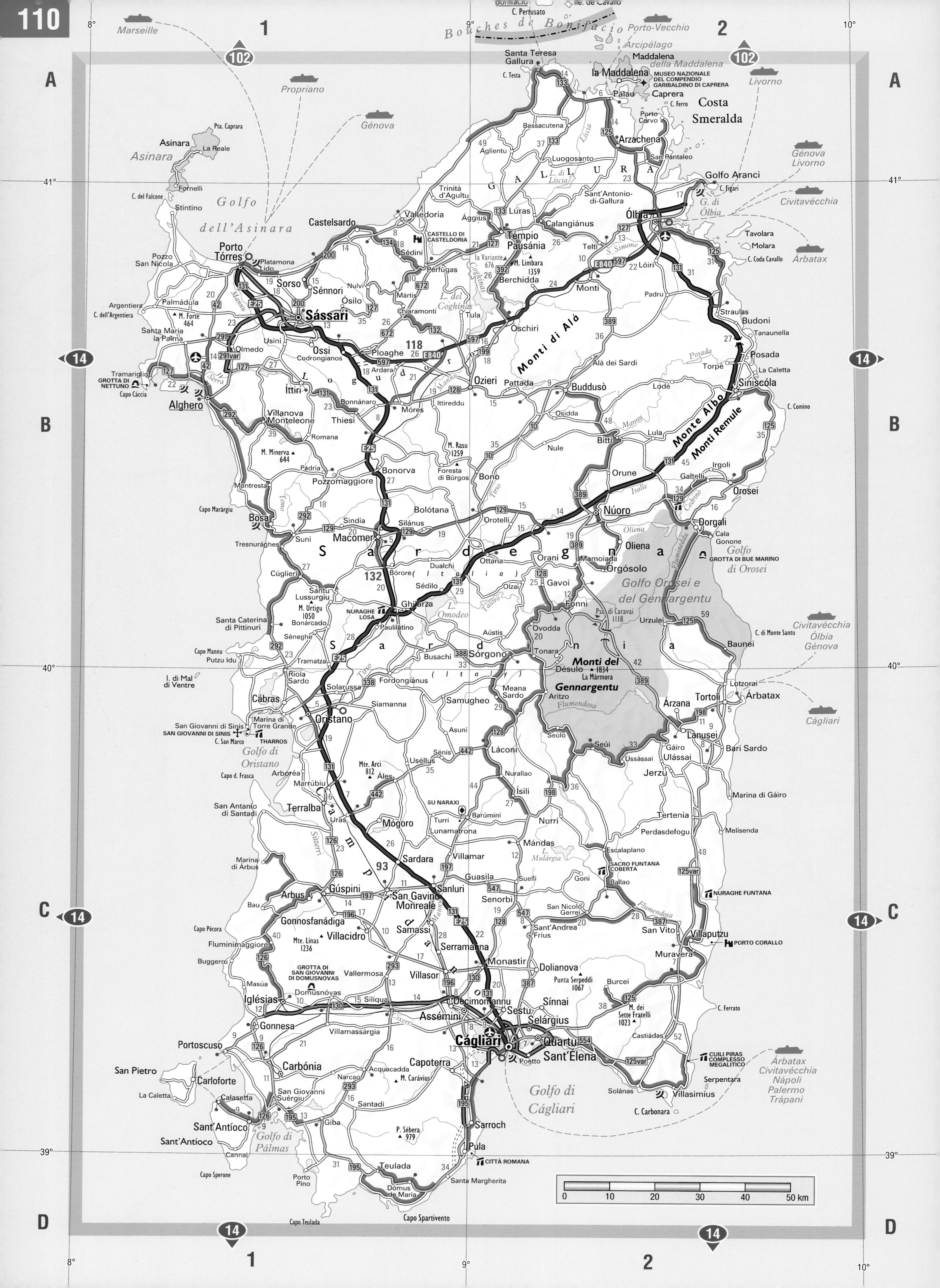
Bouches de Bonifacio
Porto-Vecchio
Marseille
Propriano
Génova
Livorno
Civitavécchia
Árbatax
Cágliari
Asinara
Pta. Caprara
La Reale
Fornelli
C. del Falcone
Stintino
Golfo dell'Asinara
Porto Tórres
Platamona Lido
Pozzo San Nicola
Castelsardo
Valledoria
Sorso
Sénnori
Sássari
Argentiera
C. dell'Argentiera
Palmádula
M. Forte 464
Santa Maria la Palma
Olmedo
Usini
Ossi
Codrongianos
Ploaghe
Ardara
Tramariglio
GROTTA DI NETTUNO
Capo Cáccia
Alghero
Íttiri
Bonnánaro
Mores
Thiesi
Villanova Monteleone
Romana
M. Minerva 644
Padria
Pozzomaggiore
Bonorva
Montresta
Capo Marárgiu
Bosa
Suni
Sindia
Macomer
Tresnuraghes
Cúglieri
Santu Lussurgiu
M. Urtigu 1050
Bonárcado
Séneghe
Santa Caterina di Pittinuri
Capo Mannu
Putzu Idu
I. di Mal di Ventre
Riola Sardo
Tramatza
Cábras
Marina di Torre Grande
San Giovanni di Sinis
SAN GIOVANNI DI SINIS
C. San Marco
THARROS
Golfo di Oristano
Oristano
Solarussa
Siamanna
Capo d. Frasca
Arboréa
Marrúbiu
Terralba
Uras
San Antonio di Santadi
Marina di Árbus
Árbus
Bau
Gúspini
Gonnosfanádiga
Capo Pécora
Fluminimaggiore
Buggerru
Villacidro
Mte. Linas 1236
GROTTA DI SAN GIOVANNI DI DOMUSNOVAS
Vallermosa
Masúa
Iglésias
Domusnóvas
Siliqua
Gonnesa
Villamassárgia
Portoscuso
Carbónia
San Pietro
Carloforte
La Caletta
Calasetta
Sant'Antíoco
Golfo di Pálmas
Cannai
Capo Sperone
Giba
San Giovanni Suérgiu
Narcao
Santadi
P. Sébera 979
Teulada
Porto Pino
Capo Teulada
Dómus de Maria
Capo Spartivento
Santa Margherita
Pula
CITTÀ ROMANA
Sarroch
Capoterra
Acquacadda
M. Carávius
Assémini
Decimomannu
Villasor
Samassi
Serramanna
San Gavino Monreale
Sanluri
Sardara
Mógoro
Turri
Lunamatrona
Barúmini
SU NARAXI
Villamar
Guasila
Senorbì
Suelli
Mandas
Nurri
Ísili
Nurallao
Láconi
Usséllus
Sénis
Mte. Arci 812
Áles
Asuni
Samugheo
Meana Sardo
Sórgono
Busachi
Fordongiánus
Aústis
Tonara
Désulo
Ovodda
Monti del Gennargentu
Punta La Mármora 1834
Aritzo
Seúlo
Seúi
Ussássai
Gáiro
Ulássai
Jerzu
Lanusei
Bari Sardo
Tortolì
Árbatax
Lotzorai
Árzana
Marina di Gáiro
Tertenia
Perdasdefogu
Melisenda
Escalaplano
SACRO FUNTANA COBERTA
Ballao
NURAGHE FUNTANA
Goni
San Nicolò Gerrei
Sant'Andrea Frius
San Vito
Villaputzu
PORTO CORALLO
Muravera
Dolianova
Punta Serpeddì 1067
Burcei
M. dei Sette Fratelli 1023
C. Ferrato
Castiádas
Monastir
Sestu
Sínnai
Selárgius
Cágliari
Quartu Sant'Elena
Poetto
CUILI PIRAS COMPLESSO MEGALITICO
Serpentara
Villasimíus
Solánas
C. Carbonara
Golfo di Cágliari
Ghilarza
NURAGHE LOSA
Paulilátino
Sédilo
L. Omodeo
Bórore
Dualchi
Silánus
Bolótana
Orotelli
Ottana
Olzai
Orani
Mamoiada
Gavoi
Fonni
Pso. di Caravai 1118
Orgósolo
Oliena
Núoro
Orune
Bitti
Nule
Bono
Foresta di Búrgos
M. Rasu 1259
Ittireddu
Ozieri
Pattada
Buddusò
Osidda
Alà dei Sardi
Monti di Alá
Oschiri
Tula
Chiaramonti
Mártis
Nulvi
Ósilo
Sédini
Pérfugas
L. del Coghinas
Berchidda
M. Limbara 1359
Témpio Pausánia
Calangiánus
Lúras
Ággius
CASTELLO DI CASTELDORIA
Trinità d'Agultu
Aglientu
Bassacutena
Luogosanto
L. di Liscia
GALLURA
Santa Teresa Gallura
C. Testa
la Maddalena
MUSEO NAZIONALE DEL COMPENDIO GARIBALDINO DI CAPRERA
Caprera
Arcipélago della Maddalena
Palau
C. Ferro
Porto Cervo
Costa Smeralda
Arzachena
San Pantaleo
Golfo Aranci
C. Figari
Sant'Antonio-di-Gallura
Ólbia
G. di Ólbia
Telti
Lóiri
Monti
Padru
Tavolara
Molara
C. Coda Cavallo
Straulas
Budoni
Tanaunella
Posada
Torpè
La Caletta
Siniscóla
Lodè
C. Comino
Monte Albo
Monti Remule
Lula
Irgoli
Galtelli
Orosei
Dorgali
Cala Gonone
GROTTA DI BUE MARINO
Golfo di Orosei
Golfo Orosei e del Gennargentu
Urzulei
C. di Monte Santu
Baunei
Sardegna (Italia)
Sardinia (Italy)
Logudoro
Campidano
0 10 20 30 40 50 km

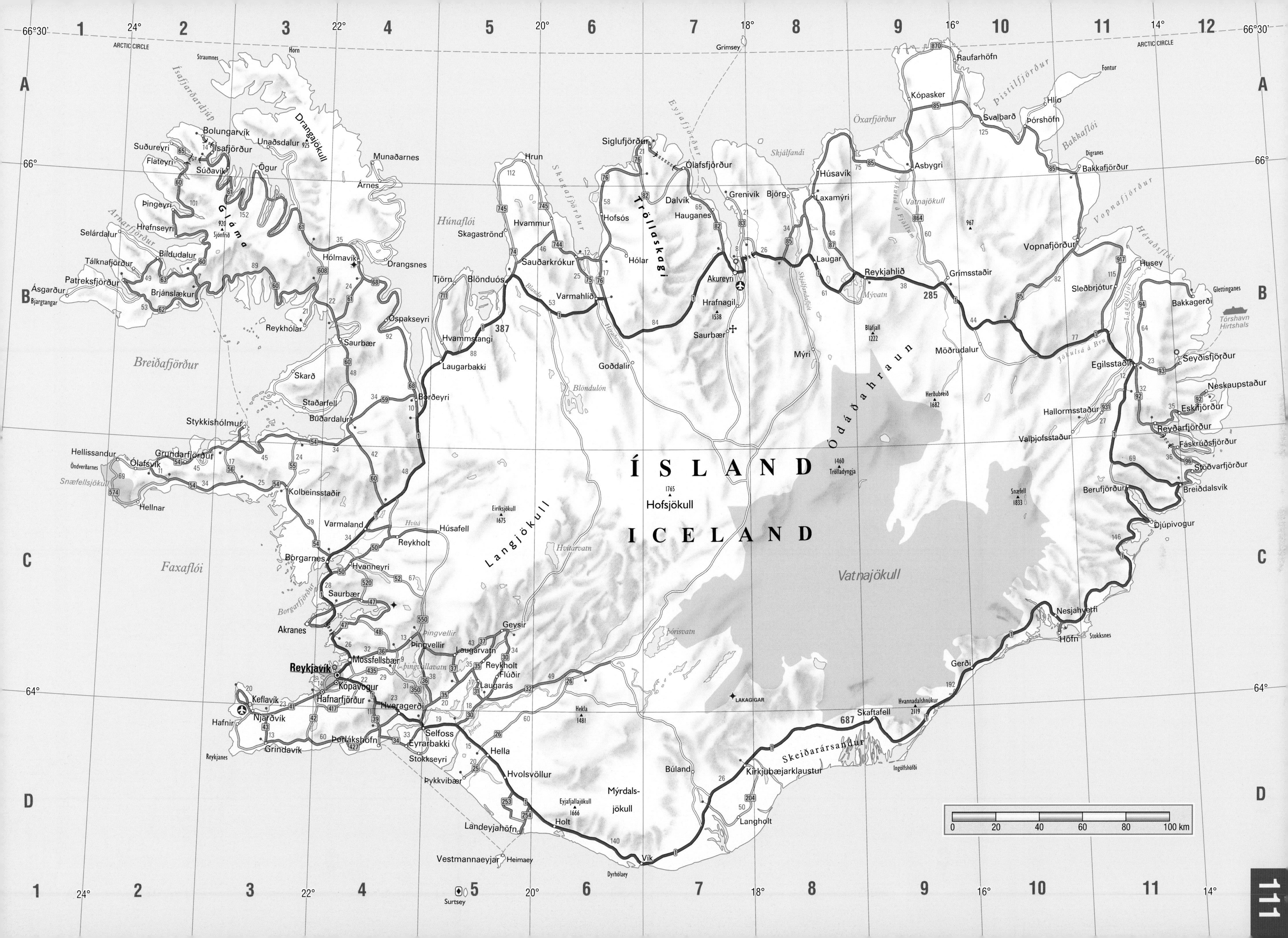
ÍSLAND
ICELAND
Vatnajökull
Hofsjökull
Langjökull
Mýrdals-
jökull
Drangajökull
Ódáðahraun
Tröllaskagi
Gláma
Skeiðarársandur
Breiðafjörður
Faxaflói
Húnaflói
Skagafjörður
Eyjafjörður
Skjálfandi
Öxarfjörður
Þistilfjörður
Bakkaflói
Vopnafjörður
Héraðsflói
Ísafjarðardjúp
Arnarfjörður
Borgarfjörður
Reykjavík
Kópavogur
Hafnarfjörður
Keflavík
Njarðvík
Hafnir
Grindavík
Reykjanes
Mosfellsbær
Akranes
Borgarnes
Hvanneyri
Saurbær
Varmaland
Reykholt
Húsafell
Þingvellir
Laugarvatn
Geysir
Flúðir
Laugarás
Hveragerði
Selfoss
Eyrarbakki
Stokkseyri
Þorlákshöfn
Þykkvibær
Hella
Hvolsvöllur
Landeyjahöfn
Vestmannaeyjar
Heimaey
Surtsey
Holt
Vík
Dyrhólaey
Búland
Kirkjubæjarklaustur
Langholt
Skaftafell
Hvannadalshnúkur
2119
Ingólfshöfði
Gerði
Höfn
Stokksnes
Nesjahverfi
Djúpivogur
Berufjörður
Breiðdalsvík
Stöðvarfjörður
Fáskrúðsfjörður
Reyðarfjörður
Eskifjörður
Neskaupstaður
Seyðisfjörður
Tórshavn
Hirtshals
Egilsstaðir
Hallormsstaður
Valþjófsstaður
Bakkagerði
Glettinganes
Húsey
Sleðbrjótur
Vopnafjörður
Bakkafjörður
Digranes
Þórshöfn
Hljo
Fontur
Svalbarð
Raufarhöfn
Kópasker
Ásbyrgi
Grímsstaðir
Möðrudalur
Herðubreið
1682
Snæfell
1833
Reykjahlíð
Mývatn
Bláfjall
1222
Trölladyngja
1460
Laugar
Laxamýri
Húsavík
Björg
Grenivík
Akureyri
Hrafnagil
1538
Saurbær
Mýri
Dalvík
Hauganes
Ólafsfjörður
Siglufjörður
Grímsey
Hofsós
Hólar
Varmahlíð
Sauðarkrókur
Hvammur
Skagaströnd
Hrun
Blönduós
Tjörn
Hvammstangi
Laugarbakki
Goðdalir
Blöndulón
Hvítárvatn
Þórisvatn
Hekla
1481
Eyjafjallajökull
1666
Eiríksjökull
1675
LAKAGÍGAR
Borðeyri
Óspakseyri
Drangsnes
Árnes
Munaðarnes
Hólmavík
Reykhólar
Skarð
Staðarfell
Búðardalur
Stykkishólmur
Kolbeinsstaðir
Grundarfjörður
Ólafsvík
Hellissandur
Öndverðarnes
Snæfellsjökull
Hellnar
Brjánslækur
Bíldudalur
Patreksfjörður
Tálknafjörður
Ásgarður
Bjargtangar
Selárdalur
Hrafnseyri
Þingeyri
Flateyri
Suðureyri
Bolungarvík
Ísafjörður
Súðavík
Ögur
Unaðsdalur
Horn
Straumnes
Sjónfríð
ARCTIC CIRCLE
66°30'
66°
64°
24°
22°
20°
18°
16°
14°
0
20
40
60
80
100 km

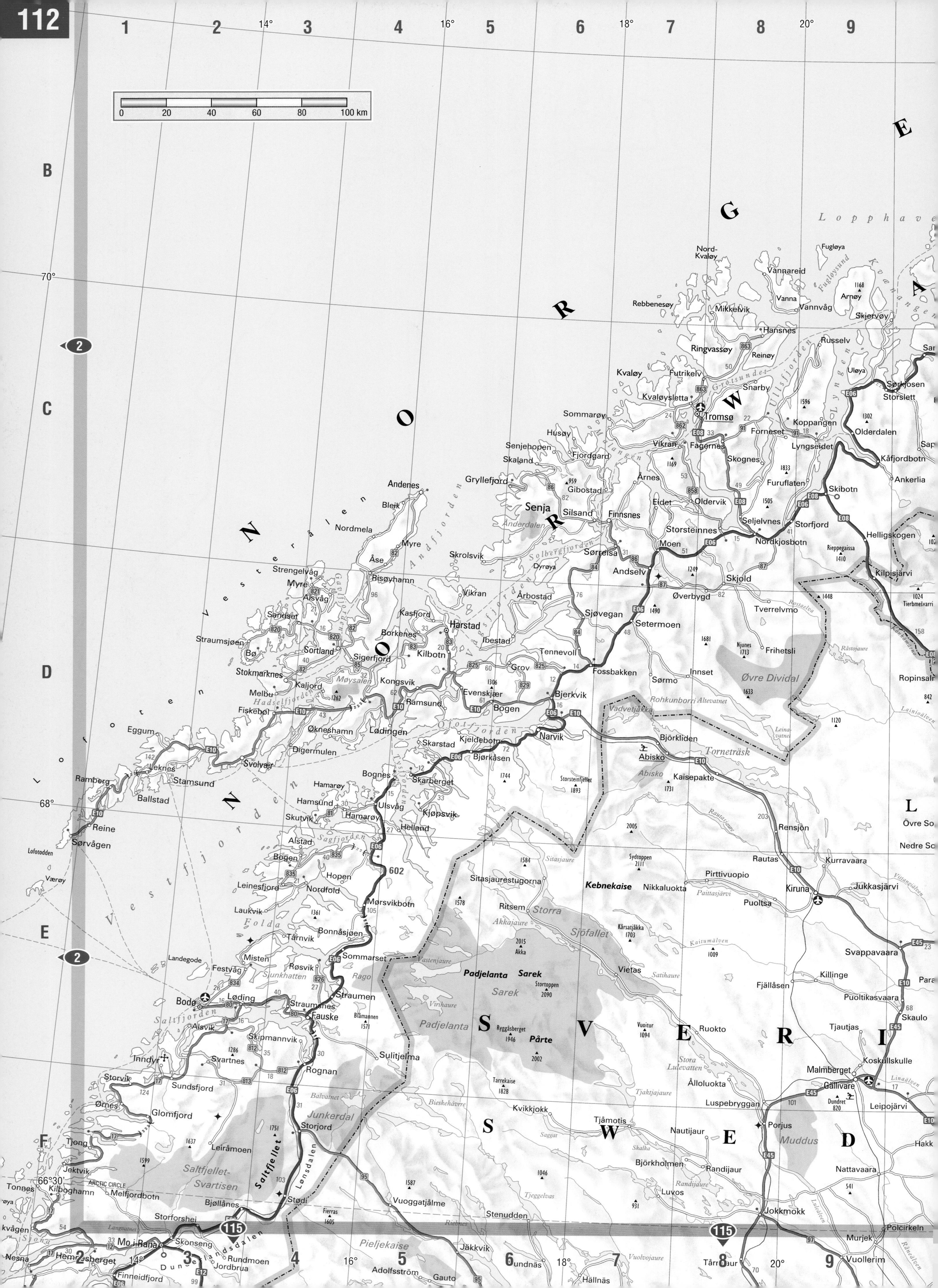

1
2
3
4
5
6
7
8
9
14°
16°
18°
20°
0
20
40
60
80
100 km
B
C
D
E
F
70°
68°
66°30'
ARCTIC CIRCLE
N O R G E
N O R W A Y
S V E R I G E
S W E D E N
Loppha ve
Lofoten
Vesterålen
Vestfjorden
Andfjorden
Nord-Kvaløy
Fugløya
Vannareid
Vanna
Vannvåg
Arnøy
Skjervøy
Rebbenesøy
Mikkelvik
Hansnes
Ringvassøy
Reinøy
Russelv
Kvaløy
Futrikelv
Grøtsundet
Ullsfjorden
Lyngen
Uløya
Sørkjosen
Storslett
Kvaløysletta
Tromsø
Snarby
Sommarøy
Koppangen
Olderdalen
Husøy
Vikran
Fagernes
Forneset
Lyngseidet
Senjehopen
Skaland
Fjordgard
Malangen
Skognes
Kåfjordbotn
Ankerlia
Gryllefjord
Gibostad
Årnes
Furuflaten
Skibotn
Andenes
Bleik
Senja
Silsand
Finnsnes
Eidet
Oldervik
Storfjord
Nordmela
Ånderdalen
Storsteinnes
Seljelvnes
Helligskogen
Myre
Skrolsvik
Sørreisa
Moen
Nordkjosbotn
Åse
Solbergfjorden
Dyrøya
Rieppegaissa
Kilpisjärvi
Strengelvåg
Andselv
Skjold
Bisøyhamn
Gavlfjorden
Vikran
Årbostad
Alsvåg
Overbygd
Tverrelvmo
Tierbmesvarri
Sandset
Kasfjord
Sjøvegan
Setermoen
Borkenes
Harstad
Straumsjøen
Sortland
Ibestad
Frihetsli
Bø
Kilbotn
Tennevoll
Njunes
Innset
Råstojaure
Sigerfjord
Grov
Fossbakken
Stokmarknes
Møysalen
Kongsvik
Evenskjær
Sørmo
Øvre Dividal
Ropinsalmi
Kaljord
Bjerkvik
Melbu
Hadselfjorden
Ramsund
Bogen
Rohkunborri
Altevatnet
Fiskebøl
Vadvetjåkka
Eggum
Økneshamn
Lødingen
Ofotfjorden
Narvik
Leinavatnet
Lainioälven
Skarstad
Kjeldebotn
Björkliden
Digermulen
Svolvær
Bjørkåsen
Abisko
Torneträsk
Leknes
Bognes
Kaisepakte
Ramberg
Stamsund
Skarberget
Storsteinfjellet
Ballstad
Hamarøy
Hamsund
Ulsvåg
Kjøpsvik
L
Övre Soppero
Reine
Skutvik
Helland
Rensjön
Sørvågen
Alstad
Sagfjorden
Nedre Soppero
Lofotodden
Bogen
Rautas
Kurravaara
Værøy
Hopen
Sitasjaure
Sydtoppen
Nordfold
Sitasjaurestugorna
Kebnekaise
Nikkaluokta
Pirttivuopio
Jukkasjärvi
Leinesfjord
Paittasjärvi
Kiruna
Mørsvikbotn
Ritsem
Storra
Puoltsa
Laukvik
Folda
Akkajaure
Sjöfallet
Kårsatjåkka
Tårnvik
Bonnåsjøen
Akka
Kaitumälven
Svappavaara
Landegode
Misten
Sommarset
Vastenjaure
Vietas
Festvåg
Røsvik
Sjunkhatten
Rago
Padjelanta
Sarek
Killinge
Stortoppen
Satihaure
Fjällåsen
Bodø
Løding
Straumen
Puoltikasvaara
Saltfjorden
Straumsnes
Fauske
Blåmannen
Virihaure
Skaulo
Alsvik
Padjelanta
Ryggåsberget
Pårte
Vuoitur
Ruokto
Tjautjas
Skipmannvik
Inndyr
Svartnes
Sulitjelma
Koskullskulle
Rognan
Stora Lulevatten
Malmberget
Storvik
Gällivare
Sundsfjord
Tarrekaise
Ålloluokta
Linaälven
Balvatnet
Tjaktjajaure
Ørnes
Bieskehávrre
Luspebryggan
Leipojärvi
Glomfjord
Kvikkjokk
Dundret
Junkerdal
Tjåmotis
Storjord
Saggat
Nautijaur
Porjus
Muddus
Tjong
Leiråmoen
Saltfjellet
Skalka
Hakk
Jektvik
Saltfjellet-Svartisen
Lønsdalen
Björkholmen
Randijaur
Nattavaara
Tonnes
Kilboghamn
Melfjordbotn
Tjeggelvas
Randijaure
Luvos
Bjøllånes
Støddi
Vuoggatjålme
Fierras
Langvatnet
Storforshei
Stenudden
Jokkmokk
Riebnes
Lulealven
Polcirkeln
kvågen
Mo i Rana
Skonseng
Dunderlandsdalen
Pieljekaise
Jäkkvik
Murjek
Rånealven
Nesna
Hemnesberget
Rundmoen
Jordbrua
Adolfsström
Gundnäs
Vuolvojaure
Tårrajaur
Vuollerim
Finneidfjord
Gauto
Hällnäs
115
2
602

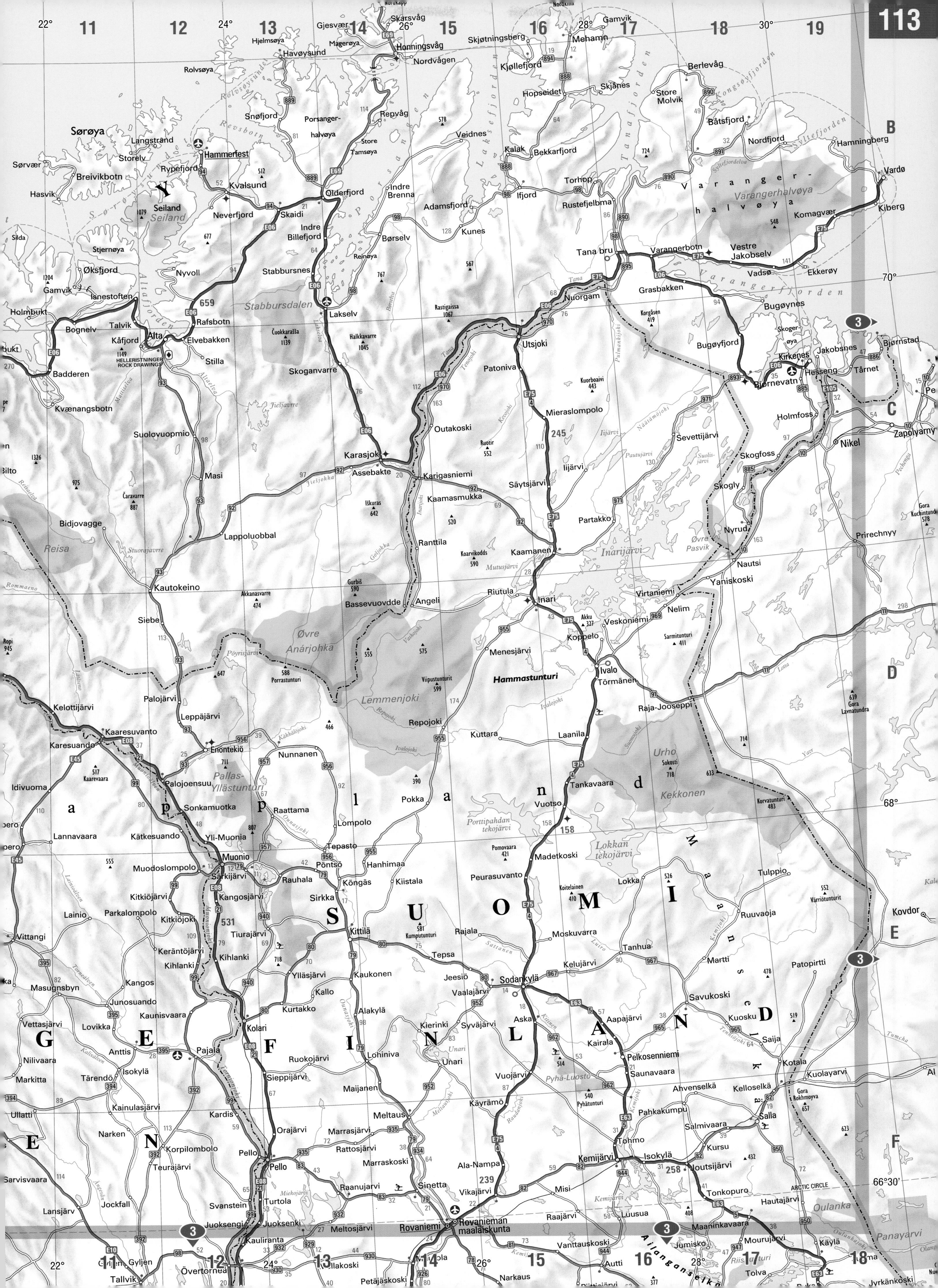

Gjesvær
Skarsvåg
Honningsvåg
Nordvågen
Hjelmsøya
Havøysund
Mågerøya
Rolvsøya
Skjøtningsberg
Mehamn
Gamvik
Kjøllefjord
Hopseidet
Skjånes
Berlevåg
Store Molvik
Båtsfjord
Nordfjord
Hamningberg
Vardø
Kiberg
Komagvær
Sørøya
Langstrand
Storelv
Hammerfest
Sørvær
Breivikbotn
Hasvik
Rypefjord
Kvalsund
Seiland
Neverfjord
Skaidi
Olderfjord
Snøfjord
Porsanger-halvøya
Repvåg
Store Tamsøya
Indre Brenna
Veidnes
Kalak
Bekkarfjord
Torhop
Ifjord
Rustefjelbma
Adamsfjord
Kunes
Børselv
Indre Billefjord
Stabbursnes
Lakselv
Stabbursdalen
Silda
Stjernøya
Øksfjord
Gamvik
Nyvoll
Isnestoften
Holmbukt
Bognelv
Talvik
Kåfjord
Alta
Rafsbotn
Elvebakken
Stilla
HELLERISTNINGER ROCK DRAWINGS
Badderen
Kvænangsbotn
Tana bru
Varangerbotn
Vestre Jakobselv
Vadsø
Ekkerøy
Varanger-halvøya
Varangerfjorden
Nuorgam
Grasbakken
Bugøynes
Bugøyfjord
Skogerøya
Jakobsnes
Bjørnstad
Kirkenes
Hesseng
Tårnet
Bjørnevatn
Holmfoss
Nikel
Zapolyarny
Skogfoss
Skogly
Nyrud
Øvre Pasvik
Prirechnyy
Nautsi
Yaniskoski
Utsjoki
Patoniva
Mieraslompolo
Outakoski
Karasjok
Assebakte
Karigasniemi
Kaamasmukka
Säytsjärvi
Iijärvi
Sevettijärvi
Partakko
Kaamanen
Inarijärvi
Ranttila
Skoganvarre
Suolovuopmio
Masi
Bidjovagge
Reisa
Lappoluobbal
Kautokeino
Siebe
Bassevuovdde
Angeli
Riutula
Inari
Virtaniemi
Nelim
Veskoniemi
Koppelo
Menesjärvi
Øvre Anárjohka
Lemmenjoki
Hammastunturi
Ivalo
Törmänen
Raja-Jooseppi
Palojärvi
Kelottijärvi
Leppäjärvi
Kaaresuvanto
Karesuando
Enontekiö
Repojoki
Kuttara
Laanila
Nunnanen
Palojoensuu
Pallas-Yllästunturi
Idivuoma
Sonkamuotka
Raattama
Lompolo
Pokka
Tankavaara
Vuotso
Urho Kekkonen
Lannavaara
Kätkesuando
Yli-Muonio
Muonio
Tepasto
Muodoslompolo
Särkijärvi
Pöntsö
Rauhala
Hanhimaa
Könkäs
Kiistala
Peurasuvanto
Madetkoski
Lokkan tekojärvi
Porttipahdan tekojärvi
Lokka
Tulppio
Kangosjärvi
Kitkiöjärvi
Lainio
Parkalompolo
Sirkka
Kittilä
Rajala
Moskuvarra
Kovdor
Vittangi
Tiurajärvi
Keräntöjärvi
Kihlanki
Tepsa
Tanhua
Martti
Patopirtti
Masugnsbyn
Kangos
Ylläsjärvi
Kaukonen
Jeesiö
Sodankylä
Kelujärvi
Junosuando
Kaunisvaara
Kallo
Kurtakko
Vaalajärvi
Alakylä
Aska
Aapajärvi
Savukoski
Kuosku
Saija
Vettasjärvi
Lovikka
Kolari
Kierinki
Syväjärvi
Kairala
Anttis
Pajala
Nilivaara
Isokylä
Ruokojärvi
Lohiniva
Unari
Pelkosenniemi
Saunavaara
Kotala
Kuolayarvi
Markitta
Tärendö
Sieppijärvi
Maijanen
Vuojärvi
Pyhä-Luosto
Ahvenselkä
Kelloselkä
Ullatti
Kainulasjärvi
Kardis
Meltaus
Käyrämö
Pahkakumpu
Salla
Narken
Korpilombolo
Orajärvi
Marrasjärvi
Rattosjärvi
Salmivaara
Tohmo
Kursu
Teurajärvi
Pello
Marraskoski
Ala-Nampa
Kemijärvi
Isokylä
Joutsijärvi
Sarvisvaara
Raanujarvi
Sinetta
Vikajärvi
Misi
Tonkopuro
ARCTIC CIRCLE
Hautajärvi
Oulanka
Lansjärv
Jockfall
Svanstein
Turtola
Luusua
Raajärvi
Juoksengi
Juoksenki
Rovaniemi
Rovanieman maalaiskunta
Meltosjärvi
Kauliranta
Vanttauskoski
Jumisko
Maaninkavaara
Mourujärvi
Käylä
Panayarvi
Gyljen
Övertorneå
Tallvik
Ailangan selkä
Autti
Tolva
Narkaus
Petäjäskoski
Jyrkänkoski
Y
a
p
p
l
a
n
d
S
U
O
M
I
F
I
N
L
A
N
D
G
E
E
N

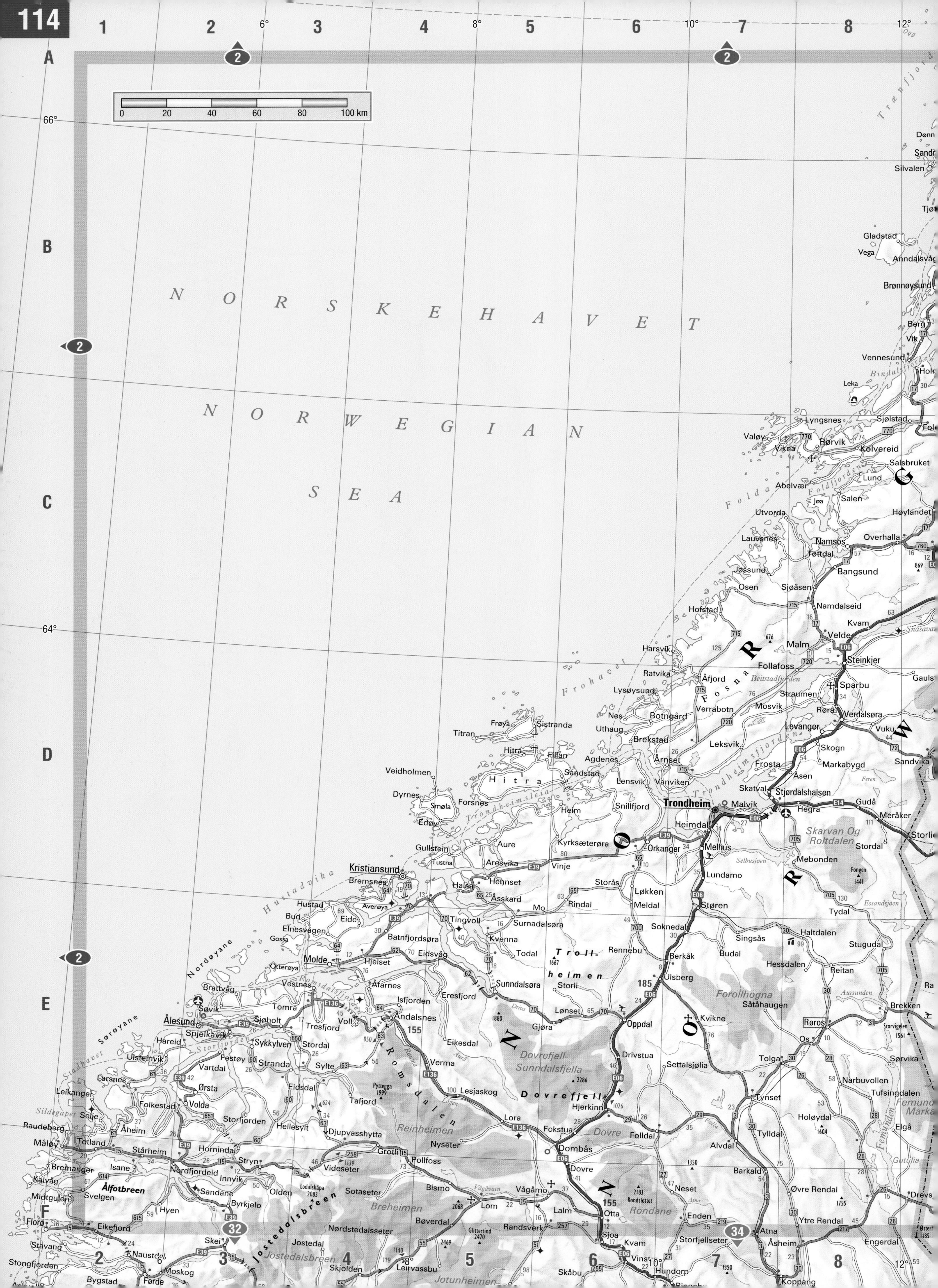

NORSKEHAVET
NORWEGIAN SEA
0 20 40 60 80 100 km
66°
64°
6°
8°
10°
12°
Trænfjorden
Dønn
Sandr
Silvalen
Tjø
Gladstad
Vega
Anndalsvåg
Brønnøysund
Berg
Vik
Vennesund
Bindalsfjorden
Holm
Leka
Lyngsnes
Sjølstad
Valøy
Vikna
Rørvik
Kolvereid
Salsbruket
Lund
Abelvær
Foldfjorden
Folda
Jøa
Salen
Utvorda
Høylandet
Lauvsnes
Namsos
Overhalla
Tøttdal
Bangsund
Jøssund
Osen
Sjøåsen
Namdalseid
Hofstad
Kvam
Velde
Snåsavatn
Harsvik
Malm
Steinkjer
Follafoss
Ratvika
Åfjord
Beitstadfjorden
Fosna
Sparbu
Lysøysund
Straumen
Verrabotn
Mosvik
Røra
Verdalsøra
Nes
Botngård
Uthaug
Levanger
Vuku
Frohavet
Frøya
Sistranda
Titran
Brekstad
Skogn
Hitra
Fillan
Agdenes
Årnset
Leksvik
Markabygd
Sandvika
Frosta
Veidholmen
Sandstad
Lensvik
Vanviken
Trondheimsfjorden
Åsen
Skatval
Stjørdalshalsen
Dyrnes
Smøla
Forsnes
Trondheimsleia
Trondheim
Malvik
Hegra
Gudå
Meråker
Edøy
Heim
Snillfjord
Heimdal
Skarvan Og Roltdalen
Storli
Gullstein
Aure
Kyrksæterøra
Orkanger
Melhus
Stordal
Tustna
Aresvika
Vinje
Selbusjøen
Mebonden
Kristiansund
Bremsnes
Hennset
Halsa
Storås
Lundamo
Fongen
Averøya
Åskard
Løkken
Hustadvika
Hustad
Rindal
Meldal
Støren
Tydal
Bud
Eide
Mo
Essandsjøen
Elnesvågen
Tingvoll
Surnadalsøra
Soknedal
Haltdalen
Gossa
Batnfjordsøra
Kvenna
Singsås
Molde
Eidsvåg
Todal
Rennebu
Budal
Stugudal
Hjelset
Trollheimen
Berkåk
Hessdalen
Nordøyane
Otterøya
Reitan
Vestnes
Romsdalsfjorden
Åfarnes
Sunndalsøra
Storli
Ulsberg
Forollhogna
Brattvåg
Eresfjord
Isfjorden
Søvik
Tomra
Åndalsnes
Lønset
Sätåhaugen
Brekken
Sørøyane
Ålesund
Sjøholt
Gjøra
Oppdal
Kvikne
Røros
Spjelkavik
Tresfjord
Voll
Os
Hareid
Sykkylven
Stordal
Eikesdal
Romsdalen
Dovrefjell-Sunndalsfjella
Storfjorden
Ulsteinvik
Festøy
Stranda
Drivstua
Settalsjølia
Tolga
Sørvika
Vartdal
Sylte
Verma
Larsnes
Narbuvollen
Stadhavet
Ørsta
Eidsdal
Lesjaskog
Dovrefjell
Tufsingdalen
Leikanger
Tafjord
Hjerkinn
Tynset
Femunden
Sildegapet
Selje
Folkestad
Volda
Lora
Holøydal
Raudeberg
Åheim
Storfjorden
Hellesylt
Reinheimen
Fokstua
Dovre
Folldal
Tylldal
Elgå
Måløy
Totland
Djupvasshytta
Nyseter
Alvdal
Bremanger
Stårheim
Hornindal
Grotli
Dombås
Isane
Stryn
Videseter
Pollfoss
Barkald
Gutulia
Kalvåg
Nordfjordeid
Innvik
Dovre
Neset
Midtgulen
Ålfotbreen
Sandane
Olden
Sotaseter
Bismo
Vågåmo
Øvre Rendal
Drevsjø
Svelgen
Lodalskåpa
Breheimen
Lom
Rondane
Hyen
Byrkjelo
Jostedalsbreen
Lalm
Otta
Ytre Rendal
Florø
Eikefjord
Bøverdal
Randsverk
Enden
Nordstedalsseter
Glittertind
Atna
Skei
Sjoa
Kvam
Storfjellseter
Stavang
Jostedal
Åsheim
Engerdal
Naustdal
Vinstra
Stongfjorden
Skjolden
Leirvassbu
Skåbu
Hundorp
Moskog
Jotunheimen
Bygstad
Førde
Koppang

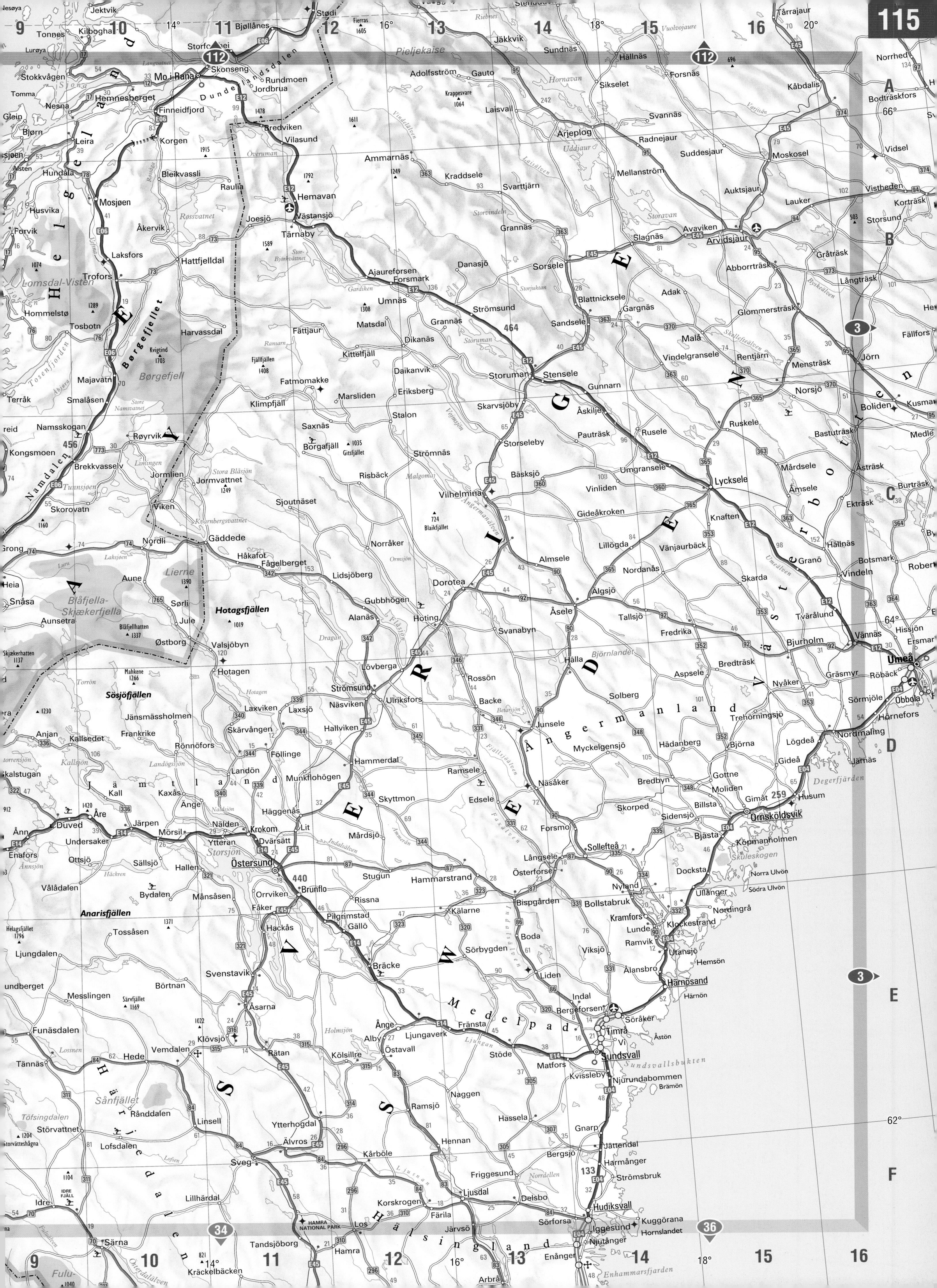
Helgeland
Västerbotten
Ångermanland
Jämtland
Medelpad
Härjedalen
Hälsingland
SVERIGE
NORGE
Børgefjellet
Børgefjell
Namdalen
Dundelandsdalen
Hotagsfjällen
Sösjöfjällen
Anarisfjällen
Blåfjella-Skjækerfjella
Lomsdal-Visten
Skuleskogen
Pieljekaise
HAMRA NATIONAL PARK
Mo i Rana
Skonseng
Rundmoen
Jordbrua
Storforshei
Bjøllånes
Kilboghamn
Tonnes
Jektvik
Stødi
Lurøya
Stokkvågen
Tomma
Nesna
Hemnesberget
Finneidfjord
Glein
Bjørn
Leira
Korgen
Alsten
Hundåla
Bleikvassli
Raulia
Mosjøen
Husvika
Forvik
Åkervik
Laksfors
Hattfjelldal
Trofors
Hommelstø
Tosbotn
Harvassdal
Majavatn
Terråk
Smalåsen
Namsskogan
Røyrvik
Kongsmoen
Brekkvasselv
Jormlien
Jormvattnet
Viken
Skorovatn
Gäddede
Nordli
Grong
Håkafot
Fågelberget
Aune
Heia
Snåsa
Ausnetra
Sørli
Jule
Østborg
Valsjöbyn
Hotagen
Jänsmässholmen
Anjan
Kallsedet
Frankrike
Rönnöfors
Skalstugan
Kall
Kaxås
Ånge
Åre
Duved
Ånn
Järpen
Undersaker
Enafors
Ottsjö
Mörsil
Nälden
Krokom
Ytteran
Dvärsätt
Sällsjö
Hallen
Östersund
Vålådalen
Bydalen
Månsåsen
Brunflo
Orrviken
Fåker
Tossåsen
Ljungdalen
Svenstavik
Börtnan
Messlingen
Åsarna
Funäsdalen
Klövsjö
Vemdalen
Tännäs
Hede
Rätan
Sånfjället
Rånddalen
Linsell
Tofsingdalen
Storvattnet
Lofsdalen
Sveg
Ytterhogdal
Älvros
Lillhärdal
Idre
Särna
Tandsjöborg
Kräckelbäcken
Hamra
Los
Fulu-
Jäkkvik
Hällnäs
Sundnäs
Forsnäs
Adolfsström
Gauto
Laisvall
Sikselet
Arjeplog
Svannäs
Radnejaur
Suddesjaur
Moskosel
Vidsel
Bredviken
Vilasund
Ammarnäs
Kraddsele
Svarttjärn
Mellanström
Auktsjaur
Vistheden
Hemavan
Västansjö
Tärnaby
Joesjö
Grannäs
Slagnäs
Avaviken
Arvidsjaur
Lauker
Storsund
Korträsk
Gråträsk
Abborrträsk
Långträsk
Danasjö
Sorsele
Ajaureforsen
Forsmark
Umnäs
Strömsund
Blattnicksele
Gargnäs
Adak
Glommersträsk
Fättjaur
Matsdal
Grannäs
Dikanäs
Kittelfjäll
Sandsele
Malå
Vindelgransele
Rentjärn
Mensträsk
Jörn
Fällfors
Daikanvik
Storuman
Stensele
Fatmomakke
Marsliden
Eriksberg
Gunnarn
Norsjö
Boliden
Kusmark
Klimpfjäll
Skarvsjöby
Åskilje
Stalon
Saxnäs
Borgafjäll
Storseleby
Pauträsk
Ruskele
Rusele
Bastuträsk
Medle
Strömnäs
Risbäck
Bäsksjö
Umgransele
Vinliden
Lycksele
Mårdsele
Åmsele
Asträsk
Burträsk
Ekträsk
Vilhelmina
Sjoutnäset
Gideåkroken
Knaften
Hällnäs
Norråker
Lillögda
Vänjaurbäck
Granö
Botsmark
Almsele
Nordanås
Skarda
Vindeln
Robertsfors
Lidsjöberg
Dorotea
Gubbhögen
Alanäs
Hoting
Åsele
Älgsjö
Tallsjö
Tvärålund
Svanabyn
Fredrika
Vännäs
Hissjö
Bjurholm
Umeå
Ersmark
Lövberga
Hälla
Bredträsk
Aspsele
Nyåker
Gräsmyr
Röbäck
Obbola
Sörmjöle
Rossön
Strömsund
Ulriksfors
Näsviken
Laxviken
Laxsjö
Backe
Solberg
Hörnefors
Trehörningsjö
Skärvången
Hallviken
Junsele
Nordmaling
Föllinge
Hammerdal
Myckelgensjö
Hädanberg
Björna
Lögdeå
Landön
Munkflohögen
Ramsele
Näsåker
Gideå
Järnäs
Gottne
Moliden
Bredbyn
Skyttmon
Edsele
Degerfjärden
Gimåt
Husum
Häggenås
Lit
Mårdsjö
Forsmo
Skorped
Sidensjö
Billsta
Örnsköldsvik
Bjästa
Köpmanholmen
Sollefteå
Långsele
Österforse
Docksta
Norra Ulvön
Södra Ulvön
Stugun
Hammarstrand
Nyland
Rissna
Bispgården
Bollstabruk
Ullånger
Nordingrå
Pilgrimstad
Gällö
Kälarne
Kramfors
Lunde
Klockestrand
Ramvik
Utansjö
Hackås
Boda
Viksjö
Hemsön
Bräcke
Sörbygden
Liden
Ålansbro
Härnösand
Härnön
Indal
Bergeforsen
Söråker
Ånge
Ljungaverk
Fränsta
Timrå
Alby
Östavall
Stöde
Vi
Åstön
Sundsvall
Matfors
Kölsillre
Kvissleby
Njurundabommen
Brämön
Sundsvallsbukten
Naggen
Ramsjö
Hassela
Gnarp
Hennan
Jättendal
Bergsjö
Harmånger
Kårböle
Friggesund
Strömsbruk
Ljusdal
Korskrogen
Delsbo
Färila
Hudiksvall
Järvsö
Sörforsa
Kuggörana
Iggesund
Hornslandet
Njutånger
Enånger
Arbrå
Enhammarsfjärden
Storsjön
Uddjaur
Storavan
Hornavan
Överuman
Storuman
Vojmsjön
Malgomaj
Flåsjön
Ormsjön
Lierne
Kallsjön
Tunnsjøen
Røssvatnet
Namsvatnet
Indalsälven
Ljungan
Ljusnan
Umeälven
Skellefteälven
Ångermanälven
Fjällsjöälven
Faxälven
Lossnen
Lofsen
Norrdellen
Vindelälven
Bjørnlandet
Dragan
Hotagen
Torrön
Ammerån
Holmsjön
Häckren
Storvindeln
Gardiken
Storjuktan
Sjona
Vefsna
Varjisån
Byskeälven
Tosenfjorden
Kvarnbergsvattnet
Stora Blåsjön
Limingen
Laksjøen
Luru
Riebnes
Vuolvojaure
Laisälven
Stor-Björkvattnet
Kvigtind 1703
Fjällfjällen 1408
Blåfjellhatten 1337
Skjækerhatten 1137
Mahkene 1266
Helagsfjället 1796
Särvfjället 1169
Fierras 1605
Krappesvare 1064
Blaikfjället
Gitsfjället
IDRE FJÄLL
Tårrajaur
Norrhed
Kåbdalis
Bodträskfors
Storbacken
Skjækerhatten
9 10 11 12 13 14 15 16
A B C D E F
14° 16° 18° 20°
62° 64° 66°
E4 E6 E10 E12 E14 E45
3 34 36 112 133 259 440 456 464

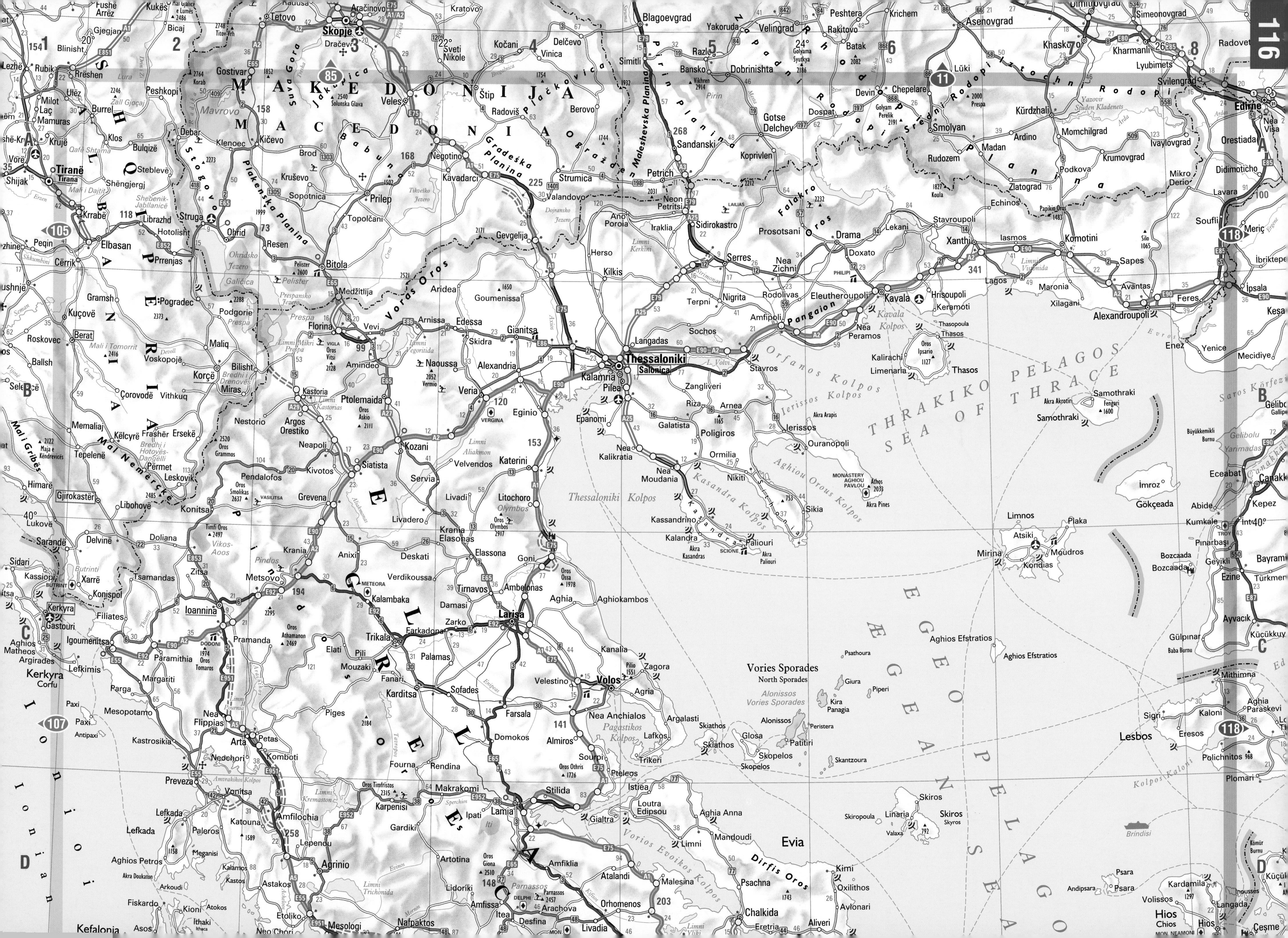

Thessaloniki
Salonica
Kavala
Drama
Serres
Xanthi
Komotini
Alexandroupoli
Thasos
Samothraki
Limnos
Lesbos
Evia
Volos
Larisa
Trikala
Kozani
Veria
Florina
Kastoria
Ioannina
Preveza
Lefkada
Kerkyra
Corfu
Agrinio
Lamia
Skopje
Ohrid
Bitola
Tiranë
Elbasan
Korçë
Berat
Gjirokastër
Edirne
Smolyan
Blagoevgrad
THRAKIKO PELAGOS
THRACE SEA OF
EGEO PELAGOS
AEGEAN SEA
MAKEDONIJA
MACEDONIA
SHQIPERIA
ELLAS
GREECE
Thessaloniki Kolpos
Kasandra
Vories Sporades
North Sporades
Skiathos
Skopelos
Alonissos
Skiros
Hios
Chalkida
Katerini
Tirnavos
Farsala
Karditsa
Arta
Metsovo
Grevena
Edessa
Naoussa
Siatista

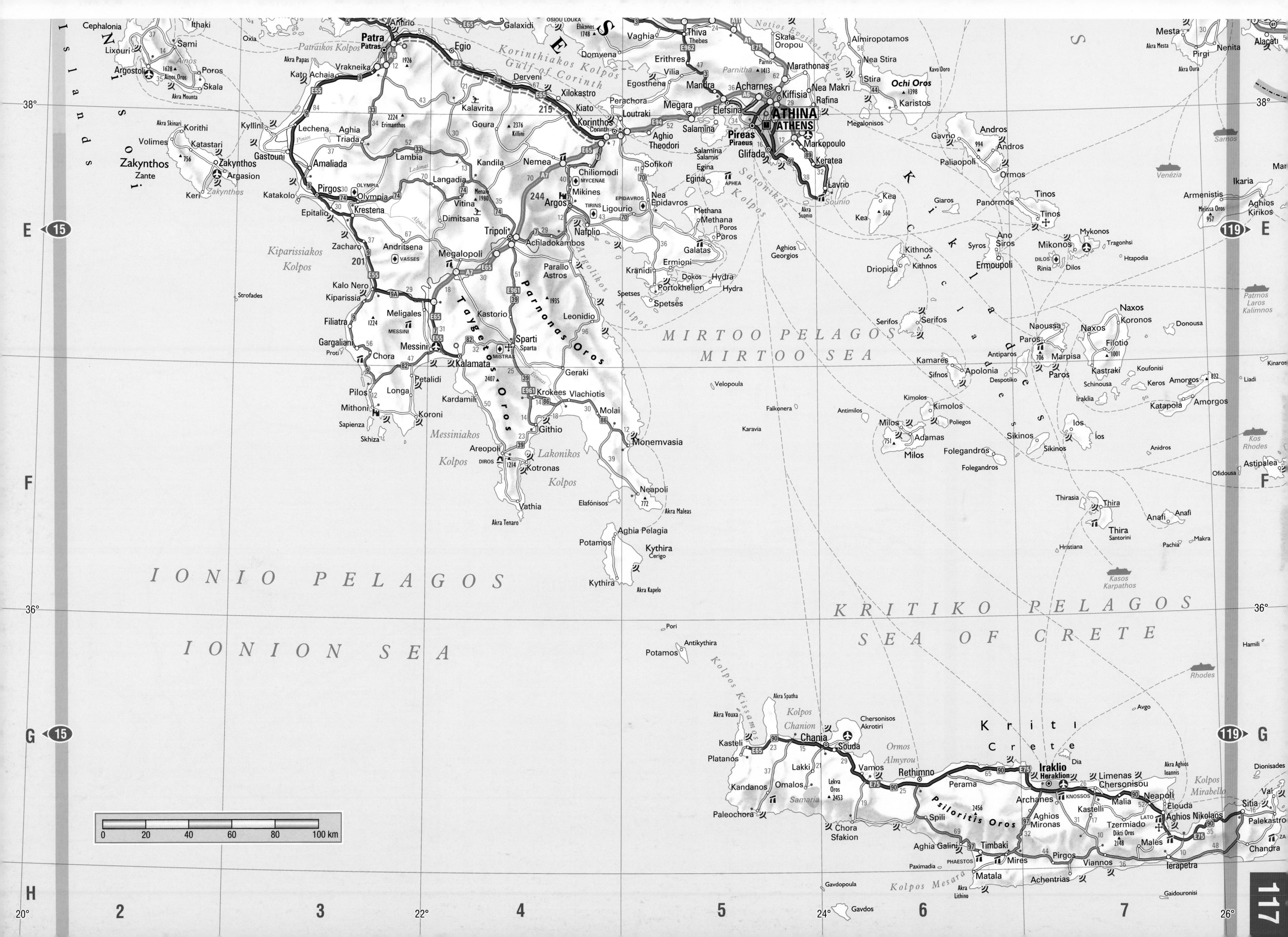
IONIO PELAGOS
IONION SEA
MIRTOO PELAGOS
MIRTOO SEA
KRITIKO PELAGOS
SEA OF CRETE
Kiklades
Kriti
Crete
Ionian Islands
ATHINA
ATHENS
Pireas
Piraeus
Glifada
Elefsina
Acharnes
Kiffisia
Marathonas
Nea Makri
Rafina
Markopoulo
Keratea
Lavrio
Sounio
Patra
Patras
Egio
Korinthos
Corinth
Loutraki
Kiato
Xilokastro
Derveni
Kalavrita
Megara
Mandra
Thiva
Thebes
Vaghia
Domvena
Galaxidi
Antirio
Argos
Nafplio
Mikines
Mycenae
Nemea
Tripoli
Megalopoli
Kalamata
Sparti
Sparta
Mistras
Githio
Monemvasia
Neapoli
Areopoli
Kotronas
Vathia
Pilos
Methoni
Koroni
Kiparissia
Filiatra
Gargaliani
Zacharo
Pirgos
Olympia
Amaliada
Gastouni
Kyllini
Lechena
Kato Achaia
Vrakneika
Zakynthos
Zante
Argostoli
Lixouri
Sami
Ithaki
Cephalonia
Kythira
Cerigo
Aghia Pelagia
Potamos
Antikythira
Elafonisos
Andros
Tinos
Syros
Ermoupoli
Mykonos
Mikonos
Dilos
Naxos
Paros
Antiparos
Sifnos
Serifos
Kithnos
Kea
Milos
Adamas
Kimolos
Folegandros
Sikinos
Ios
Thira
Santorini
Anafi
Amorgos
Katapola
Astipalea
Ikaria
Aghios Kirikos
Armenistis
Chania
Souda
Rethimno
Iraklio
Heraklion
Knossos
Malia
Aghios Nikolaos
Elouda
Neapoli
Ierapetra
Sitia
Palekastro
Chandra
Kasteli
Platanos
Kandanos
Paleochora
Chora Sfakion
Matala
Mires
Timbaki
Spili
Psiloritis Oros
Gavdos
Parnonas Oros
Taygetos Oros
Ochi Oros
Korinthiakos Kolpos
Gulf of Corinth
Saronikos Kolpos
Argolikos Kolpos
Lakonikos Kolpos
Messiniakos Kolpos
Kiparissiakos Kolpos
Patraikos Kolpos
Kolpos Kissamos
Kolpos Mesara
Kolpos Mirabello
Samaria
Samos
Venezia
Patmos
Laros
Kalimnos
Kos
Rhodes
Kasos
Karpathos
38°
36°
20°
22°
24°
26°
E
F
G
H
2
3
4
5
6
7
15
119
0
20
40
60
80
100 km

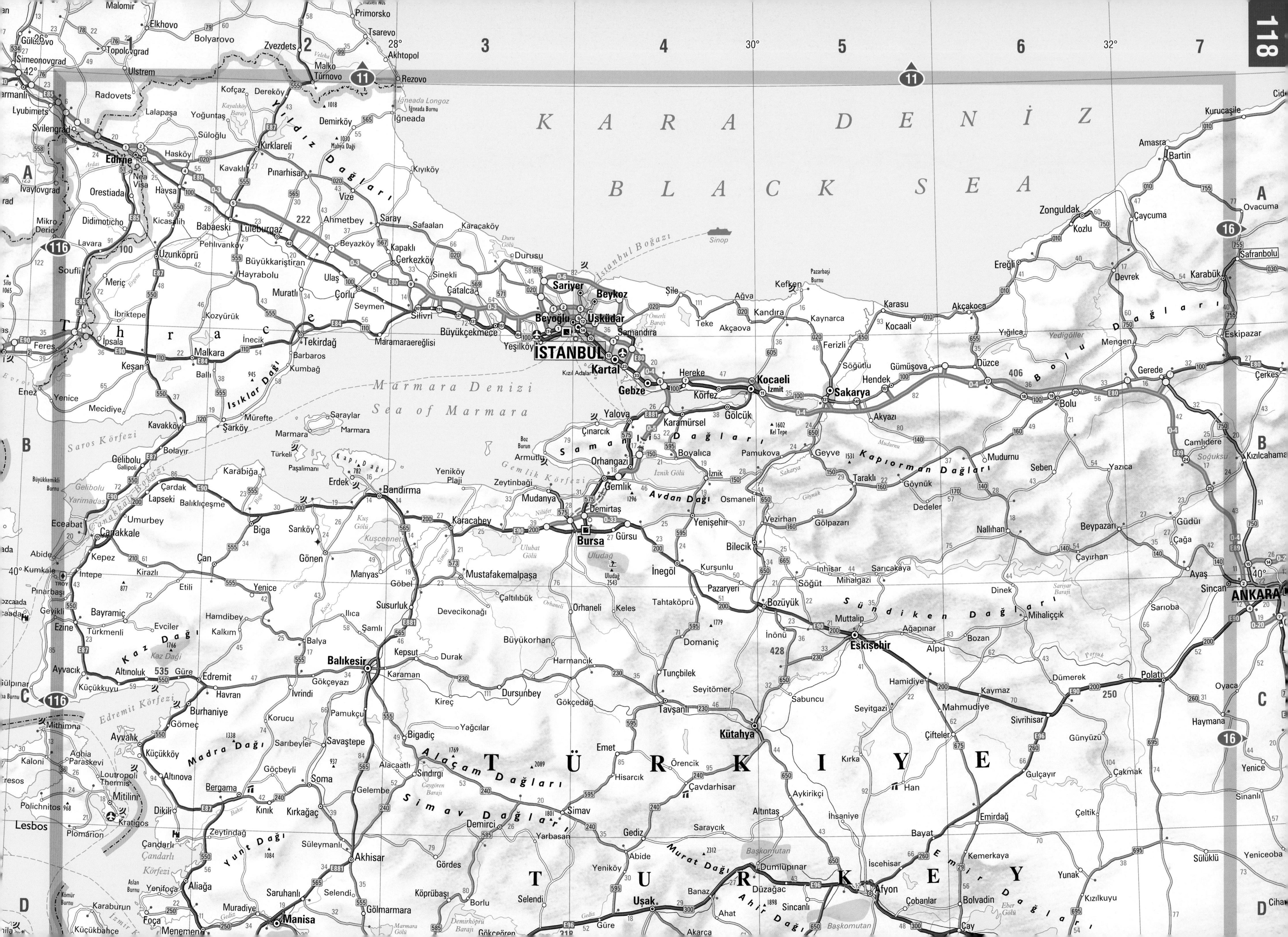
KARADENİZ
BLACK SEA
Marmara Denizi
Sea of Marmara
TÜRKİYE
TURKEY
Thrace
İSTANBUL
ANKARA
Bursa
Eskişehir
Kütahya
Balıkesir
Manisa
Uşak
Afyon
Edirne
Kırklareli
Tekirdağ
Çanakkale
Gelibolu
Kocaeli
İzmit
Sakarya
Bolu
Düzce
Zonguldak
Bartın
Karabük
Safranbolu
Gebze
Kartal
Üsküdar
Beyoğlu
Sarıyer
Beykoz
Yalova
Gemlik
Mudanya
Bandırma
Erdek
Biga
Edremit
Ayvalık
Bergama
Akhisar
Soma
Mitilini
Lesbos
Polatlı
Beypazarı
Bilecik
İnegöl
Bozüyük
Simav
Gediz
Tavşanlı
Yıldız Dağları
Uludağ
Kaz Dağı
Madra Dağı
Yunt Dağı
Murat Dağı
Sündiken Dağları
Kapıorman Dağları
Samanlı Dağları
Alaçam Dağları
Simav Dağları
Emir Dağları
Ahır Dağı
Saros Körfezi
Edremit Körfezi
Gemlik Körfezi
İstanbul Boğazı
Çanakkale Boğazı
Sinop
26°
28°
30°
32°
40°
42°
A
B
C
D
1
2
3
4
5
6
7
11
16
116

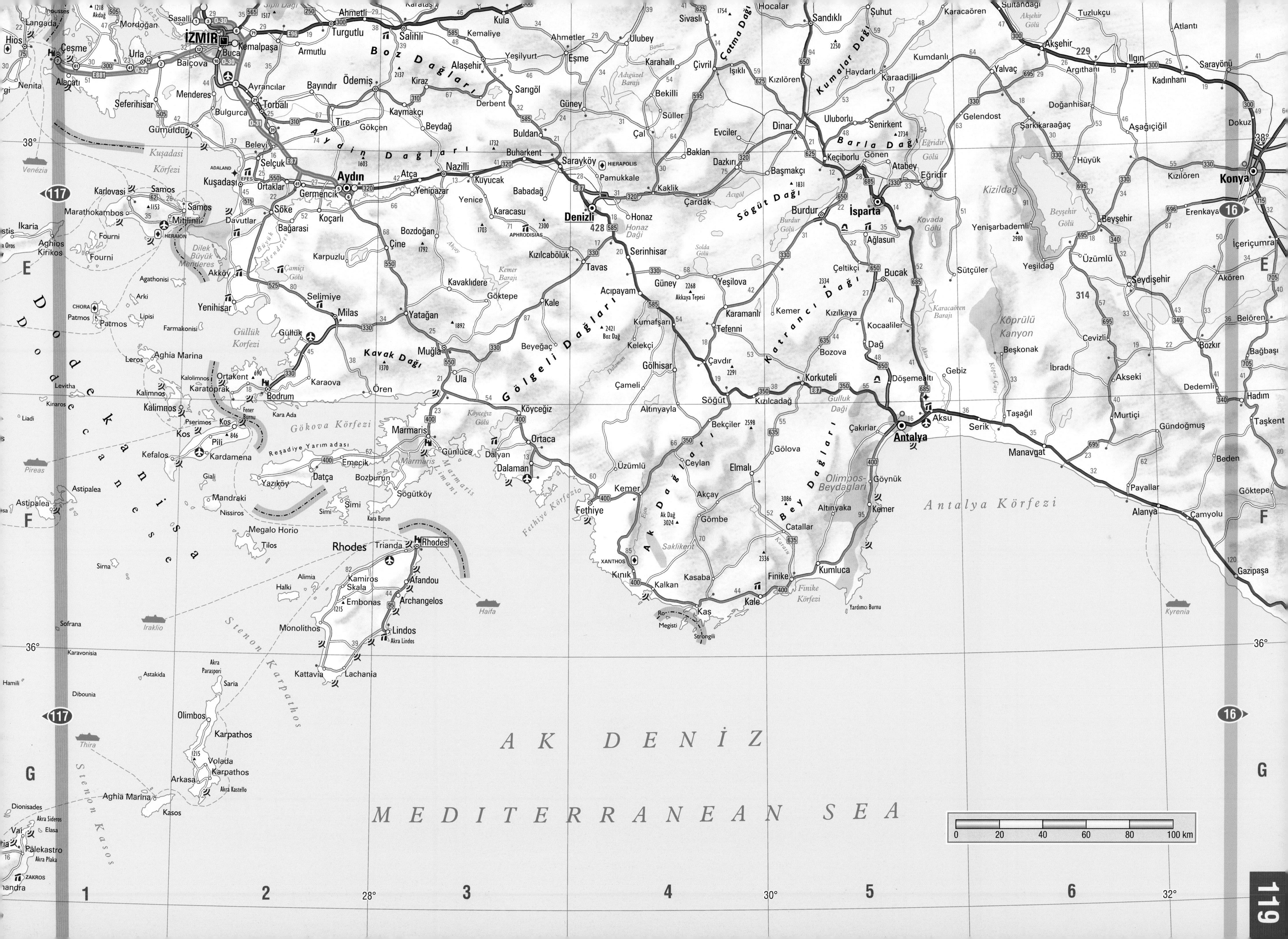

AK DENİZ
MEDITERRANEAN SEA
Antalya Körfezi
Dodekanisa
İZMİR
Konya
Antalya
Isparta
Burdur
Denizli
Aydın
Muğla
Bodrum
Marmaris
Fethiye
Kaş
Kalkan
Kemer
Finike
Kumluca
Alanya
Manavgat
Serik
Aksu
Gazipaşa
Akşehir
Ilgın
Beyşehir
Seydişehir
Eğirdir
Dinar
Sandıklı
Şuhut
Salihli
Turgutlu
Kemalpaşa
Çeşme
Urla
Seferihisar
Kuşadası
Selçuk
Söke
Milas
Yatağan
Dalaman
Ortaca
Köyceğiz
Datça
Nazilli
Tavas
Acıpayam
Elmalı
Korkuteli
Bucak
Rhodes
Lindos
Kos
Kalimnos
Leros
Patmos
Samos
Karpathos
Kasos
Tilos
Simi
Nissiros
Astipalea
Ikaria
Fourni
Boz Dağları
Aydın Dağları
Barla Dağı
Kumalar Dağı
Söğüt Dağı
Katrancı Dağı
Gölgeli Dağları
Bey Dağları
Ak Dağı
Kavak Dağı
Olimpos-Beydağları
Beyşehir Gölü
Eğirdir Gölü
Köprülü Kanyon
Gökova Körfezi
Güllük Körfezi
Kuşadası Körfezi
Fethiye Körfezi
Marmaris Limanı
Finike Körfezi
Stenon Karpathos
Stenon Kasos
E
F
G
1
2
3
4
5
6
16
117
28°
30°
32°
36°
38°
0 20 40 60 80 100 km

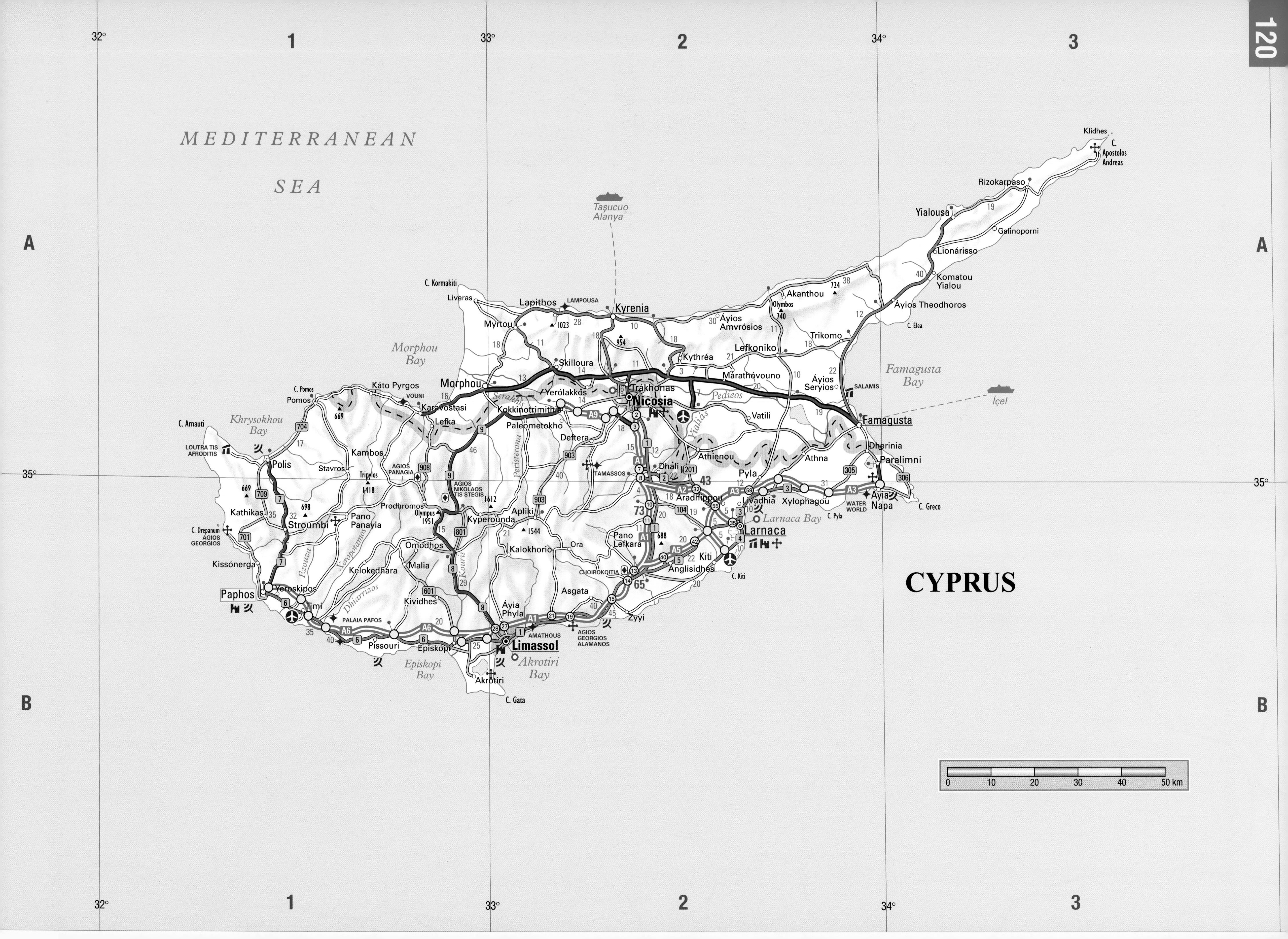

MEDITERRANEAN SEA
CYPRUS
Kyrenia
Nicosia
Famagusta
Larnaca
Limassol
Paphos
Morphou
Lapithos
LAMPOUSA
Myrtou
Liveras
C. Kormakiti
Skilloura
Yerólakkos
Kokkinotrimithia
Paleometokho
Deftera
Trakhonas
Kythréa
Lefkoniko
Marathóvouno
Áyios Amvrósios
Akanthou
Olymbos
Trikomo
Áyios Seryios
SALAMIS
Áyios Theodhoros
C. Elea
Komatou Yialou
Lionárisso
Galinoporni
Yialousa
Rizokarpaso
Klidhes
C. Apostolos Andreas
Famagusta Bay
Içel
Taşucuo Alanya
Morphou Bay
Káto Pyrgos
VOUNI
Karavostasi
Lefka
C. Pomos
Pomos
Khrysokhou Bay
C. Arnauti
LOUTRA TIS AFRODITIS
Polis
Kathikas
Stroumbi
C. Drepanum
AGIOS GEORGIOS
Kissónerga
Yeroskipos
Timi
PALAIA PAFOS
Pissouri
Episkopi
Episkopi Bay
Akrotiri
C. Gata
Akrotiri Bay
AMATHOUS
AGIOS GEORGIOS ALAMANOS
Zyyi
Áyia Phyla
Asgata
CHOIROKOITIA
Anglisidhes
Kiti
C. Kiti
Larnaca Bay
C. Pyla
WATER WORLD
Ayia Napa
C. Greco
Paralimni
Dherinia
Athna
Xylophagou
Livadhia
Pyla
Aradhippou
Athienou
Dhali
Vatili
Pedieos
Yialias
TAMASSOS
Pano Lefkara
Ora
Kalokhorio
Apliki
Kyperounda
AGIOS NIKOLAOS TIS STEGIS
Olympus 1951
Prodhromos
Pano Panayia
Omodhos
Malia
Kelokedhara
Kividhes
Kambos
Stavros
Tripylos
AGIOS PANAGIA
Serakhis
Peristerona
Kouris
Ezouza
Xeropotamos
Dhiarrizos
0 10 20 30 40 50 km

City plans • Plans de villes
Stadtpläne • Piante di città

Motorway	Autoroute	Autobahn	Autostrada			
Major through route	Route principale majeur	Hauptstrecke	Strada di grande communicazione			
Through route	Route principale	Schnellstrasse	Strada d'importanza regionale			
Secondary road	Route secondaire	Nebenstrasse	Strada d'interesse locale			
Dual carriageway	Chaussées séparées	Zweispurig Schnellstrasse	Strada a carreggiate doppie			
Other road	Autre route	Nebenstrecke	Altra strada			
Tunnel	Tunnel	Tunnel	Galleria stradale			
Limited access / pedestrian road	Rue réglementée / rue piétonne	Beschränkter Zugang / Fussgängerzone	Strada pedonale / a accesso limitato			
One-way street	Sens unique	Einbahnstrasse	Senso unico			
Parking	Parc de stationnement	Parkplatz	Parcheggio			
Motorway number	Numéro d'autoroute	Autobahnnummer	Numero di autostrada			
National road number	Numéro de route nationale	Nationalstrassennummer	Numero di strada nazionale			
European road number	Numéro de route européenne	Europäische Strassennummer	Numero di strada europea			
Destination	Destination	Ziel	Destinazione			
Car ferry	Bac passant les autos	Autofähre	Traghetto automobili			
Railway	Chemin de fer	Eisenbahn	Ferrovia			
Rail / bus station	Gare / gare routière	Bahnhof / Busstation	Stazione ferrovia / pullman			
Underground, metro station	Station de métro	U-Bahnstation	Metropolitano			
Cable car	Téléférique	Drahtseilbahn	Funivia			
Abbey, cathedral	Abbaye, cathédrale	Abtei, Kloster, Kathedrale	Abbazia, duomo			
Church of interest	Église intéressante	Interessante Kirche	Chiesa da vedere			
Synagogue	Synagogue	Synagoge	Sinagoga			
Hospital	Hôpital	Krankenhaus	Ospedale			
Police station	Police	Polizeiwache	Polizia			
Post office	Bureau de poste	Postamt	Ufficio postale			
Tourist information	Office de tourisme	Informationsbüro	Ufficio informazioni turistiche			
Place of interest	Autre curiosité	Sonstige Sehenswürdigkeit	Luogo da vedere			

Approach maps • Agglomérations
Carte régionale • Regionalkarte

Toll motorway – with motorway number	Autoroute à péage – avec numéro d'autoroute	Gebührenpflichtige Autobahn – mit Autobahnnummer	Autostrada a pedaggio – con numero
Toll-free motorway – with European road number	Autoroute – avec numéro de route européenne	Gebührenfreie Autobahn – Europäische Strassennummer	Autostrada – con numero di strada europea
Pre-pay motorway – vignette required	Autoroute – 'vignette'	Autobahn – 'vignette'	Autostrada – 'vignette'
Motorway services	Aire de service	Autobahnservice	Area di servizio autostradale
Motorway junction full access, restricted access	Échangeur d'autoroute accès libre, accès réglementé	Autobahnkreuz – voller/begrenzter Zugang	Raccordi autostradali – completo/parziali
Under construction	En construction	Im Bau	In construzione
Tunnel	Tunnel	Tunnel	Galleria stradale
Major route dual carriageway single carriageway	Route principale chausées séparées chausée sans séparation	Hauptstrecke – zweispurige Schnellstrasse	Strada di grande communicazione carreggiata doppia carreggiata unica
Secondary route dual carriageway single carriageway	Route secondaire chausées séparées chausées sans séparation	Nebenstrasse – zweispurige Schnellstrasse	Strada d'interesse locale – carreggiata doppia carreggiata unica
Other road	Autre route	Nebenstrecke	Altra strada
Car ferry	Bac passant les autos	Autofähre	Traghetto automobili
Destination	Destination	Ziel	Destinazione
Railway	Chemin de fer	Eisenbahn	Ferrovia
Railway station	Gare	Hauptbahnhof	Stazione ferrovia
Height – in metres	Altitude – en mètres	Höhe – über dem Meeresspiegel	Altezza in metri
Airport	Aéroport principal	Flughafen	Aeroporto
Airfield	Autre aéroport	Flugplatz	Aerodromo/ campo d'aviazione
City plan coverage area	Région de plan de ville	Vom Stadtplan abgedecktes Gebiet	Area della pianta della città

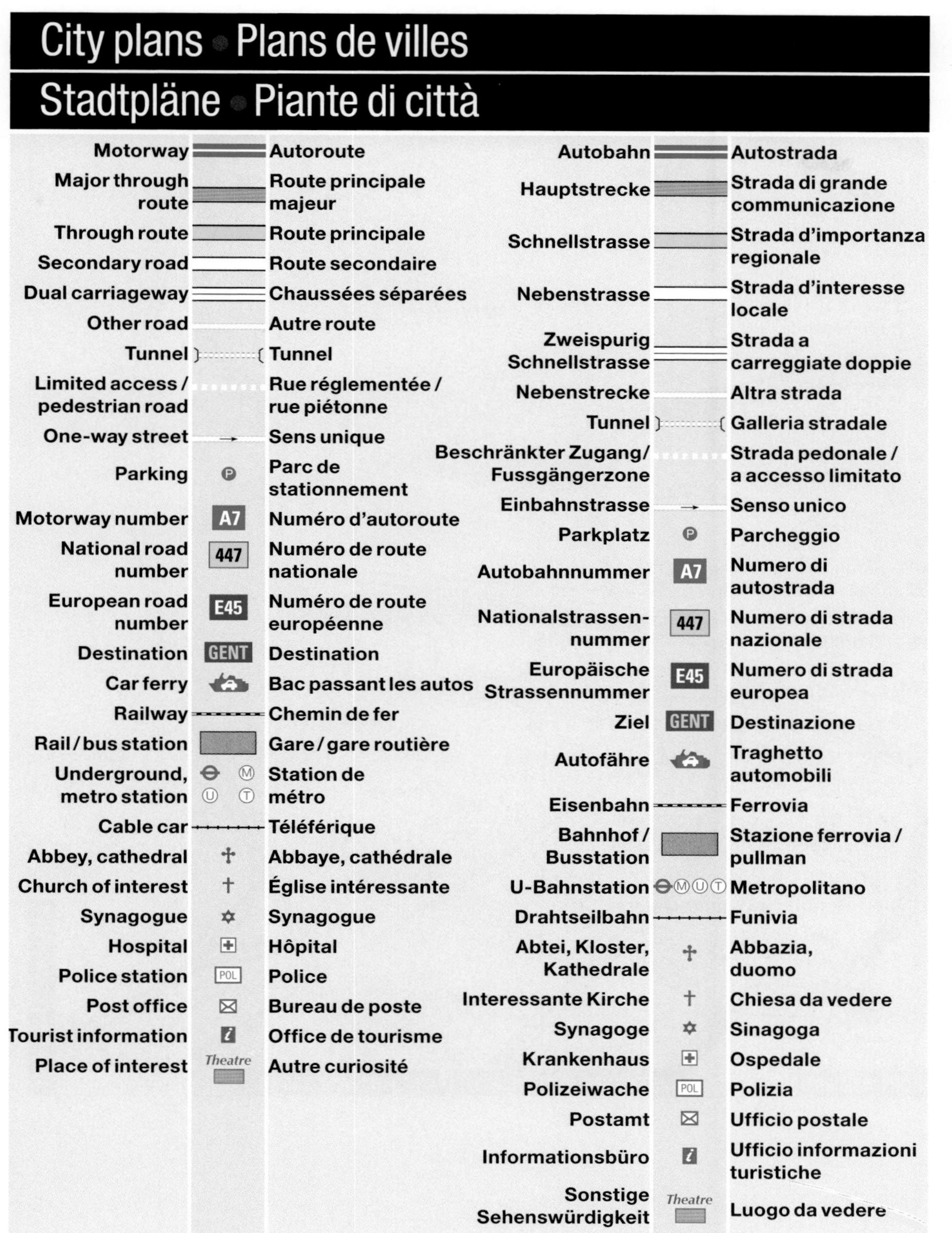

Alicante

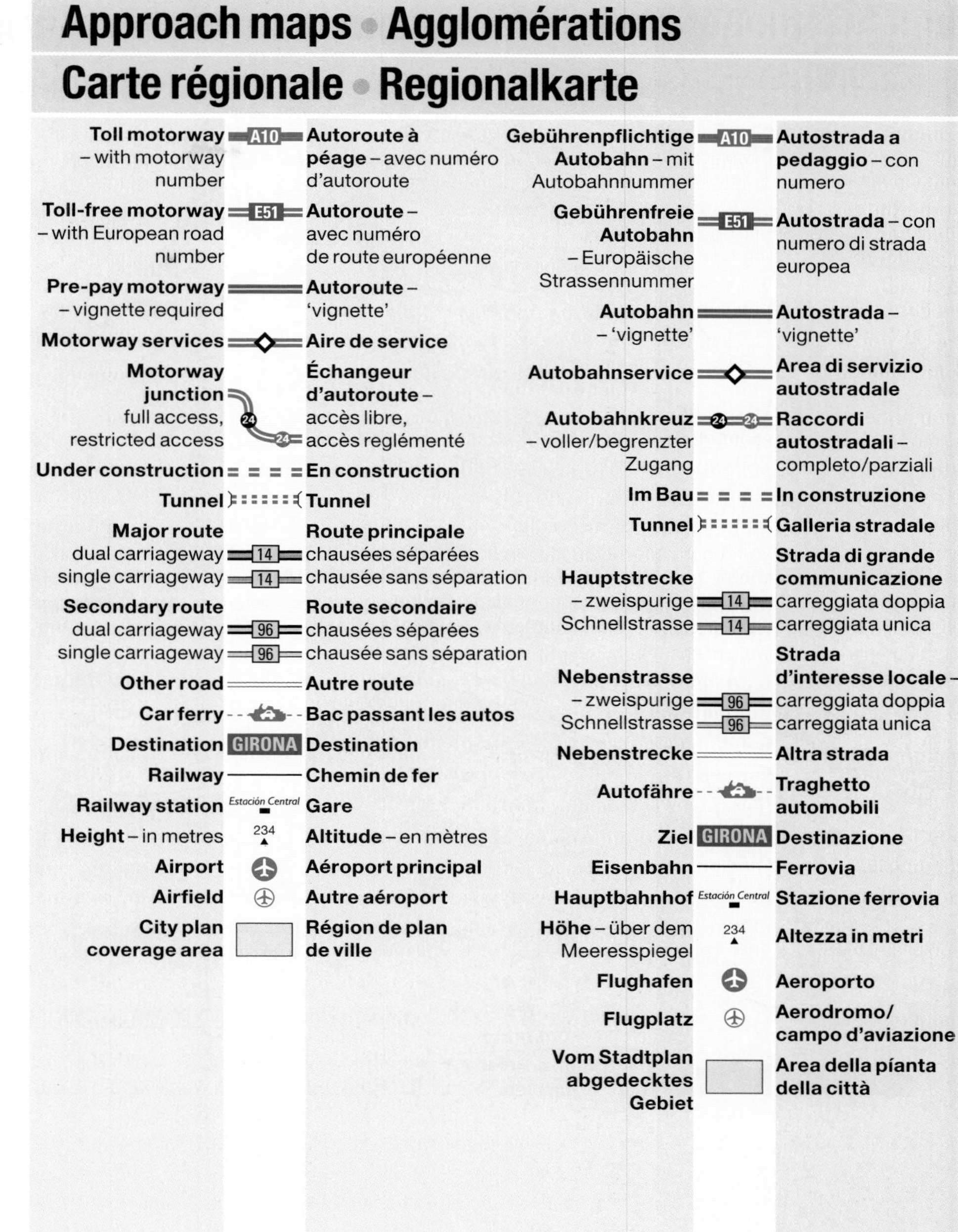

Antwerpen Antwerp

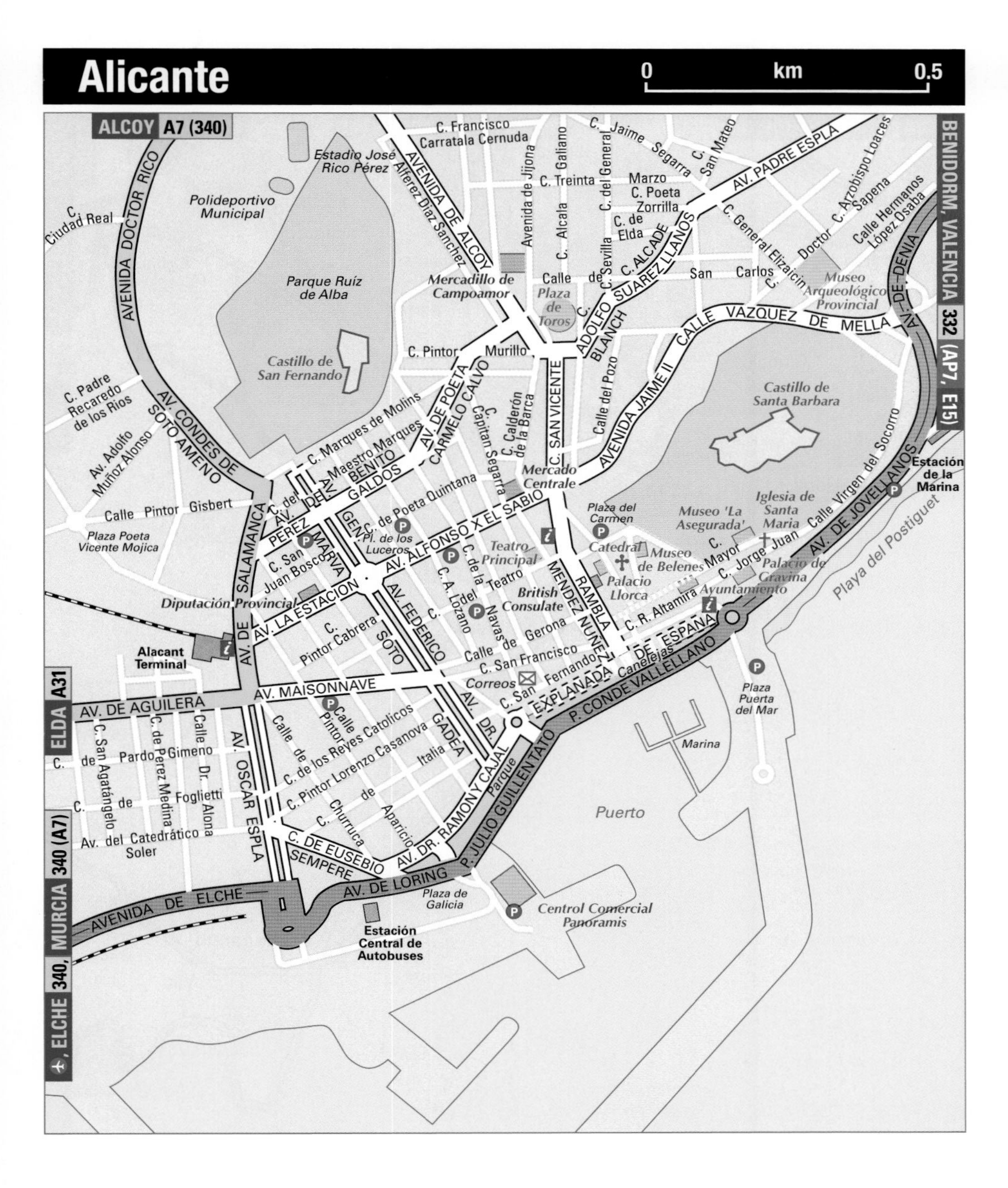

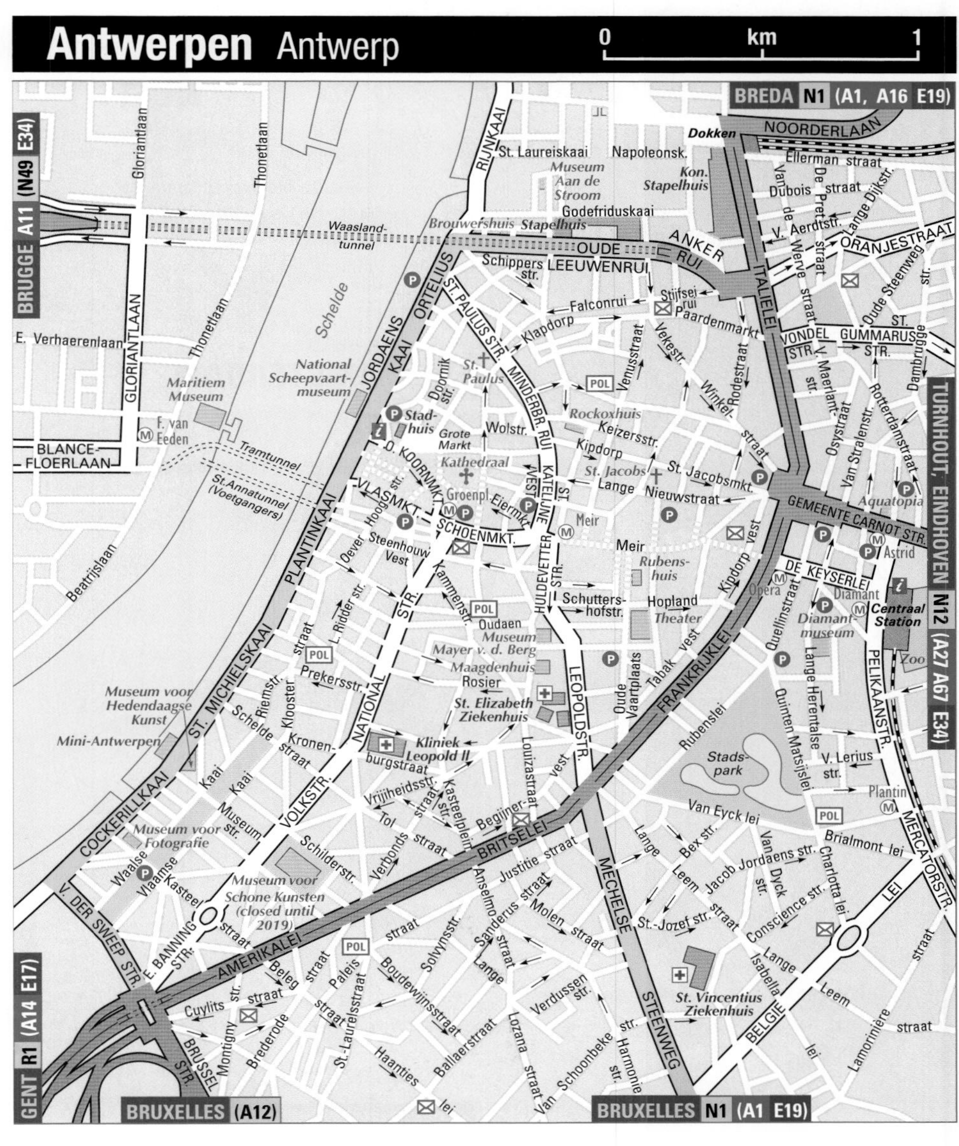

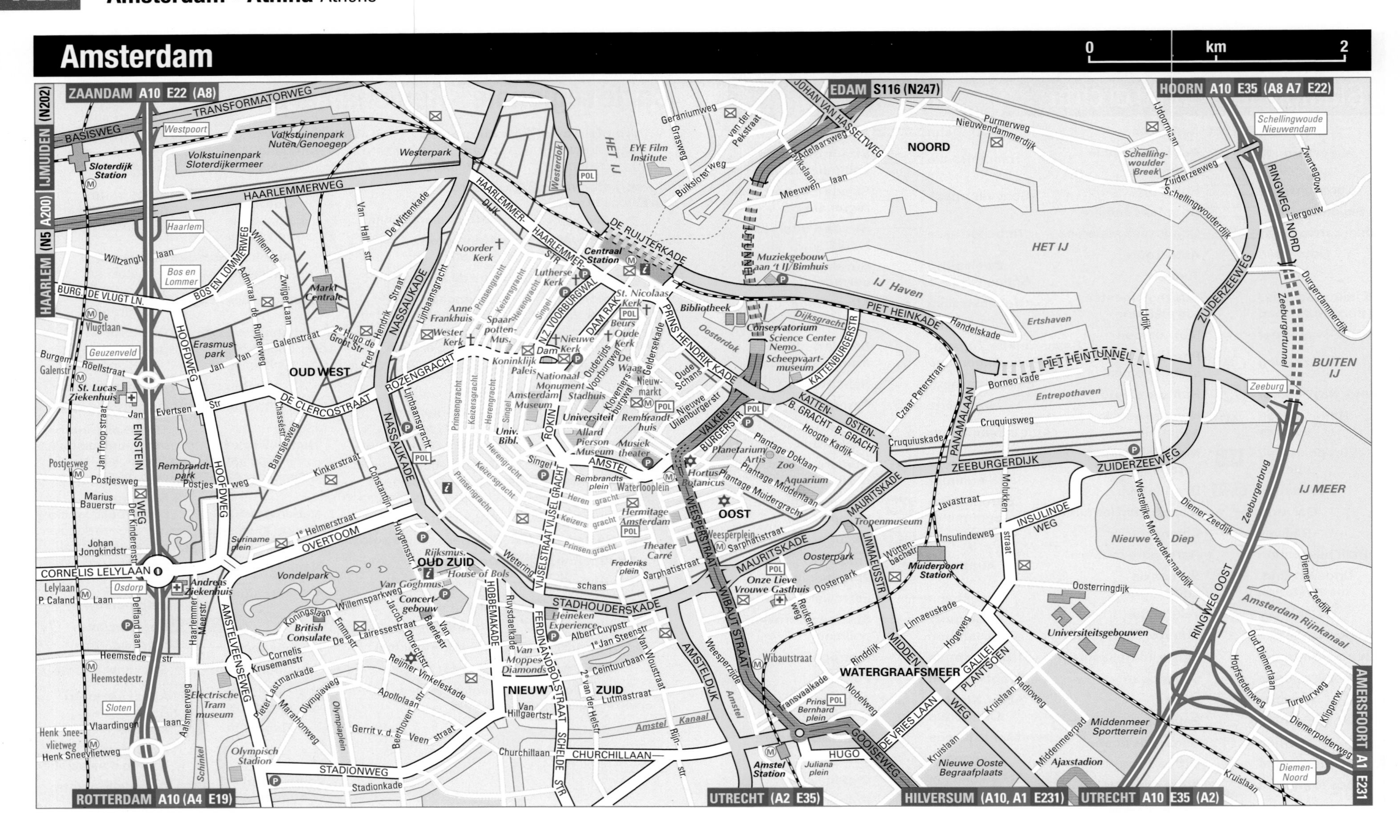

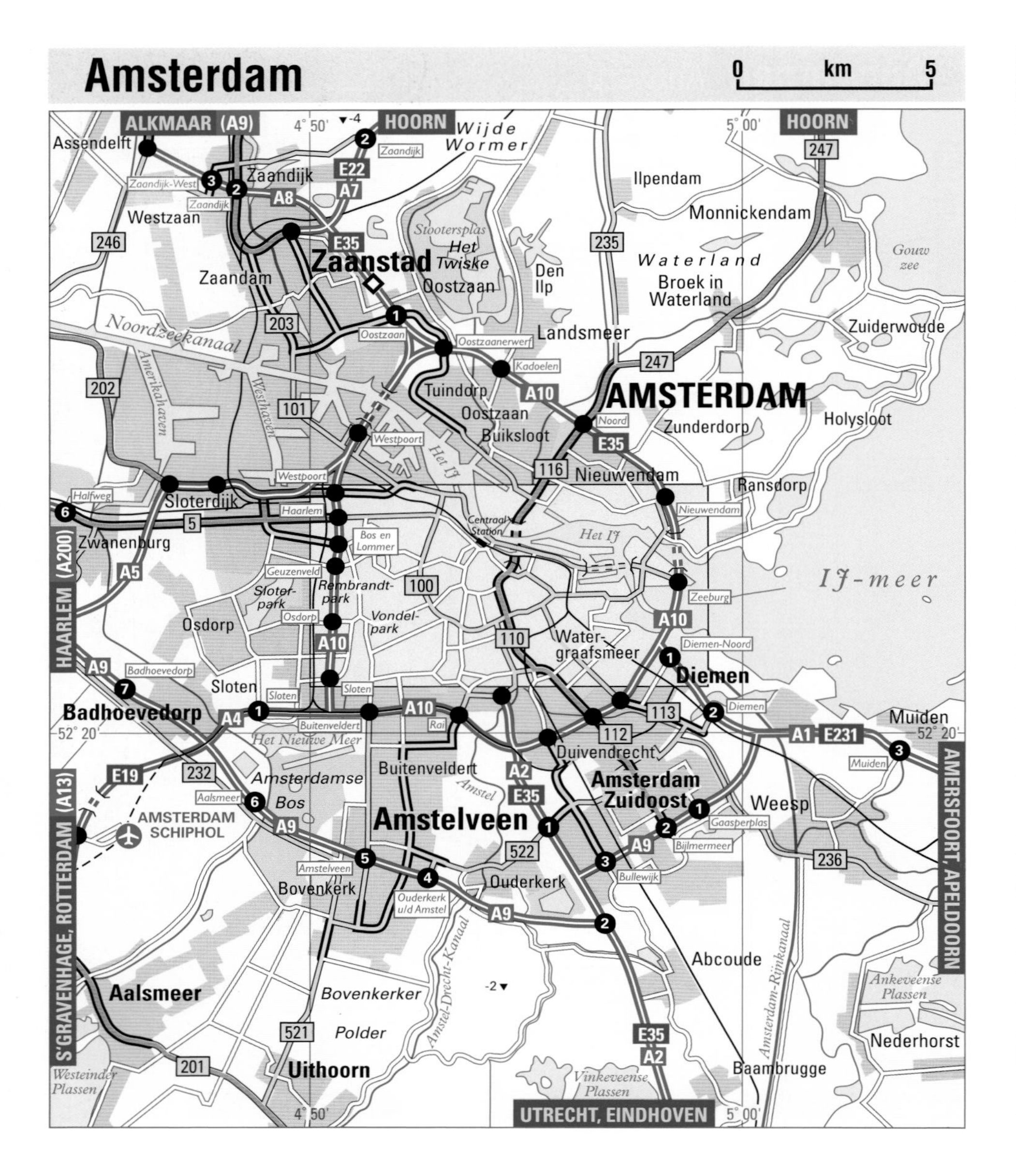

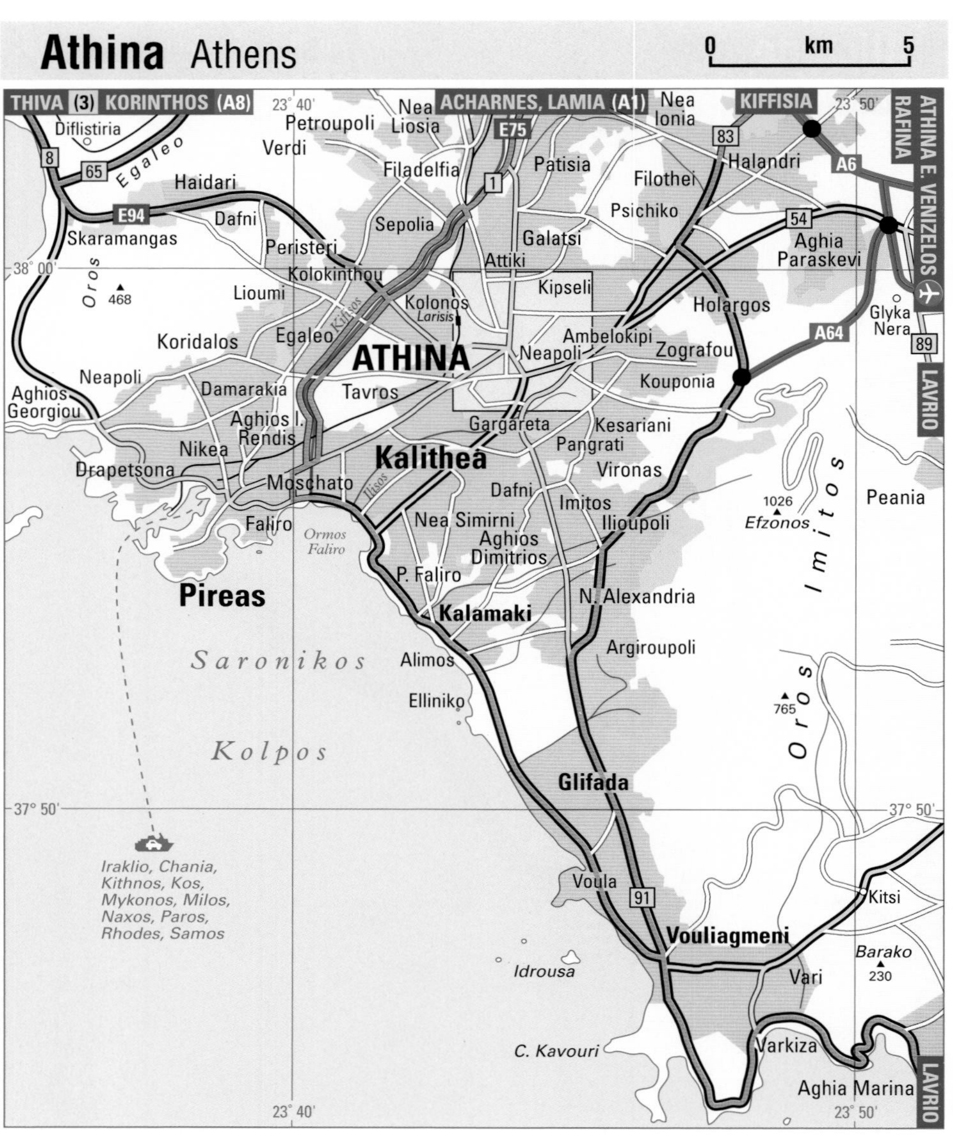

Athina Athens

0 km 1

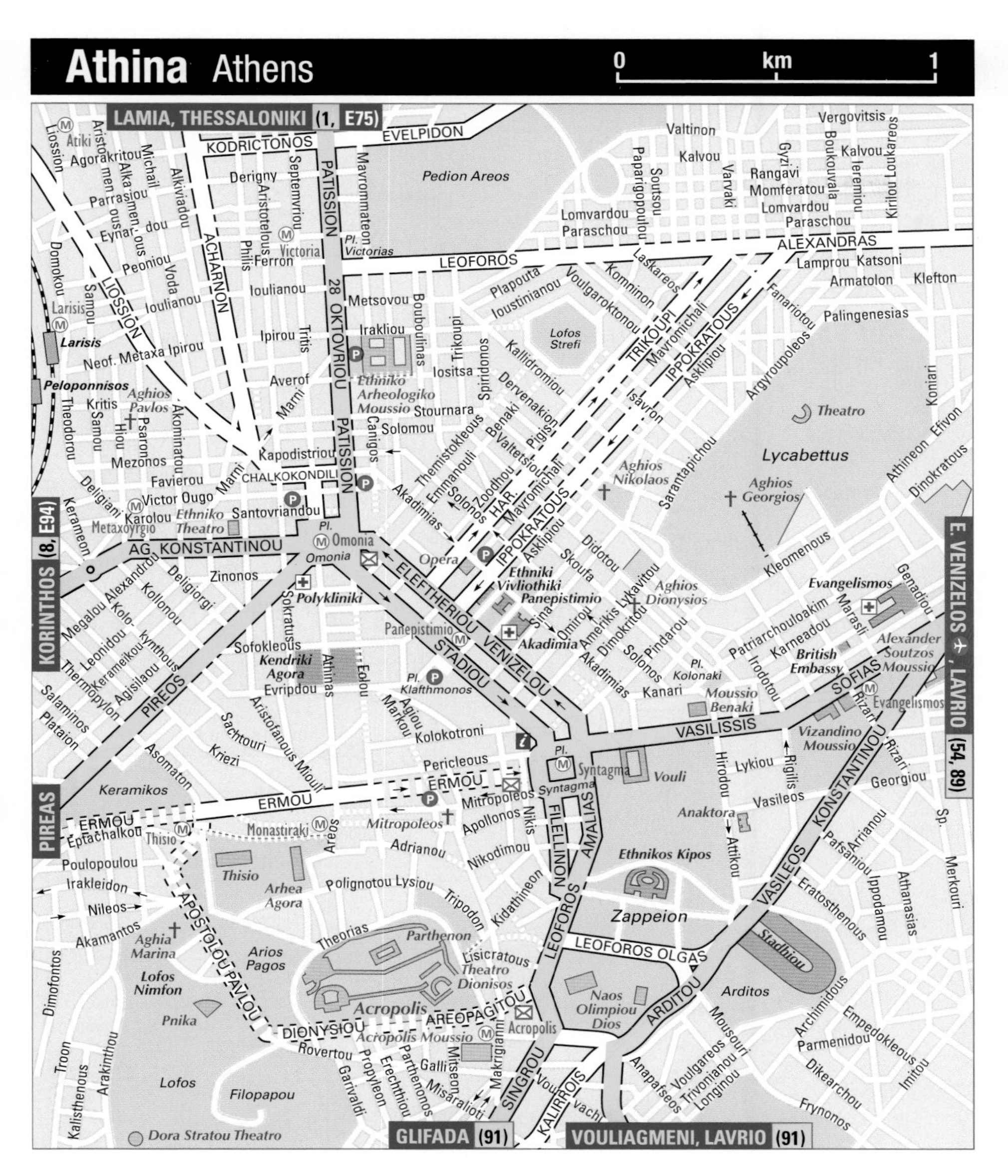

Basel

0 km 0.5

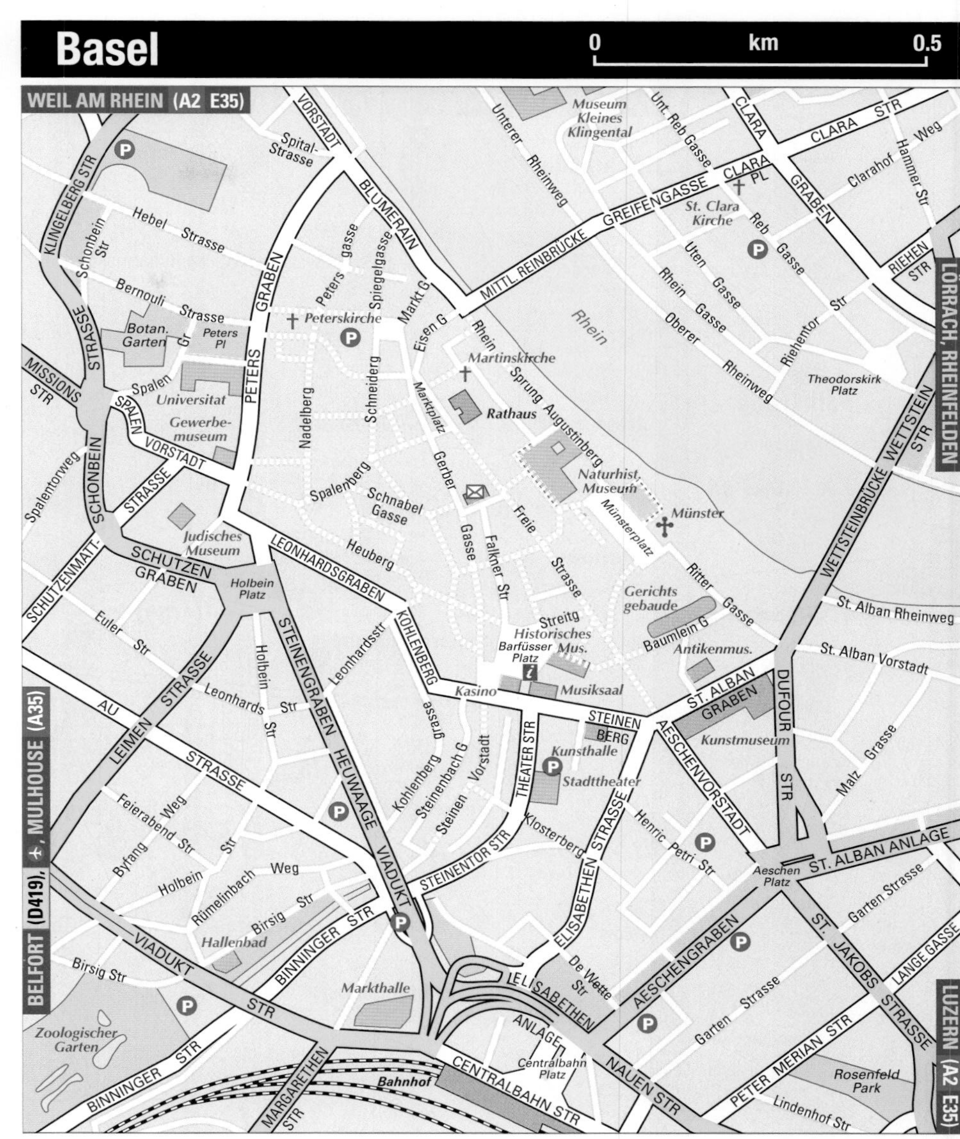

Barcelona

0 km 5

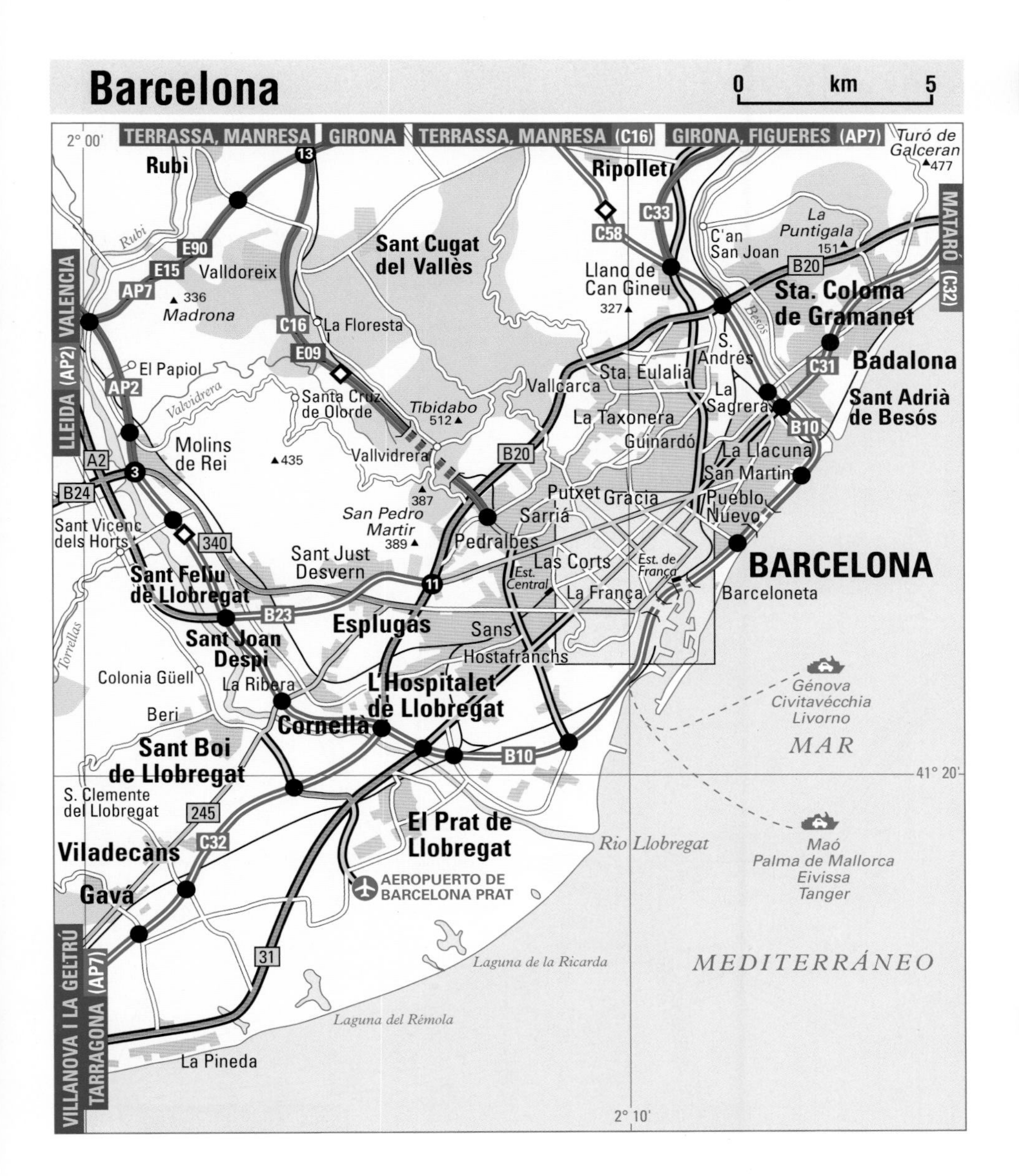

Barcelona

0 km 1

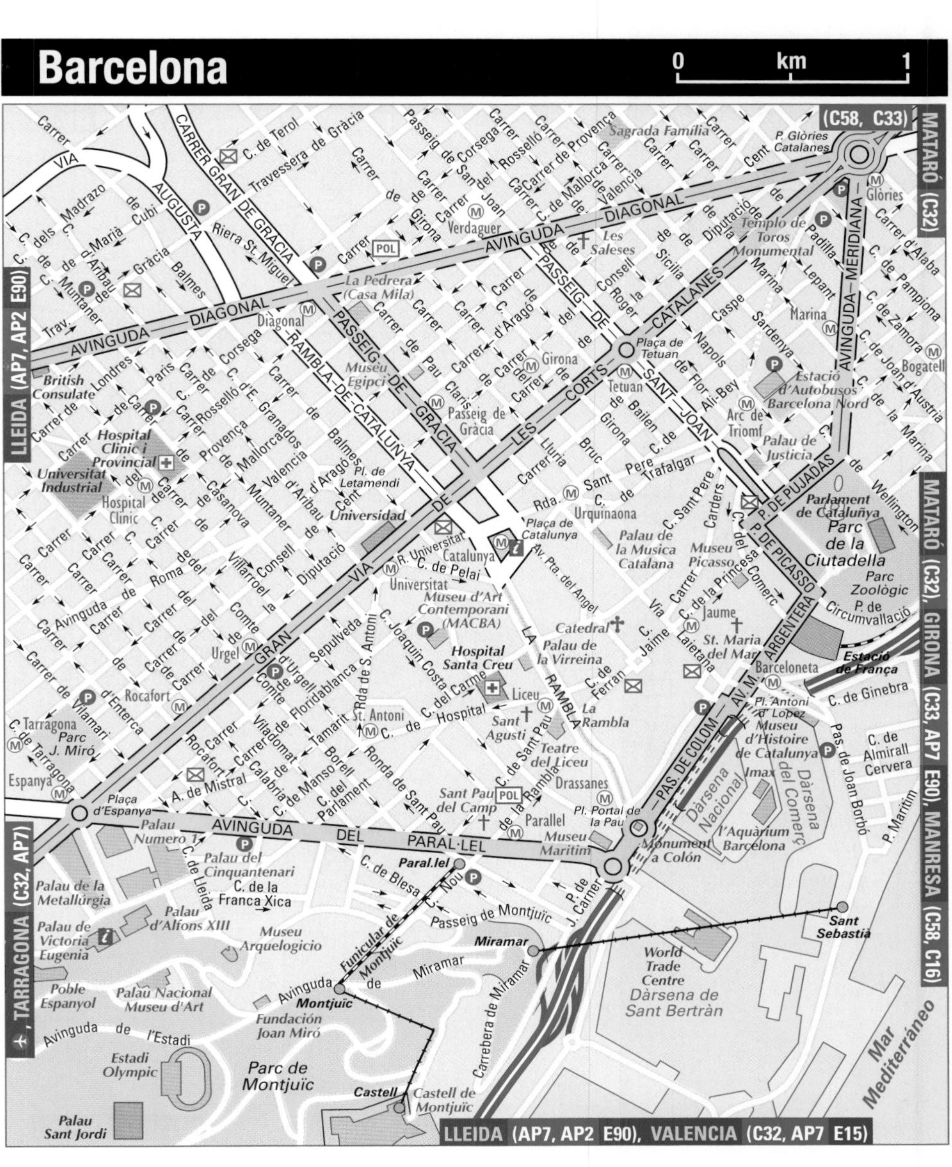

Berlin

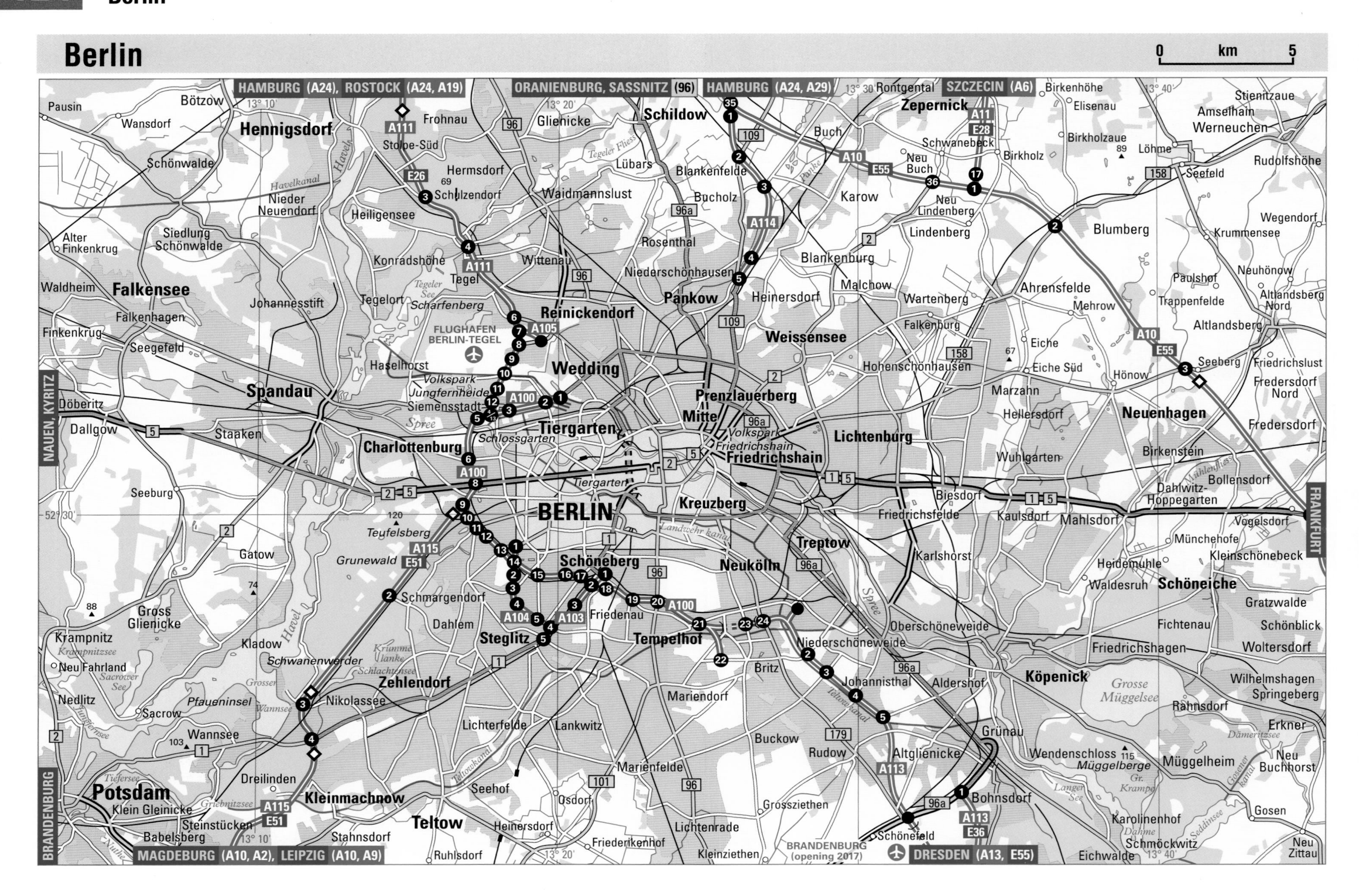

0 km 5
HAMBURG (A24), ROSTOCK (A24, A19)
ORANIENBURG, SASSNITZ (96)
HAMBURG (A24, A29)
SZCZECIN (A6)
NAUEN, KYRITZ
BRANDENBURG
FRANKFURT
MAGDEBURG (A10, A2), LEIPZIG (A10, A9)
DRESDEN (A13, E55)
BRANDENBURG (opening 2017)
Hennigsdorf
Falkensee
Spandau
Charlottenburg
Tiergarten
Wedding
Reinickendorf
Pankow
Weissensee
Prenzlauerberg
Mitte
Friedrichshain
Lichtenberg
Kreuzberg
BERLIN
Schöneberg
Neukölln
Treptow
Steglitz
Tempelhof
Zehlendorf
Köpenick
Potsdam
Kleinmachnow
Teltow
Zepernick
Blumberg
Neuenhagen
Schöneiche
Schildow
FLUGHAFEN BERLIN-TEGEL
Grunewald
Wannsee
Schönefeld
Marzahn
Hellersdorf
Müggelheim
Grosse Müggelsee

Berlin

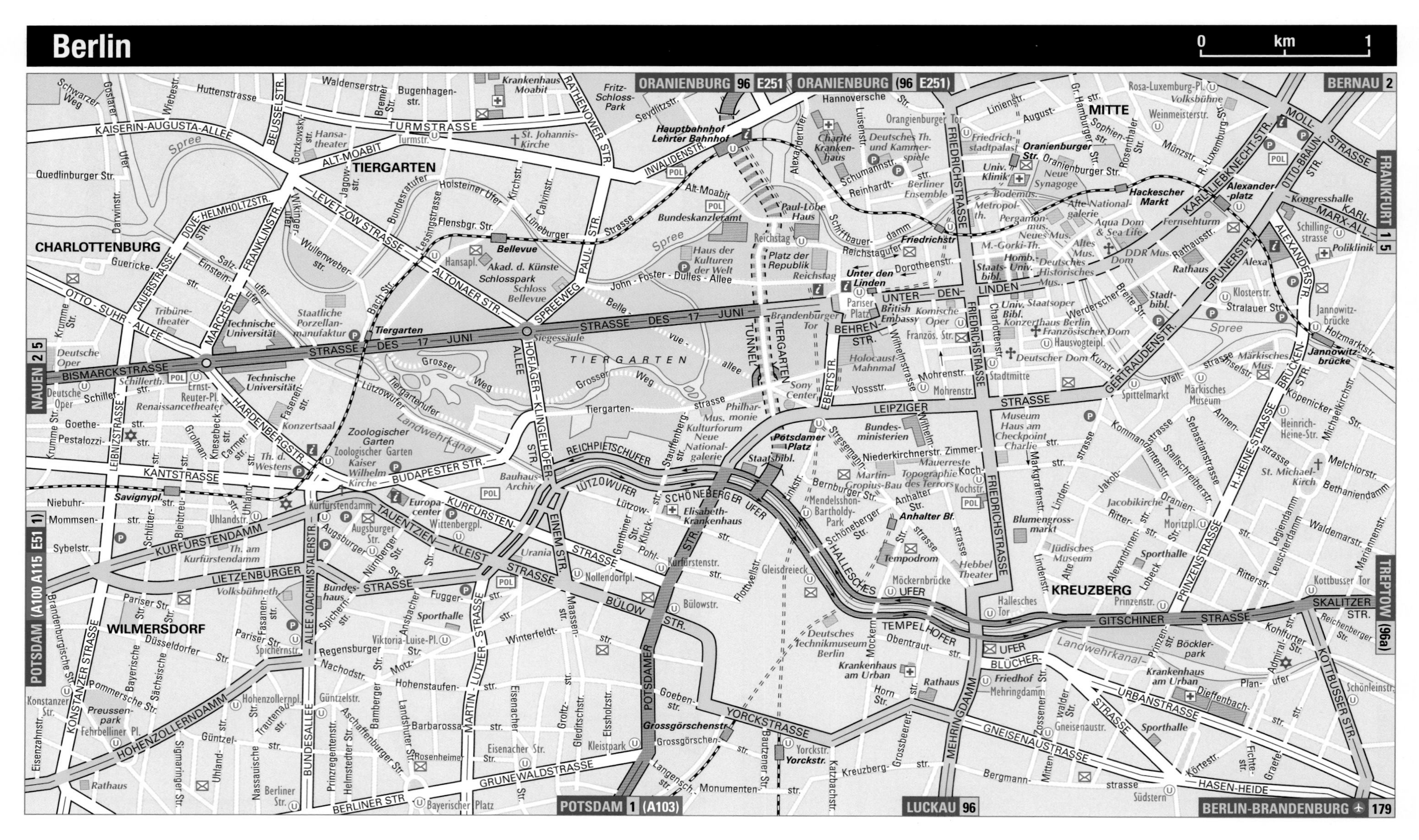

0 km 1
ORANIENBURG 96 E251
ORANIENBURG (96 E251)
BERNAU 2
FRANKFURT 1 5
TREPTOW (96a)
NAUEN 2 5
POTSDAM (A100 A115 E51 1)
POTSDAM 1 (A103)
LUCKAU 96
BERLIN-BRANDENBURG 179
CHARLOTTENBURG
TIERGARTEN
MITTE
KREUZBERG
WILMERSDORF
Hauptbahnhof Lehrter Bahnhof
Alexanderplatz
Hackescher Markt
Friedrichstr.
Unter den Linden
Brandenburger Tor
Reichstag
Potsdamer Platz
Anhalter Bf.
Zoologischer Garten
Kaiser Wilhelm Kirche
Bellevue
Siegessäule
STRASSE DES 17. JUNI
KURFÜRSTENDAMM
KANTSTRASSE
BISMARCKSTRASSE
LEIPZIGER STRASSE
FRIEDRICHSTRASSE
GITSCHINER STRASSE
YORCKSTRASSE
Tempelhofer Ufer
Landwehrkanal
Spree

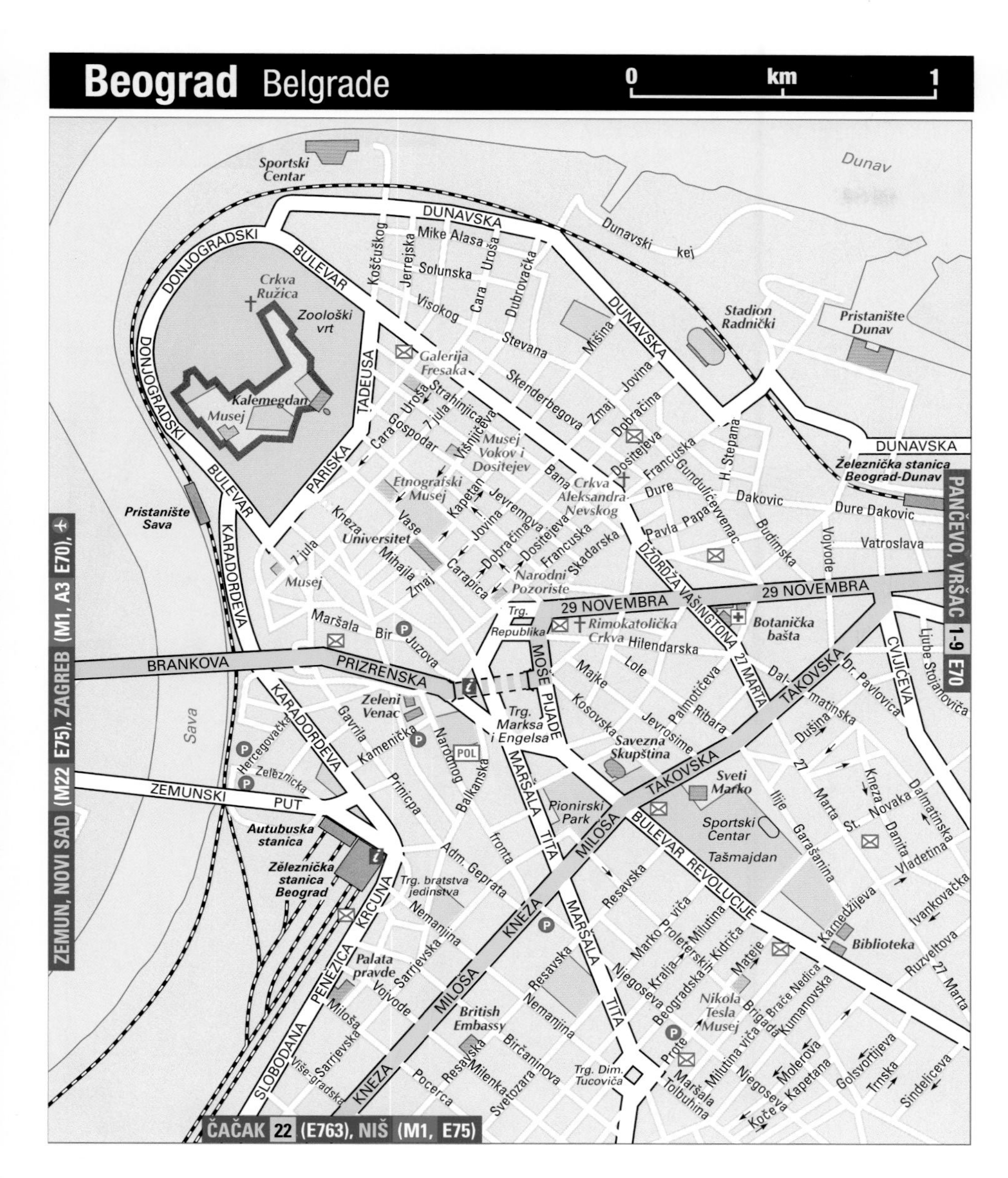

Beograd Belgrade

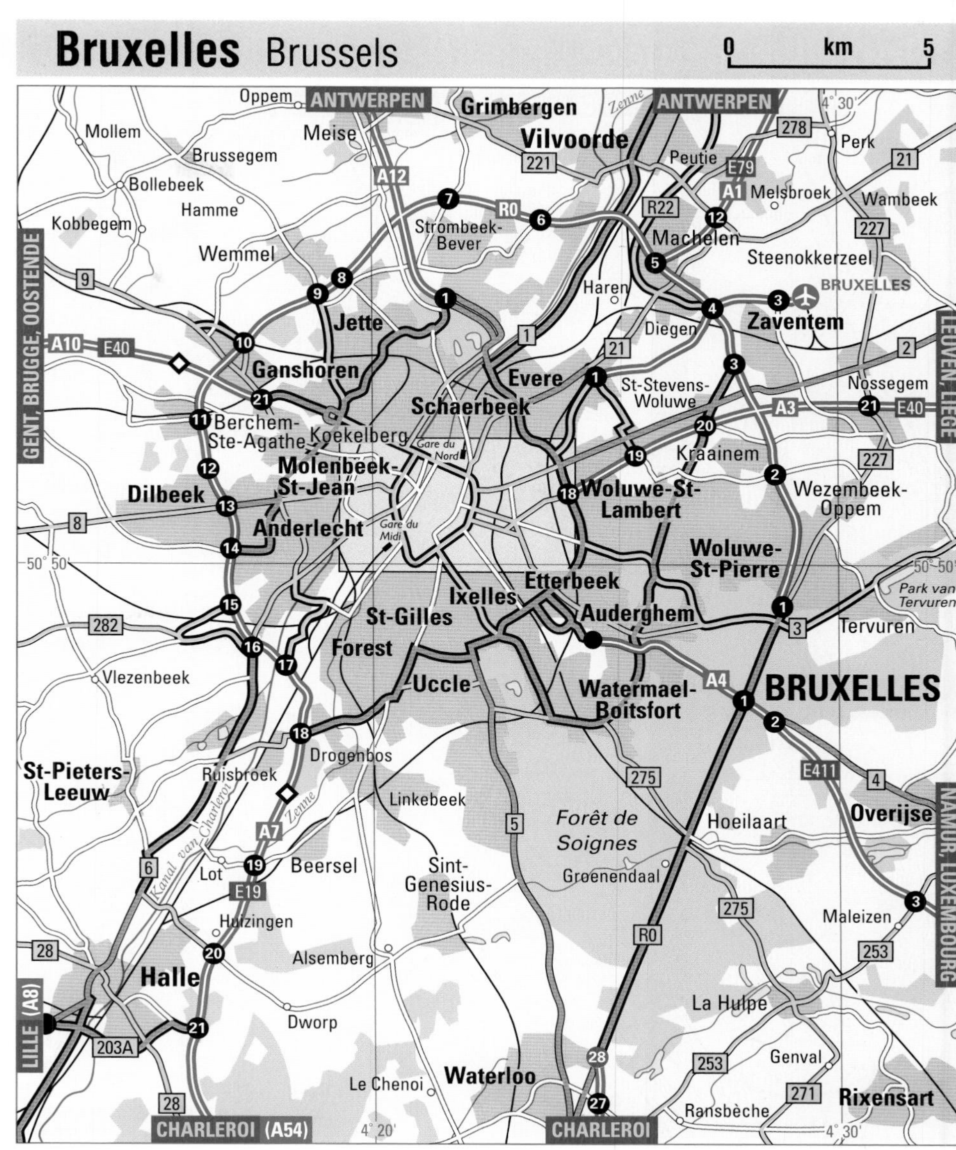

Bruxelles Brussels

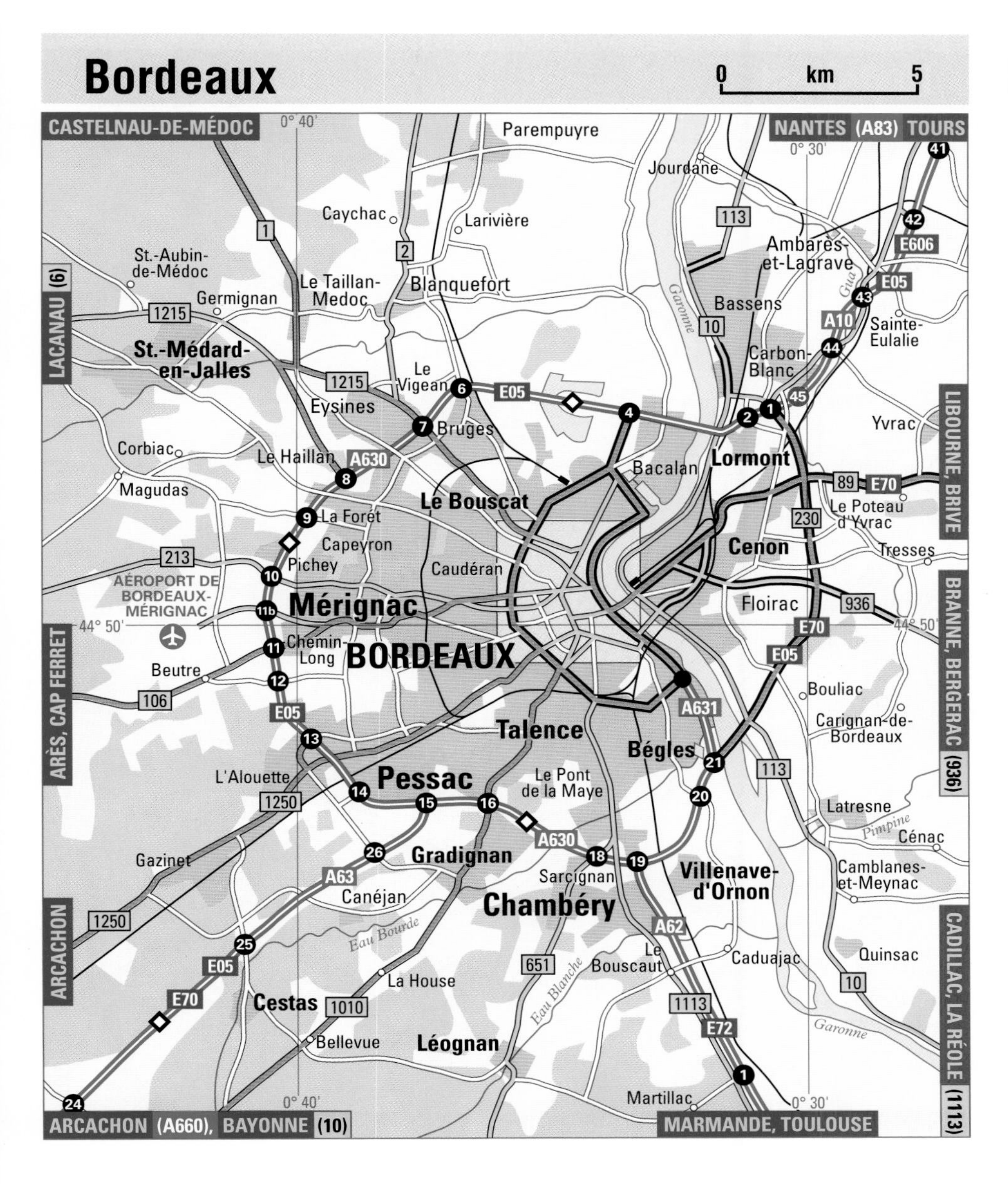

Bordeaux

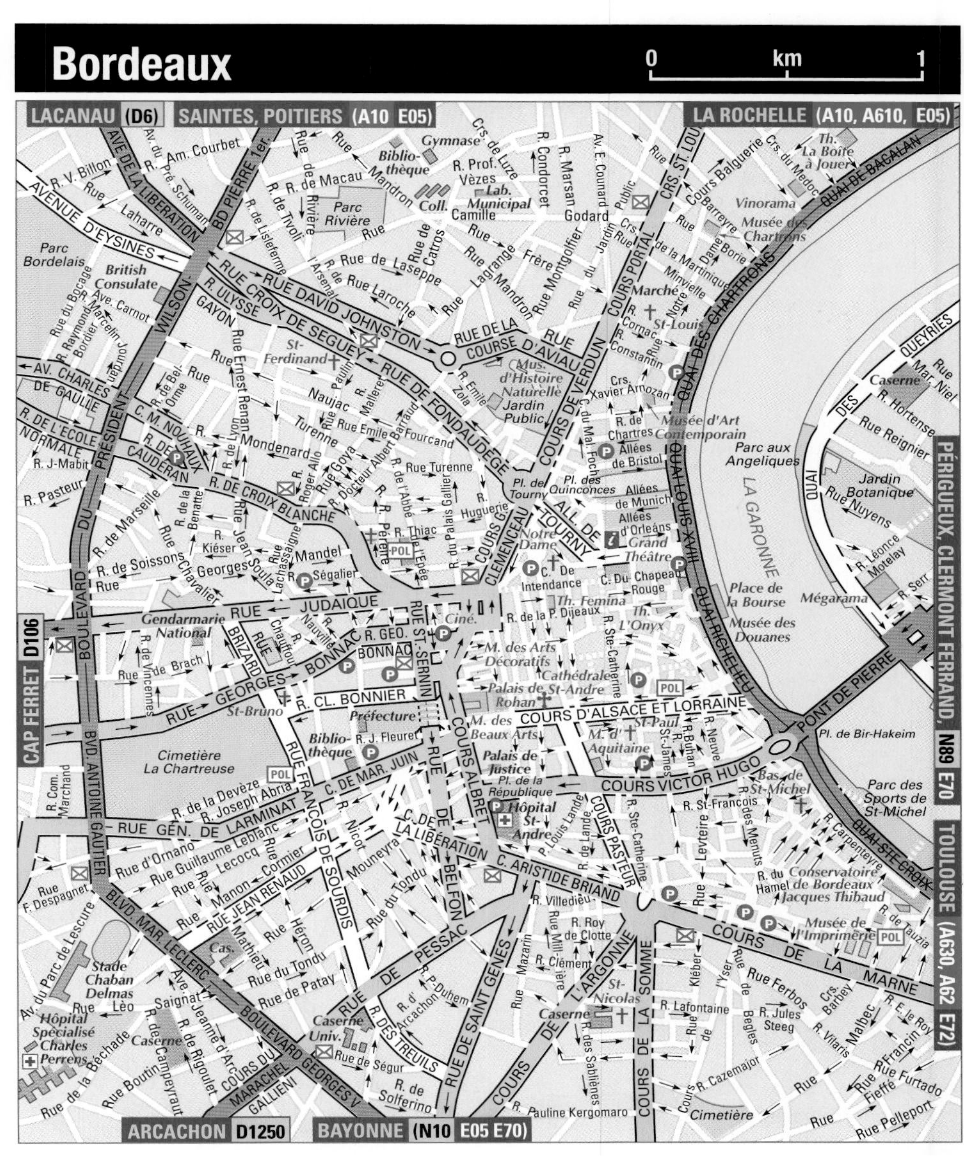

Bordeaux

Bruxelles Brussels

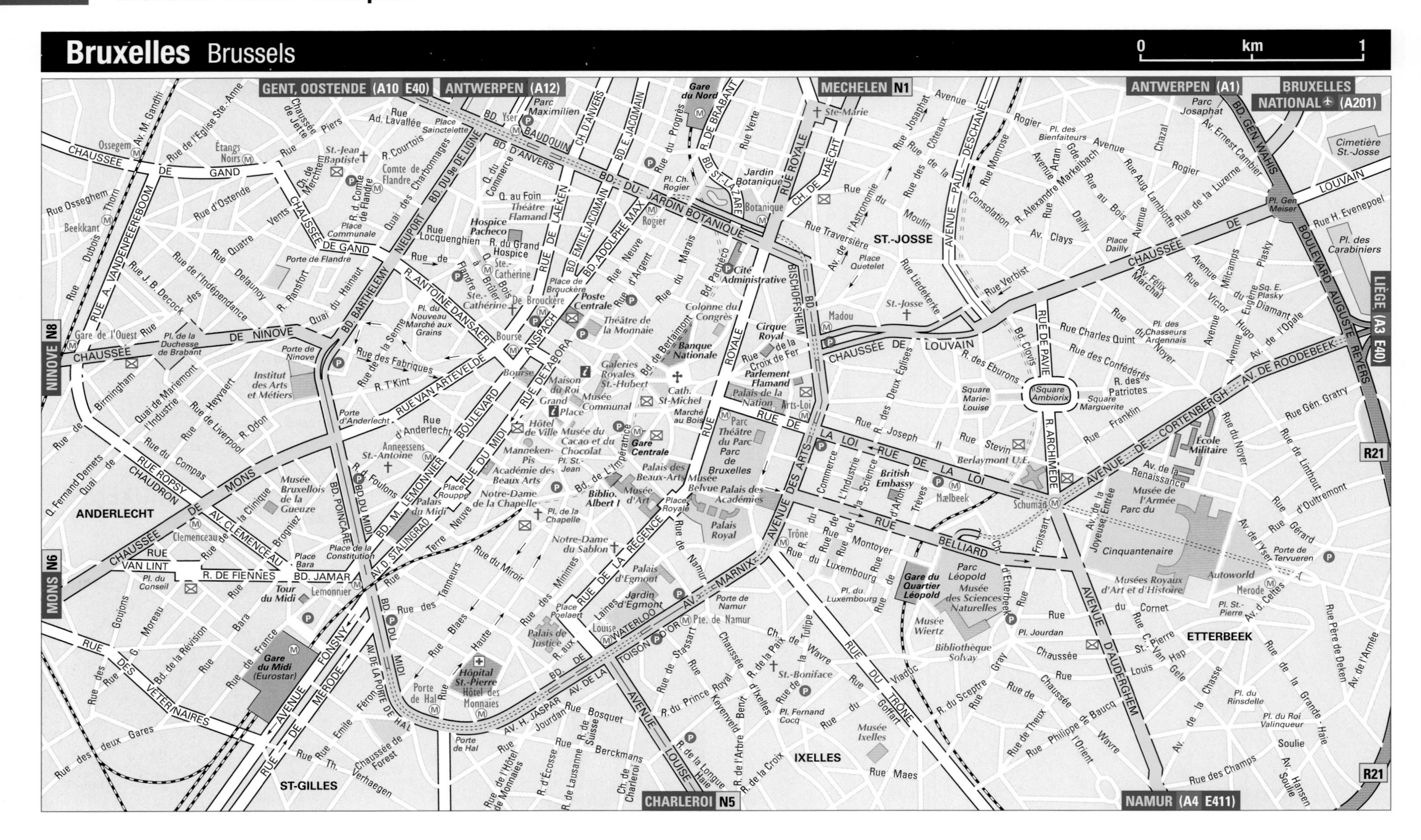
0 km 1
GENT, OOSTENDE (A10 E40)
ANTWERPEN (A12)
MECHELEN N1
ANTWERPEN (A1)
BRUXELLES NATIONAL (A201)
LIÈGE (A3 E40)
NINOVE N8
MONS N6
CHARLEROI N5
NAMUR (A4 E411)
R21
ANDERLECHT
ST.-JOSSE
ETTERBEEK
IXELLES
ST-GILLES
Gare du Nord
Gare Centrale
Gare du Midi (Eurostar)
Parc de Bruxelles
Palais Royal
Parc Léopold
Parc du Cinquantenaire
Jardin Botanique
Grand Place
Cimetière St.-Josse
Square Ambiorix

Budapest

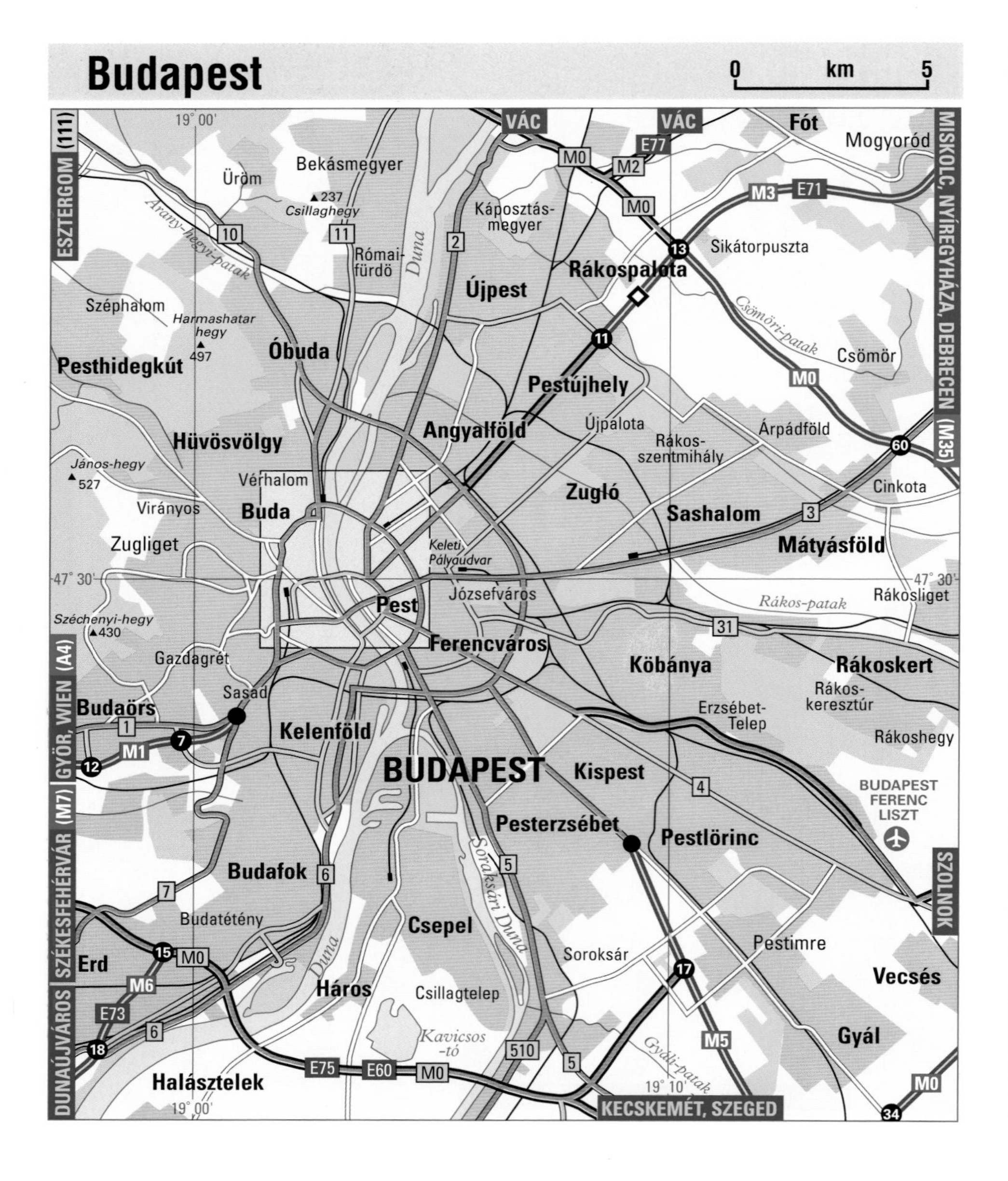
0 km 5
VÁC
Fót
Mogyoród
ESZTERGOM (111)
MISKOLC, NYÍREGYHÁZA, DEBRECEN (M35)
Üröm
Békásmegyer
Újpest
Rákospalota
Sikátorpuszta
Óbuda
Pesthidegkút
Pestújhely
Csömör
Hűvösvölgy
Angyalföld
Újpalota
Árpádföld
Rákosszentmihály
Buda
Zugló
Sashalom
Cinkota
Mátyásföld
Zugliget
Pest
Józsefváros
Rákosliget
Ferencváros
Kőbánya
Rákoskert
Gazdagrét
Budaörs
Kelenföld
BUDAPEST
Kispest
Rákoshegy
Pesterzsébet
Pestlőrinc
BUDAPEST FERENC LISZT
Budafok
Csepel
Pestimre
Vecsés
Erd
Háros
Soroksár
Csillagtelep
Gyál
Halásztelek
GYŐR, WIEN (A4)
SZÉKESFEHÉRVÁR (M7)
DUNAÚJVÁROS
SZOLNOK
KECSKEMÉT, SZEGED
Duna

Budapest

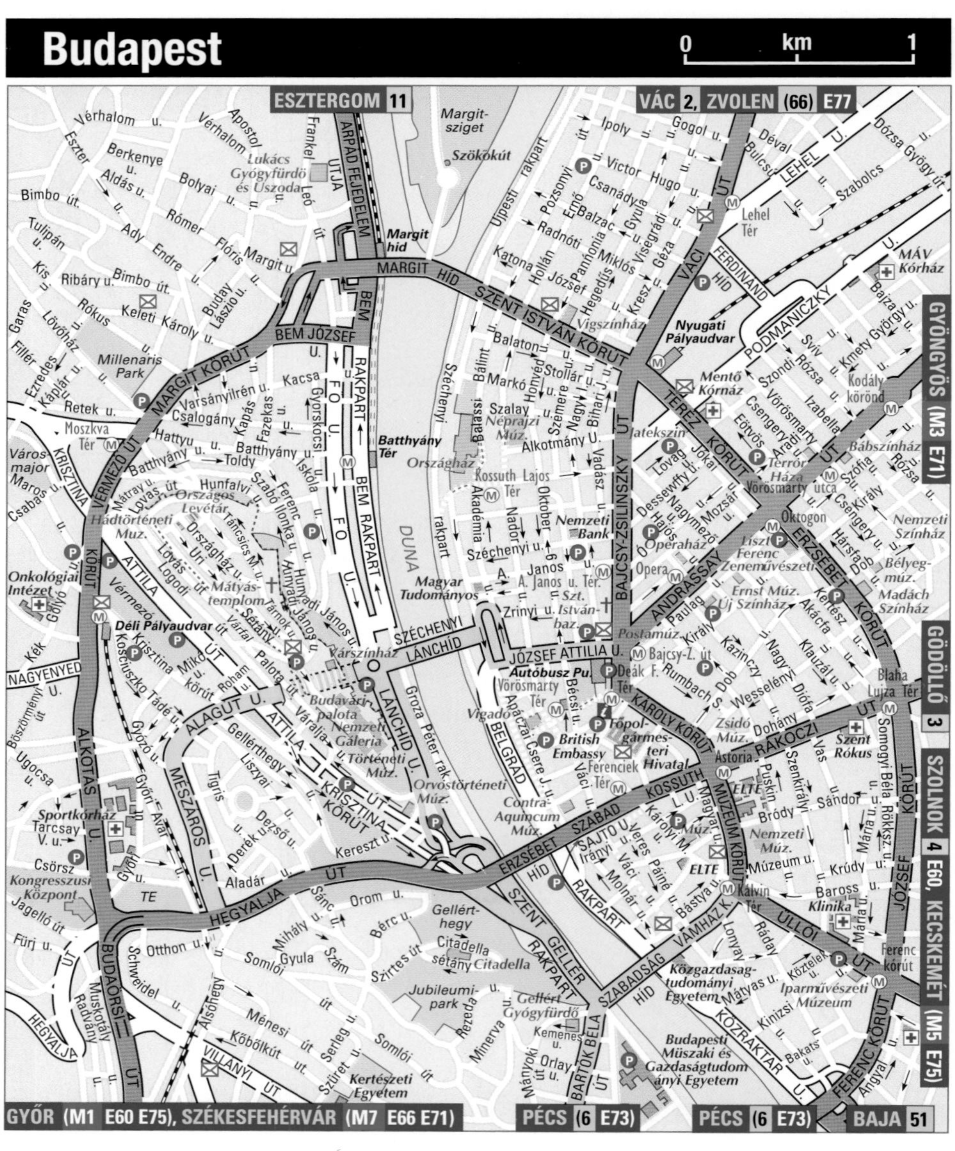
0 km 1
ESZTERGOM 11
VÁC 2, ZVOLEN (66) E77
GYÖNGYÖS (M3 E71)
GÖDÖLLŐ 3
SZOLNOK 4 E60, KECSKEMÉT (M5 E75)
GYŐR (M1 E60 E75), SZÉKESFEHÉRVÁR (M7 E66 E71)
PÉCS (6 E73)
BAJA 51
Margit-sziget
MARGIT HÍD
SZENT ISTVÁN KÖRÚT
Nyugati Pályaudvar
Déli Pályaudvar
Keleti Pályaudvar
Batthyány Tér
Országház
DUNA
Magyar Tudományos
LÁNCHÍD
Szépművészeti
Gellért-hegy
Citadella
Erzsébet híd
SZABADSÁG HÍD
Nemzeti Múzeum
Városliget
Népliget

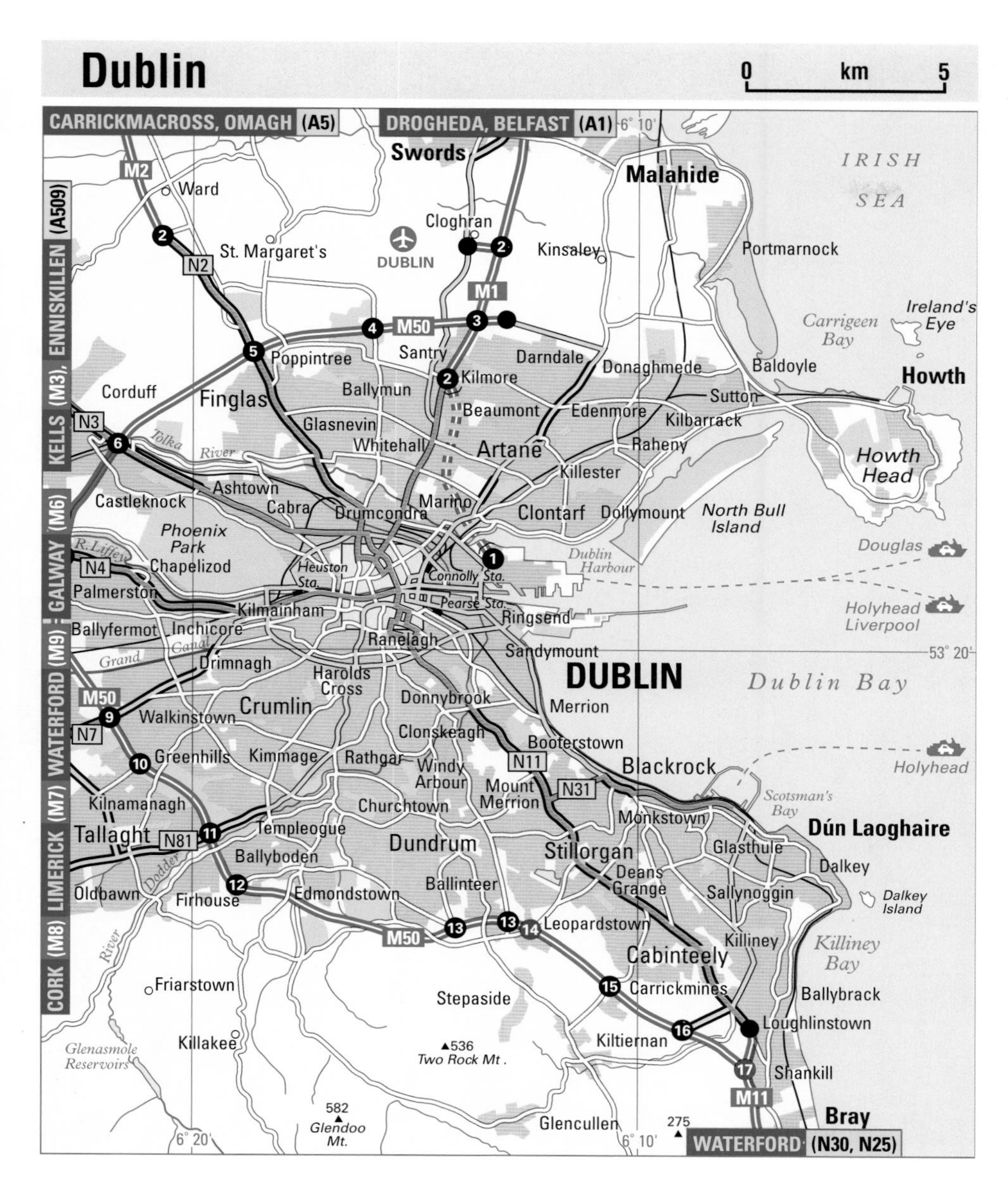

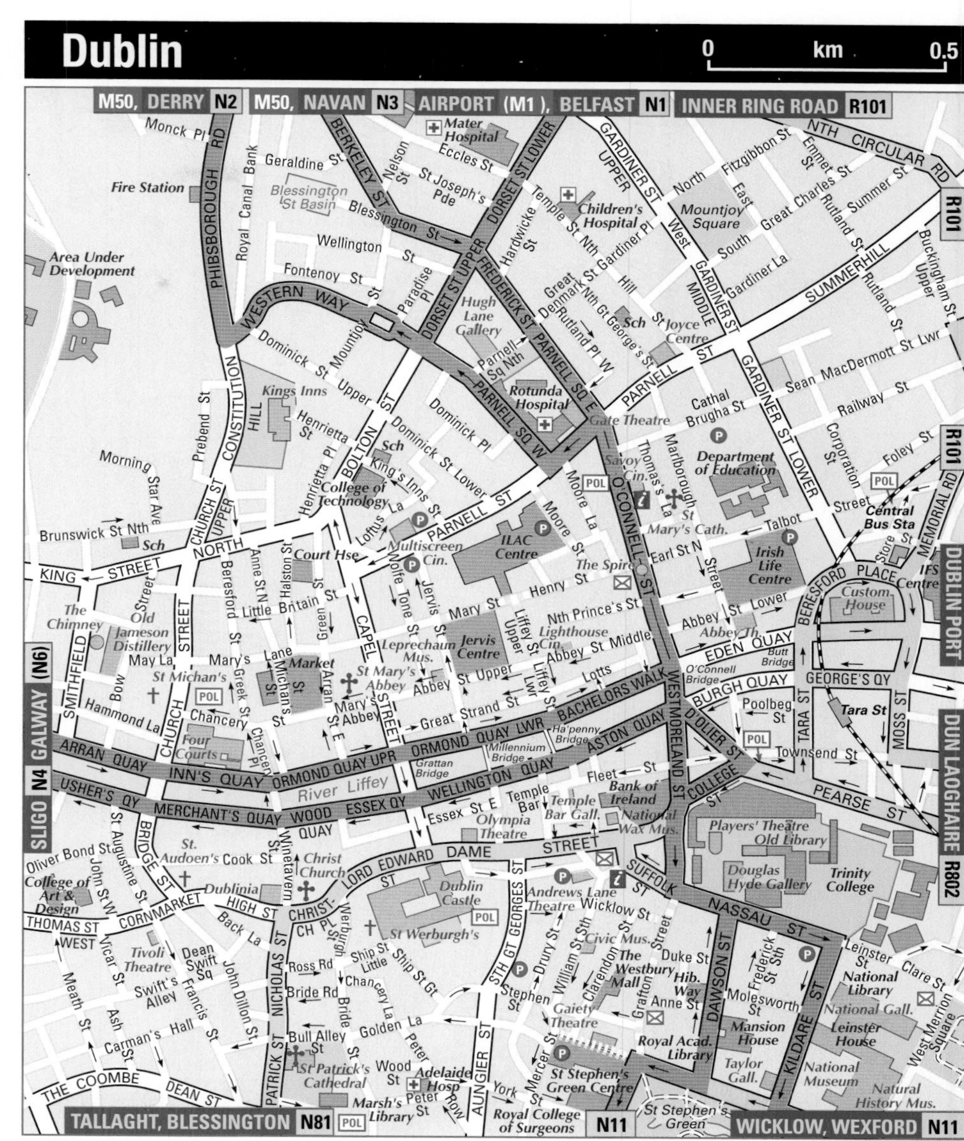

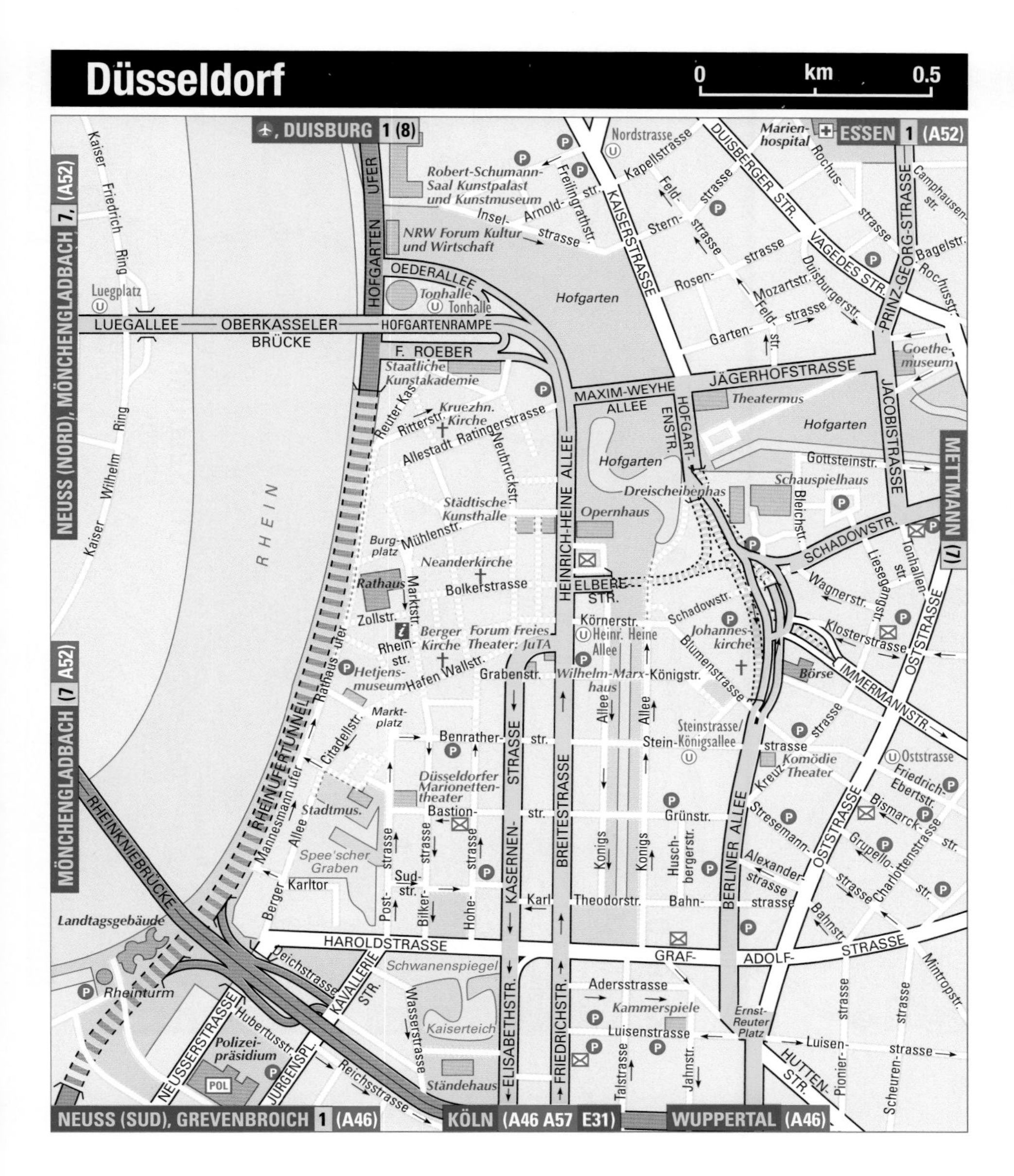

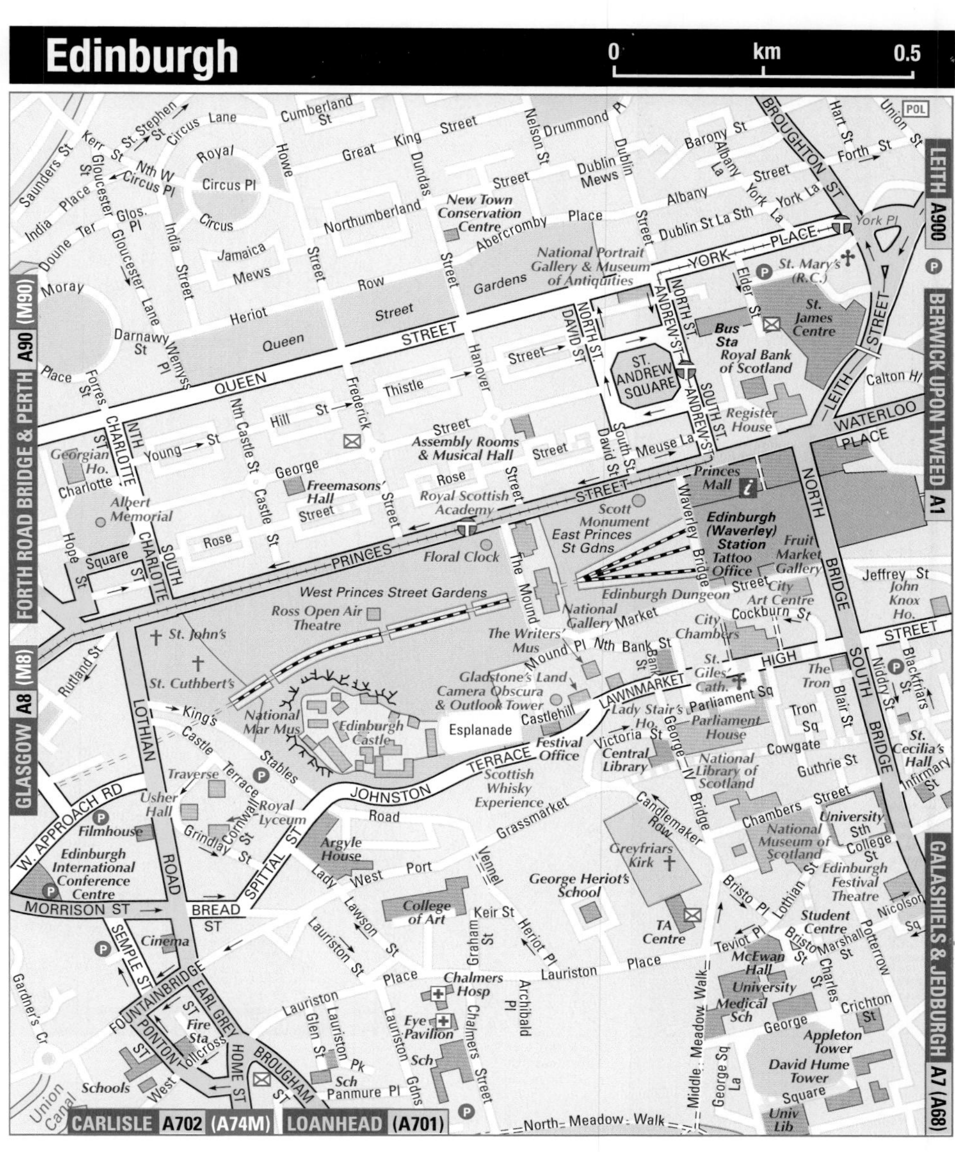

For **Cologne** see page 132
For **Copenhagen** see page 132

Düsseldorf (Ruhrgebiet)

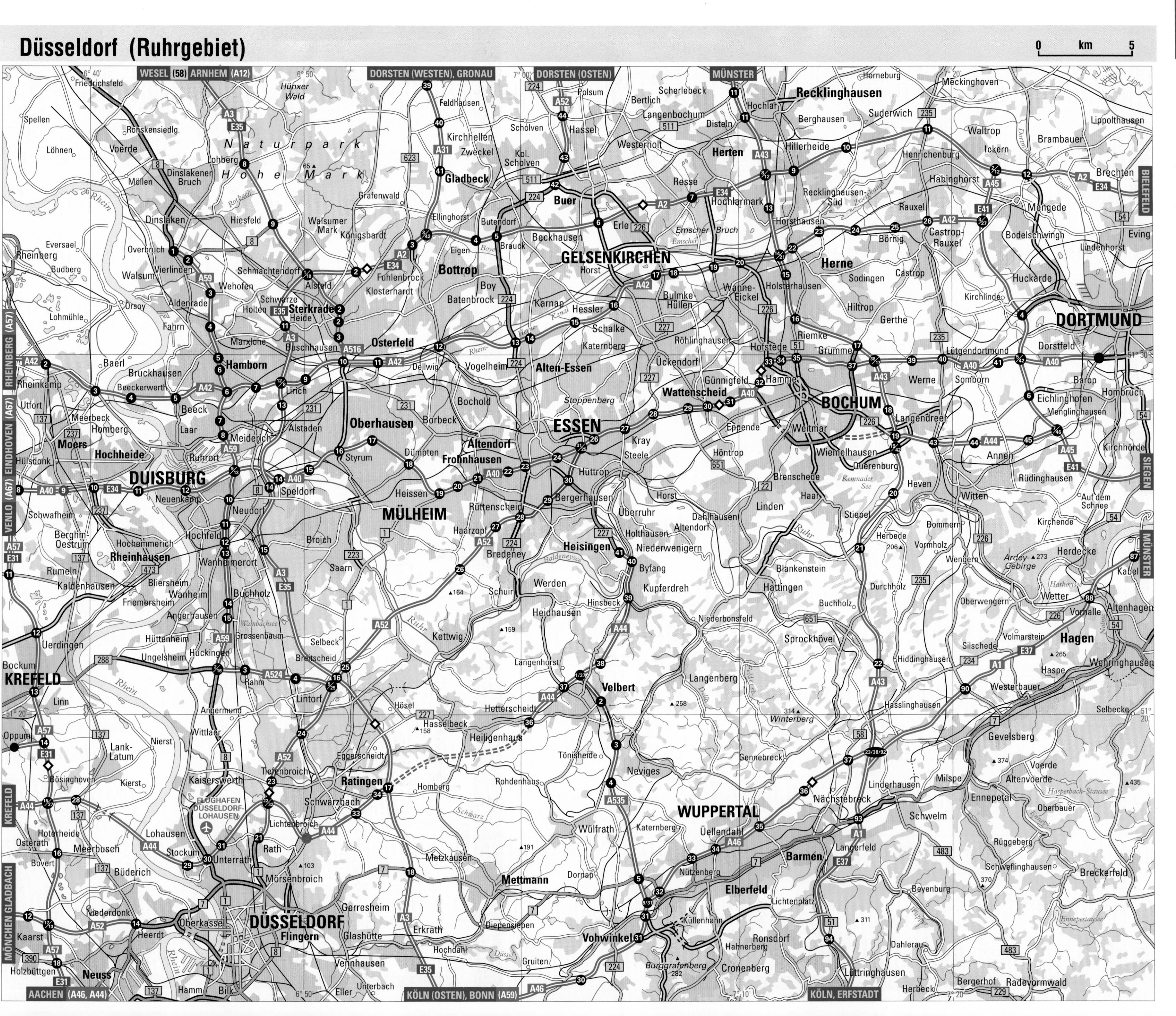
0 km 5
WESEL (58) ARNHEM (A12)
DORSTEN (WESTEN), GRONAU
DORSTEN (OSTEN)
MÜNSTER
BIELEFELD
SIEGEN
MÜNSTER
KÖLN, ERFSTADT
KÖLN (OSTEN), BONN (A59)
AACHEN (A46, A44)
MÖNCHEN GLADBACH
KREFELD
VENLO (A67) EINDHOVEN (A67)
RHEINBERG (A57)
Recklinghausen
Herten
Gladbeck
Buer
Bottrop
GELSENKIRCHEN
Herne
DORTMUND
Sterkrade
Osterfeld
Hamborn
Alten-Essen
Wattenscheid
BOCHUM
ESSEN
Oberhausen
Altendorf
Frohnhausen
Moers
Hochheide
DUISBURG
MÜLHEIM
Heisingen
Rheinhausen
KREFELD
Velbert
Hagen
Ratingen
WUPPERTAL
Barmen
Elberfeld
Mettmann
Vohwinkel
DÜSSELDORF
Flingern
Neuss
Naturpark Hohe Mark
FLUGHAFEN DÜSSELDORF-LOHAUSEN
Castrop-Rauxel
Witten
Rhein
Ruhr

Firenze Florence

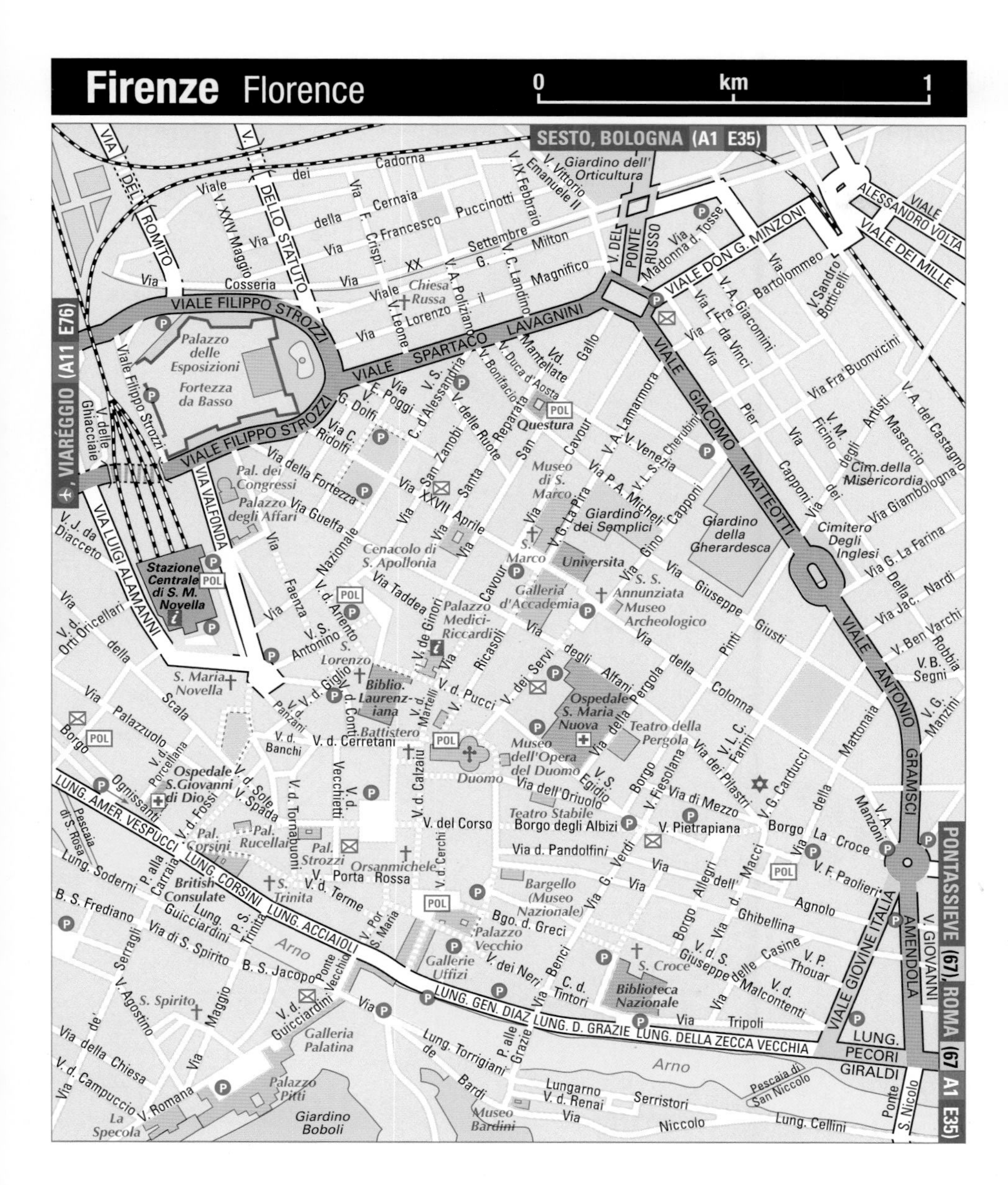

Frankfurt

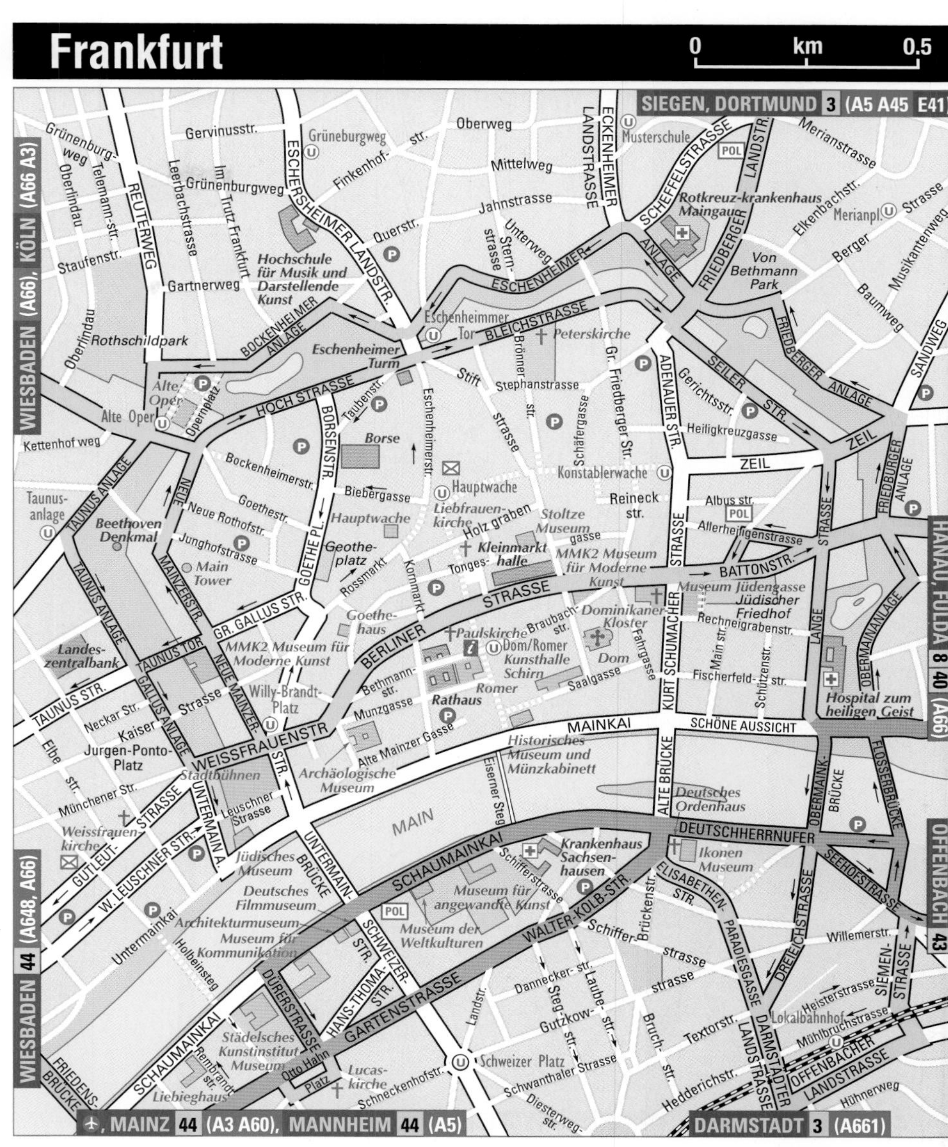

Genève Geneva

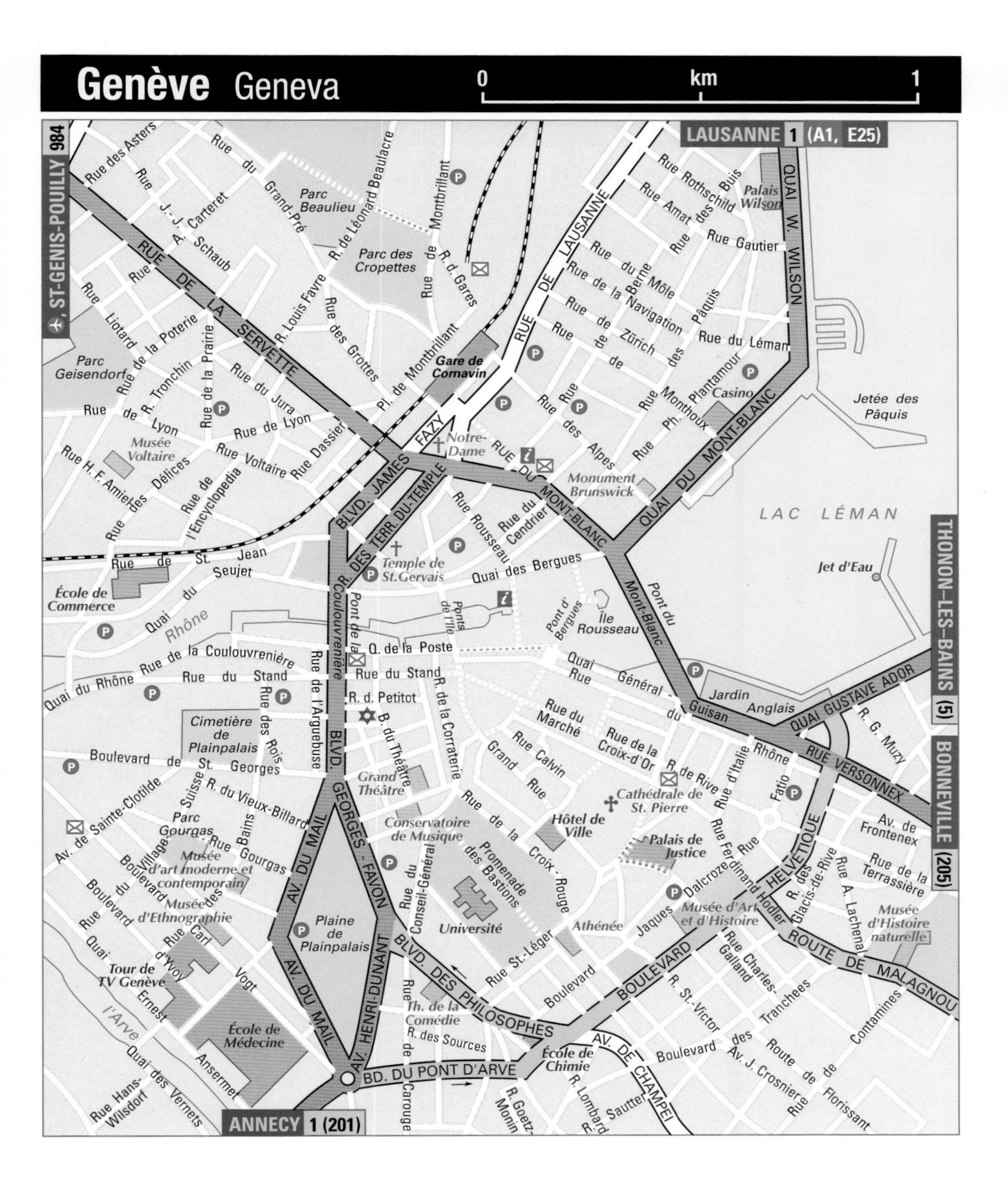

Génova Genoa

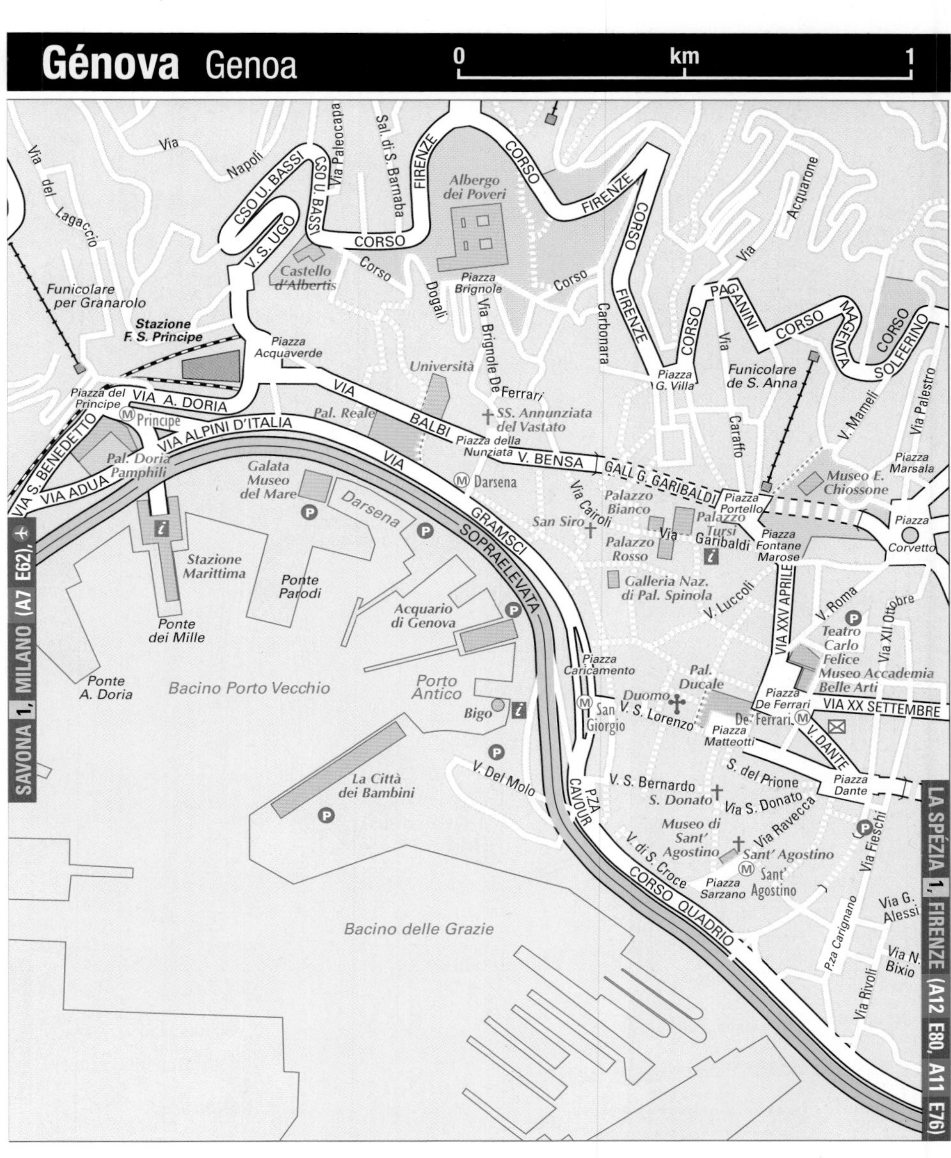

Granada

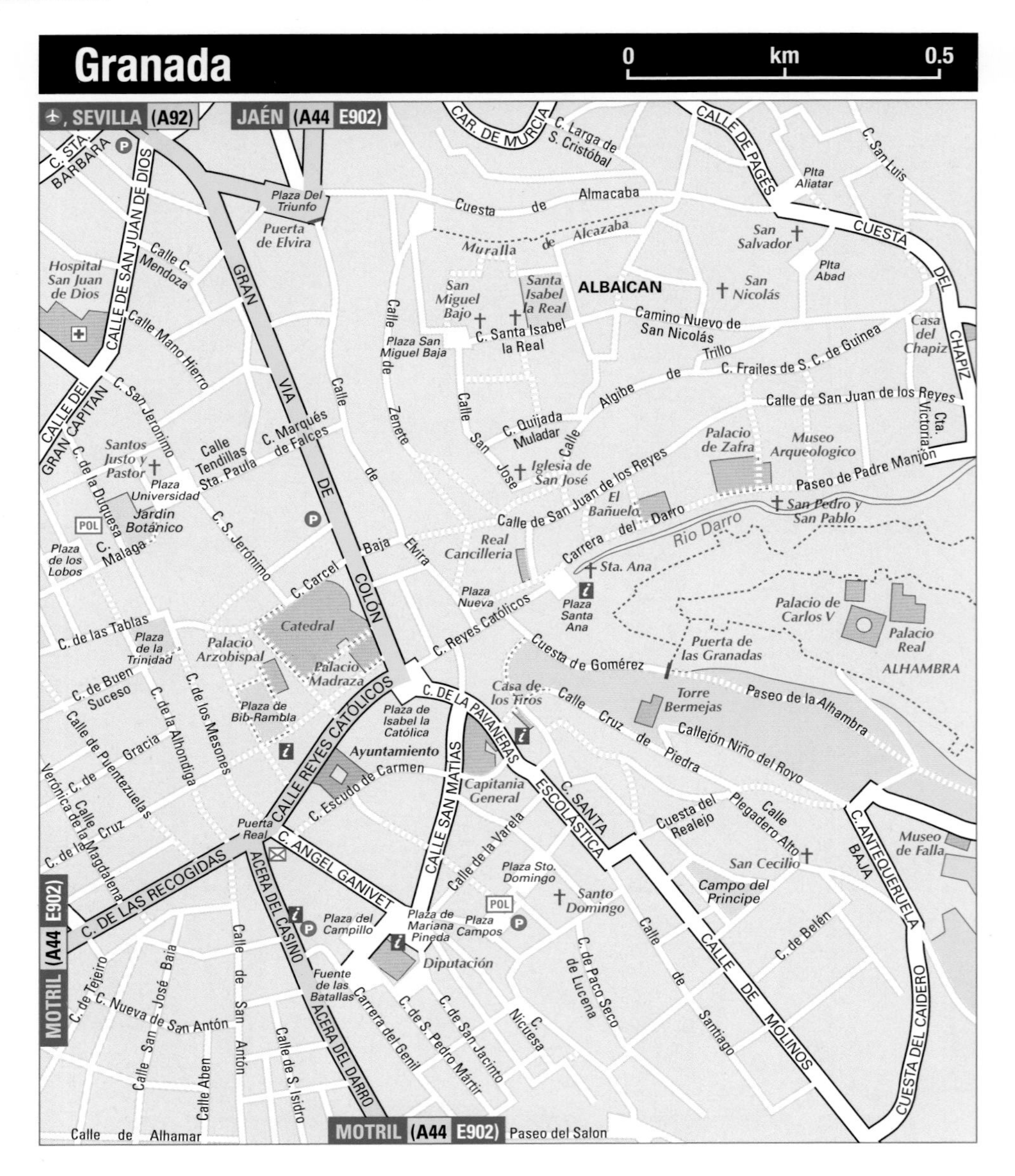

Göteborg Gothenburg

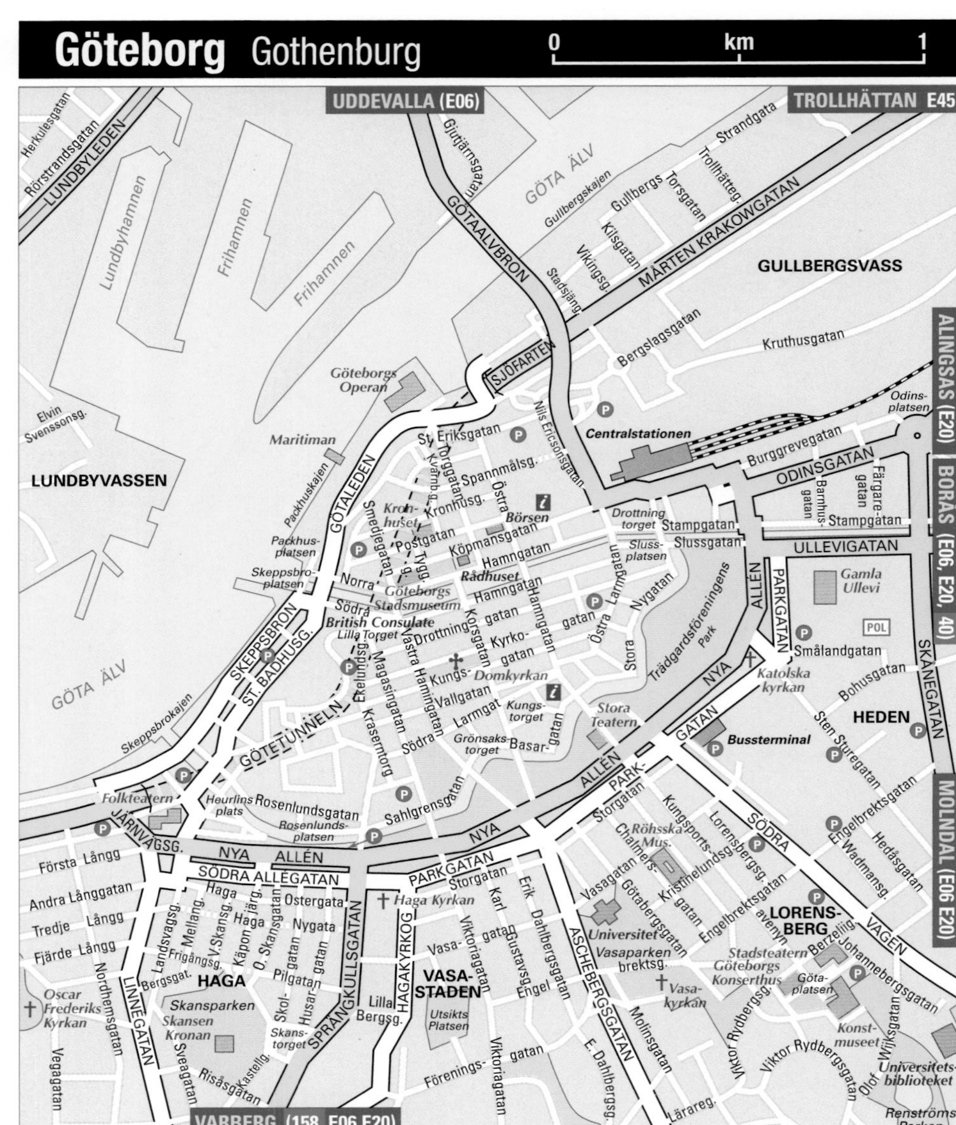

Hamburg

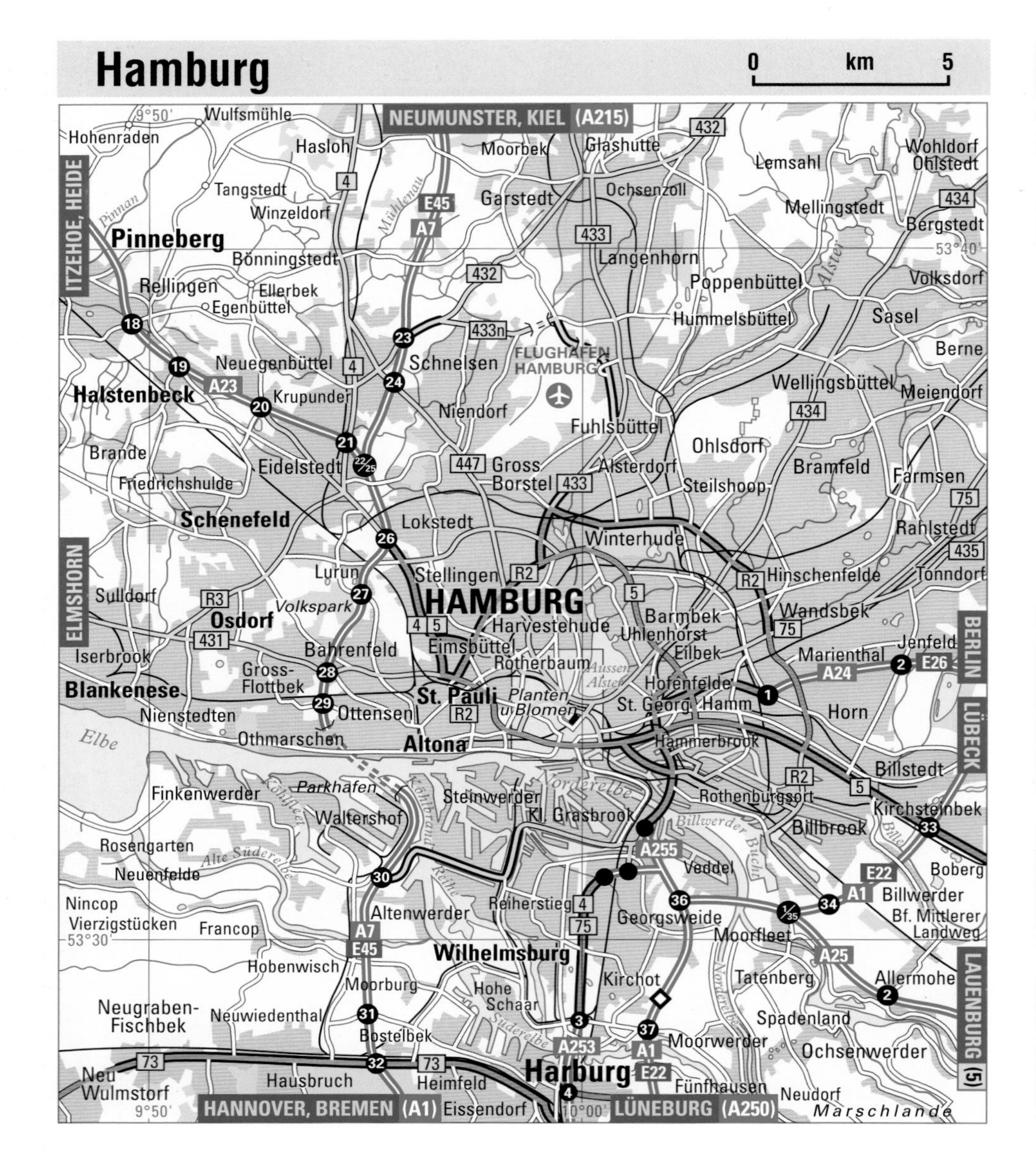

Hamburg

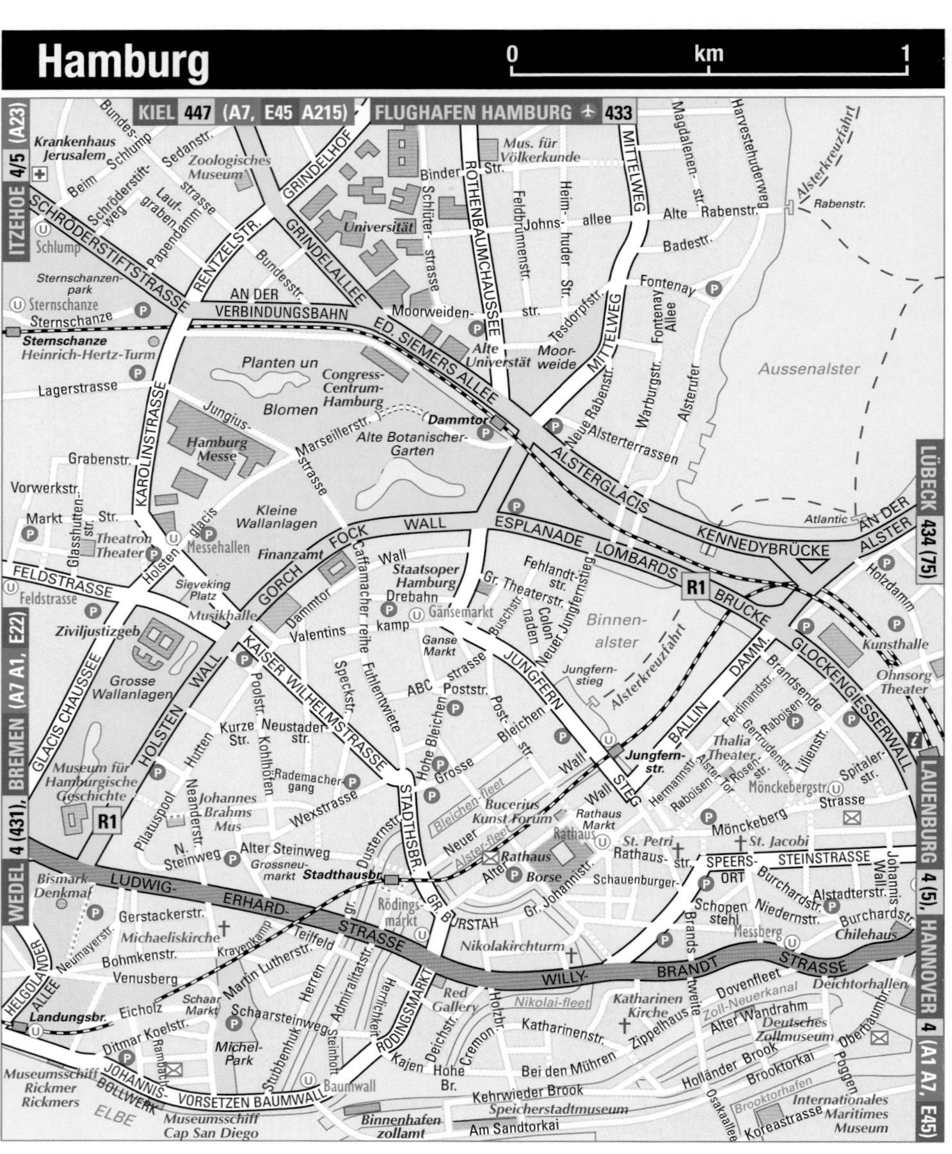

Helsinki

0 km 1

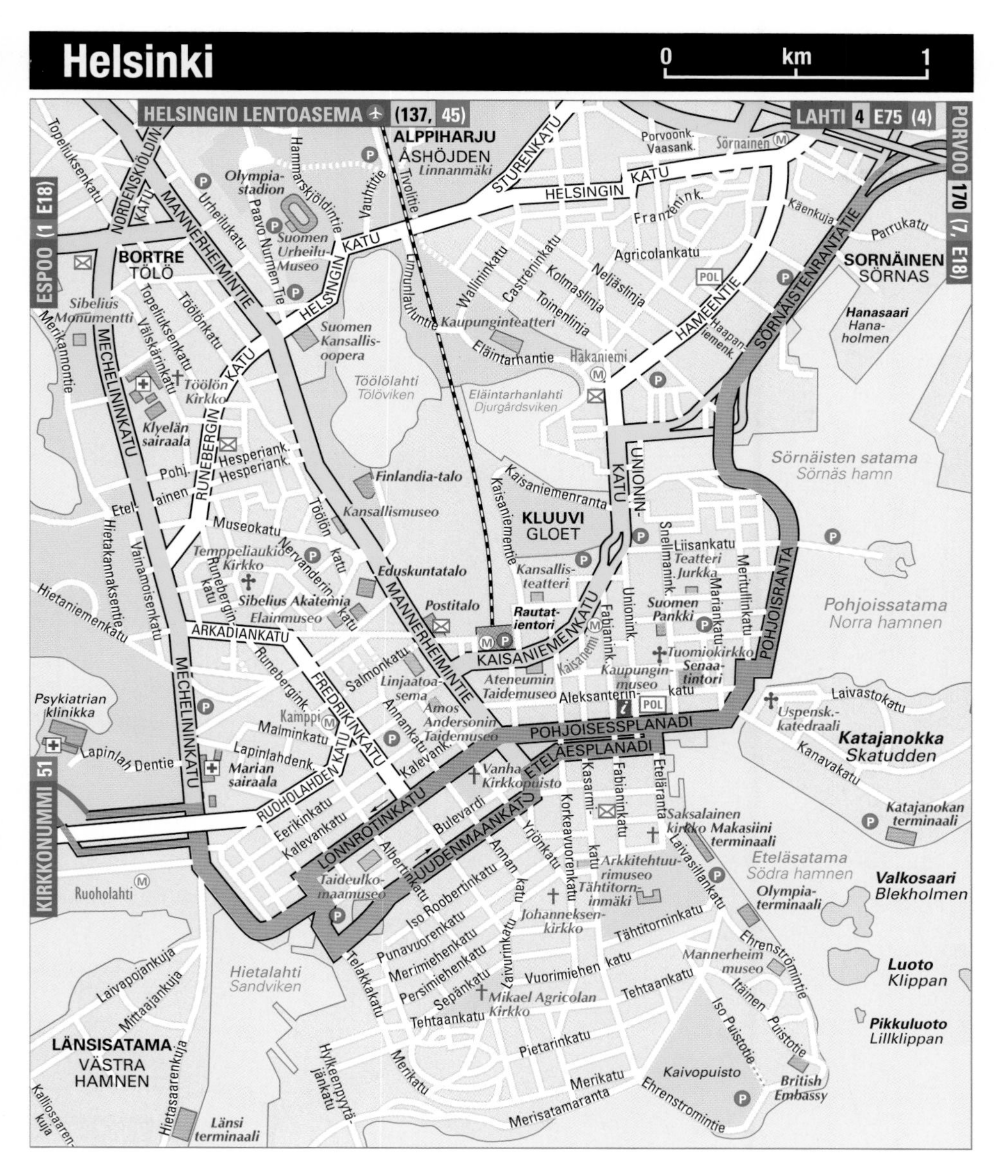
HELSINGIN LENTOASEMA (137, 45)
LAHTI 4 E75 (4)
PORVOO 170 (7, E18)
ESPOO (1 E18)
KIRKKONUMMI 51
ALPPIHARJU
ÅSHÖJDEN
BORTRE
TÖLÖ
SORNÄINEN
SÖRNÄS
KLUUVI
GLOET
Katajanokka
Skatudden
LÄNSISATAMA
VÄSTRA
HAMNEN
MANNERHEIMINTIE
MECHELININKATU
POHJOISESPLANADI
ETELÄESPLANADI
KAISANIEMENKATU
HELSINGINKATU
STURENKATU
SÖRNÄISTENRANTATIE
HÄMEENTIE
UNIONINKATU
POHJOISRANTA
LÖNNROTINKATU
BULEVARDI
ARKADIANKATU
FREDRIKINKATU
RUNEBERGINKATU
Pohjoissatama
Norra hamnen
Eteläsatama
Södra hamnen
Sörnäisten satama
Sörnäs hamn
Hietalahti
Sandviken
Töölönlahti
Tölöviken
Finlandia-talo
Kansallismuseo
Eduskuntatalo
Temppeliaukion Kirkko
Sibelius Akatemia
Sibelius Monumentti
Olympiastadion
Suomen Urheilu-Museo
Suomen Kansallisooppera
Kaupunginteatteri
Tuomiokirkko
Ateneumin Taidemuseo
Uspensk.-katedraali
Valkosaari
Blekholmen
Luoto
Klippan
Pikkuluoto
Lillklippan
Hanasaari
Hanaholmen
Kaivopuisto
British Embassy
Länsi terminaali

İstanbul

0 km 5

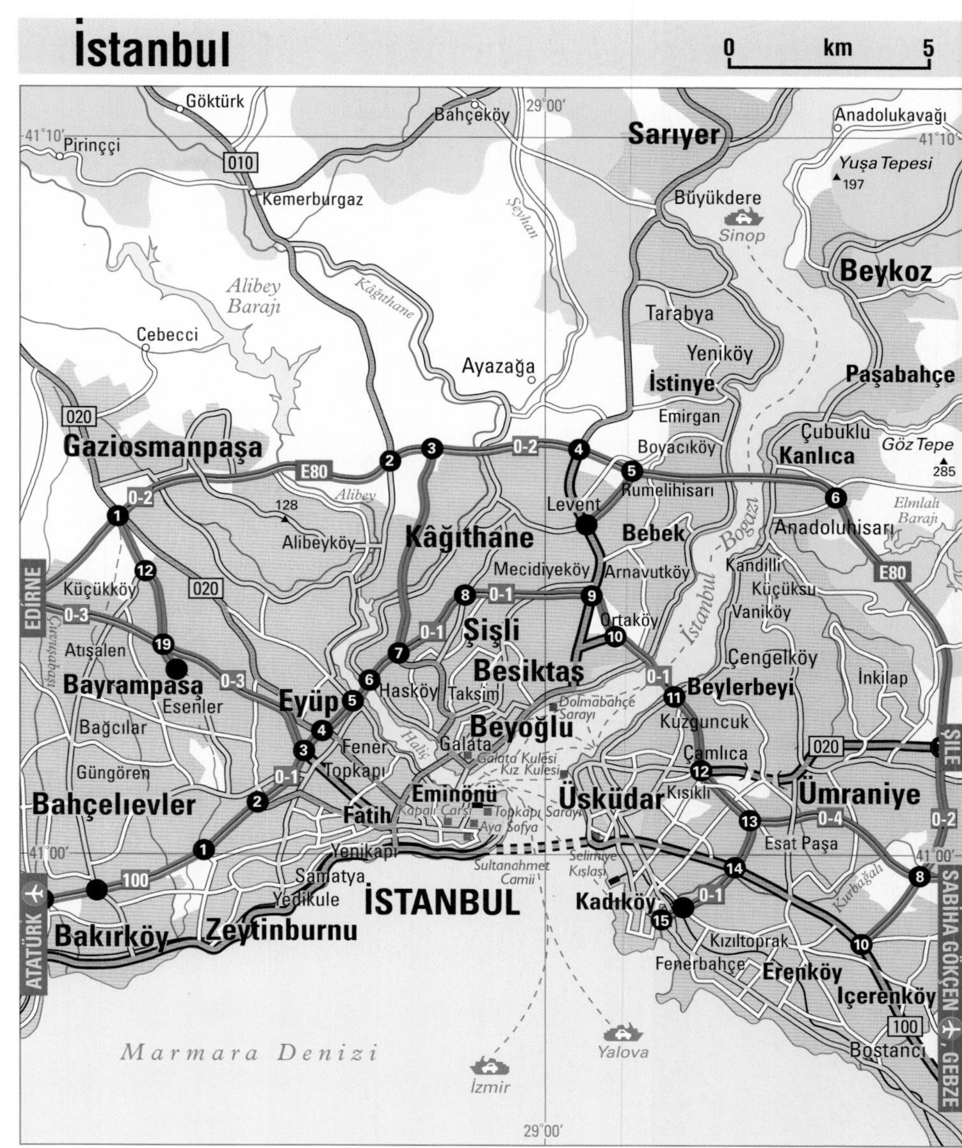
Göktürk
Bahçeköy
Sarıyer
Anadolukavağı
Yuşa Tepesi
Büyükdere
Kemerburgaz
Alibey Barajı
Tarabya
Yeniköy
İstinye
Beykoz
Paşabahçe
Cebecci
Ayazağa
Emirgan
Boyacıköy
Çubuklu
Kanlıca
Göz Tepe
Gaziosmanpaşa
Rumelihisarı
Anadoluhisarı
Levent
Bebek
Kâğıthane
Alibeyköy
Mecidiyeköy
Arnavutköy
Kandilli
Küçüksu
Vaniköy
Küçükköy
Şişli
Ortaköy
Beşiktaş
Çengelköy
İnkilap
Atışalen
Bayrampaşa
Esenler
Eyüp
Hasköy
Taksim
Dolmabahçe Sarayı
Beylerbeyi
Kuzguncuk
Bağcılar
Fener
Beyoğlu
Galata
Çamlıca
Güngören
Topkapı
Ümraniye
Bahçelievler
Fatih
Eminönü
Üsküdar
Kısıklı
Esat Paşa
Yenikapı
Samatya
Yedikule
İSTANBUL
Kadıköy
Bakırköy
Zeytinburnu
Kızıltoprak
Fenerbahçe
Erenköy
Içerenköy
Bostancı
Marmara Denizi
İzmir
Yalova
EDİRNE
ATATÜRK
SABİHA GÖKÇEN
GEBZE
ŞİLE

Helsinki

0 km 10

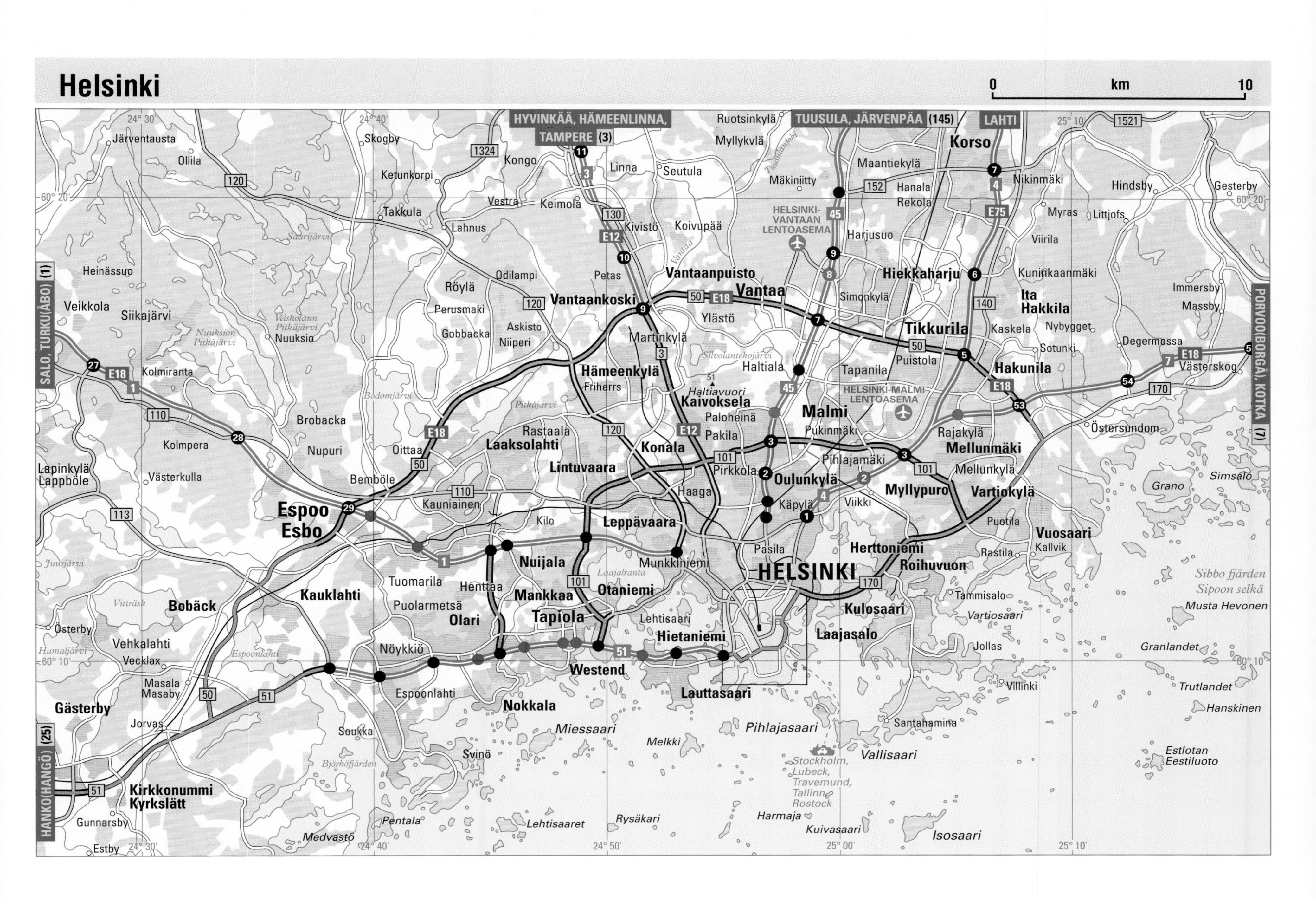
HYVINKÄÄ, HÄMEENLINNA, TAMPERE (3)
TUUSULA, JÄRVENPÄÄ (145)
LAHTI
SALO, TURKU(ÅBO) (1)
PORVOO(BORGÅ), KOTKA (7)
HANKO(HANGÖ) (25)
Järventausta
Ollila
Skogby
Kongo
Ketunkorpi
Linna
Seutula
Ruotsinkylä
Myllykylä
Korso
Maantiekylä
Mäkiniitty
Hanala
Rekola
Nikinmäki
Hindsby
Gesterby
Takkula
Vestra
Keimola
Lahnus
Kivistö
Koivupää
HELSINKI-VANTAAN LENTOASEMA
Harjusuo
Myras
Littjofs
Viirila
Heinässuo
Odilampi
Petas
Vantaanpuisto
Hiekkaharju
Kuninkaanmäki
Veikkola
Siikajärvi
Röylä
Perusmaki
Vantaankoski
Vantaa
Simonkylä
Ita Hakkila
Immersby
Massby
Nuuksio
Gobbacka
Askisto
Niiperi
Ylästö
Martinkylä
Tikkurila
Kaskela
Nybygget
Degermossa
Kolmiranta
Hämeenkylä
Friherrs
Haltiala
Tapanila
Puistola
Sotunki
Hakunila
Västerskog
HELSINKI-MALMI LENTOASEMA
Kaivoksela
Malmi
Brobacka
Rastaala
Paloheinä
Pukinmäki
Rajakylä
Östersundom
Kolmpera
Nupuri
Oittaa
Laaksolahti
Konala
Pakila
Pihlajamäki
Mellunmäki
Lapinkylä
Lappböle
Västerkulla
Bemböle
Lintuvaara
Pirkkola
Oulunkylä
Myllypuro
Vartiokylä
Mellunkylä
Simsalö
Grano
Espoo
Esbo
Kauniainen
Haaga
Käpylä
Viikki
Kilo
Leppävaara
Puotila
Vuosaari
Kallvik
Pasila
Nuijala
Munkkiniemi
HELSINKI
Herttoniemi
Rastila
Roihuvuori
Sibbo fjärden
Sipoon selkä
Musta Hevonen
Tuomarila
Kauklahti
Henttaa
Otaniemi
Bobäck
Puolarmetsä
Mankkaa
Tammisalo
Kulosaari
Vartiosaari
Olari
Tapiola
Lehtisaari
Hietaniemi
Laajasalo
Östersby
Vehkalahti
Nöykkiö
Jollas
Granlandet
Vecklax
Westend
Masala
Masaby
Espoonlahti
Lauttasaari
Villinki
Trutlandet
Gästerby
Nokkala
Hanskinen
Jorvas
Soukka
Miessaari
Santahamina
Melkki
Pihlajasaari
Svinö
Vallisaari
Estlotan
Eestiluoto
Stockholm, Lubeck, Travemund, Tallinn, Rostock
Kirkkonummi
Kyrkslätt
Gunnarsby
Pentala
Lehtisaaret
Rysäkari
Harmaja
Kuivasaari
Isosaari
Medvastö
Estby

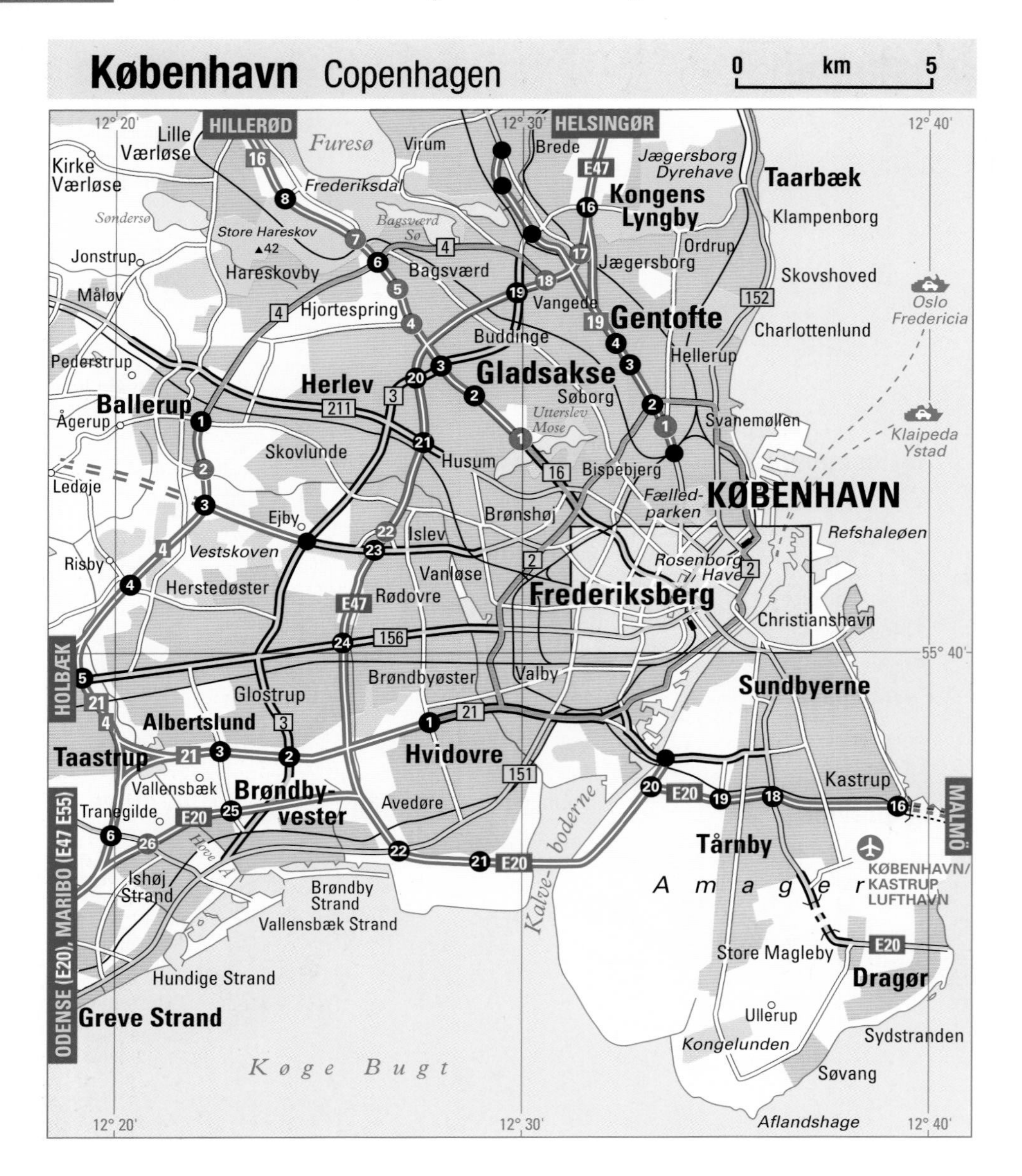
København Copenhagen
0 km 5
HILLERØD
HELSINGØR
Furesø
Virum
Brede
Lille Værløse
Kirke Værløse
Frederiksdal
Jægersborg Dyrehave
Kongens Lyngby
Taarbæk
Klampenborg
Store Hareskov
Bagsværd Sø
Bagsværd
Hareskovby
Jægersborg
Ordrup
Skovshoved
Jonstrup
Måløv
Hjortespring
Vangede
Gentofte
Charlottenlund
Oslo
Fredericia
Buddinge
Hellerup
Pederstrup
Gladsakse
Herlev
Søborg
Ballerup
Ågerup
Utterslev Mose
Svanemøllen
Klaipeda
Ystad
Skovlunde
Husum
Bispebjerg
Ledøje
Fælledparken
KØBENHAVN
Ejby
Brønshøj
Islev
Refshaleøen
Risby
Vestskoven
Vanløse
Rosenborg Have
Herstedøster
Rødovre
Frederiksberg
Christianshavn
HOLBÆK
Brøndbyøster
Valby
Glostrup
Sundbyerne
Albertslund
Taastrup
Hvidovre
Vallensbæk
Brøndbyvester
Kastrup
Tranegilde
Avedøre
MALMÖ
Kalvebøderne
Tårnby
Ishøj Strand
Brøndby Strand
Vallensbæk Strand
Amager
KØBENHAVN/KASTRUP LUFTHAVN
ODENSE (E20), MARIBO (E47 E55)
Store Magleby
Dragør
Hundige Strand
Greve Strand
Ullerup
Kongelunden
Sydstranden
Søvang
Køge Bugt
Aflandshage
12° 20'
12° 30'
12° 40'
55° 40'

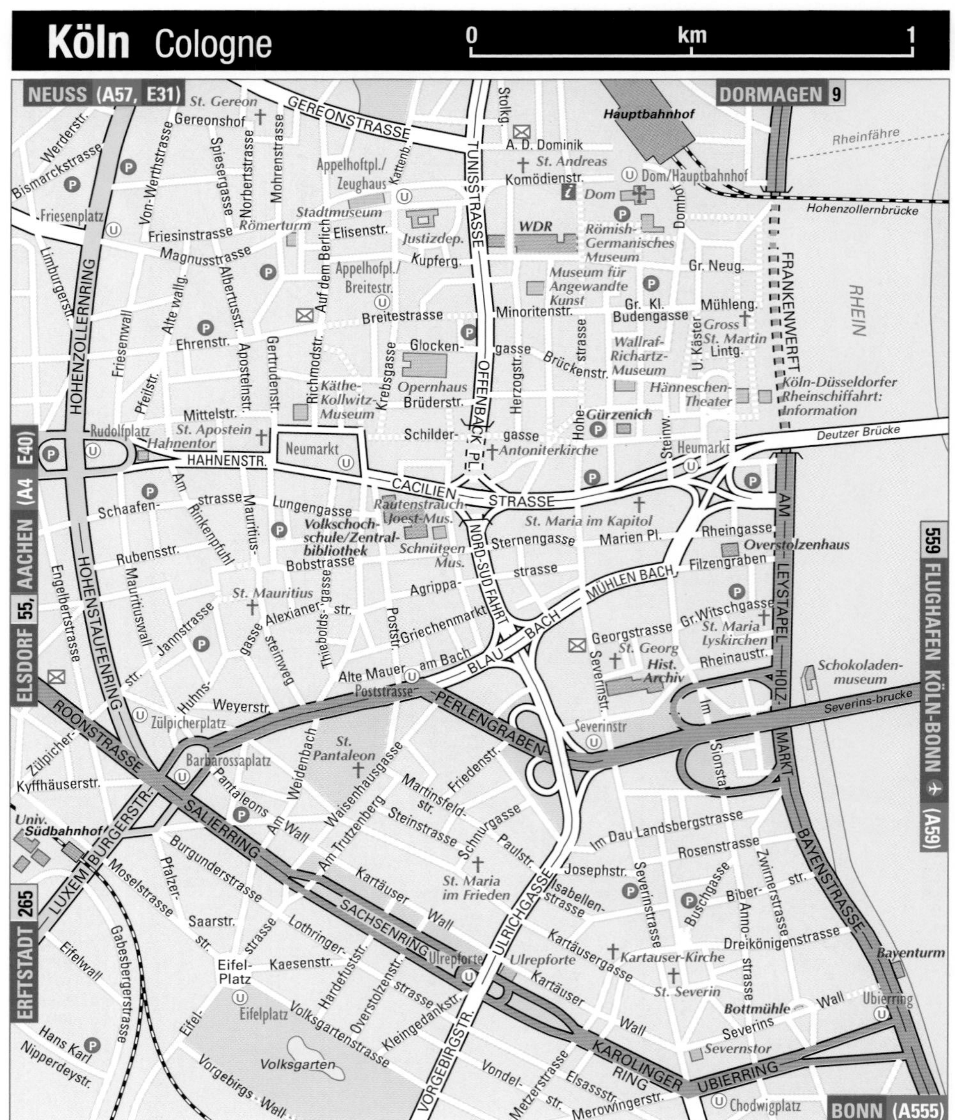
Köln Cologne
0 km 1
NEUSS (A57, E31)
DORMAGEN 9
Hauptbahnhof
Rheinfähre
Hohenzollernbrücke
St. Gereon
Gereonshof
GEREONSTRASSE
A. D. Dominik
St. Andreas
Komödienstr.
Dom/Hauptbahnhof
Dom
Appelhofpl./Zeughaus
Stadtmuseum
Römerturm
Friesenplatz
Friesinstrasse
Magnusstrasse
Elisenstr.
Justizdep.
WDR
Römisch-Germanisches Museum
Kupferg.
Appelhofpl./Breitestr.
Breitestrasse
Museum für Angewandte Kunst
Gr. Neug.
FRANKENWERFT
RHEIN
Minoritenstr.
Budengasse
Mühleng.
Gross St. Martin
Ehrenstr.
Glocken-gasse
Wallraf-Richartz-Museum
Käthe-Kollwitz-Museum
Opernhaus
Brüderstr.
Hänneschen-Theater
Köln-Düsseldorfer Rheinschiffahrt: Information
Mittelstr.
St. Apostein
Schilder-gasse
Gürzenich
Rudolfplatz
Hahnentor
HAHNENSTR.
Neumarkt
Antoniterkirche
Heumarkt
Deutzer Brücke
CACILIENSTRASSE
HOHENZOLLERNRING
Schaafenstrasse
Lungengasse
Rautenstrauch-Joest-Mus.
Volkshochschule/Zentralbibliothek
St. Maria im Kapitol
Marien Pl.
Rheingasse
Overstolzenhaus
Rubensstr.
Bobstrasse
Schnütgen Mus.
Sternengasse
Filzengraben
559 FLUGHAFEN KÖLN-BONN (A59)
ELSDORF 55, AACHEN (A4 E40)
St. Mauritius
Alexianerstr.
Agrippa-strasse
NORD-SÜD-FAHRT
MÜHLEN BACH
Griechenmarkt
Georgstrasse
St. Georg
Witschgasse
St. Maria Lyskirchen
Rheinaustr.
Hist. Archiv
Schokoladenmuseum
Weyerstr.
Alte Mauer am Bach
Poststrasse
PERLENGRABEN
Severinsbrücke
Zülpicherplatz
Barbarossaplatz
St. Pantaleon
Severinstr.
Kyffhäuserstr.
Univ. Südbahnhof
HOHENSTAUFENRING
SALIERRING
LUXEMBURGERSTR.
Martinsfeld
Landsbergstrasse
Rosenstrasse
Josephstr.
ERFTSTADT 265
Kartäuser Wall
St. Maria im Frieden
SACHSENRING
ULRICHGASSE
Ulrepforte
Kartäuser-Kirche
Dreikönigenstrasse
Bayenturm
BAYENSTRASSE
Eifel-Platz
Kaesenstr.
St. Severin
Bottmühle
Severins Wall
Ubierring
Eifelplatz
Severinstor
Hans Karl Nipperdeystr.
Volksgarten
VORGEBIRGSSTR.
KAROLINGER RING
UBIERRING
Chlodwigplatz
BONN (A555)
Merowingerstr.

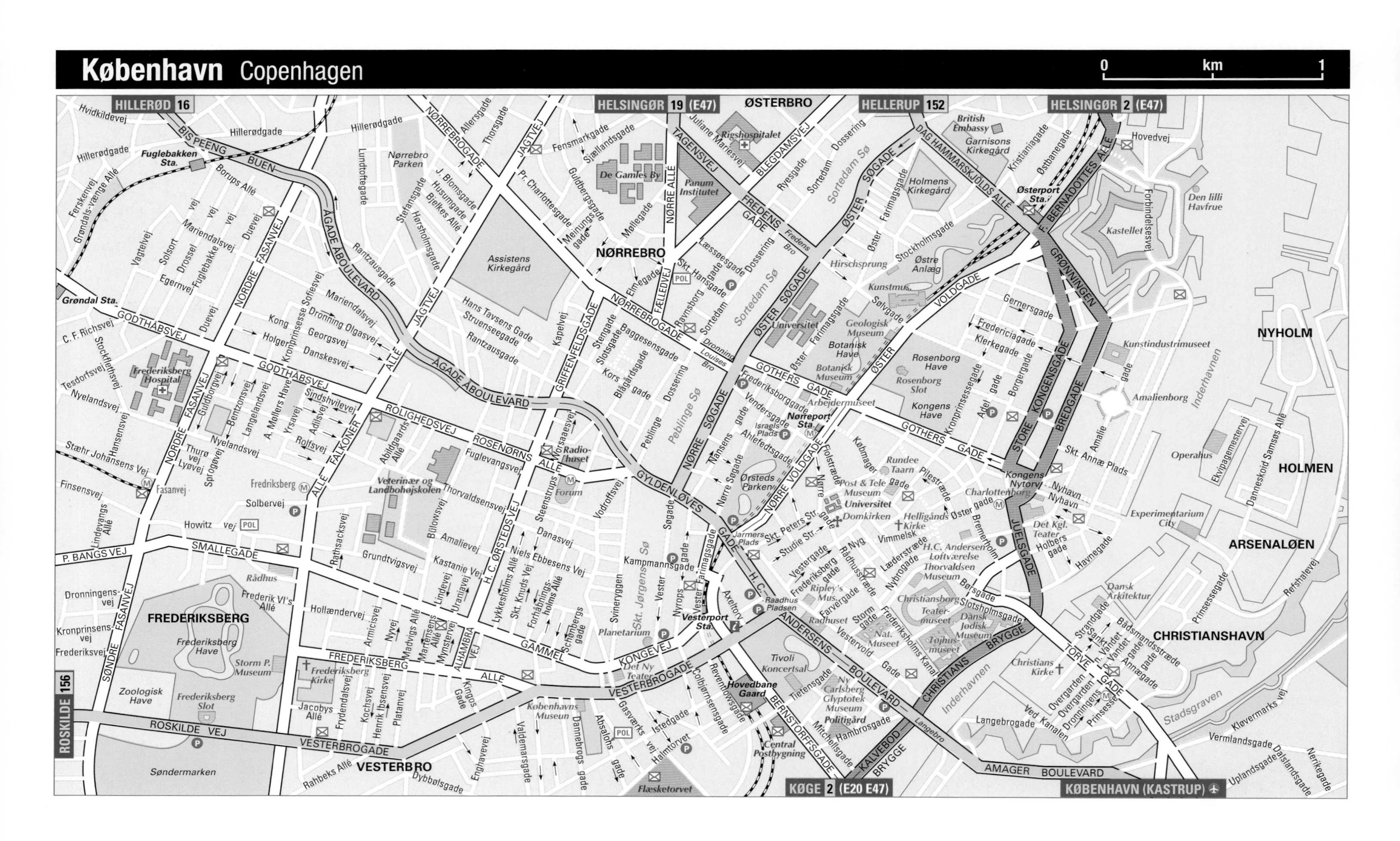
København Copenhagen
0 km 1
HILLERØD 16
HELSINGØR 19 (E47)
ØSTERBRO
HELLERUP 152
HELSINGØR 2 (E47)
Hvidkildevej
Hillerødgade
Fuglebakken Sta.
BISPEENGBUEN
Nørrebro Parken
Rigshospitalet
British Embassy
Garnisons Kirkegård
De Gamles By
Panum Instituttet
BLEGDAMSVEJ
Holmens Kirkegård
Østerport Sta.
Kastellet
Den lilli Havfrue
Assistens Kirkegård
NØRREBRO
ÅGADE ÅBOULEVARD
Østre Anlæg
Grøndal Sta.
GODTHÅBSVEJ
Sortedam Sø
Peblinge Sø
Universitet
Geologisk Museum
Botanisk Have
Rosenborg Have
Rosenborg Slot
Kongens Have
NYHOLM
Frederiksberg Hospital
Kunstindustrimuseet
Amalienborg
ROLIGHEDSVEJ
ROSENØRNS ALLÉ
Radiohuset
Nørreport Sta.
Ørsteds Parken
Operahus
HOLMEN
Veterinær og Landbohøjskolen
Forum
GYLDENLØVESGADE
Kongens Nytorv
Nyhavn
Charlottenborg
Det Kgl. Teater
Experimentarium City
ARSENALØEN
Universitet
Domkirken
Helligånds Kirke
H.C. Andersen Loftværelse
Thorvaldsen Museum
Christiansborg Slot
Teatermuseet
Dansk Arkitektur
SMALLEGADE
P. BANGS VEJ
FREDERIKSBERG
Frederiksberg Have
Storm P. Museum
Planetarium
Vesterport Sta.
Rådhus Pladsen
Ripley's Mus.
Nat. Museet
Jødisk Museum
Tøjhusmuseet
CHRISTIANSHAVN
Christians Kirke
Tivoli Koncertsal
Frederiksberg Kirke
Zoologisk Have
Frederiksberg Slot
VESTERBROGADE
Københavns Museum
Hovedbane Gaard
Ny Carlsberg Glyptotek Museum
Politigård
Central Postbygning
H.C. ANDERSENS BOULEVARD
CHRISTIANS BRYGGE
Langebrogade
Stadsgraven
ROSKILDE 156
ROSKILDE VEJ
Søndermarken
VESTERBRO
Rahbeks Allé
Dybbølsgade
Flæsketorvet
KALVEBOD BRYGGE
AMAGER BOULEVARD
KØGE 2 (E20 E47)
KØBENHAVN (KASTRUP)

Lisboa Lisbon

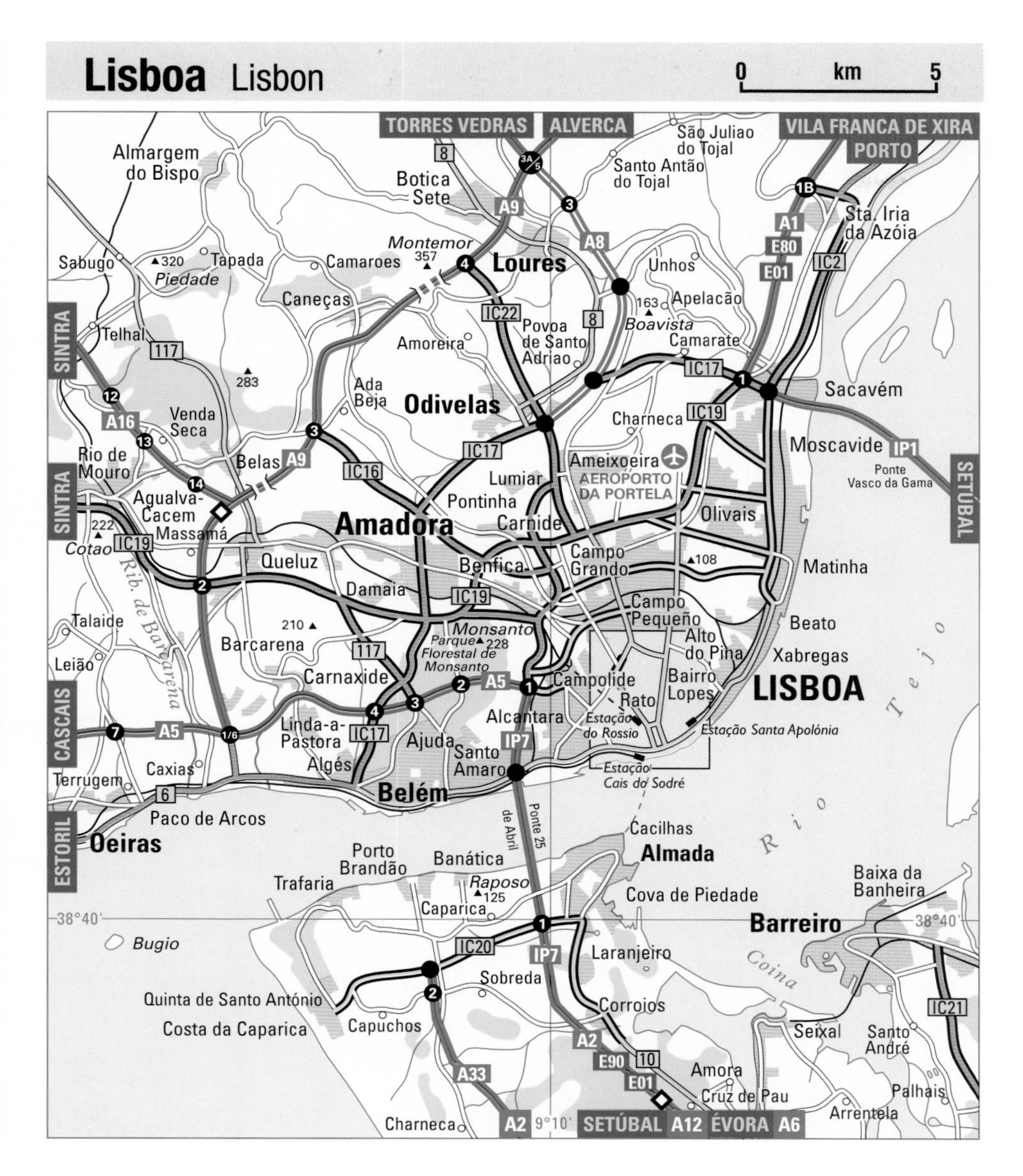
0 km 5
TORRES VEDRAS
ALVERCA
VILA FRANCA DE XIRA
PORTO
SINTRA
CASCAIS
ESTORIL
SETÚBAL
Almargem do Bispo
Botica Sete
São Juliao do Tojal
Santo Antão do Tojal
Sta. Iria da Azóia
Montemor
Loures
Sabugo
Tapada
Piedade
Camaroes
Unhos
Caneças
Apelacão
Boavista
Camarate
Telhal
Póvoa de Santo Adriao
Amoreira
Ada Beja
Odivelas
Sacavém
Venda Seca
Charneca
Moscavide
Ponte Vasco da Gama
Rio de Mouro
Belas
Lumiar
Ameixoeira
AEROPORTO DA PORTELA
Agualva-Cacem
Massamá
Pontinha
Amadora
Carnide
Olivais
Cotão
Queluz
Benfica
Campo Grande
Matinha
Damaia
Campo Pequeño
Beato
Talaide
Barcarena
Monsanto
Parque Florestal de Monsanto
Alto do Pina
Xabregas
Leião
Carnaxide
Campolide
Bairro Lopes
LISBOA
Rato
Linda-a-Pastora
Alcântara
Estação do Rossio
Estação Santa Apolónia
Ajuda
Santo Amaro
Terrugem
Caixas
Algés
Belém
Estação Cais do Sodré
Paco de Arcos
Oeiras
Ponte 25 de Abril
Cacilhas
Almada
Rio Tejo
Porto Brandão
Banática
Trafaria
Raposo
Baixa da Banheira
Caparica
Cova de Piedade
Barreiro
Bugio
Laranjeiro
Coina
Sobreda
Quinta de Santo António
Costa da Caparica
Capuchos
Corroios
Seixal
Santo André
Amora
Cruz de Pau
Palhais
Arrentela
Charneca
SETÚBAL A12
ÉVORA A6

Lisboa Lisbon

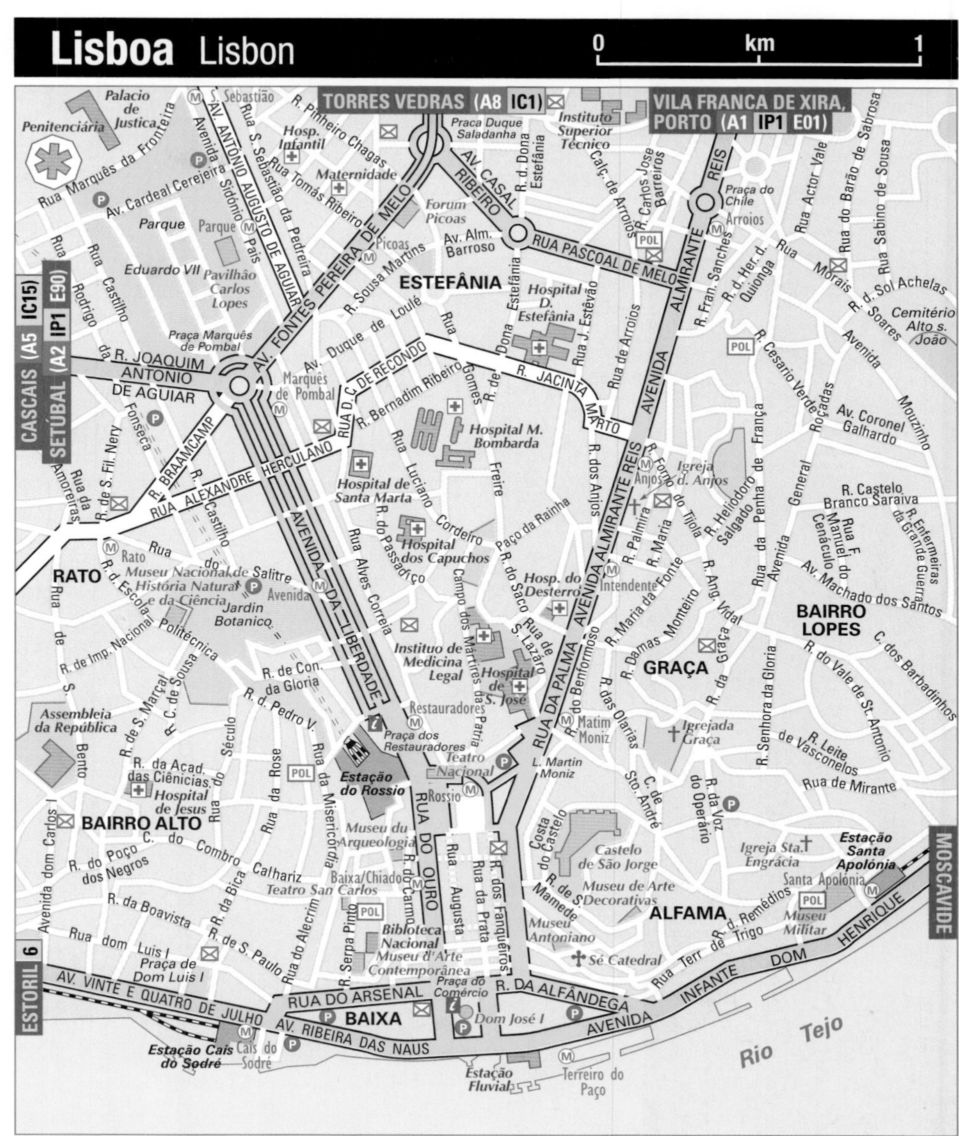
0 km 1
TORRES VEDRAS (A8 IC1)
VILA FRANCA DE XIRA, PORTO (A1 IP1 E01)
CASCAIS (A5 IC15)
SETÚBAL (A2 IP1 E90)
ESTORIL 6
MOSCAVIDE
Palácio de Justiça
Penitenciária
Instituto Superior Técnico
Praça Duque Saldanha
Maternidade
Parque
Eduardo VII
Forum Picoas
Praça do Chile
Arroios
ESTEFÂNIA
Hospital D. Estefânia
Praça Marquês de Pombal
Hospital M. Bombarda
Hospital de Santa Marta
Hospital dos Capuchos
RATO
Museu Nacional de História Natural e da Ciência
Jardim Botanico
Avenida da Liberdade
Instituto de Medicina Legal
Hospital de S. José
Hosp. do Desterro
BAIRRO LOPES
GRAÇA
Assembleia da República
Praça dos Restauradores
Estação do Rossio
Teatro Nacional
Igreja da Graça
BAIRRO ALTO
Hospital de Jesus
Museu do Arqueologia
Castelo de São Jorge
Museu de Arte Decorativas
Estação Santa Apolónia
Igreja Sta. Engrácia
Museu Militar
ALFAMA
Teatro San Carlos
Biblioteca Nacional
Museu d'Arte Contemporânea
Praça do Comércio
Sé Catedral
Museu Antoniano
BAIXA
Praça de Dom Luís I
Estação Cais do Sodré
Estação Fluvial
Terreiro do Paço
Rio Tejo
AVENIDA INFANTE DOM HENRIQUE
AV. RIBEIRA DAS NAUS
RUA DO ARSENAL

London

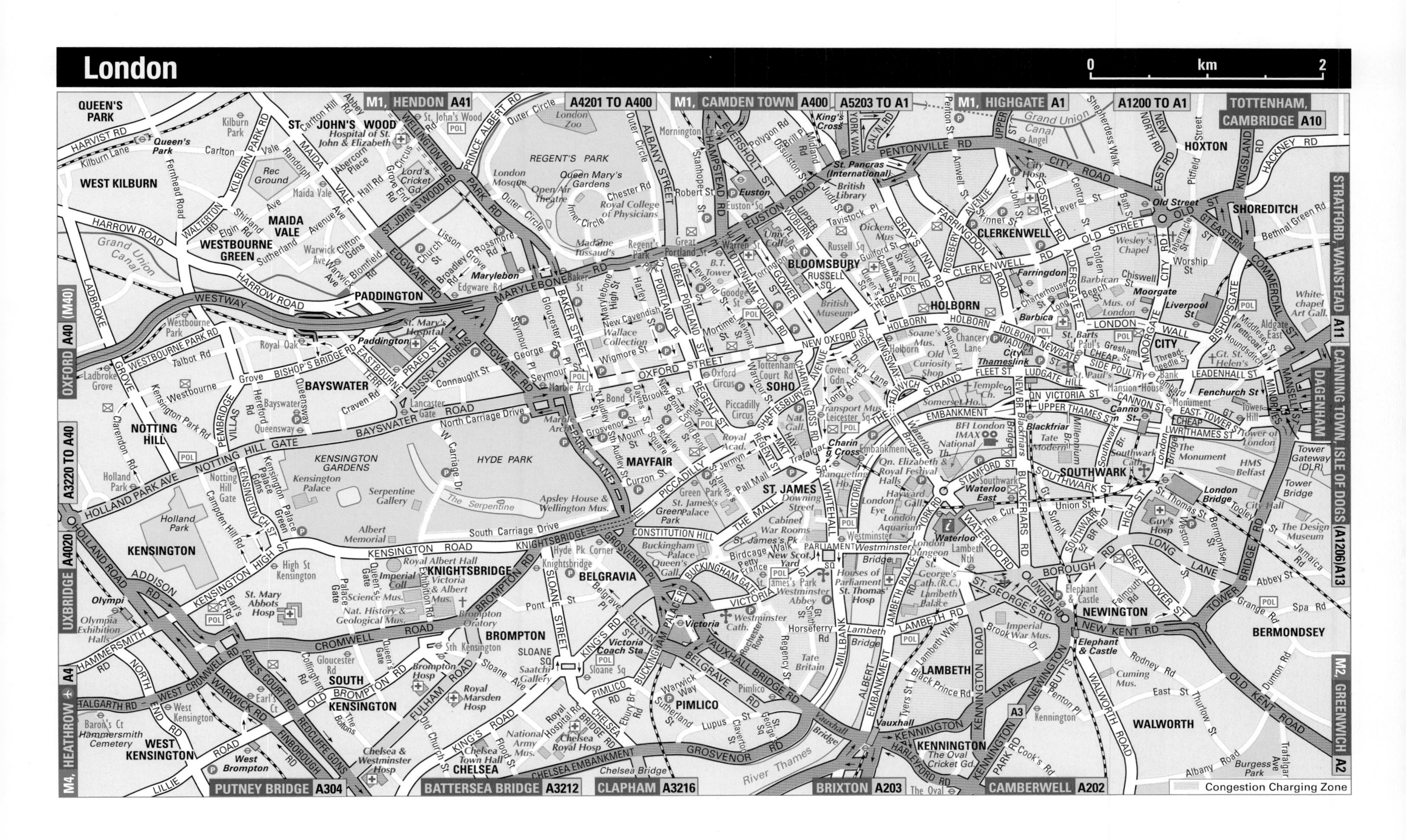
0 km 2
M1, HENDON A41
A4201 TO A400
M1, CAMDEN TOWN A400
A5203 TO A1
M1, HIGHGATE A1
A1200 TO A1
TOTTENHAM, CAMBRIDGE A10
STRATFORD, WANSTEAD A11
CANNING TOWN, ISLE OF DOGS (A1206) A13
DAGENHAM
M2, GREENWICH A2
OXFORD A40 (M40)
A3220 TO A40
UXBRIDGE A4020
M4, HEATHROW A4
PUTNEY BRIDGE A304
BATTERSEA BRIDGE A3212
CLAPHAM A3216
BRIXTON A203
CAMBERWELL A202
QUEEN'S PARK
ST. JOHN'S WOOD
WEST KILBURN
MAIDA VALE
WESTBOURNE GREEN
PADDINGTON
REGENT'S PARK
London Zoo
HOXTON
SHOREDITCH
CLERKENWELL
BLOOMSBURY
HOLBORN
CITY
BAYSWATER
NOTTING HILL
SOHO
MAYFAIR
HYDE PARK
KENSINGTON GARDENS
ST. JAMES
SOUTHWARK
KENSINGTON
KNIGHTSBRIDGE
BELGRAVIA
BROMPTON
SOUTH KENSINGTON
WEST KENSINGTON
CHELSEA
PIMLICO
LAMBETH
KENNINGTON
NEWINGTON
WALWORTH
BERMONDSEY
British Museum
British Library
St. Pancras (International)
Euston
King's Cross
Marylebone
Tower of London
Tower Bridge
London Bridge
Waterloo
Victoria
Buckingham Palace
Houses of Parliament
Westminster Abbey
Tate Britain
Tate Modern
River Thames
Congestion Charging Zone

London

0 km 10

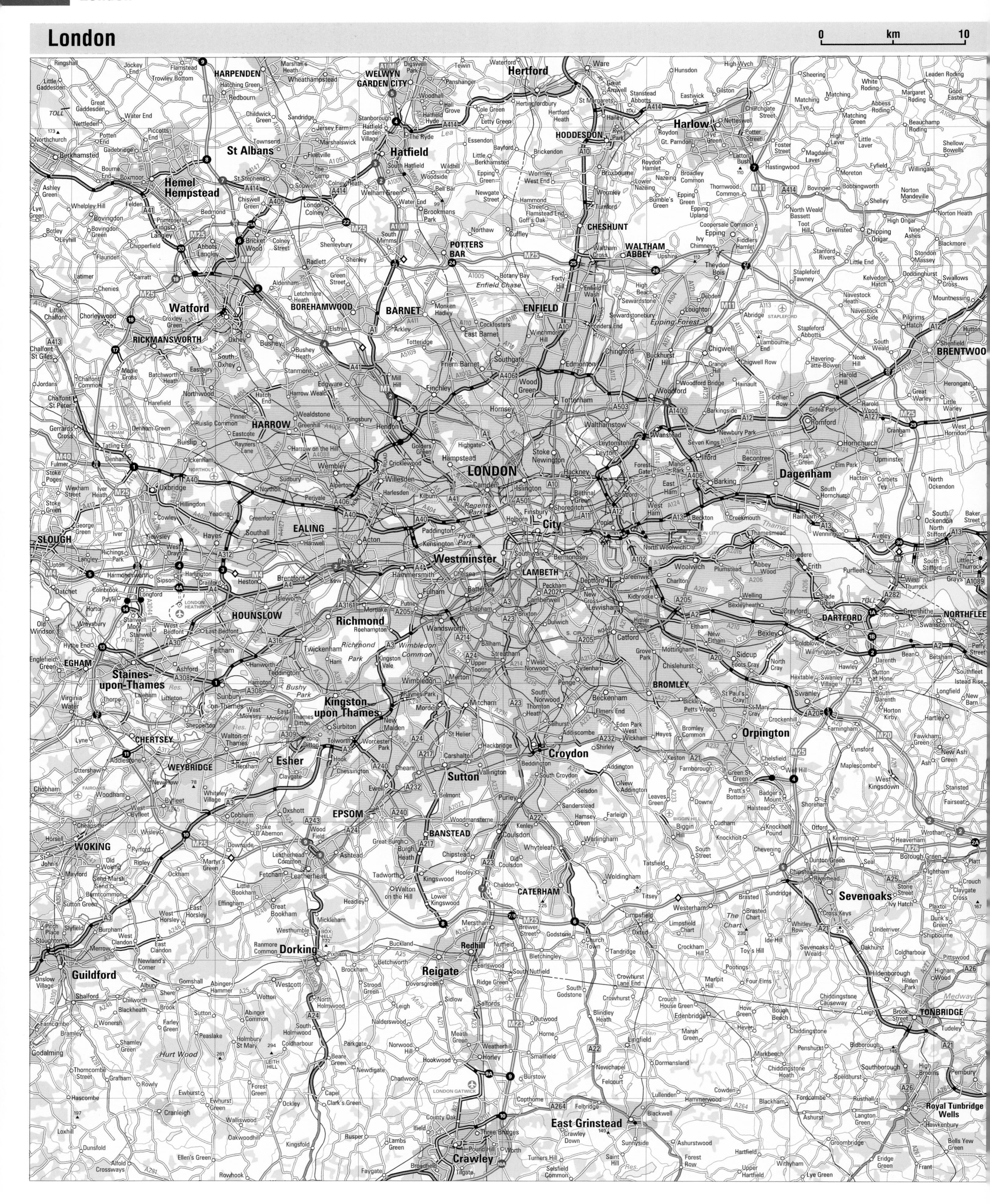
HARPENDEN
WELWYN GARDEN CITY
Hertford
Ware
Harlow
HODDESDON
St Albans
Hatfield
Hemel Hempstead
Berkhamsted
POTTERS BAR
CHESHUNT
WALTHAM ABBEY
Watford
BOREHAMWOOD
BARNET
ENFIELD
RICKMANSWORTH
BRENTWOOD
HARROW
LONDON
Romford
Dagenham
Uxbridge
SLOUGH
EALING
City
Westminster
LAMBETH
HOUNSLOW
Richmond
EGHAM
Staines-upon-Thames
DARTFORD
NORTHFLEET
Kingston upon Thames
BROMLEY
Croydon
CHERTSEY
WEYBRIDGE
Esher
Sutton
Orpington
EPSOM
BANSTEAD
WOKING
CATERHAM
Sevenoaks
Dorking
Reigate
Redhill
Guildford
TONBRIDGE
East Grinstead
Royal Tunbridge Wells
Crawley
Epping Forest
Thames
M25
M1
M11
M4
M3
M23
M20
M26
M40
A1(M)

Lyon

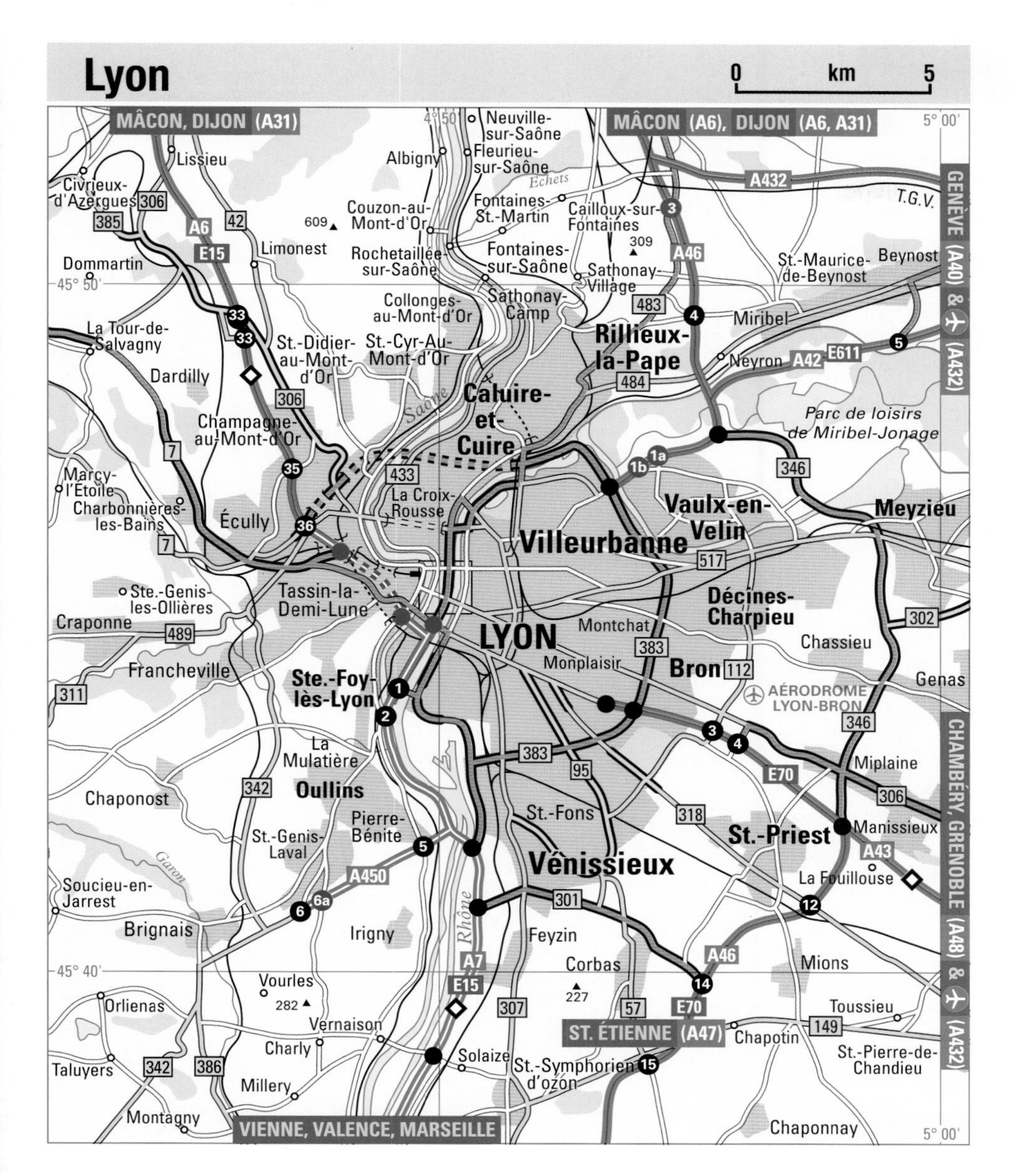
Lyon
0 km 5
MÂCON, DIJON (A31)
MÂCON (A6), DIJON (A6, A31)
GENÈVE (A40) & (A432)
CHAMBÉRY, GRENOBLE (A48) & (A432)
VIENNE, VALENCE, MARSEILLE
ST. ÉTIENNE (A47)
Neuville-sur-Saône
Fleurieu-sur-Saône
Albigny
Lissieu
Civrieux-d'Azergues
Limonest
Couzon-au-Mont-d'Or
Fontaines-St.-Martin
Cailloux-sur-Fontaines
Fontaines-sur-Saône
Rochetaillée-sur-Saône
Sathonay-Village
Sathonay-Camp
St.-Maurice-de-Beynost
Beynost
Dommartin
Collonges-au-Mont-d'Or
La Tour-de-Salvagny
St.-Didier-au-Mont-d'Or
St.-Cyr-Au-Mont-d'Or
Rillieux-la-Pape
Miribel
Neyron
Dardilly
Champagne-au-Mont-d'Or
Caluire-et-Cuire
Parc de loisirs de Miribel-Jonage
Marcy-l'Étoile
Charbonnières-les-Bains
Écully
La Croix-Rousse
Vaulx-en-Velin
Meyzieu
Villeurbanne
Ste.-Genis-les-Ollières
Tassin-la-Demi-Lune
Craponne
Montchat
Décines-Charpieu
LYON
Monplaisir
Chassieu
Francheville
Ste.-Foy-lès-Lyon
Bron
AÉRODROME LYON-BRON
Genas
La Mulatière
Oullins
Chaponost
Miplaine
St.-Genis-Laval
Pierre-Bénite
St.-Fons
St.-Priest
Manissieux
Vénissieux
Soucieu-en-Jarrest
La Fouillouse
Brignais
Irigny
Feyzin
Corbas
Mions
Vourles
Orliénas
Vernaison
Toussieu
Charly
Solaize
Chapotin
St.-Pierre-de-Chandieu
Taluyers
Millery
St.-Symphorien-d'Ozon
Montagny
Chaponnay

Lyon

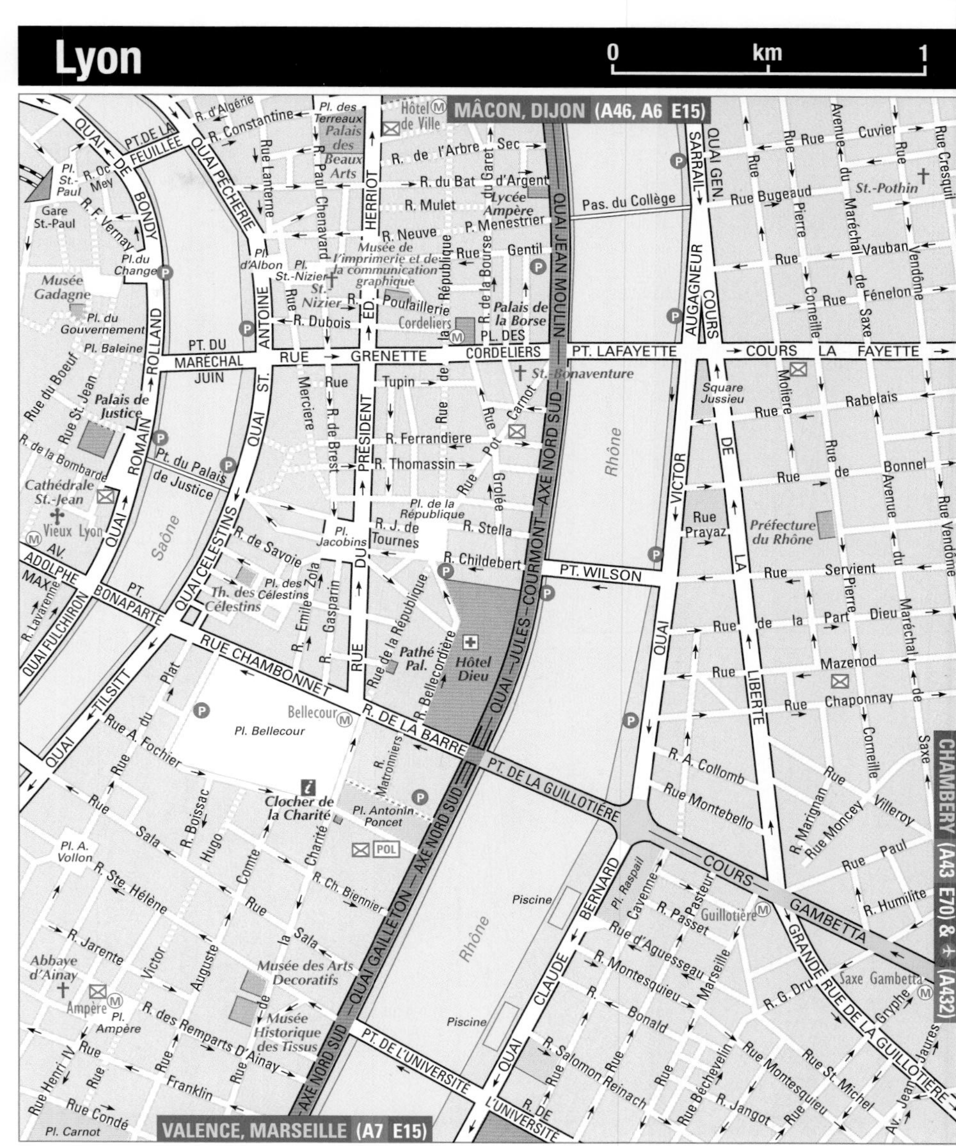
Lyon
0 km 1
MÂCON, DIJON (A46, A6 E15)
VALENCE, MARSEILLE (A7 E15)
CHAMBÉRY (A43 E70) & (A432)
QUAI DE BONDY
QUAI ST. VINCENT
QUAI PIERRE SCIZE
QUAI DE LA PÊCHERIE
Hôtel de Ville
PL. DES TERREAUX
Palais des Beaux Arts
R. de l'Arbre Sec
R. du Bât d'Argent
R. Mulet
Lycée Ampère
PL. DE LA COMÉDIE
QUAI JEAN MOULIN
Pas. du Collège
QUAI SARRAIL
QUAI GÉN.
Rue Cuvier
Rue Bugeaud
Rue Vauban
Gare St.-Paul
Musée Gadagne
Pl. du Gouvernement
Pl. du Change
R. Neuve
Musée de l'imprimerie et de la communication graphique
Rue Gentil
St. Nizier
Poulaillerie
Cordeliers
Palais de la Bourse
PL. DES CORDELIERS
PT. LAFAYETTE
COURS LAFAYETTE
PT. DU MARÉCHAL JUIN
QUAI ROMAIN ROLLAND
RUE GRENETTE
Tupin
St. Bonaventure
Square Jussieu
Rabelais
Palais de Justice
Rue du Bœuf
Cathédrale St.-Jean
Vieux Lyon
R. Thomassin
R. Ferrandière
R. de Brest
RUE DU PRÉSIDENT ÉDOUARD HERRIOT
Pl. de la République
Rhône
QUAI VICTOR AUGAGNEUR
Préfecture du Rhône
Rue Servient
QUAI FULCHIRON
QUAI ST. ANTOINE
QUAI DES CÉLESTINS
Th. des Célestins
Pl. des Jacobins
R. Stella
R. Childebert
PT. WILSON
PT. BONAPARTE
RUE CHAMBONNET
Pathé Pal.
Hôtel Dieu
QUAI TILSITT
Bellecour
Pl. Bellecour
R. DE LA BARRE
PT. DE LA GUILLOTIÈRE
Clocher de la Charité
Pl. Antonin Poncet
Pl. A. Vollon
R. Ste. Hélène
QUAI GAILLETON
AXE NORD SUD
R. Marronniers
COURS GAMBETTA
Guillotière
Saxe Gambetta
Abbaye d'Ainay
Ampère
Pl. Ampère
Musée des Arts Décoratifs
Musée Historique des Tissus
R. des Remparts d'Ainay
QUAI CLAUDE BERNARD
GRANDE RUE DE LA GUILLOTIÈRE
PT. DE L'UNIVERSITÉ
Piscine
Rue Franklin
Rue Condé
Pl. Carnot

Luxembourg

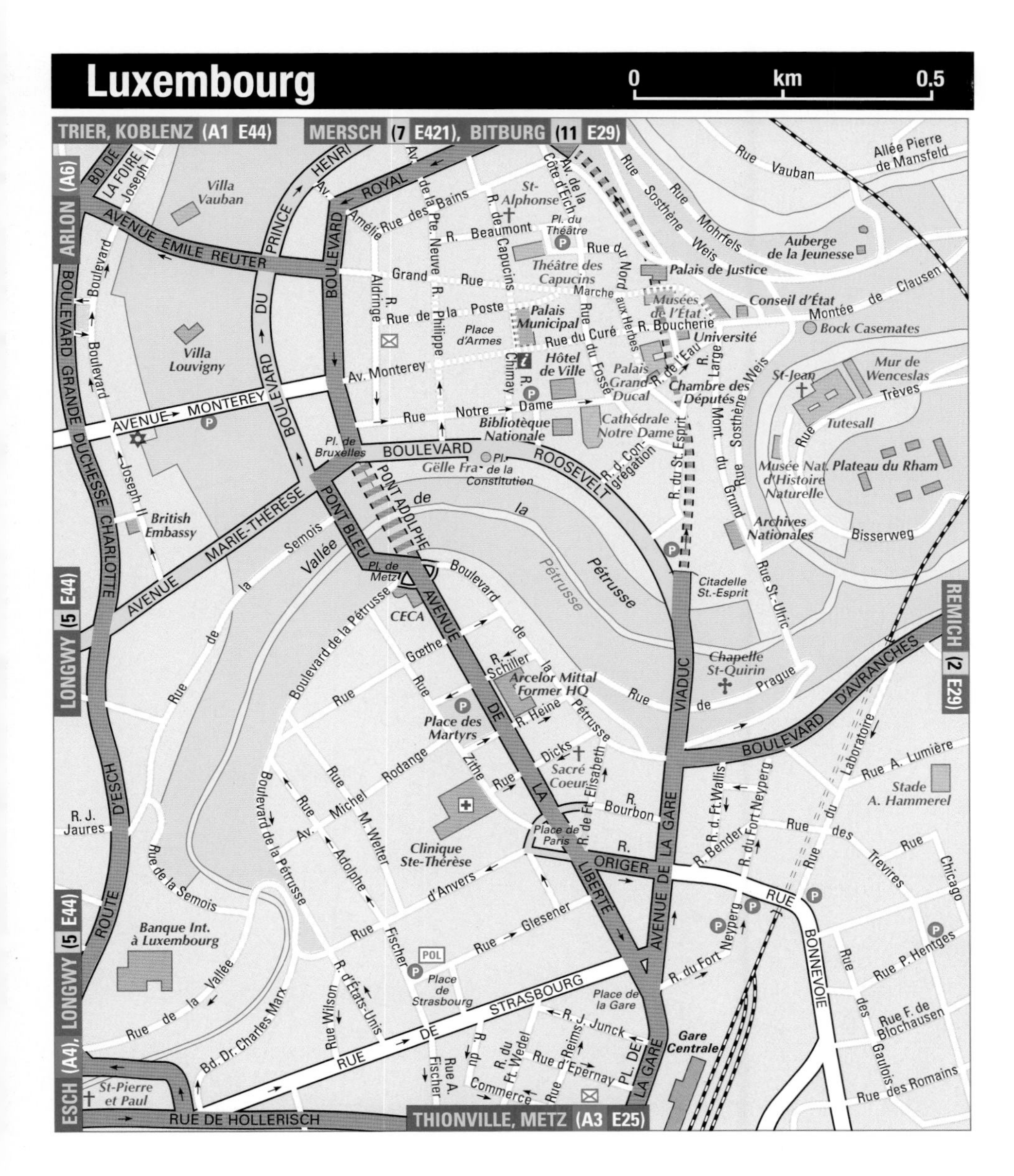
Luxembourg
0 km 0.5
TRIER, KOBLENZ (A1 E44)
MERSCH (7 E421), BITBURG (11 E29)
ARLON (A6)
LONGWY (5 E44)
ESCH (A4), LONGWY (5 E44)
THIONVILLE, METZ (A3 E25)
REMICH (2 E29)
Villa Vauban
AVENUE EMILE REUTER
BOULEVARD ROYAL
Villa Louvigny
BOULEVARD GRANDE DUCHESSE CHARLOTTE
BOULEVARD DU PRINCE HENRI
AVENUE MONTEREY
Rue Vauban
Allée Pierre de Mansfeld
Auberge de la Jeunesse
Palais de Justice
Théâtre des Capucins
Conseil d'État
Bock Casemates
Palais Municipal
Hôtel de Ville
Université
Palais Grand Ducal
Chambre des Députés
Mur de Wenceslas
Cathédrale Notre Dame
Bibliothèque Nationale
Pl. de Bruxelles
Gëlle Fra
Musée Nat. d'Histoire Naturelle
Plateau du Rham
Archives Nationales
British Embassy
AVENUE MARIE-THÉRÈSE
PONT ADOLPHE
BOULEVARD ROOSEVELT
Pétrusse
Citadelle St.-Esprit
Pl. de Metz
CECA
Arcelor Mittal Former HQ
Chapelle St.-Quirin
VIADUC
BOULEVARD D'AVRANCHES
Place des Martyrs
Sacré Cœur
Clinique Ste-Thérèse
AVENUE DE LA LIBERTÉ
AVENUE DE LA GARE
Place de Paris
RUE ORIGER
Banque Int. à Luxembourg
ROUTE D'ESCH
R. J. Jaures
Stade A. Hammerel
Place de Strasbourg
RUE DE STRASBOURG
Place de la Gare
Gare Centrale
RUE BONNEVOIE
RUE DE HOLLERISCH
St-Pierre et Paul

Madrid

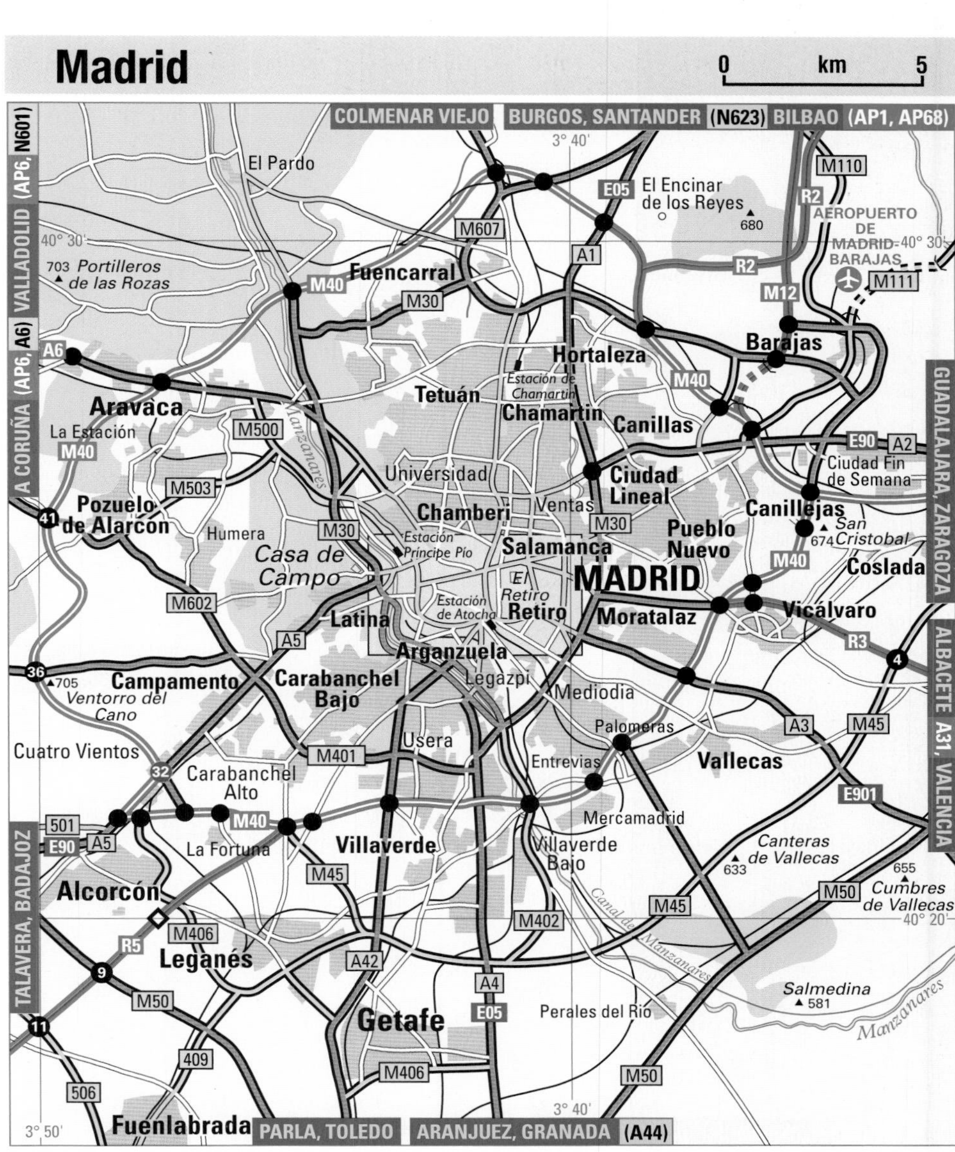
Madrid
0 km 5
COLMENAR VIEJO
BURGOS, SANTANDER (N623)
BILBAO (AP1, AP68)
VALLADOLID (AP6, N601)
A CORUÑA (AP6, A6)
TALAVERA, BADAJOZ
GUADALAJARA, ZARAGOZA
ALBACETE A31, VALENCIA
PARLA, TOLEDO
ARANJUEZ, GRANADA (A44)
El Pardo
El Encinar de los Reyes
AEROPUERTO DE MADRID-BARAJAS
Portilleros de las Rozas
Fuencarral
Hortaleza
Barajas
Aravaca
La Estación
Tetuán
Chamartín
Canillas
Pozuelo de Alarcón
Universidad
Ciudad Lineal
Ciudad Fin de Semana
Canillejas
San Cristobal
Humera
Casa de Campo
Chamberí
Salamanca
Pueblo Nuevo
Coslada
MADRID
Retiro
Moratalaz
Vicálvaro
Latina
Arganzuela
Campamento
Carabanchel Bajo
Legazpi
Ventorro del Cano
Mediodía
Cuatro Vientos
Usera
Palomeras
Vallecas
Carabanchel Alto
Entrevías
Mercamadrid
La Fortuna
Villaverde
Villaverde Bajo
Canteras de Vallecas
Cumbres de Vallecas
Alcorcón
Leganés
Salmedina
Getafe
Perales del Río
Manzanares
Fuenlabrada

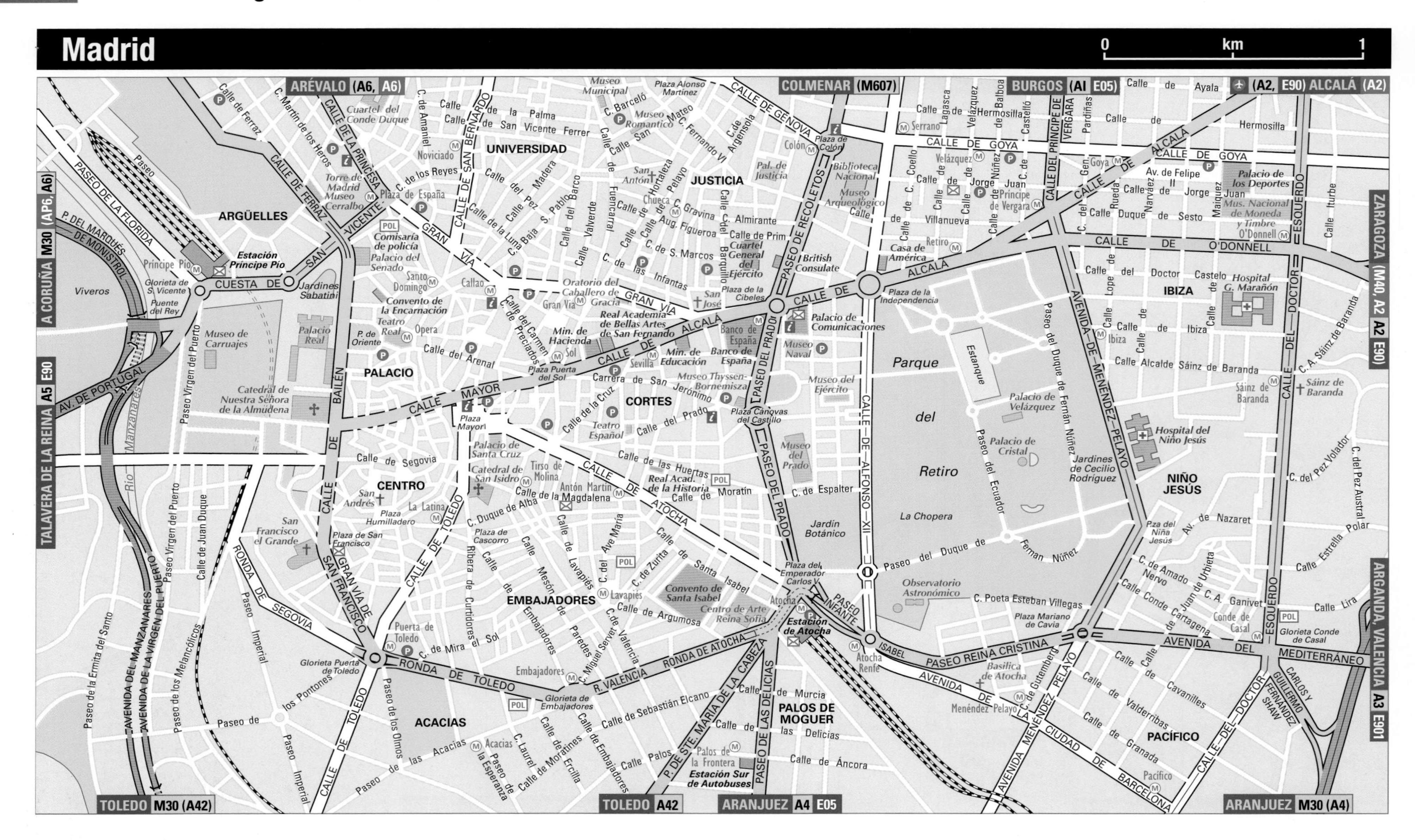

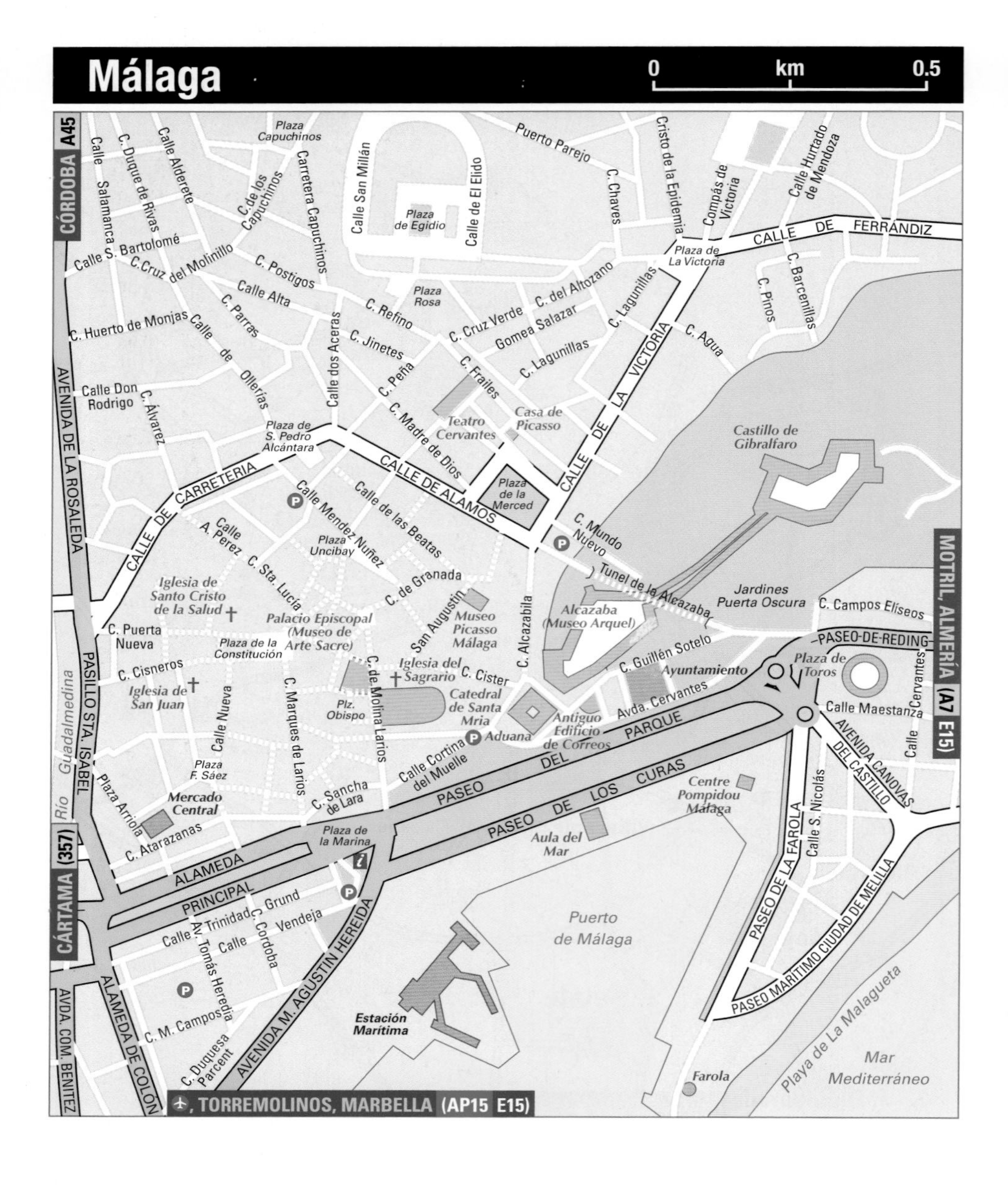

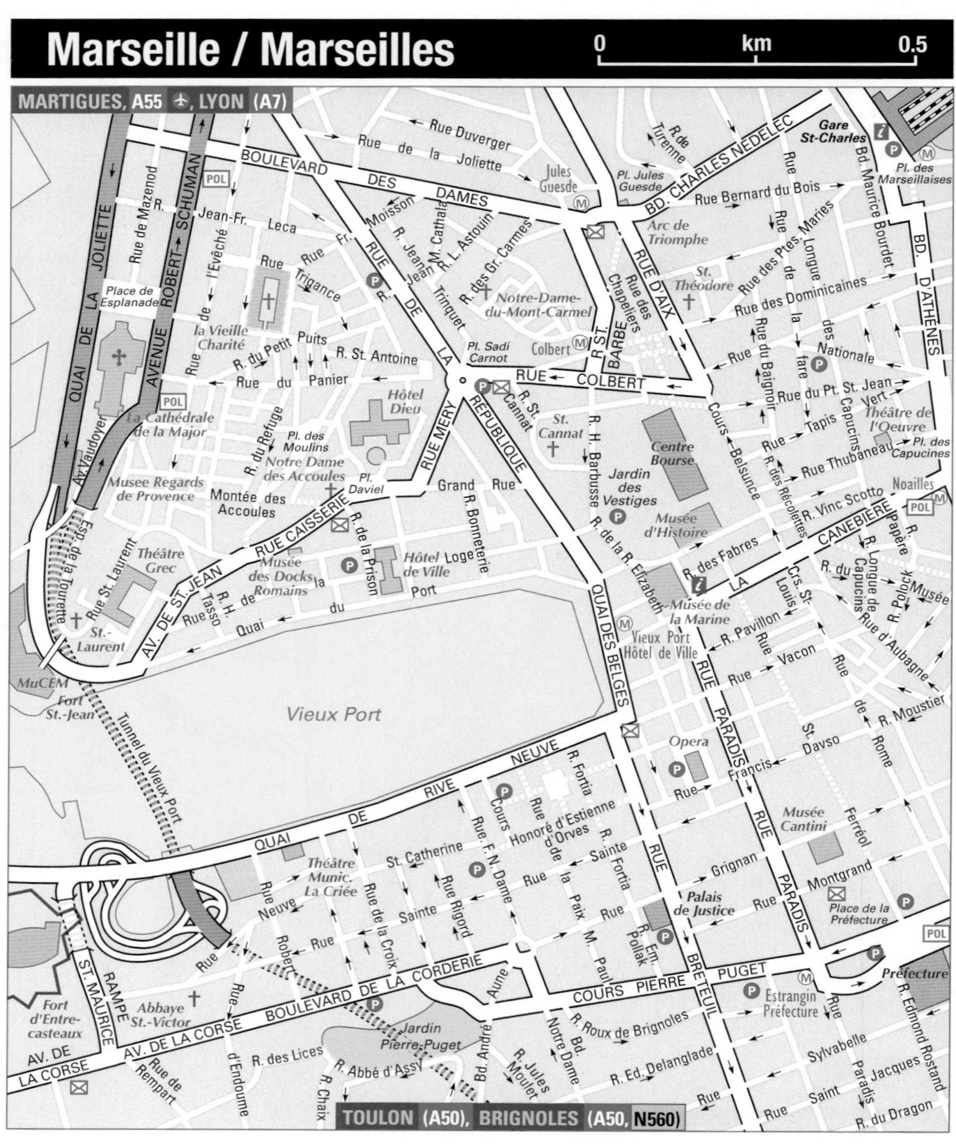

Milano Milan

0 km 5

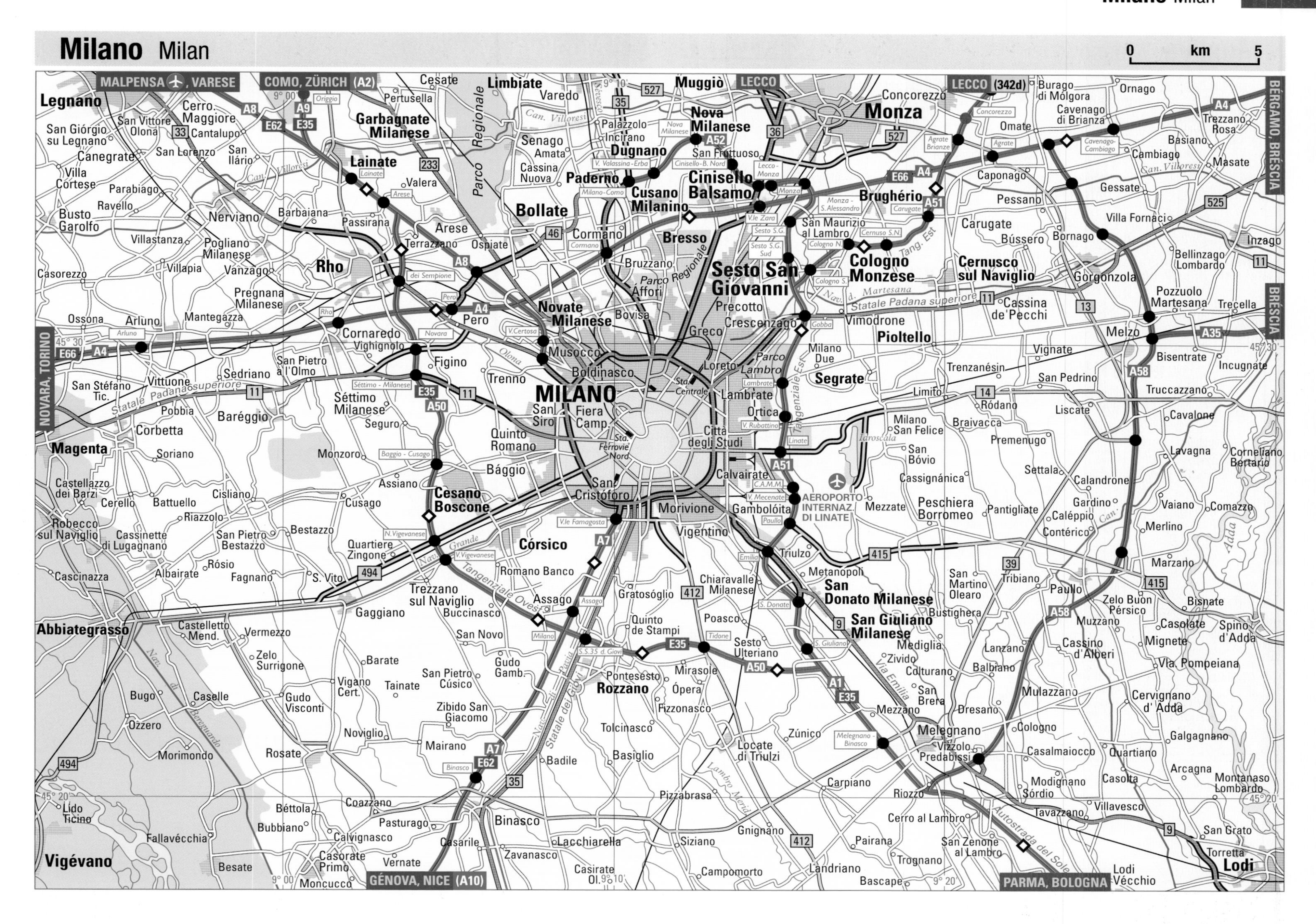
MALPENSA, VARESE
COMO, ZÜRICH (A2)
LECCO
LECCO (342d)
BERGAMO, BRESCIA
BRESCIA
NOVARA, TORINO
GÉNOVA, NICE (A10)
PARMA, BOLOGNA
Legnano
Lainate
Garbagnate Milanese
Limbiate
Muggiò
Nova Milanese
Monza
Concorezzo
Dugnano
Paderno
Cinisello Balsamo
Cusano Milanino
Bollate
Bresso
Rho
Sesto San Giovanni
Cologno Monzese
Brughério
Cernusco sul Naviglio
Novate Milanese
Pero
Pioltello
Segrate
MILANO
Magenta
Cesano Boscone
Córsico
San Donato Milanese
San Giuliano Milanese
Rozzano
Abbiategrasso
Vigévano
Melegnano
Lodi
AEROPORTO INTERNAZ. DI LINATE

Milano Milan

0 km 1

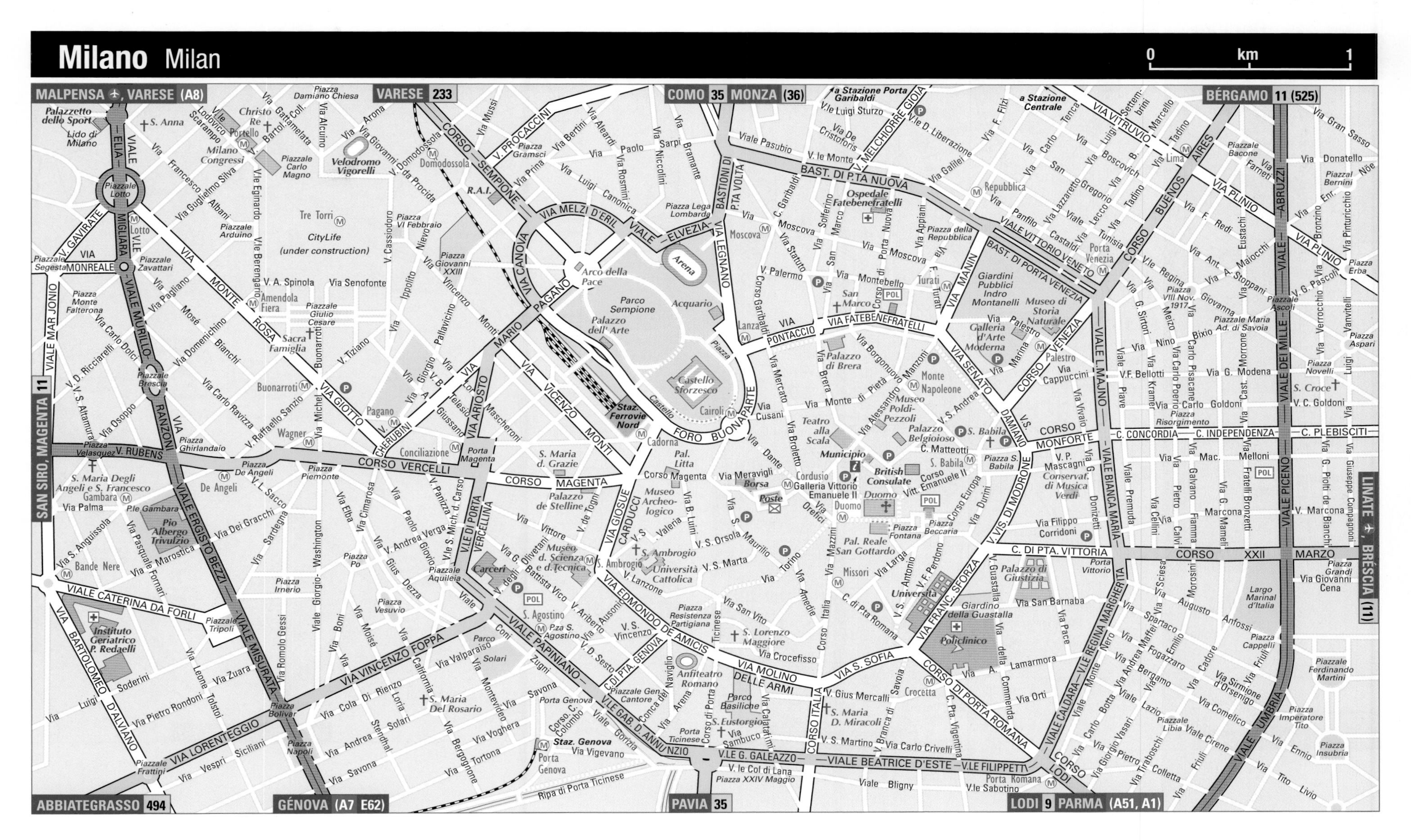
MALPENSA, VARESE (A8)
VARESE 233
COMO 35 MONZA (36)
BÉRGAMO 11 (525)
SAN SIRO, MAGENTA 11
LINATE, BRESCIA (11)
ABBIATEGRASSO 494
GÉNOVA (A7 E62)
PAVIA 35
LODI 9 PARMA (A51, A1)
Castello Sforzesco
Parco Sempione
Arco della Pace
Arena
Staz. Ferrovie Nord
Duomo
Pal. Reale
Università Cattolica
Policlinico
Giardini Pubblici Indro Montanelli
Staz. Genova
Stazione Centrale
Stazione Porta Garibaldi

Moskva Moscow

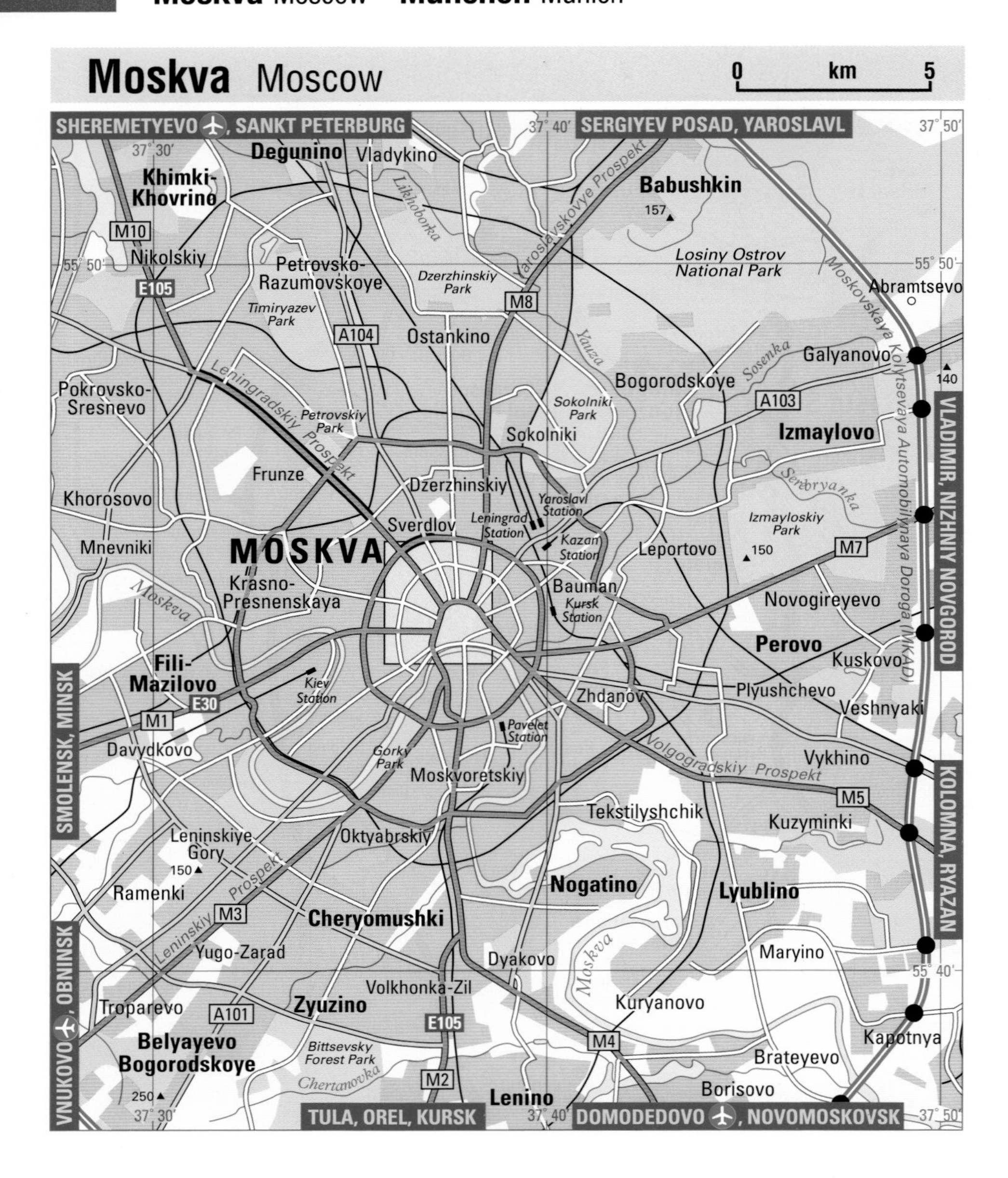

Moskva Moscow

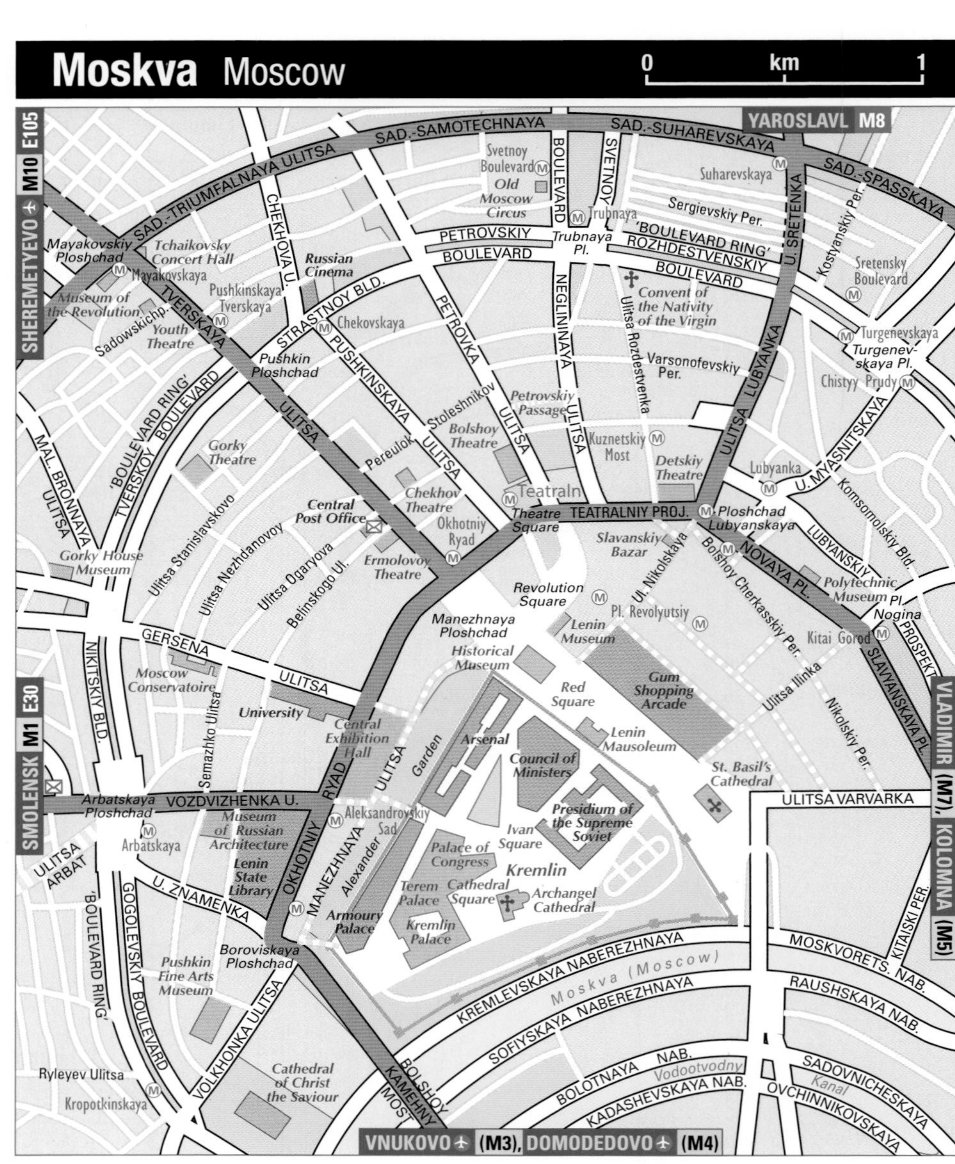

München Munich

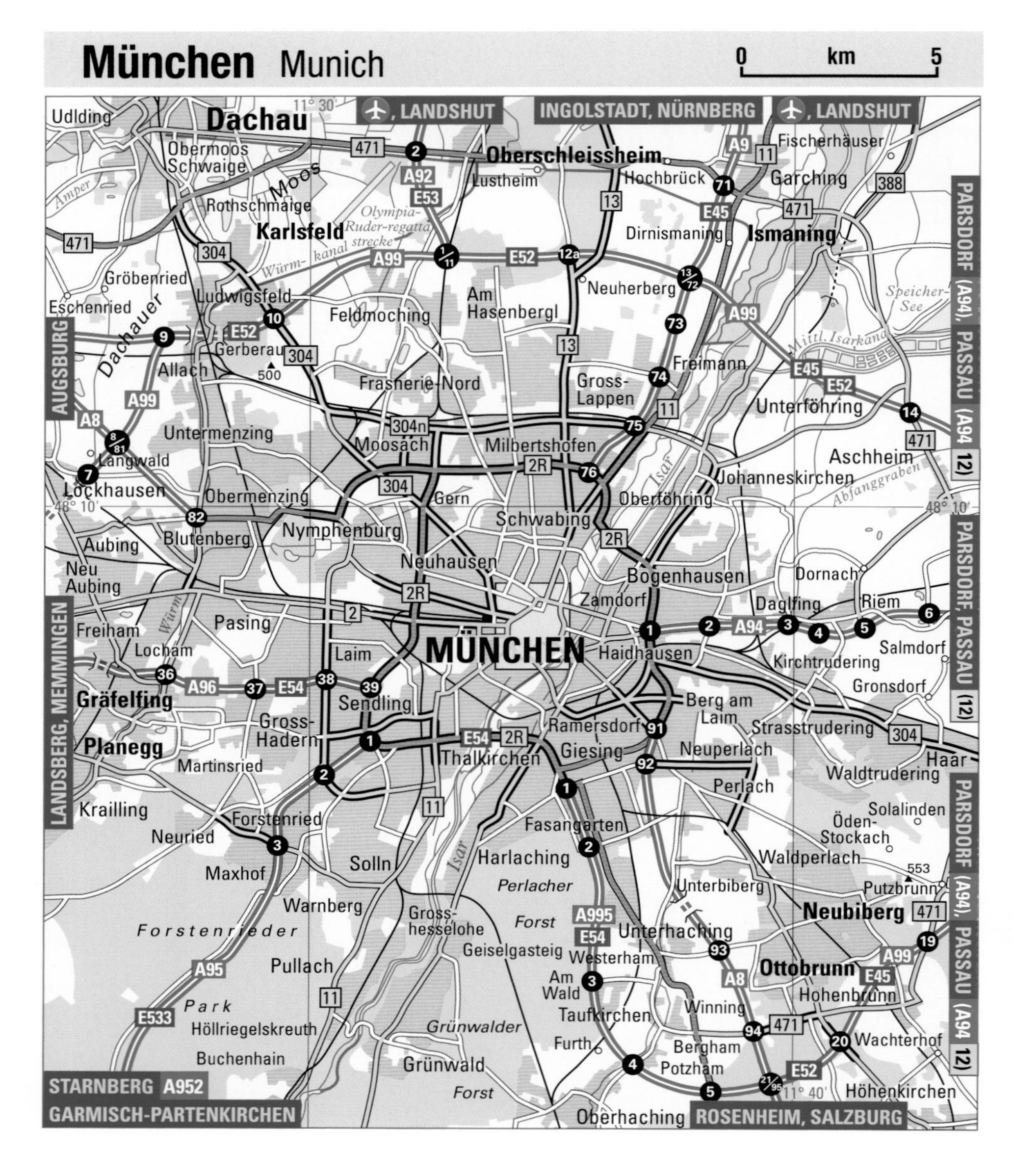

München Munich

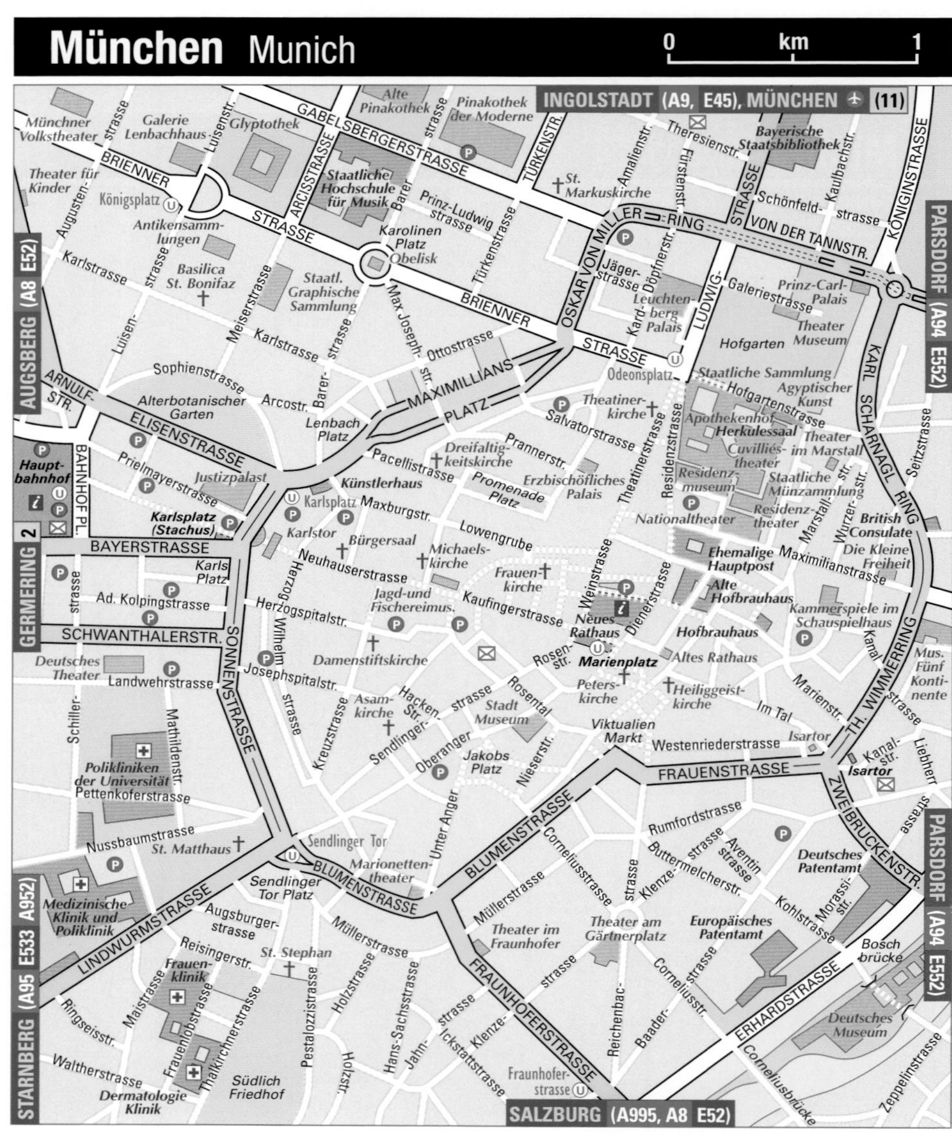

Nápoli Naples

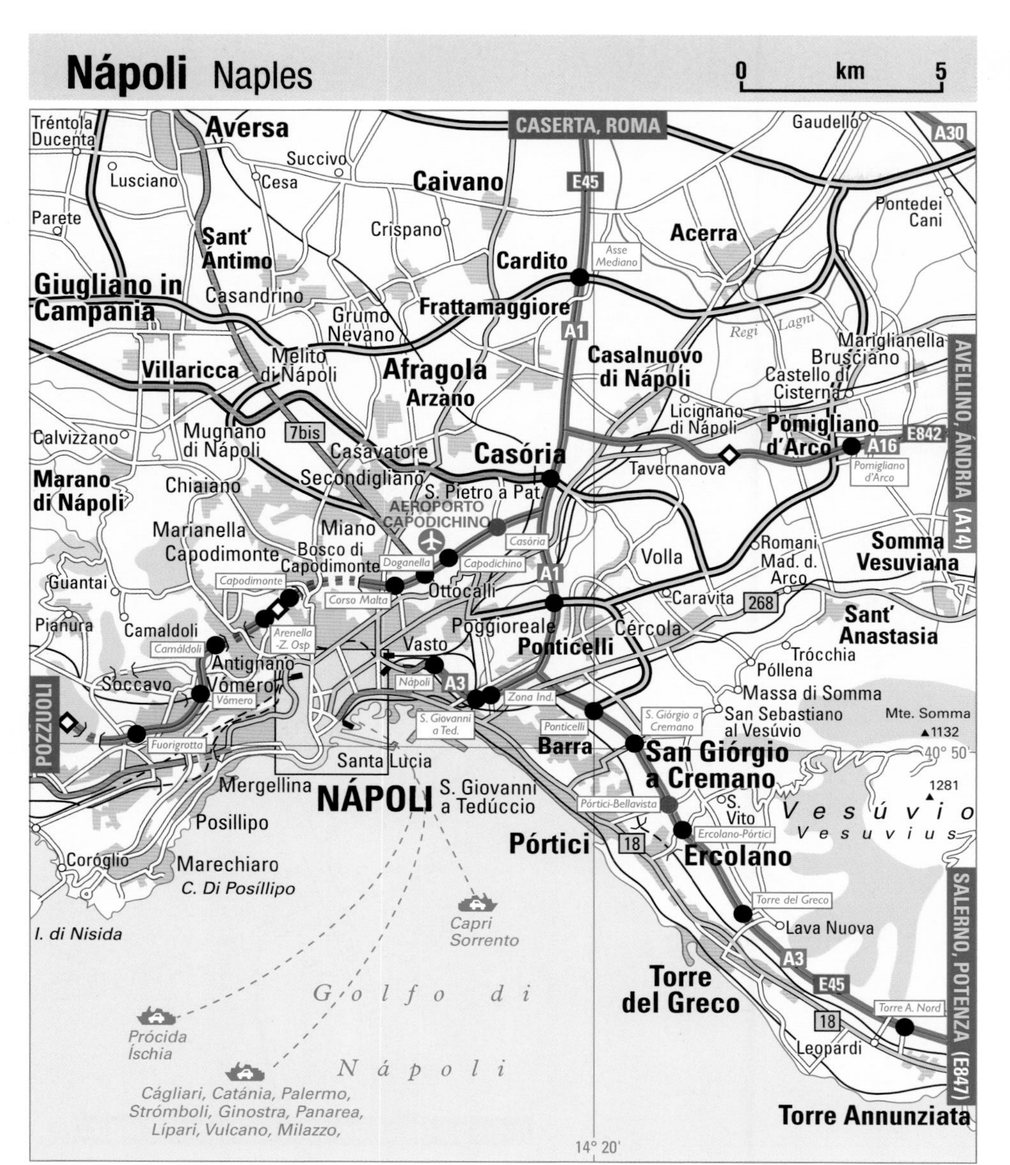
0 km 5
CASERTA, ROMA
AVELLINO, ÁNDRIA (A14)
SALERNO, POTENZA (E847)
POZZUOLI
Tréntola Ducenta
Aversa
Succivo
Cesa
Lusciano
Caivano
Gaudello
A30
E45
Pontedei Cani
Parete
Sant' Antimo
Crispano
Cardito
Acerra
Giugliano in Campania
Casandrino
Grumo Nevano
Frattamaggiore
A1
Villaricca
Melito di Nápoli
Afragola
Arzano
Casalnuovo di Nápoli
Marigliánella
Brusciano
Castello di Cisterna
Calvizzano
Mugnano di Nápoli
7bis
Casavatore
Casória
Licignano di Nápoli
Pomigliano d'Arco
A16
E842
Marano di Nápoli
Chiaiano
Secondigliano
S. Pietro a Patierno
Tavernanova
Marianella
Capodimonte
Miano
AEROPORTO CAPODICHINO
Bosco di Capodimonte
Volla
Romani
Mad. d. Arco
Somma Vesuviana
Guantai
Ottocalli
Caravita
268
Sant' Anastasia
Pianura
Camaldoli
Poggioreale
Ponticelli
Cercola
Trócchia
Póllena
Antignano
Vómero
Vasto
A3
Massa di Somma
Soccavo
San Sebastiano al Vesúvio
Mte. Somma 1132
Santa Lucia
Barra
San Giórgio a Cremano
Mergellina
NÁPOLI
S. Giovanni a Tedúccio
1281
Posillipo
S. Vito
Vesúvio
Vesuvius
Pórtici
18
Ercolano
Coroglio
Marechiaro
C. Di Posíllipo
I. di Nisida
Capri Sorrento
Lava Nuova
Golfo di Nápoli
Torre del Greco
E45
Prócida Ischia
Leopardi
Cágliari, Catánia, Palermo, Strómboli, Ginostra, Panarea, Lípari, Vulcano, Milazzo,
Torre Annunziata
14° 20'
40° 50'

Nápoli Naples

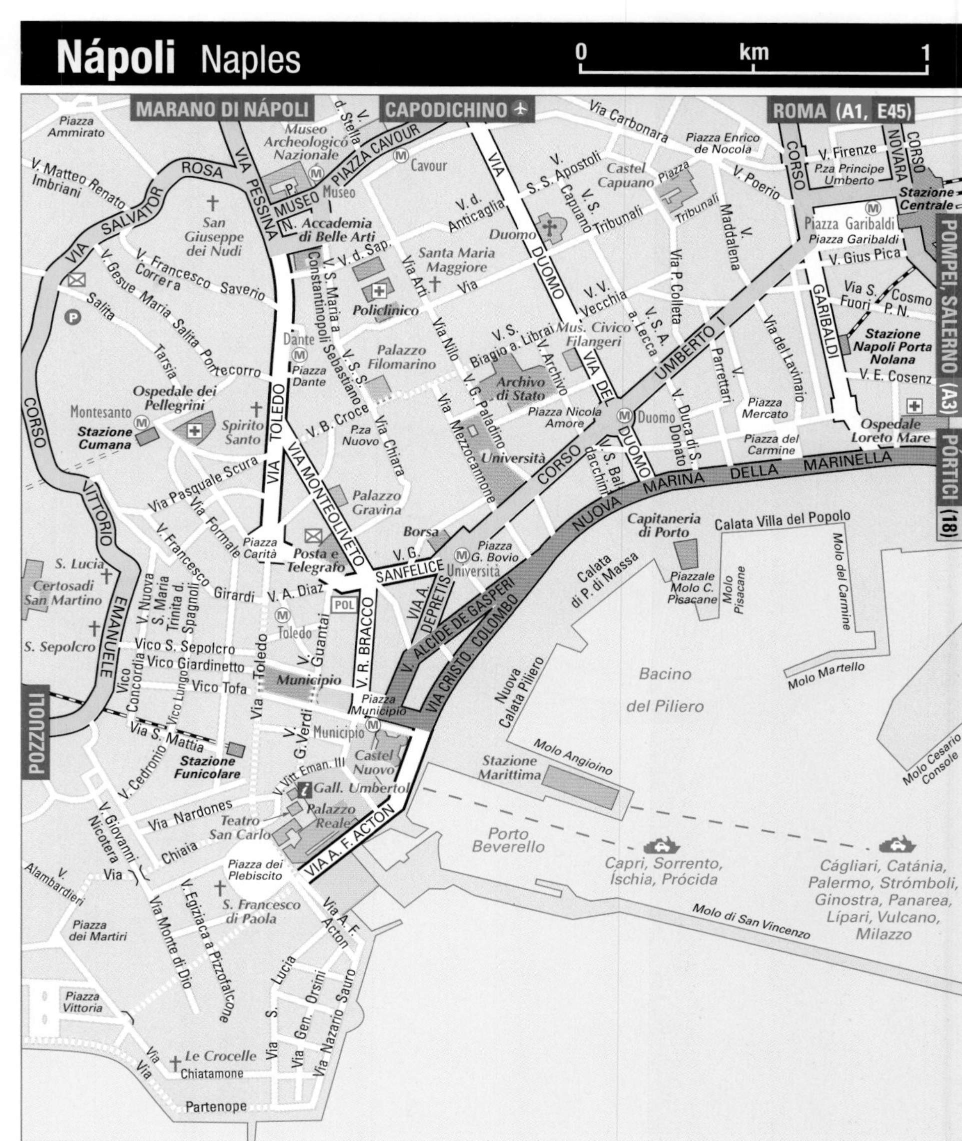
0 km 1
MARANO DI NÁPOLI
CAPODICHINO
ROMA (A1, E45)
POMPEI, SALERNO (A3)
PÓRTICI (18)
POZZUOLI
Piazza Ammirato
Museo Archeologico Nazionale
Via Carbonara
Piazza Enrico de Nocola
V. Firenze
Pza Principe Umberto
Stazione Centrale
Piazza Garibaldi
V. Gius Pica
Cavour
San Giuseppe dei Nudi
N. Accademia di Belle Arti
Castel Capuano
Tribunali
Duomo
Santa Maria Maggiore
Policlinico
Palazzo Filomarino
Mus. Civico Filangeri
Archivio di Stato
Piazza Nicola Amore
Piazza Mercato
Piazza del Carmine
Ospedale Loreto Mare
Stazione Napoli Porta Nolana
Ospedale dei Pellegrini
Montesanto
Stazione Cumana
Spirito Santo
Pza Nuovo
Dante
Piazza Dante
Università
Palazzo Gravina
Borsa
Capitaneria di Porto
Calata Villa del Popolo
Molo del Carmine
S. Lucia
Certosa di San Martino
S. Sepolcro
Piazza Carità
Posta e Telegrafo
G. Bovio Università
Piazzale Molo C. Pisacane
Bacino del Piliero
Molo Martello
Municipio
Piazza Municipio
Castel Nuovo
Stazione Funicolare
Stazione Marittima
Molo Angioino
Molo Cesario Console
Porto Beverello
Teatro San Carlo
Palazzo Reale
Gall. Umberto I
Piazza del Plebiscito
S. Francesco di Paola
Capri, Sorrento, Ischia, Prócida
Cágliari, Catánia, Palermo, Strómboli, Ginostra, Panarea, Lipari, Vulcano, Milazzo
Molo di San Vincenzo
Piazza dei Martiri
Piazza Vittoria
Le Crocelle Chiatamone
Partenope
VIA TOLEDO
VIA MONTEOLIVETO
VIA NUOVA MARINA
CORSO UMBERTO I
CORSO GARIBALDI
CORSO VITTORIO EMANUELE
VIA DUOMO
VIA A. DEPRETIS
VIA CRISTO COLOMBO
VIA A. F. ACTON
Chiaia

Oslo

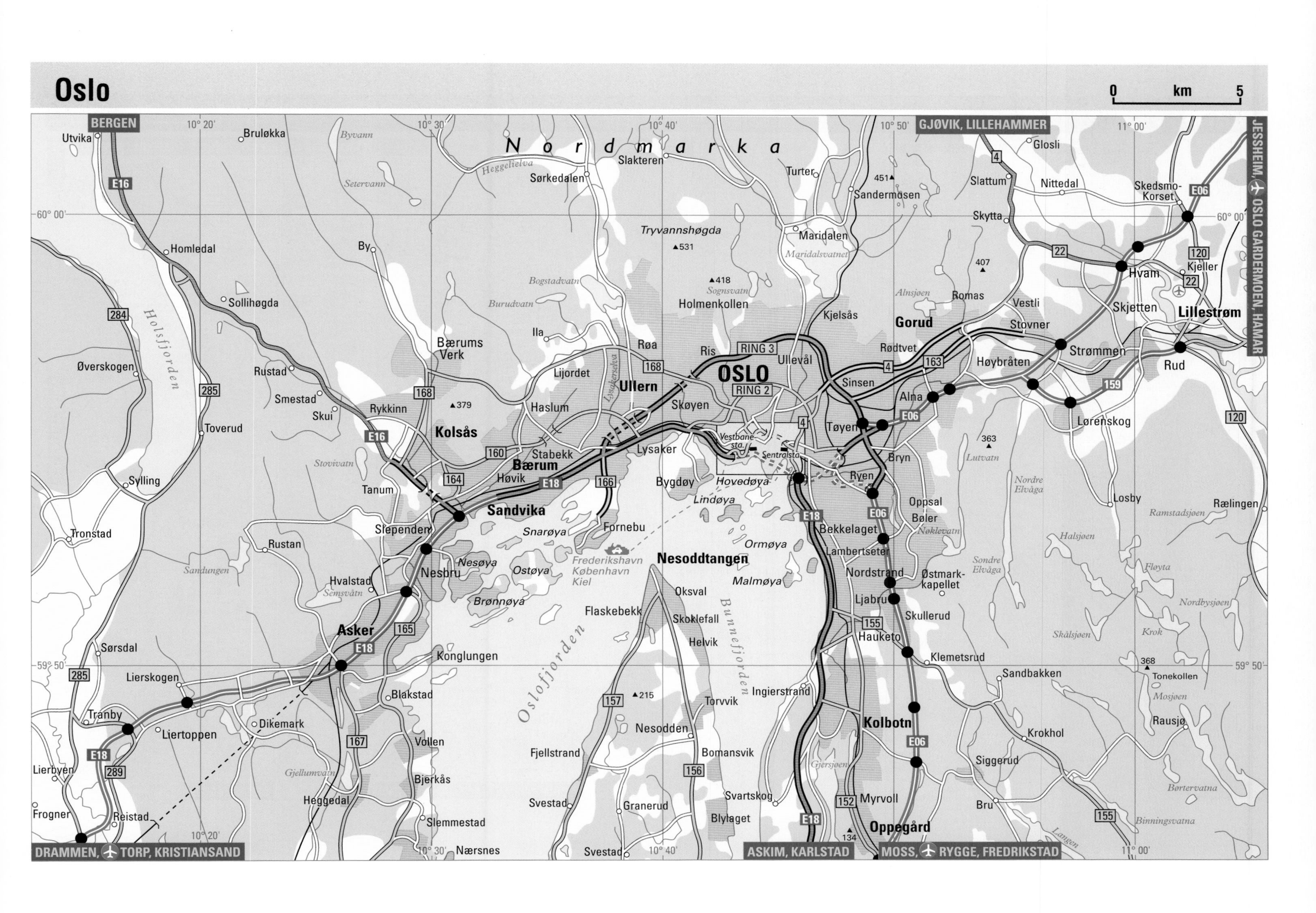
0 km 5
BERGEN
GJØVIK, LILLEHAMMER
JESSHEIM, OSLO GARDERMOEN, HAMAR
DRAMMEN, TORP, KRISTIANSAND
ASKIM, KARLSTAD
MOSS, RYGGE, FREDRIKSTAD
10° 20'
10° 30'
10° 40'
10° 50'
11° 00'
60° 00'
59° 50'
Nordmarka
Utvika
Bruløkka
Bywann
Heggelielva
Sørkedalen
Slakteren
Turter
451
Sandermosen
Glosli
Slattum
Nittedal
Skedsmo-Korset
Skytta
E16
E06
Setervann
Tryvannshøgda
531
Maridalen
Maridalsvatnet
Homledal
By
418
Sognsvatn
407
Hvam
120
Kjeller
22
Bogstadvatn
Alnsjøen
Romas
Vestli
Skjetten
Lillestrøm
Sollihøgda
Burudvann
Holmenkollen
Kjelsås
Gorud
Stovner
284
Holsfjorden
Ila
Bærums Verk
Røa
RING 3
Ris
Rødtvet
Strømmen
Rud
Øverskogen
Lijordet
Ullevål
OSLO
RING 2
Sinsen
Høybråten
Rustad
285
168
Ullern
159
Smestad
Skui
Rykkinn
379
Haslum
Skøyen
Alna
Tøyen
Lørenskog
Toverud
Kolsås
Vestbane-stasj.
Sentralstasjon
363
120
E18
Stabekk
Lysaker
Bryn
Lutvann
Stovivatn
Bærum
160
Høvik
164
166
Bygdøy
Hovedøya
Ryen
Nordre Elvåga
Losby
Sylling
Tanum
Sandvika
Lindøya
Oppsal
Bøler
Rælingen
Ramstadsjøen
Nøklevatn
Tronstad
Slependen
Snarøya
Fornebu
Bekkelaget
Halsjøen
Rustan
Ormøya
Nesøya
Østøya
Frederikshavn København Kiel
Nesoddtangen
Lambertseter
Sondre Elvåga
Fløyta
Sandungen
Hvalstad
Semsvatn
Nesbru
Malmøya
Nordstrand
Østmark-kapellet
Brønnøya
Oksval
Flaskebekk
Ljabru
Skullerud
Nordbysjøen
Asker
165
Skoklefall
Bunnefjorden
155
Hauketo
Skålsjøen
Krok
Sørsdal
Helvik
Konglungen
Klemetsrud
368
Tonekollen
285
Lierskogen
Sandbakken
Blakstad
157
215
Ingierstrand
Mosjøen
Oslofjorden
Torvvik
Tranby
Dikemark
Kolbotn
Rausjø
Liertoppen
Nesodden
Krokhol
167
Vollen
Fjellstrand
Bomansvik
Siggerud
Lierbyen
289
Gjellumvann
Bjerkås
156
Gjersjøen
Børtervatna
Frogner
Heggedal
Svartskog
Svestad
Granerud
Myrvoll
152
Bru
155
Reistad
Slemmestad
Blylaget
Oppegård
134
Binningsvatna
Nærsnes
Svestad

Oslo

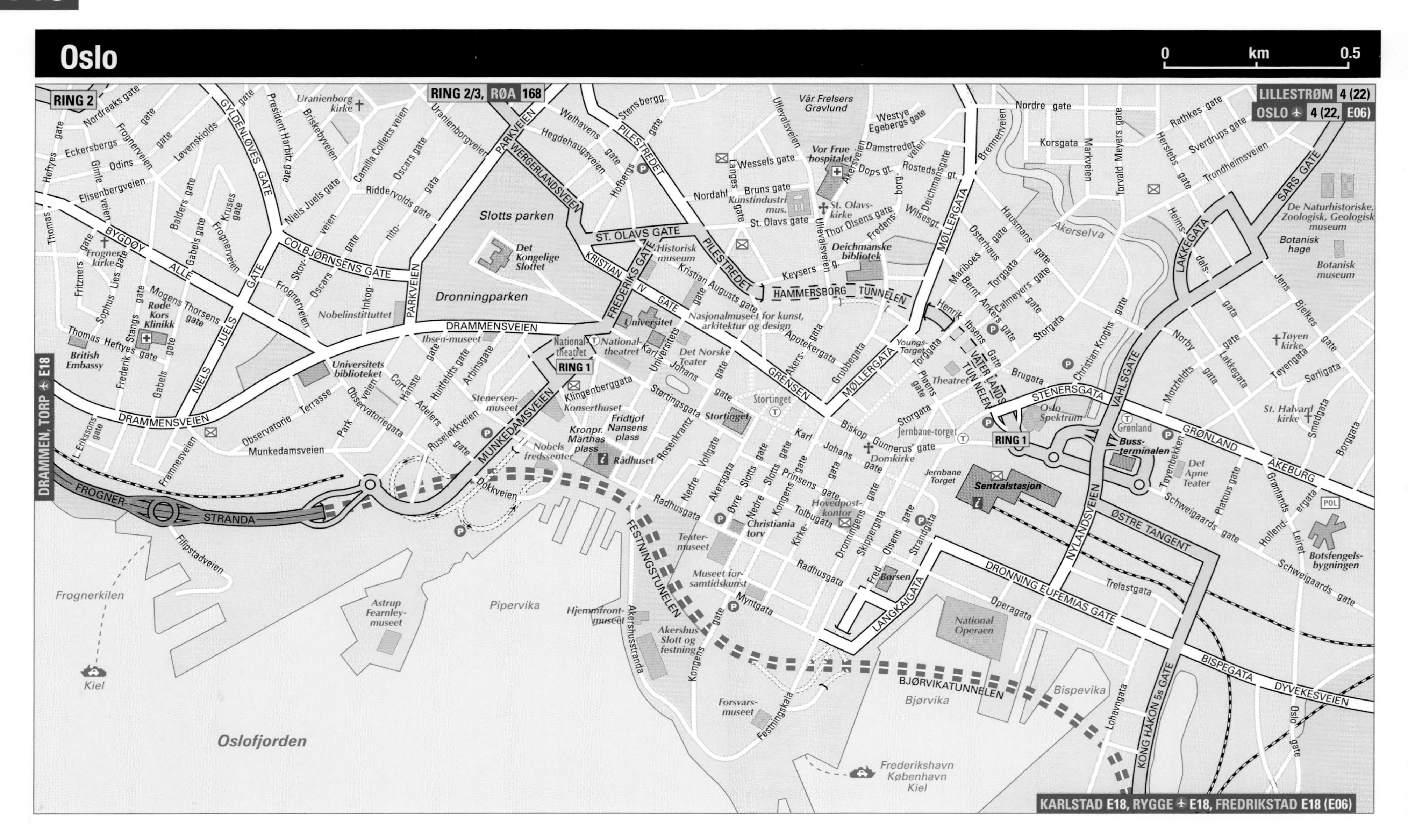
0 km 0.5
RING 2
RING 2/3, RØA 168
LILLESTRØM 4 (22)
OSLO 4 (22, E06)
DRAMMEN, TORP E18
KARLSTAD E18, RYGGE E18, FREDRIKSTAD E18 (E06)
Slotts parken
Det Kongelige Slottet
Dronningparken
DRAMMENSVEIEN
BYGDØY ALLÉ
PARKVEIEN
ST. OLAVS GATE
PILESTREDET
HAMMERSBORG TUNNELEN
RING 1
GRENSEN
MØLLERGATA
STENERSGATA
GRØNLAND
Sentralstasjon
Oslo Spektrum
Buss-terminalen
MUNKEDAMSVEIEN
FROGNER
STRANDA
FESTNINGSTUNELEN
Rådhuset
Christiania torv
Akershus Slott og festning
Astrup Fearnley-museet
Pipervika
Frognerkilen
Oslofjorden
Kiel
Bjørvika
BJØRVIKATUNNELEN
National Operaen
DRONNING EUFEMIAS GATE
BISPEGATA
DYVEKESVEIEN
KONG HAKON 5s GATE
NYLANDSVEIEN
Frederikshavn København Kiel
Akerselva
Botanisk hage
Universitetet
Nationaltheatret
Stortinget
Domkirke
Deichmanske bibliotek
Vår Frelsers Gravlund
Botsfengels-bygningen
Forsvars-museet
Nobelinstituttet
British Embassy
Frogner kirke
Røde Kors Klinikk
Tøyen kirke
St. Halvard kirke

Paris

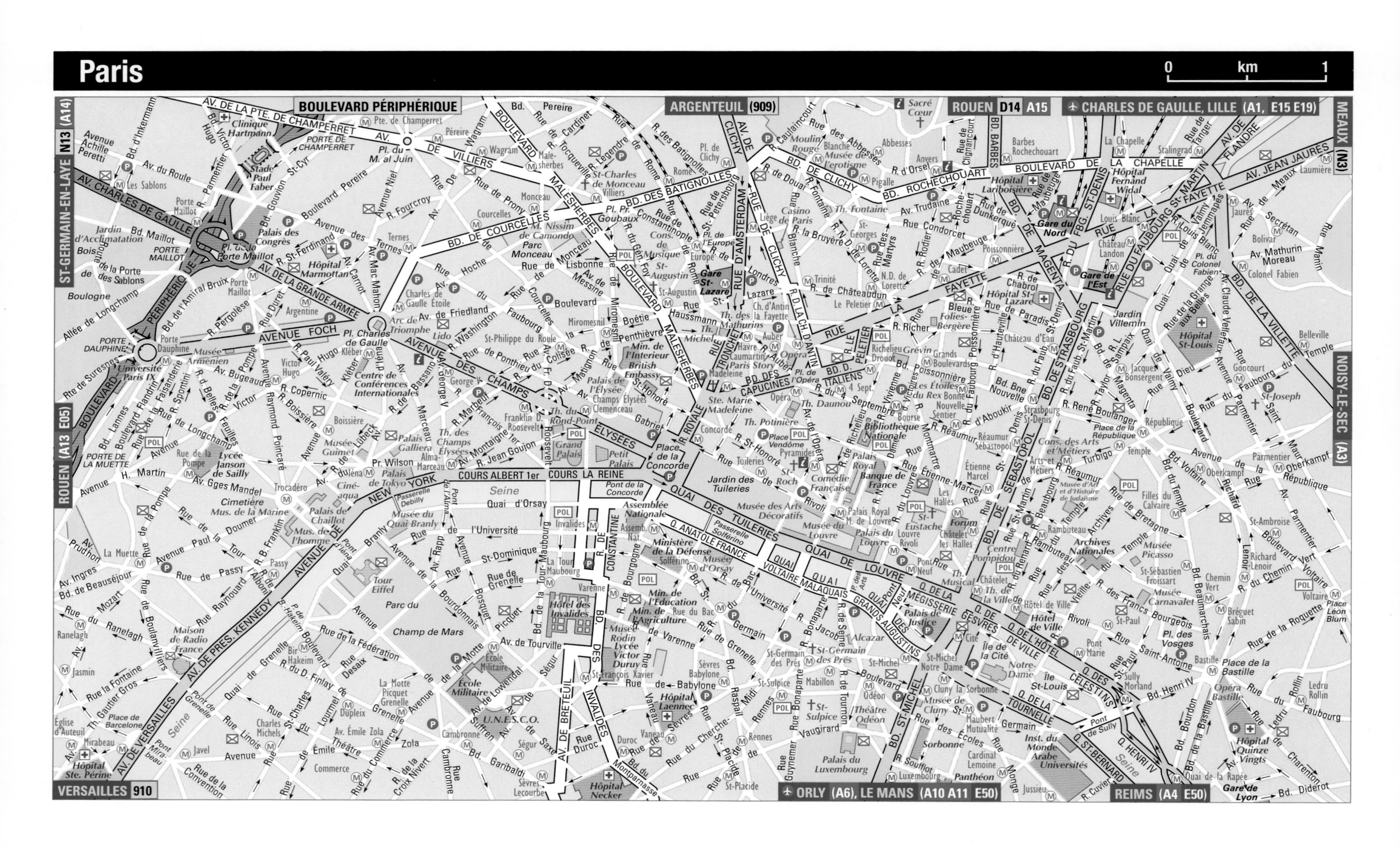
0 km 1
BOULEVARD PÉRIPHÉRIQUE
ARGENTEUIL (909)
ROUEN D14 A15
CHARLES DE GAULLE, LILLE (A1, E15 E19)
MEAUX (N3)
ST-GERMAIN-EN-LAYE N13 (A14)
ROUEN (A13 E05)
NOISY-LE-SEC (A3)
VERSAILLES 910
ORLY (A6), LE MANS (A10 A11 E50)
REIMS (A4 E50)
AV. DE LA GRANDE ARMÉE
AVENUE FOCH
Pl. Charles de Gaulle
Arc de Triomphe
AVENUE DES CHAMPS ELYSÉES
Place de la Concorde
BD. DE COURCELLES
BD. DES BATIGNOLLES
BD. DE CLICHY
BD. ROCHECHOUART
BOULEVARD DE LA CHAPELLE
Gare du Nord
Gare de l'Est
Gare St-Lazare
Gare de Lyon
Sacré Cœur
Parc Monceau
Opéra
QUAI DES TUILERIES
QUAI DE LOUVRE
Seine
Tour Eiffel
Parc du Champ de Mars
Hôtel des Invalides
Musée d'Orsay
Palais de Chaillot
Trocadéro
Île de la Cité
Notre-Dame
Hôtel de Ville
Place de la Bastille
Palais du Luxembourg
Panthéon
Sorbonne
Centre Pompidou
Forum des Halles
Place de la République
Hôpital St-Louis
U.N.E.S.C.O.
École Militaire
AV. DE VERSAILLES
AV. DE PRES. KENNEDY
AV. DE NEW YORK
BD. ST-MICHEL
BD. DE SÉBASTOPOL
BD. DE MAGENTA
BD. DE STRASBOURG
BD. DE LA VILLETTE
AV. JEAN JAURÈS
Porte Maillot
Porte Dauphine
Bois de Boulogne

Paris

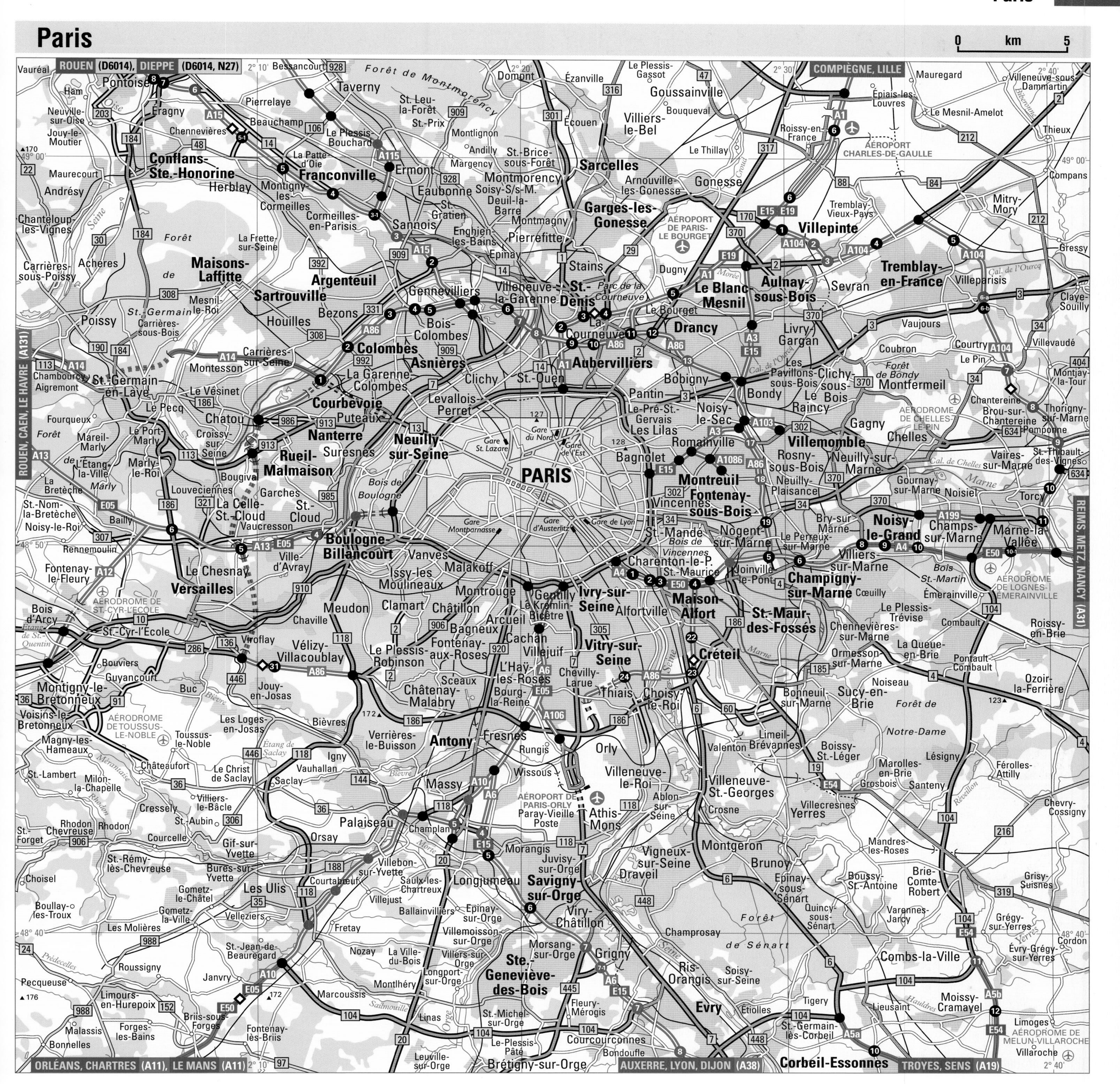

0 km 5
ROUEN (D6014), DIEPPE (D6014, N27)
COMPIÈGNE, LILLE
ROUEN, CAEN, LE HAVRE (A131)
REIMS, METZ, NANCY (A31)
ORLÉANS, CHARTRES (A11), LE MANS (A11)
AUXERRE, LYON, DIJON (A38)
TROYES, SENS (A19)
PARIS
Gare St. Lazare
Gare du Nord
Gare de l'Est
Gare Montparnasse
Gare d'Austerlitz
Gare de Lyon
Bois de Boulogne
Bois de Vincennes
AÉROPORT CHARLES-DE-GAULLE
AÉROPORT DE PARIS-LE BOURGET
AÉROPORT DE PARIS-ORLY
AÉRODROME DE ST.-CYR-L'ÉCOLE
AÉRODROME DE TOUSSUS-LE-NOBLE
AÉRODROME DE CHELLES-LE-PIN
AÉRODROME DE LOGNES-ÉMERAINVILLE
AÉRODROME DE MELUN-VILLAROCHE
Forêt de Montmorency
Forêt de St.-Germain
Forêt de Notre-Dame
Forêt de Sénart
Pontoise
Taverny
Conflans-Ste.-Honorine
Franconville
Ermont
Eaubonne
Sannois
Montmorency
Sarcelles
Garges-lès-Gonesse
Goussainville
Villiers-le-Bel
Gonesse
Villepinte
Tremblay-en-France
Aulnay-sous-Bois
Le Blanc-Mesnil
Drancy
Sevran
Maisons-Laffitte
Sartrouville
Argenteuil
Houilles
Bezons
Gennevilliers
Villeneuve-la-Garenne
St.-Denis
La Courneuve
Aubervilliers
Colombes
Asnières
Bois-Colombes
La Garenne-Colombes
Courbevoie
Puteaux
Nanterre
Neuilly-sur-Seine
Levallois-Perret
Clichy
St.-Ouen
St.-Germain-en-Laye
Le Vésinet
Chatou
Rueil-Malmaison
Suresnes
Bobigny
Pantin
Bondy
Noisy-le-Sec
Les Lilas
Bagnolet
Romainville
Montreuil
Villemomble
Rosny-sous-Bois
Fontenay-sous-Bois
Vincennes
St.-Mandé
Nogent-sur-Marne
Neuilly-Plaisance
Noisy-le-Grand
Champs-sur-Marne
Marne-la-Vallée
Chelles
Gagny
Montfermeil
Clichy-sous-Bois
Livry-Gargan
Champigny-sur-Marne
Joinville-le-Pont
Charenton-le-P.
St.-Maurice
Maisons-Alfort
Alfortville
St.-Maur-des-Fossés
Créteil
Ivry-sur-Seine
Vitry-sur-Seine
Villejuif
Gentilly
Le Kremlin-Bicêtre
Arcueil
Cachan
Montrouge
Malakoff
Vanves
Issy-les-Moulineaux
Boulogne-Billancourt
St.-Cloud
Sèvres
Meudon
Clamart
Châtillon
Bagneux
Fontenay-aux-Roses
Le Plessis-Robinson
Châtenay-Malabry
Sceaux
L'Haÿ-les-Roses
Bourg-la-Reine
Antony
Fresnes
Rungis
Thiais
Choisy-le-Roi
Orly
Villeneuve-le-Roi
Athis-Mons
Versailles
Le Chesnay
Vélizy-Villacoublay
Viroflay
Chaville
Montigny-le-Bretonneux
Guyancourt
Jouy-en-Josas
Bièvres
Massy
Palaiseau
Orsay
Les Ulis
Gif-sur-Yvette
Longjumeau
Savigny-sur-Orge
Juvisy-sur-Orge
Draveil
Vigneux-sur-Seine
Montgeron
Villeneuve-St.-Georges
Yerres
Brunoy
Boissy-St.-Léger
Sucy-en-Brie
Combs-la-Ville
Ste.-Geneviève-des-Bois
Grigny
Ris-Orangis
Evry
Corbeil-Essonnes
Brétigny-sur-Orge
Moissy-Cramayel
Lieusaint
Torcy
Noisiel
Lognes
Pontault-Combault
Ozoir-la-Ferrière
Roissy-en-Brie
Poissy
Carrières-sous-Poissy
Achères
Chambourcy
Marly-le-Roi
Bougival
La Celle-St.-Cloud
Vaucresson
Garches
St.-Cyr-l'École
Bois-d'Arcy
Roissy-en-France

Praha Prague

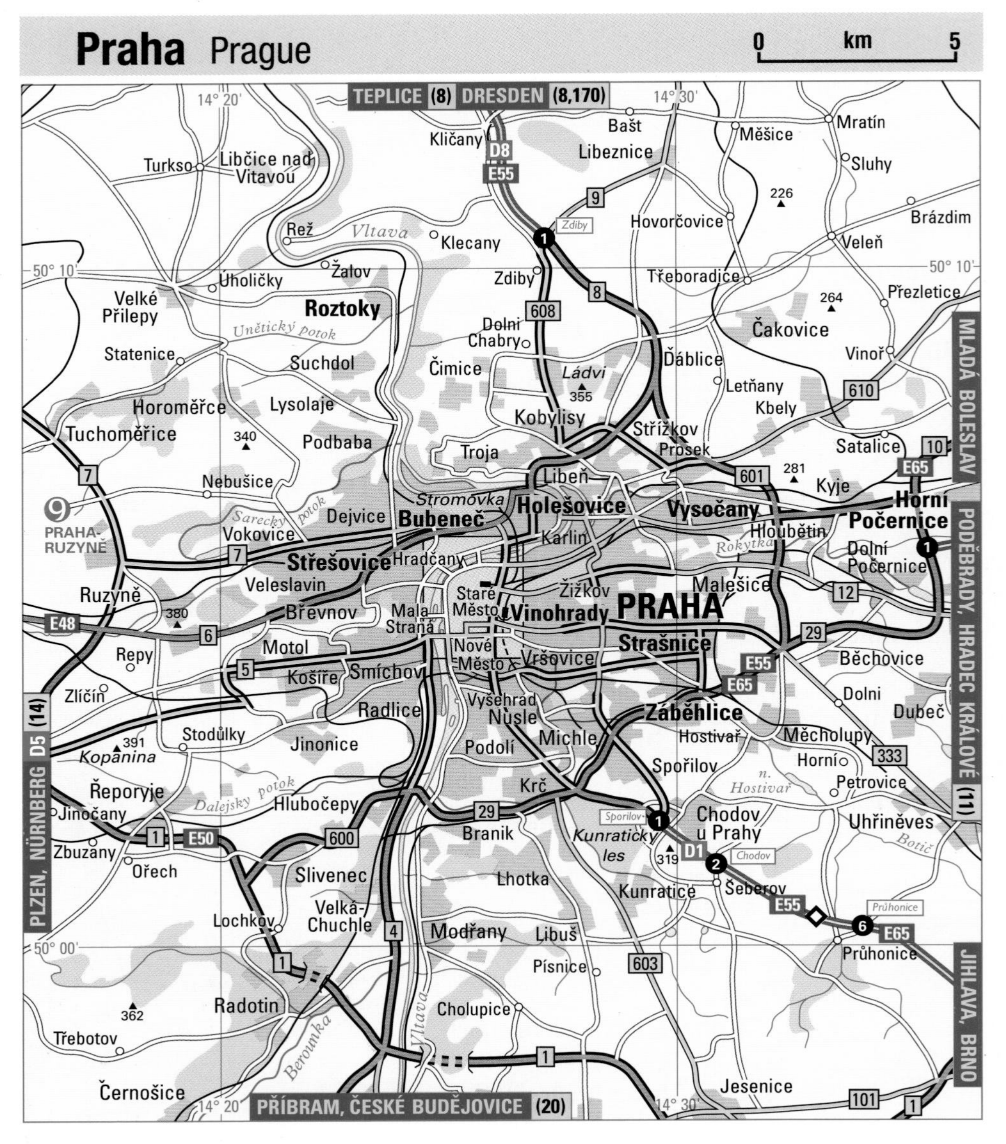

Praha Prague

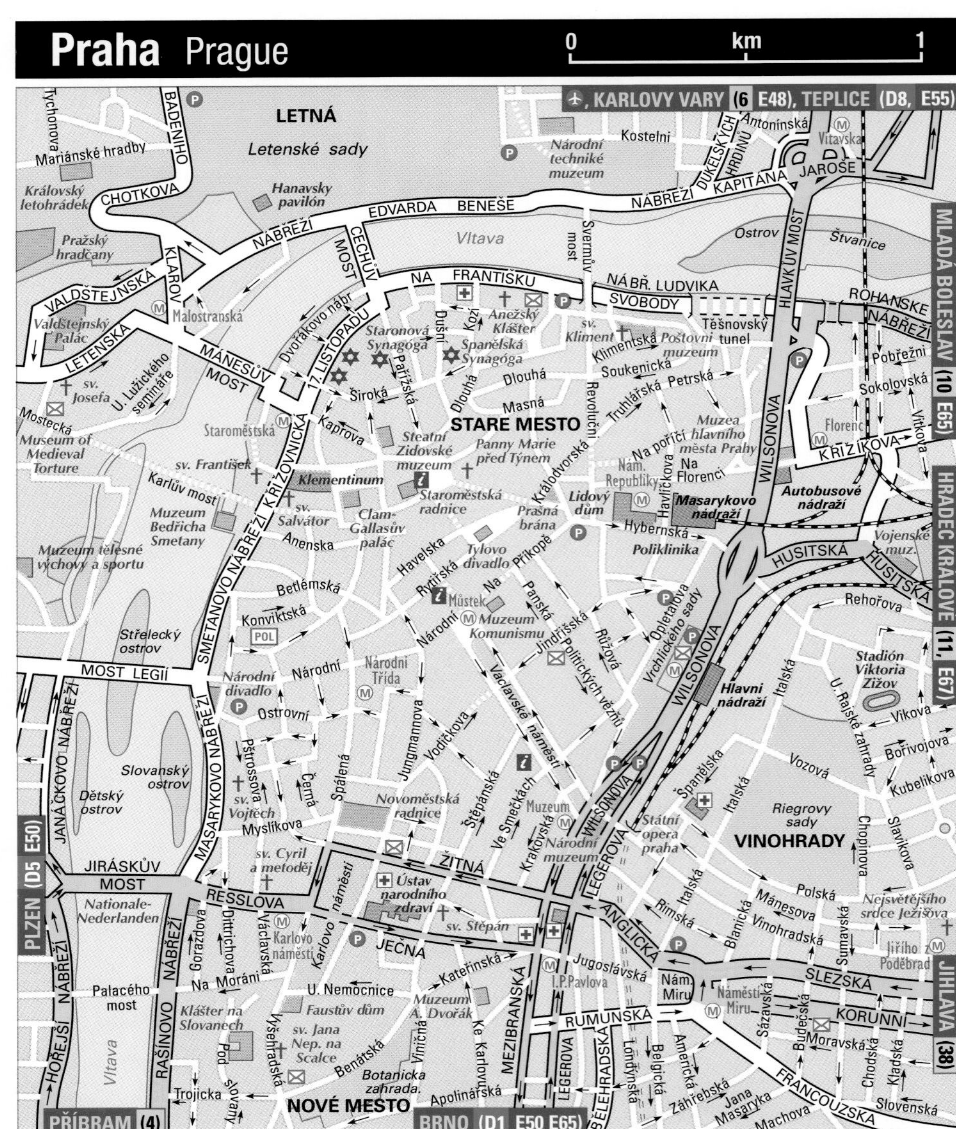

Rotterdam

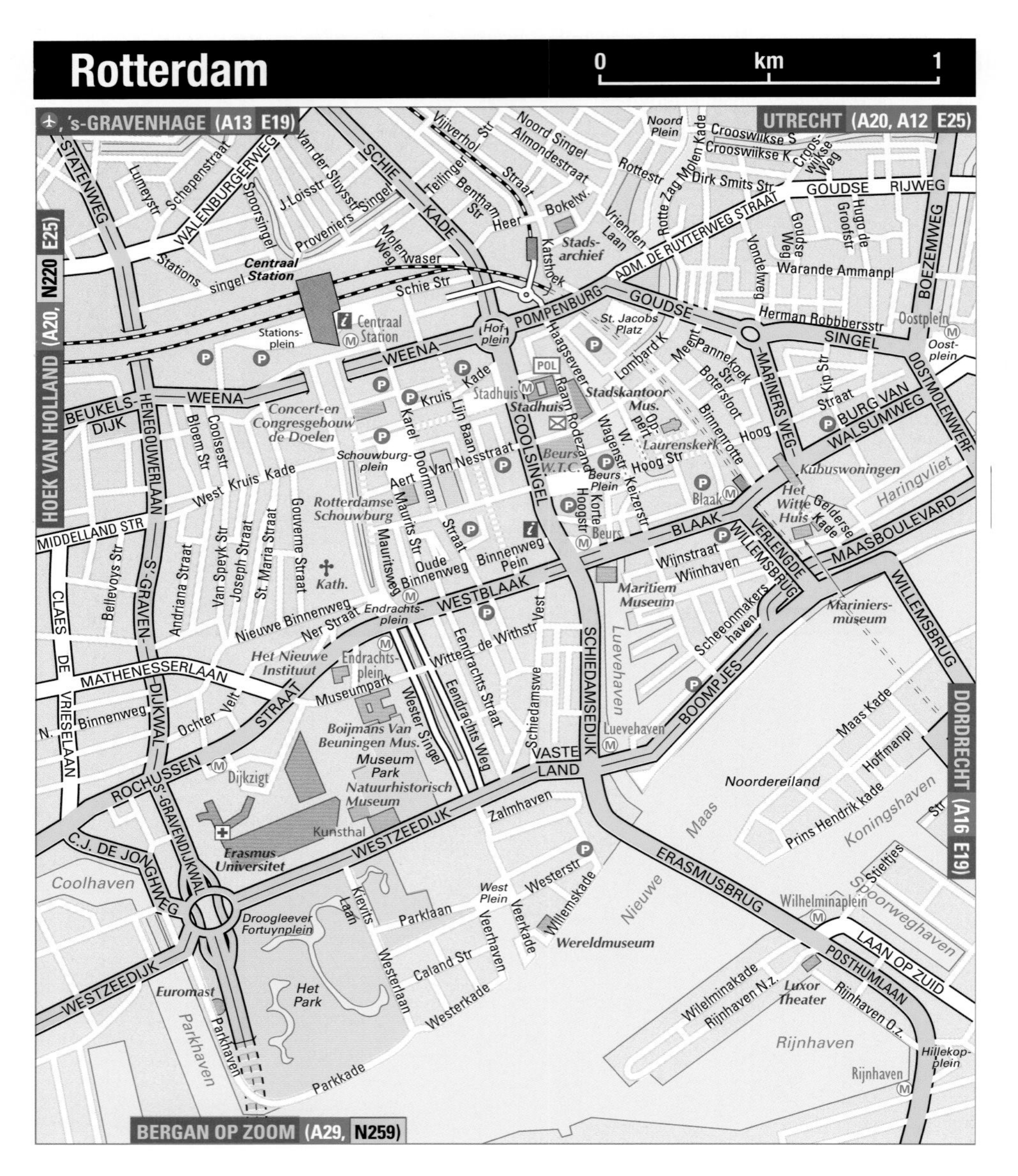

Sankt-Peterburg St. Petersburg

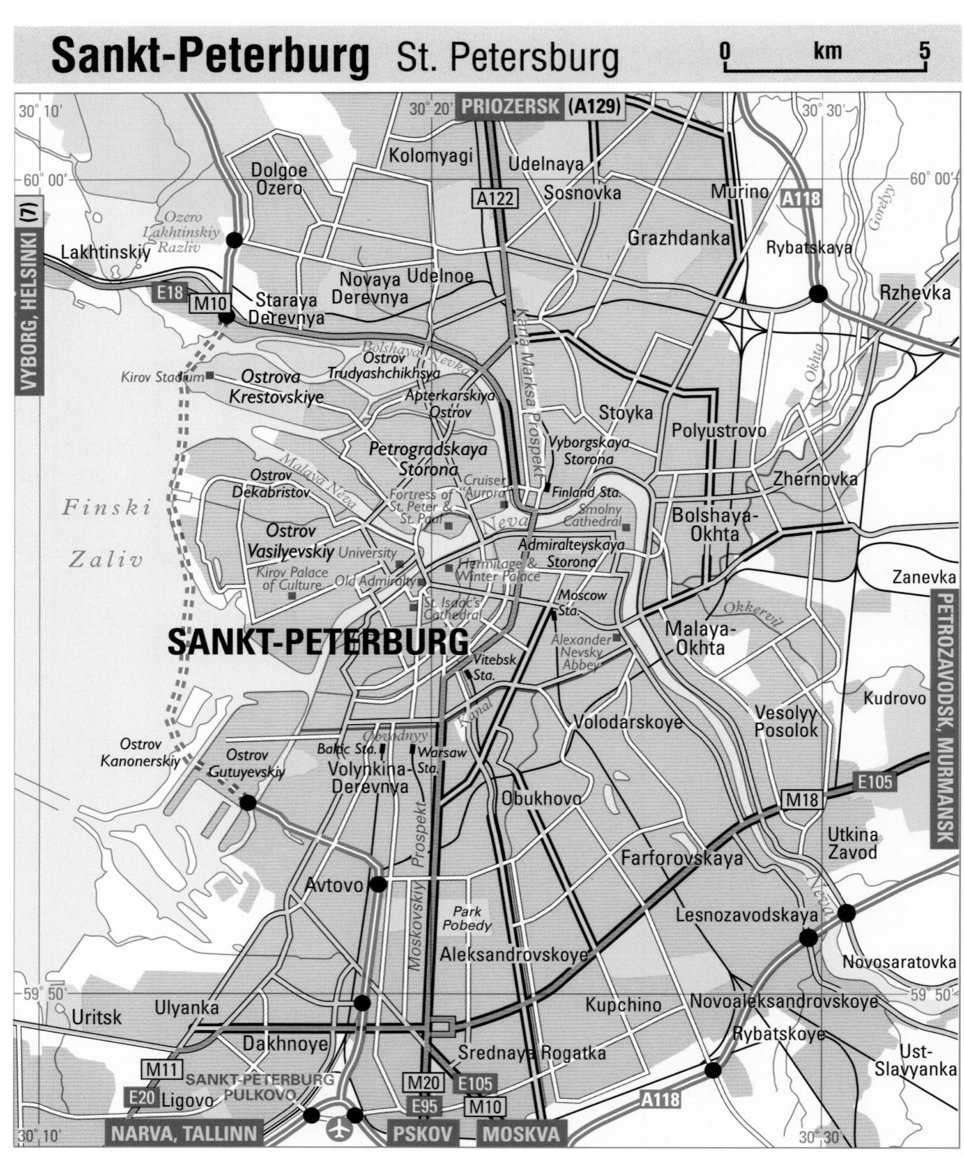

For **Rome** see page 143

Roma Rome

0 km 5

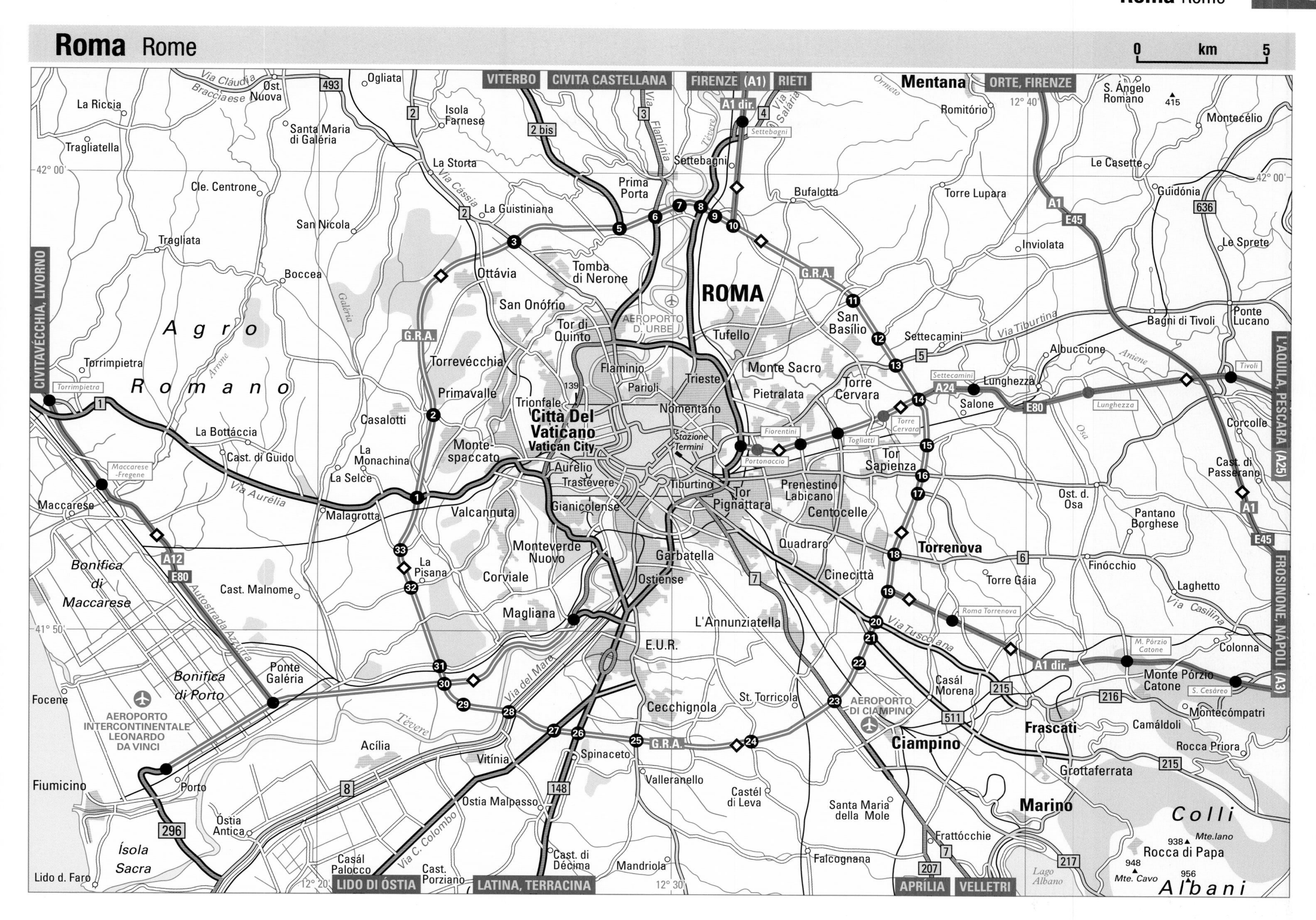
VITERBO
CIVITA CASTELLANA
FIRENZE (A1)
RIETI
Mentana
ORTE, FIRENZE
S. Ángelo Romano
Romitório
Montecélio
Le Casette
Guidónia
Le Sprete
Ogliata
Ost. Nuova
Isola Farnese
La Riccia
Santa Maria di Galéria
Tragliatella
La Storta
Settebagni
Prima Porta
Bufalotta
Torre Lupara
Cle. Centrone
La Guistiniana
San Nicola
Inviolata
Tragliata
Tomba di Nerone
Ottávia
Boccea
San Onófrio
ROMA
San Basílio
Bagni di Tivoli
Ponte Lucano
Agro Romano
Tor di Quinto
AEROPORTO D. URBE
Tufello
Settecamini
Torrimpietra
Torrevécchia
Flaminio
Trieste
Monte Sacro
Albuccione
Parioli
Torre Cervara
Lunghezza
Primavalle
Trionfale
Pietralata
Salone
Città Del Vaticano
Vatican City
Nomentano
Corcolle
La Bottáccia
Casalotti
Stazione Termini
Cast. di Guido
La Monachina
Monte-spaccato
Tor Sapienza
Cast. di Passerano
La Selce
Aurelio
Trastevere
Tiburtino
Tor Pignattara
Prenestino Labicano
Ost. d. Osa
Maccarese
Malagrotta
Valcannuta
Gianicolense
Centocelle
Pantano Borghese
Quadraro
Monteverde Nuovo
Garbatella
Torrenova
Bonifica di Maccarese
La Pisana
Corviale
Ostiense
Cinecittà
Finócchio
Cast. Malnome
Torre Gáia
Laghetto
Magliana
L'Annunziatella
E.U.R.
Colonna
Ponte Galéria
Bonifica di Porto
Casál Morena
Monte Pórzio Catone
Focene
AEROPORTO INTERCONTINENTALE LEONARDO DA VINCI
Cecchignola
St. Torricola
AEROPORTO DI CIAMPINO
Montecómpatri
Camáldoli
Acília
Ciampino
Frascati
Rocca Priora
Vitínia
Spinaceto
Grottaferrata
Fiumicino
Porto
Valleranello
Ostia Malpasso
Castél di Leva
Santa Maria della Mole
Marino
Colli Albani
Ostia Antica
Frattócchie
Ísola Sacra
Casál Palocco
Cast. di Décima
Mandriola
Falcognana
Rocca di Papa
Lido d. Faro
Cast. Porziano
Lago Albano
LIDO DI OSTIA
LATINA, TERRACINA
APRÍLIA
VELLETRI
CIVITAVÉCCHIA, LIVORNO
L'AQUILA, PESCARA (A25)
FROSINONE, NÁPOLI (A3)
G.R.A.

Roma Rome

0 km 1

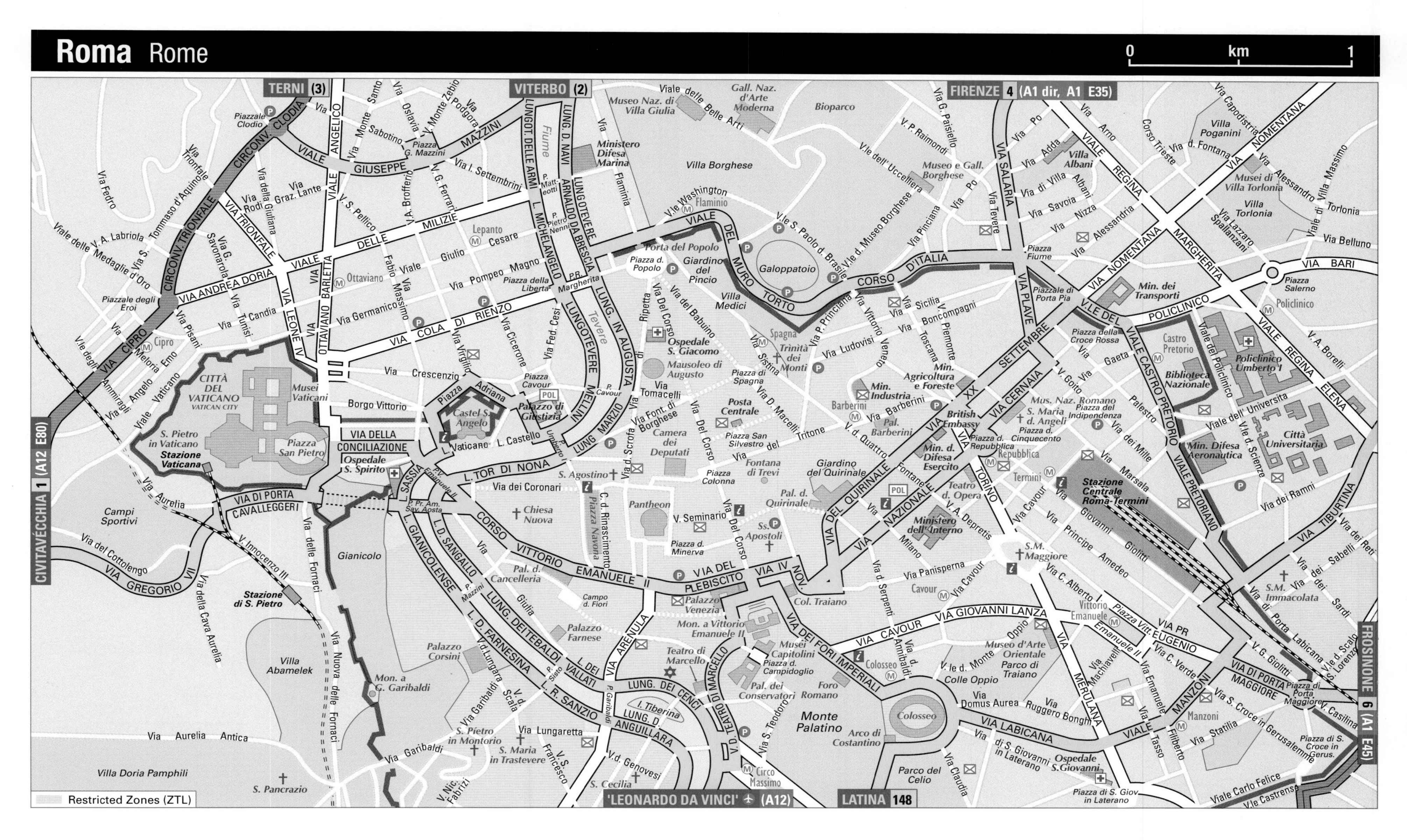
TERNI (3)
VITERBO (2)
FIRENZE 4 (A1 dir, A1 E35)
Museo Naz. di Villa Giulia
Gall. Naz. d'Arte Moderna
Bioparco
Villa Borghese
Museo e Gall. Borghese
Villa Poganini
Villa Albani
Villa Torlonia
Piazzale Clodio
Ministero Difesa Marina
Piazza del Popolo
Galoppatoio
Porta Pia
Min. dei Trasporti
Policlinico
Castro Pretorio
Biblioteca Nazionale
Policlinico Umberto I
Città Universitaria
Min. Difesa Aeronautica
Ottaviano
Lepanto
Piazza della Libertà
Piazza Cavour
Castel S. Angelo
Mausoleo di Augusto
Villa Medici
Trinità dei Monti
Piazza di Spagna
Borgo Vittorio
Musei Vaticani
CITTÀ DEL VATICANO
VATICAN CITY
S. Pietro in Vaticano
Stazione Vaticana
Piazza San Pietro
Ospedale S. Spirito
Campi Sportivi
Gianicolo
Stazione di S. Pietro
Villa Abamelek
Mon. a G. Garibaldi
Villa Doria Pamphili
S. Pancrazio
Palazzo Corsini
Palazzo Farnese
Campo d. Fiori
Pal. d. Cancelleria
Chiesa Nuova
Pantheon
Piazza Navona
Fontana di Trevi
Pal. d. Quirinale
Giardino del Quirinale
Ministero dell'Interno
Teatro d. Opera
Stazione Centrale Roma-Termini
S.M. Maggiore
Piazza Venezia
Mon. a Vittorio Emanuele II
Musei Capitolini
Teatro di Marcello
Foro Romano
Monte Palatino
Colosseo
Arco di Costantino
Parco del Celio
S. Pietro in Montorio
S. Maria in Trastevere
Circo Massimo
Colle Oppio
Domus Aurea
Museo d'Arte Orientale
Parco di Traiano
Piazza di Porta Maggiore
Piazza di S. Croce in Gerus.
Piazza di S. Giov. in Laterano
S.M. Immacolata
'LEONARDO DA VINCI' (A12)
LATINA 148
CIVITAVECCHIA 1 (A12 E80)
FROSINONE 6 (A1 E45)
Restricted Zones (ZTL)

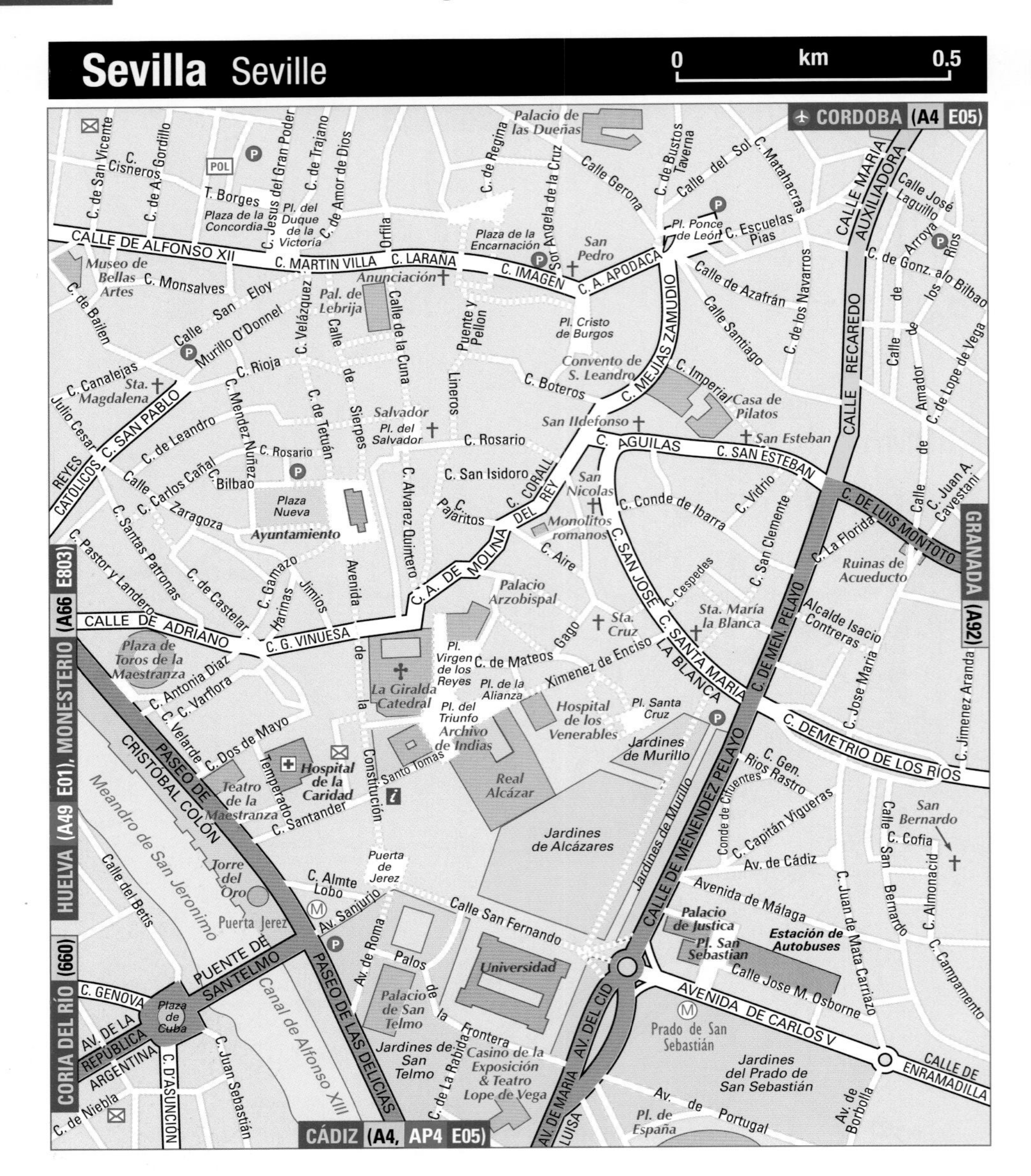
Sevilla Seville
0 km 0,5
CORDOBA (A4 E05)
GRANADA (A92)
CÁDIZ (A4, AP4 E05)
HUELVA (A49 E01), MONESTERIO (A66 E803)
CORIA DEL RÍO (660)
Palacio de las Dueñas
Museo de Bellas Artes
CALLE DE ALFONSO XII
C. MARTIN VILLA
C. LARAÑA
C. IMAGEN
C. A. APODACA
CALLE MARÍA AUXILIADORA
CALLE RECAREDO
Anunciación
Pal. de Lebrija
Plaza de la Encarnación
San Pedro
Pl. Cristo de Burgos
Convento de S. Leandro
Casa de Pilatos
San Ildefonso
San Esteban
C. AGUILAS
C. SAN ESTEBAN
C. DE LUIS MONTOTO
Salvador
C. Rosario
C. San Isidoro
Plaza Nueva
Ayuntamiento
San Nicolás
Monolitos romanos
C. SAN JOSÉ
Palacio Arzobispal
Sta. María la Blanca
Ruinas de Acueducto
CALLE DE ADRIANO
Plaza de Toros de la Maestranza
La Giralda
Catedral
Pl. Virgen de los Reyes
Archivo de Indias
Hospital de los Venerables
Jardines de Murillo
C. DEMETRIO DE LOS RÍOS
Hospital de la Caridad
Teatro de la Maestranza
Real Alcázar
Jardines de Alcázares
Torre del Oro
Puerta Jerez
Palacio de Justicia
Estación de Autobuses
Universidad
Palacio de San Telmo
Jardines de San Telmo
Casino de la Exposición & Teatro Lope de Vega
Prado de San Sebastián
Jardines del Prado de San Sebastián
AVENIDA DE CARLOS V
CALLE DE ENRAMADILLA
PASEO DE CRISTÓBAL COLÓN
PASEO DE LAS DELICIAS
PUENTE DE SAN TELMO
Canal de Alfonso XIII
Meandro de San Jerónimo
Plaza de Cuba
Pl. de España

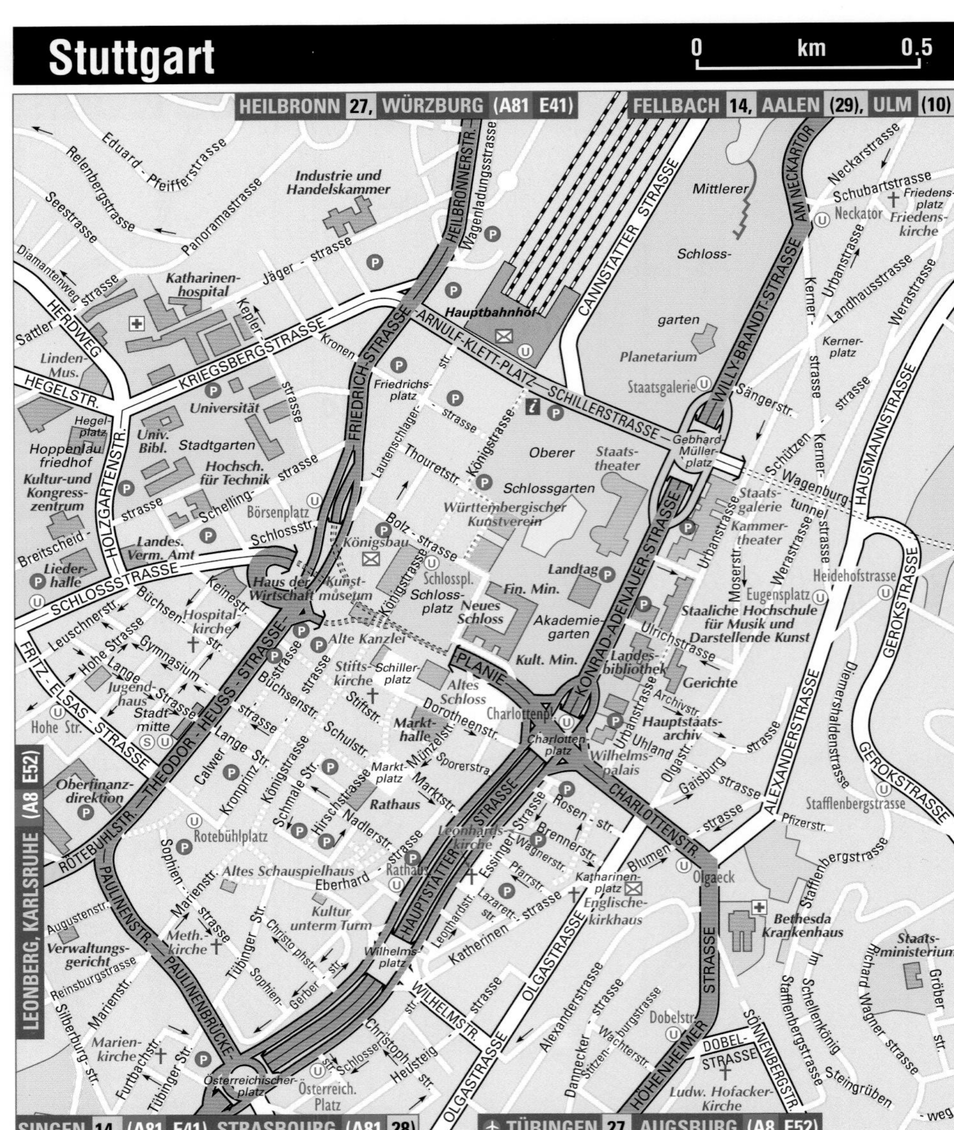
Stuttgart
0 km 0,5
HEILBRONN 27, WÜRZBURG (A81 E41)
FELLBACH 14, AALEN (29), ULM (10)
LEONBERG, KARLSRUHE (A8 E52)
SINGEN 14, (A81 E41), STRASBOURG (A81 28)
TÜBINGEN 27, AUGSBURG (A8 E52)
Industrie und Handelskammer
Katharinen-hospital
Hauptbahnhof
Schloss-garten
Mittlerer
Planetarium
Staatsgalerie
Universität
KRIEGSBERGSTRASSE
SCHILLERSTRASSE
ARNULF-KLETT-PLATZ
HEILBRONNERSTR.
CANNSTATTER STRASSE
WILLY-BRANDT-STRASSE
AM NECKARTOR
Linden-Mus.
Hoppenlau friedhof
Kultur-und Kongress-zentrum
Univ. Bibl.
Stadtgarten
Hochsch. für Technik
Oberer Schlossgarten
Württembergischer Kunstverein
Staats-theater
Landtag
Landes. Verm. Amt
Haus der Wirtschaft
Linden-museum
Königsbau
Neues Schloss
Akademie-garten
Staaliche Hochschule für Musik und Darstellende Kunst
Landes-bibliothek
Gerichte
Hauptstaats-archiv
Wilhelms-palais
SCHLOSSSTRASSE
THEODOR-HEUSS-STRASSE
KONRAD-ADENAUER-STRASSE
PLANIE
Altes Schloss
Stifts-kirche
Markt-halle
Rathaus
Altes Schauspielhaus
Kultur unterm Turm
Verwaltungs-gericht
Oberfinanz-direktion
Bethesda Krankenhaus
Staats-ministerium
CHARLOTTENSTR.
HAUPTSTÄTTER STRASSE
OLGASTRASSE
ALEXANDERSTRASSE
HOHENHEIMER STRASSE
Österreich. Platz
GEROKSTRASSE
HAUSMANNSTRASSE

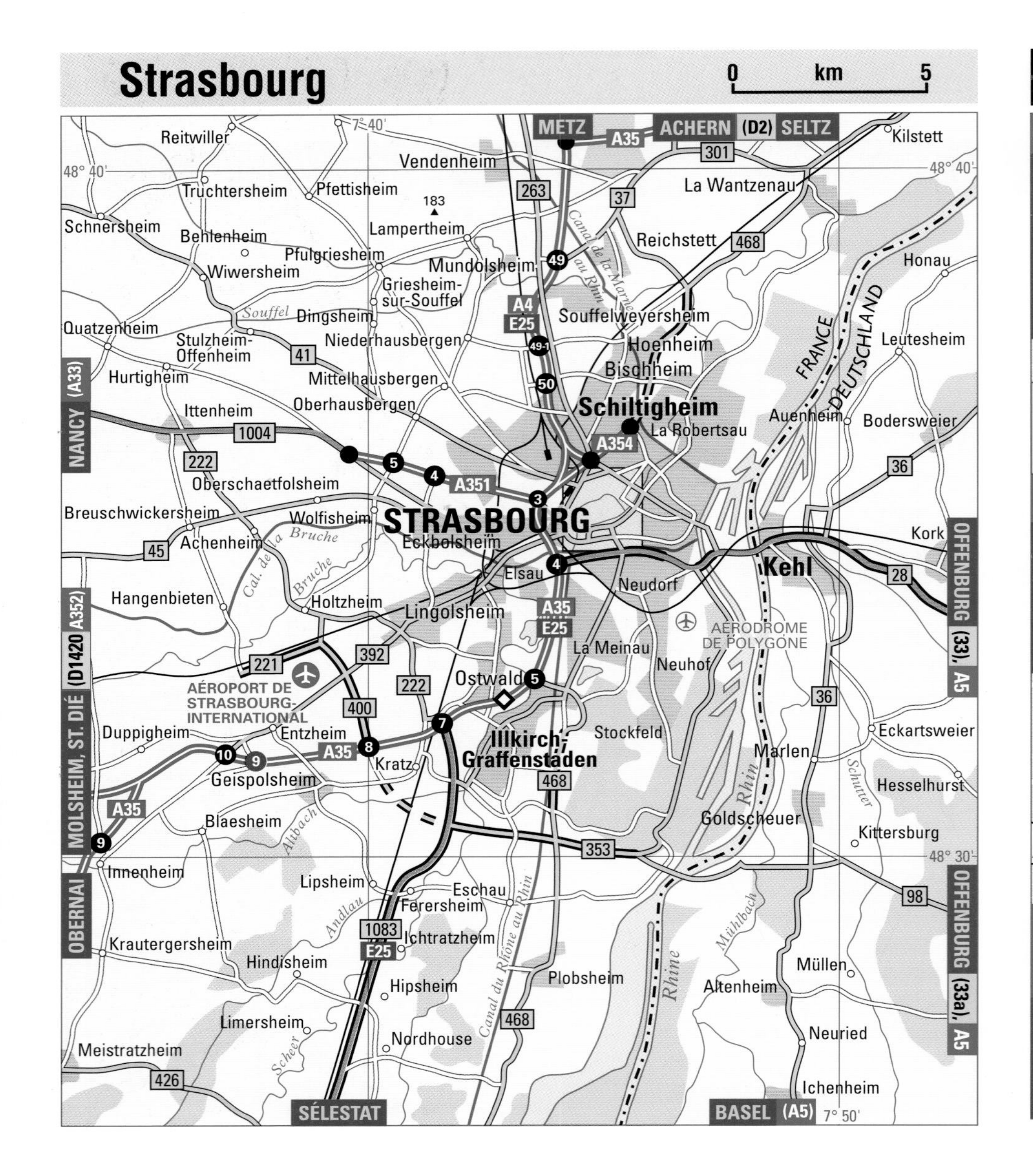
Strasbourg
0 km 5
METZ A35
ACHERN (D2) SELTZ
NANCY (A33)
MOLSHEIM, ST. DIÉ (D1420 A352)
OBERNAI
OFFENBURG (33), A5
OFFENBURG (33a), A5
SÉLESTAT
BASEL (A5)
STRASBOURG
Schiltigheim
Kehl
Illkirch-Graffenstaden
Reitwiller
Vendenheim
Kilstett
Truchtersheim
Pfettisheim
Lampertheim
La Wantzenau
Schnersheim
Behlenheim
Pfulgriesheim
Wiwersheim
Mundolsheim
Reichstett
Honau
Griesheim-sur-Souffel
Quatzenheim
Dingsheim
Souffelweyersheim
Hoenheim
Bischheim
Stulzheim-Offenheim
Niederhausbergen
Leutesheim
Hurtigheim
Mittelhausbergen
Ittenheim
Oberhausbergen
La Robertsau
Auenheim
Bodersweier
Oberschaeffolsheim
Breuschwickersheim
Wolfisheim
Eckbolsheim
Achenheim
Elsau
Neudorf
Kork
Hangenbieten
Holtzheim
Lingolsheim
AÉRODROME DE POLYGONE
AÉROPORT DE STRASBOURG-INTERNATIONAL
La Meinau
Neuhof
Ostwald
Duppigheim
Entzheim
Stockfeld
Eckartsweier
Kratz
Geispolsheim
Marlen
Hesselhurst
Blaesheim
Goldscheuer
Kittersburg
Innenheim
Lipsheim
Eschau
Fegersheim
Ichtratzheim
Krautergersheim
Hindisheim
Plobsheim
Müllen
Hipsheim
Altenheim
Limersheim
Nordhouse
Neuried
Meistratzheim
Ichenheim
FRANCE
DEUTSCHLAND
Rhin
Rhein
Canal du Rhône au Rhin
48° 40'
48° 30'
7° 40'
7° 50'

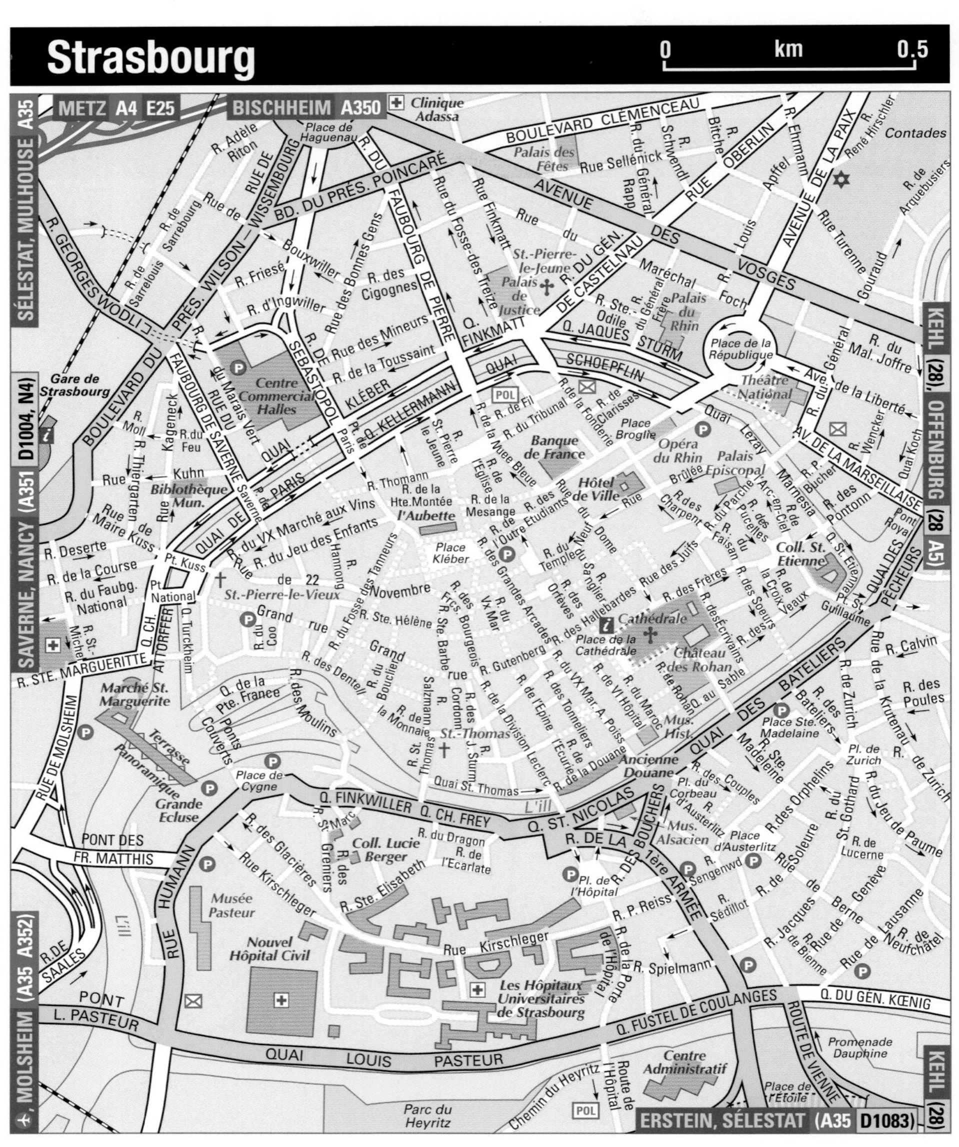
Strasbourg
0 km 0,5
METZ A4 E25
BISCHHEIM A350
Clinique Adassa
SÉLESTAT, MULHOUSE A35
SAVERNE, NANCY (A351 D1004, N4)
MOLSHEIM (A35 A352)
KEHL (28), OFFENBURG (28 A5)
KEHL (28)
ERSTEIN, SÉLESTAT (A35 D1083)
Contades
BOULEVARD CLEMENCEAU
AVENUE DES VOSGES
AVENUE DE LA PAIX
Place de la République
Théâtre National
BD. DU PRÉS. POINCARÉ
BOULEVARD DU PRÉS. WILSON
Gare de Strasbourg
Centre Commercial Halles
QUAI KLÉBER
QUAI DE PARIS
QUAI JACQUES STURM
QUAI SCHOEPFLIN
Banque de France
Opéra du Rhin
Palais Episcopal
Hôtel de Ville
Bibliothèque Mun.
Place Kléber
L'Aubette
St.-Pierre-le-Vieux
Place Gutenberg
Cathédrale
Place de la Cathédrale
Château des Rohan
Coll. St. Etienne
QUAI DES BATELIERS
Marché St. Marguerite
Terrasse Panoramique
Grande Ecluse
Place du Cygne
Q. FINKWILLER
Q. CH. FREY
Q. ST. NICOLAS
Ancienne Douane
Mus. Alsacien
Place Ste. Madeleine
Place d'Austerlitz
Coll. Lucie Berger
Musée Pasteur
Nouvel Hôpital Civil
Les Hôpitaux Universitaires de Strasbourg
QUAI LOUIS PASTEUR
Centre Administratif
Promenade Dauphine
Parc du Heyritz
L'Ill

Stockholm

0 km 5

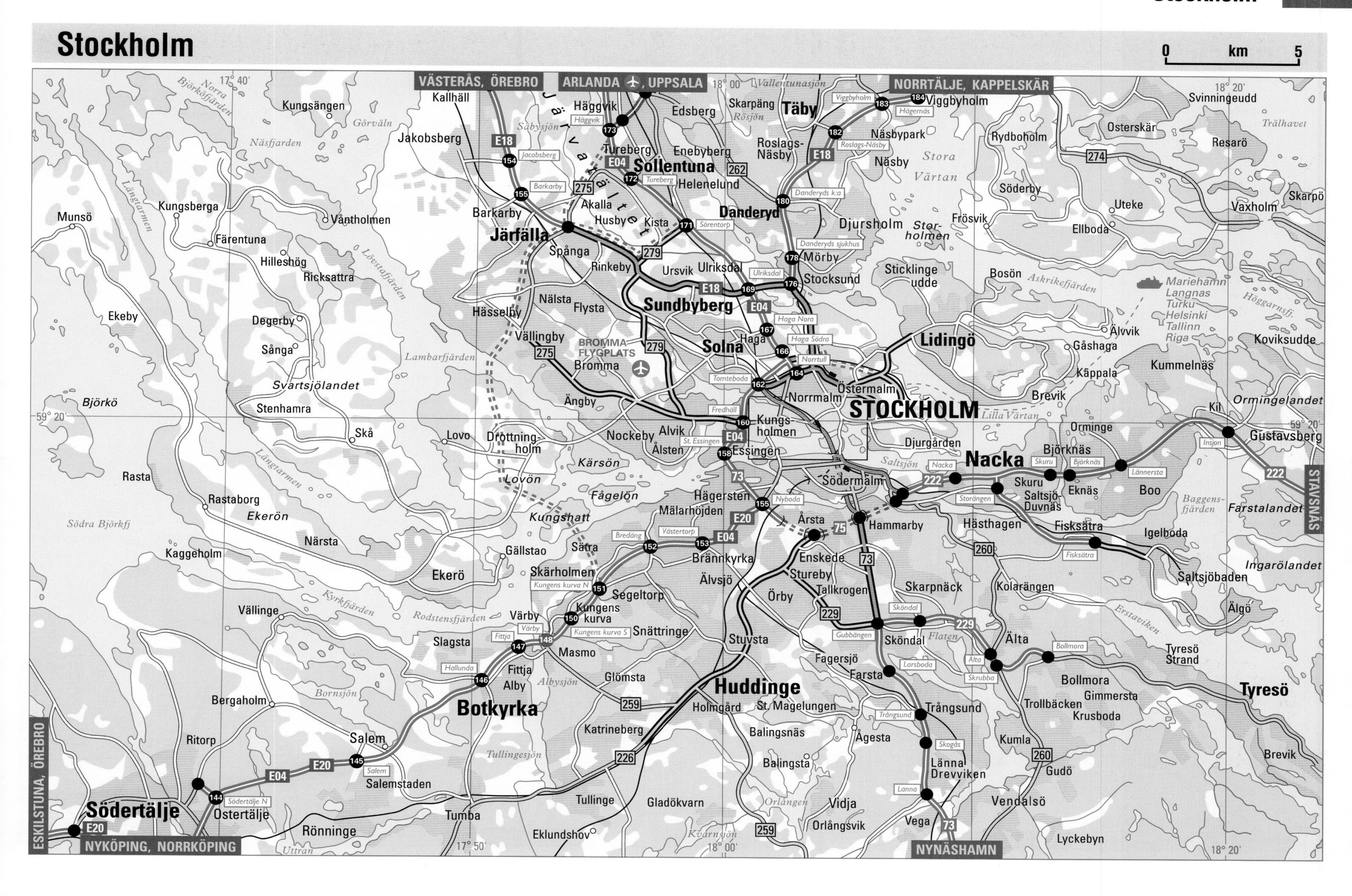
VÄSTERÅS, ÖREBRO
ARLANDA, UPPSALA
NORRTÄLJE, KAPPELSKÄR
ESKILSTUNA, ÖREBRO
NYKÖPING, NORRKÖPING
NYNÄSHAMN
STAVSNÄS
Kungsängen
Jakobsberg
Kallhäll
Häggvik
Sollentuna
Täby
Viggbyholm
Näsbypark
Roslags-Näsby
Näsby
Edsberg
Enebyberg
Helenelund
Tureberg
Järfälla
Barkarby
Akalla
Husby
Kista
Danderyd
Djursholm
Stora Värtan
Svinningeudd
Rydboholm
Österskär
Resarö
Söderby
Vaxholm
Skarpö
Uteke
Ellboda
Frösvik
Munsö
Kungsberga
Vantholmen
Färentuna
Hilleshög
Ricksattra
Spånga
Rinkeby
Ursvik
Ulriksdal
Mörby
Stocksund
Sticklinge udde
Bosön
Sundbyberg
Solna
Haga
Lidingö
Ekeby
Degerby
Sånga
Nälsta
Flysta
Hässelby
Vällingby
BROMMA FLYGPLATS
Bromma
Älvvik
Gåshaga
Käppala
Kummelnäs
Koviksudde
Svartsjölandet
Björkö
Stenhamra
Ängby
Östermalm
Norrmalm
STOCKHOLM
Lilla Värtan
Brevik
Ormingelandet
Skå
Lovö
Drottningholm
Nockeby
Alvik
Ålsten
Kungsholmen
Essingen
Djurgården
Orminge
Gustavsberg
Rasta
Kärsön
Lovön
Nacka
Björknäs
Skuru
Saltsjö-Duvnäs
Eknäs
Boo
Fågelön
Hägersten
Mälarhöjden
Södermalm
Hammarby
Rastaborg
Ekerön
Kungshatt
Årsta
Hästhagen
Fisksätra
Igelboda
Farstalandet
Södra Björkfj
Närsta
Kaggeholm
Gällstao
Sätra
Skärholmen
Ekerö
Bredäng
Västertorp
Brännkyrka
Älvsjö
Enskede
Stureby
Tallkrogen
Skarpnäck
Kolarängen
Saltsjöbaden
Ingarölandet
Segeltorp
Kungens kurva
Vällinge
Örby
Älgö
Värby
Slagsta
Snättringe
Stuvsta
Sköndal
Älta
Tyresö Strand
Masmo
Fittja
Alby
Glömsta
Fagersjö
Farsta
Bollmora
Gimmersta
Tyresö
Bergaholm
Botkyrka
Huddinge
Holmgård
St. Magelungen
Trångsund
Trollbäcken
Krusboda
Ritorp
Salem
Katrineberg
Balingsnäs
Ågesta
Kumla
Brevik
Salemstaden
Balingsta
Länna
Drevviken
Gudö
Södertälje
Östertälje
Tullinge
Gladökvarn
Vidja
Vendalsö
Rönninge
Tumba
Eklundshov
Orlångsvik
Vega
Lyckebyn

Stockholm

0 km 1

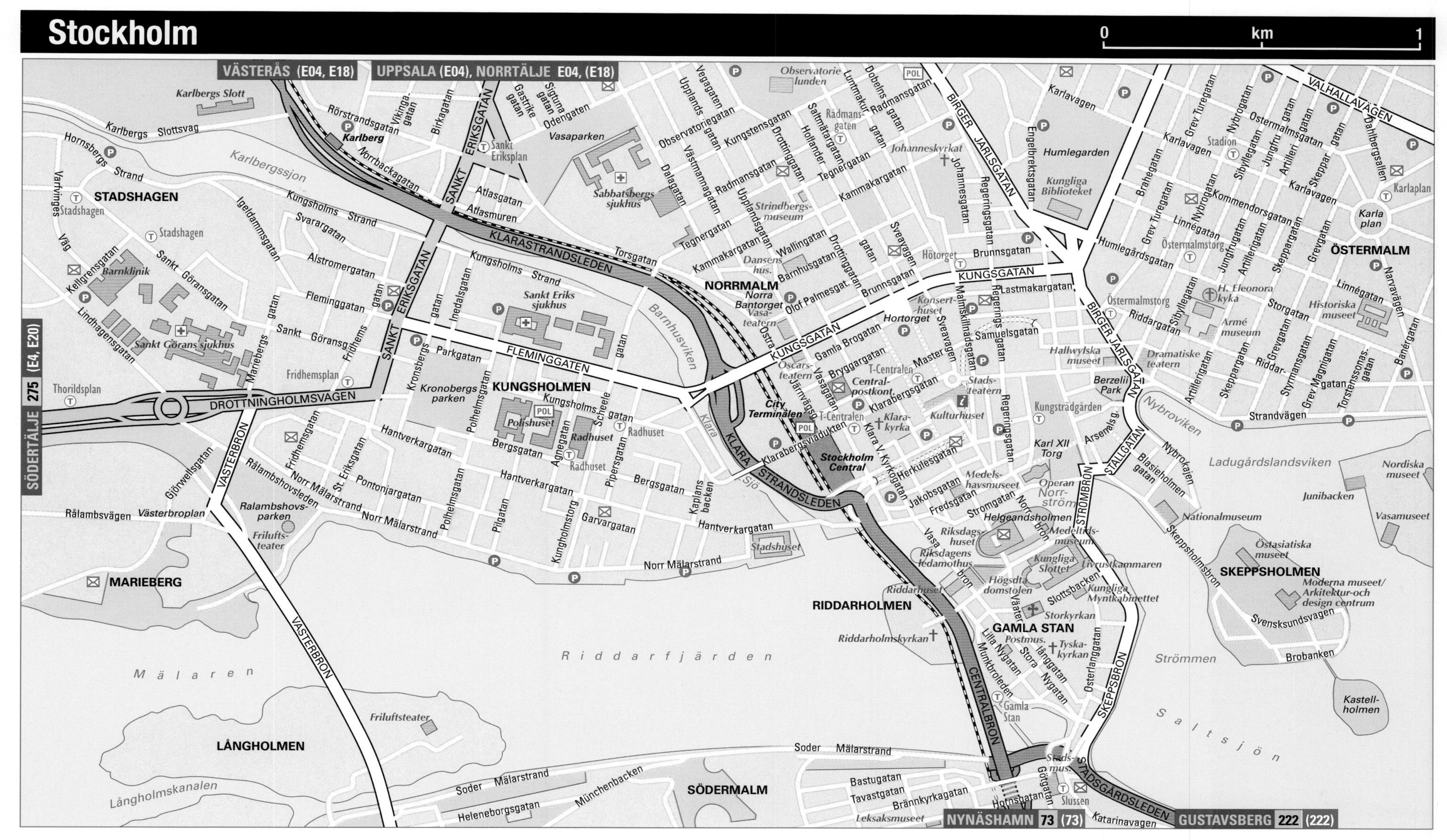
VÄSTERÅS (E04, E18)
UPPSALA (E04), NORRTÄLJE E04, (E18)
VALHALLAVÄGEN
SÖDERTÄLJE 275 (E4, E20)
NYNÄSHAMN 73 (73)
GUSTAVSBERG 222 (222)
Karlbergs Slott
Karlberg
Karlbergssjön
STADSHAGEN
Sankt Görans sjukhus
Thorildsplan
DROTTNINGHOLMSVÄGEN
VÄSTERBRON
Rålambsvägen
Västerbroplan
Rålambshovsparken
MARIEBERG
Mälaren
LÅNGHOLMEN
Långholmskanalen
KLARASTRANDSLEDEN
Sabbatsbergs sjukhus
Vasaparken
Observatorielunden
Sankt Eriks sjukhus
FLEMINGGATAN
KUNGSHOLMEN
Kronobergsparken
Polishuset
Radhuset
Barnhusviken
NORRMALM
KUNGSGATAN
City Terminalen
Stockholm Central
Humlegården
Kungliga Biblioteket
ÖSTERMALM
Karlaplan
Historiska museet
Berzelii Park
Kungsträdgården
Nybroviken
Ladugårdslandsviken
Nordiska museet
Junibacken
Vasamuseet
Nationalmuseum
SKEPPSHOLMEN
Moderna museet/ Arkitektur-och design centrum
Östasiatiska museet
Riksdagshuset
Kungliga Slottet
Helgeandsholmen
RIDDARHOLMEN
Riddarholmskyrkan
GAMLA STAN
Storkyrkan
Tyska kyrkan
Riddarfjärden
Strömmen
Saltsjön
CENTRALBRON
SKEPPSBRON
STRÖMBRON
Kastellholmen
SÖDERMALM
Slussen
Stadsmuseet
Norr Mälarstrand
Söder Mälarstrand
Heleneborgsgatan
Münchenbacken
Katarinavägen
STADSGÅRDSLEDEN

Torino Turin

0 km 5

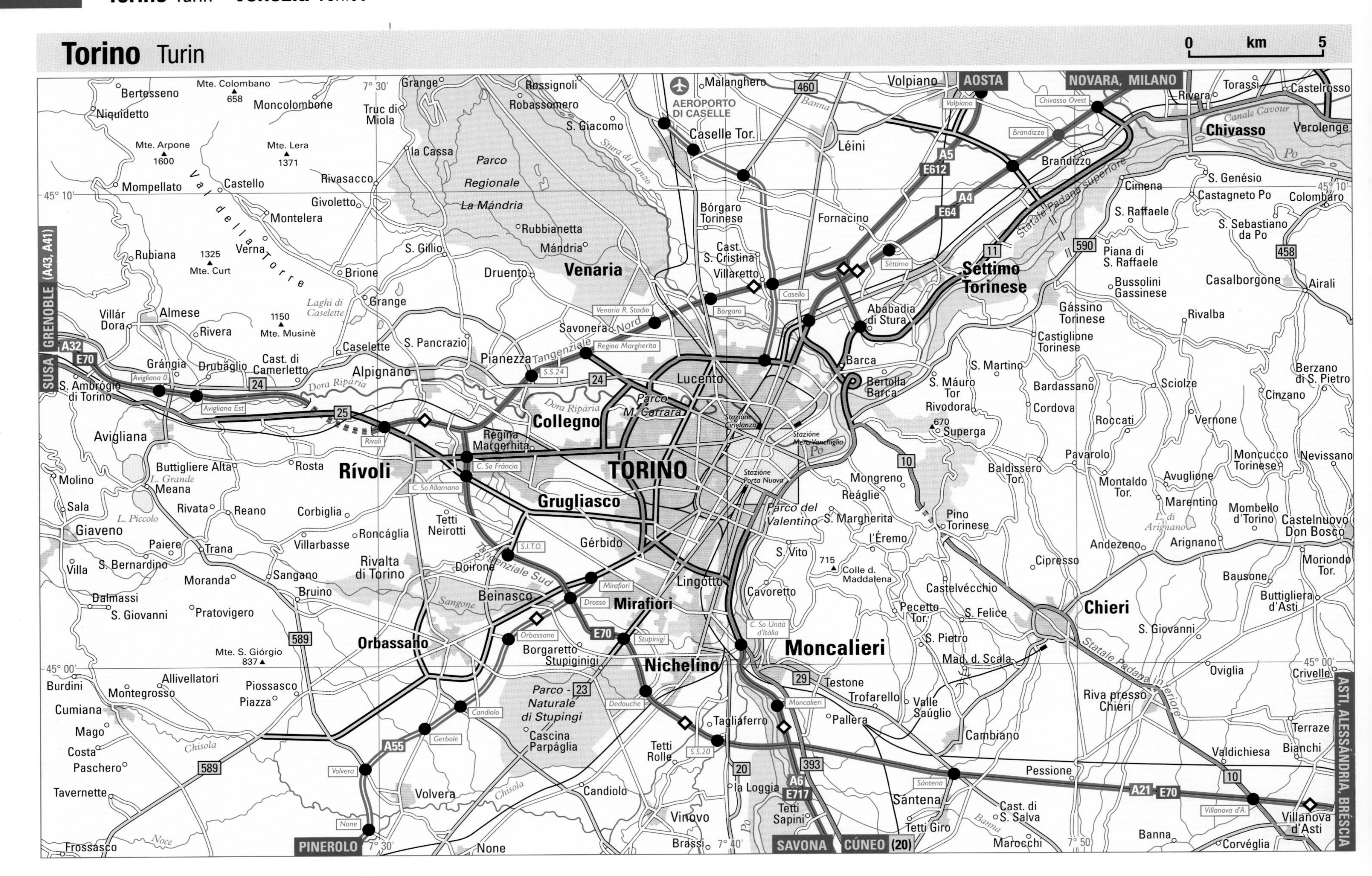
TORINO
Venaria
Settimo Torinese
Collegno
Rívoli
Grugliasco
Mirafiori
Nichelino
Moncalieri
Chieri
Chivasso
Orbassano
Beinasco
Lingotto
Lucento
Caselle Tor.
AEROPORTO DI CASELLE
Léini
Volpiano
Bórgaro Torinese
Alpignano
Pianezza
Druento
Avigliana
Giaveno
Rivalta di Torino
Piossasco
Volvera
Candiolo
Vinovo
Santena
Cambiano
Pino Torinese
Superga
Parco Regionale La Mándria
Parco Naturale di Stupinigi
AOSTA
NOVARA, MILANO
SUSA, GRENOBLE (A43, A41)
PINEROLO
SAVONA
CÚNEO (20)
ASTI, ALESSÁNDRIA, BRÉSCIA
Po

Venézia Venice

0 km 0.5

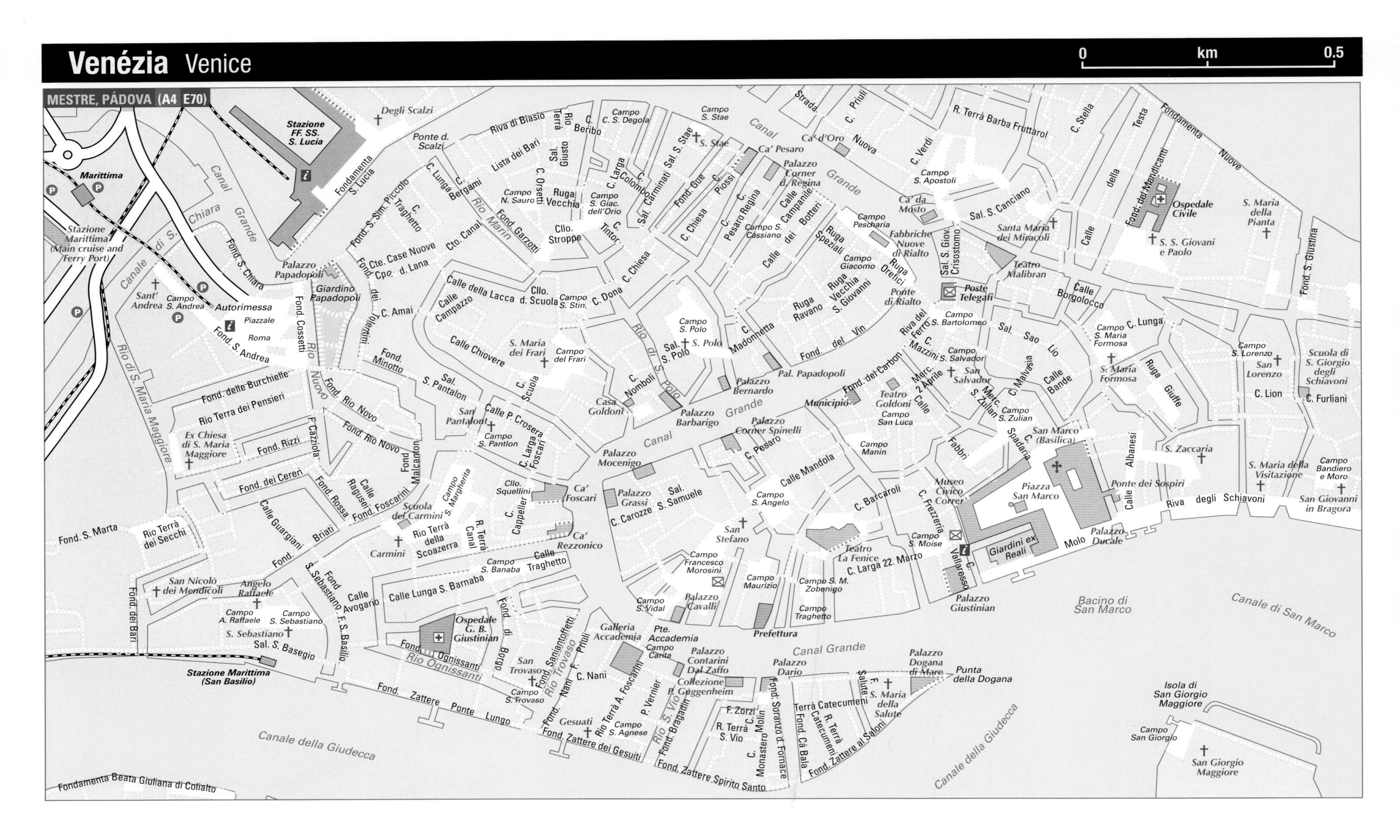
MESTRE, PÁDOVA (A4 E70)
Stazione FF. SS. S. Lucia
Canal Grande
Canale della Giudecca
Bacino di San Marco
Canale di San Marco
Piazza San Marco
S. Marco (Basilica)
Ponte dei Sospiri
Riva degli Schiavoni
Ponte di Rialto
Ca' d'Oro
Ca' Pesaro
Palazzo Ducale
Giardini ex Reali
Punta della Dogana
Galleria Accademia
Collezione P. Guggenheim
Teatro La Fenice
Isola di San Giorgio Maggiore
San Giorgio Maggiore
Stazione Marittima (Main cruise and Ferry Port)
Stazione Marittima (San Basilio)
Piazzale Roma
Ospedale Civile
Ospedale G. B. Giustinian
Fondamenta Nuove
Fond. Zattere Ponte Lungo

Torino Turin

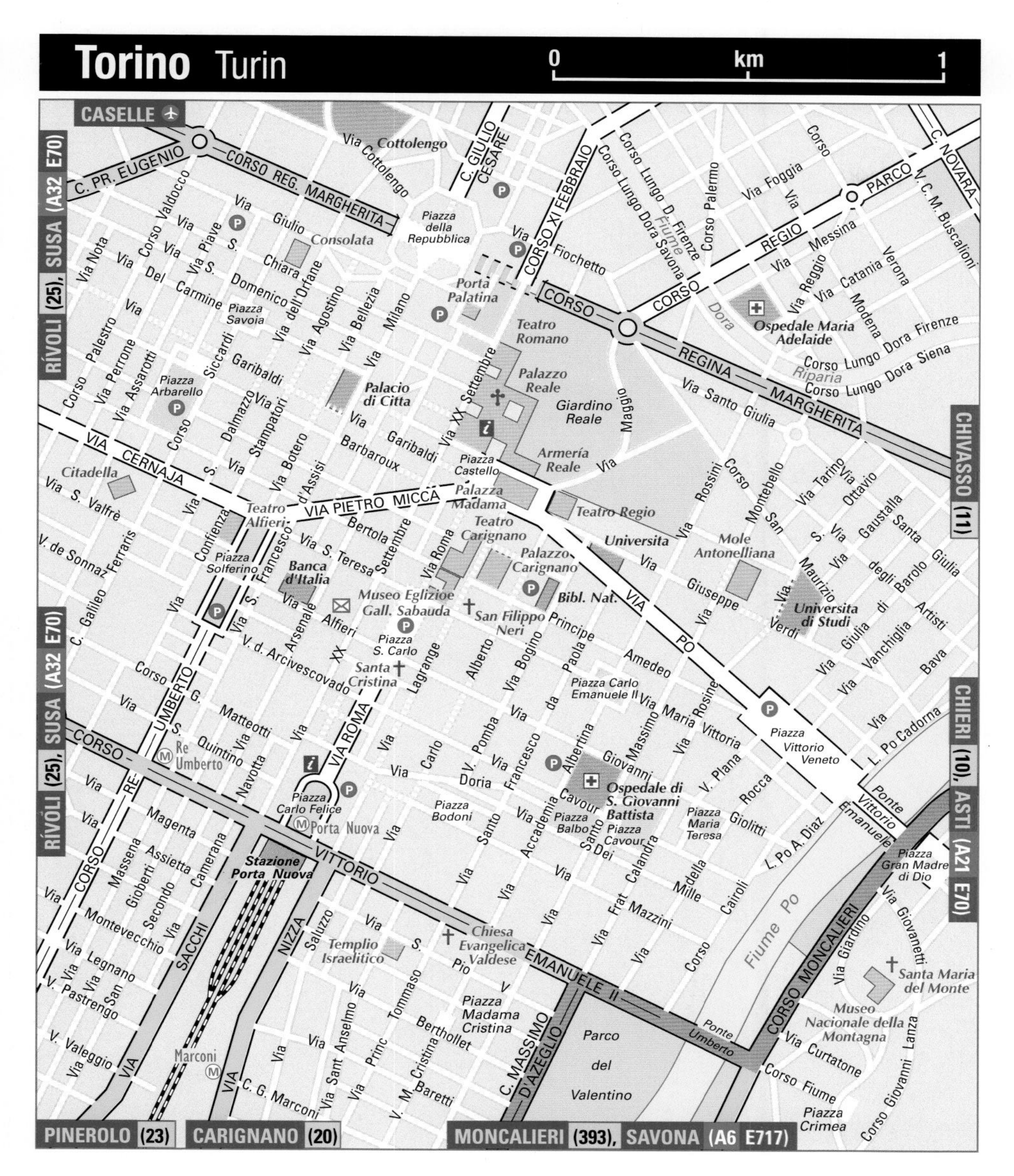

Wien Vienna

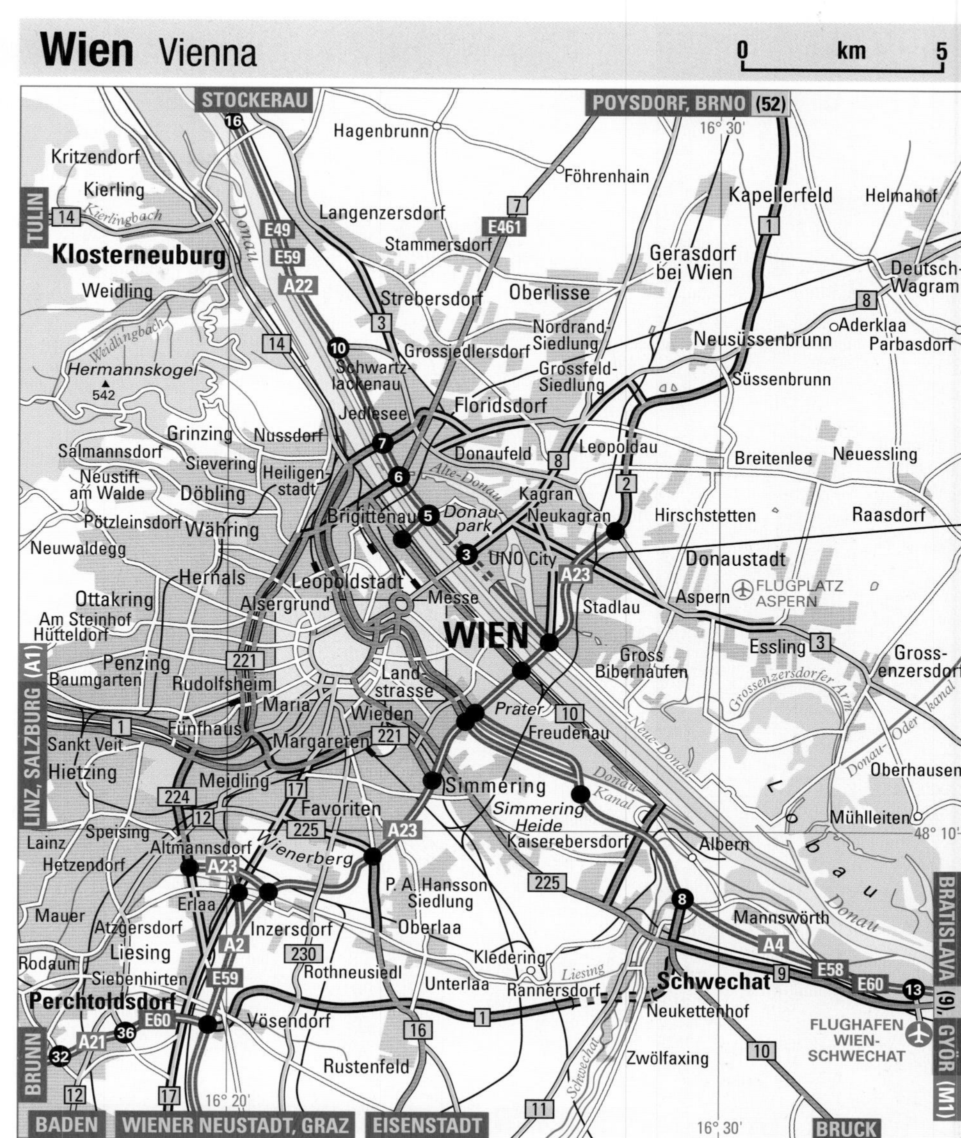

Warszawa Warsaw

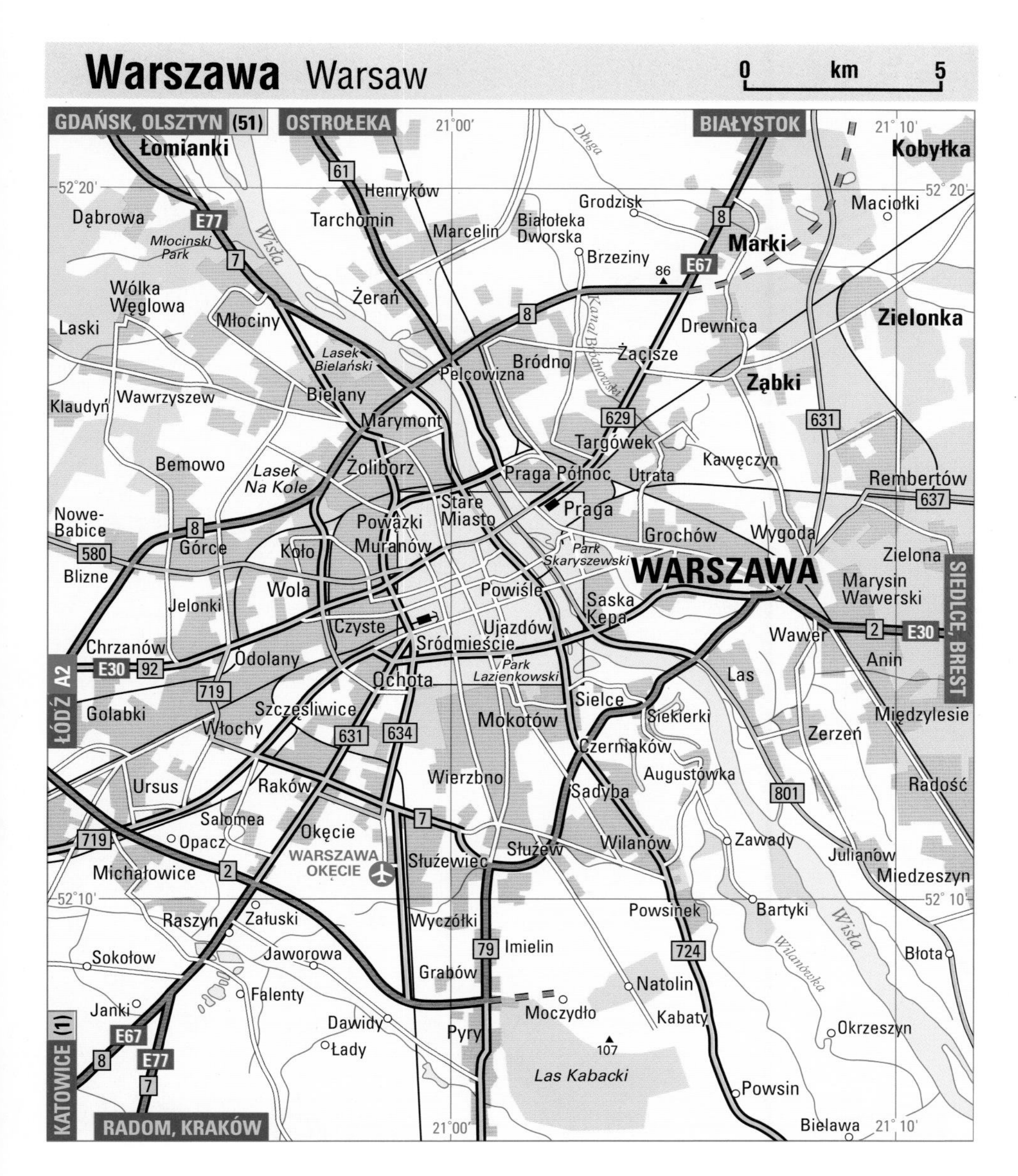

Warszawa Warsaw

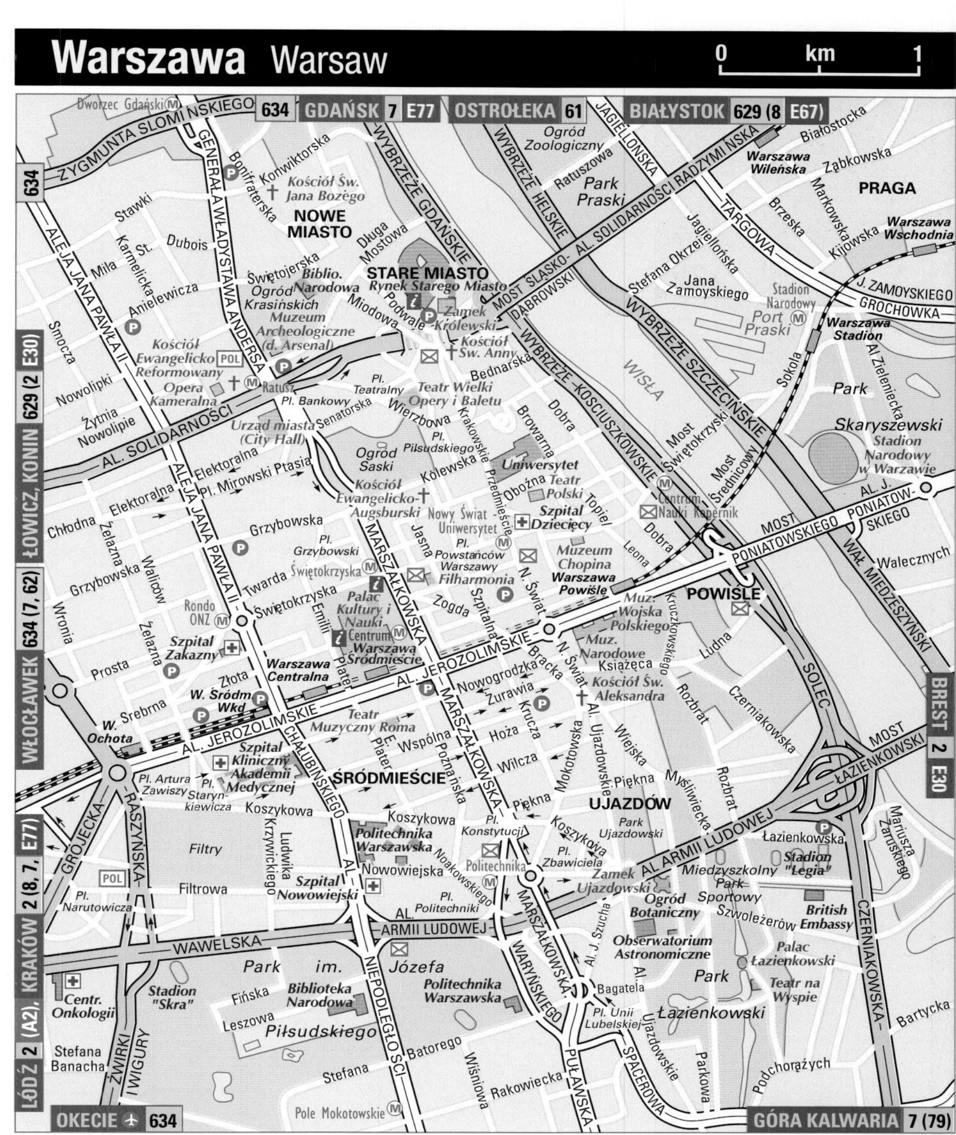

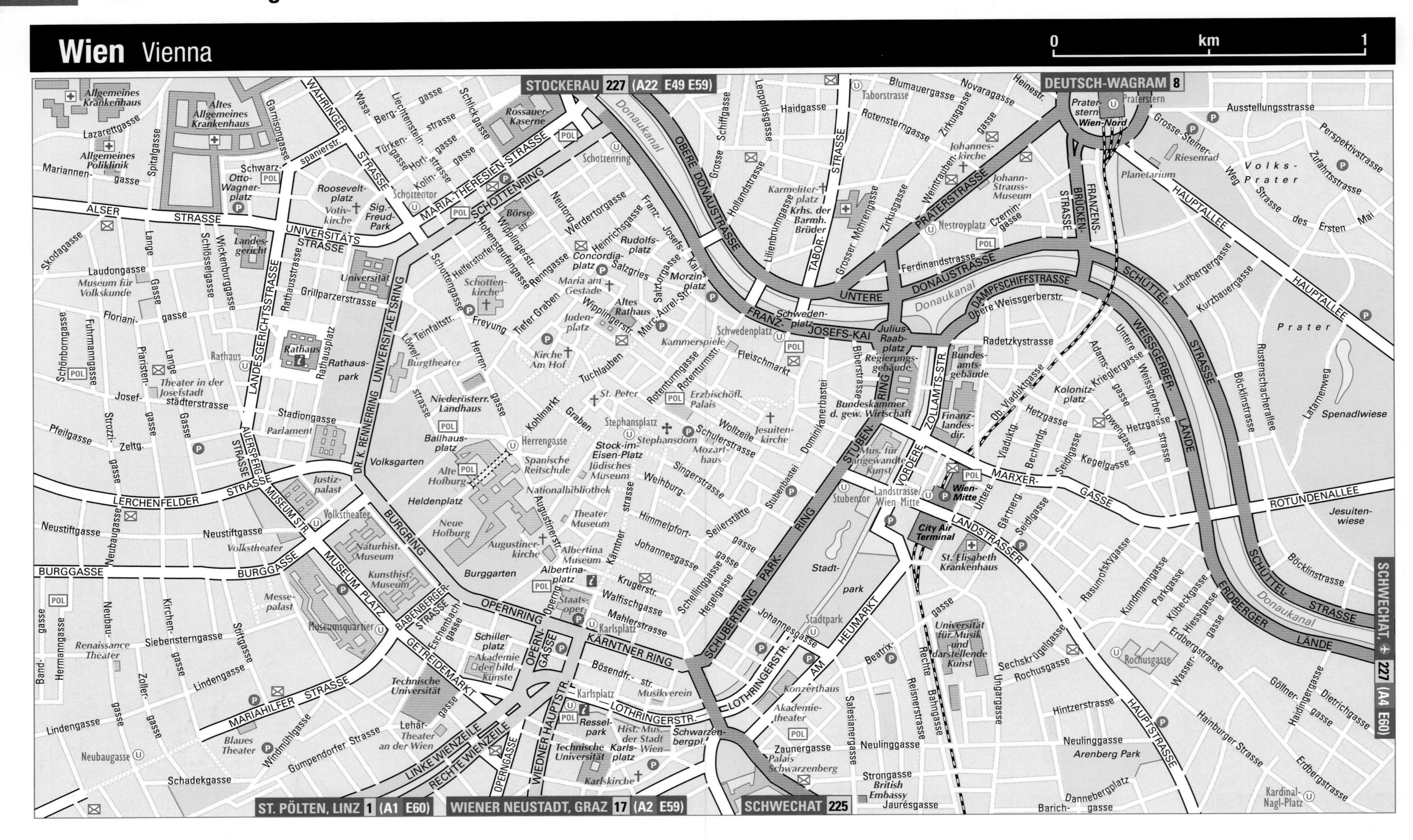

Wien Vienna

0 km 1

STOCKERAU 227 (A22 E49 E59)
DEUTSCH-WAGRAM 8

ST. PÖLTEN, LINZ 1 (A1 E60) | WIENER NEUSTADT, GRAZ 17 (A2 E59) | SCHWECHAT 225

SCHWECHAT 227 (A4 E60)

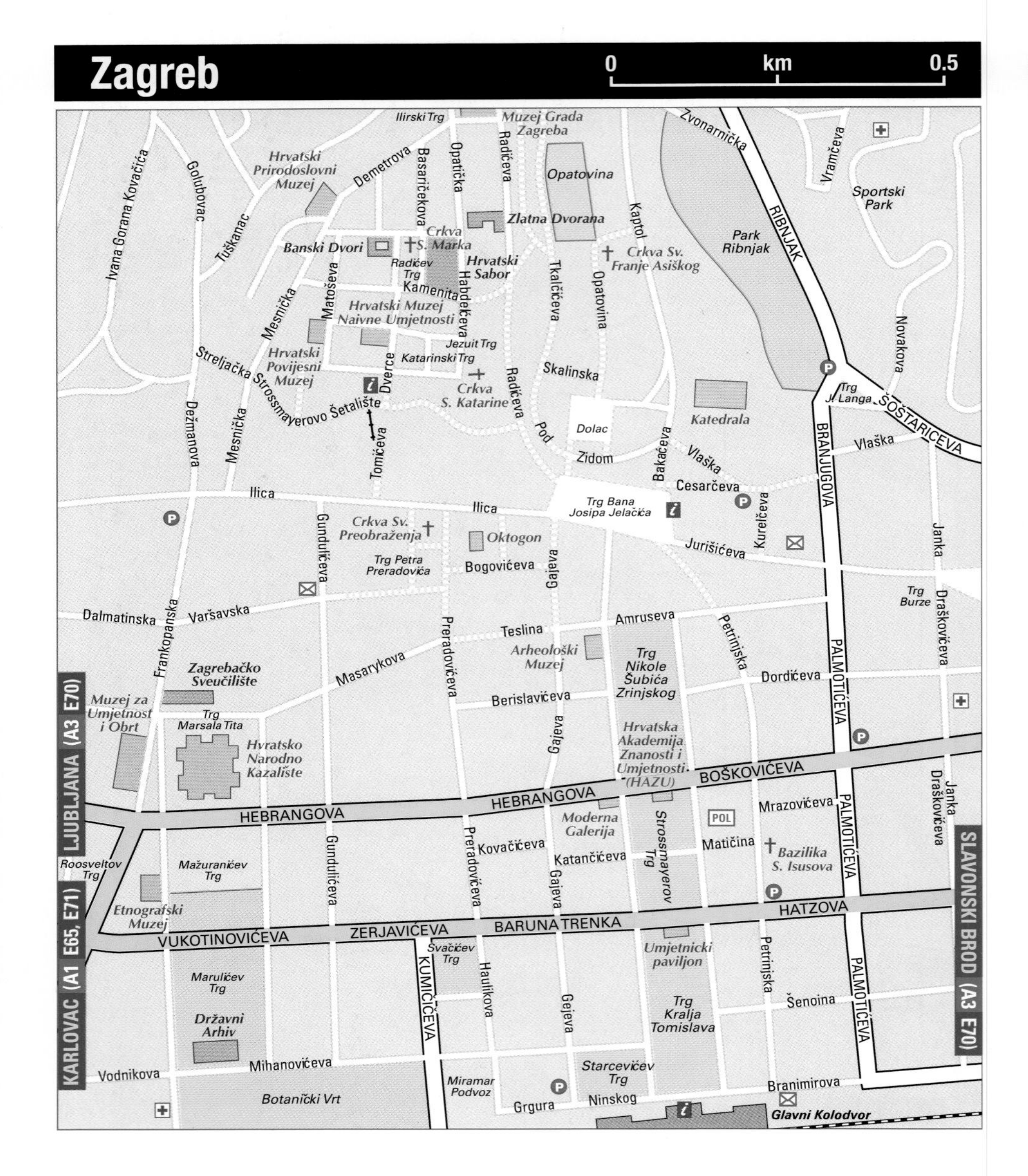

Zagreb

0 km 0.5

KARLOVAC (A1 E65, E71) | LJUBLJANA (A3 E70)

SLAVONSKI BROD (A3 E70)

Glavni Kolodvor

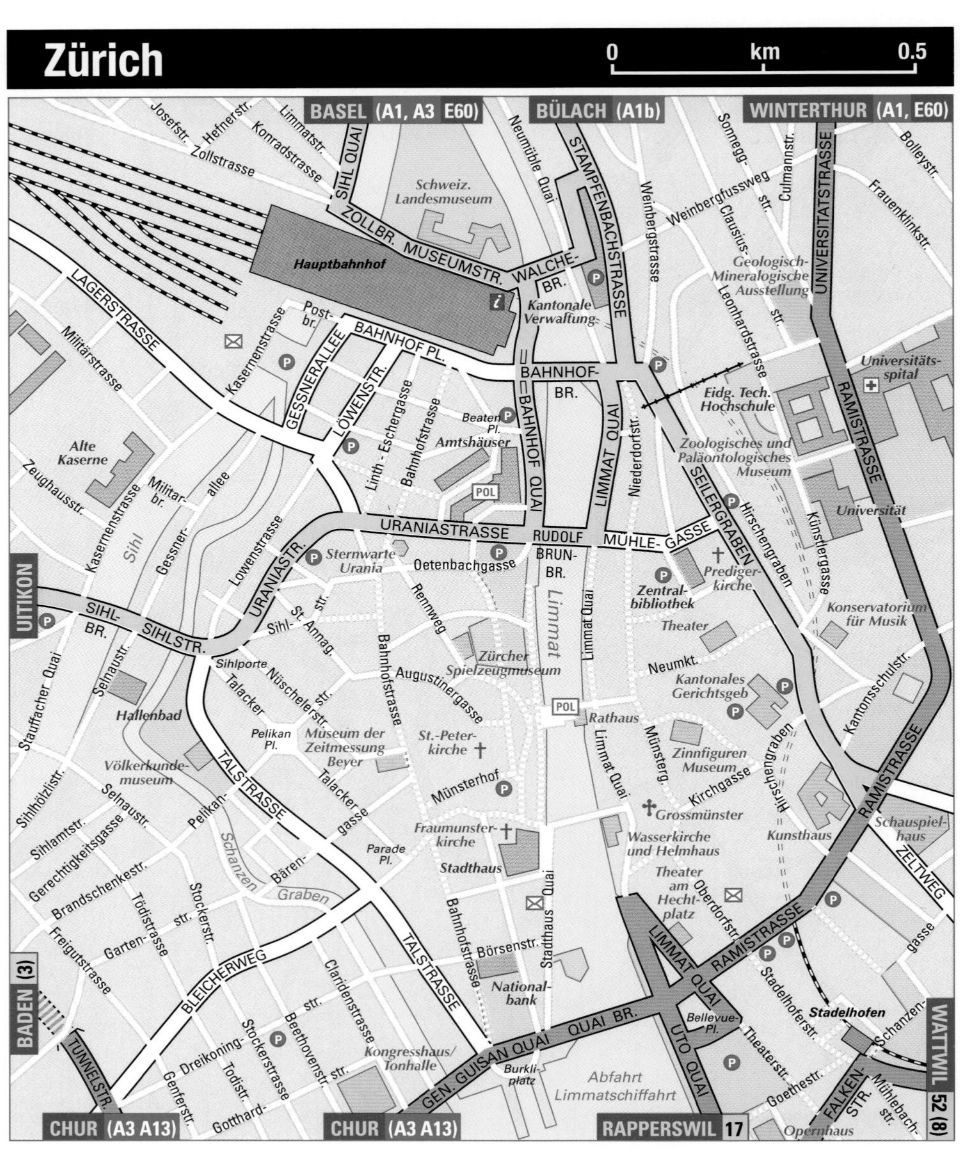

Zürich

0 km 0.5

BASEL (A1, A3 E60) | BÜLACH (A1b) | WINTERTHUR (A1, E60)

BADEN (3)

CHUR (A3 A13) | CHUR (A3 A13) | RAPPERSWIL 17

WATTWIL 52 (8)

Code	English	Français	Deutsch	Italiano
A	Austria	Autriche	Österreich	Austria
AL	Albania	Albanie	Albanien	Albania
AND	Andorra	Andorre	Andorra	Andorra
B	Belgium	Belgique	Belgien	Belgio
BG	Bulgaria	Bulgarie	Bulgarien	Bulgaria
BIH	Bosnia-Herzegovin	Bosnia-Herzegovine	Bosnien-Herzegowina	Bosnia-Herzogovina
BY	Belarus	Belarus	Weissrussland	Bielorussia
CH	Switzerland	Suisse	Schweiz	Svizzera
CY	Cyprus	Chypre	Zypern	Cipro
CZ	Czechia	République Tchèque	Tschechische Republik	Repubblica Ceca
D	Germany	Allemagne	Deutschland	Germania
DK	Denmark	Danemark	Dänemark	Danimarca
E	Spain	Espagne	Spanien	Spagna
EST	Estonia	Estonie	Estland	Estonia
F	France	France	Frankreich	Francia
FIN	Finland	Finlande	Finnland	Finlandia

Code	English	Français	Deutsch	Italiano
FL	Liechtenstein	Liechtenstein	Liechtenstein	Liechtenstein
FO	Faeroe Islands	Îles Féroé	Färöer-Inseln	Isole Faroe
GB	United Kingdom	Royaume Uni	Grossbritannien und Nordirland	Regno Unito
GBZ	Gibraltar	Gibraltar	Gibraltar	Gibilterra
GR	Greece	Grèce	Greichenland	Grecia
H	Hungary	Hongrie	Ungarn	Ungheria
HR	Croatia	Croatie	Kroatien	Croazia
I	Italy	Italie	Italien	Italia
IRL	Ireland	Irlande	Irland	Irlanda
IS	Iceland	Islande	Island	Islanda
KOS	Kosovo	Kosovo	Kosovo	Kosovo
L	Luxembourg	Luxembourg	Luxemburg	Lussemburgo
LT	Lithuania	Lituanie	Litauen	Lituania
LV	Latvia	Lettonie	Lettland	Lettonia
M	Malta	Malte	Malta	Malta
MC	Monaco	Monaco	Monaco	Monaco

Code	English	Français	Deutsch	Italiano
MD	Moldova	Moldavie	Moldawien	Moldavia
MK	Macedonia	Macédoine	Makedonien	Macedonia
MNE	Montenegro	Monténégro	Montenegro	Montenegro
N	Norway	Norvège	Norwegen	Norvegia
NL	Netherlands	Pays-Bas	Niederlande	Paesi Bassi
P	Portugal	Portugal	Portugal	Portogallo
PL	Poland	Pologne	Polen	Polonia
RO	Romania	Roumanie	Rumanien	Romania
RSM	San Marino	Saint-Marin	San Marino	San Marino
RUS	Russia	Russie	Russland	Russia
S	Sweden	Suède	Schweden	Svezia
SK	Slovakia	République Slovaque	Slowak Republik	Repubblica Slovacca
SLO	Slovenia	Slovénie	Slowenien	Slovenia
SRB	Serbia	Serbie	Serbien	Serbia
TR	Turkey	Turquie	Türkei	Turchia
UA	Ukraine	Ukraine	Ukraine	Ucraina

A

Aabenraa DK 39 D2
Aabybro DK 38 B2
Aach D 71 A4
Aachen D 50 C2
Aalborg DK 38 B2
Aalen D 61 B6
Aalestrup DK 38 C2
Aalsmeer NL 49 A5
Aalst B 49 C5
Aalten NL 50 B2
Aalter B 49 B4
Äänekoski FIN 3 E26
Aapajärvi FIN 113 E16
Ağapınar TR 118 C5
Aarau CH 70 A3
Aarberg CH 70 A2
Aarburg CH 70 A2
Aardenburg NL 49 B4
Aars DK 38 C2
Aarschot B 49 C5
Aarup DK 39 D3
Aba H 74 A3
Abádanes E 95 B4
Abades E 94 B2
Abadin E 86 A3
Abádszalók H 75 A5
Abaliget H 74 B3
Abana TR 16 A7
A Baña E 86 B2
Abanilla E 101 A4
Abano Terme I 72 C1
Abarán E 101 A4
Abasár H 65 C6
Abbadia San Salvatore I 81 D5
Abbaue D 45 B5
Abbehausen D 43 B5
Abbekäs S 41 D3
Abbeville F 48 C2
Abbey IRL 20 A3
Abbeydorney IRL 20 B2
Abbeyfeale IRL 20 B2
Abbeyleix IRL 21 B4
Abbey Town GB 25 D4
Abbiategrasso I 70 C3
Abborrträsk S 115 B16
Abbots Bromley GB 27 C4
Abbotsbury GB 29 C5
Abda H 64 C3
Abejar E 89 C4
Abela P 98 B2
Abelvær N 114 C8
Abenberg D 62 A1
Abenójar E 100 A1
Abensberg D 62 B2
Aberaeron GB 28 A3
Abercarn GB 29 B4
Aberchirder GB 23 D6
Aberdare GB 29 B4
Aberdaron GB 26 C1
Aberdeen GB 23 D6
Aberdulais GB 28 B4
Aberdyfi GB 26 C1
Aberfeldy GB 25 B4
Aberffraw GB 26 B1
Aberfoyle GB 24 B3
Abergavenny GB 29 B4
Abergele GB 26 B2
Abergynolwyn GB 26 C2
Aberporth GB 28 A3
Abersoch GB 26 C1
Abertillery GB 29 B4
Abertura E 93 B5
Aberystwyth GB 26 C1
Abetone I 81 B4
Abfaltersbach A 72 B2
Abide
Çanakkale TR 118 B1
Kütahya TR 118 D4
Abiego E 90 A2
Abild DK 39 E1
Abingdon-on-Thames GB 31 C2
Abington GB 25 C4
Abisko S 112 D7
Abiul P 92 B2
Abla E 101 B3
Ablis F 58 B2
A Bola E 87 B3
Abondance F 70 B1
Abony H 75 A5
Aboyne GB 23 D6
Abrantes P 92 B2
Abreiro P 87 C3
Abreschviller F 60 B3
Abrest F 68 B3
Abriès F 79 B5
Abrud RO 11 C7
Absdorf A 64 B1
Abtenau A 72 A3
Abtsgmünd D 61 B5
Abusejo E 93 A4
Åby
Kronoberg S 40 B4
Östergötland S 37 D3
Åbyggeby S 36 B4
Åbytorp S 37 C2
A Cañiza E 87 B2
A Capela E 86 A2
Acate I 109 B3
Accadia I 103 B8
Accéglio I 79 B5
Accettura I 104 C2
Acciaroli I 106 A2
Accous F 76 D2
Accrington GB 26 B3
Accúmoli I 82 D2
Acedera E 93 B5
Acehuche E 93 B4
Acered E 95 A5
Acerenza I 104 C1
Acerno I 103 C8
Acerra I 103 C7
Aceuchal E 93 C4
Acharacle GB 24 B2
Acharnes GR 117 D5
Achavanich GB 23 C5
Achene B 49 C6
Achenkirch A 72 A1
Achensee A 72 A1
Achenthal A 72 A1
Achentrias GR 117 H7
Achern D 61 B4
Acheux-en-Amienois F 48 C3
Achiltibuie GB 22 C3
Achim D 43 B6
Achladokambos GR 117 E4
Achnasheen GB 22 D3
Achnashellach GB 22 D3
Achosnich GB 24 B1
Aci Castello I 109 B4
Aci Catena I 109 B4
Acilia I 102 B5
Acıpayam TR 119 E4
Acireale I 109 B4
Acle GB 30 B5
A Coruña E 86 A2
Acquacadda I 110 C1
Acqua Doria F 102 B1
Acquanegra sul Chiese I 71 C5
Acquapendente I 81 D5
Acquasanta Terme I 82 D2
Acquasparta I 102 A5
Acquaviva I 81 C5
Acquaviva delle Fonti I 104 C2
Acquaviva Picena I 82 D2
Acquigny F 58 A2
Ácqui Terme I 80 B2
Acri I 106 B3
Acs H 64 C4
Acsa H 65 C5
Ácsteszér H 74 A2
Acy-en-Multien F 59 A3
Ada SRB 75 C5
Adak S 115 B15
Ådalsbruk N 34 B3
Adamas GR 117 F6
Adamsfjord N 113 B15
Adamuz E 100 A1
Adana TR 16 C7
Ádánd H 74 B3
Adanero E 94 B2
Adare IRL 20 B3
Adaševci SRB 85 A4
Adeanueva de Ebro E 89 B5
Adelboden CH 70 B2
Adelebsen D 51 B5
Adélfia I 104 B2
Adelmannsfelden D 61 B6
Adelsheim D 61 A5
Adelsö S 37 C4
Ademuz E 96 A1
Adenau D 50 C2
Adendorf D 44 B2
Adinkerke B 48 B3
Adjud RO 11 C9
Adliswil CH 70 A3
Admont A 63 C5
Ådneram N 33 C3
Adolfsström S 115 A13
Adony H 74 A3
Adorf
Hessen D 51 B4
Sachsen D 52 C2
Adra E 100 C2
Adradas E 89 C4
Adrall E 91 A4
Adrano I 109 B3
Ádria I 82 A1
Adrigole IRL 20 C2
Adwick le Street GB 27 B4
Adzaneta E 96 A2
Aesch CH 70 A2
A Estrada E 86 B2
Afandou GR 119 F3
Åfarnes N 114 E4
Affing D 62 B1
Affoltern CH 70 A3
Affric Lodge GB 22 D3
Åfjord N 114 D7
Aflenz Kurort A 73 A5
A Fonsagrada E 86 A3
Afragóla I 103 C7
Afritz A 72 B3
Afyon TR 118 D5
Ágasegyháza H 75 B4
Agay F 79 C5
Agazzano I 80 B3
Agde F 78 C2
Agdenes N 114 D6
Agen F 77 B3
Ager E 90 B3
Agerbæk DK 39 D1
Agerskov DK 39 D2
Ageyevo RUS 7 D14
Agger DK 38 C1
Aggersund DK 38 B2
Äggius I 110 B2
Aggsbach Dorf A 63 B6
Aggsbach Markt A 63 B6
Aggtelek H 65 B6
Aghalee GB 19 B5
Aghia GR 116 C4
Aghia Anna GR 116 D5
Aghia Galini GR 117 G6
Aghia Marina GR 119 G1
Aghia Paraskevi GR 118 C1
Aghia Pelagia GR 117 F4
Aghia Triada GR 117 E3
Aghiokambos GR 116 C4
Aghios Efstratios GR 116 C6
Aghios Kirikos GR 119 E1
Aghios Matheos GR 116 C1
Aghios Mironas GR 117 G7
Aghios Nikolaos GR 117 G7
Aghios Petros GR 116 D2
Aghio Theodori GR 117 E5
Agiči BIH 83 B5
Agira I 109 B3
Aglientu I 110 A2
Agnières F 79 B4
Agno CH 70 C3
Agnone I 103 B7
Agolada E 86 B2
Agon Coutainville F 57 A4
Ágordo I 72 B2
Agost E 96 C2
Agramón E 101 A4
Agramunt E 91 B4
Agreda E 89 C5
Agria GR 116 C5
Agrigento I 108 B2
Agrinio GR 116 D3
Agrón E 100 B2
Agrópoli I 103 C7
Aguadulce
Almería E 101 C3
Sevilla E 100 B1
Agualada E 86 A2
Agua Longa P 87 C2
A Guarda E 87 C2
Aguarón E 89 C5
Aguas E 90 A2
Aguas Belas P 92 B2
Aguas de Busot E 96 C2
Aguas de Moura P 92 C2
Águas Frias P 87 C3
Aguas Santas P 87 C2
Aguaviva E 90 C2
Aguaviva de la Vega E 89 C4
A Gudiña E 87 B3
Agudo E 94 D2
Águeda P 92 A2
Aguessac F 78 B2
Agugliano I 82 C2
Aguiar P 92 C3
Aguiàr da Beira P 87 D3
Aguilafuente E 94 A2
Aguilar de Campóo E 88 B2
Aguilar de la Frontera E 100 B1
Aguilas E 101 B4
Agunnaryd S 40 C4
Ahat TR 118 D4
Ahaus D 50 A2
Aheim N 114 E2
Ahigal E 93 A4
Ahigal de Villarino E 87 C4
Ahillones E 99 A5
Ahlbeck
Mecklenburg-Vorpommern D 45 B6
Mecklenburg-Vorpommern D 45 B6
Ahlen D 50 B3
Ahlhorn D 43 C5
Ahmetbey TR 118 A2
Ahmetler TR 119 D4
Ahmetli TR 119 D2
Ahoghill GB 19 B5
Ahrensbök D 44 A2
Ahrensburg D 44 B2
Ahrenshoop D 44 A4
Ahun F 68 B2
Åhus S 41 D4
Ahvenselkä FIN 113 F17
Aibar E 89 B5
Aich D 62 B3
Aicha D 63 B4
Aichach D 62 B2
Aidone I 109 B3
Aiello Cálabro I 106 B3
Aigen im Mühlkreis A 63 B4
Aigle CH 70 B1
Aignan F 76 C3
Aignay-le-Duc F 59 C5
Aigre F 67 C5
Aigrefeuille-d'Aunis F 66 B4
Aigrefeuille-sur-Maine F 66 A3
Aiguablava E 91 B6
Aiguebelle F 69 C6
Aigueperse F 68 B3
Aigues-Mortes F 78 C3
Aigues-Vives F 78 C1
Aiguilles F 79 B5
Aiguillon F 77 B3
Aigurande F 68 B1
Ailefroide F 79 B5
Aillant-sur-Tholon F 59 C4
Ailly-sur-Noye F 58 A3
Ailly-sur-Somme F 58 A3
Aimargues F 78 C3
Aime F 69 C6
Ainaži LV 6 C8
Ainet A 72 B2
Ainhoa F 76 C1
Ainsa E 90 A3
Airaines F 48 D2
Aird GB 24 B2
Aird Asaig Tairbeart GB 22 D2
Airdrie GB 25 C4
Aire-sur-l'Adour F 76 C2
Aire-sur-la-Lys F 48 C3
Airole I 80 C1
Airolo CH 70 B3
Airvault F 67 B4
Aisey-sur-Seine F 59 C5
Aïssey F 69 A6
Aisy-sur-Armançon F 59 C5
Aiterhofen D 62 B3
Aith
Orkney GB 23 B6
Shetland GB 22 A7
Aitona E 90 B3
Aitrach D 61 C6
Aiud RO 11 C7
Aix-en-Othe F 59 B4
Aix-en-Provence F 79 C4
Aixe-sur-Vienne F 67 C6
Aix-les-Bains F 69 C5
Aizenay F 66 B3
Aizkraukle LV 7 C8
Aizpute LV 6 C6
Ajac F 77 C5
Ajaccio F 102 B1
Ajain F 68 B1
Ajaureforsen S 115 B12
Ajdovščina SLO 72 C3
Ajka H 74 A2
Ajo E 89 A3
Ajofrin E 94 C3
Ajuda P 93 C3
Akanthou CY 120 A2
Akarca TR 118 D4
Akasztó H 75 B4
Akçakoca TR 118 A6
Akçaova TR 118 A4
Akçay TR 119 F4
Aken D 52 B2
Åkerby S 36 B4
Åkernes N 33 D4
Åkersberga S 37 C5
Åkers Styckebruk S 37 C4
Åkervik N 115 B10
Akhisar TR 118 D2
Åkirkeby DK 41 D4
Akköy TR 119 E2
Akkrum NL 42 B2
Akören TR 119 E7
Åkra N 32 C3
Akranes IS 111 C3
Åkrehamn N 33 C2
Akrotiri CY 120 B1
Aksaray TR 16 B7
Akşehir TR 119 D6
Akseki TR 119 E6
Aksla N 32 A3
Aksu TR 119 F5
Aktsyabrski BY 7 E10
Akureyri IS 111 B7
Åkvåg N 33 D6
Akyazı TR 118 B5
Ål N 32 B5
Ala I 71 C6
Alaca TR 16 A7
Alacaatlı TR 118 C3
Alaçam TR 16 A7
Alaçatı TR 119 D1
Alàdei Sardi I 110 B2
Ala di Stura I 70 C2
Alaejos E 88 C1
Alagna Valsésia I 70 C2
Alagón E 90 B1
Alaior E 97 B4
Alájar E 99 B4
Alakurtti RUS 3 C29
Alakylä FIN 113 E13
Alameda E 100 B1
Alameda de la Sagra E 94 B3
Alamedilla E 100 B2
Alamillo E 100 A1
Alaminos E 95 B4
Ala-Nampa FIN 113 F15
Alanäs S 115 C12
Alandroal P 92 C3
Alange E 93 C4
Alanís E 99 A5
Alanno I 103 A6
Ålansbro S 115 E14
Alanya TR 119 F7
Alap H 74 B3
Alaquáso E 96 B2
Alaraz E 94 B1
Alarcón E 95 C4
Alar del Rey E 88 B2
Alaró E 97 B2
Alaşehir TR 119 D3
Alássio I 80 B2
Ağlasun TR 119 E5
Alatoz E 96 B1
Alatri I 103 B6
Alavus FIN 3 E25
Alba
E 95 B5
I 80 B2
Alba Adriática I 82 D2
Albacete E 95 D5
Alba de Tormes E 94 B1
Alba de Yeltes E 93 A4
Albaida E 96 C2
Alba-Iulia RO 11 C7
Ålbæk DK 38 B3
Albaladejo E 101 A3
Albala del Caudillo E 93 B4
Albalat E 96 B2
Albalate de Cinca E 90 B3
Albalate del Arzobispo E 90 B2
Albalate de las Nogueras E 95 B4
Albalete de Zorita E 95 B4
Alban F 77 C5
Albánchez E 101 B3
Albanchez de Ubeda E 100 B2
Albano Laziale I 102 B5
Albanyà E 91 A5
Albaredo d'Adige I 71 C6
Albares E 95 B3
Albarracín E 95 B5
Albatana E 101 A4
Albatarrec E 90 B3
Albatera E 101 A5
Albbruck D 61 C4
Albedin E 100 B1
Albelda de Iregua E 89 B4
Albenga I 80 B2
Albens F 69 C5
Ålberga
Södermanland S 37 C3
Södermanland S 37 D3
Albergaria-a-Nova P 87 D2
Albergaria-a-Velha P 92 A2
Albergaria dos Doze P 92 B2
Alberge P 92 C2
Alberic E 96 B2
Albernoa P 98 B3
Alberobello I 104 C3
Alberoni I 72 C2
Albersdorf D 43 A6
Albersloh D 50 B3
Albert F 48 C3
Albertirsa H 75 A4
Albertville F 69 C6
Alberuela de Tubo E 90 B2
Albi F 77 C5
Albidona I 106 B3
Albínia I 102 A4
Albino I 71 C4
Albinshof D 45 B5
Albires E 88 B1
Albisola Marina I 80 B2
Albocácer E 90 C3
Albolote E 100 B2
Albondón E 100 C2
Alborea E 96 B1
Albox E 101 B3
Albrechtice nad Vitavou CZ 63 A5
Albstadt D 61 B5
Albufeira P 98 B2
Albuñol E 100 C2
Albuñuelas E 100 C2
Alburquerque E 93 B3
Alby
Öland S 41 C6
Västernorrland S 115 E12
Alcácer do Sal P 92 C2
Alcáçovas P 92 C2
Alcadozo E 101 A4
Alcafoces P 93 B3
Alcains P 92 B3
Alcaláde Guadaira E 99 B5
Alcaláde Gurrea E 90 A2
Alcaláde Henares E 95 B3
Alcaláde la Selva E 90 C2
Alcaládel Júcar E 96 B1
Alcaláde los Gazules E 99 C5
Alcaládel Río E 99 B5
Alcaládel Valle E 99 C5
Alcaláde Xivert E 90 C3
Alcalála Real E 100 B2
Álcamo I 108 B1
Alcampell E 90 B3
Alcanadre E 89 B4
Alcanar E 90 C3
Alcanede P 92 B2
Alcanena P 92 B2
Alcañices E 87 C4
Alcántara E 93 B4
Alcantarilha P 98 B2
Alcantarilla E 101 B4
Alcañiz E 90 B2
Alcaracejos E 100 A1
Alcara il Fusi I 109 A3
Alcaraz E 101 A3
Alcaria Ruiva P 98 B3
Alcarraz E 90 B3
Alcaudete E 100 B1
Alcaudete de la Jara E 94 C2
Alcázar de San Juan E 95 C3
Alcazarén E 88 C2
Alcester GB 29 A6
Alcoba E 94 C2
Alcobaça P 92 B1
Alcobendas E 94 B3
Alcocer E 95 B4
Alcochete P 92 C2
Alcoentre P 92 B2
Alcolea
Almería E 100 C3
Córdoba E 100 B1
Alcolea de Calatrava E 94 D2
Alcolea de Cinca E 90 B3
Alcolea del Pinar E 95 A4
Alcolea del Rio E 99 B5
Alcolea de Tajo E 93 B5
Alcollarin E 93 B5
Alconchel E 93 C3
Alconera E 93 C4
Alcontar E 101 B3
Alcora E 96 A2
Alcorcón E 94 B3
Alcorisa E 90 C2
Alcossebre E 96 A3
Alcoutim P 98 B3
Alcover E 91 B4
Alcoy E 96 C2
Alcsútdoboz H 74 A3
Alcubierre E 90 B2
Alcubilla de Avellaneda E 89 C3
Alcubilla de Nogales E 88 B1
Alcubillas E 100 A2
Alcublas E 96 B2
Alcúdia E 97 B3
Alcudia de Guadix E 100 B2
Alcuéscar E 93 B4
Aldbrough GB 27 B5
Aldeacentenera E 93 B5
Aldeadávila de la Ribera E 87 C4
Aldea del Cano E 93 B4
Aldea del Fresno E 94 B2
Aldea del Obispo E 87 D4
Aldea del Rey E 100 A2
Aldea de Trujillo E 93 B5
Aldealcorvo E 94 A3
Aldealuenga de Santa Maria E 89 C3
Aldeamayor de San Martin E 88 C2
Aldeanueva de Barbarroya E 94 C1
Aldeanueva del Camino E 93 A5
Aldeanueva del Codonal E 94 A2
Aldeanueva de San Bartolomé E 94 C1
Aldeapozo E 89 C4
Aldeaquemada E 100 A2
Aldea Real E 94 A2
Aldearrubia E 94 A1
Aldeaseca de la Frontera E 94 B1
Aldeasoña E 88 C2
Aldeatejada E 94 B1
Aldeavieja E 94 B2
Aldeburgh GB 30 B5
Aldehuela E 96 A1
Aldehuela de Calatañazor E 89 C4
Aldeia da Serra P 92 C3
Aldeia do Bispo P 93 A4
Aldeia do Mato P 92 B2
Aldeia Gavinha P 92 B1
Aldeire E 100 B2
Aldenhoven D 50 C2
Aldersbach D 62 B4
Aldershot GB 31 C3
Aldudes F 76 C1
Åled S 40 C2
Aledo E 101 B4
Alegria E 89 B4
Aleksandrovac
Srbija SRB 85 B6
Srbija SRB 85 C6
Aleksandrów Kujawski PL 47 C4
Aleksandrów Łódżki PL 55 B4
Aleksa Šantić SRB 75 C4
Aleksin RUS 7 D14
Älem S 40 C6
Alençon F 57 B6
Alenquer P 92 B1
Alenya F 91 A5
Aléria F 102 A2
Alès F 78 B3
Áles I 110 C1
Alessándria I 80 B2
Alessándria della Rocca I 108 B2
Alessano I 107 B5
Ålesund N 114 E3
Alet-les-Bains F 77 D5
Alexandria
GB 24 C3
GR 116 B4
RO 11 E8
Alexandroupoli GR 116 B7
Aleyrac F 78 B3
Alézio I 107 A5
Alfacar E 100 B2
Alfaiates P 93 A4
Alfajarin E 90 B2
Alfambra
E 90 C1
P 98 B2
Alfândega da Fé P 87 C4
Alfarela de Jafes P 87 C3
Alfarelos P 92 A2
Alfarim P 92 C1
Alfarnate E 100 C1
Alfaro E 89 B5
Alfarrás E 90 B3
Alfaz del Pi E 96 C2
Alfedena I 103 B7
Alfeizarão P 92 B1
Alfeld
Bayern D 62 A2
Niedersachsen D 51 B5
Alfena P 87 C2
Alferce P 98 B2
Alfhausen D 43 C4
Alfonsine I 81 B6
Alford
Aberdeenshire GB 23 D6
Lincolnshire GB 27 B6
Alforja E 90 B3
Alfoz E 86 A3
Alfreton GB 27 B4
Alfta S 36 A3
Alfundão P 98 A2
Algaida E 97 B2
Algar E 99 C5
Älgarås S 35 D6
Ålgård N 33 D2
Algarinejo E 100 B1
Algarrobo E 100 C1
Algatocin E 99 C5
Algeciras E 99 C5
Algemesí E 96 B2
Algés P 92 C1
Algete E 95 B3
Alghero I 110 B1
Älghult S 40 B5
Alginet E 96 B2
Algodonales E 99 C5
Algodor
E 94 C3
P 98 B3
Algora E 95 B4
Algoso P 87 C4
Algoz P 98 B2
Älgsjö S 115 C14
Alguaire E 90 B3
Alguazas E 101 A4
Algutsrum S 41 C6
Algyö H 75 B5
Alhama de Almería E 101 C3
Alhama de Aragón E 89 C5
Alhama de Granada E 100 C2
Alhama de Murcia E 101 B4
Alhambra E 100 A2
Alhandra P 92 C1
Alhaurin de la Torre E 100 C1
Alhaurín el Grande E 100 C1
Alhendin E 100 B2
Alhóndiga E 95 B4
Alia E 93 B5
Ália I 108 B2
Aliağa TR 118 D1
Aliaga E 90 C2
Alibunar SRB 85 A5
Alicante E 96 C2
Alicún de Ortega E 100 B2
Alife I 103 B7
Alija del Infantado E 88 B1
Alijó P 87 C3
Alimena I 109 B3
Alingsås S 40 B2
Alinyà E 91 A4
Aliseda E 93 B4
Ali Terme I 109 A4
Aliveri GR 116 D6
Alixan F 79 B4
Aljaraque E 99 B3
Aljezur P 98 B2
Aljorra E 101 B4
Aljubarrota P 92 B2
Aljucen E 93 B4
Aljustrel P 98 B2
Alken B 49 C6
Alkmaar NL 42 C1
Alkoven A 63 B5
Allaines F 58 B2
Allaire F 57 C3
Allanche F 68 C2
Alland A 64 B2
Allariz E 87 B3
Allassac F 67 C6
Allauch F 79 C4
Alleen N 33 D4
Allègre F 68 C3
Allemont F 69 C6
Allendale Town GB 25 D5
Allendorf D 51 C4
Allentsteig A 63 B6
Allepuz E 90 C2
Allersberg D 62 A2
Allershausen D 62 B2
Alles E 88 A2
Allevard F 69 C6
Allgunnen S 40 B5
Allihies IRL 20 C1
Allingåbro DK 38 C3
Allmannsdorf D 61 C5
Allo E 89 B4
Alloa GB 25 B4
Allogny F 68 A2
Ålloluokta S 112 E8
Allones
Eure et Loire F 58 B2
Maine-et-Loire F 67 A5
Allonnes F 57 C6
Allons F 76 B2
Allos F 79 B5
Allstedt D 52 B1
Alltwalis GB 28 B3
Allumiere I 102 A4
Almaceda P 92 B3
Almacelles E 90 B3
Almachar E 100 C1
Almada P 92 C1
Almadén E 100 A1
Almadén de la Plata E 99 B4
Almadenejos E 100 A1
Almadrones E 95 B4
Almagro E 100 A2
Almajano E 89 C4
Almansa E 96 C1
Almansil P 98 B2
Almanza E 88 B1
Almaraz E 93 B5
Almargen E 99 C5
Almarza E 89 C4
Almásfüzitő H 64 C4
Almassora E 96 B2
Almazán E 89 C4
Almazul E 89 C4
Alme D 51 B4
Almedina E 100 A3
Almedinilla E 100 B1
Almeida
E 87 C4
P 93 A4
Almeirim P 92 B2
Almelo NL 42 C3
Almenar E 90 B3
Almenara E 96 B2
Almenar de Soria E 89 C4
Almendra P 87 D3
Almendral E 93 C4
Almendral de la Cañada E 94 B2
Almendralejo E 93 C4
Almenno San Bartolomeo I 71 C4
Almere NL 42 C2
Almería E 101 C3
Almerimar E 101 C3
Almese I 70 C2
Almexial P 98 B3
Älmhult S 40 C4
Almiropotamos GR 117 D6
Almiros GR 116 C4
Almodôvar P 98 B2
Almodóvar del Campo E 100 A1
Almodóvar del Pinar E 95 C5
Almodóvar del Río E 99 B5
Almofala P 87 D3
Almogia E 100 C1
Almoharin E 93 B4
Almonacid de la Sierra E 89 C5
Almonacid de Toledo E 94 C3
Almonaster la Real E 99 B4
Almondsbury GB 29 B5
Almonte E 99 B4
Almoradí E 101 A5
Almoraima E 99 C5
Almorox E 94 B2
Almoster P 92 B2
Almsele S 115 C14
Älmsta S 36 C5
Almudena E 101 A4
Almudévar E 90 A2
Almuñécar E 100 C2
Almunge S 36 C5
Almuradiel E 100 A2
Almussafes E 96 B2
Almvik S 40 B6
Alness GB 23 D4
Alnmouth GB 25 C6
Alnwick GB 25 C6
Åloppe S 36 C4
Álora E 100 C1
Alos d'Ensil E 91 A4
Alosno E 99 B3
Alozaina E 100 C1
Alpbach A 72 A1
Alpedrete de la Sierra E 95 B3
Alpedrinha P 92 A3
Alpen D 50 B2
Alpera E 96 C1
Alphen aan de Rijn NL 49 A5
Alpiarça P 92 B2
Alpignano I 70 C2
Alpirsbach D 61 B4
Alpu TR 118 C5
Alpuente E 96 B1
Alqueva P 98 A3
Alquézar E 90 A3
Als DK 38 C3
Alsasua E 89 B4
Alsdorf D 50 C2
Alselv DK 39 D1
Alsfeld D 51 C5
Alsike S 36 C4
Alskog S 37 E5
Alsleben D 52 B1
Alsónémedi H 75 A4
Alsótold H 65 C5

Alsóújlak H 74 A1
Alstad N 112 E4
Alstätte D 50 A2
Alsterbro S 40 C5
Alstermo S 40 C5
Alston GB 25 D5
Alsvåg N 112 D4
Alsvik N 112 E3
Alta N 113 C12
Älta S 37 C5
Altamura I 104 C2
Altarejos E 95 C4
Altaussee A 63 C4
Altavilla Irpina I 103 B7
Altavilla Silentina I 103 C8
Altdöbern D 53 B4
Altdorf
CH 70 B3
D 62 B3
Altdorf bei Nürnberg
D 62 A2
Alte P 98 B2
Altea E 96 C2
Altedo I 81 B5
Altena D 50 B3
Altenau D 51 B6
Altenberg D 53 C3
Altenberge D 50 A3
Altenbruch D 43 B5
Altenburg D 52 C2
Altenfelden A 63 B4
Altengronau D 51 C5
Altenheim D 60 B3
Altenhundem D 50 B4
Altenkirchen
Mecklenburg-Vorpommern D 45 A5
Radom D 50 C3
Altenkunstadt D 52 C1
Altenmarkt
A 63 C4
D 62 B3
Altenmarkt im Pongall
A 72 A3
Altensteig D 61 B4
Altentreptow D 45 B5
Altenwalde D 43 B5
Alten-weddingen D 52 A1
Alter do Chão P 92 B3
Altfraunhofen D 62 B3
Altheim
A 63 B4
D 61 A5
Althofen A 73 B4
Altınoluk TR 118 C1
Altınova TR 118 C1
Altıntaş TR 118 C5
Altınyaka TR 119 F5
Altınyayla TR 119 E4
Altkirch F 60 C3
Altlandsberg D 45 C5
Altlewin D 45 C6
Altmannstein D 62 B2
Altmorschen D 51 B5
Altmunster A 63 C4
Altnaharra GB 23 C4
Alto Campoó E 88 A2
Altofonte I 108 A2
Altomonte I 106 B3
Alton
Hampshire GB 31 C3
Staffordshire GB 27 C4
Altopáscio I 81 C4
Altötting D 62 B3
Altreichenau D 63 B4
Alt Ruppin D 45 C4
Altshausen D 61 C5
Altstätten CH 71 A4
Altura E 96 B2
Altusried D 61 C6
Alūksne LV 7 C9
Alunda S 36 B5
Alustante E 95 B5
Alva GB 25 B4
Alvaiázere P 92 B2
Alvalade P 98 B2
Älvängen S 38 B5
Alvarenga P 87 D2
Alvares P 92 A2
Alvdal N 114 E7
Älvdalen S 34 A6
Alverca P 92 C1
Alversund N 32 B2
Alvesta S 40 C4
Alvignac F 77 B4
Alvignano I 103 B7
Alvik N 32 B3
Alvik S 36 B1
Alvimare F 58 A1
Alviobeira P 92 B2
Alvito P 98 A3
Älvkarleby S 36 B4
Älvkarleöbruk S 36 B4
Alvor P 98 B2
Alvorge P 92 B2
Alvøy N 32 B2
Älvros S 115 E11
Alvsbacka S 35 C5
Älvsbyn S 3 D24
Älvsered S 40 B2
Alwernia PL 55 C4
Alwinton GB 25 C5
Alyth GB 25 B4
Alytus LT 6 D8
Alzénau D 51 C5
Alzey D 61 A4
Alzira E 96 B2
Alzonne F 77 C5
Amadora P 92 C1
Åmål S 35 C4
Amalfi I 103 C7
Amaliada GR 117 E3
Amance F 60 C2
Amancey F 69 A6
Amándola I 82 D2
Amantea I 106 B3
Amarante P 87 C2
Amareleja P 98 A3
Amares P 87 C2
Amaseno I 103 B6
Amasra TR 118 A7
Amasya TR 16 A8
Amatrice I 103 A6
Amay B 49 C6
Ambarnyy RUS 3 D30
Ambazac F 67 C6
Ambelonas GR 116 C4
Amberg D 62 A2
Ambérieu-en-Bugey
F 69 C5
Ambérieux-en-Dombes
F 69 B4
Ambert F 68 C3
Ambès F 76 A2
Ambjörby S 34 B5
Ambjörnarp S 40 B3
Amble GB 25 C6
Ambleside GB 26 A3
Ambleteuse F 48 C2
Amboise F 67 A5
Ambrières-les-Vallées
F 57 B5
Amden CH 71 A4
Amel B 50 C2
Amélia I 102 A5
Amélie-les-Bains-Palalda
F 91 A5
Amelinghausen D 44 B2
Amendoa P 92 B2
Amendoeira P 98 B3
Améndola I 104 B1
Amendolara I 106 B3
Amer E 91 A5
A Merca E 87 B3
Amerongen NL 49 A6
Amersfoort NL 49 A6
Amersham GB 31 C3
Amesbury GB 29 B6
Amfiklia GR 116 D4
Amfilochia GR 116 D3
Amfipoli GR 116 B5
Amfissa GR 116 D4
Amièira P 98 A3
Amieira P 92 B3
Amieiro P 92 A2
Amiens F 58 A3
Amindeo GR 116 B3
Åminne S 40 B3
Åmli N 33 D5
Amlwch GB 26 B1
Ammanford GB 28 B4
Ammarnäs S 115 B13
Ammeberg S 37 D1
Amorbach D 61 A5
Amorebieta E 89 A4
Amorgos GR 117 F7
Amorosa P 87 C2
Amorosi I 103 B7
Åmot
Buskerud N 34 C1
Telemark N 33 C4
S 36 B3
Åmotfors S 34 C4
Åmotsdal N 33 C5
Amou F 76 C2
Ampezzo I 72 B2
Ampfing D 62 B3
Ampflwang A 63 B4
Amplepuis F 69 C4
Amposta E 90 C3
Ampthill GB 30 B3
Ampudia E 88 C2
Ampuero E 89 A3
Amriswil CH 71 A4
Åmsele S 115 C16
Amstelveen NL 49 A5
Amsterdam NL 42 C1
Amstetten A 63 B5
Amtzell D 61 C5
Amulree GB 25 B4
Amurrio E 89 A4
Amusco E 88 B2
Anacapri I 103 C7
Anadia P 92 A2
Anadon E 90 C1
Anafi GR 117 F7
Anagni I 102 B6
Anamur TR 16 C6
Ananyiv UA 11 C10
Anascaul IRL 20 B1
Ånäset S 3 D24
Ana-Sira N 33 D3
Anastażewo PL 47 C4
Anaya de Alba E 94 B1
Ança P 92 A2
Ancaster GB 27 C5
Ancede P 87 C2
Ancenis F 66 A3
Ancerville F 59 B6
Anchuras E 94 C2
Ancona I 82 C2
Ancora P 87 C2
Ancrum GB 25 C5
Ancy-le-Franc F 59 C5
Andalo I 71 B5
Åndalsnes N 114 E4
Andance F 69 C4
Andau A 64 C3
Andebu N 35 C2
Andeer CH 71 B4
Andelfingen CH 61 C4
Andelot-Blanchville F 59 B6
Andelot-en-Montagne
F 69 B5
Andenes N 112 C5
Andenne B 49 C6
Anderlues B 49 C5
Andermatt CH 70 B3
Andernach D 50 C3
Andernos-les-Bains F 76 B1
Anderslöv S 41 D3
Anderstorp S 40 B3
Andijk NL 42 C2
Andoain E 89 A4
Andocs H 74 B2
Andolsheim F 60 B3
Andorra E 90 C2
Andorra La Vella AND 91 A4
Andosilla E 89 B5
Andover GB 31 C2
Andratx E 97 B2
Andreapol RUS 7 C12
Andreas GB 26 A1
Andréspol PL 55 B4
Andrest F 76 C3
Andretta I 103 C8
Andrezieux-Bouthéon
F 69 C4
Ándria I 104 B2
Andrijevica MNE 85 D4
Andritsena GR 117 E3
Andros GR 117 E6
Andrychów PL 65 A5
Andselv N 112 C7
Andújar E 100 A1
Anduze F 78 B2
Aneby N 34 B2
Aneby S 40 B4
Añes E 89 A3
Anet F 58 B2
Anfo I 71 C5
Ang S 40 B4
Anga S 37 E5
Angaïs F 76 C2
Änge S 115 D11
Ånge S 115 E12
Angeja P 92 A2
Ängelholm S 41 C2
Angeli FIN 113 D14
Ängelsberg S 36 C3
Anger A 73 A5
Angera I 70 C3
Angermünde D 45 B6
Angern A 64 B2
Angers F 67 A4
Angerville F 58 B3
Anghiari I 82 C1
Angle GB 28 B2
Anglès E 91 B5
Anglés F 77 C5
Angles F 66 B3
Anglesola E 91 B4
Angles sur l'Anglin F 67 B5
Anglet F 76 C1
Anglisidhes CY 120 B2
Anglure F 59 B4
Angoulême F 67 C5
Angoulins F 66 B3
Angsö S 37 C3
Angueira P 87 C4
Angües E 90 A2
Anguiano E 89 B4
Anguillara Sabazia I 102 A5
Anguillara Véneta I 72 C1
Anhée B 49 C5
Anholt DK 38 C4
Aniane F 78 C2
Aniche F 49 C4
Animskog S 35 D4
Anina RO 10 D6
Anixi GR 116 C3
Anizy-le-Château F 59 A4
Anjalankoski FIN 3 F27
Anjan S 115 D9
Ankara TR 118 C7
Ankaran SLO 72 C3
Ankarsrum S 40 B6
Ankerlia N 112 C9
Anklam D 45 B5
Ankum D 43 C4
Anlauftal A 72 A3
Anlezy F 68 B3
Ann S 115 D9
Annaberg A 63 C6
Annaberg-Buchholz
D 52 C3
Annaberg im Lammertal
A 72 A3
Annaburg D 52 B3
Annahütte D 53 B3
Annalong GB 19 B6
Annan GB 25 D4
Anndalsvågen N 115 B9
Anneberg
Halland S 38 B5
Jönköping S 40 B4
Annecy F 69 C6
Annelund S 40 B3
Annemasse F 69 B6
Annenskiy Most RUS 7 A14
Annerstad S 40 C3
Annestown IRL 21 B4
Annevoie-Rouillon B 49 C5
Annonay F 69 C4
Annot F 79 C5
Annweiler D 60 A3
Ano Poroia GR 116 A5
Añora E 100 A1
Ano Siros GR 117 E6
Anould F 60 B2
Anquela del Ducado
E 95 B4
Anröchte D 51 B4
Ans DK 39 C2
Ansager DK 39 D1
Ansbach D 62 A1
Anse F 69 C4
Anseroeul B 49 C4
Ansfelden A 63 B5
Ansião P 92 B2
Ansó E 76 D2
Ansoain E 76 D1
Anstruther GB 25 B5
Antalya TR 119 F5
Antas E 101 B4
Antegnate I 71 C4
Antequera E 100 B1
Anterselva di Mezzo I 72 B2
Antibes F 79 C6
Antigüedad E 88 C2
Antillo I 109 B4
Antirio GR 117 D3
An t-Ob GB 22 D1
Antoing B 49 C4
Antonin PL 54 B2
Antrain F 57 B4
Antrim GB 19 B5
Antrodoco I 102 A6
Antronapiana I 70 B3
Anttis S 113 E11
Antuzede P 92 A2
Antwerp = Antwerpen
B 49 B5
Antwerpen = Antwerp
B 49 B5
Anversa d'Abruzzi I 103 B6
Anvin F 48 C3
Anzat-le-Luguet F 68 C3
Anzi I 104 C1
Ánzio I 102 B5
Anzola d'Emilia I 81 B5
Anzón E 89 C5
Aoiz E 76 D1
Aosta I 70 C2
Apalhão P 92 B3
Apátfalva H 75 B5
Apatin SRB 75 C4
Apatity RUS 3 C30
Apc H 65 C5
Apécchio I 82 C1
Apeldoorn NL 50 A1
Apen D 43 B4
Apenburg D 44 C3
Apensen D 43 B6
A Peroxa E 86 B3
Apiro I 82 C2
Apliki CY 120 B2
Apolda D 52 B1
Apolonia GR 117 F6
A Pontenova E 86 A3
Apostag H 75 B3
Äppelbo S 34 B6
Appennino I 82 D2
Appenzell CH 71 A4
Appiano I 71 B6
Appingedam NL 42 B3
Appleby-in-Westmorland
GB 26 A3
Applecross GB 22 D3
Appledore GB 28 B3
Appoigny F 59 C4
Apremont-la-Forêt F 60 B1
Aprica I 71 B5
Apricena I 103 B8
Aprigliano I 106 B3
Aprilia I 102 B5
Apt F 79 C4
Apúlia P 87 C2
Aquiléia I 72 C3
Aquilónia I 103 C8
Aquino I 103 B6
Ar S 37 E5
Arabayona E 94 A1
Arabba I 72 B1
Araç TR 16 A6
Aracena E 99 B4
Arachova GR 116 D4
Arad RO 75 B6
Aradac SRB 75 C5
Aradhippou CY 120 B2
Aragnouet F 76 D3
Aragona I 108 B2
Aramits F 76 C2
Aramon F 78 C3
Aranda de Duero E 88 C3
Aranda de Moncayo
E 89 C5
Arandjelovac SRB 85 B5
Aranjuez E 95 B3
Arantzazu E 89 B4
Aranzueque E 95 B3
Aras de Alpuente E 96 B1
Arauzo de Miel E 89 C3
Arazede P 92 A2
Arbas F 77 D3
Árbatax I 110 C2
Arbeca E 90 B3
Arberg D 62 A1
Arbesbach A 63 B5
Arboga S 37 C2
Arbois F 69 B5
Arbon CH 71 A4
Arboréa I 110 C1
Arbório I 70 C3
Årbostad N 112 D6
Arbrå S 36 A3
Arbroath GB 25 B5
Arbùcies E 91 B5
Arbuniel E 100 B2
Arbus I 110 C1
Arcachon F 76 B1
Arce I 103 B6
Arcen NL 50 B2
Arc-en-Barrois F 59 C5
Arces-Dilo F 59 B4
Arc-et-Senans F 69 A5
Arcévia I 82 C1
Arcey F 70 A1
Archanes GR 117 G7
Archangelos GR 119 F3
Archena E 101 A4
Archez E 100 C2
Archiac F 67 C4
Archidona E 100 B1
Archiestown GB 23 D5
Archivel E 101 A4
Arcidosso I 81 D5
Arcille I 81 D5
Arcis-sur-Aube F 59 B5
Arc-lès-Gray F 69 A5
Arco I 71 C5
Arcones E 94 A3
Arcos E 88 B3
Arcos de Jalón E 95 A4
Arcos de la Frontera
E 99 C5
Arcos de la Sierra E 95 B4
Arcos de las Salinas
E 96 B1
Arcos de Valdevez P 87 C2
Arcozelo P 92 A3
Arc-sur-Tille F 69 A5
Arcusa E 90 A3
Arcy-sur-Cure F 59 C4
Ardagh IRL 20 B2
Årdal N 33 C3
Ardala S 35 D5
Ardales E 100 C1
Ardalstangen N 32 A4
Ardara
I 110 B1
IRL 18 B3
Ardarroch GB 22 D3
Ardbeg GB 24 C1
Ardcharnich GB 22 D3
Ardchyle GB 24 B3
Ardee IRL 19 C5
Arden DK 38 C2
Ardentes F 68 B1
Ardenza I 81 C4
Ardersier GB 23 D4
Ardes F 68 C3
Ardessie GB 22 D3
Ardez CH 71 B5
Ardfert IRL 20 B2
Ardgay GB 23 D4
Ardglass GB 19 B6
Ardgroom IRL 20 C2
Ardhasig GB 22 D2
Ardino BG 116 A7
Ardisa E 90 A2
Ardkearagh IRL 20 C1
Ardlui GB 24 B3
Ardlussa GB 24 B2
Ardón E 88 B1
Ardooie B 49 C4
Ardore I 106 C3
Ardre S 37 E5
Ardres F 48 C2
Ardrishaig GB 24 B2
Ardrossan GB 24 C3
Are N 33 C2
Åre S 115 D10
Areia Branca P 92 B1
Aremark N 35 C3
Arenales de San Gregorio
E 95 C3
Arenas E 100 C1
Arenas de Iguña E 88 A2
Arenas del Rey E 100 C2
Arenas de San Juan
E 95 C3
Arenas de San Pedro
E 94 B1
Arendal N 33 D5
Arendonk B 49 B6
Arengosse F 76 B2
Arentorp S 35 D4
Arenys de Mar E 91 B5
Arenys de Munt E 91 B5
Arenzano I 80 B2
Areo E 91 A4
Areopoli GR 117 F4
Ares E 86 A2
Arès F 76 B1
Ares del Maestrat E 90 C2
Aresvika N 114 D5
Arette F 76 C2
Aretxabaleta E 89 A4
Arevalillo E 93 A5
Arévalo E 94 A2
Arez P 92 B3
Arezzo I 81 C5
Arfeuilles F 68 B3
Argalasti GR 116 C5
Argallón E 99 A5
Argamasilla de Alba
E 95 C3
Argamasilla de Calatrava
E 100 A1
Arganda E 95 B3
Arganil P 92 A2
Argasion GR 117 E2
Argegno I 71 C4
Argelès-Gazost F 76 C2
Argelès-sur-Mer F 91 A6
Argenta I 81 B5
Argentan F 57 B5
Argentat F 77 A4
Argentera I 79 B5
Argenteuil F 58 B3
Argenthal D 50 D3
Argentiera I 110 B1
Argentona E 91 B5
Argenton-Château F 67 B4
Argenton-sur-Creuse
F 67 B6
Argentré F 57 B5
Argentré-du-Plessis
F 57 B4
Argent-sur-Sauldre F 68 A2
Argirades GR 116 C1
Argithani TR 119 D6
Argos GR 117 E4
Argos Orestiko GR 116 B3
Argostoli GR 117 D2
Argote E 89 B4
Arguedas E 89 B5
Argueil F 58 A2
Arholma S 36 C6
Århus DK 39 C3
Ariano Irpino I 103 B8
Ariano nel Polésine I 82 B1
Aribe E 76 D1
Aridea GR 116 B4
Arienzo I 103 B7
Arild S 41 C2
Arileod GB 24 B1
Arinagour GB 24 B1
Ariño E 90 B2
Arinthod F 69 B5
Arisaig GB 24 B2
Arisgotas E 94 C3
Aritzo I 110 C2
Ariza E 89 C4
Årjäng S 35 C4
Arjeplog S 115 A14
Arjona E 100 B1
Arjonilla E 100 B1
Arkasa GR 119 G2
Arkelstorp S 41 C4
Arklow IRL 21 B5
Arkösund S 37 D3
Ärla S 37 C3
Arlanc F 68 C3
Arlanzón E 89 B3
Arlebosc F 78 A3
Arlena di Castro I 102 A4
Arles F 78 C3
Arles-sur-Tech F 91 A5
Arló H 65 B6
Arlon B 60 A1
Armação de Pera P 98 B2
Armadale
Highland GB 22 D3
West Lothian GB 25 C4
Armagh GB 19 B5
Armamar P 87 C3
Armenistis GR 117 E8
Armeno I 70 C3
Armenteros E 93 A5
Armentières F 48 C3
Armilla E 100 B2
Armiñón E 89 B4
Armoy GB 19 A5
Armuña de Tajuña E 95 B3
Armutlu
Bursa TR 118 B3
İzmir TR 119 D2
Arnac-Pompadour F 67 C6
Arnafjord N 32 A3
Arnage F 57 C6
Arnas F 69 B4
Årnäs S 35 D5
Arnay-le-Duc F 69 A4
Arnborg DK 39 C2
Arnbruck D 62 A3
Arnea GR 116 B5
Arneberg
Hedmark N 34 A2
Hedmark N 34 B4
Arneburg D 44 C4
Arnedillo E 89 B4
Arnedo E 89 B4
Arneguy F 76 C1
Arnés E 90 C3
Árnes IS 111 A4
Årnes
Akershus N 34 B3
Troms N 112 C7
Arnfels A 73 B5
Arnhem NL 50 B1
Arnissa GR 116 B3
Arno S 37 D4
Arnold GB 27 B4
Arnoldstein A 72 B3
Arnsberg D 50 B4
Arnschwang D 62 A3
Arnsdorf D 53 B3
Årnset N 114 D6
Arnside GB 26 A3
Arnstadt D 51 C6
Arnstein D 51 D5
Arnstorf D 62 B3
Arnum DK 39 D1
Aroche E 99 B4
Arolla CH 70 B2
Arolsen D 51 B5
Arona I 70 C3
Åros N 35 C2
Arosa
CH 71 B4
P 87 C2
Ærøskøbing DK 39 E3
Arøsund DK 39 D2
Arouca P 87 D2
Årøysund N 35 C2
Arpajon F 58 B3
Arpajon-sur-Cère F 77 B5
Arpino I 103 B6
Arquata del Tronto I 82 D2
Arques F 48 C3
Arques-la-Bataille F 58 A2
Arquillos E 100 A2
Arraia-Maeztu E 89 B4
Arraiolos P 92 C2
Arrancourt F 60 B2
Arras F 48 C3
Arrasate E 89 A4
Ärre DK 39 D1
Arreau F 77 D3
Arredondo E 89 A3
Arrens-Marsous F 76 D2
Arriate E 99 C5
Arrifana P 98 B2
Arrigorriaga E 89 A4
Arriondas E 88 A1
Arroba de los Montes
E 94 C2
Arrochar GB 24 B3
Arromanches-les-Bains
F 57 A5
Arronches P 92 B3
Arroniz E 89 B4
Arrou F 58 B2
Arroya E 88 B2
Arroya de Cuéllar E 88 C2
Arroyal E 88 B2
Arroyo de la Luz E 93 B4
Arroyo del Ojanco E 100 A3
Arroyo de San Servan
E 93 C4
Arroyomolinos de León
E 99 A4
Arroyomolinos de
Montánchez E 93 B4
Arruda dos Vinhos P 92 C1
Arsac F 76 B2
Ars-en-Ré F 66 B3
Arsiè I 72 C1
Arsiero I 71 C6
Årslev DK 39 D3
Ärsoli I 102 A6
Ars-sur-Moselle F 60 A2
Arsunda S 36 B3
Artà E 97 B3
Arta GR 116 C3
Artajona E 89 B5
Artegna I 72 B3
Arteixo E 86 A2
Artemare F 69 C5
Arten I 72 B1
Artena I 102 B5
Artenay F 58 B2
Artern D 52 B1
Artés E 91 B4
Artesa de Segre E 91 B4
Arth CH 70 A3
Arthez-de-Béarn F 76 C2
Arthon-en-Retz F 66 A3
Arthurstown IRL 21 B5
Artieda E 90 A2
Artix F 76 C2
Artotina GR 116 D4
Artsyz UA 11 C10
Artziniega E 89 A3
A Rúa E 87 B3
Arudy F 76 C2
Arundel GB 31 D3
Arveyres F 76 B2
Arvidsjaur S 115 B16
Arvieux F 79 B5
Arvika S 35 C4
Aryd
Blekinge S 41 C5
Kronoberg S 40 C4
Arzachena I 110 A2
Arzacq-Arraziguet F 76 C2
Árzana I 110 C2
Arzano F 56 C2
Aržano HR 84 C1
Arzberg D 52 C2
Arzignano I 71 C6
Arzila P 92 A2
Arzl im Pitztal A 71 A5
Arzúa E 86 B2
As B 49 B6
Aš CZ 52 C2
Ås N 35 C2
Åsa S 40 B2
Asaa DK 38 B3
Aşağıçiğil TR 119 D6
Ašanja SRB 85 B5
Asarna S 115 E11
Asarøy N 33 C3
Asarp S 40 A3
Asasp F 76 C2
Åsbro S 37 C2
Åsby S 40 B2
Åsby S 40 B3
Asbygri IS 111 A9
Ascain F 76 C1
Ascea I 106 A2
Ascha D 62 A3
Aschach an der Donau
A 63 B5
Aschaffenburg D 51 D5
Aschbach Markt A 63 B5
Ascheberg
Nordrhein-Westfalen
D 50 B3
Schleswig-Holstein D 44 A2
Aschendorf D 43 B4
Aschersleben D 52 B1
Asciano I 81 C5
Ascó E 90 B3
Asco F 102 A2
Áscoli Piceno I 82 D2
Áscoli Satriano I 104 B1
Ascona CH 70 B3
Ascot GB 31 C3
Ascoux F 58 B3
Åse N 112 C4
Åseda S 40 B5
Åsele S 115 C14
Åsen
N 114 D8
S 34 A5
Asendorf D 43 C6
Asenovgrad BG 11 E8
Åsensbruk S 35 D4
Åseral N 33 D4
Asfeld F 59 A5
Åsgårdstrand N 35 C2
Ásgarður IS 111 B1
Asgate CY 120 B2
Ash
Kent GB 31 C5
Surrey GB 31 C3
Åshammar S 36 B3
Ashbourne
GB 27 B4
IRL 21 A5
Ashburton GB 28 C4
Ashby-de-la-Zouch
GB 27 C4
Ashchurch GB 29 B5
Åsheim N 114 F8
Ashford GB 31 C4
Ashington GB 25 C6
Ashley GB 26 C3
Ashmyany BY 7 D8
Ashton Under Lyne
GB 26 B3
Ashwell GB 30 B3
Asiago I 71 C6
Asipovichy BY 7 E10
Aska FIN 113 E15
Askam-in-Furness
GB 26 A2
Askeaton IRL 20 B3
Asker N 34 C2
Askersund S 37 D1
Åskilje S 115 C14
Askim N 35 C3
Askland N 33 D5
Äsköping S 37 C3
Askvoll N 32 A2
Asljunga S 41 C3
Asnæs DK 39 D4
As Neves E 87 B2
As Nogais E 86 B3
Ásola I 71 C5
Asolo I 72 C1
Asos GR 116 D2
Asotthalom H 75 B4
Aspach A 63 B4
Aspang Markt A 64 C2
Aspariegos E 88 C1
Asparn an der Zaya A 64 B2
Aspatria GB 26 A2
Aspberg S 35 C5
Aspe E 101 A5
Aspet F 77 C3
Äspö S 41 C5
As Pontes de Garcia
Rodriguez E 86 A3
Aspres-sur-Buëch F 79 B4
Aspsele S 115 D15
Assafora P 92 C1
Asse B 49 C5
Assebakte N 113 C14
Assel D 43 B6
Asselborn L 50 C1
Assémini I 110 C1
Assen NL 42 C3
Assenede B 49 B4
Assens
Aarhus Amt. DK 38 C3
Fyns Amt. DK 39 D2
Assesse B 49 C6
Assisi I 82 C1
Åsskard N 114 D5
Assling D 62 C3
Asso I 71 C4
Asson F 76 C2
Ássoro I 109 B3
Assumar P 92 B3
Åsta N 34 A3
Astaffort F 77 B3
Astakos GR 116 D3
Asten NL 50 B1
Asti I 80 B2
Astipalea GR 119 F1
Astorga E 86 B4
Åstorp S 41 C2
Åsträsk S 115 C16
Astudillo E 88 B2
Asuni I 110 C1
Asványráró H 64 C3
Aszód H 65 C5
Aszófő H 74 B2
Atabey TR 119 E5
Atalaia P 92 B3
Atalandi GR 116 D4
Atalho P 92 C2
Átány H 65 C6
Atanzón E 95 B3
Ataquines E 94 A2
Atarfe E 100 B2
Atça TR 119 E3
Ateca E 89 C5
A Teixeira E 87 B3
Atella I 104 C1
Atessa I 103 A7
Ath B 49 C4
Athboy IRL 19 C5
Athea IRL 20 B2
Athenry IRL 20 A3
Athens = Athina GR 117 E5
Atherstone GB 27 C4
Athienou CY 120 A2
Athies F 59 A3
Athies-sous-Laon F 59 A4
Athina = Athens GR 117 E5
Athleague IRL 20 A3
Athlone IRL 21 A4
Athna CY 120 A2
Athy IRL 21 B5
Atienza E 95 A4
Atina I 103 B6
Átkár H 65 C5
Atna N 114 F7
Åtorp S 37 C1
Atrå N 32 C5
Ätran S 40 B2
Atri I 103 A6
Atripalda I 103 C7
Atsiki GR 116 C7
Attendorn D 50 B3
Attichy F 59 A4
Attigliano I 102 A5
Attigny F 59 A5
Attleborough GB 30 B5
Åtvidaberg S 37 D2
Atzendorf D 52 B1
Au
Steiermark A 63 C6
Vorarlberg A 71 A4
Bayern D 62 B2
Bayern D 62 C2
Aub D 61 A6
Aubagne F 79 C4
Aubange B 60 A1
Aubel B 50 C1
Aubenas F 78 B3
Aubenton F 59 A5
Auberive F 59 C6
Aubeterre-sur-Dronne
F 67 C5
Aubiet F 77 C3
Aubigné F 67 B4
Aubigny F 66 B3
Aubigny-au-Bac F 49 C4
Aubigny-en-Artois F 48 C3
Aubigny-sur-Nère F 68 A2
Aubin F 77 B5
Aubonne CH 69 B6
Aubrac F 78 B1
Aubusson F 68 C2
Auch F 77 C3
Auchencairn GB 25 D4
Auchinleck GB 24 C3
Auchterarder GB 25 B4
Auchtermuchty GB 25 B4
Auchtertyre GB 22 D3
Auchy-au-Bois F 48 C3
Audenge F 76 B1
Auderville F 57 A4
Audierne F 56 B1
Audincourt F 70 A1
Audlem GB 26 C3
Audruicq F 48 C3
Audun-le-Roman F 60 A1
Audun-le-Tiche F 60 A1
Aue
Nordrhein-Westfalen
D 50 B4
Sachsen D 52 C2
Auerbach
Bayern D 62 A2
Sachsen D 52 C2
Auffach A 72 A2
Augher GB 19 B4
Aughnacloy GB 19 B5
Aughrim IRL 21 B5
Augignac F 67 C5
Augsburg D 62 B1
Augusta I 109 B4
Augusten-borg DK 39 E2
Augustfehn D 43 B4
Augustów PL 6 E7
Aukrug D 44 A1
Auktsjaur S 115 B16
Auldearn GB 23 D5
Aulendorf D 61 C5
Auletta I 103 C8
Aulla I 81 B3
Aullène F 102 B2
Aulnay F 67 B4
Aulnoye-Aymeries F 49 C4
Ault F 48 C2
Aultbea GB 22 D3
Aulum DK 39 C1
Aulus-les-Bains F 77 D4
Auma D 52 C1
Aumale F 58 A2
Aumetz F 60 A1
Aumont-Aubrac F 78 B2
Aunay-en-Bazois F 68 A3
Aunay-sur-Odon F 57 A5
Aune N 115 C10
Auneau F 58 B2
Auneuil F 58 A2
Auning DK 39 C3
Aunsetra N 115 C9
Aups F 79 C5
Aura D 51 C5
Auray F 56 C3
Aurdal N 34 B1
Aure N 114 D5
Aurich D 43 B4
Aurignac F 77 C3
Aurillac F 77 B5
Auriol F 79 C4
Auritz-Burguette E 76 D1
Aurlandsvangen N 32 B4
Auronzo di Cadore I 72 B2
Auros F 76 B2
Auroux F 78 B2
Aurskog N 34 C3
Aursmoen N 34 C3
Ausónia I 103 B6
Ausservillgraton A 72 B2
Austad N 33 D4
Austbygda N 32 B5
Aústis I 110 B2
Austmarka N 34 B4
Austre Moland N 33 D5
Austre Vikebygd N 33 C2
Austrheim N 32 B1
Auterive F 77 C4
Autheuil-Authouillet
F 58 A2
Authon F 79 B5
Authon-du-Perche F 58 B1
Autol E 89 B5
Autreville F 60 B1
Autrey-lès-Gray F 69 A5
Autti FIN 113 F15
Autun F 69 B4
Auty-le-Châtel F 58 C3
Auvelais B 49 C5
Auvillar F 77 B3
Auxerre F 59 C4
Auxi-le-Château F 48 C3
Auxon F 59 B4
Auxonne F 69 A5
Auxy F 69 B4
Auzances F 68 B2
Auzon F 68 C3
Ağva TR 118 A4
Availles-Limouzine F 67 B5
Avaldsnes N 33 C2
Avallon F 68 A3
Avantas GR 116 B7
Avaviken S 115 B15
Avebury GB 29 B6
A Veiga E 87 B3
Aveiras de Cima P 92 B2
Aveiro P 92 A2
Avelgem B 49 C4
Avellino I 103 C7
Avenches CH 70 B2
A-Ver-o-Mar P 87 C2
Aversa I 103 C7
Avesnes-le-Comte F 48 C3
Avesnes-sur-Helpe F 49 C4
Avesta S 36 B3
Avetrana I 105 C3
Avezzano I 103 A6
Avià E 91 A4
Aviano I 72 B2
Aviemore GB 23 D5
Avigliana I 80 A1
Avigliano I 104 C1
Avignon F 78 C3
Ávila E 94 B2
Avilés E 88 A1
Avilley F 69 A6
Avintes P 87 C2
Avinyo E 91 B4
Àvio I 71 C5
Avioth F 59 A6
Avis P 92 B3
Avize F 59 B5
Avlonari GR 116 D6
Ávola I 109 C4
Avon F 58 B3
Avonmouth GB 29 B5
Avord F 68 A2
Avranches F 57 B4
Avrillé F 67 A4
Avtovac BIH 84 C3
Awans B 49 C6
Axams A 71 A6
Axat F 77 D5
Axbridge GB 29 B5
Axel NL 49 B4
Ax-les-Thermes F 77 D4
Axmarby S 36 B4
Axmarsbruk S 36 A4
Axminster GB 29 C5
Axvall S 35 D5
Ay F 59 A5
Aya E 89 A4
Ayamonte E 98 B3
Ayancık TR 16 A7
Ayaş TR 118 B7
Aydın TR 119 E2
Ayelo de Malferit E 96 C2
Ayer CH 70 B2
Ayerbe E 90 A2
Ayette F 48 C3
Ayia Napa CY 120 B2
Ayia Phyla CY 120 B2
Áyios Amvrósios
CY 120 A2
Áyios Seryios CY 120 A2
Áyios Theodhoros
CY 120 A3
Aykırikçi TR 118 C5
Aylesbury GB 31 C3
Ayllón E 89 C3
Aylsham GB 30 B5
Ayna E 101 A3
Ayódar E 96 B2
Ayora E 96 B1
Ayr GB 24 C3
Ayrancı TR 16 C6
Ayrancılar TR 119 D2
Ayron F 67 B5
Aysgarth GB 27 A4
Ayton GB 25 C5
Aytos BG 11 E9
Ayvacık TR 118 C1
Ayvalık TR 118 C1
Aywaille B 49 C6
Azaila E 90 B2
Azambuja P 92 B2
Azambujeira P 92 B2
Azanja SRB 85 B5
Azannes-et-Soumazannes
F 60 A1
Azanúy-Alins E 90 B3
Azaruja P 92 C3
Azay-le-Ferron F 67 B6
Azay-le-Rideau F 67 A5
Azcoitia E 89 A4
Azé F 69 B4
Azeiteiros P 92 B3
Azenhas do Mar P 92 C1
Azinhaga P 92 B2
Azinhal P 98 B3
Azinheira dos Bairros
P 98 A2
Aznalcázar E 99 B4
Aznalcóllar E 99 B4
Azóia P 92 B2
Azpeitia E 89 A4
Azuaga E 99 A5
Azuara E 90 B2
Azuqueca de Henares
E 95 B3
Azur F 76 C1
Azzano Décimo I 72 C2

B

Baad A 71 A5
Baamonde E 86 A3
Baar CH 70 A3
Bağarasi TR 119 E2
Baarle-Nassau B 49 B5
Baarn NL 49 A6
Babadağ TR 119 E3
Babadag RO 11 D10
Babaeski TR 118 A2
Babayevo RUS 7 B13
Babenhausen
Bayern D 61 B6
Hessen D 51 D4
Babiak PL 54 A3
Babice PL 55 C4
Babigoszcz PL 45 B6
Babimost PL 53 A5
Babina Greda HR 84 A3
Babócsa H 74 B2
Bábolna H 64 C3
Baborów PL 54 C2
Baboszewo PL 47 C6
Babót H 64 C3
Babruysk BY 7 E10
Babsk PL 55 B5
Bac GB 22 C2
Bač
MNE 85 D5
SRB 75 C4
Bacares E 101 B3
Bacău RO 11 C9
Baccarat F 60 B2
Bacharach D 50 C3
Bačina SRB 85 C6
Backa S 36 B2
Bačka Palanka SRB 75 C4
Backaryd S 41 C5
Bačka Topola SRB 75 C4
Backe S 115 D13
Bäckebo S 40 C6
Bäckefors S 35 D4
Bäckhammar S 35 C6
Bački Breg SRB 75 C3
Bački-Brestovac SRB 75 C4
Bački Monoštor SRB 75 C3
Bački Petrovac SRB 75 C4
Bački Sokolac SRB 75 C4
Backnang D 61 B5
Bačko Gradište SRB 75 C5
Bačko Novo Selo
SRB 75 C4
Bačko Petrovo Selo
SRB 75 B5
Bácoli I 103 C7
Bacqueville-en-Caux
F 58 A2
Bácsalmás H 75 B4
Bácsbokod H 75 B4
Bad Abbach D 62 B3
Badacsonytomaj H 74 B2
Bad Aibling D 62 C3
Badajoz E 93 C4
Badalona E 91 B5
Badalucco I 80 C1
Bad Aussee A 63 C4
Bad Bederkesa D 43 B5
Bad Bentheim D 50 A3
Bad Bergzabern D 60 A3
Bad Berka D 52 C1
Bad Berleburg D 51 B4
Bad Berneck D 52 C1
Bad Bevensen D 44 B2
Bad Bibra D 52 B1
Bad Birnbach D 62 B4
Bad Blankenburg D 52 C1
Bad Bleiberg A 72 B3
Bad Brambach D 52 C2
Bad Bramstedt D 44 B1
Bad Breisig D 50 C3
Bad Brückenau D 51 C5
Bad Buchau D 61 B5
Bad Camberg D 50 C4
Badderen N 113 C11
Bad Doberan D 44 A3
Bad Driburg D 51 B5
Bad Düben D 52 B2
Bad Dürkheim D 61 A4
Bad Dürrenberg D 52 B2
Bad Dürrheim D 61 B4
Bad Elster D 52 C2
Bad Ems D 50 C3
Baden
A 64 B2
CH 70 A3
Bådenas E 90 B1
Baden-Baden D 61 B4
Bad Endorf D 62 C3
Badenweiler D 60 C3
Baderna HR 72 C3
Bad Essen D 50 A4
Bad Fischau A 64 C2
Bad Frankenhausen
D 52 B1
Bad Freienwalde D 45 C6
Bad Friedrichshall D 61 A5
Bad Füssing D 63 B4
Bad Gandersheim D 51 B6
Bad Gastein A 72 A3
Bad Gleichenberg A 73 B5
Bad Goisern A 63 C4
Bad Gottleuba D 53 C3
Bad Grund D 51 B6
Bad Hall A 63 B5
Bad Harzburg D 51 B6
Bad Herrenalb D 61 B4
Bad Hersfeld D 51 C5
Bad Hofgastein A 72 A3
Bad Homburg D 51 C4
Bad Honnef D 50 C3
Bad Hönningen D 50 C3
Badia Calavena I 71 C6
Badia Polésine I 81 A5
Badia Pratáglia I 81 C5
Badia Tedalda I 82 C1
Bad Iburg D 50 A4
Bad Innerlaterns A 71 A4
Bad Ischl A 63 C4
Bad Karlshafen D 51 B5
Bad Kemmeriboden
CH 70 B2
Bądki PL 47 B4
Bad Kissingen D 51 C6
Bad Kleinen D 44 B3
Bad Kohlgrub D 62 C2
Bad König D 61 A5
Bad Königshofen D 51 C6
Bad Köstritz D 52 C2
Badkowo PL 47 C4
Bad Kreuzen A 63 B5

Bad Kreuznach D 60 A3
Bad Krozingen D 60 C3
Bad Laasphe D 51 C4
Bad Langensalza D 51 B6
Bad Lauchstädt D 52 B1
Bad Lausick D 52 B2
Bad Lauterberg D 51 B6
Bad Leonfelden A 63 B5
Bad Liebenwerda D 52 B3
Bad Liebenzell D 61 B4
Bad Lippspringe D 51 B4
Badljevina HR 74 C2
Bad Meinberg D 51 B4
Bad Mergentheim D 61 A5
Bad Mitterndorf A 72 A3
Bad Münder D 51 A5
Bad Münstereifel D 50 C2
Bad Muskau D 53 B4
Bad Nauheim D 51 C4
Bad Nenndorf D 43 C6
Bad Neuenahr-Ahrweiler D 50 C3
Bad Neustadt D 51 C6
Bad Oeynhausen D 51 A4
Badolato I 106 C3
Badolatosa E 100 B1
Bad Oldesloe D 44 B2
Badonviller F 60 B2
Bad Orb D 51 C5
Badovinci SRB 85 B4
Bad Peterstal D 61 B4
Bad Pyrmont D 51 B5
Bad Radkersburg A 73 B5
Bad Ragaz CH 71 B4
Bad Rappenau D 61 A5
Bad Reichenhall D 62 C3
Bad Saarow-Pieskow D 53 A4
Bad Sachsa D 51 B6
Bad Säckingen D 70 A2
Bad Salzdetfurth D 51 A6
Bad Salzig D 50 C3
Bad Salzuflen D 51 A4
Bad Salzungen D 51 C6
Bad Sankt Leonhard A 73 B4
Bad Sassendorf D 50 B4
Bad Schandau D 53 C4
Bad Schmiedeberg D 52 B2
Bad Schönborn D 61 A4
Bad Schussenried D 61 B5
Bad Schwalbach D 50 C4
Bad Schwartau D 44 B2
Bad Segeberg D 44 B2
Bad Soden D 51 C4
Bad Soden-Salmünster D 51 C5
Bad Sooden-Allendorf D 51 B5
Bad Sulza D 52 B1
Bad Sülze D 45 A4
Bad Tatzmannsdorf A 73 A6
Bad Tennstedt D 51 B6
Bad Tölz D 62 C2
Badules E 90 B1
Bad Urach D 61 B5
Bad Vellach A 73 B4
Bad Vilbel D 51 C4
Bad Vöslau A 64 C2
Bad Waldsee D 61 C5
Bad Wiessee D 62 C2
Bad Wildungen D 51 B5
Bad Wilsnack D 44 C3
Bad Windsheim D 61 A6
Bad Wörishafen D 62 B1
Bad Wurzach D 61 C5
Bad Zwesten D 51 B5
Bad Zwischenahn D 43 B5
Baells E 90 B3
Baena E 100 B1
Baesweiler D 50 C2
Baeza E 100 B2
Baflo NL 42 B3
Bafra TR 16 A7
Baga E 91 A4
Bagaladi I 106 C2
Bagenkop DK 39 E3
Baggetorp S 37 C3
Bagh a Chaisteil GB 22 E1
Bagheria I 108 A2
Bagn N 32 B6
Bagnacavallo I 81 B5
Bagnáia I 102 A5
Bagnara Cálabra I 106 C2
Bagnasco I 80 B2
Bagnères-de-Bigorre F 76 C3
Bagnères-de-Luchon F 77 D3
Bagni del Másino I 71 B4
Bagni di Lucca I 81 B4
Bagni di Rabbi I 71 B5
Bagni di Tivoli I 102 B5
Bagno di Romagna I 81 C5
Bagnoles-de-l'Orne F 57 B5
Bagnoli dei Trigno I 103 B7
Bagnoli di Sopra I 72 C1
Bagnoli Irpino I 103 C8
Bagnolo Mella I 71 C5
Bagnols-en-Forêt F 79 C5
Bagnols-sur-Cèze F 78 B3
Bagnorégio I 102 A5
Bagolino I 71 C5
Bagrationovsk RUS 47 A6
Bagrdan SRB 85 B6
Báguena E 95 A5
Bahabón de Esgueva E 88 C3
Bahillo E 88 B2
Báia delle Zágare I 104 B2
Báia Domizia I 103 B6
Baia Mare RO 11 C7
Baiano I 103 C7
Baião P 87 C2
Baiersbronn D 61 B4
Baiersdorf D 62 A2
Baignes-Ste Radegonde F 67 C4
Baigneux-les-Juifs F 59 C5
Baildon GB 27 B4
Bailén E 100 A2
Băileşti RO 11 D7
Baileux B 49 C5
Bailieborough IRL 19 C5
Bailleul F 48 C3
Baillonville B 49 C6
Bailó E 90 A2
Bain-de-Bretagne F 57 C4
Bains F 78 A2
Bains-les-Bains F 60 B2
Bainton GB 27 B5
Baio E 86 A2
Baiona E 87 B2
Bais F 57 B5
Baiso I 81 B4
Baiuca P 92 A3
Baja H 75 B3
Bajánsenye H 73 B6
Bajina Bašta SRB 85 C4
Bajmok SRB 75 C4
Bajna H 65 C4
Bajovo Polje MNE 84 C3
Bajram Curri AL 105 A6
Bajša SRB 75 C4
Bajzë AL 105 A5
Bak H 74 B1
Bakar HR 73 C4
Bakewell GB 27 B4
Bakhmach UA 7 F12
Bakio E 89 A4
Bakırdaği TR 16 B7
Bakka N 32 C6
Bakkafjörður IS 111 A11
Bakkagerði IS 111 B12
Bække DK 39 D2
Bakken N 34 B3
Baklan TR 119 E4
Bækmarksbro DK 39 C1
Bakonybél H 74 A2
Bakonycsernye H 74 A3
Bakonyjákó H 74 A2
Bakonyszentkirály H 74 A2
Bakonyszombathely H 74 A2
Bakov nad Jizerou CZ 53 C4
Bąkowiec PL 55 B6
Baks H 75 B5
Baksa H 74 C3
Bakum D 43 C5
Bala GB 26 C2
Bâlâ TR 16 B6
Balaguer E 90 B3
Balassagyarmat H 65 B5
Balástya H 75 B5
Balatonakali H 74 B2
Balatonalmádi H 74 A3
Balatonboglár H 74 B2
Balatonbozsok H 74 B3
Balatonederics H 74 B2
Balatonfenyves H 74 B2
Balatonföldvár H 74 B2
Balatonfüred H 74 B2
Balatonfüzfö H 74 A3
Balatonkenese H 74 A3
Balatonkiliti H 74 B3
Balatonlelle H 74 B2
Balatonszabadi H 74 B3
Balatonszemes H 74 B2
Balatonszentgyörgy H 74 B2
Balazote E 101 A3
Balbeggie GB 25 B4
Balbigny F 69 C4
Balboa E 86 B4
Balbriggan IRL 19 C5
Balchik BG 11 E10
Balçova TR 119 D2
Baldock GB 31 C3
Bale HR 82 A2
Baleira E 86 A3
Baleizao P 98 A3
Balen B 49 B6
Balerma E 100 C3
Balestrand N 32 A3
Balestrate I 108 A2
Balfour GB 23 B6
Bälganet S 41 C5
Balıkesir TR 118 C2
Balıklıçeşme TR 118 B2
Bälinge S 36 C4
Balingen D 61 B4
Balingsta S 36 C4
Balintore GB 23 D5
Balizac F 76 B2
Baljevac SRB 85 C5
Balk NL 42 C2
Balkbrug NL 42 C3
Balla IRL 18 C2
Ballachulish GB 24 B2
Ballaghaderreen IRL 18 C3
Ballancourt-sur-Essonne F 58 B3
Ballantrae GB 24 C3
Ballao I 110 C2
Ballasalla GB 26 A1
Ballater GB 23 D5
Ballen DK 39 D3
Ballenstedt D 52 B1
Ballerias E 90 B2
Balleroy F 57 A5
Ballerup DK 41 D2
Ballesteros de Calatrava E 100 A2
Ballı TR 118 B2
Ballina IRL 18 B2
Ballinalack IRL 19 C4
Ballinamore IRL 19 B4
Ballinascarty IRL 20 C3
Ballinasloe IRL 20 A3
Ballindine IRL 18 C3
Balling DK 38 C1
Ballingarry
Limerick IRL 20 B3
Tipperary IRL 21 B4
Ballingeary IRL 20 C2
Ballinhassig IRL 20 C3
Ballinluig GB 25 B4
Ballino I 71 C5
Ballinrobe IRL 18 C2
Ballinskelligs IRL 20 C1
Ballinspittle IRL 20 C3
Ballintra IRL 18 B3
Ballivor IRL 21 A5
Ballobar E 90 B3
Ballon
F 58 B1
IRL 21 B5
Ballószög H 75 B4
Ballsh AL 105 C5
Ballstad N 112 D2
Ballum DK 39 D1
Ballybay IRL 19 B5
Ballybofey IRL 19 B4
Ballybunion IRL 20 B2
Ballycanew IRL 21 B5
Ballycarry GB 19 B6
Ballycastle
GB 19 A5
IRL 18 B2
Ballyclare GB 19 B6
Ballyconneely IRL 18 C1
Ballycotton IRL 20 C3
Ballycroy IRL 18 B2
Ballydehob IRL 20 C2
Ballyferriter IRL 20 B1
Ballygawley GB 19 B4
Ballygowan GB 19 B6
Ballyhaunis IRL 18 C3
Ballyheige IRL 20 B2
Ballyjamesduff IRL 19 C4
Ballylanders IRL 20 B3
Ballylynan IRL 21 B4
Ballymahon IRL 21 A4
Ballymena GB 19 B5
Ballymoe IRL 18 C3
Ballymoney GB 19 A5
Ballymore IRL 21 A4
Ballymote IRL 18 B3
Ballynacorra IRL 20 C3
Ballynagore IRL 21 A4
Ballynahinch GB 19 B6
Ballynure GB 19 B6
Ballyragget IRL 21 B4
Ballysadare IRL 18 B3
Ballyshannon IRL 18 B3
Ballyvaughan IRL 20 A2
Ballyvourney IRL 20 C2
Ballywalter GB 19 B6
Balmaclellan GB 24 C3
Balmaseda E 89 A3
Balme I 70 C2
Balmedie GB 23 D6
Balmuccia I 70 C3
Balna-paling GB 23 D4
Balneario de Panticosa E 76 D2
Balotaszállás H 75 B4
Balsa P 87 C3
Balsareny E 91 B4
Balsorano-Nuovo I 103 B6
Bålsta S 37 C4
Balsthal CH 70 A2
Balta UA 11 B10
Baltanás E 88 C2
Baltar E 87 C3
Baltasound GB 22 A8
Bălţi MD 11 C9
Baltimore IRL 20 C2
Baltinglass IRL 21 B5
Baltiysk RUS 47 A5
Baltów PL 55 B6
Balugães P 87 C2
Bælum DK 38 C3
Balve D 50 B3
Balvi LV 7 C9
Balvicar GB 24 B2
Balya TR 118 C2
Balzo I 82 D2
Bamberg D 62 A1
Bamburgh GB 25 C6
Banatska Palanka SRB 85 B6
Banatski Brestovac SRB 85 B5
Banatski Despotovac SRB 75 C5
Banatski Dvor SRB 75 C5
Banatski-Karlovac SRB 85 A6
Banatsko Arandjelovo SRB 75 B5
Banatsko-Novo Selo SRB 85 B5
Banaz TR 118 D4
Banbridge GB 19 B5
Banbury GB 30 B2
Banchory GB 23 D6
Bande
B 49 C6
E 87 B3
Bandholm DK 39 E4
Bandırma TR 118 B2
Bandol F 79 C4
Bandon IRL 20 C3
Bañeres E 96 C2
Banff GB 23 D6
Bangor
F 66 A1
Down GB 19 B6
Gwynedd GB 26 B1
IRL 18 B2
Bangsund N 114 C8
Banie PL 45 B6
Banja SRB 85 C4
Banja Koviljača SRB 85 B4
Banjaloka SLO 73 C4
Banja Luka BIH 84 B2
Banjani SRB 85 B4
Banja Vručica BIH 84 B2
Banje KOS 85 D5
Banjska KOS 85 D5
Banka SK 64 B3
Bankekind S 37 D2
Bankend GB 25 C4
Bankeryd S 40 B4
Bankfoot GB 25 B4
Banloc RO 75 C6
Bannalec F 56 C2
Bannes F 59 B4
Bannockburn GB 25 B4
Bañobárez E 87 D4
Bañon E 90 C1
Banon F 79 B4
Baños E 93 A5
Baños de Gigonza E 99 C5
Baños de la Encina E 100 A2
Baños de Molgas E 87 B3
Baños de Rio Tobia E 89 B4
Baños de Valdearados E 89 C3
Bánov CZ 64 B3
Banova Jaruga HR 74 C1
Bánovce nad Bebravou SK 64 B4
Banovići BIH 84 B3
Banovići Selo BIH 84 B3
Bánréve H 65 B6
Bansin D 45 B6
Banská Belá SK 65 B4
Banská Bystrica SK 65 B5
Banská Štiavnica SK 65 B4
Banstead GB 31 C3
Banteer IRL 20 B3
Bantheville F 59 A6
Bantry IRL 20 C2
Bantzenheim F 60 C3
Banyalbufar E 97 B2
Banyoles E 91 A5
Banyuls-sur-Mer F 91 A6
Bapaume F 48 C3
Bar
MNE 105 A5
UA 11 B9
Barabhas GB 22 C2
Barači BIH 84 B1
Baracs H 74 B3
Baracska H 74 A3
Barahona E 89 C4
Barajes de Melo E 95 B4
Barakaldo E 89 A4
Baralla E 86 B3
Barañain E 76 D1
Baranavichy BY 7 E9
Báránd H 75 A6
Baranda SRB 85 A5
Baranello I 103 B7
Baranów Sandomierski PL 55 C6
Baraqueville F 77 B5
Barasoain E 89 B5
Barbacena P 92 C3
Barbadás E 87 B3
Barbadillo E 94 B1
Barbadillo de Herreros E 89 B3
Barbadillo del Mercado E 89 B3
Barbadillo del Pez E 89 B3
Barban HR 82 A3
Barbarano Vicento I 71 C6
Barbariga HR 82 B2
Barbaros TR 118 B2
Barbastro E 90 A3
Barbate E 99 C5
Barbatona E 95 A4
Barbâtre F 66 B2
Barbazan F 77 C3
Barbeitos E 86 A3
Barbentane F 78 C3
Barberino di Mugello I 81 B5
Barbezieux-St Hilaire F 67 C4
Barbonne-Fayel F 59 B4
Barbotan-les-Thermes F 76 C2
Barby D 52 B1
Bárcabo E 90 A3
Barca de Alva P 87 C4
Barcarrota E 93 C4
Barcellona-Pozzo di Gotto I 109 A4
Barcelona E 91 B5
Barcelonette F 79 B5
Barcelos P 87 C2
Bárcena del Monasterio E 86 A4
Barcena de Pie de Concha E 88 A2
Barchfeld D 51 C6
Barcin PL 46 C3
Barcino PL 46 A2
Bárcis I 72 B2
Barco P 92 A3
Barcones E 89 C4
Barcs H 74 C2
Barcus F 76 C2
Barczewo PL 47 B6
Bardejov SK 10 B6
Bårdesø DK 39 D3
Bardi I 81 B3
Bardney GB 27 B5
Bardo PL 54 C1
Bardolino I 71 C5
Bardonécchia I 79 A5
Bardoňovo SK 65 B4
Barèges F 76 D3
Barenstein D 52 C3
Barentin F 58 A1
Barenton F 57 B5
Barevo BIH 84 B2
Barfleur F 57 A4
Barga I 81 B4
Bargas E 94 C2
Barge I 79 B6
Bargemon F 79 C5
Barghe I 71 C5
Bargoed GB 29 B4
Bargrennan GB 24 C3
Bargteheide D 44 B2
Barham GB 31 C5
Bari I 104 B2
Barič Draga HR 83 B4
Barilović HR 73 C5
Bari Sardo I 110 C2
Barisciano I 103 A6
Barjac F 78 B3
Barjols F 79 C4
Barjon F 59 C5
Bårkåker N 35 C2
Barkald N 114 F7
Barkowo
Dolnośląskie PL 54 B1
Pomorskie PL 46 B3
Bârlad RO 11 C9
Bar-le-Duc F 59 B6
Barles F 79 B5
Barletta I 104 B2
Barlinek PL 45 C7
Barmouth GB 26 C1
Barmstedt D 43 B6
Barnard Castle GB 27 A4
Barnarp S 40 B4
Bärnau D 62 A3
Bärnbach A 73 A5
Barneberg D 52 A1
Barnenitz D 45 C4
Barnet GB 31 C3
Barnetby le Wold GB 27 B5
Barneveld NL 49 A6
Barneville-Carteret F 57 A4
Barnoldswick GB 26 B3
Barnowko PL 45 C6
Barnsley GB 27 B4
Barnstädt D 52 B1
Barnstaple GB 28 B3
Barnstorf D 43 C5
Barntrup D 51 B5
Baron F 58 A3
Baronissi I 103 C7
Barqueiro P 92 B2
Barquinha P 92 B2
Barr
F 60 B3
GB 24 C3
Barra P 92 A2
Barracas E 96 A2
Barraco E 94 B2
Barrado E 93 A5
Barrafranca I 109 B3
Barranco do Velho P 98 B3
Barrancos P 99 A4
Barrax E 95 C4
Barrbaar D 62 B1
Barre-des-Cevennes F 78 B2
Barreiro P 92 C1
Barreiros E 86 A3
Barrême F 79 C5
Barret-le-Bas F 79 B4
Barrhead GB 24 C3
Barrhill GB 24 C3
Barrio de Nuesra Señora E 88 B1
Barrowford GB 26 B3
Barrow-in-Furness GB 26 A2
Barrow upon Humber GB 27 B5
Barruecopardo E 87 C4
Barruelo de Santullán E 88 B2
Barruera E 90 A3
Barry GB 29 B4
Bårse DK 39 D4
Barsinghausen D 51 A5
Barssel D 43 B4
Bar-sur-Aube F 59 B5
Bar-sur-Seine F 59 B5
Barth D 45 A4
Bartholomä D 61 B5
Bartin TR 118 A7
Barton upon Humber GB 27 B5
Bartoszyce PL 47 A6
Barúmini I 110 C1
Baruth D 52 A3
Barvaux B 49 C6
Barver D 43 C5
Barwatd PL 65 A5
Barwice PL 46 B2
Barysaw BY 7 D10
Barzana E 88 A1
Bârzava RO 10 C6
Bárzio I 71 C4
Bas E 91 A5
Bašaid SRB 75 C5
Basaluzzo I 80 B2
Basarabeasca MD 11 C10
Basauri E 89 A4
Baschi I 82 D1
Baschurch GB 26 C3
Basconcillos del Tozo E 88 B3
Bascones de Ojeda E 88 B2
Basécles B 49 C4
Basel CH 70 A2
Basélice I 103 B7
Basildon GB 31 C4
Basingstoke GB 31 C2
Baška
CZ 65 A4
HR 83 B3
Baška Voda HR 84 C1
Bäsksjö S 115 C14
Baslow GB 27 B4
Başmakçı TR 119 E5
Basovizza I 72 C3
Bassacutena I 110 A2
Bassano del Grappa I 72 C1
Bassano Romano I 102 A5
Bassecourt CH 70 A2
Bassella E 91 A4
Bassevuovdde N 113 D14
Bassou F 59 C4
Bassoues F 76 C3
Bassum D 43 C5
Båstad S 40 C2
Bastardo I 82 D1
Bastelica F 102 A2
Bastelicaccia F 102 B1
Bastia
F 102 A2
I 82 C1
Bastogne B 50 C1
Baston GB 30 B3
Bastuträsk S 115 C17
Bata H 74 B3
Batajnica SRB 85 B5
Batalha P 92 B2
Bátaszék H 74 B3
Batea E 90 B3
Batelov CZ 63 A6
Bath GB 29 B5
Bathgate GB 25 C4
Batida H 75 B5
Batignano I 81 D5
Batina HR 74 C3
Bátka SK 65 B6
Batković BIH 85 B4
Batlava KOS 85 D6
Batley GB 27 B4
Batnfjordsøra N 114 E4
Batočina SRB 85 B6
Bátonyterenye H 65 C5
Batrina HR 74 C2
Båtsfjord N 113 B18
Battaglia Terme I 72 C1
Bätterkinden CH 70 A2
Battice B 50 C1
Battipáglia I 103 C7
Battle GB 31 D4
Battonya H 75 B6
Batuša SRB 85 B6
Bátya H 75 B3
Bau I 110 C1
Baud F 56 C2
Baudour B 49 C4
Baugé F 67 A4
Baugy F 68 A2
Bauma CH 70 A3
Baume-les-Dames F 69 A6
Baumholder D 60 A3
Baunatal D 51 B5
Baunei I 110 B2
Bauska LV 6 C8
Bautzen D 53 B4
Bavanište SRB 85 B5
Bavay F 49 C4
Bavilliers F 60 C2
Bavorov CZ 63 A5
Bawdsey GB 31 B5
Bawinkel D 43 C4
Bawtry GB 27 B4
Bayat TR 118 D5
Bayel F 59 B5
Bayeux F 57 A5
Bayındır TR 119 D2
Bayon F 60 B2
Bayonne F 76 C1
Bayons F 79 B5
Bayramiç TR 118 C1
Bayreuth D 52 D1
Bayrischzell D 62 C3
Baza E 101 B3
Bazas F 76 B2
Baziege F 77 C4
Bazoches-les-Gallerandes F 58 B3
Bazoches-sur-Hoëne F 58 B1
Bazzano I 81 B5
Beaconsfield GB 31 C3
Beade E 87 B2
Beadnell GB 25 C6
Beaminster GB 29 C5
Bearsden GB 24 C3
Beas E 99 B4
Beasain E 89 A4
Beas de Segura E 100 A3
Beattock GB 25 C4
Beaubery F 69 B4
Beaucaire F 78 C3
Beaufort
F 69 C6
IRL 20 B2
Beaufort-en Vallée F 67 A4
Beaugency F 58 C2
Beaujeu
Alpes-de-Haute-Provence F 79 B5
Rhône F 69 B4
Beaulac F 76 B2
Beaulieu
F 68 A2
GB 31 D2
Beaulieu-sous-la-Roche F 66 B3
Beaulieu-sur-Dordogne F 77 B4
Beaulieu-sur-Mer F 80 C1
Beaulon F 68 B3
Beauly GB 23 D4
Beaumaris GB 26 B1
Beaumesnil F 58 A1
Beaumetz-lès-Loges F 48 C3
Beaumont
B 49 C5
F 77 B3
Beaumont-de-Lomagne F 77 C3
Beaumont-du-Gâtinais F 58 B3
Beaumont-en-Argonne F 59 A6
Beaumont-Hague F 57 A4
Beaumont-la-Ronce F 58 C1
Beaumont-le-Roger F 58 A1
Beaumont-sur-Oise F 58 A3
Beaumont-sur-Sarthe F 57 B6
Beaune F 69 A4
Beaune-la-Rolande F 58 B3
Beaupréau F 66 A4
Beauraing B 49 C5
Beaurepaire F 69 C5
Beaurepaire-en-Bresse F 69 B5
Beaurières F 79 B4
Beauvais F 58 A3
Beauval F 48 C3
Beauville F 77 B3
Beauvoir-sur-Mer F 66 B2
Beauvoir-sur-Niort F 67 B4
Beba Veche RO 75 B5
Bebertal D 52 A1
Bebington GB 26 B2
Bebra D 51 C5
Bebrina HR 84 A2
Beccles GB 30 B5
Becedas E 93 A5
Beceite E 90 C3
Bečej SRB 75 C5
Becerreá E 86 B3
Becerril de Campos E 88 B2
Bécherel F 57 B4
Bechhofen D 61 A6
Bechyně CZ 63 A5
Bečići MNE 105 A4
Becilla de Valderaduey E 88 B1
Beckfoot GB 25 D4
Beckingham GB 27 B5
Beckum D 50 B4
Beco P 92 B2
Bécon-les-Granits F 66 A4
Bečov nad Teplou CZ 52 C2
Becsehely H 74 B1
Bedale GB 27 A4
Bedames E 89 A3
Bédar E 101 B4
Bédarieux F 78 C2
Bédarrides F 78 B3
Bedburg D 50 C2
Beddgelert GB 26 B1
Beddingestrand S 41 D3
Bédée F 57 B4
Bedegkér H 74 B3
Beden TR 119 F7
Bedford GB 30 B3
Będków PL 55 B4
Bedlington GB 25 C6
Bedlno PL 55 A4
Bedmar E 100 B2
Bédoin F 79 B4
Bedónia I 80 B3
Bedretto CH 70 B3
Bedsted DK 38 C1
Bedum NL 42 B3
Bedwas GB 29 B4
Bedworth GB 30 B2
Będzin PL 55 C4
Beekbergen NL 50 A1
Beek en Donk NL 49 B6
Beelen D 50 B4
Beelitz D 52 A2
Beer GB 29 C4
Beerfelde D 45 C6
Beerfelden D 61 A4
Beernem B 49 B4
Beeskow D 53 A4
Beetsterzwaag NL 42 B3
Beetzendorf D 44 C3
Beflelay CH 70 A2
Begaljica SRB 85 B5
Bégard F 56 B2
Begejci SRB 75 C5
Begijar E 100 B2
Begijnendijk B 49 B5
Begndal N 34 B1
Begues E 91 B4
Beguildy GB 26 C2
Begur E 91 B6
Beho B 50 C1
Behringen D 51 B6
Beilen NL 42 C3
Beilngries D 62 A2
Beine-Nauroy F 59 A5
Beinwil CH 70 A3
Beiseförth D 51 B5
Beith GB 24 C3
Beitostølen N 32 A5
Beiuş RO 11 C7
Beja P 98 A3
Béjar E 93 A5
Bekçiler TR 119 F4
Békés H 75 B6
Békéscsaba H 75 B6
Bekilli TR 119 D4
Bekkarfjord N 113 B16
Bela SK 65 A4
Bélâbre F 67 B6
Bela Crkva SRB 85 B6
Belalcázar E 93 C5
Belánad Radbuzou CZ 62 A3
Belanovica SRB 85 B5
Bélapátfalva H 65 B6
Bělápod Bezdězem CZ 53 C4
Belcaire F 77 D4
Bełchatów PL 55 B4
Belchite E 90 B2
Bělčice CZ 63 A4
Belcoo GB 19 B4
Belecke D 51 B4
Beled H 74 A2
Belej HR 83 B3
Beleño E 88 A1
Bélesta F 77 D4
Belev RUS 7 E14
Belevi TR 119 D2
Belfast GB 19 B6
Belford GB 25 C6
Belfort F 60 C2
Belgentier F 79 C4
Belgern D 52 B3
Belgioioso I 71 C4
Belgodère F 102 A2
Belgooly IRL 20 C3
Belgorod RUS 7 F14
Belgrade = Beograd SRB 85 B5
Belhade F 76 B2
Belica HR 74 B1
Beli Manastir HR 74 C3
Belin-Bèliet F 76 B2
Belinchón E 95 B3
Belišće HR 74 C3
Bělkovice-Lašt'any CZ 64 A3
Bella I 104 C1
Bellac F 67 B6
Bellágio I 71 C4
Bellananagh IRL 19 C4
Bellano I 71 B4
Bellária I 82 B1
Bellavary IRL 18 C2
Belleau F 59 A4
Belleek GB 18 B3
Bellegarde
Gard F 78 C3
Loiret F 58 C3
Bellegarde-en-Diois F 79 B4
Bellegarde-en-Marche F 68 C2
Bellegarde-sur-Valserine F 69 B5
Belle-Isle-en-Terre F 56 B2
Bellême F 58 B1
Bellenaves F 68 B3
Bellentre F 70 C1
Bellevaux F 69 B6
Bellevesvre F 69 B5
Belleville F 69 B4
Belleville-sur-Vie F 66 B3
Bellevue-la-Montagne F 68 C3
Belley F 69 C5
Bellheim D 61 A4
Bellinge DK 39 D3
Bellingham GB 25 C5
Bellinzago Novarese I 70 C3
Bellinzona CH 70 B4
Bell-lloc d'Urgell E 90 B3
Bello E 95 B5
Bellpuig d'Urgell E 91 B4
Bellreguart E 96 C2
Bellsbank GB 24 C3
Belltall E 91 B4
Belluno I 72 B2
Bellver de Cerdanya E 91 A4
Bellvis E 90 B3
Bélmez E 93 C5
Belmez de la Moraleda E 100 B2
Belmont GB 22 A8
Belmont-de-la-Loire F 69 B4
Belmonte
Asturias E 86 A4
Cuenca E 95 C4
P 92 A3
Belmonte de San José E 90 C2
Belmonte de Tajo E 95 B3
Belmont-sur-Rance F 78 C1
Belmullet IRL 18 B2
Belobreşca RO 85 B6
Beloeil B 49 C4
Belogradchik BG 11 E7
Belokorovichi UA 11 A10
Beloljin SRB 85 C6
Belorado E 89 B3
Belotič SRB 85 B4
Bělotin CZ 64 A3
Belozersk RUS 7 B14
Belp CH 70 B2
Belpasso I 109 B3
Belpech F 77 C4
Belper GB 27 B4
Belsay GB 25 C6
Belsh AL 105 C5
Belsk Duzy PL 55 B5
Beltinci SLO 73 B6
Beltra IRL 18 C2
Belturbet IRL 19 B4
Beluša SK 64 A4
Belušić SRB 85 C6
Belvedere Maríttimo I 106 B2
Belver de Cinca E 90 B3
Belver de los Montes E 88 C1
Belvès F 77 B3
Belvezet F 78 B2
Belvis de la Jara E 94 C2
Belvis de Monroy E 93 B5
Belyy RUS 7 D12
Belz F 56 C2
Bełżec PL 11 A7
Belzig D 52 A2
Bembibre E 86 B4
Bembridge GB 31 D2
Bemmel NL 50 B1
Bemposta
Bragança P 87 C4
Santarém P 92 B2
Benabarre E 90 A3
Benacazón E 99 B4
Benaguacil E 96 B2
Benahadux E 101 C3
Benalmádena E 100 C1
Benalúa de Guadix E 100 B2
Benalúa de las Villas E 100 B2
Benalup E 99 C5
Benamargosa E 100 C1
Benamaurel E 101 B3
Benameji E 100 B1
Benamocarra E 100 C1
Benaocaz E 99 C5
Benaoján E 99 C5
Benarrabá E 99 C5
Benasque E 90 A3
Benátky nad Jizerou CZ 53 C4
Benavente
E 88 B1
P 92 C2
Benavides de Órbigo E 88 B1
Benavila P 92 B3
Bendorf D 50 C3
Benedikt SLO 73 B5
Benejama E 101 A5
Benejúzar E 101 A5
Benešov CZ 63 A5
Bénestroff F 60 B2
Benet F 67 B4
Bene Vagienna I 80 B1
Bénévent-l'Abbaye F 67 B6
Benevento I 103 B7
Benfeld F 60 B3
Benfica P 92 B2
Bengtsfors S 35 C4
Bengtsheden S 36 B2
Beničanci HR 74 C3
Benicarló E 90 C3
Benicássim E 96 A3
Benidorm E 96 C2
Benifaió E 96 B2
Beniganim E 96 C2
Benington GB 27 B6
Benisa E 96 C3
Benkovac HR 83 B4
Benllech GB 26 B1
Benneckenstein D 51 B6
Bénodet F 56 C1
Benquerencia de la Serena E 93 C5
Bensafrim P 98 B2
Bensdorf D 44 C4
Benshausen D 51 C6
Bensheim D 61 A4
Bentley GB 31 C3
Bentwisch D 44 A4
Beočin SRB 75 C4
Beograd = Belgrade SRB 85 B5
Beragh GB 19 B4
Berane MNE 85 D4
Beranga E 89 A3
Berat AL 105 C5
Bérat F 77 C4
Beratzhausen D 62 A2
Bérbaltavár H 74 A1
Berbegal E 90 B2
Berbenno di Valtellina I 71 B4
Berberana E 89 B3
Bercedo E 89 A3
Bercel H 65 C5
Bercenay-le-Hayer F 59 B4
Berceto I 81 B3
Berchem B 49 C4
Berchidda I 110 B2
Berching D 62 A2
Berchtesgaden D 62 C4
Bérchules E 100 C2
Bercianos de Aliste E 87 C4
Berck F 48 C2
Berclaire d'Urgell E 90 B3
Berdoias E 86 A1
Berducedo E 86 A4
Berdún E 90 A2
Berdychiv UA 11 B10
Bere Alston GB 28 C3
Bereguardo I 70 C4
Berehommen N 33 C4
Berehove UA 11 B7
Berek BIH 84 A2
Beremend H 74 C3
Bere Regis GB 29 C5
Berestechko UA 11 A8
Berettyóújfalu H 10 C6
Berezhany UA 11 B8
Berezivka UA 11 C11
Berezna UA 7 F11
Berg
D 62 A2
N 114 B9
S 37 D3
Berga
Sachsen-Anhalt D 51 B7
Thüringen D 52 C2
E 91 A4
S 40 B6
Bergama TR 118 C2
Bérgamo I 71 C4
Bergara E 89 A4
Bergby S 36 B4
Berge
Brandenburg D 45 C4
Niedersachsen D 43 C4
Telemark N 33 C5
Telemark N 33 C5
Bergeforsen S 115 E14
Bergen
Mecklenburg-Vorpommern D 45 A5
Niedersachsen D 44 C1
Niedersachsen D 44 C2
N 32 B2
NL 42 C1
Bergen op Zoom NL 49 B5
Bergerac F 77 B3
Bergères-lés-Vertus F 59 B5
Bergeyk NL 49 B6
Berghausen D 61 B4
Bergheim D 50 C2
Berghem S 40 B2
Berg im Gau D 62 B2
Bergisch Gladbach D 50 C3
Bergkamen D 50 B3
Bergkvara S 41 C6
Berglern D 62 B2
Bergneustadt D 50 B3
Bergsäng S 34 B5
Bergshamra S 37 C5
Bergsjö S 115 F14
Bergs slussar S 37 D2
Bergtheim D 61 A6
Bergues F 48 C3
Bergum NL 42 B2
Bergün Bravuogn CH 71 B4
Bergwitz D 52 B2
Berhida H 74 A3
Beringel P 98 A3
Beringen B 49 B6
Berja E 100 C3
Berkåk N 114 E7
Berkeley GB 29 B5
Berkenthin D 44 B2
Berkhamsted GB 31 C3
Berkheim D 61 B6
Berkhof D 43 C6
Berkovići BIH 84 C3
Berkovitsa BG 11 E7
Berlanga E 99 A5
Berlanga de Duero E 89 C4
Berlevåg N 113 B18
Berlikum NL 42 B2
Berlin D 45 C5
Berlstedt D 52 B1
Bermeo E 89 A4
Bermillo de Sayago E 87 C4
Bern CH 70 B2
Bernalda I 104 C2
Bernardos E 94 A2
Bernartice
Jihočeský CZ 63 A5
Vychodočeský CZ 53 C5
Bernau
Baden-Württemberg D 61 C4
Bayern D 62 C3
Brandenburg D 45 C5
Bernaville F 48 C3
Bernay F 58 A1
Bernburg D 52 B1
Berndorf A 64 C2
Berne D 43 B5
Bernecebarati H 65 B4
Bernhardsthal A 64 B2
Bernkastel-Kues D 60 A3
Bernolakovo SK 64 B3
Bernsdorf D 53 B4
Bernstadt D 53 B4
Bernstein A 73 A6
Bernués E 90 A2
Beromünster CH 70 A3
Beroun CZ 53 D4
Berovo MK 116 A4
Berre-l'Etang F 79 C4
Berriedale GB 23 C5
Berriew GB 26 C2
Berrocal E 99 B4
Bersenbrück D 43 C4
Bershad' UA 11 B10
Bertamiráns E 86 B2
Berthåga S 36 C4
Berthelming F 60 B2
Bertincourt F 48 C3
Bertinoro I 82 B1
Bertogne B 49 C6
Bertrix B 59 A6
Berufjörður IS 111 C11
Berville-sur-Mer F 58 A1
Berwick-upon-Tweed GB 25 C5
Berzasca RO 10 D6
Berzence H 74 B2
Berzocana E 93 B5
Besalú E 91 A5
Besançon F 69 A6
Besenfeld D 61 B4
Besenyötelek H 65 C6
Besenyszög H 75 A5
Beshenkovichi BY 7 D10
Besigheim D 61 B5
Běšiny CZ 63 A4
Beška SRB 75 C5
Beşkonak TR 119 E6
Besle F 57 C4
Besnyö H 74 A3
Bessais-le-Fromental F 68 B2
Bessan F 78 C2
Besse-en-Chandesse F 68 C2
Bessèges F 78 B3
Bessé-sur-Braye F 58 C1
Bessines-sur-Gartempe F 67 B6
Best NL 49 B6
Bestorp S 37 D2
Betanzos E 86 A2
Betelu E 76 C1
Bétera E 96 B2
Beteta E 95 B4
Béthenville F 59 A5
Bethesda GB 26 B1
Béthune F 48 C3
Beton-Bazoches F 59 B4
Bettembourg L 60 A2
Betterdorf L 60 A2
Bettna S 37 D3
Béttola I 80 B3
Bettona I 82 C1
Bettyhill GB 23 C4
Betws-y-Coed GB 26 B2
Betxi E 96 B2
Betz F 59 A3
Betzdorf D 50 C3
Beuil F 79 B5
Beulah GB 29 A4
Beuzeville F 58 A1
Bevagna I 82 D1
Bevens-bruk S 37 C2
Beveren B 49 B5
Beverley GB 27 B5
Bevern D 51 B5
Beverstedt D 43 B5
Beverungen D 51 B5
Beverwijk NL 42 C1
Bex CH 70 B2
Bexhill GB 31 D4
Beyazköy TR 118 A2
Beychevelle F 76 A2
Beydağ TR 119 D3
Beyeğaç TR 119 E3
Beykoz TR 118 A4
Beynat F 68 C1
Beyoğlu TR 118 A4
Beypazarı TR 118 B6
Beyşehir TR 119 E6
Bezas E 95 B5
Bezau A 71 A4
Bezdan SRB 75 C3
Bèze F 69 A5
Bezenet F 68 B2
Bezhetsk RUS 7 C14
Béziers F 78 C2
Bezzecca I 71 C5
Biadki PL 54 B2
Biała
Łódzkie PL 55 B4
Opolskie PL 54 C2
Białaczów PL 55 B5
Biała Podlaska PL 6 E7
Biała Rawska PL 55 B5
Biale Błota PL 46 B3
Białobłoty PL 54 A2
Białobrzegi PL 55 B5
Białogard PL 46 B1
Bialośliwie PL 46 B3
Białowąs PL 46 B2
Biały Bór PL 46 B2
Białystok PL 6 E7
Biancavilla I 109 B3
Bianco I 106 C3
Biandrate I 70 C3
Biar E 101 A5
Biarritz F 76 C1
Bias F 76 B1
Biasca CH 70 B3
Biatorbágy H 74 A3
Bibbiena I 81 C5
Bibbona I 81 C4
Biberach
Baden-Württemberg D 61 B4
Baden-Württemberg D 61 B5
Bibinje HR 83 B4
Bibione I 72 C3
Biblis D 61 A4
Bibury GB 29 B6
Bíccari I 103 B8
Bicester GB 31 C2
Bichl D 62 C2
Bichlbach A 71 A5
Bicorp E 96 B2
Bicos P 98 B2
Bicske H 74 A3
Bidache F 76 C1
Bidart F 76 C1
Biddinghuizen NL 42 C2
Biddulph GB 26 B3
Bideford GB 28 B3
Bidford-on-Avon GB 29 A6
Bidjovagge N 113 C11
Bie S 37 C3
Bieber D 51 C5
Biebersdorf D 53 B3
Biedenkopf D 51 C4
Biel E 90 A2
Bielany Wroclawskie PL 54 B1
Bielawa PL 54 C1
Bielawy PL 55 A4
Biel/Bienne CH 70 A2
Bielefeld D 51 A4
Biella I 70 C3
Bielsa E 90 A3
Bielsk PL 47 C5
Bielsko-Biała PL 65 A5
Bielsk Podlaski PL 6 E7
Bienenbuttel D 44 B2
Bieniow PL 53 B5
Bienservida E 101 A3
Bienvenida E 93 C4
Bierdzany PL 54 C3
Bierné F 57 C5
Biersted DK 38 B2
Bierun PL 55 C4
Bierutów PL 54 B2
Bierwart B 49 C6
Bierzwina PL 46 B1
Bierzwnik PL 46 B1
Biescas E 90 A2
Biesenthal D 45 C5
Biesiekierz PL 46 A2

Bietigheim-Bissingen
D 61 B5
Bièvre B 49 D6
Bieżuń PL 47 C5
Biga TR 118 B2
Bigadiç TR 118 C3
Biganos F 76 B2
Bigas P 87 D3
Bigastro E 101 A5
Bigbury GB 28 C4
Biggar GB 25 C4
Biggin Hill GB 31 C4
Biggleswade GB 30 B3
Bignasco CH 70 B3
Biguglia F 102 A2
Bihać BIH 83 B4
Biharnagybajom H 75 A6
Bijela MNE 105 A4
Bijeljani BIH 84 C3
Bijeljina BIH 85 B4
Bijelo Polje MNE 85 C4
Bijuesca E 89 C5
Bilaj HR 83 B4
Bila Tserkva UA 11 B11
Bilbao E 89 A4
Bilcza PL 55 C5
Bildudalur IS 111 B2
Bileća BIH 84 D3
Bilecik TR 118 B4
Biled RO 75 C5
Biłgoraj PL 11 A7
Bilhorod-Dnistrovskyy
UA 11 C11
Bílina CZ 53 C3
Bilisht AL 116 B2
Bilje HR 74 C3
Billdal S 38 B4
Billerbeck D 50 B3
Billericay GB 31 C4
Billesholm S 41 C2
Billingborough GB 30 B3
Billinge S 41 D3
Billingham GB 27 A4
Billinghay GB 27 B5
Billingsfors S 35 D4
Billingshurst GB 31 C3
Billom F 68 C3
Billsta S 115 D15
Billund DK 39 D2
Bilopillya UA 7 F13
Bílovec CZ 64 A4
Bilstein D 50 B4
Bilthoven NL 49 A6
Bilto N 112 C10
Bilzen B 49 C6
Biňa SK 65 C4
Binaced E 90 B3
Binasco I 71 C4
Binbrook GB 27 B5
Binche B 49 C5
Bindlach D 52 D1
Bindslev DK 38 B3
Binefar E 90 B3
Bingen D 50 D3
Bingham GB 27 C5
Bingley GB 27 B4
Bingsjö S 36 A2
Binic F 56 B3
Binz D 45 A5
Bioče MNE 105 A5
Biograd na Moru HR 83 C4
Bionaz I 70 C2
Bioska SRB 85 C4
Birda RO 75 C6
Birdlip GB 29 B5
Biri N 34 B2
Birkeland N 33 D5
Birkenfeld
Baden-Württemberg
D 61 B4
Rheinland-Pfalz D 60 A3
Birkenhead GB 26 B2
Birkerød DK 41 D2
Birkfeld A 73 A5
Birkirkara M 107 C5
Birmingham GB 27 C4
Birr IRL 21 A4
Birresborn D 50 C2
Birstein D 51 C5
Biržai LT 6 C8
Birzebbugia M 107 C5
Bisáccia I 103 B8
Bisacquino I 108 B2
Bisbal de Falset E 90 B3
Biscarosse F 76 B1
Biscarosse Plage F 76 B1
Biscarrués E 90 A2
Biscéglie I 104 B2
Bischheim F 60 B3
Bischofsheim D 51 C5
Bischofshofen A 72 A3
Bischofswerda D 53 B4
Bischofswiesen D 62 C3
Bischofszell CH 71 A4
Bischwiller F 60 B3
Bisenti I 103 A6
Bishop Auckland GB 27 A4
Bishop's Castle GB 26 C3
Bishops Lydeard GB 29 B4
Bishop's Stortford
GB 31 C4
Bishop's Waltham
GB 31 D2
Bisignano I 106 B3
Bisingen D 61 B4
Biskupice-Oławskie
PL 54 B2
Biskupiec PL 47 B5
Bismark D 44 C3
Bismo N 114 F5
Bispgården S 115 D13
Bispingen D 44 B1
Bissen L 60 A2
Bissendorf D 50 A4
Bisserup DK 39 D4
Bistango I 80 B2
Bistarac Donje BIH 84 B3
Bistrica
BIH 84 B2
MNE 85 D4
SRB 85 C4
Bistrica ob Sotli SLO 73 B5
Bistrița RO 11 C8
Bisztynek PL 47 A6
Bitburg D 50 D2
Bitche F 60 A3
Bitetto I 104 B2
Bitola MK 116 A3
Bitonto I 104 B2
Bitschwiller F 60 C3
Bitterfeld D 52 B2
Bitti I 110 B2
Biville-sur-Mer F 48 D2
Bivona I 108 B2
Biwer L 60 A2
Bizeljsko SLO 73 B5
Bizovac HR 74 C3
Bjåen N 33 C4
Bjärnum S 41 C3
Bjärred S 41 D3
Bjästa S 115 D15
Bjelland
Vest-Agder N 33 D3
Vest-Agder N 33 D4
Bjelovar HR 74 C1
Bjerkreim N 33 D3
Bjerkvik N 112 D6
Bjerreby DK 39 E3
Bjerregrav DK 38 C2
Bjerringbro DK 39 C2
Bjøberg N 32 B5
Bjøllånes N 112 F3
Björbo S 36 B1
Bjordal N 32 A2
Björg IS 111 B8
Björkåsen N 112 D5
Björke
Gävleborg S 36 B4
Östergötland S 37 D2
Bjørkelangen N 34 C3
Björketorp S 40 B2
Björkholmen S 112 F8
Björkliden S 112 D7
Björklinge S 36 B4
Björko S 36 C6
Björkö S 38 B4
Björköby S 40 B4
Björkvik S 37 D3
Bjørn N 115 A9
Björna S 115 D15
Björneborg S 35 C6
Björnerod S 35 C3
Bjørnevatn N 113 C18
Bjørnlunda S 37 C4
Bjørnstad N 113 C19
Björsäter S 37 D3
Bjurberget S 34 B4
Bjurholm S 115 D16
Bjursås S 36 B2
Bjurtjärn S 35 C6
Bjuv S 41 C2
Blace SRB 85 C6
Blachownia PL 54 C3
Blackburn GB 26 B3
Blackpool GB 26 B2
Blackstad S 40 B6
Blackwater IRL 21 B5
Blackwaterfoot GB 24 C2
Blacy F 59 B5
Bladåker S 36 B5
Blaenau Ffestiniog
GB 26 C2
Blaenavon GB 29 B4
Blaengarw GB 29 B4
Blagaj
BIH 83 A5
BIH 84 C2
Blagdon GB 29 B5
Blagnac F 77 C4
Blagoevgrad BG 11 E7
Blaichach D 61 C6
Blain F 66 A3
Blainville-sur-l'Eau F 60 B2
Blair Atholl GB 25 B4
Blairgowrie GB 25 B4
Blajan F 77 C3
Blakeney GB 29 B5
Blakstad N 33 D5
Blâmont F 60 B2
Blanca E 101 A4
Blancos E 87 C3
Blandford Forum GB 29 C5
Blanes E 91 B5
Blangy-sur-Bresle F 58 A2
Blankaholm S 40 B6
Blankenberge B 49 B4
Blankenburg D 51 B6
Blankenfelde D 45 C5
Blankenhain D 52 C1
Blankenheim D 50 C2
Blanquefort F 76 B2
Blansko CZ 64 A2
Blanzac F 67 C5
Blanzy F 69 B4
Blaricum NL 49 A6
Blarney IRL 20 C3
Blascomillán E 94 B1
Blascosancho E 94 B2
Błaszki PL 54 B3
Blatná CZ 63 A4
Blatné SK 64 B3
Blatnice CZ 64 B3
Blatnika BIH 84 B2
Blato HR 84 D1
Blato na Cetini HR 84 C1
Blatten CH 70 B2
Blattnicksele S 115 B14
Blatzheim D 50 C2
Blaubeuren D 61 B5
Blaufelden D 61 A5
Blaustein D 61 B5
Blaydon GB 25 D6
Blaye F 76 A2
Blaye-les-Mines F 77 B5
Blázquez E 93 C5
Bleckede D 44 B2
Blecua E 90 A2
Bled SLO 73 B4
Bleiburg A 73 B4
Bleichenbach D 51 C5
Bleicherode D 51 B6
Bleik N 112 C4
Bleikvassli N 115 B10
Bléneau F 59 C3
Blentarp S 41 D3
Blera I 102 A5
Blérancourt F 59 A4
Bléré F 67 A5
Blesle F 68 C3
Blessington IRL 21 A5
Blet F 68 B2
Bletchley GB 31 C3
Bletterans F 69 B5
Blidö S 37 C5
Blidsberg S 40 B3
Blieskastel D 60 A3
Bligny-sur-Ouche F 69 A4
Blikstorp S 35 D6
Blinisht AL 105 B6
Blinja HR 73 C6
Blizanówek PL 54 B3
Bliżyn PL 55 B5
Blois F 58 C2
Blokhus DK 38 B2
Blokzijl NL 42 C2
Blombacka S 35 C5
Blomberg D 51 B5
Blomskog S 35 C4
Blomstermåla S 40 C6
Blomvåg N 32 B1
Blönduós IS 111 B5
Błonie PL 55 A5
Blonville-sur-Mer F 57 A6
Blötberget S 36 B2
Blovice CZ 63 A4
Bloxham GB 31 B2
Blšany CZ 52 C3
Bludenz A 71 A4
Bludov CZ 64 A2
Blumberg D 61 C4
Blyberg S 34 A6
Blyth
Northumberland
GB 25 C6
Nottinghamshire GB 27 B4
Blyth Bridge GB 25 C4
Blythburgh GB 30 B5
Blythe Bridge GB 26 C3
Bø
Nordland N 112 D3
Telemark N 33 C6
Boal E 86 A4
Boan MNE 85 D4
Boario Terme I 71 C5
Boat of Garten GB 23 D5
Boa Vista P 92 B2
Boğazkale TR 16 A7
Boğazlıyan TR 16 B7
Boba H 74 A2
Bobadilla
Logroño E 89 B4
Málaga E 100 B1
Bobadilla del Campo
E 94 A1
Bobadilla del Monte
E 94 B3
Bóbbio I 80 B3
Bóbbio Pellice I 79 B6
Bobigny F 58 B3
Bobingen D 62 B1
Böblingen D 61 B5
Bobolice PL 46 B2
Boboras E 87 B2
Bobowa PL 65 A6
Bobrinets UA 11 B12
Bobrová CZ 64 A2
Bobrovitsa UA 11 A11
Bobrowice PL 53 B5
Bobrówko PL 46 C1
Boca de Huérgano E 88 B2
Bocairent E 96 C2
Bočar SRB 75 C5
Bocchigliero I 106 B3
Boceguillas E 89 C3
Bochnia PL 55 D5
Bocholt
B 49 B6
D 50 B2
Bochov CZ 52 C3
Bochum D 50 B3
Bockara S 40 B6
Bockenem D 51 A6
Bockfliess A 64 B2
Bockhorn D 43 B5
Bočna SLO 73 B4
Bocognano F 102 A2
Boconád H 65 C6
Boczów PL 45 C6
Boda S 36 A3
Böda S 41 B7
Boda
Stockholm S 36 B5
Värmland S 35 C5
Västernorrland S 115 E13
Bodafors S 40 B4
Boda Glasbruk S 40 C5
Bodajk H 74 A3
Boddam
Aberdeenshire GB 23 D7
Shetland GB 22 B7
Boddin D 44 B3
Bödefeld-Freiheit D 51 B4
Boden S 3 D24
Bodenmais D 62 A4
Bodenteich D 44 C2
Bodenwerder D 51 B5
Bodiam GB 31 C4
Bodinnick GB 28 C3
Bodio CH 70 B3
Bodjani SRB 75 C4
Bodmin GB 28 C3
Bodø N 112 E3
Bodonal de la Sierra
E 99 A4
Bodrum TR 119 E2
Bodstedt D 45 A4
Bodzanów PL 47 C6
Bodzanowice PL 54 C3
Bodzechów PL 55 C6
Bodzentyn PL 55 C5
Boecillo E 88 C2
Boëge F 69 B6
Boën F 68 C3
Bogács H 65 C6
Bogadmindszent H 74 C3
Bogajo E 87 D4
Bogarra E 101 A3
Bogarre E 100 B2
Bogatić SRB 85 B4
Bogatynia PL 53 C4
Bogdaniec PL 45 C7
Bogë AL 105 A5
Boge S 37 E5
Bogen
D 62 B3
Nordland N 112 D4
Nordland N 112 E4
S 34 B4
Bogense DK 39 D3
Bogetići MNE 84 D3
Bognanco Fonti I 70 B3
Bognelv N 113 B11
Bognes N 112 D5
Bogno CH 70 B4
Bognor Regis GB 31 D3
Bogoria PL 55 C6
Bograngen S 34 B4
Boguchwaly PL 47 B6
Bogumiłowice PL 55 B4
Boguslav UA 11 B11
Boguszów-Gorce PL 53 C6
Bogutovac SRB 85 C5
Bogyiszló H 74 B3
Bohain-en-Vermandois
F 49 D4
Böheimkirchen A 64 B1
Bohinjska Bistrica
SLO 72 B3
Böhlen D 52 B2
Böhmenkirch D 61 B5
Böhmte D 43 C5
Bohonal de Ibor E 93 B5
Böhönye H 74 B2
Bohumin CZ 65 A4
Boiro E 86 B2
Bois-d'Amont F 69 B6
Boisseron F 78 C3
Boitzenburg D 45 B5
Boixols E 91 A4
Boizenburg D 44 B2
Bojadła PL 53 B5
Bojano I 103 B7
Bojanowo PL 54 B1
Bøjden DK 39 D3
Bojkovice CZ 64 A3
Bojná SK 64 B4
Bojnice SK 65 B4
Boka SRB 75 C5
Böklund D 43 A6
Bokod H 74 A3
Böksholm S 40 B4
Boksitogorsk RUS 7 B12
Bol HR 83 C5
Bolaños de Calatrava
E 100 A2
Bolayır TR 118 B1
Bolbec F 58 A1
Bölcske H 75 B3
Bolderslev DK 39 E2
Boldog H 65 C5
Boldva H 65 B6
Bolea E 90 A2
Bolekhiv UA 11 B7
Bolesławiec PL 53 B5
Boleszkowice PL 45 C6
Bolewice PL 46 C2
Bólgheri I 81 C4
Bolhrad UA 11 D10
Boliden S 3 D24
Bolimów PL 55 A5
Boliqueime P 98 B2
Boljevci SRB 85 B5
Boljkovci SRB 85 B5
Bolkhov RUS 7 E14
Bolków PL 53 C6
Bollebygd S 40 B2
Bollène F 78 B3
Bólliga E 95 B4
Bollnäs S 36 A3
Bollstabruk S 115 E14
Bollullos E 99 B4
Bollullos par del Condado
E 99 B4
Bologna I 81 B5
Bologne F 59 B6
Bolognetta I 108 B2
Bolognola I 82 D2
Bologoye RUS 7 C13
Bolótana I 110 B1
Bolsena I 102 A4
Bolshaya Vradiyevka
UA 11 C11
Bolsover GB 27 B4
Bolstad S 35 D4
Bolsward NL 42 B2
Boltaña E 90 A3
Boltenhagen D 44 B3
Boltigen CH 70 B2
Bolton GB 26 B3
Bolu TR 118 B6
Bolungarvík IS 111 A2
Bolvadin TR 118 D6
Bóly H 74 C3
Bolzaneto I 80 B2
Bolzano I 71 B6
Bomba I 103 A7
Bombarral P 92 B1
Bömenzien D 44 C3
Bomlitz D 43 C6
Bømlo N 33 C2
Bøn N 34 B3
Bona F 68 A3
Bonaduz CH 71 B4
Bonanza E 99 C4
Boñar E 88 B1
Bonarbridge GB 23 D4
Bonárcado I 110 B1
Bonares E 99 B4
Bonäs S 36 A1
Bonassola I 80 B3
Bonawe GB 24 B2
Bondal N 32 C5
Bondeno I 81 B5
Bondorf D 61 B4
Bondstorp S 40 B3
Bon-Encontre F 77 B3
Bo'ness GB 25 B4
Bonete E 101 A4
Bonifacio F 102 B2
Bonigen CH 70 B2
Bonin PL 46 A2
Bonn D 50 C3
Bonnánaro I 110 B1
Bonnåsjøen N 112 E4
Bonnat F 68 B1
Bonndorf D 61 C4
Bonnétable F 58 B1
Bonnétage F 70 A1
Bonneuil-les-Eaux F 58 A3
Bonneuil-Matours F 67 B5
Bonneval F 58 B2
Bonneval-sur-Arc F 70 C2
Bonneville F 69 B6
Bonnières-sur-Seine
F 58 A2
Bonnieux F 79 C4
Bönnigheim D 61 A5
Bonnyrigg GB 25 C4
Bonny-sur-Loire F 68 A2
Bono
E 90 A3
I 110 B2
Bonorva I 110 B1
Bønsnes N 34 B2
Bonyhád H 74 B3
Boom B 49 B5
Boos F 58 A2
Boostedt D 44 A2
Bootle
Cumbria GB 26 A2
Merseyside GB 26 B2
Bopfingen D 61 B6
Boppard D 50 C3
Boqueixón E 86 B2
Bor
CZ 62 A3
S 40 B4
SRB 11 D7
TR 16 C7
Boran-sur-Oise F 58 A3
Borås S 40 B2
Borba P 92 C3
Borbona I 102 A6
Borča SRB 85 B5
Borci BIH 84 C3
Borculo NL 50 A2
Bordány H 75 B4
Bordeaux F 76 B2
Bordeira P 98 B2
Bordesholm D 44 A2
Borðeyri IS 111 B4
Bordighera I 80 C1
Bording DK 39 C2
Bordón E 90 C2
Bore I 81 B3
Borehamwood GB 31 C3
Borek Strzeliński PL 54 C2
Borek Wielkopolski
PL 54 B2
Boreland GB 25 C4
Borello I 82 B1
Borensberg S 37 D2
Borgafjäll S 115 C12
Borgarnes IS 111 C4
Borgentreich D 51 B5
Börger D 43 C4
Borger NL 42 C3
Borggård S 37 D2
Borghamn S 37 D1
Borghetta di Vara I 81 B3
Borghetto d'Arróscia
I 80 B1
Borghetto Santo Spirito
I 80 B2
Borgholm S 41 C6
Borghorst D 50 A3
Bórgia I 106 C3
Borgloon B 49 C6
Børglum DK 38 B2
Borgo F 102 A2
Borgo alla Collina I 81 C5
Borgo a Mozzano I 81 C4
Borgoforte I 81 A4
Borgofranco d'Ivrea I 70 C2
Borgomanero I 70 C3
Borgomasino I 70 C2
Borgonovo Val Tidone
I 80 A3
Borgo Pace I 82 C1
Borgorose I 102 A6
Borgo San Dalmazzo
I 80 B1
Borgo San Lorenzo I 81 C5
Borgosésia I 70 C3
Borgo Val di Taro I 81 B3
Borgo Valsugana I 71 B6
Borgo Vercelli I 70 C3
Borgstena S 40 B3
Borgue GB 24 D3
Borgund N 32 A4
Borgvik S 35 C4
Borisovka RUS 7 F14
Borja E 89 C5
Bork D 50 B3
Borken D 50 B2
Borkenes N 112 D5
Børkop DK 39 D2
Borkowice PL 55 B5
Borkowo PL 47 C6
Borkum D 42 B3
Borlänge S 36 B2
Borlu TR 118 D3
Bormes-les-Mimosas
F 79 C5
Bórmio I 71 B5
Bormujos E 99 B4
Borna D 52 B2
Borne NL 50 A2
Bornes P 87 C3
Borne Sulinowo PL 46 B2
Bornheim D 50 C2
Bornhöved D 44 A2
Börnicke D 45 C4
Bornos E 99 C5
Borobia E 89 C5
Borodino RUS 7 D13
Borohrádek CZ 53 C6
Boronów PL 54 C3
Bórore I 110 B1
Borosżow PL 54 C3
Borota H 75 B4
Boroughbridge GB 27 A4
Borovany CZ 63 B5
Borovichi RUS 7 B12
Borovnica SLO 73 C4
Borovo HR 75 C3
Borovsk RUS 7 D14
Borovy CZ 63 A4
Borowa PL 54 B2
Borowie PL 55 B6
Borox E 94 B3
Borrby S 41 D4
Borre
DK 41 E2
N 35 C2
Borredá E 91 A4
Borrenes E 86 B4
Borriol E 96 A2
Borris
DK 39 D1
IRL 21 B5
Borris-in-Ossory IRL 21 B4
Borrisokane IRL 20 B3
Borrisoleigh IRL 21 B4
Borrowdale GB 26 A2
Børrud N 34 C4
Borşa RO 11 C8
Borsdorf D 52 B2
Børselv N 113 B14
Borsfa H 74 B1
Borský Mikuláš SK 64 B3
Borsodivánka H 65 C6
Borsodnádasd H 65 B6
Börte N 33 C4
Borth GB 26 C1
Bort-les-Orgues F 68 C2
Börtnan S 115 E10
Børtnes N 32 B6
Borup DK 39 D4
Boryslav UA 11 B7
Boryspil UA 11 A11
Boryszyn PL 46 C1
Borzęciczki PL 54 B2
Borzęcin PL 55 A5
Borzna UA 7 F12
Borzonasca I 80 B3
Borzyszkowy PL 46 A3
Borzytuchom PL 46 A3
Bosa I 110 B1
Bošáca SK 64 B3
Bosanci HR 73 C5
Bosanska Dubica BIH 74 C1
Bosanska Gradiška
BIH 74 C2
Bosanska Kostajnica
BIH 74 C1
Bosanska Krupa BIH 83 B5
Bosanski Brod BIH 84 A2
Bosanski Novi BIH 83 A5
Bosanski Petrovac
BIH 83 B5
Bosanski Šamac BIH 84 A3
Bosansko Grahovo
BIH 83 B5
Bošany SK 64 B4
Bösárkány H 64 C3
Bosau D 44 A2
Bósca H 75 B4
Boscastle GB 28 C3
Bosco I 80 B2
Bosco Chiesanuova I 71 C6
Bösdorf D 44 A2
Bösel D 43 B4
Bosham GB 31 D3
Bösingfeld D 51 A5
Bosjön S 34 C5
Boskoop NL 49 A5
Boskovice CZ 64 A2
Bošnjaci HR 84 A3
Bošnjane SRB 85 C6
Bossast E 77 D3
Bossolasco I 80 B2
Boštanj SLO 73 B5
Boston GB 27 C5
Bostrak N 33 C5
Böszénfa H 74 B2
Bot E 90 B3
Botajica BIH 84 B3
Bøte By DK 44 A3
Bothel GB 26 A2
Boticas P 87 C3
Botilsäter S 35 C5
Botngård N 114 D6
Botoš SRB 75 C5
Botoşani RO 11 C9
Botricello I 107 C3
Bottendorf D 51 B4
Bottesford GB 27 C5
Bottnaryd S 40 B3
Bottrop D 50 B2
Botunje SRB 85 B6
Boturić SRB 85 C5
Bötzingen D 60 B3
Bouaye F 66 A3
Bouça P 87 C3
Boucau F 76 C1
Bouchain F 49 C4
Bouchoir F 58 A3
Boudreville F 59 C5
Boudry CH 70 B1
Bouesse F 67 B6
Bouguenais F 66 A3
Bouhy F 68 A3
Bouillargues F 78 C3
Bouillon B 59 A6
Bouilly F 59 B4
Bouin F 66 B3
Boulay-Moselle F 60 A2
Boulazac F 67 C5
Boule-d'Amont F 91 A5
Bouligny F 60 A1
Boulogne-sur-Gesse
F 77 C3
Boulogne-sur-Mer F 48 C2
Bouloire F 58 C1
Bouquemaison F 48 C3
Bourbon-Lancy F 68 B3
Bourbon-l'Archambault
F 68 B3
Bourbonne-les-Bains
F 60 C1
Bourbourg F 48 C3
Bourbriac F 56 B2
Bourcefranc-le-Chapus
F 66 C3
Bourdeaux F 79 B4
Bouresse F 67 B5
Bourg F 76 A2
Bourg-Achard F 58 A1
Bourganeuf F 68 C1
Bourg-Argental F 69 C4
Bourg-de-Péage F 79 A4
Bourg-de-Thizy F 69 B4
Bourg-de-Visa F 77 B3
Bourg-en-Bresse F 69 B5
Bourges F 68 A2
Bourg-et-Comin F 59 A4
Bourg-Lastic F 68 C2
Bourg-Madame F 91 A4
Bourgneuf-en-Retz F 66 A3
Bourgogne F 59 A5
Bourgoin-Jallieu F 69 C5
Bourg-St Andéol F 78 B3
Bourg-St Maurice F 70 C1
Bourgtheroulde F 58 A1
Bourgueil F 67 A5
Bourmont F 60 B1
Bourne GB 30 B3
Bournemouth GB 29 C6
Bourneville F 58 A1
Bournezeau F 66 B3
Bourran F 77 B3
Bourret F 77 C4
Bourron-Marlotte F 58 B3
Bourton-on-The-Water
GB 29 B6
Boussac F 68 B2
Boussens F 77 C4
Boutersem B 49 C5
Bouttencourt F 48 D2
Bouvières F 79 B4
Bouvron F 66 A3
Bouxwiller F 60 B3
Bouzas E 87 B2
Bouzonville F 60 A2
Bova I 106 D2
Bovalino Marina I 106 C3
Bovallstrand S 35 D3
Bova Marina I 106 D2
Bovec SLO 72 B3
Bóveda E 86 B3
Bóvegno I 71 C5
Bovenau D 44 A1
Bovenden D 51 B5
Bøverdal N 114 F5
Boves F 58 A3
Bóves I 80 B1
Bovey Tracey GB 28 C4
Bovino I 103 B8
Bøvlingbjerg DK 38 C1
Bovolenta I 72 C1
Bovolone I 71 C6
Bowes GB 27 A4
Bowmore GB 24 C1
Bowness-on-Windermere
GB 26 A3
Box GB 29 B5
Boxberg
Baden-Württemberg
D 61 A5
Sachsen D 53 B4
Boxholm S 37 D2
Boxmeer NL 50 B1
Boxtel NL 49 B6
Boyabat TR 16 A7
Boyalıca TR 118 B4
Boyle IRL 18 C3
Bozan TR 118 C6
Božava HR 83 B3
Bozburun TR 119 F3
Bozcaada TR 116 C8
Bozdoğan TR 119 E3
Božepole Wielkie PL 46 A3
Boževac SRB 85 B6
Božice CZ 64 B2
Boži Dar CZ 52 C2
Bozkır TR 119 E7
Bozouls F 78 B1
Bozova TR 119 E5
Bozüyük TR 118 C5
Bózzolo I 81 A4
Bra I 80 B1
Braås S 40 B5
Brabrand DK 39 C3
Bracadale GB 22 D2
Bracciano I 102 A5
Bracieux F 67 A6
Bräcke S 115 E12
Brackenheim D 61 A5
Brackley GB 30 B2
Bracklin IRL 19 C5
Bracknell GB 31 C3
Brackwede D 51 B4
Braco GB 25 B4
Brad RO 11 C7
Bradford GB 27 B4
Bradford on Avon GB 29 B5
Bradina BIH 84 C3
Brådland N 33 D3
Brædstrup DK 39 D2
Brae GB 22 A7
Braemar GB 23 D5
Braemore GB 22 D3
Braga P 87 C2
Bragança P 87 C4
Brăila RO 11 D9
Braine F 59 A4
Braine-le-Comte B 49 C5
Braintree GB 31 C4
Braives B 49 C6
Brake D 43 B5
Brakel
B 49 C4
D 51 B5
Bräkne-Hoby S 41 C5
Brålanda S 35 D4
Bralin PL 54 B2
Brallo di Pregola I 80 B3
Bram F 77 C5
Bramafan F 79 C5
Bramberg am Wildkogel
A 72 A2
Bramdrupdam DK 39 D2
Bramming DK 39 D1
Brampton GB 25 D5
Bramsche D 43 C4
Branca I 82 C1
Brancaleone Marina
I 106 D3
Brancaster GB 30 B4
Brand
Nieder Östereich A 63 B6
Vorarlberg A 71 A4
Brandbu N 34 B2
Brande DK 39 D2
Brande-Hornerkirchen
D 43 B6
Brandenberg A 72 A1
Brandenburg D 45 C4
Brand-Erbisdorf D 52 C3
Brandis D 52 B2
Brando F 102 A2
Brandomil E 86 A2
Brandon GB 30 B4
Brandshagen D 45 A5
Brandval N 34 B4
Brandýs nad Labem
CZ 53 C4
Branice PL 54 C2
Braničevo SRB 85 B6
Braniewo PL 47 A5
Branik SLO 72 C3
Brankovina SRB 85 B4
Branky CZ 64 A3
Branne F 76 B2
Brannenburg-Degerndorf
D 62 C3
Brantôme F 67 C5
Branzi I 71 B4
Bras d'Asse F 79 C5
Braskereidfoss N 34 B3
Braslaw BY 7 D9
Brașov RO 11 D8
Brasparts F 56 B2
Brassac F 77 C5
Brassac-les-Mines F 68 C3
Brasschaat B 49 B5
Brastad S 35 D3
Břasy CZ 63 A4
Brąszewice PL 54 B3
Brataj AL 105 C5
Bratislava SK 64 B3
Brattfors S 35 C6
Brattvåg N 114 E3
Bratunac BIH 85 B4
Braubach D 50 C3
Braunau A 62 B4
Braunfels D 51 C4
Braunlage D 51 B6
Braunsbedra D 52 B1
Braunschweig D 51 A6
Bray IRL 21 A5
Bray Dunes F 48 B3
Bray-sur-Seine F 59 B4
Bray-sur-Somme F 48 D3
Brazatortas E 100 A1
Brazey-en-Plaine F 69 A5
Brbinj HR 83 B4
Brčko BIH 84 B3
Brdani SRB 85 C5
Brdów PL 47 C4
Brea de Tajo E 95 B3
Brécey F 57 B4
Brechen D 50 C4
Brechin GB 25 B5
Brecht B 49 B5
Brecketfeld D 50 B3
Břeclav CZ 64 B2
Brecon GB 29 B4
Brécy F 68 A2
Breda
E 91 B5
NL 49 B5
Bredaryd S 40 B3
Bredbyn S 115 D15
Breddin D 44 C4
Bredebro DK 39 D1
Bredelar D 51 B4
Bredenfelde D 45 B5
Bredsjö S 36 C1
Bredstedt D 43 A5
Bredsten DK 39 D2
Bredträsk S 115 D15
Bredviken S 115 A11
Bree B 49 B6
Bregana HR 73 C5
Breganze I 72 C1
Bregenz A 71 A4
Bréhal F 57 B4
Brehna D 52 B2
Breiðdalsvík IS 111 C11
Breidenbach F 60 A3
Breil-sur-Roya F 80 C1
Breisach D 60 B3
Breitenbach
CH 70 A2
D 51 C5
Breitenberg D 63 B4
Breitenfelde D 44 B2
Breitengussbach D 51 D6
Breivikbotn N 113 B11
Brejning DK 39 D2
Brekke N 32 A2
Brekken N 114 E8
Brekkestø N 33 E5
Brekkvasselv N 115 C10
Brekstad N 114 D6
Breland N 33 D4
Bremanger N 114 F1
Bremen D 43 B5
Bremerhaven D 43 B5
Bremervörde D 43 B6
Bremgarten CH 70 A3
Bremsnes N 114 D4
Brem-sur-Mer F 66 B3
Brenderup DK 39 D2
Brenes E 99 B5
Brengova SLO 73 B5
Brenna PL 65 A4
Breno I 71 C5
Brénod F 69 B5
Brensbach D 61 A4
Brentwood GB 31 C4
Brescello I 81 B4
Bréscia I 71 C5
Breskens NL 49 B4
Bresles F 58 A3
Bresnica SRB 85 C5
Bressana I 80 A3
Bressanone I 72 B1
Bressuire F 67 B4
Brest
BY 6 E7
F 56 B1
HR 72 C3
Brestač SRB 85 B4
Brestanica SLO 73 B5
Brestova HR 82 A3
Brestovac HR 74 C2
Bretenoux F 77 B4
Breteuil
Eure F 58 B1
Oise F 58 A3
Brétigny-sur-Orge F 58 B3
Bretten D 61 A4
Bretteville-sur-Laize
F 57 A5
Brettheim D 61 A6
Breuil-Cervinia I 70 C2
Breukelen NL 49 A6
Brevik
N 35 C1
Stockholm S 37 C5
Västra Götaland S 37 D1
Breza BIH 84 B3
Brežice SLO 73 C5
Bréziers F 79 B5
Brezna SRB 85 C5
Breznica HR 73 B6
Breznica Našička HR 74 C3
Březnice CZ 63 A4
Brezno SK 65 B5
Brezojevice MNE 85 D4
Brezolles F 58 B2
Březovánad Svitavou
CZ 64 A2
Brezovápod Bradlom
SK 64 B3
Brezovica
SK 65 A6
SLO 73 B4
Brezovo Polje Selo
BIH 84 B3
Briançon F 79 B5
Brianconnet F 79 C5
Briare F 58 C3
Briatexte F 77 C4
Briático I 106 C3
Briaucourt F 59 B6
Bribir HR 73 C4
Bricquebec F 57 A4
Bridgend
Argyll & Bute GB 24 C1
Bridgend GB 29 B4
Bridge of Cally GB 25 B4
Bridge of Don GB 23 D6
Bridge of Earn GB 25 B4
Bridge of Orchy GB 24 B3
Bridgnorth GB 26 C3
Bridgwater GB 29 B5
Břidličná CZ 64 A3
Bridlington GB 27 A5
Bridport GB 29 C5
Briec F 56 B1
Brie-Comte-Robert F 58 B3
Brienne-le-Château F 59 B5
Brienon-sur-Armançon
F 59 C4
Brienz CH 70 B3
Brienza I 104 C1
Briesen D 45 C6
Brieskow Finkenheerd
D 53 A4
Brietlingen D 44 B2
Brieva de Cameros E 89 B4
Briey F 60 A1
Brig CH 70 B3
Brigg GB 27 B5
Brighouse GB 27 B4
Brightlingsea GB 31 C5
Brighton GB 31 D3
Brignogan-Plage F 56 B1
Brignoles F 79 C5
Brigstock GB 30 B3
Brihuega E 95 B4
Brijuni HR 82 B2
Brillon-en-Barrois F 59 B6
Brilon D 51 B4
Brimnes N 32 B3
Brinches P 98 A3
Brindisi I 105 C3
Brinje HR 83 A4
Brinon-sur-Beuvron
F 68 A3
Brinon-sur-Sauldre F 68 A2
Brinyan GB 23 B5
Brión E 86 B2
Briones E 89 B4
Brionne F 58 A1
Brioude F 68 C3
Brioux-sur-Boutonne
F 67 B4
Briouze F 57 B5
Briscous F 76 C1
Brisighella I 81 B5
Brissac-Quincé F 67 A4
Brissago CH 70 B3
Bristol GB 29 B5
Brive-la-Gaillarde F 67 C6
Briviesca E 89 B3
Brixham GB 29 C4
Brixlegg A 72 A1
Brjánslækur IS 111 B2
Brka BIH 84 B3
Brnaze HR 83 C5
Brněnec CZ 64 A2
Brno CZ 64 A2
Bro S 37 C4
Broadclyst GB 29 C4
Broadford
GB 22 D3
IRL 20 B3
Broad Haven GB 28 B2
Broadstairs GB 31 C5
Broadstone GB 29 C5
Broadway GB 29 A6
Broager DK 39 E2
Broaryd S 40 B3
Broby S 41 C4
Brobyværk DK 39 D3
Bročanac BIH 84 C2
Bročanac MNE 84 D3
Brocas F 76 B2
Brock D 50 A3
Brockel D 43 B6
Brockenhurst GB 31 D2
Broczyno PL 46 B2
Brod MK 116 A3
Brodalen S 35 D3
Brodarevo SRB 85 C4
Broddbo S 36 C3
Brodek u Přerova CZ 64 A3
Broden-bach D 50 C3
Brodick GB 24 C2
Brod na Kupi HR 73 C4
Brodnica PL 47 B5
Brodnica Graniczna
PL 47 A4
Brody
Lubuskie PL 53 A5
Lubuskie PL 53 B4
Mazowieckie PL 47 C6
UA 11 A8
Broglie F 58 B1
Brójce PL 53 A5
Brokind S 37 D2
Brolo I 109 A3
Brome D 44 C2
Bromley GB 31 C4
Bromölla S 41 C4
Bromont-Lamothe F 68 C2
Brömsebro S 41 C5
Bromsgrove GB 29 A5
Bromyard GB 29 A5
Bronchales E 95 B5
Bronco E 93 A4
Brønderslev DK 38 B2
Broni I 80 A3
Brønnøysund N 114 B9
Brøns DK 39 D1
Bronte I 109 B3
Bronzani Mejdan BIH 84 B1
Bronzolo I 71 B6
Broons F 57 B3
Broquies F 78 B1
Brora GB 23 C5
Brørup DK 39 D2
Brösarp S 41 D4
Brossac F 67 C4
Brostrud N 32 B5
Brotas P 92 C2
Brötjärna S 36 B2
Broto E 90 A2
Brottby S 37 C5
Brøttum N 34 A2
Brou F 58 B2
Brouage F 66 C3
Brough GB 26 A3
Broughshane GB 19 B5
Broughton GB 25 C4
Broughton-in-Furness
GB 26 A2
Broumov CZ 53 C6
Broût-Vernet F 68 B3
Brouvelieures F 60 B2
Brouwershaven NL 49 B4
Brovary UA 11 A11
Brovst DK 38 B2
Brownhills GB 27 C4
Brozas E 93 B4
Brozzo I 71 C5
Brtnice CZ 63 A6
Brtonigla HR 72 C3
Bruay-la-Buissière F 48 C3
Bruchhausen-Vilsen
D 43 C6
Bruchsal D 61 A4
Bruck D 62 A3
Brück D 52 A2
Bruck an der
Grossglocknerstrasse
A 72 A2
Bruck an der Leitha A 64 B2
Bruck an der Mur A 73 A5
Brückl A 73 B4
Bruckmühl D 62 C2
Brue-Auriac F 79 C4
Brüel D 44 B3
Bruen CH 70 B3
Bruère-Allichamps F 68 B2
Bruff IRL 20 B3
Bruflat N 32 B6
Brugg CH 70 A3
Brugge B 49 B4
Brüggen D 50 B2
Brühl D 50 C2
Bruinisse NL 49 B5
Brûlon F 57 C5
Brumano I 71 C4
Brumath F 60 B3
Brummen NL 50 A2
Brumov-Bylnice CZ 64 A4
Brumunddal N 34 B2
Brunau D 44 C3
Brunehamel F 59 A5
Brünen D 50 B2
Brunete E 94 B2
Brunflo S 115 D11
Brunico I 72 B1
Brunkeberg N 33 C5
Brunn D 45 B5
Brunnen CH 70 B3
Brunsbüttel D 43 B6
Brunssum NL 50 C1
Bruntál CZ 64 A3
Brus SRB 85 C6
Brušane HR 83 B4
Brusasco I 70 C3
Brusio CH 71 B5
Brusno SK 65 B5
Brusque F 78 C1
Brussels = Bruxelles
B 49 C5
Brusson I 70 C2
Brüssow D 45 B6
Brusy PL 46 B3
Bruton GB 29 B5
Bruvno HR 83 B4
Bruvoll N 34 B3
Bruxelles = Brussels
B 49 C5
Bruyères F 60 B2
Bruz F 57 B4
Bruzaholm S 40 B5
Brwinów PL 55 A5
Bryansk RUS 7 E13
Brynamman GB 28 B4
Bryncrug GB 26 C1
Bryne N 33 D2
Brynmawr GB 29 B4
Bryrup DK 39 C2
Brzeće SRB 85 C5
Brzeg PL 54 C2
Brzeg Dolny PL 54 B1
Brześć Kujawski PL 47 C4
Brzesko PL 55 D5
Brzeszcze PL 55 D4
Brzezie PL 46 B2
Brzeziny
Łódzkie PL 55 B4
Wielkopolskie PL 54 B3
Brzeźnica PL 53 B5
Brzeźnica Nowa PL 55 B4
Brzeżno PL 46 B1
Brzotin SK 65 B6
Brzozie Lubawskie
PL 47 B5
Bua S 40 B2
Buarcos P 92 A2
Buaveg N 33 C2
Bubbio I 80 B2
Bubry F 56 C2
Buca TR 119 D2
Bucak TR 119 E5
Bučany SK 64 B3
Buccheri I 109 B3
Buccino I 103 C8
Bucelas P 92 C1
Buch
Bayern D 61 B6
Bayern D 62 B3
Buchach UA 11 B8
Bucharest = București
RO 11 D9
Buchbach D 62 B3
Buchboden A 71 A4
Buchen D 61 A5
Büchen D 44 B2
Buchenberg D 61 C6
Buchères F 59 B5
Buchholz D 44 B1
Buchloe D 62 B1
Buchlovice CZ 64 A3

Buchlyvie GB 24 B3
Bucholz D 44 B4
Buchs CH 71 A4
Buchy F 58 A2
Bückeburg D 51 A5
Buckfastleigh GB 28 C4
Buckhaven GB 25 B4
Buckie GB 23 D6
Buckingham GB 31 B3
Buckley GB 26 B2
Bückwitz D 44 C4
Bučovice CZ 64 A3
Bucsa H 75 A6
Bucureşti = Bucharest RO 11 D9
Bucy-lés-Pierrepont F 59 A4
Buczek PL 55 B4
Bud N 114 E3
Budakalasz H 65 C5
Budakeszi H 75 A3
Budal N 114 E7
Budaörs H 75 A3
Budapest H 75 A4
Búðardalur IS 111 B4
Budča SK 65 B5
Buddusò I 110 B2
Bude GB 28 C3
Budeč CZ 63 A6
Büdelsdorf D 43 A6
Budens P 98 B2
Budia E 95 B4
Budimlić-Japra BIH 83 B5
Büdingen D 51 C5
Budinšćina HR 73 B6
Budišov CZ 64 A3
Budleigh Salterton GB 29 C4
Budmerice SK 64 B3
Budoni I 110 B2
Búdrio I 81 B5
Budva MNE 105 A4
Budyněnad Ohří CZ 53 C4
Budziszewice PL 55 B4
Budzyń PL 46 C2
Bue N 33 D2
Bueña E 95 B5
Buenache de Alarcón E 95 C4
Buenache de la Sierra E 95 B5
Buenaventura E 94 B2
Buenavista de Valdavia E 88 B2
Buendia E 95 B4
Bueu E 87 B2
Buezo E 89 B3
Bugac H 75 B4
Bugarra E 96 B2
Bugeat F 68 C1
Buggerru I 110 C1
Bugojno BIH 84 B2
Bugøyfjord N 113 C18
Bugøynes N 113 C18
Bugyi H 75 A4
Buharkent TR 119 E3
Bühl
Baden-Württemberg D 61 B4
Bayern D 61 C6
Bühlertal D 61 B4
Bühlertann D 61 A5
Buia I 72 B3
Builth Wells GB 29 A4
Buin N 32 B6
Buis-les-Baronnies F 79 B4
Buitenpost NL 42 B3
Buitrago del Lozoya E 94 B3
Bujalance E 100 B1
Bujaraloz E 90 B2
Buje HR 72 C3
Bujedo E 89 B3
Bük H 74 A1
Buk PL 46 C2
Bükkösd H 74 B2
Bükkzsérc H 65 C6
Bukovci SLO 73 B5
Bukowiec PL 53 A6
Bukowina Tatrzańska PL 65 A6
Bukownica PL 54 B3
Bukowno PL 55 C4
Bülach CH 70 A3
Búland IS 111 D7
Buldan TR 119 D3
Bulgari BG 11 E9
Bulgnéville F 60 B1
Bulgurca TR 119 D2
Bülkau D 43 B5
Bulken N 32 B3
Bulkowo PL 47 C6
Bullas E 101 A4
Bulle CH 70 B2
Büllingen B 50 C2
Bulqizë AL 116 A2
Buna BIH 84 C2
Bunahowen IRL 18 B2
Bunbeg IRL 18 A3
Bunclody IRL 21 B5
Buncrana IRL 19 A4
Bunde D 43 B4
Bünde D 51 A4
Bundoran IRL 18 B3
Bunessan GB 24 B1
Bungay GB 30 B5
Bunge S 37 E6
Bunić HR 83 B4
Bunmahon IRL 21 B4
Bunnyconnellan IRL 18 B2
Buño E 86 A2
Buñol E 96 B2
Bunratty IRL 20 B3
Bunsbeek B 49 C5
Buñuel E 89 C5
Bünyan TR 16 B7
Bunyola E 97 B2
Buonabitácolo I 104 C1
Buonalbergo I 103 B7
Buonconvento I 81 C5
Buonvicino I 106 B2
Burano I 72 C2
Burbach D 50 C4
Burcei I 110 C2
Burdons-sur-Rognon F 59 B6
Burdur TR 119 E5
Bureå S 3 D24
Burela E 86 A3
Büren D 51 B4
Büren an der Aare CH 70 A2
Burford GB 29 B6
Burg
Cottbus D 53 B4
Magdeburg D 52 A1
Schleswig-Holstein D 43 B6
Burgas BG 11 E9
Burgau
A 73 A6
D 61 B6
P 98 B2
Burg auf Fehmarn D 44 A3
Burgbernheim D 61 A6
Burgdorf
CH 70 A2
D 44 C2
Burgebrach D 62 A1
Bürgel D 52 C1
Burgess Hill GB 31 D3
Burghaslach D 61 A6
Burghausen D 62 B3
Burghead GB 23 D5
Burgheim D 62 B2
Burgh le Marsh GB 27 B6
Búrgio I 108 B2
Burgkirchen D 62 B3
Burgkunstadt D 52 C1
Burglengenfeld D 62 A3
Burgo P 87 D2
Burgoberbach D 61 A6
Burgohondo E 94 B2
Burgos E 88 B3
Burgsinn D 51 C5
Burgstädt D 52 C2
Burgstall D 44 C3
Burg Stargard D 45 B5
Burgsvik S 37 E5
Burgui E 76 D2
Burguillos E 99 B5
Burguillos del Cerro E 93 C4
Burguillos de Toledo E 94 C3
Burhaniye TR 118 C1
Burhave D 43 B5
Burie F 67 C4
Burjassot E 96 B2
Burk D 61 A6
Burkhardtsdorf D 52 C2
Burlada E 76 D1
Burladingen D 61 B5
Burlage D 43 B4
Burness GB 23 B6
Burnham GB 31 C3
Burnham Market GB 30 B4
Burnham-on-Crouch GB 31 C4
Burnham-on-Sea GB 29 B5
Burniston GB 27 A5
Burnley GB 26 B3
Burntisland GB 25 B4
Burón E 88 A1
Buronzo I 70 C3
Burovac SRB 85 B6
Burow D 45 B5
Burravoe GB 22 A7
Burrel AL 105 B6
Burret F 77 D4
Burriana E 96 B2
Burry Port GB 28 B3
Bürs A 71 A4
Bursa TR 118 B4
Burseryd S 40 B3
Bürstadt D 61 A4
Burton GB 26 A3
Burton Agnes GB 27 A5
Burton Bradstock GB 29 C5
Burton Latimer GB 30 B3
Burton upon Stather GB 27 B5
Burton upon Trent GB 27 C4
Burujón E 94 C2
Burwell GB 30 B4
Burwick GB 23 C6
Bury GB 26 B3
Buryn UA 7 F12
Bury St Edmunds GB 30 B4
Burzenin PL 54 B3
Busachi I 110 B1
Busalla I 80 B2
Busana I 81 B4
Busano I 70 C2
Busca I 80 B1
Busch D 44 C3
Buševec HR 73 C6
Bushat AL 105 B5
Bushey GB 31 C3
Bushmills GB 19 A5
Bušince SK 65 B5
Buskhyttan S 37 D3
Busko-Zdrój PL 55 C5
Busot E 96 C2
Busovača BIH 84 B2
Busquistar E 100 C2
Bussang F 60 C2
Busseto I 81 B4
Bussière-Badil F 67 C5
Bussière-Poitevine F 67 B5
Bussolengo I 71 C5
Bussoleno I 70 C2
Bussum NL 49 A6
Busto Arsizio I 70 C3
Büsum D 43 A5
Butera I 109 B3
Butgenbach B 50 C2
Butler's Bridge IRL 19 B4
Butryny PL 47 B6
Bütschwil CH 70 A4
Buttermere GB 26 A2
Buttevant IRL 20 B3
Buttle S 37 E5
Buttstädt D 52 B1
Butzbach D 51 C4
Bützfleth D 43 B6
Bützow D 44 B3
Buxières-les-Mines F 68 B2
Buxtehude D 43 B6
Buxton GB 27 B4
Buxy F 69 B4
Büyükçekmece TR 118 A3
Büyükkariştiran TR 118 A2
Büyükorhan TR 118 C3
Buzançais F 67 B6
Buzancy F 59 A5
Buzău RO 11 D9
Buzet HR 72 C3
Buzsák H 74 B2
Buzy F 76 C2
By S 36 B3
Byala BG 11 E8
Byaroza BY 6 E8
Byczyna PL 54 B3
Bydalen S 115 D10
Bydgoszcz PL 47 B4
Bygdin N 32 A5
Bygland N 33 D4
Byglandsfjord N 33 D4
Bygstad N 32 A2
Bykhaw BY 7 E11
Bykle N 33 C4
Bylderup-Bov DK 39 E2
Byrkjedal N 33 D3
Byrkjelo N 114 F3
Byrum DK 38 B3
Byšice CZ 53 C4
Byske S 3 D24
Býškovice CZ 64 A3
Bysław PL 46 B3
Bystré CZ 64 A2
Bystřice CZ 63 A5
Bystřice CZ 65 A4
Bystřice nad Pernštejnem CZ 64 A2
Bystřice pod Hostýnem CZ 64 A3
Bystrzyca Kłodzka PL 54 C1
Bytča SK 65 A4
Bytnica PL 53 A5
Bytom PL 54 C3
Bytom Odrzański PL 53 B5
Bytów PL 46 A3
Byxelkrok S 41 B7
Bzenec CZ 64 B3
Bzince SK 64 B3

C

Çağa TR 118 B7
Cabacos P 92 B2
Cabaj-Čápor SK 64 B4
Cabana E 86 A2
Cabanac-et-Villagrains F 76 B2
Cabañaquinta E 88 A1
Cabanas P 98 B3
Cabañas del Castillo E 93 B5
Cabañas de Yepes E 95 C3
Cabanelles E 91 A5
Cabanes E 96 A3
Cabanillas E 89 B5
Čabar HR 73 C4
Cabasse F 79 C5
Cabdella E 91 A4
Cabeceiras de Basto P 87 C2
Cabeço de Vide P 92 B3
Cabella Ligure I 80 B3
Cabeza del Buey E 93 C5
Cabeza la Vaca E 99 A4
Cabezamesada E 95 C3
Cabezarados E 100 A1
Cabezarrubias del Puerto E 100 A1
Cabezas del Villar E 94 B1
Cabezas Rubias E 98 B3
Cabezón E 88 C2
Cabezón de la Sal E 88 A2
Cabezón de Liébana E 88 A2
Cabezuela E 94 A3
Cabezuela del Valle E 93 A5
Cabo de Gata E 101 C3
Cabo de Palos E 101 B5
Cabolafuenta E 95 A4
Cabourg F 57 A5
Cabra
E 100 B1
P 92 A3
Cabrach GB 23 D5
Cabra del Santo Cristo E 100 B2
Cábras I 110 C1
Cabreiro P 87 C2
Cabreiros E 86 A3
Cabrejas E 95 B4
Cabrela P 92 C2
Cabrillas E 87 D4
Cabuna HR 74 C2
Cacabelos E 86 B4
Čačak SRB 85 C5
Cáccamo I 108 B2
Caccuri I 107 B3
Cacela P 98 B3
Cacém P 92 C1
Cáceres E 93 B4
Cachafeiro E 86 B2
Cachopo P 98 B3
Čachtice SK 64 B3
Cacin E 100 B2
Čačinci HR 74 C2
Cadafais P 92 C1
Cadalen F 77 C5
Cadalso E 93 A4
Cadaqués E 91 A6
Cadaval P 92 B1
Cadavedo E 86 A4
Čadavica BIH 84 B1
Čadca SK 65 A4
Cadéac F 77 D3
Cadelbosco di Sopra I 81 B4
Cadenazzo CH 70 B3
Cadenberge D 43 B6
Cadenet F 79 C4
Cadeuil F 66 C4
Cádiar E 100 C2
Cadillac F 76 B2
Cádiz E 99 C4
Čadjavica HR 74 C2
Cadouin F 77 B3
Cadours F 77 C4
Cadrete E 90 B2
Caen F 57 A5
Caerleon GB 29 B5
Caernarfon GB 26 B1
Caerphilly GB 29 B4
Caersws GB 26 C2
Cafede P 92 B3
Caggiano I 104 C1
Cagli I 82 C1
Cágliari I 110 C2
Caglin HR 74 C2
Cagnano Varano I 104 B1
Cagnes-sur-Mer F 79 C6
Caher IRL 21 B4
Caherciveen IRL 20 C1
Caherdaniel IRL 20 C1
Cahors F 77 B4
Cahul MD 11 D10
Caiazzo I 103 B7
Caion E 86 A2
Cairndow GB 24 B3
Cairnryan GB 24 D2
Cairo Montenotte I 80 B2
Caister-on-Sea GB 30 B5
Caistor GB 27 B5
Caivano I 103 C7
Cajarc F 77 B4
Čajetina SRB 85 C4
Čajniče BIH 84 C4
Çakırlar TR 119 F5
Çakmak TR 118 C6
Čakovec HR 73 B6
Çakran AL 105 C5
Çal TR 119 D4
Cala E 99 B4
Calabritto I 103 C8
Calaceite E 90 C3
Calacuccia F 102 A2
Cala d'Or E 97 B3
Calaf E 91 B4
Calafat RO 11 D7
Calafell E 91 B4
Cala Galdana E 97 B3
Cala Gonone I 110 B2
Calahonda
Granada E 100 C2
Málaga E 100 C1
Calahorra E 89 B5
Calais F 48 C2
Cala Llonga E 97 C1
Calalzo di Cadore I 72 B2
Cala Millor E 97 B3
Calamocha E 95 B5
Calamonte E 93 C4
Cala Morell E 97 A3
Calanais GB 22 C2
Calañas E 99 B4
Calanda E 90 C2
Calangiánus I 110 B2
Călăraşi RO 11 D9
Cala Ratjada E 97 B3
Calascibetta I 109 B3
Calasetta I 110 C1
Calasparra E 101 A4
Calatafimi I 108 B1
Calatayud E 89 C5
Calatorao E 89 C5
Calau D 53 B3
Calbe D 52 B1
Calcena E 89 C5
Calcinelli I 82 C1
Calco I 71 C4
Caldarola I 82 C2
Caldaro sulla strada del Vino I 71 B6
Caldas da Rainha P 92 B1
Caldas de Boi E 90 A3
Caldas de Malavella E 91 B5
Caldas de Reis E 86 B2
Caldas de San Jorge P 87 D2
Caldas de Vizela P 87 C2
Caldaso de los Vidrios E 94 B2
Caldbeck GB 26 A2
Caldearenas E 90 A2
Caldelas P 87 C2
Calders E 91 B4
Caldes de Montbui E 91 B5
Caldicot GB 29 B5
Caldirola I 80 B3
Caledon GB 19 B5
Calella
Barcelona E 91 B5
Girona E 91 B6
Calenzana F 102 A1
Calera de León E 99 A4
Calera y Chozas E 94 C2
Caleruega E 89 C3
Caleruela E 93 B5
Cales de Mallorca E 97 B3
Calestano I 81 B4
Calfsound GB 23 B6
Calgary GB 24 B1
Calimera I 105 C4
Calitri I 103 C8
Calizzano I 80 B2
Callac F 56 B2
Callan IRL 21 B4
Callander GB 24 B3
Callas F 79 C5
Calliano
Piemonte I 80 A2
Trentino Alto Adige I 71 C6
Callington GB 28 C3
Callosa de Ensarriá E 96 C2
Callosa de Segura E 101 A5
Callús E 91 B4
Čalma SRB 85 A4
Calmbach D 61 B4
Calne GB 29 B6
Calolziocorte I 71 C4
Calonge E 91 B6
Čalovec SK 64 C3
Calpe E 96 C3
Caltabellotta I 108 B2
Caltagirone I 109 B3
Caltanissetta I 109 B3
Caltavuturo I 108 B2
Çaltılıbük TR 118 C3
Caltojar E 89 C4
Caluire-et-Cuire F 69 C4
Caluso I 70 C2
Calvello I 104 C1
Calvi F 102 A1
Calviá E 97 B2
Calvinet F 77 B5
Calvisson F 78 C3
Calvörde D 44 C3
Calw D 61 B4
Calzada de Calatrava E 100 A2
Calzada de Valdunciel E 94 A1
Calzadilla de los Barros E 93 C4
Cam GB 29 B5
Camaiore I 81 C4
Camarasa E 90 B3
Camarena E 94 B2
Camarès F 78 C1
Camaret-sur-Aigues F 78 B3
Camaret-sur-Mer F 56 B1
Camarillas E 90 C2
Camariñas E 86 A1
Camarma E 95 B3
Camarzana de Tera E 87 B4
Camas E 99 B4
Camastra I 108 B2
Cambados E 86 B2
Cambarinho P 92 A2
Camberley GB 31 C3
Cambil E 100 B2
Cambligeu F 48 C3
Cambo-les-Bains F 76 C1
Camborne GB 28 C2
Cambrai F 49 C4
Cambre E 86 A2
Cambridge GB 30 B4
Cambrils E 91 B4
Cambs D 44 B3
Camburg D 52 B1
Camden GB 31 C3
Cameleño E 88 A2
Camelford GB 28 C3
Çameli TR 119 E4
Camelle E 86 A1
Camerano I 82 C2
Camerino I 82 C2
Camerota I 106 A2
Camigliatello Silano I 106 B3
Caminha P 87 C2
Caminomorisco E 93 A4
Caminreal E 95 B5
Camisano Vicentino I 72 C1
Camlidere TR 118 B7
Cammarata I 108 B2
Camogli I 80 B3
Camors F 56 C3
Camp IRL 20 B2
Campagna I 103 C8
Campagnano di Roma I 102 A5
Campagnático I 81 D5
Campan F 77 C3
Campana I 107 B3
Campanario E 93 C5
Campanillas E 100 C1
Campano E 99 C4
Campaspero E 88 C2
Campbeltown GB 24 C2
Campello E 96 C2
Campelos P 92 B1
Campi Bisénzio I 81 C5
Campico López E 101 B4
Campiglia Maríttima I 81 C4
Campillo de Altobuey E 95 C5
Campillo de Aragón E 95 A5
Campillo de Arenas E 100 B2
Campillo de Llerena E 93 C5
Campillos E 100 B1
Câmpina RO 11 D8
Campi Salentina I 105 C4
Campli I 82 D2
Campo E 90 A3
Campobasso I 103 B7
Campobello di Licata I 108 B2
Campobello di Mazara I 108 B1
Campo da Feira E 86 A3
Campodársego I 72 C1
Campo de Bacerros E 87 B3
Campo de Caso E 88 A1
Campo de Criptana E 95 C3
Campodolcino I 71 B4
Campofelice di Roccella I 108 B2
Campofiorito I 108 B2
Campofórmido I 72 B3
Campofranco I 108 B2
Campofrio E 99 B4
Campogalliano I 81 B4
Campo Ligure I 80 B2
Campolongo I 72 B2
Campo Lugar E 93 B5
Campo Maior P 93 B3
Campomanes E 88 A1
Campomarino I 103 B8
Campo Molino I 79 B6
Campomono F 102 B1
Campo Real E 95 B3
Camporeale I 108 B2
Camporeggiano I 82 C1
Camporrells E 90 B3
Camporrobles E 96 B1
Campos P 87 C3
Camposa P 87 C2
Camposampiero I 72 C1
Camposanto I 81 B5
Campos del Port E 97 B3
Camposines E 90 B3
Campotéjar E 100 B2
Campotosto I 103 A6
Campo Túres I 72 B1
Camprodón E 91 A5
Campsegret F 77 B3
Camrose GB 28 B2
Camuñas E 95 C3
Çamyolu TR 119 F7
Çan TR 118 B2
Cana I 81 D5
Cañada del Hoyo E 95 C5
Cañadajuncosa E 95 C4
Cañada Rosal E 99 B5
Čaňak HR 83 B4
Çanakkale TR 118 B1
Canale I 80 B1
Canales
Asturias E 88 B1
Castellón de la Plana E 96 B2
Canals E 96 C2
Canal San Bovo I 72 B1
Cañamares E 95 B4
Cañamero E 93 B5
Cañar E 100 C2
Cañate la Real E 99 C5
Cañaveral E 93 B4
Cañaveral de León E 99 A4
Cañaveras E 95 B4
Cañaveruelas E 95 B4
Canazei I 72 B1
Cancale F 57 B4
Cancellara I 104 C1
Cancello ed Arnone I 103 B7
Cancon F 77 B3
Canda E 87 B4
Candamil E 86 A3
Candanchu E 76 D2
Çandarlı TR 118 D1
Candas E 88 A1
Candasnos E 90 B3
Candé F 66 A3
Candela I 104 B1
Candelario E 93 A5
Candeleda E 93 A5
Candia Lomellina I 70 C3
Candide Casamazzagno I 72 B2
Candin E 86 B4
Candosa P 92 A3
Canecas P 92 C1
Canelli I 80 B2
Canena E 100 A2
Canencia E 94 B3
Canero E 86 A4
Canet F 78 C2
Canet de Mar E 91 B5
Canet d'en Berenguer E 96 B2
Cañete E 95 B5
Cañete de las Torres E 100 B1
Canet-Plage F 91 A6
Canfranc E 76 D2
Cangas
Lugo E 86 A3
Pontevedra E 87 B2
Cangas de Narcea E 86 A4
Cangas de Onís E 88 A1
Canha P 92 C2
Canhestros P 98 A2
Canicattì I 108 B2
Canicattini Bagni I 109 B4
Canicosa de la Sierra E 89 C3
Caniles E 101 B3
Canillas de Aceituno E 100 C1
Canino I 102 A4
Canisy F 57 A4
Cañizal E 94 A1
Cañizo E 88 C1
Canjáyar E 101 C3
Çankırı TR 16 A6
Cannai I 110 C1
Cannara I 82 C1
Cánnero Riviera I 70 B3
Cannes F 79 C6
Canneto
Sicilia I 106 C1
Toscana I 81 C4
Canneto sull'Oglio I 71 C5
Cannich GB 22 D4
Cannóbio I 70 B3
Cannock GB 26 C3
Canonbie GB 25 C5
Canosa di Púglia I 104 B2
Can Pastilla E 97 B2
C'an Picafort E 97 B3
Cantalapiedra E 94 A1
Cantalejo E 94 A3
Cantalgallo E 99 A4
Cantalice I 102 A5
Cantalpino E 94 A1
Cantalupo in Sabina I 102 A5
Cantanhede P 92 A2
Cantavieja E 90 C2
Čantavir SRB 75 C4
Canterbury GB 31 C5
Cantiano I 82 C1
Cantillana E 99 B5
Cantiveros E 94 B2
Cantoria E 101 B3
Cantù I 71 C4
Canvey GB 31 C4
Cany-Barville F 58 A1
Canyet de Mar E 91 B5
Caol GB 24 B2
Cáorle I 72 C2
Caorso I 81 A3
Capáccio I 103 C8
Capaci I 108 A2
Capálbio I 102 A4
Capánnori I 81 C4
Caparde BIH 84 B3
Caparroso E 89 B5
Capbreton F 76 C1
Capdenac-Gare F 77 B5
Capdepera E 97 B3
Cap-de-Pin F 76 B2
Capel Curig GB 26 B2
Capellades E 91 B4
Capena I 102 A5
Capendu F 77 C5
Capestang F 78 C2
Capestrano I 103 A6
Cap Ferret F 76 B1
Capileira E 100 C2
Capinha P 92 A3
Ca'Pisani I 82 B1
Capistrello I 103 B6
Capizzi I 109 B3
Čaplje BIH 83 B5
Čapljina BIH 84 C2
Capo di Ponte I 71 B5
Caposile I 72 C2
Capoterra I 110 C1
Cappamore IRL 20 B3
Cappeln D 43 C5
Cappoquin IRL 21 B4
Capracotta I 103 B7
Capránica I 102 A5
Caprarola I 102 A5
Capretta I 82 D1
Capri I 103 C7
Capriati a Volturno I 103 B7
Caprino Veronese I 71 C5
Captieux F 76 B2
Cápua I 103 B7
Capurso I 104 B3
Capvern F 77 C3
Carabaña E 95 B3
Carabias E 88 C3
Caracal RO 11 D8
Caracenilla E 95 B4
Caráglio I 80 B1
Caraman F 77 C4
Caramánico Terme I 103 A7
Caranga E 86 A4
Caranguejeira P 92 B2
Caransebeş RO 11 D7
Carantec F 56 B2
Carapelle I 104 B1
Carasco I 80 B3
Carate Brianza I 71 C4
Caravaca de la Cruz E 101 A4
Caravággio I 71 C4
Carbajal E 100 C1
Carbajo E 93 B3
Carballeda E 86 B3
Carballeda de Avia E 87 B2
Carballo E 86 A2
Carbis Bay GB 28 C2
Carbon-Blanc F 76 B2
Carbonera de Frentes E 89 C4
Carboneras E 101 C4
Carboneras de Guadazaón E 95 C5
Carbonero el Mayor E 94 A2
Carboneros E 100 A2
Carbónia I 110 C1
Carbonin I 72 B2
Carbonne F 77 C4
Carbost
Highland GB 22 D2
Highland GB 22 D2
Carcaboso E 93 A4
Carcabuey E 100 B1
Carcaixent E 96 B2
Carcans F 76 A1
Carcans-Plage F 76 A1
Carção P 87 C4
Carcar E 89 B5
Cárcare I 80 B2
Carcassonne F 77 C5
Carcastillo E 89 B5
Carcedo de Burgos E 89 B3
Carcelén E 96 B1
Carcès F 79 C5
Carchelejo E 100 B2
Çardak
Çanakkale TR 118 B1
Denizli TR 119 E4
Cardedeu E 91 B5
Cardeña E 100 A1
Cardenete E 95 C5
Cardeñosa E 94 B2
Cardeto I 109 A4
Cardiff GB 29 B4
Cardigan GB 28 A3
Cardona E 91 B4
Cardosos P 92 B2
Carei RO 11 C7
Carentan F 57 A4
Carentoir F 57 C3
Careri I 106 C3
Carevdar HR 74 B1
Cargèse F 102 A1
Carhaix-Plouguer F 56 B2
Caria P 92 A3
Cariati I 107 B3
Carignan F 59 A6
Carignano I 80 B1
Cariñena E 90 B1
Carini I 108 A2
Cariño E 86 A3
Carinola I 103 B6
Carisbrooke GB 31 D2
Carlabhagh GB 22 C2
Carlepont F 59 A4
Carlet E 96 B2
Carlingford IRL 19 B5
Carlisle GB 25 D5
Carloforte I 110 C1
Carlópoli I 106 B3
Carlow
D 44 B2
IRL 21 B5
Carlton GB 27 C4
Carluke GB 25 C4
Carmagnola I 80 B1
Carmarthen GB 28 B3
Carmaux F 77 B5
Carmena E 94 C2
Cármenes E 88 B1
Carmine I 80 B1
Carmona E 99 B5
Carmonita E 93 B4
Carmyllie GB 25 B5
Carnac F 56 C2
Carndonagh IRL 19 A4
Carnew IRL 21 B5
Carnforth GB 26 A3
Cárnia I 72 B3
Carnlough GB 19 B6
Carno GB 26 C2
Carnon Plage F 78 C2
Carnota E 86 B1
Carnoustie GB 25 B5
Carnwath GB 25 C4
Carolei I 106 B3
Carolinensiel D 43 B4
Carolles F 57 B4
Carona I 71 B4
Caronía I 109 A3
Carovigno I 104 C3
Carovilli I 103 B7
Carpaneto Piacentino I 81 B3
Carpegna I 82 C1
Carpenédolo I 71 C5
Carpentras F 79 B4
Carpi I 81 B4
Carpignano Sésia I 70 C3
Carpineti I 81 B4
Carpineto Romano I 102 B6
Carpinis RO 75 C5
Carpino I 104 B1
Carpinone I 103 B7
Carpio E 94 A1
Carquefou F 66 A3
Carqueiranne F 79 C5
Carral E 86 A2
Carranque E 94 B3
Carrapichana P 92 A3
Carrara I 81 B4
Carraroe IRL 20 A2
Carrascalejo E 93 B5
Carrascosa del Campo E 95 B4
Carratraca E 100 C1
Carrazeda de Ansiães P 87 C3
Carrazedo de Montenegro P 87 C3
Carrbridge GB 23 D5
Carregal do Sal P 92 A2
Carreña E 88 A2
Carrick IRL 18 B3
Carrickart IRL 19 A4
Carrickfergus GB 19 B6
Carrickmacross IRL 19 C5
Carrick-on-Shannon IRL 18 C3
Carrick-on-Suir IRL 21 B4
Carrigallen IRL 19 C4
Carrión E 99 B4
Carrión de Calatrava E 94 C3
Carrión de los Condes E 88 B2
Carrizo de la Ribera E 88 B1
Carrizosa E 100 A3
Carro F 79 C4
Carrocera E 88 B1
Carros F 79 C6
Carrouge CH 70 B1
Carrouges F 57 B5
Carrù I 80 B1
Carryduff GB 19 B6
Carry-le-Rouet F 79 C4
Carsóli I 102 A6
Carsphairn GB 24 C3
Cartagena E 101 B5
Cártama E 100 C1
Cartaxo P 92 B2
Cartaya E 98 B3
Carteret F 57 A4
Cartes E 88 A2
Carúnchio I 103 B7
Carviçais P 87 C4
Carvin F 48 C3
Carvoeiro P 98 B2
Casabermeja E 100 C1
Casa Branca
Portalegre P 92 C3
Setúbal P 98 A2
Casacalenda I 103 B7
Casa Castalda I 82 C1
Casaio E 87 B4
Casa l'Abate I 105 C4
Casalarreina E 89 B4
Casalbordino I 103 A7
Casalborgone I 70 C2
Casalbuono I 104 C1
Casalbuttano ed Uniti I 71 C4
Casàl di Principe I 103 B7
Casalécchio di Reno I 81 B5
Casale Monferrato I 70 C3
Casalina I 82 D1
Casalmaggiore I 81 B4
Casalnuovo Monterotaro I 103 B8
Casaloldo I 71 C5
Casalpusterlengo I 71 C4
Casamássima I 104 C2
Casamicciola Terme I 103 C6
Casamozza F 102 A2
Casarabonela E 100 C1
Casarano I 107 A5
Casar de Cáceres E 93 B4
Casar de Palomero E 93 A4
Casarejos E 89 C3
Casares E 99 C5
Casares de las Hurdes E 93 A4
Casariche E 100 B1
Casarrubios del Monte E 94 B2
Casas de Don Pedro E 93 B5
Casas de Fernando Alonso E 95 C4
Casas de Haro E 95 C4
Casas de Juan Gil E 96 B1
Casas del Juan Núñez E 95 C5
Casas del Puerto E 101 A4
Casas del Rio E 96 B1
Casas de Millán E 93 B4
Casas de Reina E 99 A5
Casas de Ves E 96 B1
Casas-Ibáñez E 96 B1
Casasimarro E 95 C4
Casas Nuevas E 101 B4
Casasola E 94 B2
Casasola de Arión E 88 C1
Casasuertes E 88 A2
Casatejada E 93 B5
Casavieja E 94 B2
Casazza I 71 C4
Cascais P 92 C1
Cascante E 89 C5
Cascante del Rio E 96 A1
Cáscia I 82 D2
Casciana Terme I 81 C4
Cáscina I 81 C4
Cáseda E 89 B5
Casekow D 45 B6
Casella I 80 B3
Caselle Torinese I 70 C2
Casemurate I 82 B1
Casenove I 82 D1
Caseres E 90 B3
Caserio Benali E 96 B2
Caserta I 103 B7
Casével P 98 B2
Cashel IRL 21 B4
Casillas E 94 B2
Casillas de Coria E 93 B4
Casina I 81 B4
Casinos E 96 B2
Čáslav CZ 63 A6
Cásola Valsénio I 81 B5
Cásole d'Elsa I 81 C5
Cásoli I 103 A7
Casória I 103 C7
Caspe E 90 B2
Cassàde la Selva E 91 B5
Cassagnas F 78 B2
Cassagnes-Bégonhès F 77 B5
Cassano allo Iónio I 106 B3
Cassano d'Adda I 71 C4
Cassano delle Murge I 104 C2
Cassano Magnago I 70 C3
Cassano Spinola I 80 B2
Cassel F 48 C3
Cassíbile I 109 C4
Cassine I 80 B2
Cassino I 103 B6
Cassis F 79 C4
Cassolnovo I 70 C3
Cassuéjouls F 78 B1
Castá SK 64 B3
Castagnaro I 71 C6
Castagneto Carducci I 81 C4
Castagnola CH 70 B3
Castalla E 96 C2
Castañar de Ibor E 93 B5
Castanheira de Pêra P 92 A2
Cástano Primo I 70 C3
Castasegna CH 71 B4
Castéggio I 80 A3
Casteição P 87 D3
Castejón E 89 B5
Castejón de Monegros E 90 B2
Castejón de Sos E 90 A3
Castejón de Valdejasa E 90 B2
Castèl Baronia I 103 B8
Castel Bolognese I 81 B5
Castelbuono I 109 B3
Casteldáccia I 108 A2
Castel d'Aiano I 81 B4
Castel d'Ario I 71 C5
Castel de Cabra E 90 C2
Casteldelfino I 79 B6
Castél del Monte I 103 A6
Castel del Piano I 81 D5
Castel di Iúdica I 109 B3
Castel di Rio I 81 B5
Castèl di Sangro I 103 B7
Castél di Tora I 102 A5
Castelfidardo I 82 C2
Castelfiorentino I 81 C4
Castelforte I 103 B6
Castelfranco Emília I 81 B5
Castelfranco in Miscano I 103 B8
Castelfranco Véneto I 72 C1
Castèl Frentano I 103 A7
Casteljaloux F 76 B3
Castellabate I 103 C7
Castellammare del Golfo I 108 A1
Castellammare di Stábia I 103 C7
Castellamonte I 70 C2
Castellana Grotte I 104 C3
Castellane F 79 C5
Castellaneta I 104 C2
Castellaneta Marina I 104 C2
Castellar E 100 A2
Castellarano I 81 B4
Castellar de la Frontera E 99 C5
Castellar de la Ribera E 91 A4
Castellar del Vallés E 91 B5
Castellar de Santiago E 100 A2
Castell Arquato I 81 B3
Castell'Azzara I 81 D5
Castellbell i Villar E 91 B4
Castelldans E 90 B3
Castell de Cabres E 90 C3
Castell de Castells E 96 C2
Castelldefels E 91 B4
Castell de Ferro E 100 C2
Castelleone I 71 C4
Castellet E 91 B4
Castelletto di Brenzone I 71 C5
Castellfollit de la Roca E 91 A5
Castellfollit de Riubregos E 91 B4
Castellfort E 90 C2
Castellina in Chianti I 81 C5
Castellina Maríttima I 81 C4
Castellóde Farfaña E 90 B3
Castellóde la Plana E 96 B2
Castello d'Empùries E 91 A6
Castello di Fiemme I 71 B6
Castelloli E 91 B4
Castellón de Rugat E 96 C2
Castellote E 90 C2
Castello Tesino I 72 B1
Castellterçol E 91 B5
Castellúcchio I 71 C5
Castellúccio de'Sáuri I 103 B8
Castelluccio Inferiore I 106 B2
Castelmassa I 81 A5
Castelmáuro I 103 B7
Castelmoron-sur-Lot F 77 B3
Castelnaudary F 77 C4
Castelnau-de-Médoc F 76 A2
Castelnau-de-Montmirail F 77 C4
Castelnau-Magnoac F 77 C3
Castelnau-Montratier F 77 B4
Castelnou E 90 B2
Castelnovo ne'Monti I 81 B4
Castelnuovo Berardenga I 81 C5
Castelnuovo della Dáunia I 103 B8
Castelnuovo di Garfagnana I 81 B4
Castelnuovo di Val di Cécina I 81 C4
Castelnuovo Don Bosco I 80 A1
Castelnuovo Scrivia I 80 B2
Castelo Branco
Bragança P 87 C4
Castelo Branco P 92 B3
Castelo de Paiva P 87 C2
Castelo de Vide P 92 B3
Castelo do Neiva P 87 C2
Castelo Mendo P 93 A4
Castelraimondo I 82 C2
Castel San Gimignano I 81 C5
Castèl San Giovanni I 80 A3
Castèl San Pietro Terme I 81 B5
Castelsantángelo I 82 D2
Castél Sant'Elía I 102 A5
Castelsaraceno I 106 A2
Castelsardo I 110 B1
Castelsarrasin F 77 B4
Castelserás E 90 C2
Casteltérmini I 108 B2
Castelvecchio Subéquo I 103 A6
Castelvetrano I 108 B1
Castél Volturno I 103 B6
Castenédolo I 71 C5
Castets F 76 C1
Castiádas I 110 C2
Castiglioncello I 81 C4
Castiglione I 102 A6
Castiglione Chiavarese I 80 B3
Castiglione d'Adda I 71 C4
Castiglione dei Pepoli I 81 B5
Castiglione del Lago I 81 C6
Castiglione della Pescáia I 81 D4
Castiglione delle Stiviere I 71 C5
Castiglione di Sicilia I 109 B4
Castiglione d'Órcia I 81 C5
Castiglione Messer Marino I 103 B7
Castiglione Messer Raimondo I 103 A6
Castiglion Fibocchi I 81 C5
Castiglion Fiorentino I 81 C5
Castilblanco E 94 C1
Castilblanco de los Arroyos E 99 B5
Castil de Peones E 89 B3
Castilfrío de la Sierra E 89 C4
Castilgaleu E 90 A3
Castilisar E 90 A1
Castilleja E 99 B4
Castillejar E 101 B3
Castillejo de Martin Viejo E 93 A4
Castillejo de Mesleón E 89 C3
Castillejo de Robledo E 89 C3
Castillo de Bayuela E 94 B2
Castillo de Locubín E 100 B2
Castillonès F 77 B3
Castillon-la-Bataille F 76 B2
Castillon-Len-Couserans F 77 D4
Castillonroy E 90 B3
Castilruiz E 89 C4
Castione CH 70 B4
Castions di Strada I 72 C3
Castirla F 102 A2
Castlebar IRL 18 C2
Castlebellingham IRL 19 C5
Castleblaney IRL 19 B5
Castlebridge IRL 21 B5
Castle Cary GB 29 B5
Castlecomer IRL 21 B4
Castlederg GB 19 B4
Castledermot IRL 21 B5
Castle Douglas GB 25 D4
Castleford GB 27 B4
Castleisland IRL 20 B2
Castlemaine IRL 20 B2
Castlemartyr IRL 20 C3
Castlepollard IRL 19 C4
Castlerea IRL 18 C3
Castleton GB 27 B4
Castletown
Highland GB 23 C5
Isle of Man GB 26 A1
Castletown Bearhaven IRL 20 C2
Castletownroche IRL 20 B3
Castlewellan GB 19 B6
Casto I 71 C5
Castrejón E 88 C1
Castrelo del Valle E 87 B3
Castres F 77 C5
Castricum NL 42 C1
Castries F 78 C2
Castrignano del Capo I 107 B5
Castril E 101 B3
Castrillo de Duero E 88 C3
Castrillo de la Vega E 88 C3
Castrillo de Onielo E 88 C2
Castro
E 88 A2
I 107 A5
Castrocabón E 88 B1
Castro-Caldelas E 87 B3
Castrocaro Terme I 81 B5
Castrocontrigo E 87 B4
Castro Daire P 87 D3
Castro dei Volsci I 103 B6
Castro del Río E 100 B1
Castro de Rey E 86 A3
Castrofilippo I 108 B2
Castrogonzaio E 88 B1
Castrojeriz E 88 B2
Castro Laboreiro P 87 B2
Castro Marim P 98 B3
Castromonte E 88 C1

Castromudarra E 88 B1
Castronuevo E 88 C1
Castronuño E 88 C1
Castropol E 86 A3
Castroreale I 109 A4
Castroserracin E 88 C3
Castro-Urdiales E 89 A3
Castroverde E 86 A3
Castro Verde P 98 B2
Castroverde de Campos E 88 C1
Castroverde de Cerrato E 88 C2
Castrovillari I 106 B3
Castuera E 93 C5
Catadau E 96 B2
Cataéggio I 71 B4
Çatalca TR 118 A3
Catallar TR 119 F5
Çatalzeytin TR 16 A7
Catánia I 109 B4
Catanzaro I 106 C3
Catanzaro Marina I 106 C3
Catarroja E 96 B2
Catarruchos P 92 A2
Catcleugh GB 25 C5
Catenanuova I 109 B3
Caterham GB 31 C3
Cati E 90 C3
Čatići BIH 84 B3
Catignano I 103 A6
Catillon F 49 C4
Catoira E 86 B2
Caton GB 26 A3
Catral E 101 A5
Catterick GB 27 A4
Cattólica I 82 C1
Cattólica Eraclea I 108 B2
Catton GB 25 D5
Caudebec-en-Caux F 58 A1
Caudete E 101 A5
Caudete de las Fuentes E 96 B1
Caudiel E 96 B2
Caudiès-de-Fenouillèdes F 77 D5
Caudry F 49 C4
Caulkerbush GB 25 D4
Caulnes F 57 B3
Caulónia I 106 C3
Caumont-l'Evente F 57 A5
Caunes-Minervois F 77 C5
Cauro F 102 B1
Caussade F 77 B4
Causse-de-la-Selle F 78 C2
Cauterets F 76 D2
Cava de Tirreni I 103 C7
Cavaglia I 70 C3
Cavaillon F 79 C4
Cavalaire-sur-Mer F 79 C5
Cavaleiro P 98 B2
Cavalese I 71 B6
Cavallermaggiore I 80 B1
Cavallino I 72 C2
Cavan IRL 19 C4
Cavárzere I 72 C2
Çavdarhisar TR 118 C4
Çavdır TR 119 E4
Cavernães P 87 D3
Cavezzo I 81 B5
Cavignac F 76 A2
Cavle HR 73 C4
Cavo I 81 D4
Cavour I 80 B1
Cavtat HR 84 D3
Cawdor GB 23 D5
Çay TR 118 D6
Çaycuma TR 118 A7
Cayeux-sur-Mer F 48 C2
Cayiralan TR 16 B7
Çayırhan TR 118 B6
Caylus F 77 B4
Cayres F 78 B2
Cazalilla E 100 B2
Cazalla de la Sierra E 99 B5
Cazals F 77 B4
Cazanuecos E 88 B1
Cazaubon F 76 C2
Cazaux F 76 B1
Cazavet F 77 C4
Cazères F 77 C4
Cazin BIH 83 B4
Cazis CH 71 B4
Čazma HR 74 C1
Cazo E 88 A1
Cazorla E 100 B3
Cazouls-lès-Béziers F 78 C2
Cea
León E 88 B1
Orense E 86 B3
Ceánuri E 89 A4
Ceauce F 57 B5
Cebolla E 94 C2
Čebovce SK 65 B5
Cebreros E 94 B2
Čečava BIH 84 B2
Ceccano I 103 B6
Cece H 74 B3
Cecenowo PL 46 A3
Čechtice CZ 63 A6
Čechtín CZ 64 A1
Cécina I 81 C4
Ceclavín E 93 B4
Cedégolo I 71 B5
Cedeira E 86 A2
Cedillo E 92 B3
Cedillo del Condado E 94 B3
Cedrillas E 90 C2
Cedynia PL 45 C6
Cée E 86 B1
Cefalù I 109 A3
Céggia I 72 C2
Cegléd H 75 A4
Ceglédbercel H 75 A4
Céglie Messápica I 104 C3
Cehegín E 101 A4
Ceilhes-et-Rocozels F 78 C2
Ceinos de Campos E 88 B1
Ceira P 92 A2
Čejč CZ 64 B2
Cekcyn PL 47 B4
Čela BIH 83 B5
Čelákovice CZ 53 C4
Celano I 103 A6
Celanova E 87 B3
Celbridge IRL 21 A5
Čelebič BIH 83 C5
Celenza Valfortore I 103 B7
Čelić BIH 84 B3
Čelinac BIH 84 B2
Celje SLO 73 B5
Cella E 95 B5
Celldömölk H 74 A2
Celle D 44 C2
Celle Ligure I 80 B2
Celles B 49 C5
Celles-sur-Belle F 67 B4
Cellino San Marco I 105 C3
Celorico da Beira P 92 A3
Celorico de Basto P 87 C2
Çeltik TR 118 C6
Çeltikçi TR 119 E5
Cemaes GB 26 B1
Cembra I 71 B6
Čemerno BIH 84 C3
Cenad RO 75 B5
Cencenighe Agordino I 72 B1
Cenei RO 75 C5
Ceneselli I 81 A5
Cenicero E 89 B4
Cenicientos E 94 B2
Censeau F 69 B6
Čenta SRB 85 A5
Centallo I 80 B1
Centelles E 91 B5
Cento I 81 B5
Centúripe I 109 B3
Cepeda la Mora E 94 B1
Cépet F 77 C4
Čepin HR 74 C3
Čepinski Martinci HR 74 C3
Cepovan SLO 72 B3
Ceprano I 103 B6
Čeralije HR 74 C2
Cerami I 109 B3
Cerano I 70 C3
Cérans Foulletourte F 57 C6
Ceraso I 106 A2
Cerbaia I 81 C5
Cerbère F 91 A6
Cercadillo E 95 A4
Cercal
Lisboa P 92 B1
Setúbal P 98 B2
Čerčany CZ 63 A5
Cerceda E 94 B3
Cercedilla E 94 B2
Cercemaggiore I 103 B7
Cercs E 91 A4
Cercy-la-Tour F 68 B3
Cerda I 108 B2
Cerdedo E 86 B2
Cerdeira P 93 A3
Cerdon F 58 C3
Cerea I 71 C6
Ceres
GB 25 B5
I 70 C2
Cerese I 81 A4
Ceresole-Reale I 70 C2
Cereste F 79 C4
Céret F 91 A5
Cerezo de Abajo E 95 A3
Cerezo de Riotirón E 89 B3
Cerfontaine B 49 C5
Cergy F 58 A3
Cerignola I 104 B1
Cérilly F 68 B2
Cerisiers F 59 B4
Cerizay F 67 B4
Çerkeş TR 16 A6
Çerkezköy TR 118 A3
Cerkije SLO 73 B4
Cerknica SLO 73 C4
Cerkno SLO 72 B3
Cerkwica PL 45 A7
Çermë-Proshkë AL 105 B5
Černa HR 74 C3
Černá Hora CZ 64 A2
Cernavodă RO 11 D10
Cernay F 60 C3
Cerne Abbas GB 29 C5
Cernégula E 89 B3
Cernik HR 74 C2
Cernóbbio I 70 C4
Černošín CZ 62 A3
Cernovice CZ 63 A5
Cérons F 76 B2
Cerovlje HR 73 C4
Cerovo SK 65 B5
Cerqueto I 82 D1
Cerralbo E 87 D4
Cerreto d'Esi I 82 C1
Cerreto Sannita I 103 B7
Cerrigydrudion GB 26 B2
Çerrik AL 105 B5
Cerro Muriano E 100 A1
Certaldo I 81 C5
Certosa di Pésio I 80 B1
Cerva P 87 C3
Cervaro I 103 B6
Cervatos de la Cueza E 88 B2
Červena Řečice CZ 63 A6
Červená-Skala SK 65 B6
Cervená Voda CZ 54 C1
Cerveny Kostelec CZ 53 C6
Cervera E 91 B4
Cervera de la Cañada E 89 C5
Cervera del Llano E 95 C4
Cervera del Río Alhama E 89 B5
Cervera de Pisuerga E 88 B2
Cervéteri I 102 B5
Cérvia I 82 B1
Cerviáde les Garriques E 90 B3
Cervignano del Friuli I 72 C3
Cervinara I 103 B7
Cervione F 102 A2
Cervo E 86 A3
Cervon F 68 A3
Cesana Torinese I 79 B5
Cesarica HR 83 B4
Cesarò I 109 B3
Cesena I 82 B1
Cesenático I 82 B1
Cēsis LV 7 C8
Česká Belá CZ 63 A6
Česká Kamenice CZ 53 C4
Česká Lípa CZ 53 C4
Česká Třebová CZ 64 A2
České Budějovice CZ 63 B5
České Velenice CZ 63 B5
Český Brod CZ 53 C4
Český Dub CZ 53 C4
Český Krumlov CZ 63 B5
Český Těšín CZ 65 A4
Češljeva Bara SRB 85 B6
Çeşme TR 119 D1
Cessenon F 78 C2
Cesson-Sévigné F 57 B4
Cestas F 76 B2
Čestobrodica SRB 85 C5
Cesuras E 86 A2
Cetina E 89 C5
Cetin Grad HR 73 C5
Cetinje MNE 105 A4
Cetraro I 106 B2
Ceuta E 99 D5
Ceuti E 101 A4
Ceva I 80 B2
Cevico de la Torre E 88 C2
Cevico Navero E 88 C2
Cevins F 69 C6
Cévio CH 70 B3
Cevizli TR 119 E6
Cevo MNE 105 A4
Cewice PL 46 A3
Ceyhan TR 16 C7
Ceylan TR 119 F4
Ceyrat F 68 C3
Ceyzériat F 69 B5
Chaam NL 49 B5
Chabanais F 67 C5
Chabeuil F 79 B4
Chabielice PL 55 B4
Chablis F 59 C4
Châbons F 69 C5
Chabówka PL 65 A5
Chabreloche F 68 C3
Chabris F 67 A6
Chagford GB 28 C4
Chagny F 69 B4
Chagoda RUS 7 B13
Chaherrero E 94 B2
Chailland F 57 B5
Chaillé-les-Marais F 66 B3
Chailles F 67 A6
Chailley F 59 B4
Chalabre F 77 D5
Chalais F 67 C5
Chalamont F 69 C5
Châlette-sur-Loing F 58 B3
Chalindrey F 59 C6
Chalkida GR 116 D5
Challacombe GB 28 B4
Challans F 66 B3
Challes-les-Eaux F 69 C5
Chalmazel F 68 C3
Chalmoux F 68 B3
Chalonnes-sur-Loire F 66 A4
Châlons-en-Champagne F 59 B5
Châlon-sur-Saône F 69 B4
Chalupy PL 47 A4
Châlus F 67 C5
Cham
CH 70 A3
D 62 A3
Chamberet F 68 C1
Chambéry F 69 C5
Chambilly F 68 B4
Chamblet F 60 A1
Chambly F 58 A3
Chambois F 57 B6
Chambon-sur-Lac F 68 C2
Chambon-sur-Voueize F 68 B2
Chambord F 58 C2
Chamborigaud F 78 B2
Chamboulive F 68 C1
Chamerau D 62 A3
Chamonix-Mont Blanc F 70 C1
Chamoux-sur-Gelon F 69 C6
Champagnac-le-Vieux F 68 C3
Champagney F 60 C2
Champagnole F 69 B5
Champagny-Mouton F 67 B5
Champaubert F 59 B4
Champdeniers-St Denis F 67 B4
Champdieu F 68 C4
Champdôtre F 69 A5
Champeix F 68 C3
Champéry CH 70 B1
Champigne F 57 C5
Champignelles F 59 C4
Champigny-sur-Veude F 67 A5
Champlitte-et-le-Prelot F 60 C1
Champoluc I 70 C2
Champoly F 68 C3
Champorcher I 70 C2
Champrond-en-Gâtine F 58 B2
Champs-sur-Tarentaine F 68 C2
Champs-sur-Yonne F 59 C4
Champtoceaux F 66 A3
Chamrousse F 69 C5
Chamusca P 92 B2
Chanac F 78 B2
Chanaleilles F 78 B2
Chandler's Ford GB 31 D2
Chandra GR 117 G8
Chandrexa de Queixa E 87 B3
Chañe E 88 C2
Changy F 68 B3
Chania GR 117 G6
Channes F 59 C5
Chantada E 86 B3
Chantelle F 68 B3
Chantenay-St Imbert F 68 B3
Chanteuges F 78 A2
Chantilly F 58 A3
Chantonnay F 66 B3
Chão de Codes P 92 B2
Chaource F 59 B5
Chapa E 86 B2
Chapareillan F 69 C5
Chapel en le Frith GB 27 B4
Chapelle Royale F 58 B2
Chapelle-St Laurent F 67 B4
Charbonnat F 68 B4
Chard GB 29 C5
Charenton-du-Cher F 68 B2
Charlbury GB 31 C2
Charleroi B 49 C5
Charlestown
GB 28 C3
IRL 18 C3
Charlestown of Aberlour GB 23 D5
Charleville IRL 20 B3
Charleville-Mézières F 59 A5
Charlieu F 68 B4
Charlottenberg S 34 C4
Charlton Kings GB 29 B5
Charly F 59 B4
Charmes F 60 B2
Charmes-sur-Rhône F 78 B3
Charmey CH 70 B2
Charminster GB 29 C5
Charmont-en-Beauce F 58 B3
Charny F 59 C4
Charolles F 69 B4
Chârost F 68 B2
Charquemont F 70 A1
Charrin F 68 B3
Charroux F 67 B5
Chartres F 58 B2
Charzykow PL 46 B3
Chasseneuil-sur-Bonnieure F 67 C5
Chassigny F 59 C6
Château-Arnoux F 79 B5
Châteaubernard F 67 C4
Châteaubourg F 57 B4
Châteaubriant F 57 C4
Château-Chinon F 68 A3
Château-d'Oex CH 70 B2
Château-d'Olonne F 66 B3
Château-du-Loir F 58 C1
Châteaudun F 58 B2
Chateaugiron F 57 B4
Château-Gontier F 57 C5
Château-Landon F 58 B3
Château-la-Vallière F 67 A5
Château-l'Evêque F 67 C5
Châteaulin F 56 B1
Châteaumeillant F 68 B2
Châteauneuf
Nièvre F 68 A3
Saône-et-Loire F 69 B4
Châteauneuf-de-Randon F 78 B2
Châteauneuf-d'Ille-et-Vilaine F 57 B4
Châteauneuf-du-Faou F 56 B2
Châteauneuf-du-Pape F 78 B3
Châteauneuf-en-Thymerais F 58 B2
Châteauneuf la-Forêt F 67 C6
Châteauneuf-le-Rouge F 79 C4
Châteauneuf-sur-Charente F 67 C4
Châteauneuf-sur-Cher F 68 B2
Châteauneuf-sur-Loire F 58 C3
Châteauneuf-sur-Sarthe F 57 C5
Châteauponsac F 67 B6
Château-Porcien F 59 A5
Châteauredon F 79 B5
Châteaurenard
Bouches du Rhône F 78 C3
Loiret F 59 C3
Château-Renault F 58 C1
Châteauroux F 68 B1
Châteauroux-les-Alpes F 79 B5
Château-Salins F 60 B2
Château-Thierry F 59 A4
Châteauvillain F 59 B5
Châtel F 70 B1
Châtelaillon-Plage F 66 B3
Châtelaudren F 56 B3
Châtel-Censoir F 68 A3
Châtel-de-Neuvre F 68 B3
Châtelet B 49 C5
Châtelguyon F 68 C3
Châtellerault F 67 B5
Châtel-Montagne F 68 B3
Châtel-St Denis CH 70 B1
Châtel-sur-Moselle F 60 B2
Châtelus-Malvaleix F 68 B2
Châtenois F 60 B1
Châtenois-les-Forges F 70 A1
Chatham GB 31 C4
Châtillon I 70 C2
Châtillon-Coligny F 59 C3
Châtillon-en-Bazois F 68 A3
Châtillon-en-Diois F 79 B4
Châtillon-sur Chalaronne F 69 B4
Châtillon-sur-Indre F 67 B6
Châtillon-sur-Loire F 58 C3
Châtillon-sur-Marne F 59 A4
Châtillon-sur-Seine F 59 C5
Châtres F 59 B4
Chatteris GB 30 B4
Chatton GB 25 C6
Chauchina E 100 B2
Chaudes-Aigues F 78 B2
Chaudrey F 59 B5
Chauffailles F 69 B4
Chaulnes F 58 A3
Chaument Gistoux B 49 C5
Chaumergy F 69 B5
Chaumont F 59 B6
Chaumont-en-Vexin F 58 A2
Chaumont-Porcien F 59 A5
Chaumont-sur-Aire F 59 B6
Chaumont-sur-Loire F 67 A6
Chaunay F 67 B5
Chauny F 59 A4
Chaussin F 69 B5
Chauvigny F 67 B5
Chavagnes-en-Paillers F 66 B3
Chavanges F 59 B5
Chaves P 87 C3
Chavignon F 59 A4
Chazelles-sur-Lyon F 69 C4
Chazey-Bons F 69 C5
Cheadle
Greater Manchester GB 26 B3
Staffordshire GB 27 C4
Cheb CZ 52 C2
Chebsara RUS 7 B15
Checa E 95 B5
Chęciny PL 55 C5
Cheddar GB 29 B5
Cheddleton GB 26 B3
Chef-Boutonne F 67 B4
Chekalin RUS 7 D14
Chekhovo RUS 47 A6
Cheles E 93 C3
Chella E 96 B2
Chelles F 58 B3
Chełm PL 11 A7
Chełmno
Kujawsko-Pomorskie PL 47 B4
Wielkopolskie PL 54 A3
Chelmsford GB 31 C4
Chelmża PL 47 B4
Cheltenham GB 29 B5
Chelva E 96 B1
Chémery F 67 A6
Chemery-sur-Bar F 59 A5
Chemillé F 67 A4
Chemin F 69 B5
Chemnitz D 52 C2
Chénerailles F 68 B2
Cheniménil F 60 B2
Chenonceaux F 67 A6
Chenôve F 69 A4
Chepelare BG 116 A6
Chepstow GB 29 B5
Chera E 96 B2
Cherasco I 80 B1
Cherbonnières F 67 C4
Cherbourg F 57 A4
Cherchiara di Calábria I 106 B3
Cherepovets RUS 7 B14
Cherkasy UA 11 B12
Chernihiv UA 11 A11
Chernivtsi UA 11 B8
Chernobyl = Chornobyl UA 7 F11
Chernyakhovsk RUS 6 D6
Chéroy F 59 B3
Cherven BY 7 E10
Chervonohrad UA 11 A8
Cherykaw BY 7 E11
Chesham GB 31 C3
Cheshunt GB 31 C3
Chessy-lès-Pres F 59 B4
Cheste E 96 B2
Chester GB 26 B3
Chesterfield GB 27 B4
Chester-le-Street GB 25 D6
Chevagnes F 68 B3
Chevanceaux F 67 C4
Chevillon F 59 B6
Chevilly F 58 B2
Chew Magna GB 29 B5
Chézery-Forens F 69 B5
Chialamberto I 70 C2
Chiampo I 71 C6
Chianale I 79 B6
Chianciano Terme I 81 C5
Chiaramonte Gulfi I 109 B3
Chiaramonti I 110 B1
Chiaravalle I 82 C2
Chiaravalle Centrale I 106 C3
Chiaréggio I 71 B4
Chiari I 71 C4
Chiaromonte I 106 A3
Chiasso CH 70 C4
Chiávari I 80 B3
Chiavenna I 71 B4
Chiché F 67 B4
Chichester GB 31 D3
Chiclana de la Frontera E 99 C4
Chiclana de Segura E 100 A2
Chiddingfold GB 31 C3
Chieri I 80 A1
Chiesa in Valmalenco I 71 B4
Chieti I 103 A7
Chieti Scalo I 103 A7
Chiéuti I 103 B8
Chigirin UA 11 B12
Chigwell GB 31 C4
Chiliomodi GR 117 E4
Chillarón de Cuenca E 95 B4
Chillarón del Rey E 95 B4
Chilleurs-aux-Bois F 58 B3
Chillón E 100 A1
Chilluévar E 100 B2
Chiloeches E 95 B3
Chimay B 49 C5
Chimeneas E 100 B2
Chinchilla de Monte Aragón E 96 C1
Chinchón E 95 B3
Chingford GB 31 C4
Chinon F 67 A5
Chióggia I 72 C2
Chiomonte I 79 A5
Chippenham GB 29 B5
Chipping Campden GB 29 A6
Chipping Norton GB 31 C2
Chipping Ongar GB 31 C4
Chipping Sodbury GB 29 B5
Chirac F 78 B2
Chirbury GB 26 C2
Chirens F 69 C5
Chirivel E 101 B3
Chirk GB 26 C2
Chirnside GB 25 C5
Chişinău = Khisinev MD 11 C10
Chişineu Criş RO 10 C6
Chissey-en-Morvan F 69 A4
Chiusa I 71 B6
Chiusa di Pésio I 80 B1
Chiusaforte I 72 B3
Chiusa Scláfani I 108 B2
Chiusi I 81 C5
Chiva E 96 B2
Chivasso I 70 C2
Chlewiska PL 55 B5
Chludowo PL 46 C2
Chlumec nad Cidlinou CZ 53 C5
Chlum u Třeboně CZ 63 B5
Chmielnik PL 55 C5
Chobienia PL 54 B1
Chobienice PL 53 A5
Choceň CZ 53 D6
Choceń PL 47 C5
Chochołow PL 65 A5
Chocianów PL 53 B5
Chociw PL 55 B4
Chociwel PL 46 B1
Choczewo PL 46 A3
Chodaków PL 55 A5
Chodecz PL 47 C5
Chodov CZ 52 C2
Chodzież PL 46 C2
Chojna PL 45 C6
Chojnice PL 46 B3
Chojno
Kujawsko-Pomorskie PL 47 C5
Wielkopolskie PL 46 C2
Chojnów PL 53 B5
Cholet F 66 A4
Chomérac F 78 B3
Chomutov CZ 52 C3
Chop UA 11 B7
Chora GR 117 E3
Chora Sfakion GR 117 G6
Chorges F 79 B5
Chorley GB 26 B3
Chornobyl = Chernobyl UA 7 F11
Chortkiv UA 11 B8
Chorzew PL 54 B3
Chorzów PL 54 C3
Choszczno PL 46 B1
Chotcza-Józefów PL 55 B6
Chotěboř CZ 63 A6
Chouilly F 59 A5
Chouto P 92 B2
Chouzy-sur-Cisse F 67 A6
Chozas de Abajo E 88 B1
Chrast CZ 64 A1
Chrást CZ 63 A4
Chrastava CZ 53 C4
Chříbská CZ 53 C4
Christchurch GB 29 C6
Christiansfeld DK 39 D2
Chroberz PL 55 C5
Chropyně CZ 64 A3
Chrudim CZ 53 D5
Chrzanów PL 55 C4
Chtelnica SK 64 B3
Chudovo RUS 7 B11
Chueca E 94 C3
Chulmleigh GB 28 C4
Chur CH 71 B4
Church Stretton GB 26 C3
Churriana E 100 C1
Churwalden CH 71 B4
Chvalšiny CZ 63 B5
Chwaszczyno PL 47 A4
Chynava CZ 53 C4
Chýnov CZ 63 A5
Ciacova RO 75 C6
Ciadîr-Lunga MD 11 C10
Ciadoncha E 88 B3
Cianciana I 108 B2
Ciano d'Enza I 81 B4
Ciążen PL 54 A2
Cibakhaza H 75 B5
Ciborro P 92 C2
Cicagna I 80 B3
Cicciano I 103 C7
Čičevac SRB 85 C6
Ciciliano I 102 B5
Cicognolo I 71 C5
Cidadelhe P 87 D3
Cide TR 16 A6
Cidones E 89 C4
Ciechanów
Dolnośląskie PL 54 B1
Mazowieckie PL 47 C6
Ciechocinek PL 47 C4
Cielądz PL 55 B5
Ciemnik PL 46 B1
Ciempozuelos E 95 B3
Ciepielów PL 55 B6
Čierny Balog SK 65 B5
Cierp-Gaud F 77 D3
Cierpice PL 47 C4
Ciervana E 89 A3
Cierznie PL 46 B3
Cieslé PL 47 C6
Cieszyn PL 65 A4
Cieutat F 76 C3
Cieza E 101 A4
Cífer SK 64 B3
Çifteler TR 118 C6
Cifuentes E 95 B4
Cigales E 88 C2
Cigliano I 70 C3
Cihanbeyli TR 16 B6
Cilipi HR 105 A4
Cillas E 95 B5
Cilleros E 93 A4
Cilleruelo de Arriba E 88 C3
Cilleruelo de Bezana E 88 B3
Cimalmotto CH 70 B3
Cimanes del Tejar E 88 B1
Ciminna I 108 B2
Cimişlia MD 11 C10
Cimoláis I 72 B2
Cîmpulung RO 11 D8
Çınarcık TR 118 B4
Cinctorres E 90 C2
Cinderford GB 29 B5
Çine TR 119 E3
Činěves CZ 53 C5
Ciney B 49 C6
Cinfães P 87 C2
Cingia de Botti I 81 A4
Cíngoli I 82 C2
Cinigiano I 81 D5
Cinobaňa SK 65 B5
Cinq-Mars-la-Pile F 67 A5
Cinquefrondi I 106 C3
Cintegabelle F 77 C4
Cintruénigo E 89 B5
Ciółkowo PL 47 C5
Ciperez E 87 D4
Cirat E 96 A2
Cirella I 106 B2
Cirencester GB 29 B6
Cirey-sur-Vezouze F 60 B2
Ciria E 89 C5
Ciriè I 70 C2
Cirigliano I 104 C2
Cirò I 107 B4
Cirò Marina I 107 B4
Ciry-le-Noble F 69 B4
Cislău RO 11 D9
Cismon del Grappa I 72 C1
Cisneros E 88 B2
Cissac-Médoc F 66 C4
Čista CZ 52 C3
Cisterna di Latina I 102 B5
Cistérniga E 88 C2
Cisternino I 104 C3
Cistierna E 88 B1
Čitluk BIH 84 C2
Citov CZ 53 C4
Cittadella I 72 C1
Città della Pieve I 81 D6
Città del Vaticano = Vatican City I 102 B5
Città di Castello I 82 C1
Cittaducale I 102 A5
Cittanova I 106 C3
Città Sant'Angelo I 103 A7
Ciudadela de Menorca E 97 B3
Ciudad Real E 94 D3
Ciudad Rodrigo E 93 A4
Ciutadilla E 91 B4
Cividale del Friuli I 72 B3
Cívita I 102 A6
Cívita Castellana I 102 A5
Civitanova Alta I 82 C2
Civitanova Marche I 82 C2
Civitavécchia I 102 A4
Civitella di Romagna I 81 B5
Civitella di Tronto I 82 D2
Civitella Roveto I 103 B6
Civray F 67 B5
Çivril TR 119 D4
Cizur Mayor E 76 D1
Clabhach GB 24 B1
Clachan GB 22 D2
Clachan na Luib GB 22 D1
Clacton-on-Sea GB 31 C5
Cladich GB 24 B2
Claggan GB 24 B2
Clairvaux-les-Lacs F 69 B5
Clamecy F 68 A3
Claonaig GB 24 C2
Clarecastle IRL 20 B3
Claregalway IRL 20 A3
Claremorris IRL 18 C2
Clarinbridge IRL 20 A3
Clashmore
GB 23 D4
IRL 21 B4
Claudy GB 19 B4
Clausthal-Zellerfeld D 51 B6
Cláut I 72 B2
Clay Cross GB 27 B4
Claye-Souilly F 58 B3
Cléder F 56 B1
Cleethorpes GB 27 B5
Clefmont F 60 B1
Cléguérec F 56 B2
Clelles F 79 B4
Clenze D 44 C2
Cleobury Mortimer GB 29 A5
Cléon-d'Andran F 78 B3
Cléré-les-Pins F 67 A5
Clères F 58 A2
Clermont F 58 A3
Clermont-en-Argonne F 59 A6
Clermont-Ferrand F 68 C3
Clermont-l'Hérault F 78 C2
Clerval F 69 A6
Clervaux L 50 C2
Cléry-St André F 58 C2
Cles I 71 B6
Clevedon GB 29 B5
Cleveleys GB 26 B2
Cley GB 30 B5
Clifden IRL 18 C1
Clifford GB 29 A4
Clisson F 66 A3
Clitheroe GB 26 B3
Clogh IRL 21 B4
Cloghan
Donegal IRL 19 B4
Offaly IRL 21 A4
Clogheen IRL 21 B4
Clogher GB 19 B4
Cloghjordan IRL 20 B3
Clohars-Carnoët F 56 C2
Clonakilty IRL 20 C3
Clonaslee IRL 21 A4
Clondalkin IRL 21 A5
Clones IRL 19 B4
Clonmany IRL 19 A4
Clonmel IRL 21 B4
Clonmellon IRL 19 C4
Clonord IRL 21 A4
Clonroche IRL 21 B5
Cloone IRL 19 C4
Cloppenburg D 43 C5
Closeburn GB 25 C4
Clough GB 19 B6
Clova GB 25 B4
Clovelly GB 28 C3
Clowne GB 27 B4
Cloyes-sur-le-Loir F 58 C2
Cloyne IRL 20 C3
Cluis F 68 B1
Cluj-Napoca RO 11 C7
Clun GB 26 C2
Clunes GB 24 B3
Cluny F 69 B4
Cluses F 69 B6
Clusone I 71 C4
Clydach GB 28 B4
Clydebank GB 24 C3
Coachford IRL 20 C3
Coagh GB 19 B5
Coalisland GB 19 B5
Coalville GB 27 C4
Coaña E 86 A4
Çobanlar TR 118 D5
Cobas E 86 A2
Cobertelade E 89 C4
Cobeta E 95 B4
Cóbh IRL 20 C3
Cobreces E 88 A2
Coburg D 51 C6
Coca E 94 A2
Cocentaina E 96 C2
Cochem D 50 C3
Cockburnspath GB 25 C5
Cockermouth GB 26 A2
Codigoro I 82 B1
Codogno I 71 C4
Codos E 89 C5
Codróipo I 72 C2
Codrongianos I 110 B1
Coelhoso P 87 C4
Coesfeld D 50 B3
Coevorden NL 42 C3
Cofrentes E 96 B1
Cogeces del Monte E 88 C2
Coggeshall GB 31 C4
Cognac F 67 C4
Cogne I 70 C2
Cognin F 69 C5
Cogolin F 79 C5
Cogollos de Guadix E 100 B2
Cogollos-Vega E 100 B2
Cogolludo E 95 B3
Coimbra P 92 A2
Coín E 100 C1
Coirós E 86 A2
Čoka SRB 75 C5
Col SLO 73 C4
Colares P 92 C1
Cölbe D 51 C4
Colbitz D 52 A1
Colchester GB 31 C4
Coldingham GB 25 C5
Colditz D 52 B2
Coldstream GB 25 C5
Colebrooke GB 28 C4
Colera E 91 A6
Coleraine GB 19 A5
Colfiorito I 82 C1
Cólico I 71 B4
Coligny F 69 B5
Colindres E 89 A3
Collado-Mediano E 94 B2
Collado Villalba E 94 B3
Collagna I 81 B4
Collanzo E 88 A1
Collat F 68 C3
Coll de Nargó E 91 A4
Collécchio I 81 B4
Colledimezzo I 103 B7
Colle di Val d'Elsa I 81 C5
Colleferro I 102 B6
Colle Isarco I 71 B6
Collelongo I 103 B6
Collepasso I 107 A5
Collepepe I 82 D1
Collesalvetti I 81 C4
Colle Sannita I 103 B7
Collesano I 108 B2
Colli a Volturno I 103 B7
Collin GB 25 C4
Collinée F 56 B3
Collingham
Nottinghamshire GB 27 B5
West Yorkshire GB 27 B4
Collinghorst D 43 B4
Cóllio I 71 C5
Collobrières F 79 C5
Collon IRL 19 C5
Collooney IRL 18 B3
Colmar F 60 B3
Colmars F 79 B5
Colmenar E 100 C1
Colmenar de la Sierra E 95 A3
Colmenar de Oreja E 95 B3
Colmenar Viejo E 94 B3
Colmonel GB 24 C3
Colne GB 26 B3
Colobraro I 106 A3
Cologna Véneta I 71 C6
Cologne = Köln D 50 C2
Cologne F 77 C3
Cologne al Serio I 71 C4
Colombey-les-Belles F 60 B1
Colombey-les-deux-Églises F 59 B5
Colombres E 88 A2
Colomera E 100 B2
Colomers E 91 A5
Colomiers F 77 C4
Colònia de Sant Jordi E 97 B3
Colorno I 81 B4
Colos P 98 B2
Cölpin D 45 B5
Colpy GB 23 D6
Colsterworth GB 30 B3
Coltishall GB 30 B5
Colunga E 88 A1
Colwell GB 25 C5
Colwyn Bay GB 26 B2
Colyford GB 29 C4
Comácchio I 82 B1
Coma-ruga E 91 B4
Combarros E 86 B4
Combeaufontaine F 60 C1
Comber GB 19 B6
Comblain-au-Pont B 49 C6
Combloux F 70 C1
Combourg F 57 B4
Combronde F 68 C3
Comeglians I 72 B2
Comillas E 88 A2
Comines F 49 C4
Cómiso I 109 C3
Comloşu Mare RO 75 C5
Commensacq F 76 B2
Commentry F 68 B2
Commerau D 53 B4
Commercy F 60 B1
Como I 71 C4
Cómpeta E 100 C2
Compiègne F 58 A3
Comporta P 92 C2
Comps-sur-Artuby F 79 C5
Comrat MD 11 C10
Comrie GB 25 B4
Comunanza I 82 D2
Cona
Emilia Romagna I 81 B5
Veneto I 72 C2
Concarneau F 56 C2
Conceição P 98 B2
Conches-en-Ouche F 58 B1
Concordia Sagittária I 72 C2
Concordia sulla Sécchia I 81 B4
Concots F 77 B4
Condat F 68 C2
Condé-en-Brie F 59 B4
Condeixa P 92 A2
Condemios de Abajo E 95 A3
Condemios de Arriba E 95 A3
Condé-sur-l'Escaut F 49 C4
Conde-sur-Marne F 59 A5
Condé-sur-Noireau F 57 B5
Condino I 71 C5
Condom F 77 C3
Condove I 70 C2
Condrieu F 69 C4
Conegliano I 72 C2
Conflans-sur-Lanterne F 60 C2
Confolens F 67 B5
Conforto E 86 A3
Cong IRL 18 C2
Congleton GB 26 B3
Congosto E 86 B4
Congosto de Valdavia E 88 B2
Congostrina E 95 A3
Conil de la Frontera E 99 C4
Coningsby GB 27 B5
Coniston GB 26 A2
Conlie F 57 B5
Conliège F 69 B5
Conna IRL 20 C3
Connah's Quay GB 26 B2
Connantre F 59 B4
Connaugh IRL 20 B3
Connaux F 78 B3
Connel GB 24 B2
Connerré F 58 B1
Connonbridge GB 23 D4
Čonoplja SRB 75 C4
Conques F 77 B5
Conques-sur-Orbiel F 77 C5
Conquista E 100 A1
Conquista de la Sierra E 93 B5
Consándolo I 81 B5
Consélice I 81 B5
Conselve I 72 C1
Consenvoye F 59 A6
Consett GB 25 D6
Consolação P 92 B1
Constancia P 92 B2
Constanco E 86 A2
Constanța RO 11 D10
Constanti E 91 B4
Constantina E 99 B5
Consuegra E 95 C3
Consuma I 81 C5
Contarina I 82 A1
Contay F 48 D3
Conthey CH 70 B2
Contigliano I 102 A5
Contis-Plage F 76 B1
Contrada I 103 C7
Contres F 67 A6
Contrexéville F 60 B1
Controne I 103 C8
Contursi Termi I 103 C8
Conty F 58 A3
Conversano I 104 C3
Conwy GB 26 B2
Cookstown GB 19 B5
Coole F 59 B5
Coolgreany IRL 21 B5
Cooneen GB 19 B4
Cootehill IRL 19 B4
Cope E 101 B4
Copenhagen = København DK 41 D2
Copertino I 105 C4
Copparo I 81 B5
Coppenbrugge D 51 A5
Corabia RO 11 E8
Córaci I 106 B3
Coralići BIH 83 B4
Corato I 104 B2
Coray F 56 B2
Corbeil-Essonnes F 58 B3
Corbeny F 59 A4
Corbera E 96 B2
Corbie F 58 A3
Corbigny F 68 A3
Corbion B 59 A5
Corbridge GB 25 D5
Corby GB 30 B3
Corconte E 88 A3
Corcubión E 86 B1
Corcumello I 103 A6
Cordenòns I 72 C2
Cordes-sur-Ciel F 77 B4
Córdoba E 100 B1
Cordobilla de Lácara E 93 B4
Cordovado I 72 C2
Corella E 89 B5
Coreses E 88 C1
Corfe Castle GB 29 C5
Corga de Lobão P 87 D2
Cori I 102 B5
Coria E 93 B4
Coria del Río E 99 B4
Corigliano Cálabro I 106 B3
Corinaldo I 82 C1
Corinth = Korinthos GR 117 E4
Cório I 70 C2
Coripe E 99 C5
Cork IRL 20 C3
Corlay F 56 B2
Corleone I 108 B2
Corleto Monforte I 103 C8
Corleto Perticara I 104 C2
Çorlu TR 118 A2
Cormainville F 58 B2
Cormatin F 69 B4
Cormeilles F 58 A1
Cormery F 67 A5
Cormòns I 72 C3
Cormoz F 69 B5
Cornago E 89 B4
Cornberg D 51 B5
Cornellana E 86 A4
Cornești MD 11 C10
Corniglio I 81 B4
Cornimont F 60 C2
Corniolo I 81 C5
Cornuda I 72 C2
Cornudella de Montsant E 90 B3
Cornudilla E 89 B3
Cornus F 78 C2
Čorovodë AL 116 B2
Corpach GB 24 B2
Corps F 79 B4
Corps Nuds F 57 C4
Corral de Almaguer E 95 C3
Corral de Ayllon E 89 C3
Corral de Calatrava E 100 A1
Corrales E 88 C1
Corral-Rubio E 101 A4
Corran GB 24 B2
Corredoiras E 86 A2
Corréggio I 81 B4
Corrèze F 68 C1
Corridónia I 82 C2
Corris GB 26 C2
Corrubedo E 86 B1
Córsico I 71 C4
Corsock GB 25 C4
Corte F 102 A2
Corteconcepción E 99 B4
Corte de Peleas E 93 C4
Cortegaca P 87 D2
Cortegada E 87 B2
Cortegana E 99 B4
Cortemaggiore I 81 B3
Cortemilia I 80 B2
Corte Pinto P 98 B3
Cortes E 89 C5
Cortes de Aragón E 90 C2
Cortes de Arenoso E 96 A2
Cortes de Baza E 101 B3
Cortes de la Frontera E 99 C5
Cortes de Pallás E 96 B2
Cortiçadas P 92 C2
Cortico P 87 C3
Cortijo de Arriba E 94 C2
Cortijos Nuevos E 101 A3
Cortina d'Ampezzo I 72 B2
Corton GB 30 B5
Cortona I 81 C5
Coruche P 92 C2
Corullón E 86 B4
Çorum TR 16 A7
Corvara in Badia I 72 B1
Corvera E 101 B4
Corwen GB 26 C2
Cosenza I 106 B3
Cosham GB 31 D2
Coslada E 95 B3
Cosne-Cours-sur-Loire F 68 A2
Cosne d'Allier F 68 B2
Cospeito E 86 A3
Cossato I 70 C3
Cossaye F 68 B3
Cossé-le-Vivien F 57 C5
Cossonay CH 69 B6
Costa da Caparica P 92 C1
Costa de Santo André P 98 A2
Costalpino I 81 C5
Costa Nova P 92 A2
Costaros F 78 B2
Costeşti RO 11 D8
Costigliole d'Asti I 80 B2
Costigliole Saluzzo I 80 B1
Coswig
Sachsen D 52 B3
Sachsen-Anhalt D 52 B2
Cotherstone GB 27 A4
Cotronei I 107 B3
Cottbus D 53 B4
Cottenham GB 30 B4
Cottingham GB 27 B5
Coublanc F 60 C1
Couches F 69 B4
Couço P 92 C2
Coucouron F 78 B2
Coucy-le-Château-Auffrique F 59 A4
Couëron F 66 A3
Couflens F 77 D4
Couhé F 67 B5
Couiza F 77 D5
Coulags GB 22 D3
Coulanges F 68 B3
Coulanges-la-Vineuse F 59 C4
Coulanges-sur-Yonne F 68 A3
Couleuvre F 68 B2
Coulmier-le-Sec F 59 C5
Coulommiers F 59 B4
Coulonges-sur-l'Autize F 67 B4
Coulounieix-Chamiers F 67 C5
Coulport GB 24 B3
Coupar Angus GB 25 B4
Coupéville F 59 B5
Couptrain F 57 B5
Coura P 87 C2
Courcelles B 49 C5
Courcelles-Chaussy F 60 A2

Courchevel F 70 C1
Cour-Cheverny F 67 A6
Courcôme F 67 C5
Courçon F 66 B4
Cour-et-Buis F 69 C4
Courgenay CH 70 A2
Courmayeur I 70 C1
Courniou F 78 C1
Cournon d'Auvergne
F 68 C3
Cournonterral F 78 C2
Courpière F 68 C3
Coursan F 78 C2
Courseulles-sur-Mer
F 57 A5
Cours-la-Ville F 69 B4
Courson-les-Carrières
F 59 C4
Courtalain F 58 B2
Courtenay F 59 B4
Courtomer F 58 B1
Courville
Eure-et-Loire F 58 B2
Marne F 59 A4
Coussac-Bonneval F 67 C6
Coutances F 57 A4
Couterne F 57 B5
Coutras F 76 A2
Couvet CH 70 B1
Couvin B 49 C5
Couzon F 68 B3
Covadonga E 88 A1
Covaleda E 89 C4
Covarrubias E 89 B3
Covas P 87 C2
Cove GB 22 D3
Coventry GB 30 B2
Coverack GB 28 C2
Covigliáio I 81 B5
Covilhã P 92 A3
Cowbridge GB 29 B4
Cowdenbeath GB 25 B4
Cowes GB 31 D2
Cox F 77 C4
Cózar E 100 A2
Cozes F 66 C4
Cozzano F 102 B2
Craco I 104 C2
Cracow = Kraków PL 55 C4
Craibstone GB 23 D6
Craighouse GB 24 C2
Craignure GB 24 B2
Crail GB 25 B5
Crailsheim D 61 A6
Craiova RO 11 D7
Cramlington GB 25 C6
Cranleigh GB 31 C3
Craon F 57 C5
Craonne F 59 A4
Craponne F 69 C4
Craponne-sur-Arzon
F 68 C3
Crathie GB 23 D5
Crato P 92 B3
Craughwell IRL 20 A3
Craven Arms GB 26 C3
Crawford GB 25 C4
Crawinkel D 51 C6
Crawley GB 31 C3
Creag Ghoraidh GB 22 D1
Crecente E 87 B2
Crèches-sur-Saône F 69 B4
Crécy-en-Ponthieu F 48 C2
Crécy-la-Chapelle F 59 B3
Crécy-sur-Serre F 59 A4
Crediton GB 29 C4
Creeslough IRL 19 A4
Creetown GB 24 D3
Creeve GB 19 B5
Creglingen D 61 A6
Creil F 58 A3
Creissels F 78 B2
Crema I 71 C4
Cremeaux F 68 C3
Crémenes E 88 B1
Crémieu F 69 C5
Cremlingen D 51 A6
Cremona I 81 A4
Črenev F 59 B5
Črenšovci SLO 73 B6
Créon F 76 B2
Crepaja SRB 85 A5
Crépey F 60 B1
Crépy F 59 A4
Crépy-en-Valois F 59 A3
Cres HR 83 B3
Crescentino I 70 C3
Crespino I 81 B5
Crespos E 94 B2
Cressage GB 26 C3
Cressensac F 77 A4
Cressia F 69 B5
Crest F 79 B4
Cresta CH 71 B4
Créteil F 58 B3
Creully F 57 A5
Creussen D 62 A2
Creutzwald F 60 A2
Creuzburg D 51 B6
Crevalcore I 81 B5
Crèvecoeur-le-Grand
F 58 A3
Crevillente E 101 A5
Crévola d'Ossola I 70 B3
Crewe GB 26 B3
Crewkerne GB 29 C5
Criales E 89 B3
Crianlarich GB 24 B3
Criccieth GB 26 C1
Crickhowell GB 29 B4
Cricklade GB 29 B6
Crieff GB 25 B4
Criel-sur-Mer F 48 C2
Crikvenica HR 73 C4
Crillon F 58 A2
Crimmitschau D 52 C2
Crimond GB 23 D7
Crinitz D 53 B3
Cripán E 89 B4
Criquetot-l'Esneval F 57 A6
Crispiano I 104 C3
Crissolo I 79 B6
Cristóbal E 93 A5
Crivitz D 44 B3
Črna SLO 73 B4
Crna Bara
Srbija SRB 85 B4
Vojvodina SRB 75 C5
Crnac HR 74 C2
Crnča SRB 85 B4
Crni Lug
BIH 83 B5
HR 73 C4
Črni Vrh SLO 73 C4
Crnjelovo Donje BIH 85 B4
Črnomelj SLO 73 C5
Crocketford GB 25 C4
Crocq F 68 C2
Crodo I 70 B3
Croglin GB 25 D5
Crolly IRL 18 A3
Cromarty GB 23 D4
Cromer GB 30 B5
Cronat F 68 B3
Crookhaven IRL 20 C2
Crookstown IRL 20 C3
Croom IRL 20 B3
Cropalati I 106 B3
Crópani I 107 C3
Crosbost GB 22 C2
Crosby GB 26 B2
Crosía I 106 B3
Crossakiel IRL 19 C4
Cross-Hands GB 28 B3
Crosshaven IRL 20 C3
Crosshill GB 24 C3
Crossmolina IRL 18 B2
Crotone I 107 B4
Crottendorf D 52 C2
Crouy F 59 A4
Crowborough GB 31 C4
Crowland GB 30 B3
Crowthorne GB 31 C3
Croyde GB 28 B3
Croydon GB 31 C3
Crozon F 56 B1
Cruas F 78 B3
Cruceni RO 75 B6
Crúcoli I 107 B4
Cruden Bay GB 23 D7
Crudgington GB 26 C3
Cruis F 79 B4
Crumlin GB 19 B5
Cruseilles F 69 B6
Crusheen IRL 20 B3
Cruz de Incio E 86 B3
Črvenka SRB 75 C4
Črveny Kamen SK 64 A4
Csabacsüd H 75 B5
Csabrendek H 74 A2
Csákánydoroszló H 74 B1
Csákvár H 74 A3
Csanádapáca H 75 B5
Csanádpalota H 75 B5
Csány H 65 C5
Csanytelek H 75 B5
Csapod H 74 A1
Császár H 74 A3
Császártöltés H 75 B4
Csávoly H 75 B4
Csemö H 75 A4
Csengöd H 75 B4
Csépa H 75 B5
Csepreg H 74 A1
Cserkeszölö H 75 B5
Csernely H 65 B6
Csesztreg H 74 B1
Csökmö H 75 A6
Csököly H 74 B2
Csokonyavisonta H 74 B2
Csólyospálos H 75 B4
Csongrád H 75 B5
Csopak H 74 B2
Csorna H 64 C3
Csorvás H 75 B5
Csurgo H 74 B2
Cuacos de Yuste E 93 A5
Cualedro E 87 C3
Cuanca de Campos E 88 B1
Cuba P 98 A3
Cubel E 95 A5
Cubelles E 91 B4
Cubillos E 89 C4
Cubillos del Sil E 86 B4
Cubjac F 67 C5
Cubo de la Solana E 89 C4
Çubuk TR 16 A6
Cuckfield GB 31 C3
Cucuron F 79 C4
Cudillero E 86 A4
Cuéllar E 88 C2
Cuenca E 95 B4
Cuers F 79 C5
Cuerva E 94 C2
Cueva de Agreda E 89 C5
Cuevas Bajas E 100 B1
Cuevas del Almanzora
E 101 B4
Cuevas del Becerro E 99 C5
Cuevas del Campo
E 100 B3
Cuevas del Valle E 94 B1
Cuevas de San Clemente
E 89 B3
Cuevas de San Marcos
E 100 B1
Cuges-les-Pins F 79 C4
Cúglieri I 110 B1
Cugnaux F 77 C4
Cuijk NL 50 B1
Cuinzier F 69 B4
Cuiseaux F 69 B5
Cuisery F 69 B5
Culan F 68 B2
Culemborg NL 49 B6
Cúllar E 101 B3
Cullaville GB 19 B5
Cullera E 96 B2
Cullivoe GB 22 A7
Cullompton GB 29 C4
Cully CH 70 B1
Culoz F 69 C5
Cults GB 23 D6
Cumbernauld GB 25 C4
Cumbres de San
Bartolomé E 99 A4
Cumbres Mayores E 99 A4
Cumiana I 80 B1
Čumić SRB 85 B5
Cumnock GB 24 C3
Çumra TR 16 C6
Cuneo I 80 B1
Cunlhat F 68 C3
Čunski HR 83 B3
Cuntis E 86 B2
Cuorgnè I 70 C2
Cupar GB 25 B4
Cupello I 103 A7
Cupra Marittima I 82 C2
Cupramontana I 82 C2
Ćuprija SRB 85 C6
Curinga I 106 C3
Currelos E 86 B3
Currie GB 25 C4
Curtea de Argeș RO 11 D8
Curtici RO 75 B6
Curtis E 86 A2
Curtis Santa Eulalia E 86 A2
Čurug SRB 75 C5
Cusano Mutri I 103 B7
Cushendall GB 19 A5
Cusset F 68 B3
Cussy-les-Forges F 68 A4
Custines F 60 B2
Cutanda E 90 C1
Cutro I 107 B3
Cutrofiano I 107 A5
Cuts F 59 A4
Cuvilly F 58 A3
Cuxhaven D 43 B5
Cvikov CZ 53 C4
Cwmbran GB 29 B4
Cybinka PL 53 A4
Czacz PL 54 A1
Czajków PL 54 B3
Czaplinek PL 46 B2
Czarlin PL 47 A4
Czarna-Dąbrówka PL 46 A3
Czarna Woda PL 47 B4
Czarnca PL 55 C4
Czarne PL 46 B2
Czarnków PL 46 C2
Czarnowo PL 47 B4
Czarnozyly PL 54 B3
Czarny Bór PL 53 C6
Czarny-Dunajec PL 65 A5
Czarzy Las PL 54 B2
Czchow PL 65 A6
Czechowice-Dziedzice
PL 65 A4
Czempiń PL 54 A1
Czermno PL 55 B5
Czernichow PL 55 D4
Czerniejewo PL 46 C3
Czernikowo PL 47 C4
Czersk PL 46 B3
Czerwieńsk PL 53 A5
Czerwionka-Leszczyny
PL 54 C3
Czerwonka PL 47 B6
Częstochowa PL 55 C4
Czeszewo PL 46 C3
Człopa PL 46 B2
Człuchów PL 46 B3
Czołpino PL 46 A3

D

Dağ TR 119 E5
Daaden D 50 C3
Dabas H 75 A4
Dąbie PL 54 A3
Dąbki PL 46 A2
Dabo F 60 B3
Dabrowa PL 46 C3
Dąbrowa Górnicza
PL 55 C4
Dąbrowa Tarnowska
PL 55 C5
Dąbrowice PL 55 A4
Dabrowno PL 47 B6
Dachau D 62 B2
Dačice CZ 63 A6
Daday TR 16 A6
Dagali N 32 B5
Dägebüll D 39 E1
Dagmersellen CH 70 A2
Dahlen D 52 B2
Dahlenburg D 44 B2
Dahme D 52 B3
Dahn D 60 A3
Dähre D 44 C2
Daikanvik S 115 B13
Dail bho Dheas GB 22 C2
Dailly GB 24 C3
Daimiel E 95 C3
Daingean IRL 21 A4
Đakovica KOS 10 E6
Đakovo HR 74 C3
Dal
Akershus N 34 B3
Telemark N 32 C5
Dalaas A 71 A5
Dalabrog GB 22 D1
Dala-Floda S 36 B1
Dala-Husby S 36 B2
Dala-Järna S 36 B1
Dalaman TR 119 F3
Dalarö S 37 C5
Dalbeattie GB 25 D4
Dalby
DK 39 D3
Skåne S 41 D3
Uppsala S 37 C4
Värmland S 34 B4
Dale
Pembrokeshire GB 28 B2
Shetland GB 22 A7
Hordaland N 32 B2
Sogn og Fjordane N 32 A2
Dalen
Akershus N 34 C3
Telemark N 33 C5
Daleszyce PL 55 C5
Dalhalvaig GB 23 C5
Dalheim L 60 A2
Dalhem S 37 E5
Dalias E 100 C3
Dalj HR 75 C3
Dalkeith GB 25 C4
Dalkey IRL 21 A5
Dalmally GB 24 B3
Dalmellington GB 24 C3
Dalmose DK 39 D4
Daløy N 32 A1
Dalry
Dumfries & Galloway
GB 24 C3
North Ayrshire GB 24 C3
Dalrymple GB 24 C3
Dalseter N 32 A6
Dalsjöfors S 40 B3
Dals Långed S 35 D4
Dals Rostock S 35 D4
Dalston GB 25 D5
Dalstorp S 40 B3
Dalton-in-Furness GB 26 A2
Daluis F 79 B5
Dalum
D 43 C4
S 40 B3
Dalvík IS 111 B7
Dalwhinnie GB 24 B3
Dalyan TR 119 F3
Damasi GR 116 C4
Damasławek PL 46 C3
Damazan F 76 B3
Damës AL 105 C5
Damgan F 56 C3
Dammarie-les-Lys F 58 B3
Dammartin-en-Goële
F 58 A3
Damme D 43 C5
Damnica PL 46 A3
Dampierre F 69 A5
Dampierre-sur-Salon
F 69 A5
Damüls A 71 A4
Damville F 58 B2
Damvillers F 59 A6
Damwoude NL 42 B2
Danasjö S 115 B13
Danbury GB 31 C4
Dångebo S 40 C5
Dangers F 58 B2
Dangé-St Romain F 67 B5
Dargun D 45 B4
Danilovgrad MNE 105 A5
Danischenhagen D 44 A2
Daniszyn PL 54 B2
Danjoutin F 60 C2
Dannas S 40 B3
Dannemarie F 60 C3
Dannemora S 36 B4
Dannenberg D 44 B3
Dánszentmiklós H 75 A4
Dány H 75 A4
Daoulas F 56 B1
Darabani RO 11 B9
Darány H 74 C2
Darda HR 74 C3
Dardesheim D 51 B6
Darfeld D 50 A3
Darfo I 71 C5
Dargiń PL 46 A2
Dargun D 45 B4
Darlington GB 27 A4
Darłowo PL 46 A2
Darmstadt D 61 A4
Darney F 60 B2
Daroca E 95 A5
Darque P 87 C2
Darragh IRL 20 B2
Dartford GB 31 C4
Dartington GB 28 C4
Dartmouth GB 29 C4
Darton GB 27 B4
Daruvar HR 74 C2
Darvas H 75 A6
Darvel GB 24 C3
Darwen GB 26 B3
Dassel D 51 B5
Dassow D 44 B2
Datça TR 119 F2
Datteln D 50 B3
Dattenfeld D 50 C3
Daugard DK 39 D2
Daugavpils LV 7 D9
Daumeray F 57 C5
Daun D 50 C2
Daventry GB 30 B2
Davle CZ 63 A5
Davor HR 74 C2
Davos CH 71 B4
Davutlar TR 119 E2
Davyd Haradok BY 7 E9
Dawlish GB 29 C4
Dax F 76 C1
Dazkırı TR 119 E4
Deal GB 31 C5
Deauville F 57 A6
Deba E 89 A4
Debar MK 116 A2
Debe Wielkie PL 55 A6
Dębica PL 55 C6
Dębnica Kaszubska
PL 46 A3
Dębno PL 45 C6
Dębolęka PL 54 B3
Dębowa Łaka PL 47 B5
Debrc SRB 85 B4
Debrecen H 10 C6
Debrznica PL 53 A5
Debrzno PL 46 B3
Debstedt D 43 B5
Decazeville F 77 B5
Dechtice SK 64 B3
Decima I 102 B5
Decimomannu I 110 C1
Děčín CZ 53 C4
Decize F 68 B3
De Cocksdorp NL 42 B1
Decollatura I 106 B3
Decs H 74 B3
Deda RO 11 C8
Dedaj AL 105 A5
Deddington GB 31 C2
Dedeler TR 118 B5
Dedelow D 45 B5
Dedemli TR 119 E7
Dedemsvaart NL 42 C3
Dédestapolcsány H 65 B6
Dedovichi RUS 7 C10
Deeping St Nicholas
GB 30 B3
Deftera CY 120 A2
Dég H 74 B3
Degaña E 86 B4
Degeberga S 41 D4
Degerby FIN 36 B7
Degerfors S 37 C1
Degerhamn S 41 C6
Degernes N 35 C3
Deggendorf D 62 B3
Deggingen D 61 B5
Dego I 80 B2
Degolados P 93 B3
De Haan B 49 B4
Dehesas de Guadix
E 100 B2
Dehesas Viejas E 100 B2
Deia E 97 B2
Deining D 62 A2
Deinze B 49 C4
Déiva Marina I 80 B3
Dej RO 11 C7
Deje S 35 C5
De Koog NL 42 B1
Delabole GB 28 C3
Delary S 40 C3
Delbrück D 51 B4
Delčevo MK 116 A5
Delden NL 50 A2
Deleitosa E 93 B5
Delekovec HR 74 B1
Delémont CH 70 A2
Delft NL 49 A5
Delfzijl NL 42 B3
Délia I 108 B2
Delianuova I 106 C2
Deliblato SRB 85 B6
Delice TR 16 B6
Deliceto I 103 B8
Delitzsch D 52 B2
Dellach A 72 B3
Delle F 70 A2
Delme F 60 B2
Delmen-horst D 43 B5
Delnice HR 73 C4
Delsbo S 115 F13
Delvin IRL 19 C4
Delvinë AL 116 C2
Demandice SK 65 B4
Demen D 44 B3
Demidov RUS 7 D11
Demigny F 69 B4
Demirci TR 118 C3
Demirköy TR 118 A2
Demirtaş TR 118 B4
Demmin D 45 B5
Demonte I 79 B6
Demyansk RUS 7 C12
Denain F 49 C4
Denbigh GB 26 B2
Den Burg NL 42 B1
Dender-monde B 49 B5
Denekamp NL 42 C3
Den Ham NL 42 C3
Den Helder NL 42 C1
Denholm GB 25 C5
Denia E 96 C3
Denizli TR 119 E4
Denkendorf D 62 B2
Denklingen D 50 C3
Denny GB 25 B4
Den Oever NL 42 C2
Denta RO 75 C6
Déols F 68 B1
De Panne B 48 B3
Derbent TR 119 D3
Derby GB 27 C4
Dereköy TR 118 A2
Derenberg D 51 B6
Derinkuyu TR 16 B7
Dermbach D 51 C6
Dermulo I 71 B6
Deronje SRB 75 C4
Derrygonnelly GB 19 B4
Derrylin GB 19 B4
Derry/Londonderry
GB 19 B4
Dersingham GB 30 B4
Deruta I 82 D1
Dervaig GB 24 B1
Derval F 57 C4
Derveni GR 117 D4
Derventa BIH 84 B2
Dervock GB 19 A5
Desana I 70 C3
Descartes F 67 B5
Desenzano del Garda
I 71 C5
Deset N 34 A3
Deševa BIH 84 C3
Desfina GR 116 D4
Desimirovac SRB 85 B5
Désio I 71 C4
Deskati GR 116 C3
Deskle SLO 72 B3
Desná CZ 53 C5
Dešov CZ 63 B6
Despotovac SRB 85 B6
Despotovo SRB 75 C4
Dessau D 52 B2
Deštná CZ 63 A5
Destriana E 87 B4
Désulo I 110 B2
Desvres F 48 C2
Deszk H 75 B5
Deta RO 75 C6
Detmold D 51 B4
Dětřichov CZ 64 A3
Dettelbach D 61 A6
Dettingen
Baden-Württemberg
D 61 B5
Baden-Württemberg
D 61 C5
Dettwiller F 60 B3
Detva SK 65 B5
Deurne NL 50 B1
Deutschkreutz A 64 C2
Deutschlandsberg A 73 B5
Deutsch Wagram A 64 B2
Deva RO 11 D7
Dévaványa H 75 A5
Devecikonağı TR 118 C3
Devecser H 74 A2
Develi TR 16 B7
Deventer NL 50 A2
Devil's Bridge GB 28 A4
Devin BG 116 A6
Devinska Nova Ves
SK 64 B2
Devizes GB 29 B6
Devonport GB 28 C3
Devrek TR 118 A6
Devrekâni TR 16 A6
Ðevrske HR 83 C4
De Wijk NL 42 C3
Dewsbury GB 27 B4
Deza E 89 C4
Dežanovac HR 74 C2
Dezzo I 71 C5
Dhali CY 120 A2
Dherinia CY 120 A2
Dhërmi AL 105 C5
Diamante I 106 B2
Dianalund DK 39 D4
Diano d'Alba I 80 B2
Diano Marina I 80 C2
Dicomano I 81 C5
Didcot GB 31 C2
Didimoticho GR 118 A1
Die F 79 B4
Diebling F 60 A2
Dieburg D 61 A4
Diego del Carpio E 93 A5
Diekirch L 60 A2
Diélette F 57 A4
Diémoz F 69 C5
Dienten am Hochkönig
A 72 A2
Diepenbeck B 49 C6
Diepholz D 43 C5
Dieppe F 58 A2
Dierberg D 45 B4
Dierdorf D 50 C3
Dieren NL 50 A2
Dierhagen D 44 A4
Diesdorf D 44 C2
Diessen D 62 C2
Diest B 49 C6
Dietenheim D 61 B6
Dietfurt D 62 A2
Dietikon CH 70 A3
Dietzenbach D 51 C4
Dieue-sur-Meuse F 60 A1
Dieulefit F 79 B4
Dieulouard F 60 B2
Dieuze F 60 B2
Diever NL 42 C3
Diez D 50 C4
Diezma E 100 B2
Differdange L 60 A1
Digermulen N 112 D4
Dignac F 67 C5
Dignano I 72 B2
Digne-les-Bains F 79 B5
Digny F 58 B2
Digoin F 68 B3
Dijon F 69 A5
Dikanäs S 115 B13
Dikili TR 118 C1
Diksmuide B 48 B3
Dilar E 100 B2
Dillenburg D 50 C4
Dillingen
Bayern D 61 B6
Saarland D 60 A2
Dilsen B 50 B1
Dimaro I 71 B5
Dimitrovgrad BG 11 E8
Dimitsana GR 117 E4
Dinami I 106 C3
Dinan F 57 B3
Dinant B 49 C5
Dinar TR 119 D5
Dinard F 57 B3
Dinek TR 118 C6
Dingden D 50 B2
Dingelstädt D 51 B6
Dingle
IRL 20 B1
S 35 D3
Dingolfing D 62 B3
Dingtuna S 37 C3
Dingwall GB 23 D4
Dinkelsbühl D 61 A6
Dinkelscherben D 62 B1
Dinklage D 43 C5
Dinslaken D 50 B2
Dinxperlo NL 50 B2
Diö S 40 C4
Diósgyör H 65 B6
Diósjeno H 65 C5
Diou F 68 B3
Dippen GB 24 C2
Dipperz D 51 C5
Dippoldiswalde D 53 C3
Dirdal N 33 D3
Dirksland NL 49 B5
Dirlewang D 61 C6
Dischingen D 61 B6
Disentis CH 70 B3
Diso I 107 A5
Diss GB 30 B5
Dissen D 50 A4
Distington GB 26 A2
Ditzingen D 61 B5
Ditzum D 43 B4
Divača SLO 72 C3
Dives-sur-Mer F 57 A5
Divin SK 65 B5
Divion F 48 C3
Divišov CZ 63 A5
Divjakë AL 105 C5
Divonne les Bains F 69 B6
Dixmont F 59 B4
Dizy-le-Gros F 59 A5
Djúpivogur IS 111 C11
Djupvasshytta N 114 E4
Djura S 36 B1
Djurås S 36 B2
Djurmo S 36 B2
Djursdala S 40 B5
Dlouhá Loucka CZ 64 A3
Długowola PL 55 B6
Dmitriyev Lgovskiy
RUS 7 E13
Dmitrov RUS 7 C14
Dmitrovsk-Orlovskiy
RUS 7 E13
Dno RUS 7 C10
Doade E 86 B3
Doğanhisar TR 119 D6
Dobanovci SRB 85 B5
Dobbertin D 44 B4
Dobbiaco I 72 B2
Dobczyce PL 65 A6
Dobele LV 6 C7
Döbeln D 52 B3
Doberlug-Kirchhain D 52 B3
Dobern D 53 B4
Dobersberg A 63 B6
Dobiegniew PL 46 C1
Dobieszyn PL 55 B6
Doboj BIH 84 B3
Dobošnica BIH 84 B3
Doboz H 75 B6
Dobrá CZ 65 A4
Dobra
Wielkopolskie PL 54 B3
Zachodnio-Pomorskie
PL 45 B6
Zachodnio-Pomorskie
PL 45 B7
Dobrá Niva SK 65 B5
Dobřany CZ 63 A4
Dobre
Kujawsko-Pomorskie
PL 47 C4
Mazowieckie PL 55 A6
Dobre Miasto PL 47 B6
Dobreta-Turnu-Severin
RO 11 D7
Dobri H 74 B1
Dobrica SRB 75 C5
Dobrich BG 11 E9
Dobri Do SRB 85 D6
Dobříš CZ 63 A5
Dobro E 89 B3
Dobrodzień PL 54 C3
Döbröközi H 74 B3
Dobromierz PL 53 C6
Dobrosołowo PL 47 C4
Dobroszyce PL 54 B2
Dobrota MNE 105 A4
Dobrovnik SLO 73 B6
Dobrush BY 7 E11
Dobruška CZ 53 C6
Dobrzany PL 46 B1
Dobrzen Wielki PL 54 C2
Dobrzyca
Wielkopolskie PL 46 B2
Wielkopolskie PL 54 B2
Zachodnio-Pomorskie
PL 46 A1
Dobrzyńad Wisłą
PL 47 C5
Dobšiná SK 65 B6
Dobwalls GB 28 C3
Dochamps B 49 C6
Docking GB 30 B4
Docksta S 115 D15
Doddington GB 25 C5
Döderhult S 40 B6
Doesburg NL 50 A2
Doetinchem NL 50 B2
Dogliani I 80 B1
Dogueno P 98 B3
Doische B 49 C5
Dois Portos P 92 B1
Dojč SK 64 B3
Dokka N 34 B2
Dokkedal DK 38 C3
Dokkum NL 42 B2
Dokležovje SLO 73 B6
Doksy CZ 53 C4
Dokuz TR 119 D7
Dolancourt F 59 B5
Dolceácqua I 80 C1
Dol-de-Bretagne F 57 B4
Dole F 69 A5
Dølemo N 33 D5
Dolenja vas SLO 73 C4
Dolenjske Toplice
SLO 73 C5
Dolfor GB 26 C2
Dolgarrog GB 26 B2
Dolgellau GB 26 C2
Doliana GR 116 C2
Dolianova I 110 C2
Dolice PL 45 B7
Doljani HR 83 B5
Döllach im Mölltal A 72 B2
Dolle D 44 C3
Dollnstein D 62 B2
Dollot F 59 B4
Döllstadt D 51 B6
Dolná Strehová SK 65 B5
Dolné Saliby SK 64 B3
Dolni Benešov CZ 64 A4
Dolni Bousov CZ 53 C5
Dolni Kounice CZ 64 A2
Dolni Kralovice CZ 63 A6
Dolni Újezd CZ 64 A2
Dolni Žandov CZ 52 C2
Dolný Kubín SK 65 A5
Dolo I 72 C2
Dolores E 96 C2
Dolovo SRB 85 B5
Dölsach A 72 B2
Dolsk PL 54 B2
Dolwyddelan GB 26 B2
Dolynska UA 11 B12
Domaljevac BIH 84 A3
Domaniç TR 118 C4
Domaniža SK 65 A4
Domanovići BIH 84 C2
Domašov CZ 54 C2
Domaszék H 75 B4
Domaszków PL 54 C1
Domaszowice PL 54 B2
Domat-Ems CH 71 B4
Domažlice CZ 62 A3
Dombås N 114 E6
Dombasle-sur-Meurthe
F 60 B2
Dombegyház H 75 B6
Dombóvár H 74 B3
Domène F 69 C5
Domérat F 68 B2
Domfessel F 60 B3
Domfront F 57 B5
Domfront-en-Champagne
F 57 B6
Domingão P 92 B2
Domingo Pérez
Granada E 100 B2
Toledo E 94 C2
Dömitz D 44 B3
Dommartin F 59 B5
Dommartin-le-Franc
F 59 B5
Domme F 77 B4
Dommitzsch D 52 B2
Domodóssola I 70 B3
Domokos GR 116 C4
Domoszló H 65 C6
Dompaire F 60 B2
Dompierre-du-Chemin
F 57 B4
Dompierre-sur-Besbre
F 68 B3
Dompierre-sur-Mer F 66 B3
Domrémy-la-Pucelle
F 60 B1
Dömsöd H 75 A4
Domsure F 69 B5
Dómus de Maria I 110 D1
Domusnóvas I 110 C1
Domvena GR 117 D4
Domžale SLO 73 B4
Donado E 87 B4
Donaghadee GB 19 B6
Don Alvaro E 93 C4
Doña Mencía E 100 B1
Donaueschingen D 61 C4
Donauwörth D 62 B1
Don Benito E 93 C5
Doncaster GB 27 B4
Donegal IRL 18 B3
Donestebe-Santesteban
E 76 C1
Donges F 66 A2
Dongo I 71 B4
Donington GB 30 B3
Doniños E 86 A2
Donja Bebrina HR 84 A3
Donja Brela HR 84 C2
Donja Dubica BIH 84 A3
Donja Dubrava HR 74 B1
Donja Kupčina HR 73 C5
Donja Šatornja SRB 85 B5
Donja Stubica HR 73 C5
Donje Brišnik BIH 84 C2
Donje Ljupče KOS 85 D6
Donje Stative HR 73 C5
Donji-Andrijevci HR 74 C3
Donji Kazanci BIH 83 C5
Donji Koričáni BIH 84 B2
Donji Lapac HR 83 B4
Donji Malovan BIH 84 C2
Donji Miholjac HR 74 C3
Donji Mosti HR 74 B2
Donji Poloj HR 73 C5
Donji-Rujani BIH 83 C5
Donji Srb HR 83 B5
Donji Svilaj BIH 84 A3
Donji Tovarnik SRB 85 B4
Donji Vakuf BIH 84 B2
Donnalucata I 109 C3
Donnemarie-Dontilly
F 59 B4
Donnersbach A 73 A4
Donnersbachwald A 73 A4
Donnerskirchen A 64 C2
Donorático I 81 C4
Donostia-San Sebastián
E 76 C1
Donovaly SK 65 B5
Donzenac F 67 C6
Donzère F 78 B3
Donzy F 68 A3
Doonbeg IRL 20 B2
Doorn NL 49 A6
Dor E 86 A1
Dorchester GB 29 C5
Dørdal N 33 D6
Dordrecht NL 49 B5
Dörenthe D 50 A3
Dores GB 23 D4
Dorfen D 62 B3
Dorfgastein A 72 A3
Dorfmark D 43 C6
Dorf Mecklenburg D 44 B3
Dorgali I 110 B2
Dorking GB 31 C3
Dormagen D 50 B2
Dormánd H 65 C6
Dormans F 59 A4
Dornava SLO 73 B5
Dornbirn A 71 A4
Dornburg D 52 B1
Dorndorf D 51 C6
Dornecy F 68 A3
Dornes F 68 B3
Dornhan D 61 B4
Dornie GB 22 D3
Dornoch GB 23 D4
Dornum D 43 B4
Dorog H 65 C4
Dorogobuzh RUS 7 D12
Dorohoi RO 11 C9
Dorotea S 115 C13
Dorotowo PL 47 B6
Dörpen D 43 C4
Dorsten D 50 B2
Dortan F 69 B5
Dortmund D 50 B3
Doruchów PL 54 B3
Dorum D 43 B5
Dörverden D 43 C6
Dörzbach D 61 A5
Dos Aguas E 96 B2
Dosbarrios E 95 C3
Döşemealtı TR 119 E5
Dos Hermanas E 99 B5
Dospat BG 116 A6
Dos-Torres E 100 A1
Dötlingen D 43 C5
Dottignies B 49 C4
Döttingen CH 70 A3
Douai F 49 C4
Douarnenez F 56 B1
Douchy F 59 C4
Douchy-les-Mines F 49 C4
Doucier F 69 B5
Doudeville F 58 A1
Doué-la-Fontaine F 67 A4
Douglas
Isle of Man GB 26 A1
South Lanarkshire
GB 25 C4
Doulaincourt-Saucourt
F 59 B6
Doulevant-le-Château
F 59 B5
Doullens F 48 C3
Dounby GB 23 B5
Doune GB 24 B3
Dounreay GB 23 C5
Dour B 49 C4
Dourdan F 58 B3
Dourgne F 77 C5
Dournazac F 67 C5
Douro Calvo P 87 D3
Douvaine F 69 B6
Douvres-la-Délivrande
F 57 A5
Douzy F 59 A6
Dover GB 31 C5
Dovje SLO 72 B3
Dovre N 114 F6
Downham Market GB 30 B4
Downhill GB 19 A5
Downpatrick GB 19 B6
Dowra IRL 18 B3
Doxato GR 116 A6
Doyet F 68 B2
Dozule F 57 A5
Drača SRB 85 B5
Dračevo BIH 84 D3
Drachten NL 42 B3
Draga SLO 73 C4
Drăgășani RO 11 D8
Dragatuš SLO 73 C5
Dragichyn BY 7 E8
Draginja SRB 85 B4
Dragobi AL 105 A5
Dragocvet SRB 85 C6
Dragolovci BIH 84 B2
Dragoni I 103 B7
Dragør DK 41 D2
Dragotina HR 73 C6
Dragotinja BIH 83 A5
Dragozetići HR 82 A3
Draguignan F 79 C5
Drahnsdorf D 52 B3
Drahonice CZ 63 A5
Drahovce SK 64 B3
Drama GR 116 A6
Drammen N 35 C2
Drangedal N 33 C6
Drangsnes IS 111 B4
Dransfeld D 51 B5
Dranske D 45 A5
Draperstown GB 19 B5
Drassburg A 64 C2
Drávaszabolcs H 74 C3
Dravograd SLO 73 B5
Drawno PL 46 B1
Drawsko Pomorskie
PL 46 B1
Drayton GB 30 B5
Draženov CZ 62 A3
Draževac SRB 85 B5
Dražice HR 73 C4
Drebkau D 53 B4
Dreieich D 51 C4
Dreisen D 61 A4
Drem KOS 85 C5
Drenovac SRB 85 C6
Drenovci HR 84 B3
Drensteinfurt D 50 B3
Dresden D 53 B3
Dretyń PL 46 A2
Dreux F 58 B2
Dřevohostice CZ 64 A3
Drevsjø N 114 F9
Drewitz D 52 A2
Drezdenko PL 46 C1
Drežnica HR 83 A4
Drežnik-Grad HR 83 B4
Drietona SK 64 B3
Driffield GB 27 A5
Drimnin GB 24 B2
Drimoleague IRL 20 C2
Dringenberg D 51 B5
Drinić BIH 83 B5
Drinjača BIH 85 B4
Drinovci BIH 84 C2
Driopida GR 117 E6
Drivstua N 114 E6
Drlače SRB 85 B4
Drnholec CZ 64 B2
Drniš HR 83 C5
Drnje HR 74 B1
Drnovice CZ 64 A2
Dro I 71 C5
Drøbak N 35 C2
Drobin PL 47 C6
Drochia MD 11 B9
Drochtersen D 43 B6
Drogheda IRL 19 C5
Drohobych UA 11 B7
Droitwich Spa GB 29 A5
Droltowice PL 54 B2
Dromahair IRL 18 B3
Dromcolliher IRL 20 B3
Dromore
Down GB 19 B5
Tyrone GB 19 B4
Dromore West IRL 18 B3
Dronero I 79 B6
Dronfield GB 27 B4
Drongan GB 24 C3
Dronninglund DK 38 B3
Dronrijp NL 42 B2
Dronten NL 42 C2
Drosendorf A 63 B6
Drösing A 64 B2
Drottningholm S 37 C4
Droué F 58 B2
Drulingen F 60 B3
Drumbeg GB 22 C3
Drumcliff IRL 18 B3
Drumgask GB 23 D4
Drumkeeran IRL 18 B3
Drummore GB 24 D3
Drumnadrochit GB 23 D4
Drumquin GB 19 B4
Drumshanbo IRL 18 B3
Drumsna IRL 19 C4
Drunen NL 49 B6
Druskininkai LT 6 D7
Druten NL 49 B6
Druya BY 7 D9
Družetići SRB 85 B5
Drvar BIH 83 B5
Drvenik HR 84 C2
Drwalew PL 55 B6
Drymen GB 24 B3
Drynoch GB 22 D2
Drzewce PL 54 A2
Drzewiany PL 46 B2
Drzewica PL 55 B5
Dualchi I 110 B1
Duas Igrejas P 87 C4
Dub SRB 85 C4
Dubá CZ 53 C4
Dubăsari MD 11 C10
Duben D 53 B3
Dübendorf CH 70 A3
Dubi CZ 53 C3
Dubica HR 74 C1
Dublin IRL 21 A5
Dubna RUS 7 C14
Dubňany CZ 64 B3
Dubnica nad Váhom
SK 64 B4
Dubnik SK 64 C4
Dubno UA 11 A8
Dubodiel SK 64 B4
Dubona SRB 85 B5
Dubovac SRB 85 B6
Dubovic BIH 83 B5
Dubranec HR 73 C5
Dubrava HR 74 C1
Dubrave BIH 84 B3
Dubravica
HR 73 C5
SRB 85 B6
Dubrovnik HR 84 D3
Dubrovytsya UA 7 F9
Ducey F 57 B4
Duchcov CZ 53 C3
Ducherow D 45 B5
Dučina SRB 85 B5
Duclair F 58 A1
Dudar H 74 A2
Duddington GB 30 B3
Duderstadt D 51 B6
Dudeștii Vechi RO 75 B5
Dudley GB 26 C3
Dueñas E 88 C2
Duesund N 32 B2
Dueville I 72 C1
Duffel B 49 B5
Duffield GB 27 C4
Dufftown GB 23 D5
Duga Poljana SRB 85 C5
Duga Resa HR 73 C5
Dugi Rat HR 83 C5
Dugny-sur-Meuse F 59 A6
Dugopolje HR 83 C5
Dugo Selo HR 73 C6
Duino I 72 C3
Duisburg D 50 B2
Dukat AL 105 C5
Dukhovshchina RUS 7 D12
Dukla PL 64 A2
Duleek IRL 19 C5
Dülken D 50 B2
Dülmen D 50 B3
Dulovo BG 11 E9
Dulpetorpet N 34 B4
Dulverton GB 29 B4
Dumbarton GB 24 C3
Dümerek TR 118 C6
Dumfries GB 25 C4
Dumlupınar TR 118 D4
Dümpelfeld D 50 C2
Dunaalmás H 65 C4
Dunabogdány H 65 C5
Dunafalva H 74 B3
Dunaföldvár H 74 B3
Dunaharaszti H 75 A4
Dunajská Streda SK 64 C3
Dunakeszi H 65 C5
Dunakiliti H 64 C3
Dunakömlöd H 74 B3
Dunapataj H 75 B3
Dunaszekcsö H 74 B3
Dunaszentgyorgy H 74 B3
Dunatetétlen H 75 B4
Dunaújváros H 74 B3
Dunavecse H 75 B3
Dunbar GB 25 B5
Dunbeath GB 23 C5
Dunblane GB 25 B4
Dunboyne IRL 21 A5
Dundalk IRL 19 B5
Dundee GB 25 B5
Dundrennan GB 25 D4
Dundrum GB 19 B6
Dunfanaghy IRL 19 A4
Dunfermline GB 25 B4
Dungannon GB 19 B5
Dungarvan IRL 21 B4
Dungiven GB 19 B5
Dunglow IRL 18 B3
Dungourney IRL 20 C3
Duninowo PL 46 A2
Dunis SRB 85 C6
Dunkeld GB 25 B4
Dunker S 37 C3
Dunkerque = Dunkirk
F 48 B3
Dunkineely IRL 18 B3
Dunkirk = Dunkerque
F 48 B3
Dun Laoghaire IRL 21 A5
Dunlavin IRL 21 A5
Dunleer IRL 19 C5
Dun-le-Palestel F 67 B6
Dun-les-Places F 68 A4
Dunlop GB 24 C3
Dunloy GB 19 A5
Dunmanway IRL 20 C2
Dunmore IRL 18 C3
Dunmore East IRL 21 B5
Dunmurry GB 19 B5
Dunnet GB 23 C5
Dunningen D 61 B4
Dunoon GB 24 C3
Duns GB 25 C5
Dunscore GB 25 C4
Dunsford GB 28 C4
Dunshaughlin IRL 21 A5
Dunstable GB 31 C3
Dunster GB 29 B4
Dun-sur-Auron F 68 B2
Dun-sur-Meuse F 59 A6
Dunvegan GB 22 D2
Duplek SLO 73 B5
Dupnitsa BG 11 E7
Durağan TR 16 A7
Durach D 61 C6
Durak TR 118 C3
Đurakovac KOS 85 D5
Durana E 89 B4
Durance F 76 B3
Durango E 89 A4
Durankulak BG 11 E10
Duras F 76 B3
Durban-Corbières F 78 D1
Dürbheim D 61 B4
Durbuy B 49 C6
Dúrcal E 100 C2
Đurđenovac HR 74 C3
Đurdjevac HR 74 B2
Đurdjevik BIH 84 B3
Düren D 50 C2
Durham GB 25 D6
Đurinci SRB 85 B5
Durlach D 61 B4
Đurmanec HR 73 B5
Durness GB 22 C4
Dürnkrut A 64 B2
Dürrboden CH 71 B4

Dürrenboden CH 70 B3
Durrës AL 105 B5
Durrow IRL 21 B4
Durrus IRL 20 C2
Dursunbey TR 118 C3
Durtal F 57 C5
Durup DK 38 C1
Durusu TR 118 A3
Dusina BIH 84 C2
Dusnok H 75 B3
Dusocin PL 47 B4
Düsseldorf D 50 B2
Dusslingen D 61 B5
Duszniki PL 46 C2
Duszniki-Zdrój PL 54 C1
Dutovlje SLO 72 C3
Duvebo S 40 A4
Duved S 115 D9
Düzağac TR 118 D5
Düzce TR 118 B6
Dvärsätt S 115 D11
Dvor HR 83 A5
Dvorce CZ 64 A3
Dvorníky SK 64 B3
Dvory nad Žitavou SK 64 C4
Dvůr Královénad Labem CZ 53 C5
Dyatkovo RUS 7 E13
Dybvad DK 38 B3
Dyce GB 23 D6
Dygowo PL 46 A1
Dykehead GB 25 B4
Dymchurch GB 31 C5
Dymer UA 11 A11
Dyrnes N 114 D4
Dywity PL 47 B6
Džanići BIH 84 C2
Dziadowa Kłoda PL 54 B2
Działdowo PL 47 B6
Działoszyce PL 55 C5
Działoszyn PL 54 B3
Dziemiany PL 46 A3
Dzierząźnia PL 47 C6
Dzierzgoń PL 47 B5
Dzierzgowo PL 47 B6
Dzierżoniów PL 54 C1
Dzisna BY 7 D10
Dziwnów PL 45 A6
Dzyarzhynsk BY 7 E9
Dzyatlava BY 7 E8

E

Ea E 89 A4
Eaglesfield GB 25 C4
Ealing GB 31 C3
Eardisley GB 29 A4
Earls Barton GB 30 B3
Earl Shilton GB 30 B2
Earlston GB 25 C5
Easington GB 27 B6
Easky IRL 18 B3
Eastbourne GB 31 D4
East Calder GB 25 C4
East Dereham GB 30 B4
Easter Skeld GB 22 A7
East Grinstead GB 31 C4
East Ilsley GB 31 C2
East Kilbride GB 24 C3
Eastleigh GB 31 D2
East Linton GB 25 C5
East Markham GB 27 B5
Easton GB 29 C5
East Wittering GB 31 D3
Eaton Socon GB 30 B3
Eaux-Bonnes F 76 D2
Eauze F 76 C3
Ebberup DK 39 D2
Ebbs A 62 C3
Ebbw Vale GB 29 B4
Ebeleben D 51 B6
Ebeltoft DK 39 C3
Ebene Reichenau A 72 B3
Eben im Pongau A 72 A3
Ebensee A 63 C4
Ebensfeld D 51 C6
Eberbach D 61 A4
Ebergötzen D 51 B6
Ebermann-Stadt D 62 A2
Ebern D 51 C6
Eberndorf A 73 B4
Ebersbach D 53 B4
Ebersberg D 62 B2
Ebersdorf
Bayern D 52 C1
Niedersachsen D 43 B6
Eberstein A 73 B4
Eberswalde D 45 C5
Ebnat-Kappel CH 71 A4
Éboli I 103 C8
Ebrach D 61 A6
Ebreichsdorf A 64 C2
Ebreuil F 68 B3
Ebstorf D 44 B2
Ecclefechan GB 25 C4
Eccleshall GB 26 C3
Eceabat TR 118 B1
Echallens CH 69 B6
Echauri E 76 D1
Echinos GR 116 A7
Échiré F 67 B4
Échirolles F 69 C5
Echourgnac F 76 A3
Echt NL 50 B1
Echte D 51 B6
Echternach L 60 A2
Ecija E 99 B5
Ečka SRB 75 C5
Eckartsberga D 52 B1
Eckelshausen D 51 C4
Eckental D 62 A2
Eckernförde D 44 A1
Eckerö FIN 36 B6
Eckington GB 27 B4
Éclaron F 59 B5
Écommoy F 58 C1
Écouché F 57 B5
Ecouis F 58 A2
Ecséd H 65 C5
Ecsegfalva H 75 A5
Écueillé F 67 A6
Ed S 35 D3
Eda S 34 C4
Eda glasbruk S 34 C4
Edam NL 42 C2
Edane S 35 C4
Edderton GB 23 D4
Ede NL 49 A6
Edebäck S 34 B5
Edebo S 36 B5
Edelény H 65 B6
Edelschrott A 73 A5
Edemissen D 44 C2
Edenbridge GB 31 C4
Edenderry IRL 21 A4
Edenkoben D 61 A4
Edesheim D 61 A4
Edessa GR 116 B4
Edewecht D 43 B4
Edgeworthstown IRL 19 C4
Edinburgh GB 25 C4
Edinet MD 11 B9
Edirne TR 118 A1
Edland N 33 C4
Edolo I 71 B5
Edøy N 114 D5
Edremit TR 118 C2
Edsbro S 36 C5
Edsbruk S 40 A6
Edsbyn S 36 A2
Edsele S 115 D13
Edsleskog S 35 C4
Edsvalla S 35 C5
Eekloo B 49 B4
Eemshaven NL 42 B3
Eerbeek NL 50 A2
Eersel NL 49 B6
Eferding A 63 B5
Effiat F 68 B3
Efteløt N 35 C1
Egeln D 52 B1
Eger H 65 C6
Egerbakta H 65 C6
Egernsund DK 39 E2
Egersund N 33 D3
Egerszólát H 65 C6
Egervár H 74 B1
Egg
A 71 A4
D 61 B6
Eggby S 35 D5
Eggedal N 32 B6
Eggenburg A 64 B1
Eggenfelden D 62 B3
Eggesin D 45 B6
Eggum N 112 D2
Egham GB 31 C3
Eghezée B 49 C5
Egiertowo PL 47 A4
Egilsstaðir IS 111 B11
Egina GR 117 E5
Eginio GR 116 B4
Egio GR 117 D4
Égletons F 68 C2
Egling D 62 C2
Eglinton GB 19 A4
Eglisau CH 61 C4
Égliseneuve-d'Entraigues F 68 C2
Eglofs D 61 C5
Egmond aan Zee NL 42 C1
Egna I 71 B6
Egosthena GR 117 D5
Egremont GB 26 A2
Egtved DK 39 D2
Eguilles F 79 C4
Eguilly-sous-Bois F 59 B5
Éguzon-Chantôme F 67 B6
Egyek H 65 C6
Egyházasrádóc H 74 A1
Ehekirchen D 62 B2
Ehingen D 61 B5
Ehra-Lessien D 44 C2
Ehrang D 60 A2
Ehrenfriedersdorf D 52 C2
Ehrenhain D 52 C2
Ehrenhausen A 73 B5
Ehringshausen D 51 C4
Ehrwald A 71 A5
Eibar E 89 A4
Eibelstadt D 61 A6
Eibenstock D 52 C2
Eibergen NL 50 A2
Eibiswald A 73 B5
Eichenbarleben D 52 A1
Eichendorf D 62 B3
Eichstätt D 62 B2
Eickelborn D 50 B4
Eide
Hordaland N 32 B3
Møre og Romsdal N 114 E4
Eidet N 112 C7
Eidfjord N 32 B4
Eidsberg N 35 C3
Eidsbugarden N 32 A5
Eidsdal N 114 E4
Eidsfoss N 35 C2
Eidskog N 34 B4
Eidsvåg
Hordaland N 32 B2
Møre og Romsdal N 114 E5
Eidsvoll N 34 B3
Eikefjord N 114 F2
Eikelandsosen N 32 B2
Eiken N 33 D4
Eikesdal N 114 E5
Eikstrand N 35 C1
Eilenburg D 52 B2
Eilsleben D 52 A1
Eina N 34 B2
Einbeck D 51 B5
Eindhoven NL 49 B6
Einsiedeln CH 70 A3
Einville-au-Jard F 60 B2
Eisenach D 51 C6
Eisenberg
Rheinland-Pfalz D 61 A4
Thüringen D 52 C1
Eisenerz A 73 A4
Eisenhüttenstadt D 53 A4
Eisenkappel A 73 B4
Eisenstadt A 64 C2
Eisentratten A 72 B3
Eisfeld D 51 C6
Eisleben D 52 B1
Eislingen D 61 B5
Eitensheim D 62 B2
Eiterfeld D 51 C5
Eitorf D 50 C3
Eivindvik N 32 B2
Eivissa = Ibiza E 97 C1
Eixo P 92 A2
Ejby DK 39 D2
Ejea de los Caballeros E 90 A1
Ejstrupholm DK 39 D2
Ejulve E 90 C2
Eke B 49 C4
Ekeby
Gotland S 37 E5
Skåne S 41 D2
Uppsala S 36 B5
Ekeby-Almby S 37 C2
Ekenäs S 35 D5
Ekenässjön S 40 B5
Ekerö S 37 C4
Eket S 41 C3
Eketorp S 41 C6
Ekevik S 40 A6
Ekkerøy N 113 B19
Ekshärad S 34 B5
Eksingedal N 32 B2
Eksjö S 40 B4
Eksta S 37 E5
Ekträsk S 115 C16
El Alamo
Madrid E 94 B3
Sevilla E 99 B4
El Algar E 101 B5
El Almendro E 98 B3
El Alquián E 101 C3
Élancourt F 58 B2
El Arahal E 99 B5
El Arenal E 94 B1
El Arguellite E 101 A3
Elassona GR 116 C4
El Astillero E 88 A3
Elati GR 116 C3
Želazno PL 54 C1
El Ballestero E 101 A3
El Barco de Ávila E 93 A5
Elbasan AL 116 A2
El Berrón E 88 A1
El Berrueco E 95 B3
Elbeuf F 58 A1
Elbingerode D 51 B6
Elbląg PL 47 A5
El Bodón E 93 A4
El Bonillo E 95 D4
El Bosque E 99 C5
El Bullaque E 94 C2
Elburg NL 42 C2
El Burgo E 100 C1
El Burgo de Ebro E 90 B2
El Burgo de Osma E 89 C3
El Burgo Ranero E 88 B1
El Buste E 89 C5
El Cabaco E 93 A4
El Callejo E 89 A3
El Campillo E 99 B4
El Campillo de la Jara E 94 C1
El Cañavete E 95 C4
El Carpio E 100 B1
El Carpio de Tajo E 94 C2
El Casar E 95 B3
El Casar de Escalona E 94 B2
El Castillo de las Guardas E 99 B4
El Centenillo E 100 A2
El Cerro E 93 A5
El Cerro de Andévalo E 99 B4
Elche E 96 C2
Elche de la Sierra E 101 A3
Elchingen D 61 B6
El Comenar E 99 C5
El Coronil E 99 B5
El Crucero E 86 A4
El Cubo de Tierra del Vino E 88 C1
El Cuervo E 99 C4
Elda E 101 A5
Eldena D 44 B3
Eldingen D 44 C2
Elefsina GR 117 D5
El Ejido E 101 C3
Elek H 75 B6
Elemir SRB 75 C5
El Escorial E 94 B2
El Espinar E 94 B2
Eleutheroupoli GR 116 B6
El Frago E 90 A2
El Franco E 86 A4
El Frasno E 89 C5
Elgå N 114 E8
El Garrobo E 99 B4
El Gastor E 99 C5
Elgin GB 23 D5
Elgoibar E 89 A4
Elgol GB 22 D2
El Gordo E 93 B5
El Grado E 90 A3
El Granado E 98 B3
El Grao de Castelló E 96 B3
El Grau E 96 C2
Elgshøa N 34 A4
El Higuera E 100 B1
El Hijate E 101 B3
El Hontanar E 96 A1
El Hoyo E 100 A2
Elie GB 25 B5
Elizondo E 76 C1
Ełk PL 6 E7
Elkhovo BG 11 E9
Ellenberg D 61 A6
Ellesmere GB 26 C3
Ellesmere Port GB 26 B3
Ellezelles B 49 C4
Ellingen D 62 A1
Ellmau A 72 A2
Ellon GB 23 D6
Ellös S 35 D3
Ellrich D 51 B6
Ellwangen D 61 B6
Elm
CH 71 B4
D 43 B6
Elmadağ TR 16 B6
El Madroño E 99 B4
El Maillo E 93 A4
Elmalı TR 119 F4
El Masnou E 91 B5
El Mirón E 93 A5
El Molar E 95 B3
El Molinillo E 94 C2
El Morell E 91 B4
Elmshorn D 43 B6
Elmstein D 60 A3
El Muyo E 89 C3
Elne F 91 A5
Elnesvågen N 114 E4
El Olmo E 88 C3
Elorrio E 89 A4
Elöszállás H 74 B3
Elouda GR 117 G7
Éloyes F 60 B2
El Palo E 100 C1
El Pardo E 94 B3
El Payo E 93 A4
El Pedernoso E 95 C4
El Pedroso E 99 B5
El Peral E 95 C5
El Perelló
Tarragona E 90 C3
Valencia E 96 B2
Elphin GB 22 C3
El Picazo E 95 C4
El Pinell de Bray E 90 B3
El Piñero E 88 C1
El Pla de Santa Maria E 91 B4
El Pobo E 90 C2
El Pobo de Dueñas E 95 B5
El Pont d'Armentera E 91 B4
El Port de la Selva E 91 A6
El Port de Llançà E 91 A6
El Port de Sagunt E 96 B2
El Prat de Llobregat E 91 B5
El Provencio E 95 C4
El Puente E 89 A3
El Puente del Arzobispo E 93 B5
El Puerto E 86 A4
El Puerto de Santa María E 99 C4
El Real de la Jara E 99 B4
El Real de San Vincente E 94 B2
El Robledo E 94 C2
El Rocío E 99 B4
El Rompido E 99 B3
El Ronquillo E 99 B4
El Royo E 89 C4
El Rubio E 100 B1
El Sabinar E 101 A3
El Saler E 96 B2
El Salobral E 101 A4
El Saucejo E 99 B5
Els Castells E 91 A4
Elsdorf D 50 C2
Elsenfeld D 61 A5
El Serrat AND 91 A4
Elsfleth D 43 B5
Elspeet NL 50 A1
Elst NL 50 B1
Elstead GB 31 C3
Elster D 52 B2
Elsterberg D 52 C2
Elsterwerda D 52 B3
Elstra D 53 B4
El Temple E 90 B2
El Tiemblo E 94 B2
Eltmann D 51 D6
El Toboso E 95 C4
El Tormillo E 90 B2
El Torno E 93 A5
Eltville D 50 C4
El Valle de las Casas E 88 B1
Elvas P 93 C3
Elvebakken N 113 C12
El Vellón E 95 B3
Elven F 56 C3
El Vendrell E 91 B4
Elverum N 34 B3
El Villar de Arnedo E 89 B4
Elvington GB 27 B5
El Viso E 100 A1
El Viso del Alcor E 99 B5
Elxleben D 51 B6
Ely GB 30 B4
Elzach D 61 B4
Elze D 51 A5
Emådalen S 36 A1
Embleton GB 25 C6
Embonas GR 119 F2
Embrun F 79 B5
Embún E 90 A2
Emden D 43 B4
Emecik TR 119 F2
Emet TR 118 C4
Emirdağ TR 118 C6
Emlichheim D 42 C3
Emmaboda S 40 C5
Emmaljunga S 41 C3
Emmeloord NL 42 C2
Emmen
CH 70 A3
NL 42 C3
Emmendingen D 60 B3
Emmer-Compascuum NL 43 C4
Emmerich D 50 B2
Emmern D 51 A5
Emöd H 65 C6
Émpoli I 81 C4
Emsbüren D 43 C4
Emsdetten D 50 A3
Emsfors S 40 B6
Emskirchen D 62 A1
Emstek D 43 C5
Emsworth GB 31 D3
Emyvale IRL 19 B5
Enafors S 115 D9
Enånger S 115 F14
Encamp AND 91 A4
Encarnação P 92 C1
Encinas de Abajo E 94 B1
Encinas de Esgueva E 88 C2
Encinasola E 99 A4
Encinas Reales E 100 B1
Encio E 89 B3
Enciso E 89 B4
Enden N 114 F7
Endingen D 60 B3
Endrinal E 93 A5
Endröd H 75 B5
Enebakk N 34 C3
Eneryda S 40 C4
Enese H 64 C3
Enez TR 116 B8
Enfield IRL 21 A5
Eng A 72 A1
Engelberg CH 70 B3
Engelhartszell A 63 B4
Engelskirchen D 50 C3
Engen D 61 C4
Enger N 34 B2
Engerdal N 114 F8
Engerneset N 34 A4
Enge-sande D 39 E1
Engesvang DK 39 C2
Enghien B 49 C5
Engstingen D 61 B5
Engter D 43 C5
Enguera E 96 C2
Enguidanos E 95 C5
Enkenbach D 60 A3
Enkhuizen NL 42 C2
Enklinge FIN 36 B7
Enköping S 37 C4
Enna I 109 B3
Ennezat F 68 C3
Ennigerloh D 50 B4
Enningdal N 35 D3
Ennis IRL 20 B3
Enniscorthy IRL 21 B5
Enniskean IRL 20 C3
Enniskillen GB 19 B4
Ennistimon IRL 20 B2
Enns A 63 B5
Eno FIN 3 E29
Enontekiö FIN 113 D12
Ens NL 42 C2
Enschede NL 50 A2
Ensdorf D 62 A2
Ensisheim F 60 C3
Enstaberga S 37 D3
Enstone GB 31 C2
Entlebuch CH 70 A3
Entrácque I 80 B1
Entradas P 98 B2
Entrains-sur-Nohain F 68 A3
Entrambasaguas E 88 A3
Entrambasmestas E 88 A3
Entraygues-sur-Truyère F 77 B5
Entre-os-Rios P 87 C2
Entrevaux F 79 C5
Entrin Bajo E 93 C4
Entroncamento P 92 B2
Entzheim F 60 B3
Envermeu F 58 A2
Enviken S 36 B2
Enying H 74 B3
Enzingerboden A 72 A2
Enzklösterle D 61 B4
Épagny F 59 A4
Epalinges CH 70 B1
Epannes F 67 B4
Epanomi GR 116 B4
Epe
D 50 A3
NL 42 C2
Épernay F 59 A4
Épernon F 58 B2
Epfig F 60 B3
Épierre F 69 C6
Épila E 90 B1
Épinac F 69 B4
Épinal F 60 B2
Episcopia I 106 A3
Episkopi CY 120 B1
Epitalio GR 117 E3
Epoisses F 69 A4
Eppenbrunn D 60 A3
Eppendorf D 52 C3
Epping GB 31 C4
Eppingen D 61 A4
Epsom GB 31 C3
Epworth GB 27 B5
Eraclea I 72 C2
Eraclea Mare I 72 C2
Erba I 71 C4
Erbach
Baden-Württemberg D 61 B5
Hessen D 61 A4
Erbalunga F 102 A2
Erbendorf D 62 A3
Érchie I 105 C3
Ercolano I 103 C7
Ercsi H 74 A3
Érd H 74 A3
Erdek TR 118 B2
Erdemli TR 16 C7
Erdevik SRB 85 A4
Erding D 62 B2
Erdötelek H 65 C6
Erdut HR 75 C4
Erdweg D 62 B2
Ereğli
Konya TR 16 C7
Zonguldak TR 118 A6
Erenkaya TR 119 E7
Eresfjord N 114 E5
Eresos GR 116 C7
Eretria GR 116 D5
Erfde D 43 A6
Erfjord N 33 C3
Erfstadt D 50 C2
Erfurt D 52 C1
Ergli LV 7 C8
Ergoldsbach D 62 B3
Eriboll GB 23 C4
Érice I 108 A1
Ericeira P 92 C1
Eğridir TR 119 E5
Eriksberg S 115 B12
Eriksmåla S 40 C5
Eringsboda S 41 C5
Eriswil CH 70 A2
Erithres GR 117 D5
Erkelenz D 50 B2
Erkner D 45 C5
Erkrath D 50 B2
Erla E 90 A2
Erlangen D 62 A2
Erli I 80 B2
Erlsbach A 72 B2
Ermelo NL 49 A6
Ermenak TR 16 C6
Ermenonville F 58 A3
Ermezinde P 87 C2
Ermidas P 98 A2
Ermioni GR 117 E5
Ermoupoli GR 117 E6
Erndtebrück D 50 C4
Ernée F 57 B5
Ernestinovo HR 74 C3
Ernstbrunn A 64 B2
Erolzheim D 61 B6
Erquelinnes B 49 C5
Erquy F 56 B3
Erra P 92 C2
Erratzu E 76 C1
Errindlev DK 44 A3
Erro E 76 D1
Ersa F 102 A2
Érsekcsanád H 75 B3
Ersekë AL 116 B2
Érsekvadkert H 65 C5
Erstein F 60 B3
Erstfeld CH 70 B3
Ertebølle DK 38 C2
Ertingen D 61 B5
Ervedal
Coimbra P 92 A2
Portalegre P 92 B3
Ervenik HR 83 B4
Ervidel P 98 B2
Ervy-le-Châtel F 59 B4
Erwitte D 51 B4
Erxleben D 52 A1
Erzsébet H 74 B3
Esbjerg DK 39 D1
Esbly F 58 B3
Escacena del Campo E 99 B4
Escairón E 86 B3
Escalada E 88 B3
Escalante E 89 A3
Escalaplano I 110 C2
Escalona E 94 B2
Escalona del Prado E 94 A2
Escalonilla E 94 C2
Escalos de Baixo P 92 B3
Escalos de Cima P 92 B3
Escamilla E 95 B4
Es Caná E 97 B1
Escañuela E 100 B1
Es Castell E 97 B4
Escatrón E 90 B2
Eschach D 61 C5
Eschau D 61 A5
Eschede D 44 C2
Eschenau D 62 A2
Eschenbach D 62 A2
Eschenz CH 61 C4
Eschershausen D 51 B5
Esch-sur-Alzette L 60 A1
Esch-sur-Sûre L 60 A1
Eschwege D 51 B6
Eschweiler D 50 C2
Escobasa de Almazán E 89 C4
Escoeuilles F 48 C2
Escombreras E 101 B5
Escos F 76 C1
Escource F 76 B1
Escragnolles F 79 C5
Escrick GB 27 B4
Escurial E 93 B5
Escurial de la Sierra E 93 A5
Esens D 43 B4
Esgos E 87 B3
Esher GB 31 C3
Eskdalemuir GB 25 C4
Eskifjörður IS 111 B12
Eskilhem S 37 E5
Eskilsäter S 35 D5
Eskilstrup DK 39 E4
Eskilstuna S 37 C3
Eskipazar TR 118 B7
Eskişehir TR 118 C5
Eslarn D 62 A3
Eslava E 89 B5
Eslida E 96 B2
Eslohe D 50 B4
Eslöv S 41 D3
Esme TR 119 D3
Es Mercadal E 97 B4
Es Migjorn Gran E 97 B4
Espa N 34 B3
Espalion F 78 B1
Esparragalejo E 93 C4
Esparragosa del Caudillo E 93 C5
Esparragossa de la Serena E 93 C5
Esparreguera E 91 B4
Esparron F 79 C4
Espe N 32 B3
Espedal N 33 D3
Espejo
Alava E 89 B3
Córdoba E 100 B1
Espeland N 32 B2
Espelkamp D 43 C5
Espeluche F 78 B3
Espeluy E 100 A2
Espera E 99 C5
Esperança P 93 B3
Espéraza F 77 D5
Espéria I 103 B6
Espevær N 33 C2
Espiel E 99 A5
Espinama E 88 A2
Espiñaredo E 86 A3
Espinasses F 79 B5
Espinelves E 91 B5
Espinhal P 92 A2
Espinho P 87 C2
Espinilla E 88 A2
Espinosa de Cerrato E 88 C3
Espinosa de los Monteros E 89 A3
Espinoso del Rey E 94 C2
Espirito Santo P 98 B3
Espluga de Francolí E 91 B4
Esplús E 90 B3
Espolla E 91 A5
Espoo FIN 6 A8
Esporles E 97 B2
Es Port d'Alcúdia E 97 B3
Esposende P 87 C2
Espot E 91 A4
Es Pujols E 97 C1
Esquedas E 90 A2
Esquivias E 94 B3
Essay F 57 B6
Essen
B 49 B5
Niedersachsen D 43 C4
Nordrhein-Westfalen D 50 B3
Essenbach D 62 B3
Essertaux F 58 A3
Essingen D 61 B6
Esslingen D 61 B5
Es Soleràs E 90 B3
Essoyes F 59 B5
Estacas E 87 B2
Estadilla E 90 A3
Estagel F 78 D1
Estaires F 48 C3
Estang F 76 C2
Estarreja P 87 D2
Estartit E 91 A6
Estavayer-le-Lac CH 70 B1
Este I 72 C1
Esteiro E 86 A2
Estela P 87 C2
Estella E 89 B4
Estellencs E 97 B2
Estepa E 100 B1
Estépar E 88 B3
Estepona E 99 C5
Esternay F 59 B4
Esterri d'Aneu E 91 A4
Esterwegen D 43 C4
Estissac F 59 B4
Estivadas E 87 B3
Estivareilles F 68 B2
Estivella E 96 B2
Estói P 98 B3
Estopiñán E 90 B3
Estoril P 92 C1
Estoublon F 79 C5
Estrée-Blanche F 48 C3
Estrées-St Denis F 58 A3
Estrela P 98 A3
Estremera E 95 B3
Estremoz P 92 C3
Estuna S 36 C5
Esyres F 67 A5
Esztergom H 65 C4
Étables-sur-Mer F 56 B3
Étain F 60 A1
Étalans F 69 A6
Étalle B 60 A1
Étampes F 58 B3
Étang-sur-Arroux F 69 B4
Étaples F 48 C2
Étauliers F 67 C4
Etili TR 118 C1
Etna N 34 B1
Etne N 33 C2
Étoges F 59 B4
Étoliko GR 116 D3
Eton GB 31 C3
Étréaupont F 59 A4
Étréchy F 58 B3
Étrépagny F 58 A2
Étretat F 57 A6
Étroeungt F 49 C4
Étroubles I 70 C2
Ettal D 62 C2
Ettelbruck L 60 A2
Etten NL 49 B5
Ettenheim D 60 B3
Ettington GB 29 A6
Ettlingen D 61 B4
Ettringen D 62 B1
Étuz F 69 A5
Etxarri-Aranatz E 89 B4
Etyek H 74 A3
Eu F 48 C2
Euerdorf D 51 C6
Eulate E 89 B4
Eupen B 50 C2
Europoort NL 49 B5
Euskirchen D 50 C2
Eutin D 44 A2
Evanger N 32 B3
Évaux-les-Bains F 68 B2
Evciler
Afyon TR 119 D4
Çanakkale TR 118 C1
Evenskjær N 112 D5
Evenstad N 34 A3
Evercreech GB 29 B5
Evergem B 49 B4
Everöd S 41 D4
Eversberg D 51 B4
Everswinkel D 50 B3
Evertsberg S 34 A5
Evesham GB 29 A6
Évian-les-Bains F 69 B6
Evisa F 102 A1
Evje N 33 D4
Évolène CH 70 B2
Évora P 92 C3
Evoramonte P 92 C3
Evran F 57 B4
Evrecy F 57 A5
Évreux F 58 A2
Évron F 57 B5
Évry F 58 B3
Ewell GB 31 C3
Ewersbach D 50 C4
Excideuil F 67 C6
Exeter GB 29 C4
Exmes F 57 B6
Exminster GB 29 C4
Exmouth GB 29 C4
Eydehamn N 33 D5
Eye
Peterborough GB 30 B3
Suffolk GB 30 B5
Eyemouth GB 25 C5
Eyguians F 79 B4
Eyguières F 79 C4
Eygurande F 68 C2
Eylie F 77 D3
Eymet F 77 B3
Eymoutiers F 68 C1
Eynsham GB 31 C2
Eyrarbakki IS 111 D4
Eystrup D 43 C6
Ezaro E 86 B1
Ezcaray E 89 B4
Ezcároz E 76 D1
Ezine TR 118 C1
Ezmoriz P 87 D2

F

Fabara E 90 B3
Fábbrico I 81 B4
Fåberg N 34 A2
Fabero E 86 B4
Fábiánsebestyén H 75 B5
Fåborg DK 39 D3
Fabrègues F 78 C2
Fabriano I 82 C1
Fabrizia I 106 C3
Facha P 87 C2
Facinas E 99 C5
Fačkov SK 65 A4
Fadagosa P 92 B3
Fadd H 74 B3
Faédis I 72 B3
Faenza I 81 B5
Fafe P 87 C2
Fagagna I 72 B3
Făgăras RO 11 D8
Fågelberget S 115 C11
Fågelfors S 40 B5
Fågelmara S 41 C5
Fågelsta S 37 D2
Fagerås S 35 C5
Fågerheim N 32 B5
Fagerhøy N 34 A1
Fagerhult S 40 B5
Fagerlund N 34 B2
Fagernes
Oppland N 32 B6
Troms N 112 C8
Fagersanna S 35 D6
Fagersta S 36 B2
Fåglavik S 35 D5
Fagnano Castello I 106 B3
Fagnières F 59 B5
Faido CH 70 B3
Fains-Véel F 59 B6
Fairford GB 29 B6
Fairlie GB 24 C3
Fajsz H 74 B3
Fakenham GB 30 B4
Fåker S 115 D11
Fakse DK 39 D5
Fakse Ladeplads DK 41 D2
Falaise F 57 B5
Falcade I 72 B1
Falcarragh IRL 18 A3
Falces E 89 B5
Fălciu RO 11 C10
Falconara I 109 B3
Falconara Maríttima I 82 C2
Falcone I 109 A4
Faldingworth GB 27 B5
Falerum S 37 D3
Fălești MD 11 C9
Falkenberg
Bayern D 62 A3
Bayern D 62 B3
Brandenburg D 52 B3
S 40 C2
Falkensee D 45 C5
Falkenstein
Bayern D 62 A3
Sachsen D 52 C2
Falkenthal D 45 C5
Falkirk GB 25 B4
Falkland GB 25 B4
Falköping S 35 D5
Fall D 62 C2
Falla S 37 D2
Fallingbostel D 43 C6
Falmouth GB 28 C2
Falset E 90 B3
Fălticeni RO 11 C9
Falun S 36 B2
Famagusta CY 120 A2
Fammestad N 32 B2
Fana N 32 B2
Fanano I 81 B4
Fanari GR 116 C3
Fanjeaux F 77 C5
Fano I 82 C2
Fântânele RO 75 B6
Fão P 87 C2
Fara in Sabina I 102 A5
Faramontanos de Tábara E 88 C1
Fara Novarese I 70 C3
Farasdues E 90 A1
Fårbo S 40 B6
Fareham GB 31 D2
Färentuna S 37 C4
Färgelanda S 35 D3
Färila S 115 F12
Faringdon GB 31 C2
Faringe S 36 C5
Farini I 80 B3
Fariza E 87 C4
Färjestaden S 41 C6
Farkadona GR 116 C4
Farkasfa H 73 B6
Farlete E 90 B2
Färlöv S 41 C4
Farmos H 75 A4
Farnă SK 65 C4
Färnäs S 36 B1
Farnborough GB 31 C3
Farnese I 102 A4
Farnham GB 31 C3
Farnroda D 51 C6
Faro P 98 B3
Fårö S 37 E6
Fårösund S 37 E6
Farra d'Alpago I 72 B2
Farranfore IRL 20 B2
Farre DK 39 C2
Farsala GR 116 C4
Farsø DK 38 C2
Farsund N 33 D3
Farum DK 41 D2
Fårup DK 38 C2
Fasana I 103 C8
Fasano I 104 C3
Fáskrúðsfjörður IS 111 C11
Fassberg D 44 C2
Fastiv UA 11 A10
Fastnäs S 34 B5
Fatesh RUS 7 E13
Fátima P 92 B2
Fatnomakke S 115 B12
Fättjaur S 115 B12
Faucogney-et-la-Mer F 60 C2
Fauguerolles F 76 B3
Faulenrost D 45 B4
Faulquemont F 60 A2
Fauquembergues F 48 C3
Fauske N 112 E4
Fauville-en-Caux F 58 A1
Fauvillers B 60 A1
Fåvang N 34 A2
Favara
E 96 B2
I 108 B2
Faverges F 69 C6
Faverney F 60 C2
Faversham GB 31 C4
Favignana I 108 B1
Fawley GB 31 D2
Fay-aux-Loges F 58 C3
Fayence F 79 C5
Fayet F 78 C1
Fayl-Billot F 60 C1
Fayón E 90 B3
Fearn GB 23 D5
Fécamp F 58 A1
Feda N 33 D3
Fedje N 32 B1
Feeny GB 19 B4
Fegen S 40 B3
Fegyvernek H 75 A5
Fehrbellin D 45 C4
Fehring A 73 B6
Feichten A 71 A5
Feiring N 34 B3
Feistritz im Rosental A 73 B4
Feke TR 16 C7
Feketić SRB 75 C4
Felanitx E 97 B3
Feld am See A 72 B3
Feldbach A 73 B5
Feldberg D 45 B5
Feldkirch A 71 A4
Feldkirchen in Kärnten A 73 B4
Feldkirchen-Westerham D 62 C2
Felgueiras P 87 C2
Felitto I 103 C8
Félix E 101 C3
Felixstowe GB 31 C5
Felletin F 68 C2
Fellingsbro S 37 C2
Felnac RO 75 B6
Felnémet H 65 C6
Felpéc H 74 A2
Fels am Wagram A 64 B1
Felsberg D 51 B5
Felsönyék H 74 B3
Felsöszentiván H 75 B4
Felsöszentmárton H 74 C2
Felsözsolca H 65 B6
Felsted DK 39 E2
Feltre I 72 B1
Femsjö S 40 C3
Fenagh IRL 19 B4
Fene E 86 A2
Fenestrelle I 79 A6
Fénétrange F 60 B3
Feneu F 57 C5
Fengersfors S 35 D4
Fenit IRL 20 B2
Fensmark DK 39 D4
Fenwick GB 24 C3
Feolin Ferry GB 24 C1
Ferbane IRL 21 A4
Ferdinandovac HR 74 B2
Ferdinandshof D 45 B5
Fère-Champenoise F 59 B4
Fère-en-Tardenois F 59 A4
Ferentillo I 102 A5
Ferentino I 103 B6
Feres GR 116 B8
Feria E 93 C4
Feričanci HR 74 C2
Ferizli TR 118 B5
Ferla I 109 B3
Ferlach A 73 B4
Ferleiten A 72 A2
Fermil P 87 C3
Fermo I 82 C2
Fermoselle E 87 C4
Fermoy IRL 20 B3
Fernancabellero E 94 C3
Fernán Nuñéz E 100 B1
Fernán Peréz E 101 C3
Fernão Ferro P 92 C1
Fernay-Voltaire F 69 B6
Ferndown GB 29 C6
Ferness GB 23 D5
Fernhurst GB 31 C3
Ferns IRL 21 B5
Ferpécle CH 70 B2
Ferrals-les-Corbières F 78 C1
Ferrandina I 104 C2
Ferrara I 81 B5
Ferrara di Monte Baldo I 71 C5
Ferreira E 86 A3
Ferreira do Alentejo P 98 A2
Ferreira do Zêzere P 92 B2
Ferreras de Abajo E 87 C4
Ferreras de Arriba E 87 C4
Ferreries E 97 B4
Ferreruela E 90 B1
Ferreruela de Tabara E 87 C4
Ferret CH 70 C2
Ferrette F 70 A2
Ferriere I 80 B3
Ferrière-la-Grande F 49 C4
Ferrières
Hautes-Pyrénées F 76 C2
Loiret F 58 B3
Oise F 58 A3
Ferrières-sur-Sichon F 68 B3
Ferrol E 86 A2
Ferryhill GB 27 A4
Fertőrákos H 64 C2
Fertőszentmiklós H 64 C2
Ferwerd NL 42 B2
Festieux F 59 A4
Festøy N 114 E3
Festvåg N 112 E3
Fetești RO 11 D9
Fethard
Tipperary IRL 21 B4
Wexford IRL 21 B5
Fethiye TR 119 F4
Fetsund N 34 C3
Fettercairn GB 25 B5
Feucht D 62 A2
Feuchtwangen D 61 A6
Feudingen D 50 C4
Feuges F 59 B5
Feuquières F 58 A2
Feurs F 69 C4
Fevik N 33 D5
Ffestiniog GB 26 C2
Fiamignano I 102 A6
Fiano I 70 C2
Ficarazzi I 108 A2
Ficarolo I 81 B5
Fichtelberg D 52 C1
Ficulle I 82 D1
Fidenza I 81 B4
Fidjeland N 33 D3
Fieberbrunn A 72 A2
Fier AL 105 C5
Fiera di Primiero I 72 B1
Fierzë AL 105 A6
Fiesch CH 70 B3
Fiesso Umbertiano I 81 B5
Figari F 102 B2
Figeac F 77 B5
Figeholm S 40 B6
Figgjo N 33 D2
Figline Valdarno I 81 C5
Figols E 90 A3
Figueira da Foz P 92 A2
Figueira de Castelo Rodrigo P 87 D4
Figueira dos Caveleiros P 98 A2
Figueiredo P 92 B3
Figueiredo de Alva P 87 D3
Figueiródos Vinhos P 92 B2
Figueres E 91 A5
Figueroles E 96 A2
Figueruela de Arriba E 87 C4
Filadélfia I 106 C3
Fil'akovo SK 65 B5
Filderstadt D 61 B5
Filey GB 27 A5
Filiași RO 11 D7
Filiates GR 116 C2
Filiatra GR 117 E3
Filipstad S 35 C6
Filisur CH 71 B4
Fillan N 114 D5
Filotio GR 117 E7
Filottrano I 82 C2
Filskov DK 39 D2
Filton GB 29 B5
Filtvet N 35 C2
Filzmoos A 72 A3
Finale Emília I 81 B5
Finale Ligure I 80 B2
Fiñana E 101 B3
Finby FIN 36 B7
Fincham GB 30 B4
Finchingfield GB 31 C4
Findhorn GB 23 D5
Findochty GB 23 D6
Finike TR 119 F5
Finkenberg A 72 A1
Finnea IRL 19 C4
Finneidfjord N 115 A10
Finnerödja S 37 D1
Finnskog N 34 B4
Finnsnes N 112 C7
Finntorp S 35 C4
Finócchio I 102 B5
Finsjö S 40 B6
Finsland N 33 D4
Finspång S 37 D2
Finsterwalde D 53 B3
Finsterwolde NL 43 B4
Finstown GB 23 B5
Fintona GB 19 B4
Fionnphort GB 24 B1
Fiorenzuola d'Arda I 81 B3
Firenze = Florence I 81 C5
Firenzuola I 81 B5
Firmi F 77 B5
Firminy F 69 C4
Firmo I 106 B3
Fischamend Markt A 64 B2
Fischbach
A 73 A5
D 60 A3
Fischbeck D 44 C4
Fischen D 71 A5
Fishbourne GB 31 D2
Fishguard GB 28 B3
Fiskardo GR 116 D2
Fiskebäckskil S 35 D3
Fiskebøl N 112 D3
Fismes F 59 A4
Fisterra E 86 B1
Fitero E 89 B5
Fitjar N 32 C2
Fiuggi I 103 B6
Fiumata I 102 A6
Fiumefreddo Brúzio I 106 B3
Fiumefreddo di Sicília I 109 B4
Fiumicino I 102 B5
Fivemiletown GB 19 B4
Fivizzano I 81 B4
Fjälkinge S 41 C4
Fjällåsen S 112 E9
Fjällbacka S 35 D3
Fjæra N 32 C3
Fjärdhundra S 36 C3
Fjellerup DK 38 C3
Fjerritslev DK 38 B2
Fjordgard N 112 C6
Fjugesta S 37 C1
Flå N 32 B6
Flåbygd N 33 C5
Flaça E 91 A5
Flace F 69 B4
Fladungen D 51 C6
Flaine F 70 B1
Flaka FIN 36 B7
Flåm N 32 B4
Flamatt CH 70 B2
Flamborough GB 27 A5

Flammersfeld D 50 C3
Flassans-sur-Issole F 79 C5
Flatdal N 33 C5
Flatebø N 32 B3
Flateby N 34 C3
Flateland N 33 C4
Flateyri IS 111 A2
Flatøydegard N 32 B6
Flatråker N 32 C2
Flattach A 72 B3
Flatvarp S 37 E3
Flauenskjold DK 38 B3
Flavigny-sur-Moselle F 60 B2
Flavy-le-Martel F 59 A4
Flawil CH 71 A4
Flayosc F 79 C5
Flechtingen D 44 C3
Fleckeby D 44 A1
Fleet GB 31 C3
Fleetmark D 44 C3
Fleetwood GB 26 B2
Flehingen D 61 A4
Flekke N 32 A2
Flekkefjord N 33 D3
Flen S 37 C3
Flensburg D 39 E2
Fleringe S 37 E5
Flerohopp S 40 C5
Flers F 57 B5
Flesberg N 32 C6
Fleurance F 77 C3
Fleuré F 67 B5
Fleurier CH 69 B6
Fleurus B 49 C5
Fleury
Hérault F 78 C2
Yonne F 59 C4
Fleury-les-Aubrais F 58 C2
Fleury-sur-Andelle F 58 A2
Fleury-sur-Orne F 57 A5
Flieden D 51 C5
Flimby GB 26 A2
Flims CH 71 B4
Flines-lèz-Raches F 49 C4
Flint GB 26 B2
Flirey F 60 B1
Flirsch A 71 A5
Flisa N 34 B4
Flisby S 40 B4
Fliseryd S 40 B6
Flix E 90 B3
Flixecourt F 48 C3
Flize F 59 A5
Flobecq B 49 C4
Floby S 35 D5
Floda S 40 B2
Flodden GB 25 C5
Flogny-la-Chapelle F 59 C4
Flöha D 52 C3
Flonheim D 61 A4
Florac F 78 B2
Floreffe B 49 C5
Florence = Firenze I 81 C5
Florennes B 49 C5
Florensac F 78 C2
Florentin F 77 C5
Florenville B 59 A6
Flores de Avila E 94 B1
Floresta I 109 B3
Floreşti MD 11 C10
Floridia I 109 B4
Florina GR 116 B3
Florø N 114 F2
Flörsheim D 51 C4
Floss D 62 A3
Fluberg N 34 B2
Flúðir IS 111 C5
Flühli CH 70 B3
Flumet F 69 C6
Fluminimaggiore I 110 C1
Flums CH 71 A4
Flyeryd S 41 C5
Flygsfors S 40 C5
Foča BIH 84 C3
Foça TR 118 D1
Fochabers GB 23 D5
Focşani RO 11 D9
Foel GB 26 C2
Foeni RO 75 C5
Fogdö S 37 C3
Fóggia I 104 B1
Foglianise I 103 B7
Föglö FIN 36 B7
Fohnsdorf A 73 A4
Foiano della Chiana I 81 C5
Foix F 77 D4
Fojnica
BIH 84 C2
BIH 84 C3
Fokino RUS 7 E13
Fokstua N 114 E6
Földeák H 75 B5
Foldereid N 114 C9
Földes H 75 A6
Folegandros GR 117 F6
Folelli F 102 A2
Folgaria I 71 C6
Folgosinho P 92 A3
Folgoso de la Ribera E 86 B4
Folgoso do Courel E 86 B3
Foligno I 82 D1
Folkärna S 36 B3
Folkestad N 114 E3
Folkestone GB 31 C5
Follafoss N 114 D8
Folldal N 114 E6
Follebu N 34 A2
Follina I 72 C2
Föllinge S 115 D11
Follónica I 81 D4
Fölsbyn S 35 C4
Foncebadón E 86 B4
Foncine-le-Bas F 69 B6
Fondevila E 87 C2
Fondi I 103 B6
Fondo I 71 B6
Fonelas E 100 B2
Fonfría
Teruel E 90 C1
Zamora E 87 C4
Fonnes N 32 B1
Fonni I 110 B2
Fontaine F 59 B5
Fontainebleau F 58 B3
Fontaine de Vaucluse F 79 C4
Fontaine-Française F 69 A5
Fontaine-le-Dun F 58 A1
Fontan F 80 B1
Fontanarejo E 94 C2
Fontane I 80 B1
Fontanélice I 81 B5
Fontanières F 68 B2
Fontanosas E 100 A1
Fonteblanda I 102 A4
Fontenay-le-Comte F 66 B4
Fontenay-Trésigny F 59 B3
Fontevrault-l'Abbaye F 67 A5
Fontiveros E 94 B2
Fontoy F 60 A1
Fontpédrouse F 91 A5
Font-Romeu F 91 A5
Fontstown IRL 21 A5
Fonyód H 74 B2
Fonz E 90 A3
Fonzaso I 72 B1
Föppolo I 71 B4
Föra S 41 B6
Forbach
D 61 B4
F 60 A2
Forcall E 90 C2
Forcalquier F 79 C4
Forcarei E 86 B2
Forchheim D 62 A2
Forchtenau A 64 C2
Forchtenberg D 61 A5
Ford GB 24 B2
Førde
Hordaland N 33 C2
Sogn og Fjordane N 32 A2
Förderstedt D 52 B1
Førdesfjorden N 33 C2
Fordham GB 30 B4
Fordingbridge GB 29 C6
Fordon PL 47 B4
Fordongiánus I 110 C1
Forenza I 104 C1
Foresta di Búrgos I 110 B1
Forfar GB 25 B5
Forges-les-Eaux F 58 A2
Foria I 106 A2
Forio I 103 C6
Forjães P 87 C2
Førland N 33 D4
Forlì I 81 B6
Forlimpopoli I 82 B1
Formazza I 70 B3
Formby GB 26 B2
Formerie F 58 A2
Fórmia I 103 B6
Formígine I 81 B4
Formigliana I 70 C3
Formiguères F 91 A5
Fornalutx E 97 B2
Fornåsa S 37 D2
Fornelli I 110 B1
Fornells E 97 A4
Fornelos de Montes E 87 B2
Fornes E 100 C2
Forneset N 112 C8
Forni Avoltri I 72 B2
Forni di Sopra I 72 B2
Forni di Sotto I 72 B2
Forno
Piemonte I 70 C3
Piemonte I 79 A6
Forno Alpi-Gráie I 70 C2
Forno di Zoldo I 72 B2
Fornos de Algodres P 92 A3
Fornovo di Taro I 81 B4
Foros do Arrão P 92 B2
Forråskut H 75 B4
Forres GB 23 D5
Forriolo E 87 B3
Fors S 36 B3
Forsand N 33 D3
Forsbacka S 36 B3
Forserum S 40 B4
Forshaga S 35 C5
Forsheda S 40 B3
Forsinain GB 23 C5
Førslev DK 39 D4
Förslöv S 41 C2
Forsmark
Uppsala S 36 B5
Västerbotten S 115 B12
Forsmo S 115 D14
Forsnäs S 115 A15
Forsnes N 114 D5
Forssa FIN 3 F25
Forssjöbruk S 37 D3
Forst D 53 B4
Forsvik S 37 D1
Fortanete E 90 C2
Fort Augustus GB 22 D4
Forte dei Marmi I 81 C4
Fortezza I 72 B1
Forth GB 25 C4
Fort-Mahon-Plage F 48 C2
Fortrie GB 23 D6
Fortrose GB 23 D4
Fortun N 32 A4
Fortuna E 101 A4
Fortuneswell GB 29 C5
Fort William GB 24 B2
Forvik N 115 B9
Fos F 77 D3
Fosdinovo I 81 B4
Foss N 32 B6
Fossacésia I 103 A7
Fossano I 80 B1
Fossato di Vico I 82 C1
Fossbakken N 112 D6
Fosse-la-Ville B 49 C5
Fossombrone I 82 C1
Fos-sur-Mer F 78 C3
Fot H 65 C5
Fouchères F 59 B5
Fouesnant F 56 C1
Foug F 60 B1
Fougères F 57 B4
Fougerolles F 60 C2
Foulain F 59 B6
Fountainhall GB 25 C5
Fouras F 66 C3
Fourchambault F 68 A3
Fourmies F 49 C5
Fourna GR 116 C3
Fournels F 78 B2
Fourni GR 119 E1
Fournols F 68 C3
Fourques F 91 A5
Fourquevaux F 77 C4
Fours F 68 B3
Fowey GB 28 C3
Foxdale GB 26 A1
Foxford IRL 18 C2
Foyers GB 23 D4
Foynes IRL 20 B2
Foz E 86 A3
Foza I 72 C1
Foz do Arelho P 92 B1
Foz do Giraldo P 92 B3
Frabosa Soprana I 80 B1
Frades de la Sierra E 93 A5
Fraga E 90 B3
Fragagnano I 104 C3
Frailes E 100 B2
Fraire B 49 C5
Fraize F 60 B2
Framlingham GB 30 B5
Frammersbach D 51 C5
Framnes N 35 C2
França P 87 C4
Francaltroff F 60 B2
Francavilla al Mare I 103 A7
Francavilla di Sicília I 109 B4
Francavilla Fontana I 104 C3
Francavilla in Sinni I 106 A3
Francescas F 77 B3
Franco P 87 C3
Francofonte I 109 B3
Francos E 89 C3
Frändefors S 35 D4
Franeker NL 42 B2
Frangy F 69 B5
Frankenau D 51 B4
Frankenberg
Hessen D 51 B4
Sachsen D 52 C3
Frankenburg A 63 B4
Frankenfels A 63 C6
Frankenmarkt A 63 C4
Frankenthal D 61 A4
Frankfurt
Brandenburg D 45 C6
Hessen D 51 C4
Frankowo PL 47 A6
Frankrike S 115 D10
Fränsta S 115 E13
Františkovy Lázně CZ 52 C2
Franzburg D 45 A4
Frascati I 102 B5
Frasdorf D 62 C3
Fraserburgh GB 23 D6
Frashër AL 116 B2
Frasne F 69 B6
Frasnes-lez-Anvaing B 49 C4
Frasseto F 102 B2
Frastanz A 71 A4
Fratel P 92 B3
Fratta Todina I 82 D1
Frauenau D 63 B4
Frauenfeld CH 70 A3
Frauenkirchen A 64 C2
Frauenstein D 52 C3
Frauental A 73 B5
Frayssinet F 77 B4
Frayssinet-le-Gélat F 77 B4
Frechas P 87 C3
Frechen D 50 C2
Frechilla E 88 B2
Freckenhorst D 50 B3
Fredeburg D 50 B4
Fredelsloh D 51 B5
Fredeng N 34 B2
Fredensborg DK 41 D2
Fredericia DK 39 D2
Frederiks DK 39 C2
Frederikshavn DK 38 B3
Frederikssund DK 39 D5
Frederiksværk DK 39 D5
Fredrika S 115 C15
Fredriksberg S 34 B6
Fredriksdal S 40 B4
Fredrikstad N 35 C2
Fregenal de la Sierra E 99 A4
Fregene I 102 B5
Freiberg D 52 C3
Freiburg
Baden-Württemberg D 60 C3
Niedersachsen D 43 B6
Freienhagen D 51 B5
Freienhufen D 53 B3
Freiensteinau D 51 C5
Freihung D 62 A2
Freilassing D 62 C3
Freisen D 60 A3
Freising D 62 B2
Freistadt A 63 B5
Freital D 52 B3
Freixedas P 93 A3
Freixo de Espada à Cinta P 87 C4
Fréjus F 79 C5
Fremdingen D 61 B6
Frenštát pod Radhoštěm CZ 64 A4
Freren D 43 C4
Freshford IRL 21 B4
Freshwater GB 31 D2
Fresnay-sur-Sarthe F 57 B6
Fresneda de la Sierra E 95 B4
Fresneda de la Sierra Tiron E 89 B3
Fresnedillas E 94 B2
Fresnes-en-Woevre F 60 A1
Fresne-St Mamès F 69 A5
Fresno Alhandiga E 94 B1
Fresno de la Ribera E 88 C1
Fresno de la Vega E 88 B1
Fresno de Sayago E 87 C5
Fresnoy-Folny F 58 A2
Fresnoy-le-Grand F 59 A4
Fressenville F 48 C2
Fresvik N 32 A3
Fréteval F 58 C2
Fretigney F 69 A5
Freudenberg
Baden-Württemberg D 61 A5
Nordrhein-Westfalen D 50 C3
Freudenstadt D 61 B4
Freux B 49 D6
Frévent F 48 C3
Freyburg D 52 B1
Freyenstein D 44 B4
Freyming-Merlebach F 60 A2
Freystadt D 62 A2
Freyung D 63 B4
Frías de Albarracín E 95 B5
Fribourg CH 70 B2
Frick CH 70 A3
Fridafors S 41 C4
Fridaythorpe GB 27 A5
Friedberg
A 73 A6
Bayern D 62 B1
Hessen D 51 C4
Friedeburg D 43 B4
Friedewald D 51 C5
Friedland
Brandenburg D 53 A4
Mecklenburg-Vorpommern D 45 B5
Niedersachsen D 51 B5
Friedrichroda D 51 C6
Friedrichsdorf D 51 C4
Friedrichshafen D 61 C5
Friedrichskoog D 43 A5
Friedrichstadt D 43 A6
Friedrichswalde D 45 B5
Friesach A 73 B4
Friesack D 44 C4
Friesenheim D 60 B3
Friesoythe D 43 B4
Friggesund S 115 F13
Frigiliana E 100 C2
Frihetsli N 112 D8
Frillesås S 40 B2
Frinnaryd S 40 B4
Frinton-on-Sea GB 31 C5
Friockheim GB 25 B5
Friol E 86 A3
Fristad S 40 B2
Fritsla S 40 B2
Fritzlar D 51 B5
Frizington GB 26 A2
Frödinge S 40 B6
Froges F 69 C5
Frohburg D 52 B2
Frohnhausen D 50 C4
Frohnleiten A 73 A5
Froissy F 58 A3
Frombork PL 47 A5
Frome GB 29 B5
Frómista E 88 B2
Fröndenberg D 50 B3
Fronsac F 76 B2
Front I 70 C2
Fronteira P 92 B3
Frontenay-Rohan-Rohan F 67 B4
Frontenhausen D 62 B3
Frontignan F 78 C2
Fronton F 77 C4
Fröseke S 40 C5
Frosinone I 103 B6
Frosolone I 103 B7
Frosta N 114 D7
Frøstrup DK 38 B1
Frosunda S 37 C5
Frouard F 60 B2
Frövi S 37 C2
Frøyset N 32 B2
Fruges F 48 C3
Frutigen CH 70 B2
Frýdek-Místek CZ 65 A4
Frýdlant CZ 53 C5
Frydlant nad Ostravicí CZ 65 A4
Frygnowo PL 47 B6
Fryšták CZ 64 A3
Fucécchio I 81 C4
Fuencaliente
Ciudad Real E 94 C3
Ciudad Real E 100 A1
Fuencemillán E 95 B3
Fuendejalón E 89 C5
Fuengirola E 100 C1
Fuenlabrada E 94 B3
Fuenlabrada de los Montes E 94 C2
Fuensalida E 94 B2
Fuensanta E 101 B4
Fuensanta de Martos E 100 B2
Fuente-Álamo E 101 A4
Fuente-Álamo de Murcia E 101 B4
Fuentealbilla E 96 B1
Fuente al Olmo de Iscar E 88 C2
Fuentecén E 88 C3
Fuente Dé E 88 A2
Fuente de Cantos E 99 A4
Fuente del Arco E 99 A5
Fuente del Conde E 100 B1
Fuente del Maestre E 93 C4
Fuente de Santa Cruz E 94 A2
Fuente el Fresno E 94 C3
Fuente el Saz de Jarama E 95 B3
Fuente el Sol E 94 A2
Fuenteguinaldo E 93 A4
Fuentelapeña E 88 C1
Fuentelcésped E 89 C3
Fuentelespino de Haro E 95 C4
Fuentelespino de Moya E 95 C5
Fuentenovilla E 95 B3
Fuente Obejuna E 99 A5
Fuente Palmera E 99 B5
Fuentepelayo E 94 A2
Fuentepinilla E 89 C4
Fuenterroble de Salvatierra E 93 A5
Fuenterrobles E 96 B1
Fuentes E 95 C4
Fuentesauco E 88 C2
Fuentesaúco E 94 A1
Fuentes de Andalucía E 99 B5
Fuentes de Ebro E 90 B2
Fuentes de Jiloca E 89 C5
Fuentes de la Alcarria E 95 B4
Fuentes de León E 99 A4
Fuentes de Nava E 88 B2
Fuentes de Oñoro E 93 A4
Fuentes de Ropel E 88 B1
Fuentespalda E 90 C3
Fuentespina E 88 C3
Fuente-Tójar E 100 B1
Fuente Vaqueros E 100 B2
Fuentidueña E 88 C3
Fuentidueña de Tajo E 95 B3
Fuerte del Rey E 100 B2
Fügen A 72 A1
Fuglebjerg DK 39 D4
Fuglevik N 35 C2
Fuhrberg D 44 C1
Fulda D 51 C5
Fulgatore I 108 B1
Fully CH 70 B2
Fulnek CZ 64 A3
Fülöpszállás H 75 B4
Fulpmes A 71 A6
Fulunäs S 34 A5
Fumay F 49 D5
Fumel F 77 B3
Funäsdalen S 115 E9
Fundão P 92 A3
Funzie GB 22 A8
Furadouro P 87 D2
Fure N 32 A2
Fürstenau D 43 C4
Fürstenau D 51 B5
Fürstenberg D 45 B5
Fürstenfeld A 73 A6
Fürstenfeldbruck D 62 B2
Fürstenstein D 63 B4
Fürstenwalde D 45 C6
Fürstenwerder D 45 B5
Fürstenzell D 63 B4
Fürth
Bayern D 62 A1
Hessen D 61 A4
Furth im Wald D 62 A3
Furtwangen D 61 B4
Furuby S 40 C5
Furudal S 36 A2
Furuflaten N 112 C9
Furulund S 41 D3
Furusjö S 40 B3
Fusa N 32 B2
Fuscaldo I 106 B3
Fusch an der Grossglocknerstrasse A 72 A2
Fushë Arrëz AL 105 A6
Fushë-Krujë AL 105 B5
Fusina I 72 C2
Fusio CH 70 B3
Füssen D 62 C1
Fustiñana E 89 B5
Futog SRB 75 C4
Futrikelv N 112 C8
Füzesabony H 65 C6
Füzesgyarmat H 75 A6
Fužine HR 73 C4
Fyllinge S 40 C2
Fynshav DK 39 E2
Fyresdal N 33 C5

G

Gaaldorf A 73 A4
Gabaldón E 95 C5
Gabarret F 76 C2
Gabčíkovo SK 64 C3
Gąbin PL 47 C5
Gabriac F 78 B1
Gabrovo BG 11 E8
Gaby I 70 C2
Gacé F 58 B1
Gacko BIH 84 C3
Gäddede S 115 C11
Gadebusch D 44 B3
Gadmen CH 70 B3
Gádor E 101 C3
Gádoros H 75 B5
Gael F 57 B3
Găeşti RO 11 D8
Gaeta I 103 B6
Gafanhoeira P 92 C2
Gaflenz A 63 C5
Gagarin RUS 7 D13
Gaggenau D 61 B4
Gagliano Castelferrato I 109 B3
Gagliano del Capo I 107 B5
Gagnet S 36 B2
Gaibanella I 81 B5
Gaildorf D 61 B5
Gaillac F 77 C4
Gaillefontaine F 58 A2
Gaillon F 58 A2
Gainsborough GB 27 B5
Gairloch GB 22 D3
Gairlochy GB 24 B3
Gáiro I 110 C2
Gaj
HR 74 C2
SRB 85 B6
Gaja-la-Selve F 77 C4
Gajanejos E 95 B4
Gajary SK 64 B2
Gajdobra SRB 75 C4
Galan F 77 C3
Galanta SK 64 B3
Galapagar E 94 B2
Galápagos E 95 B3
Galaroza E 99 B4
Galashiels GB 25 C5
Galaţi RO 11 D10
Galatina I 107 A5
Galatista GR 116 B5
Galátone I 107 A5
Galaxidi GR 117 D4
Galdakao E 89 A4
Galeata I 81 C5
Galende E 87 B4
Galéria F 102 A1
Galgamácsa H 65 C5
Galgate GB 26 B3
Galgon F 76 B2
Galinduste E 93 A5
Galinoporni CY 120 A3
Galisteo E 93 B4
Galizes P 92 A3
Galków PL 55 B4
Gallarate I 70 C3
Gallardon F 58 B2
Gallegos de Argañán E 93 A4
Gallegos del Solmirón E 93 A5
Galleguillos de Campos E 88 B1
Galleno I 81 C4
Galliate I 70 C3
Gallicano I 81 B4
Gállio I 72 C1
Gallipoli = Gelibolu TR 118 B1
Gallipoli I 107 A4
Gällivare S 112 E9
Gallizien A 73 B4
Gallneukirchen A 63 B5
Gällö S 115 E12
Gallocanta E 95 B5
Gällstad S 40 B3
Gallur E 90 B1
Galmisdale GB 24 B1
Galmpton GB 29 C4
Galston GB 24 C3
Galta N 33 C2
Galtelli I 110 B2
Galten DK 39 C2
Galtür A 71 B5
Galve de Sorbe E 95 A3
Galveias P 92 B2
Gálvez E 94 C2
Galway IRL 20 A2
Gamaches F 48 D2
Gámbara I 71 C5
Gambárie I 106 C2
Gambassi Terme I 81 C4
Gambatesa I 103 B7
Gambolò I 70 C3
Gaming A 63 C6
Gamla Uppsala S 36 C4
Gamleby S 40 B6
Gamlingay GB 30 B3
Gammelgarn S 37 E5
Gammelstad S 3 D25
Gammertingen D 61 B5
Gams CH 71 A4
Gamvik
Finnmark N 113 A17
Finnmark N 113 B11
Gan F 76 C2
Gáname E 87 C4
Ganda di Martello I 71 B5
Gandarela P 87 C2
Ganddal N 33 D2
Ganderkesee D 43 B5
Gandesa E 90 B3
Gandía E 96 C2
Gandino I 71 C4
Gandrup DK 38 B3
Ganges F 78 C2
Gånghester S 40 B3
Gangi I 109 B3
Gangkofen D 62 B3
Gannat F 68 B3
Gannay-sur-Loire F 68 B3
Gänserdorf A 64 B2
Ganzlin D 44 B4
Gap F 79 B5
Gara H 75 B4
Garaballa E 96 B1
Garaguso I 104 C2
Garbayuela E 94 C1
Garbhallt GB 24 B2
Garbsen D 43 C6
Garching D 62 B3
Garciaz E 93 B5
Garcihernández E 94 B1
Garcillán E 94 B2
Garcinarro E 95 B4
Garcisobaco E 99 C5
Garda I 71 C5
Gardanne F 79 C4
Gårdås S 40 B3
Gårdby S 41 C6
Gardeja PL 47 B4
Gardelegen D 44 C3
Gardermoen N 34 B3
Gardiki GR 116 D3
Garding D 43 A5
Gardone Riviera I 71 C5
Gardone Val Trómpia I 71 C5
Gárdony H 74 A3
Gardouch F 77 C4
Gårdsjö S 37 D1
Gårdskär S 36 B4
Gards Köpinge S 41 D4
Garein F 76 B2
Garelochhead GB 24 B3
Garéoult F 79 C5
Garešnica HR 74 C1
Garéssio I 80 B2
Garforth GB 27 B4
Gargaliani GR 117 E3
Gargaligas E 93 B5
Gargallo E 90 C2
Garganta la Olla E 93 A5
Gargantiel E 100 A1
Gargellen A 71 B4
Gargilesse-Dampierre F 67 B6
Gargnano I 71 C5
Gargnäs S 115 B14
Gárgoles de Abajo E 95 B4
Gargrave GB 26 B3
Garitz D 52 B2
Garlasco I 70 C3
Garlieston GB 24 D3
Garlin F 76 C2
Garlitos E 94 D1
Garmisch-Partenkirchen D 71 A6
Garnat-sur-Engièvre F 68 B3
Garpenberg S 36 B3
Garphyttan S 37 C1
Garray E 89 C4
Garrel D 43 C5
Garriguella E 91 A6
Garrison GB 18 B3
Garrovillas E 93 B4
Garrucha E 101 B4
Gars-am-Kamp A 63 B6
Garsås S 36 B1
Garsdale Head GB 26 A3
Gärsnäs S 41 D4
Garstang GB 26 B3
Gartow D 44 B3
Gartz D 45 B6
Gærum DK 38 B3
Garvagh GB 19 B5
Garvão P 98 B2
Garve GB 22 D4
Garwolin PL 55 B6
Garz D 45 A5
Garzyn PL 54 B1
Gąsawa PL 46 C3
Gåsborn S 34 C6
Gaschurn A 71 B5
Gascueña E 95 B4
Gasny F 58 A2
Gąsocin PL 47 C6
Gastes F 76 B1
Gastouni GR 117 E3
Gastouri GR 116 C1
Gata
E 93 A4
HR 83 C5
Gata de Gorgos E 96 C3
Gatchina RUS 7 B11
Gatehouse of Fleet GB 24 D3
Gátér H 75 B4
Gateshead GB 25 D6
Gátova E 96 B2
Gattendorf A 64 B2
Gatteo a Mare I 82 B1
Gattinara I 70 C3
Gattorna I 80 B3
Gaucín E 99 C5
Gaulstad N 114 D9
Gaupne N 32 A4
Gautefall N 33 C5
Gauting D 62 B2
Gauto S 115 A13
Gava E 91 B5
Gavardo I 71 C5
Gavarnie F 76 D2
Gávi I 80 B2
Gavião P 92 B3
Gavirate I 70 C3
Gävle S 36 B4
Gavoi I 110 B2
Gavorrano I 81 D4
Gavray F 57 B4
Gavrio GR 117 E6
Gävunda S 34 B6
Gaweinstal A 64 B2
Gaworzyce PL 53 B5
Gawroniec PL 46 B2
Gaydon GB 30 B2
Gayton GB 30 B4
Gazipaşa TR 119 F7
Gazoldo degli Ippoliti I 71 C5
Gazzuolo I 81 A4
Gbelce SK 65 C4
Gdańsk PL 47 A4
Gdinj HR 84 C1
Gdov RUS 7 B9
Gdów PL 65 A6
Gdynia PL 47 A4
Gea de Albarracin E 95 B5
Geary GB 22 D2
Géaudot F 59 B5
Geaune F 76 C2
Gebesee D 51 B6
Gebiz TR 119 E5
Gebze TR 118 B4
Géderlak H 75 B3
Gedern D 51 C5
Gedinne B 49 D5
Gediz TR 118 D4
Gèdre F 76 D3
Gedser DK 44 A3
Gedsted DK 38 C2
Geel B 49 B5
Geesthacht D 44 B2
Geetbets B 49 C6
Gefell D 52 C1
Gehrden D 51 A5
Gehren D 52 C1
Geilenkirchen D 50 C2
Geilo N 32 B5
Geinsheim D 61 A4
Geisa D 51 C5
Geiselhöring D 62 B3
Geiselwind D 61 A6
Geisenfeld D 62 B2
Geisenhausen D 62 B3
Geisenheim D 50 D4
Geising D 53 C3
Geisingen D 61 C4
Geislingen D 61 B5
Geistthal A 73 A5
Geiterygghytta N 32 B4
Geithain D 52 B2
Geithus N 34 C1
Gela I 109 B3
Geldermalsen NL 49 B6
Geldern D 50 B2
Geldrop NL 49 B6
Geleen NL 50 C1
Gelembe TR 118 C2
Gelendost TR 119 D6
Gelibolu = Gallipoli TR 118 B1
Gelida E 91 B4
Gelnhausen D 51 C5
Gelnica SK 65 B6
Gelsa E 90 B2
Gelse H 74 B1
Gelsenkirchen D 50 B3
Gelsted DK 39 D2
Geltendorf D 62 B2
Gelterkinden CH 70 A2
Gelting D 39 E2
Gelu RO 75 B6
Gelves E 99 B4
Gembloux B 49 C5
Gemeaux F 69 A5
Gémenos F 79 C4
Gemerská Poloma SK 65 B6
Gemerská Ves SK 65 B6
Gemert NL 50 B1
Gemla S 40 C4
Gemlik TR 118 B4
Gemmenich B 50 C1
Gemona del Friuli I 72 B3
Gémozac F 67 C4
Gemund D 50 C2
Gemünden
Bayern D 51 C5
Hessen D 51 C4
Rheinland-Pfalz D 60 A3
Genappe B 49 C5
Génave E 101 A3
Genazzano I 102 B5
Gençay F 67 B5
Gencsapáti H 74 A1
Gendringen NL 50 B2
Genelard F 68 B4
Genemuiden NL 42 C3
Generalski Stol HR 73 C5
Geneva = Genève CH 69 B6
Genevad S 40 C3
Genève = Geneva CH 69 B6
Genevriéres F 60 C1
Gengenbach D 61 B4
Genillé F 67 A6
Genk B 49 C6
Genlis F 69 A5
Gennep NL 50 B1
Genner DK 39 D2
Gennes F 67 A4
Genoa = Génova I 80 B2
Genola I 80 B1
Génova = Genoa I 80 B2
Genowefa PL 54 A3
Gensingen D 60 A3
Gent = Ghent B 49 B4
Genthin D 44 C4
Gentioux F 68 C1
Genzano di Lucánia I 104 C2
Genzano di Roma I 102 B5
Georgenthal D 51 C6
Georgsmarienhütte D 50 A4
Gera D 52 C2
Geraards-bergen B 49 C4
Gerace I 106 C3
Geraci Sículo I 109 B3
Geraki GR 117 F4
Gérardmer F 60 B2
Geras A 63 B6
Gerbéviller F 60 B2
Gerbini I 109 B3
Gerbstedt D 52 B1
Gerði IS 111 C9
Gerede TR 118 B7
Gerena E 99 B4
Geretsried D 62 C2
Gérgal E 101 B3
Gergy F 69 B4
Gerindote E 94 C2
Gerjen H 74 B3
Gerlos A 72 A2
Germay F 59 B6
Germencik TR 119 E2
Germering D 62 B2
Germersheim D 61 A4
Gërneç AL 105 C5
Gernika-Lumo E 89 A4
Gernrode D 52 B1
Gernsbach D 61 B4
Gernsheim D 61 A4
Geroda D 51 C5
Gerola Alta I 71 B4
Geroldsgrun D 52 C1
Gerolsbach D 62 B2
Gerolstein D 50 C2
Gerolzhofen D 61 A6
Gerovo HR 73 C4
Gerpinnes B 49 C5
Gerrards Cross GB 31 C3
Gerri de la Sal E 91 A4
Gersfeld D 51 C5
Gerstetten D 61 B6
Gersthofen D 62 B1
Gerstungen D 51 C6
Gerswalde D 45 B5
Gerzat F 68 C3
Gerze TR 16 A7
Gerzen D 62 B3
Gescher D 50 B3
Geseke D 51 B4
Geslau D 61 A6
Gespunsart F 59 A5
Gesté F 66 A3
Gestorf D 51 A5
Gesualda I 103 C8
Gesunda S 36 B1
Geta FIN 36 B6
Getafe E 94 B3
Getinge S 40 C2
Getxo E 89 A4
Geversdorf D 43 B6
Gevgelija MK 116 A4
Gevora del Caudillo E 93 C4
Gevrey-Chambertin F 69 A4
Gex F 69 B6
Gey D 50 C2
Geyikli TR 118 C1
Geysir IS 111 C5
Geyve TR 118 B5
Gföhl A 63 B6
Ghedi I 71 C5
Ghent = Gent B 49 B4
Gheorgheni RO 11 C8
Ghigo I 79 B6
Ghilarza I 110 B1
Ghisonaccia F 102 A2
Ghisoni F 102 A2
Gialtra GR 116 D4
Gianitsa GR 116 B4
Giardinetto Vécchio I 103 B8
Giardini Naxos I 109 B4
Giarratana I 109 B3
Giarre I 109 B4
Giat F 68 C2
Giaveno I 80 A1
Giazza I 71 C6
Giba I 110 C1
Gibellina Nuova I 108 B1
Gibostad N 112 C7
Gibraleón E 99 B4
Gibraltar GBZ 99 C5
Gic H 74 A2
Gideå S 115 D16
Gideåkroken S 115 C14
Gidle PL 55 C4
Giebelstadt D 61 A5
Gieboldehausen D 51 B6
Gielniów PL 55 B5
Gielow D 45 B4
Gien F 58 C3
Giengen D 61 B6
Giens F 79 C5
Giera RO 75 C5
Gieselwerder D 51 B5
Giessen D 51 C4
Gieten NL 42 B3
Giethoorn NL 42 C3
Giffaumont-Champaubert F 59 B5
Gifford GB 25 C5
Gifhorn D 44 C2
Gige H 74 B2
Giglio Porto I 102 A3
Gignac F 78 C2
Gijón = Xixón E 88 A1
Gilena E 100 B1
Gilford GB 19 B5
Gilleberga S 35 C4
Gilleleje DK 41 C2
Gilley F 69 A6
Gilley-sur-Loire F 68 B3
Gillingham
Dorset GB 29 B5
Medway GB 31 C4
Gilocourt F 58 A3
Gilserberg D 51 C5
Gilsland GB 25 D5
Gilze NL 49 B5
Gimåt S 115 D15
Gimo S 36 B5
Gimont F 77 C3
Ginasservis F 79 C4
Gingelom B 49 C6
Gingst D 45 A5
Ginosa I 104 C2
Ginzling A 72 A1
Giões P 98 B3
Gióia dei Marsi I 103 B6
Gióia del Colle I 104 C2
Gióia Sannitica I 103 B7
Gióia Tauro I 106 C2
Gioiosa Iónica I 106 C3
Gioiosa Marea I 109 A3
Giosla GB 22 C2
Giovinazzo I 104 B2
Girifalco I 106 C3
Giromagny F 60 C2
Girona E 91 B5
Gironcourt-sur-Vraine F 60 B1
Gironella E 91 A4
Gironville-sous-les-Côtes F 60 B1
Girvan GB 24 C3
Gislaved S 40 B3
Gislev DK 39 D3
Gisors F 58 A2
Gissi I 103 A7
Gistad S 37 D2
Gistel B 48 B3
Gistrup DK 38 C3
Giswil CH 70 B3
Githio GR 117 F4
Giugliano in Campania I 103 C7
Giulianova I 82 D2
Giulvăz RO 75 C5
Giurgiu RO 11 E8
Give DK 39 D2
Givet F 49 C5
Givors F 69 C4
Givry
B 49 C5
F 69 B4
Givry-en-Argonne F 59 B5
Givskud DK 39 D2
Giżalki PL 54 A2
Gizeux F 67 A5
Giżycko PL 6 D6
Gizzeria I 106 C3
Gizzeria Lido I 106 C3
Gjedved DK 39 D2
Gjegjan AL 105 B6
Gjendesheim N 32 A5
Gjerde N 32 B3
Gjerlev DK 38 C3
Gjermundshamn N 32 B2
Gjerrild DK 38 C3
Gjerstad N 33 D6
Gjesås N 34 B4
Gjesvær N 113 A14
Gjirokastër AL 116 B2
Gjøfjell N 35 C2
Gjøl DK 38 B2
Gjøra N 114 E6
Gjøvik N 34 B2
Gladbeck D 50 B2
Gladenbach D 51 C4
Gladstad N 114 B8
Glamis GB 25 B5
Glamoč BIH 84 B1
Glamsbjerg DK 39 D3
Gland CH 69 B6
Glandorf D 50 A3
Glanegg A 73 B4
Glanshammar S 37 C2
Glarus CH 70 A4
Glasgow GB 24 C3
Glashütte
Bayern D 62 C2
Sachsen D 53 C3
Glastonbury GB 29 B5
Glatzau A 73 B5
Glauchau D 52 C2
Glava S 35 C4
Glavatičevo BIH 84 C3
Glavičice BIH 85 B4
Glavnik KOS 85 D6
Gledica SRB 85 C5
Glein
A 73 A4
N 115 A9
Gleinstätten A 73 B5
Gleisdorf A 73 A5
Glenamoy IRL 18 B2
Glenarm GB 19 B6
Glenavy GB 19 B5
Glenbarr GB 24 C2
Glenbeigh IRL 20 B2
Glenbrittle GB 22 D2
Glencoe GB 24 B2
Glencolumbkille IRL 18 B3
Glendalough IRL 21 A5
Glenealy IRL 21 B5
Glenelg GB 22 D3
Glenfinnan GB 24 B2
Glengarriff IRL 20 C2
Glenluce GB 24 D3
Glennamaddy IRL 18 C3
Glenrothes GB 25 B4
Glenties IRL 18 B3
Glesborg DK 38 C3
Glesien D 52 B2
Gletsch CH 70 B3
Glewitz D 45 A4
Glifada GR 117 E5
Glimåkra S 41 C4
Glin IRL 20 B2
Glina HR 73 C6
Glinde D 44 B2
Glinojeck PL 47 C6
Glinsk IRL 20 A2
Gliwice PL 54 C3
Glödnitz A 73 B4
Gloggnitz A 64 C1
Głogoczów PL 65 A5
Glogonj SRB 85 B5
Glogovac SRB 85 B6
Głogów PL 53 B6
Głogówek PL 54 C2
Glomel F 56 B2
Glomfjord N 112 F2
Glommen S 40 C2
Glommersträsk S 115 B16
Glonn D 62 C2
Glorenza I 71 B5
Gloria P 92 B2
Glosa GR 116 C5
Glossop GB 27 B4
Gloucester GB 29 B5
Głowaczów PL 55 B6
Główczyce PL 46 A3
Glöwen D 44 C4
Głowno PL 55 B4
Gložan SRB 75 C4
Głubczyce PL 54 C2
Głuchołazy PL 54 C2
Głuchów PL 55 B5
Głuchowo PL 54 A1
Glücksburg D 39 E2
Glückstadt D 43 B6
Glumina BIH 84 B4
Glumsø DK 39 D4
Glušci SRB 85 B4
Glusk BY 7 E10
Głuszyca PL 53 C6
Glyngøre DK 38 C1
Glyn Neath GB 29 B4
Gmünd
Kärnten A 72 B3
Nieder Östereich A 63 B5
Gmund D 62 C2
Gmunden A 63 C4
Gnarp S 115 E14
Gnarrenburg D 43 B6
Gnesau A 72 B3
Gnesta S 37 C4
Gnięchowice PL 54 B1
Gniew PL 47 B4
Gniewkowo PL 47 C4
Gniezno PL 46 C3
Gnoien D 45 B4
Gnojnice BIH 84 C2
Gnojno PL 55 C5
Gnosall GB 26 C3
Gnosjö S 40 B3
Göbel TR 118 B3
Göçbeyli TR 118 C2
Goch D 50 B2
Gochsheim D 51 C6
Göd H 65 C5
Godalming GB 31 C3
Godby FIN 36 B6
Goðdalir IS 111 B6
Goddelsheim D 51 B4
Gódega di Sant'Urbano I 72 C2
Godegård S 37 D2
Godelheim D 51 B5
Goderville F 58 A1
Godiasco I 80 B3
Godič SLO 73 B4
Godkowo PL 47 A5
Godmanchester GB 30 B3
Gödöllő H 65 C5
Gödre H 74 B2
Godshill GB 31 D2
Godzikowice PL 54 C2
Godziszewo PL 47 A4
Goes NL 49 B4
Goetzenbrück F 60 B3
Góglio I 70 B3
Gogolin PL 54 C3
Göhren D 45 A5
Goirle NL 49 B6
Góis P 92 A2
Góito I 71 C5
Goizueta E 76 C1
Gojna Gora SRB 85 C5
Gójsk PL 47 C5
Gökçedağ TR 118 C3
Gökçen TR 119 D2
Gökçeören TR 119 D3
Gökçeyazı TR 118 C2
Göktepe TR 119 E3
Gol N 32 B5
Gola
HR 74 B2
N 34 A1
Gołańcz PL 46 C3
Gölbaşı TR 16 B6
Gölby FIN 36 B6
Gölcük
Kocaeli TR 118 B4
Niğde TR 16 B7
Golčův Jenikov CZ 63 A6
Gołczewo PL 45 B6
Goldach CH 71 A4
Goldbach D 51 C5
Goldbeck D 44 C3
Goldberg D 44 B4
Goldelund D 43 A6
Goldenstedt D 43 C5
Gołdopiwo PL 47 A6
Golegã P 92 B2
Goleniów PL 45 B6
Golfo Aranci I 110 B2
Gölhisar TR 119 E4
Golina PL 54 A3

Gölle H 74 B3
Göllersdorf A 64 B2
Golling an der Salzach
A 63 C4
Gölmarmara TR 118 D2
Golnice PL 53 B5
Golnik SLO 73 B4
Gölova TR 119 F5
Gölpazarı TR 118 B5
Gols A 64 C2
Golspie GB 23 D5
Golssen D 52 B3
Golubac SRB 85 B6
Golub-Dobrzyń PL 47 B5
Golubinci SRB 85 B5
Goluboviči MNE 105 A5
Gołuchów PL 54 B2
Golzow D 52 A2
Gomagoi I 71 B5
Gómara E 89 C4
Gomaringen D 61 B5
Gömbe TR 119 F4
Gömeç TR 118 C1
Gomel = Homyel BY 7 E11
Gomes Aires P 98 B2
Gómezserracín E 88 C2
Gommern D 52 A1
Gomulin PL 55 B4
Gonäs S 36 B2
Goncelin F 69 C5
Gończyce PL 55 B6
Gondomar
E 87 B2
P 87 C2
Gondrecourt-le-Château
F 60 B1
Gondrin F 76 C3
Gönen
Balıkesir TR 118 B2
Isparta TR 119 E5
Gonfaron F 79 C5
Goñi E 76 D1
Goni
GR 116 C4
I 110 C2
Gonnesa I 110 C1
Gonnosfanádiga I 110 C1
Gönyü H 64 C3
Gonzaga I 81 B4
Goodrich GB 29 B5
Goodwick GB 28 A2
Gooik B 49 C5
Goole GB 27 B5
Goor NL 50 A2
Göpfritz an der Wild
A 63 B6
Goppenstein CH 70 B2
Göppingen D 61 B5
Gor E 100 B3
Góra
Dolnośląskie PL 54 B1
Mazowieckie PL 47 C6
Gorafe E 100 B2
Góra Kalwaria PL 55 B6
Gorawino PL 46 B1
Goražde BIH 84 C3
Gordaliza del Pino E 88 B1
Gördes TR 118 D3
Gørding DK 39 D1
Górdola CH 70 B3
Gordon GB 25 C5
Gordoncillo E 88 B1
Gorebridge GB 25 C4
Gorenja Vas SLO 73 B4
Gorenje Jelenje HR 73 C4
Gorey
GB 57 A3
IRL 21 B5
Gorgonzola I 71 C4
Gorica HR 83 B4
Gorican HR 74 B1
Gorinchem NL 49 B5
Goring GB 31 C2
Goritsy RUS 7 C14
Göritz D 45 B5
Gorizia I 72 C3
Górki PL 47 C5
Gorleben D 44 B3
Gorleston-on-sea GB 30 B5
Gørlev DK 39 D4
Görlitz D 53 B4
Górliz E 89 A4
Görmin D 45 B5
Górna Grupa PL 47 B4
Gorna Oryakhovitsa
BG 11 E8
Gornja Gorevnica
SRB 85 C5
Gornja Klina KOS 85 D5
Gornja Ploča HR 83 B4
Gornja Radgona SLO 73 B5
Gornja Sabanta SRB 85 C6
Gornja Trešnjevica
SRB 85 B5
Gornja Tuzla BIH 84 B3
Gornje Polje MNE 84 D3
Gornje Ratkovo BIH 84 B1
Gornji Grad SLO 73 B4
Gornji Humac HR 83 C5
Gornji Jasenjani BIH 84 C2
Gornji Kamengrad
BIH 83 B5
Gornji Kneginec HR 73 B6
Gornji Kokoti MNE 105 A5
Gornji Kosinj HR 83 B4
Gornji Milanovac
SRB 85 B5
Gornji Podgradci BIH 84 A2
Gornji Ravno BIH 84 C2
Gornji Sjenicak HR 73 C5
Gornji Vakuf BIH 84 C2
Górno PL 55 C5
Görömböly H 65 B6
Górowo Iławeckie
PL 47 A6
Gorran Haven GB 28 C3
Gorredijk NL 42 B3
Gorron F 57 B5
Gorseinon GB 28 B3
Gort IRL 20 A3
Gortin GB 19 B4
Görzke D 52 A2
Gorzkowice PL 55 B4
Gòrzno
Kujawsko-Pomorskie
PL 47 B5
Zachodnio-Pomorskie
PL 46 B1
Gorzów Śląski PL 54 B3
Gorzów Wielkopolski
PL 45 C7
Górzyca PL 45 C6
Gorzyce PL 54 D3
Górzyn PL 53 B4
Gorzyń PL 46 C1
Gorzyno PL 46 A3
Gosaldo I 72 B1
Gosau A 63 C4
Gosberton GB 30 B3
Gościcino PL 47 A4
Gościęcin PL 54 C3
Gościm PL 46 C1
Gościno PL 46 A1
Gosdorf A 73 B5
Gosforth GB 26 A2
Goslar D 51 B6
Goslice PL 47 C5
Gospič HR 83 B4
Gosport GB 31 D2
Gössäter S 35 D5
Gossau CH 71 A4
Goss Ilsede D 51 A6
Gössnitz D 52 C2
Gössweinstein D 62 A2
Gostimë AL 105 C6
Gostkow PL 55 B4
Göstling an der Ybbs
A 63 C5
Gostomia PL 46 B2
Gostycyn PL 46 B3
Gostyń PL 54 B2
Gostynin PL 47 C5
Goszczyn PL 55 B5
Göta S 35 D4
Göteborg = Gothenburg
S 38 B4
Götene S 35 D5
Gotha D 51 C6
Gothem S 37 E5
Gothenburg = Göteborg
S 38 B4
Gotse Delchev BG 116 A5
Gottersdorf D 62 B3
Göttingen D 51 B5
Gottne S 115 D15
Götzis A 71 A4
Gouarec F 56 B2
Gouda NL 49 A5
Goudhurst GB 31 C4
Goumenissa GR 116 B4
Goura GR 117 E4
Gourdon F 77 B4
Gourgançon F 59 B5
Gourin F 56 B2
Gournay-en-Bray F 58 A2
Gourock GB 24 C3
Gouveia P 92 A3
Gouvy B 50 C1
Gouzeacourt F 49 C4
Gouzon F 68 B2
Govedari HR 84 D2
Govérnolo I 81 A4
Gowarczów PL 55 B5
Gowerton GB 28 B3
Gowidlino PL 46 A3
Gowran IRL 21 B4
Goyatz D 53 A4
Göynük
TR 118 B5
Antalya TR 119 F5
Gozdnica PL 53 B5
Gozdowo PL 47 C5
Gozee B 49 C5
Graal-Müritz D 44 A4
Grab BIH 84 D3
Grabenstätt D 62 C3
Grabhair GB 22 C2
Gråbo S 38 B5
Grabovac
HR 84 C1
SRB 85 B5
Grabovci SRB 85 B4
Grabow D 44 B3
Grabów PL 55 A4
Grabów nad Pilicą PL 55 B6
Grabów nad Prosną
PL 54 B3
Grabowno PL 46 B3
Grabs CH 71 A4
Gračac HR 83 B4
Gračanica
BIH 84 B3
KOS 85 D6
Graçay F 68 A1
Gracen AL 105 B5
Grad SLO 73 B6
Gradac
BIH 84 D3
HR 84 C2
MNE 85 C4
SRB 85 C5
Gradačac BIH 84 B3
Gradec HR 74 C1
Gradefes E 88 B1
Grades A 73 B4
Gradil P 92 C1
Gradina
HR 74 C2
MNE 85 C4
Gradisca d'Isonzo I 72 C3
Gradište HR 74 C3
Grado
E 86 A4
I 72 C3
Grafenau D 63 B4
Gräfenberg D 62 A2
Gräfenhainichen D 52 B2
Grafenschlag A 63 B6
Grafenstein A 73 B4
Gräfenthal D 52 C1
Grafentonna D 51 B6
Grafenwöhr D 62 A2
Grafing D 62 B2
Grafling D 62 B3
Gräfsnäs S 40 A2
Gragnano I 103 C7
Grahovo
MNE 84 D3
SLO 72 B3
Graiguenamanagh
IRL 21 B5
Grain GB 31 C4
Grainau D 71 A6
Graja de Iniesta E 95 C5
Grajera E 89 C3
Gram DK 39 D2
Gramais A 71 A5
Gramat F 77 B4
Gramatneusiedl A 64 B2
Grambow D 45 B6
Grammichele I 109 B3
Gramsh AL 116 B2
Gramzow D 45 B6
Gran N 34 B2
Granada E 100 B2
Granard IRL 19 C4
Grañas E 86 A3
Granátula de Calatrava
E 100 A2
Grancey-le-Château
F 59 C6
Grandas de Salime E 86 A4
Grandcamp-Maisy F 57 A4
Grand-Champ F 56 C3
Grand Couronne F 58 A2
Grand-Fougeray F 57 C4
Grândola P 98 A2
Grandpré F 59 A5
Grandrieu
B 49 C5
F 78 B2
Grandson CH 70 B1
Grandvillars F 70 A1
Grandvilliers F 58 A2
Grañén E 90 B2
Grangärde S 36 B1
Grange IRL 18 B3
Grangemouth GB 25 B4
Grange-over-Sands
GB 26 A3
Grängesberg S 36 B1
Granges-de Crouhens
F 77 D3
Granges-sur-Vologne
F 60 B2
Gräningen D 44 C4
Granitola-Torretta I 108 B1
Granja
Évora P 98 A3
Porto P 87 C2
Granja de Moreruela
E 88 C1
Granja de Torrehermosa
E 93 C5
Gränna S 40 A4
Grannäs
Västerbotten S 115 B13
Västerbotten S 115 B14
Granö S 115 C16
Granollers E 91 B5
Granowiec PL 54 B2
Granowo PL 54 A1
Gransee D 45 B5
Gransherad N 33 C6
Grantham GB 27 C5
Grantown-on-Spey
GB 23 D5
Grantshouse GB 25 C5
Granville F 57 B4
Granvin N 32 B3
Græerup Strand DK 39 D1
Gräsås S 40 C2
Grasbakken N 113 B17
Grasberg D 43 B6
Grasmere GB 26 A2
Gräsmyr S 115 D16
Grasö S 36 B5
Grassano I 104 C2
Grassau D 62 C3
Grasse F 79 C5
Grassington GB 27 A4
Græsted DK 41 C2
Gråsten DK 39 E2
Grästorp S 35 D4
Gratkorn A 73 A5
Gråträsk S 115 B16
Gratwein A 73 A5
Graulhet F 77 C4
Graus E 90 A3
Grávalos E 89 B5
Gravberget N 34 B4
Grave NL 50 B1
Gravedona I 71 B4
Gravelines F 48 B3
Gravellona Toce I 70 C3
Gravendal S 36 B1
Gravens DK 39 D2
Gravesend GB 31 C4
Graveson F 78 C3
Gravina in Púglia I 104 C2
Gray F 69 A5
Grayrigg GB 26 A3
Grays GB 31 C4
Grayshott GB 31 C3
Grayvoron RUS 7 F13
Graz A 73 A5
Grazalema E 99 C5
Grążawy PL 47 B5
Grazzano Visconti I 80 B3
Greåker N 35 C3
Great Dunmow GB 31 C4
Great Malvern GB 29 A5
Great Torrington GB 28 C3
Great Waltham GB 31 C4
Great Yarmouth GB 30 B5
Grebbestad S 35 D3
Grebenstein D 51 B5
Grębocice PL 53 B6
Grębocin PL 47 B4
Greding D 62 A2
Gredstedbro DK 39 D1
Greencastle IRL 19 A4
Greenhead GB 25 D5
Greenisland GB 19 B6
Greenlaw GB 25 C5
Greenock GB 24 C3
Greenway GB 28 B3
Greenwich GB 31 C4
Grefrath D 50 B2
Greifenburg A 72 B3
Greiffenberg D 45 B5
Greifswald D 45 A5
Grein A 63 B5
Greipstad N 33 D4
Greiz D 52 C2
Grenaa DK 39 C3
Grenade F 77 C4
Grenade-sur-l'Adour
F 76 C2
Grenchen CH 70 A2
Grendi N 33 D4
Grenivík IS 111 B7
Grenoble F 69 C5
Gréoux-les-Bains F 79 C4
Gresenhorst D 44 A4
Gressoney-la-Trinité
I 70 C2
Gressoney-St-Jean I 70 C2
Gressthal D 51 C6
Gressvik N 35 C2
Gresten A 63 C6
Gretna GB 25 D4
Greussen D 51 B6
Greve in Chianti I 81 C5
Greven
Mecklenburg-Vorpommern D 44 B2
Nordrhein-Westfalen
D 50 A3
Grevena GR 116 B3
Grevenbroich D 50 B2
Grevenbrück D 50 B4
Grevenmacher L 60 A2
Grevesmühlen D 44 B3
Grevestrand DK 41 D2
Grevie S 41 C2
Greystoke GB 26 A3
Greystones IRL 21 A5
Grez-Doiceau B 49 C5
Grèzec F 77 B4
Grez-en-Bouère F 57 C5
Grezzana I 71 C6
Grgar SLO 72 B3
Grgurevci SRB 85 A4
Gries A 71 A6
Griesbach D 63 B4
Griesheim D 61 A4
Gries in Sellrain A 71 A6
Grieskirchen A 63 B4
Griffen A 73 B4
Grignan F 78 B3
Grignano I 72 C3
Grigno I 72 B1
Grignols F 76 B2
Grignon F 69 C6
Grijota E 88 B2
Grijpskerk NL 42 B3
Gril AL 105 A5
Grillby S 37 C4
Grimaud F 79 C5
Grimbergen B 49 C5
Grimma D 52 B2
Grimmen D 45 A5
Grimmialp CH 70 B2
Grimsås S 40 B3
Grimsby GB 27 B5
Grimslöv S 40 C4
Grímsstaðir IS 111 B9
Grimstad N 33 D5
Grimstorp S 40 B4
Grindavík IS 111 D3
Grindelwald CH 70 B3
Grindheim N 33 D4
Grindsted DK 39 D1
Griñón E 94 B3
Gripenberg S 40 B4
Gripsholm S 37 C4
Grisolles F 77 C4
Grisslehamn S 36 B5
Gritley GB 23 C6
Grizebeck GB 26 A2
Grndina BIH 84 B1
Gröbming A 72 A3
Gröbzig D 52 B1
Grocka SRB 85 B5
Gröditz D 52 B3
Gródki PL 47 B6
Grodków PL 54 C2
Grodziec PL 54 A3
Grodzisk Mazowiecki
PL 55 A5
Grodzisk Wielkopolski
PL 54 A1
Groenlo NL 50 A2
Groesbeek NL 50 B1
Grohote HR 83 C5
Groitzsch D 52 B2
Groix F 56 C2
Grójec PL 55 B5
Grom PL 47 B6
Gromiljca BIH 84 C3
Grömitz D 44 A2
Gromnik PL 65 A6
Gromo I 71 C4
Gronau
Niedersachsen D 51 A5
Nordrhein-Westfalen
D 50 A3
Grønbjerg DK 39 C1
Grönenbach D 61 C6
Grong N 114 C9
Grönhögen S 41 C6
Groningen
D 52 B1
NL 42 B3
Grønnestrand DK 38 B2
Grono CH 71 B4
Grönskåra S 40 B5
Grootegast NL 42 B3
Gropello Cairoli I 70 C3
Grorud N 34 C2
Grósio I 71 B5
Grošnica SRB 85 C5
Grossalmerode D 51 B5
Grossarl A 72 A3
Gross Beeren D 45 C5
Gross Berkel D 51 A5
Grossbodungen D 51 B6
Gross-botwar D 61 B5
Grossburgwedel D 44 C1
Grosschönau D 53 C4
Gross-Dölln D 45 B5
Grossenbrode D 44 A3
Grossenehrich D 51 B6
Grossengottern D 51 B6
Grossenhain D 52 B3
Grossenkneten D 43 C5
Grossenlüder D 51 C5
Grossensee D 44 B2
Grossenzersdorf A 64 B2
Grosseto I 81 D5
Gross-Gerau D 61 A4
Grossgerungs A 63 B5
Grossglobnitz A 63 B6
Grosshabersdorf D 62 A1
Grossharras A 64 B2
Grosshartmansdorf
D 52 C3
Grosshöchstetten
CH 70 B2
Gross Kreutz D 45 C4
Grosskrut A 64 B2
Gross Lafferde D 51 A6
Gross Leutheb D 53 A4
Grosslohra D 51 B6
Grossmehring D 62 B2
Gross Muckrow D 53 A4
Gross Oesingen D 44 C2
Grossostheim D 61 A5
Grosspertholz A 63 B5
Grosspetersdorf A 73 A6
Grosspostwitz D 53 B4
Grossraming A 63 C5
Grossräschen D 53 B4
Gross Reken D 50 B3
Grossrinderfeld D 61 A5
Grossröhrsdorf D 53 B4
Gross Sarau D 44 B2
Gross Särchen D 53 B4
Grossschirma D 52 C3
Gross Schönebeck D 45 C5
Grossschweinbarth A 64 B2
Grosssiegharts A 63 B6
Grosssölk A 72 A3
Gross Umstadt D 61 A4
Grosswarasdorf A 74 A1
Gross Warnow D 44 B3
Gross-Weikersdorf A 64 B1
Gross-Welle D 44 B4
Grosswilfersdorf A 73 A5
Gross Wokern D 44 B4
Grostenquin F 60 B2
Grosuplje SLO 73 C4
Grotli N 114 E4
Grötlingbo S 37 E5
Grottáglie I 104 C3
Grottaminarda I 103 B8
Grottammare I 82 D2
Grotte di Castro I 81 D5
Grotteria I 106 C3
Gróttole I 104 C2
Grouw NL 42 B2
Grov N 112 D6
Grova N 33 C5
Grove E 86 B2
Grua N 34 B2
Grube D 44 A3
Grubišno Polje HR 74 C2
Gruda HR 105 A4
Grude BIH 84 C2
Grudusk PL 47 B6
Grudziądz PL 47 B4
Grue N 34 B4
Gruissan F 78 C2
Grullos E 86 A4
Grumo Áppula I 104 B2
Grums S 35 C5
Grünau im Almtal A 63 C4
Grünberg D 51 C4
Grünburg A 63 C5
Grundarfjörður IS 111 C2
Gründau D 51 C5
Gründelhardt D 61 A5
Grundforsen S 34 A4
Grundlsee A 63 C4
Grundsund S 35 D3
Grunewald D 53 B3
Grungedal N 33 C4
Grunow D 53 A4
Grünstadt D 61 A4
Gruvberget S 36 A3
Gruyères CH 70 B2
Gruža SRB 85 C5
Grybów PL 65 A6
Grycksbo S 36 B2
Gryfice PL 45 B7
Gryfino PL 45 B6
Gryfów Śląski PL 53 B5
Gryllefjord N 112 C6
Grymyr N 34 B2
Gryt S 37 D3
Grytgöl S 37 D2
Grythyttan S 37 C1
Grytnäs S 37 D4
Grzmiąca PL 46 B2
Grzybno PL 45 B6
Grzywna PL 47 B4
Gschnitz A 71 A6
Gschwend D 61 B5
Gstaad CH 70 B2
Gsteig CH 70 B2
Guadahortuna E 100 B2
Guadalajara E 95 B3
Guadalaviar E 95 B5
Guadalcanal E 99 A5
Guadalcázar E 100 B1
Guadalix de la Sierra
E 94 B3
Guadálmez E 100 A1
Guadalupe E 93 B5
Guadamur E 94 C2
Guadarrama E 94 B2
Guadiaro E 99 C5
Guadix E 100 B2
Guagnano I 105 C3
Guagno F 102 A1
Guajar-Faragüit E 100 C2
Gualchos E 100 C2
Gualdo Tadino I 82 C1
Gualtieri I 81 B4
Guarcino I 103 B6
Guarda P 92 A3
Guardamar del Segura
E 96 C2
Guardão P 92 A2
Guardavalle I 106 C3
Guardea I 102 A5
Guárdia I 103 C8
Guardiagrele I 103 A7
Guardiarégia I 103 B7
Guárdia Sanframondi
I 103 B7
Guardias Viejas E 100 C3
Guardiola de Bergueda
E 91 A4
Guardo E 88 B2
Guareña E 93 C4
Guaro E 100 C1
Guarromán E 100 A2
Guasila I 110 C2
Guastalla I 81 B4
Gubbhögen S 115 C12
Gúbbio I 82 C1
Guben D 53 B4
Gubin PL 53 B4
Guča SRB 85 C5
Gudå N 114 D8
Gudavac BIH 83 B5
Guddal N 32 A2
Güderup DK 39 E2
Gudhem S 35 D5
Gudhjem DK 41 D4
Gudovac HR 74 C1
Gudow D 44 B2
Güdül TR 118 B7
Gudvangen N 32 B3
Guebwiller F 60 C3
Guéjar-Sierra E 100 B2
Guéméné-Penfao F 57 C4
Guéméné-sur-Scorff
F 56 B2
Güeñes E 89 A3
Guer F 57 C3
Guérande F 66 A2
Guéret F 68 B1
Guérigny F 68 A3
Guesa E 76 D1
Gueugnon F 68 B4
Guglionesi I 103 B7
Gühlen Glienicke D 45 B4
Guia P 92 B2
Guichen F 57 C4
Guidizzolo I 71 C5
Guidónia-Montecélio
I 102 B5
Guiglia I 81 B4
Guignes F 58 B3
Guijo E 100 A1
Guijo de Coria E 93 A4
Guijo de Santa Bábera
E 93 A5
Guijuelo E 93 A5
Guildford GB 31 C3
Guillaumes F 79 B5
Guillena E 99 B4
Guillestre F 79 B5
Guillos F 76 B2
Guilsfield GB 26 C2
Guilvinec F 56 C1
Guimarães P 87 C2
Guincho P 92 C1
Guînes F 48 C2
Guingamp F 56 B2
Guipavas F 56 B1
Guisborough GB 27 A4
Guiscard F 59 A4
Guiscriff F 56 B2
Guise F 59 A4
Guisona E 91 B4
Guitiriz E 86 A3
Guîtres F 76 A2
Gujan-Mestras F 76 B1
Gulbene LV 7 C9
Gulçayır TR 118 C6
Guldborg DK 39 E4
Gullabo S 40 C5
Gullane GB 25 B5
Gullbrå N 32 B3
Gullbrandstorp S 40 C2
Gulleråsen S 36 A2
Gullhaug N 35 C2
Gullringen S 40 B5
Gullspång S 35 D6
Gullstein N 114 D5
Güllük TR 119 E2
Gülnar TR 16 C6
Gülpınar TR 116 C8
Gülşehir TR 16 B7
Gulsvik N 34 B1
Gumiel de Hizán E 88 C3
Gummersbach D 50 B3
Gümüldür TR 119 D2
Gümüşhaciköy TR 16 A7
Gümüşova TR 118 B5
Gundelfingen D 61 B6
Gundel-fingen D 60 B3
Gundelsheim D 61 A5
Gunderschoffen F 60 B3
Gundertshausen A 62 B3
Gundinci HR 74 C3
Gündoğmuş TR 119 F7
Güney
Burdur TR 119 E4
Denizli TR 119 D4
Gunja HR 84 B3
Günlüce TR 119 F3
Gunnarn S 115 B14
Gunnarskog S 34 C4
Gunnebo S 40 B6
Gunnislake GB 28 C3
Günselsdorf A 64 C2
Guntersblum D 61 A4
Guntersdorf A 64 B2
Guntin E 86 B3
Günyüzü TR 118 C6
Günzburg D 61 B6
Gunzenhausen D 62 A1
Güre
Balıkesir TR 118 C1
Uşak TR 118 D4
Gurk A 73 B4
Gurrea de Gállego E 90 A2
Gürsu TR 118 B4
Gušće HR 74 C1
Gusev RUS 6 D7
Gusinje MNE 105 A5
Gusmar AL 105 C5
Güspini I 110 C1
Gusselby S 37 C2
Güssing A 73 A6
Gusswerk A 63 C6
Gustav Adolf S 34 B5
Gustavsberg S 37 C5
Gustavsfors S 35 C4
Güstrow D 44 B4
Gusum S 37 D3
Gutcher GB 22 A7
Gutenstein A 64 C1
Gütersloh D 51 B4
Guttannen CH 70 B3
Guttaring A 73 B4
Guttau D 53 B4
Güttingen CH 61 C5
Gützkow D 45 B5
Guzów PL 55 A5
Gvardeysk RUS 6 D6
Gvarv N 33 C6
Gvozd MNE 85 D4
Gvozdansko HR 73 C6
Gwda Wielka PL 46 B2
Gwennap GB 28 C2
Gy F 69 A5
Gyál H 75 A4
Gyarmat H 74 A2
Gyékényes H 74 B2
Gyé-sur-Seine F 59 B5
Gylling DK 39 D3
Gyoma H 75 B5
Gyömöre H 74 A2
Gyömrö H 75 A4
Gyón H 75 A4
Gyöngyfa H 74 C2
Gyöngyös H 65 C5
Gyöngyöspata H 65 C5
Gyönk H 74 B3
Györ H 64 C3
Györszemere H 74 A2
Gypsera CH 70 B2
Gysinge S 36 B3
Gyttorp S 37 C1
Gyula H 75 B6
Gyulafirátót H 74 A2
Gyulaj H 74 B3

H

Haacht B 49 C5
Haag
Nieder Östereich A 63 B5
Ober Östereich A 63 B4
D 62 B3
Haaksbergen NL 50 A2
Haamstede NL 49 B4
Haan D 50 B3
Haapajärvi FIN 3 E26
Haapsalu EST 6 B7
Haarlem NL 42 C1
Habas F 76 C2
Habay B 60 A1
Habo S 40 B4
Håbol S 35 D4
Habry CZ 63 A6
Habsheim F 60 C3
Hachenburg D 50 C3
Hacıbektaş TR 16 B7
Hacılar TR 16 B7
Hacinas E 89 C3
Hackås S 115 E11
Hacketstown IRL 21 B5
Hackthorpe GB 26 A3
Hadamar D 50 C4
Hädanberg S 115 D15
Haddington GB 25 C5
Hadersdorf am Kamp
A 63 B6
Haderslev DK 39 D2
Haderup DK 39 C1
Hadım TR 119 F7
Hadleigh
Essex GB 31 C4
Suffolk GB 30 B4
Hadlow GB 31 C4
Hadmersleben D 52 A1
Hadsten DK 39 C3
Hadsund DK 38 C3
Hadyach UA 7 F13
Hadžići BIH 84 C3
Hafnarfjörður IS 111 C4
Hafnir IS 111 D3
Hafslo N 32 A4
Haganj HR 74 C1
Hagby S 40 C6
Hage D 43 B4
Hægebostad N 33 D4
Hægeland N 33 D4
Hagen
Niedersachsen D 43 B5
Nordrhein-Westfalen
D 50 B3
Hagenbach D 61 A4
Hagenow D 44 B3
Hagetmau F 76 C2
Hagfors S 34 B5
Häggenås S 115 D11
Hagondange F 60 A2
Hagsta S 36 B4
Haguenau F 60 B3
Hahnbach D 62 A2
Hahnslätten D 50 C4
Hahót H 74 B1
Haiger D 50 C4
Haigerloch D 61 B4
Hailsham GB 31 D4
Hainburg A 64 B2
Hainfeld A 64 B1
Hainichen D 52 C3
Hajdúböszörmény H 10 C6
Hajdučica SRB 75 C5
Hajdúszoboszló H 75 A6
Hajnáčka SK 65 B5
Hajnówka PL 6 E7
Hajós H 75 B4
Håkafot S 115 C11
Hakkas S 113 F10
Håksberg S 36 B2
Halaszi H 64 C3
Halberstadt D 52 B1
Halberton GB 29 C4
Hald Ege DK 39 C2
Haldem D 43 C5
Halden N 35 C3
Haldensleben D 52 A1
Halenbeck D 44 B4
Halesowen GB 26 C3
Halesworth GB 30 B5
Halfing D 62 C3
Halhjem N 32 B2
Håliden S 34 B5
Halifax GB 27 B4
Häljelöt S 37 D3
Halkirk GB 23 C5
Hall S 37 E5
Hälla S 115 D14
Hallabro S 41 C5
Hällabrottet S 37 C2
Halland GB 31 D4
Hällaryd S 41 C4
Hallaryd S 40 C3
Hällberga S 37 C3
Hällbybrunn S 37 C3
Halle
B 49 C5
Nordrhein-Westfalen
D 51 A4
Sachsen-Anhalt D 52 B1
Hålleberga S 40 C5
Hällefors S 36 C1
Hälleforsnäs S 37 C3
Hallein A 62 C4
Hällekis S 35 D5
Hallen S 115 D11
Hållen S 36 B4
Hallenberg D 51 B4
Hällestad S 37 D2
Hällevadsholm S 35 D3
Hällevik S 41 C4
Hälleviksstrand S 35 D3
Hallingby N 34 B2
Hallingeberg S 40 B6
Hallingen N 32 B6
Hall in Tirol A 71 A6
Hållnäs S 115 A15
Hållnäs S 36 B4
Hållnäs S 115 C16
Hallormsstaður IS 111 B11
Hallsberg S 37 C2
Hållsta S 37 C3
Hallstahammar S 37 C3
Hallstatt A 72 A3
Hallstavik S 36 B5
Halltorp S 40 C6
Halluin F 49 C4
Hallviken S 115 D12
Hallworthy GB 28 C3
Halmstad S 40 C2
Hals DK 38 B3
Halsa N 114 D5
Halstead GB 31 C4
Haltdalen N 114 E8
Haltern D 50 B3
Haltwhistle GB 25 D5
Halvarsgårdarna S 36 B2
Halver D 50 B3
Halvrimmen DK 38 B2
Ham F 59 A4
Hamar N 34 B3
Hamarhaug N 32 B2
Hamarøy N 112 D4
Hambach F 60 A3
Hambergen D 43 B5
Hambergsund S 35 D3
Hambledon GB 31 D2
Hambuhren D 44 C1
Hamburg D 44 B2
Hamdibey TR 118 C2
Hamdorf D 43 A6
Hämeenlinna FIN 3 F26
Hameln = Hamlin D 51 A5
Hamersleben D 52 A1
Hamidiye TR 118 C5
Hamilton GB 24 C3
Hamina FIN 7 A9
Hamlagrø N 32 B3
Hamlin = Hameln D 51 A5
Hamm D 50 B3
Hammar S 37 D1
Hammarland FIN 36 B6
Hammarö S 35 C5
Hammarstrand S 115 D13
Hamme B 49 B5
Hammel DK 39 C2
Hammelburg D 51 C5
Hammelspring D 45 B5
Hammenhög S 41 D4
Hammerdal S 115 D12
Hammerfest N 113 B12
Hammershøj DK 38 C2
Hammerum DK 39 C2
Hamminkeln D 50 B2
Hamnavoe GB 22 A7
Hamneda S 40 C3
Hamningberg N 113 B19
Hamoir B 49 C6
Hamont B 49 B6
Hámor H 65 B6
Hamra
Gävleborg S 115 F12
Gotland S 37 F5
Hamrångefjärden S 36 B4
Hamstreet GB 31 C4
Hamsund N 112 D4
Han
MNE 84 D3
TR 118 C5
Hanaskog S 41 C4
Hanau D 51 C4
Händelöp S 40 B6
Handlová SK 65 B4
Hanerau-Hademarschen
D 43 A6
Hånger S 40 B3
Hanhimaa FIN 113 E14
Han i Hotit AL 105 A5
Hanken S 37 D1
Hankensbüttel D 44 C2
Han Knežica BIH 83 A5
Hanko FIN 6 B7
Hannover D 43 C6
Hannut B 49 C6
Han Pijesak BIH 84 B3
Hansnes N 112 C8
Hanstedt D 44 B2
Hanstholm DK 38 B1
Hantsavichy BY 7 E9
Hanušovice CZ 54 C1
Haparanda S 3 D26
Haradok BY 7 D10
Harads S 3 C24
Häradsbäck S 40 C4
Häradsbygden S 36 B2
Harbo S 36 B4
Harboør DK 38 C1
Harburg
Bayern D 62 B1
Hamburg D 44 B1
Hårby DK 39 D3
Harc H 74 B3
Hardegarijp NL 42 B2
Hardegsen D 51 B5
Hardelot Plage F 48 C2
Hardenbeck D 45 B5
Hardenberg NL 42 C3
Harderwijk NL 42 C2
Hardheim D 61 A5
Hardt D 61 B4
Hareid N 114 E3
Haren
D 43 C4
NL 42 B3
Harestua N 34 B2
Harfleur F 57 A6
Harg S 36 B5
Hargicourt F 49 D4
Hargnies F 49 C5
Hargshamn S 36 B5
Härja S 40 A3
Harkány H 74 C3
Härkeberga S 37 C4
Harkebrügge D 43 B4
Harlech GB 26 C1
Harleston GB 30 B5
Hårlev DK 41 D2
Harlingen NL 42 B2
Harlösa S 41 D3
Harlow GB 31 C4
Harmancık TR 118 C4
Harmånger S 115 F14
Härnevi S 37 C4
Härnösand S 115 E14
Haro E 89 B4
Haroldswick GB 22 A8
Háromfa H 74 B2
Haroué F 60 B2
Harpenden GB 31 C3
Harplinge S 40 C2
Harpstedt D 43 C5
Harrogate GB 27 A4
Harrow GB 31 C3
Härryda S 40 B2
Harsefeld D 43 B6
Harsewinkel D 50 B4
Hârşova RO 11 D9
Harstad N 112 D5
Harsum D 51 A5
Harsvik N 114 C7
Harta H 75 B4
Hartberg A 73 A5
Hartburn GB 25 C6
Hartennes F 59 A4
Hartest GB 30 B4
Hartha D 52 B2
Hartland GB 28 C3
Hartlepool GB 27 A4
Hartmanice CZ 63 A4
Hartmannsdorf A 73 A5
Harvassdal N 115 B11
Harwell GB 31 C2
Harwich GB 31 C5
Harzgerode D 52 B1
Häselgehr A 71 A5
Haselünne D 43 C4
Hasköy TR 118 A1
Haslach D 61 B4
Haslach an der Mühl
A 63 B5
Hasle DK 41 D4
Haslemere GB 31 C3
Haslev DK 39 D4
Hasloch D 61 A5
Hasparren F 76 C1
Hassela S 115 E13
Hasselfelde D 51 B6
Hasselfors S 37 C1
Hasselt
B 49 C6
NL 42 C3
Hassfurt D 51 C6
Hassleben D 45 B5
Hässleholm S 41 C3
Hasslö S 41 C5
Hassloch D 61 A4
Hästbo S 36 B4
Hastersboda FIN 36 B7
Hästholmen S 37 D1
Hastière-Lavaux B 49 C5
Hastigrow GB 23 C5
Hastings GB 31 D4
Hästveda S 41 C3
Hasvik N 113 B11
Hatfield
Hertfordshire GB 31 C3
South Yorkshire GB 27 B5
Hatherleigh GB 28 C3
Hathersage GB 27 B4
Hatlestrand N 32 B2
Hattem NL 42 C3
Hatten
D 43 B5
F 60 B3
Hattfjelldal N 115 B10
Hatting DK 39 D2
Hattingen D 50 B3
Hattstadt F 60 B3
Hattstedt D 43 A6
Hatvan H 65 C5
Hatvik N 32 B2
Hau D 50 B2
Haudainville F 59 A6
Hauganes IS 111 B7
Haugastøl N 32 B4
Hauge N 33 D3
Haugesund N 33 C2
Haughom N 33 D3
Haugsdal N 32 B2
Haugsdorf A 64 B2
Haukedal N 32 A3
Haukeland N 32 B2
Haukeligrend N 33 C4
Haukeliseter N 32 C4
Haukipudas FIN 3 D26
Haulerwijk NL 42 B3
Haunersdorf D 62 B3
Haus N 32 B2
Hausach D 61 B4
Hausham D 62 C2
Hausmannstätten A 73 B5
Hausvik N 33 D3
Hautajärvi FIN 113 F18
Hautefort F 67 C6
Hauterives F 69 C5
Hauteville-Lompnès
F 69 C5
Haut-Fays B 49 C6
Hautmont F 49 C4
Hautrage B 49 C4
Hauzenberg D 63 B4
Havant GB 31 D3
Havdhem S 37 E5
Havdrup DK 39 D5
Havelange B 49 C6
Havelberg D 44 C4
Havelte NL 42 C3
Haverfordwest GB 28 B3
Haverhill GB 30 B4
Havering GB 31 C4
Håverud S 35 D4
Havířov CZ 65 A4
Havixbeck D 50 B3
Havlíčkův Brod CZ 63 A6
Havndal DK 38 C3
Havneby DK 39 D1
Havnebyen DK 39 D4
Havnsø DK 39 D4
Havøysund N 113 A13
Havran TR 118 C2
Havrebjerg DK 39 D4
Havsa TR 118 A1
Havstenssund S 35 D3
Havza TR 16 A7
Hawes GB 26 A3
Hawick GB 25 C5
Hawkhurst GB 31 C4
Hawkinge GB 31 C5
Haxey GB 27 B5
Hayange F 60 A2
Haydarlı TR 119 D5
Haydon Bridge GB 25 D5
Hayle GB 28 C2
Haymana TR 118 C7
Hay-on-Wye GB 29 A4
Hayrabolu TR 118 A2
Haysyn UA 11 B10
Hayvoron UA 11 B10
Haywards Heath GB 31 D3
Hazebrouck F 48 C3
Hazlov CZ 52 C2
Heacham GB 30 B4
Headcorn GB 31 C4
Headford IRL 20 A2
Heanor GB 27 B4
Héas F 76 D3
Heathfield GB 31 D4
Hebden Bridge GB 26 B3
Heberg S 40 C2
Heby S 36 C3
Hechingen D 61 B4
Hechlingen D 62 B1
Hecho E 76 D2
Hechtel B 49 B6
Hechthausen D 43 B6
Heckelberg D 45 C5
Heckington GB 27 C5
Hecklingen D 52 B1
Hed S 37 C2
Hedalen N 34 B1
Hedared S 40 B2
Heddal N 33 C6
Hédé F 57 B4
Hede S 115 E10
Hedekas S 35 D3
Hedemora S 36 B2
Hedensted DK 39 D2
Hedersleben D 52 B1
Hedesunda S 36 B4
Hedge End GB 31 D2
Hedon GB 27 B5
Heede D 43 C4
Heek D 50 A3
Heemstede NL 42 C1
Heerde NL 42 C3
Heerenveen NL 42 C2
Heerhugowaard NL 42 C1
Heerlen NL 50 C1
Heeze NL 49 B6
Heggenes N 32 A6
Hegra N 114 D8
Hegyeshalom H 64 C3
Hegyközség H 74 A1
Heia N 114 C9
Heide D 43 A6
Heidelberg D 61 A4
Heiden D 50 B2
Heidenau D 53 C3
Heidenheim D 61 B6
Heidenreichstein A 63 B6
Heikendorf D 44 A2
Heilam GB 22 C4
Heiland N 33 D5
Heilbad Heiligenstadt
D 51 B6
Heilbronn D 61 A5
Heiligenblut A 72 A2
Heiligendamn D 44 A3
Heiligendorf D 44 C2
Heiligengrabe D 44 B4
Heiligenhafen D 44 A2
Heiligenhaus D 50 B2
Heiligenkreuz A 73 B6
Heiligenstadt D 62 A2
Heiloo NL 42 C1
Heilsbronn D 62 A1
Heim N 114 D6
Heimburg D 51 B6
Heimdal N 114 D7
Heinerscheid L 50 C2
Heinersdorf D 45 C6
Heining D 63 B4
Heiningen D 61 B5
Heinola FIN 3 F27
Heinsberg D 50 B2
Heist-op-den-Berg B 49 B5
Hejde S 37 E5
Hejdeby S 37 E5
Hejls DK 39 D2
Hejnice CZ 53 C5
Hel PL 47 A4
Helchteren B 49 B6
Heldburg D 51 C6
Heldrungen D 52 B1
Helechosa E 94 C2
Helensburgh GB 24 B3
Helfenberg A 63 B5
Helgen N 33 C6
Helgeroa N 35 D1
Hella
IS 111 D5
N 32 A3
Helland N 112 D5
Hellas S 35 D4
Helle N 33 D3
Helleland N 33 D3
Hellendoorn NL 42 C3
Hellenthal D 50 C2
Hellesøy N 32 B1
Hellesylt N 114 E3
Hellevoetsluis NL 49 B5
Helligskogen N 112 C9
Hellín E 101 A4
Hellissandur IS 111 C2
Hellnar IS 111 C2
Hellum DK 38 B3
Hellvi S 37 E5
Hellvik N 33 D2
Helm-brechts D 52 C1
Helmond NL 49 B6
Helmsdale GB 23 C5
Helmsley GB 27 A4
Helmstedt D 51 A6
Hel'pa SK 65 B5
Helsa D 51 B5
Helsby GB 26 B3

Helsingborg S 41 C2
Helsinge DK 41 C2
Helsingør DK 41 C2
Helsinki FIN 6 A8
Helston GB 28 C2
Hemau D 62 A2
Hemavan S 115 B12
Hemel Hempstead GB 31 C3
Hemer D 50 B3
Héming F 60 B2
Hemmet DK 39 D1
Hemmingstedt D 43 A6
Hemmoor D 43 B6
Hemnes N 35 C3
Hemnesberget N 115 A10
Hemse S 37 E5
Hemsedal N 32 B5
Hemslingen D 43 B6
Hemsworth GB 27 B4
Hen N 34 B2
Henån S 35 D3
Hendaye F 76 C1
Hendek TR 118 B5
Hendungen D 51 C6
Henfield GB 31 D3
Hengelo
Gelderland NL 50 A2
Overijssel NL 50 A2
Hengersberg D 62 B4
Hengoed GB 29 B4
Hénin-Beaumont F 48 C3
Henley-on-Thames GB 31 C3
Hennan S 115 E12
Henneberg D 51 C6
Hennebont F 56 C2
Henne Strand DK 39 D1
Hennigsdorf D 45 C5
Hennset N 114 D5
Hennstedt
Schleswig-Holstein D 43 A6
Schleswig-Holstein D 43 A6
Henrichemont F 68 A2
Henryków PL 54 C2
Henrykowo PL 47 A6
Hensås N 32 A5
Henstedt-Ulzburg D 44 B1
Heppenheim D 61 A4
Herad
Buskerud N 32 B6
Vest-Agder N 33 D3
Heradsbygd N 34 B3
Heraklion = Iraklio GR 117 G7
Herálec CZ 64 A2
Herand N 32 B3
Herbault F 58 C2
Herbern D 50 B3
Herbertstown IRL 20 B3
Herbeumont B 59 A6
Herbignac F 66 A2
Herbisse F 59 B5
Herbitzheim F 60 A3
Herbolzheim D 60 B3
Herborn D 50 C4
Herbrechtingen D 61 B6
Herby PL 54 C3
Herceg-Novi MNE 105 A4
Hercegovać HR 74 C2
Hercegovacka Goleša SRB 85 C4
Hercegszántó H 75 C3
Herchen D 50 C3
Heréd H 65 C5
Hereford GB 29 A5
Herefoss N 33 D5
Hereke TR 118 B4
Herencia E 95 C3
Herend H 74 A2
Herent B 49 C5
Herentals B 49 B5
Hérépian F 78 C2
Herfølge DK 41 D2
Herford D 51 A4
Herguijuela E 93 B5
Héric F 66 A3
Héricourt F 60 C2
Héricourt-en-Caux F 58 A1
Hérimoncourt F 70 A1
Heringsdorf D 44 A3
Herisau CH 71 A4
Hérisson F 68 B2
Herk-de-Stad B 49 C6
Herlufmagle DK 39 D4
Hermagor A 72 B3
Hermannsburg D 44 C2
Hermansverk N 32 A3
Heřmanův Městec CZ 53 D5
Herment F 68 C2
Hermeskeil D 60 A2
Hermisende E 87 C4
Hermonville F 59 A4
Hermsdorf D 52 C1
Hernani E 76 C1
Hernansancho E 94 B2
Herne D 50 B3
Herne Bay GB 31 C5
Hernes N 34 B3
Herning DK 39 C1
Herøya N 35 C1
Herramelluri E 89 B3
Herräng S 36 B5
Herre N 33 C6
Herrenberg D 61 B4
Herrera E 100 B1
Herrera de Alcántara E 92 B3
Herrera del Duque E 94 C1
Herrera de los Navarros E 90 B1
Herrera de Pisuerga E 88 B2
Herreros del Suso E 94 B1
Herrestad S 35 D3
Herrhamra S 37 D4
Herritslev DK 44 A3
Herrlisheim F 60 B3
Herrljunga S 40 A3
Herrnhut D 53 B4
Herrsching D 62 B2
Hersbruck D 62 A2
Hersby S 37 C5
Herscheid D 50 B3
Herselt B 49 B5
Herso GR 116 A4
Herstal B 49 C6
Herstmonceux GB 31 D4
Herten D 50 B3
Hertford GB 31 C3
Hervás E 93 A5
Hervik N 33 C2
Herxheim D 61 A4
Herzberg
Brandenburg D 45 C4
Brandenburg D 52 B3
Niedersachsen D 51 B6
Herzebrock D 50 B4
Herzfelde D 45 C5
Herzlake D 43 C4
Herzogen-aurach D 62 A1
Herzogenbuchsee CH 70 A2
Herzogenburg A 63 B6
Herzsprung D 44 B4
Hesby N 33 C2
Hesdin F 48 C3
Hesel D 43 B4
Hessdalen N 114 E8
Hesselager DK 39 D3
Hesseng N 113 C18
Hessisch Lichtenau D 51 B5
Hessisch-Oldendorf D 51 A5
Hestra S 40 B3
Heswall GB 26 B2
Hetlevik N 32 B2
Hettange-Grande F 60 A2
Hetton-le-Hole GB 25 D6
Hettstedt D 52 B1
Heuchin F 48 C3
Heudicourt-sous-les-Côtes F 60 B1
Heunezel F 60 B2
Heuqueville F 57 A6
Heves H 65 C6
Héviz H 74 B2
Hexham GB 25 D5
Heysham GB 26 A3
Heytesbury GB 29 B5
Hidas H 74 B3
Hieflau A 63 C5
Hiendelaencina E 95 A4
Hiersac F 67 C5
High Bentham GB 26 A3
Highclere GB 31 C2
High Hesket GB 25 D5
Highley GB 26 C3
High Wycombe GB 31 C3
Higuera de Arjona E 100 B2
Higuera de Calatrava E 100 B1
Higuera de la Serena E 93 C5
Higuera de la Sierra E 99 B4
Higuera de Vargas E 93 C4
Higuera la Real E 99 A4
Higuers de Llerena E 93 C4
Higueruela E 96 C1
Híjar E 90 B2
Hilchenbach D 50 B4
Hildburghausen D 51 C6
Hilden D 50 B2
Hilders D 51 C5
Hildesheim D 51 A5
Hilgay GB 30 B4
Hillared S 40 B3
Hille D 51 A4
Hillegom NL 49 A5
Hillerød DK 41 D2
Hillerstorp S 40 B3
Hillesheim D 50 C2
Hillestad N 35 C2
Hillmersdorf D 52 B3
Hillsborough GB 19 B5
Hillswick GB 22 A7
Hilpoltstein D 62 A2
Hiltpoltstein D 62 A2
Hilvarenbeek NL 49 B6
Hilversum NL 49 A6
Himarë AL 116 B1
Himbergen D 44 B2
Himesháza H 74 B3
Himmelberg A 73 B4
Himmelpforten D 43 B6
Himód H 74 A2
Hinckley GB 30 B2
Hindås S 40 B2
Hindelang D 71 A5
Hindelbank CH 70 A2
Hinderavåg N 33 C2
Hindhead GB 31 C3
Hinjosa del Valle E 93 C4
Hinnerup DK 39 C3
Hinneryd S 40 C3
Hinojal E 93 B4
Hinojales E 99 B4
Hinojos E 99 B4
Hinojosa del Duque E 93 C5
Hinojosas de Calatrava E 100 A1
Hinterhornbach A 71 A5
Hinterriss A 71 A6
Hintersee
A 63 C4
D 45 B6
Hinterstoder A 63 C5
Hintertux A 72 A1
Hinterweidenthal D 60 A3
Hinwil CH 70 A3
Hios GR 116 D8
Hippolytushoef NL 42 C1
Hirschaid D 62 A1
Hirschau D 62 A2
Hirschfeld D 52 B3
Hirschhorn D 61 A4
Hirsingue F 60 C3
Hirson F 59 A5
Hirtshals DK 38 B2
Hirzenhain D 51 C5
Hisarcık TR 118 C4
Hishult S 41 C3
Hitchin GB 31 C3
Hitra N 114 D5
Hittarp S 41 C2
Hittisau A 71 A4
Hittun N 32 A1
Hitzacker D 44 B3
Hjallerup DK 38 B3
Hjällstad S 34 B5
Hjältevad S 40 B5
Hjärnarp S 41 C2
Hjartdal N 33 C5
Hjellestad N 32 B2
Hjelmeland N 33 C3
Hjelset N 114 E4
Hjerkinn N 114 E6
Hjerm DK 38 C1
Hjerpsted DK 39 D1
Hjerting DK 39 D1
Hjo S 35 D6
Hjordkær DK 39 D2
Hjørring DK 38 B2
Hjorted S 40 B6
Hjortkvarn S 37 D2
Hjortnäs S 36 B1
Hjortsberga S 40 C4
Hjukse N 33 C6
Hjuksebø N 33 C6
Hjulsjö S 36 C1
Hliník nad Hronom SK 65 B4
Hlinsko CZ 64 A1
Hlío IS 111 A10
Hlohovec SK 64 B3
Hlubokánad Vltavou CZ 63 A5
Hlučín CZ 64 A4
Hlukhiv UA 7 F12
Hlyboka UA 11 B8
Hlybokaye BY 7 D9
Hniezdne SK 65 A6
Hnilec SK 65 B6
Hnúšťa SK 65 B5
Hobol H 74 B2
Hobro DK 38 C2
Hobscheid L 60 A1
Hocalar TR 119 D4
Hochdonn D 43 A6
Hochdorf CH 70 A3
Hochfelden F 60 B3
Hochspeyer D 60 A3
Höchstädt D 61 B6
Höchstädt D 62 A1
Hochstenbach D 50 C3
Höchst im Odenwald D 61 A5
Höckendorf D 52 C3
Hockenheim D 61 A4
Hoddesdon GB 31 C3
Hodejov SK 65 B5
Hodenhagen D 43 C6
Hodkovice CZ 53 C5
Hódmezövásárhely H 75 B5
Hodnet GB 26 C3
Hodonín CZ 64 B3
Hodslavice CZ 64 A4
Hoedekenskerke NL 49 B4
Hoegaarden B 49 C5
Hoek van Holland NL 49 B5
Hoenderlo NL 50 A1
Hof
D 52 C1
N 35 C2
Hofbieber D 51 C5
Hoff GB 26 A3
Hofgeismar D 51 B5
Hofheim
Bayern D 51 C6
Hofheim *continued*
Hessen D 51 C4
Hofkirchen im Mühlkreis A 63 B4
Höfn IS 111 C10
Hofors S 36 B3
Hofsós IS 111 B6
Hofstad N 114 C7
Höganäs S 41 C2
Högbo S 36 B3
Hogdal S 35 C3
Høgebru N 32 A4
Högfors S 36 C2
Högklint S 37 E5
Högsäter S 35 D4
Högsby S 40 B6
Högsjö S 37 C2
Hogstad S 37 D2
Högyész H 74 B3
Hohenau A 64 B2
Hohenberg A 63 C6
Hohenbucko D 52 B3
Hohenburg D 62 A2
Hohendorf D 45 A4
Hohenems A 71 A4
Hohenhameln D 51 A6
Hohenhausen D 51 A4
Hohenkirchen D 43 B4
Hohenlinden D 62 B2
Hohenlockstedt D 43 B6
Hohenmölsen D 52 B2
Hohennauen D 44 C4
Hohen Neuendorf D 45 C5
Hohenseeden D 52 A2
Hohentauern A 73 A4
Hohentengen D 70 A3
Hohenwepel D 51 B5
Hohenwestedt D 43 A6
Hohenwutzen D 45 C6
Hohenzieritz D 45 B5
Hohn D 43 A6
Hohne D 44 C2
Hohnstorf D 44 B2
Højer DK 39 E1
Højslev Stby DK 38 C2
Hok S 40 B4
Hökerum S 40 B3
Hökhuvud S 36 B5
Hokksund N 34 C1
Hökön S 40 C4
Hol N 32 B5
Hola Pristan UA 11 C12
Hólar IS 111 B6
Holašovice CZ 63 B5
Holbæk
Aarhus Amt. DK 38 C3
Vestsjællands Amt. DK 39 D4
Holbeach GB 30 B4
Holdenstedt D 44 C2
Holdhus N 32 B2
Holdorf D 43 C5
Holeby DK 44 A3
Hølen N 35 C2
Hølervasseter N 32 B6
Holešov CZ 64 A3
Holguera E 93 B4
Holíč SK 64 B3
Holice
CZ 53 C5
SK 64 C3
Höljes S 34 B4
Hollabrunn A 64 B2
Hollandstoun GB 23 B6
Høllen N 33 D4
Hollfeld D 52 D1
Hollókő H 65 C5
Hollstadt D 51 C6
Hollum NL 42 B2
Höllviksnäs S 41 D2
Holm N 114 B9
Hólmavík IS 111 B4
Holmbukt N 113 B10
Holmedal S 35 C3
Holmegil N 35 C3
Holmen N 34 B2
Holme-on-Spalding-Moor GB 27 B5
Holmes Chapel GB 26 B3
Holmestrand N 35 C2
Holmfirth GB 27 B4
Holmfoss N 113 C19
Holmsbu N 35 C2
Holmsjö S 41 C5
Holmsund S 3 E24
Holmsveden S 36 A3
Holmudden S 37 E6
Hölö S 37 C4
Holøydal N 114 E8
Holsbybrunn S 40 B5
Holseter N 34 A1
Holsljunga S 40 B2
Holstebro DK 39 C1
Holsted DK 39 D1
Holsworthy GB 28 C3
Holt
D 39 E2
Norfolk GB 30 B5
Wrexham GB 26 B3
IS 111 D6
N 33 D5
Holten NL 50 A2
Holtwick D 50 A3
Holum N 33 D4
Holwerd NL 42 B2
Holycross IRL 21 B4
Holyhead GB 26 B1
Holýšov CZ 62 A4
Holywell GB 26 B2
Holywood GB 19 B6
Holzdorf D 52 B3
Holzhausen D 51 A4
Holzheim D 61 B6
Holzkirchen D 62 C2
Holzminden D 51 B5
Holzthaleben D 51 B6
Homberg
Hessen D 51 B5
Hessen D 51 C5
Homburg D 60 A3
Hommelstø N 115 B9
Hommersåk N 33 D2
Homokmegy H 75 B4
Homokszentgyörgy H 74 B2
Homrogd H 65 B6
Homyel = Gomel BY 7 E11
Honaz TR 119 E4
Hondarribia E 76 C1
Hondón de los Frailes E 101 A5
Hondschoote F 48 C3
Hönebach D 51 C5
Hønefoss N 34 B2
Honfleur F 57 A6
Høng DK 39 D4
Honiton GB 29 C4
Hönningen D 50 C2
Honningsvåg N 113 B14
Hönö S 38 B4
Honrubia E 95 C4
Hontalbilla E 88 C2
Hontheim D 50 C2
Hontianske-Nemce SK 65 B4
Hontoria de la Cantera E 88 B3
Hontoria del Pinar E 89 C3
Hontoria de Valdearados E 89 C3
Hoofddorp NL 49 A5
Hoogerheide NL 49 B5
Hoogeveen NL 42 C3
Hoogezand-Sappemeer NL 42 B3
Hoogkarspel NL 42 C2
Hoogkerk NL 42 B3
Hoogstede D 42 C3
Hoogstraten B 49 B5
Hook GB 31 C3
Hooksiel D 43 B5
Höör S 41 D3
Hoorn NL 42 C2
Hope GB 26 B2
Hopen N 112 E4
Hope under Dinmore GB 29 A5
Hopfgarten A 72 A2
Hopfgarten in Defereggen A 72 B2
Hopseidet N 113 B16
Hopsten D 43 C4
Hoptrup DK 39 D2
Hora Svatého Sebestiána CZ 52 C3
Horaždóvice CZ 63 A4
Horb am Neckar D 61 B4
Horbelev DK 39 E5
Hørby DK 38 B3
Hörby S 41 D3
Horcajada de la Torre E 95 B4
Horcajo de los Montes E 94 C2
Horcajo de Santiago E 95 C3
Horcajo-Medianero E 93 A5
Horche E 95 B3
Horda S 40 B4
Hordabø N 32 B1
Hordalia N 32 C3
Hordvik N 32 B2
Hořesedly CZ 52 C3
Horezu RO 11 D8
Horgen CH 70 A3
Horgoš SRB 75 B4
Hořice CZ 53 C5
Horjul SLO 73 B4
Horka D 53 B4
Hörken S 36 B1
Horki BY 7 D11
Hörle S 40 B4
Horn
A 63 B6
D 51 B4
N 34 B2
S 40 B5
Horna E 101 A4
Hornachos E 93 C4
Hornachuelos E 99 B5
Horná Mariková SK 64 A4
Hornanes N 32 C2
Horná Streda SK 64 B3
Horná Štrubna SK 65 B4
Horná Súča SK 64 B3
Hornbæk
Aarhus Amt. DK 38 C2
Frederiksværk DK 41 C2
Hornberg D 61 B4
Hornburg D 51 A6
Horncastle GB 27 B5
Horndal S 36 B3
Horndean GB 31 D2
Horne
Fyns Amt. DK 39 D3
Ribe Amt. DK 39 D1
Hörnebo S 35 D6
Horneburg D 43 B6
Hörnefors S 115 D16
Horní Bečva CZ 64 A4
Horní Benešov CZ 64 A3
Horní Cerekev CZ 63 A6
Horní Jiřetín CZ 52 C3
Horní Lomná CZ 65 A4
Horní Maršov CZ 53 C5
Hornindal N 114 F3
Hørning DK 39 C3
Hörningsholm S 37 C4
Horní Planá CZ 63 B5
Horní Slavkov CZ 52 C2
Horní Vltavice CZ 63 B4
Hornnes N 33 D4
Horno D 53 B4
Hornos E 101 A3
Hornoy-le-Bourg F 58 A2
Hornsea GB 27 B5
Hornsjø N 34 A2
Hornslet DK 39 C3
Hornstein A 64 C2
Hörnum D 39 E1
Hornum DK 38 C2
Horný Tisovník SK 65 B5
Horodenka UA 11 B8
Horodnya UA 7 F11
Horodok
Khmelnytskyy UA 11 B9
Lviv UA 11 B7
Horodyshche UA 11 B11
Horokhiv UA 11 A8
Horovice CZ 63 A4
Horred S 40 B2
Hörröd S 41 D4
Hörsching A 63 B5
Horsens DK 39 D2
Horsham GB 31 C3
Hørsholm DK 41 D2
Horslunde DK 39 E4
Horšovský Týn CZ 62 A3
Horst NL 50 B2
Horstel D 50 A3
Horsten D 43 B4
Horstmar D 50 A3
Hort H 65 C5
Horta P 87 C3
Horten N 35 C2
Hortezuela E 89 C4
Hortiguela E 89 B3
Hortobágy H 75 A6
Horton in Ribblesdale GB 26 A3
Hørve DK 39 D4
Hörvik S 41 C4
Horwich GB 26 B3
Hosanger N 32 B2
Hösbach D 51 C5
Hosena D 53 B4
Hosenfeld D 51 C5
Hosingen L 50 C2
Hospental CH 70 B3
Hospital IRL 20 B3
Hossegor F 76 C1
Hosszuhetény H 74 B3
Hostal de Ipiés E 90 A2
Hoštálkova CZ 64 A3
Hostalric E 91 B5
Hostens F 76 B2
Hostěradice CZ 64 B2
Hostinné CZ 53 C5
Hostomice CZ 63 A5
Hostouň CZ 62 A3
Hotagen S 115 D11
Hoting S 115 C13
Hotolisht AL 116 A2
Hotton B 49 C6
Houdain F 48 C3
Houdan F 58 B2
Houdelaincourt F 60 B1
Houeillès F 76 B3
Houffalize B 50 C1
Houghton-le-Spring GB 25 D6
Houlberg DK 39 C2
Houlgate F 57 A6
Hounslow GB 31 C3
Hourtin F 66 C3
Hourtin-Plage F 66 C3
Houthalen B 49 B6
Houyet B 49 C5
Hov
DK 39 D3
N 34 B2
Hova S 35 D6
Høvåg N 33 D5
Hovborg DK 39 D1
Hovda N 32 B6
Hovden N 33 C4
Hove GB 31 D3
Hovedgård DK 39 D2
Hovelhof D 51 B4
Hoven DK 39 D1
Hovet N 32 B5
Hovingham GB 27 A5
Hovmantorp S 40 C5
Hovsta S 37 C2
Howden GB 27 B5
Howe D 44 B2
Höxter D 51 B5
Hoya D 43 C6
Hoya de Santa Maria E 99 B4
Hoya-Gonzalo E 95 D5
Høyanger N 32 A3
Hoyerswerda D 53 B4
Høyjord N 35 C2
Hoylake GB 26 B2
Høylandet N 114 C9
Hoym D 52 B1
Høymyr N 32 C6
Hoyocasero E 94 B2
Hoyo de Manzanares E 94 B3
Hoyo de Pinares E 94 B2
Hoyos E 93 A4
Hoyos del Espino E 93 A5
Hrabušice SK 65 B6
Hradec Králové CZ 53 C5
Hradec nad Moravicí CZ 64 A3
Hrádek CZ 64 B2
Hrádek nad Nisou CZ 53 C4
Hradište SK 65 B4
Hrafnagil IS 111 B7
Hrafnseyri IS 111 B2
Hranice
Severomoravsky CZ 64 A3
Západočeský CZ 52 C2
Hranovnica SK 65 B6
Hrasnica BIH 84 C3
Hrastnik SLO 73 B5
Hrebenka UA 11 A12
Hřensko CZ 53 C4
Hriňová SK 65 B5
Hrisoupoli GR 116 B6
Hrochov CZ 64 A2
Hrochův Tynec CZ 53 D5
Hrodna BY 6 E7
Hrodzyanka BY 7 E10
Hronov CZ 53 C6
Hronský Beňadik SK 65 B4
Hrotovice CZ 64 A2
Hrtkovci SRB 85 B4
Hrun IS 111 A5
Hrušov SK 65 B5
Hrušovany nad Jevišovkou CZ 64 B2
Hřuštín SK 65 A5
Hrvaćani BIH 84 B2
Hrvace HR 83 C5
Hrymayliv UA 11 B9
Huben A 72 B2
Hückeswagen D 50 B3
Hucknall GB 27 B4
Hucqueliers F 48 C2
Huddersfield GB 27 B4
Huddinge S 37 C4
Huddunge S 36 B3
Hude D 43 B5
Hudiksvall S 115 F14
Huélago E 100 B2
Huélamo E 95 B5
Huelgoat F 56 B2
Huelma E 100 B2
Huelva E 99 B4
Huéneja E 100 B3
Huércal de Almeria E 101 C3
Huércal-Overa E 101 B4
Huerta de Abajo E 89 B3
Huerta del Rey E 89 C3
Huerta de Valdecarabanos E 95 C3
Huertahernando E 95 B4
Huesa E 100 B2
Huesca E 90 A2
Huéscar E 101 B3
Huete E 95 B4
Huétor Tájar E 100 B1
Hüfingen D 61 C4
Hufthamar N 32 B2
Hugh Town GB 28 D1
Huglfing D 62 C2
Huissen NL 50 B1
Huittinen FIN 3 F25
Huizen NL 49 A6
Hulín CZ 64 A3
Hüls D 50 B2
Hulsig DK 38 B3
Hulst NL 49 B5
Hult S 40 B5
Hulta S 40 A6
Hulteby S 35 C6
Hulterstad S 41 C6
Hultsfred S 40 B5
Humanes E 95 B3
Humberston GB 27 B5
Humble DK 39 E3
Humenné SK 10 B6
Humilladero E 100 B1
Humlebæk DK 41 D2
Humlum DK 38 C1
Hummelsta S 37 C3
Humpolec CZ 63 A6
Humshaugh GB 25 C5
Hundåla N 115 B9
Hundested DK 39 D4
Hundvåg N 33 C2
Hundvin N 32 B2
Hunedoara RO 11 D7
Hünfeld D 51 C5
Hungen D 51 C4
Hungerford GB 31 C2
Hunndalen N 34 B2
Hunnebostrand S 35 D3
Hunstanton GB 30 B4
Huntingdon GB 30 B3
Huntley GB 29 B5
Huntly GB 23 D6
Hünxe D 50 B2
Hurbanovo SK 64 C4
Hürbel D 61 B5
Hurdal N 34 B3
Hurezani RO 11 D7
Hurlford GB 24 C3
Hurstbourne Tarrant GB 31 C2
Hurstpierpoint GB 31 D3
Hürth D 50 C2
Hurum N 32 A5
Hurup DK 38 C1
Húsafell IS 111 C5
Húsavík IS 111 A8
Husbands Bosworth GB 30 B2
Husby
D 39 E2
DK 39 D1
Husey IS 111 B11
Huşi RO 11 C10
Husina BIH 84 B3
Husinec CZ 63 A4
Husinish GB 22 D1
Huskvarna S 40 B4
Husnes N 32 C2
Husøy N 112 C6
Hustad N 114 E4
Hüsten D 50 B3
Hustopeče CZ 64 B2
Hustopeče nad Bečvou CZ 64 A3
Husum
D 43 A6
S 115 D16
Husvika N 115 B9
Huta PL 46 C2
Hutovo BIH 84 D2
Hüttenberg A 73 B4
Hüttlingen D 61 B6
Huttoft GB 27 B6
Hutton Cranswick GB 27 B5
Hüttschlag A 72 A3
Huttwil CH 70 A2
Huy B 49 C6
Hüyük TR 119 E6
Hval N 34 B2
Hvåle N 32 B6
Hvaler N 35 C3
Hvalpsund DK 38 C2
Hvammstangi IS 111 B5
Hvammur IS 111 B6
Hvanneyri IS 111 C4
Hvar HR 83 C5
Hvarnes N 35 C1
Hveragerði IS 111 D4
Hvidbjerg DK 38 C1
Hvide Sande DK 39 D1
Hvittingfoss N 35 C2
Hvolsvöllur IS 111 D5
Hybe SK 65 A5
Hycklinge S 40 B5
Hydra GR 117 E5
Hyen N 114 F2
Hyères F 79 C5
Hyéres Plage F 79 C5
Hylestad N 33 C4
Hylke DK 39 D2
Hyllestad N 32 A2
Hyllstofta S 41 C3
Hyltebruk S 40 B3
Hynish GB 24 B1
Hynnekleiv N 33 D5
Hythe
Hampshire GB 31 D2
Kent GB 31 C5
Hyvinkää FIN 3 F26

I

Iam RO 85 A6
Iași RO 11 C9
Iasmos GR 116 A7
Ibahernando E 93 B5
Iballë AL 105 A5
Ibarranguelua E 89 A4
Ibbenbüren D 50 A3
Ibeas de Juarros E 89 B3
Ibestad N 112 D6
Ibi E 96 C2
Ibiza = Eivissa E 97 C1
İbradı TR 119 E6
İbriktepe TR 118 A1
Ibros E 100 A2
Ibstock GB 27 C4
İçel TR 16 C7
Ichenhausen D 61 B6
Ichnya UA 11 A12
Ichtegem B 49 B4
Ichtershausen D 51 C6
Idanha-a-Novo P 93 B3
Idar-Oberstein D 60 A3
Idd N 35 C3
Idiazábal E 89 B4
Idivuoma S 113 D10
Idkerberget S 36 B2
Idön S 36 B5
Idre S 115 F9
Idrija SLO 73 C4
Idritsa RUS 7 C10
Idstein D 50 C4
Idvor SRB 75 C5
Iecca Mare RO 75 C5
Ielsi I 103 B7
Ieper = Ypres B 48 C3
Ierapetra GR 117 G7
Ierissos GR 116 B5
Ifjord N 113 B16
Ig SLO 73 C4
Igal H 74 B2
Igalo MNE 105 A4
Igea E 89 B4
Igea Marina I 82 B1
Igelfors S 37 D2
Igersheim D 61 A5
Iggesund S 115 F14
Iglarevo KOS 85 D5
Iglesias E 88 B3
Iglésias I 110 C1
Igls A 71 A6
Igny-Comblizy F 59 A4
Igorre E 89 A4
Igoumenitsa GR 116 C2
Igries E 90 A2
Igualada E 91 B4
Igüeña E 86 B4
Iguerande F 68 B4
Iharosberény H 74 B2
Ihl'any SK 65 A6
Ihlienworth D 43 B5
Ihringen D 60 B3
Ihrlerstein D 62 B2
İhsaniye TR 118 C5
Ii FIN 3 D26
Iijärvi FIN 113 C16
Iisalmi FIN 3 E27
IJmuiden NL 42 C1
IJsselmuiden NL 42 C2
IJzendijke NL 49 B4
Ikast DK 39 C2
Ikervár H 74 A1
Ilandža SRB 75 C5
Ilanz CH 71 B4
Ilava SK 64 B4
Iława PL 47 B5
il Castagno I 81 C4
Ilche E 90 B3
Ilchester GB 29 C5
Ilfeld D 51 B6
Ilfracombe GB 28 B3
Ilgaz TR 16 A6
Ilgın TR 119 D6
Ílhavo P 92 A2
Ilica TR 118 C2
Ilidža BIH 84 C3
Ilijaš BIH 84 C3
Ilirska Bistrica SLO 73 C4
Ilkeston GB 27 C4
Ilkley GB 27 B4
Illana E 95 B4
Illano E 86 A4
Illar E 101 C3
Illas E 88 A1
Illats F 76 B2
Illertissen D 61 B6
Illescas E 94 B3
Ille-sur-Têt F 91 A5
Illfurth F 60 C3
Illichivsk UA 11 C11
Illiers-Combray F 58 B2
Illkirch-Graffenstaden F 60 B3
Illmersdorf D 52 B3
Illmitz A 64 C2
Íllora E 100 B2
Illueca E 89 C5
Ilmajoki FIN 3 E25
Ilmenau D 51 C6
Ilminster GB 29 C5
Ilok HR 75 C4
Ilomantsi FIN 3 E29
Iłow PL 47 C6
Iłowa PL 53 B5
Iłowo-Osada PL 47 B6
Ilsenburg D 51 B6
Ilshofen D 61 A5
Ilz A 73 A5
Iłża PL 55 B6
Imamoğlu TR 16 C7
Imatra FIN 3 F28
Imber GB 29 B5
Imielin PL 55 C4
Imingen N 32 B5
Immeln S 41 C4
Immenhausen D 51 B5
Immenstadt D 61 C6
Immingham GB 27 B5
Ímola I 81 B5
Imon E 95 A4
Imotski HR 84 C2
Impéria I 80 C2
Imphy F 68 B3
İmroz TR 116 B7
Imsland N 33 C2
Imst A 71 A5
Inagh IRL 20 B2
Inari FIN 113 D15
Inca E 97 B2
Inchnadamph GB 22 C4
Incinillas E 89 B3
Indal S 115 E14
Indjija SRB 85 A5
Indre Arna N 32 B2
Indre Billefjord N 113 B14
Indre Brenna N 113 B14
İğneada TR 118 A2
İnebolu TR 16 A6
İnecik TR 118 B2
İnegöl TR 118 B4
Inerthal CH 70 A3
Infiesto E 88 A1
Ingatorp S 40 B5
Ingedal N 35 C3
Ingelheim D 50 D4
Ingelmunster B 49 C4
Ingelstad S 40 C4
Ingleton GB 26 A3
Ingolfsland N 32 C5
Ingolstadt D 62 B2
Ingrandes
Maine-et-Loire F 66 A4
Vienne F 67 B5
Ingwiller F 60 B3
Inhisar TR 118 B5
Inhulec UA 11 C12
Iniesta E 95 C5
Inishannon IRL 20 C3
Inishcrone IRL 18 B2
Inke H 74 B2
Inndyr N 112 E3
Innellan GB 24 C3
Innerleithen GB 25 C4
Innermessan GB 24 D3
Innertkirchen CH 70 B3
Innervillgraten A 72 B2
Innsbruck A 71 A6
Innset N 112 D7
Innvik N 114 F3
İnönü TR 118 C5
Inowłódz PL 55 B5
Inowrocław PL 47 C4
Ins CH 70 A2
Insch GB 23 D6
Insjön S 36 B2
Ińsko PL 46 B1
Instow GB 28 B3
İntepe TR 118 B1
Interlaken CH 70 B2
Intragna CH 70 B3
Introbio I 71 C4
Inverallochy GB 23 D7
Inveran
GB 23 D4
IRL 20 A2
Inveraray GB 24 B2
Inverbervie GB 25 B5
Invergarry GB 22 D4
Invergordon GB 23 D4
Invergowrie GB 25 B4
Inverkeilor GB 25 B5
Inverkeithing GB 25 B4
Invermoriston GB 22 D4
Inverness GB 23 D4
Inveruno I 70 C3
Inverurie GB 23 D6
Ioannina GR 116 C2
Iolanda di Savoia I 81 B5
Ion Corvin RO 11 D9
Ióppolo I 106 C2
Ios GR 117 F7
Ipati GR 116 D4
Ipsala TR 118 B1
Ipswich GB 30 B5
Iraklia GR 116 A5
Iraklio = Heraklion GR 117 G7
Irdning A 73 A4
Iregszemcse H 74 B3
Irgoli I 110 B2
Irig SRB 85 A4
Ironbridge GB 26 C3
Irpin UA 11 A11
Irrel D 60 A2
Irsina I 104 C2
Irsta S 37 C3
Irthlingborough GB 30 B3
Iruela E 87 B4
Irún E 76 C1
Irurita E 76 C1
Irurzun E 76 D1
Irvine GB 24 C3
Irvinestown GB 19 B4
Isaba E 76 D2
Isabela E 100 A2
Ísafjörður IS 111 A2
Isane N 114 F2
Isaszeg H 75 A4
Isbister GB 22 A7
Iscar E 88 C2
İscehisar TR 118 D5
Ischgl A 71 A5
Ischia I 103 C6
Ischia di Castro I 102 A4
Ischitella I 104 B1
Isdes F 58 C3
Ise N 35 C3
Iselle I 70 B3
Iseltwald CH 70 B2
Isen D 62 B3
Isenbüttel D 44 C2
Iseo I 71 C5
Iserlohn D 50 B3
Isérnia I 103 B7
Isfjorden N 114 E4
Ishëm AL 105 B5
Isigny-sur-Mer F 57 A4
Işıklı TR 119 D4
Ísili I 110 C2
İskilip TR 16 A7
Isla Canela E 98 B3
Isla Cristina E 98 B3
Islares E 89 A3
Isleham GB 30 B4
Isle of Whithorn GB 24 D3
Ismaning D 62 B2
Isna P 92 B3
Isnestoften N 113 B11
Isny D 61 C6
Isoba E 88 A1
Isokylä
FIN 113 F16
S 113 E11
Isola F 79 B6
Isola d'Asti I 80 B2
Isola del Gran Sasso d'Itália I 103 A6
Ísola del Liri I 103 B6
Ísola della Scala I 71 C6
Isola delle Fémmine I 108 A2
Ísola di Capo Rizzuto I 107 C4
Isona E 91 A4
Ispagnac F 78 B2
Isparta TR 119 E5
Isperikh BG 11 E9
Íspica I 109 C3
Isselburg D 50 B2
Issigeac F 77 B3
Issogne I 70 C2
Issoire F 68 C3
Issoncourt F 59 B6
Issoudun F 68 B2
Issum D 50 B2
Is-sur-Tille F 69 A5
Issy-l'Evêque F 68 B3
Istán E 100 C1
İstanbul TR 118 A3
Istebna PL 65 A4
Ístia d'Ombrone I 81 D5
Istiea GR 116 D5
Istok KOS 85 D5
Istres F 78 C3
Istvándi H 74 B2
Itea GR 116 D4
Ithaki GR 117 D2
Itoiz E 76 D1
Itrabo E 100 C2
Itri I 103 B6
Ittireddu I 110 B1
Ittiri I 110 B1
Itzehoe D 43 B6
Ivalo FIN 113 D16
Iván H 74 A1
Ivanava BY 7 E8
Ivančice CZ 64 A2
Ivančna Gorica SLO 73 C4
Iváncsa H 74 A3
Ivanec HR 73 B6
Ivanić Grad HR 73 C6
Ivanjica SRB 85 C5
Ivanjska BIH 84 B2
Ivanka SK 64 B4
Ivankovo HR 74 C3
Ivano-Frankivsk UA 11 B8
Ivanovice na Hané CZ 64 A3
Ivanska HR 74 C1
Ivatsevichy BY 7 E8
Ivaylovgrad BG 116 A8
Iveland N 33 D4
Ivoz Ramet B 49 C6
Ivrea I 70 C2
İvrindi TR 118 C2
Ivry-en-Montagne F 69 A4
Ivry-la-Bataille F 58 B2
Ivybridge GB 28 C4
Iwaniska PL 55 C6
Iwiny PL 53 B5
Iwuy F 49 C4
Ixworth GB 30 B4
Izarra E 89 B4
Izbica Kujawska PL 47 C4
Izbište SRB 85 A6
Izeda P 87 C4
Izegem B 49 C4
Izernore F 69 B5
Izmayil UA 11 D10
İzmir TR 119 D2
İzmit = Kocaeli TR 118 B4
Iznájar E 100 B1
Iznalloz E 100 B2
Iznatoraf E 100 A2
İznik TR 118 B4
Izola SLO 72 C3
Izsák H 75 B4
Izsófalva H 65 B6
Izyaslav UA 11 A9

J

Jabalquinto E 100 A2
Jablanac HR 83 B3
Jablanica BIH 84 C2
Jablonec nad Jizerou CZ 53 C5
Jablonec nad Nisou CZ 53 C5
Jablonica SK 64 B3
Jablonka PL 65 A5
Jabłonna PL 55 A5
Jablonnénad Orlicí CZ 54 C1
Jablonne Podještědi CZ 53 C4
Jablonov nad Turňou SK 65 B6
Jabłonowo Pomorskie PL 47 B5
Jablúnka CZ 64 A3
Jablunkov CZ 65 A4
Jabučje SRB 85 B5
Jabugo E 99 B4
Jabuka
Srbija SRB 85 C4
Vojvodina SRB 85 B5
Jabukovac HR 73 C6
Jaca E 90 A2
Jáchymov CZ 52 C2
Jacobidrebber D 43 C5
Jade D 43 B5
Jäderfors S 36 B3
Jädraås S 36 B3
Jadraque E 95 B4
Jaén E 100 B2
Jagare BIH 84 B2
Jagel D 43 A6
Jagenbach A 63 B6
Jægerspris DK 39 D4
Jagodina SRB 85 C6
Jagodnjak HR 74 C3
Jagodzin PL 53 B5
Jagstheim D 61 A6
Jagstzell D 61 A6
Jahodna SK 64 B3
Jajce BIH 84 B2
Ják H 74 A1
Jakabszálbs H 75 B4
Jäkkvik S 115 A14
Jaklovce SK 65 B6
Jakobsnes N 113 C19
Jakovlje HR 73 C5
Jakšić HR 74 C2
Jakubany SK 65 A6
Jalance E 96 B1
Jalasjärvi FIN 3 E25
Jalhay B 50 C1
Jaligny-sur-Besbre F 68 B3
Jallais F 66 A4
Jalón E 96 C2
Jâlons F 59 B5
Jamena SRB 84 B4
Jamilena E 100 B2
Jämjö S 41 C5
Jamnička Kiselica HR 73 C5
Jamno PL 46 A2
Jamoigne B 59 A6
Jämsä FIN 3 F26
Jämshög S 41 C4
Janakkala FIN 3 F26
Jandelsbrunn D 63 B4
Jänickendorf D 52 A3
Janikowo PL 47 C4
Janja BIH 85 B4
Janjina HR 84 D2
Janki
Łódzkie PL 55 B4
Mazowieckie PL 55 A5
Jankov CZ 63 A5
Jankowo Dolne PL 46 C3
Jánoshalma H 75 B4
Jánosháza H 74 A2
Jánoshida H 75 A5
Jánossomorja H 64 C3
Janovice nad Uhlavou CZ 63 A4
Janów PL 55 C4
Janowiec Wielkopolski PL 46 C3
Janowo PL 47 B6
Jänsmässholmen S 115 D10
Janville F 58 B2
Janzé F 57 C4
Jarabá SK 65 B5
Jaraczewo PL 54 B2
Jarafuel E 96 B1
Jaraicejo E 93 B5
Jaraíz de la Vera E 93 A5
Jarak SRB 85 B4
Jarandilla de la Vera E 93 A5
Jaray E 89 C4
Järbo S 36 B3
Jard-sur-Mer F 66 B3
Jaren N 34 B2
Jargeau F 58 C3
Jarkovac SRB 75 C5
Järlåsa S 36 C4
Jarmen D 45 B5
Järna S 37 C4
Jarnac F 67 C4
Järnäs S 115 D16
Järnforsen S 40 B5
Jarny F 60 A1
Jarocin PL 54 B2
Jaroměř CZ 53 C5

Jaroměřice nad Rokytnou CZ 64 A1
Jaroslav CZ 53 C6
Jaroslavice CZ 64 B2
Jarosław PL 11 A7
Jarosławiec PL 46 A2
Jarošov nad Nežárkou CZ 63 A6
Järpås S 35 D4
Järpen S 115 D10
Jarrow GB 25 D6
Järso FIN 36 B6
Järvenpää FIN 7 A8
Jarvorník CZ 54 C1
Järvsö S 115 F13
Jarzé F 67 A4
Jaša Tomic SRB 75 C5
Jasenak HR 73 C5
Jasenica BIH 83 B5
Jasenice HR 83 B4
Jasenovac HR 74 C1
Jasenovo
Srbija SRB 85 C4
Vojvodina SRB 85 B6
Jasień PL 53 B5
Jasienica PL 53 B4
Jasika SRB 85 C6
Jasło PL 10 B6
Jásova SK 65 C4
Jasseron F 69 B5
Jastarnia PL 47 A4
Jastrebarsko HR 73 C5
Jastrowie PL 46 B2
Jastrzębia-Góra PL 47 A4
Jastrzębie Zdrój PL 54 D3
Jászals-Lószentgyörgy H 75 A5
Jászapáti H 75 A5
Jászárokszállás H 65 C5
Jászberény H 75 A4
Jászdózsa H 65 C6
Jászfényszaru H 75 A4
Jászjakóhalma H 75 A5
Jászkarajenő H 75 A5
Jászkisér H 75 A5
Jászladány H 75 A5
Jászszentlászló H 75 B4
Jásztelek H 75 A5
Játar E 100 C2
Jättendal S 115 F14
Jatznick D 45 B5
Jaun CH 70 B2
Jausiers F 79 B5
Jávea E 96 C3
Jävenitz D 44 C3
Javerlhac F 67 C5
Javier E 90 A1
Javorani BIH 84 B2
Javorina SK 65 A6
Javron F 57 B5
Jawor PL 53 B6
Jaworzno PL 55 C4
Jaworzyna Śl. PL 54 C1
Jayena E 100 C2
Jażow PL 53 B4
Jebel RO 75 C6
Jebjerg DK 38 C2
Jedburgh GB 25 C5
Jedlinsk PL 55 B6
Jedlnia PL 55 B6
Jedlnia Letnisko PL 55 B6
Jedovnice CZ 64 A2
Jędrychow PL 47 B5
Jędrzejów PL 55 C5
Jedwabno PL 47 B6
Jeesiö FIN 113 E15
Jegłownik PL 47 A5
Jegun F 77 C3
Jēkabpils LV 7 C8
Jektevik N 32 C2
Jektvik N 112 F2
Jelakci SRB 85 C5
Jelcz-Laskowice PL 54 B2
Jelenec SK 64 B4
Jelenia Góra PL 53 C5
Jelgava LV 6 C7
Jelka SK 64 B3
Jelling DK 39 D2
Jels DK 39 D2
Jelsa
HR 83 C5
N 33 C3
Jelšava SK 65 B6
Jemgum D 43 B4
Jemnice CZ 63 A6
Jena D 52 C1
Jenaz CH 71 B4
Jenbach A 72 A1
Jenikow PL 45 B7
Jennersdorf A 73 B6
Jenny S 40 B6
Jerchel D 44 C3
Jeres del Marquesado E 100 B2
Jerez de la Frontera E 99 C4
Jerez de los Caballeros E 99 A4
Jerica E 96 B2
Jerichow D 44 C4
Jerka PL 54 A1
Jermenovci SRB 75 C6
Jerslev DK 38 B3
Jerte E 93 A5
Jerup DK 38 B3
Jerxheim D 51 A6
Jerzmanowice PL 55 C4
Jerzu I 110 C2
Jerzwałd PL 47 B5
Jesberg D 51 C5
Jesenice
Středočeský CZ 52 C3
Středočeský CZ 53 D4
SLO 73 B4
Jeseník CZ 54 C2
Jesenské SK 65 B6
Jesi I 82 C2
Jésolo I 72 C2
Jessen D 52 B2
Jessenitz D 44 B3
Jessheim N 34 B3
Jessnitz D 52 B2
Jesteburg D 44 B1
Jeumont F 49 C5
Jeven-stedt D 43 A6
Jever D 43 B4
Jevíčko CZ 64 A2
Jevišovice CZ 64 B1
Jevnaker N 34 B2
Jezerane HR 83 A4
Jezero
BIH 84 B2
HR 83 B4
Jeziorany PL 47 B6
Jeżów PL 55 B4
Jičín CZ 53 C5
Jičíněves CZ 53 C5
Jihlava CZ 63 A6
Jijona E 96 C2
Jilemnice CZ 53 C5
Jílové CZ 53 C4
Jílovéu Prahy CZ 63 A5
Jimbolia RO 75 C5
Jimena E 100 B2
Jimena de la Frontera E 99 C5
Jimera de Libar E 99 C5
Jimramov CZ 64 A2
Jince CZ 63 A4
Jindřichovice CZ 52 C2
Jindřichův Hradec CZ 63 A6
Jirkov CZ 52 C3
Jistebnice CZ 63 A5
Joachimsthal D 45 C5
João da Loura P 92 C2
Jobbágyi H 65 C5
Jochberg A 72 A2
Jockfall S 113 F11
Jódar E 100 B2
Jodoigne B 49 C5
Joensuu FIN 3 E28
Joesjö S 115 B11
Joeuf F 60 A1
Jõgeva EST 7 B9
Johanngeorgenstadt D 52 C2
Johannishus S 41 C5
Johanniskirchen D 62 B3
Johansfors S 40 C5
John o'Groats GB 23 C5
Johnshaven GB 25 B5
Johnstone GB 24 C3
Johnstown IRL 21 B4
Jõhvi EST 7 B9
Joigny F 59 C4
Joinville F 59 B6
Jokkmokk S 112 F8
Jöllenbeck D 51 A4
Jomala FIN 36 B6
Jönåker S 37 D3
Jonava LT 6 D8
Jonchery-sur-Vesle F 59 A4
Jondal N 32 B3
Jondalen N 33 C6
Joniškis LT 6 C7
Jönköping S 40 B4
Jonkowo PL 47 B6
Jønnbu N 33 C6
Jonsberg S 37 D3
Jonsered S 38 B5
Jonstorp S 41 C2
Jonzac F 67 C4
Jorba E 91 B4
Jordanów PL 65 A5
Jordanowo PL 46 C1
Jordanów Śląski PL 54 C1
Jordbro S 37 C5
Jordbrua N 115 A11
Jördenstorf D 45 B4
Jordet N 34 A4
Jordøse DK 39 D3
Jork D 43 B6
Jörlanda S 38 B4
Jormlien S 115 C10
Jormvattnet S 115 C11
Jörn S 115 B17
Jørpeland N 33 C3
Jorquera E 96 B1
Jošan HR 83 B4
Jošanička Banja SRB 85 C5
Jošavka BIH 84 B2
Josipdol HR 73 C5
Josipovac HR 74 C3
Jössefors S 35 C4
Josselin F 56 C3
Jøssund N 114 C7
Jostedal N 114 F4
Jósvafő H 65 B6
Jou P 87 C3
Jouarre F 59 B4
Joué-lès-Tours F 67 A5
Joué-sur-Erdre F 66 A3
Joure NL 42 C2
Joutseno FIN 3 F28
Joutsijärvi FIN 113 F16
Joux-la-Ville F 59 C4
Jouy F 58 B2
Jouy-le-Châtel F 59 B4
Jouy-le-Potier F 58 C2
Joyeuse F 78 B3
Joze F 68 C3
Józefów PL 55 A6
Juankoski FIN 3 E28
Juan-les-Pins F 79 C6
Juban AL 105 A5
Jübek D 43 A6
Jubera E 89 B4
Jubrique E 99 C5
Jüchsen D 51 C6
Judaberg N 33 C2
Judenburg A 73 A4
Juelsminde DK 39 D3
Jugon-les-Lacs F 56 B3
Juillac F 67 C6
Juillan F 76 C3
Juist D 43 B4
Jukkasjärvi S 112 E9
Jule N 115 C10
Julianadorp NL 42 C1
Julianstown IRL 19 C5
Jülich D 50 C2
Jullouville F 57 B4
Jumeaux F 68 C3
Jumièges F 58 A1
Jumilhac-le-Grand F 67 C6
Jumilla E 101 A4
Juncosa E 90 B3
Juneda E 90 B3
Jung S 35 D5
Jungingen D 61 B5
Junglingster L 60 A2
Juniville F 59 A5
Junosuando S 113 E11
Junqueira P 87 C3
Junsele S 115 D13
Juoksengi S 113 F12
Juoksenki FIN 113 F12
Juprelle B 49 C6
Jurata PL 47 A4
Jurbarkas LT 6 D7
Jurjevo HR 83 B3
Jūrmala LV 6 C7
Juromenha P 93 C3
Jursla S 37 D3
Jussac F 77 B5
Jussey F 60 C1
Jussy F 59 A4
Juta H 74 B2
Jüterbog D 52 B3
Juuka FIN 3 E28
Juvigny-le-Terte F 57 B4
Juvigny-sous-Andaine F 57 B5
Juzennecourt F 59 B5
Jyderup DK 39 D4
Jyväskylä FIN 3 E26

K

Kaamanen FIN 113 C16
Kaamasmukka FIN 113 C15
Kaaresuvanto FIN 113 D11
Kaarssen D 44 B3
Kaatscheuvel NL 49 B6
Kaba H 75 A6
Kåbdalis S 115 A17
Kačarevo SRB 85 B5
Kačikol KOS 85 D6
Kács H 65 C6
Kadan CZ 52 C3
Kadarkút H 74 B2
Kadınhanı TR 119 D7
Kaduy RUS 7 B14
Kåfalla S 37 C2
Kåfjord N 113 C12
Kåfjordbotn N 112 C9
Kågeröd S 41 D3
Kahl D 51 C5
Kahla D 52 C1
Kainach bei Voitsberg A 73 A5
Kaindorf A 73 A5
Kainulasjärvi S 113 F11
Kairala FIN 113 E16
Kaisepakte S 112 D8
Kaisersesch D 50 C3
Kaiserslautern D 60 A3
Kaisheim D 62 B1
Kajaani FIN 3 D27
Kajárpéc H 74 A2
Kajdacs H 74 B3
Kakanj BIH 84 B3
Kakasd H 74 B3
Kaklik TR 119 E4
Kakolewo PL 54 B1
Kál H 65 C6
Kalače MNE 85 D5
Kalajoki FIN 3 D25
Kalak N 113 B16
Kalamata GR 117 E4
Kalambaka GR 116 C3
Kalamria GR 116 B4
Kalandra GR 116 C5
Kälarne S 115 E13
Kalavrita GR 117 D4
Kalbe D 44 C3
Kalce SLO 73 C4
Káld H 74 A2
Kale
Antalya TR 119 F4
Denizli TR 119 E3
Kalecik TR 16 A6
Kalefeld D 51 B6
Kalenić SRB 85 C5
Kalesija BIH 84 B3
Kalety PL 54 C3
Kalevala RUS 3 D29
Kalhovd N 32 B5
Kali HR 83 B4
Kalimnos GR 119 F2
Kaliningrad RUS 47 A6
Kalinkavichy BY 7 E10
Kalinovac HR 74 B2
Kalinovik BIH 84 C3
Kalinovo SK 65 B5
Kalirachi GR 116 B6
Kaliska
Pomorskie PL 47 A4
Pomorskie PL 47 B4
Kalisko PL 55 B4
Kalisz PL 54 B3
Kalisz Pomorski PL 46 B1
Kalix S 3 D25
Kaljord N 112 D4
Kalkan TR 119 F4
Kalkar D 50 B2
Kalkım TR 118 C2
Kall
D 50 C2
S 115 D10
Källby S 35 D5
Källered S 38 B5
Källerstad S 40 B3
Kallinge S 41 C5
Kallmeti i Madh AL 105 B5
Kallmünz D 62 A2
Kallo FIN 113 E13
Kallsedet S 115 D9
Källvik S 37 D4
Kalmar S 40 C6
Kalmthout B 49 B5
Kalná SK 65 B4
Kalocsa H 75 B3
Kalokhorio CY 120 B2
Kalo Nero GR 117 E3
Kaloni GR 116 C8
Káloz H 74 B3
Kals A 72 A2
Kalsdorf A 73 B5
Kaltbrunn CH 70 A4
Kaltenbach A 72 A1
Kaltenkirchen D 44 B1
Kaltennordheim D 51 C6
Kaluga RUS 7 D14
Kalundborg DK 39 D4
Kalush UA 11 B8
Kałuszyn PL 55 A6
Kalv S 40 B3
Kalvåg N 114 F1
Kalvehave DK 41 D2
Kalwang A 73 A4
Kalwaria-Zebrzydowska PL 65 A5
Kalyazin RUS 7 C14
Kam H 74 A1
Kaman TR 16 B6
Kamares GR 117 F6
Kambos CY 120 A1
Kamen D 50 B3
Kamenice CZ 64 A1
Kamenice nad Lipou CZ 63 A6
Kameničná SK 64 C4
Kamenný Most SK 65 C4
Kamenny Ujezd CZ 63 B5
Kamenska HR 74 C2
Kamensko HR 84 C1
Kamenz D 53 B4
Kamičak BIH 84 B1
Kamień PL 55 B5
Kamieniec Ząbk PL 54 C1
Kamienka SK 65 A6
Kamień Krajeński PL 46 B3
Kamienna Góra PL 53 C6
Kamień Pomorski PL 45 B6
Kamieńsk PL 55 B4
Kaminka UA 11 B12
Kamiros Skala GR 119 F2
Kamnik SLO 73 B4
Kampen NL 42 C2
Kampinos PL 55 A5
Kamp-Lintfort D 50 B2
Kampor HR 83 B3
Kamyanets-Podil's'kyy UA 11 B9
Kamyanka-Buz'ka UA 11 A8
Kamýk nad Vltavou CZ 63 A5
Kanal SLO 72 B3
Kanalia GR 116 C4
Kandalaksha RUS 3 C30
Kandanos GR 117 G5
Kandel D 61 A4
Kandern D 60 C3
Kandersteg CH 70 B2
Kandila GR 117 E4
Kandıra TR 118 A5
Kandyty PL 47 A6
Kanfanar HR 82 A2
Kangasala FIN 3 F26
Kangos S 113 E11
Kangosjärvi FIN 113 E12
Kanië AL 105 C5
Kanjiža SRB 75 B5
Kankaanpää FIN 3 F25
Kannus FIN 3 E25
Kanturk IRL 20 B3
Kaonik SRB 85 C6
Kapaklı TR 118 A2
Kapellen
A 63 C6
B 49 B5
Kapellskär S 37 C6
Kapfenberg A 73 A5
Kapfenstein A 73 B5
Kaplice CZ 63 B5
Kapljuh BIH 83 B5
Kápolna H 65 C6
Kápolnásnyék H 74 A3
Kaposfő H 74 B2
Kaposfüred H 74 B2
Kaposszekcsö H 74 B3
Kaposvár H 74 B2
Kapp N 34 B2
Kappel D 60 B3
Kappeln D 44 A1
Kappelshamn S 37 E5
Kappl A 71 A5
Kappstad S 35 C5
Kaprun A 72 A2
Kaptol HR 74 C2
Kapuvár H 64 C3
Karaadilli TR 119 D5
Karabiğa TR 118 B2
Karabük TR 118 A7
Karaburun TR 118 D1
Karacabey TR 118 B3
Karacakılavuz TR 118 A2
Karacaköy TR 118 A3
Karacaören TR 119 D5
Karacasu TR 119 E3
Karachev RUS 7 E13
Karácsond H 65 C6
Karád H 74 B2
Karahallı TR 119 D4
Karaisali TR 16 C7
Karaman
Balıkesir TR 118 C3
Karaman TR 16 C6
Karamanlı TR 119 E4
Karamürsel TR 118 B4
Karan SRB 85 C4
Karancslapujto H 65 B5
Karaova TR 119 E2
Karapınar TR 16 C6
Karasjok N 113 C14
Karasu TR 118 A5
Karataş
Adana TR 16 C7
Manisa TR 119 D3
Karatoprak TR 119 E2
Karavostasi CY 120 A1
Karbenning S 36 B3
Kårberg S 37 D1
Kårböle S 115 F12
Karbunara AL 105 C5
Karby
D 44 A1
DK 38 C1
Kårby S 40 B6
Karby S 37 C5
Karcag H 75 A5
Karczew PL 55 A6
Karczów PL 54 C2
Karczowiska PL 53 B6
Kardamena GR 119 F2
Kardamila GR 116 D8
Kardamili GR 117 F4
Kardašova Rečice CZ 63 A5
Kardis S 113 F12
Karditsa GR 116 C3
Kärdla EST 6 B7
Kardoskút H 75 B5
Karesuando S 113 D11
Kargı TR 16 A7
Kargowa PL 53 A5
Karigasniemi FIN 113 C14
Karise DK 41 D2
Karistos GR 117 D6
Karkkila FIN 6 A8
Karlholmsbruk S 36 B4
Karlino PL 46 A1
Karl Liebknecht RUS 7 F13
Karlobag HR 83 B4
Karlovac HR 73 C5
Karlovasi GR 119 E1
Karlovčic SRB 85 B5
Karlovice CZ 54 C2
Karlovo BG 11 E8
Karlovy Vary CZ 52 C2
Karłowice PL 54 C2
Karlsborg S 37 D1
Karlshamn S 41 C4
Karlshöfen D 43 B6
Karlshus N 35 C2
Karlskoga S 37 C1
Karlskrona S 41 C5
Karlsrud N 32 B5
Karlsruhe D 61 A4
Karlstad S 35 C5
Karlstadt D 51 D5
Karlstetten A 63 B6
Karlstift A 63 B5
Karlstorp S 40 B5
Karmacs H 74 B2
Karmin PL 54 B2
Kärna S 38 B4
Karnobat BG 11 E9
Karojba HR 72 C3
Karow D 44 B4
Karpacz PL 53 C5
Karpathos GR 119 G2
Karpenisi GR 116 D3
Karpuzlu TR 119 E2
Kärrbo S 37 C3
Karrebaeksminde DK 39 D4
Karshult S 40 B3
Karsin PL 46 B3
Kårsta S 37 C5
Karstädt D 44 B3
Kartitsch A 72 B2
Kartuzy PL 47 A4
Karup DK 39 C2
Karviná CZ 65 A4
Kås DK 38 B2
Kaş TR 119 F4
Kasaba TR 119 F4
Kašava CZ 64 A3
Kåseberga S 41 D4
Kasejovice CZ 63 A4
Kasfjord N 112 D5
Kashin RUS 7 C14
Kašina HR 73 C6
Kasina-Wielka PL 65 A6
Kaskinen FIN 3 E24
Kašperské Hory CZ 63 A4
Kassandrino GR 116 B5
Kassel D 51 B5
Kassiopi GR 116 C1
Kastamonu TR 16 A6
Kastav HR 73 C4
Kasteli GR 117 G5
Kastellaun D 50 C3
Kastelli GR 117 G7
Kaštel-Stari HR 83 C5
Kaštel Zegarski HR 83 B4
Kasterlee B 49 B5
Kastl D 62 A2
Kastlösa S 41 C6
Kastorf D 44 B2
Kastoria GR 116 B3
Kastorio GR 117 E4
Kastraki GR 117 F7
Kastrosikia GR 116 C2
Kastsyukovichy BY 7 E12
Kaszaper H 75 B5
Katakolo GR 117 E3
Katapola GR 117 F7
Katastari GR 117 E2
Katerbow D 45 C4
Katerini GR 116 B4
Kathikas CY 120 B1
Kätkesuando S 113 D12
Katlenburg-Lindau D 51 B6
Kato Achaia GR 117 D3
Káto Pyrgos CY 120 A1
Katouna GR 116 D3
Katovice CZ 63 A4
Katowice PL 55 C4
Katrineberg S 36 A3
Katrineholm S 37 D3
Kattarp S 41 C2
Kattavia GR 119 G2
Katthammarsvik S 37 E5
Kattilstorp S 40 A3
Katwijk NL 49 A5
Katymár H 75 B4
Kąty Wrocławskie PL 54 B1
Katzenelnbogen D 50 C3
Katzhütte D 52 C1
Kaub D 50 C3
Kaufbeuren D 62 C1
Kauhajoki FIN 3 E25
Kauhava FIN 3 E25
Kaukonen FIN 113 E13
Kaulsdorf D 52 C1
Kaunas LT 6 D7
Kaunisvaara S 113 E12
Kaupanger N 32 A4
Kautokeino N 113 C12
Kautzen A 63 B6
Kavadarci MK 116 A4
Kavajë AL 105 B5
Kavakköy TR 118 B1
Kavaklı TR 118 A2
Kavaklıdere TR 119 E3
Kavala GR 116 B6
Kavarna BG 11 E10
Kävlinge S 41 D3
Kawcze PL 46 A2
Kaxås S 115 D10
Kaxholmen S 40 B4
Käymäjärvi FIN 113 E12
Kaymakçı TR 119 D3
Kaymaz TR 118 C6
Kaynarca TR 118 A5
Käyrämö FIN 113 F15
Kayseri TR 16 B7
Kaysersberg F 60 B3
Kazanlŭk BG 11 E8
Kazár H 65 B5
Kazimierza Wielka PL 55 C5
Kazincbarcika H 65 B6
Kaźmierz PL 46 C2
Kcynia PL 46 B3
Kdyně CZ 62 A4
Kea GR 117 E6
Keadew IRL 18 B3
Keady GB 19 B5
Kecel H 75 B4
Keçiborlu TR 119 E5
Kecskemét H 75 B4
Kėdainiai LT 6 D7
Kędzierzyn-Koźle PL 54 C3
Keel IRL 18 C1
Keenagh IRL 19 C4
Keerbergen B 49 B5
Kefalos GR 119 F1
Kefken TR 118 A5
Keflavík IS 111 C3
Kegworth GB 27 C4
Kehl D 60 B3
Kehrigk D 53 A3
Keighley GB 27 B4
Keila EST 6 B8
Keillmore GB 24 C2
Keiss GB 23 C5
Keith GB 23 D6
Kelberg D 50 C2
Kelbra D 51 B7
Kelč CZ 64 A3
Kelchsau A 72 A2
Këlcyrë AL 116 B2
Keld GB 26 A3
Kelebia H 75 B4
Kelekçi TR 119 E4
Kelemér H 65 B6
Keles TR 118 C4
Kelheim D 62 B2
Kell D 60 A2
Kellas GB 23 D5
Kellinghusen D 43 B6
Kelloselkä FIN 113 F17
Kells
GB 19 B5
IRL 19 C5
Kelmis B 50 C2
Kelokedhara CY 120 B1
Kelottijärvi FIN 113 D11
Kelsall GB 26 B3
Kelso GB 25 C5
Kelsterbach D 51 C4
Keltneyburn GB 24 B3
Kelujärvi FIN 113 E16
Kemaliye TR 119 D3
Kemalpaşa TR 119 D2
Kematen A 71 A6
Kemberg D 52 B2
Kemer
Antalya TR 119 F5
Burdur TR 119 E5
Muğla TR 119 F4
Kemerkaya TR 118 D6
Kemeten A 73 A6
Kemi FIN 3 D26
Kemijärvi FIN 113 F16
Kemnath D 62 A2
Kemnay GB 23 D6
Kemnitz
Brandenburg D 52 A2
Mecklenburg-Vorpommern D 45 A5
Kempen D 50 B2
Kempsey GB 29 A5
Kempten D 61 C6
Kemptthal CH 70 A3
Kendal GB 26 A3
Kenderes H 75 A5
Kengyel H 75 A5
Kenilworth GB 30 B2
Kenmare IRL 20 C2
Kenmore GB 25 B4
Kennacraig GB 24 C2
Kenyeri H 74 A2
Kenzingen D 60 B3
Kepez TR 118 B1
Kępice PL 46 A2
Kępno PL 54 B3
Kepsut TR 118 C3
Keramoti GR 116 B6
Keräntöjärvi S 113 E12
Keratea GR 117 E5
Kerava FIN 7 A8
Kerecsend H 65 C6
Kerekegyhaza H 75 B4
Kerepestarcsa H 75 A4
Keri GR 117 E2
Kérien F 56 B2
Kerkafalva H 74 B1
Kerken D 50 B2
Kerkrade NL 50 C2
Kerkyra GR 116 C1
Kerlouan F 56 B1
Kernascléden F 56 B2
Kernhof A 63 C6
Kerns CH 70 B3
Kerpen D 50 C2
Kerrysdale GB 22 D3
Kerta H 74 A2
Kerteminde DK 39 D3
Kerzers CH 70 B2
Keşan TR 118 B1
Kesgrave GB 30 B5
Kesh GB 19 B4
Keskin TR 16 B6
Kesselfall A 72 A2
Kestenga RUS 3 D29
Keswick GB 26 A2
Keszthely H 74 B2
Kétegyháza H 75 B6
Kéthely H 74 B2
Kętrzyn PL 6 D6
Kettering GB 30 B3
Kettlewell GB 26 A3
Kęty PL 65 A5
Ketzin D 45 C4
Keula D 51 B6
Keuruu FIN 3 E26
Kevelaer D 50 B2
Kevermes H 75 B6
Kevi SRB 75 C4
Keyingham GB 27 B5
Keynsham GB 29 B5
Kežmarok SK 65 A6
Kharmanli BG 11 F8
Khaskovo BG 11 F8
Kherson UA 11 C12
Khimki RUS 7 D14
Khisinev = Chişinău MD 11 C10
Khmelnik UA 11 B9
Khmelnytskyy UA 11 B9
Khodoriv UA 11 B8
Kholm RUS 7 C11
Khorol UA 11 B12
Khotyn UA 11 B9
Khoyniki BY 7 F10
Khust UA 11 B7
Khvoynaya RUS 7 B13
Kiato GR 117 D4
Kibæk DK 39 C1
Kiberg N 113 B19
Kicasalih TR 118 A1
Kičevo MK 116 A2
Kidderminster GB 26 C3
Kidlington GB 31 C2
Kidsgrove GB 26 B3
Kidwelly GB 28 B3
Kiefersfelden D 62 C3
Kiel D 44 A2
Kielce PL 55 C5
Kiełczygłów PL 54 B4
Kielder GB 25 C5
Kiełpino PL 47 A4
Kielpiny PL 47 B5
Kierinki FIN 113 E14
Kiernozia PL 55 A4
Kierspe D 50 B3
Kietrz PL 54 C3
Kietz D 45 C6
Kiev = Kyyiv UA 11 A11
Kiezmark PL 47 A4
Kiffisia GR 117 D5
Kifino Selo BIH 84 C3
Kihlanki
FIN 113 E12
S 113 E12
Kiistala FIN 113 E14
Kije PL 55 C5
Kijevo HR 83 C5
Kikallen N 32 B2
Kikinda SRB 75 C5
Kil
N 33 D6
Örebro S 37 C2
Värmland S 35 C5
Kila S 35 C4
Kilafors S 36 A3
Kilbaha IRL 20 B2
Kilbeggan IRL 21 A4
Kilberry GB 24 C2
Kilbirnie GB 24 C3
Kilboghamn N 112 F2
Kilbotn N 112 D5
Kilb Rabenstein A 63 B6
Kilchattan GB 24 C2
Kilchoan GB 24 B1
Kilcock IRL 21 A5
Kilconnell IRL 20 A3
Kilcormac IRL 21 A4
Kilcreggan GB 24 C3
Kilcullen IRL 21 A5
Kilcurry IRL 19 B5
Kildare IRL 21 A5
Kildinstroy RUS 3 B30
Kildonan GB 23 C5
Kildorrery IRL 20 B3
Kilegrend N 33 C5
Kilen N 33 C5
Kilgarvan IRL 20 C2
Kiliya UA 11 D10
Kilkee IRL 20 B2
Kilkeel GB 19 B5
Kilkelly IRL 18 C3
Kilkenny IRL 21 B4
Kilkieran IRL 20 A2
Kilkinlea IRL 20 B2
Kilkis GR 116 A4
Kill IRL 21 B4
Killadysert IRL 20 B2
Killala IRL 18 B2
Killaloe IRL 20 B3
Killarney IRL 20 B2
Killashandra IRL 19 B4
Killashee IRL 19 C4
Killearn GB 24 B3
Killeberg S 40 C4
Killeigh IRL 21 A4
Killenaule IRL 21 B4
Killimor IRL 20 A3
Killin GB 24 B3
Killinaboy IRL 20 B2
Killinge S 112 E9
Killinick IRL 21 B5
Killorglin IRL 20 B2
Killucan IRL 21 A4
Killybegs IRL 18 B3
Killyleagh GB 19 B6
Kilmacrenan IRL 19 A4
Kilmacthomas IRL 21 B4
Kilmaine IRL 18 C2
Kilmallock IRL 20 B3
Kilmarnock GB 24 C3
Kilmartin GB 24 B2
Kilmaurs GB 24 C3
Kilmeadan IRL 21 B4
Kilmeedy IRL 20 B3
Kilmelford GB 24 B2
Kilmore Quay IRL 21 B5
Kilmuir GB 23 D4
Kilnaleck IRL 19 C4
Kilninver GB 24 B2
Kilpisjärvi FIN 112 C9
Kilrea GB 19 B5
Kilrush IRL 20 B2
Kilsmo S 37 C2
Kilsyth GB 24 C3
Kiltoom IRL 20 A3
Kilwinning GB 24 C3
Kimasozero RUS 3 D29
Kimi GR 116 D6
Kimolos GR 117 F6
Kimovsk RUS 7 D14
Kimratshofen D 61 C6
Kimry RUS 7 C14
Kimstad S 37 D2
Kinbrace GB 23 C5
Kincardine GB 25 B4
Kincraig GB 23 D5
Kindberg A 73 A5
Kindelbruck D 52 B1
Kingarrow IRL 18 B3
Kingisepp RUS 7 B10
Kingsbridge GB 28 C4
Kingsclere GB 31 C2
Kingscourt IRL 19 C5
King's Lynn GB 30 B4
Kingsteignton GB 29 C4
Kingston
Greater London GB 31 C3
Moray GB 23 D5
Kingston Bagpuize GB 31 C2
Kingston upon Hull GB 27 B5
Kingswear GB 29 C4
Kingswood GB 29 B5
Kington GB 29 A4
Kingussie GB 23 D4
Kınık
Antalya TR 119 F4
İzmır TR 118 C2
Kinloch
Highland GB 22 C4
Highland GB 22 D2
Kinlochbervie GB 22 C3
Kinlochewe GB 22 D3
Kinlochleven GB 24 B3
Kinlochmoidart GB 24 B2
Kinloch Rannoch GB 24 B3
Kinloss GB 23 D5
Kinlough IRL 18 B3
Kinn N 34 B2
Kinna S 40 B2
Kinnared S 40 B3
Kinnarp S 40 A3
Kinnegad IRL 21 A4
Kinne-Kleva S 35 D5
Kinnitty IRL 21 A4
Kinrooi B 50 B1
Kinross GB 25 B4
Kinsale IRL 20 C3
Kinsarvik N 32 B3
Kintarvie GB 22 C2
Kintore GB 23 D6
Kinvarra IRL 20 A3
Kioni GR 116 D2
Kiparissia GR 117 E3
Kipfenburg D 62 B2
Kippen GB 24 B3
Kiraz TR 119 D3
Kirazlı TR 118 B1
Kirberg D 50 C4
Kirchbach in Steiermark A 73 B5
Kirchberg
CH 70 A2
Baden-Württemberg D 61 A5
Rheinland-Pfalz D 60 A3
Kirchberg am Wechsel A 64 C1
Kirchberg an der Pielach A 63 B6
Kirchberg in Tirol A 72 A2
Kirchbichl A 72 A2
Kirchdorf
Bayern D 63 B4
Mecklenburg-Vorpommern D 44 B3
Niedersachsen D 43 C5
Kirchdorf an der Krems A 63 C5
Kirchdorf in Tirol A 72 A2
Kirchenlamitz D 52 C1
Kirchenthumbach D 62 A2
Kirchhain D 51 C4
Kirchheim
Baden-Württemberg D 61 B5
Bayern D 61 B6
Hessen D 51 C5
Kirchheimbolanden D 61 A4
Kirchhundem D 50 B4
Kirchlintein D 43 C6
Kirchschlag A 73 A6
Kirchweidach D 62 B3
Kirchzarten D 60 C3
Kircubbin GB 19 B6
Kireç TR 118 C3
Kırıkkale TR 16 B6
Kirillov RUS 7 B15
Kirishi RUS 7 B12
Kırka TR 118 C5
Kırkağaç TR 118 C2
Kirkbean GB 25 D4
Kirkbride GB 25 D4
Kirkby GB 26 B3
Kirkby Lonsdale GB 26 A3
Kirkby Malzeard GB 27 A4
Kirkbymoorside GB 27 A5
Kirkby Stephen GB 26 A3
Kirkcaldy GB 25 B4
Kirkcolm GB 24 D2
Kirkconnel GB 24 C3
Kirkcowan GB 24 D3
Kirkcudbright GB 24 D3
Kirkehamn N 33 D3
Kirke Hyllinge DK 39 D4
Kirkenær N 34 B4
Kirkenes N 113 C19
Kirkham GB 26 B3
Kirkintilloch GB 24 C3
Kirkjubæjarklaustur IS 111 D7
Kirkkonummi FIN 6 A8
Kırklareli TR 118 A2
Kirkmichael GB 25 B4
Kirk Michael GB 26 A1
Kirkoswald GB 24 C3
Kirkpatrick Fleming GB 25 C4
Kirkton of Glenisla GB 25 B4
Kirkwall GB 23 C6
Kirkwhelpington GB 25 C6
Kirn D 60 A3
Kiro AL 105 A5
Kirov RUS 7 D13
Kirovohrad UA 11 B12
Kirovsk RUS 3 C30
Kirriemuir GB 25 B5
Kırşehir TR 16 B7
Kirton GB 30 B3
Kirton in Lindsey GB 27 B5
Kirtorf D 51 C5
Kiruna S 112 E9
Kisa S 40 B5
Kisač SRB 75 C4
Kisbér H 74 A3
Kiseljak BIH 84 C3
Kisielice PL 47 B5
Kisköre H 75 A5
Kiskőrös H 75 B4
Kiskunfélegyháza H 75 B4
Kiskunhalas H 75 B4
Kiskunlacháza H 75 A3
Kiskunmajsa H 75 B4
Kisláng H 74 B3
Kisslegg D 61 C5
Kissolt H 75 B4
Kissónerga CY 120 B1
Kist D 61 A5
Kistanje HR 83 C4
Kistelek H 75 B4
Kisterenye H 65 B5
Kisújszállás H 75 A5
Kisvárda H 11 B7
Kisvejke H 74 B3
Kiszkowo PL 46 C3
Kiszombor H 75 B5
Kitee FIN 3 E29
Kithnos GR 117 E6
Kiti CY 120 B2
Kitkiöjärvi S 113 E12
Kitkiöjoki S 113 E12
Kittelfjäll S 115 B12
Kittendorf D 45 B4
Kittilä FIN 113 E13
Kittlitz D 53 B4
Kittsee A 64 B3
Kitzbühel A 72 A2
Kitzingen D 61 A6
Kiuruvesi FIN 3 E27
Kivertsi UA 11 A8
Kividhes CY 120 B1
Kivik S 41 D4
Kivotos GR 116 B3
Kiwity PL 47 A6
Kıyıköy TR 118 A3
Kızılcabölük TR 119 E4
Kızılcadağ TR 119 E4
Kızılcahamam TR 16 A6
Kızılırmak TR 16 A6
Kızılkaya TR 119 E5
Kızılkuyu TR 118 D6
Kızılören
Afyon TR 119 D5
Konya TR 119 E7
Kjeldebotn N 112 D5
Kjellerup DK 39 C2
Kjellmyra N 34 B4
Kjøllefjord N 113 B16
Kjopmannskjaer N 35 C2
Kjøpsvik N 112 D5
Kl'ačno SK 65 B4
Kladanj BIH 84 B3
Kläden D 44 C3
Klädesholmen S 38 B4
Kladnica SRB 85 C5
Kladnice HR 83 C5
Kladno CZ 53 C4
Kladruby CZ 62 A3
Klagenfurt A 73 B4
Klågerup S 41 D3
Klagstorp S 41 D3
Klaipėda LT 6 D6
Klaistow D 52 A2
Klaksvík FO 2 E10
Klana HR 73 C4
Klanac HR 83 B4
Klanjec HR 73 B5
Klardorf D 62 A3
Klarup DK 38 B3
Klašnice BIH 84 B2
Klässbol S 35 C4
Klášterec nad Ohří CZ 52 C3
Kláštor pod Znievom SK 65 B4
Klatovy CZ 63 A4
Klaus an der Pyhrnbahn A 63 C5
Klazienaveen NL 42 C3
Kłecko PL 46 C3
Kleczew PL 47 C4
Klein Plasten D 45 B4
Klein Sankt Paul A 73 B4
Kleinsölk A 72 A3
Kleinzell A 64 C1
Klejtrup DK 38 C2
Klek SRB 75 C5
Klemensker DK 41 D4
Klenak SRB 85 B4
Klenci pod Cerchovem CZ 62 A3
Klenica PL 53 B5
Klenje SRB 85 B4
Klenoec MK 116 A2
Klenovec SK 65 B5
Klenovica HR 83 A3
Klenovnik HR 73 B6
Kleppe N 33 D2
Kleppestø N 32 B2
Kleptow D 45 B5
Kletnya RUS 7 E12
Kleve D 50 B2
Klevshult S 40 B4
Klewki PL 47 B6
Kličevac SRB 85 B6
Kliening A 73 B4
Klietz D 44 C4
Klikuszowa PL 65 A5
Klimkovice CZ 64 A4
Klimontów PL 55 C6
Klimovichi BY 7 E11
Klimpfjäll S 115 B11
Klin RUS 7 C14
Klina KOS 85 D5
Klinča Sela HR 73 C5
Klingenbach A 64 C2
Klingenberg D 61 A5
Klingenmunster D 61 A4
Klingenthal D 52 C2
Klinken D 44 B3
Klintehamn S 37 E5
Klintsy RUS 7 E12
Kliny PL 55 B5
Kliplev DK 39 E2
Klippan S 41 C3
Klis HR 83 C5
Klitmøller DK 38 B1
Klitten S 34 A6
Klixbüll D 39 E1
Kljajićevo SRB 75 C4
Ključ BIH 83 B5
Klobouky CZ 64 B2
Kłobuck PL 54 C3
Klockestrand S 115 E14
Kłodawa
Lubuskie PL 45 C7
Wielkopolskie PL 54 A3
Kłodzko PL 54 C1
Kløfta N 34 B3
Klokkarvik N 32 B2
Klokkerholm DK 38 B3
Klokočov SK 65 A4
Kłomnice PL 55 C4
Klonowa PL 54 B3
Kloosterzande NL 49 B5
Kłopot PL 53 A4
Klos AL 116 A2
Kloštar Ivanić HR 73 C6
Kloster
D 45 A5
DK 39 C1
Klösterle A 71 A5
Klostermansfeld D 52 B1
Klosterneuburg A 64 B2
Klosters CH 71 B4
Kloten CH 70 A3
Klötze D 44 C3
Klövsjö S 115 E11
Kluczbork PL 54 C3
Kluczewo PL 46 B2
Kluisbergen B 49 C4
Klundert NL 49 B5
Klutz D 44 B3
Klwów PL 55 B5
Klyetsk BY 7 E9
Knaben N 33 D3
Knaften S 115 C15
Knapstad N 35 C3
Knäred S 40 C3
Knaresborough GB 27 A4
Knarvik N 32 B2
Knebel DK 39 C3
Knebworth GB 31 C3
Knesebeck D 44 C2
Knesselare B 49 B4
Knežak SLO 73 C4
Kneževi Vinogradi HR 74 C3
Kneževo HR 74 C3
Knić SRB 85 C5
Knighton GB 29 A4
Knin HR 83 B5
Knislinge S 41 C4
Knittelfeld A 73 A4
Knivsta S 37 C4
Knock IRL 18 C3
Knocktopher IRL 21 B4
Knokke-Heist B 49 B4
Knowle GB 30 B2
Knurów PL 54 C3
Knutby S 36 C5
Knutsford GB 26 B3
Kobarid SLO 72 B3
København = Copenhagen DK 41 D2
Kobenz A 73 A4
Kobersdorf A 64 C2
Kobiernice PL 65 A5
Kobierzyce PL 54 C1
Kobilje SLO 73 B6
Kobiór PL 54 C3
Koblenz
CH 61 C4
D 50 C3
Kobryn BY 6 E8
Kobylanka PL 45 B6
Kobylin PL 54 B2
Kobyłka PL 55 A6
Kobylniki PL 47 C6
Kocaali TR 118 A5
Kocaaliler TR 119 E5
Kocaeli = İzmit TR 118 B4
Kočani MK 11 F7
Koçarlı TR 119 E2
Koceljevo SRB 85 B4
Kočerin BIH 84 C2
Kočevje SLO 73 C4
Kočevska Reka SLO 73 C4
Kochel am see D 62 C2
Kocs H 64 C4
Kocsér H 75 A4
Kocsola H 74 B3
Koczala PL 46 B3
Kodal N 35 C2
Kode S 38 B4
Kodersdorf D 53 B4
Kodrab PL 55 B4
Koekelare B 48 B3
Kofçaz TR 118 A2
Köflach A 73 A5
Køge DK 41 D2
Kohlberg D 62 A3
Kohtla-Järve EST 7 B9
Köinge S 40 B2
Kojetín CZ 64 A3
Kökar FIN 36 C7
Kokava SK 65 B5
Kokkinotrimithia CY 120 A2
Kokkola FIN 3 E25
Kokori BIH 84 B2
Kokoski PL 47 A4
Koksijde B 48 B3
Kola
BIH 84 B2
RUS 3 B30
Köla S 34 C4
Kołacin PL 55 B4
Kolari FIN 113 E12
Kolárovo SK 64 C3
Kolašin MNE 85 D4
Kolbäck S 37 C3
Kolbacz PL 45 B6
Kolbeinsstaðir IS 111 C3
Kolbermoor D 62 C3
Kołbiel PL 55 A6
Kolbnitz A 72 B3
Kolbotn N 34 C2
Kolbu N 34 B2
Kolby Kås DK 39 D3
Kolczewo PL 45 B6
Kolczyglowy PL 46 A3
Kolding DK 39 D2
Kölesd H 74 B3
Kolgrov N 32 A1
Kolín CZ 53 C5
Kolind DK 39 C3
Kolinec CZ 63 A4
Koljane HR 83 C5
Kølkær DK 39 C2
Kölleda D 52 B1
Kollum NL 42 B3
Köln = Cologne D 50 C2
Koło PL 54 A3
Kołobrzeg PL 46 A1
Kolochau D 52 B3

Kolomyya UA 11 B8
Kolonje AL 105 C5
Kolonowskie PL 54 C3
Koloveč CZ 62 A4
Kolpino RUS 7 B11
Kolpny RUS 7 E14
Kolrep D 44 B4
Kölsillre S 115 E12
Kolsko PL 53 B5
Kolsva S 37 C2
Kolta SK 65 B4
Kolunič BIH 83 B5
Koluszki PL 55 B4
Kolut SRB 75 C3
Kolvereid N 114 C8
Kølvrå DK 39 C2
Komagvær N 113 B19
Koman AL 105 A5
Komarica BIH 84 B2
Komárno SK 64 C4
Komárom H 64 C4
Komatou Yialou CY 120 A3
Komboti GR 116 C3
Komen SLO 72 C3
Komin HR 84 C2
Komiža HR 83 C5
Komjáti H 65 B6
Komjatice SK 64 B4
Komletinci HR 75 C3
Komló H 74 B3
Kömlo H 65 C6
Komoča SK 64 C4
Komorane KOS 85 D5
Komorniki PL 54 A1
Komorzno PL 54 B3
Komotini GR 116 A7
Konak SRB 75 C5
Konakovo RUS 7 C14
Konary PL 55 B6
Konarzyny PL 46 B3
Kondias GR 116 C7
Kondorfa H 73 B6
Kondoros H 75 B5
Kondrovo RUS 7 D13
Køng DK 39 D4
Konga S 40 C5
Köngäs FIN 113 E13
Kongerslev DK 38 C3
Kongsberg N 35 C1
Kongshamn N 33 D5
Kongsmark DK 39 D1
Kongsmoen N 115 C9
Kongsvik N 112 D5
Kongsvinger N 34 B4
Konice CZ 64 A2
Konie PL 55 B5
Koniecpol PL 55 C4
Königsberg D 51 C6
Königsbronn D 61 B6
Königsbrück D 53 B3
Königsbrunn D 62 B1
Konigsdorf D 62 C2
Königsee D 52 C1
Königshorst D 45 C4
Königslutter D 51 A6
Königssee D 62 C3
Königstein
Hessen D 51 C4
Sachsen D 53 C4
Königstetten A 64 B2
Königswartha D 53 B4
Königswiesen A 63 B5
Königswinter D 50 C3
Königs Wusterhausen
D 52 A3
Konin PL 54 A3
Konispol AL 116 C2
Konitsa GR 116 B2
Köniz CH 70 B2
Konjevići BIH 85 B4
Konjevrate HR 83 C5
Konjic BIH 84 C2
Konjščina HR 73 B6
Könnern D 52 B1
Konnerud N 35 C2
Konopiska PL 54 C3
Konotop
PL 53 B5
UA 7 F12
Końskie PL 55 B5
Konsmo N 33 D4
Konstancin-Jeziorna
PL 55 A6
Konstantynów Łódźki
PL 55 B4
Konstanz D 61 C5
Kontich B 49 B5
Kontiolahti FIN 3 E28
Konya TR 119 E7
Konz D 60 A2
Kópasker IS 111 A9
Kópavogur IS 111 C4
Kopčany SK 64 B3
Koper SLO 72 C3
Kopervik N 33 C2
Kópháza H 64 C2
Kopice PL 54 C2
Kopidlno CZ 53 C5
Köping S 37 C2
Köpingebro S 41 D3
Köpingsvik S 41 C6
Koplik AL 105 A5
Köpmanholmen S 115 D15
Koppang N 34 A3
Koppangen N 112 C9
Kopparberg S 36 C1
Koppelo FIN 113 D16
Koppom S 35 C4
Koprivlen BG 116 A5
Koprivna BIH 84 B3
Koprivnica HR 74 B1
Kopřivnice CZ 64 A4
Köprübaşi TR 118 D3
Koprzywnica PL 55 C6
Kopstal L 60 A2
Kopychyntsi UA 11 B8
Kopytkowo PL 47 B4
Korbach D 51 B4
Körbecke D 50 B4
Korçë AL 116 B2
Korčula HR 84 D2
Korczyców PL 53 A4
Korenevo RUS 7 F13
Korenita SRB 85 B4
Korets UA 11 A9
Korfantów PL 54 C2
Körfez TR 118 B4
Korgen N 115 A10
Korinth DK 39 D3
Korinthos = Corinth
GR 117 E4
Korita
BIH 83 B5
HR 84 D2
Korithi GR 117 E2
Korkuteli TR 119 E5
Körmend H 74 A1
Korne PL 46 A3
Korneuburg A 64 B2
Kornevo RUS 47 A6
Kórnik PL 54 A2
Kornsjø N 35 D3
Környe H 74 A3
Koromačno HR 82 B3
Koroni GR 117 F3
Koronos GR 117 E7
Koronowo PL 46 B3
Körösladány H 75 B6
Köröstarcsa H 75 B6
Korosten UA 11 A10
Korostyshev UA 11 A10
Korpilombolo S 113 F12
Korsberga
Jönköping S 40 B5
Skaraborg S 35 D6
Korshavn N 35 C2
Korskrogen S 115 F12
Korsnäs S 36 B2
Korsør DK 39 D4
Korsun Shevchenkovskiy
UA 11 B11
Kortrijk B 49 C4
Korucu TR 118 C2
Koryčany CZ 64 A3
Koryukovka UA 7 F12
Korzeńsko PL 54 B1
Korzybie PL 46 A2
Kos GR 119 F2
Kosakowo PL 47 A4
Kosanica MNE 85 C4
Kosaya Gora RUS 7 D14
Kösching D 62 B2
Kościan PL 54 A1
Kościelec PL 54 A3
Kościerzyna PL 46 A3
Koserow D 45 A5
Košetice CZ 63 A6
Košice SK 10 B6
Kosjerić SRB 85 C4
Koška HR 74 C3
Koskullskulle S 112 E9
Kosovska Mitrovica
KOS 85 D5
Kosta S 40 C5
Kostajnica HR 74 C1
Kostajnik SRB 85 B4
Kostanica MNE 105 A5
Kostanjevica SLO 73 C5
Kostelec nad Černými
Lesy CZ 53 D4
Kostelec na Hané CZ 64 A3
Kostice CZ 53 C3
Kostkowo PL 47 A4
Kostojevići SRB 85 B4
Kostolac SRB 85 B6
Kostomłoty PL 54 B1
Kostopil UA 11 A9
Kostów PL 54 B3
Kostrzyn
Lubuskie PL 45 C6
Wielkopolskie PL 46 C3
Koszalin PL 46 A2
Koszęcin PL 54 C3
Kőszeg H 74 A1
Koszwaly PL 47 A4
Koszyce PL 55 C5
Kot SLO 73 C5
Kotala FIN 113 E17
Kotë AL 105 C5
Kötelek H 75 A5
Köthen D 52 B1
Kotka FIN 7 A9
Kotomierz PL 47 B4
Kotor MNE 105 A4
Kotoriba HR 74 B1
Kotorsko BIH 84 B3
Kotor Varoš BIH 84 B2
Kotovsk UA 11 C10
Kotraža SRB 85 C5
Kotronas GR 117 F4
Kötschach A 72 B2
Kötzting D 62 A3
Koudum NL 42 C2
Kouřim CZ 53 C4
Kout na Šumave CZ 62 A4
Kouvola FIN 3 F27
Kovačevac SRB 85 B5
Kovačica SRB 85 A5
Kovdor RUS 3 C29
Kovel' UA 11 A8
Kovilj SRB 75 C5
Kovin SRB 85 B5
Kovren MNE 85 C4
Kowal PL 47 C5
Kowalewo Pomorskie
PL 47 B4
Kowalów PL 45 C6
Kowary PL 53 C5
Köyceğiz TR 119 F3
Kozan TR 16 C7
Kozani GR 116 B3
Kozarac
BIH 84 B1
HR 73 C5
Kozárovce SK 65 B4
Kozelets UA 11 A11
Kozelsk RUS 7 D13
Kozica HR 84 C2
Koziegłowy PL 55 C4
Kozienice PL 55 B6
Kozina SLO 72 C3
Kozje SLO 73 B5
Kozlu TR 118 A6
Kozluk BIH 85 B4
Koźmin PL 54 B2
Koźminek PL 54 B3
Kozolupy CZ 63 A4
Kożuchów PL 53 B5
Kožuhe BIH 84 B3
Kozyatyn UA 11 B10
Kozyürük TR 118 A1
Krackow D 45 B6
Kraddsele S 115 B13
Krąg PL 46 A2
Kragenæs DK 39 E4
Kragerø N 33 D6
Kragi PL 46 B2
Kragujevac SRB 85 B5
Kraiburg D 62 B3
Krajenka PL 46 B2
Krajišnik SRB 75 C5
Krajková CZ 52 C2
Krajné SK 64 B3
Krajnik Dolny PL 45 B6
Krakača BIH 83 A4
Kräklingbo S 37 E5
Kraków = Cracow PL 55 C4
Krakow am See D 44 B4
Králiky CZ 54 C1
Kraljevica HR 73 C4
Kraljevo SRB 85 C5
Kral'ovany SK 65 A5
Král'ov Brod SK 64 B3
Kralovice CZ 52 D3
Kralupy nad Vltavou
CZ 53 C4
Králův Dvůr CZ 63 A5
Kramfors S 115 E14
Kramsach A 72 A1
Kramsk PL 54 A3
Krämvik N 32 C5
Kranenburg D 50 B2
Krania GR 116 C3
Krania Elasonas GR 116 C4
Kranichfeld D 52 C1
Kranidi GR 117 E5
Kranj SLO 73 B4
Kranjska Gora SLO 72 B3
Krapanj HR 83 C4
Krapina HR 73 B5
Krapje HR 74 C1
Krapkowice PL 54 C2
Kraselov CZ 63 A4
Krašić HR 73 C5
Krāslava LV 7 D9
Kraslice CZ 52 C2
Krasna PL 55 B5
Krasna Lipa CZ 53 C4
Kraśnik PL 11 A7
Krašnja SLO 73 B4
Krásno SK 65 A4
Krásnohorské Podhradie
SK 65 B6
Krasno Polje HR 83 B4
Krasnozavodsk RUS 7 C15
Krasnystaw PL 11 A7
Krasnyy RUS 7 D11
Krasnyy Kholm RUS 7 B14
Krasocin PL 55 C5
Kraszewice PL 54 B3
Kraszkowice PL 54 B3
Kratigos GR 118 C1
Kraubath A 73 A4
Krausnick D 53 A3
Krautheim D 61 A5
Kravaře CZ 53 C4
Kravaře CZ 64 A4
Kravarsko HR 73 C6
Kraznějov CZ 63 A4
Krčedin SRB 75 C5
Kŭrdzhali BG 116 A7
Krefeld D 50 B2
Kregme DK 39 D5
Krembz D 44 B3
Kremenchuk UA 11 B12
Kremenets UA 11 A8
Kremmen D 45 C5
Kremna SRB 85 C4
Kremnica SK 65 B4
Krempe D 43 B6
Krems A 63 B6
Kremsbrücke A 72 B3
Kremsmünster A 63 B5
Křemže CZ 63 B5
Křenov CZ 64 A2
Krepa PL 54 B3
Krępa Krajeńska PL 46 B2
Krepsko PL 46 B2
Kreševo BIH 84 C3
Kressbronn D 61 C5
Krestena GR 117 E3
Kretinga LT 6 D6
Krettsy RUS 7 B12
Kreuth D 62 C2
Kreuzau D 50 C2
Kreuzlingen CH 61 C5
Kreuztal D 50 C3
Krewelin D 45 C5
Krezluk BIH 84 B2
Krieglach A 73 A5
Kriegsfeld D 60 A3
Kriens CH 70 A3
Krimml A 72 A2
Krimpen aan de IJssel
NL 49 B5
Křinec CZ 53 C5
Kristdala S 40 B6
Kristiansand N 33 D5
Kristianstad S 41 C4
Kristiansund N 114 D4
Kristiinankaupunki
FIN 3 E24
Kristinefors S 34 B4
Kristinehamn S 35 C6
Krivaň SK 65 B5
Křivoklát CZ 53 C3
Krivoy Rog = Kryvyy Rih
UA 11 C12
Križ HR 74 C1
Křižanov CZ 64 A2
Križevci HR 74 B1
Krk HR 83 A3
Krka SLO 73 C4
Krnjača SRB 85 B5
Krnjak HR 73 C5
Krnjeuša BIH 83 B5
Krnjevo SRB 85 B6
Krnov CZ 54 C2
Krobia PL 54 B1
Kroczyce PL 55 C4
Krøderen N 34 B1
Krokees GR 117 F4
Krokek S 37 D3
Krokom S 115 D11
Krokowa PL 47 A4
Krokstad-elva N 34 C1
Kroksund N 35 C3
Krolevets UA 7 F12
Kroměříž CZ 64 A3
Krommenie NL 42 C1
Krompachy SK 65 B6
Kromy RUS 7 E13
Kronach D 52 C1
Kronshagen D 44 A2
Kronshtadt RUS 7 B10
Kröpelin D 44 A3
Kropp D 43 A6
Kroppenstedt D 52 B1
Kropstädt D 52 B2
Krościenko nad
Dunajcem PL 65 A6
Kröslin D 45 A5
Krośnice PL 54 B2
Krośniewice PL 55 A4
Krosno PL 10 B6
Krosno Odrzańskie
PL 53 A5
Krostitz D 52 B2
Krotoszyn PL 54 B2
Krottendorf A 73 A5
Krouna CZ 64 A2
Krowiarki PL 54 C3
Krrabë AL 105 B5
Kršan HR 73 C4
Krško SLO 73 C5
Krstac MNE 84 C3
Krstur SRB 75 B5
Křtiny CZ 64 A2
Kruft D 50 C3
Kruishoutem B 49 C4
Krujë AL 105 B5
Krulyewshchyna BY 7 D9
Krumbach
A 73 A6
D 61 B6
Krumovgrad BG 116 A7
Krün D 71 A6
Krupá CZ 53 C3
Krupa na Vrbasu BIH 84 B2
Krupanj SRB 85 B4
Krupina SK 65 B5
Krupka CZ 53 C3
Krupki BY 7 D10
Kruså DK 39 E2
Kruščica BIH 84 B2
Kruševac SRB 85 C6
Kruševo MK 116 A3
Kruszwica PL 47 C4
Kruszyn PL 47 C5
Krute MNE 105 A5
Krychaw BY 7 E11
Krynica PL 65 A6
Krynica Morska PL 47 A5
Kryvyy Rih = Krivoy Rog
UA 11 C12
Krzęcin PL 46 B1
Krzelów PL 54 B1
Krzepice PL 54 C3
Krzepielów PL 53 B6
Krzeszowice PL 55 C4
Krzeszyce PL 45 C7
Krzynowłoga Mała
PL 47 B6
Krzywiń PL 54 B1
Krzyżanowice PL 54 D3
Krzyżowa PL 65 A5
Krzyż Wielkopolski
PL 46 C2
Ksiaz Wielkopolski
PL 55 C5
Książ Wielkopolski
PL 54 A2
Kętbowiec PL 46 B2
Kübekháza H 75 B5
Küblis CH 71 B4
Kuç AL 105 C5
Kuchary PL 54 B2
Kuchl A 63 C4
Kucice PL 47 C6
Kuciste HR 84 D2
Kučište KOS 85 D5
Kuçovë AL 105 C5
Küçükbahçe TR 118 D1
Küçükköy TR 118 C1
Küçükkuyu TR 118 C1
Kucura SRB 75 C4
Kuczbork-Osada PL 47 B6
Kuddby S 37 D3
Kudowa-Zdrój PL 53 C6
Kufstein A 62 C3
Kuggeboda S 41 C5
Kuggörana S 115 F14
Kühbach D 62 B2
Kuhmo FIN 3 D28
Kuhmoinen FIN 3 F26
Kuhnsdorf A 73 B4
Kuhstedt D 43 B5
Kuinre NL 42 C2
Kuivastu EST 6 B7
Kukës AL 10 E6
Kuklin PL 47 B6
Kukljica HR 83 B4
Kukujevci SRB 85 A4
Kula
Srbija SRB 85 B6
Vojvodina SRB 75 C4
Kula *continued*
TR 119 D3
Kuldīga LV 6 C6
Kulen Vakuf BIH 83 B5
Kulina BIH 84 B3
Kullstedt D 51 B6
Kulmain D 62 A2
Kulmbach D 52 C1
Kulu TR 16 B6
Kumafşarı TR 119 E4
Kumane SRB 75 C5
Kumanovo MK 10 E6
Kumbağ TR 118 B2
Kumdanlı TR 119 D5
Kumkale TR 118 C1
Kumla S 37 C2
Kumlakyrkby S 36 C3
Kumlinge FIN 36 B7
Kumluca TR 119 F5
Kumrovec HR 73 B5
Kunadacs H 75 B4
Kunágota H 75 B6
Kunbaja H 75 B4
Kunda EST 7 B9
Kundl A 72 A1
Kunes N 113 B15
Kunfehértó H 75 B4
Kungälv S 38 B4
Kungsängen S 37 C4
Kungsäter S 40 B2
Kungsbacka S 38 B5
Kungsgården S 36 B3
Kungshamn S 35 D3
Kungs-Husby S 37 C4
Kungsör S 37 C3
Kunhegyes H 75 A5
Kunmadaras H 75 A5
Kunovice CZ 64 A3
Kunów PL 55 C6
Kunowo
Wielkopolskie PL 54 B2
Zachodnio-Pomorskie
PL 45 B6
Kunštát CZ 64 A2
Kunszállás H 75 B4
Kunszentmárton H 75 B5
Kunszentmiklós H 75 A4
Kunžak CZ 63 A6
Künzelsau D 61 A5
Kuolayarvi RUS 113 F18
Kuopio FIN 3 E27
Kuosku FIN 113 E17
Kup
H 74 A2
PL 54 C2
Kupa H 65 B6
Kupari HR 84 D3
Kupci SRB 85 C6
Kupferzell D 61 A5
Kupinec HR 73 C5
Kupinečki Kraljevac
HR 73 C5
Kupinovo SRB 85 B5
Kupirovo HR 83 B5
Kupjak HR 73 C4
Kupres BIH 84 C2
Küps D 52 C1
Kurbnesh AL 105 B6
Kurd H 74 B3
Küre TR 16 A6
Kuressaare EST 6 B7
Kurikka FIN 3 E25
Kuřim CZ 64 A2
Kuřivody CZ 53 C4
Kurki PL 47 B6
Kurort Oberwiesenthal
D 52 C2
Kurort Schmalkalden
D 51 C6
Kurort Stolberg D 51 B6
Kurort Wippra D 52 B1
Kurów PL 11 A7
Kurowice PL 55 B4
Kurravaara S 112 E9
Kursk RUS 7 F14
Kursu FIN 113 F17
Kuršumlija SRB 85 C6
Kuršumlijska Banja
SRB 85 C6
Kurşunlu
Bursa TR 118 B4
Çankırı TR 16 A6
Kurtakko FIN 113 E13
Kürten D 50 B3
Kurucaşile TR 16 A6
Kurzelów PL 55 C4
Kusadak SRB 85 B5
Kuşadası TR 119 E2
Kusel D 60 A3
Kusey D 44 C3
Küsnacht CH 70 A3
Kütahya TR 118 C4
Kutenholz D 43 B6
Kutina HR 74 C1
Kutjevo HR 74 C2
Kutná Hora CZ 53 D5
Kutno PL 55 A4
Kuttara FIN 113 D15
Küttingen CH 70 A3
Kúty SK 64 B3
Kuusamo FIN 3 D28
Kuusankoski FIN 3 F27
Kuvshinovo RUS 7 C13
Kuyucak TR 119 E3
Kuzmin SRB 85 A4
Kuźnia Raciborska
PL 54 C3
Kuźnica Czarnkowska
PL 46 C2
Kuźnica Żelichowska
PL 46 C2
Kvaløysletta N 112 C7
Kvalsund N 113 B12
Kvam
Nord-Trøndelag N 114 C8
Oppland N 114 F6
Kvamsøy N 32 A3
Kvænangsbotn N 113 C11
Kvanndal N 32 B3
Kvänum S 35 D5
Kværndrup DK 39 D3
Kvås N 33 D4
Kvasice CZ 64 A3
Kvelde N 35 C1
Kvenna N 114 E5
Kvernaland N 33 D2
Kvibille S 40 C2
Kvicksund S 37 C3
Kvidinge S 41 C3
Kvikkjokk S 112 F6
Kvikne N 114 E7
Kvilda CZ 63 A4
Kville S 35 D3
Kvillsfors S 40 B5
Kvinesdal N 33 D3
Kvinlog N 33 D3
Kvinnherad N 32 C3
Kvissel DK 38 B3
Kvissleby S 115 E14
Kviteseid N 33 C5
Kvitsøy N 33 C2
Kwakowo PL 46 A3
Kwidzyn PL 47 B4
Kwilcz PL 46 C2
Kyjov CZ 64 B3
Kyleakin GB 22 D3
Kyle of Lochalsh GB 22 D3
Kylerhea GB 22 D3
Kylestrome GB 22 C3
Kyllburg D 50 C2
Kyllini GR 117 E3
Kynšperk nad Ohří
CZ 52 C2
Kyperounda CY 120 B1
Kyrenia CY 120 A2
Kyritz D 44 C4
Kyrksæterøra N 114 D6
Kysucké Nové Mesto
SK 65 A4
Kythira GR 117 F4
Kythréa CY 120 A2
Kyustendil BG 11 E7
Kyyiv = Kiev UA 11 A11
Kyyjärvi FIN 3 E26

L

Laa an der Thaya A 64 B2
La Adrada E 94 B2
Laage D 44 B4
La Alameda E 100 A2
La Alberca E 93 A4
La Alberca de Záncara
E 95 C4
La Albergueria de
Argañán E 93 A4
La Albuera E 93 C4
La Aldea del Portillo del
Busto E 89 B3
La Algaba E 99 B4
La Aliseda de Tormes
E 93 A5
La Almarcha E 95 C4
La Almolda E 90 B2
La Almunia de Doña
Godina E 89 C5
Laanila FIN 113 D16
La Antillas E 98 B3
La Arena E 86 A4
Laatzen D 51 A5
La Aulaga E 99 B4
La Balme-de-Sillingy
F 69 C6
Laban IRL 20 A3
La Bañeza E 88 B1
La Barca de la Florida
E 99 C5
La Barre-de-Monts F 66 B2
La Barre-en-Ouche F 58 B1
La Barrosa E 99 C4
La Barthe-de-Neste F 77 C3
La Bassée F 48 C3
La Bastide-de-Sèrou
F 77 C4
La Bastide-des-Jourdans
F 79 C4
Labastide-Murat F 77 B4
La Bastide-Puylaurent
F 78 B2
Labastide-Rouairoux
F 77 C5
Labastide-St Pierre F 77 C4
La Bathie F 69 C6
Lábatlan H 65 C4
La Baule-Escoublac
F 66 A2
La Bazoche-Gouet F 58 B1
La Bégude-de-Mazenc
F 78 B3
Labenne F 76 C1
La Bernerie-en-Retz F 66 A2
Labin HR 82 A3
La Bisbal d'Empordà
E 91 B6
Łabiszyn PL 46 C3
Lablachère F 78 B3
Lábod H 74 B2
Laboe D 44 A2
La Boissière F 57 A6
Labouheyre F 76 B2
La Bourboule F 68 C2
La Bóveda de Toro E 88 C1
Łabowa PL 65 A6
La Brède F 76 B2
La Bresse F 60 B2
La Bridoire F 69 C5
La Brillanne F 79 C4
Labrit F 76 B2
Labros E 95 A5
La Bruffière F 66 A3
Labruguière F 77 C5
Labrujo P 87 C2
L'Absie F 67 B4
La Bussière F 58 C3
Laç AL 105 B5
La Caillère F 66 B4
Lacalahorra E 100 B2
La Caletta
Cágliari I 110 C1
Nùoro I 110 B2
La Calmette F 78 C3
La Calzada de Oropesa
E 93 B5
La Campana E 99 B5
La Cañada E 94 B2
Lacanau F 76 B1
Lacanau-Océan F 76 A1
Lacanche F 69 A4
La Canourgue F 78 B2
La Capelle F 49 D4
Lacapelle-Marival F 77 B4
Laćarak SRB 85 A4
La Cardanchosa E 99 A5
La Caridad E 86 A4
La Carlota E 100 B1
La Carolina E 100 A2
Lacaune F 78 C1
La Cava E 90 C3
La Cavalerie F 78 B2
Laceby GB 27 B5
Lacedónia I 103 B8
La Celle-en-Moravan
F 69 A4
La Celle-St Avant F 67 A5
La Cerca E 89 B3
Láces I 71 B5
La Chaise-Dieu F 68 C3
La Chaize-Giraud F 66 B3
La Chaize-le-Vicomte
F 66 B3
La Chambre F 69 C6
Lachania GR 119 G2
La Chapelaude F 68 B2
La Chapelle-d'Angillon
F 68 A2
La Chapelle-en-
Valgaudémar F 79 B5
La Chapelle-en-Vercors
F 79 B4
La Chapelle-Glain F 57 C4
La Chapelle-la-Reine
F 58 B3
La Chapelle-Laurent
F 68 C3
La Chapelle-St Luc F 59 B5
La Chapelle-sur-Erdre
F 66 A3
La Chapelle-Vicomtesse
F 58 C2
La Charce F 79 B4
La Charité-sur-Loire
F 68 A3
La Chartre-sur-le-Loir
F 58 C1
La Châtaigneraie F 67 B4
La Châtre F 68 B1
La Chaussée-sur-Marne
F 59 B5
La Chaux-de-Fonds
CH 70 A1
Lachen CH 70 A3
Lachendorf D 44 C2
La Cheppe F 59 A5
La Chèze F 56 B3
Lachowice PL 65 A5
La Ciotat F 79 C4
Łack PL 47 C5
Läckeby S 40 C6
Läckö S 35 D5
La Clayette F 69 B4
La Clusaz F 69 C6
Lacock GB 29 B5
La Codosera E 93 B3
La Concha E 88 A3
La Condamine-Châtelard
F 79 B5
Láconi I 110 C2
La Contienda E 99 A4
La Coquille F 67 C5
La Coronada E 93 C5
La Côte-St André F 69 C5
La Cotinière F 66 C3
La Courtine F 68 C2
Lacq F 76 C2
La Crau F 79 C5
La Crèche F 67 B4
La Croix F 67 A5
Lacroix-Barrez F 77 B5
Lacroix-St Ouen F 58 A3
Lacroix-sur-Meuse F 60 B1
La Croix-Valmer F 79 C5
La Cumbre E 93 B5
Łącznik PL 54 C2
Lad H 74 B2
Ladbergen D 50 A3
Lądek-Zdrój PL 54 C1
Ladelund D 39 E2
Ladendorf A 64 B2
Ladignac-le-Long F 67 C6
Ladispoli I 102 B5
Ladoeiro P 93 B3
Ladon F 58 C3
La Douze F 77 A3
Ladushkin RUS 47 A6
Ladybank GB 25 B4
Laer D 50 A3
La Espina E 86 A4
La Estrella E 94 C1
La Farga de Moles E 91 A4
La Fatarella E 90 B3
La Felipa E 95 C5
La Fère F 59 A4
La Ferrière
Indre-et-Loire F 58 C1
Vendée F 66 B3
La Ferrière-en-Parthenay
F 67 B4
La-Ferté-Alais F 58 B3
La Ferté-Bernard F 58 B1
La Ferté-Frênel F 58 B1
La Ferté-Gaucher F 59 B4
La Ferté-Imbault F 68 A1
La Ferté-Macé F 57 B5
La Ferté-Milon F 59 A4
La Ferté-sous-Jouarre
F 59 B4
La Ferté-St-Aubin F 58 C2
La Ferté-St-Cyr F 58 C2
La Ferté-Vidame F 58 B1
La Ferté Villeneuil F 58 C2
La Feuillie F 58 A2
Lafkos GR 116 C5
La Flèche F 57 C5
La Flotte F 66 B3
Lafnitz A 73 A6
La Font de la Figuera
E 101 A5
La Fouillade F 77 B5
Lafrançaise F 77 B4
La Fregeneda E 87 D4
La Fresneda E 90 C3
La Fuencubierta E 99 B6
La Fuente de San Esteban
E 87 D4
La Fulioala E 91 B4
La Gacilly F 57 C3
La Galera E 90 C3
Lagan S 40 C3
Laganadi I 109 A4
Lagarde F 77 C4
La Garde-Freinet F 79 C5
Lagares
Coimbra P 92 A3
Porto P 87 C2
La Garnache F 66 B3
Lagaro I 81 B5
La Garriga E 91 B5
La Garrovilla E 93 C4
Lagartera E 93 B5
La Gaubretière F 66 B3
Lågbol S 36 B5
Lage D 51 B4
Lägerdorf D 43 B6
Lagg GB 24 C2
Laggan GB 22 D4
Laggartorp S 35 C6
Łagiewniki PL 54 C1
La Gineta E 95 C4
Láglio I 71 C4
Lagnieu F 69 C5
Lagny-sur-Marne F 58 B3
Lago
Calabria I 106 B3
Veneto I 72 C2
Lagôa P 98 B2
Lagoaça P 87 C4
Lagonegro I 106 A2
Lagos
GR 116 A7
P 98 B2
Lagosanto I 82 B1
Łagów
Lubuskie PL 46 C1
Świętokrzyskie PL 55 C6
La Granadella
Alicante E 96 C3
Lleida E 90 B3
La Grand-Combe F 78 B3
La Grande-Croix F 69 C4
La Grande-Motte F 78 C3
La Granja d'Escarp E 90 B3
La Granjuela E 93 C5
Lagrasse F 77 C5
La Grave F 79 A5
La Gravelle F 57 B4
Laguardia E 89 B4
La Guardia E 95 C3
La Guardia de Jaén
E 100 B2
Laguarres E 90 A3
Laguenne F 68 C1
Laguépie F 77 B4
La Guerche-de-Bretagne
F 57 C4
La Guerche-sur-l'Aubois
F 68 B2
La Guérinière F 66 B2
Laguiole F 78 B1
Laguna de Duera E 88 C2
Laguna del Marquesado
E 95 B5
Laguna de Negrillos
E 88 B1
Lagundo I 71 B6
Lagunilla E 93 A4
La Haba E 93 C5
Laharie F 76 B2
La Haye-du-Puits F 57 A4
La Haye-Pesnel F 57 B4
Lahden D 43 C4
La Herlière F 48 C3
La Hermida E 88 A2
La Herrera E 95 D4
Laheycourt F 59 B6
La Higuera E 101 A4
La Hiniesta E 88 C1
Lahnstein D 50 C3
Laholm S 40 C3
La Horcajada E 93 A5
La Horra E 88 C3
Lahr D 60 B3
Lahti FIN 3 F26
La Hulpe B 49 C5
La Hutte F 57 B6
Laichingen D 61 B5
L'Aigle F 58 B1
La Iglesuela E 94 B2
La Iglesuela del Cid E 90 C2
Laignes F 59 C5
Laiguéglia I 80 C2
L'Aiguillon-sur-Mer F 66 B3
Laimbach am Ostrong
A 63 B6
Laina E 95 A4
Lainio S 113 E11
Lairg GB 23 C4
La Iruela E 100 B3
Laissac F 78 B1
Laisvall S 115 A14
Láives I 71 B6
La Javie F 79 B5
Lajkovac SRB 85 B5
La Jonchère-St Maurice
F 67 B6
La Jonquera E 91 A5
Lajoskomárom H 74 B3
Lajosmizse H 75 A4
Lak H 65 B6
Lakenheath GB 30 B4
Lakitelek H 75 B5
Lakki GR 117 G5
Lakolk DK 39 D1
Łąkorz PL 47 B5
Lakšárska Nová Ves
SK 64 B3
Lakselv N 113 B13
Laksfors N 115 B10
Laktaši BIH 84 B2
La Lantejuela E 99 B5
Lalapaşa TR 118 A1
L'Albagès E 90 B3
Lalbenque F 77 B4
L'Alcudia E 96 B2
L'Aldea E 90 C3
Lalëz AL 105 B5
Lalín E 86 B2
Lalinde F 77 B3
La Línea de la
Concepción E 99 C5
Lalizolle F 68 B3
La Llacuna E 91 B4
Lalley F 79 B4
Lalling D 62 B4
Lalm N 114 F6
La Londe-les-Maures
F 79 C5
La Loupe F 58 B2
La Louvière B 49 C5
L'Alpe-d'Huez F 79 A5
La Luisiana E 99 B5
Laluque F 76 C1
Lam D 62 A4
La Machine F 68 B3
la Maddalena I 110 A2
Lama dei Peligni I 103 A7
Lamadrid E 88 A2
Lamagistère F 77 B3
La Mailleraye-sur-Seine
F 58 A1
La Malène F 78 B2
Lama Mocogno I 81 B4
La Mamola E 100 C2
La Manresana dels Prats
E 91 B4
Lamarche F 60 B1
Lamarche-sur-Saône
F 69 A5
Lamargelle F 69 A4
Lamarosa P 92 B2
Lamarque F 76 A2
Lamas P 92 A2
La Masadera E 90 B2
Lamas de Moaro P 87 B2
Lamastre F 78 B3
La Mata E 94 C2
La Mata de Ledesma
E 94 A1
La Mata de Monteagudo
E 88 B1
Lambach A 63 B4
Lamballe F 56 B3
Lamberhurst GB 31 C4
Lambesc F 79 C4
Lambia GR 117 E3
Lambley GB 25 D5
Lambourn GB 31 C2
Lamego P 87 C3
La Meilleraye-de-Bretagne
F 66 A3
La Ménitré F 67 A4
L'Ametlla de Mar E 90 C3
Lamia GR 116 D4
Lammhult S 40 B4
La Mojonera E 101 C3
La Mole F 79 C5
La Molina E 91 A4
La Monnerie-le-Montel
F 68 C3
La Morera E 93 C4
La Mothe-Achard F 66 B3
Lamothe-Cassel F 77 B4
Lamothe-Montravel F 76 B3
La Mothe-St Héray F 67 B4
Lamotte-Beuvron F 58 C3
La Motte-Chalançon
F 79 B4
La Motte-du-Caire F 79 B5
La Motte-Servolex F 69 C5
Lampertheim D 61 A4
Lampeter GB 28 A3
L'Ampolla E 90 C3
Lamprechtshausen A 62 C3
Lamsfeld D 53 B4
Lamspringe D 51 B6
Lamstedt D 43 B6
La Mudarra E 88 C2
La Muela E 90 B1
La Mure F 79 B4
Lamure-sur-Azergues
F 69 B4
Lana I 71 B6
Lanaja E 90 B2
Lanarce F 78 B2
Lanark GB 25 C4
La Nava E 99 B4
La Nava de Ricomalillo
E 94 C2
La Nava de Santiago
E 93 B4
Lancaster GB 26 A3
Lanchester GB 25 D6
Lanciano I 103 A7
Lancing GB 31 D3
Lançon-Provence F 79 C4
Lancova Vas SLO 73 B5
Landau
Bayern D 62 B3
Rheinland-Pfalz D 61 A4
Landeck A 71 A5
Landen B 49 C6
Landerneau F 56 B1
Landeryd S 40 B3
Landesbergen D 43 C6
Landete E 96 B1
Landévant F 56 C2
Landévennec F 56 B1
Landeyjahöfn IS 111 D5
Landivisiau F 56 B1
Landivy F 57 B4
Landl A 62 C3
Landön S 115 D11
Landos F 78 B2
Landouzy-le-Ville F 59 A5
Landquart CH 71 B4
Landrecies F 49 C4
Landreville F 59 B5
Landriano I 71 C4
Landsberg D 62 B1
Lands-berg D 52 B2
Landsbro S 40 B4
Landscheid D 50 D2
Landshut D 62 B3
Landskrona S 41 D2
Landstuhl D 60 A3
Lanesborough IRL 19 C4
Lanester F 56 C2
Lanestosa E 89 A3
La Neuve-Lyre F 58 B1
La Neuveville CH 70 A2
Langå DK 39 C2
Langada GR 116 D8
Langadas GR 116 B5
Langa de Duero E 89 C3
Langadia GR 117 E4
Langangen N 35 C1
Långared S 40 A2
Långaröd S 41 D3
Långaryd S 40 B3
Långås S 40 C2
Långasjö S 40 C5
Langau A 63 B6
Langeac F 78 A2
Langeais F 67 A5
Langedijk NL 42 C1
Langeln D 51 B6
Langelsheim D 51 B6
Langemark-Poelkapelle
B 48 C3
Langen
Hessen D 51 D4
Niedersachsen D 43 B5
Langenau D 61 B6
Langenberg D 50 B4
Langenbruck CH 70 A2
Langenburg D 61 A5
Längenfeld A 71 A5
Langenfeld D 50 B2
Langenhorn D 43 A5
Langenlois A 63 B6
Langenlonsheim D 60 A3
Langennaudorf D 52 B3
Langenneufnach D 62 B1
Langenthal CH 70 A2
Langenzenn D 62 A1
Langeoog D 43 B4
Langeskov DK 39 D3
Langesund N 35 C1
Langewiesen D 51 C6
Långflon S 34 A4
Langförden D 43 C5
Langhagen D 44 B4
Länghem S 40 B3
Langhirano I 81 B4
Langholm GB 25 C5
Langholt IS 111 D7
Långlöt S 41 C6
Langnau CH 70 B2
Langø DK 39 E4
Langogne F 78 B2
Langon F 76 B2
Langquaid D 62 B3
Långrådna S 37 D3
Langreo E 88 A1
Langres F 59 C6
Långsele S 115 D14
Långserud S 35 C4
Langset N 34 B3
Långshyttan S 36 B3
Langstrand N 113 B12
Långträsk S 115 B17
Langueux F 56 B3
Languidic F 56 C2
Längvik S 37 C5
Langwarden D 43 B5
Langwathby GB 26 A3
Langwedel D 43 C6
Langweid D 62 B1
Langwies CH 71 B4
Lanheses P 87 C2
Lanięta PL 47 C5
Lanildut F 56 B1
Lanjarón E 100 C2
Lanmeur F 56 B2
Lanna
Jönköping S 40 B3
Örebro S 37 C1
Lännaholm S 36 C4
Lannavaara S 113 D10
Lannéanou F 56 B2
Lannemezan F 77 C3
Lanneuville-sur-Meuse
F 59 A6
Lannilis F 56 B1
Lannion F 56 B2
La Nocle-Maulaix F 68 B3
Lanouaille F 67 C6
Lansjärv S 113 F11
Lanškroun CZ 64 A2
Lanslebourg-Mont-Cenis
F 70 C1
Lanta F 77 C4
Lantadilla E 88 B2
Lanton F 76 B1
Lantosque F 79 C6
La Nuez de Arriba E 88 B3
Lanusei I 110 C2
Lanúvio I 102 B5
Lanvollon F 56 B3
Lánycsók H 74 B3
Lanz D 44 B3
Lanza E 86 A2
Lanzada E 86 B2
Lanzahita E 94 B2
Lanžhot CZ 64 B2
Lanzo Torinese I 70 C2
Laole SRB 85 B6
Laon F 59 A4
Laons F 58 B2
La Paca E 101 B4
La Pacaudière F 68 B3
Lapalisse F 68 B3
La Palma d'Ebre E 90 B3
La Palma del Condado
E 99 B4
La Palme F 78 D2
La Palmyre F 66 C3
La Parra E 93 C4
Łapczyna Wola PL 55 C4
La Pedraja de Portillo
E 88 C2
La Peraleja E 95 B4
La Petit-Pierre F 60 B3
Lapeyrade F 76 B2
Lapeyrouse F 68 B2
Lapford GB 28 C4
La Pinilla E 101 B4
Lapithos CY 120 A2
La Plagne F 70 C1
La Plaza E 86 A4
Laplje Selo KOS 85 D6
Laplume F 77 B3
La Pobla de Lillet E 91 A4
La Pobla de Vallbona
E 96 B2
La Pobla Llarga E 96 B2
La Pola de Gordón E 88 B1
la Porta F 102 A2
La Pouëze F 66 A4
Lapoutroie F 60 B3
La Póveda de Soria
E 89 B4
Lapovo SRB 85 B6
Läppe S 37 C2
Lappeenranta FIN 3 F28
Lappoluobbal N 113 C12
La Preste F 91 A5
La Primaube F 77 B5
Lapseki TR 118 B1
Lapua FIN 3 E25
La Puebla de Almoradie
E 95 C3
La Puebla de Cazalla
E 99 B5
La Puebla de los Infantes
E 99 B5
La Puebla del Río E 99 B4
La Puebla de Montalbán
E 94 C2
La Puebla de Roda E 90 A3
La Puebla de Valdavia
E 88 B2
La Puebla de Valverde
E 96 A2
La Pueblanueva E 94 C2
La Puerta de Segura
E 101 A3
La Punt CH 71 B4
L'Àquila I 103 A6
La Quintana E 100 B1
La Quintera E 99 B5
La Rábita
Granada E 100 C2
Jaén E 100 B1
Laracha E 86 A2
Laragh IRL 21 A5
Laragne-Montéglin F 79 B4
La Rambla E 100 B1
l'Arboç E 91 B4
L'Arbresle F 69 C4
Lärbro S 37 E5
Larceveau F 76 C1

Loc–Mas 163

Locmariaquer F 56 C3
Locminé F 56 C3
Locorotondo I 104 C3
Locquirec F 56 B2
Locri I 106 C3
Locronan F 56 B1
Loctudy F 56 C1
Lodares de Osma E 89 C4
Lodé I 110 B2
Lodeinoye Pole RUS 7 A12
Lodève F 78 C2
Lodi I 71 C4
Løding N 112 E3
Lødingen N 112 D4
Lodosa E 89 B4
Lödöse S 38 A5
Łódź PL 55 B4
Loeches E 95 B3
Løfallstrand N 32 B3
Lofer A 62 C3
Lofsdalen S 115 E10
Loftahammar S 40 B6
Lofthus N 32 B3
Loftus GB 27 A5
Loga N 33 D3
Logatec SLO 73 C4
Lögdeå S 115 D16
Lograto I 71 C5
Logroño E 89 B4
Logrosán E 93 B5
Løgstør DK 38 C2
Løgumgårde DK 39 D1
Løgumkloster DK 39 D1
Lohals DK 39 D3
Lohiniva FIN 113 E14
Lohja FIN 6 A8
Löhlbach D 51 B4
Lohmen
Mecklenburg-Vorpommern D 44 B4
Sachsen D 53 C4
Löhnberg D 50 C4
Lohne D 43 C5
Löhne D 51 A4
Lohr D 51 D5
Lohra D 51 C4
Lohsa D 53 B4
Loiano I 81 B5
Loimaa FIN 3 F25
Loiri I 110 B2
Loitz D 45 B5
Loivos P 87 C3
Loivos do Monte P 87 C3
Loja E 100 B1
Lojanice SRB 85 B4
Lojsta S 37 E5
Løjt Kirkeby DK 39 D2
Lok SK 65 B4
Lokca SK 65 A5
Løken N 34 C3
Lokeren B 49 B4
Loket CZ 52 C2
Lokhvitsa UA 11 A12
Lokka FIN 113 E16
Løkken
DK 38 B2
N 114 D6
Loknya RUS 7 C11
Lökösháza H 75 B6
Lokot RUS 7 E13
Lokve SRB 75 C6
Lollar D 51 C4
L'Olleria E 96 C2
Lölling-Graben A 73 B4
Lom
BG 11 E7
N 114 F5
SK 65 B5
Lombez F 77 C3
Lomello I 80 A2
Łomianki PL 55 A5
Lomma S 41 D3
Lommaryd S 40 B4
Lommatzsch D 52 B3
Lommel B 49 B6
Lommersum D 50 C2
Lomnice CZ 64 A2
Lomnice nad Lužnici
CZ 63 A5
Lomnice-nad Popelkou
CZ 53 C5
Lompolo FIN 113 D13
Łomza PL 6 E7
Lönashult S 40 C4
Lønborg DK 39 D1
Londerzeel B 49 B5
Londinières F 58 A2
London GB 31 C3
Lonevåg N 32 B2
Longa GR 117 F3
Longare I 72 C1
Longares E 90 B1
Longarone I 72 B2
Longastrino I 81 B6
Long Bennington GB 27 C5
Longbenton GB 25 C6
Longchamp-sur-Aujon
F 59 B5
Longchaumois F 69 B5
Long Eaton GB 27 C4
Longeau F 59 C6
Longecourt-en-Plaine
F 69 A5
Longeville-les-St Avold
F 60 A2
Longeville-sur-Mer F 66 B3
Longford IRL 19 C4
Longframlington GB 25 C6
Longhope GB 23 C5
Longhorsley GB 25 C6
Longhoughton GB 25 C6
Longi I 109 A3
Long Melford GB 30 B4
Longny-au-Perche F 58 B1
Longobucco I 106 B3
Long Preston GB 26 A3
Longré F 67 B4
Longridge GB 26 B3
Longroiva P 87 D3
Long Sutton GB 30 B4
Longtown
Cumbria GB 25 C5
Herefordshire GB 29 B5
Longueau F 58 A3
Longué-Jumelles F 67 A4
Longuyon F 60 A1
Longvic F 69 A5
Longvilly B 50 C1
Longwy F 60 A1
Lonigo I 71 C6
Löningen D 43 C4
Lonja HR 74 C1
Lönneberga S 40 B5
Lönsboda S 41 C4
Lonset N 114 E6
Lons-le-Saunier F 69 B5
Lønstrup DK 38 B2
Looe GB 28 C3
Loone-Plage F 48 B3
Loon op Zand NL 49 B6
Loosdorf A 63 B6
Lo Pagán E 101 B5
Lopar HR 83 B3
Lopare BIH 84 B3
Lopera E 100 B1
Lopigna F 102 A1
Loppersum NL 42 B3
Łopuszna PL 65 A6
Łopuszno PL 55 C5
Lor F 59 A5
Lora N 114 E5
Lora de Estepa E 100 B1
Lora del Río E 99 B5
Loranca del Campo E 95 B4
Lorbé E 86 A2
Lörby S 41 C4
Lorca E 101 B4
Lorch D 50 C3
Lørenfallet N 34 B3
Lørenskog N 34 C2
Loreo I 82 A1
Loreto I 82 C2
Lorgues F 79 C5
Lorica I 106 B3
Lorient F 56 C2
Lorignac F 67 C4
Lörinci H 65 C5
Loriol-sur-Drôme F 78 B3
Lormes F 68 A3
Loro Ciuffenna I 81 C5
Lorqui E 101 A4
Lörrach D 60 C3
Lorrez-le-Bocage F 59 B3
Lorris F 58 C3
Lorup D 43 C4
Łoś PL 55 B5
Los S 115 F12
Losacino E 87 C4
Los Alcázares E 101 B5
Los Arcos E 89 B4
Losar de la Vera E 93 A5
Los Barios de Luna E 88 B1
Los Barrios E 99 C5
Los Caños de Meca
E 99 C4
Los Cerricos E 101 B3
Los Corrales E 100 B1
Los Corrales de Buelna
E 88 A2
Los Dolores E 101 B4
Losenstein A 63 C5
Los Gallardos E 101 B4
Losheim
Nordrhein-Westfalen
D 50 C2
Saarland D 60 A2
Los Hinojosos E 95 C4
Los Isidros E 96 B1
Los Molinos E 94 B2
Los Morales E 99 B5
Los Navalmorales E 94 C2
Los Navalucillos E 94 C2
Losne F 69 A5
Los Nietos E 101 B5
Løsning DK 39 D2
Los Palacios y Villafranca
E 99 B5
Los Pozuelos de
Calatrava E 100 A1
Los Rábanos E 89 C4
Los Santos E 93 A5
Los Santos de la Humosa
E 95 B3
Los Santos de Maimona
E 93 C4
Lossburg D 61 B4
Losse F 76 B2
Losser NL 50 A3
Lossiemouth GB 23 D5
Lössnitz D 52 C2
Loštice CZ 64 A2
Los Tijos E 88 A2
Lostwithiel GB 28 C3
Los Villares E 100 B2
Los Yébenes E 94 C3
Løten N 34 B3
Lotorp S 37 D2
Lottefors S 36 A3
Löttorp S 41 B7
Lotyń PL 46 B2
Lotzorai I 110 C2
Louargat F 56 B2
Loudéac F 56 B3
Loudun F 67 A5
Loué F 57 C5
Loughborough GB 27 C4
Loughbrickland GB 19 B5
Loughrea IRL 20 A3
Louhans F 69 B5
Louisburgh IRL 18 C2
Loukhi RUS 3 C30
Loulay F 67 B4
Loulé P 98 B2
Louny CZ 53 C3
Lourdes F 76 C2
Lourenzá E 86 A3
Loures P 92 C1
Loures-Barousse F 77 C3
Louriçal P 92 A2
Lourinhã P 92 B1
Lourmarin F 79 C4
Loury F 58 C3
Lousa
Bragança P 87 C3
Castelo Branco P 92 B3
Lousã P 92 A2
Lousa P 92 C1
Lousada
E 86 B3
P 87 C2
Louth GB 27 B5
Loutra Edipsou GR 116 D5
Loutraki GR 117 E4
Loutropoli Thermis
GR 118 C1
Louverné F 57 B5
Louvie-Juzon F 76 C2
Louviers F 58 A2
Louvigné-du-Désert
F 57 B4
Louvois F 59 A5
Lova I 72 C2
Lovasberény H 74 A3
Lövåsen S 34 C5
Lovászpatona H 74 A2
Lövberga S 115 D12
Lovech BG 11 E8
Lövenich D 50 B2
Lóvere I 71 C5
Lövestad S 41 D3
Loviisa FIN 7 A9
Lovikka S 113 E11
Lovinobaňa SK 65 B5
Loviste HR 84 C2
Lovke HR 73 C4
Lovnäs S 34 A5
Lövö H 74 A1
Lovosice CZ 53 C4
Lovozero RUS 3 C31
Lovran HR 73 C4
Lovreć HR 84 C1
Lovrenc na Pohorju
SLO 73 B5
Lovrin RO 75 C5
Lövstabruk S 36 B4
Löwenberg D 45 C5
Löwenstein D 61 A5
Lowestoft GB 30 B5
Lowick GB 25 C6
Łowicz PL 55 A4
Loxstedt D 43 B5
Loyew BY 7 F11
Lož SLO 73 C4
Loza CZ 63 A4
Łozina PL 54 B2
Loznica SRB 85 B4
Lozničko Polje SRB 85 B4
Lozorno SK 64 B3
Lozovik SRB 85 B6
Lozoya E 94 B3
Lozoyuela E 94 B3
Lozzo di Cadore I 72 B2
Luanco E 88 A1
Luarca E 86 A4
Lubaczów PL 11 A7
Lubań PL 53 B5
Lubanie PL 47 C4
Lubanów PL 55 B4
Lubars D 52 A2
Lubasz PL 46 C2
Lubawa PL 47 B5
Lubawka PL 53 C6
Lübbecke D 43 C5
Lübben D 53 B3
Lübbenau D 53 B3
Lubczyna PL 45 B6
Lübeck D 44 B2
Lubenec CZ 52 C3
Lubersac F 67 C6
Lübesse D 44 B3
Lubia E 89 C4
Lubian E 87 B4
Lubiatowo PL 45 B7
Lubichowo PL 47 B4
Lubicz Dolny PL 47 B4
Lubień PL 65 A5
Lubienia PL 55 B6
Lubień Kujawski PL 47 C5
Lubieszewo PL 46 B1
Lubin
Dolnośląskie PL 53 B6
Zachodnio-Pomorskie
PL 45 B6
Lublin PL 11 A7
Lubliniec PL 54 C3
Lubmin D 45 A5
Lubniewice PL 45 C7
Lubny UA 11 A12
Lubochnia PL 55 B5
Lubomierz
Dolnośląskie PL 53 B5
Małopolskie PL 65 A6
Lubomino PL 47 A6
Luboń PL 54 A1
L'ubotín SK 65 A6
Lubowidz PL 47 B5
Łubowo
Wielkopolskie PL 46 C3
Zachodnio-Pomorskie
PL 46 B2
Lubraniec PL 47 C4
Lubrín E 101 B3
Lubrza PL 54 C2
Lubsko PL 53 B4
Lübtheen D 44 B3
Lubuczewo PL 46 A3
Luby CZ 52 C2
Lübz D 44 B4
Luc F 78 B2
Lucainena de las Torres
E 101 B3
Lucan IRL 21 A5
Lučani SRB 85 C5
Lúcar E 101 B3
Luçay-le-Mâle F 67 A6
Lucca I 81 C4
Lucciana F 102 A2
Lucé F 58 B2
Luče SLO 73 B4
Lucena
Córdoba E 100 B1
Huelva E 99 B4
Lucenay-les-Aix F 68 B3
Lucenay-l'Evéque F 69 A4
Luc-en-Diois F 79 B4
Lučenec SK 65 B5
Luceni E 90 B1
Lucens CH 70 B1
Lucera I 103 B8
Luceram F 80 C1
Lüchow D 44 C3
Luciana E 94 D2
Lucignano I 81 C5
Lucija SLO 72 C3
Lucka D 52 B2
Luckau D 53 B3
Luckenwalde D 52 A3
Lückstedt D 44 C3
Luco dei Marsi I 103 B6
Luçon F 66 B3
Luc-sur-Mer F 57 A5
Ludanice SK 64 B4
Ludbreg HR 74 B1
Lüdenscheid D 50 B3
Lüderitz D 44 C3
Lüdersdorf D 44 B2
Ludgershall GB 31 C2
Ludgo S 37 D4
Lüdinghausen D 50 B3
Ludlow GB 29 A5
Ludomy PL 46 C2
Ludvika S 36 B2
Ludweiler Warndt D 60 A2
Ludwigsburg D 61 B5
Ludwigsfelde D 52 A3
Ludwigshafen D 61 A4
Ludwigslust D 44 B3
Ludwigsstadt D 52 C1
Ludza LV 7 C9
Luesia E 90 A1
Luftkurort Arendsee
D 44 C3
Lug
BIH 84 D3
HR 74 C3
Luga RUS 7 B10
Lugagnano Val d'Arda
I 81 B3
Lugano CH 70 B3
Lugau D 52 C2
Lugnas S 35 D5
Lúgnola I 102 A5
Lugny F 69 B4
Lugo
E 86 A3
I 81 B5
Lugoj RO 10 D6
Lugones E 88 A1
Lugros E 100 B2
Luhačovice CZ 64 A3
Luhe D 62 A3
Luino I 70 C3
Luintra E 87 B3
Lújar E 100 C2
Luka nad Jihlavou CZ 63 A6
Lukavac BIH 84 B3
Lukavika BIH 84 B3
Lukovë AL 116 C1
Lukovica SLO 73 B4
Lukovit BG 11 E8
Lukovo
HR 83 B3
SRB 85 C6
Lukovo Šugorje HR 83 B4
Łuków PL 6 F7
Łukowice Brzeskie
PL 54 C2
Luksefjell N 33 C6
Łukta PL 47 B6
Lula I 110 B2
Luleå S 3 D25
Lüleburgaz TR 118 A2
Lumbarda HR 84 D2
Lumbier E 76 D1
Lumbrales E 87 D4
Lumbreras E 89 B4
Lumbres F 48 C3
Lummelunda S 37 E5
Lummen B 49 C6
Lumparland FIN 36 B7
Lumpiaque E 90 B1
Lumsås DK 39 D4
Lumsden GB 23 D6
Lumsheden S 36 B3
Lun HR 83 B3
Luna E 90 A2
Lunamatrona I 110 C1
Lunano I 82 C1
Lunas F 78 C2
Lund
N 114 C8
Skåne S 41 D3
Västra Götaland S 35 C4
Lundamo N 114 D7
Lunde
DK 39 D1
Sogn og Fjordane N 32 A3
Sogn og Fjordane N 32 A3
Telemark N 33 C6
S 115 E14
Lundebyvollen N 34 B4
Lunden D 43 A6
Lunderseter N 34 B4
Lunderskov DK 39 D2
Lundsberg S 35 C6
Lüneburg D 44 B2
Lunel F 78 C3
Lünen D 50 B3
Lunéville F 60 B2
Lungern CH 70 B3
Lungro I 106 B3
Luninyets BY 7 E9
Lünne D 43 C4
Lunner N 34 B2
Lunteren NL 49 A6
Lunz am See A 63 C6
Luogosanto I 110 A2
Łupawa PL 46 A3
Lupión E 100 A2
Lupoglav HR 73 C4
Luppa D 52 B2
Luque E 100 B1
Lurago d'Erba I 71 C4
Lúras I 110 B2
Lurcy-Lévis F 68 B2
Lure F 60 C2
Lurgan GB 19 B5
Luri F 102 A2
Lury-sur-Arnon F 68 A2
Lušci Palanka BIH 83 B5
Lusévera I 72 B3
Lushnjë AL 105 C5
Lusignan F 67 B5
Lusigny-sur-Barse F 59 B5
Lusnić BIH 84 C1
Luso P 92 A2
Lusówko PL 46 C2
Luspebryggan S 112 E8
Luss GB 24 B3
Lussac F 76 B2
Lussac-les-Châteaux
F 67 B5
Lussac-les-Eglises F 67 B6
Lussan F 78 B3
Lüssow D 44 B4
Lustenau A 71 A4
Luštěnice CZ 53 C4
Luster N 32 A4
Lutago I 72 B1
Lutherstadt Wittenberg
D 52 B2
Lütjenburg D 44 A2
Lutnes N 34 A4
Lutocin PL 47 C5
Lutomiersk PL 55 B4
Luton GB 31 C3
Lutry
CH 70 B1
PL 47 A6
Lutsk UA 11 A8
Lutter am Barenberge
D 51 B6
Lutterworth GB 30 B2
Lututów PL 54 B3
Lützen D 52 B2
Lutzow D 44 B3
Luusua FIN 113 F16
Luvos S 112 F7
Luxembourg L 60 A2
Luxeuil-les-Bains F 60 C2
Luxey F 76 B2
Luz
Évora P 92 C3
Faro P 98 B2
Faro P 98 B3
Luzarches F 58 A3
Luže CZ 64 A2
Luzech F 77 B4
Luzern CH 70 A3
Luzino PL 47 A4
Luz-St Sauveur F 76 D2
Luzy F 68 B3
Luzzi I 106 B3
L'viv UA 11 B8
Lwówek PL 46 C2
Lwówek Śląski PL 53 B5
Lyakhavichy BY 7 E9
Lybster GB 23 C5
Lychen D 45 B5
Lychkova RUS 7 C12
Lycksele S 115 C15
Lydd GB 31 D4
Lydford GB 28 C3
Lydney GB 29 B5
Lyepyel BY 7 D10
Lygna N 34 B2
Lykkja N 32 B5
Lykling N 33 C2
Lyme Regis GB 29 C5
Lymington GB 31 D2
Lympne GB 31 C5
Lyndhurst GB 31 D2
Lyneham GB 29 B6
Lyness GB 23 C5
Lyngdal
Buskerud N 32 C6
Vest-Agder N 33 D4
Lyngør N 33 D6
Lyngsa DK 38 B3
Lyngseidet N 112 C9
Lyngsnes N 114 C8
Lynmouth GB 28 B4
Lynton GB 28 B4
Lyntupy BY 7 D9
Lyon F 69 C4
Lyons-la-Forêt F 58 A2
Lyozna BY 7 D11
Lyrestad S 35 D6
Lysánad Labem CZ 53 C4
Lysápod Makytou SK 64 A4
Lysebotn N 33 C3
Lysekil S 35 D3
Lysice CZ 64 A2
Lysomice PL 47 B4
Lysøysund N 114 D6
Lyss CH 70 A2
Lystrup DK 39 C3
Lysvik S 34 B5
Łyszkowice PL 55 B4
Lytham St Anne's GB 26 B2
Lyuban RUS 7 B11
Lyubertsy RUS 7 D14
Lyubomi' UA 11 A8
Lyubytino RUS 7 B12
Lyudinovo RUS 7 E13

M

Maaninkavaara FIN 113 F17
Maarheeze NL 49 B6
Maaseik B 50 B1
Maastricht NL 50 C1
Mablethorpe GB 27 B6
Mably F 68 B4
Macael E 101 B3
Maçanet de Cabrenys
E 91 A5
Mação P 92 B2
Macau F 76 A2
Maccagno-Agra I 70 B3
Maccarese I 102 B5
Macchiagódena I 103 B7
Macclesfield GB 26 B3
Macduff GB 23 D6
Maceda E 87 B3
Macedo de Cavaleiros
P 87 C4
Maceira
Guarda P 92 A3
Leiria P 92 B2
Macelj HR 73 B5
Macerata I 82 C2
Macerata Féltria I 82 C1
Machault F 59 A5
Machecoul F 66 B3
Mchowo PL 47 B6
Machrihanish GB 24 C2
Machynlleth GB 26 C2
Macieira P 87 C2
Maciejowice PL 55 B6
Macinaggio F 102 A2
Mackenrode D 51 B6
Mačkovci SLO 73 B6
Macomer I 110 B1
Macon B 49 C5
Mâcon F 69 B4
Macotera E 94 B1
Macroom IRL 20 C3
Macugnaga I 70 C2
Madan BG 116 A6
Madängsholm S 35 D5
Madaras H 75 B4
Maddaloni I 103 B7
Made NL 49 B5
Madeley GB 26 C3
Maderuelo E 89 C3
Madetkoski FIN 113 E15
Madley GB 29 A5
Madocsa H 75 B3
Madona LV 7 C9
Madonna di Campiglio
I 71 B5
Madrid E 94 B3
Madridejos E 95 C3
Madrigal de las Altas
Torres E 94 A1
Madrigal de la Vera E 93 A5
Madrigalejo E 93 B5
Madrigalejo de Monte
E 88 B3
Madriguera E 89 C3
Madrigueras E 95 C5
Madroñera E 93 B5
Maël-Carhaix F 56 B2
Maella E 90 B3
Maello E 94 B2
Maesteg GB 29 B4
Mafra P 92 C1
Magacela E 93 C5
Magallon E 89 C5
Magaluf E 97 B2
Magán E 94 C3
Magaña E 89 C4
Magasa I 71 C5
Magaz E 88 C2
Magdeburg D 52 A1
Magenta I 70 C3
Magescq F 76 C1
Maghera GB 19 B5
Magherafelt GB 19 B5
Maghull GB 26 B3
Magilligan GB 19 A5
Magione I 82 C1
Magioto P 92 C1
Maglaj BIH 84 B3
Maglehem S 41 D4
Magliano de'Marsi I 103 A6
Magliano in Toscana
I 102 A4
Magliano Sabina I 102 A5
Maglić SRB 75 C4
Máglie I 107 A5
Maglód H 75 A4
Magnac-Bourg F 67 C6
Magnac-Laval F 67 B6
Magnieres F 60 B2
Magnor N 34 C4
Magnuszew PL 55 B6
Magny-Cours F 68 B3
Magny-en-Vexin F 58 A2
Mágocs H 74 B3
Maguilla E 93 C5
Maguiresbridge GB 19 B4
Magyarbóly H 74 C3
Magyarkeszi H 74 B3
Magyarszék H 74 B3
Mahala MNE 105 A5
Mahide E 87 C4
Mahilyow BY 7 E11
Mahmudiye TR 118 C5
Mahora E 95 C5
Mahovo HR 73 C6
Mähring D 62 A3
Maia
E 76 C1
P 87 C2
Maiaelrayo E 95 A3
Maials E 90 B3
Maîche F 70 A1
Máida I 106 C3
Maiden Bradley GB 29 B5
Maidenhead GB 31 C3
Maiden Newton GB 29 C5
Maidstone GB 31 C4
Maienfeld CH 71 A4
Maignelay Montigny
F 58 A3
Maijanen FIN 113 E14
Maillezais F 66 B4
Mailly-le-Camp F 59 B5
Mailly-le-Château F 59 C4
Mainar E 89 C5
Mainbernheim D 61 A6
Mainburg D 62 B2
Mainhardt D 61 A5
Maintal D 51 C4
Maintenon F 58 B2
Mainvilliers F 58 B2
Mainz D 50 C4
Maiorca P 92 A2
Mairena de Aljarafe E 99 B4
Mairena del Alcor E 99 B5
Maisach D 62 B2
Maishofen A 72 A2
Maison-Rouge F 59 B4
Maissau A 64 B1
Maisse F 58 B3
Maizières-lès-Vic F 60 B2
Maja HR 73 C6
Majadahonda E 94 B3
Majadas E 93 B5
Majavatn N 115 B10
Majs H 74 C3
Majšperk SLO 73 B5
Makarska HR 84 C2
Makkum NL 42 B2
Maklár H 65 C6
Makó H 75 B5
Makoszyce PL 54 C2
Makov SK 65 A4
Makovac KOS 85 D6
Maków Mazowiecka PL 6 E6
Maków Podhalański
PL 65 A5
Makrakomi GR 116 D4
Makó S 115 B15
Mala Bosna SRB 75 B4
Malacky SK 64 B3
Maladzyechna BY 7 D9
Málaga E 100 C1
Malagón E 94 C3
Malaguilla E 95 B3
Malahide IRL 21 A5
Mala Kladuša BIH 73 C5
Mala Krsna SRB 85 B6
Malalbergo I 81 B5
Malá Lehota SK 65 B4
Malanów PL 54 B3
Mala Pijace SRB 75 B4
Mala Plana SRB 85 C6
Mala Subotica HR 74 B1
Malaucène F 79 B4
Malaunay F 58 A2
Malaya Vishera RUS 7 B12
Malborghetto I 72 B3
Malbork PL 47 A5
Malborn D 60 A2
Malbuisson F 69 B6
Malcésine I 71 C5
Malchin D 45 B4
Malching D 63 B4
Malchow D 44 B4
Malcocinado E 99 A5
Malczyce PL 54 B1
Maldegem B 49 B4
Maldon GB 31 C4
Małdyty PL 47 B5
Malè I 71 B5
Malemort F 67 C6
Malente D 44 A2
Målerås S 40 C5
Males GR 117 G7
Malesherbes F 58 B3
Malesina GR 116 D5
Malestroit F 56 C3
Maletto I 109 B3
Malexander S 40 A5
Malfa I 106 C1
Malgrat de Mar E 91 B5
Malhadas P 87 C4
Malia
CY 120 B1
GR 117 G7
Malicorne-sur-Sarthe
F 57 C5
Malijai F 79 B5
Malildjoš SRB 75 C4
Mâlilla S 40 B5
Mali Lošinj HR 83 B3
Malin IRL 19 A4
Málinec SK 65 B5
Malingsbo S 36 C2
Malinec PL 54 A3
Malinska HR 83 A3
Maliq AL 116 B2
Maljevac HR 73 C5
Malkara TR 118 B1
Małki PL 47 B5
Malko Tŭrnovo BG 11 E9
Mallaig GB 22 D3
Mallaranny IRL 18 C2
Mallemort F 79 C4
Mallén E 89 C5
Malléon F 77 C4
Mallersdorf-Pfaffenberg
D 62 B3
Málles Venosta I 71 B5
Malling DK 39 C3
Mallnitz A 72 B3
Mallow IRL 20 B3
Mallwyd GB 26 C2
Malm N 114 C8
Malmbäck S 40 B4
Malmberget S 112 E9
Malmby S 37 C4
Malmédy B 50 C2
Malmesbury GB 29 B5
Malmköping S 37 C3
Malmö S 41 D3
Malmon S 35 D3
Malmslätt S 37 D2
Malnate I 70 C3
Malo I 71 C6
Małoarkhangelsk
RUS 7 E14
Małogoszcz PL 55 C5
Maloja CH 71 B4
Małomice PL 53 B5
Måløy N 114 F2
Maloyaroslovets RUS 7 D14
Malpartida E 93 B4
Malpartida de la Serena
E 93 C5
Malpartida de Plasencia
E 93 B4
Malpas
E 90 A3
GB 26 B3
Malpica P 92 B3
Malpica de Bergantiños
E 86 A2
Malpica de Tajo E 94 C2
Malsch D 61 B4
Malšice CZ 63 A5
Malta A 72 B3
Maltat F 68 B3
Maltby GB 27 B4
Malung S 34 B5
Malungsfors S 34 B5
Maluszów PL 45 C7
Maluszyn PL 55 C4
Malva E 88 C1
Malvaglia CH 70 B3
Malveira P 92 C1
Malvik N 114 D7
Malyn UA 11 A10
Mamarrosa P 92 A2
Mamer L 60 A2
Mamers F 58 B1
Mamirolle F 69 A6
Mammendorf D 62 B2
Mámmola I 106 C3
Mamoiada I 110 B2
Mamonovo RUS 47 A6
Mamuras AL 105 B5
Maňa SK 64 B4
Manacor E 97 B3
Manavgat TR 119 F6
Mancera de Abajo E 94 B1
Mancha Real E 100 B2
Manchester GB 26 B3
Manching D 62 B2
Manchita E 93 C4
Manciano I 102 A4
Manciet F 76 C3
Mandal N 33 D4
Mandanici I 109 A4
Mandas I 110 C2
Mandatoriccio I 107 B3
Mandayona E 95 B4
Mandelieu-la-Napoule
F 79 C5
Mandello del Lário I 71 C4
Mandelsloh D 43 C6
Manderfeld B 50 C2
Manderscheid D 50 C2
Mandino Selo BIH 84 C2
Mandoudi GR 116 D5
Mandra GR 117 D5
Mandraki GR 119 F2
Mandúria I 104 C3
Mane
Alpes-de-Haute-Provence F 79 C4
Haute-Garonne F 77 C3
Manérbio I 71 C4
Mañeru E 89 B5
Manetin CZ 52 D3
Manfredónia I 104 B1
Mangalia RO 11 E10
Manganeses de la
Lampreana E 88 C1
Manganeses de la
Polvorosa E 88 B1
Mangen N 34 C3
Manger N 32 B2
Mangiennes F 60 A1
Mangotsfield GB 29 B5
Mångsbodarna S 34 A5
Mangualde P 92 A3
Maniago I 72 B2
Manilva E 99 C5
Manisa TR 118 D2
Manises E 96 B2
Mank A 63 B6
Månkarbo S 36 B4
Manlleu E 91 B5
Manna DK 38 B2
Männedorf CH 70 A3
Mannersdorf am
Leithagebirge A 64 C2
Mannheim D 61 A4
Manningtree GB 31 C5
Manoppello I 103 A7
Manorbier GB 28 B3
Manorhamilton IRL 18 B3
Manosque F 79 C4
Manowo PL 46 A2
Manresa E 91 B4
Månsarp S 40 B4
Månsåsen S 115 D11
Manschnow D 45 C6
Mansfeld D 52 B1
Mansfield GB 27 B4
Mansilla de Burgos E 88 B3
Mansilla de las Mulas
E 88 B1
Manskog S 35 C4
Mansle F 67 C5
Manso F 102 A1
Manteigas P 92 A3
Mantel D 62 A3
Mantes-la-Jolie F 58 B2
Mantes-la-Ville F 58 B2
Manthelan F 67 A5
Mantorp S 37 D2
Mántova I 71 C5
Mänttä FIN 3 E26
Mäntyjärvi FIN 113 E16
Manuel E 96 B2
Manyas TR 118 B2
Manzanal de Arriba E 87 B4
Manzanares E 95 C3
Manzanares el Real E 94 B3
Manzaneda
León E 87 B4
Orense E 87 B3
Manzanedo E 88 B3
Manzaneque E 94 C3
Manzanera E 96 A2
Manzanilla E 99 B4
Manzat F 68 C2
Manziana I 102 A5
Manziat F 69 B4
Maó E 97 B4
Maoča BIH 84 B3
Maqueda E 94 B2
Mara E 89 C5
Maramaraereğlisi
TR 118 B2
Maraña E 88 A1
Maranchón E 95 A4
Maranello I 81 B4
Marano I 103 C7
Marano Lagunare I 72 C3
Marans F 66 B3
Maratea I 106 B2
Marateca P 92 C2
Marathokambos GR 119 E1
Marathonas GR 117 D5
Marathóvouno CY 120 A2
Marazion GB 28 C2
Marbach
Baden-Württemberg
D 61 B5
Hessen D 51 C5
F 60 B2
Marbäck S 40 B3
Mårbacka S 34 C5
Marbella E 100 C1
Marboz F 69 B5
Marburg D 51 C4
Marcali H 74 B2
Marčana HR 82 B2
Marcaria I 81 A4
Marcelová SK 64 C4
Marcenat F 68 C2
March GB 30 B4
Marchamalo E 95 B3
Marchaux F 69 A6
Marche-en-Famenne
B 49 C6
Marchegg A 64 B2
Marchena E 99 B5
Marchenoir F 58 C2
Marcheprime F 76 B2
Marciac F 76 C3
Marciana Marina I 81 D4
Marcianise I 103 B7
Marcigny F 68 B4
Marcilla E 89 B5
Marcillac-la-Croisille
F 68 C2
Marcillac-Vallon F 77 B5
Marcillat-en-Combraille
F 68 B2
Marcille-sur-Seine F 59 B4
Marcilloles F 69 C5
Marcilly-le-Hayer F 59 B4
Marcinkowice PL 46 B2
Marciszów PL 53 C6
Marck F 48 C2
Marckolsheim F 60 B3
Marco de Canevezes
P 87 C2
Mårdsele S 115 C16
Mårdsjö S 115 D12
Mareham le Fen GB 27 B5
Marek S 40 B5
Marennes F 66 C3
Maresquel F 48 C2
Mareuil F 67 C5
Mareuil-en-Brie F 59 B4
Mareuil-sur-Arnon F 68 B2
Mareuil-sur-Lay F 66 B3
Mareuil-sur-Ourcq F 59 A4
Margam GB 28 B4
Margariti GR 116 C2
Margate GB 31 C5
Margaux F 76 A2
Margerie-Hancourt F 59 B5
Margès F 69 C5
Margherita di Savóia
I 104 B2
Margita SRB 75 C6
Margone I 70 C2
Margonin PL 46 C3
Marguerittes F 78 C3
Margut F 59 A6
Maria E 101 B3
Mariager DK 38 C2
Mariana E 95 B4
Maria Neustift A 63 C5
Mariannelund S 40 B5
Marianópoli I 108 B2
Mariánské Lázně CZ 52 D2
Mariapfarr A 72 A3
Maria Saal A 73 B4
Mariazell A 63 C6
Maribo DK 39 E4
Maribor SLO 73 B5
Marieberg S 37 C2
Mariefred S 37 C4
Mariehamn FIN 36 B6
Marieholm S 41 D3
Mariemburg B 49 C5
Marienbaum D 50 B2
Marienberg D 52 C3
Marienheide D 50 B3
Mariental D 51 A6
Mariestad S 35 D5
Marieux F 48 C3
Marigliano I 103 C7
Marignane F 79 C4
Marigny
Jura F 69 B5
Manche F 57 A4
Marigny-le-Châtel F 59 B4
Marija Bistrica HR 73 B6
Marijampolė LT 6 D7
Marin E 87 B2
Marina HR 83 C5
Marina del Cantone
I 103 C7
Marina di Acquappesa
I 106 B2
Marina di Alberese I 81 D5
Marina di Amendolara
I 106 B3
Marina di Árbus I 110 C1
Marina di Campo I 81 D4
Marina di Carrara I 81 B4
Marina di Castagneto-
Donorático I 81 C4
Marina di Cécina I 81 C4
Marina di Gáiro I 110 C2
Marina di Ginosa I 104 C2
Marina di Gioiosa Iónica
I 106 C3
Marina di Grosseto I 81 D4
Marina di Léuca I 107 B5
Marina di Massa I 81 B4
Marina di Novaglie I 107 B5
Marina di Pisa I 81 C4
Marina di Ragusa I 109 C3
Marina di Ravenna I 82 B1
Marina di Torre Grande
I 110 C1
Marinaleda E 100 B1
Marina Romea I 82 B1
Marine de Sisco F 102 A2
Marinella I 108 B1
Marinella di Sarzana I 81 B4
Marineo I 108 B2
Marines F 58 A2
Maringues F 68 C3
Marinha das Ondas P 92 A2
Marinha Grande P 92 B2
Marinhas P 87 C2
Marino I 102 B5
Marjaliza E 94 C3
Markabygd N 114 D8
Markaryd S 40 C3
Markdorf D 61 C5
Markelo NL 50 A2
Market Deeping GB 30 B3
Market Drayton GB 26 C3
Market Harborough
GB 30 B3
Markethill GB 19 B5
Market Rasen GB 27 B5
Market Warsop GB 27 B4
Market Weighton GB 27 B5
Markgröningen D 61 B5
Markhausen D 43 C4
Marki PL 55 A6
Markina-Xemein E 89 A4
Markinch GB 25 B4
Märkische Buchholz
D 53 A3
Markitta S 113 E10
Markkleeberg D 52 B2
Marklohe D 43 C6
Marknesse NL 42 C2
Markneukirchen D 52 C2
Markopoulo GR 117 E5
Markovac SRB 85 B6
Markowice PL 54 C3
Markranstädt D 52 B2
Marksuhl D 51 C6
Markt Allhau A 73 A6
Markt Bibart D 61 A6
Marktbreit D 61 A6
Markt Erlbach D 62 A1
Markt-heidenfeld D 61 A5
Markt Indersdorf D 62 B2
Marktl D 62 B3
Marktleuthen D 52 C1
Marktoberdorf D 62 C1
Marktredwitz D 52 C2
Markt Rettenbach D 61 C6
Markt Schwaben D 62 B2
Markt-Übelbach A 73 A5
Markusica HR 74 C3
Markušovce SK 65 B6
Marl D 50 B3
Marlborough
Devon GB 28 C4
Wiltshire GB 29 B6
Marle F 59 A4
Marlieux F 69 B5
Marlow
D 45 A4
GB 31 C3
Marma S 36 B4
Marmagne F 69 B4
Marmande F 76 B3
Marmara TR 118 B2
Marmaris TR 119 F3
Marmelete P 98 B2
Marmolejo E 100 A1
Marmoutier F 60 B3
Marnay F 69 A5
Marne D 43 B6
Marnheim D 61 A4
Marnitz D 44 B3
Maroldsweisach D 51 C6
Marolles-les-Braults
F 58 B1
Maromme F 58 A2
Marone I 71 C5
Maronia GR 116 B7
Maroslele H 75 B5
Maróstica I 72 C1
Marotta I 82 C2
Marpisa GR 117 E7
Marquion F 49 C4
Marquise F 48 C2
Marradi I 81 B5
Marrasjärvi FIN 113 F14
Marraskoski FIN 113 F14
Marratxi E 97 B2
Marrúbiu I 110 C1
Marrum NL 42 B2
Marrupe E 94 B2
Marsac F 77 C5
Marsac-en-Livradois
F 68 C3
Marságlia I 80 B3
Marsala I 108 B1
Marsberg D 51 B4
Marsciano I 82 D1
Marseillan F 78 C2
Marseille = Marseilles
F 79 C4
Marseille en Beauvaisis
F 58 A2
Marseilles = Marseille
F 79 C4
Mársico Nuovo I 104 C1
Marske-by-the-Sea
GB 27 A4
Mars-la-Tours F 60 A1
Marsliden S 115 B12
Marson F 59 B5
Märsta S 37 C4
Marstal DK 39 E3
Marstrand S 38 B4
Marta I 102 A4
Martano I 107 A5
Martel F 77 B4
Martelange B 60 A1
Martfeld D 43 C6
Martfű H 75 A5
Martham GB 30 B5
Marthon F 67 C5
Martiago E 93 A4
Martigné-Briand F 67 A4
Martigné-Ferchaud F 57 C4
Martigne-sur-Mayenne
F 57 B5
Martigny CH 70 B2
Martigny-les-Bains F 60 B1
Martigues F 79 C4
Martim-Longo P 98 B3
Martin SK 65 A4
Martina CH 71 B5
Martina Franca I 104 C3
Martinamor E 94 B1
Martin de la Jara E 100 B1
Martinengo I 71 C4
Martin Muñoz de las
Posadas E 94 A2
Martinsberg A 63 B6
Martinšćica HR 82 B3
Martinshöhe D 60 A3
Martinsicuro I 82 D2
Martinszell D 61 C6
Mártis I 110 B1
Martofte DK 39 D3
Martonvásár H 74 A3
Martorell E 91 B4
Martos E 100 B2
Martres Tolosane F 77 C3
Martti FIN 113 E17
Marugán E 94 B2
Marúggio I 104 C3
Marvejols F 78 B2
Marville F 60 A1
Marwałd PL 47 B5
Marykirk GB 25 B5
Marypark GB 23 D5
Maryport GB 26 A2
Marytavy GB 28 C3
Marzabotto I 81 B5
Marzahna D 52 B2
Marzahne D 45 C4
Marzamemi I 109 C4
Marzocca I 82 C2
Masa E 89 B3
Mas-Cabardès F 77 C5
Máscali I 109 B4
Mascaraque E 94 C3
Mascarenhas P 87 C3
Mascioni I 103 A6
Mas de Barberáns E 90 C3
Mas de las Matas E 90 C2
Masegoso E 101 A3
Masegoso de Tajuña
E 95 B4
Masera I 70 B3
Masevaux F 60 C2
Masfjorden N 32 B2
Masham GB 27 A4
Masi N 113 C12
Maside E 87 B2
Maslacq F 76 C2
Maslinica HR 83 C5
Maslovare BIH 84 B2
Masone I 80 B2

Massa I 81 B4
Massa Fiscáglia I 81 B6
Massafra I 104 C3
Massa Lombarda I 81 B5
Massa Lubrense I 103 C7
Massamagrell E 96 B2
Massa Marittima I 81 C4
Massa Martana I 82 D1
Massanassa E 96 B2
Massarosa I 81 C4
Massat F 77 D4
Massay F 68 A1
Massbach D 51 C6
Masseret F 67 C6
Masseube F 77 C3
Massiac F 68 C3
Massignac F 67 C5
Massing D 62 B3
Massmechelen B 50 C1
Masterud N 34 B4
Mästocka S 40 C3
Masty BY 6 E8
Masúa I 110 C1
Masueco E 87 C4
Masugnsbyn S 113 E11
Mašun SLO 73 C4
Maszewo
Lubuskie PL 53 A4
Zachodnio-Pomorskie PL 45 B7
Mata de Alcántara E 93 B4
Matala GR 117 H6
Matalebreras E 89 C4
Matallana de Torío E 88 B1
Matamala E 89 C4
Mataporquera E 88 B2
Matapozuelos E 88 C2
Mataró E 91 B5
Matarocco I 108 B1
Mataruge MNE 85 C4
Mataruška Banja SRB 85 C5
Matélica I 82 C2
Matera I 104 C2
Mateševo MNE 85 D4
Mátészalka H 11 C7
Matet E 96 B2
Matfors S 115 E14
Matha F 67 C4
Mathay F 70 A1
Matignon F 57 B3
Matilla de los Caños del Rio E 94 B1
Matlock GB 27 B4
Matosinhos P 87 C2
Matour F 69 B4
Mátrafüred H 65 C5
Mátraterenye H 65 B5
Matre
Hordaland N 32 B2
Hordaland N 32 C2
Matrei am Brenner A 71 A6
Matrei in Osttirol A 72 A2
Matrice I 103 B7
Matsdal S 115 B12
Mattarello I 71 B6
Mattersburg A 64 C2
Mattighofen A 62 B4
Mattinata I 104 B2
Mattos P 92 B2
Mattsee A 62 C4
Mattsmyra S 36 A2
Matulji HR 73 C4
Maubert-Fontaine F 59 A5
Maubeuge F 49 C4
Maubourguet F 76 C3
Mauchline GB 24 C3
Maud GB 23 D6
Mauer-kirchen A 62 B4
Mauern D 62 B2
Mauguio F 78 C3
Maulbronn D 61 B4
Maule F 58 B2
Mauléon F 67 B4
Mauléon-Barousse F 77 D3
Mauléon-Licharre F 76 C2
Maulévrier F 67 A4
Maum IRL 18 C2
Maurach A 72 A1
Maure-de-Bretagne F 57 C4
Maureilhan F 78 C2
Mauriac F 68 C2
Mauron F 57 B3
Maurs F 77 B5
Maury F 77 D5
Maussane-les-Alpilles F 78 C3
Mautern A 63 B6
Mauterndorf A 72 A3
Mautern im Steiermark A 73 A4
Mauthausen A 63 B5
Mauthen A 72 B2
Mauvezin F 77 C3
Mauzé-sur-le-Mignon F 67 B4
Maxent F 57 C3
Maxey-sur-Vaise F 60 B1
Maxial P 92 B1
Maxieira P 92 B2
Maxwellheugh GB 25 C5
Mayalde E 88 C1
Maybole GB 24 C3
Mayen D 50 C3
Mayenne F 57 B5
Mayet F 58 C1
Mayorga E 88 B1
Mayres F 78 B3
Mayrhofen A 72 A1
Mazagón E 99 B4
Mazaleón E 90 B3
Mazamet F 77 C5
Mazan F 79 B4
Mazara del Vallo I 108 B1
Mazarambroz E 94 C2
Mazarete E 95 B4
Mazaricos E 86 B2
Mazarrón E 101 B4
Mažeikiai LT 6 C7
Mazères F 77 C4
Mazères-sur-Salat F 77 C3
Mazières-en-Gâtine F 67 B4
Mazin HR 83 B4
Mazuelo E 88 B3
Mazyr BY 7 E10
Mazzarino I 109 B3
Mazzarrà Sant'Andrea I 109 A4
Mazzo di Valtellina I 71 B5
Mdzewo PL 47 C6
Mealabost GB 22 C2
Mealhada P 92 A2
Méan B 49 C6
Meana Sardo I 110 C2
Meaulne F 68 B2
Meaux F 59 B3
Mebonden N 114 D8
Mecerreyes E 89 B3
Mechelen B 49 B5
Mechernich D 50 C2
Mechnica PL 54 C3
Mechowo PL 45 B7
Mechterstädt D 51 C6
Mecidiye TR 118 B1
Mecikal PL 46 B3
Mecina-Bombarón E 100 C2
Mecitözü TR 16 A7
Meckenbeuren D 61 C5
Meckenheim
Rheinland-Pfalz D 50 C3
Rheinland-Pfalz D 61 A4
Meckesheim D 61 A4
Mecseknádasd H 74 B3
Meda
I 71 C4
P 87 D3
Medak HR 83 B4
Mede I 80 A2
Medebach D 51 B4
Medelim P 93 A3
Medemblik NL 42 C2
Medena Selista BIH 84 B1
Medesano I 81 B4
Medevi S 37 D1
Medgidia RO 11 D10
Medgyesháza H 75 B6
Medhamn S 35 C5
Mediaş RO 11 C8
Medicina I 81 B5
Medinaceli E 95 A4
Medina de las Torres E 93 C4
Medina del Campo E 88 C2
Medina de Pomar E 89 B3
Medina de Rioseco E 88 C1
Medina Sidonia E 99 C5
Medinilla E 93 A5
Medja SRB 75 C5
Medjedja BIH 85 C4
Medulin HR 82 B2
Meduno I 72 B2
Medveda SRB 85 B6
Medvedja SRB 85 C6
Medvedov SK 64 C3
Medvide HR 83 B4
Medvode SLO 73 B4
Medzev SK 65 B6
Medžitlija MK 116 B3
Meerane D 52 C2
Meerle B 49 B5
Meersburg D 61 C5
Meeuwen B 49 B6
Megalo Horio GR 119 F2
Megalopoli GR 117 E4
Megara GR 117 D5
Megève F 69 C6
Meggenhofen A 63 B4
Megra RUS 7 A14
Mehamn N 113 A16
Mehedeby S 36 B4
Méhkerék H 75 B6
Mehun-sur-Yèvre F 68 A2
Meigle GB 25 B4
Meijel NL 50 B1
Meilen CH 70 A3
Meilhan F 76 C2
Meimôa P 93 A3
Meina I 70 C3
Meine D 44 C2
Meinersen D 44 C2
Meinerzhagen D 50 B3
Meiningen D 51 C6
Meira E 86 A3
Meiringen CH 70 B3
Meisenheim D 60 A3
Meissen D 52 B3
Meitingen D 62 B1
Meix-devant-Virton B 60 A1
Męka PL 54 B3
Meka Gruda BIH 84 C3
Mel I 72 B2
Melbu N 112 D3
Melč CZ 64 A3
Meldal N 114 D6
Méldola I 82 B1
Meldorf D 43 A6
Melegnano I 71 C4
Melenci SRB 75 C5
Melendugno I 105 C4
Melfi I 104 C1
Melfjordbotn N 112 F2
Melgaço P 87 B2
Melgar de Arriba E 88 B1
Melgar de Fernamental E 88 B2
Melgar de Yuso E 88 B2
Melhus N 114 D7
Meliana E 96 B2
Melide
CH 70 C3
E 86 B2
Melides P 98 A2
Meligales GR 117 E3
Melilli I 109 B4
Melinovac HR 83 B4
Melisenda I 110 C2
Melisey F 60 C2
Mélito di Porto Salvo I 109 B4
Melk A 63 B6
Melksham GB 29 B5
Mellanström S 115 B15
Mellbystrand S 40 C2
Melle
B 49 B4
D 50 A4
F 67 B4
Mellendorf D 43 C6
Mellerud S 35 D4
Mellieha M 107 C5
Mellösa S 37 C3
Mellrichstadt D 51 C6
Mělnické Vtelno CZ 53 C4
Mělník CZ 53 C4
Melón E 87 B2
Melrose GB 25 C5
Mels CH 71 A4
Melsungen D 51 B5
Meltaus FIN 113 F14
Meltham GB 27 B4
Melton Mowbray GB 30 B3
Meltosjärvi FIN 113 F13
Melun F 58 B3
Melvaig GB 22 D3
Melvich GB 23 C5
Mélykút H 75 B4
Melzo I 71 C4
Memaliaj AL 116 B1
Membrilla E 95 D3
Membrio E 93 B3
Memer F 77 B4
Memmelsdorf D 51 D6
Memmingen D 61 C6
Memoria P 92 B2
Mena UA 7 F12
Menággio I 71 B4
Menai Bridge GB 26 B1
Menasalbas E 94 C2
Menat F 68 B2
Mendavia E 89 B4
Mendaza E 89 B4
Mende F 78 B2
Menden D 50 B3
Menderes TR 119 D2
Mendig D 50 C3
Mendiga P 92 B2
Mendrisio CH 70 C3
Ménéac F 56 B3
Menemen TR 118 D2
Menen B 49 C4
Menesjärvi FIN 113 D15
Menetou-Salon F 68 A2
Menfi I 108 B1
Ménfőcsanak H 64 C3
Mengamuñoz E 94 B2
Mengen
D 61 B5
TR 118 B7
Mengeš SLO 73 B4
Mengíbar E 100 B2
Mengkofen D 62 B3
Menou F 68 A3
Mens F 79 B4
Menslage D 43 C4
Menstrask S 115 B16
Mentana I 102 A5
Menton F 80 C1
Méntrida E 94 B2
Méobecq F 67 B6
Méounes-les-Montrieux F 79 C4
Meppel NL 42 C3
Meppen D 43 C4
Mequinenza E 90 B3
Mer F 58 C2
Mera
Coruña E 86 A2
Coruña E 86 A3
Meråker N 114 D8
Merano I 71 B6
Merate I 71 C4
Mercadillo E 89 A3
Mercatale I 82 C1
Mercatino Conca I 82 C1
Mercato San Severino I 103 C7
Mercato Saraceno I 82 C1
Merching D 62 B1
Merchtem B 49 C5
Merdrignac F 56 B3
Merdžanići BIH 84 C2
Meré E 88 A2
Mere GB 29 B5
Méréville F 58 B3
Merfeld D 50 B3
Méribel F 69 C6
Méribel Motraret F 69 C6
Meriç TR 118 A1
Mérida E 93 C4
Mérignac F 76 B2
Měřín CZ 64 A1
Mering D 62 B1
Merkendorf D 62 A1
Merklin CZ 63 A4
Merksplas B 49 B5
Merlånna S 37 C3
Merlimont Plage F 48 C2
Mern DK 39 D5
Mernye H 74 B2
Mersch L 60 A2
Merseburg D 52 B1
Mers-les-Bains F 48 C2
Merthyr Tydfil GB 29 B4
Mertingen D 62 B1
Mértola P 98 B3
Méru F 58 A3
Merville F 87 B2
Mervans F 69 B5
Merville F 48 C3
Méry-sur-Seine F 59 B4
Merzen D 43 C4
Merzifon TR 16 A7
Merzig D 60 A2
Mesagne I 105 C3
Mesão Frio P 87 C3
Mesas de Ibor E 93 B5
Meschede D 50 B4
Meschers-sur-Gironde F 66 C4
Meshchovsk RUS 7 D13
Meslay-du-Maine F 57 C5
Mesna N 34 A2
Mesnalien N 34 A2
Mesocco CH 71 B4
Mésola I 82 B1
Mesologi GR 116 D3
Mesopotamo GR 116 C2
Mesoraca I 107 B3
Messac F 57 C4
Messancy B 60 A1
Messdorf D 44 C3
Messei F 57 B5
Messejana P 98 B2
Messelt N 34 A3
Messina I 109 A4
Messingen D 43 C4
Messini GR 117 E4
Messkirch D 61 C5
Messlingen S 115 E9
Messtetten D 61 B4
Mesta GR 117 D7
Mestanza E 100 A1
Městec Králové CZ 53 C5
Mestlin D 44 B3
Město Albrechtice CZ 54 C2
Město Libavá CZ 64 A3
Město Touškov CZ 63 A4
Mestre I 72 C2
Mesvres F 69 B4
Mesztegnyő H 74 B2
Meta I 103 C7
Metajna HR 83 B4
Metelen D 50 A3
Methana GR 117 E5
Methlick GB 23 D6
Methven GB 25 B4
Methwold GB 30 B4
Metković HR 84 C2
Metlika SLO 73 C5
Metnitz A 73 B4
Metsäkylä FIN 113 F17
Metsovo GR 116 C3
Metten D 62 B3
Mettendorf D 50 D2
Mettet B 49 C5
Mettingen D 50 A3
Mettlach D 60 A2
Mettlen CH 70 B2
Mettmann D 50 B2
Metz F 60 A2
Metzervisse F 60 A2
Metzingen D 61 B5
Meulan F 58 A2
Meung-sur-Loire F 58 C2
Meuselwitz D 52 B2
Meuzac F 67 C6
Mevagissey GB 28 C3
Mexborough GB 27 B4
Meximieux F 69 C5
Mey GB 23 C5
Meyenburg D 44 B4
Meyerhöfen D 43 C5
Meylan F 69 C5
Meymac F 68 C2
Meyrargues F 79 C4
Meyrueis F 78 B2
Meyssac F 77 A4
Meysse F 78 B3
Meyzieu F 69 C4
Mèze F 78 C2
Mézériat F 69 B5
Mežica SLO 73 B4
Mézidon-Canon F 57 A5
Mézières-en-Brenne F 67 B6
Mézières-sur-Issoire F 67 B5
Mézilhac F 78 B3
Mézilles F 59 C4
Mézin F 76 B3
Mezőberény H 75 B6
Mezőcsát H 65 C6
Mezőfalva H 74 B3
Mezőhegyes H 75 B5
Mezőkeresztes H 65 C6
Mezőkomárom H 74 B3
Mezőkövácsháza H 75 B5
Mezőkövesd H 65 C6
Mezőörs H 74 A2
Mézos F 76 B1
Mezőszilas H 74 B3
Mezőtúr H 75 A5
Mezquita de Jarque E 90 C2
Mezzano
Emilia Romagna I 82 B1
Trentino Alto Adige I 72 B1
Mezzojuso I 108 B2
Mezzoldo I 71 B4
Mezzolombardo I 71 B6
Mgarr M 107 C5
Mgarr RUS 7 E12
Miajadas E 93 B5
Miały PL 46 C2
Mianowice PL 46 A3
Miasteczko Krajeńskie PL 46 B3
Miasteczko Śl. PL 54 C3
Miastko PL 46 A2
Michalovce SK 10 B6
Michałowice PL 55 C5
Michelau D 51 C6
Michelbach D 61 A6
Micheldorf A 63 C5
Michelhausen A 64 B1
Michelsneukirchen D 62 A3
Michelstadt D 61 A5
Michendorf D 52 A3
Mickleover GB 27 C4
Midbea GB 23 B6
Middelburg NL 49 B4
Middelfart DK 39 D2
Middelharnis NL 49 B5
Middelkerke B 48 B3
Middelstum NL 42 B3
Middlesbrough GB 27 A4
Middleton GB 24 B1
Middleton Cheney GB 30 B2
Middleton-in-Teesdale GB 26 A3
Middletown GB 19 B5
Middlewich GB 26 B3
Middlezoy GB 29 B5
Midhurst GB 31 D3
Midleton IRL 20 C3
Midlum D 43 B5
Midsomer Norton GB 29 B5
Midtgulen N 114 F2
Midtskogberget N 34 A4
Midwolda NL 43 B4
Mid Yell GB 22 A7
Miechów PL 55 C5
Miedes de Aragón E 89 C5
Miedes de Atienza E 95 A3
Międzybodzie Bielskie PL 65 A5
Międzybórz PL 54 B2
Międzychód PL 46 C1
Międzylesie PL 54 C1
Międzyrzec Podlaski PL 6 F7
Międzyrzecz PL 46 C1
Międzywodzie PL 45 A6
Międzyzdroje PL 45 B6
Miejska Górka PL 54 B1
Miélan F 76 C3
Mielec PL 55 C6
Mielęcin PL 45 B6
Mielno
Warmińsko-Mazurskie PL 47 B6
Zachodnio-Pomorskie PL 46 A2
Miengo E 88 A3
Mieraslompolo FIN 113 C16
Miercurea Ciuc RO 11 C8
Mieres
Asturias E 88 A1
Girona E 91 A5
Mieroszów PL 53 C6
Mierzyn PL 55 B4
Miesau D 60 A3
Miesbach D 62 C2
Mieścisko PL 46 C3
Mieste D 44 C3
Miesterhorst D 44 C3
Mieszków PL 54 A2
Mieszkowice PL 45 C6
Mietków PL 54 C1
Migennes F 59 C4
Miggiano I 107 B5
Migliánico I 103 A7
Migliarino I 81 B5
Migliónico I 104 C2
Mignano Monte Lungo I 103 B6
Migné F 67 B6
Miguel Esteban E 95 C3
Miguelturra E 94 D3
Mihajlovac SRB 85 B5
Miháld H 74 B2
Mihalgazi TR 118 B5
Mihalıççık TR 118 C6
Mihályi H 74 A2
Mihla D 51 B6
Mihohnić HR 83 A3
Miholjsko HR 73 C5
Mihovljan HR 73 B5
Mijares E 94 B2
Mijas E 100 C1
Mijoska MNE 85 D4
Mike H 74 B2
Mikhnevo RUS 7 D14
Mikines GR 117 E4
Mikkeli FIN 3 F27
Mikkelvik N 112 B8
Mikleuš HR 74 C2
Mikołajki Pomorskie PL 47 B5
Mikolów PL 54 C3
Mikonos GR 117 E7
Mikorzyn PL 54 B3
Mikro Derio GR 116 A8
Mikstat PL 54 B2
Mikulášovice CZ 53 C4
Mikulov CZ 64 B2
Mikulovice CZ 54 C2
Milagro E 89 B5
Miłakowo PL 47 A6
Milan = Milano I 71 C4
Miland N 32 C5
Milano = Milan I 71 C4
Milano Marittima I 82 B1
Milas TR 119 E2
Milazzo I 109 A4
Mildenhall GB 30 B4
Milejewo PL 47 A5
Milelín CZ 53 C5
Miletić SRB 75 C4
Miletićevo SRB 75 C6
Mileto I 106 C3
Milevsko CZ 63 A5
Milford IRL 19 A4
Milford Haven GB 28 B2
Milford on Sea GB 31 D2
Milhão P 87 C4
Milići BIH 84 B4
Miličin CZ 63 A5
Milicz PL 54 B2
Milín CZ 63 A5
Militello in Val di Catánia I 109 B3
Miljevina BIH 84 C3
Milkowice PL 53 B6
Millançay F 68 A1
Millares E 96 B2
Millas F 91 A5
Millau F 78 B2
Millesimo I 80 B2
Millevaches F 68 C2
Millom GB 26 A2
Millport GB 24 C3
Millstatt A 72 B3
Millstreet
Cork IRL 20 B2
Waterford IRL 21 B4
Milltown
Galway IRL 18 C3
Kerry IRL 20 B1
Milltown Malbay IRL 20 B2
Milly-la-Forêt F 58 B3
Milmarcos E 95 A5
Milmersdorf D 45 B5
Milna HR 83 C5
Milnthorpe GB 26 A3
Miločaj SRB 85 C5
Milogórze PL 47 A6
Miłomłyn PL 47 B5
Milos GR 117 F6
Miloševo SRB 85 B6
Miłosław PL 54 A2
Milot AL 105 B5
Milówka PL 65 A5
Miltach D 62 A3
Miltenberg D 61 A5
Milton Keynes GB 31 B3
Miltzow D 45 A5
Milutovac SRB 85 C6
Milverton GB 29 B4
Milzyn PL 47 C4
Mimice HR 84 C1
Mimizan F 76 B1
Mimizan-Plage F 76 B1
Mimoň CZ 53 C4
Mina de Juliana P 98 B2
Mina de São Domingos P 98 B3
Minas de Riotinto E 99 B4
Minateda E 101 A4
Minaya E 95 C4
Minde P 92 B2
Mindelheim D 61 B6
Mindelstetten D 62 B2
Minden D 51 A4
Mindszent H 75 B5
Minehead GB 29 B4
Mineo I 109 B3
Minerbe I 71 C6
Minérbio I 81 B5
Minervino Murge I 104 B2
Minglanilla E 95 C5
Mingorria E 94 B2
Minnesund N 34 B3
Miño E 86 A2
Miño de San Esteban E 89 C3
Minsen D 43 B4
Minsk BY 7 E9
Mińsk Mazowiecki PL 55 A6
Minsterley GB 26 C3
Mintlaw GB 23 D6
Minturno I 103 B6
Mionica
BIH 84 B3
SRB 85 B5
Mios F 76 B2
Mira
E 96 B1
I 72 C2
P 92 A2
Mirabel E 93 B4
Mirabel-aux-Baronnies F 79 B4
Mirabella Eclano I 103 B8
Mirabella Imbáccari I 109 B3
Mirabello I 81 B5
Miradoux F 77 B3
Miraflores de la Sierra E 94 B3
Miralrio E 95 B4
Miramar P 87 C2
Miramare I 82 B1
Miramas F 78 C3
Mirambeau F 67 C4
Miramont-de-Guyenne F 77 B3
Miranda de Arga E 89 B5
Miranda de Ebro E 89 B4
Miranda do Corvo P 92 A2
Miranda do Douro P 87 C4
Mirande F 77 C3
Mirandela P 87 C3
Mirandilla E 93 C4
Mirándola I 81 B5
Miranje HR 83 B4
Mirano I 72 C2
Miras AL 116 B2
Miravet E 90 B3
Miré F 57 C5
Mirebeau F 67 B5
Mirebeau-sur-Bèze F 69 A5
Mirecourt F 60 B2
Mirepoix F 77 C4
Mires GR 117 G6
Miribel F 69 C4
Miričina BIH 84 B3
Mirina GR 116 C7
Mirna SLO 73 C5
Miroslav CZ 64 B2
Mirosławice PL 54 C1
Mirosławiec PL 46 B2
Mirošov CZ 63 A4
Mirotice CZ 63 A5
Mirovice CZ 63 A5
Mirow D 45 B4
Mirsk PL 53 C5
Mirzec PL 55 B6
Misi FIN 113 F15
Misilmeri I 108 A2
Miske H 75 B4
Miskolc H 65 B6
Mislinja SLO 73 B5
Missanello I 104 C2
Missillac F 66 A2
Mistelbach
A 64 B2
D 62 A2
Misten N 112 E3
Misterbianco I 109 B4
Misterhult S 40 B6
Mistretta I 109 B3
Misurina I 72 B2
Mitchelstown IRL 20 B3
Mithimna GR 116 C8
Mithoni GR 117 F3
Mitilini GR 118 C1
Mitilinii GR 119 E1
Mittelberg
Tirol A 71 B5
Vorarlberg A 71 A5
Mittenwald D 71 A6
Mittenwalde D 52 A3
Mitterback A 63 C6
Mitterdorf im Mürztal A 73 A5
Mitter-Kleinarl A 72 A3
Mittersheim F 60 B2
Mittersill A 72 A2
Mitterskirchen D 62 B3
Mitterteich D 62 A3
Mitton F 76 B2
Mittweida D 52 C2
Mitwitz D 52 C1
Mizhhir'ya UA 11 B7
Mjällby S 41 C4
Mjåvatn N 33 D5
Mjöbäck S 40 B2
Mjölby S 37 D2
Mjølfjell N 32 B3
Mjøndalen N 35 C2
Mjørlund N 34 B2
Mladá Boleslav CZ 53 C4
Mladá Vožice CZ 63 A5
Mladé Buky CZ 53 C5
Mladenovac SRB 85 B5
Mladenovo SRB 75 C4
Mladikovine BIH 84 B2
Mława PL 47 B6
Mlinište BIH 84 B1
Młodzieszyn PL 55 A5
Młogoszyn PL 55 A4
Młynary PL 47 A5
Mnichóvice CZ 63 A5
Mnichovo Hradiště CZ 53 C4
Mniów PL 55 B5
Mnisek nad Hnilcom SK 65 B6
Mníšek pod Brdy CZ 63 A5
Mniszek PL 55 B5
Mniszków PL 55 B5
Mo
Hedmark N 34 B3
Hordaland N 32 B2
Møre og Romsdal N 114 E5
Telemark N 33 C4
Gävleborg S 36 A3
Västra Götaland S 35 D3
Moaña E 87 B2
Moate IRL 21 A4
Mocejón E 94 C3
Močenok SK 64 B3
Mochales E 95 A4
Mochowo PL 47 C5
Mochy PL 53 A6
Mockern D 52 A1
Mockfjärd S 36 B1
Möckmühl D 61 A5
Mockrehna D 52 B2
Moclin E 100 B2
Mocsa H 64 C4
Mőcsény H 74 B3
Modane F 70 C1
Modbury GB 28 C4
Módena I 81 B4
Módica I 109 C3
Modigliana I 81 B5
Modlin PL 47 C6
Mödling A 64 B2
Modliszewice PL 55 B5
Modliszewko PL 46 C3
Modogno I 104 B2
Modra SK 64 B3
Modran BIH 84 B2
Modriča BIH 84 B3
Möðrudalur IS 111 B10
Modrý Kamen SK 65 B5
Moëlan-sur-Mer F 56 C2
Moelfre GB 26 B1
Moelv N 34 B2
Moen N 112 C7
Moena I 72 B1
Moerbeke B 49 B4
Moers D 50 B2
Móes P 87 D3
Moffat GB 25 C4
Mogadouro P 87 C4
Mogata S 37 D3
Móggio Udinese I 72 B3
Mogielnica PL 55 B5
Mogilany PL 65 A5
Mogilno PL 46 C3
Mogliano I 82 C2
Mogliano Véneto I 72 C2
Mogor E 87 B2
Mógoro I 110 C1
Moguer E 99 B4
Mohács H 74 C3
Moheda S 40 B4
Mohedas E 93 A4
Mohedas de la Jara E 93 B5
Mohelnice CZ 64 A2
Mohill IRL 19 C4
Möhlin CH 70 A2
Moholm S 35 D6
Mohorn D 52 B3
Mohyliv-Podil's'kyy UA 11 B9
Moi N 33 D3
Moià E 91 B5
Móie I 82 C2
Moimenta da Beira P 87 D3
Mo i Rana N 115 A11
Moirans F 69 C5
Moirans-en-Montagne F 69 B5
Moisaküla EST 7 B8
Moisdon-la-Rivière F 57 C4
Moissac F 77 B4
Moita
Coimbra P 92 A2
Guarda P 93 A3
Santarém P 92 B2
Setúbal P 92 C1
Moita dos Ferreiros P 92 B1
Moixent E 101 A5
Mojacar E 101 B4
Mojados E 88 C2
Mojkovac MNE 85 D4
Mojmírovce SK 64 B4
Mojtín SK 65 B4
Möklinta S 36 B3
Mokošica HR 84 D3
Mokra Gora SRB 85 C4
Mokronog SLO 73 C5
Mokro Polje HR 83 B5
Mokrzyska PL 55 C5
Møkster N 32 B2
Mol
B 49 B6
SRB 75 C5
Mola di Bari I 104 B3
Molai GR 117 F4
Molare I 80 B2
Molaretto I 70 C2
Molas F 77 C3
Molassano I 80 B2
Molbergen D 43 C4
Mold GB 26 B2
Molde N 114 E4
Møldrup DK 38 C2
Moledo do Minho P 87 C2
Molfetta I 104 B2
Molfsee D 44 A2
Moliden S 115 D15
Molières F 77 B4
Molina de Aragón E 95 B5
Molina de Segura E 101 A4
Molinar E 89 A3
Molinaseca E 86 B4
Molinella I 81 B5
Molinet F 68 B3
Molinicos E 101 A3
Molini di Tures I 72 B1
Molinos de Duero E 89 C4
Molins de Rei E 91 B5
Moliterno I 104 C1
Molkom S 35 C5
Mollas AL 105 C6
Möllbrücke A 72 B3
Mölle S 41 C2
Molledo E 88 A2
Möllenbeck D 45 B5
Mollerussa E 90 B3
Mollet de Perelada E 91 A5
Mollina E 100 B1
Mölln D 44 B2
Molló E 91 A5
Mollösund S 35 D3
Mölltorp S 37 D1
Mölnbo S 37 C4
Mölndal S 38 B5
Mölnlycke S 38 B5
Molompize F 68 C3
Moloy F 69 A4
Molsheim F 60 B3
Moltzow D 45 B4
Molve HR 74 B2
Molveno I 71 B5
Molvizar E 100 C2
Molzbichl A 72 B3
Mombaróccio I 82 C1
Mombeltrán E 94 B1
Mombris D 51 C5
Mombuey E 87 B4
Momchilgrad BG 116 A7
Mommark DK 39 E3
Momo I 70 C3
Monaghan IRL 19 B5
Monar Lodge GB 22 D4
Monasterace Marina I 106 C3
Monasterevin IRL 21 A4
Monasterio de Rodilla E 89 B3
Monastir I 110 C2
Monbahus F 77 B3
Monbazillac F 77 B3
Moncada E 96 B2
Moncalieri I 80 A1
Moncalvo I 80 A2
Monção P 87 B2
Moncarapacho P 98 B3
Moncel-sur-Seille F 60 B2
Monchegorsk RUS 3 C30
Mönchengladbach = Munchen-Gladbach D 50 B2
Mónchio della Corti I 81 B4
Monchique P 98 B2
Monclar-de-Quercy F 77 C4
Moncofa E 96 B2
Moncontour F 56 B3
Moncoutant F 67 B4
Monda E 100 C1
Mondariz E 87 B2
Mondavio I 82 C1
Mondéjar E 95 B3
Mondello I 108 A2
Mondim de Basto P 87 C3
Mondolfo I 82 C2
Mondoñedo E 86 A3
Mondorf-les-Bains L 60 A2
Mondoubleau F 58 C1
Mondovì I 80 B1
Mondragon F 78 B3
Mondragone I 103 B6
Mondsee A 63 C4
Monéglia I 80 B3
Monegrillo E 90 B2
Monein F 76 C2
Monemvasia GR 117 F5
Mónesi I 80 B1
Monesiglio I 80 B2
Monesterio E 99 A4
Monestier-de-Clermont F 79 B4
Monestiés F 77 B5
Monéteau F 59 C4
Moneygall IRL 21 B4
Moneymore GB 19 B5
Monfalcone I 72 C3
Monfero E 86 A2
Monflanquin F 77 B3
Monflorite E 90 A2
Monforte P 92 B3
Monforte da Beira
E 92 B3
P 92 B3
Monforte d'Alba I 80 B1
Monforte del Cid E 96 C2
Monforte de Lemos E 86 B3
Monforte de Moyuela E 90 B1
Monghidoro I 81 B5
Mongiana I 106 C3
Monguelfo I 72 B2
Monheim D 62 B1
Moniaive GB 25 C4
Monifieth GB 25 B5
Monikie GB 25 B5
Monistrol-d'Allier F 78 B2
Monistrol de Montserrat E 91 B4
Monistrol-sur-Loire F 68 C4
Mönkebude D 45 B5
Monkton GB 24 C3
Monmouth GB 29 B5
Monnaie F 67 A5
Monnerville F 58 B3
Monnickendam NL 42 C2
Monolithos GR 119 F2
Monópoli I 104 C3
Monor H 75 A4
Monóvar E 101 A5
Monpazier F 77 B3
Monreal
D 50 C3
E 76 D1
Monreal del Campo E 95 B5
Monreale I 108 A2
Monroy E 93 B4
Monroyo E 90 C2
Mons B 49 C4
Monsaraz P 92 C3
Monschau D 50 C2
Monségur F 76 B3
Monsélice I 72 C1
Mønshaug N 32 B3
Monster NL 49 A5
Mönsterås S 40 B6
Monsummano Terme I 81 C4
Montabaur D 50 C3
Montafia I 80 B2
Montagnac F 78 C2
Montagnana I 71 C6
Montaigu F 66 B3
Montaigu-de-Quercy F 77 B4
Montaiguët-en-Forez F 68 B3
Montaigut F 68 B2
Montaigut-sur-Save F 77 C4
Montainville F 58 B2
Montalbán E 90 C2
Montalbán de Córdoba E 100 B1
Montalbano Elicona I 109 A4
Montalbano Iónico I 104 C2
Montalbo E 95 C4
Montalcino I 81 C5
Montaldo di Cósola I 80 B3
Montalegre P 87 C3
Montalieu-Vercieu F 69 C5
Montalivet-les-Bains F 66 C3
Montallegro I 108 B2
Montalto delle Marche I 82 D2
Montalto di Castro I 102 A4
Montalto Pavese I 80 B3
Montalto Uffugo I 106 B3
Montalvão P 92 B3
Montamarta E 88 C1
Montana BG 11 E7
Montana-Vermala CH 70 B2
Montánchez E 93 B4
Montanejos E 96 A2
Montano Antilia I 106 A2
Montans F 77 C4
Montargil P 92 B2
Montargis F 58 C3
Montastruc-la-Conseillère F 77 C4
Montauban F 77 B4
Montauban-de-Bretagne F 57 B3
Montbard F 59 C5
Montbarrey F 69 A5
Montbazens F 77 B5
Montbazon F 67 A5
Montbéliard F 70 A1
Montbenoit F 69 B6
Montbeugny F 68 B3
Montblanc E 91 B4
Montbozon F 69 A6
Montbrison F 68 C4
Montbron F 67 C5
Montbrun-les-Bains F 79 B4
Montceau-les-Mines F 69 B4
Montcenis F 69 B4
Montchanin F 69 B4
Montcornet F 59 A5
Montcuq F 77 B4
Montdardier F 78 C2
Mont-de-Marsan F 76 C2
Montdidier F 58 A3
Monteagudo E 101 A4
Monteagudo de las Vicarias E 89 C4
Montealegre E 88 C2
Montealegre del Castillo E 101 A4
Montebello Iónico I 109 B4
Montebello Vicentino I 71 C6
Montebelluna I 72 C2
Montebourg F 57 A4
Montebruno I 80 B3
Monte-Carlo MC 80 C1
Montecarotto I 82 C2
Montecassiano I 82 C2
Montecastrilli I 102 A5
Montecatini Terme I 81 C4
Montécchio I 82 C1
Montécchio Emilia I 81 B4
Montécchio Maggiore I 71 C6
Montech F 77 C4
Montechiaro d'Asti I 80 A2
Monte Clara P 92 B3
Monte Clérigo P 98 B2
Montecórice I 103 C7
Montecorvino Rovella I 103 C7
Monte da Pedra P 92 B3
Monte de Goula P 92 B3
Montederramo E 87 B3
Montedoro I 108 B2
Monte do Trigo P 92 C3
Montefalco I 82 D1
Montefalcone di Val Fortore I 103 B8
Montefalcone nel Sánnio I 103 B7
Montefano I 82 C2
Montefiascone I 102 A5
Montefiorino I 81 B4
Montefortino I 82 D2
Montefranco I 102 A5
Montefrío E 100 B2
Montegiordano Marina I 106 A3
Montegiórgio I 82 C2
Monte Gordo P 98 B3
Montegranaro I 82 C2
Montehermoso E 93 A4
Montejicar E 100 B2
Montejo de la Sierra E 95 A3
Montejo de Tiermes E 89 C3
Monte Juntos P 92 C3
Montel-de-Gelat F 68 C2
Monteleone di Púglia I 103 B8
Monteleone di Spoleto I 102 A5
Monteleone d'Orvieto I 81 D6
Montelepre I 108 A2
Montelibretti I 102 A5
Montelier F 79 B4
Montélimar F 78 B3
Montella
E 91 A4
I 103 C8
Montellano E 99 B5
Montelupo Fiorentino I 81 C5
Montemaggiore Belsito I 108 B2
Montemagno I 80 B2
Montemayor E 100 B1
Montemayor de Pinilla E 88 C2
Montemésola I 104 C3
Montemilleto I 103 B7
Montemilone I 104 B1
Montemolín E 99 A4
Montemónaco I 82 D2
Montemor-o-Novo P 92 C2
Montemor-o-Velho P 92 A2
Montemurro I 104 C1
Montendre F 67 C4
Montenegro de Cameros E 89 B4
Montenero di Bisáccia I 103 B7
Monteneuf F 57 C3
Monteparano I 104 C3
Montepescali I 81 D5
Montepiano I 81 B5
Monte Porzio I 82 C2
Montepulciano I 81 C5
Monte Real P 92 B2
Montereale I 103 A6
Montereale Valcellina I 72 B2
Montereau-Faut-Yonne F 59 B3
Monte Redondo P 92 B2
Monterénzio I 81 B5
Monte Romano I 102 A4
Monteroni d'Arbia I 81 C5
Monteroni di Lecce I 105 C4
Monterosso al Mare I 80 B3
Monterosso Almo I 109 B3
Monterosso Grana I 79 B6
Monterotondo I 102 A5
Monterotondo Marittimo I 81 C4
Monterrey E 87 C3
Monterroso E 86 B3
Monterrubio de la Serena E 93 C5
Monterubbiano I 82 C2
Montesa E 96 C2
Montesalgueiro E 86 A2
Monte San Giovanni Campano I 103 B6
Montesano sulla Marcellana I 104 C1
Monte San Savino I 81 C5
Monte Sant'Ángelo I 104 B1
Montesárchio I 103 B7
Montescaglioso I 104 C2
Montesclaros E 94 B2
Montesilvano I 103 A7
Montespértoli I 81 C5
Montesquieu-Volvestre F 77 C4
Montesquiou F 77 C3
Montestruc-sur-Gers F 77 C3
Montes Velhos P 98 B2
Montevarchi I 81 C5
Montéveglio I 81 B5
Monte Vilar P 92 B1
Montfaucon F 66 A3
Montfaucon-d'Argonne F 59 A6
Montfaucon-en-Velay F 69 C4
Montferrat
Isère F 69 C5
Var F 79 C5
Montfort-en-Chalosse F 76 C2
Montfort-l'Amaury F 58 B2
Montfort-le-Gesnois F 58 B1
Montfort-sur-Meu F 57 B4
Montfort-sur-Risle F 58 A1
Montgai E 90 B3
Montgaillard F 76 C3
Montgenèvre F 79 B5
Montgiscard F 77 C4
Montgomery GB 26 C2
Montguyon F 67 C4
Monthermé F 59 A5
Monthey CH 70 B1
Monthois F 59 A5
Monthureux-sur-Saône F 60 B1
Monti I 110 B2
Monticelli d'Ongina I 81 A3
Montichiari I 71 C5
Monticiano I 81 C5
Montiel E 100 A3
Montier-en-Der F 59 B5
Montieri I 81 C5
Montiglio I 80 A2
Montignac F 77 A4
Montigny-le-Roi F 60 C1
Montigny-lès-Metz F 60 A2
Montigny-sur-Aube F 59 C5
Montijo
E 93 C4
P 92 C2
Montilla E 100 B1
Montillana E 100 B2
Montilly F 68 B3
Montivilliers F 57 A6
Montjaux F 78 B1
Montjean-sur-Loire F 66 A4
Montlhéry F 58 B3
Montlieu-la-Garde F 67 C4
Mont-Louis F 91 A5
Montlouis-sur-Loire F 67 A5
Montluçon F 68 B2
Montluel F 69 C5
Montmarault F 68 B2
Montmartin-sur-Mer F 57 B4
Montmédy F 59 A6
Montmélian F 69 C6
Montmeyan F 79 C5
Montmeyran F 78 B3
Montmirail
Marne F 59 B4
Sarthe F 58 B1
Montmiral F 69 C5
Montmirat F 78 C3
Montmirey-le-Château F 69 A5
Montmoreau-St Cybard F 67 C5
Montmorency F 58 B3
Montmorillon F 67 B5
Montmort-Lucy F 59 B4
Montoir-de-Bretagne F 66 A2
Montoire-sur-le-Loir F 58 C1
Montoito P 92 C3
Montolieu F 77 C5

Montório al Vomano
I 103 A6
Montoro E 100 A1
Montpellier F 78 C2
Montpezat-de-Quercy
F 77 B4
Montpezat-sous-Bouzon
F 78 B3
Montpon-Ménestérol
F 76 A3
Montpont-en-Bresse
F 69 B5
Montréal
Aude F 77 C5
Gers F 76 C3
Montredon-Labessonnié
F 77 C5
Montréjeau F 77 C3
Montrésor F 67 A6
Montresta I 110 B1
Montret F 69 B5
Montreuil
Pas de Calais F 48 C2
Seine St Denis F 58 B3
Montreuil-aux-Lions
F 59 A4
Montreuil-Bellay F 67 A4
Montreux CH 70 B1
Montrevault F 66 A3
Montrevel-en-Bresse
F 69 B5
Montrichard F 67 A6
Montricoux F 77 B4
Mont-roig del Camp E 90 B3
Montrond-les-Bains F 69 C4
Montrose GB 25 B5
Montroy E 96 B2
Montsalvy F 77 B5
Montsauche-les-Settons
F 68 A4
Montseny E 91 B5
Montsoreau F 67 A5
Mont-sous-Vaudrey F 69 B5
Monts-sur-Guesnes F 67 B5
Mont-St Aignan F 58 A2
Mont-St Vincent F 69 B4
Montsûrs F 57 B5
Montuenga E 94 A2
Montuïri E 97 B3
Monturque E 100 B1
Monza I 71 C4
Monzón E 90 B3
Monzón de Campos
E 88 B2
Moorbad Lobenstein
D 52 C1
Moordorf D 43 B4
Moorslede B 49 C4
Moos D 61 C4
Moosburg D 62 B2
Moosburg im Kärnten
A 73 B4
Mór H 74 A3
Mora E 94 C3
Móra P 92 C2
Mora S 36 A1
Moraby S 36 B2
Móra d'Ebre E 90 B3
Mora de Rubielos E 96 A2
Moradillo de Roa E 88 C3
Morąg PL 47 B5
Mórahalom H 75 B4
Moraime E 86 A1
Morais P 87 C4
Mòra la Nova E 90 B3
Moral de Calatrava
E 100 A2
Moraleda de Zafayona
E 100 B2
Moraleja E 93 A4
Moraleja del Vino E 88 C1
Morales del Vino E 88 C1
Morales de Toro E 88 C1
Morales de Valverde
E 88 C1
Moralina E 87 C4
Morano Cálabro I 106 B3
Mörarp S 41 C2
Morasverdes E 93 A4
Morata de Jalón E 89 C5
Morata de Jiloca E 89 C5
Morata de Tajuña E 95 B3
Moratalla E 101 A4
Moravče SLO 73 B4
Moravec CZ 64 A2
Moravița RO 75 C6
Morávka CZ 65 A4
Moravská Třebová
CZ 64 A2
Moravské Budějovice
CZ 64 A1
Moravské Lieskové
SK 64 B3
Moravske Toplice
SLO 73 B6
Moravský-Beroun CZ 64 A3
Moravský Krumlov
CZ 64 A2
Moravský Svätý Ján
SK 64 B3
Morawica PL 55 C5
Morawin PL 54 B3
Morbach D 60 A3
Morbegno I 71 B4
Morbier F 69 B6
Mörbisch am See A 64 C2
Mörbylånga S 41 C6
Morcenx F 76 B2
Morciano di Romagna
I 82 C1
Morcone I 103 B7
Morcuera E 89 C3
Mordelles F 57 B4
Mordoğan TR 119 D1
Moréac F 56 C3
Morebattle GB 25 C5
Morecambe GB 26 A3
Moreda
Granada E 100 B2
Oviedo E 88 A1
Morée F 58 C2
Moreles de Rey E 88 B1
Morella E 90 C2
Moreruela de los
Infanzones E 88 C1
Morés E 89 C5
Móres I 110 B1
Morestel F 69 C5
Moretonhampstead
GB 28 C4
Moreton-in-Marsh GB 29 B6
Moret-sur-Loing F 58 B3
Moretta I 80 B1
Moreuil F 58 A3
Morez F 69 B6
Mörfelden D 51 D4
Morgat F 56 B1
Morges CH 69 B6
Morgex I 70 C2
Morgongåva S 36 C3
Morhange F 60 B2
Morhet B 49 D6
Mori I 71 C5
Morialmé B 49 C5
Morianes P 98 B3
Moriani Plage F 102 A2
Móricháida H 74 A2
Moriles E 100 B1
Morille E 94 B1
Moringen D 51 B5
Morjärv S 3 C25
Morkarla S 36 B4
Mørke DK 39 C3
Mørkøv DK 39 D4
Morkovice-Slížany
CZ 64 A3
Morlaàs F 76 C2
Morlaix F 56 B2
Morley F 59 B6
Mörlunda S 40 B5
Mormanno I 106 B2
Mormant F 59 B3
Mornant F 69 C4
Mornay-Berry F 68 A2
Morokovo MNE 85 D4
Morón de Almazán E 89 C4
Morón de la Frontera
E 99 B5
Morović SRB 85 A4
Morozzo I 80 B1
Morpeth GB 25 C6
Morphou CY 120 A1
Mörrum S 41 C4
Morsbach D 50 C3
Mörsch D 61 B4
Mörsil S 115 D10
Morsum D 39 E1
Mørsvikbotn N 112 E4
Mortagne-au-Perche
F 58 B1
Mortagne-sur-Gironde
F 66 C4
Mortagne-sur-Sèvre
F 66 B4
Mortágua P 92 A2
Mortain F 57 B5
Mortara I 70 C3
Morteau F 69 A6
Mortegliano I 72 C3
Mortelle I 109 A4
Mortemart F 67 B5
Mortimer's Cross GB 29 A5
Mortrée F 57 B6
Mörtschach A 72 B2
Mortsel B 49 B5
Morud DK 39 D3
Morwenstow GB 28 C3
Moryń PL 45 C6
Morzeszczyn PL 47 B4
Morzewo PL 47 B5
Morzine F 70 B1
Mosalsk RUS 7 D13
Mosbach D 61 A5
Mosbjerg DK 38 B3
Mosby N 33 D4
Mosca P 87 C4
Moscavide P 92 C1
Moščenica HR 73 C6
Moščenice HR 73 C4
Moščenicka Draga
HR 73 C4
Mosciano Sant'Ángelo
I 82 D2
Mościsko PL 54 C1
Moscow = Moskva
RUS 7 D14
Mosina PL 54 A1
Mosjøen N 115 B10
Moskog N 32 A3
Moskorzew PL 55 C4
Moskosel S 115 B16
Moskuvarra FIN 113 E15
Moskva = Moscow
RUS 7 D14
Moslavina Podravska
HR 74 C2
Moșnița Nouă RO 75 C6
Moso in Passiria I 71 B6
Mosonmagyaróvár H 64 C3
Mošorin SRB 75 C5
Mošovce SK 65 B4
Mosqueruela E 90 C2
Moss N 35 C2
Mossfellsbær IS 111 C4
Mössingen D 61 B5
Mosstrand N 32 C5
Most CZ 52 C3
Mosta M 107 C5
Mostar BIH 84 C2
Mosterhamn N 33 C2
Mostki PL 53 A5
Most na Soči SLO 72 B3
Móstoles E 94 B3
Mostová SK 64 B3
Mostowo PL 46 A2
Mostuéjouls F 78 B2
Mosty PL 45 B6
Mostys'ka UA 11 B7
Mosvik N 114 D7
Mota del Cuervo E 95 C4
Mota del Marqués E 88 C1
Motala S 37 D2
Motherwell GB 25 C4
Möthlow D 45 C4
Motilla del Palancar E 95 C5
Motnik SLO 73 B4
Motovun HR 72 C3
Motril E 100 C2
Motta I 71 C6
Motta di Livenza I 72 C2
Motta Montecorvino
I 103 B8
Motta Visconti I 70 C3
Mottisfont GB 31 C2
Móttola I 104 C3
Mou DK 38 C3
Mouchard F 69 B5
Moudon CH 70 B1
Moudros GR 116 C7
Mougins F 79 C5
Mouilleron en-Pareds
F 66 B4
Mouliherne F 67 A5
Moulinet F 80 C1
Moulins F 68 B3
Moulins-Engilbert F 68 B3
Moulins-la-Marche F 58 B1
Moulismes F 67 B5
Moult F 57 A5
Mountain Ash GB 29 B4
Mountbellew IRL 20 A3
Mountfield GB 19 B4
Mountmellick IRL 21 A4
Mountrath IRL 21 A4
Mountsorrel GB 30 B2
Moura P 98 A3
Mourão P 92 C3
Mourenx F 76 C2
Mouriés F 78 C3
Mourmelon-le-Grand
F 59 A5
Mouronho P 92 A2
Mouscron B 49 C4
Mousehole GB 28 C2
Moussac F 78 C3
Moussey F 60 B2
Mousteru F 56 B2
Moustey F 76 B2
Moustiers-Ste Marie
F 79 C5
Mouthe F 69 B6
Mouthier-Haute-Pierre
F 69 A6
Mouthoumet F 77 D5
Moutier CH 70 A2
Moûtiers F 69 C6
Moutiers-les-Mauxfaits
F 66 B3
Mouy F 58 A3
Mouzaki GR 116 C3
Mouzon F 59 A6
Møvik N 32 B2
Moville IRL 19 A4
Moy
Highland GB 23 D4
Tyrone GB 19 B5
Moycullen IRL 20 A2
Moyenmoutier F 60 B2
Moyenvic F 60 B2
Moylough IRL 18 C3
Mózar E 88 C1
Mozhaysk RUS 7 D14
Mozirje SLO 73 B4
Mözs H 74 B3
Mozzanica I 71 C4
Mramorak SRB 85 B5
Mrčajevci SRB 85 C5
Mrkonjić Grad BIH 84 B2
Mrkopalj HR 73 C4
Mrmoš SRB 85 C6
Mrocza PL 46 B3
Mroczeń PL 54 B2
Mroczno PL 47 B5
Mrozy PL 55 A6
Mrzezyno PL 45 A7
Mšec CZ 53 C3
Mšeno CZ 53 C4
Mstów PL 55 C4
Mstsislaw BY 7 D11
Mszana Dolna PL 65 A6
Mszczonów PL 55 B5
Mtsensk RUS 7 E14
Muć HR 83 C5
Múccia I 82 C2
Much D 50 C3
Mücheln D 52 B1
Much Marcle GB 29 B5
Muchów PL 53 B6
Much Wenlock GB 26 C3
Mucientes E 88 C2
Muckross IRL 20 B2
Mucur TR 16 B7
Muda P 98 B2
Mudanya TR 118 B3
Mudau D 61 A5
Müden D 44 C2
Mudersbach D 50 C3
Mudurnu TR 118 B6
Muel E 90 B1
Muelas del Pan E 88 C1
Muess D 44 B3
Muff IRL 19 A4
Mugardos E 86 A2
Muge P 92 B2
Mügeln
Sachsen D 52 B3
Sachsen-Anhalt D 52 B3
Múggia I 72 C3
Mugnano I 82 C1
Mugron F 76 C2
Mugueimes E 87 C3
Muhi H 65 C6
Mühlacker D 61 B4
Mühlbach am Hochkönig
A 72 A3
Mühlberg
Brandenburg D 52 B3
Thüringen D 51 C6
Mühldorf
A 72 B3
D 62 B3
Muhleberg CH 70 B2
Mühleim D 61 B4
Muhlen-Eichsen D 44 B3
Mühlhausen
Bayern D 62 A1
Thüringen D 51 B6
Mühltroff D 52 C1
Muhos FIN 3 D27
Muhr A 72 A3
Muine Bheag IRL 21 B5
Muirkirk GB 24 C3
Muir of Ord GB 23 D4
Muitos P 92 B1
Mukacheve UA 11 B7
Muker GB 26 A3
Mula E 101 A4
Muğla TR 119 E3
Mulben GB 23 D5
Mulegns CH 71 B4
Mules I 71 B6
Mülheim D 50 B2
Mulhouse F 60 C3
Muljava SLO 73 C4
Mullanys Cross IRL 18 B3
Müllheim D 60 C3
Mullhyttan S 37 C1
Mullinavat IRL 21 B4
Mullingar IRL 21 A4
Mullion GB 28 C2
Müllrose D 53 A4
Mullsjö S 40 B3
Mulseryd S 40 B3
Munaðarnes IS 111 A4
Munana E 94 B1
Muñás E 86 A4
Münchberg D 52 C1
Müncheberg D 45 C6
München = Munich D 62 B2
Munchen-Gladbach =
Mönchengladbach
D 50 B2
Münchhausen D 51 C4
Mundaka E 89 A4
Münden D 51 B5
Munderfing A 63 B4
Munderkingen D 61 B5
Mundesley GB 30 B5
Munera E 95 C4
Mungia E 89 A4
Munich = München D 62 B2
Muñico E 94 B1
Muniesa E 90 B2
Munka-Ljungby S 41 C2
Munkebo DK 39 D3
Munkedal S 35 D3
Munkflohögen S 115 D11
Munkfors S 34 C5
Munktorp S 37 C3
Münnerstadt D 51 C6
Muñopepe E 94 B2
Muñotello E 94 B1
Münsingen
CH 70 B2
D 61 B5
Munsö S 37 C4
Münster
CH 70 B3
Hessen D 61 A4
Munster D 44 C2
Münster D 50 B3
Munster F 60 B3
Muntibar E 89 A4
Münzkirchen A 63 B4
Muodoslompolo S 113 E12
Muonio FIN 113 E12
Muotathal CH 70 B3
Muradiye TR 118 D2
Murakeresztúr H 74 B1
Murán SK 65 B6
Murano I 72 C2
Muras E 86 A3
Murat F 78 A1
Muratlı TR 118 A2
Murato F 102 A2
Murat-sur-Vèbre F 78 C1
Murau A 73 A4
Muravera I 110 C2
Murazzano I 80 B2
Murça P 87 C3
Murchante E 89 B5
Murchin D 45 B5
Murcia E 101 B4
Murczyn PL 46 C3
Mur-de-Barrez F 77 B5
Mur-de-Bretagne F 56 B2
Mur-de-Sologne F 67 A6
Mureck A 73 B5
Mürefte TR 118 B2
Muret F 77 C4
Murg CH 71 A4
Murguia E 89 B4
Muri CH 70 A3
Murias de Paredes E 86 B4
Muriedas E 88 A3
Muriel Viejo E 89 C4
Murillo de Rio Leza E 89 B4
Murillo el Fruto E 89 B5
Murino MNE 85 D4
Muriqan AL 105 A5
Murlaggan GB 22 E3
Murmansk RUS 3 B30
Murmashi RUS 3 B30
Murnau D 62 C2
Muro
E 97 B3
F 102 A1
Muro de Alcoy E 96 C2
Murol F 68 C2
Muro Lucano I 103 C8
Muron F 66 B4
Muros E 86 B1
Muros de Nalón E 86 A4
Murowana Goślina
PL 46 C3
Mürren CH 70 B2
Murrhardt D 61 B5
Murska Sobota SLO 73 B6
Mursko Središce HR 73 B6
Murtas E 100 C2
Murten CH 70 B2
Murter HR 83 C4
Murtiçi TR 119 F6
Murtosa P 87 D2
Murvica HR 83 B4
Murviel-lès-Béziers F 78 C2
Mürzsteg A 63 C6
Murzynowo PL 46 C1
Mürzzuschlag A 63 C6
Musculdy F 76 C2
Mushqeta AL 105 B5
Muskö S 37 C5
Mušov CZ 64 B2
Musselburgh GB 25 C4
Musselkanaal NL 43 C4
Mussidan F 77 A3
Mussomeli I 108 B2
Musson B 60 A1
Mussy-sur-Seine F 59 C5
Mustafakemalpaşa
TR 118 B3
Muszaki PL 47 B6
Muszyna PL 65 A6
Mut TR 16 C6
Muta SLO 73 B5
Muthill GB 25 B4
Mutné SK 65 A5
Mutriku E 89 A4
Muttalip TR 118 C5
Mutterbergalm A 71 A6
Muxía E 86 A1
Muxilka-Ugarte E 89 A4
Muzillac F 66 A2
Mužla SK 65 C4
Muzzano del Turgnano
I 72 C3
Mybster GB 23 C5
Myckelgensjö S 115 D14
Myennes F 68 A2
Myjava SK 64 B3
Myking N 32 B2
Mykland N 33 D5
Mykolayiv = Nikolayev
UA 11 C12
Myra N 33 D6
Myrdal N 32 B4
Myre
Nordland N 112 C4
Nordland N 112 D4
Myresjö S 40 B4
Myrhorod UA 11 B12
Mýri IS 111 B8
Myrtou CY 120 A2
Mysen N 35 C3
Mysłakowice PL 53 C5
Myślenice PL 65 A5
Myślibórz PL 45 C6
Mysłowice PL 55 C4
Myszków PL 55 C4
Mytishchi RUS 7 D14
Mýtna SK 65 B5
Mýtne Ludany SK 65 B4
Mýto CZ 63 A4

N

Nå N 32 B3
Naaldwijk NL 49 B5
Naantali FIN 6 A6
Naas IRL 21 A5
Nabais P 92 A3
Nabbelund S 41 B7
Nabburg D 62 A3
Načeradec CZ 63 A5
Náchod CZ 53 C6
Nacław PL 46 A2
Nadarzyce PL 46 B2
Nadarzyn PL 55 A5
Nádasd H 74 B1
Nădlac RO 75 B5
Nádudvar H 75 A6
Nadvirna UA 11 B8
Näfels CH 70 A4
Nafpaktos GR 116 D3
Nafplio GR 117 E4
Nagel D 52 D1
Nagele NL 42 C2
Naggen S 115 E13
Nagłowice PL 55 C5
Nagold D 61 B4
Nagore E 76 D1
Nagyatád H 74 B2
Nagybajom H 74 B2
Nagybaracska H 74 B3
Nagybátony H 65 C5
Nagyberény H 74 B3
Nagybörzsöny H 65 C4
Nagycenk H 64 C2
Nagydorog H 74 B3
Nagyfüged H 65 C6
Nagyhersány H 74 C3
Nagyigmánd H 64 C4
Nagyiván H 75 A5
Nagykanizsa H 74 B1
Nagykáta H 75 A4
Nagykonyi H 74 B3
Nagykörös H 75 A4
Nagykörü H 75 A5
Nagylóc H 65 B5
Nagymágocs H 75 B5
Nagymányok H 74 B3
Nagymaros H 65 C4
Nagyoroszi H 65 B5
Nagyrábé H 75 A6
Nagyréde H 65 C5
Nagyszékely H 74 B3
Nagyszénás H 75 B5
Nagyszokoly H 74 B3
Nagytöke H 75 B5
Nagyvázsony H 74 B2
Nagyvenyim H 74 B3
Naharros E 95 B4
Nahe D 44 B2
Naidăș RO 85 B6
Naila D 52 C1
Nailloux F 77 C4
Nailsworth GB 29 B5
Naintré F 67 B5
Nairn GB 23 D5
Najac F 77 B4
Nájera E 89 B4
Nak H 74 B3
Nakksjø N 33 C6
Nakło nad Notecią
PL 46 B3
Nakskov DK 39 E4
Nalda E 89 B4
Nälden S 115 D11
Nálepkovo SK 65 B6
Nalliers F 66 B3
Nallıhan TR 118 B6
Nalzen F 77 D4
Nalžouské Hory CZ 63 A4
Namdalseid N 114 C8
Náměšť nad Oslavou
CZ 64 A2
Námestovo SK 65 A5
Namnå N 34 B4
Namsos N 114 C8
Namsskogan N 115 C10
Namur B 49 C5
Namysłów PL 54 B2
Nançay F 68 A2
Nanclares de la Oca
E 89 B4
Nancy F 60 B2
Nangis F 59 B4
Nannestad N 34 B3
Nant F 78 B2
Nanterre F 58 B3
Nantes F 66 A3
Nanteuil-le-Haudouin
F 58 A3
Nantiat F 67 B6
Nantua F 69 B5
Nantwich GB 26 B3
Naoussa
Cyclades GR 117 E7
Imathia GR 116 B4
Napajedla CZ 64 A3
Napiwoda PL 47 B6
Naples = Nápoli I 103 C7
Nápoli = Naples I 103 C7
Nar S 37 E5
Nara N 32 A1
Naraval E 86 A4
Narberth GB 28 B3
Nærbø N 33 D2
Narbonne F 78 C1
Narbonne-Plage F 78 C2
Narbuvollen N 114 E8
Narcao I 110 C1
Nardò I 107 A5
Narken S 113 F11
Narmo N 34 B3
Narni I 102 A5
Naro I 108 B2
Naro Fominsk RUS 7 D14
Narón E 86 A2
Narros del Castillo E 94 B1
Narta HR 74 C1
Naruszewo PL 47 C6
Narva EST 7 B10
Narvik N 112 D6
Narzole I 80 B1
Näs FIN 36 B7
Nås S 36 B1
Näs S 37 E5
Näsåker S 115 D13
Năsăud RO 11 C8
Nasavrky CZ 64 A1
Nasbinals F 78 B2
Næsbjerg DK 39 D1
Näshull S 40 B5
Našice HR 74 C3
Nasielsk PL 47 C6
Naso I 109 A3
Nassau D 50 C3
Nassenfels D 62 B2
Nassenheide D 45 C5
Nassereith A 71 A5
Nässjö S 40 B4
Nastätten D 50 C3
Næstved DK 39 D4
Näsum S 41 C4
Näsviken S 115 D12
Natalinci SRB 85 B5
Naters CH 70 B3
Nater-Stetten D 62 B2
Nattavaara S 112 F9
Natters A 71 A6
Nattheim D 61 B6
Nättraby S 41 C5
Naturno I 71 B5
Naucelle F 77 B5
Nauders A 71 B5
Nauen D 45 C4
Naul IRL 19 C5
Naumburg D 52 B1
Naundorf D 52 C3
Naunhof D 52 B2
Naustdal N 32 A2
Nautijaur S 112 F8
Nautsi RUS 113 D18
Nava E 88 A1
Navacerrada E 94 B2
Navaconcejo E 93 A5
Nava de Arévalo E 94 B2
Nava de la Asunción
E 94 A2
Nava del Rey E 88 C1
Navafriá E 94 A3
Navahermosa E 94 C2
Navahrudak BY 7 E8
Naval E 90 A3
Navalacruz E 94 B2
Navalcán E 94 B1
Navalcarnero E 94 B2
Navaleno E 89 C3
Navalmanzano E 94 A2
Navalmoral E 94 B2
Navalmoral de la Mata
E 93 B5
Naválón E 96 C2
Navalonguilla E 93 A5
Navalperal de Pinares
E 94 B2
Navalpino E 94 C2
Navaltalgordo E 94 B2
Navaltoril E 94 C2
Navaluenga E 94 B2
Navalvillar de Pela E 93 B5
Navan IRL 19 C5
Navaperal de Tormes
E 93 A5
Navapolatsk BY 7 D10
Navarclés E 91 B4
Navarredonda de Gredos
E 93 A5
Navarrenx F 76 C2
Navarrés E 96 B2
Navarrete E 89 B4
Navarrevisca E 94 B2
Navás E 91 B4
Navascués E 76 D1
Navas del Madroño E 93 B4
Navas del Rey E 94 B2
Navas del Sepillar E 100 B1
Navas de Oro E 94 A2
Navas de San Juan
E 100 A2
Navasfrias E 93 A4
Nave I 71 C5
Nave de Haver P 93 A4
Nävekvarn S 37 D3
Navelli I 103 A6
Navenby GB 27 B5
Näverkärret S 37 C2
Naverstad S 35 D3
Navés E 91 B4
Navezuelas E 93 B5
Navia E 86 A4
Navia de Suarna E 86 B4
Navilly F 69 B5
Navlya RUS 7 E13
Năvodari RO 11 D10
Naxos GR 117 E7
Nay F 76 C2
Nazaré P 92 B1
Nazarje SLO 73 B4
Nazilli TR 119 E3
Nazza D 51 B6
Ndroq AL 105 B5
Nea Anchialos GR 116 C4
Nea Epidavros GR 117 E5
Nea Flippias GR 116 C2
Nea Kalikratia GR 116 B5
Nea Makri GR 117 D5
Nea Moudania GR 116 B5
Neap GB 22 A7
Nea Peramos GR 116 B6
Neapoli
Kozani GR 116 B3
Kriti GR 117 G7
Lakonia GR 117 F5
Nea Stira GR 117 D6
Neath GB 28 B4
Nea Visa GR 118 A1
Nea Zichni GR 116 A5
Nebljusi HR 83 B4
Neblo SLO 72 B3
Nebolchy RUS 7 B12
Nebra D 52 B1
Nebreda E 88 C3
Nechanice CZ 53 C5
Neckargemünd D 61 A4
Neckarsulm D 61 A5
Neda E 86 A2
Neded SK 64 B3
Nedelišće HR 73 B6
Nederweert NL 50 B1
Nedreberg N 34 B3
Nedre Gärdsjö S 36 B2
Nedre Soppero S 113 D10
Nedstrand N 33 C2
Nedvědice CZ 64 A2
Nędza PL 54 C3
Neede NL 50 A2
Needham Market GB 30 B5
Needingworth GB 30 B3
Neermoor D 43 B4
Neeroeteren B 50 B1
Neerpelt B 49 B6
Neesen D 51 A4
Neetze D 44 B2
Nefyn GB 26 C1
Negbina SRB 85 C4
Negotin SRB 11 D7
Negotino MK 116 A4
Negrar I 71 C5
Negredo E 95 A4
Negreira E 86 B2
Nègrepelisse F 77 B4
Negru Vodă RO 11 E10
Negueira de Muñiz E 86 A4
Neheim D 50 B3
Neila E 89 B4
Néive I 80 B2
Nejdek CZ 52 C2
Nekla PL 46 C3
Neksø DK 41 D5
Nelas P 92 A3
Nelaug N 33 D5
Nelidovo RUS 7 C12
Nelim FIN 113 D17
Nellingen D 61 B5
Nelson GB 26 B3
Neman RUS 6 D7
Nemea GR 117 E4
Nemesgörzsöny H 74 A2
Nemeskér H 74 A1
Nemesnádudvar H 75 B4
Nemesszalók H 74 A2
Németkér H 74 B3
Nemours F 58 B3
Nemška Loka SLO 73 C5
Nemšová SK 64 B4
Nenagh IRL 20 B3
Nenince SK 65 B5
Nenita GR 117 D8
Nenzing A 71 A4
Neochori GR 116 C3
Neo Chori GR 116 D3
Neon Petritsi GR 116 A5
Nepi I 102 A5
Nepomuk CZ 63 A4
Nérac F 77 B3
Neratovice CZ 53 C4
Nerchau D 52 B2
Néré F 67 C4
Neresheim D 61 B6
Nereto I 82 D2
Nerezine HR 82 B3
Nerežišća HR 83 C5
Neringa LT 6 D6
Néris-les Bains F 68 B2
Nerito I 103 A6
Nerja E 100 C2
Néronde F 69 C4
Nérondes F 68 B2
Nerpio E 101 A3
Nersingen D 61 B6
Nerva E 99 B4
Nervesa della Battáglia
I 72 C2
Nervi I 80 B3
Nes
N 114 D6
Buskerud N 34 B1
Hedmark N 34 B2
NL 42 B2
Nesbyen N 32 B6
Neset N 114 F7
Nesflaten N 33 C3
Nesjahverfi IS 111 C10
Neskaupstaður IS 111 B12
Nesland N 33 C4
Neslandsvatn N 33 D6
Nesle F 59 A3
Nesna N 115 A10
Nesoddtangen N 34 C2
Nesovice CZ 64 A3
Nesselwang D 61 C6
Nesslau CH 71 A4
Nessmersiel D 43 B4
Nesso I 71 C4
Nesterov UA 11 A7
Nestorio GR 116 B3
Nesttun N 32 B2
Nesvady SK 64 C4
Nesvatnstemmen N 33 D5
Nether Stowey GB 29 B4
Netland N 33 D3
Netolice CZ 63 A5
Netphen D 50 C4
Netstal CH 70 A4
Nettancourt F 59 B5
Nettetal D 50 B2
Nettlingen D 51 A6
Nettuno I 102 B5
Neualbenreuth D 52 D2
Neubeckum D 50 B4
Neubrandenburg D 45 B5
Neubruchhausen D 43 C5
Neubukow D 44 A3
Neuburg D 62 B2
Neuchâtel CH 70 B1
Neu Darchau D 44 B2
Neudau A 73 A6
Neudietendorf D 51 C6
Neudorf D 61 A4
Neuenbürg D 61 B4
Neuenburg D 43 B4
Neuendorf D 45 A5
Neuenhagen D 45 C5
Neuenhaus D 42 C3
Neuenkirchen
Niedersachsen D 43 B6
Niedersachsen D 43 C5
Nordrhein-Westfalen
D 50 A3
Nordrhein-Westfalen
D 50 C3
Neuenrade D 50 B3
Neuenwalde D 43 B5
Neuerburg D 50 C2
Neufahrn
Bayern D 62 B2
Bayern D 62 B3
Neuf-Brisach F 60 B3
Neufchâteau
B 60 A1
F 60 B1
Neufchâtel-en-Bray F 58 A2
Neufchâtel-sur-Aisne
F 59 A5
Neuflize F 59 A5
Neugersdorf D 53 C4
Neuhardenberg D 45 C6
Neuharlingersiel D 43 B4
Neuhaus
Bayern D 62 A2
Bayern D 63 B4
Niedersachsen D 43 B6
Niedersachsen D 44 B2
Niedersachsen D 51 B5
Neuhaus a Rennweg
D 52 C1
Neuhausen
CH 61 C4
D 52 C3
Neuhausen ob Eck D 61 C4
Neuhof
Bayern D 62 A1
Hessen D 51 C5
Neuhofen an der Krems
A 63 B5
Neuillé-Pont-Pierre F 67 A5
Neuilly-en-Thelle F 58 A3
Neuilly-le-Réal F 68 B3
Neuilly-l'Évêque F 60 C1
Neuilly-St Front F 59 A4
Neu-Isenburg D 51 C4
Neukalen D 45 B4
Neu Kaliss D 44 B3
Neukirch D 53 B4
Neukirchen
A 62 B4
Hessen D 51 C5
Schleswig-Holstein D 39 E1
Neukirchen am
Grossvenediger A 72 A2
Neukirchen bei Heiligen
Blut D 62 A3
Neukloster D 44 B3
Neulengbach A 64 B1
Neulise F 68 C4
Neu Lübbenau D 53 A3
Neum BIH 84 D2
Neumagen D 60 A2
Neumarkt D 62 A2
Neumarkt am Wallersee
A 63 C4
Neumarkt im
Hausruckkreis A 63 B4
Neumarkt im Mühlkreis
A 63 B5
Neumarkt im Steiermark
A 73 A4
Neumarkt Sankt Veit
D 62 B3
Neumünster D 44 A1
Neunburg vorm Wald
D 62 A3
Neung-sur-Beuvron F 68 A1
Neunkirch
Luzern CH 70 A3
Schaffhausen CH 61 C4
Neunkirchen
A 64 C2
Nordrhein-Westfalen
D 50 C3
Saarland D 60 A3
Neunkirchen am Brand
D 62 A2
Neuötting D 62 B3
Neupetershain D 53 B4
Neuravensburg D 61 C5
Neureut D 61 A4
Neuruppin D 45 C4
Neusäss D 62 B1
Neusiedl A 64 C2
Neuss D 50 B2
Neussargues-Moissac
F 68 C2
Neustadt
Bayern D 62 A1
Bayern D 62 A3
Bayern D 62 B2
Brandenburg D 44 C4
Hessen D 51 C5
Niedersachsen D 43 C6
Rheinland-Pfalz D 61 A4
Sachsen D 53 B4
Schleswig-Holstein D 44 A2
Thüringen D 52 C1
Thüringen D 52 C1
Neustadt-Glewe D 44 B3
Neustift im Stubaital
A 71 A6
Neustrelitz D 45 B5
Neutal A 73 A6
Neutrebbin D 45 C6
Neu-Ulm D 61 B6
Neuves-Maisons F 60 B2
Neuvic
Corrèze F 68 C2
Dordogne F 77 A3
Neuville-aux-Bois F 58 B3
Neuville-de-Poitou F 67 B5
Neuville-les-Dames F 69 B5
Neuville-sur-Saône F 69 C4
Neuvy-le-Roi F 58 C1
Neuvy-Santour F 59 B4
Neuvy-St Sépulchre
F 68 B1
Neuvy-sur-Barangeon
F 68 A2
Neuwied D 50 C3
Neuzelle D 53 A4
Névache F 79 A5
Neveklov CZ 63 A5
Nevel RUS 7 D10
Neverfjord N 113 B12
Nevers F 68 B3
Nevesinje BIH 84 C3
Névez F 56 C2
Nevlunghavn N 35 D1
Nevşehir TR 16 B7
New Abbey GB 25 D4
New Aberdour GB 23 D6
New Alresford GB 31 C2
Newark-on-Trent GB 27 B5
Newbiggin-by-the-Sea
GB 25 C6
Newbliss IRL 19 B4
Newborough GB 26 B1
Newbridge IRL 21 A5
Newbridge on Wye
GB 29 A4
Newburgh
Aberdeenshire GB 23 D6
Fife GB 25 B4
Newbury GB 31 C2
Newby Bridge GB 26 A3
Newcastle GB 19 B6
Newcastle Emlyn GB 28 A3
Newcastleton GB 25 C5
Newcastle-under-Lyme
GB 26 B3
Newcastle upon Tyne
GB 25 D6
Newcastle West IRL 20 B2
Newchurch GB 29 A4
New Costessey GB 30 B5
New Cumnock GB 24 C3
Newent GB 29 B5
New Galloway GB 24 C3
Newham GB 31 C4
Newhaven GB 31 D4
Newington GB 31 C5
Newinn IRL 21 B4
Newlyn GB 28 C2
Newmachar GB 23 D6
Newmarket
Suffolk GB 30 B4
Western Isles GB 22 C2
IRL 20 B3
Newmarket-on-Fergus
IRL 20 B3
New Mills GB 27 B4
New Milton GB 31 D2
New Pitsligo GB 23 D6
Newport
Isle of Wight GB 31 D2
Newport GB 29 B5
Pembrokeshire GB 28 A3
Telford & Wrekin GB 26 C3
Mayo IRL 18 C2
Tipperary IRL 20 B3
Newport-on-Tay GB 25 B5
Newport Pagnell GB 30 B3
Newquay GB 28 C2
New Quay GB 28 A3
New Radnor GB 29 A4
New Romney GB 31 D4
New Ross IRL 21 B5
Newry GB 19 B5
New Scone GB 25 B4
Newton Abbot GB 29 C4
Newton Arlosh GB 25 D4
Newton Aycliffe GB 27 A4
Newton Ferrers GB 28 C3
Newtonhill GB 23 D6
Newtonmore GB 23 D4
Newton Stewart GB 24 D3
Newtown
Herefordshire GB 29 A5
Powys GB 26 C2
Newtownabbey GB 19 B6
Newtownards GB 19 B6
Newtownbutler GB 19 B4
Newtown Cunningham
IRL 19 B4
Newtownhamilton GB 19 B5
Newtownmountkennedy
IRL 21 A5
Newtown St Boswells
GB 25 C5
Newtown Sands IRL 20 B2
Newtownshandrum
IRL 20 B3
Newtownstewart GB 19 B4
Nexon F 67 C6
Neyland GB 28 B3
Nibbiano I 80 B3
Nibe DK 38 C2
Nicaj-Shalë AL 105 A5
Nicastro I 106 C3
Niccone I 82 C1
Nice F 80 C1
Nickelsdorf A 64 C3
Nicolosi I 109 B4
Nicosia
CY 120 A2
I 109 B3
Nicótera I 106 C2
Nidda D 51 C5
Niğde TR 16 C7
Nidzica PL 47 B6
Niebla E 99 B4
Nieborów PL 55 A5
Niebüll D 39 E1
Niechanowo PL 46 C3
Niechorze PL 45 A7
Niedalino PL 46 A2
Niederaula D 51 C5
Niederbipp CH 70 A2
Niederbronn-les-Bains
F 60 B3
Niederfischbach D 50 C3
Niedergörsdorf D 52 B2
Niederkrüchten D 50 B2
Niederndorf A 62 C3
Nieder-Olm D 61 A4
Niedersachswerfen D 51 B6
Niederstetten D 61 A5
Niederurnen CH 70 A4
Niederwölz A 73 A4
Niedoradz PL 53 B5
Niedzica PL 65 A6
Niegosławice PL 53 B5
Nieheim D 51 B5
Niemcza PL 54 C1
Niemegk D 52 A2
Niemodlin PL 54 C2
Nienburg
Niedersachsen D 43 C6
Sachsen-Anhalt D 52 B1
Niepołomice PL 55 C5
Nierstein D 61 A4
Niesky D 53 B4
Niestronno PL 46 C3
Nieświń PL 55 B5
Nieszawa PL 47 C4
Nieul-le-Dolent F 66 B3
Nieul-sur-Mer F 66 B3
Nieuw-Amsterdam
NL 42 C3
Nieuw-Buinen NL 42 C3
Nieuwegein NL 49 A6
Nieuwe Niedorp NL 42 C1
Nieuwe-Pekela NL 42 B3
Nieuwerkerken B 49 C6
Nieuwe-schans NL 43 B4
Nieuwolda NL 42 B3
Nieuwpoort B 48 B3
Nieuw-Weerdinge NL 42 C3
Nigrita GR 116 B5
Nigüelas E 100 C2
Níjar E 101 C3
Nijemci HR 75 C4
Nijkerk NL 49 A6
Nijlen B 49 B5
Nijmegen NL 50 B1
Nijverdal NL 42 C3
Nikel RUS 113 C19
Nikinci SRB 85 B4
Nikiti GR 116 B5
Nikitsch A 74 A1
Nikkaluokta S 112 E8
Nikla H 74 B2
Niklasdorf A 73 A5
Nikolayev = Mykolayiv
UA 11 C12
Nikšić MNE 84 D3
Nilivaara S 113 E10
Nîmes F 78 C3
Nimis I 72 B3
Nimtofte DK 39 C3
Nin HR 83 B4
Nindorf D 43 A6
Ninemilehouse IRL 21 B4
Ninove B 49 C5
Niort F 67 B4
Niš SRB 10 E6
Nisa P 92 B3
Niscemi I 109 B3
Nissafors S 40 B3
Nissan-lez-Ensérune
F 78 C2
Nissedal N 33 C5
Nissumby DK 38 C1
Nisterud N 33 C6
Niton GB 31 D2
Nitra SK 64 B4
Nitrianske-Pravno SK 65 B4
Nitrianske Rudno SK 65 B4
Nitry F 59 C4
Nittedal N 34 B2
Nittenau D 62 A3
Nittendorf D 62 A2
Nivala FIN 3 E26
Nivelles B 49 C5
Nivenskoye RUS 47 A6
Nivnice CZ 64 B3
Nizhyn UA 11 A11
Nižná SK 65 A5
Nižná Boca SK 65 B5
Nižne Repaše SK 65 A6
Nizza Monferrato I 80 B2
Njarðvík IS 111 D3
Njegůsevo SRB 75 C4
Njivice HR 73 C4
Njurundabommen
S 115 E14
Njutånger S 115 F14
Noailles F 58 A3
Noain E 76 D1
Noale I 72 C2
Noalejo E 100 B2
Noblejas E 95 C3
Noceda E 86 B4
Nocera Inferiore I 103 C7
Nocera Terinese I 106 B3
Nocera Umbra I 82 C1
Noceto I 81 B4
Noci I 104 C3
Nociglia I 107 A5
Nodeland N 33 D4
Nödinge S 38 B5
Nods F 69 A6
Noé F 77 C4
Noépoli I 106 A3
Noeux-les-Mines F 48 C3
Noez E 94 C2
Nogales E 93 C4
Nogara I 71 C6
Nogarejas E 87 B4
Nogaro F 76 C2
Nogent F 59 B6
Nogent l'Artaud F 59 B4
Nogent-le-Roi F 58 B2
Nogent-le-Rotrou F 58 B1
Nogent-sur-Seine F 59 B4
Nogent-sur-Vernisson
F 58 C3
Nogersund S 41 C4
Noguera E 95 B5
Noguerones E 100 B1
Nohfelden D 60 A3
Nohn D 50 C2
Noia E 86 B2
Noicáttaro I 104 B2
Noirétable F 68 C3
Noirmoutier-en-l'Île F 66 A2
Noja E 89 A3
Nojewo PL 46 C2
Nokia FIN 3 F25
Nol S 38 B5
Nola I 103 C7

Pajares E 88 A1
Pajares de los Oteros
E 88 B1
Pajęczno PL 54 B3
Páka H 74 B1
Pakość PL 47 C4
Pakosławice PL 54 C2
Pakoštane HR 83 C4
Pakrac HR 74 C2
Paks H 74 B3
Palacios de la Sierra
E 89 C3
Palaciòs de la Valduerna
E 88 B1
Palacios del Sil E 86 B4
Palacios de Sanabria
E 87 B4
Palaciosrubios E 94 A1
Palafrugell E 91 B6
Palagiano I 104 C3
Palagonia I 109 B3
Paláia I 81 C4
Palaiseau F 58 B3
Palaj AL 105 A5
Palamas GR 116 C4
Palamós E 91 B6
Palanga LT 6 D6
Palanzano I 81 B4
Palárikovo SK 64 B4
Palas de Rei E 86 B3
Palata I 103 B7
Palatna KOS 85 C6
Palau I 110 A2
Palavas-les-Flots F 78 C2
Palazuelos de la Sierra
E 89 B3
Palazzo Adriano I 108 B2
Palazzo del Pero I 81 C5
Palazzolo Acrèide I 109 B3
Palazzolo sull Oglio I 71 C4
Palazzo San Gervàsio
I 104 C1
Palazzuolo sul Senio
I 81 B5
Paldiski EST 6 B8
Pale BIH 84 C3
Palekastro GR 117 G8
Palena I 103 B7
Palencia E 88 B2
Palenciana E 100 B1
Paleochora GR 117 G5
Paleometokho CY 120 A2
Palermo I 108 A2
Paleros GR 116 D2
Palestrina I 102 B5
Pálfa H 74 B3
Palfau A 63 C5
Palhaça P 92 A2
Palheiros da Tocha P 92 A2
Palheiros de Quiaios
P 92 A2
Paliaopoli GR 117 E6
Palić SRB 75 B4
Palidoro I 102 B5
Palinuro I 106 A2
Paliouri GR 116 C5
Paliseul B 59 A6
Pallanza I 70 C3
Pallares E 99 A4
Pallaruelo de Monegros
E 90 B2
Pallas Green IRL 20 B3
Pallerols E 91 A4
Palling D 62 B3
Palluau F 66 B3
Palma P 92 C2
Palma Campània I 103 C7
Palma del Río E 99 B5
Palma de Mallorca E 97 B2
Palma di Montechiaro
I 108 B2
Palmádula I 110 B1
Palmanova I 72 C3
Palma Nova E 97 B2
Palmela P 92 C2
Palmerola E 91 A5
Palmi I 106 C2
Pälmonostora H 75 B4
Palo del Colle I 104 B2
Palojärvi FIN 113 D12
Palojoensuu FIN 113 D12
Palomares E 101 B4
Palomares del Campo
E 95 C4
Palomas E 93 C4
Palombara Sabina I 102 A5
Palos de la Frontera
E 99 B4
Palotabozsok H 74 B3
Palotás H 65 C5
Pals E 91 B6
Pålsboda S 37 C2
Paluzza I 72 B3
Pamhagen A 64 C2
Pamiers F 77 C4
Pamietowo PL 46 B3
Pampaneira E 100 C2
Pamparato I 80 B1
Pampilhosa
Aveiro P 92 A2
Coimbra P 92 A3
Pampliega E 88 B3
Pamplona E 76 D1
Pampow D 44 B3
Pamukçu TR 118 C2
Pamukkale TR 119 E4
Pamukova TR 118 B5
Panagyurishte BG 11 E8
Pancalieri I 80 B1
Pančevo SRB 85 B5
Pancey F 59 B6
Pancorvo E 89 B3
Pancrudo E 90 C1
Pandino I 71 C4
Pandrup DK 38 B2
Panenský-Týnec CZ 53 C3
Panes E 88 A2
Panevėžys LT 6 D8
Pangbourne GB 31 C2
Panissières F 69 C4
Panki PL 54 C3
Pannes F 58 B3
Panningen NL 50 B1
Pannonhalma H 74 A2
Pano Lefkara CY 120 B2
Pano Panayia CY 120 B1
Panormos GR 117 E7
Panschwitz-Kuckau
D 53 B4
Pansdorf D 44 B2
Pantano de Cijara E 94 C2
Panteleria I 108 C1
Panticosa E 76 D2
Pantín E 86 A2
Pantoja E 94 B3
Pantón E 86 B3
Panxon E 87 B2
Páola I 106 B3
Paola M 107 C5
Pápa H 74 A2
Papasidero I 106 B2
Pápateszér H 74 A2
Papenburg D 43 B4
Paphos CY 120 B1
Pappenheim D 62 B1
Paprotnia PL 55 A5
Parábita I 107 A5
Paraćin SRB 85 C6
Parád H 65 C6
Parada
Bragança P 87 C4
Viseu P 92 A2
Paradas E 99 B5
Paradela E 86 B3
Parades de Rubiales
E 94 A1
Paradinas de San Juan
E 94 B1
Paradiso di Cevadale
I 71 B5
Paradyż PL 55 B5
Parainen FIN 6 A7
Parakhino Paddubye
RUS 7 B12
Parakka S 113 E10
Paralimni CY 120 A2
Parallo Astros GR 117 E4
Paramé F 57 B4
Paramithia GR 116 C2
Páramo E 86 A4
Páramo del Sil E 86 B4
Parandaça P 87 C3
Paravadella E 86 A3
Paray-le-Monial F 68 B4
Parceiros P 92 B2
Parcey F 69 A5
Parchim D 44 B3
Parciaki PL 47 B6
Parcice PL 54 B3
Pardilla E 88 C3
Pardubice CZ 53 C5
Paredes
E 95 B4
P 87 C2
Paredes de Coura P 87 C2
Paredes de Nava E 88 B2
Paredes de Siguenza
E 95 A4
Pareja E 95 B4
Parennes F 57 B5
Parenti I 106 B3
Parentis-en-Born F 76 B1
Parey D 44 C3
Parfino RUS 7 C11
Parga GR 116 C2
Pargny-sur-Saulx F 59 B5
Pari-Gagné F 69 B4
Parigné-l'Évêque F 58 C1
Parikkala FIN 3 F28
Paris F 58 B3
Parisot F 77 B4
Parkalompolo S 113 E11
Parkano FIN 3 E25
Parknasilla IRL 20 C2
Parla E 94 B3
Parlavà E 91 A6
Parma I 81 B4
Parndorf A 64 C2
Párnica SK 65 A5
Parnu EST 6 B8
Parolis E 101 A3
Paros GR 117 E7
Parrillas E 94 B1
Parsberg D 62 A2
Parstein D 45 C6
Partakko FIN 113 C16
Partanna I 108 B1
Parthenay F 67 B4
Partinico I 108 A2
Partizani SRB 85 B5
Partizánske SK 65 B4
Partney GB 27 B6
Påryd S 40 C5
Parysów PL 55 B6
Parzymiechy PL 54 B3
Paşcani RO 11 C9
Pasewalk D 45 B5
Pašina Voda MNE 85 C4
Påskallavik S 40 B6
Pasłęk PL 47 A5
Pašman HR 83 C4
Passage East IRL 21 B5
Passage West IRL 20 C3
Passail A 73 A5
Passais F 57 B5
Passau D 63 B4
Passegueiro P 92 A2
Passignano sul
Trasimeno I 82 C1
Passo di Tréia I 82 C2
Passopisciaro I 109 B4
Passow D 45 B6
Passy F 70 C1
Pastavy BY 7 D9
Pástena I 103 B7
Pastrana E 95 B4
Pastrengo I 71 C5
Pasym PL 47 B6
Pásztó H 65 C5
Pata SK 64 B3
Patay F 58 B2
Pateley Bridge GB 27 A4
Paterek PL 46 B3
Paterna E 96 B2
Paterna del Campo E 99 B4
Paterna del Madera
E 101 A3
Paterna de Rivera E 99 C5
Paternion A 72 B3
Paternò I 109 B3
Paternópoli I 103 C8
Patersdorf D 62 A3
Paterswolde NL 42 B3
Patitiri GR 116 C5
Patmos GR 119 E1
Patna GB 24 C3
Patnow PL 54 A3
Patoniva FIN 113 C16
Patopirtti FIN 113 E18
Patos AL 105 C5
Patra = Patras GR 117 D3
Patras = Patra GR 117 D3
Patreksfjörður IS 111 B2
Patrickswell IRL 20 B3
Patrimonio F 102 A2
Patrington GB 27 B5
Pattada I 110 B2
Pattensen
Niedersachsen D 44 B2
Niedersachsen D 51 A5
Patterdale GB 26 A3
Patti I 109 A3
Páty H 74 A3
Pau F 76 C2
Pauillac F 66 C4
Paularo I 72 B3
Paulhaguet F 68 C3
Paulhan F 78 C2
Paulilátino I 110 B1
Paullström S 40 B5
Paullo I 71 C4
Paulstown IRL 21 B4
Pausa D 52 C1
Pauträsk S 115 C14
Pavia
I 71 C4
P 92 C2
Pavias E 96 B2
Pavilly F 58 A1
Pāvilosta LV 6 C6
Pavino Polje MNE 85 C4
Pavullo nel Frignano
I 81 B4
Pawłowice PL 54 B2
Pawlowice PL 54 D3
Paxi GR 116 C2
Payallar TR 119 F6
Payerne CH 70 B1
Paymogo E 98 B3
Payrac F 77 B4
Pazardzhik BG 11 E8
Pazaryeri TR 118 B4
Pazin HR 72 C3
Paziols F 78 D1
Pčelić HR 74 C2
Peal de Becerro E 100 B2
Peasmarsh GB 31 D4
Peć KOS 85 D5
Péccioli I 81 C4
Pécel H 75 A4
Pechao P 98 B3
Pechenga RUS 3 B29
Pechenizhyn UA 11 B8
Pecica RO 75 B6
Pećinci SRB 85 B4
Pecka SRB 85 B4
Peckelsheim D 51 B5
Pečory RUS 7 C9
Pécs H 74 B3
Pécsvárad H 74 B3
Pečurice MNE 105 A5
Peczniew PL 54 B3
Pedaso I 82 C2
Pedavena I 72 B1
Pedérobba I 72 C1
Pedersker DK 41 D4
Pedescala I 71 C6
Pedrafita E 86 B3
Pedrajas de San Esteban
E 88 C2
Pedralba E 96 B2
Pedralba de la Praderia
E 87 B4
Pedraza E 94 A3
Pedreguer E 96 C3
Pedrera E 100 B1
Pedro Abad E 100 B1
Pedro Bernardo E 94 B2
Pedroche E 100 A1
Pedrógão P 98 A3
Pedrogao P 92 A3
Pedrógão P 92 B2
Pedrógão Grande P 92 B2
Pedrola E 90 B1
Pedro-Martinez E 100 B2
Pedro Muñoz E 95 C4
Pedrosa del Rey E 88 C1
Pedrosa del Rio Urbel
E 88 B3
Pedrosa de Tobalina
E 89 B3
Pedrosillo de los Aires
E 94 B1
Pedrosillo el Ralo E 94 A1
Pędzewo PL 47 B4
Peebles GB 25 C4
Peel GB 26 A1
Peenemünde D 45 A5
Peer B 49 B6
Pega P 93 A3
Pegalajar E 100 B2
Pegau D 52 B2
Peggau A 73 A5
Pegli I 80 B2
Pegnitz D 62 A2
Pego E 96 C2
Pegões-Estação P 92 C2
Pegões Velhos P 92 C2
Pęgów PL 54 B1
Pegswood GB 25 C6
Peguera E 97 B2
Pehlivanköy TR 118 A1
Peine D 51 A6
Peisey-Nancroix F 70 C1
Peissenberg D 62 C2
Peiting D 62 C1
Peitz D 53 B4
Péjo I 71 B5
Pelagićevo BIH 84 B3
Pelahustán E 94 B2
Pełczyce PL 46 B1
Pelhřimov CZ 63 A6
Pélissanne F 79 C4
Pelkosenniemi FIN 113 E16
Pellegrino Parmense
I 81 B3
Pellegrue F 76 B3
Pellérd H 74 B3
Pellestrina I 72 C2
Pellevoisin F 67 B6
Pellizzano I 71 B5
Pello
FIN 113 F13
S 113 F12
Peloche E 93 B5
Pelplin PL 47 B4
Pelussin F 69 C4
Pély H 75 A5
Pembroke GB 28 B3
Pembroke Dock GB 28 B3
Peñacerrada E 89 B4
Penacova P 92 A2
Peña de Cabra E 94 B1
Peñafiel E 88 C2
Penafiel P 87 C2
Peñaflor E 99 B5
Peñalba de Santiago
E 86 B4
Peñalsordo E 93 C5
Penalva do Castelo P 92 A3
Penamacôr P 93 A3
Peñaparda E 93 A4
Peñaranda de
Bracamonte E 94 B1
Peñaranda de Duero
E 89 C3
Peñarroya de Tastavins
E 90 C3
Peñarroya-Pueblonuevo
E 93 C5
Peñarrubla E 86 B3
Penarth GB 29 B4
Peñascosa E 101 A3
Peñas de San Pedro
E 101 A4
Peñausende E 88 C1
Penc H 65 C5
Pencoed GB 29 B4
Pendalofos GR 116 B3
Pendeen GB 28 C2
Pendine GB 28 B3
Pendueles E 88 A2
Penedono P 87 D3
Penela P 92 A2
Pénestin F 56 C3
Penhas Juntas P 87 C3
Peniche P 92 B1
Penicuik GB 25 C4
Penig D 52 C2
Penilhos P 98 B3
Peñíscola E 90 C3
Penistone GB 27 B4
Penkridge GB 26 C3
Penkun D 45 B6
Penmarch F 56 C1
Pennabilli I 82 C1
Penne I 103 A6
Penne-d'Agenais F 77 B3
Pennes I 71 B6
Pennyghael GB 24 B1
Peno RUS 7 C12
Penpont GB 25 C4
Penrhyndeudraeth
GB 26 C1
Penrith GB 26 A3
Penryn GB 28 C2
Pentraeth GB 26 B1
Penybontfawr GB 26 C2
Penygroes
Carmarthenshire
GB 28 B3
Gwynedd GB 26 B1
Penzance GB 28 C2
Penzberg D 62 C2
Penzlin D 45 B5
Pepeljevac SRB 85 C6
Pepinster B 50 C1
Peqin AL 105 B5
Pér H 64 C3
Pera Boa P 92 A3
Perachora GR 117 D4
Perafita P 87 C2
Peraleda de la Mata E 93 B5
Peraleda del Zaucejo
E 93 C5
Peraleda de San Román
E 93 B5
Perales de Alfambra
E 90 C1
Perales del Puerto E 93 A4
Perales de Tajuña E 95 B3
Peralta E 89 B5
Peralta de la Sal E 90 B3
Peralva P 98 B3
Peralveche E 95 B4
Perama GR 117 G6
Perast MNE 105 A4
Perbál H 65 C4
Perchtoldsdorf A 64 B2
Percy F 57 B4
Perdasdefogu I 110 C2
Perdiguera E 90 B2
Peredo P 87 C4
Peregu Mare RO 75 B5
Pereiro
Faro P 98 B3
Guarda P 87 D3
Pereiro *continued*
Santarém P 92 B2
Pereiro de Aguiar E 87 B3
Perelada E 91 A6
Perelejos de las Truchas
E 95 B5
Pereña E 87 C4
Pereruela E 88 C1
Pereyaslav-Khmelnytskyy
UA 11 A11
Pérfugas I 110 B1
Perg A 63 B5
Pérgine Valsugana I 71 B6
Pérgola I 82 C1
Pergusa I 109 B3
Periam RO 75 B5
Periana E 100 C1
Périers F 57 A4
Périgueux F 67 C5
Perino I 80 B3
Perjasica HR 73 C5
Perkáta H 74 A3
Perković HR 83 C5
Perleberg D 44 B3
Perlez SRB 75 C5
Përmet AL 116 B2
Pernarec CZ 62 A4
Pernek SK 64 B3
Pernes P 92 B2
Pernes-les-Fontaines
F 79 B4
Pernik BG 11 E7
Pernink CZ 52 C2
Pernitz A 64 C1
Peronnes B 49 C5
Péronne F 59 A3
Péronnes B 49 C5
Pero Pinheiro P 92 C1
Perorrubio E 94 A3
Perosa Argentina I 79 B6
Perozinho P 87 C2
Perpignan F 91 A5
Perranporth GB 28 C2
Perranzabuloe GB 28 C2
Perrecy-les-Forges F 69 B4
Perrero I 79 B6
Perrignier F 69 B6
Perros-Guirec F 56 B2
Persan F 58 A3
Persberg S 34 C6
Persenbeug A 63 B6
Pershore GB 29 A5
Persön S 113 D12
Perstorp S 41 C3
Perth GB 25 B4
Pertisau A 72 A1
Pertoča SLO 73 B6
Pertuis F 79 C4
Perućac SRB 85 C4
Perúgia I 82 C1
Perušić HR 83 B4
Péruwelz B 49 C4
Pervomaysk UA 11 B11
Perwez B 49 C5
Pesadas de Burgos E 89 B3
Pesaguero E 88 A2
Pésaro I 82 C1
Pescantina I 71 C5
Pescara I 103 A7
Pescasséroli I 103 B6
Peschici I 104 B2
Peschiera del Garda I 71 C5
Péscia I 81 C4
Pescina I 103 A6
Pescocostanzo I 103 B7
Pescopagano I 103 C8
Pesco Sannita I 103 B7
Peshkopi AL 116 A2
Pesmes F 69 A5
Pesnica SLO 73 B5
Peso da Régua P 87 C3
Pesquera de Duero E 88 C2
Pessac F 76 B2
Pestovo RUS 7 B13
Petalidi GR 117 F3
Pétange L 60 A1
Petas GR 116 C3
Peteranec HR 74 B1
Peterborough GB 30 B3
Peterculter GB 23 D6
Peterhead GB 23 D7
Peterlee GB 25 D6
Petersfield GB 31 C3
Petershagen
Brandenburg D 45 C5
Brandenburg D 45 C6
Nordrhein-Westfalen
D 43 C5
Petershausen D 62 B2
Peterswell IRL 20 A3
Pétervására H 65 B6
Petília Policastro I 107 B3
Petín E 87 B3
Pětipsy CZ 52 C3
Petkus D 52 B3
Petlovac HR 74 C3
Petlovača SRB 85 B4
Petőfiszállás H 75 B4
Petra E 97 B3
Petralia Sottana I 109 B3
Petrčane HR 83 B4
Petrella Tifernina I 103 B7
Petrer E 101 A5
Petreto-Bicchisano
F 102 B1
Petrich BG 116 A5
Petrijevci HR 74 C3
Petrinja HR 73 C6
Petrodvorets RUS 7 B10
Pétrola E 101 A4
Petronà I 107 B3
Petronell A 64 B2
Petroşani RO 11 D7
Petrovac
MNE 105 A4
SRB 85 B6
Petrovaradin SRB 75 C4
Petrovice
BIH 84 B3
CZ 53 C3
Pettenbach A 63 C5
Pettigo IRL 19 B4
Petworth GB 31 D3
Peuerbach A 63 B4
Peuntenansa E 88 A2
Peurasuvanto FIN 113 E15
Pevensey Bay GB 31 D4
Peveragno I 80 B1
Pewsey GB 29 B6
Pewsum D 43 B4
Peyrat-le-Château F 68 C1
Peyrehorade F 76 C1
Peyriac-Minervois F 77 C5
Peyrins F 79 A4
Peyrissac F 67 C6
Peyrolles-en-Provence
F 79 C4
Peyruis F 79 B4
Pézarches F 59 B3
Pézenas F 78 C2
Pezinok SK 64 B3
Pezuls F 77 B3
Pfaffenhausen D 61 B6
Pfaffenhofen
Bayern D 61 B6
Bayern D 62 B2
Pfaffenhoffen F 60 B3
Pfäffikon CH 70 A3
Pfarrkirchen D 62 B3
Pfeffenhausen D 62 B2
Pfetterhouse F 70 A2
Pforzheim D 61 B4
Pfreimd D 62 A3
Pfronten D 61 C6
Pfullendorf D 61 C5
Pfullingen D 61 B5
Pfunds A 71 B5
Pfungstadt D 61 A4
Pfyn CH 61 C4
Phalsbourg F 60 B3
Philippeville B 49 C5
Philippsreut D 63 B4
Philippsthal D 51 C5
Piacenza I 81 A3
Piacenza d'Adige I 72 C1
Piádena I 71 C5
Piana F 102 A1
Piana Crixia I 80 B2
Piana degli Albanesi
I 108 B2
Piana di Monte Verna
I 103 B7
Piancastagnáio I 81 D5
Piandelagotti I 81 B4
Pianella
Abruzzi I 103 A7
Toscana I 81 C5
Pianello Val Tidone I 80 B3
Pianoro I 81 B5
Pians A 71 A5
Pías E 87 B4
Pias P 98 A3
Piaseczno PL 55 A6
Piasek PL 45 C6
Piaski PL 47 A5
Piastów PL 55 A5
Piaszcyna PL 46 A3
Piątek PL 55 A4
Piatra Neamţ RO 11 C9
Piazza al Sérchio I 81 B4
Piazza Armerina I 109 B3
Piazza Brembana I 71 C4
Piazze I 81 D5
Piazzola sul Brenta I 72 C1
Picassent E 96 B2
Piccione I 82 C1
Picerno I 104 C1
Picher D 44 B3
Pickering GB 27 A5
Pico I 103 B6
Picón E 94 C2
Picquigny F 58 A3
Piechowice PL 53 C5
Piecnik PL 46 B2
Piedicavallo I 70 C2
Piedicroce F 102 A2
Piedimonte Etneo I 109 B4
Piedimonte Matese I 103 B7
Piedimulera I 70 B3
Piedipaterno I 82 D1
Piedrabuena E 94 C2
Piedraescrita E 94 C2
Piedrafita E 88 A1
Piedrahita E 93 A5
Piedralaves E 94 B2
Piedras Albas E 93 B4
Piedras Blancas E 88 A1
Piegaro I 82 D1
Piekary Śl. PL 54 C3
Pieksämäki FIN 3 E27
Pielenhofen D 62 A2
Pielgrzymka PL 53 B5
Pieniężno PL 47 A6
Pieńsk PL 53 B5
Pienza I 81 C5
Piera E 91 B4
Pieranie PL 47 C4
Pierowall GB 23 B6
Pierre-Buffière F 67 C6
Pierrecourt F 60 C1
Pierre-de-Bresse F 69 B5
Pierrefeu-du-Var F 79 C5
Pierrefitte-Nestalas F 76 D2
Pierrefitte-sur-Aire F 59 B6
Pierrefonds F 59 A3
Pierrefontaine-les-Varans
F 69 A6
Pierrefort F 78 B1
Pierrelatte F 78 B3
Pierrepont
Aisne F 59 A4
Meurthe-et-Moselle F 60 A1
Piesendorf A 72 A2
Piešťany SK 64 B3
Pieszkowo PL 47 A6
Pieszyce PL 54 C1
Pietarsaari FIN 3 E25
Pietragalla I 104 C1
Pietra Ligure I 80 B2
Pietralunga I 82 C1
Pietramelara I 103 B7
Pietraperzía I 109 B3
Pietrasanta I 81 C4
Pietravairano I 103 B7
Pieve del Cáiro I 80 A2
Pieve di Bono I 71 C5
Pieve di Cadore I 72 B2
Pieve di Cento I 81 B5
Pieve di Soligo I 72 C2
Pieve di Teco I 80 B1
Pievepélago I 81 B4
Pieve Santo Stefano I 82 C1
Pieve Torina I 82 C2
Piges GR 116 C3
Píglio I 102 B6
Pigna I 80 C1
Pignan F 78 C2
Pignataro Maggiore
I 103 B7
Pijnacker NL 49 A5
Pikalevo RUS 7 B13
Piła PL 46 B2
Pilar de la Horadada
E 101 B5
Pilas E 99 B4
Pilastri I 81 B5
Piława PL 55 B6
Piława Górna PL 54 C1
Piławki PL 47 B5
Pilchowice PL 54 C3
Pilea GR 116 B5
Pilgrimstad S 115 E12
Pili
Dodekanisa GR 119 F2
Trikala GR 116 C3
Pilica PL 55 C4
Pilis H 75 A4
Piliscaba H 65 C4
Pilisszántó H 65 C4
Pilisvörösvár H 65 C4
Pilos GR 117 F3
Pilsting D 62 B3
Pilszcz PL 54 C2
Pilterud N 34 C2
Pilu RO 75 B6
Pilzno PL 55 D6
Pina de Ebro E 90 B2
Piñar E 100 B2
Pınarbaşı TR 118 C1
Pınarhisar TR 118 A2
Pinas F 77 C3
Pincehely H 74 B3
Pinchbeck GB 30 B3
Pińczów PL 55 C5
Pineda de la Sierra E 89 B3
Pineda de Mar E 91 B5
Pinerella I 82 B1
Pinerolo I 79 B6
Pineta Grande I 103 C6
Pineto I 103 A7
Piney F 59 B5
Pinggau A 73 A6
Pinhal Novo P 92 C2
Pinhão P 87 C3
Pinheiro
Aveiro P 87 C2
Aveiro P 87 D2
Pinheiro Grande P 92 B2
Pinhel P 87 D3
Pinhoe GB 29 C4
Pinilla E 101 A4
Pinilla de Toro E 88 C1
Pinkafeld A 73 A6
Pinneberg D 43 B6
Pinnow D 53 B4
Pino F 102 A2
Pino del Rio E 88 B2
Pino de Val E 86 B2
Pinofranqueado E 93 A4
Pinols F 78 A2
Piñor E 86 B2
Pinos del Valle E 100 C2
Pinoso E 101 A4
Pinos Puente E 100 B2
Pinsk BY 7 E9
Pinto E 94 B3
Pinzano al Tagliamento
I 72 B2
Pinzio P 93 A3
Pinzolo I 71 B5
Pióbbico I 82 C1
Piombino I 81 D4
Pionki PL 55 B6
Pionsat F 68 B2
Pióraco I 82 C1
Piornal E 93 A5
Piotrkowice PL 55 C5
Piotrków-Kujawski
PL 47 C4
Piotrków Trybunalski
PL 55 B4
Piotrowice PL 55 A6
Piotrowo PL 46 C2
Piove di Sacco I 72 C2
Piovene I 71 C6
Piperskärr S 40 B6
Pipriac F 57 C4
Piraeus = Pireas GR 117 E5
Piran SLO 72 C3
Pireas = Piraeus GR 117 E5
Piré-sur-Seiche F 57 B4
Pirgi GR 117 D7
Pirgos
Ilia GR 117 E3
Kriti GR 117 G7
Piriac-sur-Mer F 66 A2
Piringsdorf A 73 A6
Pirmasens D 60 A3
Pirna D 53 C3
Pirnmill GB 24 C2
Pirot SRB 11 E7
Pirovac HR 83 C4
Pirttivuopio S 112 E8
Pisa I 81 C4
Pisany F 66 C4
Pisarovina HR 73 C5
Pischelsdorf in der
Steiermark A 73 A5
Pişchia RO 75 C6
Pisciotta I 106 A2
Písek CZ 63 A5
Pisogne I 71 C5
Pissos F 76 B2
Pissouri CY 120 B1
Pisticci I 104 C2
Pistóia I 81 C4
Piteå S 3 D24
Piteşti RO 11 D8
Pithiviers F 58 B3
Pitigliano I 102 A4
Pitkyaranta RUS 3 F29
Pitlochry GB 25 B4
Pitomača HR 74 C2
Pitres E 100 C2
Pittentrail GB 23 D4
Pitvaros H 75 B5
Pivka SLO 73 C4
Pivnice SRB 75 C4
Piwniczna PL 65 A6
Pizarra E 100 C1
Pizzano I 71 B5
Pizzighettone I 71 C4
Pizzo I 106 C3
Pízzoli I 103 A6
Pizzolungo I 108 A1
Pjätteryd S 40 C4
Plabennec F 56 B1
Placencia E 89 A4
Plaffeien CH 70 B2
Plaisance
Gers F 76 C3
Haute-Garonne F 77 C4
Tarn F 77 C5
Plaka GR 116 C7
Plan E 90 A3
Planá CZ 62 A3
Planánad Lužnici CZ 63 A5
Plaňany CZ 53 C5
Planchez F 68 A4
Plancoët F 57 B3
Plancy-l'Abbaye F 59 B4
Plan-de-Baix F 79 B4
Plandište SRB 75 C6
Plan-d'Orgon F 78 C3
Plánice CZ 63 A4
Planina
SLO 73 B5
SLO 73 C4
Plankenfels D 62 A2
Plasencia E 93 A4
Plasenzuela E 93 B4
Plaški HR 83 A4
Plassen
Buskerud N 32 B4
Hedmark N 34 A4
Plášťovce SK 65 B5
Plasy CZ 63 A4
Platamona Lido I 110 B1
Platania I 106 B3
Platanos GR 117 G5
Platí I 106 C3
Platičevo SRB 85 B4
Platja d'Aro E 91 B6
Plattling D 62 B3
Plau D 44 B4
Plaue
Brandenburg D 44 C4
Thüringen D 51 C6
Plauen D 52 C2
Plav MNE 85 D4
Plavecký Mikuláš SK 64 B3
Plavinas LV 7 C8
Plavna SRB 75 C4
Plavnica SK 65 A6
Plavno HR 83 B5
Plavsk RUS 7 E14
Playben F 56 B2
Pléaux F 68 C2
Pleine-Fougères F 57 B4
Pleinfeld D 62 A1
Pleinting D 62 B4
Plélan-le-Grand F 57 C3
Plémet F 56 B3
Pléneuf-Val-André F 56 B3
Plentzia E 89 A4
Plérin F 56 B3
Plešivec SK 65 B6
Plessa D 52 B3
Plessé F 66 A3
Plestin-les-Grèves F 56 B2
Pleszew PL 54 B2
Pleternica HR 74 C2
Plettenberg D 50 B3
Pleubian F 56 B2
Pleumartin F 67 B5
Pleumeur-Bodou F 56 B2
Pleurs F 59 B4
Pleven BG 11 E8
Plevlja MNE 85 C4
Plevnik-Drienové SK 65 A4
Pleyber-Christ F 56 B2
Pliego E 101 B4
Pliešovce SK 65 B5
Plitvička Jezera HR 83 B4
Plitvički Ljeskovac
HR 83 B4
Ploaghe I 110 B1
Ploče HR 84 C2
Plochingen D 61 B5
Płock PL 47 C5
Ploemeur F 56 C2
Ploërmel F 56 C3
Ploeuc-sur-Lie F 56 B3
Plogastel St Germain
F 56 C1
Plogoff F 56 B1
Ploiești RO 11 D9
Plomari GR 118 D1
Plombières-les-Bains
F 60 C2
Plomin HR 82 A3
Plön D 44 A2
Plonéour-Lanvern F 56 C1
Płonia PL 45 B6
Płońsk PL 47 C6
Płoskinia PL 47 A5
Plössberg D 62 A3
Płoty PL 45 B7
Plouagat F 56 B2
Plouaret F 56 B2
Plouarzel F 56 B1
Plouay F 56 C2
Ploubalay F 57 B3
Ploubazlanec F 56 B2
Ploudalmézeau F 56 B1
Ploudiry F 56 B1
Plouescat F 56 B1
Plouézec F 56 B3
Plougasnou F 56 B2
Plougastel-Daoulas F 56 B1
Plougonven F 56 B2
Plougonver F 56 B2
Plougrescant F 56 B2
Plouguenast F 56 B3
Plouguerneau F 56 B1
Plouha F 56 B3
Plouhinec F 56 B1
Plouigneau F 56 B2
Ploumanach F 56 B2
Plounévez-Quintin F 56 B2
Plouray F 56 B2
Plouzévédé F 56 B1
Plovdiv BG 11 E8
Plozévet F 56 C1
Plumbridge GB 19 B4
Pluméliau F 56 C3
Plumlov CZ 64 A3
Plungė LT 6 D6
Pluty PL 47 A6
Pluvigner F 56 C3
Plužine
BIH 84 C3
MNE 84 C3
Płuznica PL 47 B4
Plymouth GB 28 C3
Plymstock GB 28 C3
Płytnica PL 46 B2
Plyusa RUS 7 B10
Plzeň CZ 63 A4
Pniewy PL 46 C2
Pobes E 89 B4
Poběžovice CZ 62 A3
Pobiedziska PL 46 C3
Pobierowo PL 45 A6
Pobla de Segur E 90 A3
Pobladura del Valle E 88 B1
Pobla-Tornesa E 96 A3
Pobra de Trives E 87 B3
Pobra do Brollón E 86 B3
Pobra do Caramiñal
E 86 B2
Pobudje BIH 85 B4
Počátky CZ 63 A6
Poceirão P 92 C2
Pochep RUS 7 E12
Pochinok RUS 7 D12
Pöchlarn A 63 B6
Pociecha PL 55 B5
Pockau D 52 C3
Pocking D 63 B4
Pocklington GB 27 B5
Podą MNE 85 D4
Podbořany CZ 52 C3
Podbrdo SLO 72 B3
Podbrezová SK 65 B5
Podčetrtek SLO 73 B5
Poddębice PL 54 B3
Poděbrady CZ 53 C5
Podence P 87 C4
Podensac F 76 B2
Podenzano I 80 B3
Podersdorf am See A 64 C2
Podgaje PL 46 B2
Podgora HR 84 C2
Podgóra PL 55 B6
Podgorač HR 74 C3
Podgorica MNE 105 A5
Podgorie AL 116 B2
Podgrad SLO 73 C4
Podhájska SK 65 B4
Podkova BG 116 A7
Podlapača HR 83 B4
Podlejki PL 47 B6
Podlužany SK 65 B4
Podnovlje BIH 84 B3
Podolie SK 64 B3
Podolinec SK 65 A6
Podolsk RUS 7 D14
Podporozhy RUS 7 A13
Podromanija BIH 84 C3
Podturen HR 74 B1
Podujevo KOS 85 D6
Podvín CZ 64 B2
Podwilk PL 65 A5
Poetto I 110 C2
Poggendorf D 45 A5
Poggiardo I 107 A5
Poggibonsi I 81 C5
Póggio a Caiano I 81 C5
Poggio Imperiale I 103 B8
Póggio Mirteto I 102 A5
Póggio Moiano I 102 A5
Póggio Renatico I 81 B5
Póggio Rusco I 81 B5
Pöggstall A 63 B6
Pogny F 59 B5
Pogorzela PL 54 B2
Pogorzelice PL 46 A3
Pogradec AL 116 B2
Pogrodzie PL 47 A5
Pohořelá SK 65 B6
Pohořelice CZ 64 B2
Pohronská Polhora
SK 65 B5
Poiares P 92 A2
Poio E 86 B2
Poirino I 80 B1
Poisson F 68 B4
Poissons F 59 B6
Poissy F 58 B3
Poitiers F 67 B5
Poix-de-Picardie F 58 A2
Poix-Terron F 59 A5
Pokka FIN 113 D14
Pokój PL 54 C2
Pokupsko HR 73 C5
Pol E 86 A3
Pola RUS 7 C11
Pol a Charra GB 22 D1
Pola de Allande E 86 A4
Pola de Laviana E 88 A1
Pola de Lena E 88 A1
Pola de Siero E 88 A1
Pola de Somiedo E 86 A4
Polaincourt-et-
Clairefontaine F 60 C2
Połajewo PL 46 C2
Polán E 94 C2
Polanica-Zdrój PL 54 C1
Połaniec PL 55 C6
Polanów PL 46 A2
Polatlı TR 118 C7
Polatsk BY 7 D10
Polch D 50 C3
Polčno PL 46 A3
Polczyn-Zdrój PL 46 B2
Polegate GB 31 D4
Poleñino E 90 B2
Polesella I 81 B5
Polessk RUS 6 D6
Polgár H 65 C6
Polgárdi H 74 A3
Polhov Gradec SLO 73 B4
Police PL 45 B6
Police nad Metují CZ 53 C6
Polichnitos GR 116 C8
Polička CZ 64 A2
Poličnik HR 83 B4
Policoro I 104 C2
Policzna PL 55 B6
Poligiros GR 116 B5
Polignano a Mare I 104 C3
Poligny F 69 B5
Polis CY 120 A1
Polistena I 106 C3
Polizzi Generosa I 109 B3
Poljana SRB 85 B6
Poljanák HR 83 B4
Poljčane SLO 73 B5
Polje BIH 84 B2
Poljice
BIH 83 B5
BIH 84 B3
Poljna SRB 85 C6
Polkowice PL 53 B6
Polla I 104 C1
Pollas E 88 C1
Pöllau A 73 A5
Polleben D 52 B1
Pollença E 97 B3
Pollenfeld D 62 B2
Pollfoss N 114 F4
Póllica I 106 A2
Polminhac F 77 B5
Polná CZ 63 A6
Polna RUS 7 B10
Polne PL 46 B2
Polomka SK 65 B5
Polonne UA 11 A9
Polperro GB 28 C3
Polruan GB 28 C3
Põls A 73 A4
Polska Cerekiew PL 54 C3
Poltár SK 65 B5
Põltsamaa EST 7 B8
Polyarny RUS 3 B30
Polyarnye Zori RUS 3 C30
Polzela SLO 73 B5
Pomarance I 81 C4
Pomarez F 76 C2
Pomárico I 104 C2
Pomáz H 65 C5
Pombal P 92 B2
Pomeroy GB 19 B5
Pomézia I 102 B5
Pomichna UA 11 B11
Pommard F 69 A4
Pommelsbrunn D 62 A2
Pomonte I 81 D4
Pomorie BG 11 E9
Pomos CY 120 A1
Pompei I 103 C7
Pompey F 60 B2
Pomposa I 82 B1
Poncin F 69 B5
Pondorf D 62 B2
Ponferrada E 86 B4
Pongoma RUS 3 D31
Poniec PL 54 B1
Ponikva SLO 73 B5
Poniky SK 65 B5
Pons F 67 C4
Ponsacco I 81 C4
Pont I 70 C2
Pont-a-Celles B 49 C5
Pontacq F 76 C2
Pontailler-sur-Saône
F 69 A5
Pont-a-Marcq F 49 C4
Pont-à-Mousson F 60 B2
Pontão P 92 B2
Pontardawe GB 28 B4
Pontarddulais GB 28 B3
Pontarion F 68 C1
Pontarlier F 69 B6
Pontassieve I 81 C5
Pontaubault F 57 B4
Pont-Audemer F 58 A1
Pontaumur F 68 C2
Pont-Aven F 56 C2
Pont Canavese I 70 C2
Pontcharra F 69 C6
Pontcharra-sur-Turdine
F 69 C4
Pontchâteau F 66 A2
Pont-Croix F 56 B1
Pont-d'Ain F 69 B5
Pont de-Beauvoisin F 69 C5
Pont-de-Buis-lès-
Quimerch F 56 B1
Pont-de-Chéruy F 69 C5
Pont de Dore F 68 C3
Pont-de-Labeaume F 78 B3
Pont-de-l'Arche F 58 A2
Pont de Molins E 91 A5
Pont-de-Roide F 70 A1
Pont-de-Salars F 78 B1
Pont-d'Espagne F 76 D2
Pont de Suert E 90 A3
Pont-de-Vaux F 69 B4
Pont-de-Veyle F 69 B4
Pont d'Ouilly F 57 B5
Pont-du-Château F 68 C3
Pont-du-Navoy F 69 B5
Ponte a Moriano I 81 C4
Ponte Arche I 71 B5
Ponteareas E 87 B2
Pontebba I 72 B3
Ponte Cáffaro I 71 C5
Pontecagnano I 103 C7
Ponte-Caldelas E 87 B2
Ponteceso E 86 A2
Pontecesures E 86 B2
Pontecorvo I 103 B6
Ponte da Barca P 87 C2
Pontedássio I 80 C2
Pontedécimo I 80 B2
Ponte de Lima P 87 C2
Ponte dell'Ólio I 80 B3
Pontedera I 81 C4
Ponte de Sor P 92 B2
Pontedeume E 86 A2
Ponte di Barbarano I 71 C6
Ponte di Legno I 71 B5
Ponte di Nava I 80 B1
Ponte di Piave I 72 C2
Ponte Felcino I 82 C1
Pontefract GB 27 B4
Ponte Gardena I 71 B6
Ponteginori I 81 C4
Pontelagoscuro I 81 B5
Ponteland GB 25 C6
Pontelandolfo I 103 B7
Ponte-Leccia F 102 A2
Pontelongo I 72 C2
Ponte nelle Alpi I 72 B2
Pont-en-Royans F 79 A4
Pontenure I 81 A3
Pontenx-les-Forges F 76 B1
Ponterwyd GB 26 C2
Ponte San Giovanni I 82 C1
Ponte San Pietro I 71 C4
Pontevedra E 86 B2
Pontevico I 71 C5
Pont Farcy F 57 B4
Pontfaverger-Moronvillers
F 59 A5
Pontgibaud F 68 C2
Ponticino I 81 C5
Pontigny F 59 C4
Pontijou F 58 C2
Pontinia I 102 B6
Pontinvrea I 80 B2
Pontivy F 56 B3
Pont-l'Abbé F 56 C1
Pont-l'Évêque F 57 A6
Pontlevoy F 67 A6
Pontoise F 58 A3
Pontones E 101 A3
Pontonx-sur-l'Abour
F 76 C2
Pontoon IRL 18 C2
Pontorson F 57 B4
Pontrémoli I 81 B3
Pont-Remy F 48 C2
Pontresina CH 71 B4
Pontrhydfendigaid
GB 28 A4
Pontrieux F 56 B2
Ponts E 91 B4
Ponts-aux-Dames F 59 B3
Pont Scorff F 56 C2
Pöntsö FIN 113 E13
Pont-Ste Maxence F 58 A3
Pont-St Esprit F 78 B3

Pont-St Mamet F 77 B3
Pont-St Martin
F 66 A3
I 70 C2
Pont-St Vincent F 60 B2
Pont-sur-Yonne F 59 B4
Pontvallain F 57 C6
Pontypool GB 29 B4
Pontypridd GB 29 B4
Ponza I 102 C5
Poo E 88 A2
Poole GB 29 C6
Poolewe GB 22 D3
Poperinge B 48 C3
Pópoli I 103 A6
Popovac SRB 85 C6
Popovača HR 74 C1
Popow PL 55 A4
Poppel B 49 B6
Poppenhausen
Bayern D 51 C6
Hessen D 51 C5
Poppi I 81 C5
Poprad SK 65 A6
Popučke SRB 85 B4
Pópulo P 87 C3
Populónia I 81 D4
Pörböly H 74 B3
Porcuna E 100 B1
Pordenone I 72 C2
Pordic F 56 B3
Poręba PL 55 C4
Poreč HR 72 C3
Pori FIN 3 F24
Porjus S 112 F8
Porkhov RUS 7 C10
Porlezza I 71 B4
Porlock GB 29 B4
Pörnbach D 62 B2
Pornic F 66 A2
Pornichet F 66 A2
Porodin SRB 85 B6
Poronin PL 65 A5
Poros
Attiki GR 117 E5
Kefalonia GR 117 D2
Poroszló H 65 C6
Porozina HR 82 A3
Porquerolles F 79 D5
Porrentruy CH 70 A2
Porreres E 97 B3
Porretta Terme I 81 B4
Porsgrunn N 35 C1
Porspoder F 56 B1
Port-a-Binson F 59 A4
Portacloy IRL 18 B2
Portadown GB 19 B5
Portaferry GB 19 B6
Portaje E 93 B4
Portalegre P 92 B3
Portarlington IRL 21 A4
Port Askaig GB 24 C1
Portavadie GB 24 C2
Portavogie GB 19 B6
Portbail F 57 A4
Port Bannatyne GB 24 C2
Port-Barcarès F 78 D2
Portbou E 91 A6
Port-Camargue F 78 C3
Port Charlotte GB 24 C1
Port d'Andratx E 97 B2
Port-de-Bouc F 78 C3
Port-de-Lanne F 76 C1
Port de Pollença E 97 B3
Port-des-Barques F 66 C3
Port de Sóller E 97 B2
Portegrandi I 72 C2
Portel P 92 C3
Portela P 92 A2
Port Ellen GB 24 C1
Portelo P 87 C4
Portemouro E 86 B2
Port-en-Bessin F 57 A5
Port'Ercole I 102 A4
Port Erin GB 26 A1
Portes-lès-Valence F 78 B3
Portets F 76 B2
Port Eynon GB 28 B3
Portezuelo E 93 B4
Port Glasgow GB 24 C3
Portglenone GB 19 B5
Porthcawl GB 28 B4
Port Henderson GB 22 D3
Porthleven GB 28 C2
Porthmadog GB 26 C1
Porticcio F 102 B1
Portici I 103 C7
Portico di Romagna I 81 B5
Portilla de la Reina E 88 A2
Portillo E 88 C2
Portimao P 98 B2
Portinatx E 97 B1
Portinho da Arrabida
P 92 C1
Port Isaac GB 28 C3
Portishead GB 29 B5
Port-Joinville F 66 B2
Portknockie GB 23 D6
Port-la-Nouvelle F 78 C2
Portlaoise IRL 21 A4
Portlethen GB 23 D6
Port Logan GB 24 D3
Port Louis F 56 C2
Portmagne IRL 20 C1
Portmahomack GB 23 D5
Portman E 101 B5
Port Manech F 56 C2
Portnacroish GB 24 B2
Portnahaven GB 24 C1
Port Nan Giuran GB 22 C2
Port-Navalo F 66 A2
Port Nis GB 22 C2
Porto
F 102 A1
P 87 C2
Porto-Alto P 92 C2
Porto Azzurro I 81 D4
Portocannone I 103 B8
Porto Cerésio I 70 C3
Porto Cervo I 110 A2
Porto Cesáreo I 107 A4
Porto Colom E 97 B3
Porto Covo P 98 B2
Porto Cristo E 97 B3
Porto d'Áscoli I 82 D2
Porto de Lagos P 98 B2
Porto de Mos P 92 B2
Porto de Rei P 98 A2
Porto do Son E 86 B2
Porto Empédocle I 108 B2
Portoferráio I 81 D4
Portofino I 80 B3
Porto Garibaldi I 82 B1
Portogruaro I 72 C2
Portokhelion GR 117 E5
Portomaggiore I 81 B5
Portomarín E 86 B3
Porton GB 29 B6
Portonovo E 87 B2
Portopalo di Capo
Passero I 109 C4
Porto Petro E 97 B3
Porto Pino I 110 D1
Porto Potenza Picena
I 82 C2
Portør N 33 D6
Porto Recanati I 82 C2
Porto San Giórgio I 82 C2
Porto Sant'Elpídio I 82 C2
Porto Santo Stéfano
I 102 A4
Portoscuso I 110 C1
Porto Tolle I 82 B1
Porto Tórres I 110 B1
Porto-Vecchio F 102 B2
Portovénere I 81 B3
Portpatrick GB 24 D2
Portreath GB 28 C2
Portree GB 22 D2
Portroe IRL 20 B3
Portrush GB 19 A5
Port St Mary GB 26 A1
Portsall F 56 B1
Portsmouth GB 31 D2
Portsoy GB 23 D6
Port-Ste Marie F 77 B3
Portstewart GB 19 A5
Port-St-Louis-du-Rhône
F 78 C3
Port-sur-Saône F 60 C2
Port Talbot GB 28 B4
Portugalete E 89 A4
Portumna IRL 20 A3
Port-Vendres F 91 A6
Port William GB 24 D3
Porvoo FIN 7 A8
Porzuna E 94 C2
Posada
Oviedo E 88 A1
Oviedo E 88 A2
I 110 B2
Posada de Valdeón E 88 A2
Posadas E 99 B5
Poschiavo CH 71 B5
Posedarje HR 83 B4
Positano I 104 C1
Possagno I 72 C1
Posseck D 52 C2
Possesse F 59 B5
Pössneck D 52 C1
Posta I 102 A6
Postal I 71 B6
Posta Piana I 104 B1
Postbauer-Heng D 62 A2
Posterholt NL 50 B2
Postioma I 72 C2
Postira HR 83 C5
Postojna SLO 73 C4
Postoloprty CZ 53 C3
Postomino PL 46 A2
Posušje BIH 84 C2
Potamos
Attiki GR 117 F4
Attiki GR 117 G5
Potegowo PL 46 A3
Potenza I 104 C1
Potenza Picena I 82 C2
Potes E 88 A2
Potigny F 57 B5
Potkrajci MNE 85 C4
Potočari BIH 85 B4
Potoci
BIH 83 B5
BIH 84 C2
Potony H 74 C2
Potries E 96 C2
Potsdam D 45 C5
Potštát CZ 64 A3
Pottenbrunn A 63 B6
Pottendorf A 64 C2
Pottenstein
A 64 C2
D 62 A2
Potters Bar GB 31 C3
Pöttmes D 62 B2
Pöttsching A 64 C2
Potworów PL 55 B5
Pouancé F 57 C4
Pougues-les-Eaux F 68 A3
Pouilly-en-Auxois F 69 A4
Pouilly-sous Charlieu
F 68 B4
Pouilly-sur-Loire F 68 A2
Poujol-sur-Orb F 78 C2
Poullaouen F 56 B2
Poulton-le-Fylde GB 26 B3
Poundstock GB 28 C3
Pourcy F 59 A4
Pourrain F 59 C4
Pouyastruc F 76 C3
Pouy-de-Touges F 77 C4
Pouzauges F 66 B4
Pova de Santa Iria P 92 C1
Považská Bystrica
SK 65 A4
Povedilla E 101 A3
Povlja HR 84 C1
Povljana HR 83 B4
Póvoa
Beja P 98 A3
Santarém P 92 B2
Póvoa de Lanhoso P 87 C2
Póvoa de Varzim P 87 C2
Póvoa e Meadas P 92 B3
Powidz PL 46 C3
Poyales del Hoyo E 93 A5
Poynton GB 26 B3
Poyntz Pass GB 19 B5
Poysdorf A 64 B2
Poza de la Sal E 89 B3
Pozaldez E 88 C2
Pozán de Vero E 90 A3
Pozanti TR 16 C7
Požarevac SRB 85 B6
Požega
HR 74 C2
SRB 85 C5
Poznań PL 46 C2
Pozo Alcón E 100 B3
Pozoantiguo E 88 C1
Pozoblanco E 100 A1
Pozo Cañada E 101 A4
Pozo de Guadalajara
E 95 B3
Pozo de la Serna E 100 A2
Pozohondo E 101 A4
Pozondón E 95 B5
Poźrzadło Wielkie
PL 46 B1
Pozuel del Campo E 95 B5
Pozuelo de Alarcón
E 94 B3
Pozuelo de Calatrava
E 100 A2
Pozuelo del Páramo
E 88 B1
Pozuelo de Zarzón E 93 A4
Pozzallo I 109 C3
Pozzomaggiore I 110 B1
Pozzo San Nicola I 110 B1
Pozzuoli I 103 C7
Pozzuolo I 81 C5
Prabuty PL 47 B5
Prača BIH 84 C3
Prachatice CZ 63 A4
Prada E 87 B3
Pradelle F 79 B4
Pradelles F 78 B2
Prades
E 90 B3
F 91 A5
Pradła PL 55 C4
Prado
E 88 A1
P 87 C2
Prado del Rey E 99 C5
Pradoluengo E 89 B3
Pragelato I 79 A5
Pragersko SLO 73 B5
Prägraten A 72 A2
Prague = Praha CZ 53 C4
Praha = Prague CZ 53 C4
Prahecq F 67 B4
Praia P 92 B1
Práia a Mare I 106 B2
Praia da Rocha P 98 B2
Praia da Viera P 92 B2
Praia de Mira P 92 A2
Praiano I 103 C7
Pralboino I 71 C5
Pralognan-la-Vanoise
F 70 C1
Pramanda GR 116 C3
Pranjani SRB 85 B5
Prapatnica HR 83 C5
Præstø DK 39 D5
Praszka PL 54 B3
Prat F 77 C3
Prata I 81 C4
Prata di Pordenone I 72 C2
Pratau D 52 B2
Prat de Compte E 90 C3
Pratdip E 90 B3
Pratella I 103 B7
Prato I 81 C5
Prátola Peligna I 103 A6
Pratola Serra I 103 C7
Prats-de-Mollo-la-Preste
F 91 A5
Prauthoy F 59 C6
Pravia E 86 A4
Praxmar A 71 A6
Prayssac F 77 B4
Prazzo I 79 B6
Prebold SLO 73 B5
Préchac F 76 B2
Précy-sur-Thil F 69 A4
Predáppio I 81 B5
Predazzo I 72 B1
Předín CZ 63 A6
Preding A 73 B5
Predjame SLO 73 C4
Predlitz A 72 A3
Predmeja SLO 72 C3
Predoi I 72 A2
Pré-en-Pail F 57 B5
Prees GB 26 C3
Preetz D 44 A2
Préfailles F 66 A2
Pregarten A 63 B5
Pregrada HR 73 B5
Preignan F 77 C3
Preiļi LV 7 C9
Preitenegg A 73 B4
Prekaja BIH 83 B5
Preljina SRB 83 B4
Preljina SRB 85 C5
Prelog HR 74 B1
Prelošćica HR 74 C1
Přelouč CZ 53 C5
Prem SLO 73 C4
Premantura HR 82 B2
Prémery F 68 A3
Prémia I 70 B3
Premiàde Mar E 91 B5
Premnitz D 44 C4
Prémont F 49 C4
Prenzlau D 45 B5
Preodac BIH 83 B5
Přerov CZ 64 A3
Prerow D 45 A4
Presencio E 88 B3
Presicce I 107 B5
Presly F 68 A2
Prešov SK 10 B6
Pressac F 67 B5
Pressath D 62 A2
Pressbaum A 64 B2
Prestatyn GB 26 B2
Prestebakke N 35 D3
Presteigne GB 29 A4
Přeštice CZ 63 A4
Preston
Lancashire GB 26 B3
Scottish Borders GB 25 C5
Prestonpans GB 25 C5
Prestwick GB 24 C3
Prettin D 52 B2
Preturo I 103 A6
Pretzchendorf D 52 C3
Pretzier D 44 C3
Pretzsch D 52 B2
Preuilly-sur-Claise F 67 B5
Prevalje SLO 73 B4
Prevenchères F 78 B2
Préveranges F 68 B2
Preveza GR 116 D2
Prevršac HR 73 C6
Prezid HR 73 C4
Priaranza del Bierzo
E 86 B4
Priay F 69 B5
Pribeta SK 64 C4
Priboj
BIH 84 B3
SRB 85 C4
Přibor CZ 64 A4
Příbram CZ 63 A5
Pribylina SK 65 A5
Přibyslav CZ 63 A6
Pričević SRB 85 B4
Pridjel BIH 84 B3
Priego E 95 B4
Priego de Córdoba
E 100 B1
Priekule LV 6 C6
Prien D 62 C3
Prienai LT 6 D7
Prievidza SK 65 B4
Prigradica HR 84 D1
Prigrevica SRB 75 C4
Prijeboj HR 83 B4
Prijedor BIH 83 B5
Prijepolje SRB 85 C4
Prilep MK 116 A3
Priluka BIH 84 C1
Primda CZ 62 A3
Primel-Trégastel F 56 B2
Primišje HR 73 C5
Primorsk
Kaliningrad RUS 47 A6
Severo-Zapadnyy
RUS 7 A10
Primošten HR 83 C4
Primstal D 60 A2
Princes Risborough
GB 31 C3
Princetown GB 28 C3
Principina a Mare I 81 D5
Priolo Gargallo I 109 B4
Prioro E 88 B2
Priozersk RUS 3 F29
Prirechnyy RUS 113 C19
Prisoje BIH 84 C2
Pristen RUS 7 F14
Priština KOS 85 D6
Pritzerbe D 44 C4
Pritzier D 44 B3
Pritzwalk D 44 B4
Privas F 78 B3
Priverno I 102 B6
Privlaka
Vukovarsko-Srijemska
HR 74 C3
Zadarska HR 83 B4
Prizna HR 83 B3
Prizren KOS 10 E6
Prizzi I 108 B2
Prnjavor
BIH 84 B2
HR 73 C5
SRB 85 B4
Proaza E 86 A4
Probstzella D 52 C1
Probus GB 28 C3
Prócchio I 81 D4
Prochowice PL 54 B1
Prócida I 103 C7
Prodhromos CY 120 B1
Prodo I 82 D1
Proença-a-Nova P 92 B3
Proença-a-Velha P 92 A3
Profondeville B 49 C5
Prokuplje SRB 10 E6
Propriano F 102 B1
Prosec CZ 64 A2
Prösen D 52 B3
Prosenjakovci SLO 73 B6
Prosotsani GR 116 A5
Prostějov CZ 64 A3
Prószków PL 54 C2
Proszowice PL 55 C5
Protić BIH 84 B1
Protivanov CZ 64 A2
Protivín CZ 63 A5
Prötzel D 45 C5
Provins F 59 B4
Prozor BIH 84 C2
Prrenjas AL 116 A2
Prudhoe GB 25 D6
Prudnik PL 54 C2
Pruggern A 72 A3
Prüm D 50 C2
Pruna E 99 C5
Prunelli-di-Fiumorbo
F 102 A2
Prunetta I 81 B4
Pruniers F 68 B2
Prusice PL 54 B1
Pruské SK 64 A4
Pruszce PL 47 B4
Pruszcz Gdański PL 47 A4
Pruszków PL 55 A5
Prutz A 71 A5
Prüzen D 44 B4
Pruzhany BY 6 E8
Pružina SK 65 A4
Pryluky UA 11 A12
Pryzlęg PL 46 C1
Przechlewo PL 46 B3
Przecław PL 55 C6
Przedbórz PL 55 B4
Przedecz PL 54 A3
Przejęslav PL 53 B5
Przemków PL 53 B5
Przemocze PL 45 B6
Przemyśl PL 11 B7
Przerąb PL 55 B4
Przewodnik PL 47 B4
Przewóz PL 53 B4
Przezmark PL 47 B5
Przodkowo PL 47 A4
Przybiernów PL 45 B6
Przyborowice PL 47 C6
Przybyszew PL 55 B5
Przybyszów PL 55 B4
Przylęg PL 46 C1
Przysucha PL 55 B5
Przytóczna PL 46 C1
Przytyk PL 55 B5
Przywidz PL 47 A4
Psachna GR 116 D5
Psara GR 116 D7
Psary PL 54 B3
Pskov RUS 7 C10
Pszczew PL 46 C1
Pszczółki PL 47 A4
Pszczyna PL 54 D3
Pszów PL 54 C3
Pteleos GR 116 C4
Ptolemaida GR 116 B3
Ptuj SLO 73 B5
Ptusza PL 46 B2
Puch A 62 C4
Puchberg am Schneeberg
A 64 C1
Puchevillers F 48 C3
Puchheim D 62 B2
Púchov SK 64 A4
Pučišća HR 83 C5
Puck PL 47 A4
Puçol E 96 B2
Puconci SLO 73 B6
Pudasjärvi FIN 3 D27
Puderbach D 50 C3
Puebla de Albortón E 90 B2
Puebla de Alcocer E 93 C5
Puebla de Beleña E 95 B3
Puebla de Don Fadrique
E 101 B3
Puebla de Don Rodrigo
E 94 C2
Puebla de Guzmán E 98 B3
Puebla de la Calzada
E 93 C4
Puebla de la Reina E 93 C4
Puebla de Lillo E 88 A1
Puebla del Maestre E 99 A4
Puebla del Principe
E 100 A3
Puebla de Obando E 93 B4
Puebla de Sanabria E 87 B4
Puebla de Sancho Pérez
E 93 C4
Puente Almuhey E 88 B2
Puente de Domingo
Flórez E 86 B4
Puente de Génave E 101 A3
Puente del Congosto
E 93 A5
Puente de Montañana
E 90 A3
Puente Duero E 88 C2
Puente-Genil E 100 B1
Puente la Reina E 89 B5
Puente la Reina de Jaca
E 90 A2
Puentelarra E 89 B3
Puente Mayorga E 99 C5
Puente Viesgo E 88 A3
Puertas
Asturias E 88 A2
Salamanca E 87 C4
Puerto de Mazarrón
E 101 B4
Puerto de Santa Cruz
E 93 B5
Puerto de San Vicente
E 94 C1
Puerto-Lápice E 95 C3
Puertollano E 100 A1
Puerto Lumbreras E 101 B4
Puerto Moral E 99 B4
Puerto Real E 99 C4
Puerto Rey E 94 C1
Puerto Seguro E 87 D4
Puerto Serrano E 99 C5
Puget-Sur-Argens F 79 C5
Puget-Théniers F 79 C5
Puget-ville F 79 C5
Pugnochiuso I 104 B2
Puigcerdà E 91 A4
Puigpunyent E 97 B2
Puig Reig E 91 B4
Puillon F 76 C2
Puimichel F 79 C5
Puimoisson F 79 C5
Puiseaux F 58 B3
Puisieux F 48 C3
Puisserguier F 78 C2
Puivert F 77 D5
Pujols F 76 B2
Pukanec SK 65 B4
Pukavik S 41 C4
Pukë AL 105 A5
Pula
HR 82 B2
I 110 C1
Puławy PL 11 A7
Pulborough GB 31 D3
Pulfero I 72 B3
Pulgar E 94 C2
Pulheim D 50 B2
Pulkau A 64 B1
Pulpi E 101 B4
Pulsano I 104 C3
Pulsnitz D 53 B4
Pułtusk PL 6 E6
Pumpsaint GB 28 A4
Punat HR 83 A3
Punta Marina I 82 B1
Punta Prima E 97 B4
Punta Sabbioni I 72 C2
Puntas de Calnegre
E 101 B4
Punta Umbria E 99 B4
Puolanka FIN 3 D27
Puoltikasvaara S 112 E10
Puoltsa S 112 E8
Puračić BIH 84 B3
Purbach am Neusiedler
See A 64 C2
Purchena E 101 B3
Purfleet GB 31 C4
Purgstall A 63 B6
Purkersdorf A 64 B2
Purmerend NL 42 C1
Purullena E 100 B2
Pushkin RUS 7 B11
Pushkino RUS 7 C14
Püspökladány H 75 A6
Pusté Ulany SK 64 B3
Pustelnik PL 55 A6
Pustoshka RUS 7 C10
Puszcza Mariańska
PL 55 B5
Puszczykowo PL 54 A1
Pusztamagyaród H 74 B1
Pusztamonostor H 75 A4
Pusztaszabolcs H 74 A3
Pusztavám H 74 A3
Putanges-Pont-Ecrepin
F 57 B5
Putbus D 45 A5
Putignano I 104 C3
Putlitz D 44 B4
Putnok H 65 B6
Putte B 49 B5
Puttelange-aux-Lacs
F 60 A2
Putten NL 49 A6
Puttgarden D 44 A3
Püttlingen D 60 A2
Putzu Idu I 110 B1
Puy-Guillaume F 68 C3
Puylaroque F 77 B4
Puylaurens F 77 C5
Puy-l'Évêque F 77 B4
Puymirol F 77 B3
Puyôo F 76 C2
Puyrolland F 67 B4
Pwllheli GB 26 C1
Pyatykhatky UA 11 B12
Pyetrikaw BY 7 E10
Pyhäjärvi FIN 3 E26
Pyla CY 120 A2
Pyla-sur-Mer F 76 B1
Pyryatyn UA 11 A12
Pyrzyce PL 45 B6
Pysely CZ 63 A5
Pyskowice PL 54 C3
Pytalovo RUS 7 C9
Pyzdry PL 54 A2

Q

Quakenbrück D 43 C4
Quargnento I 80 B2
Quarré-les-Tombes F 68 A3
Quarteira P 98 B2
Quartu Sant'Élena I 110 C2
Quatre-Champs F 59 A5
Quedlinburg D 52 B1
Queensferry
Edinburgh GB 25 C4
Flintshire GB 26 B2
Queige F 69 C6
Queipo E 99 B4
Queixans E 91 A4
Quel E 89 B4
Quelaines-St-Gault F 57 C5
Queljada P 87 C2
Quemada E 89 C3
Queralbs E 91 A5
Quercianella I 81 C4
Querfurt D 52 B1
Quérigut F 77 D5
Quero
E 95 C3
I 72 C1
Querqueville F 57 A4
Quesada E 100 B2
Questembert F 56 C3
Quettehou F 57 A4
Quevauvillers F 58 A3
Quevy B 49 C5
Quiaois P 92 A2
Quiberon F 66 A1
Quiberville F 58 A1
Quickborn D 44 B1
Quiévrain B 49 C4
Quillan F 77 D5
Quillebeuf F 58 A1
Quimper F 56 B1
Quimperlé F 56 C2
Quincampoix F 58 A2
Quincoces de Yuso E 89 B3
Quincy F 68 A2
Quinéville F 57 A4
Quingey F 69 A5
Quinson F 79 C5
Quinssaines F 68 B2
Quinta-Grande P 92 C2
Quintana de la Serena
E 93 C5
Quintana del Castillo
E 86 B4
Quintana del Marco E 88 B1
Quintana del Puente
E 88 B2
Quintana-Martín Galíndez
E 89 B3
Quintanaortuño E 88 B3
Quintanapalla E 89 B3
Quintanar de la Orden
E 95 C3
Quintanar de la Sierra
E 89 C3
Quintanar del Rey E 95 C5
Quintanilla de la Mata
E 88 C3
Quintanilla del Coco
E 89 C3
Quintanilla de Onésimo
E 88 C2
Quintanilla de Somoza
E 87 B4
Quintas de Valdelucio
E 88 B2
Quintela P 87 D3
Quintin F 56 B3
Quinto E 90 B2
Quinzano d'Oglio I 71 C5
Quiroga E 86 B3
Quismondo E 94 B2
Quissac F 78 C2
Quistello I 81 A4

R

Raab A 63 B4
Raabs an der Thaya
A 63 B6
Raahe FIN 3 D26
Raajärvi FIN 113 F15
Raalte NL 42 C3
Raamsdonksveer NL 49 B5
Raanujarvi FIN 113 F13
Raattama FIN 113 D13
Rab HR 83 B3
Rabac HR 82 A3
Rábade E 86 A3
Rábafüzes H 73 B6
Rábahidvég H 74 A1
Rabanales E 87 C4
Rábapatona H 64 C3
Rabapordány H 74 A2
Rabastens F 77 C4
Rabastens-de-Bigorre
F 76 C3
Rabat = Victoria M 107 C5
Rabat M 107 C5
Rabča SK 65 A5
Rabe SRB 75 B5
Rabi CZ 63 A4
Rabino PL 46 B1
Rabka PL 65 A5
Rabrovo SRB 85 B6
Rača
Srbija SRB 85 B6
Srbija SRB 85 C6
Răcale I 107 B5
Răcalmás H 75 A3
Racalmuto I 108 B2
Racconigi I 80 B1
Rače SLO 73 B5
Rachecourt-sur-Marne
F 59 B6
Raciąż PL 47 C6
Racibórz PL 54 C3
Račinovci HR 84 B3
Ráckeve H 75 A3
Racławice PL 55 C5
Racławice Śląskie
PL 54 C2
Racot PL 54 A1
Råda
Skaraborg S 35 D5
Värmland S 34 B5
Radalj SRB 85 B4
Rădăuţi RO 11 C8
Radda in Chianti I 81 C5
Raddusa I 109 B3
Radeberg D 53 B3
Radebeul D 52 B3
Radeburg D 53 B3
Radeče SLO 73 B5
Radekhiv UA 11 A8
Radenci SLO 73 B6
Radenthein A 72 B3
Radevormwald D 50 B3
Radicófani I 81 D5
Radicóndoli I 81 C5
Radišići BIH 84 C2
Radizel SLO 73 B5
Radków PL 54 C1
Radlje ob Dravi SLO 73 B5
Radłów PL 55 C5
Radmer an der Stube
A 73 A4
Radnejaur S 115 B15
Radnice CZ 63 A4
Radohova BIH 84 B2
Radojevo SRB 75 C5
Radolfzell D 61 C4
Radom PL 55 B6
Radomice PL 47 B5
Radomin PL 47 B5
Radomsko PL 55 B4
Radomyshl UA 11 A10
Radomyśl Wielki PL 55 C6
Radošina SK 64 B3
Radošovce SK 64 B3
Radostowo PL 47 B6
Radoszewice PL 54 B3
Radoszyce PL 55 B5
Radotín CZ 53 D4
Radoviš MK 116 A4
Radovljica SLO 73 B4
Radowo Wielkie PL 46 B2
Radstadt A 72 A3
Radstock GB 29 B5
Raduc HR 83 B4
Radviliškis LT 6 D7
Radzanów
Mazowieckie PL 47 C6
Mazowieckie PL 55 B5
Radziejów PL 47 C4
Radziejowice PL 55 A5
Radzovce SK 65 B5
Radzymin PL 55 A6
Radzyń Chełmiński
PL 47 B4
Raeren B 50 C2
Raesfeld D 50 B2
Raffadali I 108 B2
Rafina GR 117 D5
Rafsbotn N 113 B12
Ragachow BY 7 E11
Ragály H 65 B6
Rågeleje DK 41 C2
Raglan GB 29 B5
Ragnitz A 73 B5
Ragusa I 109 C3
Rahden D 43 C5
Råholt N 34 B3
Raiano I 103 A6
Raigada E 87 B3
Rain D 62 B1
Rainbach im Mühlkreis
A 63 B5
Rainham GB 31 C4
Rairiz de Veiga E 87 B3
Raisdorf D 44 A2
Raisio FIN 6 A7
Raiva
Aveiro P 87 C2
Coimbra P 92 A2
Raja-Jooseppi FIN 113 D17
Rajala FIN 113 E15
Rajcza PL 65 A5
Rajec SK 65 A4
Rájec-Jestřebí CZ 64 A2
Rajecké Teplice SK 65 A4
Rajevo Selo HR 84 B3
Rajhrad CZ 64 A2
Rajić HR 74 C2
Rajka H 64 C3
Rakek SLO 73 C4
Rakhiv UA 11 B8
Rakitna SLO 73 C4
Rakkestad N 35 C3
Rákóczifalva H 75 A5
Rakoniewice PL 53 A6
Rakoszyce PL 54 B1
Raková SK 65 A4
Rakovac BIH 84 A2
Rakovica HR 83 B4
Rakovník CZ 53 C3
Rakow D 45 A5
Raków PL 55 C6
Rakvere EST 7 B9
Ralja SRB 85 B5
Rälla S 41 C6
Ramacastañas E 94 B1
Ramacca I 109 B3
Ramales de la Victoria
E 89 A3
Ramberg N 112 D2
Rambervillers F 60 B2
Rambouillet F 58 B2
Rambucourt F 60 B1
Ramdala S 41 C5
Ramerupt F 59 B5
Ramingstein A 72 A3
Ramirás E 87 B2
Ramiswil CH 70 A2
Ramkvilla S 40 B4
Ramme DK 38 C1
Rämmen S 34 B6
Ramnäs S 36 C3
Ramnes N 35 C2
Râmnicu Vâlcea RO 11 D8
Ramonville-St Agne
F 77 C4
Rampside GB 26 A2
Ramsau D 62 C3
Ramsbeck D 51 B4
Ramsberg S 36 C2
Ramsele S 115 D13
Ramsey
Cambridgeshire GB 30 B3
Isle of Man GB 26 A1
Ramseycleuch GB 25 C4
Ramsgate GB 31 C5
Ramsjö S 115 E12
Ramstein-Meisenbach
D 60 A3
Ramsund N 112 D5
Ramundberget S 114 E9
Ramvik S 115 E14
Ranalt A 71 A6
Rånäs S 36 C5
Rånäsfoss N 34 B3
Rance B 49 C5
Ránchio I 82 C1
Randaberg N 33 D2
Randalstown GB 19 B5
Randan F 68 B3
Randazzo I 109 B3
Rånddalen S 115 E10
Randegg A 63 B5
Randers DK 38 C3
Randijaur S 112 F8
Randín E 87 C3
Randsverk N 114 F6
Rånes F 57 B5
Rångedala S 40 B3
Ranis D 52 C1
Rankweil A 71 A4
Rånnaväg S 40 B3
Ränneslöv S 40 C3
Rannoch Station GB 24 B3
Ranovac SRB 85 B6
Ransäter S 34 C5
Ransbach-Baumbach
D 50 C3
Ransta S 36 C3
Ranttila FIN 113 C14
Ranua FIN 3 D27
Ranum DK 38 C2
Ranvalhal P 92 B1
Raon-l'Étape F 60 B2
Ráossi I 71 C6
Rapallo I 80 B3
Rapla EST 6 B8
Rapness GB 23 B6
Rapolano Terme I 81 C5
Rapolla I 104 C1
Raposa P 92 B2
Rapperswil CH 70 A3
Raša HR 82 A3
Rasal E 90 A2
Rascafría E 94 B3
Rasdorf D 51 C5
Raseiniai LT 6 D7
Rašica SLO 73 C4
Rasines E 89 A3
Raška SRB 85 C5
Rasquera E 90 B3
Rássina I 81 C5
Rastatt D 61 B4
Rastede D 43 B5
Rastenberg D 52 B1
Rastošnica BIH 84 B3
Rastovac MNE 84 D3
Rasueros E 94 A1
Rasy PL 55 B4
Raszków PL 54 B2
Rataje SRB 85 C6
Rätan S 115 E11
Rateče SLO 72 B3
Ratekau D 44 B2
Ratež SLO 73 C5
Rathangan IRL 21 A5
Rathcoole IRL 21 A5
Rathcormack IRL 20 B3
Rathdrum IRL 21 B5
Rathebur D 45 B5
Rathenow D 44 C4
Rathfriland GB 19 B5
Rathkeale IRL 20 B3
Rathmelton IRL 19 A4
Rathmolyon IRL 21 A5
Rathmore IRL 20 B2
Rathmullan IRL 19 A4
Rathnew IRL 21 B5
Rathvilly IRL 21 B5
Ratibořské Hory CZ 63 A5
Ratingen D 50 B2
Ratková SK 65 B6
Ratkovo SRB 75 C4
Ratne UA 6 F8
Ratoath IRL 21 A5
Rattelsdorf D 51 C6
Ratten A 73 A5
Rattosjärvi FIN 113 F13
Rattray GB 25 B4
Rättvik S 36 B2
Ratvika N 114 D7
Ratzeburg D 44 B2
Rätzlingen D 44 C3
Raucourt-et-Flaba F 59 A5
Raudeberg N 114 F2
Raufarhöfn IS 111 A10
Raufoss N 34 B2
Rauhala FIN 113 E13
Rauland N 33 C5
Raulhac F 77 B5
Raulia N 115 B11
Rauma FIN 3 F24
Raundal N 32 B3
Raunds GB 30 B3
Rauris A 72 A3
Rautas S 112 E8
Rautavaara FIN 3 E28
Rauville-la-Bigot F 57 A4
Rauzan F 76 B2
Ravanusa I 108 B2
Rava-Rus'ka UA 11 A7
Ravča HR 84 C2
Ravels B 49 B5
Rävemåla S 40 C5
Ravenglass GB 26 A2
Ravenna I 82 B1
Ravensburg D 61 C5
Rävlanda S 40 B2
Ravna Gora HR 73 C4
Ravne na Koroškem
SLO 73 B4
Ravnište SRB 85 C6
Ravnje SRB 85 B4
Ravno BIH 84 D2
Ravno Selo SRB 75 C4
Rawa Mazowiecka PL 55 B5
Rawicz PL 54 B1
Rawtenstall GB 26 B3
Rayleigh GB 31 C4
Ražana SRB 85 B4
Ražanac HR 83 B4
Razboj BIH 84 A2
Razbojna SRB 85 C6
Razes F 67 B6
Razgrad BG 11 E9
Razkrižie SLO 73 B6
Razo E 86 A2
Reading GB 31 C3
Réalmont F 77 C5
Rebais F 59 B4
Reboly RUS 3 E29
Rebordelo P 87 C3
Recanati I 82 C2
Recas
E 94 B3
RO 10 D6
Recco I 80 B3
Recess IRL 18 C2
Recey-sur-Ource F 59 C5
Recezinhos P 87 C2
Rechnitz A 73 A6
Rechytsa BY 7 E11
Recke D 43 C4
Recklinghausen D 50 B3
Recoaro Terme I 71 C6
Recogne B 59 A6
Recoules-Prévinquières
F 78 B1
Recsk H 65 C6
Recz PL 46 B1
Reda PL 47 A4
Redalen N 34 B2
Redange L 60 A1
Redcar GB 27 A4
Redditch GB 29 A6
Redefin D 44 B3
Redhill GB 31 C3
Redics H 74 B1
Redkino RUS 7 C14
Redland GB 23 B5
Redlin D 44 B4
Redon F 57 C3
Redondela E 87 B2
Redondo P 92 C3
Red Point GB 22 D3
Redruth GB 28 C2
Redzikowo PL 46 A3
Reepham GB 30 B5
Rees D 50 B2
Reeth GB 27 A4
Reetz D 44 B3
Reftele S 40 B3
Regalbuto I 109 B3
Regen D 62 B4
Regensburg D 62 A3
Regenstauf D 62 A3
Reggello I 81 C5
Réggio di Calábria I 109 A4
Reggiolo I 81 B4
Réggio nell'Emília I 81 B4
Reghin RO 11 C8
Régil E 89 A4
Regna S 37 D2
Regnéville F 57 A4
Regny F 69 C4
Rego da Leirosa P 92 A2
Regöly H 74 B3
Regueiro E 86 B2
Reguengo
Portalegre P 92 B3
Santarém P 92 B2
Reguengos de Monsaraz
P 92 C3
Rehau D 52 C2
Rehburg D 43 C6
Rehden D 43 C5
Rehna D 44 B3
Reichelsheim D 61 A4
Reichelshofen D 61 A6
Reichenau A 64 C1
Reichenbach
Sachsen D 52 C2
Sachsen D 53 B4
Reichenfels A 73 A4
Reichensachsen D 51 B6
Reichertshofen D 62 B2
Reichshoffen F 60 B3
Reiden CH 70 A2
Reigada
E 86 A4
P 87 D4
Reigate GB 31 C3
Reillanne F 79 C4
Reillo E 95 C5
Reims F 59 A5
Reinach CH 70 A3
Reinbek D 44 B2
Reinberg D 45 A5
Reine N 112 E2
Reinfeld D 44 B2
Reinheim D 61 A4
Reinli N 32 B6
Reinosa E 88 A2
Reinstorf D 44 B3
Reinsvoll N 34 B2
Reisach A 72 B3
Reiss GB 23 C5
Reitan N 114 E8
Reit im Winkl D 62 C3
Rejmyre S 37 D2
Rekavice BIH 84 B2
Rekovac SRB 85 C6
Relleu E 96 C2
Rém H 75 B4
Remagen D 50 C3
Rémalard F 58 B1
Rembercourt-aux-Pots
F 59 B6
Remedios P 92 B1
Remels D 43 B4
Remetea Mare RO 75 C6
Remich L 60 A2
Rémilly F 60 A2
Remiremont F 60 C2
Remolinos E 90 B1
Remoulins F 78 C3
Remscheid D 50 B3
Rémuzat F 79 B4
Rena N 34 A3
Renaison F 68 B3
Renazé F 57 C4
Renchen D 61 B4
Rencurel F 79 A4
Rende I 106 B3
Rendina GR 116 C3
Rendsburg D 43 A6
Renedo E 88 C2
Renens CH 69 B6
Renfrew GB 24 C3
Rengsjö S 36 A3
Reni UA 11 D10
Rennebu N 114 E6
Rennerod D 50 C4
Rennertshofen D 62 B2
Rennes F 57 B4
Rennes-les-Bains F 77 D5
Rennweg A 72 A3
Rens DK 39 E2
Rensjön S 112 D8
Renteria E 76 C1
Rentjärn S 115 B15
Répcelak H 74 A2
Repojoki FIN 113 D14
Repvåg N 113 B14
Requena E 96 B1
Réquista F 77 B5
Rerik D 44 A3
Resana I 72 C1
Resarö S 37 C5
Reschen = Résia I 71 B5
Resen MK 116 A3
Resende P 87 C3
Résia = Reschen I 71 B5
Reşiţa RO 10 D6
Resko PL 46 B1
Resnik SRB 85 B5
Ressons-sur-Matz F 58 A3
Restábal E 100 C2
Resuttano I 109 B3
Retamal E 93 C4
Retford GB 27 B5
Rethel F 59 A5
Rethem D 43 C6
Rethimno GR 117 G6
Retie B 49 B6
Retiers F 57 C4
Retortillo E 87 D4
Retortillo de Soria E 89 C3
Retournac F 68 C4
Rétság H 65 C5
Rettenegg A 73 A5
Retuerta del Bullaque
E 94 C2
Retz A 64 B1
Retzbach D 61 A5
Reuden D 52 A2
Reuilly F 68 A2
Reus E 91 B4
Reusel NL 49 B6
Reuterstadt Stavenhagen
D 45 B4
Reuth D 62 A3
Reutlingen D 61 B5
Reutte A 71 A5
Reuver NL 50 B2
Revel F 77 C5
Revello I 80 B1
Revenga E 94 B2
Revest-du-Bion F 79 B4
Révfülöp H 74 B2
Revigny-sur-Ornain F 59 B5
Revin F 59 A5
Řevnice CZ 63 A5
Řevničov CZ 53 C3
Revo I 71 B6
Revsnes N 32 A4
Revúca SK 65 B6
Rewa PL 47 A4
Rewal PL 45 A7
Rexbo S 36 B2
Reyðarfjörður IS 111 B11
Reyero E 88 B1
Reykhólar IS 111 B3
Reykholt
Árnessýsla IS 111 C5
Borgarfjarðarsýsla
IS 111 C4
Reykjahlið IS 111 B9
Reykjavík IS 111 C4
Rezé F 66 A3
Rēzekne LV 7 C9
Rezovo BG 11 F10
Rezzato I 71 C5
Rezzoáglio I 80 B3
Rhade D 43 B6
Rhaunen D 60 A3
Rhayader GB 29 A4
Rheda-Wiedenbrück
D 50 B4
Rhede
Niedersachsen D 43 B4
Nordrhein-Westfalen
D 50 B2
Rheinau D 60 B3
Rheinbach D 50 C2
Rheinberg D 50 B2
Rheine D 43 C4
Rheinfelden D 70 A2
Rheinsberg D 45 B4

Rhêmes-Notre-Dame
I 70 C2
Rhenen NL 49 B6
Rhens D 50 C3
Rheydt D 50 B2
Rhiconich GB 22 C4
Rhinow D 44 C4
Rhiw GB 26 C1
Rho I 70 C4
Rhoden D 51 B5
Rhodes GR 119 F3
Rhondda GB 29 B4
Rhosllanerchrugog
GB 26 B2
Rhosneigr GB 26 B1
Rhossili GB 28 B3
Rhubodach GB 24 C2
Rhuddlan GB 26 B2
Rhyl GB 26 B2
Rhynie GB 23 D6
Riala S 37 C5
Riallé F 66 A3
Riaño E 88 B1
Riano I 102 A5
Rians F 79 C4
Rianxo E 86 B2
Riaza E 89 C3
Riba E 89 A3
Ribadavia E 87 B2
Ribadeo E 86 A3
Riba de Saelices E 95 B4
Ribadesella E 88 A1
Ribaflecha E 89 B4
Ribaforada E 89 C5
Ribare SRB 85 B6
Ribariće SRB 85 D5
Riba-roja d'Ebre E 90 B3
Riba-Roja de Turia E 96 B2
Ribe DK 39 D1
Ribeauvillé F 60 B3
Ribécourt-Dreslincourt
F 59 A3
Ribeira da Pena P 87 C3
Ribeira de Piquín E 86 A3
Ribemont F 59 A4
Ribera I 108 B2
Ribérac F 67 C5
Ribera de Cardós E 91 A4
Ribera del Fresno E 93 C4
Ribesalbes E 96 A2
Ribes de Freser E 91 A5
Ribiers F 79 B4
Ribnica
BIH 84 B3
SLO 73 C4
SRB 85 C5
Ribnica na Potorju
SLO 73 B5
Ribnik HR 73 C5
Ribnița MD 11 C10
Ribnitz-Damgarten D 44 A4
Ribolla I 81 D5
Říčany CZ 64 A2
Říčany CZ 53 D4
Riccia I 103 B7
Riccione I 82 B1
Ricco Del Golfo I 81 B3
Richebourg F 59 B6
Richelieu F 67 A5
Richisau CH 70 A3
Richmond
Greater London GB 31 C3
North Yorkshire GB 27 A4
Richtenberg D 45 A4
Richterswil CH 70 A3
Rickling D 44 A2
Rickmansworth GB 31 C3
Ricla E 89 C5
Riddarhyttan S 36 C2
Ridderkerk NL 49 B5
Riddes CH 70 B2
Ridjica SRB 75 C4
Riec-sur-Bélon F 56 C2
Ried A 63 B4
Riedenburg D 62 B2
Ried im Oberinntal A 71 A5
Riedlingen D 61 B5
Riedstadt D 61 A4
Riegersburg A 73 B5
Riego de la Vega E 88 B1
Riego del Camino E 88 C1
Riello E 88 B1
Riemst B 49 C6
Rienne B 49 D5
Riénsena E 88 A2
Riesa D 52 B3
Riese Pio X I 72 C1
Riesi I 109 B3
Riestedt D 52 B1
Rietberg D 51 B4
Rieti I 102 A5
Rietschen D 53 B4
Rieumes F 77 C4
Rieupeyroux F 77 B5
Rieux-Volvestre F 77 C4
Riez F 79 C5
Riga LV 6 C8
Riggisberg CH 70 B2
Rignac F 77 B5
Rignano Gargánico
I 104 B1
Rigolato I 72 B2
Rigside GB 25 C4
Rigutino I 81 C5
Riihimäki FIN 3 F26
Rijeka HR 73 C4
Rijeka Crnojevića
MNE 105 A5
Rijen NL 49 B5
Rijkevorsel B 49 B5
Rijssen NL 50 A2
Rilić BIH 84 C2
Rilievo I 108 B1
Rillé F 67 A5
Rillo de Gallo E 95 B5
Rimavská Baňa SK 65 B5
Rimavská Seč SK 65 B6
Rimavská Sobota SK 65 B6
Rimbo S 36 C5
Rimforsa S 37 D2
Rímini I 82 B1
Rîmnicu Sărat RO 11 D9
Rimogne F 59 A5
Rimpar D 61 A5
Rimske Toplice SLO 73 B5
Rincón de la Victoria
E 100 C1
Rincón de Soto E 89 B5
Rindal N 114 D6
Rinde N 32 A3
Ringarum S 37 D3
Ringaskiddy IRL 20 C3
Ringe DK 39 D3
Ringebu N 34 A2
Ringkøbing DK 39 C1
Ringsaker N 34 B2
Ringsted DK 39 D4
Ringwood GB 29 C6
Rinkaby S 41 D4
Rinkabyholm S 40 C6
Rinlo E 86 A3
Rinn A 71 A6
Rinteln D 51 A5
Río E 86 B3
Riobo E 86 B2
Riodeva E 96 A1
Rio do Coures P 92 B2
Rio Douro P 87 C3
Riofrio E 94 B2
Rio Frio P 92 C2
Riofrio de Aliste E 87 C4
Rio frio de Riaza E 95 A3
Riogordo E 100 C1
Rioja E 101 C3
Riola I 81 B5
Riola Sardo I 110 C1
Riolobos E 93 B4
Riom F 68 C3
Riomaggiore I 81 B3
Rio Maior P 92 B2
Rio Marina I 81 D4
Riom-ès-Montagnes
F 68 C2
Rion-des-Landes F 76 C2
Rionegro del Puente
E 87 B4
Rionero in Vúlture I 104 C1
Riopar E 101 A3
Riós E 87 C3
Rioseco E 88 A1
Rioseco de Tapia E 88 B1
Rio Tinto P 87 C2
Riotord F 69 C4
Riotorto E 86 A3
Rioz F 69 A6
Ripač BIH 83 B4
Ripacándida I 104 C1
Ripanj SRB 85 B5
Ripatransone I 82 D2
Ripley GB 27 B4
Ripoll E 91 A5
Ripon GB 27 A4
Riposto I 109 B4
Ripsa S 37 D3
Risan MNE 105 A4
Risbäck S 115 C12
Risca GB 29 B4
Rischenau D 51 B5
Riscle F 76 C2
Risebo S 40 A6
Risnes N 32 A2
Rišňovce SK 64 B3
Risør N 33 D6
Risøyhamn N 112 D4
Rissna S 115 D12
Ritsem S 112 E6
Ritterhude D 43 B5
Riutula FIN 113 D15
Riva del Garda I 71 C5
Riva Ligure I 80 C1
Rivanazzano I 80 B3
Rivarolo Canavese I 70 C2
Rivarolo Mantovano I 81 A4
Rive-de-Gier F 69 C4
Rivedoux-Plage F 66 B3
Rivello I 106 A2
Rivergaro I 80 B3
Rives F 69 C5
Rivesaltes F 78 D1
Rivignano I 72 C3
Rivne UA 11 A9
Rivoli I 80 A1
Rivolta d'Adda I 71 C4
Rixheim F 60 C3
Rixo S 35 D3
Riza GR 116 B5
Rizokarpaso CY 120 A3
Rjukan N 32 C5
Rø DK 41 D4
Rö S 37 C5
Roa
E 88 C3
N 34 B2
Roade GB 30 B3
Roager DK 39 D1
Roaldkvam N 33 C3
Roanne F 68 B4
Robakowo PL 47 B4
Róbbio I 70 C3
Röbel D 45 B4
Roberton GB 25 C5
Robertville B 50 C2
Robin Hood's Bay GB 27 A5
Robleda E 93 A4
Robledillo de Trujillo
E 93 B5
Robledo
Albacete E 101 A3
Orense E 86 B4
Robledo de Chavela
E 94 B2
Robledo del Buey E 94 C2
Robledo del Mazo E 94 C2
Robledollano E 93 B5
Robles de la Valcueva
E 88 B1
Robliza de Cojos E 87 D5
Robres E 90 B2
Robres del Castillo E 89 B4
Rocafort de Queralt E 91 B4
Rocamadour F 77 B4
Roccabernarda I 107 B3
Roccabianca I 81 A4
Roccadáspide I 103 C8
Rocca di Mezzo I 103 A6
Rocca di Papa I 102 B5
Roccagorga I 102 B6
Rocca Imperiale I 106 A3
Roccalbegna I 81 D5
Roccalumera I 109 B4
Roccamena I 108 B2
Roccamonfina I 103 B6
Roccanova I 106 A3
Roccapalumba I 108 B2
Roccapassa I 103 A6
Rocca Priora I 82 C2
Roccaraso I 103 B7
Rocca San Casciano
I 81 B5
Roccasecca I 103 B6
Rocca Sinibalda I 102 A5
Roccastrada I 81 C5
Roccatederighi I 81 C5
Roccella Iónica I 106 C3
Rocchetta Sant'António
I 103 B8
Rocester GB 27 C4
Rochdale GB 26 B3
Rochechouart F 67 C5
Rochefort
B 49 C6
F 66 C4
Rochefort-en-Terre F 56 C3
Rochefort-Montagne
F 68 C2
Rochefort-sur-Nenon
F 69 A5
Roche-lez-Beaupré F 69 A6
Rochemaure F 78 B3
Rocheservière F 66 B3
Rochester
Medway GB 31 C4
Northumberland GB 25 C5
Rochlitz D 52 B2
Rociana del Condado
E 99 B4
Rockenhausen D 60 A3
Rockhammar S 37 C2
Rockneby S 40 C6
Ročko Polje HR 73 C4
Ročov CZ 53 C3
Rocroi F 59 A5
Rodach D 51 C6
Roda de Bara E 91 B4
Roda de Ter E 91 B5
Rodalben D 60 A3
Rødberg N 32 B5
Rødby DK 44 A3
Rødbyhavn DK 44 A3
Rødding
Sonderjyllands Amt.
DK 39 D2
Viborg Amt. DK 38 C1
Rödeby S 41 C5
Rodeiro E 86 B3
Rødekro DK 39 D2
Roden NL 42 B3
Ródenas E 95 B5
Rodenkirchen D 43 B5
Rödental D 52 C1
Rödermark D 51 D4
Rodewisch D 52 C2
Rodez F 77 B5
Rodi Gargánico I 104 B1
Roding D 62 A3
Rödjebro S 36 B4
Rødkærsbro DK 39 C2
Rodolivas GR 116 B5
Rodoñá E 91 B4
Rødvig DK 41 D2
Roermond NL 50 B1
Roesbrugge B 48 C3
Roeschwoog F 61 B4
Roeselare B 49 C4
Roetgen D 50 C2
Roffiac F 78 A2
Röfors S 37 D1
Rofrano I 106 A2
Rogač HR 83 C5
Rogačica SRB 85 B4
Rogalinek PL 54 A1
Rogaška Slatina SLO 73 B5
Rogatec SLO 73 B5
Rogatica BIH 84 C4
Rogatyn UA 11 B8
Rogätz D 52 A1
Roggendorf D 44 B3
Roggiano Gravina I 106 B3
Roghadal GB 22 D2
Rogliano
F 102 A2
I 106 B3
Rognan N 112 E4
Rogne N 32 A6
Rognes F 79 C4
Rogny-les-7-Ecluses
F 59 C3
Rogowo PL 46 C3
Rogóz PL 47 A6
Rogoznica HR 83 C4
Rogoźnica PL 53 B6
Rogoźno PL 46 C2
Rohan F 56 B3
Röhlingen D 61 B6
Rohožník SK 64 B3
Rohr D 51 C6
Rohrbach A 63 B4
Rohrbach-lès-Bitche
F 60 A3
Rohrberg D 44 C3
Rohr im Gebirge A 63 C6
Röhrnbach D 63 B4
Roisel F 59 A4
Roja LV 6 C7
Rojales E 96 C2
Röjeråsen S 36 B1
Rojewo PL 47 C4
Rokiciny PL 55 B4
Rokietnica PL 46 C2
Rokiškis LT 7 D8
Rokitki PL 53 B5
Rokitno RUS 7 F13
Rokycany CZ 63 A4
Rolampont F 59 C6
Rold DK 38 C2
Røldal N 32 C3
Rolde NL 42 C3
Rollag N 32 B6
Rollán E 94 B1
Rolle CH 69 B6
Roma = Rome I 102 B5
Roma S 37 E5
Romagnano Sésia I 70 C3
Romagné F 57 B4
Romakloster S 37 E5
Roman RO 11 C9
Romana I 110 B1
Romanèche-Thorins
F 69 B4
Romano di Lombardia
I 71 C4
Romanshorn CH 71 A4
Romans-sur-Isère F 79 A4
Rombas F 60 A2
Rome = Roma I 102 B5
Romeán E 86 B3
Romenay F 69 B5
Romeral E 95 C3
Römerstein D 61 B5
Rometta I 109 A4
Romford GB 31 C4
Romhány H 65 C5
Römhild D 51 C6
Romilly-sur-Seine F 59 B4
Romny UA 11 A12
Romodan UA 11 B12
Romont CH 70 B1
Romorantin-Lanthenay
F 68 A1
Romrod D 51 C5
Romsey GB 31 D2
Rømskog N 35 C3
Rønbjerg DK 38 C1
Roncal E 76 D2
Ronce-les-Bains F 66 C3
Ronchamp F 60 C2
Ronchi dei Legionari
I 72 C3
Ronciglione I 102 A5
Ronco Canavese I 70 C2
Ronco Scrivia I 80 B2
Ronda E 99 C5
Rønde DK 39 C3
Rone S 37 E5
Ronehamn S 37 E5
Rong N 32 B1
Rönnäng S 38 B4
Rønne DK 41 D4
Ronneburg D 52 C2
Ronneby S 41 C5
Rönneshytta S 37 D2
Rönninge S 37 C4
Rönnöfors S 115 D10
Rönö S 37 D3
Ronov nad Doubravou
CZ 63 A6
Ronse B 49 C4
Roosendaal NL 49 B5
Roosky IRL 19 C4
Ropczyce PL 55 C6
Ropeid N 33 C3
Ropinsalmi FIN 113 D10
Ropuerelos del Páramo
E 88 B1
Roquebilière F 79 B6
Roquebrun F 78 C2
Roquecourbe F 77 C5
Roquefort F 76 B2
Roquemaure F 78 B3
Roquesteron F 79 C6
Roquetas de Mar E 101 C3
Roquetes E 90 C3
Roquevaire F 79 C4
Røra N 114 D8
Rörbäcksnäs S 34 A4
Rørbæk DK 38 C2
Rore BIH 83 B5
Röro S 38 B4
Røros N 114 E8
Rorschach CH 71 A4
Rørvig DK 39 D4
Rørvik N 114 C8
Rörvik S 40 B4
Rosà I 72 C1
Rosal de la Frontera
E 98 B3
Rosalina Mare I 72 C2
Rosa Marina I 104 C3
Rosans F 79 B4
Rosário P 98 B2
Rosarno I 106 C2
Rosbach D 50 C3
Rosche D 44 C2
Rościszewo PL 47 C5
Roscoff F 56 B2
Roscommon IRL 18 C3
Roscrea IRL 21 B4
Rosdorf D 51 B5
Rose I 106 B3
Rosegg A 73 B4
Rosehall GB 22 D4
Rosehearty GB 23 D6
Rosel GB 57 A3
Rosell E 90 C3
Roselló E 90 B3
Rosendal N 32 C3
Rosenfeld D 61 B4
Rosenfors S 40 B5
Rosenheim D 62 C3
Rosenow D 45 B5
Rosenthal D 51 B4
Rosersberg S 37 C4
Roses E 91 A6
Roseto degli Abruzzi
I 103 A7
Roseto Valfortore I 103 B8
Rosheim F 60 B3
Rosia I 81 C5
Rosice CZ 64 A2
Rosières-en-Santerre
F 58 A3
Rosignano Maríttimo
I 81 C4
Rosignano Solvay I 81 C4
Roşiori-de-Vede RO 11 D8
Roskhill GB 22 D2
Roskilde DK 39 D5
Roskovec AL 105 C5
Röslau D 52 C1
Roslavl RUS 7 E12
Roslev DK 38 C1
Rosmaninhal P 93 B3
Rosmult IRL 21 B4
Rosnowo PL 46 A2
Rosolini I 109 C3
Rosova MNE 85 C4
Rosoy F 59 B4
Rosporden F 56 C2
Rosquete P 92 B2
Rosrath D 50 C3
Rossa CH 71 B4
Rossano I 106 B3
Rossas
Aveiro P 87 D2
Braga P 87 C2
Rossdorf D 51 C6
Rossett GB 26 B3
Rosshaupten D 62 C1
Rossiglione I 80 B2
Rossignol B 60 A1
Rossla D 52 B1
Rosslare IRL 21 B5
Rosslare Harbour IRL 21 B5
Rosslau D 52 B2
Rosslea GB 19 B4
Rossleben D 52 B1
Rossön S 115 D13
Ross-on-Wye GB 29 B5
Rossoszyca PL 54 B3
Rosswein D 52 B3
Röstånga S 41 C3
Roštár SK 65 B6
Rostock D 44 A4
Rostrenen F 56 B2
Røsvik N 112 E4
Rosyth GB 25 B4
Röszke H 75 B5
Rot S 34 A6
Rota E 99 C4
Rota Greca I 106 B3
Rot am See D 61 A6
Rotberget N 34 B4
Rotella I 82 D2
Rotenburg
Hessen D 51 C5
Niedersachsen D 43 B6
Roth
Bayern D 62 A2
Rheinland-Pfalz D 50 C3
Rothbury GB 25 C6
Rothemühl D 45 B5
Röthenbach D 62 A2
Rothenburg D 53 B4
Rothenburg ob der
Tauber D 61 A6
Rothéneuf F 57 B4
Rothenklempenow D 45 B6
Rothenstein D 62 B2
Rotherham GB 27 B4
Rothes GB 23 D5
Rothesay GB 24 C2
Rothwell GB 30 B3
Rotnes N 34 B2
Rotonda I 106 B3
Rotondella I 106 A3
Rotova E 96 C2
Rott
Bayern D 62 C1
Bayern D 62 C3
Rottach-Egern D 62 C2
Röttenbach D 62 A2
Rottenbuch D 62 C1
Rottenburg
Baden-Württemberg
D 61 B4
Bayern D 62 B3
Rottenmann A 73 A4
Rotterdam NL 49 B5
Rotthalmünster D 63 B4
Rottingdean GB 31 D3
Röttingen D 61 A5
Rottleberode D 51 B6
Rottne S 40 B4
Rottneros S 34 C5
Rottofreno I 80 A3
Rottweil D 61 B4
Rötz D 62 A3
Roubaix F 49 C4
Roudnice nad Labem
CZ 53 C4
Roudouallec F 56 B2
Rouen F 58 A2
Rouffach F 60 C3
Rougé F 57 C4
Rougemont F 69 A6
Rougemont le-Château
F 60 C2
Rouillac F 67 C4
Rouillé F 67 B5
Roujan F 78 C2
Roulans F 69 A6
Roundwood IRL 21 A5
Rousínov CZ 64 A2
Roussac F 67 B6
Roussennac F 77 B5
Rousses F 78 B2
Roussillon F 69 C4
Rouvroy-sur-Audry F 59 A5
Rouy F 68 A3
Rovanieman
maalaiskunta FIN 113 F14
Rovaniemi FIN 113 F14
Rovato I 71 C4
Rovensko pod Troskami
CZ 53 C5
Roverbella I 71 C5
Rovereto I 71 C6
Rövershagen D 44 A4
Roverud N 34 B4
Rovigo I 81 A5
Rovinj HR 82 A2
Rovišce HR 74 C1
Rów PL 45 C6
Rowy PL 46 A3
Royal Leamington Spa
GB 30 B2
Royal Tunbridge Wells
GB 31 C4
Royan F 66 C3
Royat F 68 C3
Roybon F 69 C5
Roybridge GB 24 B3
Roye F 58 A3
Royère-de-Vassivière
F 68 C1
Røykenvik N 34 B2
Royos E 101 B3
Røyrvik N 115 C10
Royston GB 30 B3
Rozadas E 86 A4
Rožaj MNE 85 D5
Rozalén del Monte E 95 C4
Rózańsko PL 45 C6
Rožanstvo SRB 85 C4
Rozay-en-Brie F 59 B3
Roždalovice CZ 53 C5
Rozdilna UA 11 C11
Rozental PL 47 B5
Rozhyshche UA 11 A8
Rožmitál pod Třemšínem
CZ 63 A4
Rožňava SK 65 B6
Rožnov pod Radhoštěm
CZ 64 A4
Rozoy-sur-Serre F 59 A5
Rozprza PL 55 B4
Roztoky CZ 53 C4
Rozvadov CZ 62 A3
Rozzano I 71 C4
Rranxë AL 105 B5
Rrëshen AL 105 B5
Rrogozhine AL 105 B5
Ruanes E 93 B5
Rubbestadnesset N 32 C2
Rubi E 91 B5
Rubiá E 86 B4
Rubiacedo de Abajo
E 89 B3
Rubielos Bajos E 95 C4
Rubielos de Mora E 96 A2
Rubiera I 81 B4
Rubik AL 105 B5
Rucandio E 89 B3
Rud
Akershus N 34 B3
Buskerud N 34 B2
Ruda
PL 54 B3
S 40 B6
Rudabánya H 65 B6
Ruda Maleniecka PL 55 B5
Ruda Pilczycka PL 55 B5
Ruda Śl. PL 54 C3
Ruddervorde B 49 B4
Ruden A 73 B4
Rudersberg D 61 B5
Rudersdorf A 73 A6
Rüdersdorf D 45 C5
Ruderting D 63 B4
Rüdesheim D 50 D3
Rudkøbing DK 39 E3
Rudmanns A 63 B6
Rudna
CZ 53 C4
PL 53 B6
Rudnik
KOS 85 D5
SRB 85 B5
Rudniki
Opolskie PL 54 B3
Śląskie PL 55 C4
Rudno
Dolnośląskie PL 54 B1
Pomorskie PL 47 B4
Rudnya RUS 7 D11
Rudo BIH 85 C4
Rudolstadt D 52 C1
Rudowica PL 53 B5
Rudozem BG 116 A6
Rudskoga S 35 C6
Rudston GB 27 A5
Ruds Vedby DK 39 D4
Rudy PL 54 C3
Rue F 48 C2
Rueda E 88 C2
Rueda de Jalón E 90 B1
Ruelle-sur-Touvre F 67 C5
Ruerrero E 88 B3
Ruffano I 107 B5
Ruffec F 67 B5
Rufina I 81 C5
Rugby GB 30 B2
Rugeley GB 27 C4
Ruggstrop S 40 C6
Rugles F 58 B1
Rugozero RUS 3 D30
Rühen D 44 C2
Ruhla D 51 C6
Ruhland D 53 B3
Ruhle D 43 C4
Ruhpolding D 62 C3
Ruhstorf D 63 B4
Ruidera E 95 D4
Ruillé-sur-le-Loir F 58 C1
Ruinen NL 42 C3
Ruiselede B 49 B4
Rulles B 60 A1
Rülzheim D 61 A4
Rum H 74 A1
Ruma SRB 85 A4
Rumboci BIH 84 C2
Rumburk CZ 53 C4
Rumenka SRB 75 C4
Rumia PL 47 A4
Rumigny F 59 A5
Rumilly F 69 C5
Rumma S 37 D3
Rumney GB 29 B4
Rumont F 59 B6
Rumy PL 47 B6
Runa P 92 B1
Runcorn GB 26 B3
Rundmoen N 115 A11
Rungsted DK 41 D2
Runhällen S 36 B3
Runowo PL 47 A6
Runtuna S 37 D4
Ruokojärvi FIN 113 E13
Ruokolahti FIN 3 F28
Ruokto S 112 E8
Ruoms F 78 B3
Ruoti I 104 C1
Rupa HR 73 C4
Ruppichteroth D 50 C3
Rupt-sur-Moselle F 60 C2
Rus E 100 A2
Ruse BG 11 E9
Ruše SLO 73 B5
Rusele S 115 C15
Ruševo HR 74 C3
Rush IRL 21 A5
Rushden GB 30 B3
Rusiec PL 54 B3
Rusinowo
Zachodnio-Pomorskie
PL 46 B1
Zachodnio-Pomorskie
PL 46 B2
Ruskele S 115 C15
Ruski Krstur SRB 75 C4
Ruskington GB 27 B5
Rusovce SK 64 B3
Rüsselsheim D 51 D4
Russelv N 112 C9
Russi I 81 B6
Rust A 64 C2
Rustefjelbma N 113 B17
Rustrel F 79 C4
Ruszki PL 55 A5
Ruszów PL 53 B5
Rute E 100 B1
Rüthen D 51 B4
Rutherglen GB 24 C3
Ruthin GB 26 B2
Ruthven GB 23 D4
Ruthwell GB 25 D4
Rüti CH 70 A3
Rutigliano I 104 B3
Rutledal N 32 A2
Rutoši SRB 85 C4
Ruurlo NL 50 A2
Ruuvaoja FIN 113 E17
Ruvo del Monte I 104 C1
Ruvo di Púglia I 104 B2
Ruynes-en-Margeride
F 78 B2
Ružic HR 83 C5
Ružomberok SK 65 A5
Ruzsa H 75 B4
Ry DK 39 C2
Rybany SK 64 B4
Rybina PL 47 A5
Rybinsk RUS 7 B15
Rybnik PL 54 C3
Rychliki PL 47 B5
Rychlocice PL 54 B3
Rychnov nad Kněžnou
CZ 53 C6
Rychnowo PL 47 B6
Rychtal PL 54 B2
Rychwał PL 54 A3
Ryczywół PL 55 B6
Ryczywól PL 46 C2
Ryd S 40 C4
Rydaholm S 40 C4
Rydal S 40 B2
Rydbo S 37 C5
Rydboholm S 40 B2
Ryde GB 31 D2
Rydöbruk S 40 C3
Rydsgård S 41 D3
Rydsnäs S 40 B5
Rydultowy PL 54 C3
Rydzyna PL 54 B1
Rye GB 31 D4
Rygge N 35 C2
Ryjewo PL 47 B4
Rykene N 33 D5
Rylsk RUS 7 F13
Rymań PL 46 B1
Rýmařov CZ 64 A3
Rynarzewo PL 46 B3
Ryomgård DK 39 C3
Rypefjord N 113 B12
Rypin PL 47 B5
Rysjedalsvika N 32 A2
Ryssby S 40 C4
Rytel PL 46 B3
Rytro PL 65 A6
Rywociny PL 47 B6
Rzeczenica PL 46 B3
Rzeczniów PL 55 B6
Rzeczyca PL 55 B5
Rzęgnowo PL 47 B6
Rzejowice PL 55 B4
Rzemień PL 55 C6
Rzepin PL 45 C6
Rzesznikowo PL 46 B1
Rzeszów PL 10 A6
Rzgów PL 55 B4
Rzhev RUS 7 C13

S

Saal
Bayern D 51 C6
Bayern D 62 B2
Saalbach A 72 A2
Saalburg D 52 C1
Saales F 60 B3
Saalfeld D 52 C1
Saalfelden am Steinernen
Meer A 72 A2
Saanen CH 70 B2
Saarbrücken D 60 A2
Saarburg D 60 A2
Saarijärvi FIN 3 E26
Saarlouis D 60 A2
Saas-Fee CH 70 B2
Šabac SRB 85 B4
Sabadell E 91 B5
Sabáudia I 102 B6
Sabbioneta I 81 B4
Sabero E 88 B1
Sabiñánigo E 90 A2
Sabiote E 100 A2
Sables-d'Or-les-Pins
F 56 B3
Sablé-sur-Sarthe F 57 C5
Sabóia P 98 B2
Saborsko HR 83 A4
Sæbøvik N 32 C2
Sabres F 76 B2
Sabrosa P 87 C3
Sabugal P 93 A3
Sabuncu TR 118 C5
Sæby DK 38 B3
Săcălaz RO 75 C6
Sacecorbo E 95 B4
Saceda del Rio E 95 B4
Sacedón E 95 B4
Săcele RO 11 D8
Saceruela E 94 D2
Sachsenburg A 72 B3
Sachsenhagen D 43 C6
Sacile I 72 C2
Sacramenia E 88 C3
Sada E 86 A2
Sádaba E 90 A1
Saddell GB 24 C2
Sadernes E 91 A5
Sadki PL 46 B3
Sadkowice PL 55 B5
Sadlinki PL 47 B4
Sadów PL 53 A4
Sadská CZ 53 C4
Saelices E 95 C4
Saelices de Mayorga
E 88 B1
Saerbeck D 50 A3
Saeul L 60 A1
Safaalan TR 118 A3
Safara P 98 A3
Säffle S 35 C4
Saffron Walden GB 31 B4
Safonovo RUS 7 D12
Safranbolu TR 16 A6
Säfsnäs S 36 B1
Şag RO 75 C6
Sagard D 45 A5
S'Agaro E 91 B6
Sågmyra S 36 B2
Sagone F 102 A1
Sagres P 98 C2
Ságújfalu H 65 B5
Sagunt E 96 B2
Sagvåg N 32 C2
Ságvár H 74 B3
Sagy F 69 B5
Sahagún E 88 B1
Šahy SK 65 B4
Saignelégier CH 70 A1
Saignes F 68 C2
Saija FIN 113 E17
Saillagouse F 91 A5
Saillans F 79 B4
Sains Richaumont F 59 A4
St Abb's GB 25 C5
St Affrique F 78 C1
St Agnan F 68 B3
St Agnant F 66 C4
St Agnes GB 28 C2
St Agrève F 78 A3
St Aignan F 67 A6
St Aignan-sur-Roë F 57 C4
St Albans GB 31 C3
St Alban-sur-Limagnole
F 78 B2
St Amand-en-Puisaye
F 68 A3
St Amand-les-Eaux F 49 C4
St Amand-Longpré F 58 C2
St Amand-Montrond
F 68 B2
St Amans F 78 B2
St Amans-Soult F 77 C5
St Amant-Roche-Savine
F 68 C3
St Amarin F 60 C2
St Ambroix F 78 B3
St Amé F 60 B2
St Amour F 69 B5
St André-de-Corcy F 69 C4
St André-de-Cubzac
F 76 B2
St André-de-l'Eure F 58 B2
St André-de-
Roquepertuis F 78 B3
St André-de-Sangonis
F 78 C2
St Andre-de-Valborgne
F 78 B2
St André-les-Alpes F 79 C5
St Andrews GB 25 B5
St Angel F 68 C2
St Anthème F 68 C3
St Antoine F 102 A2
St Antoine-de-Ficalba
F 77 B3
St Antönien CH 71 B4
St Antonin-Noble-Val
F 77 B4
St Août F 68 B1
St Armant-Tallende F 68 C3
St Arnoult F 58 B2
St Asaph GB 26 B2
St Astier F 67 C5
St Athan GB 29 B4
St Auban F 79 C5
St Aubin
CH 70 B1
F 69 A5
GB 57 A3
St Aubin-d'Aubigné F 57 B4
St Aubin-du-Cormier
F 57 B4
St Aubin-sur-Aire F 60 B1
St Aubin-sur-Mer F 57 A5
St Aulaye F 67 C5
St Austell GB 28 C3
St Avit F 68 C2
St Avold F 60 A2
St Aygulf F 79 C5
St Bauzille-de-Putois
F 78 C2
St Béat F 77 D3
St Beauzély F 78 B1
St Bees GB 26 A2
St Benim-d'Azy F 68 B3
St Benoît-du-Sault F 67 B6
St Benoit-en-Woëvre
F 60 B1
St Berthevin F 57 B5
St Blaise-la-Roche F 60 B3
St Blazey GB 28 C3
St Blin F 59 B6
St Bonnet F 79 B5
St Bonnet Briance F 67 C6
St Bonnet-de-Joux F 69 B4
St Bonnet-le-Château
F 68 C4
St Bonnet-le-Froid F 69 C4
St Brévin-les-Pins F 66 A2
St Briac-sur-Mer F 57 B3
St Brice-en-Coglès F 57 B4
St Brieuc F 56 B3
St Bris-le-Vineux F 59 C4
St Broladre F 57 B4
St Calais F 58 C1
St Cannat F 79 C4
St Cast-le-Guildo F 57 B3
St Céré F 77 B4
St Cergue CH 69 B6
St Cergues F 69 B6
St Cernin F 77 A5
St Chamant F 68 C1
St Chamas F 79 C4
St Chamond F 69 C4
St Chély-d'Apcher F 78 B2
St Chély-d'Aubrac F 78 B1
St Chinian F 78 C1
St Christol F 79 B4
St Christol-lès-Alès F 78 B3
St Christoly-Médoc F 66 C4
St Christophe-du-
Ligneron F 66 B3
St Christophe-en-
Brionnais F 69 B4
St Ciers-sur-Gironde
F 67 C4
St Clair-sur-Epte F 58 A2
St Clar F 77 C3
St Claud F 67 C5
St Claude F 69 B5
St Clears GB 28 B3
St Columb Major GB 28 C3
St Come-d'Olt F 78 B1
St Cosme-en-Vairais
F 58 B1
St Cyprien
Dordogne F 77 B4
Pyrenées-Orientales
F 91 A6
St Cyr-sur-Loire F 67 A5
St Cyr-sur-Mer F 79 C4
St Cyr-sur-Methon F 69 B4
St David's GB 28 B2
St Denis F 58 B3
St Denis-d'Oléron F 66 B3
St Denis d'Orques F 57 B5
St Didier F 69 B4
St Didier-en-Velay F 69 C4
St Dié F 60 B2
St Dier-d'Auvergne F 68 C3
St Dizier F 59 B5
St Dizier-Leyrenne F 68 B1
St Dogmaels GB 28 A3
Ste Adresse F 57 A6
Ste Anne F 58 B1
Ste Anne-d'Auray F 56 C3
Ste Croix CH 69 B6
Ste Croix-Volvestre F 77 C4
Ste Engrâce F 76 C2
Ste Enimie F 78 B2
St Efflam F 56 B2
Ste Foy-de-Peyrolières
F 77 C4
Ste Foy-la-Grande F 76 B3
Ste Foy l'Argentiere
F 69 C4
Ste Gauburge-Ste
Colombe F 58 B1
Ste Gemme la Plaine
F 66 B3
Ste Geneviève F 58 A3
St Égrève F 69 C5
Ste Hélène F 76 B2
Ste Hélène-sur-Isère
F 69 C6
Ste Hermine F 66 B3
Ste Jalle F 79 B4
Ste Livrade-sur-Lot F 77 B3
St Eloy-les-Mines F 68 B2
Ste Marie-aux-Mines
F 60 B3
Ste Marie-du-Mont F 57 A4
Ste Maure-de-Touraine
F 67 A5
Ste Maxime F 79 C5
Ste Ménéhould F 59 A5
Ste Mère-Église F 57 A4
St Emiland F 69 B4
St Émilion F 76 B2
St Enoder GB 28 C3
Sainteny F 57 A4
Ste Ode B 49 C6
Saintes F 67 C4
Ste Savine F 59 B5
Ste Sévère-sur-Indre
F 68 B2
Ste Sigolène F 69 C4
St Esteben F 76 C1
St Estèphe F 66 C4
Ste Suzanne F 57 B5
St Étienne F 69 C4
St Etienne-de-Baigorry
F 76 C1
St Étienne-de-Cuines
F 69 C6
St Etienne-de-Fursac
F 67 B6
St Etienne-de-Montluc
F 66 A3
St Etienne-de-St Geoirs
F 69 C5
St Étienne-de-Tinée F 79 B5
St Étienne-du-Bois F 69 B5
St Étienne-du-Rouvray
F 58 A2
St Etienne-les-Orgues
F 79 B4
Ste Tulle F 79 C4
St Fargeau F 59 C4
St Félicien F 78 A3
St Felix-de-Sorgues F 78 C1
St Félix-Lauragais F 77 C4
Saintfield GB 19 B6
St Fillans GB 24 B3
St Firmin F 79 B5
St Florent F 102 A2
St Florentin F 59 C4
St Florent-le-Vieil F 66 A3
St Florent-sur-Cher F 68 B2
St Flour F 78 A2
St Flovier F 67 B6
St Fort-sur-le-Né F 67 C4
St Fulgent F 66 B3
St Galmier F 69 C4
St Gaudens F 77 C3
St Gaultier F 67 B6
St Gély-du-Fesc F 78 C2
St Genest-Malifaux F 69 C4
St Gengoux-le-National
F 69 B4
St Geniez F 79 B5
St Geniez-d'Olt F 78 B1
St Genis-de-Saintonge
F 67 C4
St Genis-Pouilly F 69 B6
St Genix-sur-Guiers
F 69 C5
St Georges Buttavent
F 57 B5
St Georges-d'Aurac F 68 C3
St Georges-de-Commiers
F 79 A4
St Georges-de-Didonne
F 66 C4
St Georges-de-Luzençon
F 78 B1
St Georges-de Mons
F 68 C2
St Georges-de-Reneins
F 69 B4
St Georges d'Oléron
F 66 C3
St Georges-en-Couzan
F 68 C3
St Georges-lès-
Baillargeaux F 67 B5
St Georges-sur-Loire
F 66 A4
St Georges-sur-Meuse
B 49 C6
St Geours-de-Maremne
F 76 C1
St Gérand-de-Vaux F 68 B3
St Gérand-le-Puy F 68 B3
St Germain F 60 C2
St Germain-Chassenay
F 68 B3
St Germain-de-Calberte
F 78 B2
St Germain-de-Confolens
F 67 B5
St Germain-de-Joux
F 69 B5
St Germain-des-Fossés
F 68 B3
St Germain-du-Bois F 69 B5
St Germain-du-Plain
F 69 B4
St Germain-du Puy F 68 A2
St Germain-en-Laye F 58 B3
St Germain-Laval F 68 C4
St Germain-Lembron
F 68 C3
St Germain-les-Belles
F 67 C6
St Germain-Lespinasse
F 68 B3
St Germain-l'Herm F 68 C3
St Gervais-d'Auvergne
F 68 B2
St Gervais-les-Bains
F 70 C1
St Gervais-sur-Mare
F 78 C2
St Gildas-de-Rhuys F 66 A2
St Gildas-des-Bois F 66 A2
St Gilles
Gard F 78 C3
Ille-et-Vilaine F 57 B4
St Gilles-Croix-de-Vie
F 66 B3
St Gingolph F 70 B1
St Girons
Ariège F 77 D4
Landes F 76 C1
St Girons-Plage F 76 C1
St Gobain F 59 A4
St Gorgon-Main F 69 A6
St Guénolé F 56 C1
St Harmon GB 29 A4
St Helens GB 26 B3
St Helier GB 57 A3
St Herblain F 66 A3
St Hilaire
Allier F 68 B3
Aude F 77 C5
St Hilaire-de-Riez F 66 B3
St Hilaire-des-Loges
F 67 B4
St Hilaire-de-Villefranche
F 67 C4
St Hilaire-du-Harcouët
F 57 B4
St Hilaire-du-Rosier F 79 A4
St Hippolyte
Aveyron F 77 B5
Doubs F 70 A1
St Hippolyte-du-Fort
F 78 C2
St Honoré-les-Bains
F 68 B3
St Hubert B 49 C6
St Imier CH 70 A2
St Issey GB 28 C3
St Ives
Cambridgeshire GB 30 B3
Cornwall GB 28 C2
St Izaire F 78 C1
St Jacques-de-la-Lande
F 57 B4
St Jacut-de-la-Mer F 57 B3
St James F 57 B4
St Jaume d'Enveja E 90 C3
St Jean-Brévelay F 56 C3
St Jean-d'Angély F 67 C4
St Jean-de-Belleville
F 69 C6
St Jean-de-Bournay
F 69 C5
St Jean-de-Braye F 58 C2
St Jean-de-Côle F 67 C5
St Jean-de-Daye F 57 A4
St Jean de Losne F 69 A5
St Jean-de-Luz F 76 C1
St Jean-de-Maurienne
F 69 C6
St Jean-de-Monts F 66 B2
St Jean-d'Illac F 76 B2
St Jean-du-Bruel F 78 B2
St Jean-du-Gard F 78 B2
St Jean-en-Royans F 79 A4
St Jean-la-Riviere F 79 C6
St Jean-Pied-de-Port
F 76 C1
St Jean-Poutge F 77 C3
St Jeoire F 69 B6
St Joachim F 66 A2
St Johnstown IRL 19 B4
St Jorioz F 69 C6
St Joris Winge B 49 C5
St Jouin-de-Marnes F 67 B4
St Juéry F 77 C5
St Julien F 69 B5
St Julien-Chapteuil F 78 A3
St Julien-de-Vouvantes
F 57 C4
St Julien-du-Sault F 59 B4
St Julien-du-Verdon
F 79 C5
St Julien-en-Born F 76 B1
St Julien-en-Genevois
F 69 B6
St Julien-l'Ars F 67 B5
St Julien la-Vêtre F 68 C3
St Julien-Mont-Denis
F 69 C6
St Julien-sur-Reyssouze
F 69 B5
St Junien F 67 C5
St Just
F 78 B3
GB 28 C2
St Just-en-Chaussée
F 58 A3
St Just-en-Chevalet F 68 C3
St Justin F 76 C2

170 St J–San

St Just-St Rambert F 69 C4
St Keverne GB 28 C2
St Lary-Soulan F 77 D3
St Laurent-d'Aigouze F 78 C3
St Laurent-de-Chamousset F 69 C4
St Laurent-de-Condel F 57 A5
St Laurent-de-la-Cabrerisse F 78 C1
St Laurent-de-la-Salanque F 78 D1
St Laurent-des-Autels F 66 A3
St Laurent-du-Pont F 69 C5
St Laurent-en-Caux F 58 A1
St Laurent-en-Grandvaux F 69 B5
St Laurent-Médoc F 76 A2
St Laurent-sur-Gorre F 67 C5
St Laurent-sur-Mer F 57 A5
St Laurent-sur-Sèvre F 66 B4
St Leger B 60 A1
St Léger-de-Vignes F 68 B3
St Léger-sous-Beuvray F 68 B4
St Léger-sur-Dheune F 69 B4
St Léonard-de-Noblat F 67 C6
St Leonards GB 31 D4
St Lô F 57 A4
St Lon-les-Mines F 76 C1
St Louis F 60 C3
St Loup F 68 B3
St Loup-de-la-Salle F 69 B4
St Loup-sur-Semouse F 60 C2
St Lunaire F 57 B3
St Lupicin F 69 B5
St Lyphard F 66 A2
St Lys F 77 C4
St Macaire F 76 B2
St Maclou F 58 A1
St Maixent-l'École F 67 B4
St Malo F 57 B3
St Mamet-la-Salvetat F 77 B5
St Mandrier-sur-Mer F 79 C4
St Marcel
Drôme F 78 B3
Saône-et-Loire F 69 B4
St Marcellin F 69 C5
St Marcellin sur Loire F 68 C4
St Marcet F 77 C3
St Mards-en-Othe F 59 B4
St Margaret's-at-Cliffe GB 31 C5
St Margaret's Hope GB 23 C6
St Mars-la-Jaille F 66 A3
St Martin-d'Ablois F 59 B4
St Martin-d'Auxigny F 68 A2
St Martin-de-Belleville F 69 C6
St Martin-de-Bossenay F 59 B4
St Martin-de-Crau F 78 C3
St Martin-de-Londres F 78 C2
St Martin-d'Entraunes F 79 B5
St Martin-de-Queyrières F 79 B5
St Martin-de-Ré F 66 B3
St Martin des Besaces F 57 A5
St Martin-d'Estreaux F 68 B3
St Martin-de-Valamas F 78 B3
St Martin-d'Hères F 69 C5
St Martin-du-Frêne F 69 B5
St Martin-en-Bresse F 69 B5
St Martin-en-Haut F 69 C4
St Martin-la-Méanne F 68 C1
St Martin-sur-Ouanne F 59 C4
St Martin-Valmeroux F 77 A5
St Martin-Vésubie F 79 B6
St Martory F 77 C3
St Mary's GB 23 C6
St Mathieu F 67 C5
St Mathieu-de-Tréviers F 78 C2
St Maurice CH 70 B1
St Maurice-Navacelles F 78 C2
St Maurice-sur-Moselle F 60 C2
St Mawes GB 28 C2
St Maximin-la-Ste Baume F 79 C4
St Méard-de-Gurçon F 76 B3
St Médard-de-Guizières F 76 A2
St Médard-en-Jalles F 76 B2
St Méen-le-Grand F 57 B3
St Menges F 59 A5
St Merløse DK 39 D4
St Město CZ 54 C1
St M'Hervé F 57 B4
St Michel
Aisne F 59 A5
Gers F 77 C3
St Michel-Chef-Chef F 66 A2
St Michel-de-Castelnau F 76 B2
St Michel-de-Maurienne F 69 C6
St Michel-en-Grève F 56 B2
St Michel-en-l'Herm F 66 B3
St Michel-Mont-Mercure F 66 B4
St Mihiel F 60 B1
St Monance GB 25 B5
St Montant F 78 B3
St Moritz CH 71 B4
St Nazaire F 66 A2
St Nazaire-en-Royans F 79 A4
St Nazaire-le-Désert F 79 B4
St Nectaire F 68 C2
St Neots GB 30 B3
St Nicolas-de-Port F 60 B2
St Nicolas-de-Redon F 57 C3
St Nicolas-du-Pélem F 56 B2
St Niklaas B 49 B5
St Omer F 48 C3
St Pair-sur-Mer F 57 B4
St Palais F 76 C1
St Palais-sur-Mer F 66 C3
St Pardoux-la-Rivière F 67 C5
St Paul-Cap-de-Joux F 77 C4
St Paul-de-Fenouillet F 77 D5
St Paul-de-Varax F 69 B5
St Paulien F 68 C3
St Paul-le-Jeune F 78 B3
St Paul-lès-Dax F 76 C1
St Paul-Trois-Châteaux F 78 B3
St Pé-de-Bigorre F 76 C2
St Pée-sur-Nivelle F 76 C1
St Péravy-la-Colombe F 58 C2
St Péray F 78 B3
St Père-en-Retz F 66 A2
St Peter Port GB 56 A3
St Petersburg = Sankt-Peterburg RUS 7 B11
St Philbert-de-Grand-Lieu F 66 A3
St Pierre F 78 C1
St Pierre-d'Albigny F 69 C6
St Pierre-d'Allevard F 69 C6
St Pierre-de-Chartreuse F 69 C5
St Pierre-de-Chignac F 77 A3
St Pierre-de-la-Fage F 78 C2
St Pierre-d'Entremont F 69 C5
St Pierre-d'Oléron F 66 C3
St Pierre-Eglise F 57 A4
St Pierre-en-Port F 58 A1
St Pierre-le-Moûtier F 68 B3
St Pierre Montlimart F 66 A3
St Pierre-Quiberon F 66 A1
St Pierre-sur-Dives F 57 A5
St Pierreville F 78 B3
St Pieters-Leeuw B 49 C5
St Plancard F 77 C3
St Poix F 57 C4
St Pol-de-Léon F 56 B2
St Polgues F 68 C3
St Pol-sur-Ternoise F 48 C3
St Pons-de-Thomières F 78 C1
St Porchaire F 66 C4
St Pourçain-sur-Sioule F 68 B3
St Priest F 69 C4
St Privat F 68 C2
St Quay-Portrieux F 56 B3
St Quentin F 59 A4
St Quentin-la-Poterie F 78 B3
St Quentin-les-Anges F 57 C5
St Rambert-d'Albon F 69 C4
St Rambert-en-Bugey F 69 C5
St Raphaël F 79 C5
St Rémy-de-Provence F 78 C3
St Rémy-du-Val F 57 B6
St Remy-en-Bouzemont F 59 B5
St Renan F 56 B1
St Révérien F 68 A3
St Riquier F 48 C2
St Romain-de-Colbosc F 58 A1
St Rome-de-Cernon F 78 B1
St Rome-de-Tarn F 78 B1
St Sadurní-d'Anoia E 91 B4
St Saëns F 58 A2
St Sampson GB 56 A3
St Samson-la-Poterie F 58 A2
St Saturnin-de-Lenne F 78 B2
St Saturnin-lès-Apt F 79 C4
St Sauflieu F 58 A3
St Saulge F 68 A3
St Sauveur
Finistère F 56 B2
Haute-Saône F 60 C2
St Sauveur-de-Montagut F 78 B3
St Sauveur-en-Puisaye F 59 C4
St Sauveur-en-Rue F 69 C4
St Sauveur-Lendelin F 57 A4
St Sauveur-le-Vicomte F 57 A4
St Sauveur-sur-Tinée F 79 B6
St Savin
Gironde F 76 A2
Vienne F 67 B5
St Savinien F 67 C4
St Savournin F 79 C4
St Seine-l'Abbaye F 69 A4
St Sernin-sur-Rance F 77 C5
St Sevan-sur-Mer F 57 B3
St Sever F 76 C2
St Sever-Calvados F 57 B4
St Sorlin-d'Arves F 69 C6
St Supplets F 58 B3
St Sulpice F 77 C4
St Sulpice-Laurière F 67 B6
St Sulpice-les-Feuilles F 67 B6
St Symphorien F 76 B2
St Symphorien-de-Lay F 69 C4
St Symphorien d'Ozon F 69 C4
St Symphoriensur-Coise F 69 C4
St Teath GB 28 C3
St Thégonnec F 56 B2
St Thiébault F 60 B1
St Trivier-de-Courtes F 69 B5
St Trivier sur-Moignans F 69 B4
St Trojan-les-Bains F 66 C3
St Tropez F 79 C5
St Truiden B 49 C6
St Vaast-la-Hougue F 57 A4
St Valérien F 59 B4
St Valery-en-Caux F 58 A1
St Valéry-sur-Somme F 48 C2
St Vallier
Drôme F 69 C4
Saône-et-Loire F 69 B4
St Vallier-de-Thiey F 79 C5
St Varent F 67 B4
St Vaury F 68 B1
St Venant F 48 C3
St Véran F 79 B5
St Vincent I 70 C2
St Vincent-de-Tyrosse F 76 C1
St Vit F 69 A5
St Vith B 50 C2
St Vivien-de-Médoc F 66 C3
St Yan F 68 B4
St Ybars F 77 C4
St Yorre F 68 B3
St Yrieix-la-Perche F 67 C6
Saissac F 77 C5
Saja E 88 A2
Šajan SRB 75 C5
Šajkaš SRB 75 C5
Sajókaza H 65 B6
Sajószentpéter H 65 B6
Sajóvámos H 65 B6
Şakarya TR 118 B5
Šakiai LT 6 D7
Sakskøbing DK 39 E4
Sakule SRB 75 C5
Sal'a SK 64 B3
Sala S 36 C3
Sala Baganza I 81 B4
Sala Consilina I 104 C1
Salakovac SRB 85 B6
Salamanca E 94 B1
Salamina GR 117 E5
Salandra I 104 C2
Salaparuta I 108 B1
Salar E 100 B1
Salardú E 90 A3
Salas E 86 A4
Salas de los Infantes E 89 B3
Salau F 77 D4
Salavaux CH 70 B2
Salbertrand I 79 A5
Salbohed S 36 C3
Salbris F 68 A2
Salbu N 32 A2
Salce E 86 B4
Salching D 62 B3
Salcombe GB 28 C4
Saldaña E 88 B2
Saldus LV 6 C7
Sale I 80 B2
Saleby S 35 D5
Salem D 61 C5
Salemi I 108 B1
Salen
Argyll & Bute GB 24 B2
Highland GB 24 B2
N 114 C8
Sälen S 34 A5
Salernes F 79 C5
Salerno I 103 C7
Salers F 68 C2
Salford GB 26 B3
Salgótarján H 65 B5
Salgueiro P 92 B3
Salhus N 32 B2
Sali HR 83 C4
Sálice Salentino I 105 C3
Salientes E 86 B4
Salies-de-Béarn F 76 C2
Salies-du-Salat F 77 C3
Salignac-Eyvigues F 77 B4
Saligney-sur-Roudon F 68 B3
Salihli TR 119 D3
Salihorsk BY 7 E9
Salinas
Alicante E 101 A5
Huesca E 90 A3
Salinas de Medinaceli E 95 A4
Salinas de Pisuerga E 88 B2
Salindres F 78 B3
Saline di Volterra I 81 C4
Salins-les-Bains F 69 B5
Salir P 98 B2
Salisbury GB 29 B6
Salla
A 73 A4
FIN 113 F17
Sallachy GB 23 C4
Sallanches F 70 C1
Sallent E 91 B4
Sallent de Gállego E 76 D2
Salles F 76 B2
Salles-Curan F 78 B1
Salles-sur-l'Hers F 77 C4
Sallins IRL 21 A5
Sällsjö S 115 D10
Salmerón E 95 B4
Salmiech F 77 B5
Salmivaara FIN 113 F17
Salmoral E 94 B1
Salo FIN 6 A7
Salò I 71 C5
Salobreña E 100 C2
Salon-de-Provence F 79 C4
Salonica = Thessaloniki GR 116 B4
Salonta RO 10 C6
Salorino E 93 B3
Salornay-sur-Guye F 69 B4
Salorno I 71 B6
Salou E 91 B4
Šalovci SLO 73 B6
Salsbruket N 114 C8
Salses-le-Château F 78 D1
Salsomaggiore Terme I 81 B3
Salt E 91 B5
Saltaire GB 27 B4
Saltara I 82 C1
Saltash GB 28 C3
Saltburn-by-the-Sea GB 27 A5
Saltcoats GB 24 C3
Saltfleet GB 27 B6
Salto P 87 C3
Saltrød N 33 D5
Saltsjöbaden S 37 C5
Saltvik
FIN 36 B7
S 40 B6
Saludécio I 82 C1
Salussola I 70 C3
Saluzzo I 80 B1
Salvacañete E 95 B5
Salvada P 98 B3
Salvagnac F 77 C4
Salvaleon E 93 C4
Salvaterra de Magos P 92 B2
Salvaterra do Extremo P 93 B4
Salvatierra
Avila E 89 B4
Badajoz E 93 C4
Salvatierra de Santiago E 93 B4
Salviac F 77 B4
Salzburg A 62 C4
Salzgitter D 51 A6
Salzgitter Bad D 51 A6
Salzhausen D 44 B2
Salzhemmendorf D 51 A5
Salzkotten D 51 B4
Salzmünde D 52 B1
Salzwedel D 44 C3
Samadet F 76 C2
Samandıra TR 118 B4
Samassi I 110 C1
Samatan F 77 C3
Sambiase I 106 C3
Sambir UA 11 B7
Sambuca di Sicilia I 108 B2
Samedan CH 71 B4
Samer F 48 C2
Sami GR 117 D2
Şamlı TR 118 C2
Sammichele di Bari I 104 C2
Samnaun CH 71 B5
Samobor HR 73 C5
Samoëns F 70 B1
Samogneux F 59 A6
Samokov BG 11 E7
Samora Correia P 92 C2
Šamorín SK 64 B3
Samos
E 86 B3
GR 119 E1
Samoš SRB 75 C5
Samothraki GR 116 B7
Samper de Calanda E 90 B2
Sampéyre I 79 B6
Sampieri I 109 C3
Sampigny F 60 B1
Samplawa PL 47 B5
Samproniano I 81 D5
Samtens D 45 A5
Samugheo I 110 C1
San Adrián E 89 B5
San Agustín E 101 B3
San Agustin de Guadalix E 94 B3
Sanaigmore GB 24 C1
San Alberto I 82 B1
San Amaro E 87 B2
Sânandrei RO 75 C6
San Andrés del Rabanedo E 88 B1
San Antanio di Santadi I 110 C1
San Antolín de Ibias E 86 A4
San Arcángelo I 104 C2
Sanary-sur-Mer F 79 C4
San Asensio E 89 B4
San Bartoloméde las Abiertas E 94 C2
San Bartoloméde la Torre E 99 B3
San Bartoloméde Pinares E 94 B2
San Bartolomeo in Galdo I 103 B8
San Benedetto del Tronto I 82 D2
San Benedetto in Alpe I 81 C5
San Benedetto Po I 81 A4
San Benito E 100 A1
San Benito de la Contienda E 93 C3
San Biágio Plátani I 108 B2
San Biágio Saracinisco I 103 B6
San Bonifacio I 71 C6
San Calixto E 99 B5
San Cándido I 72 B2
San Carlo
CH 70 B3
I 108 B2
San Carlos del Valle E 100 A2
San Casciano dei Bagni I 81 D5
San Casciano in Val di Pesa I 81 C5
San Cataldo
Puglia I 105 C4
Sicilia I 108 B2
San Cebrián de Castro E 88 C1
Sancergues F 68 A2
Sancerre F 68 A2
San Cesário di Lecce I 105 C4
Sancey-le-Long F 69 A6
Sanchiorian E 94 B2
San Chírico Raparo I 106 A3
Sanchonuño E 88 C2
San Cibrao das Viñas E 87 B3
San Cipirello I 108 B2
San Ciprián E 86 A3
San Clemente E 95 C4
San Clodio E 86 B3
Sancoins F 68 B2
San Colombano al Lambro I 71 C4
San Costanzo I 82 C2
San Crisóbal de Entreviñas E 88 B1
San Cristóbal de la Polantera E 88 B1
San Cristóbal de la Vega E 94 A2
San Cristovo E 87 C3
Sanct-Petri E 99 C4
Sancti-Spíritus E 87 D4
Sand
Hedmark N 34 B3
Rogaland N 33 C3
Sanda S 37 E5
San Damiano d'Asti I 80 B2
San Damiano Macra I 79 B6
Sandane N 114 F3
San Daniele del Friuli I 72 B3
Sandanski BG 116 A5
Sandared S 40 B2
Sandarne S 36 A4
Sandau D 44 C4
Sandbach
D 63 B4
GB 26 B3
Sandbank GB 24 C3
Sandbanks GB 29 C6
Sandbukt N 112 C10
Sandby DK 39 E4
Sande
D 43 B5
Sogn og Fjordane N 32 A2
Vestfold N 35 C2
Sandefjord N 35 C2
Sandeid N 33 C2
San Demétrio Corone I 106 B3
San Demétrio né Vestini I 103 A6
Sandersleben D 52 B1
Sanderstølen N 32 B6
Sandes N 33 D4
Sandesneben D 44 B2
Sandhead GB 24 D3
Sandhem S 40 B3
Sandhorst D 43 B4
Sandhurst GB 31 C3
Sandıklı TR 119 D5
Sandillon F 58 C3
Sandl A 63 B5
Sandnes N 33 D2
Sandness GB 22 A7
Sandnessjøen N 115 A9
Sando E 87 D4
Sandomierz PL 55 C6
San Dónaci I 105 C3
San Donà di Piave I 72 C2
San Donato Val di Comino I 103 B6
Sándorfalva H 75 B5
Sandown GB 31 D2
Sandøysund N 35 C2
Sandrigo I 72 C1
Sandsele S 115 B14
Sandset N 112 D3
Sandsjöfors S 40 B4
Sandstad N 114 D6
Sandvatn N 33 D3
Sandvig-Allinge DK 41 D4
Sandvika
Akershus N 34 C2
Hedmark N 34 B3
Nord-Trøndelag N 114 D9
Sandviken S 36 B3
Sandvikvåy N 32 C2
Sandwich GB 31 C5
Sandy GB 30 B3
San Emiliano E 86 B5
San Enrique E 99 C5
San Esteban E 86 A4
San Esteban de Gormaz E 89 C3
San Esteban de la Sierra E 93 A5
San Esteban de Litera E 90 B3
San Esteban del Molar E 88 C1
San Esteban del Valle E 94 B2
San Esteban de Valdueza E 86 B4
San Fele I 104 C1
San Felice Circeo I 102 B6
San Felices E 88 B3
San Felices de los Gallégos E 87 D4
San Felice sul Panaro I 81 B5
San Ferdinando di Púglia I 104 B2
San Fernando E 99 C4
San Fernando de Henares E 95 B3
San Fili I 106 B3
San Foca I 105 C4
San Fratello I 109 B3
Sangatte F 48 C2
San Gavino Monreale I 110 C1
San Gémini Fonte I 102 A5
Sangerhausen D 52 B1
San Germano Vercellese I 70 C3
San Giácomo
Trentino Alto Adige I 72 B1
Umbria I 82 D1
San Gimignano I 81 C5
San Ginésio I 82 C2
Sangineto Lido I 106 B2
San Giórgio a Liri I 103 B6
San Giorgio della Richinvelda I 72 B2
San Giórgio del Sánnio I 103 B7
San Giórgio di Lomellina I 70 C3
San Giórgio di Nogaro I 72 C3
San Giorgio di Piano I 81 B5
San Giórgio Iónico I 104 C3
San Giovanni a Piro I 106 A2
San Giovanni Bianco I 71 C4
San Giovanni di Sinis I 110 C1
San Giovanni in Croce I 81 A4
San Giovanni in Fiore I 106 B3
San Giovanni in Persiceto I 81 B5
San Giovanni Reatino I 102 A5
San Giovanni Rotondo I 104 B1
San Giovanni Suérgiu I 110 C1
San Giovanni Valdarno I 81 C5
San Giuliano Terme I 81 C4
San Giustino I 82 C1
San Godenzo I 81 C5
Sangonera la Verde E 101 B4
San Gregorio Magno I 103 C8
Sangüesa E 90 A1
Sanguinet F 76 B1
San Guiseppe Jato I 108 B2
Sanica BIH 83 B5
Sanitz D 44 A4
San Javier E 101 B5
San Jorge P 92 B2
San José E 101 C3
San Juan E 89 B3
San Juan de Alicante E 96 C2
San Juan de la Nava E 94 B2
San Justo de la Vega E 86 B4
Sankt Aegyd am Neuwalde A 63 C6
Sankt Andrä A 73 B4
Sankt Andreasberg D 51 B6
Sankt Anna S 37 D3
Sankt Anna am Aigen A 73 B5
Sankt Anton am Arlberg A 71 A5
Sankt Anton an der Jessnitz A 63 C6
Sankt Augustin D 50 C3
Sankt Blasien D 61 C4
Sankt Englmar D 62 A3
Sankt Gallen
A 63 C5
CH 71 A4
Sankt Gallenkirch A 71 A4
Sankt Georgen
A 63 B5
D 61 B4
Sankt Georgen am Reith A 63 C5
Sankt Georgen ob Judenburg A 73 A4
Sankt Georgen ob Murau A 73 A4
Sankt Gilgen A 63 C4
Sankt Goar D 50 C3
Sankt Goarshausen D 50 C3
Sankt Ingbert D 60 A3
Sankt Jacob A 73 B4
Sankt Jakob in Defereggen A 72 B2
Sankt Johann am Tauern A 73 A4
Sankt Johann am Wesen A 63 B4
Sankt Johann im Pongau A 72 A3
Sankt Johann in Tirol A 72 A2
Sankt Katharein an der Laming A 73 A5
Sankt Kathrein am Hauenstein A 73 A5
Sankt Lambrecht A 73 A4
Sankt Leonhard am Forst A 63 B6
Sankt Leonhard im Pitztal A 71 A5
Sankt Lorenzen A 72 B2
Sankt Marein
Steiermark A 73 A5
Steiermark A 73 A5
Sankt Margarethen im Lavanttal A 73 B4
Sankt Margrethen CH 71 A4
Sankt Michael A 73 A5
Sankt Michael im Burgenland A 73 A6
Sankt Michael im Lungau A 72 A3
Sankt Michaelisdonn D 43 B6
Sankt Niklaus CH 70 B2
Sankt Nikolai im Sölktal A 73 A4
Sankt Olof S 41 D4
Sankt Oswald D 63 B4
Sankt Paul
A 73 B4
F 79 B5
Sankt Peter D 61 B4
Sankt Peter am Kammersberg A 73 A4
Sankt-Peterburg = St Petersburg RUS 7 B11
Sankt Peter-Ording D 43 A5
Sankt Pölten A 63 B6
Sankt Radegund A 73 A5
Sankt Ruprecht an der Raab A 73 A5
Sankt Salvator A 73 B4
Sankt Stefan A 73 B4
Sankt Stefan an der Gail A 72 B3
Sankt Stefan im Rosental A 73 B5
Sankt Valentin A 63 B5
Sankt Veit an der Glan A 73 B4
Sankt Veit an der Gölsen A 63 B6
Sankt Veit in Defereggen A 72 B2
Sankt Wendel D 60 A3
Sankt Wolfgang
A 63 C4
D 62 B3
San Lazzaro di Sávena I 81 B5
San Leo I 82 C1
San Leonardo de Yagüe E 89 C3
San Leonardo in Passiria I 71 B6
San Lorenzo al Mare I 80 C1
San Lorenzo a Merse I 81 C5
San Lorenzo Bellizzi I 106 B3
San Lorenzo de Calatrava E 100 A2
San Lorenzo de El Escorial E 94 B2
San Lorenzo de la Parrilla E 95 C4
San Lorenzo di Sebato I 72 B1
San Lorenzo in Campo I 82 C1
San Lorenzo Nuovo I 81 D5
San Lourenco P 98 A2
San Luca I 106 C3
Sanlúcar de Barrameda E 99 C4
Sanlúcar de Guadiana E 98 B3
Sanlúcar la Mayor E 99 B4
San Lúcido I 106 B3
Sanluri I 110 C1
San Marcello I 82 C2
San Marcello Pistoiese I 81 B4
San Marcial E 88 C1
San Marco I 103 C7
San Marco Argentano I 106 B3
San Marco dei Cavoti I 103 B7
San Marco in Lámis I 104 B1
San Marino RSM 82 C1
San Martín de Castañeda E 87 B4
San Martín de la Vega E 95 B3
San Martin de la Vega del Alberche E 93 A5
San Martín del Tesorillo E 99 C5
San Martín de Luiña E 86 A4
San Martín de Montalbán E 94 C2
San Martín de Oscos E 86 A4
San Martín de Pusa E 94 C2
San Martín de Unx E 89 B5
San Martín de Valdeiglesias E 94 B2
San Martino di Campagna I 72 B2
San Martino di Castrozza I 72 B1
San-Martino-di-Lota F 102 A2
San Martino in Pénsilis I 103 B8
San Mateo de Gallego E 90 B2
San Máuro Forte I 104 C2
San Michele all'Adige I 71 B6
San Michele di Ganzaria I 109 B3
San Michele Mondovì I 80 B1
San Miguel de Aguayo E 88 A2
San Miguel de Bernuy E 88 C3
San Miguel del Arroyo E 88 C2
San Miguel de Salinas E 101 B5
Sânmihaiu Roman RO 75 C6
San Millán de la Cogolla E 89 B4
San Miniato I 81 C4
San Muñoz E 87 D4
Sänna S 37 D1
Sannazzaro de'Burgondi I 80 A2
Sanne D 44 C3
Sannicandro di Bari I 104 B2
Sannicandro Gargánico I 104 B1
San Nicola del'Alto I 107 B3
San Nicolás del Puerto E 99 B5
Sânnicolau Mare RO 75 B5
San Nicolò I 81 B5
San Nicolò Gerrei I 110 C2
Sannidal N 33 D6
Sanniki PL 47 C5
Sanok PL 11 B7
San Pablo de los Montes E 94 C2
San Pancrázio Salentino I 105 C3
San Pantaleo I 110 A2
San Páolo di Civitate I 103 B8
San Pawl il-Bahar M 107 C5
San Pedro
Albacete E 101 A3
Oviedo E 86 A4
San Pedro de Alcántara E 100 C1
San Pedro de Ceque E 87 B4
San Pedro del Arroyo E 94 B2
San Pedro de Latarce E 88 C1
San Pedro del Pinatar E 101 B5
San Pedro del Romeral E 88 A3
San Pedro de Merida E 93 C4
San Pedro de Valderaduey E 88 B2
San Pedro Manrique E 89 B4
San Pellegrino Terme I 71 C4
San Piero a Sieve I 81 C5
San Piero in Bagno I 81 C5
San Piero Patti I 109 A3
San Pietro I 109 B3
San Pietro in Casale I 81 B5
San Pietro in Gu I 72 C1
San Pietro in Palazzi I 81 C4
San Pietro in Volta I 72 C2
San Pietro Vara I 80 B3
San Pietro Vernótico I 105 C3
San Polo d'Enza I 81 B4
Sanquhar GB 25 C4
San Quírico d'Órcia I 81 C5
San Rafael del Rio E 90 C3
San Remo I 80 C1
San Román de Cameros E 89 B4
San Roman de Hernija E 88 C1
San Román de la Cuba E 88 B2
San Roman de los Montes E 94 B2
San Romao P 92 C3
San Roque E 99 C5
San Roque de Riomera E 88 A3
San Rufo I 104 C1
San Sebastián de los Ballesteros E 100 B1
San Salvador de Cantamuda E 88 B2
San Salvo I 103 A7
San Salvo Marina I 103 A7
San Sebastián de los Reyes E 94 B3
San Sebastiano Curone I 80 B3
San Secondo Parmense I 81 B4
Sansepolcro I 82 C1
San Serverino Marche I 82 C2
San Severino Lucano I 106 A3
San Severo I 103 B8
Sanski Most BIH 83 B5
San Sosti I 106 B3
San Stéfano di Cadore I 72 B2
San Stino di Livenza I 72 C2
Santa Agnès E 97 B1
Santa Amalia E 93 B4
Santa Ana
Cáceres E 93 B5
Jaén E 100 B2
Santa Ana de Pusa E 94 C2
Santa Barbara E 90 C3
Santa Bárbara P 98 B2
Santa Barbara de Casa E 98 B3
Santa Bárbara de Padrões P 98 B3
Santacara E 89 B5
Santa Catarina P 98 B3
Santa Caterina di Pittinuri I 110 B1
Santa Caterina Villarmosa I 109 B3
Santa Cesárea Terme I 107 A5
Santa Clara-a-Nova P 98 B2
Santa Clara-a-Velha P 98 B2
Santa Clara de Louredo P 98 B3
Santa Coloma de Farners E 91 B5
Santa Coloma de Gramenet E 91 B5
Santa Coloma de Queralt E 91 B4
Santa Colomba de Curueño E 88 B1
Santa Colomba de Somoza E 86 B4
Santa Comba E 86 A2
Santa Comba Dáo P 92 A2
Santa Comba de Rossas P 87 C4
Santa Cristina I 71 C4
Santa Cristina de la Polvorosa E 88 B1
Santa Croce Camerina I 109 C3
Santa Croce di Magliano I 103 B7
Santa Cruz
E 86 A2
P 92 B1
Santa Cruz de Alhama E 100 B2
Santa Cruz de Campezo E 89 B4
Santa Cruz de Grio E 89 C5
Santa Cruz de la Salceda E 89 C3
Santa Cruz de la Sierra E 93 B5
Santa Cruz de la Zarza E 95 C3
Santa Cruz del Retamar E 94 B2
Santa Cruz del Valle E 94 B1
Santa Cruz de Moya E 96 B1
Santa Cruz de Mudela E 100 A2
Santa Cruz de Paniagua E 93 A4
Santadi I 110 C1
Santa Doménica Talao I 106 B2
Santa Doménica Vittória I 109 B3
Santa Elena E 100 A2
Santa Elena de Jamuz E 88 B1
Santaella E 100 B1
Santa Eufemia E 100 A1
Santa Eufémia d'Aspromonte I 106 C2
Santa Eulalia E 95 B5
Santa Eulália P 92 C3
Santa Eulália de Oscos E 86 A3
Santa Eulàlia des Riu E 97 C1
Santa Fe E 100 B2
Santa Fiora I 81 D5
Sant'Ágata dei Goti I 103 B7
Sant'Ágata di Ésaro I 106 B2
Sant'Ágata di Puglia I 103 B8
Sant'Agata Feltria I 82 C1
Sant'Ágata Militello I 109 A3
Santa Gertrude I 71 B5
Santa Giustina I 72 B2
Sant Agustíde Lluçanès E 91 A5
Santa Iria P 98 B3
Santa Leocadia P 87 C2
Santa Lucia del Mela I 109 A4
Santa Lucia-de-Porto-Vecchio F 102 B2
Santa Luzia P 98 B2
Santa Maddalena Vallalta I 72 B2
Santa Magdalena de Polpís E 90 C3
Santa Margalida E 97 B3
Santa Margarida P 92 B2
Santa Margarida do Sado P 98 A2
Santa Margaridao de Montbui E 91 B4
Santa Margherita I 110 D1
Santa Margherita di Belice I 108 B2
Santa Margherita Ligure I 80 B3
Santa Maria
CH 71 B5
E 90 A2
Santa Maria al Bagno I 107 A4
Santa Maria Cápua Vétere I 103 B7
Santa Maria da Feira P 87 D2
Santa Maria de Cayón E 88 A3
Santa Maria de Corco E 91 A5
Santa Maria de Huerta E 95 A4
Santa Maria de la Alameda E 94 B2
Santa Maria de las Hoyas E 89 C3
Santa Maria del Camí E 97 B2
Santa Maria del Campo E 88 B3
Santa Maria del Campo Rus E 95 C4
Santa Maria della Versa I 80 B3
Santa Maria del Páramo E 88 B1
Santa Maria del Taro I 80 B3
Santa Maria de Mercadillo E 89 C3
Santa Maria de Nieva E 101 B4
Santa Maria de Trassierra E 100 B1
Santa Maria di Licodia I 109 B3
Santa Maria-di-Rispéscia I 81 D5
Santa Maria la Palma I 110 B1
Santa María la Real de Nieva E 94 A2
Santa Maria Maggiore I 70 B3
Santa Maria Ribarredonda E 89 B3
Santa Marina del Rey E 88 B1
Santa Marinella I 102 A4
Santa Marta
Albacete E 95 C4
Badajoz E 93 C4
Santa Marta de Magasca E 93 B4
Santa Marta de Penaguião P 87 C3
Santa Marta de Tormes E 94 B1
Santana
Évora P 92 C2
Setúbal P 92 C1
Santana da Serra P 98 B2
Sant'Ana de Cambas P 98 B3
Santana do Mato P 92 C2
Sant'Anastasia I 103 C7
Santander E 88 A3
Sant'Andrea Frius I 110 C2
Sant'Ángelo dei Lombardi I 103 C8
Sant'Angelo in Vado I 82 C1
Sant'Angelo Lodigiano I 71 C4
Santa Ninfa I 108 B1
Sant'Antíoco I 110 C1
Sant Antoni de Calonge E 91 B6
Sant Antoni de Portmany E 97 C1
Sant'Antonio-di-Gallura I 110 B2
Santanyí E 97 B3
Santa Olalla
Huelva E 99 B4
Toledo E 94 B2
Santa Pau E 91 A5
Santa Pola E 96 C2
Santa Ponça E 97 B2
Santarcángelo di Romagna I 82 B1
Santarém P 92 B2
Santa Severa
F 102 A2
I 102 A4
Santa Severina I 107 B3
Santas Martas E 88 B1
Santa Sofia I 81 C5
Santa Susana P 92 C2
Santa Suzana P 92 C3
Santa Teresa di Riva I 109 B4
Santa Teresa Gallura I 110 A2
Santa Uxía E 86 B2
Santa Valburga I 71 B5
Santa Vittória in Matenano I 82 C2
Sant Boi de Llobregat E 91 B5
Sant Carles de la Ràpita E 90 C3
Sant Carlos E 97 B1
Sant'Caterina I 81 C5
Sant Celoni E 91 B5
Sant Climent E 97 B4
Santed E 95 A5
Sant'Egidio alla Vibrata I 82 D2
Sant'Elia a Pianisi I 103 B7
Sant'Elia Fiumerapido I 103 B6
Santelices E 88 A3
San Telmo E 99 B4
Sant'Elpídio a Mare I 82 C2
Santéramo in Colle I 104 C2
Santervas de la Vega E 88 B2
Sant' Eufemia Lamezia I 106 C3
Sant Feliu E 91 B5
Sant Feliu de Codines E 91 B5
Sant Feliu de Guíxols E 91 B6
Sant Feliu Sasserra E 91 B5
Sant Ferran E 97 C1
Sant Francesc de Formentera E 97 C1
Sant Francesc de ses Salines E 97 C1
Santhià I 70 C3
Sant Hilari Sacalm E 91 B5
Sant Hipòlit de Voltregà E 91 A5
Santiago de Alcántara E 92 B3
Santiago de Calatrava E 100 B1
Santiago de Compostela E 86 B2
Santiago de la Espade E 101 A3
Santiago de la Puebla E 94 B1
Santiago de la Ribera E 101 B5
Santiago del Campo E 93 B4
Santiago de Litem P 92 B2
Santiago do Cacém P 98 B2
Santiago do Escoural P 92 C2
Santiago Maior P 92 C3
Santibáñez de Béjar E 93 A5
Santibáñez de la Peña E 88 B2
Santibáñez de Murias E 88 A1
Santibáñez de Vidriales E 87 B4
Santibáñez el Alto E 93 A4
Santibáñez el Bajo E 93 A4
Santillana E 88 A2
Santiponce E 99 B4
San Tirso de Abres E 86 A3
Santisteban del Puerto E 100 A2
Santiuste de San Juan Bautiste E 94 A2
Santiz E 94 A1
Sant Jaume dels Domenys E 91 B4
Sant Joan Baptista E 97 B1
Sant Joan de les Abadesses E 91 A5
Sant Jordi E 90 C3
Sant Josep de sa Talaia E 97 C1
Sant Juliáde Loria AND 91 A4
Sant'Ilario d'Enza I 81 B4
Sant Llorençde Morunys E 91 A4
Sant Llorençdes Carctassar E 97 B3
Sant Llorenç Savall E 91 B5
Sant Luis E 97 B4
Sant Martíde Llemaná E 91 A5
Sant Marti de Maldá E 91 B4
Sant Marti Sarroca E 91 B4
Sant Mateu E 90 C3
Sant Miquel E 97 B1
Santo Aleixo P 98 A3
Santo Amado P 98 A3
Santo Amaro P 92 C3
Santo André P 98 A2
Santo Domingo E 93 C3

Santo Domingo de la Calzada E 89 B4
Santo Domingo de Silos E 89 C3
Santo Estêvão
Faro P 98 B3
Santarém P 92 C2
Santok PL 46 C1
Santomera E 101 A4
Santoña E 89 A3
Santo-Pietro-di Tenda F 102 A2
Sant'Oreste I 102 A5
Santo Spirito I 104 B2
Santo Stefano d'Aveto I 80 B3
Santo Stéfano di Camastra I 109 B3
Santo Stefano di Magra I 81 B3
Santo Stéfano Quisquina I 108 B2
Santo Tirso P 87 C2
Santotis E 88 A2
Santo Tomé E 100 A2
Santovenia
Burgos E 89 B3
Zamora E 88 C1
Sant Pau de Seguries E 91 A5
Santpedor E 91 B4
Sant Pere de Riudebitles E 91 B4
Sant Pere Pescador E 91 A6
Sant Pere Sallavinera E 91 B4
Sant Quirze de Besora E 91 A5
Sant Rafel E 97 C1
Sant Ramon E 91 B4
Santu Lussurgiu I 110 B1
Santutzi E 89 A3
Sant Vincençde Castellet E 91 B4
San Valentino alla Muta I 71 B5
San Venanzo I 82 D1
San Vicente de Alcántara E 93 B3
San Vicente de Arana E 89 B4
San Vicente de la Barquera E 88 A2
San Vicente de la Sonsierra E 89 B4
San Vicente de Toranzo E 88 A3
San Vietro E 87 C4
San Vigilio I 72 B1
San Vincente del Raspeig E 96 C2
San Vincenzo I 81 C4
San Vito I 110 C2
San Vito al Tagliamento I 72 C2
San Vito Chietino I 103 A7
San Vito dei Normanni I 104 C3
San Vito di Cadore I 72 B2
San Vito lo Capo I 108 A1
San Vito Romano I 102 B5
Sanxenxo E 86 B2
Sanza I 104 C1
São Aleixo P 92 C3
São Barnabé P 98 B2
São Bartoloméda Serra P 98 A2
São Bartolomeu de Messines P 98 B2
São Bento P 87 C2
São Brás P 98 B3
São Brás de Alportel P 98 B3
São Braz do Reguedoura P 92 C2
São Cristóvão P 92 C2
São Domingos P 98 B2
São Geraldo P 92 C2
São Jacinto P 92 A2
São João da Madeira P 87 D2
São João da Pesqueira P 87 C3
São João da Ribeira P 92 B2
São João da Serra P 87 D2
São João da Venda P 98 B3
São João dos Caldeireiros P 98 B3
São Julião P 92 B3
São Leonardo P 92 C3
São Luis P 98 B2
São Manços P 92 C3
São Marcos da Ataboeira P 98 B3
Saõ Marcos da Serra P 98 B2
São Marcos de Campo P 92 C3
São Martinho da Cortiça P 92 A2
São Martinho das Amoreiras P 98 B2
São Martinho do Porto P 92 B1
São Matias
Beja P 98 A3
Évora P 92 C2
São Miguel d'Acha P 92 A3
São Miguel de Machede P 92 C3
São Pedro da Torre P 87 C2
São Pedro de Cadeira P 92 B1
São Pedro de Moel P 92 B1
São Pedro de Solis P 98 B3
São Pedro do Sul P 87 D2
Saorge F 80 C1
São Romão P 92 C2
São Sebastião dos Carros P 98 B3
São Teotónio P 98 B2
São Torcato P 87 C2
Sapataria P 92 C1
Sapes GR 116 A7
Sapiãos P 87 C3
Sa Pobla E 97 B3
Sappada I 72 B2
Sappen N 112 C10
Sapri I 106 A2
Sarajevo BIH 84 C3
Saramon F 77 C3
Sarandë AL 116 C2
Saranovo SRB 85 B5
Saraorci SRB 85 B6
Sa Rapita E 97 B3
Saray TR 118 A2
Saraycık TR 118 C4
Sarayköy TR 119 E3
Saraylar TR 118 B2
Sarayönü TR 119 D7
Sarbia PL 46 C2
Sarbinowo
Zachodnio-Pomorskie PL 45 C6
Zachodnio-Pomorskie PL 46 A1
Sárbogárd H 74 B3
Sarcelles F 58 A3
Sarche I 71 B5
Sardara I 110 C1
Sardoal P 92 B2
Sardón de Duero E 88 C2
Sare F 76 C1
S'Arenal E 97 B2
Šarengrad HR 75 C4
Sarentino I 71 B6
Sarezzo I 71 C5
Sargans CH 71 A4
Sári H 75 A4
Sarıbeyler TR 118 C2
Sarıcakaya TR 118 B5
Sari-d'Orcino F 102 A1
Sarıgöl TR 119 D3
Sarıkaya TR 16 B7
Sarıköy TR 118 B2
Sarilhos Grandes P 92 C2
Sariñena E 90 B2
Sarıoba TR 118 C7
Sárisáp H 65 C4
Sariyer TR 118 A4
Sarkad H 75 B6
Sárkeresztes H 74 A3
Sárkeresztúr H 74 A3
Särkijärvi FIN 113 E12
Şarkikaraağaç TR 119 D6
Şarköy TR 118 B2
Sarlat-la-Canéda F 77 B4
Sarliac-sur-l'Isle F 67 C5
Sármellék H 74 B2
Särna S 115 F10
Sarnadas P 92 B3
Sarnano I 82 C2
Sarnen CH 70 B3
Sarnesfield GB 29 A5
Sárnico I 71 C4
Sarno I 103 C7
Sarnonico I 71 B6
Sarnow D 45 B5
Sarny UA 11 A9
Särö S 38 B4
Saronno I 70 C4
Sárosd H 74 A3
Šarovce SK 65 B4
Sarpoil F 68 C3
Sarpsborg N 35 C3
Sarracín E 88 B3
Sarral E 91 B4
Sarralbe F 60 A3
Sarrancolin F 77 D3
Sarras F 69 C4
Sarre I 70 C2
Sarreaus E 87 B3
Sarrebourg F 60 B3
Sarreguemines F 60 A3
Sárrétudvari H 75 A6
Sarre-Union F 60 B3
Sarria E 86 B3
Sarriàde Ter E 91 A5
Sarrión E 96 A2
Sarroca de Lleida E 90 B3
Sarroch I 110 C2
Sarron F 76 C2
Sársina I 82 C1
Særslev DK 39 D3
Sarstedt D 51 A5
Sárszentlörinc H 74 B3
Sárszentmihaly H 74 A3
Sárszentmiklós H 74 B3
Sarteano I 81 D5
Sartène F 102 B1
Sartilly F 57 B4
Sartirana Lomellina I 80 A2
Saruhanlı TR 118 D2
Sárvár H 74 A1
Sarvisvaara S 113 F10
Sarzana I 81 B3
Sarzeau F 66 A2
Sarzedas P 92 B3
Sasalli TR 119 D1
Sasamón E 88 B2
Sa Savina E 97 C1
Sásd H 74 B3
Sasino PL 46 A3
Sássari I 110 B1
Sassello I 80 B2
Sassenberg D 50 B4
Sassetta I 81 C4
Sassnitz D 45 A5
Sassocorvaro I 82 C1
Sasso d'Ombrone I 81 D5
Sassoferrato I 82 C1
Sassoleone I 81 B5
Sasso Marconi I 81 B5
Sassuolo I 81 B4
Šástago E 90 B2
Šaštinske Stráže SK 64 B3
Sas van Gent NL 49 B4
Såtåhaugen N 114 E7
Satão P 87 D3
Sätenäs S 35 D4
Säter S 36 B2
Sätila S 40 B2
Satillieu F 69 C4
Satnica Đakovačka HR 74 C3
Sátoraljaújhely H 10 B6
Satow D 44 B3
Sätra-brunn S 36 C3
Sætre N 35 C2
Satrup D 43 A6
Satteins A 71 A4
Satu Mare RO 11 C7
Saturnia I 102 A4
Saucats F 76 B2
Saucelle E 87 C4
Sauda N 33 C3
Sauðarkrókur IS 111 B6
Saudasjøen N 33 C3
Sauerlach D 62 C2
Saugues F 78 B2
Sauherad N 33 C6
Saujon F 66 C4
Sauland N 33 C5
Saulces Monclin F 59 A5
Saulgau D 61 B5
Saulgrub D 62 C2
Saulieu F 69 A4
Saulnot F 60 C2
Sault F 79 B4
Sault-Brénaz F 69 C5
Sault-de-Navailles F 76 C2
Saulx F 60 C2
Saulxures-sur-Moselotte F 60 C2
Saulzais-le-Potier F 68 B2
Saumos F 76 B1
Saumur F 67 A4
Saunavaara FIN 113 E16
Saundersfoot GB 28 B3
Saurat F 77 D4
Saurbær
Borgarfjarðarsýsla IS 111 C4
Dalasýsla IS 111 B4
Eyjafjarðarsýsla IS 111 B7
Sáuris I 72 B2
Sausset-les-Pins F 79 C4
Sauteyrargues F 78 C2
Sauvagnat F 68 C2
Sauve F 78 C2
Sauveterre-de-Béarn F 76 C2
Sauveterre-de-Guyenne F 76 B2
Sauviat-sur-Vige F 67 C6
Sauxillanges F 68 C3
Sauzet
Drôme F 78 B3
Lot F 77 B4
Sauzé-Vaussais F 67 B5
Sauzon F 66 A1
Sava I 104 C3
Sævareid N 32 B2
Savarsin RO 11 C7
Savaştepe TR 118 C2
Savci SLO 73 B6
Säve S 38 B4
Savelletri I 104 C3
Savelli I 107 B3
Savenay F 66 A3
Saverdun F 77 C4
Saverne F 60 B3
Savières F 59 B4
Savigliano I 80 B1
Savignac-les-Eglises F 67 C5
Savignano Irpino I 103 B8
Savignano sul Rubicone I 82 B1
Savigny-sur-Braye F 58 C1
Saviñán E 89 C5
Savines-le-lac F 79 B5
Savino Selo SRB 75 C4
Savio I 82 B1
Šávja S 36 C4
Šavnik MNE 85 D4
Savognin CH 71 B4
Savona I 80 B2
Savonlinna FIN 3 F28
Savournon F 79 B4
Sævråsvåg N 32 B2
Sävsjö S 40 B4
Savsjön S 36 C1
Sävsjöström S 40 B5
Savudrija HR 72 C3
Savukoski FIN 113 E17
Sawbridgeworth GB 31 C4
Sawtry GB 30 B3
Sax E 101 A5
Saxdalen S 36 B1
Saxilby GB 27 B5
Saxmundham GB 30 B5
Saxnäs S 115 C12
Saxthorpe GB 30 B5
Sayalonga E 100 C1
Sayatón E 95 B4
Sayda D 52 C3
Säytsjärvi FIN 113 C16
Šazava CZ 64 A1
Sázava CZ 63 A5
Scaër F 56 B2
Scafa I 103 A7
Scalasaig GB 24 B1
Scalby GB 27 A5
Scalea I 106 B2
Scaletta Zanclea I 109 A4
Scalloway GB 22 A7
Scamblesby GB 27 B5
Scandale I 107 B3
Scandiano I 81 B4
Scandicci I 81 C5
Scandolara Ravara I 81 A4
Scanno I 103 B6
Scansano I 81 D5
Scanzano Jónico I 104 C2
Scarborough GB 27 A5
Scardovari I 82 B1
Scardoy GB 22 D4
Scarinish GB 24 B1
Scarperia I 81 C5
Scarriff IRL 20 B3
Scey-sur-Saône et St Albin F 60 C1
Schachendorf A 73 A6
Schaffhausen CH 61 C4
Schafstädt D 52 B1
Schafstedt D 43 A6
Schäftlarn D 62 C2
Schagen NL 42 C1
Schalkau D 51 C7
Schangnau CH 70 B2
Schapbach D 61 B4
Scharbeutz D 44 A2
Schärding A 63 B4
Scharnitz A 71 A6
Scharrel D 43 B4
Schattendorf A 64 C2
Scheemda NL 42 B3
Scheessel D 43 B6
Schéggia I 82 C1
Scheibbs A 63 B6
Scheibenberg D 52 C2
Scheidegg D 61 C5
Scheifling A 73 A4
Scheinfeld D 61 A6
Schelklingen D 61 B5
Schenefeld
Schleswig-Holstein D 43 A6
Schleswig-Holstein D 44 B1
Schenklengsfeld D 51 C5
Scherfede D 51 B5
Schermbeck D 50 B2
Scherpenzeel NL 49 A6
Schesslitz D 52 D1
Scheveningen NL 49 A5
Schiedam NL 49 B5
Schieder-Schwalenberg D 51 B5
Schierling D 62 B3
Schiers CH 71 B4
Schildau D 52 B2
Schillingen D 60 A2
Schillingsfürst D 61 A6
Schilpário I 71 B5
Schiltach D 61 B4
Schiltigheim F 60 B3
Schio I 71 C6
Schirmeck F 60 B3
Schirnding D 52 C2
Schkeuditz D 52 B2
Schkölen D 52 B1
Schlabendorf D 53 B3
Schladen D 51 A6
Schladming A 72 A3
Schlangen D 51 B4
Schleiden D 50 C2
Schleiz D 52 C1
Schleswig D 43 A6
Schleusingen D 51 C6
Schlieben D 52 B3
Schliengen D 60 C3
Schliersee D 62 C2
Schlitz D 51 C5
Schloss Neuhans D 51 B4
Schlossvippach D 52 B1
Schlotheim D 51 B6
Schluchsee D 61 C4
Schlüchtern D 51 C5
Schmallenberg D 50 B4
Schmelz D 60 A2
Schmidmühlen D 62 A2
Schmiedeberg D 53 C3
Schmiedefeld D 51 C6
Schmirn A 72 A1
Schmölln
Brandenburg D 45 B6
Sachsen D 52 C2
Schnaittach D 62 A2
Schneeberg D 52 C2
Schneizlreuth D 62 C3
Schneverdingen D 44 B1
Schöder A 73 A4
Schoenburg B 50 C2
Schollene D 44 C4
Schöllkrippen D 51 C5
Schomberg D 61 B4
Schönach D 62 B3
Schönau
Baden-Württemberg D 60 C3
Bayern D 62 B3
Schönbeck D 45 B5
Schönberg
Bayern D 63 B4
Mecklenburg-Vorpommern D 44 B2
Schleswig-Holstein D 44 A2
Schönebeck D 52 A1
Schöneck D 52 C2
Schönecken- D 50 C2
Schönermark D 45 B5
Schönewalde D 52 B3
Schongau D 62 C1
Schöngrabern A 64 B2
Schönhagen D 51 B5
Schönhausen D 44 C4
Schöningen D 51 A6
Schönkirchen D 44 A2
Schönsee D 62 A3
Schöntal D 61 A5
Schönthal D 62 A3
Schonungen D 51 C6
Schönwalde D 44 A2
Schoondijke NL 49 B4
Schoonebeek NL 42 C3
Schoonhoven NL 49 B5
Schopfheim D 60 C3
Schöppenstedt D 51 A6
Schörfling A 63 C4
Schorndorf D 61 B5
Schortens D 43 B4
Schotten D 51 C5
Schramberg D 61 B4
Schraplau D 52 B1
Schrattenberg A 64 B2
Schrecksbach D 51 C5
Schrems A 63 B6
Schrobenhausen D 62 B2
Schröcken A 71 A5
Schrozberg D 61 A5
Schruns A 71 A4
Schüpfheim CH 70 B3
Schüttorf D 50 A3
Schwaan D 44 B4
Schwabach D 62 A2
Schwäbisch Gmünd D 61 B5
Schwäbisch Hall D 61 A5
Schwabmünchen D 62 B1
Schwadorf A 64 B2
Schwagstorf D 43 C4
Schwaigern D 61 A5
Schwalmstadt D 51 C5
Schwanberg A 73 B5
Schwanden CH 70 B4
Schwandorf D 62 A3
Schwanebeck D 52 B1
Schwanenstadt A 63 B4
Schwanewede D 43 B5
Schwanfeld D 61 A6
Schwangau D 62 C1
Schwarmstedt D 43 C6
Schwarza D 51 C6
Schwarzach im Pongau A 72 A3
Schwarzau im Gebirge A 63 C6
Schwarzenau A 63 B6
Schwarzenbach D 52 C1
Schwarzenbach am Wald D 52 C1
Schwarzenbek D 44 B2
Schwarzenberg D 52 C2
Schwarzenburg CH 70 B2
Schwarzenfeld D 62 A3
Schwarz-heide D 53 B3
Schwaz A 72 A1
Schwechat A 64 B2
Schwedt D 45 B6
Schwei D 43 B5
Schweich D 60 A2
Schweighausen D 60 B3
Schweinfurt D 51 C6
Schweinitz D 52 B3
Schweinrich D 45 B4
Schwelm D 50 B3
Schwemsal D 52 B2
Schwendt A 62 C3
Schwenningen D 61 B4
Schwepnitz D 53 B3
Schwerin D 44 B3
Schwerte D 50 B3
Schweskau D 44 C3
Schwetzingen D 61 A4
Schwyz CH 70 A3
Sciacca I 108 B2
Scicli I 109 C3
Ściechów PL 45 C6
Scigliano I 106 B3
Scilla I 109 A4
Ścinawa PL 54 B1
Scionzier F 69 B6
Scoglitti I 109 C3
Scole GB 30 B5
Sconser GB 22 D2
Scopello
Piemonte I 70 C3
Sicilia I 108 A1
Scordia I 109 B3
Scorzè I 72 C2
Scotch Corner GB 27 A4
Scotter GB 27 B5
Scourie GB 22 C3
Scousburgh GB 22 B7
Scrabster GB 23 C5
Screeb IRL 20 A2
Scremerston GB 25 C6
Scritto I 82 C1
Scunthorpe GB 27 B5
Scuol CH 71 B5
Scúrcola Marsicana I 103 A6
Seaford GB 31 D4
Seaham GB 25 D6
Seahouses GB 25 C6
Seascale GB 26 A2
Seaton GB 29 C4
Sebazac-Concourès F 77 B5
Sebečevo SRB 85 C5
Seben TR 118 B6
Sebersdorf A 73 A5
Sebezh RUS 7 C10
Sebnitz D 53 C4
Seborga I 80 C1
Seby S 41 C6
Seč
Vychodočeský CZ 63 A6
Západočeský CZ 63 A4
Sečanj SRB 75 C5
Secemin PL 55 C4
Séchault F 59 A5
Seckau A 73 A4
Seclin F 49 C4
Secondigny F 67 B4
Seda P 92 B3
Sedan F 59 A5
Sedano E 88 B3
Sedbergh GB 26 A3
Sedella E 100 C1
Séderon F 79 B4
Sedgefield GB 27 A4
Sedico I 72 B2
Sédilo I 110 B1
Sédini I 110 B1
Sedlarica HR 74 C2
Sedlčany CZ 63 A5
Sedlec-Prčice CZ 63 A5
Sedlice CZ 63 A4
Sędziejowice PL 55 B4
Sędziszów PL 55 C5
Sędziszów Małapolski PL 55 C6
Seebach F 60 B3
Seeboden A 72 B3
Seefeld
Brandenburg D 45 C5
Niedersachsen D 43 B5
Seefeld in Tirol A 71 A6
Seeg D 62 C1
Seehausen
Sachsen-Anhalt D 44 C3
Sachsen-Anhalt D 52 A1
Seeheim-Jugenheim D 61 A4
Seelbach D 60 B3
Seelow D 45 C6
Seelze D 43 C6
Seerhausen D 52 B3
Sées F 57 B6
Seesen D 51 B6
Seeshaupt D 62 C2
Seewalchen A 63 C4
Seferihisar TR 119 D1
Sefkerin SRB 85 A5
Segård N 34 B2
Segerstad S 35 C5
Segesd H 74 B2
Seglinge FIN 36 B7
Segmon S 35 C5
Segonzac F 67 C4
Segorbe E 96 B2
Segovia E 94 B2
Segré F 57 C5
Segura
E 89 B4
P 93 B3
Segura de León E 99 A4
Segura de los Baños E 90 C2
Ségur-les-Villas F 68 C2
Segurrilla E 94 B2
Sehnde D 51 A5
Seia P 92 A3
Seiches-sur-le-Loir F 67 A4
Seifhennersdorf D 53 C4
Seignelay F 59 C4
Seijo E 87 C2
Seilhac F 68 C1
Seilles B 49 C6
Seim N 32 B2
Seinäjoki FIN 3 E25
Seissan F 77 C3
Seitenstetten Markt A 63 B5
Seixal P 92 C1
Seiz A 73 A4
Seizthal A 73 A4
Sejerslev DK 38 C1
Seksna RUS 7 B15
Selárdalur IS 111 B1
Selárgius I 110 C2
Selb D 52 C2
Selby GB 27 B4
Selca HR 84 C1
Selcë AL 105 A5
Selce HR 73 C4
Selçuk TR 119 E2
Selde DK 38 C2
Selenča SRB 75 C4
Selendi
Manisa TR 118 D2
Manisa TR 118 D3
Selenicë AL 105 C5
Sélestat F 60 B3
Seleuš SRB 75 C5
Selevac SRB 85 B5
Selfoss IS 111 D5
Selgua E 90 B3
Selice SK 64 B3
Seligenstadt D 51 C4
Seligenthal D 51 C6
Selimiye TR 119 E2
Selizharovo RUS 7 C12
Selja S 36 A1
Selje N 114 E2
Seljelvnes N 112 C8
Seljord N 33 C5
Selkirk GB 25 C5
Sellano I 82 D1
Selles-St Denis F 68 A1
Selles-sur-Cher F 67 A6
Sellières F 69 B5
Sellin D 45 A5
Sellye H 74 C2
Selm D 50 B3
Selnica ob Dravi SLO 73 B5
Selongey F 59 C6
Selonnet F 79 B5
Selow D 44 B3
Selsey GB 31 D3
Selsingen D 43 B6
Selters D 50 C3
Seltso RUS 7 E13
Seltz F 61 B4
Selva E 97 B2
Selva di Cadore I 72 B2
Selva di Val Gardena I 72 B1
Selvik
Sogn og Fjordane N 32 A2
Vestfold N 35 C2
Selvino I 71 C4
Selyatyn UA 11 C8
Sem N 35 C2
Semeljci HR 74 C3
Semenovka
Chernihiv UA 7 E12
Kremenchuk UA 11 B12
Semič SLO 73 C5
Semide
F 59 A5
P 92 A2
Semily CZ 53 C5
Seminara I 106 C2
Semlac RO 75 B5
Semmen-stedt D 51 A6
Šempeter SLO 73 B5
Semriach A 73 A5
Semur-en-Auxois F 69 A4
Sena E 90 B2
Sena de Luna E 88 B1
Senarpont F 58 A2
Sénas F 79 C4
Senćanski Trešnjevac SRB 75 C4
Sencelles E 97 B2
Senčur SLO 73 B4
Senden
Bayern D 61 B6
Nordrhein-Westfalen D 50 B3
Sendenhorst D 50 B3
Sendim P 87 C4
Senec SK 64 B3
Seneffe B 49 C5
Séneghe I 110 B1
Senés E 101 B3
Senez F 79 C5
Senftenberg D 53 B3
Sengouagnet F 77 D3
Sengwarden D 43 B5
Senica SK 64 B3
Senice na Hané CZ 64 A3
Senigállia I 82 C2
Senirkent TR 119 D5
Sénis I 110 C1
Senise I 106 A3
Senj HR 83 B3
Senje SRB 85 C6
Senjehopen N 112 C6
Senjski Rudnik SRB 85 C6
Senlis F 58 A3
Sennan S 40 C2
Sennecey-le-Grand F 69 B4
Sennen GB 28 C2
Senno BY 7 D10
Sénnori I 110 B1
Sennwald CH 71 A4
Sennybridge GB 29 B4
Senohrad SK 65 B5
Senonches F 58 B2
Senones F 60 B2
Senorb ì I 110 C2
Senovo SLO 73 B5
Senožeče SLO 73 C4
Senožeti SLO 73 B4
Sens F 59 B4
Sens-de-Bretagne F 57 B4
Senta SRB 75 C5
Senterada E 90 A3
Šentilj SLO 73 B5
Šentjernej SLO 73 C5
Šentjur SLO 73 B5
Senumstad N 33 D5
Seoane E 86 B3
Seon CH 70 A3
Sépeaux F 59 C4
Sépey CH 70 B2
Sepino I 103 B7
Sępólno Krajeńskie PL 46 B3
Seppenrade D 50 B3
Seppois F 70 A2
Septeuil F 58 B2
Sepúlveda E 88 C3
Sequals I 72 B2
Sequeros E 93 A4
Seraincourt F 59 A5
Seraing B 49 C6
Seravezza I 81 C4
Sered' SK 64 B3
Seredka RUS 7 B10
Şereflikoçhisar TR 16 B6
Seregélyes H 74 A3
Seregno I 71 C4
Sérent F 56 C3
Serfaus A 71 A5
Sergiyev Posad RUS 7 C15
Seriate I 71 C4
Sérifontaine F 58 A2
Serifos GR 117 E6
Sérignan F 78 C2
Serik TR 119 F6
Serina I 71 C4
Serinhisar TR 119 E4
Sermaises F 58 B3
Sermaize-les-Bains F 59 B5
Sérmide I 81 B5
Sermoneta I 102 B5
Sernache de Bonjardim P 92 B2
Sernancelhe P 87 D3
Serón E 101 B3
Serón de Najima E 89 C4
Serooskerke NL 49 B4
Seròs E 90 B3
Serpa P 98 B3
Serpukhov RUS 7 D14
Serracapriola I 103 B8
Serrada E 88 C2
Serra de Outes E 86 B2
Serradifalco I 108 B2
Serradilla E 93 B4
Serradilla del Arroyo E 93 A4
Serradilla del Llano E 93 A4
Serramanna I 110 C1
Serramazzoni I 81 B4
Serranillos E 94 B2
Serrapetrona I 82 C2
Serra San Bruno I 106 C3
Serra San Quírico I 82 C2
Serrastretta I 106 B3
Serravalle
Piemonte I 70 C3
Umbria I 82 D2
Serravalle di Chienti I 82 C1
Serravalle Scrívia I 80 B2
Serre I 103 C8
Serrejón E 93 B5
Serres
F 79 B4
GR 116 A5
Serrières F 69 C4
Serrières-de-Briord F 69 C5
Sersale I 106 B3
Sertã P 92 B2
Sertig Dörfli CH 71 B4
Servance F 60 C2
Serverette F 78 B2
Servia GR 116 B4
Servian F 78 C2
Serviers F 78 B3
Servigliano I 82 C2
Serzedelo P 87 C2
Seseña Nuevo E 95 B3
Sesimbra P 92 C1
Seskinore GB 19 B4
Sesma E 89 B4
Sessa Aurunca I 103 B6
Ses Salines E 97 B3
Sesta Godano I 80 B3
Šestanovac HR 84 C1
Sestao E 89 A4
Sestino I 82 C1
Sesto I 72 B2
Sesto Calende I 70 C3
Sesto Fiorentino I 81 C5
Séstola I 81 B4
Sesto San Giovanni I 71 C4
Sestriere I 79 B5
Sestri Levante I 80 B3
Sestroretsk RUS 7 A11
Sestu I 110 C2
Sesvete HR 73 C6
Setcases E 91 A5
Sète F 78 C2
Setenil E 99 C5
Setermoen N 112 D7
Šetonje SRB 85 B6
Setskog N 34 C3
Settalsjølia N 114 E7
Séttimo Torinese I 70 C2
Settimo Vittone I 70 C2
Settle GB 26 A3
Setúbal P 92 C2
Seubersdort D 62 A2
Seúi I 110 C2
Seúlo I 110 C2
Seurre F 69 B5
Sevaster AL 105 C5
Sevel DK 38 C1
Sevenoaks GB 31 C4
Sévérac-le-Château F 78 B2
Sever do Vouga P 87 D2
Severin HR 73 C5
Severomorsk RUS 3 B30
Séveso I 71 C4
Ševětín CZ 63 A5
Sevettijärvi FIN 113 C17
Sévigny F 59 A5
Sevilla = Seville E 99 B5
Sevilla la Nueva E 94 B2
Seville = Sevilla E 99 B5
Sevilleja de la Jara E 94 C2
Sevlievo BG 11 E8
Sevnica SLO 73 B5
Sevojno SRB 85 C4
Sevrier F 69 C6
Sevsk RUS 7 E13
Sexdrega S 40 B3
Seyches F 76 B3
Seyda D 52 B2
Seydişehir TR 119 E6
Seyðisfjörður IS 111 B12
Seyitgazi TR 118 C5
Seyitömer TR 118 C4
Seymen TR 118 A2
Seyne F 79 B5
Seynes F 78 B3
Seyssel F 69 C5
Sežana SLO 72 C3
Sézanne F 59 B4
Sezulfe P 87 C3
Sezze I 102 B6
Sfântu Gheorghe RO 11 D8
Sforzacosta I 82 C2
Sgarasta Mhor GB 22 D1
's-Gravendeel NL 49 B5
's-Gravenhage = The Hague NL 49 A5
's-Gravenzande NL 49 B5
Shaftesbury GB 29 B5
Shaldon GB 29 C4
Shanagolden IRL 20 B2
Shanklin GB 31 D2
Shannon IRL 20 B3
Shap GB 26 A3
Sharpness GB 29 B5
Shawbury GB 26 C3
Shchekino RUS 7 D14
Shchigry RUS 7 F14
Shchors UA 7 F11
's-Heerenberg NL 50 B2
Sheerness GB 31 C4
Sheffield GB 27 B4
Shefford GB 31 B3
Shenfield GB 31 C4
Shëngjergj AL 116 A2
Shëngjin AL 105 B5
Shepetivka UA 11 A9
Shepshed GB 27 C4
Shepton Mallet GB 29 B5
Sherborne GB 29 C5
Shercock IRL 19 C5
Sheringham GB 30 B5
's-Hertogenbosch NL 49 B6
Shiel Bridge GB 22 D3
Shieldaig GB 22 D3
Shijak AL 105 B5
Shillelagh IRL 21 B5
Shimsk RUS 7 B11
Shipston-on-Stour GB 29 A6
Shirgjan AL 105 B6
Shklow BY 7 D11
Shkodër AL 105 A5
Shoeburyness GB 31 C4
Shoreham-by-Sea GB 31 D3
Shostka UA 7 F12
Shotley Gate GB 31 C5
Shpola UA 11 B11
Shrewsbury GB 26 C3
Shugozero RUS 7 B13
Shumen BG 11 E9
Siabost GB 22 C2
Siamanna I 110 C1
Sianów PL 46 A2
Siatista GR 116 B3
Šiauges-St Romain F 78 A2
Šiauliai LT 6 D7
Sibari I 106 B3
Šibbhult S 41 C4
Šibenik HR 83 C4
Siberstedt D 43 A6
Sibinj HR 74 C2
Sibiu RO 11 D8
Sibnica SRB 85 B5
Sibsey GB 27 B6
Šiculiana I 108 B2
Šid SRB 85 A4
Sidari GR 116 C1
Siddeburen NL 42 B3
Sidensjö S 115 D15
Siderno I 106 C3
Sidirokastro GR 116 A5
Sidmouth GB 29 C4
Sidzina PL 65 A5
Siebe N 113 D12
Siebenlehn D 52 B3
Siedlce PL 6 E7
Siedlice PL 46 B1
Siedlinghausen D 51 B4
Siedlisko PL 46 C2
Siegburg D 50 C3
Siegen D 50 C4
Siegenburg D 62 B2
Sieghartskirchen A 64 B2
Siegsdorf D 62 C3
Siekierki PL 45 C6
Sielpia PL 55 B5
Siemiany PL 47 B5
Siena I 81 C5
Sieniawka PL 53 C4
Siennica PL 55 A6
Sienno PL 55 B6
Sieppijärvi FIN 113 E13
Sieradz PL 54 B3
Sieraków
Śląskie PL 54 C3
Wielkopolskie PL 46 C2
Sierakowice PL 46 A3
Sierck-les-Bains F 60 A2
Sierentz F 60 C3
Sierning A 63 B5
Sierpc PL 47 C5
Sierra de Fuentes E 93 B4
Sierra de Luna E 90 A2
Sierra de Yeguas E 100 B1
Sierre CH 70 B2
Siestrzeń PL 55 A5
Sietamo E 90 A2
Siewierz PL 55 C4
Sigdal N 34 B1
Sigean F 78 C1
Sigerfjord N 112 D4
Sighetu-Marmatiei RO 11 C7
Sighişoara RO 11 C8
Sigillo I 82 C1
Siglufjörður IS 111 A7
Sigmaringen D 61 B5
Signa I 81 C5
Signes F 79 C4
Signy-l'Abbaye F 59 A5
Signy-le-Petit F 59 A5
Sigogne F 67 C4
Sigri GR 116 C7
Sigtuna S 37 C4
Sigueiro E 86 B2
Sigüenza E 95 A4
Sigües E 90 A1
Sigulda LV 6 C8
Siilinjärvi FIN 3 E27
Sikenica SK 65 B4
Sikia GR 116 B5
Sikinos GR 117 F7
Sikkilsdalseter N 32 A6
Siklós H 74 C3
Sikórz PL 47 C5
Sikselet S 115 A14
Silandro I 71 B5
Silánus I 110 B1
Silbaš SRB 75 C4
Şile TR 118 A4
Siles E 101 A3
Silgueiros P 92 A3
Silifke TR 16 C6
Silíqua I 110 C1
Silistra BG 11 D9
Silivri TR 118 A3
Siljan N 35 C1
Siljansnäs S 36 B1
Silkeborg DK 39 C2
Silla E 96 B2
Sillamäe EST 7 B9
Silleda E 86 B2
Sillé-le-Guillaume F 57 B5
Sillenstede D 43 B4
Sillerud S 35 C4
Sillian A 72 B2
Silloth GB 25 D4
Silno PL 46 B3
Silnowo PL 46 B2
Silo HR 73 C4
Sils E 91 B5
Silsand N 112 C6
Šilte S 37 E5
Šilute LT 6 D6
Silvalen N 114 B9
Silvaplana CH 71 B4
Silvares P 92 A3
Silvberg S 36 B2
Silverdalen S 40 B5
Silvermines IRL 20 B3
Silverstone GB 30 B2
Silverton GB 29 C4
Silves P 98 B2
Silvi Marina I 103 A7
Šimandre F 69 B4
Šimanovci SRB 85 B5
Simard F 69 B5
Simat de Valldigna E 96 B2
Simav TR 118 C3
Simbach
Bayern D 62 B3
Bayern D 62 B4
Simbário I 106 C3
Simeria RO 11 D7
Simi GR 119 F2
Simićevo SRB 85 B6
Simlångsdalen S 40 C3
Simmerath D 50 C2
Simmerberg D 61 C5
Simmern D 50 D3
Šimo FIN 3 D26
Šimonovce SK 65 B6
Simonsbath GB 28 B4
Simonstorp S 37 D3
Simontornya H 74 B3
Simplon CH 70 B3
Simrishamn S 41 D4
Sinaia RO 11 D8
Sinalunga I 81 C5
Sinanaj AL 105 C5
Sinarcas E 96 B1
Sincan TR 118 C7
Sincanlı TR 118 D5
Sindal DK 38 B3
Sindelfingen D 61 B5
Sindia I 110 B1
Sındırgı TR 118 C3
Sinekli TR 118 A3
Sines P 98 B2
Sinetta FIN 113 F14
Sineu E 97 B3
Singen D 61 C4
Singleton GB 31 D3
Singsås N 114 E7
Siniscóla I 110 B2
Sinj HR 83 C5
Sinlabajos E 94 A2
Sinn D 50 C4
Sinnai I 110 C2
Sinnes N 33 D3
Sinop TR 16 A7
Sins CH 70 A3
Sinsheim D 61 A4
Sint Annaland NL 49 B5
Sint Annaparochie NL 42 B2
Sint Athonis NL 50 B1
Sint Nicolaasga NL 42 C2
Sint Oedenrode NL 49 B6
Sintra P 92 C1
Sinzheim D 61 B4
Sinzig D 50 C3
Siófok H 74 B3
Sion CH 70 B2
Sion Mills GB 19 B4
Siorac-en-Périgord F 77 B3
Šipanska Luka HR 84 D2
Šipovo BIH 84 B2
Sira N 33 D3
Siracusa I 109 B4
Siret RO 11 C9
Sirevåg N 33 D2
Sirig SRB 75 C4
Sirkka FIN 113 E13
Sirmione I 71 C5
Široki H 65 C6
Široké SK 65 B6
Široki Brijeg BIH 84 C2
Sirolo I 82 C2
Siruela E 94 D1
Sisak HR 73 C6
Sisante E 95 C4
Šišljavić HR 73 C5
Sissach CH 70 A2
Sissonne F 59 A4
Sistelo P 87 C2
Sisteron F 79 B4
Sistiana I 72 C3
Sistranda N 114 D5
Sitasjaurestugorna S 112 E6
Sitges E 91 B4
Sitia GR 117 G8
Sittard NL 50 B1
Sittensen D 43 B6
Sittingbourne GB 31 C4
Sitzenroda D 52 B2
Sivac SRB 75 C4
Sivaslı TR 119 D4
Siverić HR 83 C5
Sivrihisar TR 118 C6
Sixt-Fer-á-Cheval F 70 B1
Siziano I 71 C4
Sizun F 56 B1
Sjenica SRB 85 C5
Sjoa N 114 F6
Sjøåsen N 114 C8
Sjöbo S 41 D3
Sjøenden
Hedmark N 34 A3
Hedmark N 34 B3
Sjøholt N 114 E3
Sjøli N 34 A3
Sjølstad N 114 C9
Sjölunda S 37 C2
Sjømarken S 40 B2
Sjørring DK 38 C1
Sjötofta S 40 B3
Sjötorp S 35 D5
Sjoutnäset S 115 C11
Sjøvegan N 112 D6
Sjuntorp S 35 D4
Skåbu N 32 A6
Skadovsk UA 11 C12
Skafså N 33 C5
Skaftafell IS 111 D9
Skagaströnd IS 111 B5
Skagen DK 38 B3
Skagersvik S 35 D6
Skaiå N 33 D4
Skaidi N 113 B13
Skala GR 117 D2
Skała PL 55 C4
Skaland N 112 C6
Skala Oropou GR 117 D5
Skala-Podilska UA 11 B9
Skalat UA 11 B8
Skalbmierz PL 55 C5
Skålevik N 33 D5
Skalica SK 64 B3
Skalité SK 65 A4
Skällinge S 40 B2
Skalná CZ 52 C2
Skals DK 38 C2
Skælskør DK 39 D4
Skalstugan S 114 D9
Skanderborg DK 39 C2
Skånes-Fagerhult S 41 C3
Skåne-Tranås S 41 D3
Skånevik N 33 C2
Skänninge S 37 D2
Skanör med Falsterbo S 41 D2
Skåpafors S 35 C4
Skąpe PL 53 A5
Skara S 35 D5
Skærbæk DK 39 D1
Skarberget N 112 D5
Skärblacka S 37 D2
Skarð IS 111 B3
Skarda S 115 C15
Skare N 32 C3
Skåre S 35 C5
Skärhamn S 38 B4
Skarnes N 34 B3
Skärplinge S 36 B4
Skarpnatö FIN 36 B6
Skarp Salling DK 38 C2
Skarrild DK 39 D1
Skarstad N 112 D5
Skärstad S 40 B4
Skarsvåg N 113 A14
Skarszewy PL 47 A4
Skårup DK 39 D3
Skärvången S 115 D11
Skarvsjöby S 115 C14
Skaryszew PL 55 B6
Skarżysko-Kamienna PL 55 B5
Skarzysko Ksiazece PL 55 B5
Skatøy N 33 D6
Skattkärr S 35 C5
Skattungbyn S 36 A1
Skatval N 114 D7
Skaulo S 112 E10
Skave DK 39 C1
Skawina PL 55 D4
Skebobruk S 36 C5
Skebokvarn S 37 C3
Skedala S 40 C2
Skedevi S 37 D2
Skedsmokorset N 34 B3
Skee S 35 D3
Skegness GB 27 B6
Skela SRB 85 B5
Skelani BIH 85 C4
Skellefteå S 3 D24
Skelleftehamn S 3 D24
Skelmersdale GB 26 B3
Skelmorlie GB 24 C3
Skelund DK 38 C3
Skender Vakuf BIH 84 B2
Skene S 40 B2
Skępe PL 47 C5
Skepplanda S 40 B2
Skeppshult S 40 B3
Skerries IRL 19 C5
Ski N 35 C2
Skiathos GR 116 C5
Skibbereen IRL 20 C2
Skibotn N 112 C9
Skidra GR 116 B4
Skien N 35 C1
Skierniewice PL 55 B5
Skillingaryd S 40 B4
Skillinge S 41 D4
Skillingmark S 34 C4
Skilloura CY 120 A2
Skinnardai S 37 C5
Skinnskatteberg S 36 C2

Sulzbach
Baden-Württemberg
D 61 A5
Baden-Württemberg
D 61 B5
Bayern D 61 A5
Saarland D 60 A3
Sulzbach-Rosenberg
D 62 A2
Sülze D 44 C2
Sulzfeld D 51 C6
Sumartin HR 84 C1
Sumburgh GB 22 B7
Sümeg H 74 B2
Šumiswald CH 70 A2
Šumná CZ 64 B1
Šumperk CZ 54 D1
Šumvald CZ 64 A3
Sumy UA 7 F13
Sunbilla E 76 C1
Sünching D 62 B3
Sund
FIN 36 B7
S 35 C3
Sundborn S 36 B2
Sundby DK 38 C1
Sunde N 32 C2
Sunde bru N 33 D6
Sunderland GB 25 D6
Sundern D 50 B4
Sundhultsbrunn S 40 B4
Sundnäs S 115 A14
Sunds DK 39 D2
Sundsfjord N 112 F3
Sundsvall S 115 E14
Sungurlu TR 16 A7
Suni I 110 B1
Sunja HR 74 C1
Sunnansjö S 36 B1
Sunnaryd S 40 B3
Sunndalsøra N 114 E5
Sunne S 34 C5
Sunnemo S 34 C6
Sunnersberg S 35 D5
Suolovuopmio N 113 C12
Suomussalmi FIN 3 D28
Suoyarvi RUS 3 E30
Super Sauze F 79 B5
Supetar HR 83 C5
Supetarska Draga HR 83 B3
Supino I 102 B6
Šuplja Stijena MNE 84 C4
Surahammar S 37 C3
Šurany SK 64 B4
Surazh
BY 7 D11
RUS 7 E12
Surbo I 105 C4
Surčin SRB 85 B5
Surgères F 66 B4
Surhuisterveen NL 42 B3
Súria E 91 B4
Surin F 67 B5
Surka N 34 B2
Surnadalsøra N 114 E5
Sursee CH 70 A3
Surte S 38 B5
Surwold D 43 C4
Sury-le-Comtal F 69 C4
Susa I 70 C2
Šušara SRB 85 B6
Susch CH 71 B5
Susegana I 72 C2
Süsel D 44 A2
Šušice CZ 63 A4
Šušnjevica HR 73 C4
Sussen D 61 B5
Susurluk TR 118 C3
Susz PL 47 B5
Sütçüler TR 119 E5
Sutivan HR 83 C5
Sutjeska SRB 75 C5
Sutomore MNE 105 A5
Sutri I 102 A5
Sutton GB 31 C3
Sutton Coldfield GB 27 C4
Sutton-in-Ashfield
GB 27 B4
Sutton-on-Sea GB 27 B6
Sutton-on-Trent GB 27 B5
Sutton Scotney GB 31 C2
Sutton Valence GB 31 C4
Suvaja BIH 83 B5
Suvereto I 81 C4
Suvorov RUS 7 D14
Suwałki PL 6 D7
Suze-la-Rousse F 78 B3
Suzzara I 81 B4
Svabensverk S 36 A2
Svalbarð IS 111 A10
Svalöv S 41 D3
Svanabyn S 115 C13
Svanberga S 36 C5
Svaneke DK 41 D5
Svanesund S 35 D3
Svängsta S 41 C4
Svannäs S 115 A15
Svanskog S 35 C4
Svanstein S 113 F12
Svappavaara S 112 E10
Svärdsjö S 36 B2
Svarstad N 35 C1
Svartå S 37 C1
Svärta S 37 D4
Svartå S 34 C5
Svärtinge S 37 D3
Svartnäs S 36 B3
Svartnes N 112 E3
Svarttjärn S 115 B13
Svatsum N 34 A1
Svätý Jur SK 64 B3
Svätý Peter SK 64 C4
Svedala S 41 D3
Sveg S 115 E11
Sveindal N 33 D4
Sveio N 33 C2
Svejbæk DK 39 C2
Svelgen N 114 F2
Svelvik N 35 C2
Svendborg DK 39 D3
Svene N 32 C6
Svenljunga S 40 B3
Svennevad S 37 C2
Svenstavik S 115 E11
Švenstrup DK 38 C2
Švermov CZ 53 C4
Sveti Ivan Zabno HR 74 C1
Sveti Ivan Zelina HR 73 C6
Sveti Nikola MNE 105 B5
Sveti Rok HR 83 B4
Sveti Stefan MNE 105 A4
Světla nad Sázavou
CZ 63 A6
Svetlyy RUS 47 A6
Švetvinčenat HR 82 A2
Švica HR 83 B4
Švidník SK 10 B6
Švihov CZ 63 A4
Svilajnac SRB 85 B6
Svilengrad BG 11 F9
Svindal N 35 C3
Svinhult S 40 B5
Svinna SK 64 B4
Svinninge
DK 39 D4
S 37 C5
Sviritsa RUS 7 A12
Svishtov BG 11 E8
Svislach BY 6 E8
Svit SK 65 A6
Svitavy CZ 64 A2
Svitlovodsk UA 11 B12
Svodín SK 65 C4
Svolvær N 112 D3
Svortemyr N 32 A2
Svortland N 32 C2
Svratka CZ 64 A2
Svrčinovec SK 65 A4
Svullrya N 34 B4
Svyetlahorsk BY 7 E10
Swadlincote GB 27 C4
Swaffham GB 30 B4
Swanage GB 29 C6
Swanley GB 31 C4
Swanlinbar IRL 19 B4
Swansea GB 28 B4
Swarzędz PL 46 C3
Swatragh GB 19 B5
Świątki PL 47 B6
Świdnica
Dolnośląskie PL 54 C1
Lubuskie PL 53 B5
Świdnik PL 11 A7
Świdwin PL 46 B1
Świebodzice PL 53 C6
Świebodzin PL 53 A5
Świecie PL 47 B4
Świedziebnia PL 47 B5
Świeradów Zdrój PL 53 C5
Świerki PL 54 C1
Swierzawa PL 53 B5
Swierzno PL 45 B6
Swięta PL 45 B6
Swięta Anna PL 55 C4
Świętno PL 53 A6
Swifterbant NL 42 C2
Swindon GB 29 B6
Swineshead GB 30 B3
Swinford IRL 18 C3
Świnoujście PL 45 B6
Swinton GB 25 C5
Swobnica PL 45 B6
Swords IRL 21 A5
Swornegacie PL 46 B3
Sya S 37 D2
Syasstroy RUS 7 A12
Sycewice PL 46 A2
Sychevka RUS 7 D13
Syców PL 54 B2
Sycowice PL 53 A5
Sydnes N 33 C2
Syfteland N 32 B2
Syke D 43 C5
Sykkylven N 114 E3
Sylling N 34 C2
Sylte N 114 E4
Symbister GB 22 A7
Symington GB 25 C4
Symonds Yat GB 29 B5
Sypniewo
Kujawsko-Pomorskie
PL 46 B3
Wielkopolskie PL 46 B2
Sysserum S 40 B6
Sysslebäck S 34 B4
Syväjärvi FIN 113 E14
Szabadbattyán H 74 A3
Szabadegyháza H 74 A3
Szabadszállás H 75 B4
Szadek PL 54 B3
Szajol H 75 A5
Szakály H 74 B3
Szakcs H 74 B3
Szakmár H 75 B4
Szalánta H 74 C3
Szałas PL 55 B5
Szalkszentmárton H 75 B4
Szalonna H 65 B6
Szamocin PL 46 B3
Szamotuły PL 46 C2
Szany H 74 A2
Szarvas H 75 B5
Szarvaskő H 65 C6
Szászvár H 74 B3
Százhalombatta H 74 A3
Szczawa PL 65 A6
Szczawnica PL 65 A6
Szczecin PL 45 B6
Szczecinek PL 46 B2
Szczekociny PL 55 C4
Szczerców PL 55 B4
Szczucin PL 55 C6
Szczuczarz PL 46 B2
Szczurkowo PL 47 A6
Szczurowa PL 55 C5
Szczyrk PL 65 A5
Szczytna PL 54 C1
Szczytno PL 6 E6
Szczyty PL 54 B3
Szécsény H 65 B5
Szederkény H 74 C3
Szedres H 74 B3
Szeged H 75 B5
Szeghalom H 75 A6
Szegvár H 75 B5
Székesfehérvár H 74 A3
Székkutas H 75 B5
Szekszárd H 74 B3
Szemplino Czarne PL 47 B6
Szemud PL 47 A4
Szendehely H 65 C5
Szendrő H 65 B6
Szentendre H 65 C5
Szentes H 75 B5
Szentgotthárd H 73 B6
Szentlászló H 74 B2
Szentlőrinc H 74 B2
Szentmártonkáta H 75 A4
Szenyér H 74 B2
Szeremle H 74 B3
Szerep H 75 A6
Szigetszentmiklós H 75 A4
Szigetvár H 74 B2
Szikáncs H 75 B5
Szikszó H 65 B6
Szil H 74 A2
Szilvásvárad H 65 B6
Szklarska Poreba PL 53 C5
Szlichtyngowa PL 53 B6
Szob H 65 C4
Szolnok H 75 A5
Szombathely H 74 A1
Szorosad H 74 B3
Szpetal Graniczny PL 47 C5
Szprotawa PL 53 B5
Szreńsk PL 47 B6
Sztum PL 47 B5
Sztutowo PL 47 A5
Szubin PL 46 B3
Szücsi H 65 C5
Szulmierz PL 47 C6
Szulok H 74 B2
Szumanie PL 47 C5
Szwecja PL 46 B2
Szydłów
Łódzkie PL 55 B4
Świętokrzyskie PL 55 C6
Szydłowiec PL 55 B5
Szydlowo PL 47 B6
Szydłowo PL 46 B2
Szymanów PL 55 A5
Szynkielów PL 54 B3
Szynwald PL 55 D6

T

Taastrup DK 41 D2
Tab H 74 B3
Tabanera la Luenga E 94 A2
Tabaqueros E 96 B1
Tábara E 88 C1
Tabenera de Cerrato
E 88 B2
Taberg S 40 B4
Tabernas E 101 B3
Tabiano Bagni I 81 B4
Taboada E 86 B3
Taboadela E 87 B3
Tábor CZ 63 A5
Táborfalva H 75 A4
Taborište HR 73 C6
Tábua P 92 A2
Tabuaco P 87 C3
Tabuenca E 89 C5
Tabuyo del Monte E 87 B4
Täby S 37 C5
Tác H 74 A3
Tachov CZ 62 A3
Tadcaster GB 27 B4
Tadley GB 31 C2
Tafalla E 89 B5
Tafjord N 114 E4
Taganheira P 98 B2
Tågarp S 41 D2
Tággia I 80 C1
Tagliacozzo I 102 A6
Táglio di Po I 82 A1
Tagnon F 59 A5
Tahal E 101 B3
Tahitótfalu H 65 C5
Tahtaköprü TR 118 C4
Tailfingen D 61 B5
Taillis F 57 B4
Tain GB 23 D4
Tain-l'Hermitage F 78 A3
Taipadas P 92 C2
Taivalkoski FIN 3 D28
Takene S 35 C5
Takovo SRB 85 B5
Taksony H 75 A4
Tal E 86 B2
Talachyn BY 7 D10
Talamello I 82 C1
Talamone I 102 A4
Talant F 69 A4
Talarrubias E 93 B5
Talas TR 16 B7
Talaván E 93 B4
Talavera de la Reina
E 94 C2
Talavera la Real E 93 C4
Talayuela E 93 B5
Talayuelas E 96 B1
Talgarth GB 29 B4
Talgje N 33 C2
Talhadas P 92 A2
Táliga E 93 C3
Talizat F 78 A2
Tálknafjörður IS 111 B2
Talla I 81 C5
Talladale GB 22 D3
Tallaght IRL 21 A5
Tallard F 79 B5
Tällberg S 36 B1
Tallinn EST 6 B8
Talloires F 69 C6
Tallow IRL 21 B4
Tallsjö S 115 C15
Talmay F 69 A5
Talmont-St Hilaire F 66 B3
Talmont-sur-Gironde
F 66 C4
Talne UA 11 B11
Talsano I 104 C3
Talsi LV 6 C7
Talvik N 113 B11
Talybont GB 26 C2
Tal-Y-Llyn GB 26 C2
Tamajón E 95 B3
Tamame E 88 C1
Tamames E 93 A4
Tamarit de Mar E 91 B4
Tamarite de Litera E 90 B3
Tamariu E 91 B6
Tamási H 74 B3
Tambach-Dietharz D 51 C6
Tameza E 86 A4
Tammisaari FIN 6 A7
Tampere FIN 3 F25
Tamsweg A 72 A3
Tamurejo E 94 D2
Tamworth GB 27 C4
Tana bru N 113 B17
Tañabueyes E 89 B3
Tanakajd H 74 A1
Tananger N 33 D2
Tanaunella I 110 B2
Tancarville F 58 A1
Tandsjöborg S 115 F11
Tånga S 41 C2
Tangelic H 74 B3
Tangen N 34 B3
Tangerhütte D 44 C3
Tangermünde D 44 C3
Tanhua FIN 113 E16
Taninges F 69 B6
Tankavaara FIN 113 D16
Tann D 51 C6
Tanna D 52 C1
Tannadice GB 25 B5
Tannåker S 40 C3
Tännäs S 115 E9
Tannay
Ardennes F 59 A5
Nièvre F 68 A3
Tannenbergsthal D 52 C2
Tännesberg D 62 A3
Tannheim A 71 A5
Tanowo PL 45 B6
Tanum S 35 D3
Tanumshede S 35 D3
Tanus F 77 B5
Tanvald CZ 53 C5
Taormina I 109 B4
Tapa EST 7 B8
Tapfheim D 62 B1
Tapia de Casariego E 86 A4
Tapio F 77 C4
Tápióbicske H 75 A4
Tápiógyörgye H 75 A4
Tápióság H 75 A4
Tápiószecső H 75 A4
Tápiószele H 75 A4
Tápiószentmárton H 75 A4
Tapolca H 74 B2
Tapolcafő H 74 A2
Tar HR 72 C3
Tarabo S 40 B2
Taradell E 91 B5
Taraklı TR 118 B5
Taramundi E 86 A3
Tarancón E 95 B3
Táranto I 104 C3
Tarare F 69 C4
Tarascon F 78 C3
Tarascon-sur-Ariège
F 77 D4
Tarashcha UA 11 B11
Tarazona E 89 C5
Tarazona de la Mancha
E 95 C5
Tarbena E 96 C2
Tarbert
GB 24 C2
IRL 20 B2
Tarbes F 76 C3
Tarbet GB 24 B3
Tarbolton GB 24 C3
Tarcento I 72 B3
Tarčin BIH 84 C3
Tarczyn PL 55 B5
Tardajos E 88 B3
Tardelcuende E 89 C4
Tardets-Sorholus F 76 C2
Tardienta E 90 B2
Tärendö S 113 E11
Targon F 76 B2
Târgoviște 11 D8
Târgu-Jiu RO 11 D7
Târgu Mureș RO 11 C8
Târgu Ocna RO 11 C9
Târgu Secuiesc RO 11 D9
Tarifa E 99 C5
Tariquejas E 98 B3
Tarján H 65 C4
Tárkany H 64 C4
Tarland GB 23 D6
Tarłów PL 55 B6
Tarm DK 39 D1
Tarmstedt D 43 B6
Tärnaby S 115 B12
Tarnalelesz H 65 B6
Tarnaörs H 65 C6
Târnăveni RO 11 C8
Tärnet N 113 C19
Tarnobrzeg PL 55 C6
Tarnos F 76 C1
Tarnów
Lubuskie PL 45 C6
Małopolskie PL 55 C5
Tarnowo Podgórne
PL 46 C2
Tarnowskie Góry PL 54 C3
Tärnsjö S 36 B3
Tärnvik N 112 E4
Tarouca P 87 C3
Tarp D 43 A6
Tarquínia I 102 A4
Tarquínia Lido I 102 A4
Tarragona E 91 B4
Tàrrega E 91 B4
Tarrenz A 71 A5
Tårs
Nordjyllands DK 38 B3
Storstrøms DK 39 E4
Tarsia I 106 B3
Tarsus TR 16 C7
Tartas F 76 C2
Tartu EST 7 B9
Tarussa RUS 7 D14
Tarves GB 23 D6
Tarvísio I 72 B3
Taşağıl TR 119 F6
Täsch CH 70 B2
Taşköprü TR 16 A7
Tasov CZ 64 A2
Tasovčići BIH 84 C2
Taşucu TR 16 C6
Tát H 65 C4
Tata H 65 C4
Tatabánya H 74 A3
Tataháza H 75 B4
Tatarbunary UA 11 D10
Tatárszentgyörgy H 75 A4
Tatranská-Lomnica
SK 65 A6
Tau N 33 C2
Tauberbischofsheim
D 61 A5
Taucha D 52 B2
Taufkirchen D 62 B3
Taufkirchen an der Pram
A 63 B4
Taulé F 56 B2
Taulignan F 78 B3
Taulov DK 39 D2
Taunton GB 29 B4
Taunusstein D 50 C4
Tauragė LT 6 D7
Taurianova I 106 C3
Taurisano I 107 B5
Tauste E 90 B1
Tauves F 68 C2
Tavankut SRB 75 B4
Tavannes CH 70 A2
Tavarnelle val di Pesa
I 81 C5
Tavas TR 119 E4
Tavaux F 69 A5
Tävelsås S 40 C4
Taverna I 106 B3
Taverne CH 70 B3
Tavernelle I 82 C1
Tavernes de la Valldigna
E 96 B2
Tavérnola Bergamasca
I 71 C5
Taverny F 58 A3
Tavescan E 91 A4
Taviano I 107 B5
Tavira P 98 B3
Tavistock GB 28 C3
Tavnik SRB 85 C5
Tavşanlı TR 118 C4
Tayinloan GB 24 C2
Taynuilt GB 24 B2
Tayport GB 25 B5
Tázlár H 75 B4
Tazones E 88 A1
Tczew PL 47 A4
Tczów PL 55 B6
Teangue GB 22 D3
Teano I 103 B7
Teba E 100 C1
Tebay GB 26 A3
Techendorf A 72 B3
Tecklenburg D 50 A3
Tecko-matorp S 41 D3
Tecuci RO 11 D9
Tefenni TR 119 E4
Tegelsmora S 36 B4
Tegernsee D 62 C2
Teggiano I 104 C1
Tegoleto I 81 C5
Teichel D 52 C1
Teignmouth GB 29 C4
Teillay F 57 C4
Teillet F 77 C5
Teisendorf D 62 C3
Teistungen D 51 B6
Teixeiro E 86 A2
Tejada de Tiétar E 93 A5
Tejado E 89 C4
Tejares E 94 B1
Tejn DK 41 D4
Teke TR 118 A4
Tekirdağ TR 118 B2
Tekovské-Lužany SK 65 B4
Telavåg N 32 B1
Telč CZ 63 A6
Telese Terme I 103 B7
Telford GB 26 C3
Telfs A 71 A6
Telgárt SK 65 B6
Telgte D 50 B3
Tellingstedt D 43 A6
Telšiai LT 6 D7
Telti I 110 B2
Teltow D 45 C5
Tembleque E 95 C3
Temelin CZ 63 A5
Temerin SRB 75 C4
Temiño E 89 B3
Témpio Pausânia I 110 B2
Templederry IRL 20 B3
Templemore IRL 21 B4
Temple Sowerby GB 26 A3
Templin D 45 B5
Temse B 49 B5
Tenay F 69 C5
Ten Boer NL 42 B3
Tenbury Wells GB 29 A5
Tenby GB 28 B3
Tence F 78 A3
Tende F 80 B1
Tenhult S 40 B4
Tenja HR 74 C3
Tenneville B 49 C6
Tennevoll N 112 D6
Tensta S 36 B4
Tenterden GB 31 C4
Teo E 86 B2
Teora I 103 C8
Tepasto FIN 113 E13
Tepelenë AL 116 B2
Teplá CZ 52 D2
Teplice CZ 53 C3
Teplička nad Váhom
SK 65 A4
Tepsa FIN 113 E14
Tera E 89 C4
Téramo I 103 A6
Ter Apel NL 43 C4
Terborg NL 50 B2
Terchová SK 65 A5
Terebovlya UA 11 B8
Teremia Mare RO 75 C5
Terena P 92 C3
Teresa de Cofrentes
E 96 B1
Terešov CZ 63 A4
Terezín CZ 53 C4
Terezino Polje HR 74 C2
Tergnier F 59 A4
Teriberka RUS 3 B31
Terlizzi I 104 B2
Termas de Monfortinho
P 93 A4
Terme di Súio I 103 B6
Terme di Valdieri I 79 B6
Termens E 90 B3
Termes F 78 B2
Términi Imerese I 108 B2
Terminillo I 102 A5
Térmoli I 103 B8
Termonfeckin IRL 19 C5
Ternberg A 63 C5
Terndrup DK 38 C3
Terneuzen NL 49 B4
Terni I 102 A5
Ternitz A 64 C2
Ternopil UA 11 B8
Terpan AL 105 C6
Terpni GR 116 B5
Terracina I 102 B6
Terråk N 115 B9
Terralba I 110 C1
Terranova di Pollino
I 106 B3
Terranova di Sibari I 106 B3
Terras do Bouro P 87 C2
Terrasini I 108 A2
Terrassa E 91 B5
Terrasson-la-Villedieu
F 77 A4
Terrazos E 89 B3
Terriente E 95 B5
Terrugem P 92 C3
Tertenia I 110 C2
Teruel E 90 C1
Tervola FIN 3 C26
Tervuren B 49 C5
Terzaga E 95 B5
Tešanj BIH 84 B2
Tesáske-Mlyňany SK 65 B4
Teslić BIH 84 B2
Tessin D 44 A4
Tessy-sur-Vire F 57 B4
Tét H 74 A2
Tetbury GB 29 B5
Teterchen F 60 A2
Teterow D 45 B4
Teteven BG 11 E8
Tetiyev UA 11 B10
Tetovo MK 10 E6
Tettau D 52 C1
Tettnang D 61 C5
Teublitz D 62 A3
Teuchern D 52 B2
Teulada
E 96 C3
I 110 D1
Teupitz D 52 A3
Teurajärvi S 113 F11
Teutschenthal D 52 B1
Tevel H 74 B3
Teviothead GB 25 C5
Tewkesbury GB 29 B5
Thale D 52 B1
Thalfang D 60 A2
Thalgau A 63 C4
Thalkirch CH 71 B4
Thalmässing D 62 A2
Thalwil CH 70 A3
Thame GB 31 C3
Thann F 60 C3
Thannhausen D 61 B6
Thaon-les-Vosges F 60 B2
Tharandt D 52 C3
Tharsis E 99 B3
Thasos GR 116 B6
Thatcham GB 31 C2
Thaxted GB 31 C4
Thayngen CH 61 C4
Theale GB 31 C2
The Barony GB 23 B5
Thebes = Thiva GR 117 D5
Theding-hausen D 43 C6
Theessen D 52 A2
The Hague = 's-
Gravenhage NL 49 A5
Themar D 51 C6
The Mumbles GB 28 B4
Thénezay F 67 B4
Thenon F 67 C6
Therouanne F 48 C3
Thessaloniki = Salonica
GR 116 B4
Thetford GB 30 B4
Theth AL 105 A5
Theux B 50 C1
Thézar-les-Corbières
F 78 C1
Thèze F 76 C2
Thiberville F 58 A1
Thibie F 59 B5
Thiéblemont-Farémont
F 59 B5
Thiendorf D 53 B3
Thiene I 71 C6
Thierrens CH 70 B1
Thiers F 68 C3
Thiesi I 110 B1
Thiessow D 45 A5
Thiezac F 77 A5
Þingeyri IS 111 B2
Þingvellir IS 111 C4
Thionville F 60 A2
Thira GR 117 F7
Thiron-Gardais F 58 B1
Thirsk GB 27 A4
Thisted DK 38 C1
Thiva = Thebes GR 117 D5
Thivars F 58 B2
Thiviers F 67 C5
Thizy F 69 B4
Tholen NL 49 B5
Tholey D 60 A3
Thomas Street IRL 20 A3
Thomastown IRL 21 B4
Thônes F 69 C6
Thonnance-les-Joinville
F 59 B6
Thonon-les-Bains F 69 B6
Thorame-Basse F 79 B5
Thorame-Haute F 79 B5
Thorens-Glières F 69 C6
Thorigny-sur-Oreuse
F 59 B4
Thörl A 73 A5
Þorlákshöfn IS 111 D4
Thornaby on Tees GB 27 A4
Thornbury GB 29 B5
Thorne GB 27 B5
Thornhill
Dumfries & Galloway
GB 25 C4
Stirling GB 24 B3
Thornthwaite GB 26 A2
Thornton-le-Dale GB 27 A5
Þórshöfn IS 111 A10
Thouarcé F 67 A4
Thouars F 67 B4
Thrapston GB 30 B3
Threlkeld GB 26 A2
Thrumster GB 23 C5
Thueyts F 78 B3
Thuin B 49 C5
Thuir F 91 A5
Thumau D 52 C1
Thun CH 70 B2
Thuret F 68 C3
Thurey F 69 B5
Thüringen A 71 A4
Thurins F 69 C4
Thürkow D 45 B4
Thurles IRL 21 B4
Thurmaston GB 30 B2
Thurø By DK 39 D3
Thursby GB 25 D4
Thurso GB 23 C5
Thury-Harcourt F 57 B5
Thusis CH 71 B4
Thyborøn DK 38 C1
Þykkvibær IS 111 D5
Thyregod DK 39 D2
Tibi E 96 C2
Tibro S 35 D6
Tidaholm S 35 D5
Tidan S 35 D6
Tidersrum S 40 B5
Tiedra E 88 C1
Tiefenbach D 62 A3
Tiefencastel CH 71 B4
Tiefenort D 51 C6
Tiefensee D 45 C5
Tiel NL 49 B6
Tielmes E 95 B3
Tielt B 49 B4
Tienen B 49 C5
Tiengen D 61 C4
Tiercé F 57 C5
Tierga E 89 C5
Tiermas E 90 A1
Tierp S 36 B4
Tierrantona E 90 A3
Tighina MD 11 C10
Tighnabruaich GB 24 C2
Tignes F 70 C1
Tigy F 58 C3
Tihany H 74 B2
Tijnje NL 42 B2
Tijola E 101 B3
Tikhvin RUS 7 B12
Tilburg NL 49 B6
Til Châtel F 69 A5
Tilh F 76 C2
Tillac F 76 C3
Tillberga S 37 C3
Tille F 58 A3
Tillicoultry GB 25 B4
Tilloy Bellay F 59 A5
Tilly F 67 B6
Tilly-sur-Seulles F 57 A5
Tim DK 39 C1
Timau I 72 B3
Timbaki GR 117 G6
Timi CY 120 B1
Timișoara RO 75 C6
Timmele S 40 B3
Timmendorfer Strand
D 44 B2
Timmernabben S 40 C6
Timmersdala S 35 D5
Timoleague IRL 20 C3
Timolin IRL 21 B5
Timrå S 115 E14
Timsfors S 40 C3
Timsgearraidh GB 22 C1
Tinajas E 95 B4
Tinalhas P 92 B3
Tinchebray F 57 B5
Tincques F 48 C3
Tineo E 86 A4
Tinglev DK 39 E2
Tingsryd S 40 C4
Tingstäde S 37 E5
Tingvoll N 114 E5
Tinlot B 49 C6
Tinnoset N 33 C6
Tinos GR 117 E7
Tintagel GB 28 C3
Tinténiac F 57 B4
Tintern GB 29 B5
Tintigny B 60 A1
Tione di Trento I 71 B5
Tipperary IRL 20 B3
Tiptree GB 31 C4
Tirana = Tiranë AL 105 B5
Tiranë = Tirana AL 105 B5
Tirano I 71 B5
Tiraspol MD 11 C10
Tire TR 119 D2
Tires I 71 B6
Tiriez E 95 D4
Tirig E 90 C3
Tiriolo I 106 C3
Tirnavos GR 116 C4
Tirrénia I 81 C4
Tirschenreuth D 62 A3
Tirstrup DK 39 C3
Tirteafuera E 100 A1
Tishono RUS 47 A6
Tisno HR 83 C4
Tišnov CZ 64 A2
Tisovec SK 65 B5
Tisselskog S 35 D4
Tistedal N 35 C3
Tistrup DK 39 D1
Tisvildeleje DK 39 C5
Tiszaalpár H 75 B4
Tiszabő H 75 A5
Tiszadorogma H 65 C6
Tiszaföldvár H 75 B5
Tiszafüred H 65 C6
Tiszajenő H 75 A5
Tiszakécske H 75 B5
Tiszakürt H 75 B5
Tiszanána H 75 A5
Tiszaörs H 75 A5
Tiszaroff H 75 A5
Tiszasüly H 75 A5
Tiszasziget H 75 B5
Tiszaszőlős H 75 A5
Titaguas E 96 B1
Titel SRB 75 C5
Titisee-Neustadt D 61 C4
Tito I 104 C1
Titova Korenica HR 83 B4
Titran N 114 D5
Tittling D 63 B4
Tittmoning D 62 B3
Titz D 50 B2
Tiurajärvi FIN 113 E13
Tivat MNE 105 A4
Tived S 37 D1
Tiverton GB 29 C4
Tivisa E 90 B3
Tívoli I 102 B5
Tjällmo S 37 D2
Tjåmotis S 112 F7
Tjæreborg DK 39 D1
Tjautjas S 112 E9
Tjøme N 35 C2
Tjong N 112 F2
Tjonnefoss N 33 D5
Tjörn IS 111 B5
Tjörnarp S 41 D3
Tjøtta N 115 B9
Tkon HR 83 C4
Tleń PL 47 B4
Tlmače SK 65 B4
Tłuchowo PL 47 C5
Tlumačov CZ 64 A3
Tóalmas H 75 A4
Toano I 81 B4
Toba D 51 B6
Tobarra E 101 A4
Tobermore GB 19 B5
Tobermory GB 24 B1
Toberonochy GB 24 B2
Tobha Mor GB 22 D1
Tobo S 36 B4
Tocane-St Apre F 67 C5
Tocha P 92 A2
Tocina E 99 B5
Töcksfors S 35 C3
Tocón E 100 B2
Todal N 114 E5
Todi I 82 D1
Todmorden GB 26 B3
Todorici BIH 84 B2
Todtmoos D 61 C3
Todtnau D 60 C3
Toén E 87 B3
Tofta
Gotland S 37 E5
Skaraborg S 35 D5
Toftbyn S 36 B2
Tofte N 35 C2
Töftedal S 35 D3
Tofterup DK 39 D1
Toftlund DK 39 D2
Tófü H 74 B3
Tohmo FIN 113 F16
Tokarnia PL 55 C5
Tokary PL 54 A3
Tokod H 65 C4
Tököl H 75 A3
Tolastadh bho Thuath
GB 22 C2
Toledo E 94 C2
Tolentino I 82 C2
Tolfa I 102 A4
Tolg S 40 B4
Tolga N 114 E8
Tolkmicko PL 47 A5
Tolko PL 47 A6
Tollarp S 41 D3
Tollered S 40 B2
Tølløse DK 39 D4
Tolmachevo RUS 7 B10
Tolmezzo I 72 B3
Tolmin SLO 72 B3
Tolna H 74 B3
Tolnanémedi H 74 B3
Tolob GB 22 B7
Tolosa
E 89 A4
P 92 B3
Tolox E 100 C1
Tolpuddle GB 29 C5
Tolva E 90 A3
Tolve I 104 C2
Tomar P 92 B2
Tomarza TR 16 B7
Tomaševac SRB 75 C5
Tomašica BIH 83 B5
Tomášikovo SK 64 B3
Tomašouka BY 6 F7
Tomášovce SK 65 B5
Tomaszów Mazowiecki
PL 55 B5
Tomatin GB 23 D5
Tombeboeuf F 77 B3
Tomdoun GB 22 D3
Tomelilla S 41 D3
Tomellosa E 95 B4
Tomelloso E 95 C3
Tomiño E 87 C2
Tomintoul GB 23 D5
Tomislavgrad BIH 84 C2
Tomisław PL 53 B5
Tomisławice PL 47 C4
Tomnavoulin GB 23 D5
Tompa H 75 B4
Tompaládony H 74 A1
Tomra N 114 E3
Tomter N 35 C2
Tona E 91 B5
Tonara I 110 B2
Tonbridge GB 31 C4
Tondela P 92 A2
Tønder DK 39 E1
Tongeren B 49 C6
Tongue GB 23 C4
Tönisvorst D 50 B2
Tønjum N 32 A4
Tonkopuro FIN 113 F17
Tonnay-Boutonne F 67 C4
Tonnay-Charente F 66 C4
Tonneins F 77 B3
Tonnerre F 59 C4
Tonnes N 115 A10
Tönning D 43 A5
Tonsåsen N 32 B6
Tønsberg N 35 C2
Tonstad N 33 D3
Toomyvara IRL 20 B3
Toormore IRL 20 C2
Topares E 101 B3
Topas E 94 A1
Toplița RO 11 C8
Topola SRB 85 B5
Topolčani MK 116 A3
Topoľčany SK 64 B4
Topoľčianky SK 65 B4
Topolje HR 73 C6
Topólka PL 47 C4
Topoľníky SK 64 C3
Topolovățu Mare RO 75 C6
Toponár H 74 B2
Toporów PL 53 A5
Topsham GB 29 C4
Topusko HR 73 C5
Toques E 86 B3
Torà E 91 B4
Toral de los Guzmanes
E 88 B1
Toral de los Vados E 86 B4
Torbalı TR 119 D2
Torbjörntorp S 35 D5
Torbole I 71 C5
Torchiarolo I 105 C4
Torcross GB 29 C4
Torcy-le-Petit F 58 A2
Torda SRB 75 C5
Tørdal N 33 C5
Tordehumos E 88 C1
Tordera E 91 B5
Tordesillas E 88 C1
Tordesilos E 95 B5
Töre S 3 D25
Töreboda S 35 D6
Toreby DK 39 E4
Torekov S 41 C2
Torella dei Lombardi
I 103 C8
Torellò E 91 A5
Toreno E 86 B4
Torfou F 66 A3
Torgau D 52 B3
Torgelow D 45 B6
Torgueda P 87 C3
Torhamn S 41 C5
Torhop N 113 B16
Torhout B 49 B4
Torigni-sur-Vire F 57 A5
Torija E 95 B3
Toril E 95 B5
Torino = Turin I 80 A1
Toritto I 104 C2
Torkovichi RUS 7 B11
Torla E 90 A2
Tormänen FIN 113 D16
Tormestorp S 41 C3
Tórmini I 71 C5
Tornada P 92 B1
Tornal'a SK 65 B6
Tornavacas E 93 A5
Tornby DK 38 B2
Tornesch D 43 B6
Torness GB 23 D4
Torniella I 81 C5
Tornimparte I 103 A6
Torning DK 39 C2
Tornio FIN 3 D26
Tornjoš SRB 75 C4
Tornos E 95 B5
Toro E 88 C1
Törökszentmiklós H 75 A5
Toropets RUS 7 C11
Torpa S 40 C3
Torpè I 110 B2
Torphins GB 23 D6
Torpo N 32 B5
Torpoint GB 28 C3
Torpsbruk S 40 B4
Torquay GB 29 C4
Torquemada E 88 B2
Torralba de Burgo E 89 C4
Torralba de Calatrava
E 94 C3
Torrão P 98 A2
Torre Annunziata I 103 C7
Torreblacos E 89 C4
Torreblanca E 96 A3
Torreblascopedro E 100 B2
Torrecaballeros E 94 A2
Torrecampo E 100 A1
Torre Canne I 104 C3
Torre Cardela E 100 B2
Torrecilla E 95 B4
Torrecilla de la Jara
E 94 C2
Torrecilla de la Orden
E 94 A1
Torrecilla del Pinar E 88 C2
Torrecilla en Cameros
E 89 B4
Torrecillas de la Tiesa
E 93 B5
Torre das Vargens P 92 B3
Torre de Coelheiros
P 92 C3
Torre de Dom Chama
P 87 C3
Torre de Juan Abad
E 100 A2
Torre de la Higuera E 99 B4
Torre del Bierzo E 86 B4
Torre del Burgo E 95 B3
Torre del Campo E 100 B2
Torre del Greco I 103 C7
Torre del Lago Puccini
I 81 C4
Torre dell'Orso I 105 C4
Torre del Mar E 100 C1
Torredembarra E 91 B4
Torre de Miguel Sesmero
E 93 C4
Torre de Moncorvo P 87 C3
Torre de Santa Maria
E 93 B4
Torredonjimeno E 100 B2
Torre do Terranho P 87 D3
Torre Faro I 109 A4
Torregrosa E 90 B3
Torreira P 87 D2
Torrejoncillo E 93 B4
Torrejón de Ardoz E 95 B3
Torrejón de la Calzada
E 94 B3
Torrejón del Rey E 95 B3
Torrejon el Rubio E 93 B4
Torrelaguna E 95 B3
Torrelapaja E 89 C5
Torre la Ribera E 90 A3
Torrelavega E 88 A2
Torrelobatón E 88 C1
Torrelodones E 94 B3
Torre los Negros E 90 C1
Torremaggiore I 103 B8
Torremanzanas E 96 C2
Torremayor E 93 C4
Torremezzo di Falconara
I 106 B3
Torremocha E 93 B4
Torremolinos E 100 C1
Torrenieri I 81 C5
Torrenostra E 96 A3
Torrenova I 102 B5
Torrent E 96 B2
Torrente de Cinca E 90 B3
Torrenueva
Ciudad Real E 100 A2
Granada E 100 C2
Torreorgaz E 93 B4
Torre Orsáia I 106 A2
Torre-Pacheco E 101 B5
Torre Péllice I 79 B6
Torreperogil E 100 A2
Torres E 100 B2
Torresandino E 88 C3
Torre Santa Susanna
I 105 C3
Torres-Cabrera E 100 B1
Torres de la Alameda
E 95 B3
Torres Novas P 92 B2
Torres Vedras P 92 B1
Torrevieja E 96 D2
Torricella I 104 C3
Torri del Benaco I 71 C5
Torridon GB 22 D3
Torriglia I 80 B3
Torrijos E 94 C2
Tørring DK 39 D2
Torrita di Siena I 81 C5
Torroal P 92 C2
Torroella de Montgrì
E 91 A6
Torrox E 100 C2
Torsåker S 36 B3
Torsås S 41 C6
Torsby S 34 B4
Torsetra N 34 B2
Torshälla S 37 C3
Tórshavn FO 2 E10
Torslanda S 38 B4
Torsminde DK 39 C1
Torsnes N 32 B3
Törtel H 75 A4
Tórtoles E 93 A5
Tórtoles de Esgueva
E 88 C2
Tortol I 110 C2
Tortona I 80 B2
Tórtora I 106 B2
Tortoreto Lido I 82 D2
Tortorici I 109 A3
Tortosa E 90 C3
Tortosendo P 92 A3
Tortuera E 95 B5
Tortuero E 95 B3
Toruń PL 47 B4
Torup S 40 C3
Tor Vaiánica I 102 B5
Torver GB 26 A2
Tørvikbygde N 32 B3
Torviscón E 100 C2
Torzhok RUS 7 C13
Torzym PL 53 A5
Tosbotn N 115 B9
Toscolano-Maderno
I 71 C5
Tosno RUS 7 B11
Tossa de Mar E 91 B5
Tossåsen S 115 E10
Tosse F 76 C1
Tösse S 35 D4
Tossicia I 103 A6
Tostedt D 43 B6
Tosya TR 16 A7
Tószeg H 75 A5
Toszek PL 54 C3
Totana E 101 B4
Totebo S 40 B6
Tôtes F 58 A2
Tótkomlós H 75 B5
Totland N 114 F2
Tøtlandsvik N 33 C3
Totnes GB 28 C4
Tótszerdahely H 74 B1
Tøttdal N 114 C8
Totton GB 31 D2
Touça P 87 C3
Toucy F 59 C4
Toul F 60 B1
Toulon F 79 C4
Toulon-sur-Allier F 68 B3
Toulon-sur-Arroux F 68 B4
Toulouse F 77 C4
Tourcoing F 49 C4
Tour de la Parata F 102 A1
Tourlaville F 57 A4
Tournai B 49 C4
Tournan-en-Brie F 58 B3
Tournay F 76 C3
Tournon-d'Agenais F 77 B3
Tournon-St Martin F 67 B5
Tournon-sur-Rhône
F 78 A3
Tournus F 69 B4
Touro
E 86 B2
P 87 D3
Tourouvre F 58 B1
Tourriers F 67 C5
Tours F 67 A5
Tourteron F 59 A5
Tourves F 79 C4
Toury F 58 B2
Touvedo P 87 C2
Touvois F 66 B3
Toužim CZ 52 C2
Tovačov CZ 64 A3
Tovariševo SRB 75 C4
Tovarnik HR 75 C4
Tovdal N 33 D5
Tovrljane SRB 85 C6
Towcester GB 30 B3
Town Yetholm GB 25 C5
Tråastølen N 32 B4
Trabada E 86 A3
Trabadelo E 86 B4
Trabanca E 87 C4
Trabazos E 87 C4
Traben-Trarbach D 60 A3
Trabia I 108 B2
Tradate I 70 C3

Trädet S 40 B3
Trafaria P 92 C1
Tragacete E 95 B5
Tragwein A 63 B5
Traiguera E 90 C3
Trainel F 59 B4
Traisen A 63 B6
Traismauer A 64 B1
Traitsching D 62 A3
Trákhonas CY 120 A2
Tralee IRL 20 B2
Tramacastilla de Tena E 76 D2
Tramagal P 92 B2
Tramariglio I 110 B1
Tramatza I 110 B1
Tramelan CH 70 A2
Tramonti di Sopra I 72 B2
Tramore IRL 21 B4
Trampot F 60 B1
Trana I 80 A1
Tranås S 40 A4
Tranbjerg DK 39 C3
Tranby N 34 C2
Trancoso P 87 D3
Tranebjerg DK 39 D3
Tranekær DK 39 E3
Tranemo S 40 B3
Tranent GB 25 C5
Tranevåg N 33 D3
Trängslet S 34 A5
Tranhult S 40 B3
Trani I 104 B2
Trans-en-Provence F 79 C5
Transtrand S 34 A5
Tranum DK 38 B2
Tranvik S 37 C5
Trápani I 108 A1
Trappes F 58 B3
Traryd S 40 C3
Trasacco I 103 B6
Trasierra E 99 A4
Träslövsläge S 40 B2
Trasmiras E 87 B3
Traspinedo E 88 C2
Trate SLO 73 B5
Trauchgau D 62 C1
Traun A 63 B5
Traunreut D 62 C3
Traunstein D 62 C3
Traunwalchen D 62 C3
Trävad S 35 D5
Travemünde D 44 B2
Traversétolo I 81 B4
Travnik
BIH 84 B2
SLO 73 C4
Travo
F 102 B2
I 80 B3
Trawsfynydd GB 26 C2
Trbovlje SLO 73 B5
Trbušani SRB 85 C5
Treban F 68 B3
Třebařov CZ 64 A2
Trebatsch D 53 A4
Trebbin D 52 A3
Třebechovice pod Orebem CZ 53 C5
Trebel D 44 C3
Třebenice CZ 53 C3
Trébeurden F 56 B2
Třebíč CZ 64 A1
Trebinje BIH 84 D3
Trebisacce I 106 B3
Trebitz D 52 B2
Trebnje SLO 73 C5
Třeboň CZ 63 A5
Třebovice CZ 64 A2
Trebsen D 52 B2
Trebujena E 99 C4
Trecastagni I 109 B4
Trecate I 70 C3
Trecenta I 81 A5
Tredegar GB 29 B4
Tredózio I 81 B5
Treffen A 72 B3
Treffort F 69 B5
Treffurt D 51 B6
Trefnant GB 26 B2
Tregaron GB 28 A4
Trégastel-Plage F 56 B2
Tregnago I 71 C6
Tregony GB 28 C3
Tréguier F 56 B2
Trégunc F 56 C2
Treharris GB 29 B4
Trehörningsjö S 115 D15
Tréia I 82 C2
Treignac F 68 C1
Treignat F 68 B2
Treignes B 49 C5
Treis-Karden D 50 C3
Trekanten S 40 C6
Trélazé F 67 A4
Trelech GB 28 B3
Trélissac F 67 C5
Trelleborg S 41 D3
Trélon F 49 C5
Trélou-sur-Marne F 59 A4
Tremblay-le-Vicomte F 58 B2
Tremés P 92 B2
Tremezzo I 71 C4
Třemošná CZ 63 A4
Tremp E 90 A3
Trenčianska Stankovce SK 64 B3
Trenčianska Turná SK 64 B4
Trenčianske Teplá SK 64 B4
Trenčianske Teplice SK 64 B4
Trenčín SK 64 B4
Trendelburg D 51 B5
Trengereid N 32 B2
Trensacq F 76 B2
Trent D 45 A5
Trento I 71 B6
Treorchy GB 29 B4
Trepča KOS 85 D5
Trept F 69 C5
Trepuzzi I 105 C4
Trescore Balneário I 71 C4
Tresenda I 71 B5
Tresfjord N 114 E4
Tresigallo I 81 B5
Trešnjevica SRB 85 C6
Tresnurághes I 110 B1
Trespaderne E 89 B3
Třešť CZ 63 A6
Trestina I 82 C1
Tretower GB 29 B4
Trets F 79 C4
Tretten N 34 A2
Treuchtlingen D 62 B1
Treuen D 52 C2
Treuenbrietzen D 52 A2
Treungen N 33 C5
Trevelez E 100 C2
Trevi I 82 D1
Treviana E 89 B3
Treviglio I 71 C4
Trevignano Romano I 102 A5
Trevi nel Lázio I 102 B6
Treviso I 72 C2
Trévoux F 69 C4
Treysa D 51 C5
Trézelles F 68 B3
Trezzo sull'Adda I 71 C4
Trhová Kamenice CZ 64 A1
Trhové Sviny CZ 63 B5
Triacastela E 86 B3
Triaize F 66 B3
Trianda GR 119 F3
Triaucourt-en-Argonne F 59 B6
Tribanj Kruščica HR 83 B4
Triberg D 61 B4
Tribsees D 45 A4
Tribuče SLO 73 C5
Tricárico I 104 C2
Tricase I 107 B5
Tricésimo I 72 B3
Trieben A 73 A4
Triebes D 52 C2
Triepkendorf D 45 B5
Trier D 60 A2
Trieste I 72 C3
Trie-sur-Baïse F 77 C3
Triggiano I 104 B2
Triglitz D 44 B4
Trignac F 66 A2
Trigueros E 99 B4
Trigueros del Valle E 88 C2
Trijebine SRB 85 C4
Trikala GR 116 C3
Trikeri GR 116 C5
Trikomo CY 120 A2
Trilj HR 83 C5
Trillo E 95 B4
Trilport F 59 B3
Trim IRL 21 A5
Trimdon GB 25 D6
Trindade
Beja P 98 B3
Bragança P 87 C3
Třinec CZ 65 A4
Tring GB 31 C3
Trinità d'Agultu I 110 B1
Trinitápoli I 104 B2
Trino I 70 C3
Trinta P 92 A3
Triora I 80 C1
Tripoli GR 117 E4
Triponzo I 82 D1
Triptis D 52 C1
Triste E 90 A2
Trittau D 44 B2
Trivento I 103 B7
Trivero I 70 C3
Trivigno I 104 C1
Trn BIH 84 B2
Trnava
HR 74 C3
SK 64 B3
Trnovec SK 64 B3
Trnovo BIH 84 C3
Trnovska vas SLO 73 B5
Troarn F 57 A5
Trochtelfingen D 61 B5
Trödje S 36 B4
Troense DK 39 D3
Trofa P 87 C2
Trofaiach A 73 A5
Trofors N 115 B10
Trogir HR 83 C5
Trøgstad N 35 C3
Tróia I 103 B8
Troia P 92 C2
Troina I 109 B3
Troisdorf D 50 C3
Trois-Ponts B 50 C1
Troisvierges L 50 C2
Trojane SLO 73 B4
Trojanów PL 55 B6
Troldhede DK 39 D1
Trollhättan S 35 D4
Trolog BIH 84 C1
Tromello I 70 C3
Tromøy N 33 D5
Tromsø N 112 C8
Trondheim N 114 D7
Tronget F 68 B3
Trönninge S 40 C2
Trönningeby S 40 B2
Trönö S 36 A3
Tronzano-Vercellese I 70 C3
Trôo F 58 C1
Troon GB 24 C3
Tropea I 106 C2
Tropojë AL 105 A6
Tropy Sztumskie PL 47 B5
Trosa S 37 D4
Trösken S 36 B3
Trosly-Breuil F 59 A4
Trossingen D 61 B4
Trostberg D 62 B3
Trostyanets UA 7 F13
Trouville-sur-Mer F 57 A6
Trowbridge GB 29 B5
Troyes F 59 B5
Trpanj HR 84 C2
Trpezi MNE 85 D5
Trpinja HR 74 C3
Tršće HR 73 C4
Tršice CZ 64 A3
Trstená SK 65 A5
Trstenci BIH 84 A2
Trstenik
KOS 85 D5
SRB 85 C6
Trsteno HR 84 D2
Trstice SK 64 B3
Trstín SK 64 B3
Trubchevsk RUS 7 E12
Trubia E 88 A1
Trubjela MNE 84 D3
Truchas E 87 B4
Trujillanos E 93 C4
Trujillo E 93 B5
Trumieje PL 47 B5
Trun
CH 70 B3
F 57 B6
Truro GB 28 C2
Trusetal D 51 C6
Truskavets' UA 11 B7
Trustrup DK 39 C3
Trutnov CZ 53 C5
Tryserum S 37 D3
Trysil N 34 A4
Tryszczyn PL 46 B3
Trzcianka PL 46 B2
Trzciel PL 46 C1
Trzcińsko Zdrój PL 45 C6
Trzebiatów PL 45 A7
Trzebiel PL 53 B4
Trzebielino PL 46 A3
Trzebień PL 53 B5
Trzebiez PL 45 B6
Trzebinia PL 55 C4
Trzebnica PL 54 B2
Trzebnice PL 53 B6
Trzeciewiec PL 47 B4
Trzemeszno PL 46 C3
Trzemeszno-Lubuskie PL 46 C1
Trzetrzewina PL 65 A6
Tržič SLO 73 B4
Tsamandas GR 116 C2
Tschagguns A 71 A4
Tschernitz D 53 B4
Tsebrykove UA 11 C11
Tsvetkovo UA 11 B11
Tsyelyakhany BY 7 E8
Tua P 87 C3
Tuam IRL 20 A3
Tubbercurry IRL 18 B3
Tubbergen NL 42 C3
Tubilla del Lago E 89 C3
Tübingen D 61 B5
Tubize B 49 C5
Tučapy CZ 63 A5
Tučepi HR 84 C2
Tuchan F 78 D1
Tüchen D 44 B4
Tuchola PL 46 B3
Tuchomie PL 46 A3
Tuchów PL 65 A7
Tuczno PL 46 B2
Tuddal N 32 C5
Tudela E 89 B5
Tudela de Duero E 88 C2
Tudweiliog GB 26 C1
Tuejar E 96 B1
Tuffé F 58 B1
Tufsingdalen N 114 E8
Tuhaň CZ 53 C4
Tui E 87 B2
Tukums LV 6 C7
Tula
I 110 B1
RUS 7 D14
Tulcea RO 11 D10
Tul'chyn UA 11 B10
Tulette F 78 B3
Tuliszków PL 54 A3
Tulla IRL 20 B3
Tullamore IRL 21 A4
Tulle F 68 C1
Tullins F 69 C5
Tulln A 64 B2
Tullow IRL 21 B5
Tułowice PL 54 C2
Tulppio FIN 113 E18
Tulsk IRL 18 C3
Tumba S 37 C4
Tummel Bridge GB 24 B3
Tun S 35 D4
Tuna
Kalmar S 40 B6
Uppsala S 36 B5
Tuna Hästberg S 36 B2
Tunçbilek TR 118 C4
Tunes P 98 B2
Tungelsta S 37 C5
Tunje AL 105 C6
Tunnerstad S 40 A4
Tunnhovd N 32 B5
Tunstall GB 30 B5
Tuohikotti FIN 3 F27
Tuoro sul Trasimeno I 82 C1
Tupadły PL 47 C4
Tupanari BIH 84 B3
Tupik RUS 7 D12
Tuplice PL 53 B4
Tura H 65 C5
Turanj HR 83 C4
Turany SK 65 A5
Turbe BIH 84 B2
Turbenthal CH 70 A3
Turcia E 88 B1
Turčianske Teplice SK 65 B4
Turcifal P 92 B1
Turckheim F 60 B3
Turda RO 11 C7
Turégano E 94 A3
Turek PL 54 A3
Tŭrgovishte BG 11 E9
Turgutlu TR 119 D2
Turi I 104 C3
Turin = Torino I 80 A1
Turis E 96 B2
Türje H 74 B2
Turka UA 11 B7
Túrkeve H 75 A5
Türkheim D 62 B1
Türkmenli TR 118 C1
Turku FIN 6 A7
Turleque E 94 C3
Turňa nad Bodvou SK 65 B6
Turnberry GB 24 C3
Turnhout B 49 B5
Türnitz A 63 C6
Turnov CZ 53 C5
Turnu RO 75 B6
Turnu Măgurele RO 11 E8
Turón E 100 C2
Turoszów PL 53 C4
Turowo PL 47 B6
Turquel P 92 B1
Turri I 110 C1
Turries F 79 B5
Turriff GB 23 D6
Tursi I 104 C2
Turtmann CH 70 B2
Turtola FIN 113 F12
Turze PL 54 B2
Turzovka SK 65 A4
Tusa I 109 B3
Tuscánia I 102 A4
Tuse DK 39 D4
Tušilovic HR 73 C5
Tuszyn PL 55 B4
Tutin SRB 85 D5
Tutow D 45 B5
Tutrakan BG 11 D9
Tuttlingen D 61 C4
Tutzing D 62 C2
Tuzi MNE 105 A5
Tuzla
BIH 84 B3
TR 16 C7
Tuzlukçu TR 119 D6
Tvååker S 40 B2
Tvärålund S 115 C16
Tvärskog S 40 C6
Tvedestrand N 33 D5
Tveit
Hordaland N 32 B4
Rogaland N 33 C3
Tver RUS 7 C13
Tverrelvmo N 112 D8
Tversted DK 38 B3
Tving S 41 C5
Tvrdošín SK 65 A5
Tvrdošovce SK 64 B4
Twardogóra PL 54 B2
Twatt GB 23 B5
Twello NL 50 A2
Twimberg A 73 B4
Twist D 43 C4
Twistringen D 43 C5
Tworóg PL 54 C3
Twyford
Hampshire GB 31 C2
Wokingham GB 31 C3
Tyachiv UA 11 B7
Tychówka PL 46 B2
Tychowo PL 46 B2
Tychy PL 54 C3
Tydal N 114 D8
Týec nad Labem CZ 53 C5
Tyfors S 34 B6
Tygelsjö S 41 D2
Tylldal N 114 E7
Tylstrup DK 38 B2
Tymbark PL 65 A6
Tymowa PL 65 A6
Tyndrum GB 24 B3
Týnec nad Sázavou CZ 63 A5
Tynemouth GB 25 C6
Tyngsjö S 34 B5
Týniště nad Orlicí CZ 53 C6
Týn nad Vltavou CZ 63 A5
Tynset N 114 E7
Tyresö S 37 C5
Tyringe S 41 C3
Tyrislöt S 37 D3
Tyristrand N 34 B2
Tyrrellspass IRL 21 A4
Tysnes N 32 B2
Tysse N 32 B2
Tyssebotn N 32 B2
Tyssedal N 32 B3
Tystberga S 37 D4
Tysvær N 33 C2
Tywyn GB 26 C1
Tzermiado GR 117 G7
Tzummarum NL 42 B2

U

Ub SRB 85 B5
Ubby DK 39 D4
Úbeda E 100 A2
Überlingen D 61 C5
Ubidea E 89 A4
Ubli
HR 84 D1
MNE 105 A5
Ubrique E 99 C5
Ucero E 89 C3
Uchaud F 78 C3
Uchte D 43 C5
Uckerath D 50 C3
Uckfield GB 31 D4
Ucklum S 38 A4
Uclés E 95 C4
Ucria I 109 A3
Udbina HR 83 B4
Uddebo S 40 B3
Uddeholm S 34 B5
Uddevalla S 35 D3
Uddheden S 34 C4
Uden NL 49 B6
Uder D 51 B6
Udiča SK 65 A4
Údine I 72 B3
Udvar H 74 C3
Ueckermünde D 45 B6
Uelsen D 42 C3
Uelzen D 44 C2
Uetendorf CH 70 B2
Uetersen D 43 B6
Uetze D 44 C2
Uffculme GB 29 C4
Uffenheim D 61 A6
Ugarana E 89 A4
Ugento I 107 B5
Ugerldse DK 39 D4
Uggerby DK 38 B3
Uggerslev DK 39 D3
Uggiano la Chiesa I 107 A5
Ugíjar E 100 C2
Ugine F 69 C6
Uglejevik BIH 84 B4
Uglenes N 32 B2
Uglich RUS 7 C15
Ugljane HR 84 C1
Ugod H 74 A2
Uherské Hradiště CZ 64 A3
Uherský Brod CZ 64 A3
Uherský Ostroh CZ 64 B3
Uhingen D 61 B5
Uhliřské-Janovice CZ 63 A6
Uhřiněves CZ 53 C4
Uhyst D 53 B4
Uig GB 22 D2
Uitgeest NL 42 C1
Uithoorn NL 49 A5
Uithuizen NL 42 B3
Uithuizermeeden NL 42 B3
Uivar RO 75 C5
Ujazd
Łódzkie PL 55 B4
Opolskie PL 54 C3
Ujezd u Brna CZ 64 A2
Ujhartyán H 75 A4
Újkígyós H 75 B6
Ujpetre H 74 C3
Ujście PL 46 B2
Ujsolt H 75 B4
Újszász H 75 A5
Újué E 89 B5
Ukanc SLO 72 B3
Ukmergė LT 6 D8
Ukna S 40 A6
Ula TR 119 E3
Ul'anka SK 65 B5
Ulaş TR 118 A2
Ulássai I 110 C2
Ulbjerg DK 38 C2
Ulbster GB 23 C5
Ulceby GB 27 B5
Ulcinj MNE 105 B5
Uldum DK 39 D2
Ulefoss N 33 C6
Uleila del Campo E 101 B3
Ulëz AL 105 B5
Ulfborg DK 39 C1
Uljma SRB 85 A6
Ullånger S 115 D15
Ullapool GB 22 D3
Ullared S 40 B2
Ullatti S 113 E10
Ullatun N 33 C3
Ulldecona E 90 C3
Ulldemolins E 90 B3
Ullerslev DK 39 D3
Ullervad S 35 D5
Üllés H 75 B4
Üllő H 75 A4
Ulm D 61 B5
Ulme P 92 B2
Ulmen D 50 C2
Ulnes N 32 B6
Ulog BIH 84 C3
Ulricehamn S 40 B3
Ulrichstein D 51 C5
Ulrika S 37 D2
Ulriksfors S 115 D12
Ulrum NL 42 B3
Ulsberg N 114 E6
Ulsta GB 22 A7
Ulsted DK 38 B3
Ulsteinvik N 114 E2
Ulstrup
Vestsjællands Amt. DK 39 D3
Viborg Amt. DK 39 C2
Ulsvåg N 112 D4
Ulubey TR 119 D4
Uluborlu TR 119 D5
Ulukışla TR 16 C7
Ulverston GB 26 A2
Ulvik N 32 B3
Umag HR 72 C3
Uman UA 11 B11
Umba RUS 3 C31
Umbértide I 82 C1
Umbriático I 107 B3
Umčari SRB 85 B5
Umeå S 115 D17
Umgransele S 115 C15
Umhausen A 71 A5
Umka SRB 85 B5
Umljanovic HR 83 C5
Umnäs S 115 B13
Umurbey TR 118 B1
Unaðsdalur IS 111 A3
Unapool GB 22 C3
Unari FIN 113 E14
Uncastillo E 90 A1
Undenäs S 37 D1
Undersaker S 115 D10
Undredal N 32 B4
Unecha RUS 7 E12
Unešić HR 83 C5
Úněšov CZ 62 A4
Ungheni MD 11 C9
Unhais da Serra P 92 A3
Unhošt CZ 53 C4
Unichowo PL 46 A3
Uničov CZ 64 A3
Uniejów PL 54 B3
Unisław PL 47 B4
Unkel D 50 C3
Unken A 62 C3
Unna D 50 B3
Unnaryd S 40 C3
Unquera E 88 A2
Unterach A 63 C4
Unterägeri CH 70 A3
Unterammergau D 62 C2
Unterhaching D 62 B2
Unteriberg CH 70 A3
Unterkochen D 61 B6
Unter Langkampfen A 72 A2
Unterlaussa A 63 C5
Unterlüss D 44 C2
Untermünkheim D 61 A5
Unterschächen CH 70 B3
Unterschleissheim D 62 B2
Unterschwaningen D 62 A1
Untersiemau D 51 C6
Unter-steinbach D 61 A6
Unterweissenbach A 63 B5
Unterzell D 62 A3
Upavon GB 29 B6
Úpice CZ 53 C6
Upiłka PL 46 B3
Upphärad S 35 D4
Uppingham GB 30 B3
Upplands-Väsby S 37 C4
Uppsala S 36 C4
Uppsjøhytta N 34 A1
Upton-upon-Severn GB 29 A5
Ur F 91 A4
Ura e Shtrenjte AL 105 A5
Uras I 110 C1
Ura-Vajgurorë AL 105 C5
Uraz PL 54 B1
Urbánia I 82 C1
Urbino I 82 C1
Urçay F 68 B2
Urda E 94 C3
Urdax E 76 C1
Urdilde E 86 B2
Urdos F 76 D2
Urk NL 42 C2
Úrkút H 74 A2
Urla TR 119 D1
Urlingford IRL 21 B4
Urnäsch CH 71 A4
Urnes N 32 A4
Uroševac KOS 10 E6
Urracal E 101 B3
Urries E 90 A1
Urroz E 76 D1
Ursensollen D 62 A2
Urshult S 40 C4
Uršna Sela SLO 73 C5
Urszulewo PL 47 C5
Ury F 58 B3
Urziceni RO 11 D9
Urzulei I 110 B2
Usagre E 93 C4
Uşak TR 118 D4
Ušće SRB 85 C5
Usedom D 45 B5
Useldange L 60 A1
Uséllus I 110 C1
Ushakovo RUS 47 A6
Usingen D 51 C4
Usini I 110 B1
Usk GB 29 B5
Uskedal N 32 C2
Üsküdar TR 118 A4
Uslar D 51 B5
Úsov CZ 64 A3
Usquert NL 42 B3
Ussássai I 110 C2
Ussé F 67 A5
Usséglio I 70 C2
Ussel
Cantal F 78 A1
Corrèze F 68 C2
Usson-du-Poitou F 67 B5
Usson-en-Forez F 68 C3
Usson-les-Bains F 77 D5
Ustaoset N 32 B5
Ustaritz F 76 C1
Úštěk CZ 53 C4
Uster CH 70 A3
Ústí CZ 64 A3
Ustibar BIH 85 C4
Ustikolina BIH 84 C3
Ústí nad Labem CZ 53 C4
Ústí nad Orlicí CZ 54 D1
Ustipračà BIH 84 C4
Ustka PL 46 A2
Ust Luga RUS 7 B10
Ustroń PL 65 A4
Ustronie Morskie PL 46 A1
Ustyuzhna RUS 7 B14
Uszód H 74 B3
Utåker N 32 C2
Utansjö S 115 E14
Utebo E 90 B2
Utena LT 7 D8
Utery CZ 62 A4
Uthaug N 114 D6
Utiel E 96 B1
Utne N 32 B3
Utö S 37 D5
Utrecht NL 49 A6
Utrera E 99 B5
Utrillas E 90 C2
Utsjoki FIN 113 C16
Utstein kloster N 33 C2
Uttendorf A 72 A2
Uttenweiler D 61 B5
Utterslev DK 39 E4
Uttoxeter GB 27 C4
Utvälinge S 41 C2
Utvorda N 114 C7
Uusikaarlepyy FIN 3 E25
Uusikaupunki FIN 3 F24
Uvac BIH 85 C4
Uvaly CZ 53 C4
Uvdal N 32 B5
Uza F 76 B1
Uzdin SRB 75 C5
Uzdowo PL 47 B6
Uzein F 76 C2
Uzel F 56 B3
Uzerche F 68 C1
Uzès F 78 B3
Uzhhorod UA 11 B7
Uzhok UA 11 B7
Užice SRB 85 C4
Uznach CH 70 A3
Üznovë AL 105 C6
Üzümlü
Konya TR 119 E6
Muğla TR 119 F4
Uzunköprü TR 118 A1

V

Vaalajärvi FIN 113 E15
Vaas F 58 C1
Vaasa FIN 3 E24
Vaasen NL 50 A1
Vabre F 77 C5
Vác H 65 C5
Vacha D 51 C6
Váchartyán H 65 C5
Väckelsång S 40 C4
Vacqueyras F 78 B3
Vad S 36 B2
Vada I 81 C4
Väddö S 36 C5
Väderstad S 37 D1
Vadheim N 32 A2
Vadillo de la Sierra E 93 A5
Vadillos E 95 B4
Vadla N 33 C3
Vado I 81 B5
Vado Lígure I 80 B2
Vadsø N 113 B18
Vadstena S 37 D1
Vadum DK 38 B2
Vaduz FL 71 A4
Vafos N 33 D6
Vág H 74 A2
Vågåmo N 114 F6
Væggerløse DK 44 A3
Vaggeryd S 40 B4
Vaghia GR 117 D5
Vaglia I 81 C5
Váglio Basilicata I 104 C1
Vagney F 60 B2
Vagnhärad S 37 D4
Vagnsunda S 37 C5
Vagos P 92 A2
Vai GR 117 G8
Vaiano I 81 C5
Vaiges F 57 B5
Vaihingen D 61 B4
Vaillant F 59 C6
Vailly-sur-Aisne F 59 A4
Vailly-sur Sauldre F 68 A2
Vairano Scalo I 103 B7
Vaison-la-Romaine F 79 B4
Vaite F 60 C1
Väjern S 35 D3
Vajszló H 74 C2
Vaksdal N 32 B2
Vál H 74 A3
Valaam RUS 3 F29
Valada P 92 B2
Vålådalen S 115 D10
Valadares P 87 C2
Valado P 92 B1
Valandovo MK 116 A4
Valaská SK 65 B5
Valaská Belá SK 65 B4
Valaská Dubová SK 65 A5
Valašská Polanka CZ 64 A3
Valašské Klobouky CZ 64 A4
Valašské Meziříčí CZ 64 A3
Valberg F 79 B5
Vålberg S 35 C5
Valbo S 36 B4
Valbom P 87 C2
Valbondione I 71 B5
Valbonë AL 105 A5
Valbonnais F 79 B4
Valbuena de Duero E 88 C2
Vălcani RO 75 C5
Valdagno I 71 C6
Valdahon F 69 A6
Valdaracete E 95 B3
Valday RUS 7 C12
Valdealgorfa E 90 C2
Valdecaballeros E 93 B5
Valdecabras E 95 B4
Valdecarros E 94 B1
Valdeconcha E 95 B4
Valdeflores E 99 B4
Valdefresno E 88 B1
Valdeganga E 95 C5
Valdelacasa E 93 A5
Valdelacasa de Tajo E 93 B5
Valdelarco E 99 B4
Valdelosa E 94 A1
Valdeltormo E 90 C3
Valdelugeros E 88 B1
Valdemanco de Esteras E 94 D2
Valdemarsvik S 37 D3
Valdemorillo E 94 B2
Valdemoro E 94 B3
Valdemoro Sierra E 95 B5
Valdenoceda E 89 B3
Valdeobispo E 93 A4
Valdeolivas E 95 B4
Valdepeñas E 100 A2
Valdepeñas de Jaén E 100 B2
Valdepiélago E 88 B1
Valdepolo E 88 B1
Valderas E 88 B1
Valdérice I 108 A1
Valderrobres E 90 C3
Valderrueda E 88 B2
Val de San Lorenzo E 86 B4
Val de Santo Domingo E 94 B2
Val d'Esquières F 79 C5
Valdestillas E 88 C2
Valdetorres E 93 C4
Valdetorres de Jarama E 95 B3
Valdeverdeja E 93 B5
Valdevimbre E 88 B1
Valdieri I 80 B1
Valdilecha E 95 B3
Val-d'Isère F 70 C1
Valdobbiádene I 72 C1
Valdocondes E 89 C3
Valdoviño E 86 A2
Valea lui Mihai RO 11 C7
Vale de Açor
Beja P 98 B3
Portalegre P 92 B3
Vale de Água P 98 B2
Vale de Cambra P 87 D2
Vale de Lobo P 98 B2
Vale de Prazeres P 92 A3
Vale de Reis P 92 C2
Vale de Rosa P 98 B3
Vale de Santarém P 92 B2
Vale de Vargo P 98 B3
Vale do Peso P 92 B3
Valega P 87 D2
Valéggio sul Mincio I 71 C5
Valeiro P 92 C2
Valença P 87 B2
Valençay F 67 A6
Valence
Charente F 67 C5
Drôme F 78 B3
Valence d'Agen F 77 B3
Valence-d'Albigeois F 77 B5
Valence-sur-Baise F 77 C3
Valencia E 96 B2
Valencia de Alcántara E 93 B3
Valencia de Don Juan E 88 B1
Valencia de las Torres E 93 C4
Valencia del Ventoso E 99 A4
Valencia de Mombuey E 99 A3
Valenciennes F 49 C4
Valensole F 79 C4
Valentano I 102 A4
Valentigney F 70 A1
Valentine F 77 C3
Valenza I 80 A2
Valenzuela E 100 B1
Valenzuela de Calatrava E 100 A2
Våler
Hedmark N 34 B3
Østfold N 35 C2
Valera de Abajo E 95 C4
Valeria E 95 C4
Valestrand N 33 C2
Valestrandsfossen N 32 B2
Valevåg N 33 C2
Valfabbrica I 82 C1
Valflaunes F 78 C2
Valga EST 7 C9
Valgorge F 78 B3
Valgrisenche I 70 C2
Valguarnera Caropepe I 109 B3
Valhelhas P 92 A3
Valjevo SRB 85 B4
Valka LV 7 C8
Valkeakoski FIN 3 F26
Valkenburg NL 50 C1
Valkenswaard NL 49 B6
Valkó H 75 A4
Valla S 37 C3
Vallada E 96 C2
Vallado E 86 A4
Valladolid E 88 C2
Vallåkra S 41 D2
Vallata I 103 B8
Vallberga S 40 C3
Vall d'Alba E 96 A2
Valldemossa E 97 B2
Valle N 33 C4
Valle Castellana I 82 D2
Valle de Abdalajís E 100 C1
Valle de Cabuérniga E 88 A2
Valle de la Serena E 93 C5
Valle de Matamoros E 93 C4
Valle de Santa Ana E 93 C4
Valledolmo I 108 B2
Valledoria I 110 B1
Vallelado E 88 C2
Vallelunga Pratameno I 108 B2
Valle Mosso I 70 C3
Vallendar D 50 C3
Vallentuna S 37 C5
Vallerås S 34 B5
Valleraugue F 78 B2
Vallermosa I 110 C1
Vallet F 66 A3
Valletta M 107 C5
Valley GB 26 B1
Vallfogona de Riucorb E 91 B4
Valli del Pasúbio I 71 C6
Vallo della Lucánia I 103 C8
Valloire F 69 C6
Vallombrosa I 81 C5
Vallon-Pont-d'Arc F 78 B3
Vallorbe CH 69 B6
Vallouise F 79 B5
Valls E 91 B4
Vallset N 34 B3
Vallsta S 36 A3
Vallstena S 37 E5
Valmadrid E 90 B2
Valmiera LV 7 C8
Valmojado E 94 B2
Valmont F 58 A1
Valmontone I 102 B5
Valö S 36 B5
Valognes F 57 A4
Valonga P 92 A2
Valongo P 87 C2
Válor E 100 C2
Valoria la Buena E 88 C2
Valøy N 114 C7
Valozhyn BY 7 D9
Valpaços P 87 C3
Valpelline I 70 C2
Valpiana I 81 C4
Valpovo HR 74 C3
Valras-Plage F 78 C2
Valréas F 78 B3
Vals CH 71 B4
Valsavarenche I 70 C2
Vålse DK 39 E4
Valsequillo E 93 C5
Valsjöbyn S 115 C11
Vals-les-Bains F 78 B3
Valsonne F 69 C4
Valstagna I 72 C1
Val-Suzon F 69 A4
Valtablado del Rio E 95 B4
Valþjofsstaður IS 111 B11
Val Thorens F 69 C6
Valtice CZ 64 B2
Valtiendas E 88 C3
Valtierra E 89 B5
Valtopina I 82 C1
Valtorta I 71 C4
Valtournenche I 70 C2
Valverde E 89 C5
Valverde de Burguillos E 93 C4
Valverde de Júcar E 95 C4
Valverde de la Vera E 93 A5
Valverde de la Virgen E 88 B1
Valverde del Camino E 99 B4
Valverde del Fresno E 93 A4
Valverde de Llerena E 99 A5
Valverde de Mérida E 93 C4
Vamberk CZ 53 C6
Vamdrup DK 39 D2
Våmhus S 34 A6
Vamlingbo S 37 F5
Vammala FIN 3 F25
Vamos GR 117 G6
Vámosmikola H 65 C4
Vámosszabadi H 64 C3
Vanault-les-Dames F 59 B5
Vandel DK 39 D2
Vandenesse F 68 B3
Vandenesse-en-Auxois F 69 A4
Vandóies I 72 B1
Väne-Åsaka S 35 D4
Vänersborg S 35 D4
Vänersnäs S 35 D4
Vang N 32 A5
Vänge S 36 C4
Vangsnes N 32 A3
Vänjaurbäck S 115 C15
Vännacka S 35 C4
Vannareid N 112 B8
Vännäs S 115 D16
Vannes F 56 C3
Vannsätter S 36 A3
Vannvåg N 112 B8
Vansbro S 34 B6
Vanse N 33 D3
Vantaa FIN 6 A8
Vanviken N 114 D7
Vanyarc H 65 C5
Vaour F 77 B4
Vapnyarka UA 11 B10
Vaprio d'Adda I 71 C4
Vaqueiros P 98 B3
Vara S 35 D4
Varacieux F 69 C5
Varades F 66 A3
Varages F 79 C4
Varaldsøy N 32 B2
Varallo I 70 C3
Varangerbotn N 113 B17
Varano de'Melegari I 81 B4
Varaždin HR 73 B6
Varaždinske Toplice HR 73 B6
Varazze I 80 B2
Varberg S 40 B2
Vardal N 34 B2
Varde DK 39 D1
Vårdö FIN 36 B7
Vardø N 113 B20
Vardomb H 74 B3
Varel D 43 B5
Varėna LT 6 D8
Vårenes N 33 C2
Varengeville-sur-Mer F 58 A1
Varenna I 71 B4
Varennes-en-Argonne F 59 A6
Varennes-le-Grand F 69 B4
Varennes-St Sauveur F 69 B5
Varennes-sur-Allier F 68 B3
Varennes-sur-Amance F 60 C1
Vareš BIH 84 B3
Varese I 70 C3
Varese Ligure I 80 B3
Vârfurile RO 11 C7
Vårgårda S 40 A2
Vargas
E 88 A3
P 92 B2
Vargön S 35 D4
Varhaug N 33 D2
Variaş RO 75 B5
Variaşu Mic RO 75 B6
Varilhes F 77 C4
Varin SK 65 A4
Väring S 35 D5
Váriz P 87 C4
Varkaus FIN 3 E27
Varmahlíð IS 111 B6
Varmaland IS 111 C4
Värmlands Bro S 35 C5
Värmskog S 35 C4
Varna
BG 11 E9
SRB 85 B4
Värnamo S 40 B4
Varnhem S 35 D5
Varnsdorf CZ 53 C4
Värö S 40 B2
Varoška Rijeka BIH 83 A5
Városlöd H 74 A2
Várpalota H 74 A3
Varreddes F 59 B3
Vars F 79 B5
Varsi I 81 B3
Varsseveld NL 50 B2
Vårsta S 37 C4
Vartdal N 114 E3
Vartofta S 40 A3
Vårvarin SRB 85 C6
Vårvik S 35 C4
Värvölgy H 74 B2
Varzi I 80 B3
Varzjelas P 92 A2
Varzo I 70 B3
Varzy F 68 A3
Vasad H 75 A4
Väse S 35 C5
Vašica SRB 85 A4
Vasilevichi BY 7 E10
Väskinde S 37 E5
Vaskút H 75 B3
Vaslui RO 11 C9
Vassbotn N 33 D5
Vassenden N 32 A6
Vassieux-en-Vercors F 79 B4
Vassmolösa S 40 C6
Vassy F 57 B5
Västansjö S 115 B12
Västanvik S 36 B1
Västerås S 37 C3
Västerby S 36 B2
Västerfärnebo S 36 C3
Västergarn S 37 E5
Västerhaninge S 37 C5
Västervik S 40 B6
Vasto I 103 A7
Västra Ämtervik S 35 C5
Västra-Bodarne S 40 B2
Västra Karup S 41 C2
Vasvár H 74 A1
Vasylkiv UA 11 A11
Vát H 74 A1
Vatan F 68 A1
Väte S 37 E5
Vathia GR 117 F4
Vatican City = Cittádel Vaticano I 102 B5
Vatili CY 120 A2
Vatin SRB 75 C6
Vatland N 33 D4
Vatnar N 33 C6
Vatnås N 32 C6
Vatne N 33 D4
Vatnestrøm N 33 D5
Vätö S 36 C5
Vatra-Dornei RO 11 C8
Vatry F 59 B5
Vattholma S 36 B4
Vättis CH 71 B4
Vauchamps F 59 B4
Vauchassis F 59 B4
Vaucouleurs F 60 B1
Vaudoy-en-Brie F 59 B4
Vaulen N 33 D2
Vaulruz CH 70 B1
Vaulx Vraucourt F 48 C3
Vaumas F 68 B3
Vausseroux F 67 B4
Vauvenargues F 79 C4
Vauvert F 78 C3
Vauvillers F 60 C2
Vaux-sur-Sure B 60 A1
Vawkavysk BY 6 E8
Vaxholm S 37 C5
Växjö S 40 C4
Våxtorp S 41 C3
Vayrac F 77 B4
Važec SK 65 A5
Veberöd S 41 D3
Vechelde D 51 A6
Vechta D 43 C5
Vecinos E 94 B1
Vecsés H 75 A4
Vedavågen N 33 C2
Veddige S 40 B2
Vedersø DK 39 C1
Vedeseta I 71 C4
Vedevåg S 37 C2
Vedra E 86 B2
Vedum S 35 D5
Veendam NL 42 B3
Veenendaal NL 49 A6
Vega
Asturias E 88 A1
Asturias E 88 A1
Vega de Espinareda E 86 B4
Vega de Infanzones E 88 B1
Vegadeo E 86 A3
Vega de Pas E 88 A3
Vega de Valcarce E 86 B4
Vega de Valdetronco E 88 C1
Vegårshei N 33 D5
Vegas de Coria E 93 A4
Vegas del Condado E 88 B1
Vegby S 40 B3
Vegger DK 38 C2
Veggli N 32 B6
Veghel NL 49 B6
Veglast D 45 A4
Véglie I 105 C3
Veguillas E 95 B3
Vegusdal N 33 D5
Veidholmen N 114 D4
Veidnes N 113 B15
Veikåker N 34 B1
Veinge S 40 C3
Vejbystrand S 41 C2
Vejen DK 39 D2
Vejer de la Frontera E 99 C5
Vejle DK 39 D2
Vejprty CZ 52 C3
Velada E 94 B2
Vela Luka HR 83 D5
Velayos E 94 B2
Velbert D 50 B3
Velburg D 62 A2
Velde N 114 C8
Velden
Bayern D 62 A2
Bayern D 62 B3
Velden am Worther See A 73 B4
Velefique E 101 B3
Velen D 50 B2
Velenje SLO 73 B5
Veles MK 116 A3
Velesevec HR 73 C6
Velešin CZ 63 B5
Velestino GR 116 C4
Velez Blanco E 101 B3
Vélez de Benaudalla E 100 C2
Vélez-Málaga E 100 C1
Vélez Rubio E 101 B3
Veliiki Radinci SRB 85 A4
Velika
HR 74 C2
MNE 85 D4
Velika Drenova SRB 85 C6
Velika Gorica HR 73 C6
Velika Grdevac HR 74 C2
Velika Greda SRB 75 C6
Velika Ilova BIH 84 B2
Velika Kladuša BIH 73 C5
Velika Kopanica HR 74 C3
Velika Krsna SRB 85 B5
Velika Obarska BIH 85 B4
Velika Pisanica HR 74 C2
Velika Plana
Srbija SRB 85 B6
Srbija SRB 85 C6
Velika Zdenci HR 74 C2
Velike Lašče SLO 73 C4
Veliki Gaj SRB 75 C6
Veliki Popović SRB 85 B6
Veliki Šiljegovac SRB 85 C6
Velikiye Luki RUS 7 C11
Veliko Gradište SRB 85 B6
Veliko Orašje SRB 85 B6
Veliko Selo SRB 85 B6
Veliko Tŭrnovo BG 11 E8
Velilla del Río Carrió E 88 B2
Velilla de San Antonio E 95 B3
Veli Lošinj HR 83 B3
Velipojë AL 105 B5
Velizh RUS 7 D11
Veljun HR 73 C5
Velká Bíteš CZ 64 A2
Velká Hleďsebe CZ 52 D2

Velká Lomnica SK 65 A6
Velkánad Veličkou CZ 64 B3
Velké Bystřice CZ 64 A3
Velké Heraltice CZ 54 D2
Velké Karlovice CZ 64 A4
Vel'ke'Kostol'any SK 64 B3
Vel'ké Leváre SK 64 B3
Velké Losiny CZ 54 C2
Velké Meziříčí CZ 64 A2
Velké Pavlovice CZ 64 B2
Vel'ké Rovné SK 65 A4
Vel'ké Uherce SK 65 B4
Vel'ké Zálužie SK 64 B3
Vel'ký Blahovo SK 65 B6
Velky Bor CZ 63 A4
Vel'ký Cetin SK 64 B4
Vel'ký Krtíš SK 65 B5
Vel'ký Meder SK 64 C3
Velky Ujezd CZ 64 A3
Vellahn D 44 B2
Vellberg D 61 A5
Velles F 67 B6
Velletri I 102 B5
Vellinge S 41 D3
Vellisca E 95 B4
Velliza E 88 C2
Vellmar D 51 B5
Velp NL 50 A1
Velten D 45 C5
Velvary CZ 53 C4
Velvendos GR 116 B4
Vemb DK 39 C1
Vemdalen S 115 E10
Veme N 34 B2
Véménd H 74 B3
Vemmedrup DK 39 D5
Vena S 40 B5
Venaco F 102 A2
Venafro I 103 B7
Venarey-les-Laumes F 69 A4
Venaría I 70 C2
Venasca I 80 B1
Venčane SRB 85 B5
Vence F 79 C6
Venda Nova
Coimbra P 92 A2
Leiria P 92 B2
Vendas Novas P 92 C2
Vendays-Montalivet F 66 C3
Vendel S 36 B4
Vendelso S 37 C5
Vendeuil F 59 A4
Vendeuvre-sur-Barse F 59 B5
Vendoeuvres F 67 B6
Vendôme F 58 C2
Venelles F 79 C4
Veness GB 23 B6
Venézia = Venice I 72 C2
Venialbo E 88 C1
Venice = Venézia I 72 C2
Vénissieux F 69 C4
Venjan S 34 B5
Venlo NL 50 B2
Vennesla N 33 D4
Vennesund N 114 B9
Vennezey F 60 B2
Venn Green GB 28 C3
Venosa I 104 C1
Venray NL 50 B1
Vent A 71 B5
Venta de Baños E 88 C2
Venta del Moro E 96 B1
Venta de los Santos E 100 A2
Venta las Ranas E 88 A1
Ventanueva E 86 A4
Ventas de Huelma E 100 B2
Ventas de Zafarraya E 100 C1
Ventavon F 79 B4
Ventimíglia I 80 C1
Ventnor GB 31 D2
Ventosa de la Sierra E 89 C4
Ventosilla E 89 C4
Ventspils LV 6 C6
Venturina I 81 C4
Venzolasca F 102 A2
Venzone I 72 B3
Vép H 74 A1
Vera
E 101 B4
N 115 D9
Vera Cruz P 98 A3
Vera de Bidasoa E 76 C1
Vera de Moncayo E 89 C5
Verbánia I 70 C3
Verberie F 58 A3
Verbicaro I 106 B2
Verbier CH 70 B2
Vercelli I 70 C3
Vercel-Villedieu-le-Camp F 69 A6
Verchen D 45 B4
Vercheny F 79 B4
Verclause F 79 B4
Verdalsøra N 114 D8
Verden D 43 C6
Verdens Ende N 35 C2
Verdikoussa GR 116 C3
Verdille F 67 C4
Verdú E 91 B4
Verdun F 59 A6
Verdun-sur-Garonne F 77 C4
Verdun-sur-le-Doubs F 69 B5
Veresegyház H 65 C5
Verfeil F 77 C4
Vergato I 81 B5
Vergel E 96 C3
Vergeletto CH 70 B3
Verges E 91 A6
Vergiate I 70 C3
Vergt F 77 A3
Veria GR 116 B4
Verín E 87 C3
Veringenstadt D 61 B5
Verkhovye RUS 7 E14
Verl D 51 B4
Verma N 114 E5
Vermand F 59 A4
Vermelha P 92 B1
Vermenton F 59 C4
Vermosh AL 85 D4
Vernago I 71 B5
Vernante I 80 B1
Vernantes F 67 A5
Vernár SK 65 B6
Vernasca I 81 B3
Vernayaz CH 70 B2
Vernazza I 81 B3
Vern-d'Anjou F 57 C5
Verneřice CZ 53 C4
Vernet F 77 C4
Vernet-les-Bains F 91 A5
Verneuil F 59 A4
Verneuil-sur-Avre F 58 B1
Vernier CH 69 B6
Vérnio I 81 B5
Vérnole I 105 C4
Vernon F 58 A2
Vernoux-en-Vivarais F 78 B3
Veróce H 65 C5
Verolanuova I 71 C5
Véroli I 103 B6
Verona I 71 C6
Verpelét H 65 C6
Verrabotn N 114 D7
Verrès I 70 C2
Verrey-sous-Salmaise F 69 A4
Verrières F 67 B5
Versailles F 58 B3
Versam CH 71 B4
Verseg H 65 C5
Versmold D 50 A4
Versoix CH 69 B6
Verteillac F 67 C5
Vértesacsa H 74 A3
Vertou F 66 A3
Vertus F 59 B4
Verviers B 50 C1
Vervins F 59 A4
Verwood GB 29 C6
Veryan GB 28 C3
Veržej SLO 73 B6
Verzuolo I 80 B1
Verzy F 59 A5
Vescovato F 102 A2
Vése H 74 B2
Veselínad Lužnicí CZ 63 A5
Veselínad Moravou CZ 64 B3
Veseliy BG 11 E9
Vésime I 80 B2
Veskoniemi FIN 113 D16
Vesoul F 60 C2
Vespolate I 70 C3
Vessigebro S 40 C2
Vestbygd N 33 D3
Vestenanova I 71 C6
Vester Husby S 37 D3
Vester Nebel DK 39 D2
Vesterøhavn DK 38 B3
Vester Torup DK 38 B2
Vester Vedsted DK 39 D1
Vestervig DK 38 C1
Vestfossen N 35 C1
Vestmannaeyjar IS 111 D5
Vestmarka N 34 C3
Vestnes N 114 E4
Vestone I 71 C5
Vestre Gausdal N 34 A2
Vestre Jakobselv N 113 B18
Vestre Slidre N 32 A5
Vesyegonsk RUS 7 B14
Veszprém H 74 A2
Veszprémvarsány H 74 A2
Vésztő H 75 B6
Vetlanda S 40 B5
Vetovo HR 74 C2
Vetralla I 102 A5
Větrný Jeníkov CZ 63 A6
Vétroz CH 70 B2
Vetschau D 53 B4
Vettasjärvi S 113 E10
Vetto I 81 B4
Vetulónia I 81 D4
Veules-les-Roses F 58 A1
Veulettes-sur-Mer F 58 A1
Veum N 33 C5
Veurne B 48 B3
Veverská Bítýška CZ 64 A2
Vevey CH 70 B1
Vevi GR 116 B3
Vevring N 32 A2
Vex CH 70 B2
Veynes F 79 B4
Veyre-Monton F 68 C3
Veyrier F 69 C6
Vézelay F 68 A3
Vézelise F 60 B2
Vézenobres F 78 B3
Vezins F 67 A4
Vézins-de-Lévézou F 78 B1
Vezirhan TR 118 B5
Vezirköprü TR 16 A7
Vezza di Óglio I 71 B5
Vezzani F 102 A2
Vezzano I 71 B6
Vezzano sul Cróstolo I 81 B4
Vi S 115 E14
Viadana I 81 B4
Via Gloria P 98 B3
Viana E 89 B4
Viana do Alentejo P 92 C2
Viana do Bolo E 87 B3
Viana do Castelo P 87 C2
Vianden L 60 A2
Viannos GR 117 G7
Viaréggio I 81 C4
Viator E 101 C3
Vibble S 37 E5
Viborg DK 38 C2
Vibo Valéntia I 106 C3
Vibraye F 58 B1
Vic E 91 B5
Vícar E 101 C3
Vicarello I 81 C4
Vicari I 108 B2
Vicchio I 81 C5
Vicdesses F 77 D4
Vic-en-Bigorre F 76 C3
Vicenza I 71 C6
Vic-Fézensac F 76 C3
Vichy F 68 B3
Vickan S 38 B5
Vickerstown GB 26 A2
Vic-le-Comte F 68 C3
Vico F 102 A1
Vico del Gargano I 104 B1
Vico Equense I 103 C7
Vicopisano I 81 C4
Vicosoprano CH 71 B4
Vicovaro I 102 A5
Vic-sur-Aisne F 59 A4
Vic-sur-Cère F 77 B5
Victoria = Rabat M 107 C5
Vidago P 87 C3
Vidauban F 79 C5
Vide P 92 A3
Videbæk DK 39 C1
Videm SLO 73 C4
Videseter N 114 F4
Vidigueira P 98 A3
Vidin BG 11 E7
Vidlin GB 22 A7
Vidzy BY 7 D9
Viechtach D 62 A3
Vieille-Brioude F 68 C3
Vieira P 92 B2
Vieira do Minho P 87 C2
Vieiros P 92 C3
Vielha E 90 A3
Vielle-Aure F 77 D3
Viellespesse F 68 C3
Viellevigne F 66 B3
Vielmur-sur-Agout F 77 C5
Vielsalm B 50 C1
Viels Maison F 59 B4
Vienenburg D 51 B6
Vienna = Wien A 64 B2
Vienne F 69 C4
Vieritz D 44 C4
Viernheim D 61 A4
Vierraden D 45 B6
Viersen D 50 B2
Vierville-sur-Mer F 57 A5
Vierzon F 68 A2
Vieselbach D 52 C1
Vieste I 104 B2
Vietas S 112 E7
Vieteren B 48 C3
Vietri di Potenza I 104 C1
Vietri sul Mare I 103 C7
Vieux-Boucau-les-Bains F 76 C1
Vif F 79 A4
Vig DK 39 D4
Vigásio I 71 C5
Vigaun A 63 C4
Vigeland N 33 D4
Vigeois F 67 C6
Vigévano I 70 C3
Viggianello I 106 B3
Viggiano I 104 C1
Vigliano I 102 A6
Vigmostad N 33 D4
Vignale I 80 A2
Vignanello I 102 A5
Vigneulles-lès-Hattonchâtel F 60 B1
Vignevieille F 77 D5
Vignola I 81 B5
Vignory F 59 B6
Vignoux-sur Barangeon F 68 A2
Vigo E 87 B2
Vigo di Fassa I 72 B1
Vigone I 80 B1
Vigrestad N 33 D2
Vihiers F 67 A4
Viitasaari FIN 3 E26
Vík IS 111 D6
Vik
Nordland N 114 B9
Rogaland N 33 D2
Sogn og Fjordane N 32 A3
S 41 D4
Vika S 36 B2
Vikajärvi FIN 113 F15
Vikane N 35 C2
Vikarbyn S 36 B2
Vike N 32 B2
Vikedal N 33 C2
Vikeland N 33 D4
Viken
Jämtland S 115 C10
Skåne S 41 C2
Viker N 34 B2
Vikersund N 34 C1
Vikeså N 33 D3
Vikevåg N 33 C2
Vikingstad S 37 D2
Vikmanshyttan S 36 B2
Vikna N 114 C7
Vikøy N 32 B3
Vikran
Troms N 112 C7
Troms N 112 D5
Viksjö S 115 E14
Viksøyri N 32 A3
Viksta S 36 B4
Vila Boim P 92 C3
Vila Chãde Ourique P 92 B2
Viladamat E 91 A6
Vila de Cruces E 86 B2
Vila de Rei P 92 B2
Vila do Bispo P 98 B2
Vila do Conde P 87 C2
Viladrau E 91 B5
Vila Flor P 87 C3
Vila Franca das Navas P 87 D3
Vilafranca del Maestrat E 90 C2
Vilafranca del Penedès E 91 B4
Vila Franca de Xira P 92 C1
Vila Fresca P 92 C1
Vilagarcía de Arousa E 86 B2
Vilajuiga E 91 A6
Vilamarin E 86 B3
Vilamartín de Valdeorras E 86 B3
Vila Nogueira P 92 C1
Vila Nova da Baronia P 98 A2
Vilanova de Castelló E 96 B2
Vila Nova de Cerveira P 87 C2
Vila Nova de Famalicão P 87 C2
Vila Nova de Foz Côa P 87 C3
Vila Nova de Gaia P 87 C2
Vila Nova de Milfontes P 98 B2
Vila Nova de Paiva P 87 D3
Vila Nova de São Bento P 98 B3
Vilanova de Sau E 91 B5
Vilanova i la Geltrú E 91 B4
Vilapedre E 86 A3
Vila Pouca de Aguiar P 87 C3
Vila Praja de Ancora P 87 C2
Vilarandelo P 87 C3
Vilar de Santos E 87 B3
Vilardevós E 87 C3
Vila Real P 87 C3
Vila-real de los Infantes E 96 B2
Vila Real de Santo António P 98 B3
Vilar Formosa P 93 A4
Vila-Rodona E 91 B4
Vila Ruiva P 98 A3
Vilasantar E 86 A2
Vilaseca E 91 B4
Vila Seca P 92 A2
Vilassar de Mar E 91 B5
Vilasund S 115 A11
Vila Velha de Ródão P 92 B3
Vila Verde
Braga P 87 C2
Lisboa P 92 B1
Vila Verde de Filcalho P 98 B3
Vila Viçosa P 92 C3
Vilches E 100 A2
Vildbjerg DK 39 C1
Vilémov CZ 63 A6
Vileyka BY 7 D9
Vilhelmina S 115 C13
Vilia GR 117 D5
Viljandi EST 7 B8
Villabáñez E 88 C2
Villablanca E 98 B3
Villablino E 86 B4
Villabona E 89 A4
Villabragima E 88 C1
Villabuena del Puente E 88 C1
Villacadima E 95 A3
Villacañas E 95 C3
Villacarriedo E 88 A3
Villacarrillo E 100 A2
Villa Castelli I 104 C3
Villacastín E 94 B2
Villach A 72 B3
Villacidro I 110 C1
Villaconejos E 95 B3
Villaconejos de Trabaque E 95 B4
Villa Cova de Lixa P 87 C2
Villada E 88 B2
Villadangos del Páramo E 88 B1
Villadecanes E 86 B4
Villa del Prado E 94 B2
Villa del Rio E 100 B1
Villadepera E 87 C4
Villa de Peralonso E 87 C4
Villa di Chiavenna I 71 B4
Villadiego E 88 B2
Villadompardo E 100 B1
Villadóssola I 70 B3
Villaeles de Valdavia E 88 B2
Villaescusa de Haro E 95 C4
Villafáfila E 88 C1
Villafeliche E 95 A5
Villaflores E 94 A1
Villafrades de Campos E 88 B2
Villafranca
Avila E 93 A5
Navarra E 89 B5
Villafranca de Córdoba E 100 B1
Villafranca del Bierzo E 86 B4
Villafranca de los Barros E 93 C4
Villafranca de los Caballeros E 95 C3
Villafranca di Verona I 71 C5
Villafranca in Lunigiana I 81 B3
Villafranca-Montes de Oca E 89 B3
Villafranca Tirrena I 109 A4
Villafranco del Campo E 95 B5
Villafranco del Guadalquivir E 99 B4
Villafrati I 108 B2
Villafrechós E 88 C1
Villafruela E 88 C3
Villagarcia de las Torres E 93 C4
Villaggio Mancuso I 106 B3
Villagonzalo E 93 C4
Villagotón E 86 B4
Villagrains F 76 B2
Villaharta E 100 A1
Villahermosa E 100 A3
Villaherreros E 88 B2
Villahoz E 88 B3
Villaines-la-Juhel F 57 B5
Villajoyosa E 96 C2
Villalago I 103 B6
Villalba
E 86 A3
I 108 B2
Villalba de Calatrava E 100 A2
Villalba de Guardo E 88 B2
Villalba del Alcor E 99 B4
Villalba de la Sierra E 95 B4
Villalba de los Alcores E 88 C2
Villalba de los Barros E 93 C4
Villalba del Rey E 95 B4
Villalcampo E 87 C4
Villalcázar de Sirga E 88 B2
Villalengua E 89 C5
Villalgordo del Júcar E 95 C4
Villalgordo del Marquesado E 95 C4
Villalmóndar E 89 B3
Villalón de Campos E 88 B1
Villalonga E 96 C2
Villalonso E 88 C1
Villalpando E 88 C1
Villaluenga E 94 B3
Villalumbroso E 88 B2
Villálvaro E 89 C3
Villamalea E 95 C5
Villamanán E 88 B1
Villamanín E 88 B1
Villamanrique E 100 A3
Villamanrique de la Condesa E 99 B4
Villamanta E 94 B2
Villamantilla E 94 B2
Villamar I 110 C1
Villamartín E 99 C5
Villamartin de Campos E 88 B2
Villamartin de Don Sancho E 88 B1
Villamassárgia I 110 C1
Villamayor E 88 A1
Villamayor de Calatrava E 100 A1
Villamayor de Campos E 88 C1
Villamayor de Santiago E 95 C4
Villamblard F 77 A3
Villamejil E 86 B4
Villamesias E 93 B5
Villaminaya E 94 C3
Villa Minozzo I 81 B4
Villamor de los Escuderos E 88 C1
Villamoronta E 88 B2
Villamuelas E 94 C3
Villamuriel de Cerrato E 88 C2
Villandraut F 76 B2
Villanova I 104 C3
Villanova d'Asti I 80 B1
Villanova del Battista I 103 B8
Villanova Mondov ì I 80 B1
Villanova Monteleone I 110 B1
Villante E 88 B3
Villantério I 71 C4
Villanubla E 88 C2
Villanueva de Alcardete E 95 C3
Villanueva de Alcorón E 95 B4
Villanueva de Algaidas E 100 B1
Villanueva de Argaña E 88 B3
Villanueva de Bogas E 95 C3
Villanueva de Córdoba E 100 A1
Villanueva de Gállego E 90 B2
Villanueva del Aceral E 94 A2
Villanueva de la Concepcion E 100 C1
Villanueva de la Fuente E 101 A3
Villanueva de la Jara E 95 C5
Villanueva de la Reina E 100 A2
Villanueva del Arzobispo E 100 A3
Villanueva de la Serena E 93 C5
Villanueva de la Sierra E 93 A4
Villanueva de las Manzanas E 88 B1
Villanueva de las Peras E 88 C1
Villanueva de las Torres E 100 B2
Villanueva de la Vera E 93 A5
Villanueva del Campo E 88 C1
Villanueva del Duque E 100 A1
Villanueva del Fresno E 93 C3
Villanueva del Huerva E 90 B1
Villanueva de los Castillejos E 98 B3
Villanueva de los Infantes E 100 A3
Villanueva del Rey E 99 A5
Villanueva del Rio E 99 B5
Villanueva del Río y Minas E 99 B5
Villanueva del Rosario E 100 C1
Villanueva del Trabuco E 100 B1
Villanueva de Mesia E 100 B2
Villanueva de Nía E 88 B2
Villanueva de Oscos E 86 A4
Villanueva de San Carlos E 100 A2
Villanueva de San Juan E 99 B5
Villanueva de Tapia E 100 B1
Villanueva de Valdegovia E 89 B3
Villány H 74 C3
Villaputzu I 110 C2
Villaquejida E 88 B1
Villaquilambre E 88 B1
Villaquiran de los Infantes E 88 B2
Villaralto E 100 A1
Villarcayo E 89 B3
Villard-de-Lans F 79 A4
Villar de Barrio E 87 B3
Villar de Cañas E 95 C4
Villar de Chinchilla E 96 C1
Villar de Ciervo E 87 D4
Villardeciervos E 87 C4
Villar de Domingo Garcia E 95 B4
Villardefrades E 88 C1
Villar del Arzobispo E 96 B2
Villar del Buey E 87 C4
Villar del Cobo E 95 B5
Villar del Humo E 95 C5
Villar de los Navarros E 90 B1
Villar del Pedroso E 93 B5
Villar del Rey E 93 B4
Villar del Rio E 89 B4
Villar del Saz de Navalón E 95 B4
Villar de Rena E 93 B5
Villarejo E 95 A3
Villarejo de Fuentes E 95 C4
Villarejo de Orbigo E 88 B1
Villarejo de Salvanes E 95 B3
Villarejo-Periesteban E 95 C4
Villares del Saz E 95 C4
Villaretto I 79 A6
Villargordo del Cabriel E 96 B1
Villarino E 87 C4
Villarino de Conso E 87 B3
Villarluengo E 90 C2
Villarobe E 89 B3
Villarosa I 109 B3
Villar Perosa I 79 B6
Villarramiel E 88 B2
Villarrasa E 99 B4
Villarreal de San Carlos E 93 B4
Villarrin de Campos E 88 C1
Villarrobledo E 95 C4
Villarroya de la Sierra E 89 C5
Villarroya de los Pinares E 90 C2
Villarrubia de los Ojos E 95 C3
Villarrubia de Santiago E 95 C3
Villarrubio E 95 C4
Villars-les-Dombes F 69 B5
Villarta E 95 C5
Villarta de los Montes E 94 C2
Villarta de San Juan E 95 C3
Villasana de Mena E 89 A3
Villasandino E 88 B2
Villa San Giovanni I 109 A4
Villa Santa Maria I 103 B7
Villasante E 89 A3
Villa Santina I 72 B2
Villasarracino E 88 B2
Villasayas E 89 C4
Villasdardo E 87 C4
Villaseca de Henares E 95 B4
Villaseca de Laciana E 86 B4
Villaseca de la Sagra E 94 C3
Villaseco de los Gamitos E 87 C4
Villaseco de los Reyes E 87 C4
Villasequilla de Yepes E 94 C3
Villasimíus I 110 C2
Villasmundo I 109 B4
Villasor I 110 C1
Villastar E 90 C1
Villastellone I 80 B1
Villatobas E 95 C3
Villatorp E 93 A5
Villatoya E 96 B1
Villavaliente E 96 B1
Villavelayo E 89 B4
Villavella E 87 B3
Villaver de de Guadalimar E 101 A3
Villaverde del Rio E 99 B5
Villaviciosa E 88 A1
Villaviciosa de Córdoba E 99 A6
Villaviciosa de Odón E 94 B3
Villavieja de Yeltes E 87 D4
Villayón E 86 A4
Villé F 60 B3
Villebois-Lavalette F 67 C5
Villecerf F 59 B3
Villecomtal F 77 B5
Villedieu-les-Poêles F 57 B4
Villedieu-sur-Indre F 67 B6
Ville-di-Pietrabugno F 102 A2
Villedômain F 67 A6
Villefagnan F 67 B5
Villefontaine F 69 C5
Villefort F 78 B2
Villefranche-d'Albigeois F 77 C5
Villefranche-d'Allier F 68 B2
Villefranche-de-Lauragais F 77 C4
Villefranche-de-Lonchat F 76 B3
Villefranche-de-Panat F 78 B1
Villefranche-de-Rouergue F 77 B5
Villefranche-du-Périgord F 77 B4
Villefranche-sur-Cher F 68 A1
Villefranche-sur-Mer F 80 C1
Villefranche-sur-Saône F 69 B4
Villegenon F 68 A2
Villel E 96 A1
Villemaur-sur-Vanne F 59 B4
Villemontais F 68 C3
Villemur-sur-Tarn F 77 C4
Villena E 101 A5
Villenauxe-la-Grande F 59 B4
Villenave-d'Ornon F 76 B2
Villeneuve
CH 70 B1
F 77 B5
Villeneuve-d'Ascq F 49 C4
Villeneuve-de-Berg F 78 B3
Villeneuve-de-Marsan F 76 C2
Villeneuve-de-Rivière F 77 C3
Villeneuve-la-Guyard F 59 B4
Villeneuve-l'Archevêque F 59 B4
Villeneuve-le-Comte F 58 B3
Villeneuve-lès-Avignon F 78 C3
Villeneuve-les-Corbières F 78 D1
Villeneuve-St Georges F 58 B3
Villeneuve-sur-Allier F 68 B3
Villeneuve-sur-Lot F 77 B3
Villeneuve-sur-Yonne F 59 B4
Villeréal F 77 B3
Villerias E 88 C2
Villeromain F 58 C2
Villers-Bocage
Calvados F 57 A5
Somme F 48 D3
Villers-Bretonneux F 58 A3
Villers-Carbonnel F 59 A3
Villers-Cotterêts F 59 A4
Villersexel F 60 C2
Villers-Farlay F 69 B5
Villers-le-Gambon B 49 C5
Villers-le-Lac F 70 A1
Villers-sur-Mer F 57 A6
Villerupt F 60 A1
Villerville F 57 A6
Villeseneux F 59 B5
Ville-sous-la-Ferté F 59 B5
Ville-sur-Illon F 60 B2
Ville-sur-Tourbe F 59 A5
Villetrun F 58 C2
Villetta Barrea I 103 B6
Villeurbanne F 69 C4
Villeveyrac F 78 C2
Villevocance F 69 C4
Villiers-St Benoit F 59 C4
Villiers-St Georges F 59 B4
Villingen D 61 B4
Villmar D 50 C4
Villoldo E 88 B2
Villon F 59 C5
Villoria E 94 B1
Vilnes N 32 A1
Vilnius LT 7 D8
Vils
A 62 C1
DK 38 C1
Vilsbiburg D 62 B3
Vilseck D 62 A2
Vilshofen D 63 B4
Vilshult S 41 C4
Vilusi MNE 84 D3
Vilvestre E 87 C4
Vilvoorde B 49 C5
Vimeiro P 92 B1
Vimercate I 71 C4
Vimianzo E 86 A1
Vimieiro P 92 C3
Vimioso P 87 C4
Vimmerby S 40 B5
Vimoutiers F 57 B6
Vimperk CZ 63 A4
Vimy F 48 C3
Vinadi CH 71 B5
Vinadio I 79 B6
Vinaixa E 90 B3
Vinarós E 90 C3
Vinäs S 36 B1
Vinay F 69 C5
Vinberg S 40 C2
Vinca F 91 A5
Vinča SRB 85 B5
Vinchiaturo I 103 B7
Vinci I 81 C4
Vindeby DK 39 D3
Vindelgransele S 115 B15
Vindeln S 115 C16
Vinderup DK 38 C1
Vindsvik N 33 C3
Vinets F 59 B5
Vineuil F 58 C2
Vinga RO 75 B6
Vingåker S 37 C2
Vingnes N 34 A2
Vingrau F 78 D1
Vingrom N 34 A2
Vinhais P 87 C4
Vinica
HR 73 B6
SK 65 B5
SLO 73 C5
Vinicka MNE 85 D4
Viniegra de Arriba E 89 B4
Vinje
Hordaland N 32 B3
Sør-Trøndelag N 114 D6
Telemark N 33 C4
Vinkovci HR 74 C3
Vinliden S 115 C14
Vinninga S 35 D5
Vinnytsya UA 11 B10
Vinon F 68 A2
Vinon-sur-Verdon F 79 C4
Vinslöv S 41 C3
Vintjärn S 36 B3
Vintrosa S 37 C1
Viñuela E 100 C1
Viñuela de Sayago E 87 C5
Viñuelas E 95 B3
Vinuesa E 89 C4
Vinzelberg D 44 C3
Viöl D 43 A6
Viola I 80 B1
Violay F 69 C4
Vipava SLO 72 C3
Vipiteno I 71 B6
Vipperow D 45 B4
Vir
BIH 84 C2
HR 83 B4
Vira CH 70 B3
Vire F 57 B5
Vireda S 40 B4
Vireux F 49 C5
Virgen A 72 A2
Virgen de la Cabeza E 100 A1
Virginia IRL 19 C4
Virieu F 69 C5
Virieu-le-Grand F 69 C5
Virje HR 74 B1
Virklund DK 39 C2
Virovitica HR 74 C2
Virpazar MNE 105 A5
Virsbo S 36 C3
Virserum S 40 B5
Virtaniemi FIN 113 D17
Virton B 60 A1
Virtsu EST 6 B7
Viry F 69 B6
Vis HR 83 C5
Visbek D 43 C5
Visby
DK 39 D1
S 37 E5
Visé B 50 C1
Višegrad BIH 85 C4
Viserba I 82 B1
Viseu P 92 A3
Visiedo E 90 C1
Viskafors S 40 B2
Visland N 33 D3
Vislanda S 40 C4
Visnes N 33 C2
Višnja Gora SLO 73 C4
Višnjan HR 72 C3
Višnové CZ 64 B2
Visnums-Kil S 35 C6
Viso del Marqués E 100 A2
Visoko
BIH 84 C3
SLO 73 B4
Visone I 80 B2
Visp CH 70 B2
Vissefjärda S 40 C5
Visselhövede D 43 C6
Vissenbjerg DK 39 D3
Visso I 82 D2
Vistabella del Maestrat E 96 A2
Vita I 108 B1
Vitanje SLO 73 B5
Vitanovac SRB 85 C5
Vitebsk = Vitsyebsk BY 7 D11
Viterbo I 102 A5
Vitez BIH 84 B2
Vithkuq AL 116 B2
Vitigudino E 87 C4
Vitina
BIH 84 C2
GR 117 E4
Vitis A 63 B6
Vítkov CZ 64 A3
Vitkovac SRB 85 C5
Vitomirica KOS 85 D5
Vitoria-Gasteiz E 89 B4
Vitré F 57 B4
Vitrey-sur-Mance F 60 C1
Vitry-en-Artois F 48 C3
Vitry-le-François F 59 B5
Vitry-sur-Seine F 58 B3
Vitsand S 34 B4
Vitsyebsk = Vitebsk BY 7 D11
Vittangi S 113 E10
Vittaryd S 40 C3
Vitteaux F 69 A4
Vittel F 60 B1
Vittinge S 36 C4
Vittória I 109 C3
Vittório Véneto I 72 C2
Vittsjö S 41 C3
Viù I 70 C2
Viul N 34 B2
Vivario F 102 A2
Viveiro E 86 A3
Vivel del Rio Martin E 90 C2
Viver E 96 B2
Viverols F 68 C3
Viveros E 101 A3
Viviers F 78 B3
Vivonne F 67 B5
Vivy F 67 A4
Vize TR 118 A2
Vizille F 79 A4
Viziñada HR 72 C3
Viziru RO 11 D9
Vizovice CZ 64 A3
Vizvár H 74 B2
Vizzavona F 102 A2
Vizzini I 109 B3
Vlachiotis GR 117 F4
Vlachovice CZ 64 A3
Vlachovo SK 65 B6
Vláchovo Březi CZ 63 A4
Vladimirci SRB 85 B4
Vladimirovac SRB 85 A5
Vladislav CZ 64 A1
Vlagtwedde NL 43 B4
Vlajkovac SRB 85 A6
Vlasenica BIH 84 B3
Vlašim CZ 63 A5
Vlatkovići BIH 84 B2
Vledder NL 42 C3
Vlissingen NL 49 B4
Vlkolínec SK 65 A5
Vlorë AL 105 C5
Vlotho D 51 A4
Vnanje Gorice SLO 73 C4
Vobarno I 71 C5
Voćin HR 74 C2
Vöcklabruck A 63 B4
Vöcklamarkt A 63 C4
Vodanj SRB 85 B5
Voderady SK 64 B3
Vodice
Istarska HR 73 C4
Šibenska HR 83 C4
SLO 73 B4
Vodňany CZ 63 A5
Vodnjan HR 82 B2
Vodskov DK 38 B3
Voe GB 22 A7
Voerså DK 38 B3
Voghera I 80 B3
Vogogna I 70 B3
Vogošća BIH 84 C3
Vogué F 78 B3
Vohburg D 62 B2
Vohenstrauss D 62 A3
Vöhl D 51 B4
Vöhrenbach D 61 B4
Vöhringen D 61 B6
Void-Vacon F 60 B1
Voiron F 69 C5
Voise F 58 B2
Voisey F 60 C1
Voiteg RO 75 C6
Voiteur F 69 B5
Voitsberg A 73 A5
Vojens DK 39 D2
Vojka SRB 85 B5
Vojlovica SRB 85 B5
Vojnić HR 73 C5
Vojnice SK 65 C4
Vojnik SLO 73 B5
Vojvoda Stepa SRB 75 C5
Volada GR 119 G2
Volargne I 71 C5
Volary CZ 63 B4
Volče SLO 72 B3
Volda N 114 E3
Volendam NL 42 C2
Volga RUS 7 B15
Volimes GR 117 E2
Volissos GR 116 D7
Volkach D 61 A6
Völkermarkt A 73 B4
Volkhov RUS 7 B12
Völklingen D 60 A2
Volkmarsen D 51 B5
Voll N 114 E4
Vollenhove NL 42 C2
Vollore-Montagne F 68 C3
Vollsjö S 41 D3
Volodymyr-Volyns'kyy UA 11 A8
Volokolamsk RUS 7 C13
Volos GR 116 C4
Volosovo RUS 7 B10
Volovets UA 11 B7
Voltággio I 80 B2
Volta Mantovana I 71 C5
Volterra I 81 C4
Voltri I 80 B2
Volturara Áppula I 103 B8
Volturara Irpina I 103 C7
Volvic F 68 C3
Volx F 79 C4
Volyně CZ 63 A4
Vonitsa GR 116 D2
Vönöck H 74 A2
Vonsild DK 39 D2
Voorschoten NL 49 A5
Vopnafjörður IS 111 B11
Vorau A 73 A5
Vorbasse DK 39 D2
Vorchdorf A 63 C4
Vorden
D 43 C5
NL 50 A2
Vordernberg A 73 A4
Vordingborg DK 39 D4
Vorë AL 105 B5
Voreppe F 69 C5
Vorey F 68 C3
Vorgod DK 39 C1
Vormsund N 34 B3
Voronezh UA 7 F12
Vöru EST 7 C9
Voskopojë AL 116 B2
Voss N 32 B3
Votice CZ 63 A5
Voué F 59 B5
Vouillé F 67 B5
Voulx F 59 B3
Voussac F 68 B3
Vouvray F 67 A5
Vouvry CH 70 B1
Vouzela P 87 D2
Vouziers F 59 A5
Voves F 58 B2
Voxna S 36 A2
Voy GB 23 B5
Voynitsa RUS 3 D29
Voznesensk UA 11 C11
Voznesenye RUS 7 A13
Vrå
DK 38 B2
S 40 C3
Vráble SK 64 B4
Vračenovići MNE 84 D3
Vračev Gaj SRB 85 B6
Vraćevsnica SRB 85 B5
Vrådal N 33 C5
Vrakneika GR 117 D3
Vrana HR 83 B3
Vranduk BIH 84 B2
Vrångö S 38 B4
Vrani RO 85 A6
Vranić SRB 85 B5
Vraniči BIH 84 C3
Vranja HR 73 C4
Vranjak BIH 84 B3
Vranje SRB 10 E6
Vranovice CZ 64 B2
Vranov nad Dyje CZ 64 B1
Vransko SLO 73 B4
Vrapčići BIH 84 C2
Vratimov CZ 64 A4
Vratsa BG 11 E7
Vrbanja HR 84 B3
Vrbanjci BIH 84 B2
Vrbas SRB 75 C4
Vrbaška BIH 84 A2
Vrbnik
Primorsko-Goranska HR 83 A3
Zadarsko-Kninska HR 83 B5
Vrbno pod Pradědem CZ 54 C2
Vrboska HR 83 C5
Vrbov SK 65 A6
Vrbovce SK 64 B3
Vrbové SK 64 B3
Vrbovec HR 73 C6
Vrbovski SRB 85 B5
Vrbovsko HR 73 C5
Vrchlabí CZ 53 C5
Vrčin SRB 85 B5
Vrdy CZ 63 A6
Vrebac HR 83 B4
Vreden D 50 A2
Vrela KOS 85 D5
Vreoci SRB 85 B5
Vretstorp S 37 C1
Vrginmost HR 73 C5
Vrgorac HR 84 C2
Vrhnika SLO 73 C4
Vrhovine HR 83 B4
Vrhpolie SRB 85 B4
Vriezenveen NL 42 C3
Vrigne-aux-Bois F 59 A5
Vrigstad S 40 B4
Vrlika HR 83 C5
Vrmbaje SRB 85 C5
Vrnjačka Banja SRB 85 C5
Vrnograč BIH 73 C5
Vron F 48 C2
Vroomshoop NL 42 C3
Vroutek CZ 52 C3
Vrpolje HR 74 C3
Vršac SRB 85 A6
Vrsar HR 82 A2
Vrsi HR 83 B4
Vrtoče BIH 83 B5
Vrútky SK 65 A4
Všeruby CZ 62 A3
Všestary CZ 53 C5
Vsetín CZ 64 A3
Vuča MNE 85 D5
Vučitrn KOS 85 D5
Vučkovica SRB 85 C5
Vught NL 49 B6
Vuillafans F 69 A6
Vukovar HR 75 C4
Vuku N 114 D8
Vulcan RO 11 D7
Vulcăneşti MD 11 D10
Vuoggatjålme S 112 F5
Vuojärvi FIN 113 E15
Vuolijoki FIN 3 D27
Vuotso FIN 113 D16
Vuzenica SLO 73 B5
Vyartsilya RUS 3 E29
Vyazma RUS 7 D13
Vyborg RUS 3 F28
Výčapy CZ 64 A1
Výčapy-Opatovce SK 64 B4
Východna SK 65 A5
Vydrany SK 64 B3
Vyerkhnyadzvinsk BY 7 D9
Vyhne SK 65 B4
Vy-lès Lure F 60 C2
Vylkove UA 11 D10
Vynohradiv UA 11 B7
Vyshniy Volochek RUS 7 C13
Vyškov CZ 64 A3
Vysokánad Kysucou SK 65 A4
Vysoké Mýto CZ 53 D6
Vysokovsk RUS 7 C14
Vyšší Brod CZ 63 B5
Vytegra RUS 7 A14

W

Waabs D 44 A1
Waalwijk NL 49 B6
Waarschoot B 49 B4
Wabern D 51 B5
Wąbrzeźno PL 47 B4
Wąchock PL 55 B6
Wachow D 45 C4
Wachów PL 54 C3
Wächtersbach D 51 C5
Wackersdorf D 62 A3
Waddington GB 27 B5
Wadebridge GB 28 C3
Wadelsdorf D 53 B4
Wädenswil CH 70 A3
Wadern D 60 A2
Wadersloh D 50 B4
Wadlew PL 55 B4
Wadowice PL 65 A5
Wagenfeld D 43 C5
Wageningen NL 49 B6
Waghäusel D 61 A4
Waging D 62 C3
Wagrain A 72 A3
Wagrowiec PL 46 C3
Wahlsdorf D 52 B3
Wahlstedt D 44 B2
Wahrenholz D 44 C2
Waiblingen D 61 B5
Waidhaus D 62 A3
Waidhofen an der Thaya A 63 B6
Waidhofen an der Ybbs A 63 C5
Waimes B 50 C2
Wainfleet All Saints GB 27 B6
Waizenkirchen A 63 B4
Wakefield GB 27 B4
Wałbrzych PL 53 C6
Walchensee D 62 C2
Walchsee A 62 C3
Wałcz PL 46 B2
Wald CH 70 A3
Waldaschaff D 51 D5
Waldbach A 73 A5
Waldböckelheim D 60 A3
Waldbröl D 50 C3
Waldeck D 51 B5
Waldenburg D 52 C2
Waldfischbach-Burgalben D 60 A3
Waldheim D 52 B3
Waldkappel D 51 B5
Waldkirch D 60 B3
Waldkirchen D 63 B4
Waldkirchen am Wesen A 63 B4
Waldkraiburg D 62 B3
Wald-Michelbach D 61 A4
Waldmohr D 60 A3
Waldmünchen D 62 A3
Waldring A 62 C3
Waldsassen D 52 C2
Waldshut D 61 C4